Finding Ella Briggs

Finding Ella Briggs

The Life and Work of an Unconventional Architect

Despina Stratigakos and Elana Shapira

with contributors Megan Brandow-Faller, Celina Kress, Dörte Kuhlmann, Ulrike Matzer, Christine Oertel, Eva B. Ottillinger, Barbara Penner, Sabine Plakolm-Forsthuber, Monika Platzer, Ursula Prokop, Sabrina Rahman, Katrin Stingl, Carmen Trifina, Christine Zwingl

PRINCETON UNIVERSITY PRESS
Princeton and Oxford

Published by Princeton University Press, 41 William Street, Princeton, New Jersey 08540
In the United Kingdom: Princeton University Press, 99 Banbury Road, Oxford OX2 6JX

press.princeton.edu

Jacket images: Portrait of Ella Briggs, 1921. Architekturzentrum Wien, Collection, Bert Singer and Angela Kimberk Archive (Cambridge, MA). Pestalozzi-Hof in Vienna, 1925–27, designed by Ella Briggs. Wiener Stadt- und Landesarchiv.

ISBN 978-0-691-26395-3
ISBN (ebook) 978-0-691-26508-7

Library of Congress Control Number: 2025939755

British Library Cataloging-in-Publication Data is available

Editorial: Michelle Komie and Annie Miller
Production Editorial: Jaden Young
Text and Jacket/Cover Design: Heather Hansen
Production: Steven Sears
Publicity: Jodi Price
Copyeditor: Lachlan Brooks

This book has been composed in Adobe Text Pro with Loos

Printed in the United States of America

1 3 5 7 9 10 8 6 4 2

CONTENTS

PART II: REFLECTIONS ON ELLA BRIGGS

PREFACE

For a long time, we searched for Ella Briggs. The talented artist, designer, and architect appeared at the turning points and places of history: she studied with the Secessionists in Vienna, created luminous rooms in Gilded Age New York, erected social housing in Red Vienna, and designed modernist buildings in Weimar Berlin. By the time Adolf Hitler came to power in Germany and Briggs fled to London, she had attained an international profile. In exile she remained active, contributing to England's postwar reconstruction. Yet after her death, historians lost sight of her.

Still, her name and work were never entirely forgotten. Time and again, a determined historian or student would write about her. Their efforts, however, were always by necessity incomplete. Briggs led a peripatetic life, and retracing her footsteps presents a challenge for any writer. This difficulty goes beyond geography: everywhere she went, Briggs skillfully navigated and built new professional networks. A lone historian would struggle to master these many different contexts across place, time, and culture. What was needed to compose Briggs's biography, we realized, was a team.

Our desire to know her story launched an audacious idea. We would invite to Vienna historians from around the world who had unearthed fragments of Briggs's career, to see if we as a group could piece together a larger whole. On a warm, rainy summer morning, we converged on the Architekturzentrum Wien, Austria's national architecture museum, for a day-long workshop. By day's end, we realized we had found a pathway to reach Ella Briggs.

Over the ensuing months, many of the workshop's participants as well as newly invited partners began an international adventure. Each investigating in place, from New York to London to Vienna to Munich and Berlin, we searched libraries, archives, and sometimes even attics for clues. Over many hours of conversation, we compared notes and shared discoveries. We became obsessed with finding the next tantalizing morsel. We began to think of this project as a proverbial stone soup: starting with what little we had, we each added ingredients until a rich and satisfying brew emerged. At the end of this book, we will come back to our process to examine what we learned from this unusual form of collaborative storytelling. But in the meantime, what follows is the exciting and revealing history of Ella Briggs, told here for the first time.

Despina Stratigakos and Elana Shapira

PART I

A Biography of Ella Briggs

Section I.
EARLY YEARS IN VIENNA AND NEW YORK: A DESIGNER EMERGES, 1880–1907

1.
Family Life in an Imperial Capital
Dreams of Belonging

Elana Shapira

Our story begins in a city obsessed with building monuments to its own glory. In 1880, the year of Ella Briggs's birth, Vienna bristled with construction activity. Magnificent structures designed in historical styles rose along the Ringstrasse, the grand boulevard occupying the imperial capital's long-outgrown city walls. The population had boomed, as the peoples of the Habsburg Empire arrived in the city, drawn by the excitement and the promise of a growing metropolis. To his citizens, Emperor Franz Joseph represented security and continuity. The last war—with Prussia, in 1866—had become a distant memory, and the popular monarch was credited with having brought peace and prosperity to a vast and diverse empire. The *Ausgleich* (political compromise) with Hungary of 1867 had strengthened Habsburg rule in Central Europe, and the Austrian Constitution of the same year, which guaranteed equal rights for all nationalities and ethnic minorities within the Austro-Hungarian Empire, fostered hopes for a new era of freedom. The grand public buildings of the Ringstrasse—the opera house, parliament, city hall, university, and many others—unabashedly proclaimed Vienna's immense pride, as well as its emergence as a capital of modern governance, education, and culture (plate 1).

Josef Baumfeld and Karoline Bryk, Ella's parents, were among the young people who came to Vienna wanting to partake of the capital's vitality and prestige. New railway expansion projects provided easy access to Vienna from the provincial parts of the empire. This encouraged ambitious men such as Josef, trained in white-collar professions, to move to the empire's capital in search of better employment opportunities and higher living standards.[1]

Josef and his brother Isidor Theodor, as well as Karoline Bryk and her brothers, emigrated from the province of Galicia (today spanning southeastern Poland and northwestern Ukraine) just a few years before Jews received equal rights in the empire in 1867. Josef was born in 1840 in Lesko, a small town on the Sian River. He arrived in Vienna eager to launch his career as a lawyer. There he partnered with Ignaz Pisko (an authority on commercial law) and prospered, earning the title of Hof- und Gerichts-Advokat (Imperial Court Lawyer).[2] Josef's father and grandfather were medical doctors and therefore belonged to the bourgeoisie in Galicia.[3] Karoline, born in 1845 in the city of Rzeszów, also came from a well-to-do family.[4] Karoline's father, Salomon Bryk, had been a successful jeweler.[5] His work as a diamond trader took him frequently to London, where he became so proficient in English that he translated a "famous English novel" into German.[6] Affluent Jews often embraced the processes of modernization and Germanization in the region, and this appears to have been the case for both Josef's and Karoline's families.

When the couple married in a Jewish ceremony, those families undoubtedly bestowed blessings on them for children to come. And come they did: Moritz, in 1868; Friedrich, in 1870; and Friederike, in 1873. Then, on the day Friederike turned seven years old—March 5, 1880—Elsa arrived, the little sister who would become known as Ella. Perhaps Ella's conception had come as a surprise to Josef and Karoline, who at the time of their daughter's birth were forty and thirty-four, respectively. Close familial bonds likely developed as the older siblings helped care for the youngest one. As was the custom among Jewish families in the Habsburg Empire, Ella's parents gave each child a German and a Hebrew name.[7]

Ella was born at her family's apartment on Schottenbastei, a street in a wealthy new neighborhood to which her family had recently moved (plate 2). Their building, erected in 1870, was owned by the banker Nathaniel Rothschild and was designed by Jewish architect Wilhelm Fränkel.[8] It was located near the financial center of Vienna's first district, where several prominent Jewish families lived. Among them were the Ephrussi family, part of the grain and banking dynasty celebrated in Edmund de Waal's family memoir *The Hare with Amber Eyes*.[9] By the time Ella arrived in 1880, the Baumfeld family was living, and thriving, among Vienna's elites.

Although Ella grew up in the comfort of a bourgeois household, the family experienced changes small and large that shifted its internal dynamics and external situation. Moritz left home in 1888 for his mandatory year of military service, and Friedrich followed suit the next year.[10] Far more destabilizing was Josef Baumfeld's prolonged illness, which became severe around 1890, when he resigned from legal practice.[11] That summer, Josef's deteriorating condition precipitated a move to healthier climes. After a long trip on the Brenner Railway heading south from Vienna toward Italy, he arrived at the city of Merano (then part of Austrian South Tyrol), accompanied by Karoline and their two daughters.[12] He may have rented an apartment for his family in Villa Gothensitz, an elegant pension.[13] Surrounded by mountains, Merano offered uplifting walks along its beautiful promenades. After visits from Empress Elisabeth in the early 1870s, it had become a popular spa destination for the Viennese aristocracy, who enjoyed not only its sun and mild temperatures but also its famous thermal baths.[14] The city had a growing and prosperous Jewish community, and a number of prominent Jewish figures stayed there hoping to improve their health.[15] Sadly, for Josef there would be no recovery: he passed away in October of 1892, when Ella was just twelve.[16]

After Josef Baumfeld's death, his widow and two daughters returned to their life in Vienna, now changed forever. From a financial standpoint, it is unclear how this painful turn of events impacted the family. Here and there we glimpse signs of continued affluence. Yet from a number of moves the family made over the ensuing years to less desirable neighborhoods within Vienna, it appears that money was a concern.[17]

The children could not have helped much financially. Moritz was then the only child in the family to have finished *Gymnasium* and completed his *Matura* (an exam taken at the end of secondary school that students must pass in order to enter university).[18] Before his father's death, Moritz had been studying law at the University of Vienna; afterward, perhaps freed from paternal expectations, he pursued a journalistic career. He established himself as the editor of several liberal newspapers in Vienna, namely the *Neues Wiener Journal* (New Vienna Journal), *Wiener Sonn- und Montagszeitung* (Vienna Sunday and Monday Paper), and *Capitalist*.[19] Once Moritz, in his late twenties, married Angelika "Ange" Dorothea Hanss in 1895, he would have needed his income to support his own growing family.[20] Friedrich, unlike Moritz, attended a *Realschule* (vocational secondary school).[21] When he lost his father, he was in his early twenties and just starting to launch a career in timber sales. In time, he accumulated substantial wealth, but he could not have contributed much to the family coffers in the early years after his mother was widowed. Sister Friederike, who was nineteen when her father died, does not seem to have been employed, and Ella, of course, was still a child.

If Karoline did need assistance, as many widows would, she may have turned to relatives for help. By then, Josef's brother Isidor Theodor was a wealthy bank director, but having the means to help is not necessarily the same as having the inclination to do so.[22] It seems more likely that Karoline's own family would have offered financial support if she found herself in reduced circumstances. The Bryk family resided in the predominantly Jewish second district of Leopoldstadt and occupied a socially prominent place in Viennese society. Adolph and Philipp Bryk, Karoline's brothers, had successfully integrated into Viennese economic and cultural life.[23] Adolph had earned the title of Imperial Court Lawyer, like Ella's father.

In adolescence and beyond, Ella found important role models among her mother's family as she crafted her own sense of professional identity. Her late grandfather Salomon Bryk's prowess at crossing frontiers and learning new languages became a part of Ella's cultural and family heritage, remaining a source of pride throughout her life. His story likely encouraged her own frontier crossings, which began at the turn of the twentieth century. Although Salomon died about ten years before Ella was born, Ella kept his portrait, painted in miniature, as a prized possession. Other Bryk relatives may have similarly provided her with inspiration. Karoline's brother Philipp was an acclaimed pianist and directed his own music school in Leopoldstadt.[24] He also led the musical society Lyra in Vienna, and counted among his friends Franz Lehár, famous for his operetta *Die lustige Witwe* (*The Merry Widow*). Philipp's son Hugo (Ella's cousin) was a conductor and composer who worked in cities across Europe, including Berlin.[25] Other members of the Bryk family were involved in the Viennese liberal publishing world.[26]

For the Bryks and for many other Jewish newcomers, attaining a leading position within the arts and culture of Vienna meant not only achieving social integration but also playing a critical role as producers of Austrian culture. It is telling, for example, that outside the courtroom, Adolph Bryk positioned himself as a Macher (mover and shaker) in Viennese bohemian circles. A dandy, he was immortalized in Johan Strauss's 1873 operetta *Der Karneval in Rom* (*The Carnival in Rome*) in the character of the eccentric painter Arthur Bryk.[27] But the very success of Jewish newcomers such as the Bryks would come to have unintended consequences—ones that in many important ways would affect Ella's own future as an upper-middle-class Jewish woman in Vienna. As the Jewish population grew and prospered, they became a thorn in the side of Austria's conservative Christian majority, and members of emerging German nationalist movements threatened to undercut their success. Vehement antisemites in political and cultural circles attacked prominent Jewish individuals, especially those with origins in Galicia and Bukovina, criticizing their contributions to Viennese culture as presumptuous attempts by "outsiders" to teach locals their own German culture.[28]

Galicia was considered the poorest and most backward province of Austro-Hungary. Many Galician Jews lived a marginal existence as *luftmenschen* (unanchored people), a Yiddish word, meaning to live in and from the air as a transient, indigent person, used to describe Jewish small-town traders, peddlers, and vagrants.[29] Many well-to-do Galician Jewish residents in Vienna who feared being tainted by the dubious reputations of Galician Jewish peddlers avoided associating with them.[30] We do not know how Ella related to her own family's Galician Jewish roots. In 1932 she would misrepresent her family's origins, stating they had come to Austria from Germany. This declaration was made, however, in the context of her application for German citizenship, and at a time when the contributions of all Jews were coming under increasingly violent antisemitic attack.[31]

Efforts to undermine claims made by Jewish men and women that they belonged to German culture grew stronger—even fashionable—around the turn of the twentieth century. In 1897 a seventeen-year-old Ella would have watched as Emperor Franz Joseph was compelled to approve the election of the antisemite Karl Lueger as mayor of Vienna. Lueger's hateful rhetoric included a call to boycott Jewish businesses, rants against other sources of Jewish wealth and power, and promises to "liberate" German culture from Jewish influence.

Lueger's antisemitism shook Vienna's Jewish residents, long-term and newly arrived alike. Jewish voices rose to protest his threats of violence. Felix Salten, best known as the author of Walt Disney's *Bambi*, pilloried the dangerous speeches Lueger made after his election: "Then this man comes and slaughters a Jew . . . in front of the howling crowd. On the rostrum he slaughters him with words, stabs him to death with words, tears him to shreds, hurls him to the people as a sacrifice . . . [It is his first act in power]: showing the general discontent the way to the Jewish alleys, where it can run riot."[32] In this climate, some Jewish residents left in search of more hospitable environs. This may have factored into Ella's brother Moritz's decision around this time to seek his fortune in New York. Similarly, it may have motivated Ella's cousin (Adolph Bryk's son) Siegfried to pursue his journalistic career in Berlin, where he would rise to the top echelons of the city's press scene.[33] In Vienna Jewish patrons, who had largely funded the development of the Ringstrasse, endeavored more than ever to support liberal-modernist cultural institutions and art movements as a progressive alternative to Mayor Lueger's xenophobic politics.

For young Ella, Moritz served as the conduit to the worlds of contemporary politics and culture. After suffering the loss of her father, it seems she turned to her oldest brother to fill the lingering void. The two siblings became close. As Ella grew to adolescence, Moritz introduced her to the richness of the imperial capital's arts and society, which he actively cultivated. He wrote broadly on politics and legal affairs, as well as on art, literature, and theater. In articles appearing in the *Wiener Montags-Journal* he supported modernism, even going so far as to call for a cultural renewal.[34] Moritz's passion for art and modern culture apparently rubbed off on Ella, who would continue to explore them both throughout her own life.

From her earliest days, when her mother or perhaps her nanny took her for walks around the neighborhood, Ella witnessed firsthand modern Vienna's institutional, artistic, and cultural emergence as made manifest in the construction of its many impressive new buildings along the Ringstrasse. The neoclassical Parlamentsgebäude (Austrian Parliament Building) was completed when Ella was three. The majestic, neobaroque Burgtheater (Court Theater) opened when she was eight (see plate 1). As she neared her tenth birthday, she would have noticed that the palatial Kunsthistorisches Museum (Museum of Fine Arts), which would house the Habsburgs' art collections, was almost finished. Ella's escorted walks through turn-of-the-century Vienna would no doubt have provided her with an inspiring view of life in a constant state of improvement. Given her family's involvement in Viennese culture, perhaps the young Ella even began to anticipate joining its exciting world of art.

But at the same time, with the rise of German nationalism and the proliferation of narrow-minded, antisemitic campaigns in Austria, Ella must also have sensed a danger. For families like the Baumfelds, the Ringstrasse represented the collective efforts of an earlier generation of Jewish patrons and leaders to shape Viennese life and culture; for conservative Catholics and populist German nationalists, it represented a threat to Viennese life and culture as they knew it. If Ella, like other Jewish residents of Vienna at the time, recognized that maintaining cultural aspirations would be critical to their continued integration and success in the city, she must have also realized that achieving those aspirations would not come without a fight.

2. Art and Design Studies: A Beginning

Elana Shapira

Raised in the heart of Austria's art and music scene, Ella Briggs came of age in a period when exciting developments of lasting significance were taking place. In May 1897 the new conductor of the Vienna Court Opera, composer Gustav Mahler, made his debut performance with Richard Wagner's *Lohengrin*, thrilling Viennese audiences.[1] Mahler's innovative productions were much admired by the members of the new Secession movement, who rejected academic styles and hierarchies in favor of a new synthesis of painting, sculpture, and architecture. In March 1898, the first Secession exhibition opened in the rented halls of the Viennese Horticultural Society, featuring experimental work by leading artists from around the world, including the German symbolist sculptor and painter Max Klinger, the French modernist sculptor Auguste Rodin, the Belgian symbolist painter Fernand Khnopff, and the American painter and printmaker James McNeill Whistler.[2] Fifty-seven thousand visitors attended, heightening expectations for the new movement. The show's financial windfall went toward constructing a permanent Secession Building.[3] Inaugurated in November of the same year, the building's Jugendstil decorative motifs and striking golden dome of interweaving laurel branches instantly made it a city icon. We can imagine Ella accompanying her brother Moritz to events such as these, bedazzled by the presence of artistic luminaries. By the time she reached the age of seventeen, she had begun to exhibit her very own artistic talents, as well as her independent spirit.

In 1897 the teenager began her art studies at the newly established Kunstschule für Frauen und Mädchen (Art School for Women and Girls).[4] Founded as a private institution by a group of progressive women, including artists Tina Blau-Lang and Olga Prager (both Jewish) and women's rights campaigner Rosa Mayreder, the school provided education to aspiring female artists at a time when it was highly unusual for middle-class girls to train for a profession.

Details surrounding Ella's primary and secondary schooling, prior to her study of art, remain somewhat murky. We know only that she attended public schools in Vienna and Merano.[5] Middle-class Jewish families in Vienna typically valued and sought out quality education for their daughters. Although the city's Jewish population at the time represented about 10 percent of Vienna's total population, Jewish girls made up half of those enrolled in private girls' lyceums.[6]

If educating Ella was important from a cultural standpoint at this time, it may also have been desirable within a familial context. At least one member of Ella's extended family is known to have supported institutions that advanced girls' education. During the years in which Ella studied art, her maternal cousin—the engineer, editor, and philosopher of science Otto Bryk—taught at and financially supported the girls' lyceum run by the Jewish women's rights activist and education reformer Eugenie Schwarzwald.[7] Schwarzwald was among the prominent Austrian feminists who recognized the importance of girls' education for the emancipation of women. Bryk's receptiveness to Schwarzwald's progressive ideas about girls' schooling may signal a general familial receptiveness to educating young women—one that may have benefited the adolescent Ella as she pleaded her case for undertaking an education in art.

Advocates of women's rights at this time emphasized the pressing need to educate girls. Yet despite the fact that more opportunities to do so began emerging by the end of the nineteenth century, a common pattern persisted: girls from bourgeois homes ended their schooling while still adolescents and then waited, sometimes for years, for a groom to materialize.[8] Alice Salomon, a German supporter of women's education, wrote about the excruciating boredom "young ladies" of her generation faced at a time when they were expected to "feed the canary, embroider doilies, and wait for marriage."[9] This appears to have been the path taken by Friederike, who neither pursued higher education nor married. Perhaps Ella—having experienced the loss of her family's main financial provider and having watched as her sister "fed the canary," so to speak—felt compelled to choose a different, less conventional path. Ella's widowed mother may also have understood how important it was for Ella to establish her economic independence. Or perhaps Ella found inspiration to pursue a professional career in her cousin, Elsa Bryk. Eight years Ella's senior, Elsa was an accomplished pianist. Reports of concerts she performed as a youngster with her brother Hugo frequently appeared in newspapers during Ella's childhood. In the early 1900s, Elsa became a notable music teacher.[10] However it came about, Ella seems to have set her sights on establishing her own successful career.

Just as Ella was starting her second year of art school, tragedy struck the Baumfeld family once more. In November 1898, Moritz's twenty-six-year-old wife Ange died suddenly, leaving him a widower with two young children.[11] Ella temporarily suspended her studies, presumably to help her brother. By the end of 1899, she had re-enrolled in art school and continued with her classes.[12]

In the art schools of the day, choosing a professor with whom to study essentially meant committing oneself to that person's artistic style. Ella, instead, showed signs of an independent mind. For two years she studied under the history painter Adalbert Franz Seligmann, who painted in a naturalistic style.[13] One of the original cofounders of the Art School for Women and Girls, Seligmann was an enthusiastic supporter of Impressionist artists Olga Wisinger-Florian and Tina Blau-Lang. Yet in other ways, he was conservative. He adhered to the academic doctrine in art education, which meant that his art students learned by copying from antiquity and the Old Masters. He also maintained a traditional hierarchy between the fine arts and the applied arts.[14] As an academic painter, he was skeptical of the Secession movement. In his 1898 review of the first Secession exhibition, published in the liberal journal *Die Wage* (The Scales), he praised much of the art, but he questioned the Secession artists' insistence that their modernity required slaying past traditions or that they had discovered novel artistic truths.[15]

Seligmann's doubts about the Secession movement were countered by journalists and art critics who strongly advocated for such a break from tradition and for the pursuit of new forms of artistic expression and education. Berta Zuckerkandl, for example, championed architect Josef Hoffmann and designer Koloman Moser, key members of the Secession, in newspaper columns and journal articles. At the forefront of the Viennese art scene, the Jewish journalist, art critic, and hostess of a famed Viennese literary salon expressed a common interest shared among the liberal bourgeoisie (Jews and non-Jews alike) in promoting the ideal of pluralism and inclusive modernism as the pathway to a better future.[16]

Weighing the alternatives, Ella would decide for herself whom to follow. She aligned herself with the Secessionists' more radical approach. In her last year at the Art School for Women and Girls she chose to study under one of its leading artists, Adolf Böhm, a founding member of the Secession and strong proponent of women artists.[17] Yet Ella would not forget Seligmann's doubts about radical artistic claims to "true" modernism; like her former teacher, she would never blindly follow such dictates.

The curriculum of Vienna's art schools was closely coordinated with contemporary exhibitions at the Künstlerhaus (Artists' House), Wiener Secession (Secession Building), and Österreichisches Museum für Kunst und Industrie (Austrian Museum of Art and Industry; today Museum für angewandte Kunst Wien, or MAK). Students were encouraged to seek inspiration outside the classroom proper, and there is no question that these exhibitions would have formed an important part of Ella's education. Although we do not know exactly which exhibitions she saw, it is probable that in the spring of 1901 she visited the Austrian Museum of Art and Industry. There she would have encountered the impressive modern decorative art created by female students of the Kunstgewerbeschule (School of Applied Arts). It was around this time that Ella decided to continue her studies at that school, which enabled her to pursue a more progressive agenda in her art education.

Not only did Ella's move to the School of Applied Arts in the fall of 1901 secure the young artist's involvement with the Secessionist movement, which by then had established itself as a leading avant-garde force in Vienna, but it also inserted her into a vibrant and ambitious community of female students at the school. For example, the future artist Marianne Pisko, daughter of Ignaz Pisko, Ella's father's law partner, joined Ella in her first-year anatomy class. The two young, Jewish women would enjoy a lifelong friendship.[18]

In her busy first year, Ella also enrolled in technical drawing and painting classes, as well as in a specialist course in art embroidery and lacework taught by Johann Hrdlička, whose own work featured elegant botanical patterns. In subsequent semesters she took, among other topics, art history, chemistry, and figure modeling.[19] By her second year, Ella had decided on painting as her concentration, choosing to study under Koloman Moser. She excelled under his tutelage, earning high grades for her course work.[20] Moser was intensely interested in Japanese art, and Ella's graphic work of this time reveals the influence of Japanese prints that she absorbed through her teacher. In her first-ever published work, undertaken for Moser's class, Ella created a design pattern for embroidery in silk and metal threads (plate 3).[21] She chose a fish motif popular in Japanese art and placed it in a composition that lacks depth to evoke the flat space characteristic of Japanese prints. This work also may have been influenced by a delicate cabinet designed by Marietta Peyfuss, a student of Moser, included in the student work displayed at the spring 1901 exhibition of the Austrian Museum of Art and Industry. The cabinet was ornamented with an embroidery of descending fish, somewhat like Ella's swimming fish.[22]

It is more likely, however, that Ella had a different source of inspiration for her embroidery design, which also suggests a sly and critical sense of humor. Gustav Klimt published his allegorical *Fischblut* (Fish Blood) in the March 1898 issue of the Secessionist journal *Ver Sacrum* (Sacred Spring) (fig. 2.1).[23] Seductive women with long, flowing hair merge into an erotic, viscous force, while a large fish, looking back at the viewer, intrudes at the left. In Ella's work there is also a large fish (or perhaps a sea lion) peering at the viewer from the right. But here, Klimt's female figures have been transformed back into small, colorful fish, depicted in a palette of ochre, white, and red against the turquoise water. Putting the works of Briggs and Klimt side by side, it is hard not to read her version as a blatant critique that drolly and effectively punctures Klimt's sexist views of women as animalistic, seductive, and even dangerous.

Another humorous, if gentler, critique can be seen in an early student print of frogs (plate 4). Although not definitively attributed to Briggs, the work is almost certainly by her.[24] Here the artist (presumably Briggs) picks up the flat, decorative Japanese influences of Moser's prints and reworks them. Moser transformed Japanese sources into aesthetically pleasing Jugendstil patterns. The creator of the frog print realized that this process, when applied to certain motifs, could deflate the seriousness of the artist's intent. Created as a decorative pattern, the print illustrates green frogs standing upright and jumping over small green squares. The repetitive aspect of the design and formal posture of the frogs playfully convey the silliness potentially generated by reducing the organic shape of a natural source into a Jugendstil pattern.

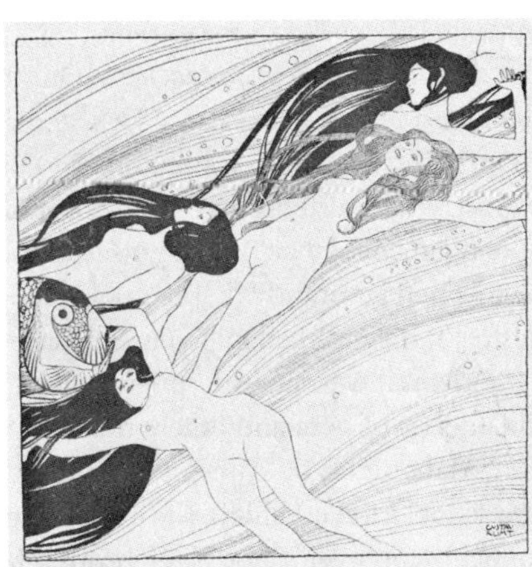

Fig. 2.1 Gustav Klimt, *Fischblut*, illustration for the journal *Ver Sacrum*, ink on paper, 1898.

The frog pattern was published in 1904 in the innovative journal *Die Fläche* as part of an issue featuring Moser's students.[25] But even prior to this time, Briggs's student work had begun to draw recognition. Her submission for a student competition to design the cover of the German monthly *Dekorative Kunst* (Decorative Arts), a leading design journal read widely throughout the German-speaking world, was published in its

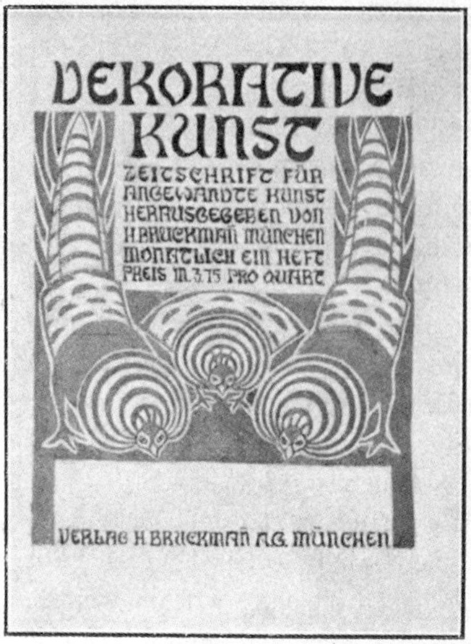

Fig. 2.2 Ella Baumfeld [Briggs], submission (honorable mention) for the cover of the German monthly *Dekorative Kunst*, 1903.

pages in 1903. Ella's graphic design, which received an honorable mention, offers another kind of metamorphosis of the natural world (fig. 2.2). The fantasy animal—a cross between a lizard, a bird, and a peacock with a long tail—pulses with the dynamic movement of alternating decorative patterns in nature.[26]

Briggs's interest in natural imagery may have been stimulated by the time she spent early on in her studies in the fashionable resort town of Hinterbrühl, a short distance from Vienna, where her mother was living in 1901.[27] In addition to tourists, it attracted Viennese artists and writers, such as Secessionist architect Joseph Maria Olbrich (who in 1898 designed the Villa Friedmann there) and the famous author and dramatist Arthur Schnitzler (who, vacationing with his family, could be seen bicycling around town).[28] On walks in the forest, Ella would have had many opportunities to explore the natural world and its inhabitants.

By 1902, Ella's mother had rented an apartment in Vienna.[29] Within Vienna's urban context, Ella would have observed a different type of phenomenon: specifically, the feminist groundswell taking place within the Austrian capital. Popular media openly discussed women's changing lives and questioned their fate as wives and mothers exclusively. Newspapers reported on feminist publications written by women, some of which provoked a backlash from conservative critics. The 1902 bestselling novel *Eine für Viele: Aus dem Tagebuche eines Mädchens* (One for many: From a girl's diary), published under the pseudonym "Vera," caused a scandal with its devastating portrayal of bourgeois women's hopelessness as unfulfilled and idle objects of male desire.[30] Bemoaning the hypocrisy of social norms and the profound inequality between the sexes, the author openly lamented that "young girls from affluent circles . . . approach their life's purpose blindly and ignorantly."[31] The book's supporters demanded recognition of girls' own desires and their freedom to pursue lives of creativity and happiness.

Perhaps it was the widespread debates about the constraints on women's lives and the urgings of Vera and others that women face their destinies head-on that pushed Ella to take a truly bold next step. Although she must have been sad to leave her mother and school friends behind, she likely felt that there was a bigger world out there, ready for her to discover. Her trusted brother Moritz had taken a job in New York City, and his letters home would surely have shared the excitement of the bustling American metropolis. And so, in late 1903, Ella decided to join him in the New World.

3.
New World Encounters: The First Transatlantic Crossing

Despina Stratigakos

Ella Briggs sailed into New York in style. On November 18, 1903, the luxurious transatlantic ocean liner SS *Kaiser Wilhelm der Grosse* entered New York Harbor with the twenty-three-year-old Austrian on board.[1] We can imagine Ella, bundled against the wind rising off the cold waters of New York Harbor, standing at the rails with other first-class passengers and watching with excitement as Manhattan's skyline came into view. But what that vision meant to her—what hopes she had for her new life in this vibrant American city—is harder to decipher.

Ship manifests contain various sorts of information about their passengers, from their marital status to the amount of money they carried, but they do not record aspirations. Unlike passengers travelling in steerage on the decks below hers, Ella had had a comfortable—even enviable—life. Her family, despite having lost its main breadwinner, remained part of Vienna's cultural elite. This afforded Ella opportunities that were then rare for young women, such as enrollment in art school. And as a student interested in design reform, Ella had already found herself in arguably the most exciting place on earth: the heart of the Vienna Secession. What, then, did New York have to offer her that Vienna did not?

The most obvious answer is her brother Moritz. In 1899, not long after the death of his wife Ange, he departed for New York, with his two young children, Angela and Joseph, in tow. The thirty-one-year-old widower began a new life in the United States, working as a special correspondent for the leading Viennese newspaper *Neue Freie Presse* (New Free Press). In his adopted city, he used the name Maurice Baumfeld, an Anglicized version of the German.

In June 1901, Moritz sailed again to New York. He had returned to Europe to bring back with him twenty-four-year-old Ida Hutter, born in the small Jewish village of Zabłocie in Austrian Silesia (later Poland). Three months later, on September 5, Moritz and Ida wed in Manhattan. In June 1902, the couple welcomed a baby boy, Theodore, and in July 1903, Ida gave birth to a daughter, Elisabeth Ellen. Now caring for four children, the couple may have felt overwhelmed, even with the help of servants. Perhaps they urged Ella to come lend a hand (enticing her with a first-class ticket), which would account for her abandoning her classes at the Vienna School of Applied Arts midway through her fifth semester. The family's life took a tragic turn one year later, when on November 6, 1904, the fourteen-month-old Elisabeth Ellen died, possibly a victim of the meningitis epidemic then sweeping New York. Of the thousands who died, two-thirds were children, with the youngest having the highest mortality rates. Was Ella present at her niece's burial at Woodlawn Cemetery on November 7, 1904, comforting her grieving sister-in-law, who was only a few years older than Ella herself? It is impossible to know for sure. In May 1905, Ida gave birth to the couple's last child, Beatrice.[2]

Yet joining Moritz and his family may not have been Ella's sole, or even primary, reason for moving to New York: the city had something else—or rather, someone else—that Vienna did not. His name was Walter Briggs. He was born in Vienna in 1865 as Walter Brix to Jewish parents, although he converted to Protestantism at the age of eighteen (becoming Walter Johannes). After earning his law degree at the University of Vienna he worked as an Imperial Court Lawyer and also held political office as an elected representative on Vienna's *Gemeinderat* (City Council).[3] By the time he reached his early thirties, Brix had begun patronizing Secessionist artists. The interior of his law office, decorated with furniture by Josef Hoffmann, was featured in the Viennese design monthly *Das Interieur* (The Interior).[4]

In addition to being a follower of the avant-garde art movement, the five-foot-nine, brown-eyed bachelor may also have been a fast-talking swindler. Or so claimed Olga Wisinger-Florian, an older and accomplished artist who regularly exhibited with the Secessionists (and who was much admired by Ella Briggs's first art teacher, Adalbert Franz Seligmann). Wisinger-Florian maintained that Brix urged her to invest in a company that he assured her would yield high profits, even though he already knew, because of his own involvement, that the company was in poor financial straits. Wisinger-Florian not only lost her initial investment but also found herself liable for the company's debts, ultimately losing a fortune. In gleeful coverage of the ensuing scandal and trial, which took place in February 1903, the tabloid-like *Illustrirtes Wiener Extrablatt* (Vienna Illustrated Extra) reported that Brix fled Vienna to avoid imprisonment. The satirical *Die Fackel* (The Torch), seizing an opportunity to mock both a politician and the Secessionists, joked that Brix could not serve his sentence because he was only capable of living in a one-room cell if it were furnished by Josef Hoffmann. For several years thereafter, Viennese newspapers kept track of the fugitive Brix. In 1904, the popular *Neues Wiener Tagblatt* (New Vienna Daily) reported on a rumor that he had married a rich American, the daughter of the multimillionaire owner of a large New York department store.[5]

Although the marriage rumor proved false, Brix had indeed settled in New York. Rather than surrender himself to authorities in Vienna to begin his sentence, he had boarded a ship in Antwerp and sailed for the United States, arriving on March 4, 1903. The thirty-eight-year-old told the immigration inspector that he was only visiting New York. But unable to return to Vienna, he quickly set about making a new life for himself under the Anglicized name Briggs. Despite having been disbarred in Austria, he organized an office for Austrian and international legal matters while also studying American law.[6] An exposé in the *Neues Wiener Tagblatt*, published after Walter fled to the United States, portrayed him as a talented but lackadaisical lawyer, who sought to make money quickly and lived beyond his means. A gifted entertainer and violinist, and avid joiner of clubs and committees (including for Vienna's famous ball season), he was popular and shone brilliantly in social gatherings.[7] It did not take long for this gregarious figure to find his social footing in New York.

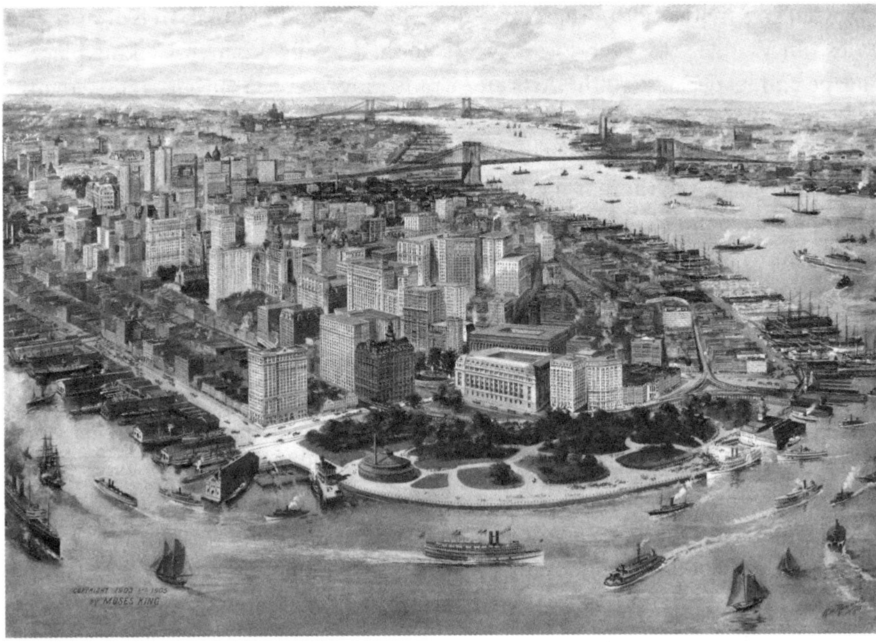

Fig. 3.1 R. W. Rummell, *New York City: The Business Center of the Borough of Manhattan*, engraving, 1903.

Ella arrived in New York eight months after Walter had sailed. She may have known Walter from Secessionist circles, or through family connections, and perhaps had even fallen in love with him before she made the journey. Or, she may have met him for the first time in New York, through the Austrian émigré social set. What Ella thought about his legal troubles, which prevented him from returning to Austria, remains a mystery. One thing we do know for certain: in the coming years, their lives would entangle.

Ella did not leave behind letters or diaries about her New York experiences, so we can only wonder about how an artist steeped in the imperial grandeur of turn-of-the-century Vienna perceived her new environs. On the day Ella's ship passed Lower Manhattan on its way to North German Lloyd's new piers in Hoboken, New Jersey, the passengers would have seen the jagged outline of New York's tall new buildings—a sight unlike any other in the world (fig. 3.1). Most large American corporations and banking institutions were headquartered in this city of three million people—the nation's capital of business and finance.[8] For many observers, Manhattan's skyscrapers symbolized New York's vast economic power and human energies, as well as American ambition more generally. American architects such as Louis Sullivan, seeking a modern, native form of building, saw in the skyscraper a novel type of beauty, born of rationalism, entrepreneurialism, and democracy. In 1896 Sullivan published "The Tall Office Building Artistically Considered" in *Lippincott's Magazine*, the widely read American monthly that boasted contributors such as Arthur Conan Doyle and Oscar Wilde. Sullivan's essay, in which he famously issued the building dictum "form follows function," resonated with progressive designers seeking to break free of historical styles.[9] In Vienna, however, Secessionists looked to developments taking place in Europe and, especially, to the Arts and Crafts movement in Britain, rather than to the United States, for design inspiration. Thus, Ella might have been little prepared for the shock of seeing this radical new urban form. Whether she found the skyscrapers ugly or beautiful, there is no doubt this encounter would have excited a young artist immersed in discussions about art and modernity.

Skyscrapers were not the only attention-grabbing construction projects underway in New York in 1903. When Ella disembarked from the SS *Kaiser Wilhelm der Grosse*, she headed to the Upper West Side, where she lived with Moritz and his family in a building facing Central Park.[10] Until the 1880s, this area of Manhattan had been considered a rough backwater best avoided by New York's elite. By the time Ella arrived, it had transformed into a thriving neighborhood of largely upper-middle-class professionals and businesspeople as well as a magnet for Gilded Age millionaires, whose palatial mansions sprouted up along Riverside Drive. Heterogeneity characterized the architecture of the Upper West Side, in terms of both style and type, and walking its streets provided lessons not only in the eclectic tastes of New Yorkers but also in the rampant speculative real estate market driving development. Some of the new buildings in Ella's neighborhood were striking, even dramatic. In 1903 the Ansonia, a massive residential hotel inspired by the grandeur of Parisian boulevards, began offering its wealthy tenants myriad luxuries and services, including filtered air cooled with frozen brine and a roof garden where orchestras played in the summer months. The building attracted thousands of visitors daily, who "passed though the arched entranceways of the hotel to gawk at the mahogany-paneled lobbies and watch the live seals barking in the lobby fountain."[11]

Just across Central Park, on the east side of town, less noisy splendors of a different sort awaited Ella. In December 1902, visitors streamed into the Metropolitan Museum of Art's new entrance on Fifth Avenue to marvel at the Great Hall, which recalled the ancient Roman baths. Designed by Richard Morris Hunt, the vast structure was one of the most resplendent of all monumental, highly ornamented buildings erected in this period. Incorporating historical, often classical, elements and motifs, these "Beaux-Arts" buildings (so-called after the École des Beaux-Arts in Paris, where many of the style's originators trained) emerged from the efforts of Gilded Age elites to give the city an architectural and civic grandeur comparable to Europe's finest cultural capitals—grandeur befitting their own status as citizens of the world.

The fast-paced architectural developments of the Gilded Age, however, were not exclusively luxurious or marble clad. Gilded Age New York was sharply divided by geography and class. Ella may have already sensed these disparities aboard the SS *Kaiser Wilhelm der Grosse*, where a limited number of first-class passengers enjoyed luxury cabins, grand staircases, lavish salons, and a covered promenade on the upper decks, while eight hundred steerage passengers crowded the lower decks.[12] Steerage passengers who settled in New York typically lived on the Lower East Side, then one of the most densely inhabited places on the planet. As the wave of immigrants surged, speculative developers erected purpose-built tenements to meet the housing demand. Concerns about crowded and unsanitary living conditions led to the 1901 New York Tenement House Act, which mandated provisions for water, lighting, ventilation, and indoor bathrooms—a substantial victory for housing reformers.

In the late nineteenth century, New York's housing reform movement had attracted a broad spectrum of advocates, including pioneering women architects. In 1895 Alice Hands and Mary Gannon became a sensation by "solving" the tenement problem with a model design that promised "to revolutionize the whole vile, wretched tenement system of New York." Gannon and Hands emphasized that theirs was not a theoretical effort, and their methods supported this. They planned to erect sixteen model buildings in New York and Jersey City with the help of an investor. As preparation, they spent a year living in a dilapidated tenement, experiencing for themselves the privations of their neighbors, so that their design would fully address future occupants' actual needs and desires. No evidence suggests that Ella knew of these architects in New York celebrated for their "women's wits" and moxie.[13] Yet she undoubtedly would have been aware of the broader issue housing posed, a topic covered extensively in the city's newspapers.

Such was the urban landscape that Ella Briggs encountered in New York in 1903: a vast laboratory of ideas and experiences for a young artist. Over the course of her long career, Ella mined various aspects of her American encounters for her projects, especially in housing. But newly arrived in New York, she understandably drew on her training at the Vienna School of Applied Arts in her efforts to launch an artistic career within a vastly different social and cultural milieu. As time would reveal, this was a smart strategy.

Ella was among the first artists—perhaps even *the* first—trained by Vienna Secessionists to arrive in New York, presenting a unique professional opportunity. To exploit it, she had to build connections to the city's cultural elite who might become her patrons—not an easy task for a twenty-three-year-old newcomer. She was aided in this effort by Moritz, whose work provided entry into prominent circles both in New York and beyond. For example, a 1902 story in the *Boston Daily Globe* described Moritz's visit on a quiet Sunday morning with the philanthropist and patron of the arts Isabella Stewart Gardner, who gave him a personal tour of her house and art collection.[14] Moritz's relationships with art patrons such as Gardner, as well as politicians, publishers, and other American elites, surely proved useful as Ella established her career.

At the same time that Ella pursued new professional networks in New York, she maintained her connection to her former art classmates and instructors through exhibitions, which helped publicize her work and identify it with the most radical design movements in Europe. Specifically, she participated in two important international exhibitions, both of which took place during her first year in New York: the Children's World's Fair in St. Petersburg (1903–1904), and the Louisiana Purchase Exposition in St. Louis (1904).

Her Imperial Highness the Grand Duchess Elizabeth Mavrikievna of Russia opened the Children's World's Fair in St. Petersburg on December 5, 1903. The fair received enthusiastic reviews from the international press including the *New York Times*, which noted, “This is the first international exposition devoted exclusively to the life of children ever held, and is unique in every respect.” Countries from around the world participated, with Austria having the fourth largest exhibit, behind Russia, France, and Germany. The exposition covered many different subjects related to children, such as newborn care, model nurseries, playground design, education, hygiene, and more.[15]

Swarmed by Austrian dignitaries and exhibitors, the Grand Duchess toured the Austrian section, which the *London Standard* described as “brilliant,” noting also that its “artistic decorations were universally admired.” The section included the category of the fine and applied arts in the life of the child, which encompassed artwork with children as subjects as well as the child’s aesthetic environment and education. Else Unger, a graduate of the Vienna School of Applied Arts, curated this category, which was prominently situated in the layout of the Austrian section. Among other applied artists and designers, Josef Hoffmann exhibited silver objects, Koloman Moser contributed glassware, and Ella Briggs showed ceramic work. As noted in an Austrian government report, exposition visitors lauded the fine and applied arts category and purchased many of the objects on display.[16]

As the St. Petersburg fair came to a close in February 1904, another, even greater showcase for the young artist loomed. For the last half of that year, Ella’s work was on exhibit at the Louisiana Purchase Exposition in St. Louis, which brought Austrian modern design to the world stage on an unprecedented scale. When the Austrian Pavilion opened on June 2, a month after the official start of the fair, its novel appearance attracted attention. For its design, the state architect Ludwig Baumann had drawn inspiration from the Secessionist group, though tempering its more radical tendencies. Even so, the pavilion struck visitors as starkly modern, especially when compared to the historicizing styles of the fair’s main buildings.[17]

Inside the pavilion and across from the main entrance, a large hall celebrated the achievements of Austrian and Bohemian arts and crafts schools. The Vienna School of Applied Arts had its own, striking room decorated by Hoffmann according to the latest Secessionist principles (fig. 3.2). The black-and-white space with its geometrically patterned carpet provided a spare but elegant framework for the display of the students’ objects. The room’s austere geometry also revealed the new direction taken by Secessionist designers, away from the curvilinear decorative forms associated with Jugendstil.

Reporters heralded the artistic merits of the Austrian pavilion. On the day the building opened, the *St. Louis Republic* called it an “architectural triumph.” The *Boston Evening Transcript* enthusiastically described the pavilion, inside and out, as “magnificent and audacious.” The exhibit of the arts and crafts schools garnered special praise. A writer for the Chicago-based art journal *Pen and Brush* remarked that “a new world” had been revealed to him when viewing the students’ work. Many reporters singled out the Austrian pavilion as one of the most beautiful and modern of the exposition. Yet it may have been their insistence on the pavilion’s “uniqueness,”

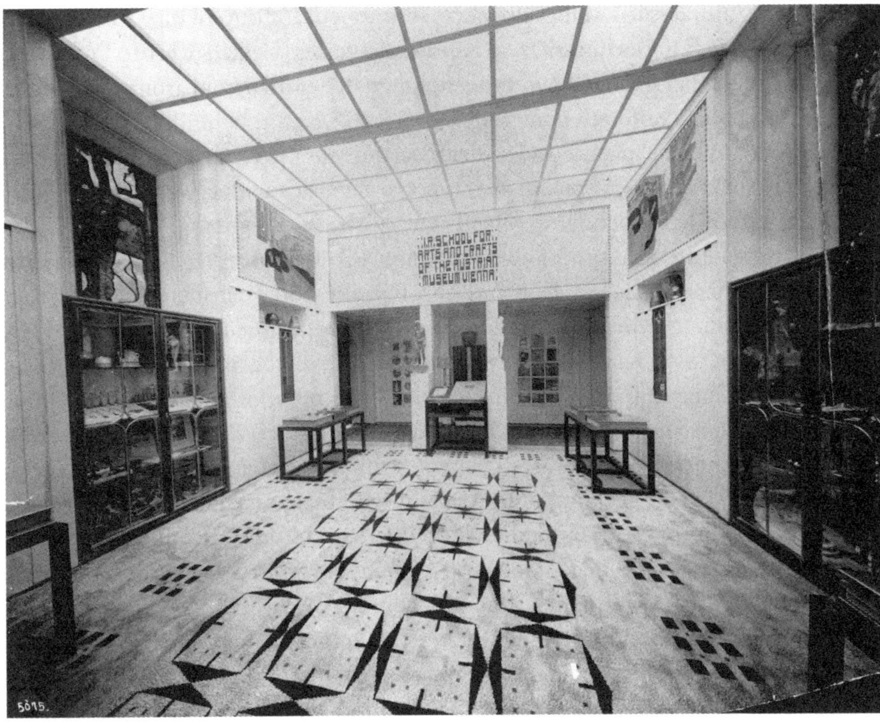

Fig. 3.2 Josef Hoffmann, display space for the Vienna School of Applied Arts in the Austrian Pavilion at the Louisiana Purchase Exposition in St. Louis, 1904.

along with references to a mysterious new Secession style, that piqued the interest of fairgoers most. Here, finally, was something different.[18]

In late fall the exposition's international jury awarded prizes to exhibitors, who received local and national news coverage. To the pleasure of Austrian government officials, its exhibitors received a disproportionately large share. The Vienna School of Applied Arts collectively won a grand prize, and many of its professors, including Hoffmann and Moser, also earned individual gold medals. Ella, too, received good news: she was awarded a bronze medal for work exhibited in the Austrian Pavilion. Her artwork had also appeared elsewhere in the fair, in the East Pavilion of the Art Palace, where Austria was assigned two galleries. There, a section had been set aside for instructors and students of Austria's arts and crafts schools as an extension of the exhibit in the Austrian Pavilion, thus allowing for more work to be shown. Ella was included with other pupils from the School of Applied Arts. In keeping with her interest in animal motifs, she exhibited a frog modeled in lead.[19]

Did Ella attend the St. Louis World's Fair? Over the course of its duration, from April to December, nearly 20 million people visited the largest world's fair ever organized at the time. Everyone, it seemed, was making plans to meet in St. Louis. Beyond the excitement of seeing the fair and her own work on display, there is a particular reason why Ella's attendance seems probable: Moritz. He covered the fair in his role as a cultural critic and political correspondent for the Viennese newspaper *Neue Freie Presse*.[20] If Ella did travel to St. Louis, it raises the question of whether the experience of the fair changed her understanding of her own work, having seen it in a broader and vastly different context.

Despite the public exposure and critical acclaim modern Austrian design received at the 1904 World's Fair, its immediate impact on American tastes was minimal. Nevertheless, a door had opened, especially for Austrian designers practicing in the United States. In the months following the fair, Ella continued to look for ways to reach an American audience, this time through the booming sector of American magazine publishing, which was predominantly headquartered in New York. In 1905 she published artwork in the February, March, and November issues of *The American Printer*, a trade journal for the printing industry (plate 5). Although the journal was worlds away from *Ver Sacrum*, the Secession's own organ, it nevertheless offered access to an important market—publishers, printers, lithographers, bookmakers, advertisers, and others seeking to stay current with business, technical, and artistic developments within the printing industry. The March issue introduced Ella to its readers with a short note that stated, "Miss Baumfeld, who is located in New York City, studied in Austria at the Imperial Art School. Her work shows originality, and is sure to attract attention." Whether Moritz, with his publishing connections, helped to facilitate introductions is unknown. Publishing in this journal was a shrewd choice on Ella's part and anticipates her later success in using the power of the magazine industry to reach a targeted audience.[21]

By the time the November issue of *The American Printer* appeared, Ella was back in Vienna and once again studying at the School of Applied Arts.[22] But she would not be away from New York for long. This chapter of her life, lasting less than two years, proved formative. When Ella sailed into New York Harbor on that chilly November day in 1903, she began a long love affair with the city and a lifelong pattern of seeking opportunities in new places.

4.
A Return to Design Education in Vienna, In and Out of School

Elana Shapira

Returning to Vienna from New York in 1905, Ella Briggs moved back in with her mother and reenrolled in the Kunstgewerbeschule (School of Applied Arts) to continue her studies.[1] Her commute was a fifteen-minute walk south through a bustling commercial and residential neighborhood, along streets lined with buildings swathed in neoclassical and neobaroque ornamentation. The historicist fever that had been raging among Viennese architects for decades made of Ella's walk a veritable survey course in eclectic historical designs. The teachers with whom she studied vehemently opposed such backward-looking design tendencies, and perhaps Ella pondered their opinions as she passed each building. Years later, when she became a practicing architect herself, she would prove to be more open to stylistic diversity than her Secessionist professors and modernist peers.

As she neared her destination, if she had time before class began, Ella might have been tempted to stop by the Austrian Museum of Art and Industry, located next door to the School of Applied Arts. In November 1905, the museum opened the *Ausstellung Österreichischer Hausindustrie und Volkskunst* (Austrian House Industry and Folk Art Exhibition) to the public. On display was the material culture of the myriad ethnic groups forming the Austro-Hungarian Empire, reinforcing the state's official ideology of pluralism in modernity. Walking the halls of the exhibition, design students such as Briggs would have encountered a wealth of objects, including Styrian folk art, Salzburg religious art, South Tyrolean woodcuts, Bohemian wooden toys, Galician basketry, Romanian embroidery, and Polish and Ruthenian folk costumes. Among the long list of exhibitors were many female designers.[2] The following year, the museum building itself would have become an object of curiosity for budding design students. Between 1906 and 1909, it underwent an expansion by the architect Ludwig Baumann—the designer of the much discussed 1904 Austrian pavilion in St. Louis, where Ella's student projects had been exhibited. Baumann's work was known for its fashionable mix of Baroque and Jugendstil elements.

At school Briggs continued to learn from her former teacher, Koloman Moser.[3] Although how familiar she was with him remains unclear, Briggs may have seen Moser as a mentor of sorts. Ideological tensions affecting the school's faculty around this time may have led her to identify more closely with him, at least philosophically. In June 1905 these tensions, reported on by journalists, led to a definitive split among the artists of the Secession. According to art critic Berta Zuckerkandl, the conflict between the painter Josef Engelhart's group, identified as the *Stilisten* (stylists), and Gustav Klimt's group, the *Raumkünstler* (spatial artists), placed those who demanded the promotion of purely fine art at odds with those who ascribed equal status to the fine and applied arts.[4] Moser and other prominent artists, including the architect Josef Hoffmann, left the Secession as a result of their colleagues' rejection of their *Raumkunst* ideology. As students in a small school, Briggs and her peers certainly would have talked about the artistic battles being waged by their teachers and likely developed their own loyalties. That Moser's alignment with the *Raumkünstler* and his definitive break with the *Stilisten* may have had a lasting impact on Ella may be inferred by her subsequent pursuit of interior design and architectural space as integrated artistic ensembles—the very definition of *Raumkunst.*

Moser's life at this time was turbulent not only professionally but also personally. He experienced religious discrimination when he converted to Protestantism (from Catholicism) for his marriage in 1905.[5] At the time he was working on a prestigious commission with the leading architect Otto Wagner: the Catholic Church at Steinhof, in Vienna's fourteenth district. Although Moser's designs for a series of stained glass windows were completed and installed in the church, he was unable to realize his artistic concept for the altarpiece because a Catholic Church representative overseeing the project objected to his conversion.[6] Witnessing her mentor's professional struggles, Briggs would have received an early lesson in the destructive power of religious prejudice and strict ideological boundaries. This may have strengthened the pragmatic approach she would later develop as a practitioner.

In this period of homegrown discord, the growing recognition of Secessionist design abroad must have been both balm and inspiration to the school's students, including Ella. In the spring of 1906, local newspapers reported on the enthusiastic reception of the Imperial Royal Austrian Exhibition held at London's Earl's Court, which promoted Austrian arts and tourism. British critics hailed the Secessionist-style designs included in the exhibition as representing the best of Austrian art and as an inspiration to the design world internationally.[7] Reading the glowing reviews and thinking back to her earlier participation in exhibitions of Austrian design in St. Louis and St. Petersburg, Briggs must have been more convinced than ever that she could use her schooling to her advantage abroad.

At home, whatever tensions existed within the various factions of Vienna's contemporary art scene, the city itself offered Briggs manifold opportunities to enrich her education. Did Ella attend the immensely popular *Allgemeine Hygienische Ausstellung* (General Hygienic Exhibition) that opened in May 1906 inside the Prater's large exhibition hall? If so, it may have influenced the careful attention she would later devote in her architectural work to the proper installation of domestic hygienic facilities. The exhibition sought to educate visitors on how to maintain hygienic conditions within the home, as well as in schools, hospitals, and other urban infrastructure.[8] They learned about the various tools and methods available to promote good hygiene and the latest contemporary scientific developments relating to general healthcare. Most striking were the modernist interiors of children's rooms, kitchens, and other spaces.[9] In the autumn of 1906, Ella may have attended the *Möbelausstellung* (Furniture Exhibition) hosted by the Klub der Industriellen für Wohnungseinrichtung (Home Furnishing Manufacturers Association) and cocurated by Hoffmann and

Wagner, which displayed the latest interior design trends.[10] Exhibitions such as these would have exposed Briggs to a broad range of developments happening in various design fields and perhaps planted seeds for her future professional growth.

At this point in her career, however, Briggs continued to work and publish in a graphic format. In 1906 Briggs's illustration of children in a horse-drawn sleigh was published in the journal *Die Woche für die Deutsche Jugend* (German Weekly for German Youth) (plate 6). A Christmas poem by German poet Anna Ritter titled "Schlittenfahrt" (Sleighride) accompanied the image. It is unclear whether Briggs created the picture specifically for the poem or if it was chosen separately by the editor. In style, the image is similar to the illustration of a girl Briggs published the previous year in *The American Printer* (see plate 5). Perhaps Briggs had created both images depicting children a few years earlier, in hopes that they would be included in the 1903 Children's World's Fair in St. Petersburg; or it is possible she created them as part of her student work, as a *Bilderbuch* (picture book). The "naive" style of both illustrations is reminiscent of a drawing from a similar picture book by Alice Korvin-Müller, a student at the School of Applied Arts, exhibited in the 1901 Austrian Museum of Art and Industry exhibition.[11] Regardless of exactly why and when "Schlittenfahrt" was created by Briggs, it is plausible that her cousin Siegfried Bryk, active in Berlin's publishing world, encouraged her to send her work to various German journals.

It is interesting to note that the mood of Ritter's poem, which ends with the hopeful words "Santa Claus is coming tomorrow," is somewhat at odds with Briggs's illustration. Seated side by side in the sleigh are a young girl in a red hat with long brown hair and a boy in a grey cap. The boy holds the reins and drives the sleigh toward an unseen destination. With the snow falling and the low winter light, the mood is quiet, even melancholic. Rather than evoke the joyous arrival of Santa Claus, the image elicits a feeling of suspension, similar to that characterizing Briggs's seated girl of 1905. One is tempted to read into this image the lingering influence of the artist's own past, when as a girl of twelve her childhood was interrupted by the loss of her father. Or perhaps this image looks forward, to a time when, as a young woman of twenty-seven, Ella would bid farewell to childhood by returning to New York and marrying the Viennese lawyer Walter Briggs. We cannot know for sure.

Section II.
INTERIOR DESIGN IN NEW YORK AND VIENNA, AND A TURN TO ARCHITECTURE, 1907–1920

5. A Viennese Designer Takes Manhattan

Despina Stratigakos

On April 9, 1907, Ella Briggs returned to New York, sailing on the newly built SS *Kaiserin Auguste Victoria*. It was a difficult voyage, with stormy weather that sent waves breaking over the ship's highest decks and made almost all of the passengers seasick. Slushy, pelting rain reduced visibility as the ship arrived in New York Harbor, causing the great steamship to nearly ram a crowded ferryboat, averting disaster only at the last moment. Other mayhem occurred on board: a fistfight broke out among gamblers in the first-class smoking room over a lost wager, and a blind concert singer who had entertained the first-class passengers claimed that someone had stolen her diamond. New York police greeted the ship as she docked, due to the reported presence of a kidnapper onboard.[1]

This was not the reception first-class passengers were accustomed to receiving. First-class passengers such as Ella were typically given a cursory inspection by a US immigration officer who boarded the ship. The passenger manifest gives no hint of any unruliness, or of the presence of thieves or kidnappers; it contains only routine entries. Under the category of "calling or occupation," the officer who processed the first-class passengers listed the men's professions, while identifying female passengers as "wife" or "daughter." In some cases, the officer jotted "none" when describing a woman's calling or occupation, or—as in Ella's case—simply made a nullifying slash. As she had done in 1903, Ella indicated that she would live with her brother Moritz.[2] Within months of her arrival in New York, however, much of what the officer had written about Ella would change profoundly.

On Friday, September 7, 1907, the twenty-seven-year-old Ella Baumfeld married the forty-two-year-old Walter Briggs. A short notice in the *New York Times* mentioned that the couple had wed at their home in Mount Vernon, a small city about thirty minutes north of Manhattan by train. Westchester County communities such as Mount Vernon were developing rapidly during this period, as New York City residents sought suburban homes and train companies promised commuters better and faster lines.[3] In contrast to wealthy settlements such as Larchmont and Briarcliff Manor, Mount Vernon offered "inexpensive dwellings that provide homes for people of modest means who wish to get away from the flats and tenements of Manhattan."[4] Ten years hence, Ella would benefit directly from the professional opportunities created by this growing desire to leave the city, as her American writings and building commissions of the 1920s would focus on suburban living.

The couple's decision to hold their marriage ceremony in their modest residence suggests that it was a small affair, despite the groom's growing social visibility. Within a few years of arriving in New York in 1903, and despite the scandal he had left behind in Vienna, Walter began making a name for himself among the city's Austrian elite.

On February 10, 1907, the Austrian Society of New York hosted a European-style cabaret at the Hotel Astor, introducing New Yorkers to this new form of entertainment. Moritz Baumfeld was the master of ceremonies, and Walter Briggs composed the prologue, sung by the tenor Andreas Dippel, a former member of the Vienna Court Opera and frequent performer with the New York Metropolitan Opera. The audience included Austrian dignitaries such as Baron Hengelmüller von Hengervár, the Austro-Hungarian ambassador to the United States.[5]

The cabaret event reveals that the future brothers-in-law Walter and Moritz had a preexisting relationship, but its nature and origins are unclear. They may have known each other in Vienna, or met later as émigrés. In April 1907, just as Ella was returning to the United States, Moritz dramatically switched careers to become director of New York's German-language Irving Place Theater, located near Union Square. Perhaps this prompted a closer friendship between Moritz and Walter, who was a theater devotee.[6] It certainly created a new professional bond between Moritz and Ella, as it launched her career as an interior designer.

By the late nineteenth century, New York was the third-largest German-speaking city in the world, surpassed only by Berlin and Vienna. German-language newspapers and publications, societies and clubs, eateries, shops, and cultural institutions catered to the German community. When Moritz took over as director of Irving Place Theater, he committed in the short term to bringing the finest German actors and productions to New York. But he also expressed a grander ambition: to open a new playhouse uptown to provide the facilities needed to raise the standards of German theater in New York beyond what was possible at Irving Place. He wanted the new theater to rank among the nation's best—in terms not only of performance but also of architectural beauty. True to his word, the new German Theater opened in October 1908, in a building on Madison Avenue at 59th Street, with Moritz as the inaugural director.[7]

Critics lauded the design of the German Theater. One emphasized its importance for American interior decorators, who could now experience "a complete scheme of modern German decoration."[8] This impression of a *Gesamtkunstwerk*, or total work of art that integrated numerous art forms, had been achieved through the ingenious reuse of a preexisting structure. Since 1886 the building had served a variety of entertainment purposes. Originally constructed as a cyclorama, it was converted in 1890 into the Lenox Lyceum, a music hall with a round auditorium reflecting the building's original purpose.[9] The Lenox Lyceum interior was decorated in an early Italian Renaissance style, with vivid reds and abundant gold-leaf ornamentation.[10] In March 1908, Moritz announced the complete renovation of the building's interior. The young Brooklyn architect Eugene Schoen, who shared a practice with Swedish-born architect Axel Hedman, prepared the plans. Henry Beaumont Herts, of the New York architectural firm Herts and Tallant celebrated for its New York theater designs, served as consulting architect.[11] Herts and Hugh Tallant had trained in Paris and brought Beaux-Arts and Art Nouveau influences to their New York projects.[12] Czech artist Alphonse Mucha directed the artistic decoration of the renovated interior, with a focus on the auditorium. Ella Briggs designed a series of rooms adjacent to the performance space.

Despite the various artistic hands at work on the design, a strong Viennese current ran through it. Schoen was born in New York in 1880 to Jewish Hungarian parents and studied architecture at Columbia University. In 1904, two years after his graduation, he took a combined honeymoon and study tour to Europe, ending in Vienna. There he met Otto Wagner, who introduced him to Josef Hoffmann and Mucha.[13] Mucha, who trained and lived in Paris, earned fame in the 1890s for his Art Nouveau poster designs for stage actress Sarah Bernhardt. He subsequently became a founding member of the Vienna Secession, his work featured in the group's exhibitions and publications. His impact on Secessionist artists—especially Koloman Moser—was considerable, although their styles diverged after the turn of the century when Viennese artists moved away from the ornate curvilinearity of Mucha's Art Nouveau style. In 1904 Mucha sailed to New York to find new artistic opportunities and patrons, renting "a big, sunny studio" near Central Park; he would live in the United States off and on until 1910, staying for extended periods of time.[14] As a Secessionist-trained artist and contributor to Viennese modern art movements, Briggs shared Mucha's and Schoen's direct ties to the Vienna Secession. Briggs and Mucha—the two principal decorators—were intimately involved with the movement. The new German Theater on Madison Avenue may not have been a Secessionist space per se, but it was arguably the closest thing to one then existing in New York.

A large and glittering crowd attended the theater's opening night, October 1, 1908. The *New York Times* theater critic admired the pleasant restfulness of the theater's design (figs. 5.1–5.2). Cantilevered balconies eliminated the need for columns, producing straight sightlines—a hallmark of the new theater design introduced to New York by Herts and Tallant. Critics also lauded safety innovations, such as the wide promenades that enabled the easy movement of audience members, in addition to the respite and delight provided by the ladies' parlors and gentlemen's smoking rooms (fig. 5.3; and see figs. 5.7–5.10). The architects developed these features through the thoughtful reuse of the cavernous space provided by the former music hall. They had ample room to experiment with a theater design model that afforded new levels of comfort, safety, and enjoyment. Architectural critics emphasized that the project represented an advance in theater typology.[15]

In keeping with Secessionist principles, the designers rejected historicizing ornamentation. They hung textiles woven in neutral colors and stenciled with abstract patterns on the wall surfaces of the auditorium, emphasizing their flatness. Simple planar moldings framed the wall expanses. Relocating the proscenium boxes behind the orchestra seats further accentuated the flat surfaces and created the opportunity for a decorative scheme that "gives a dignity and grandeur not usually possible in theatre interiors."[16] The dominant colors were "neutral yellows and écru, with counter tones in gray, green and vermillion, with here and there a suspicion of blue and gold, which serves as a foil to the general color schemes employed and echoes the predominating colors of the figure decoration."[17] The novel, harmonious color scheme impressed the

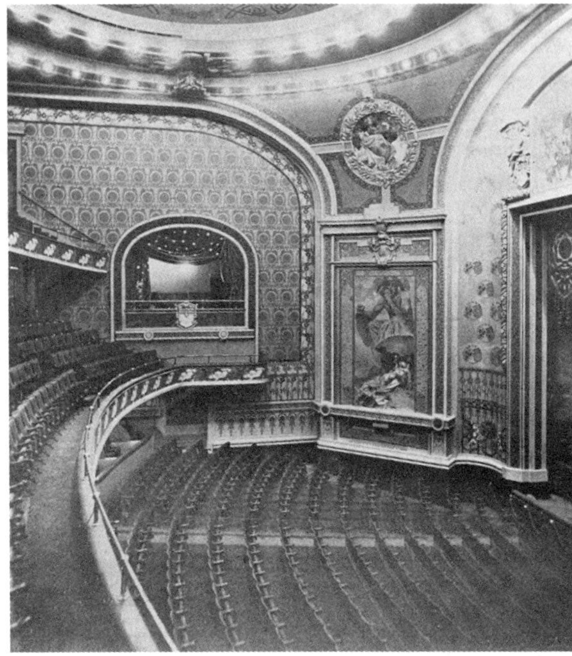

Fig. 5.1 (right) View across the auditorium of the German Theater, New York, facing the arched opening of a side promenade and the paintings of *Tragedy* and *German Girl* (above) beside the proscenium.

Fig. 5.2 (opposite) View of the German Theater galleries from the stage, with the boxes at the back of the orchestra seats.

critics. "Thank God," a German writer exclaimed, that the gold and red typical of theaters (including the former Lenox Lyceum) were nowhere to be found.[18]

Rather than serving as a distraction, the auditorium's decorative scheme heightened the focus on the stage. "The interior decoration, as a whole," noted a critic, "forms a great frame for the stage picture. This frame itself is again a series of framed pictures." Above and to the sides of the proscenium opening, Mucha arranged five large paintings he had created especially for the theater. He placed two canvases, each measuring twelve by twenty-four feet, on either side: *Tragedy* (to the left, when facing the stage) and *Comedy* (to the right, fig. 5.4; and fig. 5.5 for comparison). Above them he positioned medallions: *The German Girl* (left) and *The American Girl* (right). *The Quest for Beauty* hung directly above the proscenium arch. These paintings not only formed a second artistic frame for the stage but also functioned as the climax of the auditorium's decorative story. Stated differently, "the entire scheme of color and design acts as a background for the mural paintings."[19]

To awed critics, the German Theater elevated interior design to an art form and distinguished it from the gilt- and plaster-filled theaters of the day. Henry W. Frohne, associate editor of *Architectural Record*, wrote that "One misses with extreme pleasure the prolific Rococo plaster ornament and the lurid painty expressions of the contractor-decorator. This individual, whose efforts are so plentiful in American buildings and especially in our theater auditoriums, clearly had nothing to do with designing the exceptional decorative treatment of this room. Here we have the hand of the artist, and not less his cooperation with the architect."[20] That collaboration reached its luxurious

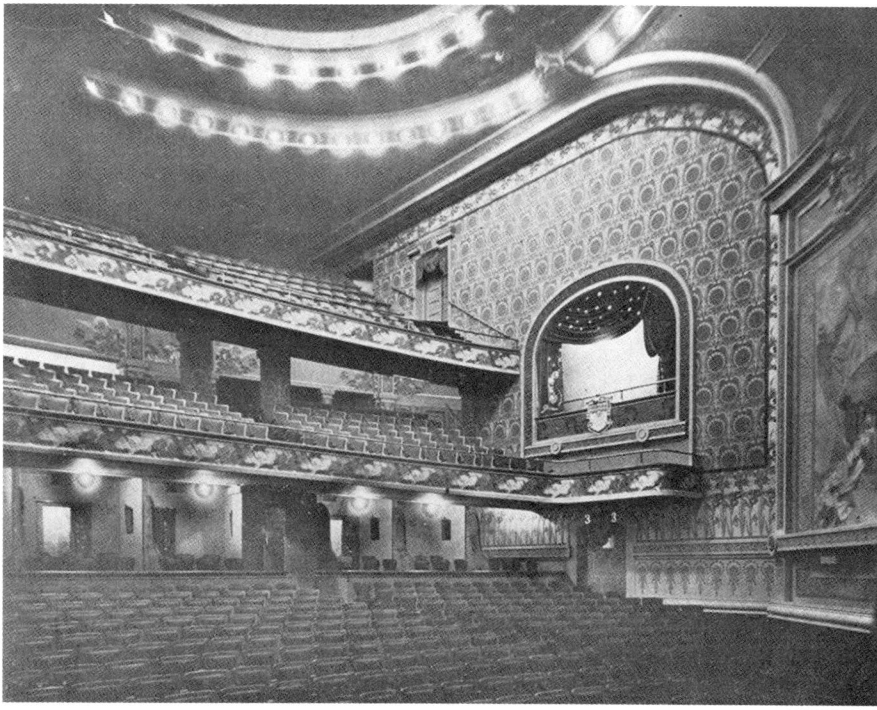

apogee in the "rusty yellow silk velvet" stage curtain, which spanned forty-five feet and was decorated with hand-colored satin appliqué. Frohne hailed the curtain, executed under Mucha's direction by his female students at the New York School of Applied Design for Women, as "a remarkable piece of work" (fig. 5.6).[21]

The rooms designed by Ella Briggs impressed critics then, as they have more recent writers. Each of the German Theater's three tiers included a smoking room for men (to the left of the auditorium, when facing the stage) and a ladies' parlor (to the right). Briggs decorated these six rooms, giving each a unique look and employing furnishings in some cases of her own making (figs. 5.7–5.10). She also designed a dining room (fig. 5.11). The rooms echoed the theater's broader color schemes while also remaining distinct. A contemporary description published in *The Master Painter*, an American magazine for painters and decorators, makes clear the influence of modern Viennese and British design trends:

> One of the parlors is to be all in pale grays, with white woodwork, while the materials and curtains will be in soft purple. The stenciled designs for the wall spaces are done in purple and silver white, while touches of orange in the curtain embroideries and a green mantel designed by Mrs. Briggs furnish the note of contrast.
>
> Another dressing room is all in dull yellow, with a dull blue and white decoration of the walls, gray woodwork and blue materials. A touch of deeper orange in stained glass windows and in the mirror frames gives the contrasting note.

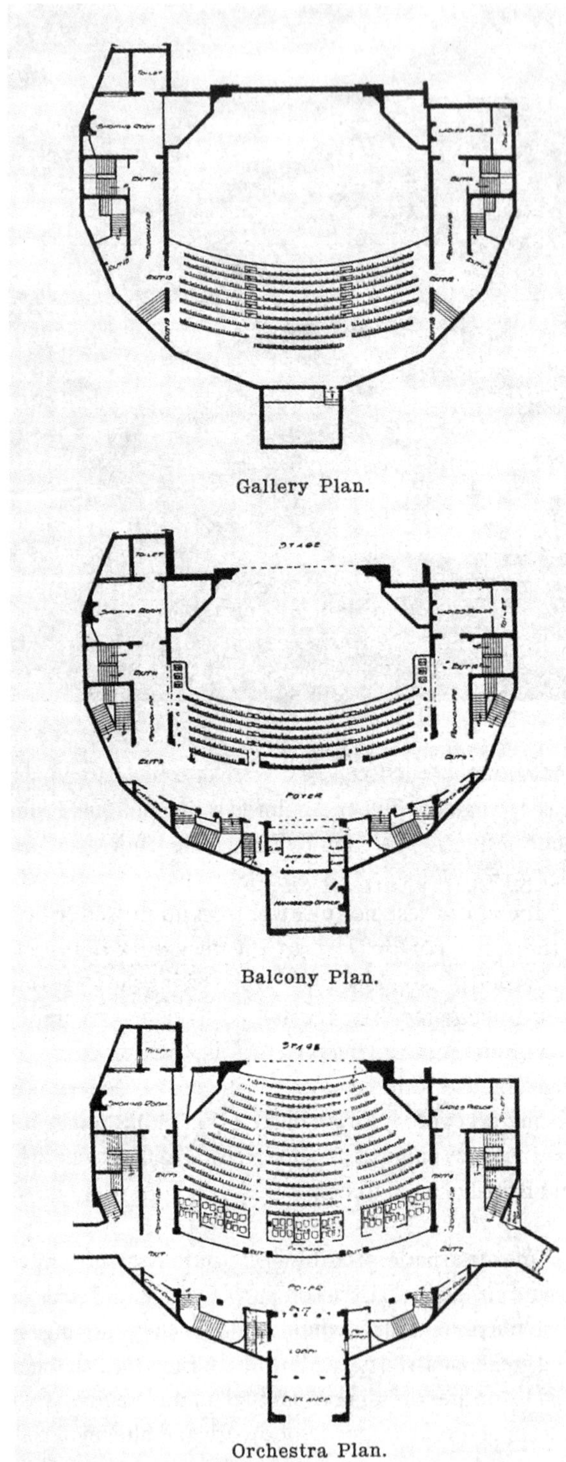

Fig. 5.3 German Theater, plans, c. 1908.

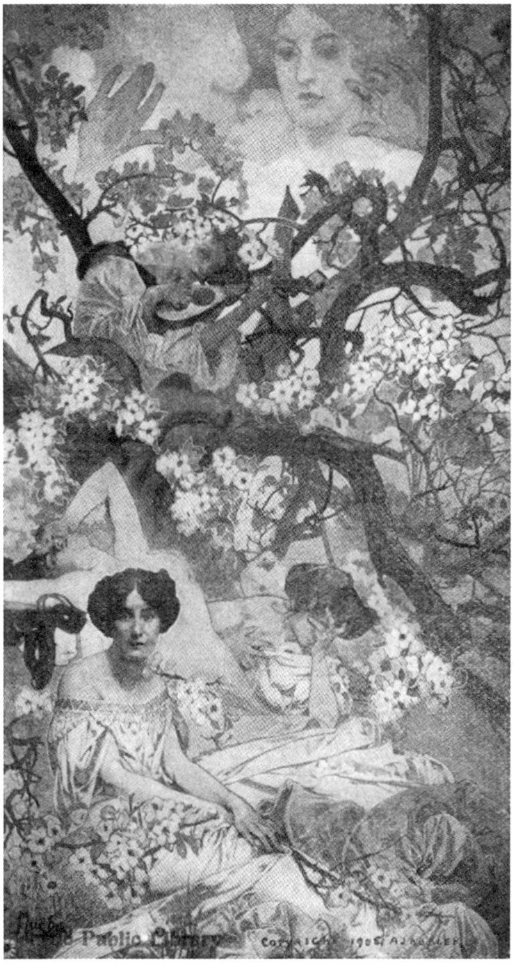

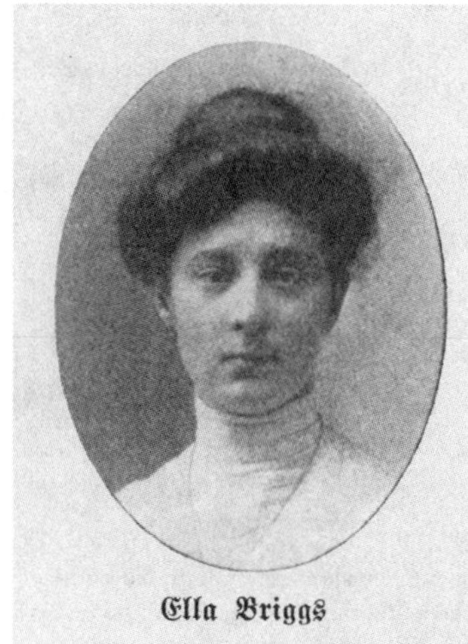

Fig. 5.4 (left) Alphonse Mucha, *Comedy*, 1908, originally hung in the German Theater (lost).

Fig. 5.5 (above) Portrait of Ella Briggs, 1908.

> The smoking rooms will be wainscoted in a Cuban wood, hitherto unknown in this country, which is of a natural grayish green. Tiles set in this wainscoting will make vivid color splashes. Above are stenciled frescoes, and still above the wall is covered by silver gray Japanese matting. Blue materials will be used in one smoking room, while another will be in rich shades of brown, with brown mantel and stencils. All the silks used will be printed by hand and entirely individual.[22]

The Austrian Museum of Art and Industry's journal *Kunst und Kunsthandwerk* (Art and Craft), an important organ for modern design, published images of a ladies' parlor, smoking room, and dining room of the German Theater. The accompanying text, by Austrian American writer and painter Klara Ruge, praised Briggs's designs for the theater as "a great success." Ruge described the exquisite color harmonies of the rooms and the use of textiles, as well as the natural motifs favored by Briggs in her work, including here butterflies, birds, and flowers.[23]

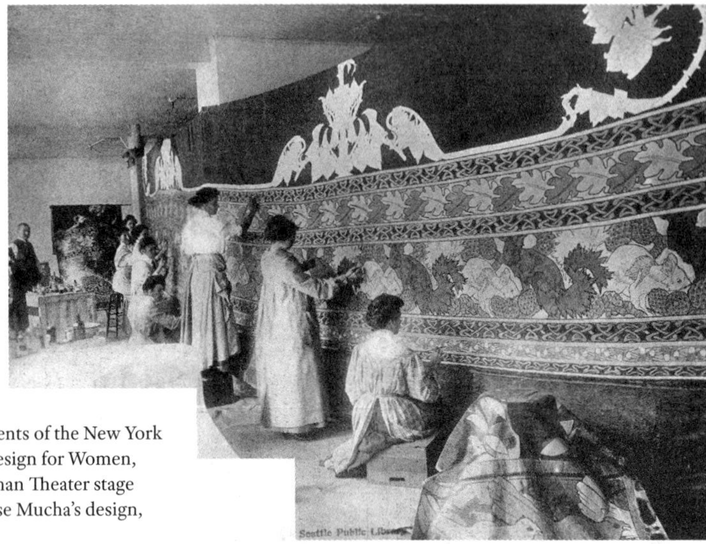

Fig. 5.6 Female students of the New York School of Applied Design for Women, working on the German Theater stage curtain after Alphonse Mucha's design, 1908.

Robert A. M. Stern, in his 1983 coauthored book *New York 1900*, praised the German Theater, including the ladies' parlors. He wrote, "The ladies' parlors were extraordinarily sophisticated and virtually unique in New York as examples of the influence of the Glasgow School of Art Nouveau. Details such as bare electric light bulbs hanging from wire hoops, stencil patterns on the walls and curtains, segmental arches cut in thin planes of white-painted wood, and exposed tile surrounding the fireplace laid in a stack bond pattern were all integrated with custom-designed furniture." Stern credited these rooms to Herts and Tallant and does not seem to have been aware of Briggs, thus also missing the Viennese influence, perhaps because the 1908 sources he used—Frohne's article in *Architectural Record* and a review published in *Architects' and Builders' Magazine*—also did not mention Briggs.[24] It must have frustrated Briggs to see her work misattributed, but other contemporary publications gave her credit and praised her for venturing into new professional realms for women. "Mrs. Ella Briggs," wrote *Master Painter*, "is the first woman to have the decoration of a theater entrusted to her supervision."[25]

Although there can be no doubt that Ella's connection to Moritz helped her to secure a role in designing the German Theater's spaces, it appears that she had branched out into interior decoration before this time. Ruge, in her review, mentioned that Briggs not only designed furniture but also whole interiors—and, indeed, that this was her primary focus.[26] The sophistication of Briggs's German Theater designs also suggests both talent and experience. Unfortunately, no previous interior design projects are known, leaving us with scant information as to how she arrived at this point in her career.

Little is also known about Briggs's relationship to Mucha, although there are hints of its depths. By the time he arrived in New York, Mucha was a world-famous artist

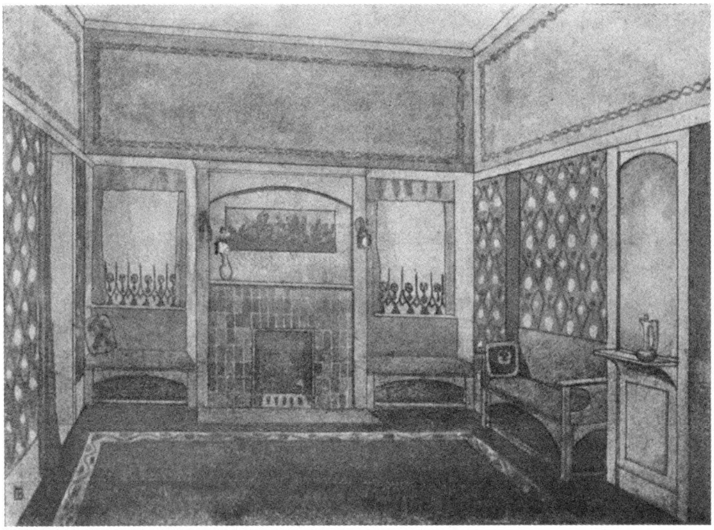

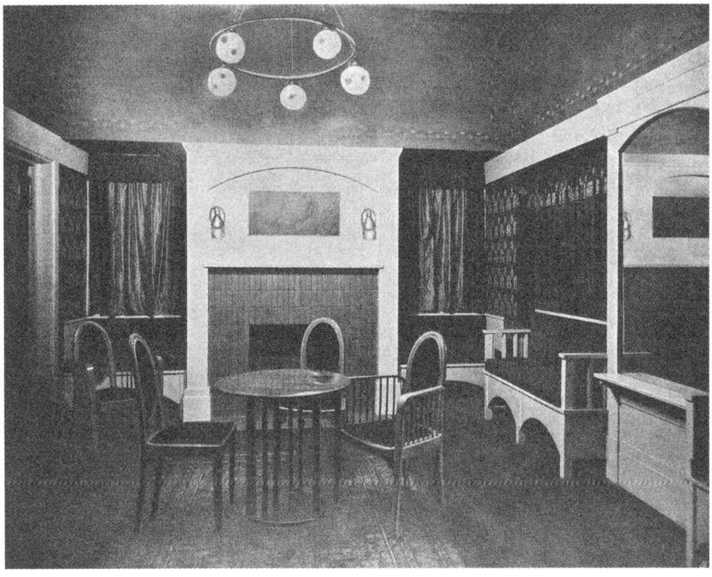

Fig. 5.7 (top) Ella Briggs, drawing of a ladies' parlor at the German Theater, 1908.

Fig. 5.8 (left) Ella Briggs, photograph of a ladies' parlor at the German Theater, 1908.

known primarily for his posters. His previous work in interior decoration and stage sets had been carried out in the ornate style of Art Nouveau and continued in this vein even after Viennese Secessionists turned toward simpler geometrical abstraction. The German Theater was Mucha's most significant American commission, and Mucha scholars attribute it to the intervention of Ella Briggs.[27]

Typically, when there is a difference in age and experience between artists, we expect the younger to be mentored by the elder. Undoubtedly, Briggs learned a great deal from

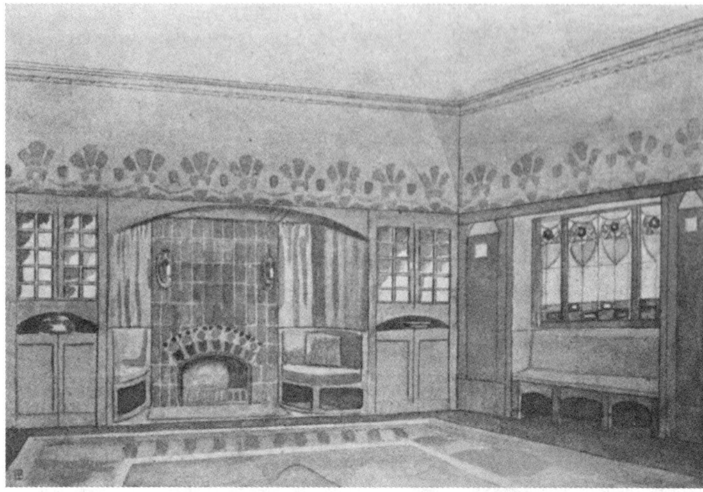

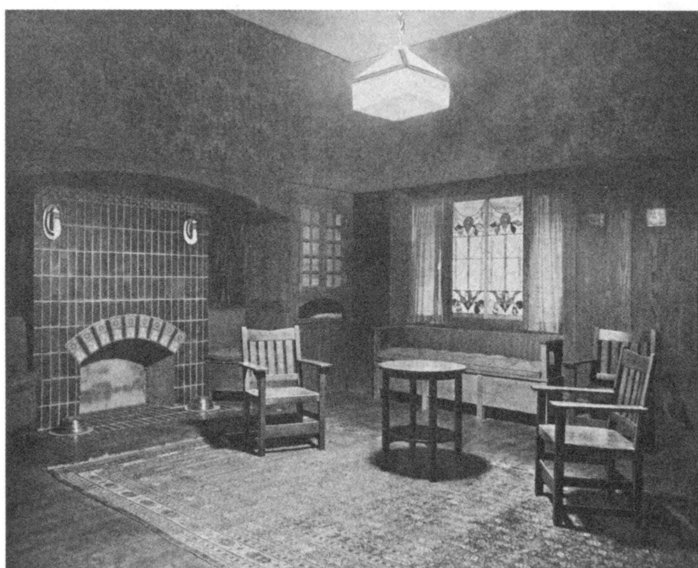

Fig. 5.9 (top) Ella Briggs, drawing of a smoking room at the German Theater, 1908.

Fig. 5.10 (right) Ella Briggs, photograph of a smoking room at the German Theater, 1908.

working with Mucha and Herts, two enormously successful, older artists. At the same time, we must also consider Briggs's influence on the artists with whom she collaborated, especially given how much the German Theater auditorium aligns with Viennese design trends, how different it is from Mucha's previous decorative work, and the fact that, according to Stern, it represents the most "distinguished and comprehensive interior" ever created by Herts and Tallant. Did Briggs push Mucha and Herts toward a Viennese modernist sensibility, perhaps with Schoen's assistance?

Remarkably, there is evidence—once visible for all to see—that Briggs acted as muse to the forty-eight-year-old Mucha. In *Comedy*, the large painting to the prosce-

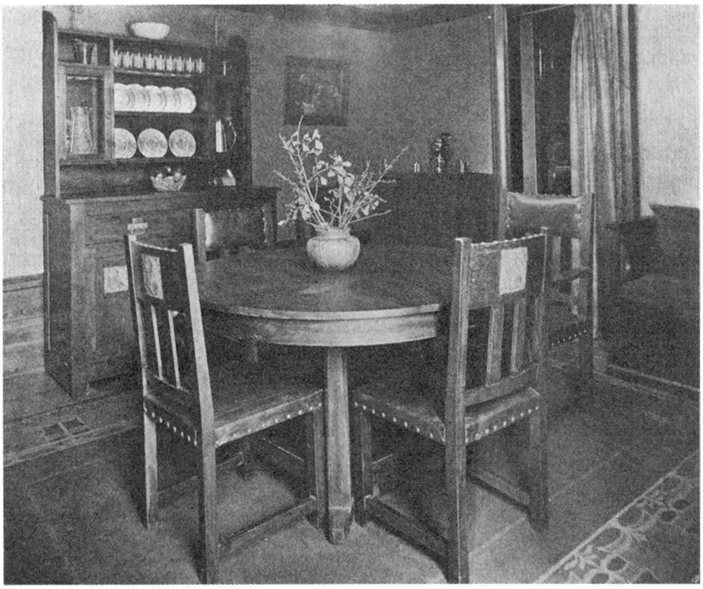

Fig. 5.11
Ella Briggs, dining room at the German Theater, 1908.

nium's right, a serene and self-possessed Ella Briggs looked out at the audience (see figs. 5.4 and 5.5). Briggs served as the model for the foreground figure, who sits under a tree. A young man perched on the branches above plays the lute. Two women below him appear overwhelmed by the music.[28] Compared to these emotional women, Briggs is a figure of stillness, communicating directly with the audience and drawing the viewer with her gaze into the allegorical world of the painting, which foreshadows the make-believe world of the theater. How Briggs came to model for Mucha is unknown, but it reveals that their relationship extended beyond the theater, to the artist's studio itself, and suggests an intense dedication to the project by two creative partners.

Indeed, it must have been a heady experience for Briggs to work on the German Theater, which represented her big brother's greatest dream and brought together an exceptional artistic team around a common, lofty goal—to create a modern space like no other in New York. Moritz Baumfeld met with Mucha to discuss the commission in the spring of 1908, which gave the artist a very short timeframe to complete the work before the theater's October 1 opening. In a letter he wrote to his sister Anna, Mucha described the intense period of work that followed in order to meet the deadline, and even then, only at the last moment.[29] As the accolades poured in on opening night, the entire artistic team must have felt euphoric to see their vision realized.

Sadly, the dream did not last for long. Although Moritz had obtained a twenty-one-year lease, the German Theater closed at the end of its first season. His original intention had been to absorb Irving Place into the new German Theater, but the merger did not occur, leaving two competing German-language theater companies. Despite the city's sizeable German-speaking population, there was insufficient demand to sustain both theaters. The German-language New York journal *Der deutsche*

Vorkämpfer (The German Pioneer), in an article about the new theater that highlighted Ella Briggs's contributions (see fig. 5.5), warned that if New York Germans did not rise to the occasion, the next season would see the German Theater taken over by an American troupe performing "idiotic" musical comedies. In fact, this is exactly what happened. The vaudeville agent William Morris obtained the building's lease and transformed the theater into the Plaza Music Hall. On opening night, April 19, 1909, the promenades were filled with flowers and the program featured top-tier vaudeville performers such as Saharet, an Australian dancer, and the comedic duo Rice and Cady. Soon after, Marcus Loew, a show business entrepreneur, took over the management and introduced moving pictures, combined with cheaper vaudeville entertainments. In 1919 theater manager Milton Gosdorfer converted the auditorium into a cinema, which brought the space back to the attention of New Yorkers. It became one of the city's most popular film venues for the next decade.[30]

Despite its various incarnations, much of the original theater design, including Mucha's paintings, remained intact and continued to impress New York audiences for more than two decades. A 1919 article described the theater as "splendid" and its twelve-piece orchestra as one of the finest in the country, claiming the Plaza "draws not only wealthy but cultured, prominent and refined people. Its mailing list reads like the social register, and contains names with which to conjure."[31] The building was ultimately demolished in 1929, but even after its physical disappearance, the German Theater's stunningly modern interiors retained their significance. In their influential design history book of 1948, *The Story of Modern Applied Art*, Rudolph Rosenthal and Helena Ratzka described the German Theater as "one of the first buildings free of any style influence," which they attributed to Eugene Schoen and his encounter with Otto Wagner and the Secession.[32] This claim of a lack of stylistic influences is not entirely accurate: Art Nouveau influences lingered in Mucha's and Herts's work, and Stern was right about the impact of the Glasgow School of Art on Briggs's (unacknowledged) designs as filtered through a Secessionist lens. But even if exaggerated, Rosenthal and Ratzka's claim indicates how the designs impressed contemporary critics as something new and fresh, shorn of old traditions. Rosenthal and Ratzka wrote their book as international modernism—which also insisted on its own stylelessness—was becoming a global phenomenon, and it is significant that they saw the German Theater interiors as a precedent. Their exclusion of Briggs from the narrative also demonstrates how female designers disappeared from modernist history.

Such erasures aside, Briggs's career received an enormous boost from the German Theater project. As Moritz watched his professional dreams evaporate, Ella launched onto New York's design scene. Another major commission quickly followed: in 1909 architectural journals published the news that Briggs had been selected to decorate the interiors of a newly erected ten-story building—the home of the New York Press Club (fig. 5.12). Founded in the nineteenth century, the New York Press Club was a social club for journalists. It hosted prominent speakers and provided its members with valuable resources, including meeting rooms, a library, and access to politicians and publishers. The new club building stood on the corner of William and Spruce streets, in the heart of Manhattan's newspaper district, and was designed by New York architect Ernest Greene.

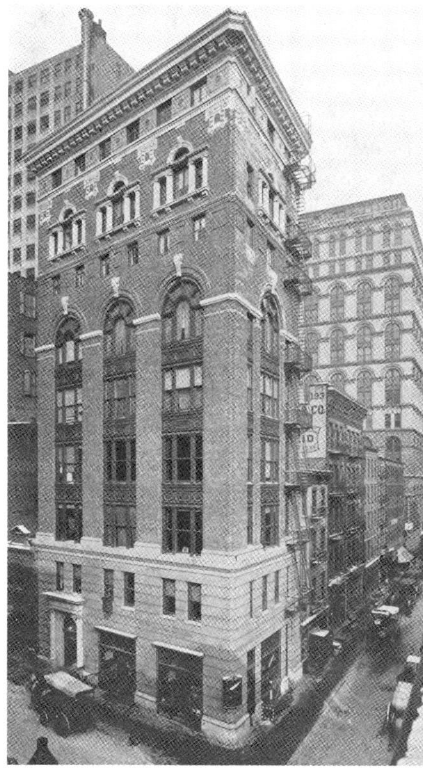

Fig. 5.12 Ernest Greene, New York Press Club, New York, 1909.

It is easy to assume that Moritz Baumfeld used the professional connections he developed as a journalist to help his sister obtain the commission. Or we might surmise that Walter Briggs used his influence to support her selection. In addition to his business activities, Walter worked as a correspondent for several European newspapers. He contributed to *Austria*, a weekly devoted to Austrian interests in America, eventually becoming its editor. He was also a member of the American Association of Foreign Language Newspapers.[33] It appears, however, that Ella found a winning strategy of her own to obtain the commission.

As a 1910 review in *The New York Architect* magazine notes, Briggs had competed with "several large Fifth Avenue firms" for the contract to decorate and furnish the club building. Intriguingly, she entered this competition with a partner: Minna Leigh Mercer. If Mercer is remembered today, it is as the mother of Lucy Mercer, the woman who had a long-standing affair with President Franklin D. Roosevelt. At the time, however, Minna Leigh Mercer was known as the blue-blooded Washington socialite who had entertained the nation's political elite at her home before depleting her inheritance, separating from her husband (Carroll Mercer), and moving to New York. A 1908 article about Mercer noted that the socialite who Queen Victoria had once called "the most beautiful American woman" had been compelled by "financial reverses" to become a decorator. "Her extensive travels and association with the nobility and wealth of Europe and America," the article continued, "have made her services of great value to a New York firm of decorators."[34] Like the unnamed firm of decorators, Ella Briggs also clearly realized the benefits of choosing a well-connected society member as her professional partner.

What Mercer, who had no formal training, contributed to the interior designs is unclear; the glowing reviews published once the club opened highlighted Briggs. *The New York Architect* informed readers that Briggs was "already known here as an interior decorator of original and modern ideas." Her influence was credited with delivering interiors "on entirely new lines," in keeping with "a modern applied art, which heretofore has not sufficiently been used in this country." At the same time, Briggs

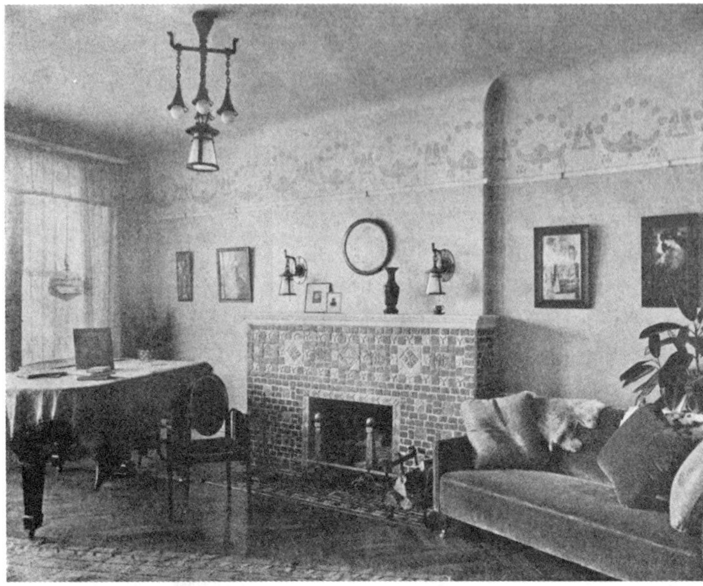

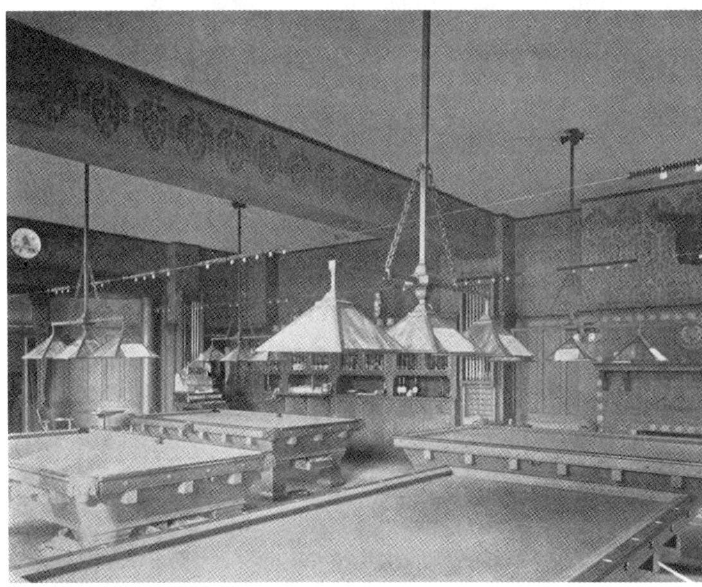

Fig. 5.13 (top) Ella Briggs and Minna Leigh Mercer, reading room in the New York Press Club, 1909. Note the stencil design by Briggs along the upper wall.

Fig. 5.14 (right) Ella Briggs and Minna Leigh Mercer, billiard room, New York Press Club, 1909.

was applauded for knowing her clientele: "In America since 1903, [she] has adapted the modern principles of color harmony, simplicity, truthfulness of applied material and comfort to the American taste." Unfortunately, readers were not given more details about that process or what, exactly, about modern principles required adjustment to American tastes.[35]

The decorated rooms varied in function according to club member needs; they included a high-ceilinged assembly room, boardroom, club office, library, reading

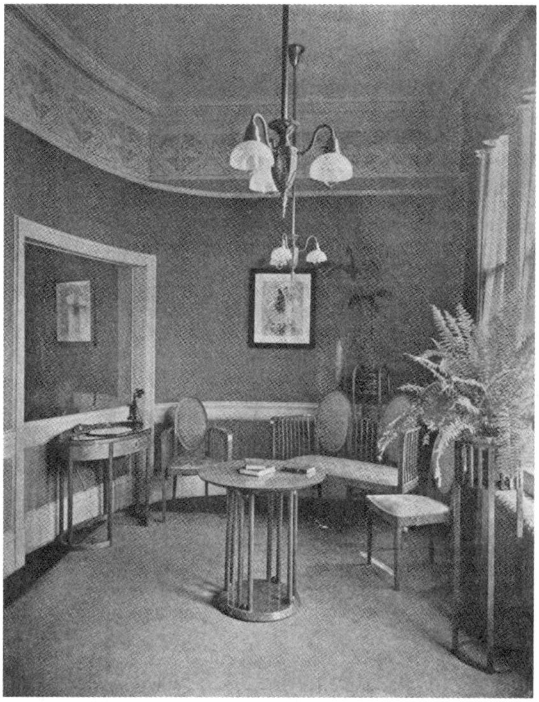

Fig. 5.15 Ella Briggs and Minna Leigh Mercer, ladies' reception room, New York Press Club, 1909.

room (fig. 5.13), billiard room (fig. 5.14), ladies' reception room (fig. 5.15), ladies' dining room, main dining room, guest bedrooms (for members), and service rooms. *The New York Architect* claimed that Briggs's "particular strength is in color schemes and in the designs for stenciled friezes and patterns for wall coverings, all of which in the New York Press Club are her originals. The skillful use of good textiles, tiles, etc., combined with tasteful and comfortable furniture produces an artistic and harmonious effect." An example of this approach, and one that suggests how Briggs adapted modern principles to American tastes, is the billiard room, which was on the fourth floor. A black-and-white photograph gives a misleadingly conservative impression of heavy furniture and dark, somber colors—the norm for these spaces of male sociability (see fig. 5.14). *The New York Architect* reviewer conveys a better sense of how the room would have struck contemporary observers: "Lively coloring prevails in the billiard room. The green of the billiard tables and of the wainscoting is sharply contrasted by red stencils in heraldic patterns and red curtains. The room has a remarkable fireplace in Moravian (Mercer) tiles." Briggs employed Japanese grass cloth (a woven fabric made from plant fibers) to cover the walls above the wainscoting, which she then stenciled in bold red designs. The Arts and Crafts fireplace tiles by Henry .Chapman Mercer added a further colorful, artistic note to the room. Briggs had created a billiard room recognizable from other male clubs but created along "new lines."[36]

Briggs's decorative schemes for the club created visual rhythms across different rooms. For example, the ladies' reception and dining rooms, which shared the fifth floor, displayed contrasting but complementary color schemes. The ladies' dining room achieved a "light and airy effect" with gray walls and a light green, white, and silver-gray combination for the wall stencils and the room's textiles, including the curtains decorated with bird and tree motifs. The adjacent ladies' reception room created a joyous mood with its yellows and deep violets, the furniture covered with "a beautiful silk in modern patterns, imported from Vienna" (see fig. 5.15). The excitement of the new interiors attracted more press attention than the architecture of the building itself, which may have annoyed the architect. In a 1910 article he published describing his architectural plans, Greene made clear that he was fully in charge: "The decorating and furnishing were done by Mr. [*sic*] Ella Briggs and Mrs. Carroll Mercer, under the architects' personal supervision."[37] One wonders, was the misgendering of Briggs intentional, meant as an insult to the designer's strong will or perceived lack of femininity?

From a professional standpoint, Ella was thriving. She joined the National Arts Club, which included prominent artists and patrons, and obtained a studio in its Gramercy Park clubhouse.[38] Her work for the German Theater and the New York Press Club had been universally acclaimed. Future commissions seemed assured. And yet not all was well in her life. Her marriage to Walter Briggs was unravelling; in the spring of 1910, less than three years after their wedding, Walter was living alone on the Upper West Side in a boarding house run by a young German widow with two daughters.[39]

In marrying Walter, a man who could not return to Austria without being arrested, Ella had made the decision to make New York her home. The presence of her beloved Moritz and her nieces and nephews must have cemented that feeling. She now had to confront the possibility that she would lose all of that. In late fall of 1910, Ella sailed away from New York, leaving behind a husband, a blossoming career, and growing social circles. Was this departure meant to be a temporary respite from a failing relationship or the stresses of work? Or was she truly abandoning New York and all she had built there? If so, where was home? Could she feel welcome again in Vienna, where the embarrassment of her husband's scandal awaited her? If we understand all that Ella sailed away from in New York, what, then, was she sailing toward?

6.
Paris: A Detour

Despina Stratigakos

Ella Briggs's destination as she left New York in 1910 was not Vienna, at least not at first. On November 10, she arrived in Paris, where she would spend the next half-year.[1] What was she doing there? One possible explanation appears in a *New York Tribune* article from 1924, which mentions that Briggs "studied architecture" in Paris.[2] Since architecture and other types of design were often conflated in this period, perhaps she was there to study interior or furniture design. Her successes in New York with the German Theater and the New York Press Club may have encouraged her to expand her skills. But if so, why choose the French capital over other possible design destinations?

Briggs's arrival on November 10 meant that she missed attending the famous 1910 Salon d'Automne by just two days. Held at the Grand Palais des Champs-Élysées, the exhibition outraged Parisian audiences with a new artistic movement that would become known as cubism, and that explored the representation of geometry, time, and space. Cubist artists' rejection of naturalistic conventions was attacked as a German-influenced attempt to destroy the elegance and harmony of French art. The German designers who participated in the show also caused a scandal with their designs for furniture and interiors. They belonged to the Deutscher Werkbund, a powerful alliance of artists, craftspeople, architects, and industrialists founded in Germany in 1907, which sought to strengthen the design quality of German goods and boost exports. Architect Frantz Jourdain had specifically invited Werkbund artists to participate, hoping to provoke a healthy debate about the state of French design, which lagged behind developments in other European countries. His aim was more than realized. French critics, already enflamed by growing nationalism, expressed their outrage at the German "invasion." But the threat posed by German designers and by the public's exposure to the high-quality work produced abroad galvanized French designers to strengthen their own traditions.[3] Briggs thus landed in Paris at a time of fervor and reassessment in the local design world, when her "German" identity may have been perceived as a professional asset—or hindrance—depending on the context.

Despite the months she spent in Paris, Briggs's subsequent work reveals no discernible influence of French Art Nouveau; instead, American and Austrian trends remain prominent. It might be that she did not find anything in Paris particularly striking, when compared to the American and Viennese innovations she already knew. Or perhaps she was not fully engaged in her milieu, her mind and heart elsewhere. Although we do not know the reason for Briggs's presence in Paris, it was quite possibly her failing marriage. Why else abandon her rising stardom in New York, if not to put her husband and their problems behind her? With the earnings from two large commissions, she would have had the financial independence that, perhaps for the first time in her life, allowed her to fully determine her own path.

Even though we may not perceive French influence in her post-Parisian designs, her French sojourn may nevertheless have left a powerful trace. In Paris, Briggs would have stood out, and not only because of her association with the Austrian and German design movements that had French critics up in arms: her gender would also have made her highly visible, as the decorative arts industry in France at that time was dominated almost entirely by men.[4] As a female interior designer, Briggs's success certainly was notable in any country. But in New York other women, such as Elsie de Wolfe, were making names for themselves, and in Vienna female designers had fostered their own growing and supportive community.[5] In Paris, Briggs would have felt "othered" in a way that likely surpassed anything she had ever experienced before. Could this be the reason that, upon her return to Vienna, she became more engaged with the world of Austrian feminism? For it is after she leaves Paris, her divorce from Walter Briggs pending, that she seems to have had a definitive feminist awakening.

At the end of April 1911, Briggs left the City of Light and returned to her family in Vienna. What this chapter in Paris meant to her we may never know, but there are signs that it left her a changed woman.

7.
Opening an Interior Design Firm in Vienna

Elana Shapira

After Ella Briggs returned to Vienna in the spring of 1911, she set out to conquer new frontiers. Her experience in Paris of seeing how the French anxiously defended their decorative arts traditions from Germanic influence apparently bolstered her belief in the desirability and strength of modern Austrian design. She now embarked on an astonishing new course.

That summer, Briggs sought the support of Eduard Leisching, director of the Austrian Museum of Art and Industry, and Adolf Vetter, director of the Austrian Office for the Promotion of the Trades, to open a retail outlet selling the best of Austrian arts and crafts in the United States on a commission basis. Briggs asked Leisching to recommend design companies that she might represent, and he provided her with names of manufacturers from whom the Austrian Museum of Art and Industry had recently purchased modernist work. Items such as the pottery of Gmundner Keramik, silverware by Eduard Friedmann, and Jugendstil-decorated tablecloths and upholstery by Herrburger and Rhomberg would be offered for sale through her design store in New York.[1]

It is possible that the idea of opening an American sales outlet for Austrian design predated Briggs's Paris sojourn, germinating while she was in New York executing commissions for the German Theater and New York Press Club. Briggs incorporated Austrian furniture in these projects and perhaps wished that she had access to a larger selection of Austrian goods. The critical success of these projects may also have encouraged Briggs to believe that American interior decorators and consumers would be receptive to such an enterprise. Whereas individual Austrian manufacturers such as Jacob & Josef Kohn maintained their own shops in New York, the idea to open a retail outlet representing several furniture and design companies was novel.[2] Briggs saw this as an opportunity to corner a developing market.

In a second letter to Leisching, written two weeks after her first, Briggs updated the museum director on the progress of her plan, and enclosed a copy of the application she had made to Adolf Vetter. Since 1910, Vetter had been director of the national Office for the Promotion of the Trades, which offered small businesses various types of support to help them survive in the face of increasing industrialization. According to Briggs, Vetter said he intended to pass her proposal on "to his Ministry of Labor advising that the Office for the Promotion of the Trades would be prepared to grant part of the necessary amount, provided the Ministry of Commerce would contribute the greater share." Briggs remarked that she also had had success obtaining agreements with new design firms, concluding, "the readiness with which almost all the men and women accepted my proposal seems to me to be proof that the planned enterprise would indeed meet an existing need."[3]

When the Ministry of Commerce asked Briggs to provide a reference to support her subvention request, she directed them to Leisching. At the end of October, Leisching received a letter from the Ministry of Commerce asking him to give his assessment of Briggs's "personal suitability" to opening a design retail store and wholesale agency in New York, stating, "The lady makes a very good impression and reveals a great selection in the arts and crafts firms she has taken on." The Ministry also suggested, "Perhaps you could also comment in some way on the prospects or necessity of such a venture."[4] How Leisching responded to the Ministry's inquiry we do not know.

In hindsight, we can see how truly pathbreaking Briggs's plan was. A year later, the Austrian Werkbund would be founded (along lines similar to its German predecessor) and her idea of promoting Austrian design abroad would be taken up and explored by others.[5] In 1922, the Wiener Werkstätte (Vienna Workshops), a design cooperative founded by Josef Hoffmann and Koloman Moser in 1903, would extend the reach of Austrian design by opening up its own store in New York City.[6] That her application predated these endeavors underscores the audacity of Briggs's vision, as well as her desire to serve as an international player in promoting the transatlantic flow of modernist design ideas.

Perhaps fearing she would be branded a materialistic "Jewish merchant"—a negative stereotype prevalent in antisemitic circles at the time—Briggs was careful to emphasize her artistic activities in her initial letter to Leisching: "I am currently working on a small collection of embroidery and batik work, and hope . . . to exhibit these at the Christmas exhibition of the Austrian Museum of Art and Industry—I do not want to be considered, especially at the moment, as just a retailer."[7] In November, Ella's handicrafts were indeed on view in the vast Christmas exhibition featuring more than two thousand objects, in forty halls spanning the museum's old and newly completed galleries. The show included the work of instructors, students, and alumni of the School of Applied Arts, with special attention given to Josef Hoffmann's modernist interiors. Other female applied artists also exhibited their designs, among them the future architect Liane Zimbler. As newspaper reports reviewing the exhibition reveal, Ella now used the surname Briggs-Baumfeld, reflecting her new independence and evolving identity.[8]

While she was waiting to hear back about support for establishing a New York design retail store, Briggs departed for a commission in Breslau (today Wrocław, Poland) at the end of January 1912.[9] Breslau was the capital of Silesia, an ethnically diverse region populated by Germans, Poles, and Jews, which prospered from coal mining and steel production. Briggs's patron there was Lilly Pringsheim (née Hutter), the sister of Ida Baumfeld (the second wife of Ella's brother Moritz).[10] Lilly was married to the national economist Otto Pringsheim, and the couple lived in a house designed by the architect Curt Brandt in 1910.[11] Otto must have been an interesting interlocutor for Ella. He published widely, on subjects ranging from culture to economic history, and was a friend of the renowned sociologist Werner Sombart.[12] A progressive intellectual, Otto was interested in the ideas of German feminist Marie Stritt, who advocated

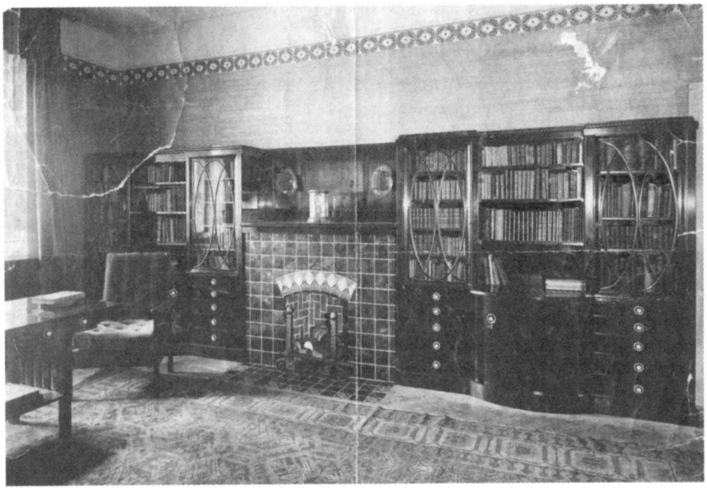

Fig 7.1 Ella Briggs's living room design for Lilly and Otto Pringsheim, Breslau (today Wrocław, Poland), c. 1912

equality and legal protection for women.[13] The Pringsheims commissioned Briggs to decorate their home. The living room was elegantly furnished with a tiled chimneypiece adorned with abstract leaf motifs, a large Persian rug, glass-front bookcases with a Biedermeier-like oval pane decoration, and a stenciled border placed high along the wall: the style was in keeping with design trends in both Vienna and Breslau at the time (fig. 7.1).[14]

The Pringsheims's upper-class social networks may have helped Briggs obtain the prestigious and no doubt lucrative commission to design the public rooms of the Schützendorf Palace, owned by Felix and Elisabeth Schottländer and located in the small German town of Wilamowice (today in southern Poland) in 1912. Both Otto Pringsheim and Felix Schottländer supported charities in Breslau's Jewish community and perhaps had come to know each other in this way.[15] Proud of her interior design work and eager to have it more widely seen, Briggs would exhibit photographs of the Schützendorf Palace music room, library, and dining room in an exhibition that she organized at the Neuer Wiener Frauenklub (New Vienna Women's Club) in 1914.[16]

But back in the spring of 1912, as she waited for her future to gel, Briggs seems to have been unsettled. By mid-March she was staying with her brother Friedrich in Berlin.[17] Her sister Friederike, who may have shared the apartment with Friedrich, was then enjoying a brief career writing on design and culture for women's magazines.[18] As with her Paris sojourn, we know little about Ella's time in the German capital, including how long she stayed. Friedrich's work importing Hungarian wood may have enticed her there with its potential to bring the interior designer new clients. Or perhaps she went there to expand her training. In an interview Briggs gave to the German women's magazine *Frau und Gegenwart* (Woman and Contemporary Times) fifteen years later, she mentions volunteering in a furniture factory and learning carpentry skills while in Berlin.[19]

It was around the time she spent in Berlin that her plans for returning to New York and opening a retail store appear to have derailed. On March 10, 1912, she wrote again to museum director Leisching, telling him about her interior design commission in Breslau and thanking him for his kind support. She said that the American project was now in limbo and asked him not to hold it against her if it did not materialize.[20] The letter did not explain why her plans had not advanced; perhaps it was because she was having trouble securing the necessary financing.

Or maybe the reason was more personal. Just as her New York plans were coming to an end, she signed divorce papers.[21] Having a design store in New York would have meant spending time there on a regular basis, and perhaps wrapped up in those business plans was some hope about keeping her marriage alive. Conversely, from the little we know about the divorce, it does not sound like Ella pined for her husband Walter. Decades later, she told her grandniece Phylis Morrison that she had thrown him out of the house for being an unemployed good-for-nothing.[22] As a divorced woman, she would refocus her sights on Vienna.

During that restless year, which saw Ella move from one city to another, she found a home of sorts at the Lehrerhaus (Teachers' House) in Vienna. The residence had opened in 1906 to serve as temporary accommodations for teachers during their training. Ella rented a room there, off and on, for over a year.[23] She probably chose it because it was cheap and convenient, but it also might be a sign that she was now considering a teaching career. In the summer of 1912, an announcement in a women's journal informed readers that Briggs would offer a course on *Wohnkultur* (dwelling culture), instructing women on how to arrange their domestic environment in a practical way.[24] The course was planned as part of the offerings of the Athenäum (Athenaeum), an association founded by historian Ludo Hartmann, feminist educator Olly Schwarz, and professor of anatomy Emil Zuckerkandl. The Athenaeum hosted advanced lectures for women given by experts in various fields. (Attendees did not earn college credit or a diploma for these courses.) Zuckerkandl, husband of journalist Berta Zuckerkandl, offered his anatomy institute's lecture halls for Athenaeum classes. In the fall of 1912, Briggs taught her *Wohnkultur* course at the institute.[25]

Although Ella never lost interest in educating the public—indeed, her future work in exhibitions and publications indicates a natural inclination to teach—her life took a different and decisive turn during the summer of 1912. After her March 10 letter to Leisching, we hear no more about her plans for a New York design retail store. But as that door closed, Leisching played an important role in opening another. In June 1912, Briggs applied for a grant funded by the Obersthofmeisteramt (Office of the Grand Master of the Court), the body responsible for managing the imperial estates. Grants to individuals and institutions supported various initiatives promoting the applied arts. A committee of the Austrian Museum of Art and Industry made recommendations from the applicant pool, with the final decision resting with the Office of the Grand Master. At the end of August, Briggs received a letter from Leisching informing her that she had received a grant of 4,000 kronen (crowns)—a generous sum.[26] After a period of uncertainty, Ella's future now took shape.

Ella used the funds to open an interior design studio of her own. She chose an address on Taubstummengasse, a short walk from the magnificent Belvedere palace and gardens.[27] Beyond its beauty and elegance, the neighborhood had the advantage of being close in proximity to Vienna's center. It was also home to prominent patrons of the Vienna Secession and the Wiener Werkstätte; clients of Josef Hoffmann and Koloman Moser, including the Wittgenstein and Gallia families, resided nearby. Briggs's studio was located on the top floor of a newly constructed, elegantly modern building with neobaroque and Jugendstil decorative elements (plate 7).

A special issue on contemporary interiors that ran in *Das Interieur* featured Briggs's studio design in 1914. One of the photographs reveals a writing room with a desk, chairs, small round table, and sofa flanked by two side cabinets (plate 8).[28] These pieces are visually brought together through a floral decorative stencil on the upper part of the light-yellow walls and a harmonious interplay of colors, patterns, and materials used for the fabrics and furniture: the green carpet and curtains and the yellow-green upholstery (in a Biedermeier-style striped pattern) complemented the cabinet's reddish cherrywood and white ivory handles.[29] In this skillful mixture of elements, Briggs demonstrated a joyous creative freedom. Compared to the work of other leading designers such as Hoffmann and Dagobert Peche contained in the issue, she clearly reworked and updated the Secessionist's *Raumkunst* ideology of integrated architecture, fine art, and interior decoration according to her own tastes. Specifically, her interior challenged the idea of a dominant decorative scheme, done according to a strict stylistic hegemony; instead, it offered an elegant interior that was comfortable and reflective of the user's needs and personality.

Karl Walde's accompanying article, "The Woman as an Interior Designer," focused on Briggs's recent work and picked up on this shift, implying that her approach represented a new development within the modernist design scene. Rather than force clients to conform to a total work of art, as leading artists of the Wiener Werkstätte had done, she focused on people's needs. Walde praised Briggs's awareness and respect for the habits and living conditions of the people for whom her interiors were intended: "A simple, modest person will not feel comfortable in a splendid room; for those who are accustomed to use their furniture without special care, delicate furniture with a glossy polish is a source of annoyance and discomfort." Walde concluded his endorsement of Briggs's work with the following insight and prediction: "Since the artist starts from the correct premise that it cannot be the task of modern arts and crafts to erect mere showrooms, but rather and above all to bring comfortable *Wohnkultur* to broader strata of the population—which in turn is only possible if the production costs are in proper proportion to the purchasing power of the public—we are likely to see many fine works come out of the artist's studio."[30] In its attention to Briggs's user-friendly approach, the article helped raise awareness among readers that they need not bow down to fashionable designers but instead could choose their interior design according to their own needs.

Examining the writing room further, we note the careful curation and display of its contents (see plate 8). Two electric lamps, likely purchased commercially, light the space: a practical one on a tall stand for the desk, and a fabric-covered one for ambient light hanging from the ceiling. Historical objects (perhaps Ella's family heirlooms) such as a Biedermeier clock on the desk balance with modernist ones, like the portrait of a pensive figure on the far wall. The menorah also speaks to family heritage, as well as cultural identity. Next to the window hangs a print of Japanese artist Katsushika Hokusai's woodcut *The Great Wave off Kanagawa* (1831), revealing Briggs's interest in Far Eastern art, which she shared with the Secessionists including her former teacher Koloman Moser. Two female figurines—one resembling a prehistoric Venus and the other a contemporary dancer—may allude to this working room as a woman's space.[31] Although we cannot know for sure the specific associations she intended to create, the objects in this room (which likely functioned as her own personal writing room, as well as part of her studio) appear to have been deeply meaningful to Briggs. As she moved from city to city in subsequent years, she took many of these with her. She also kept a photograph of the writing room as it appeared in *Das Interieur*—a representation perhaps of her ideal "room of one's own."[32]

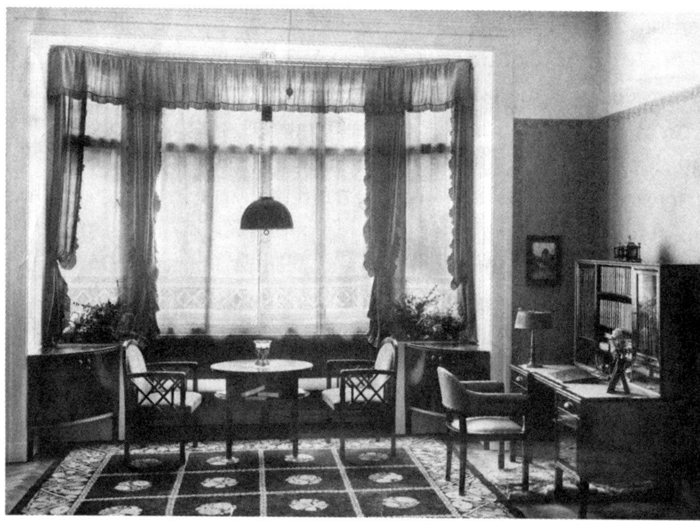

Fig. 7.2 (right) Ella Briggs's living room design for Dr. Wengraf in Vienna, 1912.

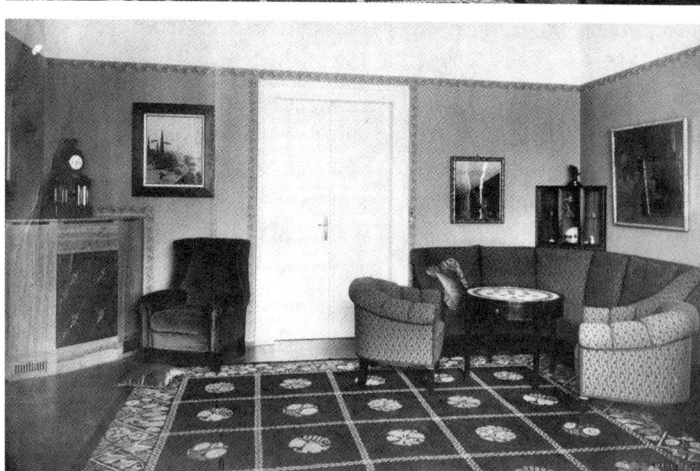

Fig. 7.3 (below) Ella Briggs, living room for Dr. Wengraf in Vienna, 1912. The carpet, produced by the Ginzkey carpet factory, was to her own design. This photograph was published in *Das Interieur* in 1914.

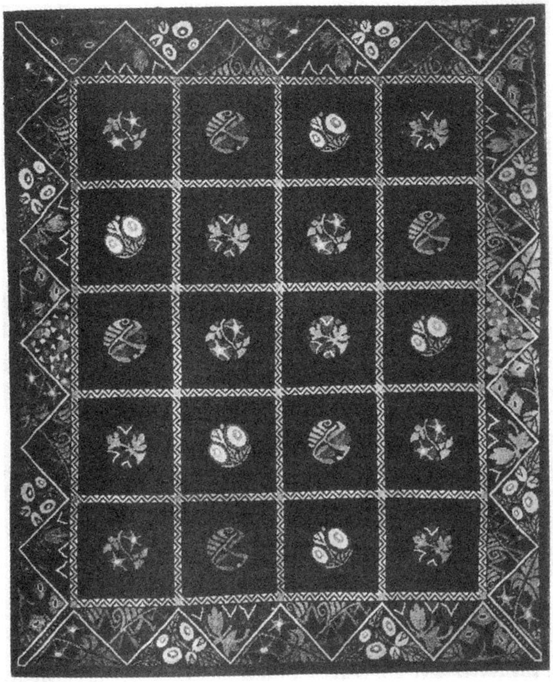

Fig. 7.4 Ella Briggs, carpet design produced by I. Ginzkey, 1912.

The furniture illustrated in *Das Interieur* was created after Briggs's own designs, possibly revealing the impact of her training as a furniture maker in Berlin.[33] Although some of the furnishings in her New York projects had been designed by her, she also used furniture created by others. In this period in Vienna, Briggs emerges as a furniture designer of note. Indeed, she used the imperial grant she received in part to commission the production of the furniture she designed and showcased in her studio. Briggs also displayed her furniture in a number of Viennese exhibitions in this period.[34]

One of Briggs's first clients was a Dr. Wengraf, for whom she designed a living room in 1912 (figs. 7.2–7.3).[35] Who this Dr. Wengraf might be—there are four listed in the Vienna address book that year—remains a mystery.[36] For the commission, Briggs worked with the prestigious I. Ginzkey carpet factory in Maffersdorf, in northern Bohemia.[37] The knotted carpet she designed is notable for its playful, Jugendstil-influenced abstract beetles and flowers. In 1914 the same carpet was featured in the journal *Textile Kunst und Industrie* (Textile Art and Industry) (fig. 7.4).[38]

By early 1913, Briggs had gotten to know Jewish feminist Yella Hertzka, cofounder and president of the New Vienna Women's Club. Hertzka was actively involved in women's rights and peace movements, in Austria as well as internationally. She had recently established the Higher Horticultural School for Women, which opened the fields of horticulture and landscape architecture to women in Austria. Briggs's relationship with Hertzka deepened the architect's engagement with women's spaces. In New York, Briggs's commissions had offered women private spaces within public venues. With Hertzka's support Briggs aspired to develop such private realms into worlds of their own.

Briggs may have come into contact with Hertzka through a group of women designers, including former classmate Marietta Peyfuss, who had joined Hertzka's club years earlier. But what originally brought the two together also could have been a family connection: Moritz Baumfeld and Hertzka's husband Emil shared acquaintances, including the composer Gustav Mahler. No less charismatic than his wife Yella, Emil Hertzka was an influential music publisher. Brought in to save the classical music publishing house Universal Edition from becoming obsolete in 1907, he managed to do so in just a few years by refocusing the company on contemporary music.[39] Around 1913 Emil commissioned Briggs to decorate his office in the couple's new home, and his support for modernism may have challenged Briggs to create one of her most unique interior designs (figs. 7.5–7.6).

The Hertzka office project promised Briggs significant exposure within Vienna's art circles. The couple resided in the Kaasgraben villa colony in the Döbling district, planned by Josef Hoffmann and constructed between 1912 and 1913. Many artists and writers lived in the development, and leading Viennese art personalities were known to attend the Hertzkas' parties. In Emil's office, bold columns of floral decorative stencils vertically segmented the walls. A monochromatic avant-gardist sofa and armchair were arranged in a niche with a striped textile background. It may have been with an eye to catching the attention of this bohemian set that Briggs included her unusual design of a sofa and armchairs that recall lips.

A photograph of the office illustrated her 1917 article "Selbst ist die Frau!" (The self-reliant woman!).[40] Its title, a play on the German saying "Selbst ist der Mann" urging men to depend on themselves when something needs to be done, serves as its own rallying cry, encouraging women to take charge of designing their own home interiors. The article appeared in *Blatt der Hausfrau* (Housewife's Journal), a women's magazine published in Vienna and Berlin that offered its female readers short stories, sewing patterns, and advice on raising children and keeping house. Briggs's contribution fit the program of encouraging women to direct and cultivate their home environment in a conscious way.

In the article, Briggs provided instructions on how best to use patterns and colors in crafting an interior environment. For example, she recommended considering how the width of a decorative frieze in relation to the positioning of furniture affects the experience of the space. Her design for Hertzka's office, with its harmonious relationship between decorated walls and modernist furniture, illustrates this lesson well. She also noted the importance of color schemes in evoking a warm or cool atmosphere and pointed out the way different levels and directions of daylight entering a room affect color. This detailed discussion of the various aspects of interior design served as a kind of "do-it-yourself" manual for artistic creativity. In her New York designs, Briggs had shifted her focus from the flat surfaces of graphic works of art to the more expansive surfaces of a building's interior. When she published her article in 1917, female artists of the Wiener Werkstätte were also expanding their fields of creativity,

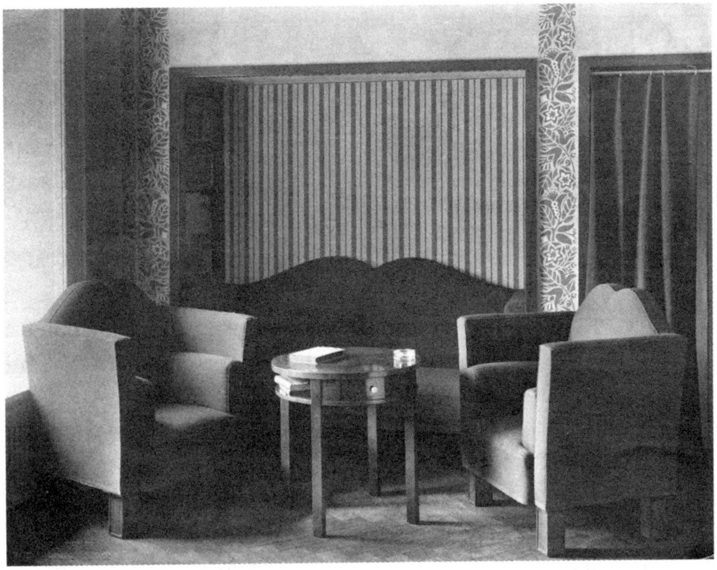

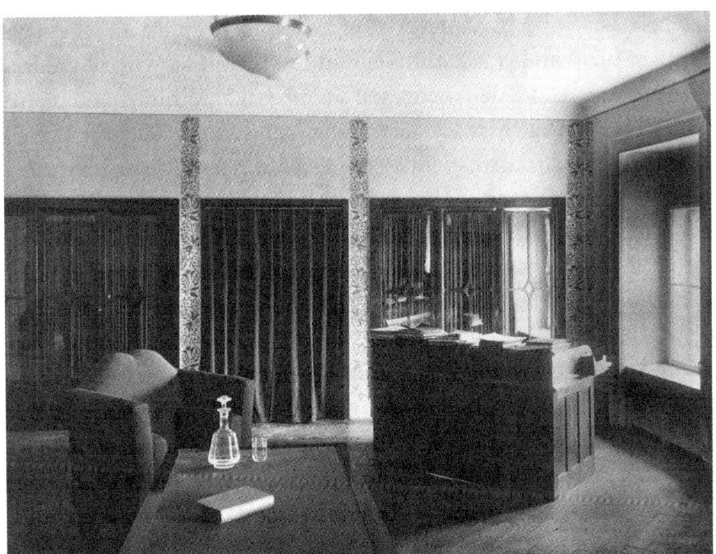

Fig. 7.5 (top) Ella Briggs, photograph of the home office of Emil Hertzka, Kaasgrabengasse 19, Vienna, 1913. The striking lip-shaped upper back of the sofa and armchairs is unique in her oeuvre.

Fig. 7.6 (left) Ella Briggs, photograph of the home office of Emil Hertzka, Kaasgrabengasse 19, Vienna, 1913.

moving from the graphic arts to the walls of homes, exhibitions, and shops to create a kind of Viennese feminist design trend in mural appropriation.[41] Briggs, in her way, invited readers of *Blatt der Hausfrau* to join in this wave of spatial self-expression.

On March 4, 1913, tragedy once again struck the Baumfeld family. Ella's beloved brother Moritz died suddenly from appendicitis, just as the curtain was about to rise on a performance at the Irving Place Theater in New York where he had returned as director.[42] In Vienna, where Moritz was a well-known and respected figure, his death was reported in the newspapers, and his lavish memorial in New York, held at the

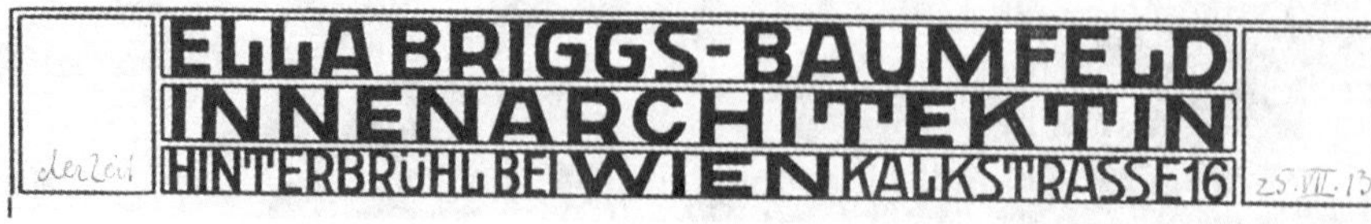
ELLA BRIGGS-BAUMFELD
INNENARCHITEKTIN
HINTERBRÜHL BEI WIEN KALKSTRASSE 16

Fig. 7.7 Ella Briggs-Baumfeld used this letterhead, which she may have designed herself, when she wrote to Eduard Leisching, director of the Austrian Museum of Art and Industry, in July 1913. Underneath her name it states: "Interior Architect," followed below by her address in Hinterbrühl bei Wien, which was also her mother's residence.

theater, was a star-studded affair.[43] Ella was undoubtedly devastated by this loss. She moved temporarily to Hinterbrühl, where her mother had relocated, to give and receive support in their time of shared grief.[44]

Yet even as she mourned her brother, Briggs kept busy. In July 1913, she wrote again to Leisching, asking him to recommend her to his acquaintance Franz Trenner. As the mayor of Baden bei Wien, a spa town near Vienna, Trenner had the power to approve architects. Briggs wanted the mayor to give Otto von Aufschnaiter, chief physician and director of the grand Sanatorium Gutenbrunn, the go-ahead to hire her as interior designer of his casino rooms. Aufschnaiter had already approached Briggs with requests to prepare plans and cost estimates and, well-satisfied with her work, wanted to move forward, but he needed the mayor's approval.[45] Although it remains unclear whether or not Leisching recommended Briggs and she received the commission, the letterhead she used to correspond with Leisching speaks to her maturing professional self-confidence one year after her divorce (fig. 7.7). As opposed to a personal calling card, the letterhead identifying Briggs as an "Interior Architect" testifies to a seriousness of intent. It marks a difference between conceiving of oneself as an interior designer who works only sporadically and one who heads up a fledgling professional firm.

Briggs's identity and reputation as a female designer continued to grow. In January 1914, Archduke Karl Franz Josef toured the fifth exhibition of the Vereinigung bildender Künstlerinnen Österreichs (Association of Austrian Women Artists), where he praised Briggs's Biedermeier-style ladies' room for its choice of colors—a remark reported by the influential newspaper *Neue Freie Presse*.[46] Her work was also singled out by others, including two female critics. Ida Mauthner noted the harmonious effect of Briggs's furniture designs, while Daisy Minor welcomed the work of "architect Ella Briggs-Baumfeld" and encouraged more women to enter the field of interior design.[47]

Despite such recognition, Briggs ran into financial difficulties with her studio. In February 1914 she approached Leisching with an application for another large grant. In requesting the sum of 8,000 kronen (crowns), double the original subvention, she pointed out that her costs had exceeded her income as recent economic downturns in Austria and Germany had discouraged customers from placing orders. She was confident that, with help, her studio could thrive. In May 1914, however, her application was rejected.[48] Two other female graduates of the School of Applied Arts were awarded smaller grants in this same round of applications, indicating the Office of the Grand Master remained interested in supporting women designers.[49] Perhaps it was the size of Briggs's request, or her entreaty not to calculate the amount in too puny a manner ("nicht zu klein zu bemessen"), that resulted in the Grand Master's decision to deny her funding.

In the context of this setback, which threatened the survival of Briggs's studio, the support of Yella Hertzka proved decisive. Earlier that year, and at Hertzka's instigation, Briggs accepted a new and highly visible role as organizer of what was intended to be a series of arts and crafts exhibitions, planned on a small scale and designed for intimate effect, for the New Vienna Women's Club. The purpose of the shows was to acquaint the public with the achievements of female craft artists and interior designers. The inaugural exhibition opened on April 30 to press acclaim and attention, much of it focused on Briggs.

A broad range of work by twenty women was represented, from jewelry, embroidery, and ceramics to furniture and complete interiors. The furniture and interiors were by Briggs, with the interiors illustrated through watercolor sketches and photographs. Briggs designed the exhibition space itself, which, although small, drew admiring reviews. A critic for the newspaper *Fremden-Blatt* (Foreign News), well impressed by what he saw, provided readers with an overview of Briggs's educational and professional background, including her work in New York, and complimented her on the success she had achieved so soon after returning to Vienna; he also noted the many different kinds of formats and materials in which she worked, from pillows to furniture to whole rooms.[50] Another writer, who published an article titled "Originelle Frauenberufe" (Original women's professions) in *Blatt der Hausfrau*, expressed astonishment that female interior architects remained so rare, noting that Briggs was the first to become known in this capacity in Vienna.[51] This publicity presented Briggs as a role model for other Austrian women. Yet the impact she could have at this moment was limited by forces far beyond her control.

In July 1914, Ella's life—indeed, the lives of all Austrian citizens—changed profoundly. Emperor Franz Joseph declared war on Serbia, and the conflict quickly escalated. Motivated perhaps by the patriotic fervor that initially greeted the war, or by the desire to aid the incoming casualties, in August Briggs took a month-long course in hospital practice at the Wiedener Hospital in the fourth district, a ten-minute walk from her studio. She also volunteered as a nurse at the newly established Red Cross Reserve Hospital No. 2.[52] But this lasted only a few months, as she must have realized her skills as a designer and exhibit organizer could be better utilized to raise money for the war effort and care of wounded soldiers. Briggs participated on the organizing committee of an art lottery exhibition, held at the military casino on Schwarzenbergplatz in February 1915, for which she arranged the applied arts section and donated her own work. The committee, chaired by cofounder of the Art School for Women and Girls Tina Blau-Lang, included prominent Viennese artists and patrons such as Broncia Koller and Serena Lederer. Briggs thus appeared once again as part of an evolving Viennese women's modernism.[53] Later that spring, Briggs created a poster for a music

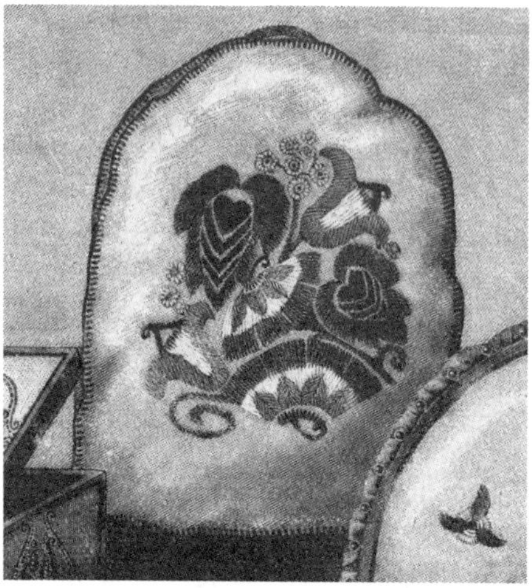

Fig. 7.8 Ella Briggs, coffee pot warmer embroidery pattern, c. 1915, offered for sale through *Das Blatt der Frau* in October 1915.

exhibition raising money for musicians impacted by the war.[54] At the bottom of the poster, Briggs drew a drum, directly under which she placed her name—a confident patriotic gesture.

Once the war started, Briggs would have found it increasingly difficult to maintain her independent design studio. Hoping perhaps that there might be more of a market for everyday objects, she tried a direct sales approach that she would return to in the postwar period: offering her designs through women's magazines (fig. 7.8). Yet such efforts could not stem the flow of expenses and the lack of revenue. The year 1916 appears to have been a turning point. By then she had moved out of Taubstummengasse and taken employment at other firms.[55] Nevertheless, she continued to design whole ensembles when the opportunity arose.[56] In February 1917, her interior designs shown at the Association of Austrian Women Artists' annual exhibition were praised for demonstrating taste and skill in harmonizing antique and modern objects.[57]

By the time the war finally came to an end in November 1918, the Austria of Briggs's youth and adolescence had been destroyed. Prejudice against Jews in Austria and Germany had intensified and become more mainstream. It was now not only reflected in the vicious caricatures portrayed in literature and the press, but also encountered in an increasingly violent physical world.[58] Witnessing the rise of German nationalism, and perhaps taking a lesson from the disappointments of her teacher Koloman Moser, who had earlier battled religion-based prejudice and lost, Briggs made a practical decision to step up her career. In October 1918, with the support of a patron, Judge Adolf Böhm, she converted to the Protestant faith.[59] For many Jews conversion provided a means of self-protection against growing discrimination and persecution.

If the war brought tremendous social upheaval, it also ushered in new opportunities. Lacking major commissions, Briggs decided to undertake a professional makeover. While she would continue to mine her experience and skills in interior decoration, furniture design, and exhibition design during the years to come, by the time the fighting ceased on the battlefields of Europe, Briggs was setting herself new challenges—ones that only a woman with enormous ambition and self-determination could ever meet.

8.
The Fight to Integrate Architecture Studies

Christine Zwingl, Carmen Trifina, and Christine Oertel

In times of war, clients interested in undertaking lavish interior design projects are hard to find. While Ella Briggs continued to design objects and spaces and to organize exhibitions, she also sought employment within architectural offices. The conscription of men to fight in the trenches created openings for women in many offices, and Briggs's extensive design experience made her a desirable hire.

Beginning in 1916, Briggs worked briefly for the architectural office of Alfred Keller, a figure well connected in Viennese artistic circles. Then acting president of the Hagenbund, a modernist artists' association, he later became a vice president of the Zentralvereinigung der Architekten Österreichs (Central Association of Austrian Architects). During Briggs's employment, Keller's firm was planning workers' housing in the southeastern Austrian state of Styria. Briggs then joined the architectural office of Karl Holey, who taught at the Technische Hochschule Wien (Vienna Technical University) and served as general conservator of the K. K. Zentralkommission für Denkmalpflege (Austro-Hungarian Office for the Preservation of Monuments). As an architect, Holey was mainly active in the field of sacral buildings. Within both of these offices, Briggs served as an interior decorator and assistant architect.[1] The diverse work undertaken by these firms provided experience that Briggs was able to use to her advantage.

Around this time, and seemingly inspired by this new milieu, Briggs made the extraordinary decision to pursue an architecture degree. To appreciate how outlandish this would have appeared to many of her contemporaries, as well as how much raw determination it would have required, it is important to understand that until 1919, women were not admitted to architecture programs at the Vienna Technical University or the Academy of Fine Arts. In certain countries, such as Germany, women had previously fought for and acquired access to higher technical education.[2] But only with the founding of the First Austrian Republic in 1918 and the passage of ministerial legislation in April 1919 were women permitted to matriculate as regular students at Austrian technical universities, beginning with the 1919–1920 winter semester. Even so, their presence was countenanced only if it did not "impair" the studies of their male colleagues.[3]

Even before these changes took place, Briggs set her mind on auditing architecture lectures at the Vienna Technical University. Yet it was not an easy decision to make. A decade later, Briggs opened up in an interview about her personal struggles in taking this step. It was not only societal hurdles that gave her pause about pursuing architectural studies as a woman; her own heart and mind were conflicted. A voice within her whispered to stick with interior design. But another, louder voice "demanded that she turn away from half measures and aim for the whole thing—the whole that could result from combining her interior design skills and architectural work."[4]

Perhaps it was also her connection to Holey, who was teaching at the technical university, that convinced her to make this bold attempt. In November 1916 Briggs approached Hermann Daub, a professor on the architecture faculty, to ask if she could be admitted as a guest to his (and others') lectures. Although women before Briggs had audited courses at the Vienna Technical University, they had yet to be admitted to architecture. Seeking guidance, the cautious Daub sent a letter to the university rector, explaining that he was reluctant to decide on "something completely new" by himself. Rector Max Bamberger, who supported women's higher technical education, realized that the university needed to clarify its policy toward female auditors. This resulted in Briggs's request being put on the agenda of the professors' council meeting of December 6, 1916, where it was decided after a long discussion that "each professor shall be permitted, at his own discretion, to admit women as guests to lectures and tutorials."[5]

In 1917, in her mid-thirties, Briggs joined the small cohort of women who audited classes at the Vienna Technical University.[6] As the first woman granted permission to attend architecture lectures there, her presence would have been highly conspicuous in the otherwise all-male auditoriums. The accounts of women who integrated other architecture schools stress the courage and determination their presence required. One apocryphal story, repeated to this day, maintains that Briggs dressed up as a male student in order to pass undetected.[7] More likely, she cloaked herself in the steely resolve she displayed on many other challenging occasions.

Whatever the hurdles she faced, Briggs persisted, returning for additional semesters. Because of her status as an auditor, she left few academic records behind. What remains suggests that the former arts and crafts school student decided to forego artistic course offerings such as freehand drawing in favor of more technical subjects. We also glimpse her broader developing interests in architecture in the requests she made to audit classes, which ostensibly brought her into the classrooms of Max Fabiani, a former student of Otto Wagner and representative of modern architecture, and of Leopold Simony, a pioneer of social housing.[8]

As the war years progressed, the Vienna Technical University witnessed a steady influx of women drawn to technical subjects. With male students off at the front, female students filled the empty seats. But war was not the only precipitator of this change; women increasingly sought to lead lives of self-determination and independence. They used this time of social and political disruption to forge new science, technology, and engineering-focused career paths through higher education that had once been off limits.

Briggs was soon joined by two other female students taking architecture courses. Eighteen-year-old Margarethe von Heimerich began auditing courses in the summer of 1917; she attended for several semesters before being admitted, after some ministerial resistance, as a regular student in September 1919.[9] Melitta Urbanek, a construction technician in her mid-twenties who had already completed a lengthy

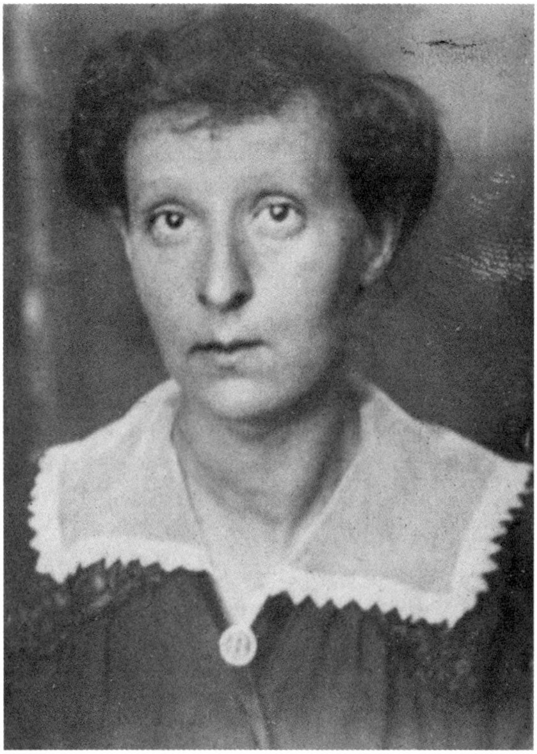

Fig. 8.1 Photograph of Ella Briggs, c. 1918, included with her student application to the Munich Technical University.

education, successfully applied to audit architecture lectures in December 1917.[10] Given their unique status, the female auditors must have known of each other and perhaps even met in the corridors or lecture halls to compare notes.

Even though women became more visible within the university during this period, their status remained tenuous. After two years as an auditor at the Vienna Technical University, Briggs decided to advance her architectural studies elsewhere. Across the border in Germany, at the Technische Hochschule München (Munich Technical University), women had been allowed to matriculate since 1905.[11] Briggs applied for admission to the architecture department in August 1918 but was accepted only as an auditor (fig. 8.1). Nevertheless, she moved to Munich and began to audit courses at the technical university that fall.[12]

A few months later, in December 1918, Briggs applied to the Technische Hochschule Charlottenburg (Charlottenburg Technical University, later Berlin Technical University) for admission as a regular student, intending to transfer there from Munich. For Briggs, Berlin had several advantages as a place to study architecture. She would have been able to live with her mother, who had relocated to Berlin, lessening the need to support herself while attending school. Additionally, and as she stated in her application letter, she found the Berlin architecture curriculum particularly well suited to her interests. In January 1919 Briggs learned that she had been admitted, but again only as an auditor.[13] The reason was that she lacked a *Matura* (school-leaving exam), a requirement for matriculation. Most women at the time did not have this qualification. Girls were not expected to attend university, and few girls' schools prepared them for this path. Middle-class parents overwhelmingly favored sons over daughters when deciding whose higher education to finance. And as a young woman, Briggs had not needed a *Matura* to enter the Vienna School of Applied Arts.

Because she could not matriculate at Berlin's Technical University, Briggs stayed in Munich and prepared to take the school-leaving exam, while also continuing to audit university architecture courses. Her workload as a student in the spring of 1919 must have been exceptionally high. In July 1919, she passed her *Matura* successfully at a school in the nearby Austrian city of Salzburg.[14] With certificate in hand, she could finally enroll as a regular student at the Munich Technical University. She managed to receive credit in Munich for courses she had taken in Vienna, which shortened the length of her architecture diploma studies. She was less successful, however, in her request to receive financial support as a war veteran, since her service at a Red Cross reserve hospital in Vienna in 1914 did not qualify her as a veteran.[15]

In the nineteenth century, Munich had emerged as Germany's art capital, and it continued to be an exciting place for art students as the war ended and regular life resumed. The architectural training at the Munich Technical University, and particularly the courses of architect Theodor Fischer, enjoyed a strong reputation. The program attracted a good number of female students: during the 1918–1919 winter term, a total of seventeen women attended architecture courses. Briggs thus found herself in a larger female cohort than she had experienced in Vienna.[16]

Officially enrolled by the fall of 1919, Briggs accelerated the pace of her studies. Having deferred her ambitions for so long, she now pushed herself to finish as quickly as possible when the goal was finally in sight. Astonishingly, she took the preliminary state architecture exam in June 1920, and the final examination (for the diploma) later that summer, which she passed with *Gut* (merit). Her diploma certificate, issued in August 1920, confirmed her eight semesters of university study, which earned her the long-coveted *Diplom-Ingenieur*, the degree awarded to academically trained architects in Germany and Austria.[17] Briggs proudly joined the pioneering cohort of women to graduate from academic architecture programs in Germany.

Valuing the qualifications that came with her new degree (and mindful of the potential doors they would open), Briggs returned to Vienna and pursued the recognition of professional organizations. She applied for membership in the Österreichischer Ingenieur- und Architektenverein, or ÖIAV (Austrian Association of Engineers and Architects) and in April 1921 was accepted as its first female member. In the meeting during which her admission was decided, her colleagues acknowledged her considerable achievements. They resolved to send a "special letter of welcome to Mrs. Briggs."[18]

When Ella Briggs opened that letter, she held in her hands proof that her colleagues recognized and appreciated the successful completion of her years-long struggle to attain qualifications that permitted her to join their professional ranks. But whether she would be fully accepted as their peer remained to be seen.

Section III.
ARCHITECTURE PROJECTS IN NEW YORK AND VIENNA, 1920–1927

9.
The Vienna Settler Movement and Early Architectural Work

Sabine Plakolm-Forsthuber

With her architecture degree in hand, Ella Briggs left Munich in 1920 to return to her homeland (plate 9). She arrived in a country profoundly different from the one she had left—a country that had undergone tremendous political, territorial, and economic upheaval in the span of only a few years. Following the First World War, the Austro-Hungarian monarchy had ceased to exist, transforming Vienna from a royal seat of power into the capital of a newly formed republic. The monarchy's most important industrial and agricultural production sites now lay outside the Republic of Austria's borders. Plagued by high inflation and a catastrophic housing shortage, Austria's people (especially in Vienna) grew hungry and malnourished. Briggs moved back to Vienna "full of creative energy" and determination to contribute her new architectural skills to improving these conditions.[1]

In Vienna, the housing situation after 1918 was calamitous and confusing. Soldiers returning from the war, disabled veterans, unemployed workers, widows, and displaced persons illegally appropriated land in the capital's green belt, on which they built simple huts and planted vegetable gardens in desperate attempts at self-sufficiency. Tens of thousands of Viennese lived in the margins of the city in these spontaneously proliferating self-help communities. The so-called wild settlements manifested the starving population's sheer will to survive.

Officials attempted to steer this uncontrolled land grab into structured, cooperative channels. Following the 1919 municipal election and their landslide victory, Social Democrats governed Vienna and would continue to do so until 1934. As of 1922, the city would possess the status of a separate federal state, giving Viennese officials a high degree of independence and the resources to pursue a radical program of social reforms centered on architecture that would become known as Red Vienna. Vienna's first Social Democratic mayor, Jakob Reumann, was a powerful ally of the settlers. Reumann was advised on housing matters by his friend and fellow Social Democratic city councilor Gustav Scheu, who guided the city's response to the housing crisis toward a grassroots approach in support of the settlers' desire for self-sufficiency. At the same time, the settlers were growing more political, vocal, and organized. By setting up their own cooperative associations, they created administrative and financial structures to help them construct their own homes and grow their own food.[2]

Based on Scheu's efforts, in 1921 the city established the Siedlungsamt (Settlement Office) to allocate land, distribute subsidies, provide design and building assistance, and generally coordinate efforts between municipal agencies and the settlers' cooperative associations. Hans Kampffmeyer, a leading protagonist of the prewar German garden city movement, became its director.[3] Adolf Loos, a close friend of Scheu, was hired as its chief architect. Even before his appointment, Loos had been vocally supportive of the settlers, attending public demonstrations and defending the movement in the Viennese press. As chief architect, Loos established design and construction guidelines for housing on the settlements, which in the early years of wild development had ignored building codes. Loos was also directly involved in the design of new settlements and experimented with methods to simplify construction and reduce costs.[4]

Other architects employed by the Settlement Office and the cooperative societies also developed architectural models for the new urban form of living desired by the settlers, which brought together dwelling, community, and cultivation of the soil. Josef Frank, a professor at the Kunstgewerbeschule (School of Applied Arts), was hired in 1920 by a cooperative association to design the Hoffingergasse Siedlung (settlement) at the southwestern edge of the city, which was hailed by the *Arbeiter-Zeitung* (Workers' Newspaper), an organ of the Social Democrats, as ideal proletarian housing.[5]

Margarete (Grete) Schütte-Lihotzky, who had studied architecture at the School of Applied Arts under Oskar Strnad during the war, played an important role in the settler movement with her simple adaptable furniture designs and studies in the optimal organization of the kitchen, which culminated in her renowned standardized kitchen models of the mid-1920s.[6] Schütte-Lihotzky also created several types of very simple, one-room *Siedlerhütten*, or settler huts, that contained basic cooking and sleeping facilities and were meant to serve as provisional structures for families awaiting a permanent dwelling. Along these lines, she and other architects developed variations of a *Kernhaus*, or core-house, a phased-construction house type that could be built in stages and finished by the settlers. Schütte-Lihotzky recognized that these bare-minimum types did not represent an ideal but instead were meant to be modified as settlers' circumstances allowed.[7]

The simplicity of forms produced by Frank, Loos, and Schütte-Lihotzky emerged from their efforts to make house construction as economical and easy as possible, recognizing that working-class residents had limited resources, time, and skills. It was also symbolic: in settlements intended for a new kind of communal life, defined by mutual support and self-government, the similarity and simplicity of the houses spoke to an ethos of equality and democracy.[8] Yet different streams of thought shaped the settler movement's early years, and some architects took other approaches. The garden city movement, which had begun in England at the turn of the twentieth century and then spread to other countries, including Germany, played an important role in the settler movement; particularly, in the centrality of the garden and the preference for low-rise, low-density suburban housing estates. Debates that had animated the prewar German garden city movement lingered after the war, such as how to accommodate different social classes. The response from architects to the wild settlements was hardly uniform or static, even within progressive circles and with the regulations laid out by Loos.

Hugo Mayer, a Viennese municipal architect, had studied English and German garden colonies before the war. In his 1921 design for the Rosenhügel Siedlung, southwest of Vienna's city center, he followed the standards set by the Settlement Office, and organizationally, his houses were similar to those of Loos. Yet unlike Loos, he decorated the facades with neo-Biedermeier ornament, influenced by prewar bourgeois housing settlements and garden city design. Originally developed in Austria and Germany in the eighteenth century, this classicizing style was closely associated with bourgeois urban culture. Even though the language of middle-class ornament was arguably a poor choice for proletariat housing, some kind of decorative touch was preferred by settlers; when Frank's Hoffingergasse Siedlung welcomed its first residents in 1921, those unhappy with the plainness and sameness of the new houses took it upon themselves to decorate the exteriors.[9]

It was within this intense environment of architects' and intellectuals' engagement with the settlers' predicament that Briggs may have first heard about the economist Otto Neurath. A garden city enthusiast and key organizer of Vienna's settler movement, he united groups with different interests into powerful umbrella associations. Among them was the Österreichischer Verband für Siedlungs- und Kleingartenwesen, or ÖVSK (Austrian Association for Settlement and Allotment Gardens), which he founded in 1921. Neurath placed great emphasis on the educational aspect of the garden city, and the ÖVSK quickly started a settler school to teach residents the practical skills they needed to succeed at gardening and construction, as well as theoretical instruction in subjects such as social organization, the economy, and law as it pertained to settlement housing.[10] Loos, Frank, and Schütte-Lihotzky were among the architects who offered courses. Although Briggs did not meet Neurath until later in the 1920s, she must have been exposed to his ideas about the self-empowerment of workers through self-education, self-organization, and cooperative house construction. She absorbed and later reworked these ideas as part of her professional ideology regarding the role of the architect as teacher and mediator in her residential projects and exhibition designs.[11]

In Vienna, Briggs drew on her extensive professional networks to look for work. It would have been clear to her that in this immediate postwar period, commissions were more likely to come from the public sector—in particular, the City of Vienna—than from the private sector. Her numerous contacts, which included prominent architects, may have proven helpful here. For example, Alfred Keller, for whom she had worked during the First World War, was one of the architects invited by Scheu in 1920 to compete for the development of a model settlement plan for the city to lay the foundation for the new housing to come.[12]

In the early phase of the settler movement, Briggs worked for a while for Josef Frank within the Grundstein architectural office, where Frank was a consultant.[13] Grundstein (meaning "foundation stone") was a large building cooperative established in 1921 by the construction unions in Vienna to erect houses in conjunction with settlers, who would participate in building their own homes.[14] Members of this anti-capitalist organization, which opened branches in the provinces, were labeled as "veiled communists" by competing private companies.[15] While Briggs was employed there, the office was working on the planning of Frank's Hoffingergasse Siedlung as well as Hugo

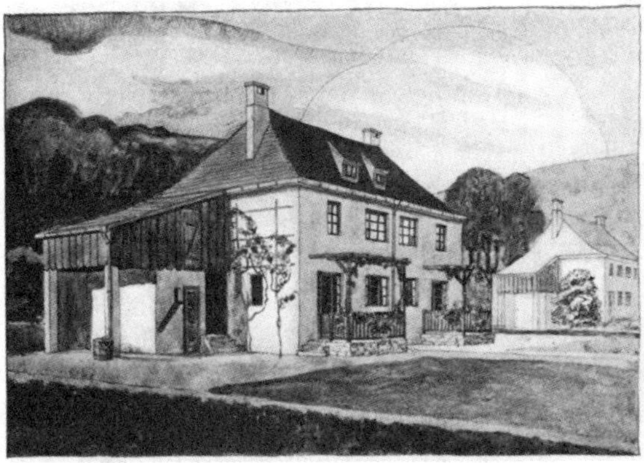

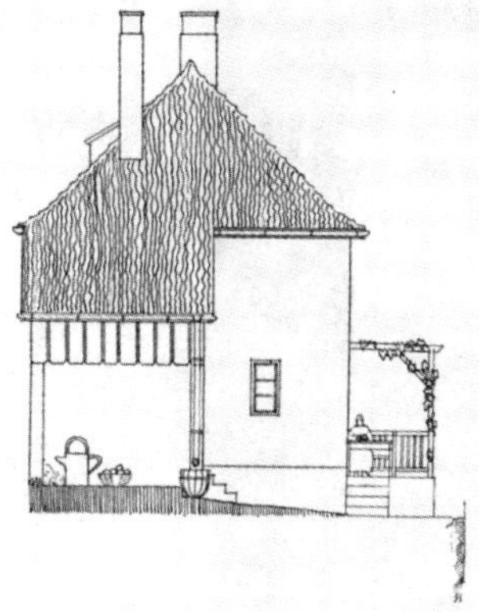

Fig. 9.1 (left) Ella Briggs, exterior view of a semidetached house designed for an Austrian government housing development, c. 1922.

Fig. 9.2 (right) Ella Briggs, side elevation of the semidetached house shown in fig. 9.1.

Mayer's Rosenhügel Siedlung—both self-sufficient settlements but with different approaches in accommodating petit bourgeois tastes.[16]

Some of the work Briggs did in these early years in Vienna appears to be preserved in an article she published in *Architecture* magazine in 1922 (figs. 9.1–9.4).[17] Written by Briggs for an American audience, the article gives us our first glimpse of her work as an architect. The text explains the Austrian government's response to the wild settlement and the development of regulated new housing projects in Vienna's outer districts. The illustrations include a site plan showing the layout of an (unidentified) "housing development near Vienna," as well as sections, plans, and drawings of houses.

The two-story, semidetached houses appear in a verdant landscape, with the dark rectangle of a garden plot in the immediate foreground. The houses have basements and hipped roofs, and the entrances project from the side elevations (see figs. 9.1 and 9.4). Notably, the exteriors are unornamented except for trellised vines and shrubbery. From the entrance, a vestibule leads into a *Wohnküche* (a traditional type of kitchen with space for family living) with a separate dining alcove (figs. 9.3 and 9.4). Three bedrooms are accessible via a staircase from the *Wohnküche* to the upper floor. On the ground floor, Briggs planned a separate living room with a small, covered terrace in front (imagined as an outdoor workspace for the housewife), a scullery with its own bathtub (which Briggs recommended covering and using as a worktable when not in use), and a separate toilet (figs. 9.2 and 9.4). Briggs noted that the "thoughtful architect" must aim "to save the housewife every superfluous step." In her own design, she pointed out how she provided "a small window from the kitchen to the scullery to allow the housewife, while doing her work there, to peep at her cooking-pots."[18] This attention to laborsaving approaches to design, and her insistence that this was an architectural imperative, is the first instance we have of a theme that would remain and grow dominant in Briggs's subsequent architectural work.

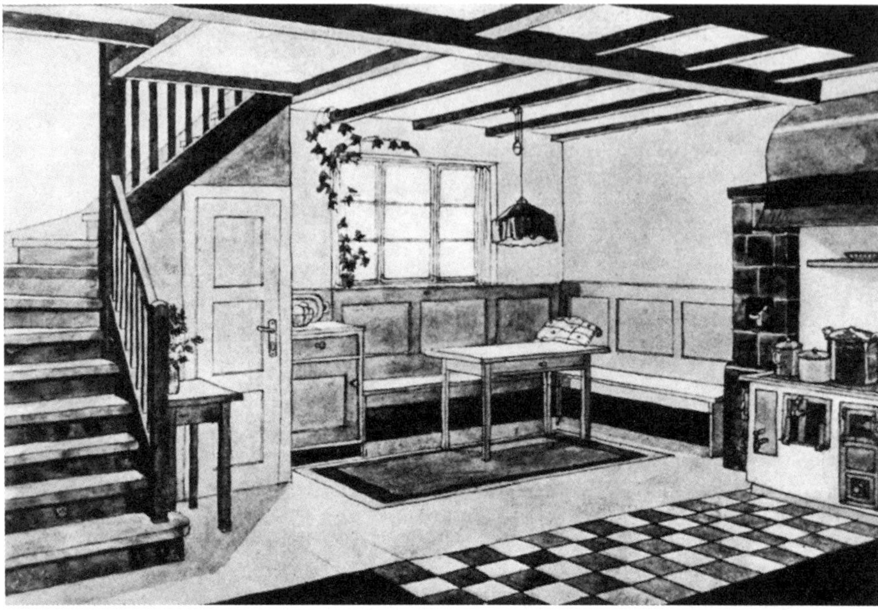

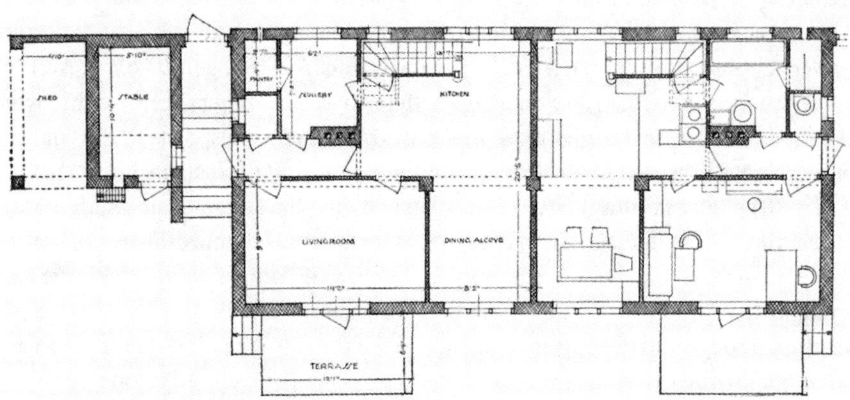

Fig. 9.3 (top) Ella Briggs, live-in kitchen for the semidetached house planned for an Austrian government housing development, c. 1922.

Fig. 9.4 (bottom) Ella Briggs, first-floor plan of the semidetached house designed for an Austrian government housing development, c. 1922.

Many elements of Briggs's design were standard features of the settler house, required by Loos's design specifications: the *Wohnküche*, with its direct access to the garden plot; the scullery, for "dirty" housework; the upper floor reserved for bedrooms; a stable (with hayloft above), connected to the entrance porch; a small shed. But the addition in Briggs's design of separate living and dining areas, the covered terrace, and the proper bathtub—not to mention the generous spatial dimensions of the project overall—suggest that Briggs did not have the working classes in mind.

Whereas Schütte-Lihotzky's settler huts and core-house types had an extremely functional layout on a minimal ground plan, Briggs's designs evoked the spatial arrangement of a middle-class, single-family house.

Briggs's rejection of the simple rowhouse typologies developed by Loos, Frank, and Schütte-Lihotzky may result here from her desire to accommodate the expectations of American audiences. But it may also be a strategic move. Through her work for Grundstein, Briggs would have been well aware of various strands within the settler movement. Briggs's semidetached houses recall prewar German garden city settlements, which, despite their similar emphasis on communal life, mixed housing types to accommodate different social classes. Perhaps this reflects the influence of her teacher Theodor Fischer at the Munich Technical University, who was active in the German garden city movement. Was she aligning herself here with more centrist garden city protagonists in Vienna?[19] If so, Briggs was prescient. Around this time, the City of Vienna began shifting its approach to settlement housing, moving closer to what Briggs had in mind. Franz Schacherl and Franz Schuster's Siedlung Wasserturm (Water Tower Settlement), which began construction in 1923, exemplifies this change toward settlement housing that appealed to a middle-class ideal of the more autonomous, private household.[20]

The fact that Briggs, at least in this design, sidestepped the settlers' needs and requirements may have been the reason that she does not appear to have built independently (outside of her work for Grundstein) in this period. In addition to this professional disappointment, other conditions such as the municipality's extreme poverty and yet-to-be-resolved strategies for regulating and financing new housing policy contributed to Briggs's decision to leave Vienna in 1922 and return to the United States.[21]

Within the architectural profession, the drastically reduced presence of a wealthy private clientele in Red Vienna elicited a shift toward urban planning; indeed, Vienna's city planning department dominated building activity. In the United States, on the other hand, single-family house construction soared after the war and provided manifold opportunities for an up-and-coming architect like Briggs. New York also suited Briggs's aspirations as an architect at this moment—in particular, her desire to go beyond strictly functional housing typologies. Both the American housing market and its architectural culture would prove more amenable to Briggs's enterprising spirit. At the same time, seeds had been planted during this early period in Vienna that would reemerge and grow as Briggs matured as an architect.

10.
Building Clients and Avid Readers in New York and Beyond

Despina Stratigakos

In the decade after the First World War, the United States emerged as a global powerhouse. New York, the nation's largest city, thrived culturally and financially. This contrasted sharply with Vienna, where in the wake of the collapse of the Austro-Hungarian Empire, the city struggled to find a new political identity and to revive its gutted economy. Work in Vienna, Ella Briggs would later maintain, had been difficult to find. Lured by greater opportunities, and perhaps needing a change after her mother's death in 1921, the forty-two-year-old architect sought her fortune elsewhere.[1]

Briggs arrived in New York aboard the SS *Yorck* on May 5, 1922. More than ten years had passed since her last visit. For the first time, she travelled second class, instead of first, indicating a need to economize. Her brother Moritz now deceased, she gave the US immigration officer a friend's name as her local contact and address (the friend was Hella Bernays, a niece of Sigmund Freud). She also told the officer that she was divorced (although before boarding the ship in Bremen, she claimed she was widowed when questioned by German authorities). Under profession, the officer noted "engineer" (she may have told him she was a *Diplom-Ingenieur*, the qualification awarded by architecture departments in German and Austrian technical universities).[2] New York had always been good to Ella Briggs, and she must have hoped that she would once again find her path forward in this city of self-reinvention.

And indeed, in New York Briggs would find her footing as an architect. Here she experienced two significant career milestones, both related to domestic architecture: her first independent house commissions, and her emergence as a magazine writer focused on the design of the home. These professional developments would prove to be foundational. Her attention to the needs of the home's occupants, and especially of the housewife, would shape her career for the next three decades.

In November 1922, Briggs published two articles in American journals. Although addressing different case studies, the articles shared a common ideology. The first, which appeared in *Architecture* magazine, concerned attempts by the Austrian government to alleviate acute housing and food shortages, then threatening the stability of the newly formed republic.[3] Briggs explained the political and economic strategies behind the settler movement in Vienna to her American readers, including the provision of affordable mortgages, the allocation of leased land, and the establishment of work requirements, such as joint cultivation of agricultural plots. Possibly anticipating that an American readership would find the communal aspects of the Vienna homeownership plan disconcerting, she headed off criticism by stating: "The owning of personal property is the safest way to keep people from going into communistic excesses."[4] She also proposed her own designs (see figs. 9.1–9.4), which she attempted

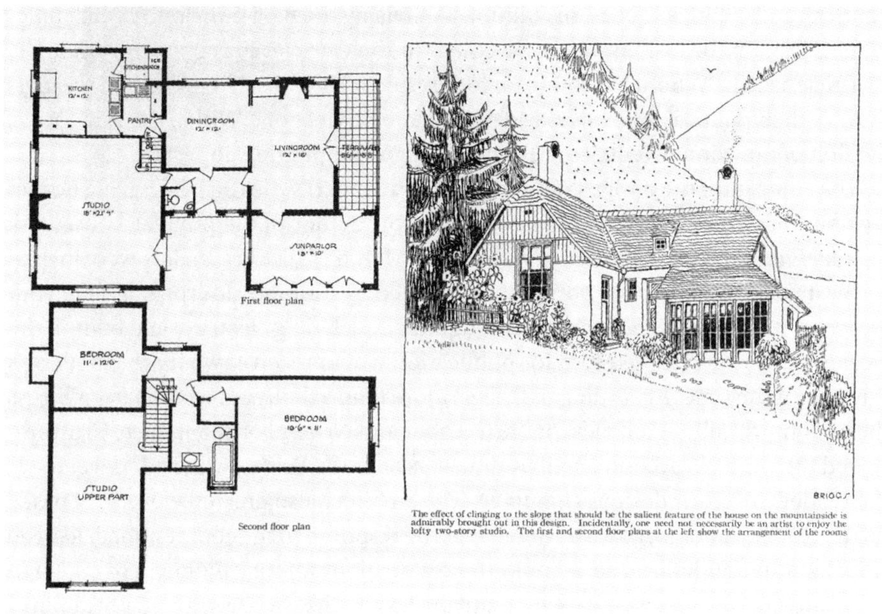

Fig. 10.1 Ella Briggs, plans and elevation for a mountain house, 1922.

to normalize for her readers: of the illustrated *Wohnküche* (combined living room and kitchen), Briggs maintained that despite the small size, it made for "a most intimate and homelike impression."

The second article appeared in *Country Life*, a magazine published by Doubleday and devoted to the lifestyles of the wealthy. It featured Briggs's designs for modest mountain homes, which she noted could work just as well in suburban settings. Unlike what she had proposed for a Viennese housing settlement, these country homes included luxuries such as a maid's room and a two-story artist's studio (fig. 10.1). Here she appealed to an aspirational audience: the reader who dreams of owning a small piece of nature. The article's title indicated as much in emphasizing the affordability of these artful yet "simple Swiss chalets."[5] Although Briggs's two essays differ sharply in their offerings—a charming cottage for prospering Americans versus self-help settlements for impoverished Viennese—both convey a strong belief in the desirability, and attainability, of the small, thoughtfully organized home, designed by an architect and set within a green environment.

If Briggs was not alone among architects in promoting such beliefs, she stands out in terms of the audiences she engaged as well as how she engaged them. As an interior designer in Vienna, she had addressed female audiences through her teaching, writings, and exhibitions. Now, as a credentialed architect, she continued that outreach. In 1923 Briggs collaborated with *Pictorial Review* on a design competition directed at housewives. One of the leading women's magazines in the United States at the time, *Pictorial Review* had built its publishing success on stimulating its readers' intellectual, political, and creative agency, in addition to advising them on more traditional topics such as fashion, beauty, and housekeeping. In the October 1923 issue, for example, an article asked, "Whom Do You Want for President Next Year?," encouraging readers to voice their political opinions ahead of the national election.[6] Within this same issue, the first of the winning entries in Briggs's design competition appeared.

The context for the design competition was a six-part series on laborsaving houses written for *Pictorial Review* by Mae Savell Croy, author of the popular housework manual *Putnam's Household Handbook*. In the March 1923 issue, readers were invited to "write us a letter of 200 words, accompanied by a simple floorplan, giving your ideas of a step-saving arrangement of equipment, including electrical and built-in devices, etc." The entries selected for publication would receive twenty-five dollars, a tidy sum at the time. According to Briggs, more than a thousand women from across the country submitted entries. In the October and November 1923 issues, Croy presented the winners, accompanied by drawings made by Briggs, who had "developed" the readers' original designs (fig. 10.2). The architect also created elevations based on the readers' floor plans. Croy noted that the response to the competition had been "most gratifying, indicating as it did the tremendous interest women are taking in the planning of homes to systematize and professionalize housework." Only minimal changes, she claimed, had been made to the original submissions for the sake of adapting them to the requirements of most users and to ideas of architectural beauty.[7]

How or why Briggs accepted this project for *Pictorial Review* is unknown. Her willingness to let the housewife lead the design process is at odds with how her male contemporaries set out to define the relationship between architect and housewife. Although in the 1920s, modernist architects such as Bruno Taut proclaimed the necessity of a design partnership with housewives in recognition of their influence, they assumed the architect would lead the innovation of domestic forms and practices.[8] At least in the context of the magazine contest, Briggs was willing to publicly serve as the medium channeling the housewife's vision and expertise. This proffered a different approach to the creative partnership between architect and housewife, positioning the latter as her own design authority—even if she still needed the architect to transcribe her ideas. Based on the response, *Pictorial Review* readers found the chance to generate their own designs empowering, and perhaps Briggs hoped the competition would bring her new clients. From the broader perspective of Briggs's career, it gives us an early glimpse of her interest in user-driven architectural design.

For Briggs, centering a user's needs and desires also entailed building flexibility into a design to allow for changes over time. In May 1923 she published an article in *Country Life* that demonstrated how a young couple could plan to grow their family in place with a design she called "the house with a future." This house was planned in three phases, with the early phases supporting subsequent phases of development, if desired. The first phase encompasses the construction of a small bungalow, appropriate for a couple of "modest means"; it features a large living room that will remain the core of the house in later expansions (fig. 10.3). The second phase, timed to the arrival of children, sees an expansion of the house into two stories. New bedrooms are located

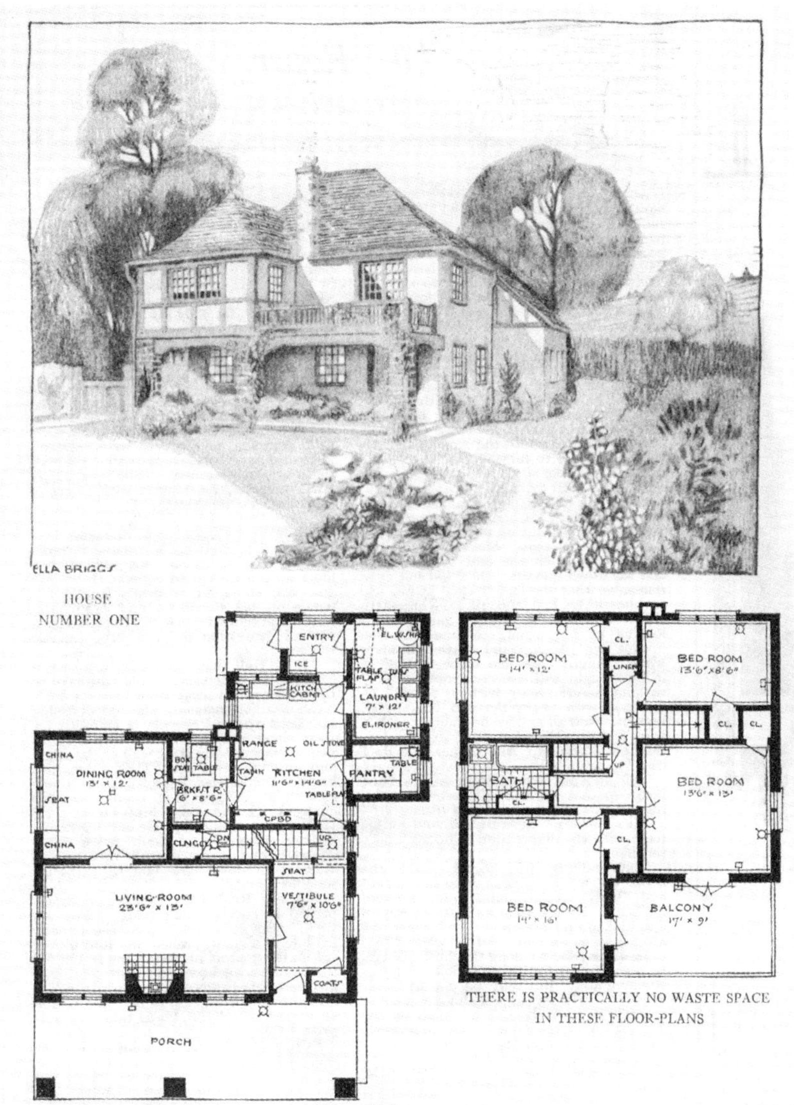

Fig. 10.2 Ella Briggs, elevation and plans based on the submission of Mrs. G. B. Porter of Kingsport, Tennessee, to the 1923 *Pictorial Review* competition for a laborsaving house.

on the second floor and the ground-floor bedroom converted into a library, further enlarging the living space (fig. 10.4). The third and final phase, accommodating an elderly parent or young couple, reintroduces a bedroom on the ground floor through an addition, which houses a sleeping porch above (fig. 10.5). The expanding design also provides discrete spaces and circulation pathways for a growing staff of servants.[9]

As Briggs maintained, the design offered numerous advantages compared to conventional ways of building. Although the article did not provide technical

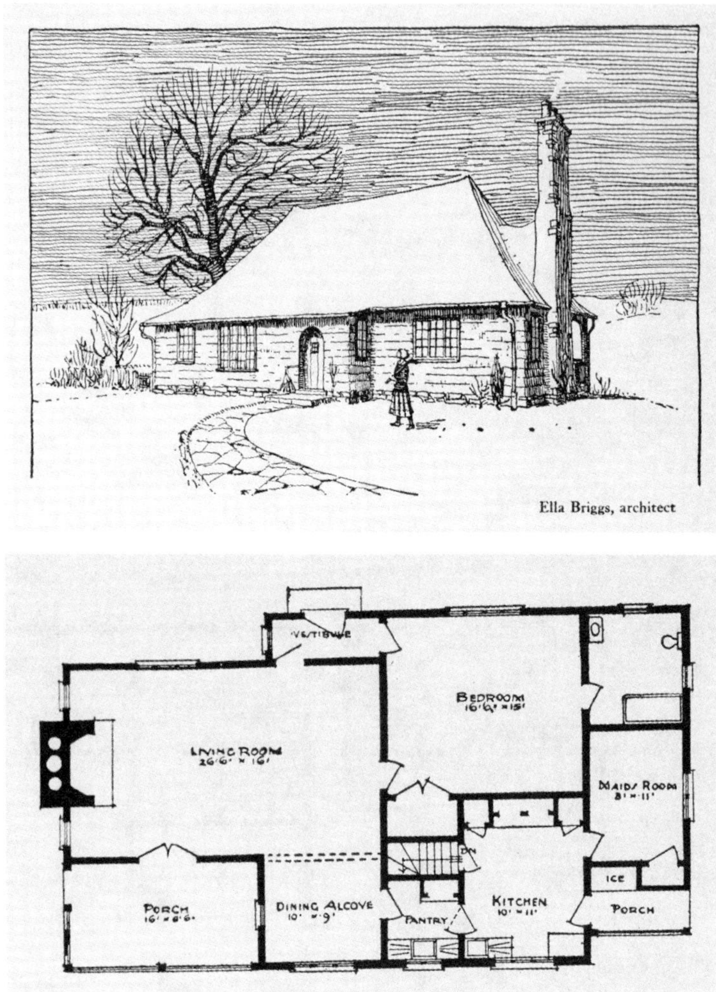

Fig. 10.3 Ella Briggs, elevation (top) and plan (bottom) of the first stage of the house with a future, 1923.

specifications, Briggs noted that structurally the ceiling beams, columns, and foundations were engineered to carry the weight of the house as it grew, facilitating the growth process. At the same time, she emphasized that aesthetically, the house would appear complete and beautiful at every stage. And "at no time" during its incremental construction would "the strain of building [be] too heavy on the purse." Careful planning, Briggs contended, could produce a design that seamlessly metamorphosed from "the chrysalis of a humble bungalow . . . into a really substantial country home of the man with means, with ample room for servants and guests." On a more sentimental level, Briggs wrote that the house would have "grown with the growth of the family and become a part of the life that has been lived within its walls."[10] Yet perhaps the biggest advantage of Briggs's design was that it introduced readers to new and important ideas

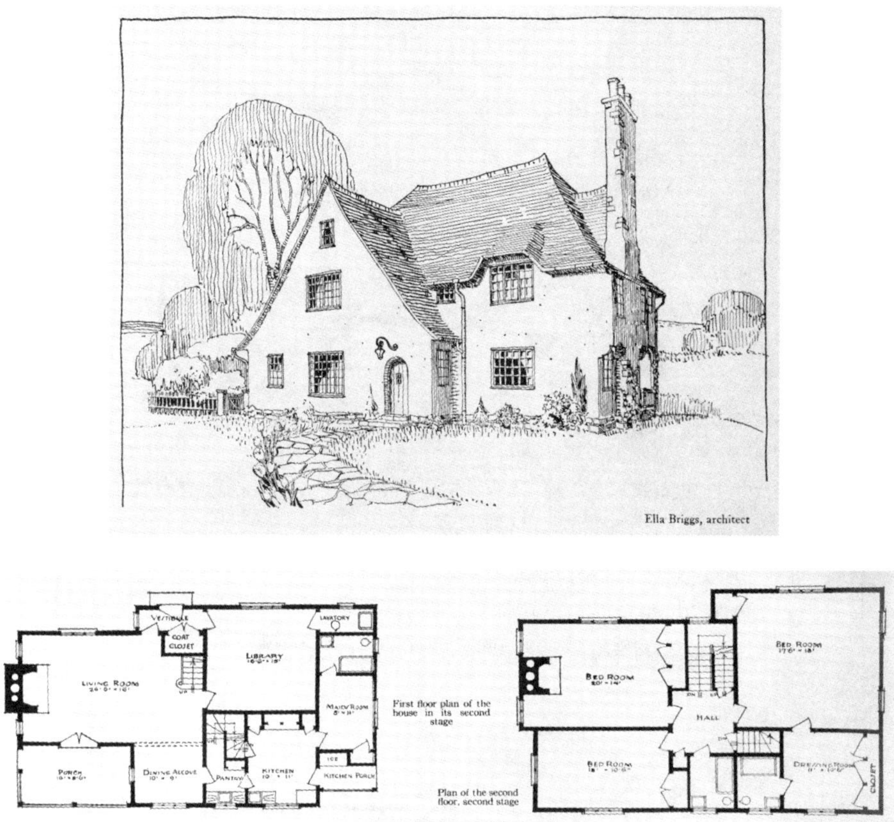

Fig. 10.4 Ella Briggs, elevation (top) and floor plans (bottom) of the second stage of the house with a future, 1923. The floor plan to the left is of the first floor, and to the right of the second floor.

about the long-term lifecycle of domestic environments, which could accommodate changing family configurations through thoughtful design.

Briggs's article about "the house with a future" appeared just as Grete Schütte-Lihotzky began publishing about her core-house types, which aimed to provide Viennese workers with a method for creating their homes in stages, as they could afford to expand.[11] The contemporaneousness of these two developments raises fascinating questions about the circulation of ideas in this period: how did Schütte-Lihotzky and Briggs, on different sides of the Atlantic, simultaneously arrive at such similar conceptions, if for very different audiences with disparate class aspirations? It seems likely that Briggs drew on radical discussions that were taking place within Vienna's architectural circles while she worked for the settler movement, but then transformed those ideas to suit a middle-class American audience.

A similar adaptation of European precedents—drawing on settlement housing in Vienna and prewar German garden cities—appears in an article she wrote later that same fall. In October 1923, Briggs offered readers of *The Ladies' Home Journal* a different approach to domestic architecture—one that again promised greater comfort

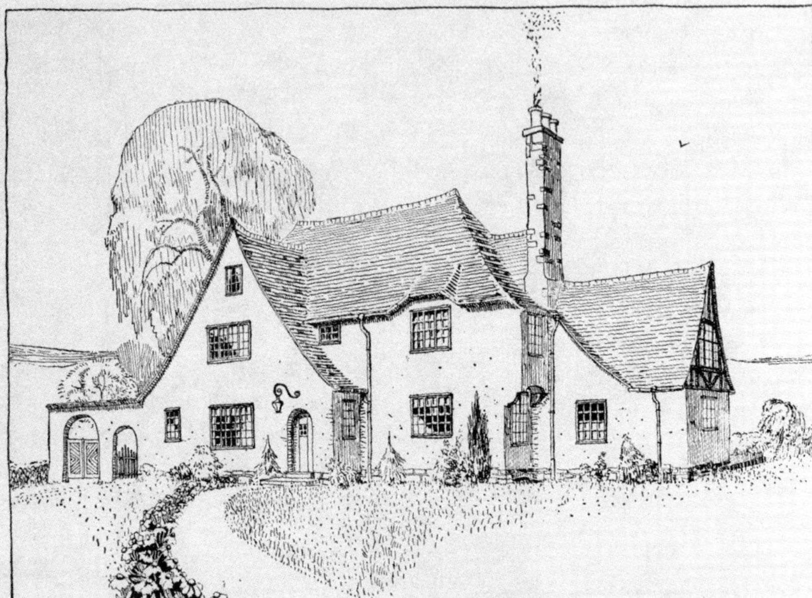

Ella Briggs, architect

In the final stage the house develops into a roomy, inviting country home—a home that has grown with the growth of the family and become a part of the life that has been lived within its walls

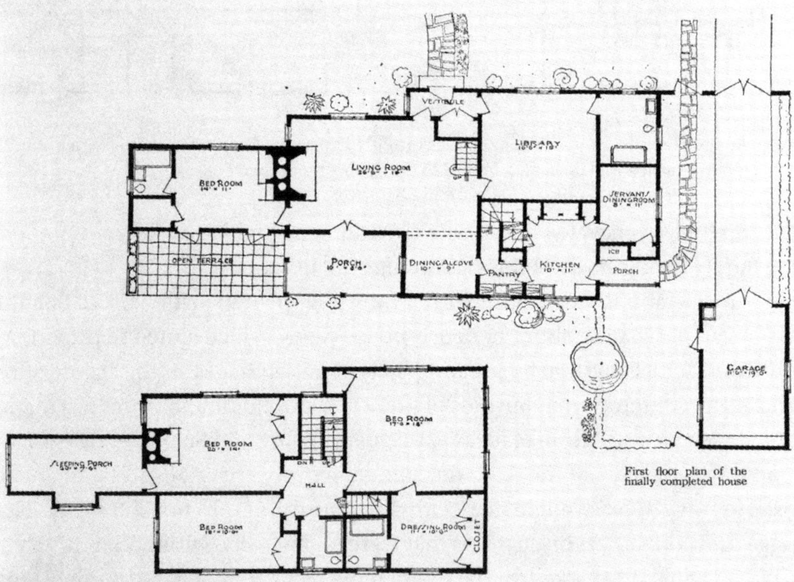

First floor plan of the finally completed house

The only change on the second floor of the finally completed house is the addition of a sleeping porch over the new bedroom on the first floor

Fig. 10.5 Ella Briggs, elevation (top) and floor plans (bottom) of the third stage of the house with a future, 1923. The floor plan above is of the first (ground) floor, and the floor plan below is of the second floor (as the architect notes, the only change to occur on the second floor is the addition of a sleeping porch above the new bedroom on the first floor).

and beauty with lower costs through an innovative design process. In this case, she focused on the advantages of cooperative building in the creation of apartments and townhouses (fig. 10.6). Specifically, she argued that instead of families building on individual plots, as was then the norm and resulted in "houses of mediocre design set in undeveloped or badly planned garden plots," they come together to build as a group. Building together would lower construction costs, and the savings could be put toward laborsaving devices that otherwise would be out of reach to individual homeowners. This coordinated approach, Briggs further noted, would allow the designer to maximize the building's health benefits—for example, by ensuring good cross-ventilation, enlarging communal greenspaces, and providing a children's playground. Compact kitchens in the individual units lowered building costs and reduced "the steps of the housewife to a minimum"—an approach that anticipates by a few years Schütte-Lihotzky's kitchen designs for mass housing in Frankfurt, Germany. Onsite communal laundry facilities would offer an electric washer, irons, and indoor and outdoor drying spaces. Briggs made extensive suggestions about the type and location of plantings that could provide privacy and beauty to the spaces—even the utilitarian ones, such as the drying yards, which she envisioned "surrounded by a 7-foot lattice covered with climbing roses and separated from the nearest tenants by a stretch of lawn softened with shrubbery." Although Briggs emphasized the advantages of constructing in this manner, she notably omitted any mention of communal life more broadly, which defined Austrian settler and German garden city movements; she must have sensed this would not resonate with middle-class American audiences. She also did not explain how families would come together to cooperate; she instead left unprobed the institutional frameworks for such activity, which she knew had been instrumental to achieving progress in Vienna. The questions of new communal and political forms that filled the socialist *Arbeiter-Zeitung* in Vienna during this period were less easily explored in *The Ladies' Home Journal*.[12]

Briggs's articles in *The Ladies' Home Journal* and *Pictorial Review*, among others, raised her profile and attracted work from other publishers. The *New York Tribune*, calling Briggs "one of the foremost practicing women architects in New York," hired her in 1924 "to design a number of unique and economical plans of small homes" for its Small House Page, a Sunday feature published in collaboration with the Home Owners Service Institute. This architects' organization, formed in response to the popularity of mass-produced mail-order houses, sought "to create the desire for and to educate the prospective home owner to build better homes, where happiness and contentment will reign." On February 17, 1924, the Small House Page featured Briggs's "laborsaving" house plan (no. 94 in the *Tribune* series), which she based on one of the winning entries from the 1923 *Pictorial Review* competition (see fig. 10.2). The design, as she described it, demonstrated thoughtful, laborsaving efficiencies, not just in the service areas but also throughout the house, leading to greater comfort and enjoyment for the occupants. Briggs informed readers that her blueprint working drawings and detailed specifications for the design could be purchased through the Home Owners Service Institute. At between $14,000 and $18,000, the projected cost of

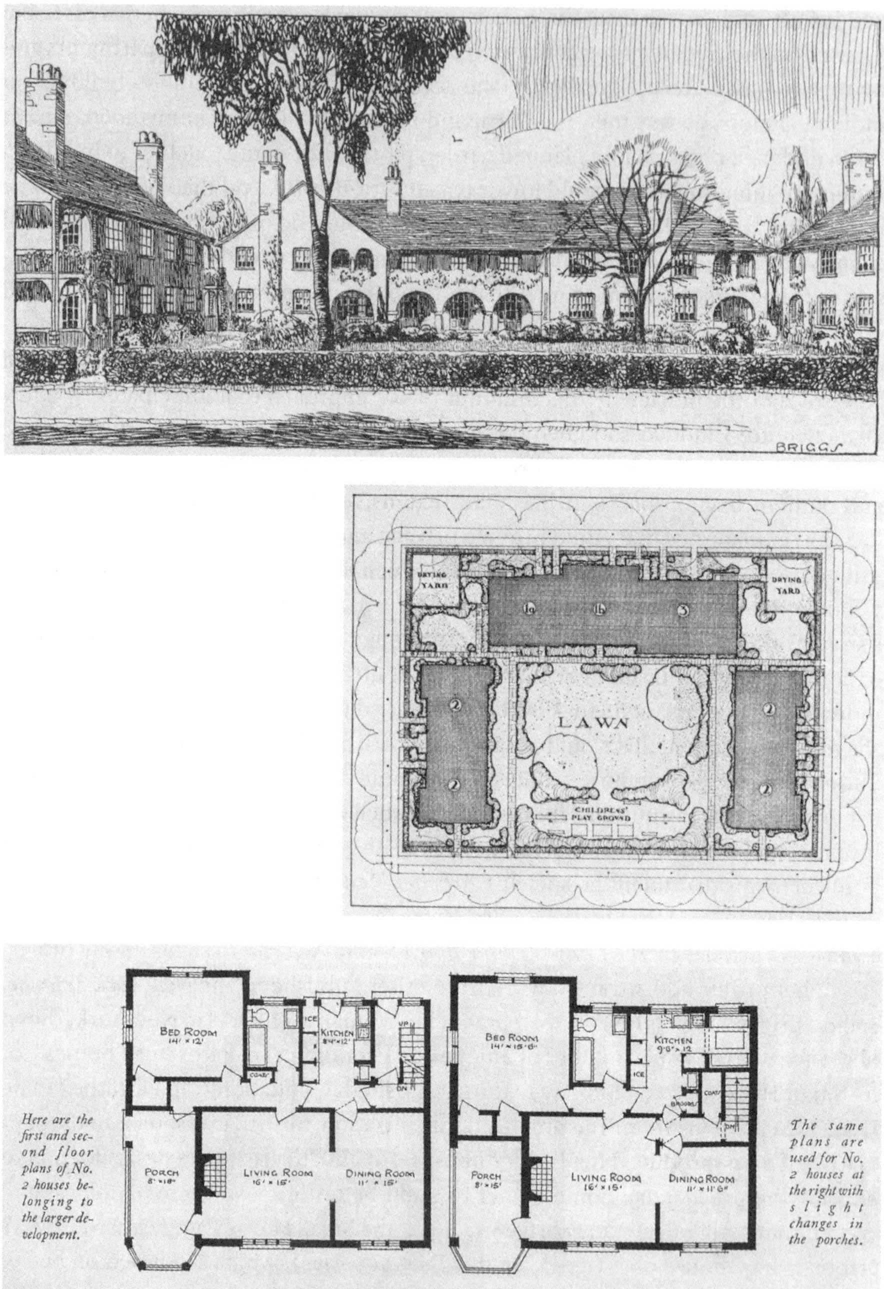

Fig. 10.6 Ella Briggs, apartment house complex, 1923: elevation (top), site plan (middle), and "No. 2 houses" floor plans (bottom). The floor plans are for the buildings (marked with small number 2s) located to the left and right of the lawn in the site plan. The floor plans depict the arrangement of the first (ground) and second floors of these "no. 2" duplexes. The planting arrangement and playground on the site plan were credited to Richard H. Pratt, Jr. Although not illustrated here, Briggs included floor plans for the other apartment houses in this complex as well as for laundry and storage spaces (in the basement of house no. 3, to the top right of the lawn).

building the house was many times higher than that of the cheapest house kits sold by mail-order companies, but the amount was in line with comparable four-bedroom house plans published by the *Tribune*.[13]

The *Tribune*'s description of Briggs as "one of the foremost practicing women architects in New York" raises the question of how she saw herself, both within a profession that was stridently masculine and in relation to broader societal norms about gender roles. Reading Briggs's articles in the context of contemporary women's magazines—with their attention to husbands and children and housework but also romance and pleasure—reveals that she attempted to relate to readers in more conventional terms, even as she asserted her own authority as an expert. For example, in a 1924 article published in *The Designer and the Woman's Magazine*, titled "A Little House That Grew," Briggs revisited the theme of the adaptable house. In this version, however, she expanded on the connection between marital happiness and the home, especially for a newlywed couple:

> Often one hears young people say that rather than live squeezed into a tiny apartment where the housewife cooks on the corner of the bathtub that part of the meal not bought at the delicatessen store they would like to have a little house of their own. But—they continue—the house they could build or buy now would be such a tiny thing that in later years, when the family will have grown, when they will have become more prosperous, they would be obliged to sell it and build a new one, and so had better wait for the time when they could afford to have the big house.
>
> Is this wise? I don't think so. Very often the first years of marriage are the ones that decide whether it is to be harmonious or not. And a real home offers many more opportunities for husband and wife to share work and pleasure than the life in an apartment. For a child to grow up in rural surroundings means not only additional health—it means a happier childhood.[14]

This style of writing, reminiscent of advice columns, positioned the woman architect as both family counselor and design consultant. Other women architects in the early twentieth century similarly adopted a strategy of presenting themselves as domestic architecture experts, claiming that their gender gave them an insider's perspective that their male colleagues lacked, which resulted in better design. Some chafed at the idea, however, that their gender best suited them to domestic projects, and they fought against the association of female architects with domesticity reinforced by the press.[15]

Beyond Briggs's public persona, details of her life in New York remain scarce. In 1924 Briggs lived at 112 East 19th Street.[16] The twelve-story, prewar building had a simple modern facade and large windows, in keeping with its commercial function: it primarily housed the offices of publishers, businesses, and educational and other organizations. The surrounding neighborhood of Gramercy Park, familiar to Briggs from her time as a member of the National Arts Club and her brother's stint at the

Irving Place Theater, attracted writers, artists, actors, and musicians, as well as independent and outspoken women pioneering new professional roles. Ethel Doty Brown, a physician who fought for equal opportunity for women doctors, lived at 26 Gramercy Park, and Beatrice Moses Hinkle, a feminist and Jungian psychoanalyst who criticized the modern institution of marriage and argued for a new sexual morality based on women's economic independence, lived at 10 Gramercy Park.[17] Did Briggs engage her neighbors on women's challenges to social and professional norms and on how she, as an architect, might contribute to the cause?

Briggs's first known building commission, also from 1924, came from a client who fell outside traditional ideas of the new homeowner, at least as presented in women's magazines.[18] Mary Knox Chapin was the forty-eight-year-old widow of H. Gerald Chapin, a professor at the Fordham School of Law. In 1920 she and her eighteen-year-old son were living in a Hamilton Heights apartment near the Hudson River, and like many widows, she took in lodgers. Chapin was a potter and a member of the New York Society of Craftsmen. She may have known Briggs through the National Arts Club or from the days when both had spouses working in law. Chapin decided to move out of the city, prompted perhaps by a desire for more natural surroundings, an in-home pottery studio, or her son's departure and her transition to a new stage of her life—we do not know. An announcement in the *New York Times* real estate section on March 9, 1924, accompanied by a drawing, revealed that Briggs was building a residence for Chapin in Larchmont Gardens, a neighborhood in the town of Mamaroneck, in Westchester County (fig. 10.7).[19]

The *Times* article reported that ground had been broken for the construction and described the project: "The design of the house, of the rural English type, which is situated on a picturesque site of solid rock, has been inspired by the formation of the land. The blasting of the rock for the garage, which is incorporated in the house, produced fine building material. The first story is built of stone, while the second will show a rough stucco treatment."[20] What happened subsequently with the construction—and how much of Briggs's design was completed—is unclear. Chapin passed away in January 1927 and may have fallen ill before the house was finished.[21] In 1926 she sold the property to a builder, who then sold "a stone and stucco English type dwelling" to an executive of the George A. Fuller Company, which erected many New York skyscrapers, including their own headquarters in the Flatiron Building.[22]

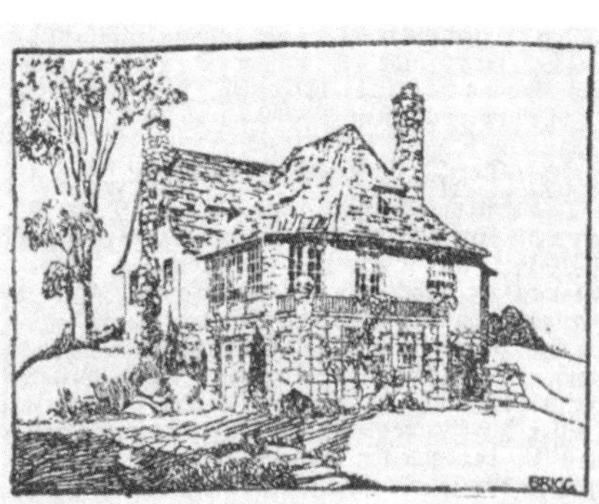

Fig. 10.7 Ella Briggs, elevation of residence planned for Mary Knox Chapin in Larchmont Gardens, New York, 1924.

The attention to site, both in terms of topography and materials, noted by the *New York Times* also appears in Briggs's writings of this period. The Chapin house exemplifies Briggs's desire to keep the house low to the site so that it could "ramble" across the lot. This characteristic, more than any other, "effectively conveys the impression of the spaciousness and freedom of country life" as opposed to "the cramped, narrow facades of city houses," she maintained. Beyond the physical and psychological expression of expansiveness, the outer appearance of the house should have a pleasing variety. One of her design principles, she wrote, "is that no detached house should have a front. It is the built-in house which logically requires a front and rear view, while the detached house should have as many fronts as sides—in other words, it should be agreeable to look at from all sides." Notably, this picturesque aspect of the house was not produced "for the sake of being picturesque"; rather, it emerged from the honest expression of function: "The unpretentious picturesqueness of the house is the result of the fact that it frankly expresses in its exterior the arrangement of the rooms inside." Briggs acknowledged that the picturesque opportunities driven "naturally" by the floor plans required the designer's thoughtful intervention, especially in bringing the massing of the house together in a pleasing manner.[23]

Function also determined the inner layout of the house plan, which Briggs compared to biology: "The good house is as purposeful as a living organism. I like to think that the different rooms of the house are so many departments, each with a main purpose to carry out." Briggs was proud that "every bit of space is put to some useful purpose" and that her house designs not only accommodated the occupants' present needs but also anticipated those of the future, including those structures that were not planned to grow in stages. As she told readers, the flow of air, the sunlight that fell on the interior, the feelings evoked by passages and rooms, the needs of the body while at work or rest, and the economies of the purse all factored into her design decisions. Briggs's explanations about site integration, purposeful layout, the body's needs, and plasticity (potential for adaptation) helped to make accessible the idea of organic design—previously explored by Frank Lloyd Wright and other architects—to her female readers. More broadly, by walking readers through her decisions and encouraging them to "wander in imagination through these rooms," she educated them about what a "good house" meant.[24]

Around 1924, Briggs designed a house for local bank executive Alfred L. Hammett and his wife Elizabeth Burdick Oxx at 1024 Clay Avenue in Pelham Manor, an affluent village in Westchester County (fig. 10.8). The two-and-a-half story, wood-frame house, completed around 1925, had nine rooms, three bathrooms, a fireplace, shingled exterior, hip roof, stone chimney, and detached garage. The Hammetts, then in their seventies, lived next door with their unmarried daughter in a nineteenth-century house, where all three continued to reside. The property at 1024 Clay Avenue, which still stands today, was rented to various tenants until it was sold by the Hammett family in 1943. Although the Hammetts' reason for building the house is unknown, they may have intended it for their son, Alfred D. Hammett, who was then living with his wife and three children in New Jersey. The children had been born in the early-to-late 1920s, and perhaps the family had planned to move to Pelham Manor to be next door to the aging grandparents.[25]

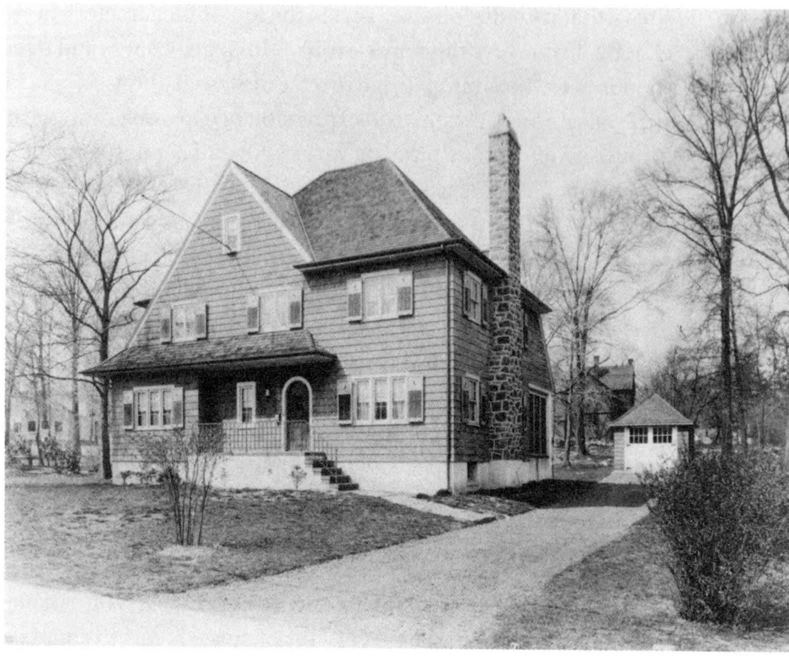

Fig. 10.8 Ella Briggs, Alfred L. Hammett House, Pelham Manor, New York, c. 1924.

How the Hammetts came to hire Ella Briggs is a mystery, but the connection may have been an article she published in the March 1924 issue of *Good Housekeeping*. Briggs began the article by recounting that the magazine's editor had asked her "to design the best house you possibly can for a family that wants a beautiful home, one with lasting value, but can't pay a big price for it." Briggs jumped at the opportunity and expressed her "hope that among the readers of the magazine there will be many who will want this house for themselves." It appears that the Hammetts were just such readers. A comparison of the house illustrated in the article with that built by the Hammetts reveals a striking similarity (fig. 10.9; and see fig. 10.8, respectively). The article encouraged readers to make further inquiries: "If you think this is the house of your dreams come true, ask us what a set of blueprints and specifications will cost you."[26]

According to *Good Housekeeping*, the response to "a charming small house" featured in the March 1924 issue had been so strong that, a year later, the magazine again commissioned Briggs to develop a house design that was "a bit larger" for its readers.[27] A photograph of a built version of this "bit larger" house, in an unspecified location, as well as of the Hammett residence were included in a 1928 article entitled "American Single-Family Homes," which Briggs published in an Austrian building magazine. In the text she claimed the *Good Housekeeping* plans had been built "over and over in different places in the United States." The architect would repeat this claim late into her life.[28] This raises a tantalizing question of whether Briggs's designs still stand elsewhere in the American landscape.

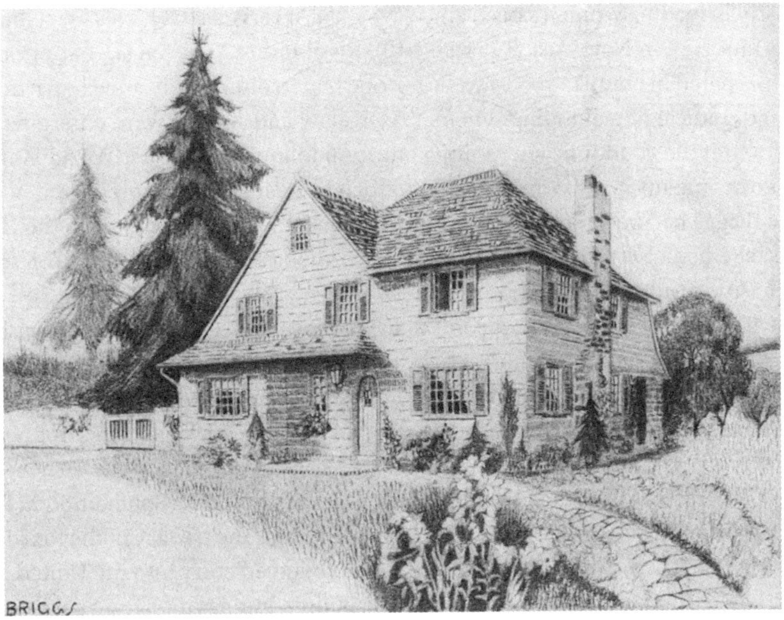

Fig. 10.9 Ella Briggs, elevation of a house designed for *Good Housekeeping*, 1924.

That Briggs herself did not seem to know their locations raises a potential drawback: if the magazine served as a vehicle for the broad implementation of Briggs's ideas, it also left the architect out of a decision-making process that could impact the successful execution of those ideas. The architect warned, "This magazine is read in so many parts of the country that no definite suggestion for the placing [of the house] on the lot can be made."[29] She nonetheless offered considerations that readers might keep in mind for optimally siting their home that factored in local conditions.

In the 1928 Austrian article, Briggs acknowledged the need to take into consideration local traditions and client tastes regarding the appearance of the home. Perhaps anticipating that her Austrian peers might find her designs old-fashioned, she noted that, "the exterior could not stray too far from the conventional type." But modernity, she also made clear to these colleagues, went beyond the facade: she emphasized her rationalization of the floor plans and introduction of new technologies intended to minimize the housewife's labor and maximize the occupants' comfort (even as, here too, she noted she had adapted her designs to American conditions).[30] In Briggs's description of her design approach to Austrian architects, we see an emerging profile of the architect's work. Briggs's emphasis on four elements—contextualization, rationalization, technologically advanced features, and user-focused designs—formed her definition of good modern design. Some of the elements already present in her prewar interior designs (in particular, contextualization and user-focused design), coalesce here as she finds her architectural footing.

By the mid-1920s, Briggs could boast of domestic commissions in the New York, Chicago, New Jersey, and Philadelphia areas.[31] Her essays and designs were published regularly in leading women's magazines, which also served as vehicles for selling her blueprints. Life in New York was rich with possibilities. Yet even so, her options at this time paled in comparison to what Europe had to offer: the chance to participate in grand, radical new building schemes. Germany and Austria were emerging from the worst of the economic and political turmoil following the First World War, and their governments made commitments to social housing on an unprecedented scale. While Briggs had been engaging with American audiences and clients in the United States, she had also travelled and exhibited in Austria to maintain her professional relationships and seek new opportunities.

By the time her big break came in Vienna in 1925, Briggs had made the decision to make a definitive, permanent move back to Europe. In addition to meaningful work, living in Vienna or Berlin would bring her in closer proximity to family and friends, and as she reached middle age this undoubtedly took on a deeper significance for her. But there was also something else to consider. On November 2, 1927, while arriving back in New York on the White Star liner RMS *Majestic* from Berlin via Southampton, Briggs was unexpectedly detained by US immigration officials. The passage of the 1924 Immigration Act restricted the number of immigrants allowed entry into the United States on the basis of quotas determined country by country. Immigration from southern and eastern Europe was sharply limited: almost all of the passengers detained on that day hailed from those regions.[32]

Unlike some of the other detainees, Briggs was admitted to the United States that same day. But this encounter with immigration officials, which foreshadows the immense difficulty that Jewish refugees would have in finding safe harbor in the United States a decade later, perhaps reinforced Briggs's conviction that she was better off in Europe. Despite New York's ample opportunities, the city had changed since her younger days. Upon her initial return in 1922, she must have noticed that New York's once-vibrant German-language culture had all but disappeared in the wake of postwar anti-German sentiment.[33] More broadly, nativism and xenophobia in the United States was on the rise, resulting in anti-immigration policies that contributed directly to Briggs's 1927 detention. And although 1920s New York hummed with new artistic energies, Briggs may have missed the older version of the city, which had also been home to her husband, since divorced, and brother, now deceased.

When Briggs briefly returned to New York in 1927, it was to undertake a research tour of the United States. The German government had commissioned her to design a modern American kitchen for a 1928 Berlin exhibition. While in New York, she visited the American Gas Association headquarters to ask for help in obtaining a new type of gas range for the model kitchen. Briggs still clearly appreciated some aspects of the United States, such as its advanced technologies, which she sought to bring to European homes.[34] When at the end of her tour she set sail to return to Berlin, she was in her late forties and had spent long stretches of time during the preceding three decades in the city, developing her career from applied artist to interior designer to architect. New York held many memories, but new horizons beckoned. She would never return.

11.
Return to Vienna and a Big Break

Sabine Plakolm-Forsthuber

While still living in New York, Briggs submitted eight photographs of buildings and projects she had designed in America to the autumn exhibition of the Künstlerhaus in Vienna, which would open on November 14, 1923. The Künstlerhaus, Austria's oldest artists' association, still excluded women from membership, but it did permit female artists to participate in its shows. Briggs's entries included two examples of a "growing house" for which several phases of expansion were planned, a conversion of existing single houses into a residential courtyard project in Philadelphia, four dwellings with laborsaving features, and one other residence. The jury of architects deciding architectural entries accepted four of her photographs corresponding to one of the "growing" houses and three of the dwellings with laborsaving devices.[1] Her inclusion was significant, as the architecture segment of the show included the work of only two other Austrian architects, in addition to Briggs: the up-and-coming Karl Dirnhuber, and the aging historicist Friedrich Ohmann.[2] Appearing in the 1923 exhibition no doubt raised Briggs's visibility within Vienna and its architectural community. Having moved to New York a year earlier but perhaps already anticipating a return, she fostered professional ties and opportunities in her hometown. Briggs would submit work to the Künstlerhaus in 1924 and 1926 as well, although neither of these future attempts to exhibit were successful.[3]

Because she would be living in New York in the fall of 1923 when the Künstlerhaus exhibit took place, Briggs noted in her application that her photographs should be returned to Melanie Langer.[4] This detail gives us a glimpse into Briggs's social circles in Vienna and how the worlds of art and affluence intermingled. Melanie was born into the wealthy and prominent Jewish Gallia family in Vienna. Her parents Moriz and Hermine Gallia were leading patrons of modernist art, architecture, and design, commissioning work from Gustav Klimt, Josef Hoffmann, and the Wiener Werkstätte. Melanie and her husband Jakob Langer, as well as Jakob's brother Leopold Langer, were among Adolf Loos's most important early clients.[5] Although Briggs had left the Jewish community and converted to Protestantism at the end of 1918, she continued to rely on Jewish support networks and to socialize with Jewish friends and colleagues (some of whom, like the Gallias, had also converted). Perhaps Ella thought that staying in touch with the well-connected Melanie would improve her chances of reintegrating quickly into the Viennese architectural scene if she decided to return. Yet the modernist arena was changing in Red Vienna, ushering in a new set of players.

After spending only two years in New York, Briggs was back in Vienna by the end of 1924. Following a work-related trip to Italy, Briggs deployed her prewar women's network to find a place to live.[6] In March 1925 she took up residence at Hofzeile 29 in Vienna-Döbling, in the Hortensium, a horticultural school for girls and boys founded in the early 1920s by Grete Salzer, a former student of Briggs's friend Yella Hertzka.[7] Salzer had converted her family's property into a spacious school building and laid out extensive school gardens on an adjacent lot.

In January 1926, Briggs moved to Weimarer Strasse 1.[8] This dynamic corner building designed by Karl Dirnhuber was part of the municipal social housing program (fig. 11.1). Its attic-lofts were offered as artists' studios (which some, like Briggs, also used as their living quarters) in an attempt to draft artists' support for the city's socialist agenda. Perhaps Briggs landed this desirable unit through the architect himself, whom she may have known through mutual friends or professional associations.[9] Briggs certainly would have had to use her networks to find places to live. As a single, divorced woman, she would not have found it easy to rent a good apartment. According to a 1924 report by journalist Gisela Urban, the general opinion among Viennese landlords was that "A woman is an undesirable lodger. She stays too much at home. And she does all the little jobs, washing, ironing, cooking little meals herself, so that there is not much profit to be got out of her."[10] Yet the situation was evolving with the city's new buildings, which included apartments for single people (a development to which Briggs would soon contribute). By choosing a studio, she defined herself not as a single woman but rather as an artist and architect. This domestic camouflaging hints at a desire to avoid the stigma in her milieu of being a divorced woman. Perhaps more importantly, it was a thrifty choice, allowing her to minimize her expenses as she sought to establish her architectural practice in Vienna. For a self-reliant woman, financial concerns were also front and center.

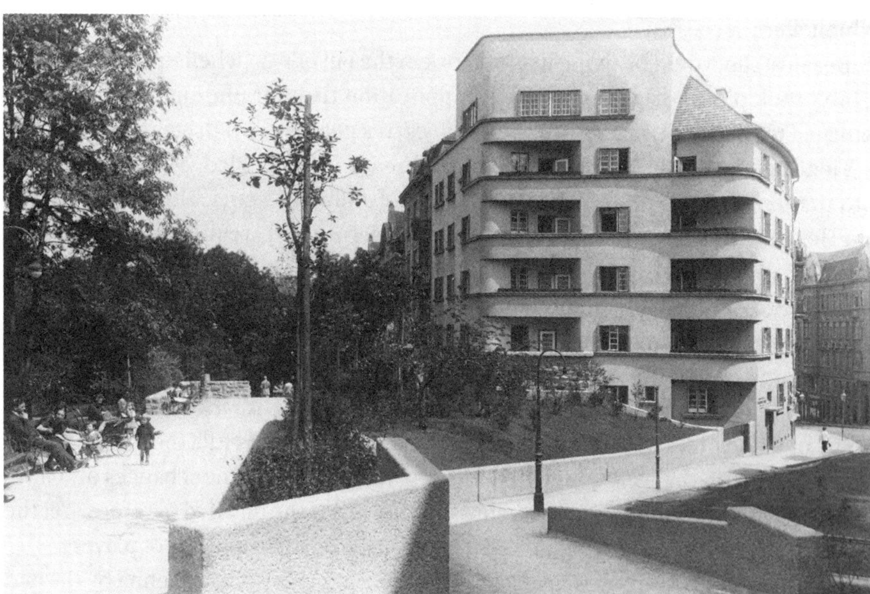

Fig. 11.1 Karl Dirnhuber, Weimarer Strasse 1 (near Schubertpark) in Vienna, 1924–1925. Ella Briggs rented an artist's studio, where she also lived, on the top (American sixth or Austrian fifth) floor. (Photograph by Martin Gerlach, Jr., c. 1926.)

Yet even as such societal prejudices lingered, more enlightened attitudes about women were emerging in the newly founded Austrian republic. In 1918 and 1919 the Social Democrats introduced women's suffrage as well as women's right to higher education in their efforts to promote gender equality. The party envisioned a working-class woman who would be employed, politically active, and independent.[11] The city's social housing program was key to realizing this vision. As a credentialed architect and socially engaged woman, Briggs saw an opportunity. But how to deploy it posed a problem, especially since gendered stereotypes—and male power networks—did not change overnight. A significant transformation in Vienna's housing policy, however, created an opening that the enterprising Briggs could exploit.

After several years supporting low-scale, low-density cooperative settlements in outlying green areas, the Vienna City Council shifted its strategy for residential development to large-scale public housing and municipal settlements in urban settings. Vienna's sweeping municipal housing program, adopted by the Social Democrats in 1923, envisioned the construction of 25,000 apartments by 1927. A second five-year program received approval in 1927. Together the programs made it possible to build 64,000 apartments to rehouse 200,000 people by 1934. The City of Vienna had recognized that the housing crisis could not be overcome with the settler movement initiatives alone and planned for the construction of multistory residential buildings. Its target group was working-class families, who were to be given access to small modern apartments that were affordable and hygienic. A tax on goods and property introduced in 1923 provided the funding for the rapidly progressing construction program.[12]

Although during the first phase of construction the majority of the architects were civil servants from the city planning department, private firms increasingly came on board, including a considerable number of architects who had studied under Otto Wagner. Since Briggs had not yet made a name for herself as an architect in Vienna, and in addition, was a woman in a male-dominated field, it undoubtedly would have been extremely difficult for her to gain the attention and trust of the city's hierarchically structured city planning department. Without intervention from male colleagues, desirable commissions for large-scale construction projects would probably have remained out of reach for her. So the question becomes, who helped Briggs in her efforts to receive commissions from the city planning department? Dirnhuber, who during the 1920s built multiple communal housing projects, in addition to the one at Weimarer Strasse 1 where Briggs lived, is a possible contender.[13]

Yet Briggs's strategic approach to obtaining a large municipal commission was likely carried out on additional fronts. We can infer her intent from her application for membership to the Zentralvereinigung der Architekten Österreichs (Central Association of Austrian Architects) (fig. 11.2). Recommendations from two members and "at least five years of work in the studio of a recognized architect" were required to join this professional association of independent architects. Because the association's files have been lost, it is no longer possible to find out who served as her advocates. She had worked for Alfred Keller and Karl Holey during the war, so perhaps one or both of them took

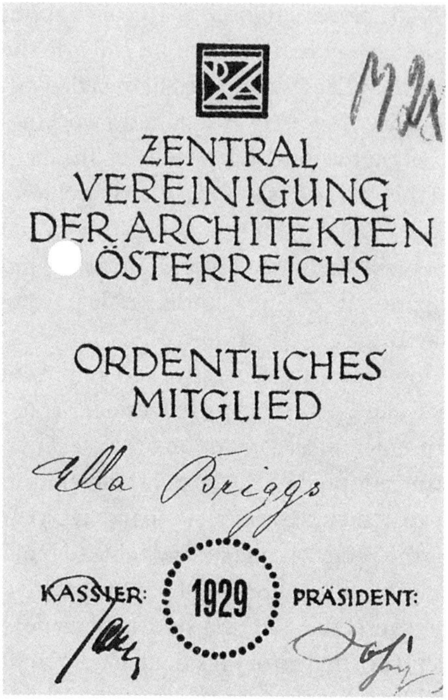

Fig. 11.2 Ella Briggs's membership card (front side) from 1929 for the Central Association of Austrian Architects. Briggs submitted this card for her restitution claim after World War II as evidence of her professional standing and accomplishments as an architect before she was forced into exile.

on this role; or maybe Dirnhuber, again, was involved. Briggs's application was successful, and in 1925 she became the first female member of the Central Association of Austrian Architects.[14]

Later that same year Leonie Pilewski also joined the association. Like Briggs, Pilewski had attempted during the First World War to matriculate as a regular student at the Vienna Technical University, but to no avail. Pilewski then studied in Darmstadt, where she completed her studies in 1922.[15] Both women had gained their initial professional experience as architects abroad—Pilewski in Germany and the Soviet Union; Briggs in the United States—which they were permitted to put toward their admission to the Central Association of Austrian Architects. Once received, this membership gave them access to public building contracts.

Though membership in the Central Association of Austrian Architects was not a prerequisite for receiving a contract from the municipality, hiring a member offered some legal security for the client—in this case, the city. Members committed to upholding the laws and duties of the architectural profession. In this sense, membership represented a certain standard of quality and professionalism—a stamp of approval, one could say, for an elite cohort of freelance architects.

Around the time that Briggs became a member of the Central Association of Austrian Architects, she also worked to raise and define her public profile. The opportunity to do so arose because of a major exhibition and the public conversations it spurred on the topic of household rationalization. At the end of April 1925, the blockbuster *Hygiene-Ausstellung Wien* (Vienna Hygiene Exhibition) opened at the Messepalast, the large exhibition building in the Prater, a vast popular park in the city center that had once been royal hunting grounds. The exhibition encompassed three parts: *Hygiene*, offering a sweeping view of health from the individual to society; *Der Mensch* (The Human Being), exploring the human body; and *Der neue Haushalt* (The New Housekeeping), surveying modern housekeeping. The Bund Österreichischer Frauenvereine (Federation of Austrian Women's Associations) coordinated the housekeeping section, which featured displays on all aspects of the modern household, including different sizes and types of kitchens, some with electrical appliances. The exhibition drew huge crowds—100,000 in the first week alone—with women particularly well represented.[16]

Among architects in Austria and Germany, interest was growing in household reform, and particularly in American developments led by figures such as Christine Frederick, a housewife who applied the principles of Taylorism or scientific management to housekeeping to economize on time, labor, space, and costs.[17] In 1921 Frederick's enormously successful 1913 book *The New Housekeeping: Efficiency Studies in Home Management* was translated into German as *Die rationelle Haushaltsführung* (Rational housekeeping).[18] Although Frederick's reliance on electric gadgetry was out of the price range of most Viennese, her experiments applying time and motion studies developed for the factory workplace to the home found an eager audience. Grete Schütte-Lihotzky claimed her Taylorized kitchen designs were directly inspired by reading Frederick's book in 1921.[19] In 1924 Berlin architect Bruno Taut, also influenced by Frederick, published *Die neue Wohnung: Die Frau als Schöpferin* (The new dwelling: The woman as creator), a guidebook to help the housewife rid herself of old habits and embrace her role in the creation of more efficient and beautiful dwellings.[20]

The Hygiene Exhibition and the public conversations that unfolded in its wake brought the significance of the new housekeeping to a broad audience in Vienna. Newspapers and magazines across the political spectrum discussed the topic, encouraging women to absorb the exhibit's lessons in order to help themselves and society, with the tone vacillating between patronizing and emancipatory. *Der freie Genossenschafter* (The Free Cooperator), the journal of Austria's cooperative movement, pleaded with proletariat women to buy themselves an electric iron, reasoning that they could afford it if they just went to the cinema less often.[21] Gisela Urban, who participated on the women's committee for *Der neue Haushalt*, brought attention to conversations about the new housekeeping that the exhibition had prompted among women themselves, including in their associations. Urban called for women to have a stronger voice in housing policy so that the requirements of the new housekeeping were considered when building new homes.[22]

Others also brought attention to the significance of the new housekeeping for the social housing then being planned and erected by the City of Vienna. In an April 1925 radio address about the upcoming exhibition, an organizer of *Der neue Haushalt* noted that the housing shortage posed the challenge of how to accommodate "many people in small spaces." A solution could only be found, the speaker maintained, if housewives and architects worked together to determine how to live comfortably even under such conditions.[23]

Seeing the interest in modern housekeeping generated by the exhibition and the connections being made to the new social housing, Briggs grasped that this angle would be the most favorable way to present her American work to her Viennese colleagues. Many of her projects in the United States had involved single-family homes in a suburban setting, in contrast to the shift toward denser, urban forms of living in Vienna. The wildly disparate economic and political contexts of the United States and Austria would have made it hard to argue for the suitability of the American house type—no matter how innovative—for Vienna. Yet by highlighting her efforts to reduce household labor through thoughtful architectural design, Briggs could portray herself as an expert in a field that was about to take center stage in the city's housing discussions. Thanks to American writers such as Frederick as well as innovations in domestic technologies, Europeans viewed the United States as a leader in the field of housework modernization. All considered, this was a brilliant move on Briggs's part.

In June of 1925, as the exhibition entered its last month, Briggs launched a public campaign to insert herself into the unfolding new housekeeping discussions. To begin, she presented a slide lecture on June 16 on "How the American Dwelling Eases Household Management" at the Messepalast as part of the Hygiene Exhibition programming.[24] In addition, that month she published two articles on related themes in Viennese newspapers.[25] One of them, on the Taylorization of the American kitchen, appeared in the *Arbeiter-Zeitung*, the daily of the Social Democratic Party (fig. 11.3). Publishing in this venue allowed Briggs to engage a critical and influential audience on the subject of the society which they were all in the process of constructing.

In these various forms of public dialogue, Briggs drew on her own American experiences and architectural projects to advocate for greater efficiency in domestic design in order to lessen the energy and time that housework required. Thoughtful arrangement of floorplans to minimize labor saved the housewife steps and fatigue. But Briggs also advocated for the mechanization of the kitchen through appliances: "What can be done by a machine should be removed from the realm of manual work." In particular, she praised the American electrical washing machine, which transformed doing laundry from a daylong torment into an occasional task. "Anyone who knows the horrors of a laundry day in Vienna," she wrote, would admire how "painlessly" the American housewife could do her family's weekly laundry "in just a few hours."[26]

And yet even as Briggs advocated for electrical machines, she admitted in her *Arbeiter-Zeitung* article that such laborsaving devices were "out of the question" for the individual consumer "in our poor country." Instead, she praised as "a brilliant social idea" Emmy Freundlich's proposal to make such appliances available as part of "working groups" within the new social housing.[27] Freundlich, a Social Democratic parliamentarian and staunch advocate of the cooperative movement, was also one of the main exhibition organizers of *Der neue Haushalt*.[28] As much as Freundlich admired the advances in domestic technologies on display in Vienna as aids in lessening a housewife's burden, she did not view them as a solution to women's emancipation. This was not only because of their prohibitive cost but also because such change was ultimately social in nature. Freundlich thus proposed the creation of "working groups" for housewives, cooperatives that would be formed in the new social housing that would enable women to pool their resources to buy appliances together. She imagined a communal room set up with bread machines and laundry equipment, among other things, that could be used by all the housewives in a building. These groups could also organize daily activities, such as shopping and childcare, so that women did not have to do everything themselves. With this free time, a housewife might go for an excursion or join in political work. Appliances had their purpose, but for Freundlich, "the housewife's freedom and equality can only be gained through organization."[29]

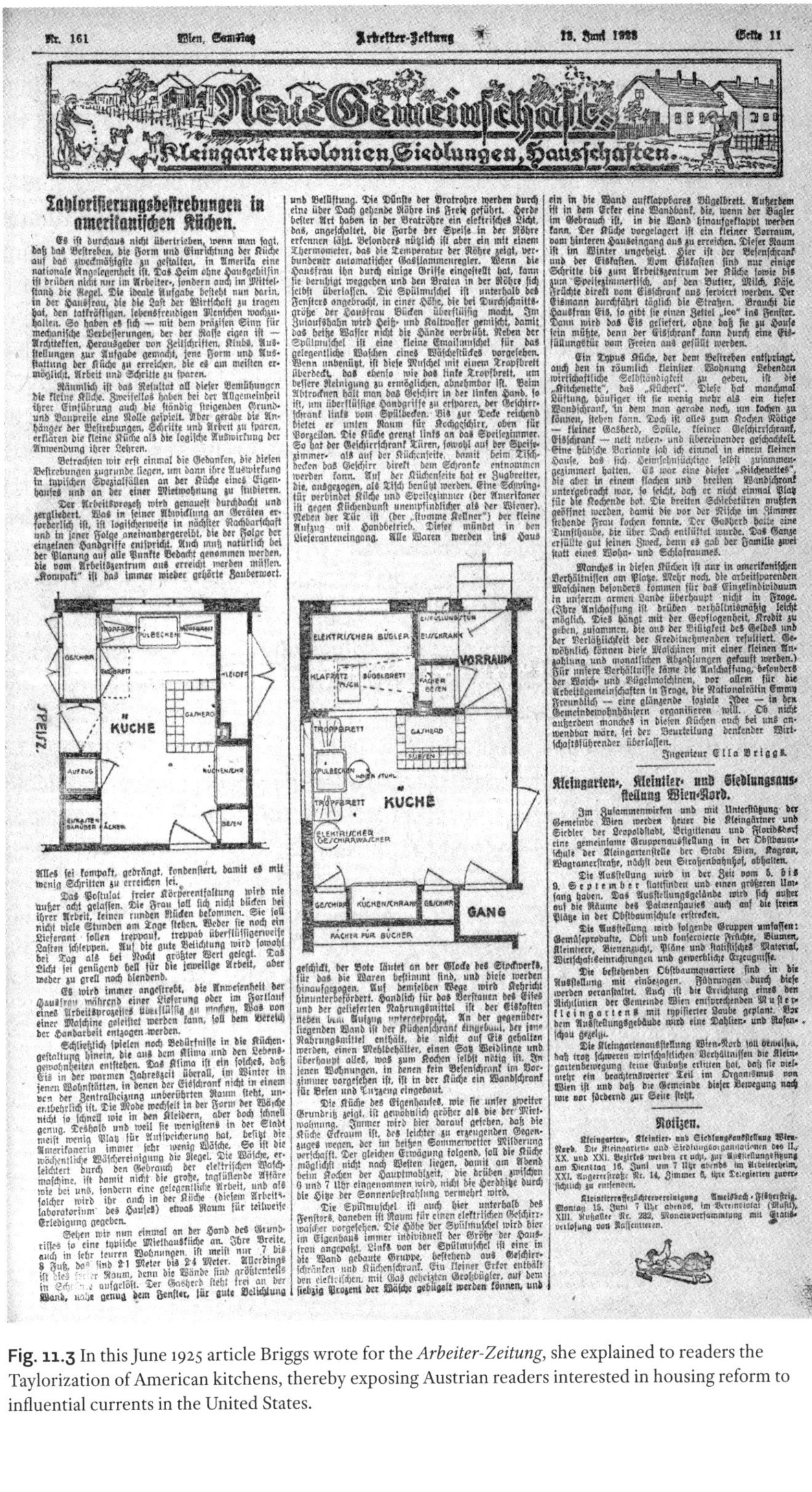

Nr. 161 Wien, Samstag Arbeiter-Zeitung 13. Juni 1925 Seite 11

Neue Gemeinschaft

Kleingartenkolonien, Siedlungen, Hausschaften.

Taylorisierungsbestrebungen in amerikanischen Küchen.

Es ist durchaus nicht übertrieben, wenn man sagt, daß das Bestreben, die Form und Einrichtung der Küche auf das zweckmäßigste zu gestalten, in Amerika eine nationale Angelegenheit ist. Das Heim ohne Hausgehilfin ist drüben nicht nur im Arbeiter-, sondern auch im Mittelstand die Regel. Die ideale Aufgabe besteht nun darin, in der Hausfrau, die die Last der Wirtschaft zu tragen hat, den tatkräftigen, lebensfreudigen Menschen wachzuhalten. So haben es sich — mit dem präzisen Sinn für mechanische Verbesserungen, der der Rasse eigen ist — Architekten, Herausgeber von Zeitschriften, Klubs, Ausstellungen zur Aufgabe gemacht, jene Form und Ausstattung der Küche zu erreichen, die es am meisten ermöglicht, Arbeit und Schritte zu sparen.

Räumlich ist das Resultat all dieser Bemühungen die kleine Küche. Zweifellos haben bei der Allgemeinheit ihrer Einführung auch die ständig steigenden Grund- und Baupreise eine Rolle gespielt. Aber gerade die Anhänger der Bestrebungen, Schritte und Arbeit zu sparen, erklären die kleine Küche als die logische Auswirkung der Anwendung ihrer Lehren.

Betrachten wir erst einmal die Gedanken, die diesen Bestrebungen zugrunde liegen, um dann ihre Auswirkung in typischen Spezialfällen an der Küche eines Eigenhauses und an der einer Mietwohnung zu studieren.

Der Arbeitsprozeß wird genauest durchdacht und zergliedert. Was in seiner Abwicklung an Geräten erforderlich ist, ist logischerweise in nächster Nachbarschaft und in jener Folge aneinandergereiht, die der Folge der einzelnen Handgriffe entspricht. Auch muß natürlich bei der Planung auf alle Punkte Bedacht genommen werden, die vom Arbeitszentrum aus erreicht werden müssen. „Kompakt" ist das immer wieder gehörte Zauberwort.

Alles sei kompakt, gedrängt, kondensiert, damit es mit wenig Schritten zu erreichen sei.

Das Postulat freier Körperentfaltung wird nie außer acht gelassen. Die Frau soll sich nicht bücken bei ihrer Arbeit, keinen runden Rücken bekommen. Sie soll nicht viele Stunden am Tage stehen. Weder sie noch ein Lieferant sollen treppauf, treppab überflüssigerweise Lasten schleppen. Auf die gute Belichtung wird sowohl bei Tag als bei Nacht größter Wert gelegt. Das Licht sei genügend hell für die jeweilige Arbeit, aber weder zu grell noch blendend.

Es wird immer angestrebt, die Anwesenheit der Hausfrau während einer Lieferung oder im Fortlauf eines Arbeitsprozesses überflüssig zu machen. Was von einer Maschine geleistet werden kann, soll dem Bereich der Handarbeit entzogen werden.

Schließlich spielen noch Bedürfnisse in die Küchengestaltung hinein, die aus dem Klima und den Lebensgewohnheiten entstehen. Das Klima ist ein solches, daß Eis in der warmen Jahreszeit überall, im Winter in jenen Wohnstätten, in denen der Eisschrank nicht in einem von der Zentralheizung unberührten Raum steht, unentbehrlich ist. Die Mode wechselt in der Form der Wäsche nicht so schnell wie in den Kleidern, aber doch schnell genug. Deshalb und weil sie wenigstens in der Stadt meist wenig Platz für Aufspeicherung hat, besitzt die Amerikanerin immer sehr wenig Wäsche. So ist die wöchentliche Wäschereinigung die Regel. Die Wäsche, erleichtert durch den Gebrauch der elektrischen Waschmaschine, ist damit nicht die große, tagfüllende Affäre wie bei uns, sondern eine gelegentliche Arbeit, und als solcher wird ihr auch in der Küche (diesem Arbeitslaboratorium des Hauses) etwas Raum für teilweise Erledigung gegeben.

Sehen wir nun einmal an der Hand des Grundrisses so eine typische Miethausküche an. Ihre Breite, auch in sehr teuren Wohnungen, ist meist nur 7 bis 8 Fuß, das sind 2·1 Meter bis 2·4 Meter. Allerdings ist dies freier Raum, denn die Wände sind größtenteils in Schränke aufgelöst. Der Gasherd steht frei an der Wand, nahe genug dem Fenster, für gute Belichtung und Belüftung. Die Dünste der Bratrohre werden durch eine über Dach gehende Röhre ins Freie geführt. Herde bester Art haben in der Bratröhre ein elektrisches Licht, das, angeschaltet, die Farbe der Speise in der Röhre erkennen läßt. Besonders nützlich ist aber ein mit einem Thermometer, das die Temperatur der Röhre zeigt, verbundener automatischer Gasflammenregler. Wenn die Hausfrau ihn durch einige Griffe eingestellt hat, kann sie beruhigt weggehen und den Braten in der Röhre sich selbst überlassen. Die Spülmuschel ist unterhalb des Fensters angebracht, in einer Höhe, die bei Durchschnittsgröße der Hausfrau Bücken überflüssig macht. Im Zulaufshahn wird Heiß- und Kaltwasser gemischt, damit das heiße Wasser nicht die Hände verbrüht. Neben der Spülmuschel ist eine kleine Emailmuschel für das gelegentliche Waschen eines Wäschestückes vorgesehen. Wenn unbenützt, ist diese Muschel mit einem Tropfbrett überdeckt, das ebenso wie das linke Tropfbrett, um bessere Reinigung zu ermöglichen, abnehmbar ist. Beim Abtrocknen hält man das Geschirr in der linken Hand, so ist, um überflüssige Handgriffe zu ersparen, der Geschirrschrank links vom Spülbecken. Bis zur Decke reichend bietet er unten Raum für Kochgeschirr, oben für Porzellan. Die Küche grenzt links an das Speisezimmer. So hat der Geschirrschrank Türen, sowohl auf der Speisezimmer- als auf der Küchenseite, damit beim Tischdecken das Geschirr direkt dem Schranke entnommen werden kann. Auf der Küchenseite hat er Zugbretter, die, ausgezogen, als Tisch benützt werden. Eine Schwingtür verbindet Küche und Speisezimmer (der Amerikaner ist gegen Küchendunst unempfindlicher als der Wiener). Neben der Tür ist (der „stumme Kellner") der kleine Aufzug mit Handbetrieb. Dieser mündet in den Lieferanteneingang. Alle Waren werden ins Haus

geschickt, der Bote läutet an der Glocke des Stockwerks, für das die Waren bestimmt sind, und diese werden hinaufgezogen. Auf demselben Wege wird Kehricht hinunterbefördert. Handlich für das Verstauen des Eises und der gelieferten Nahrungsmittel ist der Eiskasten neben dem Aufzug untergebracht. An der gegenüberliegenden Wand ist der Küchenschrank eingebaut, der jene Nahrungsmittel enthält, die nicht auf Eis gehalten werden, einen Mehlbehälter, einen Satz Weidlinge und überhaupt alles, was zum Kochen selbst nötig ist. In jenen Wohnungen, in denen kein Besenschrank im Vorzimmer vorgesehen ist, ist in der Küche ein Wandschrank für Besen und Putzzeug eingebaut.

Die Küche des Eigenhauses, wie sie unser zweiter Grundriß zeigt, ist gewöhnlich größer als die der Mietwohnung. Immer wird hier darauf gesehen, daß die Küche Eckraum ist, des leichter zu erzeugenden Gegenzuges wegen, der im heißen Sommerwetter Milderung verschafft. Der gleichen Erwägung folgend, soll die Küche möglichst nicht nach Westen liegen, damit am Abend beim Kochen der Hauptmahlzeit, die drüben zwischen 6 und 7 Uhr eingenommen wird, nicht die Herdhitze durch die Hitze der Sonnenbestrahlung vermehrt wird.

Die Spülmuschel ist auch hier unterhalb des Fensters, daneben ist Raum für einen elektrischen Geschirrwascher vorgesehen. Die Höhe der Spülmuschel wird hier im Eigenhaus immer individuell der Größe der Hausfrau angepaßt. Links von der Spülmuschel ist eine in die Wand gebaute Gruppe, bestehend aus Geschirrschränken und Küchenschrank. Ein kleiner Erker enthält den elektrischen, mit Gas geheizten Großbügler, auf dem siebzig Prozent der Wäsche gebügelt werden können, und ein in die Wand aufklappbares Bügelbrett. Außerdem ist in dem Erker eine Wandbank, die, wenn der Bügler im Gebrauch ist, in die Wand hinaufgeklappt werden kann. Der Küche vorgelagert ist ein kleiner Vorraum, vom hinteren Hauseingang aus zu erreichen. Dieser Raum ist im Winter ungeheizt. Hier ist der Besenschrank und der Eiskasten. Vom Eiskasten sind nur einige Schritte bis zum Arbeitszentrum der Küche sowie bis zum Speisezimmertisch, auf den Butter, Milch, Käse, Früchte direkt vom Eisschrank aus serviert werden. Der Eismann durchfährt täglich die Straßen. Braucht die Hausfrau Eis, so gibt sie einen Zettel „ice" ins Fenster. Dann wird das Eis geliefert, ohne daß sie zu Hause sein müßte, denn der Eisschrank kann durch eine Eisfüllungstür vom Freien aus gefüllt werden.

Ein Typus Küche, der dem Bestreben entspringt, auch den in räumlich kleinster Wohnung Lebenden wirtschaftliche Selbständigkeit zu geben, ist die „Kitchenette", das „Kücherl". Diese hat manchmal Lüftung, häufiger ist sie wenig mehr als ein tiefer Wandschrank, in dem man gerade noch, um kochen zu können, stehen kann. Doch ist alles zum Kochen Nötige — kleiner Gasherd, Spüle, kleiner Geschirrschrank, Eisschrank — nett neben- und übereinander geschachtelt. Eine hübsche Variante sah ich einmal in einem kleinen Hause, das sich Heimsehnsüchtige selbst zusammengezimmert hatten. Es war eine dieser „Kitchenettes", die aber in einem flachen und breiten Wandschrank untergebracht war, so seicht, daß er nicht einmal Platz für die Kochende bot. Die breiten Schiebetüren mußten geöffnet werden, damit die vor der Nische im Zimmer stehende Frau kochen konnte. Der Gasherd hatte eine Dunsthaube, die über Dach entlüftet wurde. Das Ganze erfüllte gut seinen Zweck, denn es gab der Familie zwei statt eines Wohn- und Schlafraumes.

Manches in diesen Küchen ist nur in amerikanischen Verhältnissen am Platze. Mehr noch, die arbeitsparenden Maschinen besonders kommen für das Einzelindividuum in unserem armen Lande überhaupt nicht in Frage. (Ihre Anschaffung ist drüben verhältnismäßig leicht möglich. Dies hängt mit der Gepflogenheit, Kredit zu geben, zusammen, die aus der Billigkeit des Geldes und der Verläßlichkeit der Kreditnehmenden resultiert. Gewöhnlich können diese Maschinen mit einer kleinen Anzahlung und monatlichen Abzahlungen gekauft werden.) Für unsere Verhältnisse käme die Anschaffung, besonders der Wasch- und Bügelmaschinen, vor allem für die Arbeitsgemeinschaften in Frage, die Nationalrätin Emmy Freundlich — eine glänzende soziale Idee — in den Gemeindewohnhäusern organisieren will. Ob nicht außerdem manches in diesen Küchen auch bei uns anwendbar wäre, sei der Beurteilung denkender Wirtschaftsführender überlassen.

Ingenieur Ella Briggs.

Kleingarten-, Kleintier- und Siedlungsausstellung Wien-Nord.

Im Zusammenwirken und mit Unterstützung der Gemeinde Wien werden heuer die Kleingärtner und Siedler der Leopoldstadt, Brigittenau und Floridsdorf eine gemeinsame Gruppenausstellung in der Obstbaumschule der Kleingartenstelle der Stadt Wien, Kagran, Wagramerstraße, nächst dem Straßenbahnhof, abhalten.

Die Ausstellung wird in der Zeit vom 5. bis 9. September stattfinden und einen größeren Umfang haben. Das Ausstellungsgelände wird sich außer auf die Räume des Palmenhauses auch auf die freien Plätze in der Obstbaumschule erstrecken.

Die Ausstellung wird folgende Gruppen umfassen: Gemüseprodukte, Obst und konservierte Früchte, Blumen, Kleintiere, Bienenzucht, Pläne und statistisches Material, Wirtschaftseinrichtungen und gewerbliche Erzeugnisse.

Die bestehenden Obstbaumquartiere sind in die Ausstellung mit einbezogen. Führungen durch diese werden veranstaltet. Auch ist die Errichtung eines den Richtlinien der Gemeinde Wien entsprechenden Musterkleingartens mit typisierter Laube geplant. Vor dem Ausstellungsgebäude wird eine Dahlien- und Rosenschau gezeigt.

Die Kleingartenausstellung Wien-Nord soll beweisen, daß trotz schweren wirtschaftlichen Verhältnissen die Kleingartenbewegung keine Einbuße erlitten hat, daß sie vielmehr ein beachtenswerter Teil im Organismus von Wien ist und daß die Gemeinde dieser Bewegung nach wie vor fördernd zur Seite steht.

Notizen.

Kleingarten-, Kleintier- und Siedlungsausstellung Wien-Nord. Die Kleingarten- und Siedlungsorganisationen des II., XX. und XXI. Bezirkes werden ersucht, zur Ausstellungssitzung am Dienstag 16. Juni um 7 Uhr abends im Arbeiterheim, XXI. Angererstraße Nr. 14, Zimmer 6, ihre Delegierten zuversichtlich zu entsenden.

Kleintierrassezüchtervereinigung Ameisbach-Fischerstieg. Montag 15. Juni 7 Uhr abends, im Vereinslokal (Musil), XIII. Auhofstraße Nr. 232, Monatsversammlung mit Gratisverlosung von Rassentieren.

Fig. 11.3 In this June 1925 article Briggs wrote for the *Arbeiter-Zeitung*, she explained to readers the Taylorization of American kitchens, thereby exposing Austrian readers interested in housing reform to influential currents in the United States.

It is significant that Briggs, as an architect, actively and openly engaged with advances in domestic reform led by home economists such as Christine Frederick. Although her male colleagues benefited from research in this field, with a few exceptions (such as Bruno Taut) they did not acknowledge their debt. Briggs, by contrast, unapologetically leveraged such female-led domestic design expertise.[30] She publicly and emphatically aligned her architectural practice with the domestic reform movement, a gambit that was sincere as well as strategic. By 1925 Briggs already had a history of engaging with such concerns as an architect. And as she occasionally let seep through in her writings—in referring, for example, to knowing the "horrors" of Vienna's washdays—it was also a subject that she knew from personal experience, as a single woman who ran her own household. Bruno Taut, as much as he wanted to help housewives (and to have housewives help architects), probably never did his own laundry.

Briggs's efforts to raise her professional visibility through the exhibition *Der neue Haushalt* may also have served another purpose. In 1925 Briggs's expertise in rationalization was still grounded in the generously proportioned American single-family house rather than in the cramped Viennese apartment. By engaging with Viennese audiences on this topic through conversation and writing, she may also have begun to more fully translate her American-formed ideas into a Viennese context. This period of activity might thus also be considered as a way that Briggs provided herself with an intellectual testing ground to check where adjustment was needed as she brought concepts and experiences from the other side of the Atlantic to bear on a different place and context.

Shortly after initiating her public outreach strategy, Briggs had her big break. On July 29, 1925, Vienna's city council passed a resolution in favor of building a residential complex in Vienna-Döbling on a site bordered by Felix Mottlstrasse (renamed Philippovichgasse in 1927), Lissbauergasse, and Billrothstrasse.[31] The commission to design and construct the Pestalozzi-Hof, as it would be named, was awarded to Briggs.[32] This was a tremendous personal and professional achievement for the forty-five-year-old. Here was an opportunity to harness years of practice as an interior designer and lately, architect, to explore—at a scale beyond anything she had attempted before—a new way of living. Briggs thus found herself at the heart of a vast social housing experiment that she herself would now have a hand in shaping.

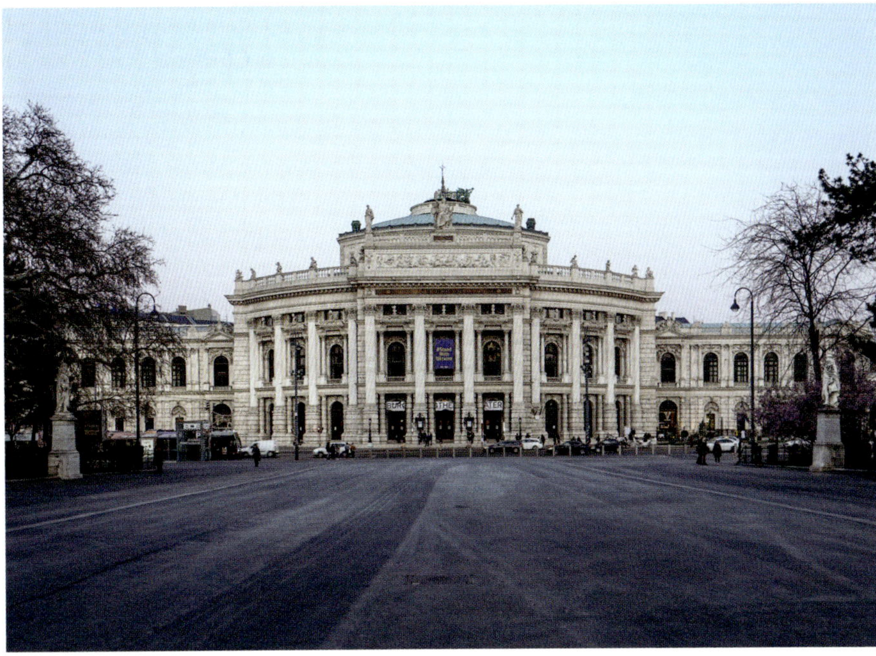

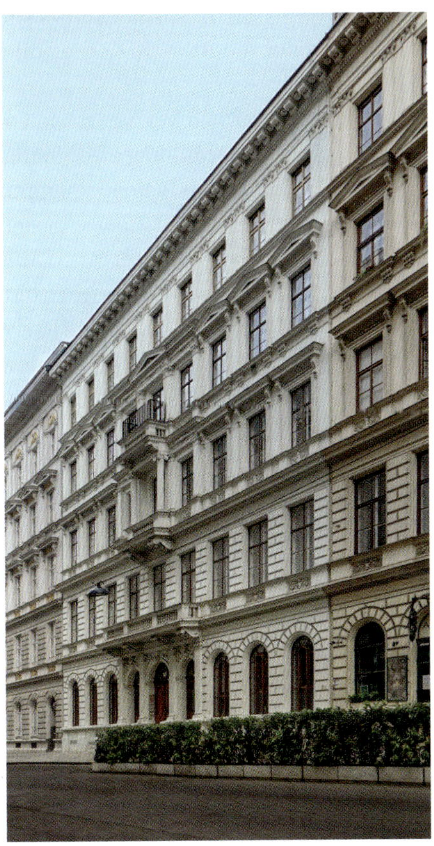

Plate 1 (above) Contemporary view of the Burgtheater (Court Theater), on Vienna's renowned Ringstrasse. (Photograph by Benjamin von Radom, 2024.)

Plate 2 (left) Ella Briggs's birthplace and first family home: Schottenbastei 6, in Vienna's prestigious first district. (Photograph by Benjamin von Radom, 2024.)

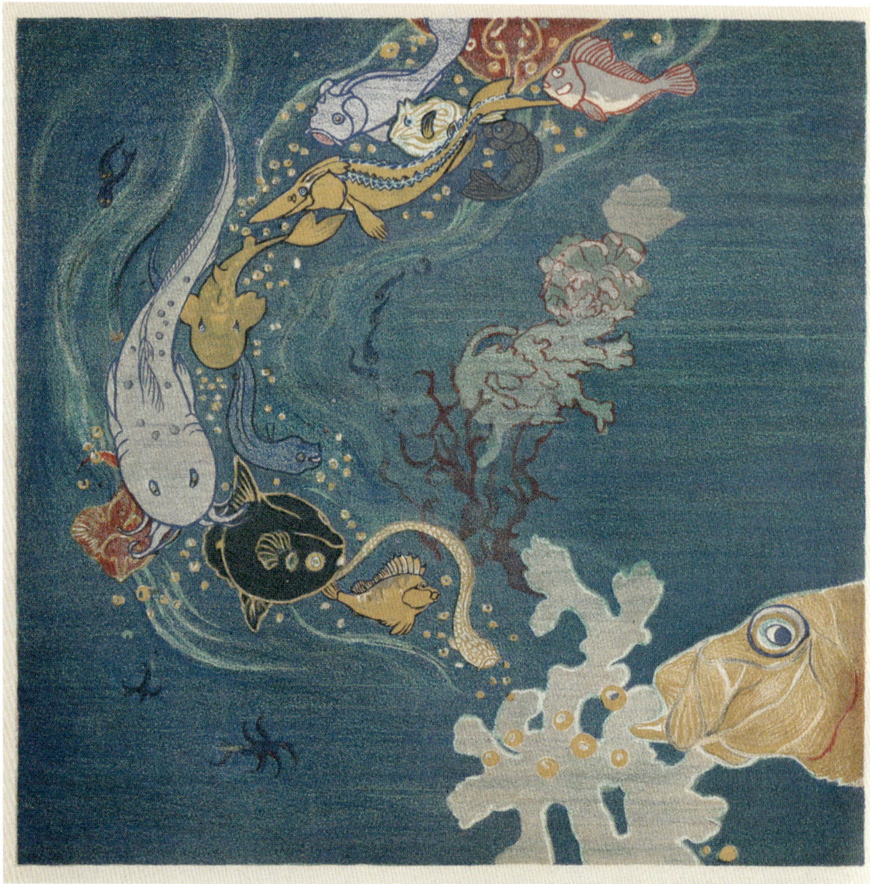

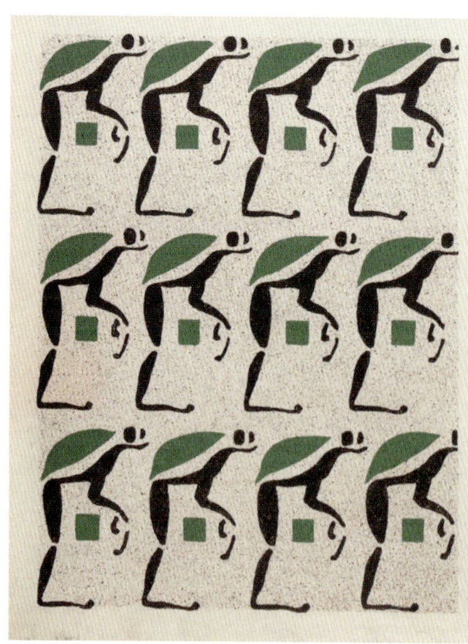

Plate 3 (above) Ella Baumfeld [Briggs], design for embroidery in silk and metal threads, color lithograph, c. 1902.

Plate 4 (right) Decorative pattern with frogs, c. 1904. This design may have been created by Ella Briggs.

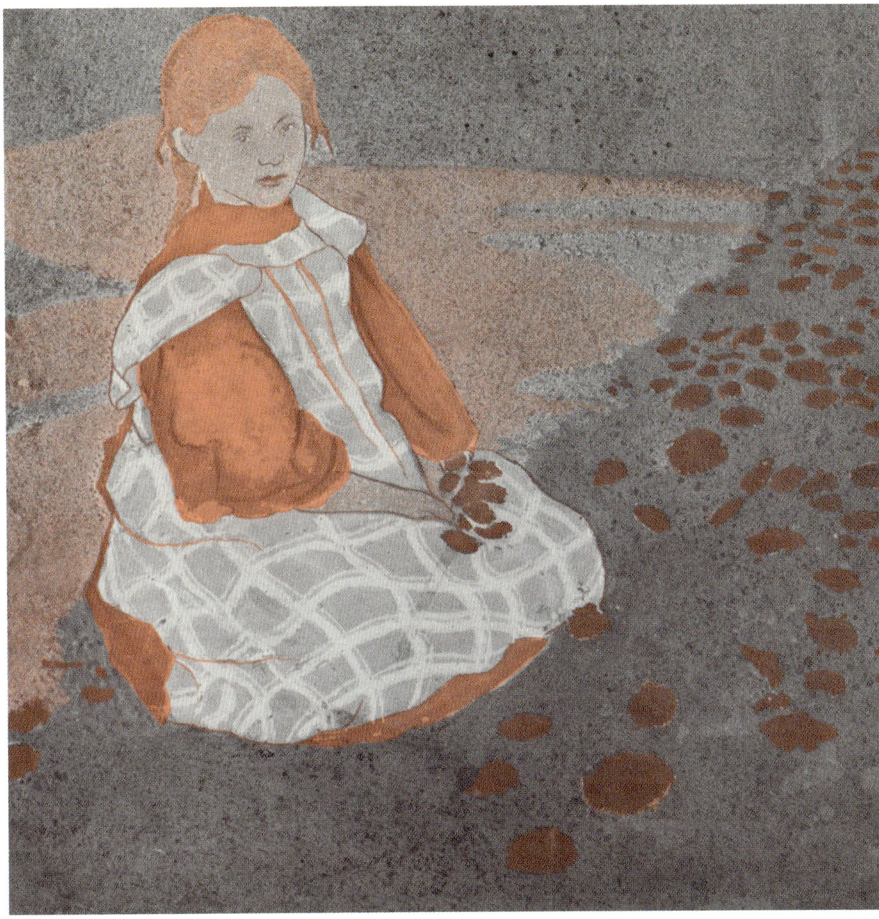

Plate 5 Ella Baumfeld [Briggs], illustration of a girl, published in *The American Printer* in 1905. The caption was composed of the concluding lines of William Wordsworth's poem "To a Butterfly": "Sweet childish days, that were as long / As twenty days are now." This coupling of image and text raises the question of the artwork's autobiographical significance: Was the artist reflecting on happiness shadowed by loss, the innocence of childhood ending with her father's death?

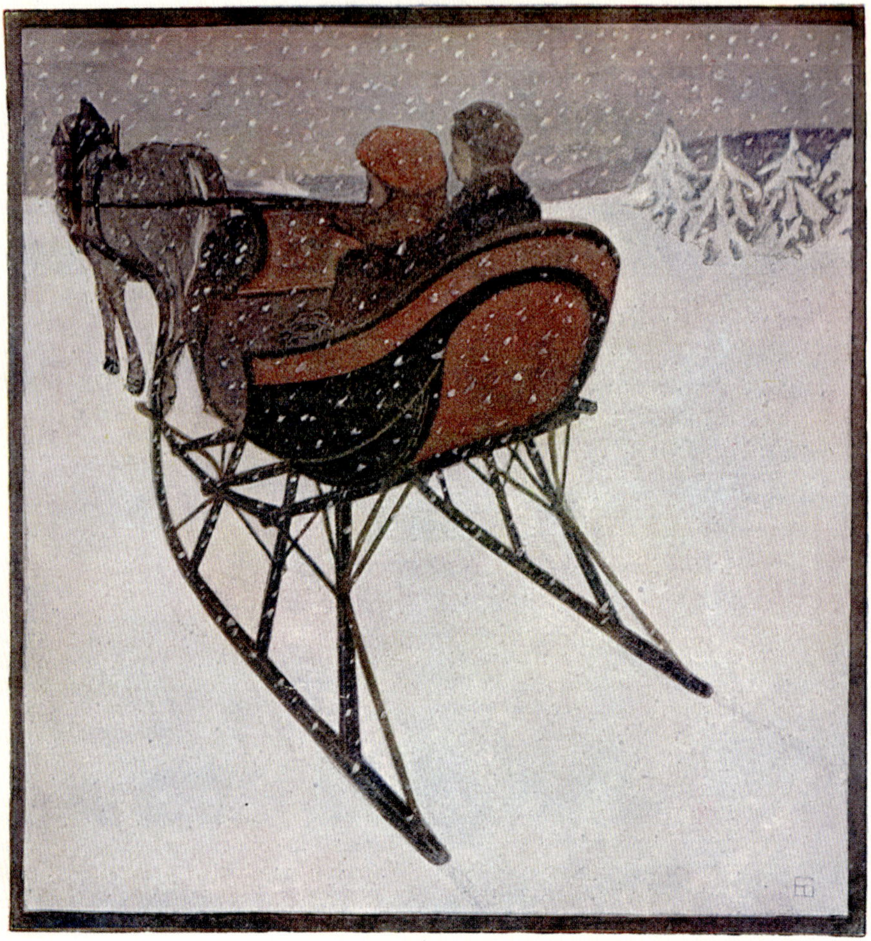

Plate 6 Ella Baumfeld [Briggs], illustration for Anna Ritter's poem "Schlittenfahrt" (Sleighride) published in 1906 in *Die Woche für die Deutsche Jugend*.

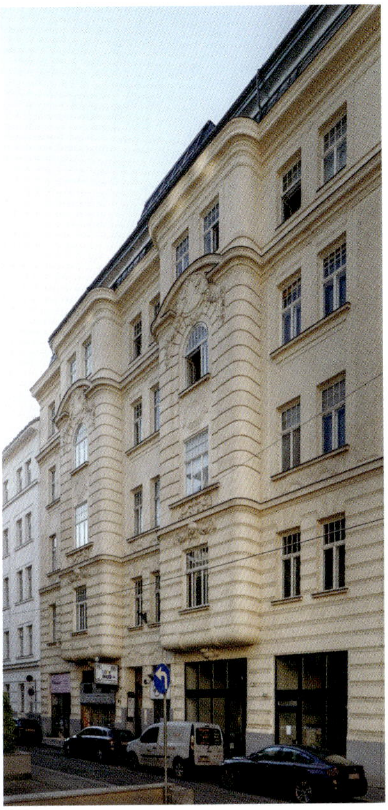

Plate 7 (left) The location of Ella Briggs's former interior design studio (on the top floor) at Taubstummengasse 13 in Vienna's fourth district, which she opened in 1912. The building was designed by Anton Schwarz and completed the same year. (Photograph by Benjamin von Radom, 2024.)

Plate 8 (below) Ella Briggs, writing room, Vienna, 1913–1914. Briggs retained this photograph her entire life. It was published in *Das Interieur* in 1914.

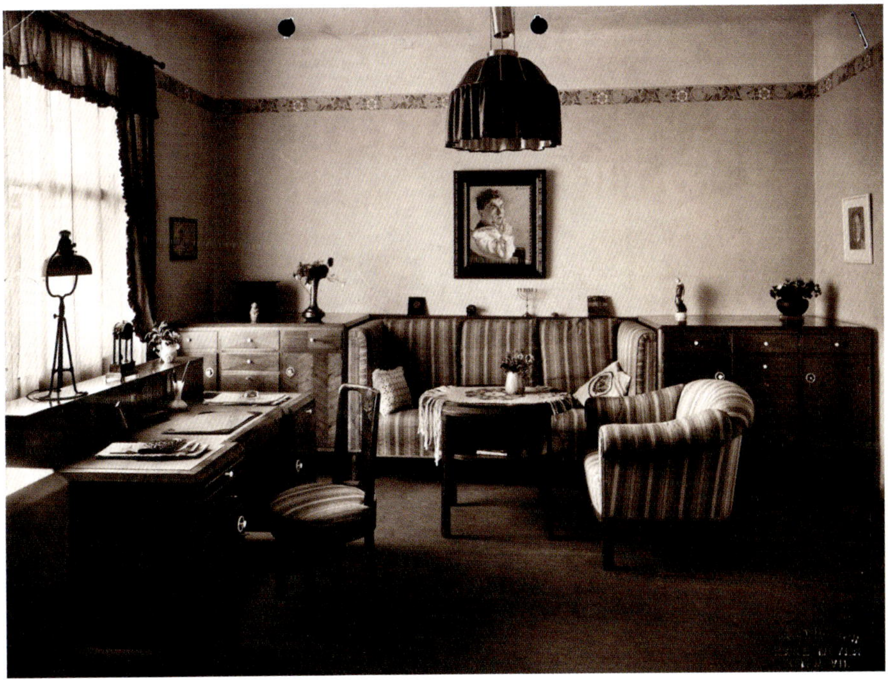

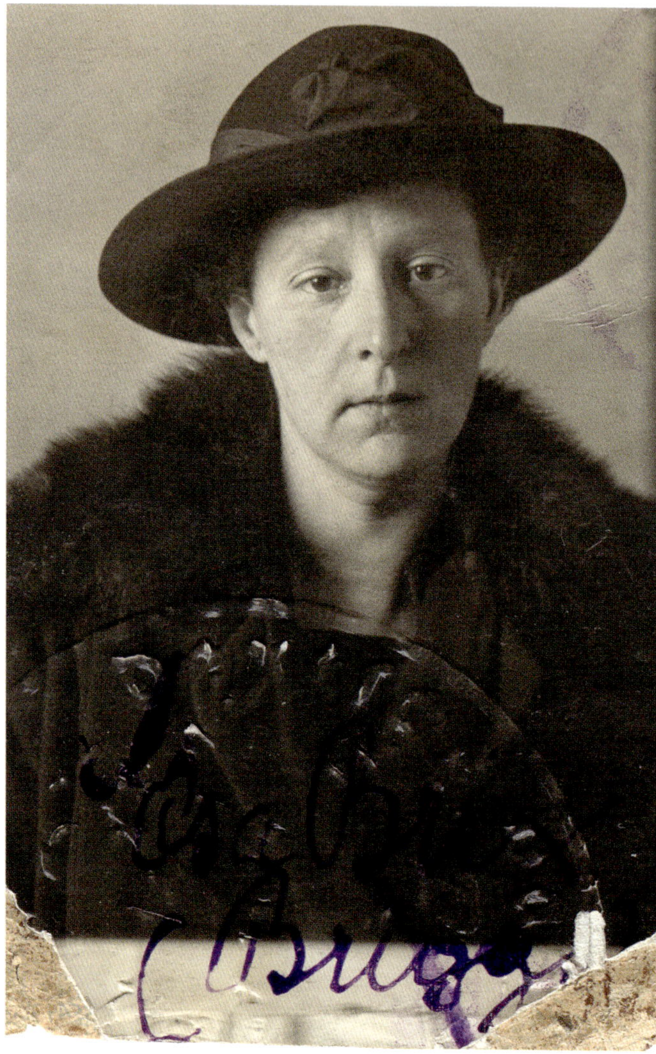

Plate 9 Ella Briggs's passport photograph, dated January 2, 1921. Her name on the front is written as "Elsa Brix (Briggs)."

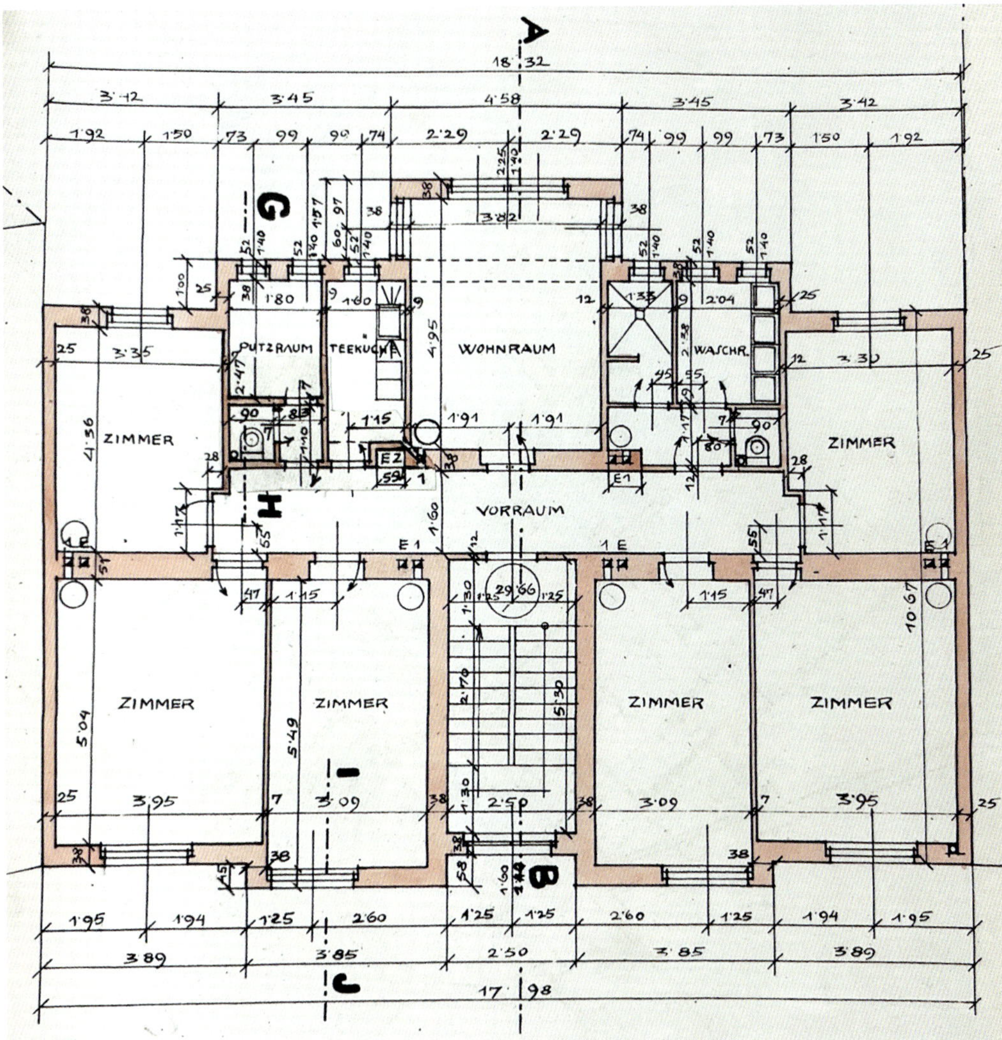

Plate 10 Ella Briggs, fourth-floor plan of the Ledigenheim dating from October 1926, showing the stairway (bottom center) and the shared living room marked *Wohnraum* (top center). To the top left, beside the living room, is a kitchenette (*Teeküche*), to the left of that a cleaning space (*Putzraum*) with a toilet, and to the right of the living room a common bathroom.

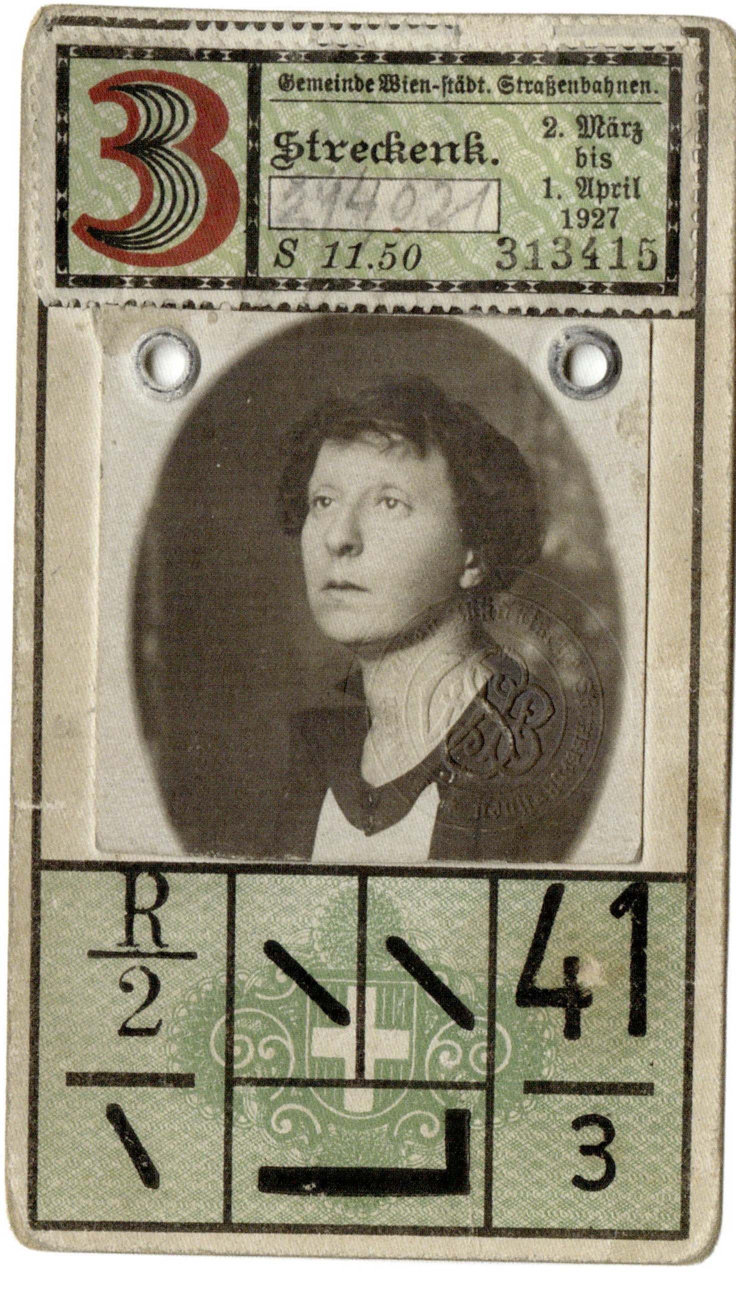

Plate 11 Photograph of Ella Briggs on her Vienna monthly tram card for March 1927. Not long afterward she would leave for Berlin.

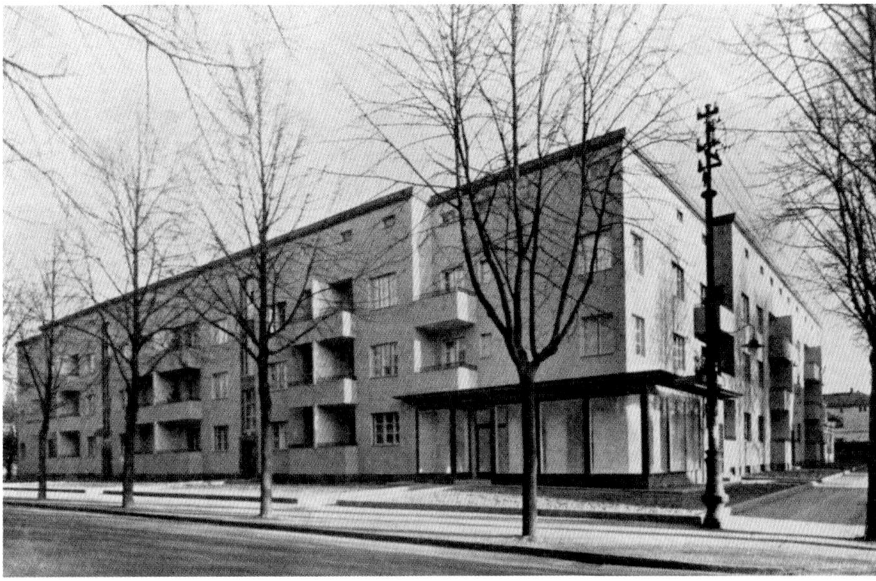

Plate 12 Ella Briggs, apartment block in Berlin-Mariendorf, 1928–1929, view toward Rathausstrasse, corner Königstrasse, with a reconstruction of the original color scheme by Katrin Stingl.

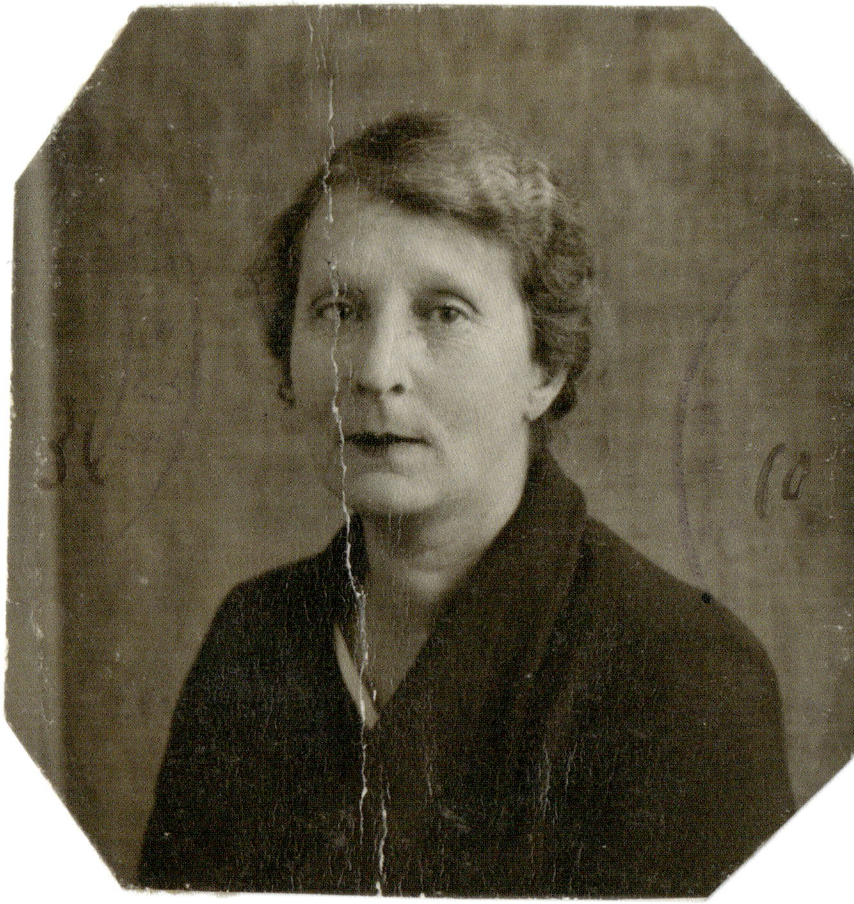

Plate 13 Photograph of Ella Briggs, c. 1936. This photograph, bearing traces of official stamps, appears to have been taken during the period when Briggs frantically sought safe harbor outside fascist Germany and Austria. The word "photograph" is printed on the back, indicating it was taken in England.

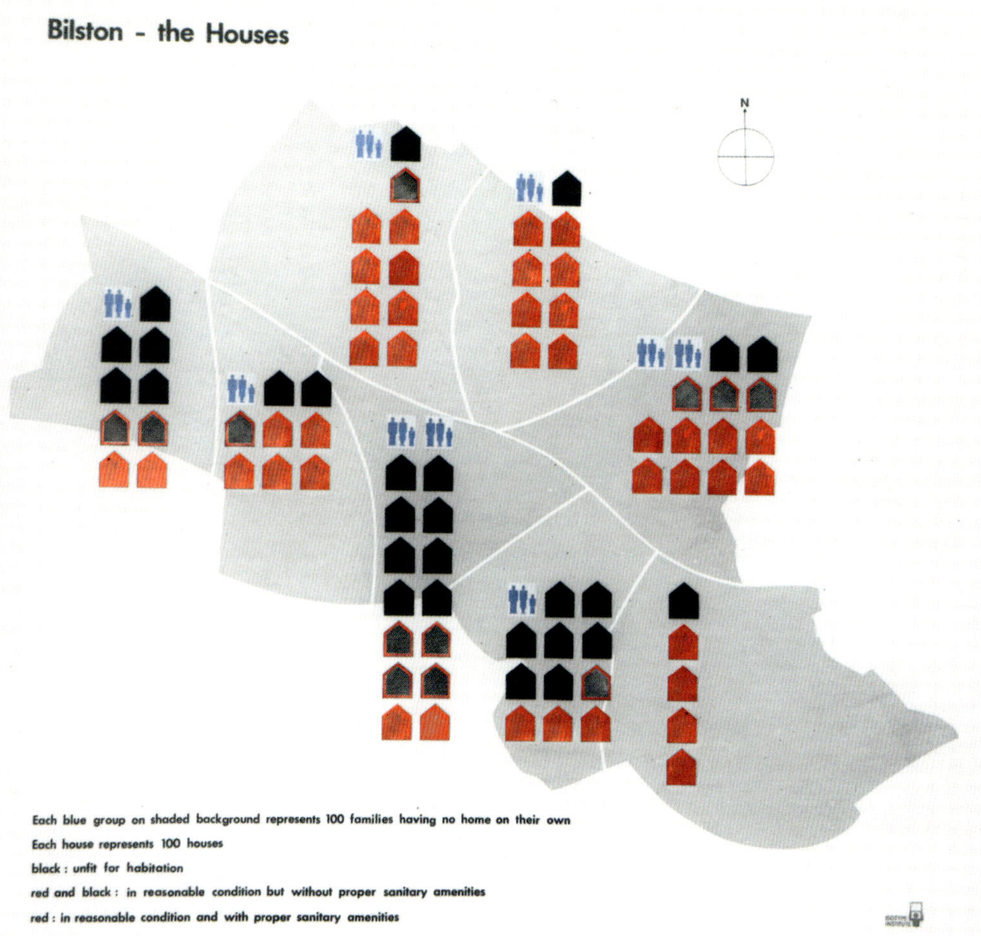

Plate 14 Isotype Institute, black and white bromide print of Isotype chart "Bilston—the Houses" displayed in the Bilston Housing Exhibition, 1946. (Digital image file colored by Pia Pedersen.) This chart shows the state of Bilston's housing stock before redevelopment. Each blue group of people represents one hundred families with no home of their own. Each house represents one hundred houses. The black houses are unfit for habitation, the gray houses (with red outlines) are in reasonable condition but without sanitary amenities, and the red houses are in reasonable condition and with sanitary amenities. Although some areas are substantially better housed than others, there is significant deprivation overall.

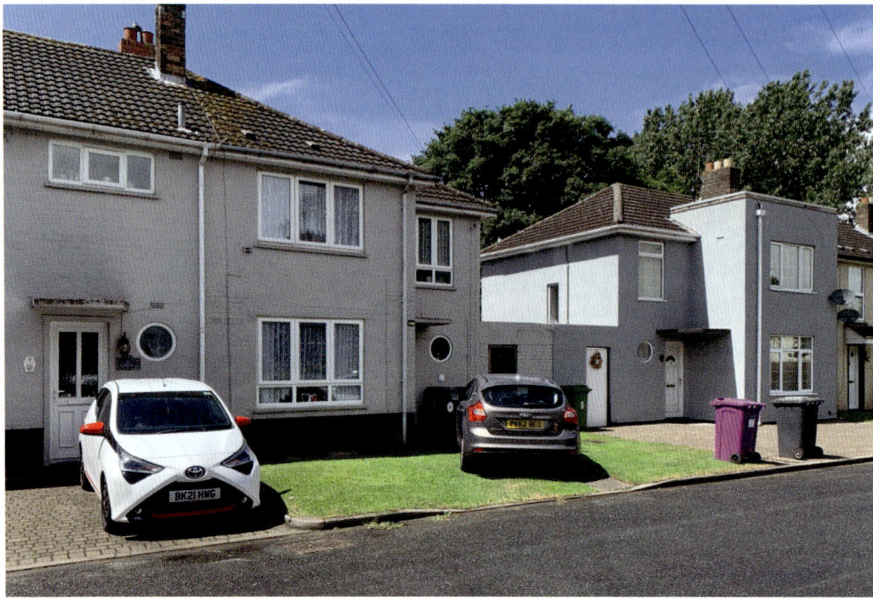

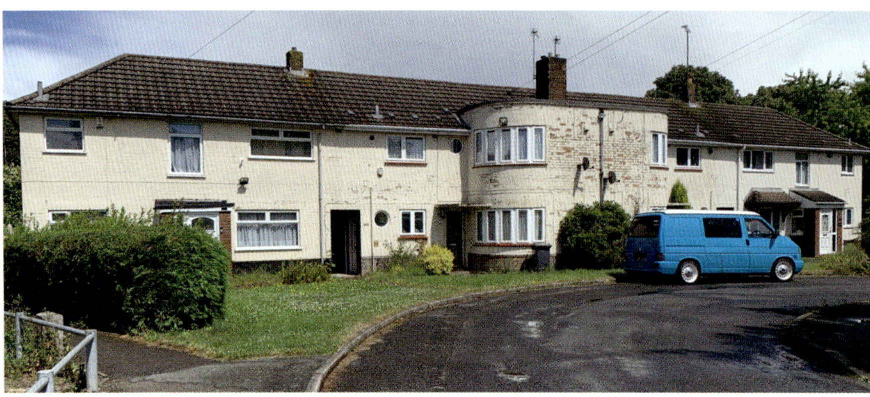

Plate 15 Lawnside Green, Stowlawn Park Estate, Bilston, showing the end houses (Type J) of two separate groups of rowhouses on the west side facing the green, linked by a low wall to give visual continuity. (Photograph by Barbara Penner, 2024.)

Plate 16 Lawnside Green, Stowlawn Park Estate, Bilston, showing a terrace enclosing the north side of the green. The central dwelling (with the curving wall) contains four Type H one-bedroom flats; it is flanked by two single-family larger Type F houses. For plans of the Type H houses, see fig. 19.6. (Photograph by Barbara Penner, 2024.)

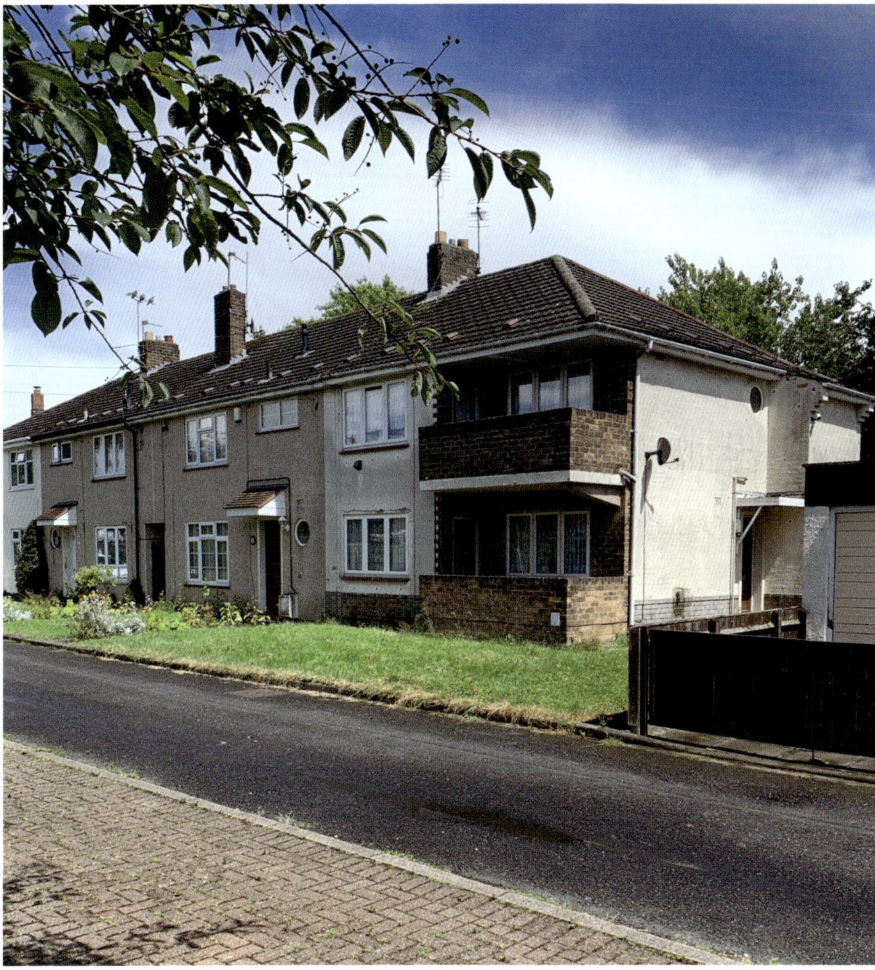

Plate 17 Lawnside Green, Stowlawn Park Estate, Bilston, showing a terrace with two Type G dwellings (each containing two flats), and two single-family Type C houses in between, on the east side of the green. Solid brick balconies allowed laundry to be dried without being visible from the street. (Photograph by Barbara Penner, 2024.)

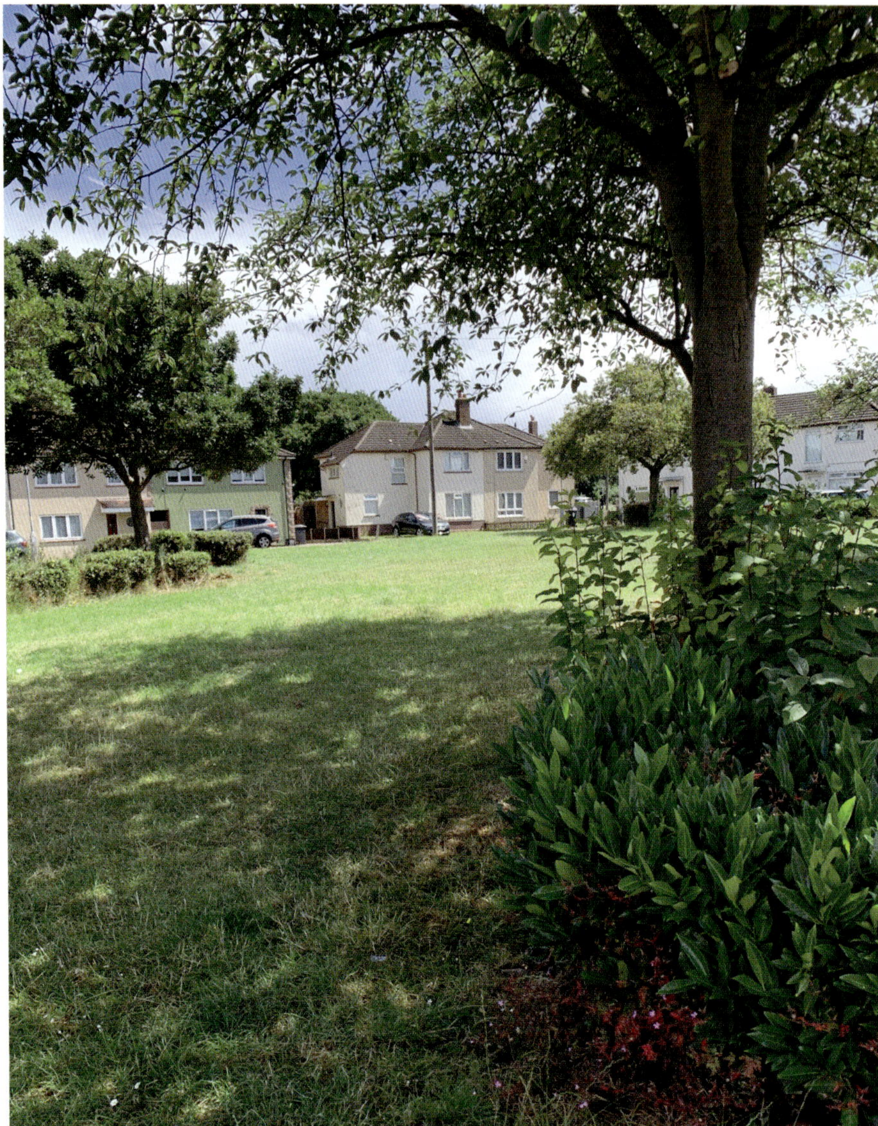

Plate 18 Lawnside Green today, looking to the semidetached houses and rowhouses enclosing the southeast side of the more recently planted, pleasant green. (Photograph by Barbara Penner, 2024.)

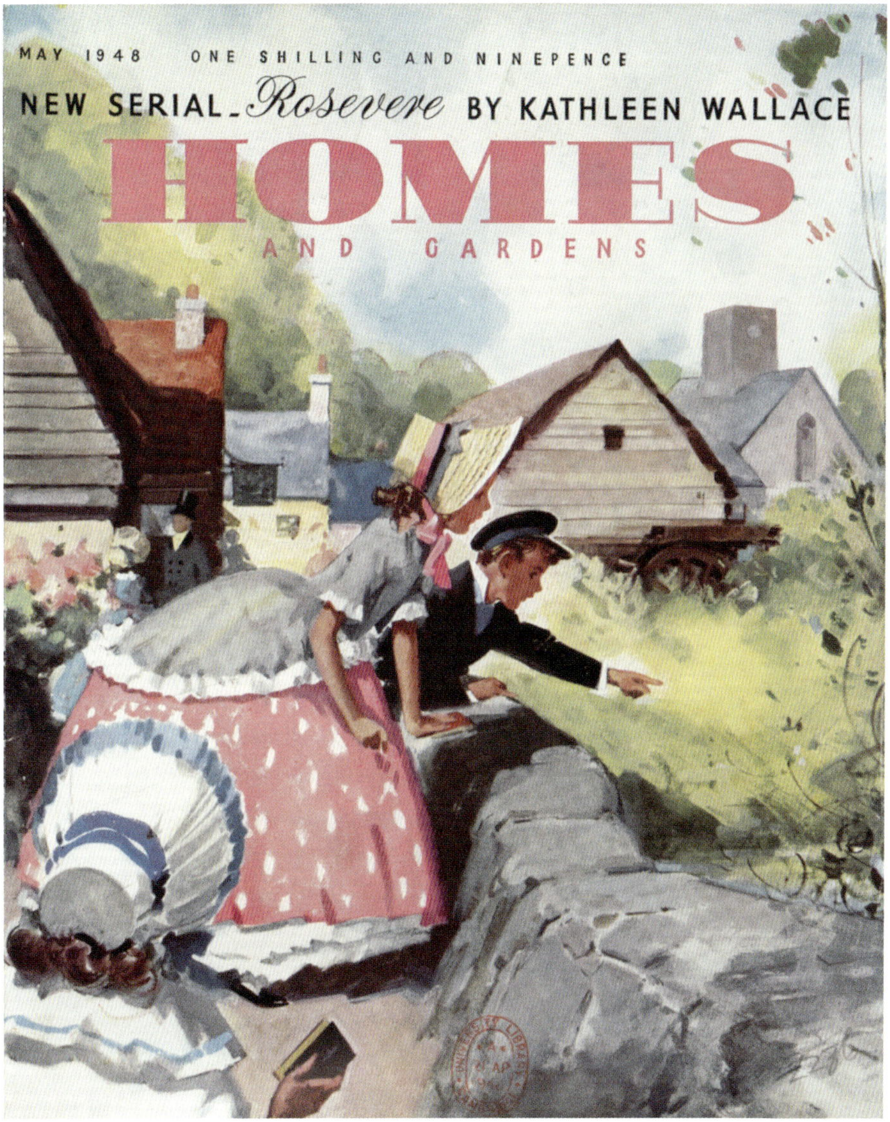

Plate 19 May 1948 cover of *Homes and Gardens*. This cover highlights the magazine's preference for full-blown romantic depictions of English cottage settings, quite at odds with Briggs's more sober, modern designs (see fig. 20.2).

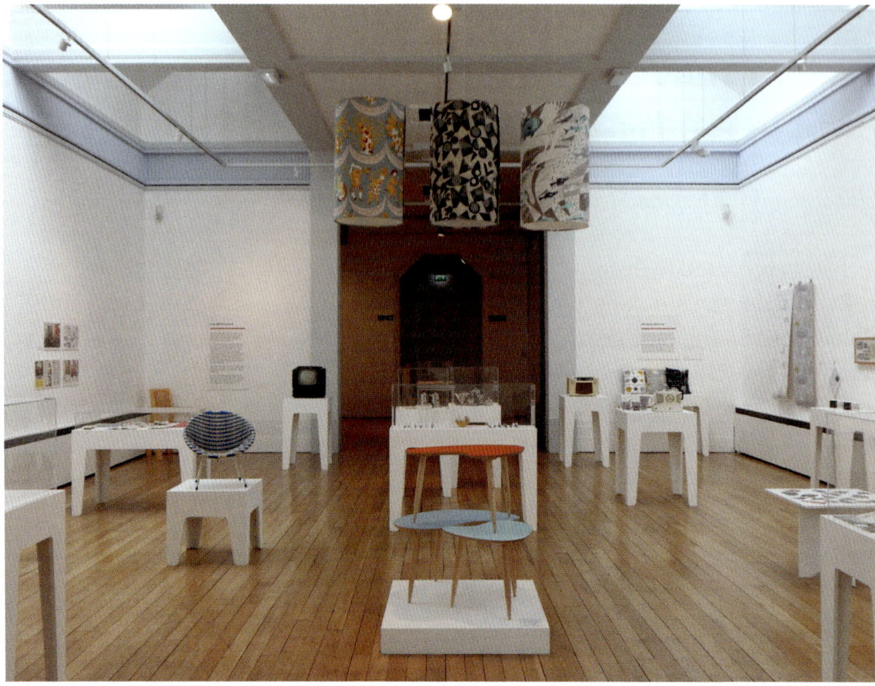

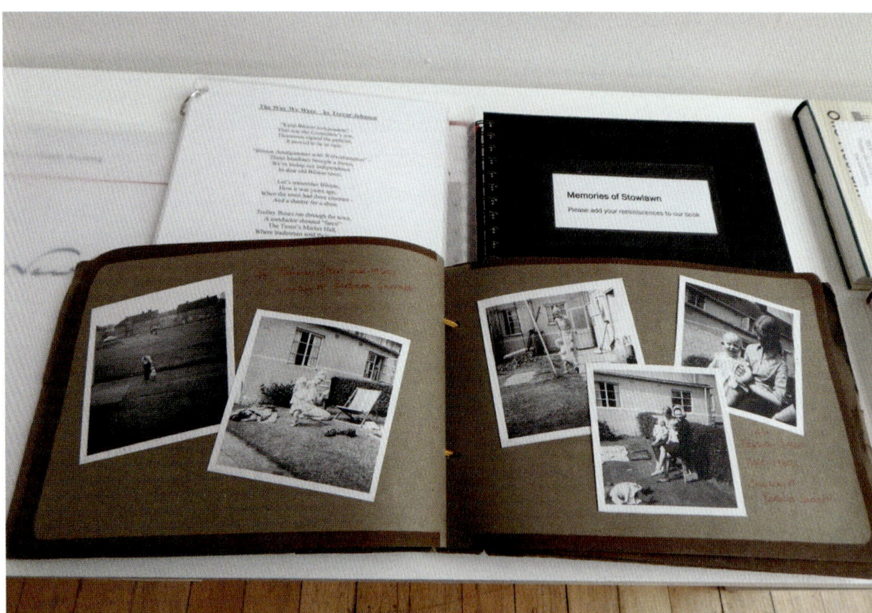

Plate 20 (top) View of *Bilston's Happy Housing: Otto Neurath's Vision for Postwar Modern Living* exhibition, Bilston Craft Gallery, cocurated by Sabrina Rahman and Carol Thompson. (Photograph taken by Sabrina Rahman in 2015.)

Plate 21 (bottom) Exhibit with early Bilston resident memories, on display in *Bilston's Happy Housing: Otto Neurath's Vision for Postwar Modern Living* exhibition, Bilston Craft Gallery, cocurated by Sabrina Rahman and Carol Thompson. (Photograph taken by Sabrina Rahman in 2015.)

12.
Italian Travels, Architectural Photography, and Jail

Elana Shapira, Despina Stratigakos, and Ulrike Matzer

As Briggs prepared to become a full-fledged member of the architectural revolution in Red Vienna, she took part in another sweeping change, this one happening on a global scale. By the mid-1920s, photographic images had become omnipresent in everyday culture. The illustrated press, which reached a vast audience with its inexpensive newspapers and popular magazines, used photography to engage readers in news stories, expose them to unfamiliar ideas and places, persuade them to support causes, and entertain them. Even with costlier price tags, books that featured high-quality images, including those on architecture, found appreciative and willing buyers. As these publishing markets expanded, the demand for photographs grew apace. It was within this context that Briggs took up her camera for an exciting new project, which would prove to be a greater adventure than she could have possibly imagined.

Around 1925, the Architectural Book Publishing Company of New York hired Briggs to take photographs for use as illustrations in a book on Sicilian architecture. Founded by Paul Wenzel, the company issued numerous volumes on minor Renaissance architecture and farmhouses in England, France, Italy, and Spain, in the 1920s.[1] Guy Lowell, an American architect, had been commissioned to write and illustrate two books on smaller Italian villas and farmhouses, and Briggs was contracted to complete the last in that series, devoted to Sicilian farmhouses.[2] Other books by the press focused on architectural and decorative details, such as the 1920 *Ornamental Details of the Italian Renaissance* and the 1925 *Portals, Doorways, and Windows of France*.[3] The photographs that Briggs would produce in Italy closely reflect the publisher's interests in these themes and included Renaissance-era churches, farmhouses, and detailed views of portals and other architectural features.

Briggs's motives for pursuing this project are open to speculation. The photographic documentation of historical architectural monuments was closely related to the establishment of art history as an academic discipline, and Italy was considered the central country in art historical research at the time. Perhaps the commission reflected Briggs's interest in extending her own involvement in publishing in a new literary direction.[4] Because photographers were compensated by publishers for their work, Briggs's photographs—economically speaking—constituted profitable media products for which she received an advance on earnings. Perhaps a financial motive was at play.

By the 1920s, travel guides featuring sites of art-historical interest had become a genre in their own right, often linked to cultural tourism. Indeed, Briggs's own brother had written one such guide some twenty years earlier. In 1905 Moritz Baumfeld published *Cruising in the Mediterranean*—an account of his voyage on the world's first steamer designed as a luxury cruise ship, the SS *Prinzessin Victoria Luise*. Emil L. Boas, general manager in the United States of the Hamburg-American Line (which owned the ship) commissioned the publication to promote his cruises. Baumfeld's lighthearted narrative of life on board and in the "exotic" cities along the ship's route are accompanied by photos featuring art-historical subjects, genre scenes, and the hustle and bustle of the streets.[5] Familiarity with her brother's work perhaps demystified the publishing process for Briggs, who brought her artistically trained eye to illustrating a different narrative project.

We do not know whether Briggs received training in photography during her student days in Vienna or learned it elsewhere. We do know, however, that women photographers had emerged on the scene at the end of the nineteenth century and worked globally in the decades that followed.[6] They were active in large numbers in Vienna, as well as in the United States, London, Paris, and Berlin, and worked across all genres of publishing, including architectural documentation and travel reportage.[7] During the post–World War I era, women photographers were considered the epitome of the New Woman—an ideal of female freedom that combined fashion, movement, and independence. For many progressive women, however, photography was more than a stylish pastime; it provided an important means of artistic expression.

The daughters of affluent, educated Jewish families, in particular, were drawn to professional photography. Writing and publishing often went hand in hand with image-making, as in the case not only of Briggs but also of Gisèle Freund and Lucia Moholy. Both began taking photographs in Germany in the 1920s. Freund received early acclaim for her social reportage, and Moholy is still well-known for her Bauhaus photographs, produced around the same time that Briggs was at work in Italy.[8] In Vienna in this period, Jewish women photographers ran most of the photo studios owned by women; some of them also took photographs outside the studio.[9] Journalist and women's rights activist Alice Schalek was by far the most highly acclaimed Viennese travel photographer of the time. Publishing illustrated travel books before the First World War, Schalek took thousands of photographs in India, Japan, and North Africa.[10] She employed an anthropological approach, typically taking casual snapshots to capture the land and its people. Briggs would develop a different style, photographing architectural motifs with an appreciation for the art-historical but with an architect's eye.

Briggs made two or three journeys to Sicily, supported by a $250 advance from the publishing company.[11] Surviving photographs reveal that she travelled widely en route to her destination. In northern Italy, she photographed the Church of Saint Ursus in Aosta, an ancient town bordering France and Switzerland. In central Italy she visited Aquilla, Aquino, Assisi, and Bagnaia, where she documented medieval and Renaissance villas and church buildings.[12] In Sicily Briggs photographed ecclesiastical and vernacular structures, passing through Taormina, Giarre, and Syracuse on the Ionian Sea; Randazzo, near Mount Etna; and the coastal towns of San Leone, Sciacca, Marsala, and Trapani.

Briggs took her images using a plate camera on a tripod. Setting up each shot required careful preparation, and to make the exposure she had to disappear under a dark cloth. Since the 1890s, travel cameras with a wooden housing (which resembled a small suitcase when folded up) had been on the market for such purposes. This bulky but portable equipment, called an English Field Camera, allowed Briggs—a slender woman who stood about five feet, five inches tall—to travel without an assistant and to work the camera on her own.[13] Exposures were made on glass negatives, ensuring remarkable detail and a broad range of sharp focus in the resulting print. The impressive depth of field captured by this technique resulted in the continued use of glass negatives in architectural photography decades after celluloid film was introduced.

Briggs carefully composed her photographs. When the vantage point permitted, she aligned the primary edges and lines of the facades and portals parallel to the image plane. But she also photographed some buildings from slightly above or below or at an oblique angle in order to emphasize their special features. The lack of distortion is evidence of a fine lens. Briggs had the equipment of a professional photographer, the large-format camera geared toward high-quality architectural documentation. To these technical advantages, Briggs brought her apparent experience as a photographer and also her shrewdness as an architect. The striking perspectives she chose placed details in high relief in the picture in such a way that they are easily discernible. The photographs seem deliberately composed in terms of how the buildings are situated in their surroundings; the distribution of the massing and the play of light and shadow are also carefully balanced (fig. 12.1). Briggs's images exhibit the clinical eye of a design professional interested in architectural details.

Although the focus is always on the architectural setting, occasionally local people are integrated into the picture. In a few cases, this makes Briggs's work seem like staged genre photographs. But most of the time, photographing villagers was likely unavoidable, as residents of these places went about their day. Onlookers often populate the edges of the pictures, sometimes peeking out of windows and doors (fig. 12.2). Their faces, however, remain mostly in shadow; in contrast to the genre of street photography, in which people share significance with their surroundings, Briggs's pictures prioritize the architectural. Even if she had wanted to create the kind of quick, casual snapshots later made possible by the hand-held camera, roll film, and rapid exposure times, her large-format plate camera would not have allowed it.

Her camera equipment alone made Briggs a conspicuous addition to any Italian urban landscape. At the time, taking a photograph in public space was, by necessity, a prolonged and highly visible endeavor. What is more, whereas using a camera was a matter of course for the culture-savvy gentleman traveler, it still entailed certain dangers for a woman. Briggs was travelling as an unescorted woman. Positioning herself with the camera on the open road represented a transgression of traditional gender roles, especially in Italy's patriarchal Catholic society. Briggs no doubt would have attracted the attention of curious—perhaps even disdainful—locals. Yet her pursuit of the Sicilian book project typifies her determination to be her own person, despite prevailing gender norms.

The precise dates of Briggs's journeys to Italy have yet to be determined. A dated sketch she made in Sicily puts her there in January 1925.[14] During her first stay in Sicily, she was welcomed in artistic circles and established good relationships with local organizations—including the architects association and the preservation office—that

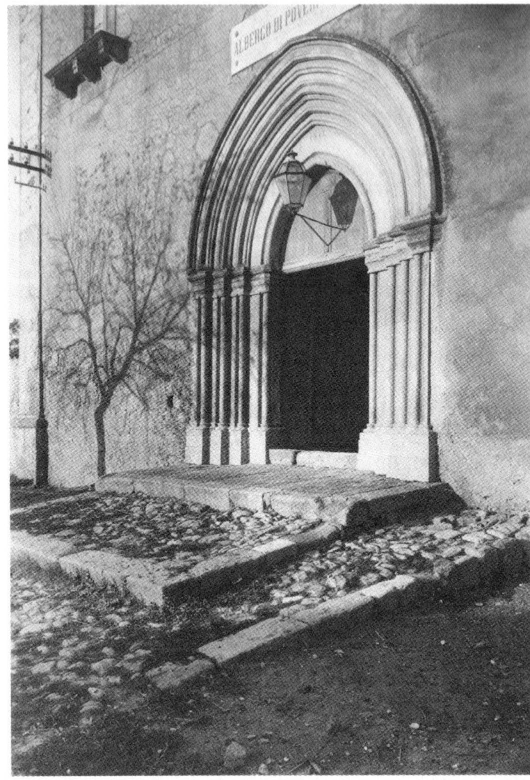

Fig. 12.1 Ella Briggs, photograph of Caltagirone: Albergo dei Poveri (formerly Santa Maria di Gesù), 1925. This photograph was among those purchased by the Victoria and Albert Museum, London.

"came in extremely handy" for her work. At the end of November, she travelled again to Sicily, with the intention of being back in Vienna by December 20. Briggs's journey started out promisingly. After arriving in Palermo, she settled into the Hotel Panormus and began making excursions with her camera into the surrounding area. All was upended, though, on the evening of December 6, when secret police turned up in Briggs's hotel room with wild accusations about her identity and activities in Italy. They subsequently placed her under room arrest and left. The next morning, they returned and took her to police headquarters, where she was interrogated, arrested, and thrown in a jail cell.[15]

The story of the photographer's detention begins earlier, in fact, and farther north, in South Tyrol. In the aftermath of the First World War, in 1919, this area had been annexed to Italy. During the 1920s, fascist authorities imposed an aggressive Italianization campaign on its majority German-speaking inhabitants. Although in October 1925, Germany, France, Belgium, Great Britain, and Italy signed the Locarno Treaties securing Germany's western border and normalizing political relations, Italy remained highly sensitive to the possibility of German espionage—especially since many Germans and Austrians hoped to reclaim South Tyrol. Two months after the Locarno Treaties were signed, Ella Briggs was arrested on espionage charges and stood accused of being a German spy.

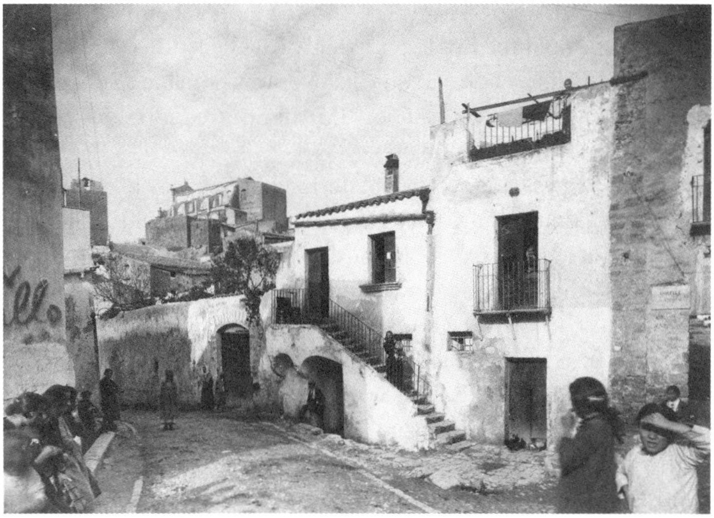

Fig. 12.2 Ella Briggs, photograph of Cortile San Nicolò, Sciacca, 1925. With her camera equipment and as a lone female traveler, Briggs would have been conspicuous on her Italian journey.

News of Briggs's arrest was reported widely. The fate of Mata Hari—the dancer executed by firing squad in France in October 1917 as a German spy—was still fresh in people's memory, perhaps heightening international interest. Briggs's name cropped up in newspapers around the world, from Los Angeles to Vienna. Bold headlines reported her detention as a spy.[16] How on earth, American readers of *The Ladies' Home Journal* must have wondered, had Briggs gone from advising on house plans to occupying a jail cell in Sicily?

As reporters speculated, Briggs may have inadvertently photographed a military zone in Palermo, provoking suspicion on the part of an "overzealous official" that led to her arrest. Briggs identified this man as Antonio Pizzuto, a commissioner of Mussolini's secret police.[17] Briggs described Pizzuto as a paranoid tormenter who interrogated her for hours, during which time she learned that she had been followed for five days by Pizzuto's undercover detectives. Pizzuto thought she was lying about her Austrian citizenship, believing instead that she was German. He also did not believe that she was an architect. In his interrogation, Pizzuto posed a difficult mathematical problem to Briggs, and when she could not immediately solve it, he said it proved she was no architect. Her protests about her identity fell on deaf ears. In his eyes she was duplicitous, like all Germans: "The more you talk," he said, "the less we believe you." The interrogation ended late in the evening with Pizzuto handing her a bar of soap "with a gallant gesture." The Catholic nuns who looked after the female prisoners then locked her up with sixteen local women.[18]

For more than two weeks, Briggs languished in jail. She did what she could to advocate for herself; when all else failed, she launched a hunger strike. A letter she wrote during her internment to a Viennese relative paints a picture of what she endured. "I am in the dungeon," she complained, surrounded by "female murderers." She pleaded with her jailers to contact the Austrian embassy in Rome as well as Vienna Mayor

Karl Seitz, but nothing came of this. She was not allowed a lawyer and saw no one from the outside. Even as she doubted this letter would be mailed, discarded like the others before it, she implored her relative to do whatever was possible to obtain her freedom. Psychologically, she was in bad shape: "If I am not free soon, pray that I die; I feel myself going insane in this nothingness."[19]

The good relationships Briggs had established during her first stay in Sicily with local architects and preservationists failed her during her imprisonment. When she asked those colleagues for help, they tread cautiously, intimidated by the fascist authorities. A letter to her brother Friedrich in Berlin went unanswered for a time; it was her sister Friederike (also in Berlin) who came to her rescue, contacting Briggs's lawyer in Vienna to seek her release.[20] Briggs's American publisher, Wenzel, campaigned publicly for her release, urging the US State Department to intercede on her behalf by claiming she was an American citizen (which she was not).[21] The Central Association of Austrian Architects also demonstrated their commitment to a member who had only recently been brought into the fold. Siegfried Theiss, then-president of the association, threw his weight behind the architect, directing media attention to her plight. He stated, "We most resolutely object to the kind of treatment being meted out to our member in Italy," and he demanded "her immediate release."[22] Behind the scenes her lawyer, Paul Pallester, a relative, appealed to the Austrian Foreign Ministry in Vienna and to the Italian ambassador to Austria. With interventions from the Austrian embassy in Rome, Briggs was freed on December 24 after eighteen soul-destroying days of captivity.[23]

Publicly, Italian authorities denied that Briggs had been held on suspicion of being a spy. Instead, they blamed passport irregularities and ordered her to leave the country. Briggs did not need to be convinced and began her journey home to Vienna as soon as she could, on December 25. In an interview she gave following her release, published on December 28, Briggs told an American reporter she was completely baffled about why she had been held: "'I suppose I am to blame,' Mrs. Briggs remarked, 'but I am so confused by the whole fuss I can't think clearly.'"[24] Others blamed the fascists unequivocally for Briggs's mistreatment: on December 31, *Münchner Neueste Nachrichten* (Munich's Latest News) condemned the episode as an act of fascist terror.[25]

Once Briggs was released, the press eagerly awaited her return to Vienna, even reporting on her location as she made her way back to the city. The *Wiener Allgemeine Zeitung* (Vienna General Newspaper) interviewed her "in her studio on Weimarer Strasse 1," making the connection between this new building and Briggs's own participation in the city's social housing program. On New Year's Eve, Briggs herself visited the offices of the *Arbeiter-Zeitung* to tell them her story. Only days after her release, the plot of that story had begun shifting, from horror to absurdity. Briggs's account featured sadistic nuns, lazy diplomats, and soap powder mistaken for explosives. The daily of the Social Democratic Party framed Briggs's experience in terms of a fascist disregard for human rights and dignity. Briggs herself seemed personally less interested in putting a political gloss on the incident and instead excoriated Austrian bureaucratic incompetence and religious hypocrisy, as much as Italian fascist cruelty. Her sharp characterizations, poignant details, and suspenseful twists point to her prodigious skill as a raconteur.[26]

Briggs never published the book on Sicilian farmhouses commissioned by the Architectural Book Publishing Company, presumably because the arrest prevented her from completing the necessary itinerary. Still, the photographic output resulting from her travels—hundreds of images—is impressive. Briggs published materials and images from her Italian journey in two separate articles, one in the American popular press and the other in a German professional journal. The two publications highlight Briggs's canny understanding of her readership, as well as of the architecture she encountered on her Italian journeys.

In the June 1926 issue of *The Ladies' Home Journal,* Briggs offered drawings from her Italian sketchbooks depicting "fragments of beautiful everyday objects from Taormina," specifically a window, door, and garden features (fig. 12.3). She praised the Italian "passion for color" revealed in its traditional houses: the "buffs, pinks, shades of cream." She also observed that "the roofs of red tiles, the black iron grills and the blue painted shutters of the old buildings supply the contrasting color notes that make them flash out like jewels against the blue of their native skies." The impact of these colors is further heightened, she pointed out, "since the walls of true Italian houses are wide expanses, unbroken except by the window and door openings." Her eye for color extended to garden features, such as the blue door or "vases of red burnt clay." Briggs also

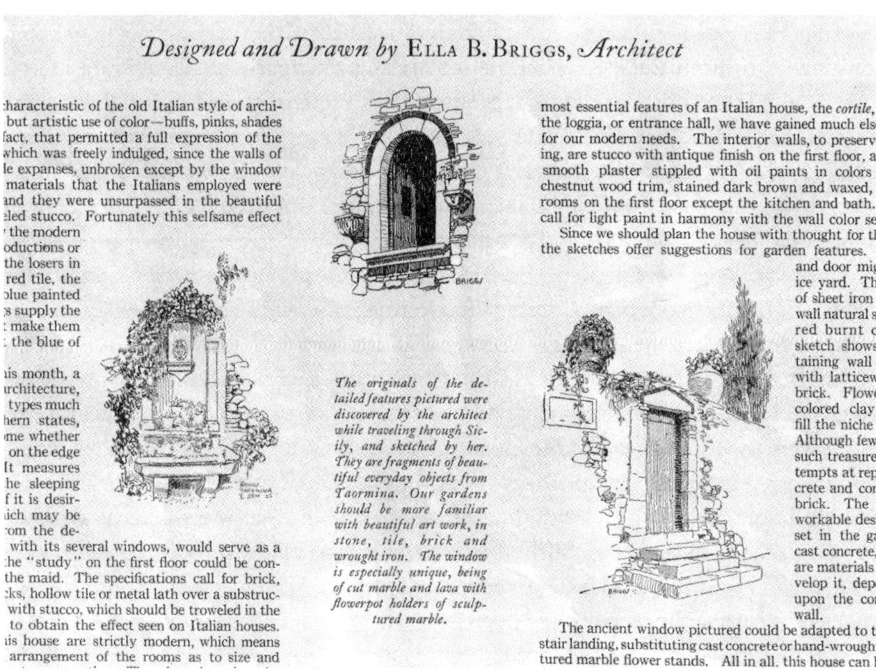

Designed and Drawn by ELLA B. BRIGGS, *Architect*

:haracteristic of the old Italian style of archi-
but artistic use of color—buffs, pinks, shades
fact, that permitted a full expression of the
which was freely indulged, since the walls of
le expanses, unbroken except by the window
materials that the Italians employed were
and they were unsurpassed in the beautiful
:led stucco. Fortunately this selfsame effect
the modern
oductions or
the losers in
red tile, the
blue painted
s supply the
make them
the blue of

is month, a
architecture,
types much
hern states,
me whether
on the edge
It measures
he sleeping
f it is desir-
ich may be
om the de-
with its several windows, would serve as a
he "study" on the first floor could be con-
the maid. The specifications call for brick,
:ks, hollow tile or metal lath over a substruc-
with stucco, which should be troweled in the
to obtain the effect seen on Italian houses.
is house are strictly modern, which means
arrangement of the rooms as to size and

The originals of the detailed features pictured were discovered by the architect while traveling through Sicily, and sketched by her. They are fragments of beautiful everyday objects from Taormina. Our gardens should be more familiar with beautiful art work, in stone, tile, brick and wrought iron. The window is especially unique, being of cut marble and lava with flowerpot holders of sculptured marble.

most essential features of an Italian house, the *cortile,* o
the loggia, or entrance hall, we have gained much else
for our modern needs. The interior walls, to preserve
ing, are stucco with antique finish on the first floor, an
smooth plaster stippled with oil paints in colors
chestnut wood trim, stained dark brown and waxed, is
rooms on the first floor except the kitchen and bath.
call for light paint in harmony with the wall color sel
Since we should plan the house with thought for the
the sketches offer suggestions for garden features.
and door migh
ice yard. The
of sheet iron
wall natural st
red burnt cl
sketch shows
taining wall
with latticew
brick. Flower
colored clay
fill the niche
Although few
such treasures,
tempts at repr
crete and com
brick. The
workable desig
set in the gar
cast concrete,
are materials f
velop it, depe
upon the con
wall.
The ancient window pictured could be adapted to th
stair landing, substituting cast concrete or hand-wrought
tured marble flower stands. All in all, this house can b

Fig. 12.3 Ella Briggs, architectural and garden features sketched in Taormina, January 1925, published in *The Ladies' Home Journal.*

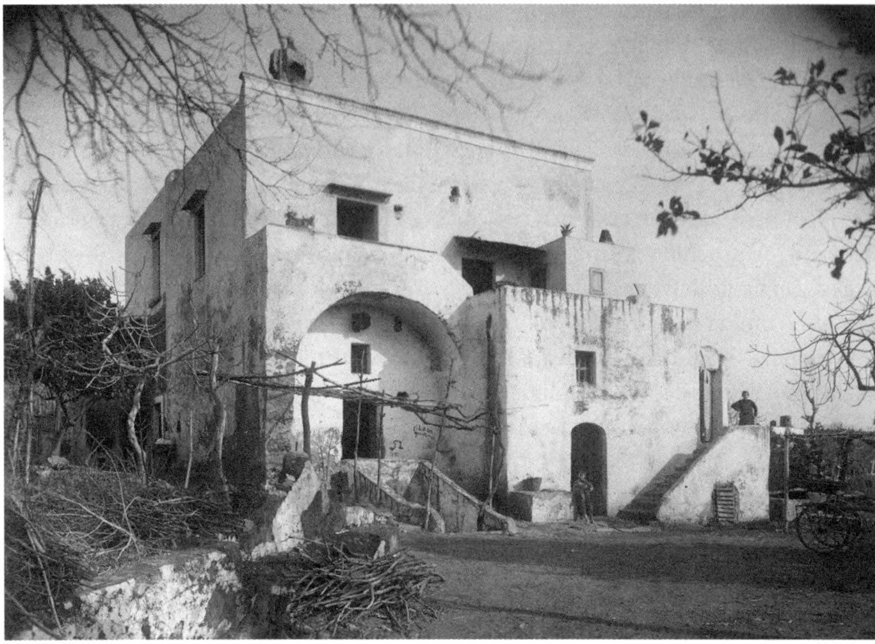

Fig. 12.4 Ella Briggs, photograph of a farmhouse at Torre del Greco near Naples, 1925. This photograph was included in Briggs's article about Sicilian architecture for *Deutsche Bauzeitung* in 1930, although it is of a farmhouse near Naples, not in Sicily.

described the "beautiful effects" of the materials, particularly the "native stone and stucco," which she noted could be reproduced by "modern craftsmen" in the United States. Indeed, she offered her own house design of "a modern version of Italian architecture . . . one of the Mediterranean types much sought after in our Southern states," available for purchase through the magazine.[27] To her American readers, Briggs thus emphasized beauty, pleasure, and consumption.

Four years later, in 1930, Briggs published an article about Sicilian architecture in *Deutsche Bauzeitung* (German Construction Journal), a technical journal read primarily by architects and civil engineers, which she illustrated with her own photographs (fig. 12.4). Although the text reveals strong continuities with Briggs's earlier writings about domestic architecture published in American magazines, the emphasis here differs from the 1926 article for *The Ladies' Home Journal*. In particular, she considered how a house's physical structure expresses domestic needs, with function driving the form and organization of the building massing—a point that she similarly made in the American articles she published in women's magazines in the 1920s. She also emphasized the local builders' "extraordinarily sensitive adaptation to the terrain." Briggs's concern for housework and hygiene can be seen in her attention to stone washing vats integrated into a village well.[28]

The Sicilian buildings Briggs documented in *Deutsche Bauzeitung* struck her as simple and honest adaptations to function and site. "The houses," she wrote, were "uninfluenced by style, an unornamented expression of living needs."[29] In taking "anonymous" building seriously, Briggs joined a long tradition in architecture of seeking original precedents in so-called primitive structures. In the late 1920s and 1930s, modernists such as Le Corbusier and Bernard Rudofsky turned to Mediterranean vernacular buildings in their search for an organic connection between modern society and architectural form. Briggs's interest in southern Italian architecture as representative of traditional ways of building is an early example of this growing discourse in modernism, which would continue until the 1960s.[30]

Briggs's final Italian trip coincided with the design of her social housing building projects for Red Vienna. Did her experience of the Sicilian houses influence her modernist conceptions? Briggs already had a deep interest in "organic" and efficient spatial arrangements of domestic space and functions, which the Sicilian architecture seemed to confirm and reinforce. Briggs understood that the "unornamented expression" of Italian vernacular architecture, which she emphasized in *Deutsche Bauzeitung* and which was also in line with modernist trends, heightened the joy in color that she also expressed in her Viennese social housing projects. In those designs, she created moments where the eye could delight in a detail that emerged seemingly organically out of the building's functional massing.

Beyond the impact of Briggs's Sicilian sojourn on her architectural production, the imprisonment itself raises the question of personal consequences and any long-term effects it may have had on her psychologically. In contemporary interviews, Briggs was open about how harrowing her internment had been, which she said had induced "crying fits" and suicidal thoughts, and how she had been left in a state of extreme depression that required treatment. Indeed, Briggs planned to sue the Italian government for damages.[31] Her candor suggests trauma, especially since such publicity about deep emotional wounds came just as she was completing construction on a major architectural commission. It is hard to imagine a Mies van der Rohe or Corbusier being so frank about their personal pain with the press. Admitting to crying fits, even in the context of fascist abuse, does not fit easily within the ideals of the master modernist architect who is always fully in control.

At the same time, Briggs had the wherewithal to skillfully parlay her traumatic experience into even more media exposure, playing to the interest in an architect who, at least temporarily, had become a household name across the world. Yet in other ways, she minimized any negative assessment of her Italian encounter, for example, by emphasizing how well treated she had been on earlier legs of the trip, or by dismissing her arrest as so much "fuss." By the time Briggs retold the story to her grandniece Phylis Morrison decades later, her Italian travels and the Sicilian jail cell had transformed from a nightmare into a "really charming adventure."[32] But we should be cautious about assuming that Briggs merely instrumentalized this experience to promote her own fame, or brushed it off as irrelevant, or turned it into fare for a good dinner story. By the time Adolf Hitler rose to power, Briggs had already suffered fascism's inhumanity; stripped of all illusions, she would do everything she could to save herself.

13.
Building for Red Vienna: Pestalozzi-Hof and Ledigenheim

Katrin Stingl and Sabine Plakolm-Forsthuber

In the 1920s, the City of Vienna grew adept at using the official openings of its new communal housing blocks for propaganda purposes. And so it was on February 27, 1927, when thousands of people reportedly gathered in Döbling to inaugurate the latest such project, a large apartment block named after the Swiss pedagogue Johann Heinrich Pestalozzi to mark the centenary of his death (fig. 13.1). Its celebrated design was the work of architect Ella Briggs, who had been given the sizeable commission despite the fact that she had never completed a building of this scale before. Designing the project—a veritable urban landmark, perched on a sloping, irregularly shaped plot of land—had proven to be a formidable task (fig. 13.2).

To realize the enormously ambitious housing program the city had adopted in 1923, it would commission more than two hundred architects to plan *Volkswohnhäuser* (housing for the people).[1] These urban projects distributed throughout the city ranged in scale, from small projects filling gaps within a city block to large complexes built on land recently cleared for development. Although diverse, the communal housing blocks of Red Vienna are still recognizable today by their inclusion of certain standardized elements specified by the municipal building authority. Rules determining apartment size, room layouts, ceiling heights, and window types contributed to a certain underlying similarity among the buildings, despite their outward stylistic variation.

The *Volkswohnhäuser* offered the working classes affordable, high-quality modern dwellings that would free them from the perennially cramped and overcrowded living conditions of Vienna's tenements. The new apartments were small, but the careful arrangement of spaces and consideration of proportion created a new housing type that had its own dignity and logic, rather than one that merely mimicked old domestic forms at reduced scale. The majority of apartments built before 1927 measured 38 square meters. Each had their own small foyer; a *Wohnküche* (living room/kitchen), which is a comfortably sized room traditional in working-class homes that allowed the family to gather; a toilet; and one additional full-size room. The ceilings were low, but windows flooded each room with fresh air and sunlight; some dwellings also had their own balconies. There was a gas cooker, electric lighting, and running water in the kitchen and toilet room. In the *Wohnküche*, some kitchen functions were located in a Taylorized work niche that could be separated from the room by a curtain. This feature drew upon Grete Schütte-Lihotzky's previous experiments with efficient kitchen and scullery design. Hardwood covered the floors except in the cooking niche, toilet, and balcony areas, where easily cleaned tiles were used instead. Although central heating

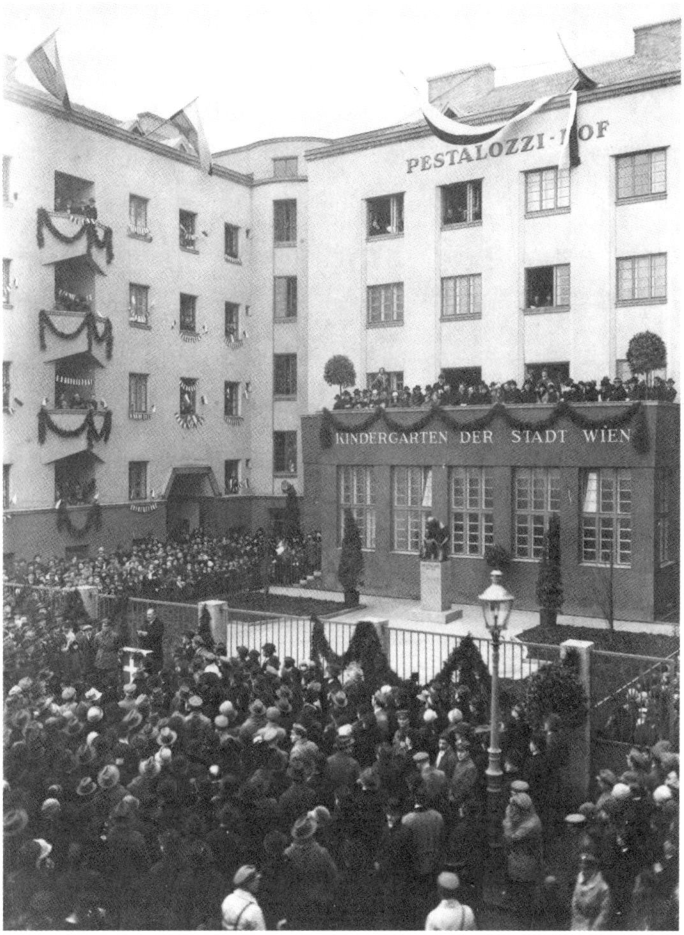

Fig. 13.1 Crowds attend the opening festivities for the Pestalozzi-Hof on February 27, 1927. The courtyard and kindergarten are visible behind the fence. (Photograph by Martin Gerlach.)

and private bathrooms (with bathtubs or showers) were not yet introduced, the new apartments represented a vast improvement in comfort and hygiene when compared to the dark, poorly ventilated, and unhygienic tenement dwellings, with their shared toilets and lack of running water.[2]

In addition to improving the living conditions of working-class families, the *Volkswohnhäuser* also promoted the Social Democrats' vision of a new proletariat society. To that end, the municipal government required the integration of numerous communal amenities meant to foster the growth of a publicly oriented social and political culture among the working classes. These included communal laundries, childcare facilities, kindergartens, libraries, theaters, lecture halls, cooperative stores, medical and dental clinics, gardens, playgrounds, pools, and other public facilities.[3] The *Volkswohnhäuser* were thus about much more than mere accommodation.

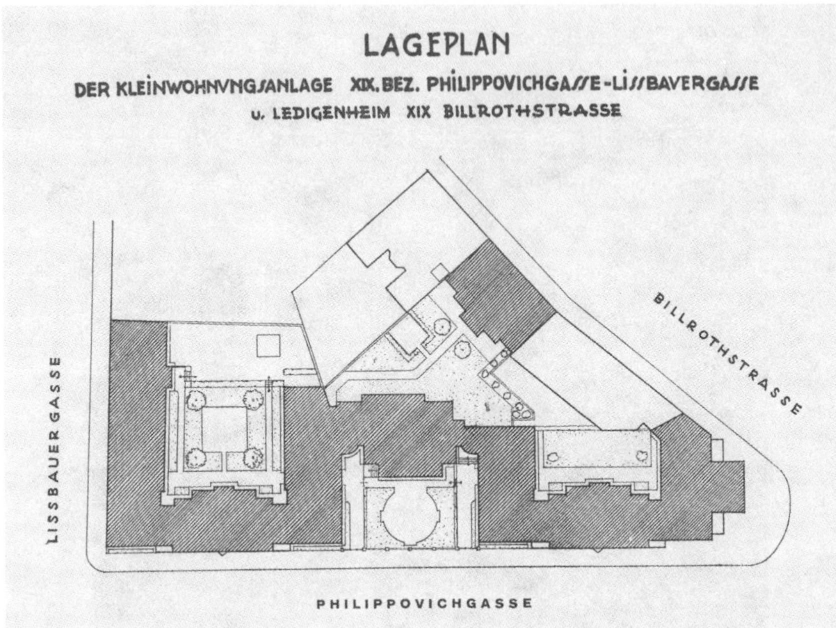

Fig. 13.2 Ella Briggs, site plan showing the location (dark hatching) of the Pestalozzi-Hof (bottom) and the Ledigenheim (top right) in Vienna, c. 1925–1927. The Pestalozzi-Hof borders Lissbauergasse (left), Philippovichgasse (bottom), and Billrothstrasse (which the Ledigenheim faces).

Critical to realizing Vienna's ambitious social housing program was its status (from 1922) as a federal state, which gave it access to federal funding and the ability to levy taxes at both the municipal and state level. The city's success in developing a new communal building culture became a source of great pride and would remain a model into the postwar period.[4] Indeed, today it continues to shape Vienna, which, compared to other European cities, has an unusually high percentage of renters in social housing from all walks of life, who enjoy affordable and secure housing in a vast urban network of municipally owned buildings.[5]

Despite the generosity of this vision of a new type of living, the various requirements and restrictions imposed by the municipality at times severely reined in the architects' latitude. How Briggs managed these, while still attempting to leave her own mark on Vienna's urban landscape, tells us much about her emerging architectural sensibilities and casts light on her perspective on what constituted essential housing reform. If previously we have seen how skillfully Briggs inserted herself into Vienna's professional cohort, here we see how she navigated the system, and we get a glimpse of how she envisioned herself as a professional working in a male-dominated field. At the time the Pestalozzi-Hof commission was awarded, Briggs was the only female architect in Vienna who had been formally qualified as a *Diplom-Ingenieur*.

Briggs's building site was in Döbling, the nineteenth district, in the north of the city. Where to locate the *Volkswohnhäuser* was a hotly debated topic among Viennese

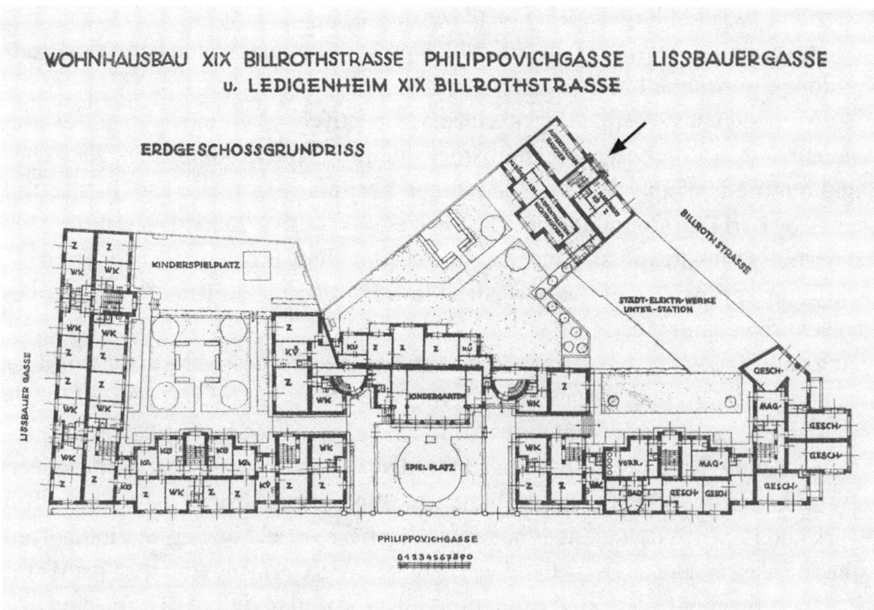

Fig. 13.3 Ella Briggs, site plan showing the ground floors of the Pestalozzi-Hof und Ledigenheim in Vienna, c. 1925–1927. The shops are at the far right. The courtyard and kindergarten are at the center of Philippovichgasse (bottom center of the plan). The Ledigenheim is at the top right (see added arrow).

politicians. Government representatives emphasized the availability of vacant lots and municipal property as well as traffic considerations. And indeed, the Pestalozzi-Hof's site had the advantage of being a parcel of land owned by the city in the immediate vicinity of public transportation. Conservative opponents, by contrast, accused the government of selecting locations for politically strategic reasons. In Döbling, the creation of *Volkswohnhäuser* brought significantly more proletarian residents into the district, consolidating the Social Democrats' position.[6]

Construction of the Pestalozzi-Hof took about one year, beginning in fall 1925.[7] The site was a challenging corner plot measuring nearly 4,000 square meters. Briggs built on a little more than half of that area, leaving extensive green spaces, as required by city regulations (fig. 13.3; and see figs. 13.1–13.2). The structure rose four to five stories above a subterranean level. It encompassed 119 apartments intended primarily for working-class families. Of these, the majority (81) had a *Wohnküche* and one additional room, as well as a small foyer and a toilet room. The remaining units—with one exception—varied slightly in size and the configuration of their plan, but they all featured two rooms (in most cases, the second room was quite small) and a separate kitchen. The exception was one sole unit, consisting of a single room and no kitchen, that was intended for a single person. Briggs had managed to carve this out of space that could not be used for a regular apartment. The Pestalozzi-Hof's communal spaces included nine laundries, bathing facilities with showers and bathtubs, shop premises, a kindergarten, and a playground.[8] In planning the site, Briggs also had to take zoning laws into account, which prescribed a streetside courtyard midway along a perimeter block.

Surprising as it may seem, Briggs's project was relatively small among Vienna's *Volkswohnhäuser*. Most of these were multistory buildings, and in some cases, they contained hundreds of apartments. The famous Karl-Marx-Hof, also in Döbling and planned by Karl Ehn around the time that Briggs was constructing the Pestalozzi-Hof, demonstrates the gargantuan scale that the largest of these projects reached. The massive, robust appearance of the new social housing became a distinctive feature of Vienna's urban landscape.

At a time of ongoing debates about what constituted the proper form for working-class housing in Vienna, Briggs's design for the Pestalozzi-Hof was praised for its simplicity and lack of ornamentation. Although her approach may indicate some influence from the Italian buildings she admired, it also aligns with what we have seen many times before: Briggs's superb ability to absorb a model from a new context and rework and improve it, making it her own. Viennese social housing was influenced by the rise of *Neues Bauen* (New Building) in Austria and Germany after the First World War. This movement advocated a functionalist approach to design that rejected historical ornament and had its roots in the radical design movements that arose at the turn of the twentieth century, including the Secession. Briggs's designs for the German Theater in New York from 1908 illustrate her longstanding familiarity with and contribution to the stylistic precursors of the *Neues Bauen*.[9] But after the war, this new direction came to hold great political weight as a symbol of the new society that German and Austrian progressives hoped would emerge from the catastrophe of war.

The design of the Pestalozzi-Hof demonstrates Briggs's ability to deploy the new architectural syntax with great sensitivity to the building's site and urban location. Briggs arranged the building's masses to forge an overall impression of a whole while simultaneously creating a sense of movement, rhythm, and articulation. To begin, she seized the dynamic possibilities of the corner plot of land that also rises in elevation from one end to the other, visually creating vertical and horizontal thrusts. Where the land slopes downward to its lowest point, at the meeting point of Philippovichgasse and Billrothstrasse (see fig. 13.2), the building surges upward (fig. 13.4). The upper residential floors of the building are painted a light tone and rest on a high-ceilinged ground floor clad in a strong shade of reddish brown. This base gives the striking impression of a colored ribbon of wall that, moving horizontally in the other direction, as Philippovichgasse rises, gradually tapers, becoming a narrow plinth. Where the building abuts one of the district's thoroughfares (at the intersection of Philippovichgasse and Billrothstrasse), large shop windows perforate the colorful base, thereby avoiding a ponderous feel. The architect's inclusion of symmetrical porticoes on either side, each with a single sculpted gray column, bolsters the urbanity of the small, finely articulated retail center.

At some distance from this commercial interface, midway along Philippovichgasse, Briggs placed the required *Strassenhof* (street courtyard) (fig. 13.5; and see figs. 13.1–13.3).

The projecting wings flanking the street courtyard act like two open arms, marking the entrance to the complex. The actual entrances are not directly in front (parallel to the street) but rather are recessed and placed to either side of the courtyard. Passing through them, residents then gain access to further interior courtyards and stairwells leading to the apartments. The street courtyard itself is enclosed by a wrought-iron fence with two clearly marked gates of entry. This ambivalence of openness and demarcation, as well as of protection and surveillance, was characteristic of the courtyard complexes of Red Vienna (see figs. 13.3 and 13.5).

Briggs situated the kindergarten—a central, single-story projecting structure with ample glazing—in the cramped, shallow street courtyard (see figs. 13.3 and 13.5). By painting the entire kindergarten facade a reddish-brown tone, the architect brought attention to it as the social and educational heart of the entire complex, in the same manner in which the color unity of the shop facades indicated an economic focus.[10] Child welfare—and especially the promotion of early childhood education—played a central role in the far-reaching, structural reforms of the Social Democratic welfare system (fig. 13.6; and see fig. 13.5). It is therefore surprising that the kindergarten was given so little room to thrive.[11]

The kindergarten's location was initially intended to house a workshop, but the idea was discarded during the planning phase; this may help to explain why the kindergarten is small in size. Other initial elements of Briggs's design were also altered over time. She originally envisioned doors leading directly from the large playroom to the adjoining courtyard to encourage outdoor play. If this had been realized, the indoor and outdoor spaces would have had a much more fluid connection. Instead, windows were placed facing onto the courtyard, and a door at the side became the entrance to the kindergarten. This change was a consequence of the decision to dedicate the new complex to Pestalozzi, the renowned educator. At that juncture, the City of Vienna pushed for a stately memorial design within the highly visible courtyard space. Instead of children tumbling out through the doors to play, a statue of the honoree (guiding a child) was placed on a high pedestal on the central axis, right in front of the kindergarten. A large, circular sandy area—more monumental rondel than child-friendly playground—adjoins it on the side nearest the street (see fig. 13.1).

A more successful interplay of indoor and outdoor space, and one that also serves to make the facades appear more dynamic, is Briggs's use of balconies and loggias. Balcony details ran the gamut from slightly outdated expressionistic triangular shapes (see fig. 13.5) to simple modern iron grilles. The appropriateness of balconies in social housing was not uniformly accepted during this period. Such features were seen by some as vestigial symbols of prestige for status-conscious urban dwellers. Yet others argued for their importance in providing private outdoor space to the working classes.[12] The Pestalozzi-Hof was unusual in how many apartments had their own balconies or loggias: about 60 percent. By comparison, other social housing projects built in this period equipped on average only a third of their apartments with similar amenities.[13]

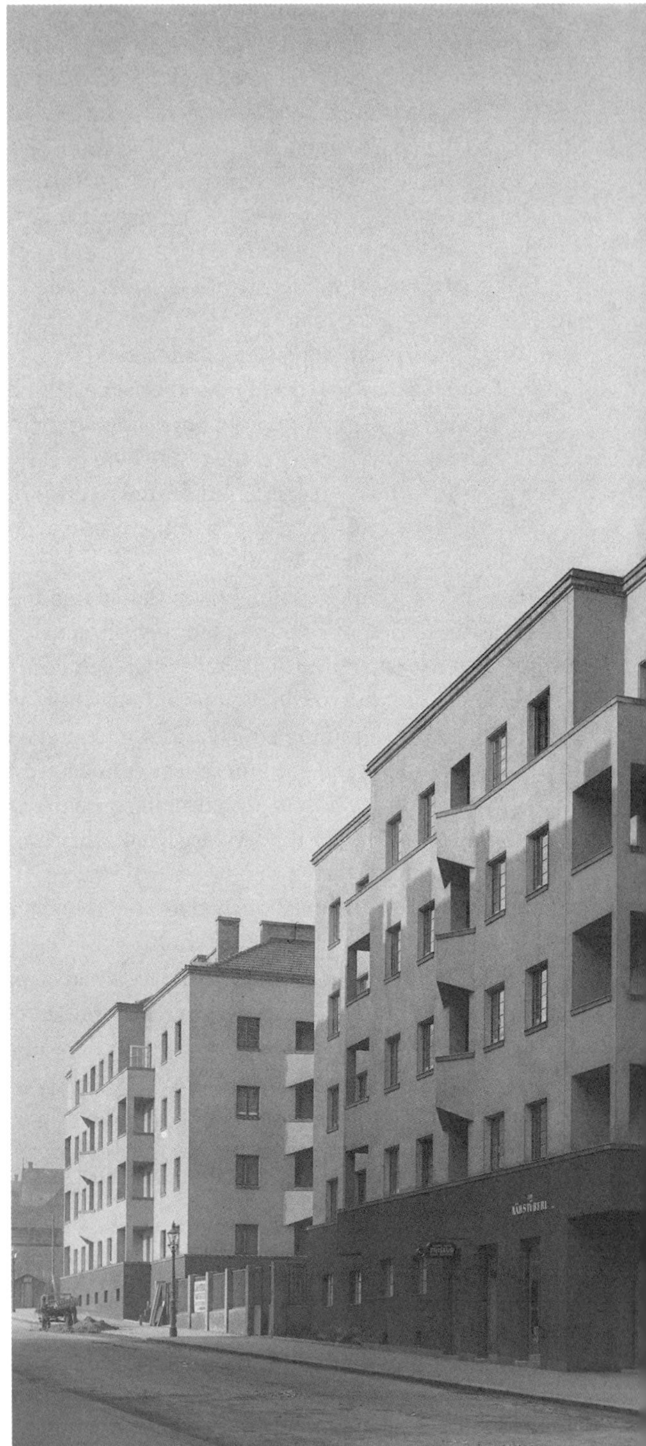

Fig. 13.4 Ella Briggs, Pestalozzi-Hof in Vienna, 1925–1927, showing the shopfronts with the gray columns (only one visible from this angle) at the intersection of Philippovichgasse and Billrothstrasse, and the broad longitudinal side of the building along the rising Philippovichgasse. The lettering at the top of the building, near the cornice, announces this is a municipal building. It reads: "Erbaut von der Gemeinde Wien in den Jahren 1925–1926 aus den Mitteln der Wohnbausteuer" (Built by the City of Vienna in the years 1925–1926 with housing tax funds). (Photograph by Martin Gerlach.)

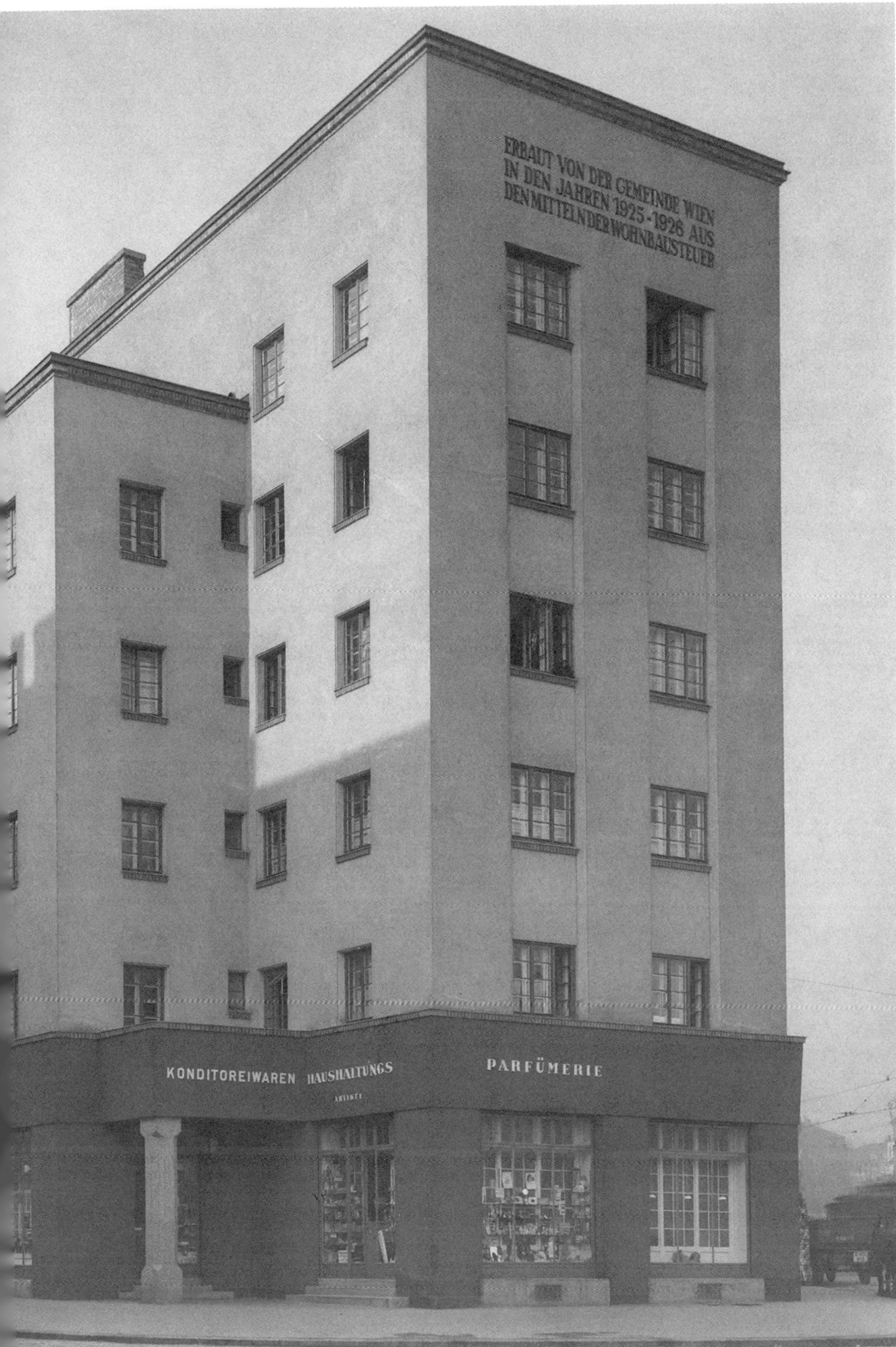
ERBAUT VON DER GEMEINDE WIEN
IN DEN JAHREN 1925-1926 AUS
DEN MITTELN DER WOHNBAUSTEUER
KONDITOREIWAREN
HAUSHALTUNGS
PARFÜMERIE

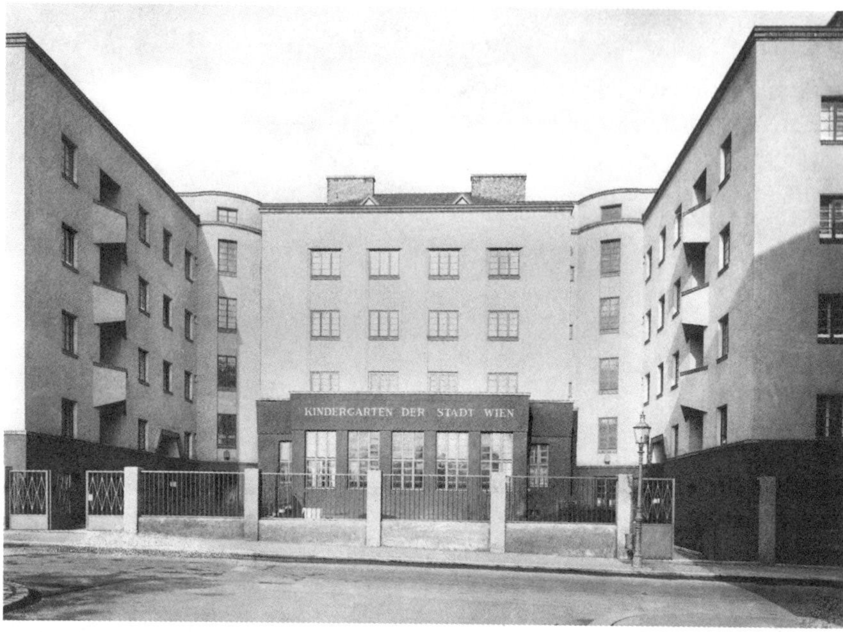

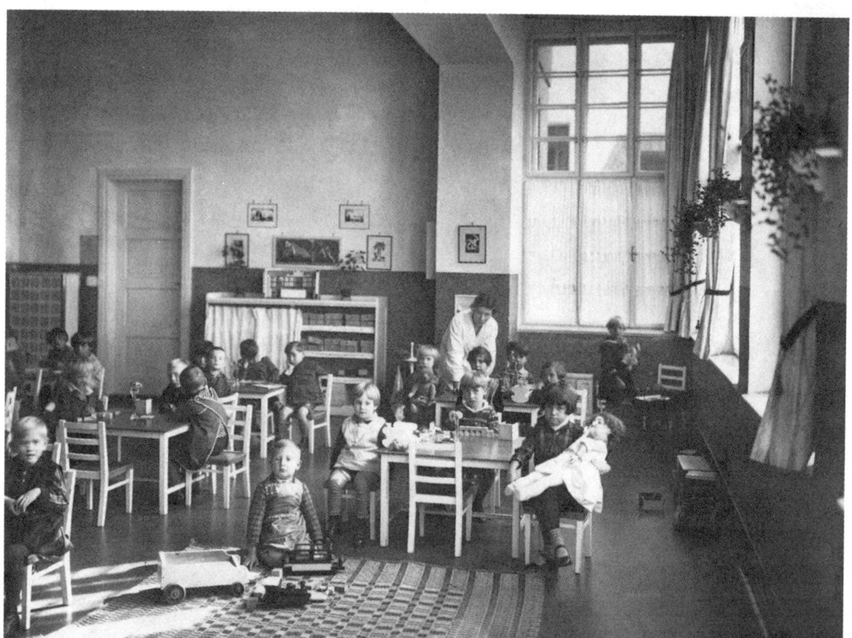

Fig. 13.5 (top) Pestalozzi-Hof street courtyard with access gates and the kindergarten, as it looked in 1926–1927, before the official opening and naming in February 1927. The name "Pestalozzi-Hof" near the cornice and Pestalozzi statue (see fig. 13.1) were not yet added. Note the triangular-shaped balconies on the wings. (Photograph by Martin Gerlach.)

Fig. 13.6 (bottom) Ella Briggs, Pestalozzi-Hof kindergarten interior, view of the large playroom with children and a teacher, c. 1928.

Despite Briggs's efforts to give the Pestalozzi-Hof the sense of a whole through such elements as color, the unifying base, and the visual cadences of balconies and loggias, none of the facades are the same, which adds to its overall dynamic effect. In her American writings on the single-family house, Briggs had argued that a building's external form should emerge honestly from the interior function of the rooms, and if the building were freestanding, this would result in no two sides being alike. As she emphasized, this picturesqueness was not produced for its own sake, although it did require the intervention of the architect to bring together the massing in a pleasing manner.[14] In the Pestalozzi-Hof, Briggs has done just that on a grand scale, and it was this sophisticated interplay of architectural forms, variety, and accents that caught critics' attention and earned their plaudits. As one journalist noted, Briggs's functionalism did not replace beauty; instead, residents were given both.[15]

The challenging plot and onerous building regulations imposed on the project required ingenuity on Briggs's part to accommodate as many apartments as possible within the complex. To realize this goal, Briggs varied the spatial arrangement of components along the building's long, zigzagging plan. Where she could, she created cross-ventilation within the dwellings, a feature strongly advocated by housing reformers at the time. Additionally, by giving many of the *Wohnküchen* their own balcony or loggia, she created a more expansive sense of space for the family and provided the housewife with convenient outdoor access.

Yet not all of Briggs's design efforts bore fruit. Phylis Morrison, the architect's grandniece, recounted how Briggs had continued to fight for better-equipped bathrooms in the Pestalozzi-Hof apartments until the time of their completion.[16] Having become acquainted with advances in domestic hygiene in the United States, Briggs strove to upgrade even the smallest municipal apartments by including a modern shower. How she envisioned doing so is captured in a small sketch she made, which a reform-minded colleague published in 1926 to illustrate a newspaper article on a variety of new apartment types being developed in Vienna by contemporary architects, including Briggs.[17] The sketch illustrates a small apartment with a foyer, *Wohnküche* with balcony, and a bedroom. The foyer has been subdivided to include a small bathroom with a toilet and shower (fig. 13.7). In comparing the sketch to the Pestalozzi-Hof apartment layouts, it becomes clear that this approach would have allowed Briggs to install a shower in only a handful of the 119 apartments: there simply was not enough space in most of the small existing foyers to add a shower beside the toilet.[18] Ultimately, Briggs was compelled to follow communal housing standards and install collective bathing facilities in the basement. Despite her efforts and a growing desire more generally, private bathrooms in the *Volkswohnhäuser* remained a rarity. Briggs's sketch was published precisely as finishing touches were being made on the Pestalozzi-Hof. Perhaps she put it out there in frustration, as a public critique of the outdated solutions still in use in new housing developments.

More broadly, restrictions imposed by Viennese city authorities meant that Briggs could not make the Pestalozzi-Hof a case study to advance the rationalization of the household that she had promoted publicly in Vienna before she received the

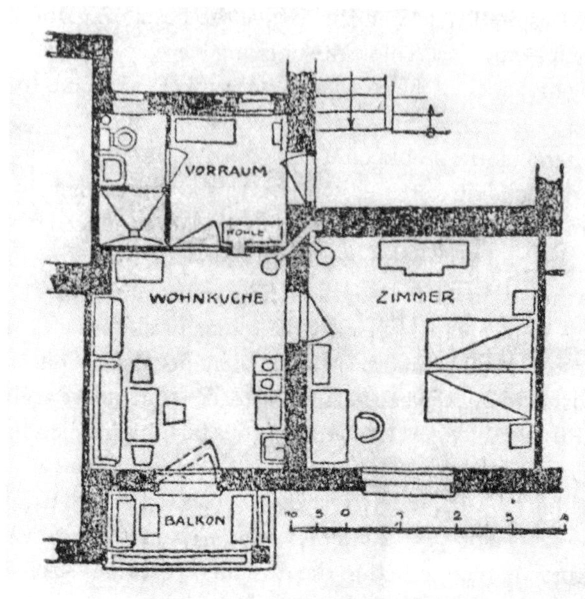

Fig. 13.7 Ella Briggs, (unrealized) sketch for a 38-square-meter apartment with bathroom, including toilet and shower stall accessed through the *Vorraum* (foyer) adjacent to the *Wohnküche* (living room/kitchen), 1926.

commission or to incorporate other developments she had experienced in the United States, beyond individual bathrooms. Regulations regarding apartment size and furnishing standards were simply too rigid to allow for much experimentation. Admittedly, some facilities to ease domestic labor were standard: large municipal housing complexes offered women central laundries with washing machines and electric irons. Yet in her writings, Briggs wanted to go beyond such communal amenities and advocated for the use of electrical appliances within the individual home, such as washing machines and dishwashers, arguing that it would liberate women from "the slavery of housework."[19]

If Briggs had to reluctantly settle for less than she wanted in amenities, she nonetheless achieved a sense of dignity in the modest homes she designed. This is perhaps best appreciated in the few images to survive of the interiors.[20] Apartments were rented unfurnished, but in a model apartment Briggs created a spare yet elegant home environment. In a published photograph, we see a small room, its walls painted in bright colors to the height of the doors and framed by simple geometric borders (fig. 13.8). The stained oak furniture, including a generously sized desk, is simple and unfussy. A curtain with a modern floral pattern and matching upholstery add to the welcoming impression. In another part of the model apartment, a room with a cooking niche contains rather spartan furniture made of dark-stained larch, including a simple wooden bench (which could be converted into a bed), a chair with a woven seat, and an oval folding table (fig. 13.9). The light walls contrast with the dark furniture. The cooking niche, equipped with the minimal furnishings typical of the time—a two-burner gas stove and a sink with running water—could be separated from its surroundings by a curtain. Home accessories such as tableware and a vase with flowers are arranged spar-

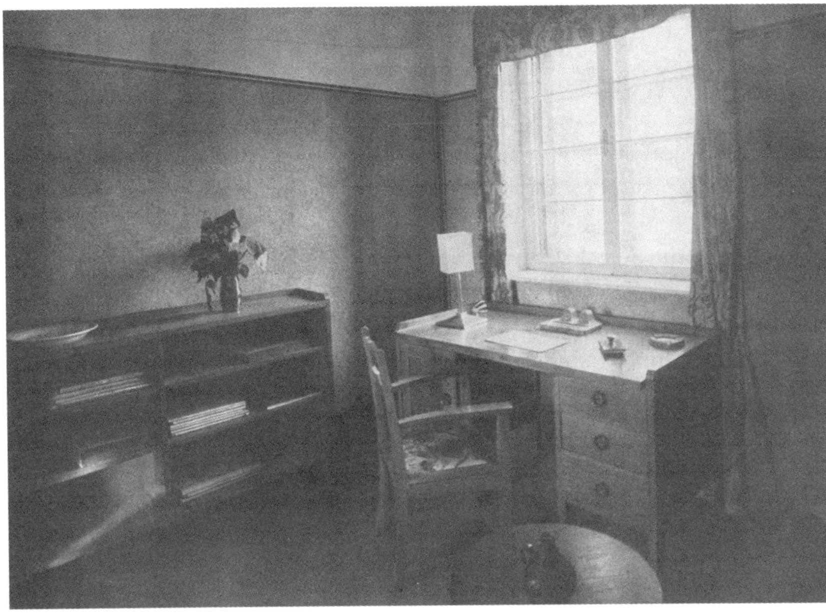

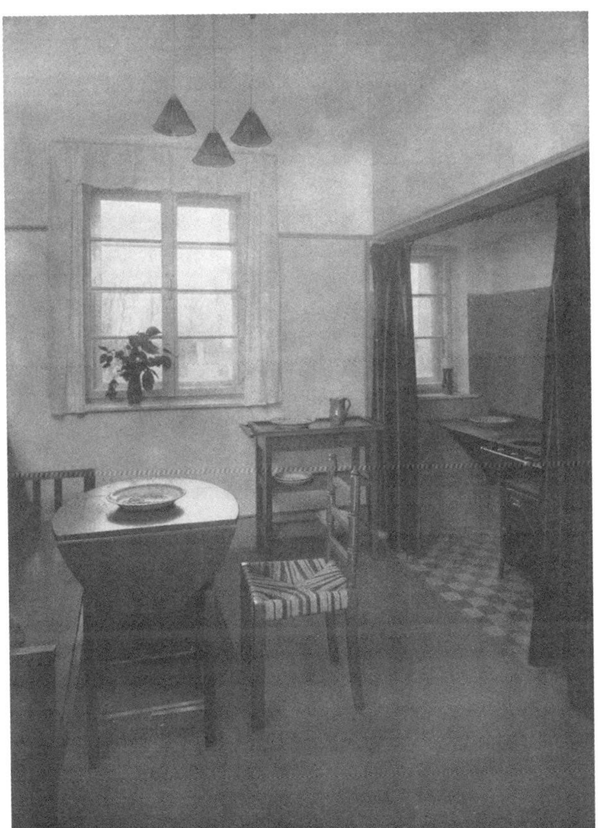

Fig. 13.8 (above) Ella Briggs, view of a small room with desk in a model apartment in the Pestalozzi-Hof in Vienna, 1926. Briggs may have designed the furniture herself (see also fig. 13.9). Additionally, the well-balanced composition of these interior photographs suggests we are encountering here yet another of Briggs's talents: her architectural photography.

Fig. 13.9 (left) Ella Briggs, view of a combined living room and kitchenette in a model apartment in the Pestalozzi-Hof in Vienna, 1926. To the left is a bench that can be transformed into a sleeping platform.

ingly. This kind of simple, small-scale furniture had long been encouraged by architects working on the new housing as appropriate for small dwellings, even though it still met with resistance from residents who wanted to be able to bring family heirlooms with them or liked heavier furniture.[21] As an experienced furniture designer from her prewar interior design days, Briggs likely designed the furniture for the model apartment. Graceful yet unpretentious, Briggs's design embraced a new way of living.

In keeping with the Social Democrats' building priorities, most of the dwellings in the Pestalozzi-Hof were allocated to small families. Yet politicians knew that other constituent groups existed in Vienna in need of attention. Single men and women, for example, had few independent housing options. A divorced, working woman herself, Briggs had personal experience living in three of these options, indicating her ability to navigate the city's resources as an independent single woman. The first was charitable institutions for single women, widows, and orphans. For a few weeks in the fall of 1902, as she was starting her second year at the School of Applied Arts, Briggs had stayed in such a home, before her mother moved back to Vienna from Hinterbrühl and rented an apartment for the two of them.[22] The second option was dormitories run by professional associations: Briggs had rented a room in Vienna's Lehrerhaus (Teachers' House) around the time of her divorce in 1912.[23] The third was one-room apartments or studios situated within the *Volkswohnhäuser*, which had the added benefit of reducing social isolation for single individuals: as of 1926 Briggs lived in a studio in one such communal social housing block, designed by her colleague Karl Dirnhuber, located at Weimarer Strasse 1.[24] As work on the Pestalozzi-Hof was progressing in 1926, the Social Democratic city government joined forces with Briggs to experiment with a new type of housing: a residence for single people, the first new communal building of this kind in Vienna (fig. 13.10).[25]

The Ledigenheim (singles' home), as it would be called, was built on a narrow plot neighboring the Pestalozzi-Hof to forge close social ties between the two resident groups (see fig. 13.3). In her design, and even more clearly than in the Pestalozzi-Hof, Briggs made the different types of communal housing spaces legible from the outside through the varied use of volume and color. On the street facade, the private units were terracotta colored; some extruded out of the facade as squarish elements. Gray was used to delineate other types of spaces: the glass-fronted stairwell, the laundry in the attic, and communal rooms and custodian's apartment on the ground floor. Reddish-brown clinker brick framed the entrance portal and accented some window corners. The windows themselves were painted blue. Briggs's Italian journey may have inspired the building's color scheme, particularly in combining light-colored walls with contrasts of red and blue.[26] At the rear, the building's shared communal areas jutted out, staggered in plan, into the garden, and the application of white paint brightened up this core area of the building. The flanking private rooms were stepped back, and, analogous to the street side, painted in a terracotta tone.[27] Thus even here where the building was not detached, Briggs strove to bring variety to different facades through an "honest" expression of internal functions as well as the use of color.

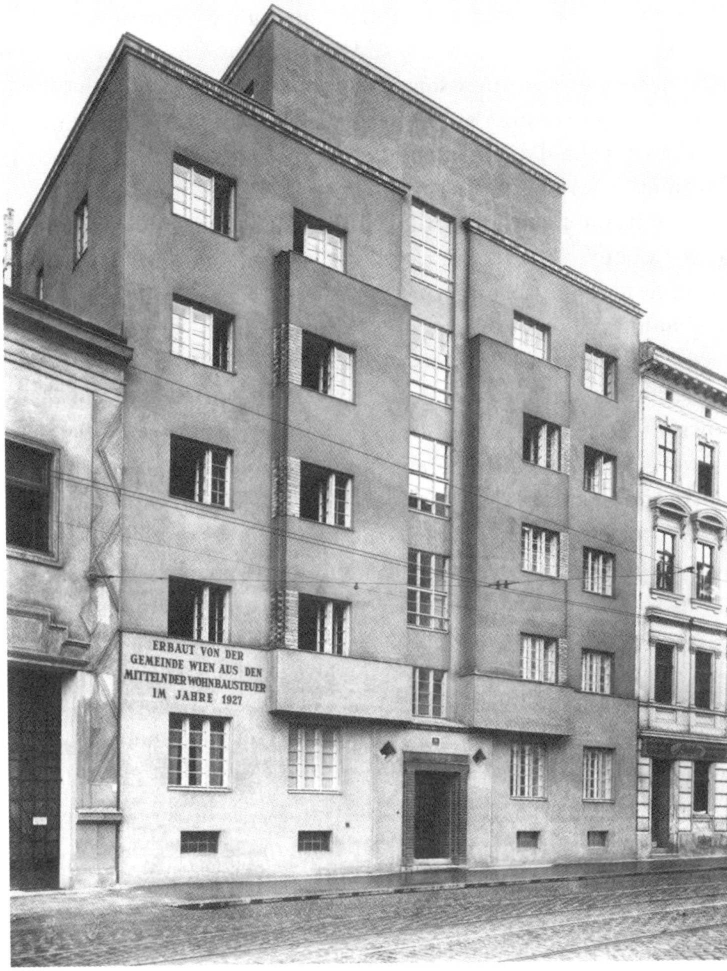

Fig. 13.10 Ella Briggs, street facade of the Ledigenheim at Billrothstrasse 9 in Vienna, 1928. (Photograph by Martin Gerlach.)

Briggs was among an early group of *Neues Bauen* architects to experiment with color as a means to enhance the visual richness of a building's facade within the broader urban landscape but also to help the user to understand and read the building.[28] That is, Briggs's use of color on the exterior went beyond the decorative, to speak of function and structure—to organize the building's components from a visual standpoint. At the same time, color added variety and points of dialogue with the surrounding urban environment in a manner similar to what Briggs had encountered in Italian vernacular architecture. Color, for Briggs, was both beautiful and functional.[29]

On the interior, four identical residential floors were stacked above the ground floor. Each of these floors formed a residential unit consisting of six private rooms and common spaces (plate 10). The residential floors were reached via a staircase; a locked door ensured that each floor was accessible only to its residents.[30] In the center of each floor, the architect placed a shared living room, which was flanked by a bathroom (with showers but no bathtubs) and a kitchenette. Briggs, who had travelled extensively on her own and knew something about the reality of such a lifestyle, emphasized organizing each story as a home, encouraging a feeling of family among the residents. This contrasted with contemporary experiments in housing types for single men and women undertaken by German architects Walter Gropius and Marcel Breuer, who in celebrating the anonymity of the "modern nomad" envisioned something more akin to a luxury hotel.[31] In articles Briggs wrote around this time on the single-family American home in American magazines, she presented the living room as the family's "spiritual center," a concept she extended to the Ledigenheim as well. She claimed that a sense of home was what was missing from the rented furnished rooms that most single people in cities were forced to accept for want of anything else available to them.[32] Briggs's own efforts to keep her furniture and other beloved possessions with her, in her many moves within and to different cities, takes on a deeper meaning here, as an insistence on her individual domestic identity.

When the Ledigenheim finally opened its doors in the spring of 1928, a target group of occupants had been specified: male students. Originally, the residence had been intended for twenty-five "single people," each with their own room. In the end, fifty students were accommodated in the rooms, most of which were now shared.[33] Two large common rooms were provided on the ground floor, one for smokers and the other for nonsmokers.[34] Although these spaces had been planned from the beginning, they were now needed more than ever to accommodate the higher density of occupants on each floor.

In the Ledigenheim, as in the Pestalozzi-Hof, Briggs did not achieve all that she had wanted. In the spirit of modern health reform movements, the architect had initially proposed adding a new flat roof above an electrical transformer station, located in between the two projects, as a place for residents to sun themselves and exercise. Unfortunately, although the building authorities gave preliminary approval, the sun terrace was not implemented, presumably because of structural concerns.[35] Less glamourous but more immediately impactful on the students' wellbeing would have been central heating, which here, as in the Pestalozzi-Hof, exceeded the city's tight budgets.

Still, and as journalists noted when the home opened, the Ledigenheim offered a tremendous improvement over the usual choices faced by male students seeking accommodation. Private landlords typically exploited them by renting shoddy rooms at expensive rates. Cheap housing could generally be found only with the antisemitic and right-wing Catholic student fraternities. Female students faced an even more difficult situation, which Briggs would have known personally from her own student days in Munich. One wonders what she thought of their exclusion from the Ledigenheim.[36]

In the fall of 1927, while the Ledigenheim was still under construction, Briggs was interviewed for *Frau und Gegenwart* (Woman and Contemporary Times), a German women's magazine that often published on pathbreaking female professionals.[37] The article, probably written by Gisela Urban, caught Briggs in a seemingly contemplative mood. By any measure, Briggs had achieved stunning career successes since earning her architecture degree in 1920—successes that were evoked by the many illustrations of Briggs's buildings that peppered the article. Not having found work that matched her ambitions after she graduated from Munich's Technical University, she had relocated to New York. There, she had not only undertaken her first independent architectural projects, but also emerged as a leading voice on domestic design in the influential world of women's magazines. Lured by even greater professional opportunities in Vienna, she had returned and against the odds, managed to breach a male bastion in obtaining two large social housing commissions. She had positioned herself as an important actor in Red Vienna, deserving recognition from the city authorities, her male colleagues, and the public. Yet in the interview she gave, she did not give the impression that her struggles were behind her.

Despite lauding her designs, the article actually focused on Briggs herself, and how she saw herself as a woman in architecture. It opened with a quote from Briggs, who stated, "I am against women's work only being valued because it was done by a woman. The details of a woman's approach might differ from those of a man, but in general, she too can only strive to do decent work. To want to derive special recognition from the fact that a woman has done a specific job—that seems to me to be unjustified."[38] Briggs insisted that she wanted her work to be judged by "objective considerations" alone, even though she had had to overcome prejudices and barriers as a woman in her education and professional advancement.[39] Yet at the time, that kind of unbiased assessment was hardly the reality for women architects. Briggs's support by the municipality of Vienna was thus a very important and public act of confidence in women's abilities.

Indeed, in his remarks at the opening of the Pestalozzi-Hof in February 1927 (see fig. 13.1), Mayor of Vienna Karl Seitz referred to Briggs's building as proof of women's calling in architecture and of the city's commitment (in having hired her) to the "principle of gender equality in business and work."[40] It is unknown if the architect was present herself at the ceremony to hear her work being praised (plate 11). By the time this celebration took place, Briggs was preparing to move to Berlin, unable, it seems—and despite the accolades—to secure further municipal commissions in her hometown.

In this context, Briggs's insistence that her work be judged only by "objective considerations" and not by the gender of the creator is revealing. Despite all she had achieved in New York and Vienna, the fact that she felt compelled to make this plea suggests that she was still looking for that elusive level playing field, where she would have the same chances as her male colleagues to succeed. In the broader horizons of Berlin's architecture world, she perhaps hoped to find it at last.

Section IV.

BUILDING COMMISSIONS AND EXHIBITIONS IN BERLIN, 1927–1935

14.
An Office in Berlin: Modernist Housing Blocks

Celina Kress, with contributions on Mariendorf by Katrin Stingl

In the spring of 1927, Ella Briggs travelled to Berlin on an express train powered by a steam locomotive.[1] *Berlin: Die Sinfonie der Großstadt* (Berlin: Symphony of a metropolis), Walther Ruttmann's classic silent film of 1927, provides a glimpse of the sights (if not the sounds) she might have encountered on her journey. From the window of the train, distant, isolated rural houses, meadows, and clusters of trees pass rapidly into and out of view, the speed of the train marked by the blur of power line poles in the foreground. Gradually, the scene becomes more densely inhabited. Allotment gardens metamorphose into residential neighborhoods. As we approach the city, industrial sites appear. Multistory apartment buildings, some under construction and scaffolded, rise beside the railroad line. The train slows, slicing through tall urban walls, and finally rolls to a stop in the center of the city at Anhalter Bahnhof.

This cross section of the topography then typical of the Prussian metropolis would constitute the scope of Briggs's work over the course of the next eight years. As an architect, she would contribute to each of the urban conditions illustrated in Ruttmann's film, from private single-family homes on the outskirts of the city to more centralized apartment blocks. Through her designs for exhibitions and trade fairs, she would explore the spaces of industrial production as well as new ways of living. Briggs would also impact the city's architectural culture through her voice as a writer, enriching the discussions about housing then gripping Berlin.

But all of that still lay in the future. As Briggs looked out the train window, we can imagine that she saw both the vast possibilities and the herculean challenges that confronted the German capital, which had parallels to those that had been consuming her as an architect in Vienna. Like Austria, Germany had been devastated economically by the defeat of World War I. In the capitals of both countries, enormous housing shortages fueled misery, and their remediation required the intervention of municipal governments as well as the coordination of agencies and offices across many different sectors. Although in Vienna the city council was responsible for the social housing projects, in Berlin—which by the 1920s far surpassed Vienna in population and size—a plethora of local authorities, cooperatives, and private building firms, working in tandem, were directly responsible for housing initiatives. To succeed as an architect in Berlin, Briggs had to learn to navigate this complex landscape and identify its key players.

The housing crisis in Berlin was decades in the making. In the second half of the nineteenth century, the city grew rapidly as it emerged as a center of business, industry, government, education, and transportation, especially after it became the capital of a unified German Empire in 1871. From 1850 to 1890, the population more than quadrupled, and by 1900 it was nearing 2 million inhabitants.[2] The government left the immense demand for housing in the hands of private developers, who made windfall profits with their speculative ventures. This led to the spread of a distinct Berlin apartment type: the so-called *Mietskaserne* (rental barracks). The typical tenement building was four or five stories tall with a massive street facade, behind which lay one or more narrow courtyards enclosed by side and back wings. For most residents, the only light and air came from the dark courtyard. This housing type came under intense criticism for its poor daylighting, unsanitary conditions, and notorious overcrowding. By the time the twentieth century began, reformers campaigned to replace the rental barracks with new forms of mass housing as well as small, single-family homes.[3]

Despite these reform efforts, municipal fragmentation thwarted any coordinated action in housing and urban development during this period; it would take the loss of World War I to break open the region's encrusted economic networks and administrative structures. In October 1920 nearly one hundred municipalities united to form Greater Berlin, which provided the political basis for innovative, socially oriented housing construction during the 1920s. Such initiatives were desperately needed after the war, as refugees, returning soldiers, and newlyweds further swelled the population of the region and exacerbated an already severe housing shortage.

Yet construction efforts initially floundered due to the economic crisis unleashed by hyperinflation. Only in 1924 did housing construction in Berlin begin to take off. This development was enabled not only by the stabilization of the German currency the previous year, but also by the establishment of a federal tax subsidy program, which covered the majority of housing construction costs.[4] The City of Berlin created the Wohnungsfürsorgegesellschaft (Housing Welfare Society) to distribute these federal funds. During the years that followed, private and public initiatives for housing projects intertwined, creating a flourishing market for architects interested in domestic innovation, including women such as Ella Briggs.

In 1925, a new building code came into force for Greater Berlin. This reduced the permissible height, buildable area, and occupancy rate of buildings in all zoning districts. At the same time, it shifted the balance from building zones with attached development or high urban density in favor of zones with detached suburban houses or lower urban density. The new building code formed the legal basis for Berlin's new urban planning model: the dispersed, green city organized by function.[5]

To ensure that well-designed, well-ventilated, and well-lit forms of housing would become the standard, Berlin's Housing Welfare Society set up a building advisory service. A 1926 book explained the new public funding in detail and presented the first projects created in Berlin with that support.[6] The volume largely focused on midsize (three- to four-story) courtyard apartment buildings as well as single- and multifamily rowhouses. It also promoted freestanding single-family homes.

These housing projects were sharply criticized by Martin Wagner, an architect and planner who had been pivotal in pushing forward the organization of Berlin's social housing sector and who in the fall of 1926 was appointed Stadtbaurat (Director of Urban Development) of Greater Berlin.[7] He rejected the typological diversity of the projects. He also believed their small-scale nature would lead to a "fragmentation of resources among small and very small building sites." Wagner advocated instead for a more consistent rationalization of housing construction through the planning and implementation of large housing estates.[8] In terms of the form these would take, he called for "new laws of design to be created according to the *rhythm of building massing*. We want to strip away all the accumulated opulence of inanimate decoration from this massing, which we need to shape today into the form of residential buildings."[9]

Ella Briggs adhered exactly to Wagner's precepts in the social housing designs she had realized in Vienna between 1925 and 1927.[10] From the scale of the buildings to the functional layout of the dwellings, these projects received high praise from contemporary experts, including those based in Germany. Leo Adler, the influential editor of *Wasmuths Monatshefte für Baukunst* (Wasmuth's Monthly Magazine for Architecture), counted the Pestalozzi-Hof among the "more pleasing examples . . . in the architectural chaos that the Viennese 'people's palaces' spread over the city."[11] Werner Hegemann, Walter Müller-Wulckow, and Hans Hildebrandt (all also German) similarly singled out the Pestalozzi-Hof, as well as Briggs's Ledigenheim, for inclusion in their architectural publications.[12] Although these accolades did not translate into further building commissions for Briggs from the City of Vienna, they may have helped her gain a foothold in Berlin.

Briggs did not have a "wait and see" personality, and when opportunities failed to materialize in Vienna, she did not hesitate to seek out brighter horizons, as she had done in the past. In the spring of 1927, Briggs put out feelers in Berlin to test the waters. With her characteristic self-confidence, it appears she inquired, portfolio in hand, at the Berlin City Council offices as to whether there were any job opportunities for an architect committed to *Neues Bauen*.[13] She had rightly identified Berlin's chief planner, Martin Wagner, as the key powerbroker in the city's architectural scene.

It is hard to overstate Wagner's importance to Berlin's interwar architectural and urban development. In 1926, while still director of the collaborative housing enterprise Gemeinnützige Heimstätten-, Spar- und Bau-Aktiengesellschaft, or GEHAG (Community Home Savings and Building Company), he had succeeded in setting in motion the city's first large-scale housing project—the Hufeisensiedlung (Horseshoe Settlement) in the former village of Britz, in the Neukölln district. GEHAG's even more extensive follow-up project, the Waldsiedlung (Forest Settlement), in the northern part of Zehlendorf, was in the planning stage. Once he became Greater Berlin's chief planner in October 1926, and for the next six years, Wagner steered the city's overall development. At his side was Ernst Reuter, the new head for urban transportation.

When Briggs got in touch with Wagner, he advised her to register as an architect in Berlin. He also supported her by writing a personal letter of recommendation, dated May 6, 1927. In the letter he expressed familiarity with her work, presented to him by the architect herself, and with her expertise, gleaned through "repeated" conversations with her on architectural questions. He also emphasized her "extremely noteworthy" talent. He deemed it desirable, he wrote, for Briggs to have the opportunity to practically apply her experience, "originating from the women's viewpoint," to Berlin housing. Whether Briggs suggested her "women's viewpoint" or Wagner conceived of it himself, we do not know.[14] But without doubt, Wagner's endorsement was a valuable ticket for any architect seeking entry into Berlin's exciting architectural world.

Yet Briggs did not rely on Wagner's help alone. She was an excellent networker and knew how to make her way in new environments. Publishing continued to be an important and reliable tool to make herself visible and to create opportunities. In late 1927 she published her first technical article in *Wohnungswirtschaft* (Housing Industry), the central organ of social housing in Germany. (The editor of the journal was none other than Martin Wagner.) The topic of the piece, "electricity in the home," was well chosen, as it enabled Briggs to distinguish herself as technologically adept, innovative, and knowledgeable, and in the very subject matter most likely to be assigned to a woman in the construction field.[15] Moreover, Briggs could boast the most up-to-date knowledge of American housing technologies, which she had refreshed that fall when she had undertaken a research tour in the United States—about a half year after moving to Berlin.[16] Likewise, her first contribution to the highly respected architectural journal *Bauwelt* (Building World), published in 1928, on residences designed for single people—a novel urban housing type—must have aroused interest in the Berlin architectural community.[17]

A month after Leo Adler lauded Briggs's Vienna social housing in the February 1928 issue of *Wasmuths Monatshefte für Baukunst*, a more critical assessment appeared in the Berlin financial newspaper *Berliner Börsen-Zeitung* (Berlin Stock Exchange News). Taking issue with Adler's favorable judgment, the anonymous reviewer found Briggs's social housing "sober and harsh." Although the reviewer praised Briggs's "excellent apartment design," he decried the building's external appearance as "monotonous barrenness."[18] This public exposure of Briggs's architecture in a leading financial newspaper may have drawn the attention of businessman Adolf Bloch, who, if he did see the article, apparently disagreed with the criticism. He was to become Briggs's most important private client in Berlin.

Unfortunately, almost nothing is known about Bloch. He was one of several managing directors of the Berlin-based firm Gesellschaft für Spezialbauausführungen (Specialized Building Construction Company), which offered engineering and construction services for concrete and reinforced concrete structures. In the fall of 1928, Bloch, acting on behalf of his firm, gave Briggs her first major housing contract in Berlin.[19] Boswau and Knauer, a leading construction company in 1920s Germany, was also involved with the project, presumably as the general contractor.[20]

Briggs was commissioned to design an apartment block in Mariendorf (fig. 14.1).[21] In 1920 the flourishing former village had been integrated into Greater Berlin as part of the borough of Tempelhof, on Berlin's southern edge. At the time, and on account of its land reserves, Tempelhof's rate of construction activity was among the city's highest. The site of Briggs's first building in Berlin was situated prominently on Rathausstrasse, Mariendorf's main thoroughfare, at the corner of Königstrasse. One street over, at the thoroughfare's intersection with Kaiserstrasse, a new local center had been established several years earlier with a city hall, fire station, police station, and high school.[22]

Berlin's 1925 zoning regulations aimed to relieve the density of new urban housing projects by forbidding the presence of rear buildings, which had characterized older tenements. Instead, the area to be developed was to be ringed with perimeter buildings, which presented an unbroken street facade on all sides. Because the 4,000-square-meter plot for Briggs's project already had older commercial structures on one side, she designed a U-shaped complex instead (fig. 14.2; and see fig. 14.1).[23] The building would have disappeared behind the dense foliage of the linden trees on Rathausstrasse had it not been for the deep setback characteristic of Berlin. Viewed from the street, two vertical elements determined the overall impression of the flat-roofed building. Groups of double balconies were stacked one on top of the other and cantilevered above the front gardens. Delicate glazed stairwells aligned with the entrance portals. The pale bluish-green loggias contrasted in color with the pale-yellow cement plaster on the wall surfaces; the reddish clinker cladding of the stairwell entrances with matching vermilion-painted front doors supplied further color accents. Green frames surrounded white window sashes (plate 12).[24] Briggs had long been attentive to the spatial impact of color, explored in innovative ways from her interior design days. Her attention to color on building facades may have been heightened by her experience of Italian vernacular architecture in the mid-1920s. In Vienna, she used color on the facades of her social housing buildings in complex ways, including to heighten their visually dynamic effect. In her Mariendorf apartment block design, she continued to explore color's rhythmic energies, perhaps influenced by contemporary modernist housing settlements such as the Waldsiedlung in Zehlendorf, which she admired.[25]

Whereas the colors gave the complex a fresh and vibrant overall expression, the three-story staggered cubic projections and recesses emphasized its clear and well-proportioned structure. This seemingly simple, rational design was the result of careful tinkering on the part of the architect. In contrast to bar-shaped building massing, it is not a simple task to offer living conditions of equal value on three sides of a courtyard. Yet this challenge also created an opportunity. Briggs was now operating in a highly competitive field with leading architects such as Bruno Taut and Walter Gro pius. To be noticed, Briggs knew she could not depend on past accomplishments, especially not in an environment where all architects were expected to innovate at the level of design and construction. Rather than try to refine the designs of her Viennese social housing, which had relied on project conditions different from those in Berlin, the apartment block in Mariendorf demonstrates her determination to explore new directions in addressing tenants' domestic needs.

The complex encompassed fifty-three apartments, which varied from two to four rooms, excluding kitchens and bathrooms, and ranged from about 50 to 80 square meters in size.[26] This was a significantly more generous arrangement than that of the Pestalozzi-Hof in Vienna, a reflection of the client's desire to ensure the rentability of the apartments in the future, once the housing shortage had eased (and, presumably,

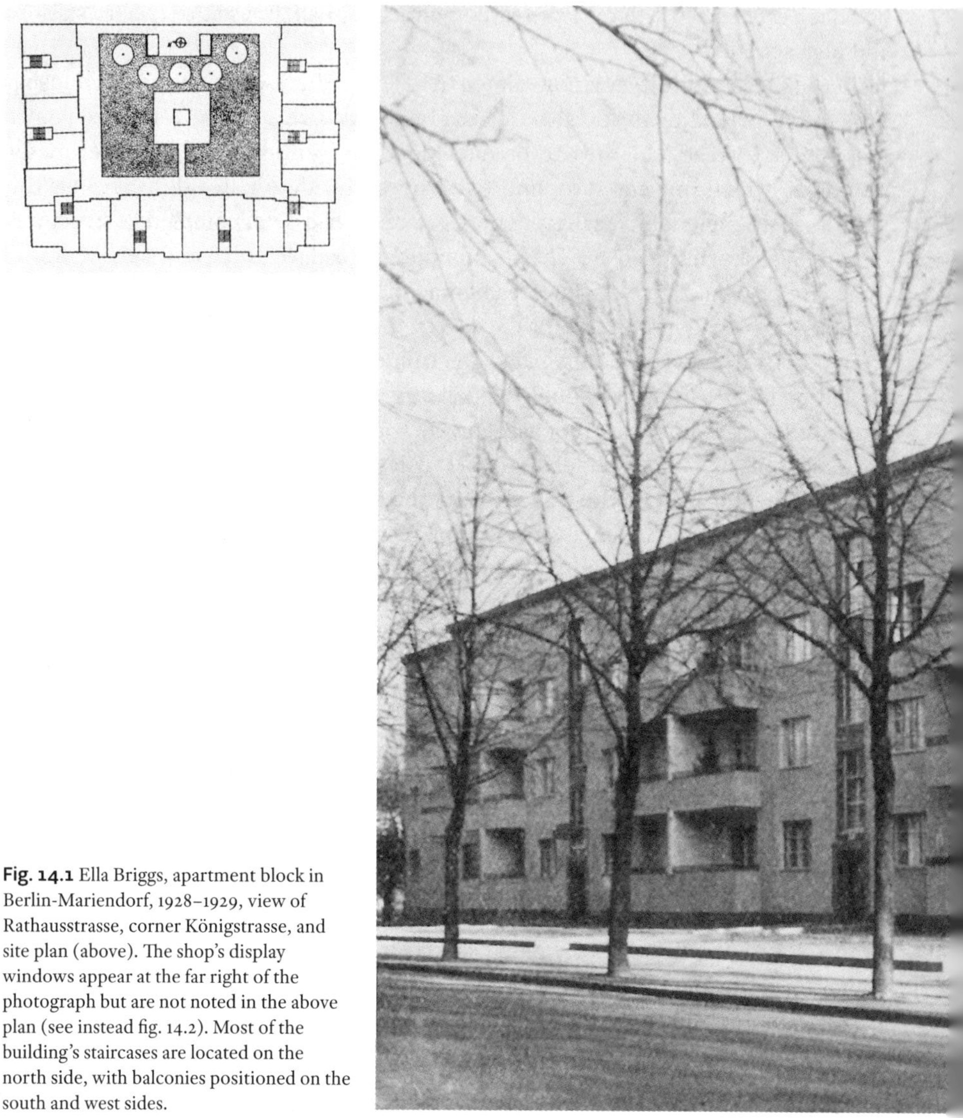

Fig. 14.1 Ella Briggs, apartment block in Berlin-Mariendorf, 1928–1929, view of Rathausstrasse, corner Königstrasse, and site plan (above). The shop's display windows appear at the far right of the photograph but are not noted in the above plan (see instead fig. 14.2). Most of the building's staircases are located on the north side, with balconies positioned on the south and west sides.

when people wanted and could afford larger dwellings). The kitchens were relatively spacious (as required by Housing Welfare Society guidelines) and equipped with a ventilated pantry, a double sink, and a well-lit seating area (fig. 14.3).[27] In accordance with her public advocacy for electrical appliances in the home, Briggs undoubtedly would have preferred to include electrical appliances in the kitchen; such a luxury, however, could not be afforded. The construction of the Mariendorf project took place during a period of economic fluctuations in Germany. This may also explain why the apartments were heated by relatively old-fashioned individual tile stoves, fueled by coal.[28]

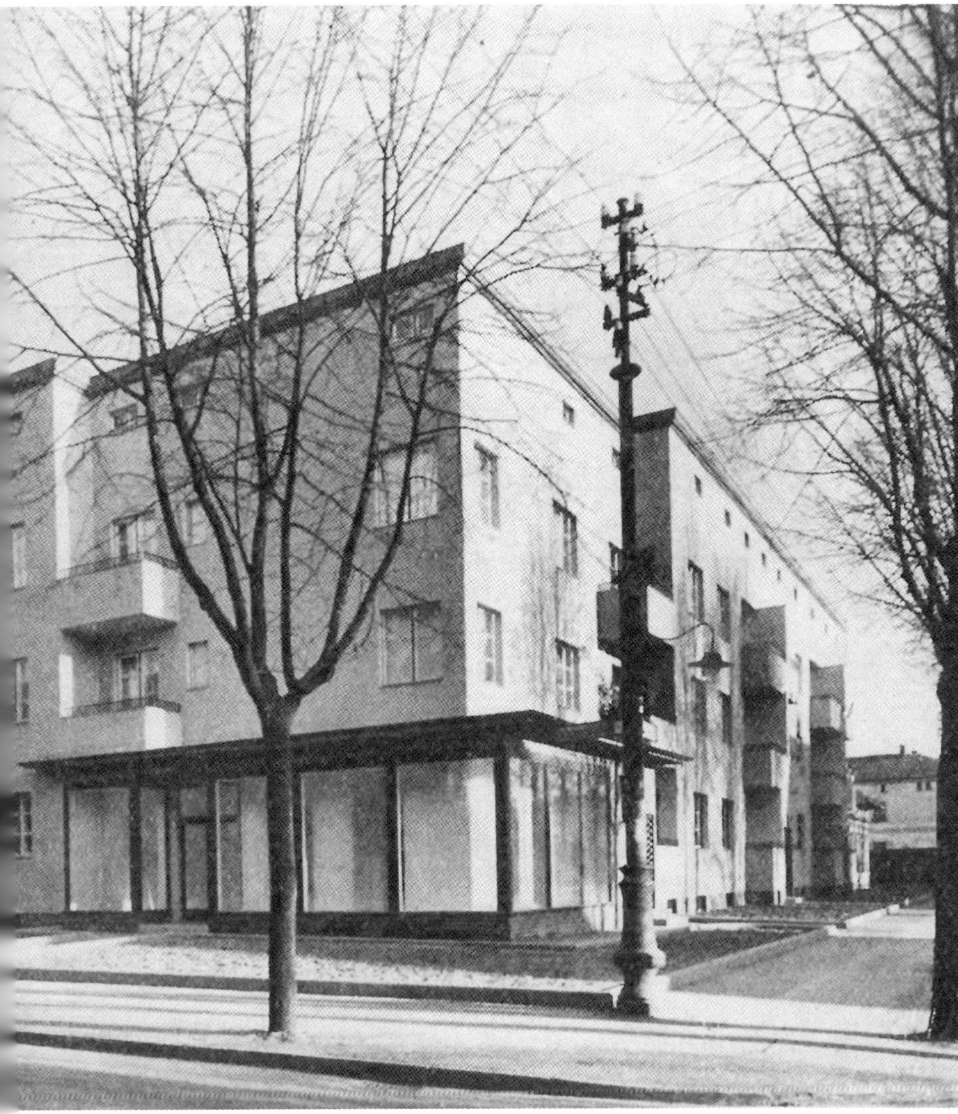

Yet if finances constrained the apartments' installed equipment, in designing the complex Briggs took advantage of a free resource. Specifically, the layout is optimally adapted to the cardinal directions in all three wings of the U-shaped complex. Briggs ensured that the apartments' larger rooms and balconies were ideally oriented with respect to the sun. The stairwells, on the other hand, were arranged on the less sunlit facades—sometimes facing the street, sometimes the courtyard (see figs. 14.1–14.2). Briggs took advantage of the greater flexibility the Mariendorf site afforded when compared to the complicated plot on which she had had to position her Vienna social housing buildings.

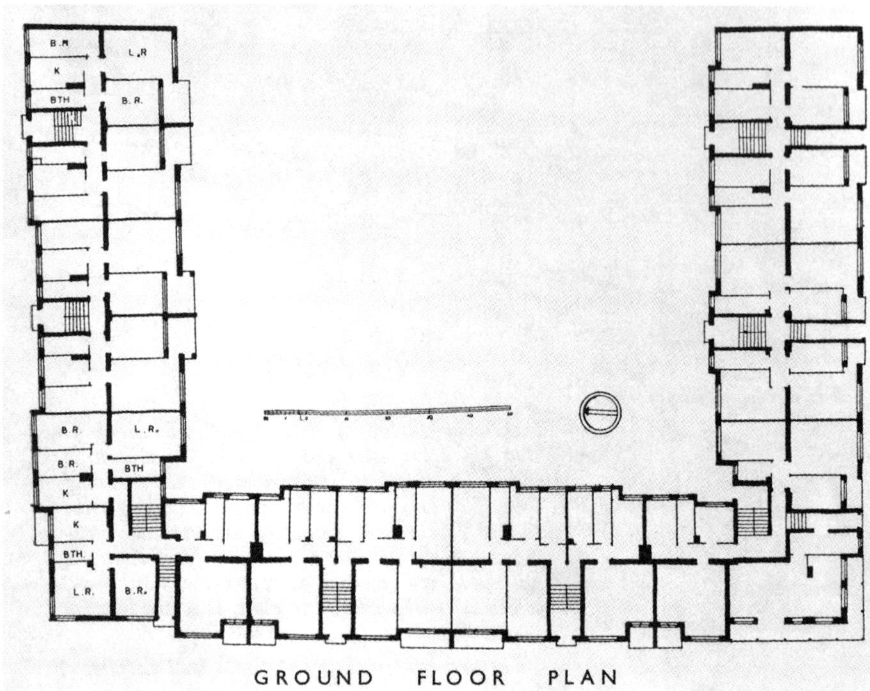

Fig. 14.2 Ella Briggs, apartment block in Berlin-Mariendorf, 1928–1929, ground floor plan. The corner shop with its surrounding glass external walls is indicated at the far right. Unlike in Vienna, Berlin mandated that all stairwells leading to apartments have direct access to the street.

At the southwest corner of the building, where Rathausstrasse and Königstrasse intersect, one ground-level structure stood out: the modern, glass-fronted shop, which a contemporary architectural critic disparaged as an alien element (see fig. 14.1, plate 12).[29] The generous sweep of its dark, canopy-like roof clearly demarcated the projecting shop front from the rest of the building; below it, large shop windows illuminated the goods on display. The integration of the corner shop came at the client's request.[30] Like at the Pestalozzi-Hof in Vienna, Briggs would have liked this commercial area of the complex to architecturally gesture to the surrounding neighborhood. For that reason, she attempted to add an additional story to that corner to clearly establish an urban, commercial accent oriented toward Mariendorf's new municipal center, but the building authorities rejected the plan as too significant a departure from the specified building height.[31]

The rhythmic effect created by Briggs's grouping of the balconies was very much of its time. Balconies were among the elements of the Weimar Republic's large housing estates that were treated as (acceptable) ornament. In Berlin, this approach is markedly evident, for example, in the Siemensstadt housing estate by Walter Gropius, Hans Scharoun, and Otto Bartning of 1929–1931, and in the color-intensive Carl Legien housing estate in Prenzlauer Berg by Bruno Taut of 1928–1930. In a 1928 review of the Waldsiedlung in Zehlendorf, Briggs praised the pleasingly "urban" image produced

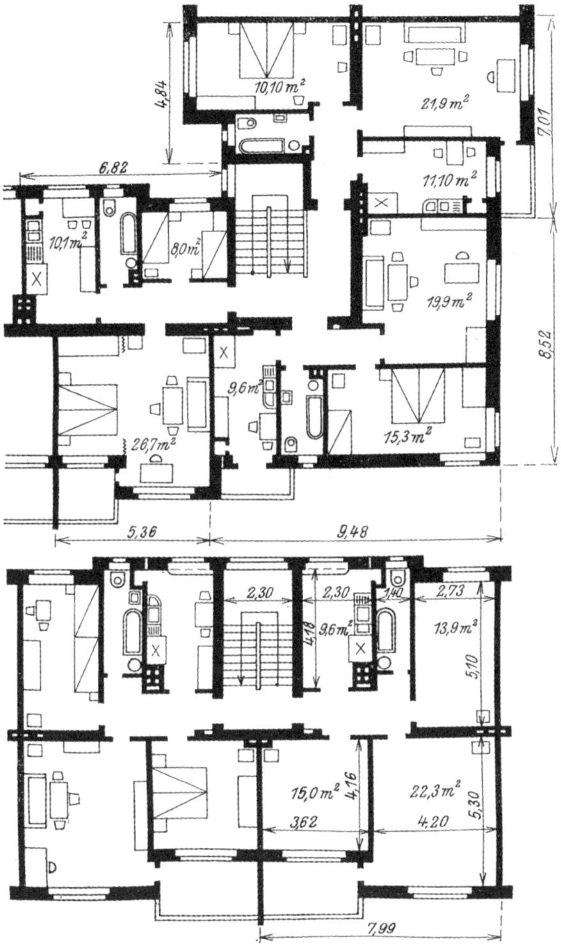

Fig. 14.3 Floor plans of the Mariendorf housing block in Berlin. The floor plan at the top illustrates three apartments that share a corner stairwell. The apartment at the bottom left of this cluster has a large living room with sleeping alcove. The bottom plan illustrates the more common two-apartment-per-stairwell approach. Unlike in Vienna, each apartment had its own bathtub.

by Taut, Hugo Häring, and Otto Rudolf Salvisberg through seriality, particularly through the "sequencing [of] numerous equivalent components."[32] Shortly after writing this, Briggs incorporated such a sequence of equivalent components (with her balconies and glazed stairwells) into her own Mariendorf design. Here she went even further than in her Viennese projects, where she had also experimented with balconies, projections, and recessing. In Berlin, these elements became more fully and boldly integrated into the buildings' massing and rhythms.

Such developments in Briggs's design approach also emerged as a creative response to the constraints she encountered in Berlin's housing codes. In the Mariendorf project, two apartments per floor were typically accessed from each stairwell (only in the building's recessed corner areas in the courtyard are there three apartments per stairwell; see fig. 14.3). This generous two-apartment-per-floor system required in Berlin contrasted with the economical four-apartment-per-floor system Briggs was familiar with from Vienna's municipal housing program. The Berlin two-apartment system permitted excellent cross-ventilation within the apartments—a hygienic improvement highly valued at the time—but it also required a higher number of stairwells. Like the grouped balconies—their sculptural counterparts on the sunny sides of the building—Briggs used the stairwells on the shady sides as rhythm-defining elements, which also characterized other *Neues Bauen* housing projects.

Briggs's attentiveness to the needs of the occupants is abundantly evident in the Mariendorf project. In addition to orientation and layout of the apartments, which maximized light and air, apartments had balconies and/or large windows. In the small corner apartments, Briggs created both a sense of spaciousness and access to plenty of light and air through a novel arrangement of balcony, living room, and sleeping alcove. A large living room (measuring almost 27 square meters) contained a sleeping alcove with a very large window opening onto a balcony, which provided fresh air for the sleeper (see fig. 14.3). Briggs recognized the significance of this sleeping alcove-balcony innovation and reused it in a later design (fig. 14.4). In the attic, tenants had use of laundry rooms as well as storage space. Briggs also added visual variety to the interiors by painting each stairwell a different color, and by allowing the residents to choose the decorative finishes used throughout their own apartments.[33]

Construction of the Mariendorf building wrapped up in the fall of 1929.[34] The attractive new structure raised Briggs's visibility and status within Berlin's architecture world. She was admitted in July 1929 to the Bund Deutscher Architekten (Association of German Architects), the main professional association for self-employed architects.[35] As in Austria, Briggs continued to pursue the status and recognition that membership in such professional organizations conferred, as well as the insider connections that could lead to clients. Also around this time, Briggs was commissioned to write two key articles for the *Handwörterbuch des Wohnungswesens* (Dictionary of Housing), a recognition of her expertise as a leading voice in the German public discourse on modern housing.[36]

Unlike in Vienna, in Berlin Briggs seemed to be on a promising trajectory leading to greater professional acceptance and new projects. Following the smooth completion of the Mariendorf project, she received a commission for eighty-four apartments as part of a larger housing complex on Müllerstrasse in the Wedding district that also involved fellow architects Jean Krämer and Otto Bartning. The complex was conceived as three wings flanking a courtyard that opened to the southwest onto a planned park. Each architect was commissioned to design one wing. The client for the project was Primus, a municipal housing association headed by Ernst Reuter, Wagner's colleague. Perhaps Wagner had some influence in Briggs receiving this commission, her earlier gambit to join a coveted circle of architects working for the city here paying dividends. At the same time, by this point Briggs had developed her own rich nexus of client relationships with city hall departments and subsidiary organizations.[37]

For the design of her wing in the Wedding complex, Briggs took the Mariendorf apartment type with the sleeping alcove as her point of departure (see fig. 14.4). She presented two apartment types, laid out side to side on one floor: an apartment with two rooms of about the same size and an apartment with one larger and one smaller

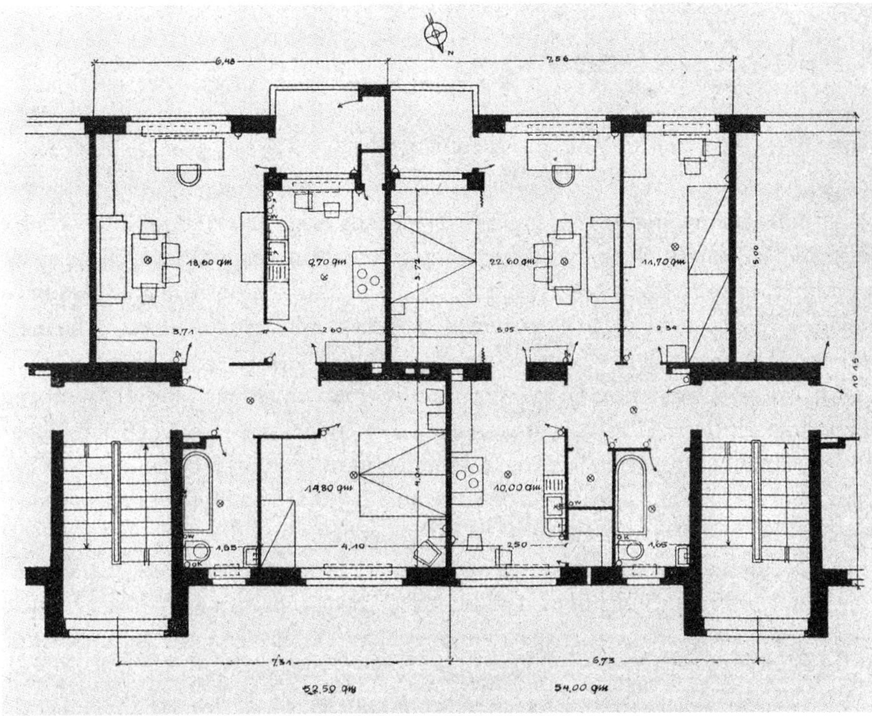

Fig. 14.4 Ella Briggs, floor plan for the unrealized apartment block on Müllerstrasse in the Wedding district of Berlin, showing two different two-room (excluding kitchen and bathroom) apartment types. The one on the right has a larger living room (top center) containing a sleeping alcove with its own window onto a balcony, a unique design that Briggs invented in her Mariendorf project.

room.[38] It was the latter type that included a sleeping alcove, located in the larger room. This modest apartment (measuring only 54 square meters) could accommodate a family of four, with the parents sleeping in the alcove. The arrangement and southwest exposure of the living areas ensured adequate sunlight and air for all occupants. Yet by the end of 1929, it had become clear that the building project was no longer feasible in view of the global economic turmoil that followed the stock market crash earlier that fall. Indeed, the architects involved had difficulty collecting their fees for the project's preliminary phase.[39] The Mariendorf project would remain Briggs's only apartment block project in Berlin.

15. Publishing Endeavors

Celina Kress, with contributions by Katrin Stingl

Living in Berlin in the late 1920s and early 1930s, Ella Briggs occupied a vibrant center of the *Neues Bauen* movement then spreading across Europe, primarily in German-speaking countries. This was an exciting time, as around this architectural quest to provide all people with well-designed and inexpensive dwellings a wealth of bold experimental approaches developed. Some of these new ideas took shape in the buildings that arose around the city; many more, however, took form in Berlin's animated publishing culture. The city functioned as an international center for publishing about modern architecture, its dailies, journals, and bound volumes read far beyond Germany's borders. Briggs actively participated in this vibrant architectural discourse—even expressing opinions that went against the grain.

Briggs emerged as a vocal critic of contemporary housing reform while in the midst of planning her Mariendorf apartment building. Specifically, in a 1928 *Bauwelt* article she critically assessed the two-apartment-per-floor system then coming into vogue within Berlin housing initiatives, which she herself had been compelled to adopt. As she explained in her article, the two-apartment-per-floor approach required the construction of more stairwells than did other layouts, and those stairwells were expensive to build. But smaller apartment building projects had to limit construction costs in order to remain affordable. The two-apartment-per-floor layout also posed potential problems in arranging the dwellings. Comfort and spaciousness were optimized by a floor plan that provided a large living room and smaller auxiliary rooms—an arrangement this approach made difficult. Consequently, Briggs proposed a four-apartment-per-floor solution employing a small light well that would be placed at the intersection of the four units and that would act as a fresh-air conduit pulling air into the adjoining kitchens and bathrooms. In her opinion this would provide the ventilation required for healthy housing while preserving the economic advantages of the four-apartment-per-floor system.[1] She put forth this pragmatic solution undaunted by the fact that her contemporaries might associate light wells with the dark courtyards of the outdated *Mietskaserne* (tenement barracks) that modern building initiatives meant to replace.

Briggs's knowledge and expertise around issues of apartment layout and planning were called upon in 1929 by the Deutscher Verein für Wohnungsreform (German Association for Housing Reform). The association commissioned experts in various fields to write a comprehensive handbook on housing, the *Handwörterbuch des Wohnungswesens* (Dictionary of Housing).[2] Briggs was enlisted to contribute two essays to this standard reference work. Her chapters on the design of the kitchen and on the gallery-access apartment building took on fundamental themes of modern housing reform. Briggs's authorship of elements in this authoritative manual testifies to the excellent reputation she had acquired in the field of housing design.

In her chapter on the kitchen, Briggs made clear that this room was the most essential expression of the new, modern attitude toward building.[3] She compared it to a "factory workspace," for which the architect must ensure the best possible lighting, a logical sequence of labor processes, and the shortest routes among workspaces and to the destination where the finished materials are delivered (in this case, dinner on the dining room table). The first fundamental decision to be made, Briggs wrote, is whether the kitchen is a workspace (*Kochküche*, or cooking kitchen) or part of the living space (*Wohnküche*, or combined kitchen and living room). The author presented both kitchen types, identified their historical genesis and regional distribution, and weighed their various advantages and disadvantages.

At the end of her article, Briggs noted that good examples of minimal kitchens within the new modernist apartments already existed. She identified a few specific designs, including the built-in kitchen developed under Ernst May in Frankfurt by her younger colleague Grete Schütte-Lihotzky (see fig. 25.1). While showcasing the Frankfurt Kitchen, Briggs also offered some criticisms. She stated that a number of items in the narrow (1.9 × 3.4 meter) layout were superfluous and that overall the design was excessively systematized: the large number of standardized food storage bins as well as the built-in furniture and fittings were unnecessarily costly and robbed the housewife of the opportunity to customize her workspace.[4] In keeping with her earlier writings and designs, Briggs here upheld her idea of adapting interiors to the specific needs of their occupants.

This chapter on the kitchen reveals an important shift from her article on the Taylorized kitchen that Briggs published in the Viennese *Arbeiter-Zeitung* in 1925. Specifically, she seems to have abandoned her earlier advocacy of electrical appliances such as washing machines and dishwashers, fostered from her time in the United States. In the handbook, her discussions of these amenities are notably absent.[5] Her experience with social housing projects in Vienna and Berlin, where she was unable to deliver such "luxuries" to residents, seems to have weaned her off of the hope that Austrian and German households could be improved through the purchase of appliances. Here, her advice falls more in line with that of her German peers, including Schütte-Lihotzky, who relied primarily on rationalization (rather than consumption) to improve the plight of housewives.

In Briggs's treatment of the gallery-accessed apartment block, a social housing type characterized by self-contained units with their own doors accessed via shared external walkways and stairs, she prefaced her remarks with a history of its origins and development in England, Holland, and France.[6] She then highlighted contemporary German examples by Paul Frank in Hamburg, Walter Gropius in Berlin's Siemensstadt, and Alexander Klein in Bad Dürrenberg. From each of these architects she solicited statements regarding specific questions of implementation. To the most important question—whether only kitchens and bathrooms should be situated along the balconies, or if other living spaces could also be placed there—her peers gave differing answers. Whereas Frank had had good experience with situating living spaces along access galleries, Gropius was strictly opposed to it; Klein considered it permissible when higher parapets prevented passers-by from glimpsing apartment interiors from the gallery.

In September of 1928, Briggs became embroiled in a controversy about modern architectural form that played out in the Berlin press. At the time of her arrival to Berlin in the spring of 1927, municipal planners Martin Wagner and Ernst Reuter were promoting the construction of large housing estates. Among them was the Waldsiedlung in the Zehlendorf district, built from 1926 onward (on land owned by the private developer Adolf Sommerfeld) by two housing companies: GEHAG (Gemeinnützige Heimstätten-, Spar- und Bau-Aktiengesellschaft, or Community Home Savings and Building Company) and GAGFAH (Gemeinnützige Aktien-Gesellschaft für Angestellten-Heimstätten, or Public Corporation for Salaried Employees Homesteads). The first phases of construction, under GEHAG, saw modernist architects Bruno Taut, Hugo Häring, and Otto Rudolf Salvisberg develop a highly rationalized planning scheme of low-rise apartment buildings and single-family rowhouses with flat roofs throughout. In response, GAGFAH acquired a narrow section of the site directly opposite and hired Heinrich Tessenow to create a model housing estate with different house types designed by himself and sixteen other architects. This more conservative housing association stipulated the use of gable roofs as a matter of principle. The two camps faced off directly on a quiet street named Am Fischtal. Its unbalanced appearance, with houses on one side of the street with gable roofs and on the other side with flat roofs, prompted the Berlin press to declare the "Zehlendorf roof war." Commentators played up the differences, seeing the flat roofs as a modernist architectural expression, and the gable roofs (associated with traditional domestic forms) as the reactionary defense of the GAGFAH housing company and its architects. Am Fischtal became a symbol of the smoldering power struggle between politically left-leaning supporters of modernity and right-leaning traditionalists.

Briggs intervened in the debate with an article in the *Berliner Tageblatt*, the influential Berlin daily that was also widely read abroad. Addressing the Zehlendorf projects from the perspective of town planning, she began by complimenting the GEHAG housing estate: "By sequencing numerous equivalent components, most attractively differentiated only through color, a pleasing urbanistic image has emerged." She went on to assess the more conservative GAGFAH section, which seemed to her to be "only united into small groups of houses, devoid of shared attributes. A textbook example of the fact that in town planning today, a spacious effect can only be achieved through the very means dictated by economic efficiency—standardized building types for the masses, not a juxtaposition of small individual houses, some of which document their individual taste all too strongly." With this, Briggs took a clear stance and openly positioned herself as a representative of modernism in Berlin. Notably, she did not define herself as pro- or anti-flat roof (both styles appear in her designs). Rather, she focused on functionality, standardization, and large-scale housing construction as the organizational principles and design leitmotifs of modern urban development. She relativized her scathing judgment of the GAGFAH model housing development only slightly at this point by referencing some successful examples by the architects

Heinrich Tessenow, Hans Poelzig, Paul Mebes and Paul Emmerich, and Alexander Klein.[7] She then ended with another round of criticisms, targeting design features that prioritized aesthetics over function—such as standardizing window sizes to give the facade an even look, even though the varied purpose of the opening in each room is thus undermined. In critiquing other major players in Berlin modernism, Briggs clearly had gained confidence in her perspective as a recognized architect. She had come into her own as a critic of contemporary architecture, demonstrating great clarity in her beliefs and command of the architectural discourses of the time.

Significantly, Briggs also expressed her architectural philosophy through the study of rural architecture and traditional housing types of the past. Travelling throughout Italy in the mid-1920s, Briggs documented structures built mostly by anonymous builders. A selection of her Sicilian photographs appeared in a May 1930 article she wrote for *Deutsche Bauzeitung* (German Construction Journal). She found many aspects of vernacular architecture instructive for modernist housing design. She appreciated how the provincial dwellings were "uninfluenced by style," had a "clear arrangement of the building volumes according to their functions," and demonstrated an "extraordinarily sensitive adaptation to the terrain." She also noted approvingly their use of natural stone, left exposed or only lightly whitewashed.[8] For Briggs, good—indeed, beautiful—design logically follows the parameters of material conditions and functional requirements. In sharing these Sicilian examples with her colleagues, who were then shaping urban and architectural developments in Berlin, Briggs was among an early group of modernists looking to vernacular Mediterranean design for guiding principles for a new architecture.[9]

For Briggs, publications were not only a means to communicate ideas; they were also a way for her to experiment beyond the real design restrictions she faced. As noted earlier, her 1928 *Bauwelt* article critiqued the two-apartment-per-floor approach she was compelled to follow in her Mariendorf complex and imagined a better alternative. In the spring of 1930, Briggs again published in *Bauwelt*, this time featuring new floor plan designs for a large housing development on Müllerstrasse in the Wedding district of Berlin.[10] In the article, she reflected on the disadvantages of mirror-image apartment floor plans—for example, in the lighting of kitchen workplaces—and presented options that creatively avoided these problems. Additionally, she adopted connecting doors between kitchen and dining room—an arrangement she had seen and used in the United States that had recently become popular among German architects seeking to increase efficiency by minimizing distances.[11] These features had not played a role in the Mariendorf apartment block: there, the floor plans were arranged in a simple mirrored fashion throughout. In compliance with building regulations, to reach the kitchen from the dining area (or, for that matter, from any other room) it was necessary to pass through the central corridor. Perhaps if the Müllerstrasse project had been completed, Briggs could have put these new solutions, devised on paper, into practice.

While Briggs was writing about, and critiquing, the work of other architects, her own work was being written about and evaluated as well. Her designs overwhelmingly received positive reviews in the architectural press. The architect, critic, and theorist Leo Adler helped to make her buildings known to a larger audience. In his function as editor of the renowned *Wasmuths Monatshefte für Baukunst*, in 1928 he presented Briggs's Pestalozzi-Hof to experts as an outstanding example of a new architectural syntax.[12] At the beginning of 1931, Adler published *Neuzeitliche Mietshäuser und Siedlungen* (Modern tenement houses and settlements), a systematic compilation of modern apartment buildings and housing estates. In it, he sought to "give an objective picture of the work of our generation" from a formal-aesthetic point of view.[13] Of the seventy or so European (and mainly German-speaking) architects to be presented, Ella Briggs was the only woman.

In publishing on vital housing issues of her day in a variety of professional journals, Briggs directly engaged with her colleagues. In continuing to write for newspapers, she helped educate the broader public. The impression her writing gives, across the many themes it explores, is of an architect deeply committed to the search for better ways of living. She brought to this search a truly impressive breadth and depth of knowledge, as well as her trademark fearlessness. Briggs's publications also reveal her incredible savvy in positioning herself within contemporary architectural discourses while at the same time extending the impact of her built projects. And yet, remarkably, publishing was not the only means through which she pursued this aim. Through her participation in exhibitions and trade fairs, she would also place herself at the center of architectural currents in Berlin.

16.
Exhibition Design: Trade Fairs in Berlin

Elana Shapira

That Briggs could cast a critical eye not only on her fellow architects but also on herself is clear from her evolution as an exhibition designer. Briggs had participated in exhibitions from the very start of her artistic career, her work being shown in venues from St. Louis to St. Petersburg. As a student at the Vienna School of Applied Arts, she had absorbed the Secessionist ideal of *Raumkunst*, a totally unifying aesthetic among architecture, interior decoration, and fine arts. When, shortly before the First World War, Briggs began to experiment with exhibition design herself, she displayed more creative freedom in her decorative schemes, seeking harmony instead of hegemony. Among the pleasingly arranged art and crafts objects, she also included photographs of interior design projects as objects worthy of contemplation in their own right.[1] After moving to Berlin in 1927, and riding the acclaim of her Vienna social housing projects, she was presented with opportunities to explore and develop new exhibition design strategies in line with the times.

Briggs obtained commissions to organize and design displays at trade fairs and municipal exhibitions devoted to a broad range of themes. In light of the increasing demand to promote industries geared toward domestic consumption, Briggs's earlier approach of creating visually appealing *Raumkunst*-inspired exhibits now seemed old-fashioned, and the presentation of photographs of architecture and interiors as self-explanatory display objects, insufficient. Instead, Briggs would advocate for a more analytical and psychological approach.

In her noteworthy article "Exhibition Designs," published in *Bauwelt* in 1931, Briggs explained her rethinking of this medium. For the journal's primary audience of students and professionals in architecture and engineering, she explored the relationships among the built environment, display, and consumption. More specifically, reviewing her own designs for commercial exhibits at Berlin trade fairs, together with those of her colleagues, Briggs recommended carefully considering the effects on viewers of spatial arrangements, materials, color, light, statistics, photomontages, and sound, and always playing to the psychology of the viewer, who was encouraged to absorb new information through direct interaction with the displays.[2]

This shift in her exhibition design approach was rooted in an important precedent. In Vienna during the 1920s, Briggs had observed how a team of graphic artists, scientists, and educators at the Gesellschafts- und Wirtschaftsmuseum (Museum of Society and Economy) translated scientific data into statistical graphic images. Heading the program was museum director and sociologist Otto Neurath. As part of his process, Neurath and his team would directly engage visitors by asking them questions on display panels, such as what they noticed when looking at a particular image. Neurath showcased his team's new approach at the 1925 Vienna Hygiene Exhibition and the

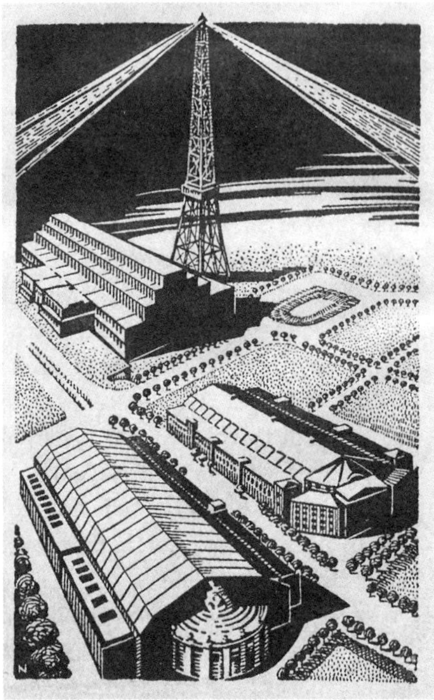

Fig. 16.1 Drawing depicting the pavilions and fairgrounds of the 1928 exhibition *Die Ernährung* (Health and Nutrition) in Berlin.

1926 *Internationale Städtebau-Ausstellung* (International Urban Planning Exhibition), both in Vienna. The principal exhibition space for the Museum of Society and Economy (created in collaboration with architect Josef Frank) opened in Vienna's City Hall in December 1927.[3] Briggs met Neurath in Vienna sometime in the late 1920s, perhaps on a return visit to her hometown to see the museum designed for a popular audience.[4]

From Neurath's work, what Briggs seems to have derived as most relevant for her new design tasks in Berlin was his emphasis on the power of statistical visual language and its ability to translate complex bureaucratic information into accessible terms for the working classes. Yet Briggs also understood that her exhibit displays needed to offer more than statistical graphics, which she regarded primarily as content for specialists, in order to engage a broader audience.[5]

By employing striking color arrangements, Briggs created an eye-catching model depicting the operations of a margarine factory for the 1928 *Die Ernährung* (Health and Nutrition) exhibition, held in the exhibition halls on Kaiserdamm in Berlin (fig. 16.1).[6] Her model was on display in the exhibition's second hall, dedicated to the theme of technology (fig. 16.2). Also included were displays on the production of bread and sugar, and on the process of oil extraction. With the help of bold colors and plain lettering, Briggs's model design gave visitors a glimpse of the margarine production process. Every container, utensil, and machine inside the model was carefully arranged, Briggs explained, "like the sober explanatory scheme of a textbook."[7] Briggs's applied lettering, labels, and colors aroused the viewer's curiosity and served as didactic tools to demonstrate the factory's production process.

In 1929 Briggs was commissioned to oversee the displays for the German Copper Institute at the *Deutsche Ausstellung Gas und Wasser* (German Gas and Water Exhibition), also held in the Kaiserdamm exhibition halls.[8] The fair, organized by the Berliner Städtische Wasserwerke Aktien-Gesellschaft (Berlin Municipal Waterworks Stock Company), showcased achievements in the fields of municipal infrastructure, as well as household appliances, heating technology, and sanitary installations. In her 1931 *Bauwelt* article, Briggs noted how the design of one space within the German Copper Institute's exhibit featured copper as a design material and included copper plates covering the walls (fig. 16.3). This material was intermixed

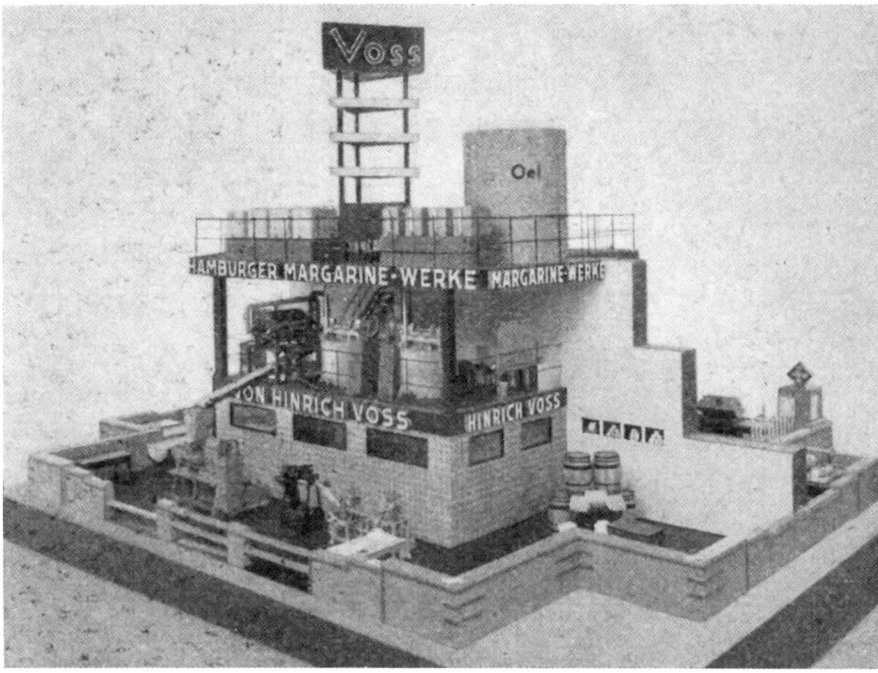

Fig. 16.2 Ella Briggs, model depicting the Hamburger Margarine-Werke von Hinrich Voss (Hinrich Voss's Hamburg Margarine Factory). The Voss company presumably commissioned the work. The model's sleek modernist appearance differs significantly from the actual factory in Hamburg, revealing how Briggs visually updated it to better align (in the viewer's mind) the modernity of the production processes with the physical plant.

with others—glass, light, photographs, and lettering—to achieve a layered complexity that animated the displays. Former Bauhaus professor László Moholy-Nagy contributed a pictorial installation on the qualities of copper pipes that integrated light and shadow. How this collaboration developed is unknown, but Briggs may have seen and admired Moholy-Nagy's work at the 1928 *Bauen und Wohnen* (Building and Housing) exhibition in Berlin, which she reviewed.[9] In a separate display, Briggs included a bathroom installation (probably created by German Copper Institute employees) that left pipes and equipment visible (fig. 16.4). Briggs's decision to include both of these displays (and to illustrate them side by side in her 1931 article) attests to her appreciation for a hybrid arrangement of "high" (the sophisticated design of Moholy-Nagy) and "low" (the straightforward presentation of bathroom fixtures) approaches to exhibition design, and the opportunity this juxtaposition provided to compare, contrast, and read across designs, heightening the viewer's engagement.

In August 1930 Briggs was hired to construct eighteen exhibits at the *Internationale Lederschau* (International Leather Show) in Berlin. She was also commissioned by a certain Dr. Auerbach to design a booth for the Reichsverband Deutscher Schuhhändler (National Association of German Shoe Retailers).[10] In her 1931 article, Briggs

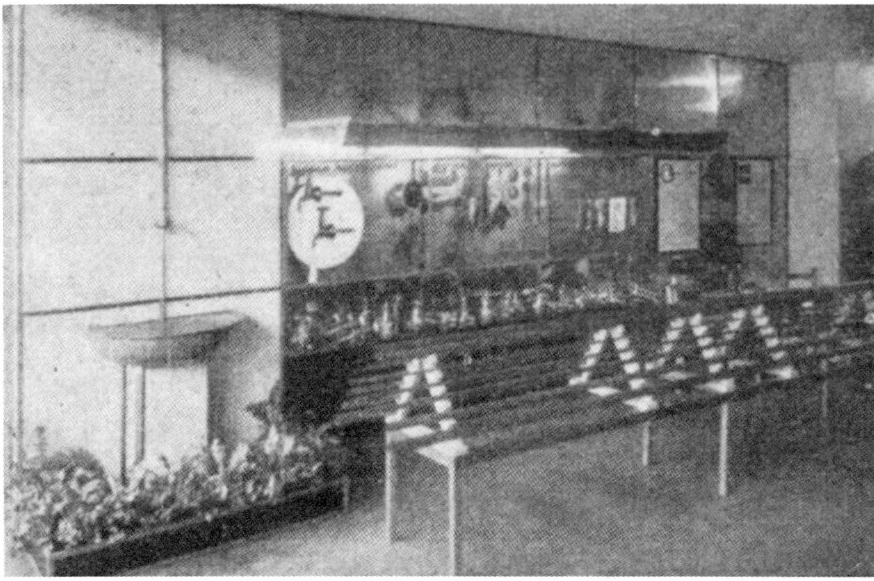

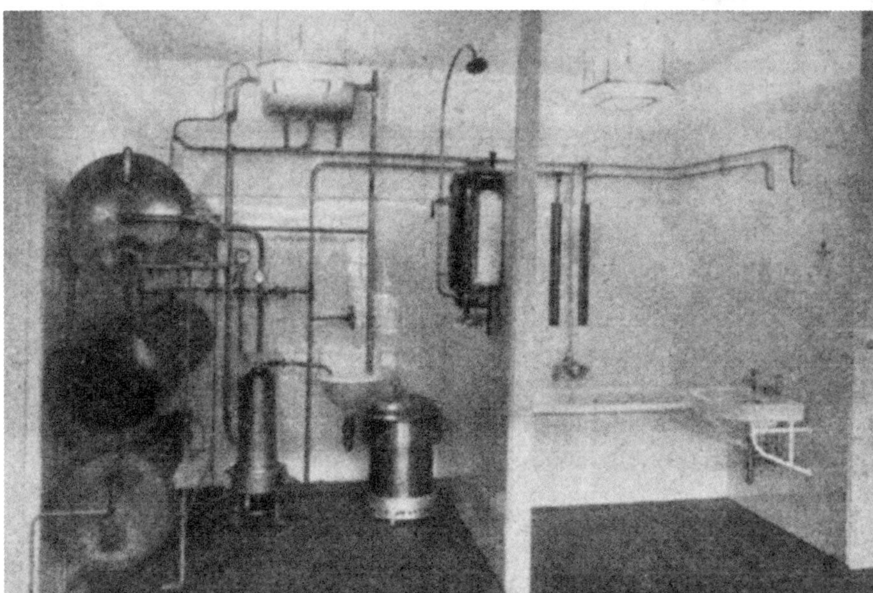

Fig. 16.3 (top) German Copper Institute display, with contributions by László Moholy-Nagy, featuring copper materials as design elements, at the 1929 German Gas and Water Exhibition in Berlin.

Fig. 16.4 (bottom) Bathroom installation with exposed copper pipes and equipment included as part of the German Copper Institute exhibit at the 1929 German Gas and Water Exhibition in Berlin.

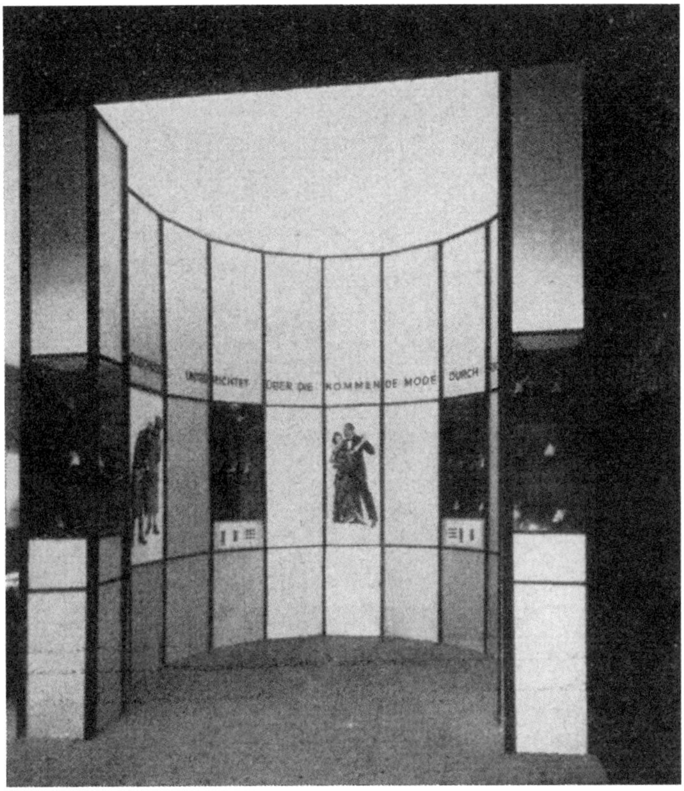

Fig. 16.5 Rounded enclosure with built-in display cases and poster-like illustrations in the International Leather Show in Berlin, 1930.

expressed admiration for an intimate, rounded enclosure erected to showcase upcoming fashions, which integrated built-in display cases (containing shoes) alongside movie-like posters, including one of a young couple dancing (fig. 16.5). This alcove-like space offered the exhibition visitor a respite from the rest of the information-laden displays. Briggs appreciated the pleasant subdivision that the curvature created and the fact that it improved the experience of the larger space.[11]

In 1931 Briggs was commissioned to design a large model for the sixth *Grüne Woche* (Green Week) in Berlin, an important international trade fair showcasing agricultural products for farmers and retailers.[12] The project also involved the presentation of statistical information. In her 1931 article, she explored various methods designers could employ to encourage visitors to read statistical graphics and absorb information, and to combat viewing fatigue more broadly. Aware of the didactic power of curiosity and play, she proposed allowing the exhibition visitors, for example, to press buttons that turned on lights or created movement.[13] By encouraging engagement with installations in this way, Briggs anticipated the interactive museum displays of today.

Her most important and, as it would turn out, final exhibition project would be her design for the 1931 *Deutsche Bauausstellung Berlin* (German Building Exhibition in Berlin), which took place between May and August. The ambitious showcase of the German building industry covered a total area of 130,000 square meters—the largest

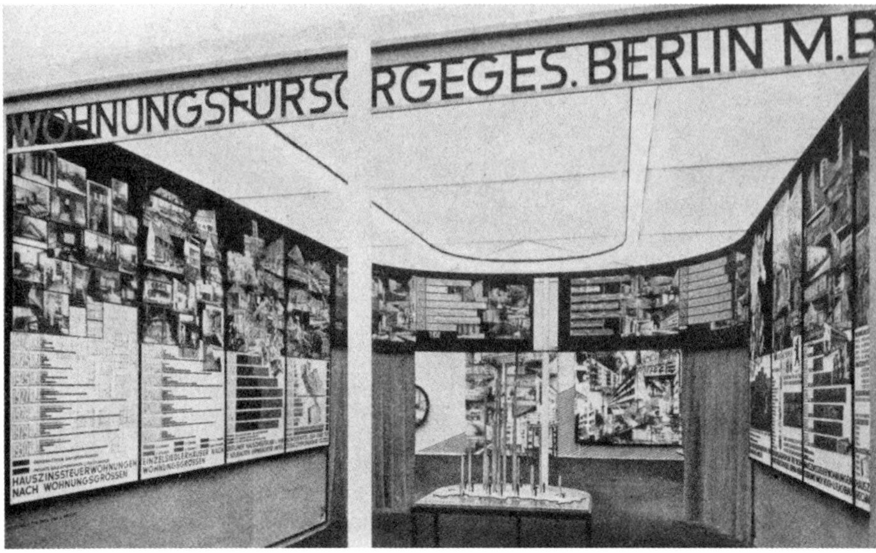

Fig. 16.6 View of Ella Briggs's exhibit design for the Housing Welfare Society, displayed in the 1931 German Building Exhibition in Berlin. Arthur Köster is credited with photographing the display space and panels (see fig. 16.7).

building exhibition in Germany since the First World War. Innovations in modern architecture and interiors, construction, and urban planning were presented to a national and international public.[14]

Briggs was commissioned to design the exhibition space of Berlin's Wohnungsfürsorgegesellschaft (Housing Welfare Society) for this mega-show. She designed a U-shaped display that provided a comprehensive overview of modern housing construction in Berlin at the time (figs. 16.6–16.7).[15] She installed large, dynamic panels consisting of photomontages and statistical charts that engagingly depicted related themes. To illustrate population growth, she included a photomontage of babies in various poses tumbling down into the statistical tables below. Another panel addressed subsidized housing according to high- and low-rise construction (fig. 16.7). Around fifteen buildings appeared in a photomontage above statistical information. The mosaic-like arrangement of images spills over into the lower part of the statistical bar charts, enlivening the numeric data. In this way Briggs helped to modernize the visual consumption of architecture, by combining captivating images with empirical information. The illuminated ceiling of the exhibition area gave the varied presentations a unified, modernist feel.

In the photomontage of fifteen buildings described above, Briggs incorporated her own Mariendorf apartment block, situating herself at the center of contemporary modernist architecture. Briggs's design presence also appeared elsewhere at the German Building Exhibition, in the section "Das Bauwerk unserer Zeit" (The building of our time), in Hall 1. Here, the section's organizers presented her Mariendorf project in greater detail, and exhibition goers could appraise it alongside the work of the most renowned German architects of the period, including Walter Gropius and Bruno Taut.[16]

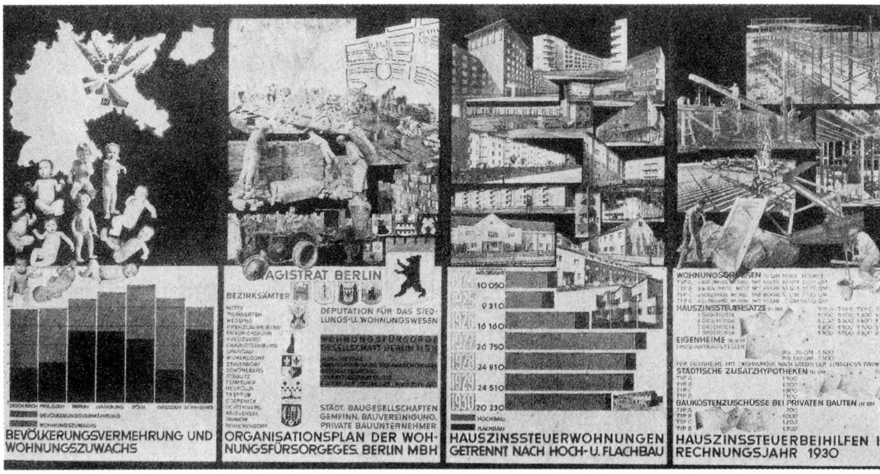

Fig. 16.7 View of panels included in Ella Briggs's exhibit design for the Housing Welfare Society, displayed in the 1931 German Building Exhibition in Berlin. The panel to the far left includes the tumbling babies. The third panel from the left includes the photomontage of about fifteen modernist buildings, including Briggs's Mariendorf project (second building from the top on the right-hand side of the panel).

Briggs understood that to fully engage the consuming public, the exhibition designer faced the challenge of finding appealing ways to present the complex relationships between consumption and modernism. In developing her own philosophy for exhibition design, she drew inspiration from Neurath and reworked it into her own distinct style. She developed a variety of design approaches that stimulated the eye with striking colors, photomontages, or cinematographic effects using light, material, and transparency; employed different typefaces and varied displays of statistical information; and added further dynamic notes through the use of electronic devices (buttons and levers), roving light effects, films, and soundtracks. Taken as a whole, the goal was to "give the public the impression that they are participating in the work."[17] Through the innovative design approaches she developed, Briggs encouraged exhibition attendees to learn more about issues driving modernism, and to critically rethink their consumption habits.

Briggs's exhibition work not only demonstrated her ability to creatively choreograph an engaging and educational relationship between the viewer and modernist design. It was also lucrative: Briggs's income from these exhibition designs was significant.[18] For Briggs was both an architect interested in contributing to the advances of her profession in terms of design and discourse, and also a businesswoman, the owner of an independent architectural firm. Here, too, Briggs was coming into her own in Berlin.

17.
Late Berlin Projects, Family Ties, and Growing Danger

Celina Kress

As the 1931 German Building Exhibition took place in Berlin, an economic disaster was unfolding outside its vast fairgrounds. After several years of prosperity and hope, Germany was feeling the financial effects of the 1929 stock market crash, as were other countries around the world. In the summer of 1931, as the exhibition was in full swing, German banks collapsed, sending the world into a global depression.[1] In Germany, the construction industry was hit particularly hard: from a statistical peak in housing completions in 1930, housing production plummeted nearly 80 percent over the following two years.[2] As a lone female entrepreneur, Briggs felt this decline in construction acutely.

With an estimated 25 percent of the German workforce unemployed—including nearly 40 percent of industrial workers—the federal government announced plans for new housing settlements for the unemployed on the outskirts of industrial cities throughout the country. Nearly two thousand houses were planned for Berlin. These settlements were meant to provide both labor for the unemployed and small plots of land for residents, who could then grow their own food. Yet the numbers were not nearly enough to meet the need; by 1933 more than 100,000 Berliners were living illegally in "wild settlements" outside the city. This recalled the situation that had prevailed in Vienna in the years immediately after the First World War, when the city's hungry and dispossessed had helped themselves through their own agricultural and building initiatives.[3] Having participated in the Vienna settler movement, Briggs now set out to put her architectural expertise to use.

In October 1931, Briggs published an article in *Bauwelt* on the housing settlements for the unemployed, offering practical advice on construction and infrastructure ranging from roads to waste collection (used to fertilize plots). She also offered her own architectural designs. These designs prioritized minimizing the cost of building materials and onsite construction, recognizing that the use of expensive machinery such as cranes would not be possible. Drawing on ideas she had published in the 1920s, as well as on concepts developed for the Vienna settlers by Grete Schütte-Lihotzky, Briggs proposed a *Wachsendes Haus* (growing house) type that could be built in stages, as resources permitted. With expansion in mind, she considered whether a flat-roof dwelling that could be expanded horizontally was cheaper in the long run than a roofed structure that could be expanded into two stories. Here the ideological politics of the "roof war" were no longer in play—only simple economics. In the flat-roofed version, in its first (core) stage, Briggs included one modest room (19 square meters) with a separate kitchen and small adjacent spaces, including a washroom beside the kitchen where clothes could be laundered in a zinc tub that

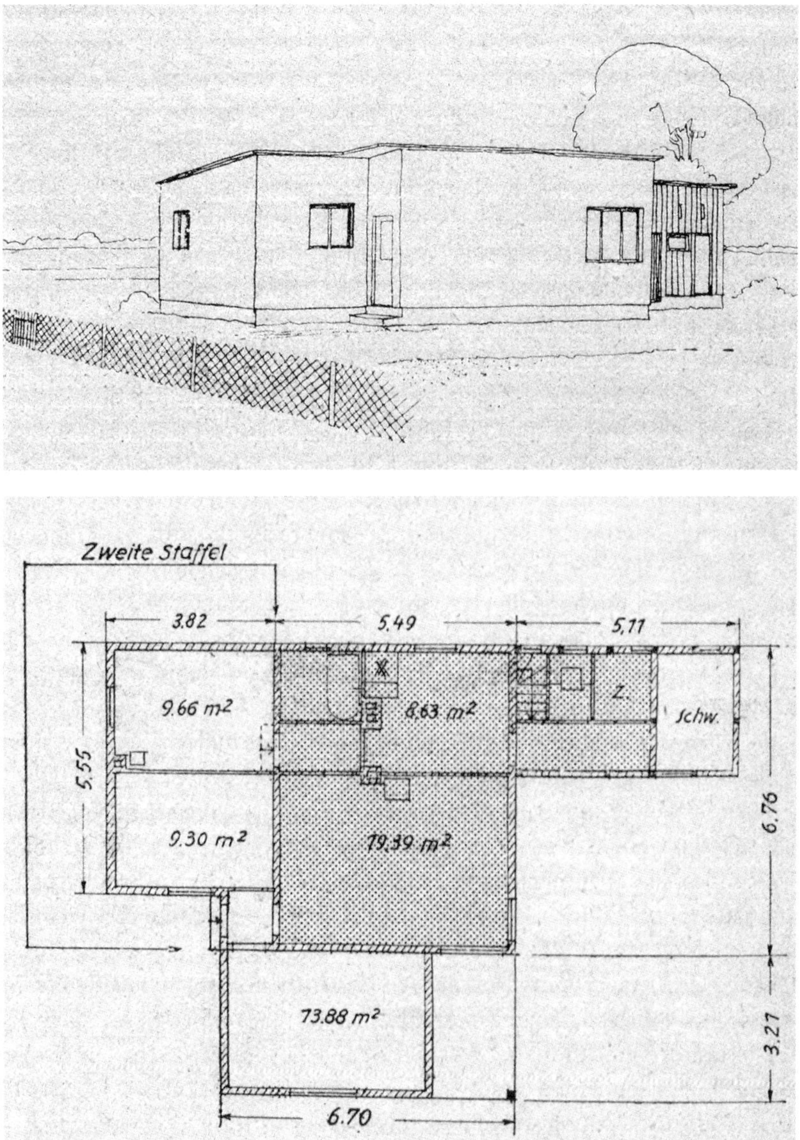

Fig. 17.1 Ella Briggs, drawings for a small house for an unemployed settlement, 1931. At top: elevation of the second stage of development. At bottom: plan showing first stage of development (shaded area), and second stage, including two additional rooms to the left (boxed in and marked "zweite Staffel") and a pig stall to the right. A third stage with an additional room and arbor (to the front) is also indicated.

could also serve for bathing (fig. 17.1). Given the severe economic and construction limitations settlements faced, proper plumbing infrastructure would have to wait; outhouses would need to suffice, for a time.[4] Compared to her impractical design for the Vienna settlements published a decade earlier, these housing types demonstrate how Briggs's later experience designing social housing in Vienna and Berlin had led her to develop minimalist solutions that could now be applied to the single-family home.[5]

Around the time that Briggs published this article, she was commissioned by the Stadt und Land Wohnbauten Gesellschaft (City and State Housing Society) to design houses for the Stadtrandsiedlung Blankenfelde (Blankenfelde Suburban Housing Estate), a housing settlement for the unemployed. Indeed, the *Bauwelt* article may have emerged directly out of Briggs's own research for this project. In a later resume, Briggs listed ninety-five houses built after her designs at the Stadtrandsiedlung Blankenfelde, which have yet to be definitively identified.[6] It is likely that these were core-house types, similar to those she explored in her article, constructed by the unemployed. By the end of 1932, 184 settlers moved into 92 houses in the Stadtrandsiedlung Blankenfelde. The location of the settlement, north of Berlin, was former municipal sewage fields, which bordered one of Berlin's oldest nature preserves. Today, the community remains tightly knit, and houses are passed down within families. It took a long time, though, for the settlement to make all the improvements that Briggs had foreseen in the early 1930s; the houses were only recently connected to a central wastewater disposal system.[7]

Other major commissions slipped through Briggs's hands during this period, as the economic crisis resulted in cancelled contracts and unpaid invoices. These unrealized projects include a housing estate extension in Friedrichshagen commissioned in 1930 by the Gemeinnützige Baugesellschaft Berlin-Ost (Building Cooperative Berlin-East), the Primus housing estate in Wedding, and a large building project for which Adolf Bloch and Briggs had signed a preliminary contract.[8]

To make ends meet and to possibly stir up new business, Briggs published a number of articles in German magazines in the early 1930s in quick succession on topics that were timely and that might appeal to a broad range of clients. In addition to the housing settlements for the unemployed, she also wrote about daycare facilities for infants and children, including those who were school-age, facilities that were desperately needed as more mothers began working (by necessity) outside the home. These facilities were being financed by public and cooperative entities. An article on built-in furniture framed the issues around cost and the impact on rental prices, speaking to developers concerned about keeping their apartments affordable. Similarly, an article on the subdividing and remodeling of large apartments in older, multistory buildings offered technical plumbing specifications together with construction and rental cost estimates. Briggs's intent here was to appeal to landlords who had spacious apartments sitting empty, their rents now beyond the means of most Berliners.[9]

Ever resourceful, Briggs shifted her focus to smaller, private commissions. Around 1931, Helene Moniac, a wealthy widow, hired Briggs for apartment renovations in the elegant apartment building she owned in Schöneberg.[10] More private projects followed: nine one- and two-family houses over the next few years.[11] Briggs also designed a housing complex named Sommer (summer), in Karlshorst (in the Berlin district of Lichtenberg), which included seven apartments, three shops, and six garages, completed in November 1935. Briggs's success in the private residential market is notable, given the economic uncertainty. It suggests that her clients were well satisfied with the architect's work and that commissions spread by word of mouth; as Briggs herself later stated, "One client recommended me to another."[12]

Of the nine one- and two-family houses Briggs designed, only two have been identified, both in Kleinmachnow. Haus Widera (1933; fig. 17.2) and Haus Hielscher (1934), both single-family houses, are functionally well wrought, adapted to the wishes of the clients, and unobtrusive in terms of design. Haus Widera was commissioned by a businessman; Haus Hielscher, by a banker. The houses incorporate elements of modernism—for example, the curved corner of Haus Widera's garden facade, or the geometric balustrade in the ground-floor entry (fig. 17.3)—but in a subdued manner. This may reflect the more conservative tastes of the clients as well as Briggs's desire, as the political winds shifted in Germany, to avoid any complications from the building authorities by employing a more overtly radical style.[13]

Despite her expanding professional visibility, not much is known about Briggs's personal life in Berlin. Various address directories and other sources reveal that she did not settle immediately in one place after she arrived in the city. Her earliest known address, from 1928, is at Emser Strasse 23, in the Wilmersdorf district, just a few minutes' walk to the fashionable boulevard Kurfürstendamm.[14] It was also within walking distance of the residence of her brother Friedrich, now a wealthy timber merchant.

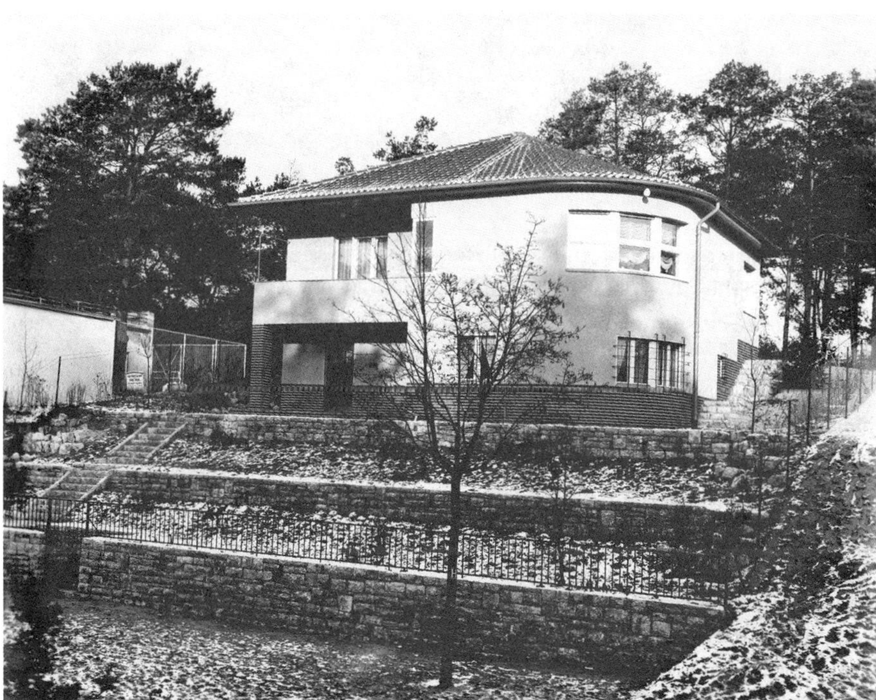

Fig. 17.2 Ella Briggs, garden facade of Haus Widera on Fontanestrasse in Kleinmachnow, Berlin, 1933. The photograph may have been taken by Briggs herself.

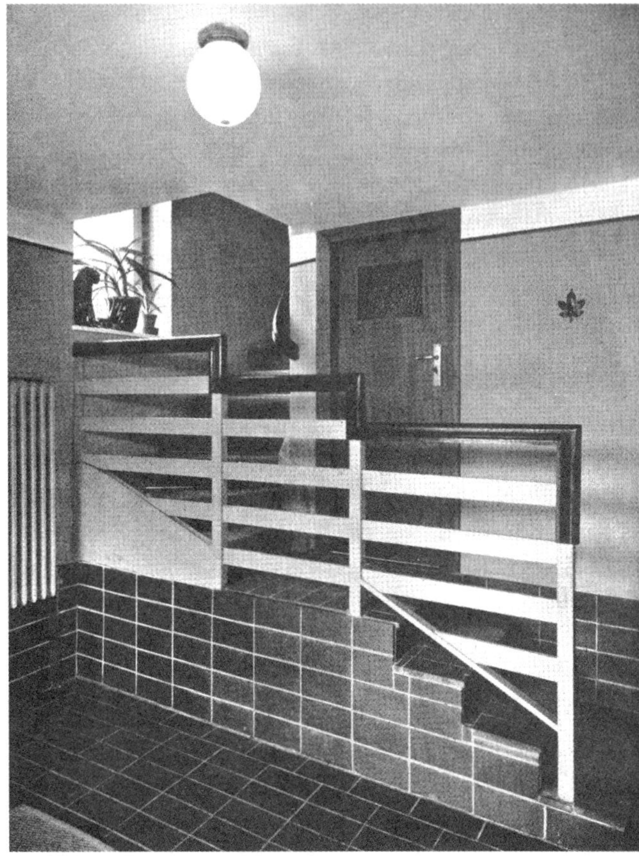

Fig. 17.3 Ella Briggs, Haus Widera ground floor entry hall (from the garden) with staircase.

Briggs had other family members in Berlin: sister Friederike, cousin Hugo Bryk (prominent in the city's music scene), and sister-in-law Ida Baumfeld, Moritz's widow.[15] Based on these close family ties, we can say that Berlin had effectively become home for the architect.

By fall 1929, Briggs had moved to the Charlottenburg neighborhood, taking up residence in an apartment at Fasanenstrasse 15.[16] This address raises an interesting question that brings back into the picture Ella's ex-husband, Walter Briggs. In 1920, Walter moved to Berlin, where he worked for the American company International Trade Developer. He was joined there by his young wife Hilda (née Landes), whom he had married in 1918. Born in Vienna in 1889, Hilda had moved to the United States as a child. She worked as a journalist in Chicago, where Walter's employer was also headquartered. In 1923, while in Berlin, Hilda died at the age of thirty-four from influenza.[17] In 1929, Walter was living at Fasanenstrasse 13—literally next door to Ella. Surely this was not a coincidence. What was their relationship? There is circumstantial evidence that the couple had reunited.[18] If so, Ella may not have appreciated the photograph of Walter published in 1929 in the weekly Berlin newspaper *Sport im Bild* (Illustrated

Sports), which shows him making merry at a costume ball held at the Esplanade Hotel, standing very close behind the chair of a beautiful young woman.[19]

Ella and Walter's status as neighbors did not last long. A year after she had relocated to Fasanenstrasse, Ella moved again. In November 1930, she went to Ravensburger Strasse 4, also in Charlottenburg. In September 1933, Ella again relocated, this time to Lauenburgstrasse 16—in Steglitz, a district to the south of Berlin's center—which also served as her architecture office.[20] In Berlin, Briggs repeated the pattern she had established in Vienna of working from home, her residence and office space combined. Although she worked in conjunction with other professionals and contractors, we know little about her own staff.[21]

In late 1931, seeking to consolidate her position in Berlin, Briggs submitted an application for naturalization to the German authorities. It was promptly denied, presumably because she could not prove *Deutschstämmigkeit* (German descent). In March 1932, she appealed the decision, this time making a case for her family's contributions to German culture as well as her own loyalty, pointing out that she had never become an American citizen because of her strong German identity. This attempt to legalize her sense of belonging came at a time when the nation's economic misery was accompanied by the growing influence of right-wing thinkers within administrative and municipal bodies. Adolf Hitler found opportunity in the 1931 banking crisis to dramatically expand his following, becoming a serious political threat. Antisemitic resentments were expressed more openly and with increasing impunity. Briggs's shift to private residential projects may be a reflection not only of the lack of larger commissions during the economic downturn but also the increasingly difficult situation Jewish architects faced in Berlin as the National Socialists consolidated power. In September 1932, Briggs's application for naturalization was again rejected after a clerk lobbied against it on the grounds that she was not German in origin, had only lived there since 1927, and was an architect—a profession already brimming with unemployed German practitioners. The correspondence between German and Austrian authorities strikes a suspicious note about this peripatetic woman, including the imputation—despite Briggs's assertion to the contrary—that she was actually an American.[22]

Where this exclusion and hostility would ultimately lead became clear in the mid-1930s, when Briggs was busy realizing a design for a client named Hans Bauer in Johannisthal, in southeast Berlin. It was a difficult situation, and not one of her choosing. Bauer was a Sturmabteilung, or SA man—that is, a member of the paramilitary wing of the Nazi Party—and Briggs had been compelled to take him on as a client. She claimed he intentionally challenged her authority as an architect, insisting on altering the design, such as reversing the house's orientation so that the street facade became the garden side. Briggs, it seems, stood up for herself, because he threatened to denounce her to the authorities.[23]

Bauer's was by no means an idle threat; Berlin's concentration camps were then filling up with the victims of such denunciations. Briggs must have been frightened by the confrontation, realizing her own helplessness. She would later blame Bauer for an accusation brought against her by an official of Berlin's Wohnungsfürsorgegesellschaft (Housing Welfare Society), who threatened her with "serious consequences" for disrespecting Hitler and his regime. Bauer seems to have been a typical SA bully, a man from a humble background who saw power as an instrument to torment women and his social betters, including "snobby" educated professionals. But the threat from the Housing Welfare Society would have hit Briggs differently, since she had worked closely with them for years. Briggs later wrote that she felt her world in Berlin had become "unbearable."[24]

In 1935 it was high time for Ella Briggs to leave Germany. She made the difficult decision to emigrate.

Section V.
FLIGHT AND EXILE, 1935–1977

18.
Desperation in Vienna

Elana Shapira

At the end of February 1935, Ella Briggs left Berlin for Vienna, where she remained for ten days perhaps to explore her options for a possible return there. She stayed in an elegant late-historicist house in the nineteenth district, not far from where she had had her art studio in the 1920s.[1] While Briggs had been working in Berlin, critics in the Viennese design scene continued to mention her in local newspapers as the creator of the Pestalozzi-Hof and Ledigenheim. In 1930 the artist and journalist Illy Kjäer highlighted Briggs's social housing projects in her lecture "Die Frau im Kunstgewerbe" ("The Woman in the Applied Arts"), which she gave in November at the Viennese adult education institute Urania.[2] All the same, Ella had been away for several years, and times had changed.

The atmosphere in Austria was becoming increasingly dangerous. After a constitutional crisis in March 1933 that effectively ended democracy, followed by a brief civil war in February 1934, Austrian Chancellor Engelbert Dollfuß cemented an authoritarian system known as Austrofascism by establishing a new constitution in May 1934. In this reactionary political context, Briggs must have realized the difficulties she would face in reactivating her old professional networks. As dictator, Dollfuß replaced socialist representatives in Vienna's municipal government with members of the far-right Christian Socialist Party, and consequently "Red Vienna" became "Black Vienna." Following Dollfuß's assassination by a Nazi terrorist in July 1934, the Austrian National Socialist Party was declared illegal. Kurt Schuschnigg became the new dictator in Austria. Having suffered from the repressive justice system in Mussolini's Italy, Briggs had more than an inkling of the loss of freedoms to come with Austria's fascist turn.[3]

The Christian Socialist Party aggressively pursued an ethno-nationalist campaign of *Blut und Boden* (blood and soil), and its racism quickly permeated Austrian society, including the architecture scene. In February 1934, Josef Hoffmann joined architects Peter Behrens and Clemens Holzmeister to found the Neuer Werkbund Österreich (New Austrian Werkbund), which they claimed represented Austrian identity, as opposed to the "old" Austrian Werkbund led by the Jewish architect Josef Frank. In a conspicuous rejection of cosmopolitan and industrial design, the New Austrian Werkbund embraced a folkish worldview centered on *Heimat* (homeland)—both formally and rhetorically. The Austrian Museum of Art and Industry, which had played a critical role in advancing Briggs's career, now refused to cooperate with the "old" Austrian Werkbund. Frank, who had employed Briggs as a newly minted architect in the early 1920s, saw his colleagues turn against him; this, just two years after he had organized the hugely successful 1932 international Werkbundsiedlung (Werkbund Housing Settlement) exhibition in Vienna. Essentially blacklisted, Frank felt compelled to leave Austria with his Swedish wife and live in exile in Stockholm.[4] If someone as respected as Frank experienced such a reversal in circumstances, what chance would Briggs have in the architectural scene?

After this short trip to Vienna, Ella returned to Berlin. She arrived back in town just as her ex-husband, Walter, then seventy years old and still a widower, departed for Chicago.[5] Walter had become a United States citizen decades earlier but had lived in Berlin since 1920, working for an American firm. Despite intending, it would seem, to live out his retirement years in Germany, he had the ability to leave, and he wisely chose to do so. We do not know if Ella saw him off, or if they still maintained a relationship. Yet surely she must have been aware that the city was losing the friends and family that had once surrounded her there.

That fall, the political situation grew more difficult and frightening. In mid-September 1935, the Nuremberg Race Laws codified Nazi Germany's racial discrimination against Jews, legalizing their difference from so-called Aryan Germans. Under the new laws, Briggs, despite her religious conversion, was defined as "racially" Jewish. This drastically limited her employment opportunities. The walls were closing in on her "as a racially persecuted person," as she would later describe herself. In the fall of 1935, she made a trip to London to seek a job and a way out.[6]

Unable, it seems, to secure an offer from a British architectural firm, Briggs traveled from London to Vienna in March 1936. She had not yet given up her Berlin residence, her eventual destination remaining uncertain. She stayed in Vienna for almost three months, searching for work and options for emigration. During this period, she took up residence in a beautiful Jugendstil building on the outskirts of the city, in a neighborhood of older villas in the eighteenth district.[7] Although Briggs still had friends in Vienna, conditions were worsening for Jewish residents: discrimination against them became more open, and new efforts sought to drive them out of the city's commercial life. In April Briggs expressed the helplessness she felt in a letter to architect Godfrey Samuel (the son of Sir Herbert Samuel, a prominent Jewish statesman and, until 1935, leader of the British Liberal Party). She lamented, "No public work of any kind is given to a Jewish person." Samuel's reply offered little encouragement. In late May Briggs wrote again to Samuel, proclaiming, "It is impossible to find any work at all in Vienna." The effort was clearly taking a toll on her: "The longer one is without work, the harder it is to bear."[8]

Briggs's age may have further hindered her professional reintegration in Vienna (plate 13). She had just turned fifty-six and found that a younger generation of mostly Jewish women architects had conquered the interior design scene. Their established professional networks provided them with work from private clients as well as recognition in Viennese journals. In 1936 the furniture of up-and-coming architect Leonie Pilewski was displayed at the *25 Jahre Vereinigung Bildender Künstlerinnen Österreichs* (25th Anniversary of the Association of Austrian Women Artists) exhibition at the Hagenbund, a modernist Viennese artists' association. Pilewski's work was also reproduced in the journal *Österreichische Kunst* (Austrian Art).[9] Even more visible in the media were the designs of architect Liane Zimbler, who in 1936 remodeled an original Adolf Loos–designed apartment for the Sabl family in Vienna's nineteenth district.[10] At the end of 1936, Hilde Blumberger (later called Jacqueline Groag), another younger colleague and graduate of the School of Applied Arts, displayed hand-printed fabrics in an exhibition of the "old" Austrian Werkbund (also at the Hagenbund).[11] Seeing younger colleagues thriving may have added to Briggs's growing resentment of her native city. Perhaps she thought that after having designed major built projects and exhibitions, small commissions were not worthy of her time. Recognizing the stiff competition that now existed in Vienna, she returned to London for a second time in June 1936. Although she secured a residency permit, work remained elusive.

In February 1937 Briggs traveled again to Vienna, where she stayed for a week with her friend Cornelia Löwenthal, the widow of the American vice-consul Max Löwenthal.[12] Life continued to deteriorate for the city's Jewish residents, as documented in letters written by prominent personalities at the time that openly addressed an imminent threat to their safety.[13] Having been unable to find her professional footing in London, Briggs may have looked for opportunities further west, in the United States, where she may have hoped to reestablish her network of American friends and colleagues. Yet Briggs had never applied for American citizenship. The memory of her detainment by US immigration authorities on her most recent visit there, in 1927, may have made her reluctant to attempt reentry. Her sister-in-law Ida Baumfeld (Moritz's widow) had recently returned to the States with one of her children.[14] But even if Briggs's American relatives had wanted to get her out of Europe, they would have been unable to offer much help. The United States was hostile to Jewish refugees, and US immigration policy sharply limited entry to Germans and Austrians.[15] Ultimately, Briggs returned to London for a third time, and this time she stayed.

In leaving Vienna Briggs lost more than most can imagine. Cornelia Löwenthal decided not to follow her friend into exile, and in 1942 she was murdered in Theresienstadt, a Nazi concentration camp where many Jewish artists perished.[16] Ella's stay with her friend was very likely the last time she ever visited her hometown.

19.
London: Struggles, New Beginnings, and a Commission

Barbara Penner

By 1937 Ella Briggs had relocated to London as a refugee, in what would be the final move of her peripatetic life. After decades of change, the fifty-six-year-old settled into what was then a jittery, fading imperial metropolis (fig. 19.1). She would soon be joined in England by her two surviving siblings, Friedrich and Friederike "Frieda" Baumfeld, who fled Germany empty-handed at the beginning of what Briggs referred to as "the Nazi terror."[1] No doubt their presence helped ease a transition Briggs found extremely difficult. Yet she was sustained by a goal: that of reestablishing herself professionally. And she would exhibit her usual determination and deftness in pursuing it, ultimately extending the horizon of what we might think possible for a Jewish female refugee architect in wartime Britain and beyond.[2]

This did not mean that Briggs lived without regret. In later years, the architect longingly recalled the thriving practice she had left behind in Berlin. To British authorities Briggs repeatedly denied any sense of personal threat, or of having been forced to emigrate by the Nazi regime's ever more restrictive laws against Jews.[3] On the contrary, she insisted she had been "able to carry on her work" and "had still quite a good practice" into the mid-1930s but had chosen to leave because of her "hatred for Hitler."[4] Although there is no doubting Briggs's hatred of Hitler, the real story is more complicated. Against the odds, she had continued to find private residential work after "non-Aryans" were excluded from public jobs. Her clash with a client who was part of the paramilitary Sturmabteilung (SA), however, imperiled both her ability to work and her safety.[5] By the autumn of 1935, she had begun exploring emigration.

We do not know exactly why Briggs selected England, but it was a logical choice on many levels. Educated Viennese Jews often had an Anglophilic bent and an affinity with English culture and design; in Briggs's case, the sense of connection was strengthened by family tales about her maternal grandfather, Salomon Bryk, a diamond trader who frequented London on business many years before. (His miniature was one of the few heirlooms she was able to bring with her to London.)[6] Practically, too, thanks to her experience in America, Briggs was able to work comfortably both in English and in imperial measurement systems, requirements that would daunt many of her fellow émigrés. But even with these advantages, England was hardly an easy option. Refugees had to show the government that they could financially maintain themselves—a challenge given that they were not granted work permits automatically even if they had a residence permit (fig. 19.2).

Briggs thus had no guarantee she could practice in England. She made an initial foray to London in September 1935 to scope out the architectural scene, assess her employment

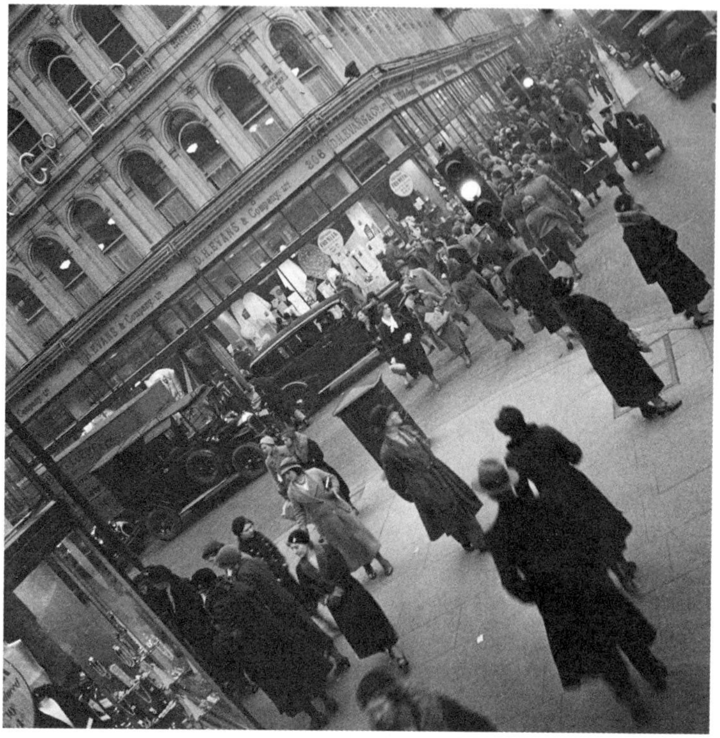

Fig. 19.1 Edith Tudor-Hart, *Oxford Street, London*, 1936. Edith Tudor-Hart was a Jewish-Austrian émigré photographer, trained at the Bauhaus, who brought strong socialist commitments to her work. Here she captures the alienating bustle of London's busiest shopping street.

prospects, and apply for a work permit.[7] What did the Home Office, the body responsible for granting or denying her that permit, make of her? Influenced by the Royal Institute of British Architects (RIBA), the Home Office favored leading architects like Walter Gropius, who could set up firms and create jobs for British citizens.[8] Briggs was internationally successful, with a mixed portfolio of work that included large projects in Red Vienna, whose housing program was much admired in England.[9] Even so, female architects were still far from usual: despite having established a Women's Committee in 1931, with the energetic architect Gertrude Leverkus as secretary, the RIBA had comparatively few qualified women as members. And given local architects' reported "apprehensiveness" about losing work to refugees, there may have been particular sensitivity around allowing a female "alien" architect to compete with men.[10] Testing the waters on her own scoping visit to England, Margarete Schütte-Lihotzky, the only other female architect to have had a housing commission in Red Vienna, found the environment inauspicious and moved on to Turkey.[11]

Briggs persisted, only to have her application rejected in a crushingly polite letter from the Home Office in March 1936. In a few lines, Briggs was told that the secretary of state had carefully considered her application, but that "on the information before him" (this information is not specified) "he regrets that he could not agree to your establishing yourself in this country as an architect or seeking work as an architectural

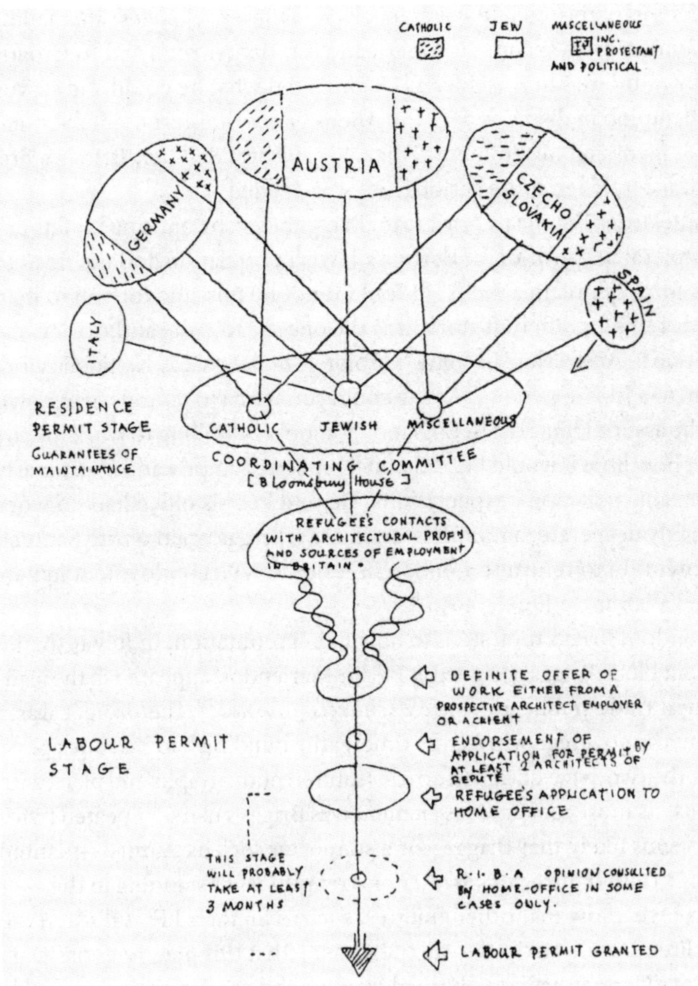

Fig. 19.2 Diagram of the "Process of Admission" by the Refugees Committee of the Royal Institute of British Architects, 1939. This chart, showing the separate "residence permit" and "labour permit" stages for UK refugees, confirms the intimidating complexity of these processes.

assistant."[12] That was all. This letter was surely a blow—to be not allowed to work, even as an assistant?[13] She retreated back to Austria, but she did not give up. The English Consulate in Vienna advised that, if she succeeded in getting a job offer, she would most likely be granted a permit.[14]

It was at this moment that Briggs reached out to London-based Jewish architect Godfrey Samuel, who with Berthold Lubetkin had been a founding member of the groundbreaking modernist architectural firm Tecton. Despite the hostility and defensiveness of some English architects, others did step forward to offer assistance to refugees, and Samuel was one of the most active, supporting both men and women. In addition to Briggs, he attempted to help at least one other German female architect, Marianne Loehnberg, as well as the Bauhausler textile designer Otti Berger. Berger's eventual fate reminds us of the terrible stakes involved in these exchanges: after failing to find work in London or to secure an American visa, Berger returned to Croatia and was eventually murdered in Auschwitz.[15] Samuel did what he could. He served as the refugees' champion in disputes with the Aliens Office or internment tribunals and was not above involving his eminent father, Sir Herbert Samuel, Britain's first Jewish Cabinet minister, when more serious heft was needed.

Writing to Samuel from Vienna in April 1936, Briggs began by quoting his father's speech on the "intolerable" position of Europe's Jewish population and the need to offer them "every form of practical help." "Would it not be possible for you to help me?" she appealed. Telling a different story than the one she told the authorities, she admitted the situation in Austria had become "absolutely hopeless. . . . No public work of any kind is given to a Jewish person." As she could count on 150 pounds of her own money per year, she assured him that in England, "I should be willing to work for any amount, no matter how little it would be."[16] Samuel replied promptly and courteously but in a manner meant to dampen expectations. He told her his office had no work to offer.[17] Increasingly desperate, a month later, in May, Briggs again wrote Samuel, announcing her intention to return to London in order to seek employment in person.[18] She departed Vienna on June 9, 1936.[19]

On arrival in London, Briggs took steps to bolster her reputation. In July 1936, the modernist apartment block Briggs designed at Berlin-Mariendorf appeared in the leading UK architectural trade publication *The Architects' Journal*.[20] The project was a substantial one, but the coverage was hardly timely: the building had been designed eight years before. The two-page unsigned article featured photographs and plans with descriptive captions; its most conspicuous element was Briggs's name, repeated twice in large letters. It seems likely that Briggs—or a supporter such as Samuel—planted this flattering piece to either attract a job offer or strengthen her standing in the eyes of the Home Office; we know that other émigrés, such as Sigmund Freud's son, the architect Ernst L. Freud, were advised to do the same.[21] That this piece was basically an English version of a German article published six years earlier suggests it was quickly repurposed.[22]

This article may well have helped soften the Home Office toward Briggs. Her second application for a work permit was approved sometime in 1937. In truth, however, it is not known why this application succeeded where the first had failed. There is no evidence that Briggs was hired by an architectural practice or had secured a client, as the process required; she would subsequently describe herself as self-employed.[23] She set up her own studio/residence in a Georgian terrace house at 3 Gower Street in Bloomsbury, a once-elegant property by then broken up into rental flats.[24] There Briggs found herself surrounded by other refugees drawn by the area's cheap accommodation and proximity to key relief organizations and cultural institutions such as the British Museum Library.[25] The country's preeminent architecture school, the Architectural Association (AA), was just around the corner in Bedford Square.[26] And Briggs's neighbor next door at number 5 was none other than Gertrude Leverkus, then in practice with the architect Eleanor Hughes.[27]

It is tantalizing to think that Leverkus and Briggs, two accomplished female housing architects, briefly had front doors mere feet apart.[28] Could it be that the German-born Leverkus offered aid of some kind to Briggs? While we cannot confirm their relationship, we know Briggs needed all the local support she could muster and was not shy in seeking it. Her position remained tenuous, as she was required to demonstrate she was working satisfactorily for the renewal of her work permit. She again turned to Samuel in March 1937, asking if she could collaborate on his small house commissions. "I should be only too willing, to release you as much as possible of the work to be done. With regard to any fee, I should leave it entirely to you." Her sole motive was to show the Home Office evidence of work.[29] Samuel wrote back to clarify he had not meant to suggest his firm had jobs to spare, promising only to "bear your position in mind as I said."[30] The archive holds no further correspondence between the two, leaving it unclear if and how he assisted her.

Nevertheless, Briggs claimed to have secured a trickle of small design projects and exhibitions in these years. In an application to the Architects' Registration Council (ARC) in 1940, she described her activities as follows: "A number of one family houses for building firms," including one displayed at the *Daily Mail* Ideal Home Exhibition; two exhibitions for the petroleum company Shell Mex Ltd.; and some consulting.[31] She tried to drum up more work. In early 1939 another article appeared in *The Architects' Journal*, this time focusing on a single-family villa Briggs had designed in Berlin six years earlier.[32] She sold 116 prints of her Italian photographs to the Victoria and Albert Museum in London for 14 pounds and 14 shillings; they remain part of its photo collection today.[33] She also sold a full set of prints to London's Courtauld Institute of Art.[34] No more sales would be forthcoming, however, as she had left behind her original photographic plates in Berlin. Happily, she did manage to ship over some furnishings, architectural tools, and her drawing board, which joined her at Gower Street.[35]

Compared to her commissions in Berlin, these jobs were modest. But it is remarkable that Briggs found any work at all given the deteriorating political and economic situation. In fact, immediately after war against Germany was declared in September 1939, the British government would class 70,000 adult Jewish refugees from Germany and Austria, including Briggs, as "enemy aliens," their specific fates to be decided by tribunals. One person who stepped forward to write Briggs a character reference at this point was Ernst Freud, who had naturalized as a British citizen earlier that year. Freud wrote that he had known Briggs for thirteen years, but that "some connection between our two families in Vienna has existed for an even longer time." (We recall Briggs had stayed with Sigmund Freud's niece, Hella Bernays, in New York in 1922.) He affirmed Briggs was "reliable" and repeated the story that she had a healthy practice in Berlin but left because of her "strongly Anti-Nazi" sentiment.[36] Whether or not Freud's letter tipped the balance, the tribunal decided that Briggs was a Category C, meaning that she did not require interning or repatriating. In 1940, however, her brother Friedrich, aged sixty-nine, would be interned for six weeks.[37]

The episode with Freud reveals Briggs's trademark resourcefulness. As she had done throughout her career, in the face of daunting challenges, Briggs managed to find her

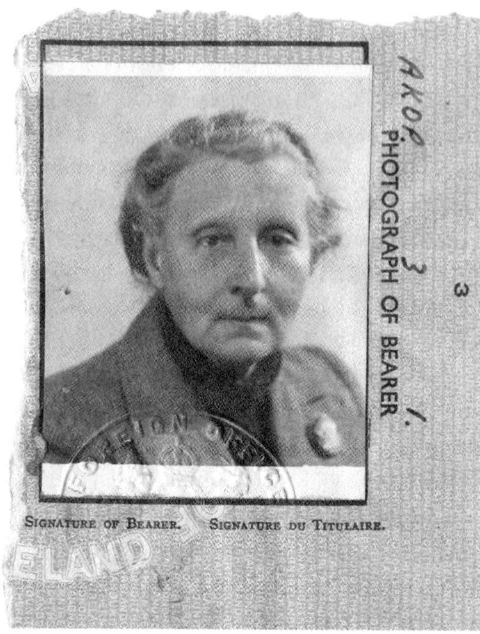

Fig. 19.3 Ella Briggs's British passport, perhaps dating to 1947, when she was naturalized as a British citizen at age 67. The photograph, which survived among the family's possessions, was torn out of the passport.

feet and to mobilize the support of influential people when it counted. This was evident when she applied to register as an architect in 1940. In her application to the ARC, she repeated the line that her practice in Berlin had been good but her opposition to Hitler forced her to leave. In this context we see why she massaged her story this way: she judged the ARC would look more favorably on a foreign architect who had left a successful practice for political reasons than one looking to better their financial prospects. After summarizing the jobs she had done since arriving in England, she audaciously cited the two articles in *The Architects' Journal*—articles she likely had some hand in planting—as proof of her "good reputation."[38] She also affirmed her intention to naturalize as a British citizen, which she was eventually able to do (fig. 19.3). But the most intriguing detail of her application is the name of the architect who endorsed it for her: Alister Gladstone MacDonald, the eldest son of former Labour prime minister Ramsay MacDonald.

Did Briggs cold-call MacDonald, as she had Samuel? Or did Samuel broker the introduction between them?[39] And what persuaded the dashing, well-connected MacDonald then to support Briggs, which he did on more than one occasion? As a noted cinema architect with firsthand experience of American innovations, did he feel a particular affinity to Briggs due to her theater work in the United States? Or did his pacifist views and civic ethos simply compel him to offer aid when he could?[40] Similarly, exactly how the other Brits were enlisted to endorse or witness Briggs's other professional applications remains obscure. This respectable but ragtag cast of characters includes architects Grahame B. Tubbs and Max R. Hofler, as well as Lettice Rathbone, author of the 1935 domestic novel *Occupation: Spinster*.[41]

More surprisingly, equally little is known about Briggs's relationships to other émigré architects and designers in London. Her decision to live in Bloomsbury put her at some distance from the best-known (and most enthusiastically welcomed) Bauhauslers such as Gropius, László Moholy-Nagy, and Egon Riss, who clustered in northwest London in areas like Hampstead and in modernist residences like Isokon.[42] Such proximate networks did not emerge by accident. They were lifelines for "aliens" trying to reestablish themselves professionally in hostile and dangerous conditions, especially during the war years when the threat of German invasion loomed. Yet Briggs seemed removed from these networks. To date, her name has not emerged in connection with the organizations frequently joined by her male counterparts; most notably, the Modern Architectural Research (MARS) Group, which Godfrey Samuel was integrally involved with, and which has been described as "a *de facto* welcoming committee for many émigrés."[43] Briggs was likely aware of the MARS Group, and some of their members were surely aware of her. Energized by new arrivals, particularly Moholy-Nagy, the MARS Group in 1938 staged a landmark show, *New Architecture: An Exhibition of the Elements of Modern Architecture*, in London's Burlington Galleries in an effort to align British modernism more closely with the Continental European model. Given her own direct contributions in Vienna and Berlin to the "new architecture" movement, Briggs would have been well positioned to participate.[44] Did she not seek the group out? Was she not invited to join?

Possibly it was the case that female émigrés were a greater source of support and solidarity for Briggs in these years. This is suggested by the one glimpse we have of her socializing from that period. Briggs appears in a letter from 1945 by Austrian émigré art historian and author Betty Kurth, based at the Warburg Institute; they were introduced to each other by Marianne Hausmann (née Pisko), a close friend of Briggs's from the Applied Arts School in Vienna. Kurth writes her daughter Gertrud Kurth about spending an afternoon with "a famous Lady-architect"—Briggs—and her brother Friedrich. Kurth was charmed by the encounter, which took place at Briggs's "nice little house in North London." Kurth would return for at least one more extended visit in 1946, excitedly telling her daughter that she had again been a guest of "the famous lady architect, who built the 'Pestalozzi-Hof' in Vienna."[45]

The "nice little house" was 9 Slades Gardens, a pleasant but ordinary semidetached residence in Enfield, Middlesex, where Briggs had recently moved and would remain almost until the end of her life. Although suburban Enfield was connected to central London via the underground, it again seems an unexpected choice for a woman like Briggs, who was more usually found in studio flats located in dense city centers. Possibly the relentless bombing of Bloomsbury during the Blitz made this area's quiet charms seem more appealing.[46] It is poignant to imagine what Briggs and Kurth talked about at their meetings. In 1902, Kurth had published the fictional diary *Eine für Viele: Aus dem Tagebuche eines Mädchens* (One for many: From a girl's diary) under the pseudonym "Vera," scandalizing the Viennese with its recognition of female desires and call for young women—like Briggs at the time—to fulfill their creative selves.[47] How did these two nonconformists now take stock of their lives compared to those earlier days of promise in Vienna?

While it may have seemed like the war had permanently derailed such grand ambitions, many female refugee artists, photographers, and designers would go on to prosper in Britain, especially the younger generation of Vienna School of Applied Arts graduates, such as textile designer Jacqueline Groag (formerly Hilde Blumberger) and ceramicist Lucie Rie.[48] Briggs was one of the only architects amongst them: of more than sixty biographical entries in Charlotte Benton's authoritative book on émigré architects in Britain, Briggs is the sole woman—something Benton notes apologetically.[49] Benton points to the presence of several other female émigré architects—Loehnberg, Olga Gemes-Forbat, Ellen Shoendorff—but explains that too little was known for them to be included in her book. More recently, details have come to light about the architect Marie Frommer, who spent several years in London before moving on to New York;[50] and also about Hedwig Adler (née Feldmann), part of Ernst May's "brigade" with Schütte-Lihotzky in Moscow, who emigrated in 1939 but never practiced in England.[51] As Kurth's description of her hostess as a "famous lady architect" underscores, Briggs was unquestionably the most high-profile of this group. Still, Briggs never took her reputation for granted; she worked hard to ensure she did not fade from view. The main reason Benton could track her career in England, for instance, was because Briggs obtained professional accreditation, which in turn meant that the ARC and RIBA retain some record of her activities.

With purposeful immodesty, Briggs would continue to evoke earlier achievements and restate her celebrity to secure new work. We see this in the byline that appeared in the British publication *Homes and Gardens*. Briggs had by 1944 become a contributor to the popular women's magazine, in which she was presented to readers either as "an architect of international fame" or as "a famous architect with international experience." With little variation, this description of Briggs would recur from the mid-1940s on, in applications, letters, and magazines. The insistent assertion of her fame is striking when we recall that, at this moment, Briggs had not built anything of consequence for over a decade. Nonetheless, Briggs seems to have always understood the way that perception influenced reality: having described herself thusly, the description was repeated by those describing her to others and so rippled outward, reaffirming itself.

This tactic was in evidence when Briggs obtained her one major UK commission. Although she reported serving as an architectural assistant in local government offices during the early war years, she apparently gave up this work in order to pursue private practice again.[52] At this time, however, commissions were scarce for all architects, let alone foreign ones. To drum up business, Briggs wrote to the influential Austrian sociologist Otto Neurath in early 1943. She reminded him that she had visited him in Vienna, sometime after her social housing projects there had been completed, and asked if she could be "of service to you in connection with exhibition work."[53]

Neurath had recently resurrected his Isotype Institute in Oxford with his wife Marie, with the aim of using their influential International System of Typographic Picture Education of pictorial statistics to inform the public about contemporary political and social issues (plate 14).[54] When he replied to Briggs with an offer of help (in

English), she thanked him (also in English), saying frankly, "I could do with it," and confessing that she had not had any jobs for seven months. She reminded him that she had previously done "a great deal of important exhibition work" for the city of Berlin. In fact, in the 1931 German Building Exhibition in Berlin, Briggs had drawn directly on Neurath's own Isotype approach.[55] By touching on their shared history, she evidently hoped to lay the groundwork for future collaborations.

While not able to deliver immediately on his promise, in July 1945 Neurath was brought in as an adviser to Bilston Borough Council in the West Midlands, a coal-mining community that was planning generous amounts of new housing to improve the degraded living conditions of local workers (see plate 14). Neurath's appointment alone underscores that this was no ordinary project. Bilston was conceived as a social experiment, and Neurath's role was to reeducate the local population, via exhibitions, so that they would fully embrace their new communities and break established habits of living formed in poverty. As he described his sociological approach: "If we wish to explain the general importance of a new architectural project or idea . . . to laymen, we must show how people live and act within buildings. . . . That is to say, it is not enough to represent location and motion of men, vehicles and other things—one must also give a picture of the factors which condition human happiness."[56] In keeping with this emphasis, Neurath's title at Bilston was Consultant for Happiness.[57]

The ambition of the Bilston project today seems remarkable, almost incredible. But the displacements and destruction of war also made possible such improbably radical conjunctions of ideas and characters. So it was that, under the stewardship of A. V. Williams, a progressive town clerk with a sociological bent, the spirit of Red Vienna was revived in the so-called "Black Country," one of the more deprived and despoiled parts of England. That Vienna was the touchstone was driven home when, presumably at Neurath's recommendation, Williams made contact with Briggs and, in late 1945, commissioned her to design dwellings for the Stowlawn Estate. And when Williams reported back to the council that he had secured her services, he described her as "a Viennese architect of international repute," almost exactly repeating *Homes and Gardens*'s formulation.[58]

After years without a big project, Briggs was undoubtedly delighted to accept the commission, which would occupy her between 1946 and 1947. By the time Briggs was appointed, the site, on reclaimed coalfields, had already been laid out and had been made ready for building. (In an ironic twist, due to the labor shortages, this preparatory work was reportedly done by German prisoners of war.)[59] Shortly thereafter, the arrival of Sir Charles Reilly—another powerful character with far-reaching social aims—resulted in the development of bolder plans that were more in tune with Neurath's vision. Reilly was one of the most eminent names in British architecture and another ally of refugees, including Austrian architect Joseph Berger and his wife and Vienna School of Applied Arts graduate, the illustrator Margarete Berger-Hamerschlag.[60] He was given the task of laying out Stowlawn again according to his own system, revolving around community centers on common land, called Reilly greens.[61] Briggs was commissioned to design 160 homes, although the actual number of units she completed seems to have been a little over half that figure.[62]

The resulting dwellings, enclosing the long oval of Lawnside Green, are hard to define stylistically (figs. 19.4–19.5). With their spare facades, they had some modernist pretensions; yet with their hipped roofs and chimneys, they also evoked English cottages, possibly to harmonize with the village feel of Reilly's greens. The same mingling of modern and vernacular further characterized the materials used, with door canopies rendered in precast reinforced concrete contrasting with roofs of handmade Stoke-on-Trent pantiles. The brick constructions were covered with cement render, either Snowcem or Cementone, and painted.[63] In early photos, Lawnside Green's bright facades stand out sharply against the raw, reclaimed site and the surrounding landscape, which Reilly described as "an angry sea of black shale."[64] This was a tough, industrial, polluted environment—a long way from a picturesque idyll.

The most critical aspect of Lawnside Green's design, however, was neither its style nor its materials: it was its effort to promote social mixing through planning. And here, even though the man himself had unexpectedly passed away in December 1945, we see the imprint of Neurath.[65] Neurath promoted mixed occupancy as a means to integrate older residents with younger ones and to counteract feelings of isolation. Briggs thus included different types of rental housing to suit many kinds of occupants. The accommodation ranged from two-, three-, and four-bedroom homes to houses made up of four flats. No building exceeded two stories, and none was freestanding; they were either semidetached or part of terraces, with passages to private backyards and gardens. Unfenced front lawns and low walls connecting end houses ensured that the whole projected a unified image, an effect we know Briggs strove for in her urban housing as well (plate 15).[66] Yet thanks to Lawnside Green's wide range of housing types and their varied rooflines, windows, and balconies, the ensemble did not have the dull conformity that so often characterized contemporary English suburban developments.

Divided into pairs of one-bedroom units on the ground and upper floors, the multi-flat dwellings in particular were well suited to the elderly, single people, and childless couples—residents normally overlooked in community plans (plate 16; fig. 19.6). In an article for *Homes and Gardens* in 1947, Briggs justified their inclusion by stating firmly, "Single persons and childless couples are valuable members of society, and they deserve something better than having to pay extortionate rents for furnished accommodation which will never be a real home."[67] Her strength of feeling on this issue may have been amplified by her own experience as a woman living outside the norms of married life, but it also was a longstanding professional concern of hers, as the designer of the Ledigenheim, Vienna's first-ever municipal residence for single people.[68] Her desire to engineer a sense of worth and connection among all residents was also fully in keeping with Neurath's principles and hopes for Bilston.

Still, and in accordance with the Bilston team's wishes, communal life was not to be forced; rather it was to be "allowed to develop naturally in those who feel the need for it."[69] Their exteriors might have been ungainly, but Briggs's dwellings were

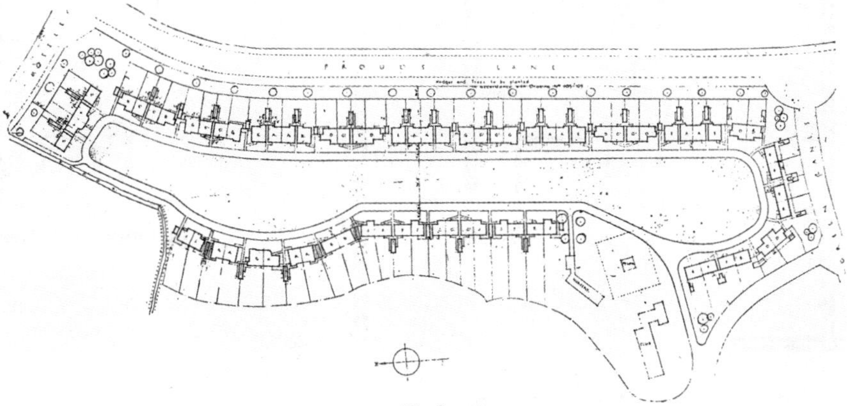

The layout.

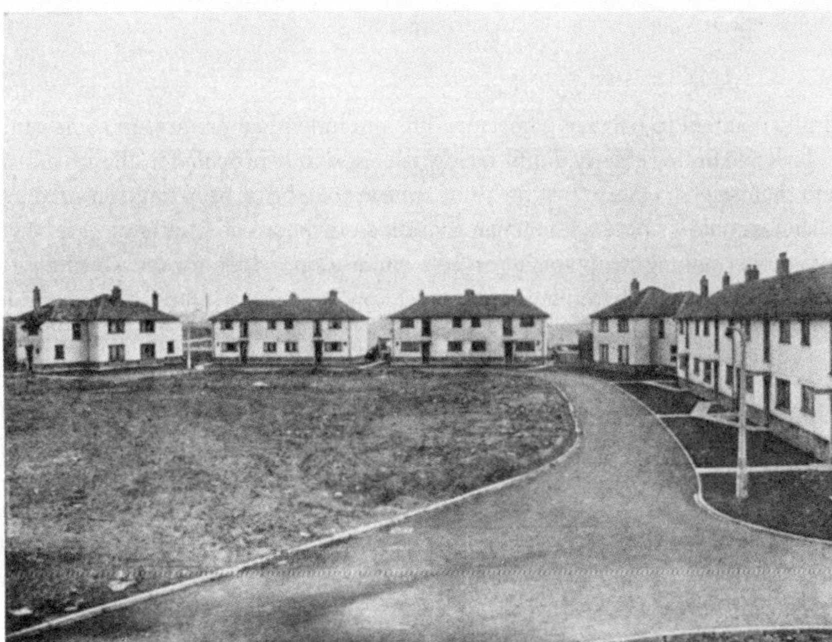

Types B and D houses.

Fig. 19.4 (top) “The Layout,” Lawnside Green, Stowlawn Park Estate, Bilston. All dwellings planned and designed by Ella Briggs around a so-called Reilly green. Note that the nursery and club buildings indicated in the southwest corner were never constructed.

Fig. 19.5 (bottom) “Types B and D houses,” Lawnside Green, Stowlawn Park Estate, Bilston, looking at single-family semidetached houses and rowhouses enclosing the south side of the green. The site had been reclaimed from use by the coal industry.

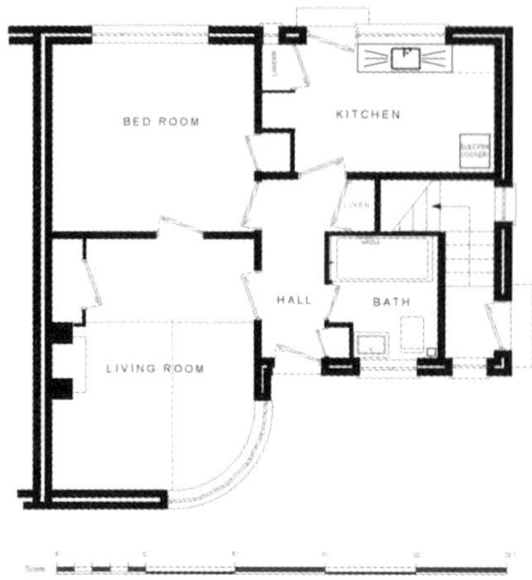

Fig. 19.6 “Plans of Type H flats for aged people,” Lawnside Green, Stowlawn Park Estate, Bilston. Left: ground-floor apartment; right: upper-floor apartment. These compact one-bedroom flats still provided a fully equipped kitchen with an electric cooking range, hot water boiler, built-in larder, and dresser (on the upper floor only). (Plans redrawn by Paul Sutliff after Ella Briggs.)

skillfully planned to balance communal life and individual privacy. In some of the flats designed for the elderly, south-facing balconies were provided to allow residents to sun themselves (plate 17); at the same time, a solid brick balustrade ensured personal items could be aired without being visible from the street. Windows were placed to avoid overlooking, with small porthole windows provided for cross-ventilation. And Briggs banished shared entrances, declaring, “It is usual all over the world for feuds between flat-tenants to start in communal places.”[70]

This statement sounds strange coming from Briggs, whose fame stemmed from socialist housing projects celebrated for their generous communal provisions. But her point was that tenants should be free to choose how much or how little interaction they had. This emphasis on choice extended to her interiors. All were designed to maximize natural light, air circulation, and outdoor access; the absence of stairs in ground floor apartments also meant they could accommodate those with mobility issues. The dwellings were well-equipped: all had built-in storage, indoor bathrooms, hot water boilers, kitchens with cooking ranges, and bedrooms with electrical outlets—novel features for residents who had previously made do in dilapidated Victorian terraces with outdoor toilets (fig. 19.7). Here we see the generous standard of domestic convenience that Briggs had advocated for, but had been unable to deliver because of economic and regulatory limitations, in her social housing projects in Vienna and Berlin.

The details further reveal Briggs’s thoughtfulness about occupants and her ability to anticipate their daily lives and routines. With her typical concern for minimizing the labor of housekeeping, she selected materials that were easily cleaned and maintained; for instance, linoleum or highly polished black or charcoal gray tiles to finish floors rather than the usual British carpeting. Living and dining rooms were open plan—no redundant formal front parlors—with plenty of space for tenants’ own furnishings and knickknacks

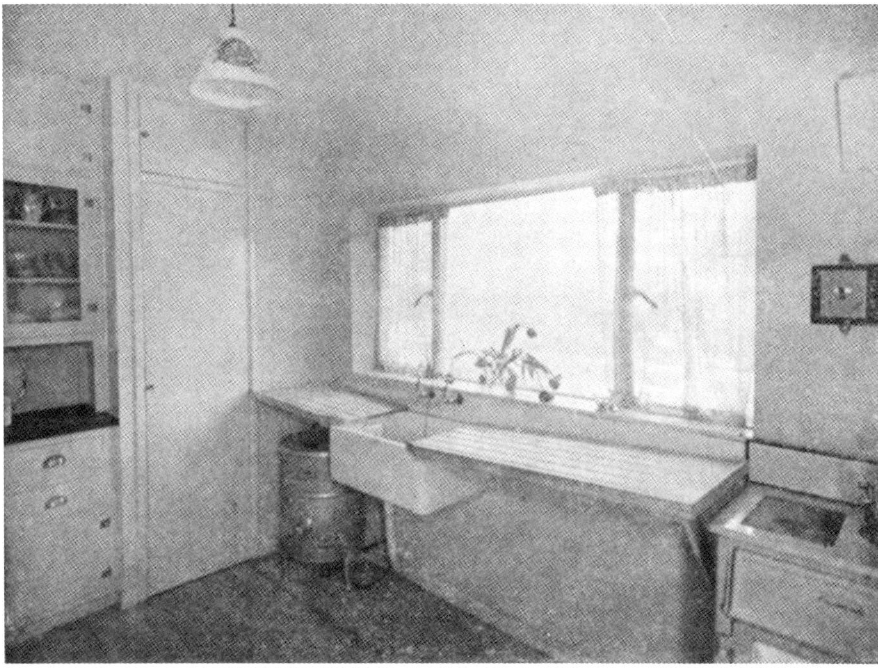

Fig. 19.7 "A kitchen in the Type H flats," Lawnside Green, Stowlawn Park Estate, Bilston, looking at the sink with attached worktops and the wide horizontal window that let in natural light and views. Note the built-in larder and attractive glass-fronted dresser on the back wall.

(fig. 19.8).[71] And when explaining why a kitchen window faced east, Briggs argued that if it did not, "The rays of the afternoon sun, combined with the heat originated by the preparation of dinner, might destroy the calm of mind desirable for turning out a good meal."[72] Here again we see the care for women's physical and psychological comfort, which had been a hallmark of her design ethos since the early 1920s.[73] Would Walter Gropius ever have thought about, let alone admitted to, such prosaic concerns?

Unfortunately, as so often happened with housing projects, the elements that were meant to support the development of communal life never materialized. With the departure of Williams in 1946 and the death of Reilly two years later, the Bilston experiment fizzled, along with the fabulous amenities that had been envisioned, such as central clubhouses from which housewives could order hot meals, twenty-four-hour children's nurseries, and an all-male staff of home help.[74] Yet what *was* built should not just be seen as a utopian fragment, a "what might have been." In the face of severe postwar material shortages and cost restrictions, Bilston Council and Briggs managed to create a new community of dwellings that went well beyond basic needs. They were "real homes," as Briggs promised, which felt like "palaces" to tenants.[75] And they have stood the test of time. Although a proportion of homes are now privately owned and modified in appearance, Lawnside Green remains a healthy mixed neighborhood, anchored by a mature and pleasant green much used by children who play in cheerful defiance of the council's "no ball games" signs (plate 18).

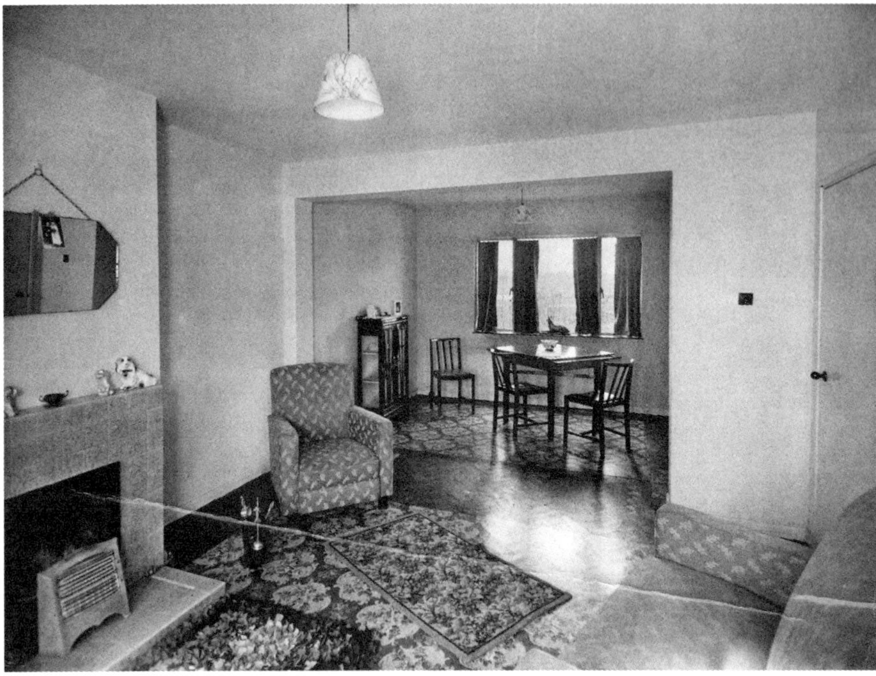

Fig. 19.8 Ella Briggs, living room of Type D house, Lawnside Green, Stowlawn Park Estate, Bilston, looking from the living room into the dining alcove. This interior has been customized (presumably by tenants) with photographs, carpets, furnishings, and ornaments on the mantle.

Stowlawn served Briggs's interests in another way: it provided her with additional coverage in the UK trade papers *The Architects' Journal* and *The Builder*.[76] It also helped her achieve another milestone. After successfully naturalizing as a British citizen, she secured her RIBA licentiate in 1947, aged sixty-seven, again with Alister MacDonald's endorsement.[77] This marked the pinnacle of Briggs's career in England. Certainly, we know of no other female refugee architect gaining an RIBA licentiate. Given how hard Briggs had worked to establish herself, and how dim the prospects must have seemed upon her arrival, it is hard to imagine that she would not have been deeply gratified at achieving professional recognition in her adopted country, especially at a time when "letters after names" really meant something.[78]

We might think that Briggs, having come through a decade of continual upheaval and precarity, would be tempted to retire. Likely compelled by a combination of financial necessity and her own drive, however, Briggs showed no immediate signs of stopping. She seemed open to accepting new jobs. We know, for instance, that in 1947 she was hired on a freelance basis to convert some requisitioned homes into flats for Holborn Borough Council (1–3 Bedford Way, since destroyed).[79] Yet even as other émigré architects became substantially involved in postwar urban reconstruction, she would receive no further commissions for large projects. Instead, she would cultivate another outlet for her designs. Appropriately enough for someone who had always toggled between architecture, exhibitions, and journalism, the magazine *Homes and Gardens* now became the focus of her still formidable creative energies.

20.
Writing, Designing, and Fighting for Restitution

Barbara Penner

Although little about Ella Briggs should surprise us by now, it is still startling to realize that, between the ages of sixty-four and seventy-five, she managed to turn out nearly thirty articles on housing for one of Britain's preeminent women's magazines. Her association with *Homes and Gardens* began in 1944, but as her architectural practice wound down, the pace of her writing accelerated. She would hit her stride in the early 1950s, producing six articles in 1952 alone.

A conventional reading would be that this return to women's magazines simply proves how her opportunities were limited by her gender: like so many female architects, Briggs would end up discussing house design for a predominantly nonprofessional readership of women. Yet even during her years of active practice, she had treated these publications as a way to experiment outside the boundaries of actual built projects and to communicate with an audience interested in the domestic matters that were her specialty.[1] At this phase of her life, as age and increasingly poor health made a building practice untenable, it made sense that Briggs would once again seek out this familiar outlet. Writing for *Homes and Gardens* provided her with a way to continue to push on her ideas and seriously explore problems of house design for a large audience well into her seventies.

That said, Briggs was not the most obvious fit for *Homes and Gardens*.[2] When she began writing in April 1944, England was still enduring the privations of war and prosperity remained years away. *Homes and Gardens* was intended as a pleasurable diversion for war-weary women: it offered articles on fashion, recipes, decor, and gardening, and it kept things chatty and bright, with heavy lashings of romance and advertisements (nylon stockings and gas cookers loomed large). By contrast, Briggs—"an architect of international fame"—contributed rather ponderous, repetitive articles that sat awkwardly alongside this lighter fare. Instead of photographs, the pieces featured Briggs's own black-and-white perspective drawings and plans. No seductive interior views were provided.

Yet the editors appeared willing to forgive her austere approach because Briggs provided authoritative advice on that most significant of topics: the postwar home.[3] Across her articles, she asked how a decent home could be achieved in a time of extreme material shortages and building restrictions—conditions that would stretch on for the next decade.[4] And who better to speak to the problem of designing in severely constrained conditions than Briggs? When practicing in Vienna and Berlin, she had also worked with stringent economic restrictions and knew well how to make the most of limited resources. She now brought this pragmatic approach and experience to the English context, working through specific sites and plans for "clients" of differing means and needs.

In her very first article, "Essentials of House Planning," Briggs advised readers to identify what was truly important to them in a home (fig. 20.1). "Do you go in for elaborate cooking?" she asked. She then illustrated a house that met a well-to-do family's preferences—a large, detached home with a hipped roof. It is telling that the debate over the traditional pitched roof versus the modernist flat one, which so exercised architects in Britain, did not trouble Briggs; her designs would feature both.[5] Possibly she was less dogmatic about external stylistic markers because, as we

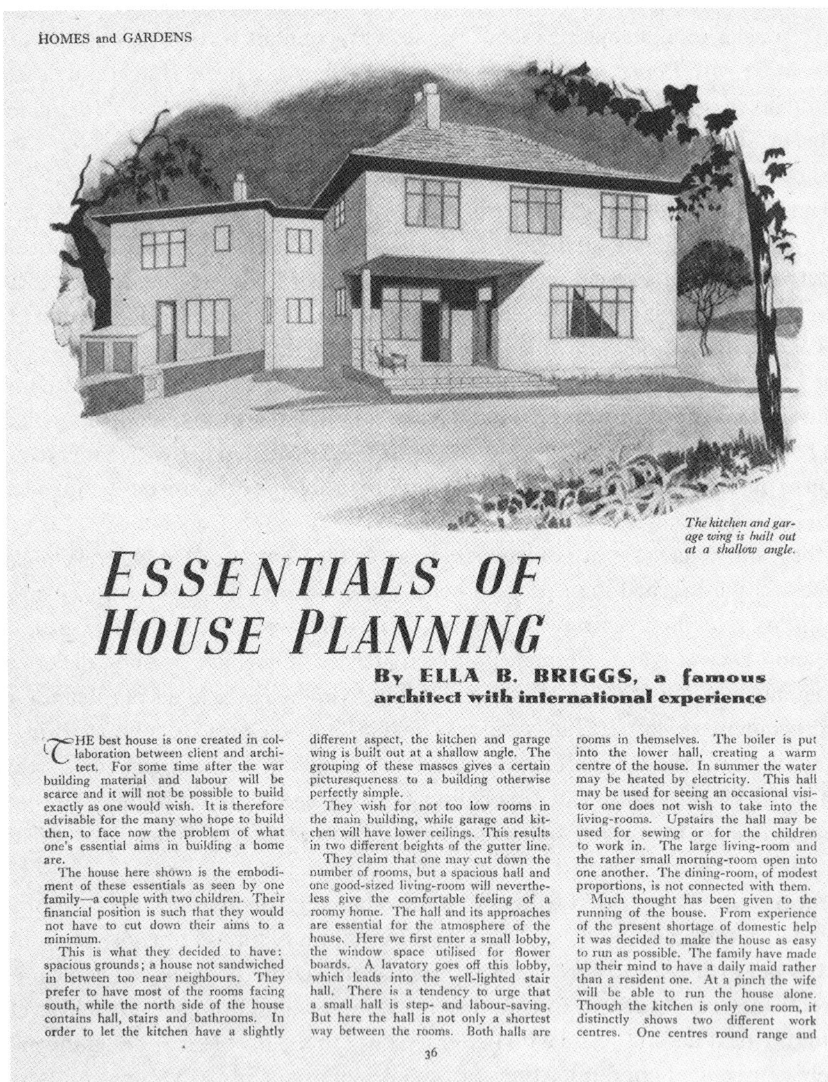

HOMES and GARDENS

The kitchen and garage wing is built out at a shallow angle.

ESSENTIALS OF HOUSE PLANNING

By ELLA B. BRIGGS, a famous architect with international experience

THE best house is one created in collaboration between client and architect. For some time after the war building material and labour will be scarce and it will not be possible to build exactly as one would wish. It is therefore advisable for the many who hope to build then, to face now the problem of what one's essential aims in building a home are.

The house here shown is the embodiment of these essentials as seen by one family—a couple with two children. Their financial position is such that they would not have to cut down their aims to a minimum.

This is what they decided to have: spacious grounds; a house not sandwiched in between too near neighbours. They prefer to have most of the rooms facing south, while the north side of the house contains hall, stairs and bathrooms. In order to let the kitchen have a slightly different aspect, the kitchen and garage wing is built out at a shallow angle. The grouping of these masses gives a certain picturesqueness to a building otherwise perfectly simple.

They wish for not too low rooms in the main building, while garage and kitchen will have lower ceilings. This results in two different heights of the gutter line.

They claim that one may cut down the number of rooms, but a spacious hall and one good-sized living-room will nevertheless give the comfortable feeling of a roomy home. The hall and its approaches are essential for the atmosphere of the house. Here we first enter a small lobby, the window space utilised for flower boards. A lavatory goes off this lobby, which leads into the well-lighted stair hall. There is a tendency to urge that a small hall is step- and labour-saving. But here the hall is not only a shortest way between the rooms. Both halls are rooms in themselves. The boiler is put into the lower hall, creating a warm centre of the house. In summer the water may be heated by electricity. This hall may be used for seeing an occasional visitor one does not wish to take into the living-rooms. Upstairs the hall may be used for sewing or for the children to work in. The large living-room and the rather small morning-room open into one another. The dining-room, of modest proportions, is not connected with them.

Much thought has been given to the running of the house. From experience of the present shortage of domestic help it was decided to make the house as easy to run as possible. The family have made up their mind to have a daily maid rather than a resident one. At a pinch the wife will be able to run the house alone. Though the kitchen is only one room, it distinctly shows two different work centres. One centres round range and

36

Fig. 20.1 Ella Briggs's April 1944 article in *Homes and Gardens* about a single-family house for a couple with two children. Note the description following her name: "a famous architect with international experience."

observed in her work at Bilston, she believed that modernism ultimately resided not in such details but in the plan. While commodious, the home she proposed in this article was designed for convenience, so the homemaker could run it without employing a live-in maid.[6] Highlighting the postwar dearth of domestic help and displaying sensitivity to housewives, Briggs addressed the topic of laborsaving in most articles, bridging the worlds of architecture and domestic science.[7] As she had done in the 1920s and 1930s, she wrote knowledgeably of the latest American technologies and innovations, championing dumbwaiters, built-in storage, central heating, and open plans.[8]

Her next article, from 1945, was more radical than her first, moving as it did away from the travails of the well-off and offering a technical solution to the specific problems confronting a less affluent middle-class family. In "Bungalow Home from Prefabricated Huts," Briggs described a home planned for a young couple with a child. It was a cozy but simple three-bedroom house: its main luxury was a "flower window," a deep double window located in a hallway where plants could grow—a signature Briggs feature.[9] Due to the scarcity of materials and labor, however, the house could not be built "for quite a time" unless the clients were willing to use prefabricated units. Despite the family's reported resistance, Briggs successfully redrew the plan to suit two factory-made huts, making only minimal modifications and utilizing a slightly more rectilinear roofline.

Briggs's article was timely. The previous year, the government had passed its Temporary Housing Programme, which relied heavily on Emergency Factory Made Houses to relieve Britain's housing shortages. Although she did not mention the program, Briggs was plainly trying to counter public prejudice against prefabs, praising their "advantages of flexibility in planning . . . [and] great rapidity of erection." Perhaps aware that her discussion of building loads and panel fillings was unlikely to move the *Homes and Gardens* readership, she also waxed poetic about how the "recurrence of the upright posts" gave prefabs the same "rhythm" as Greek temples. In her conclusion, however, she descended from the clouds to remind readers that the benefits of a private home should outweigh any concerns about materials: "You may have to curtail the proportions of your home for years to come. You may have to build in other material than you intended. But you are still free to procure for yourself and your family this most valuable commodity—space."[10]

In short, Briggs's prefab advocacy was done in the name of preserving family life. This was typical of her early articles for the magazine: while remaining true to the hallmarks of modernism—adaptable designs, advanced technologies, and laborsaving gadgets—her focus at this stage was on homes for nuclear families built on secluded garden plots. "Wait to build your own home until it is possible to build larger houses," she advised in 1946. If people did not wish to delay, she recommended building extendible houses to allow expansion once resources became available (fig. 20.2).[11] This idea of a house that could grow over time was a favored theme of hers, which she had first explored in her 1920s magazine articles geared toward young American couples with small budgets and revisited during the Depression when creating home types for the unemployed settlers and their families in Berlin.[12] Postwar material shortages in England would provide yet another compelling justification for phased construction.

Her work in Bilston in 1947, however, seemed to push Briggs to rethink her single-family focus. In an article on her own design for a four-flat house at Stowlawn, she admitted that recent research confirmed that too many three-bedroom houses were being built that did not suit the needs of single people, young childless couples, or the elderly—a category to which she, of course, now belonged. This concern prompted

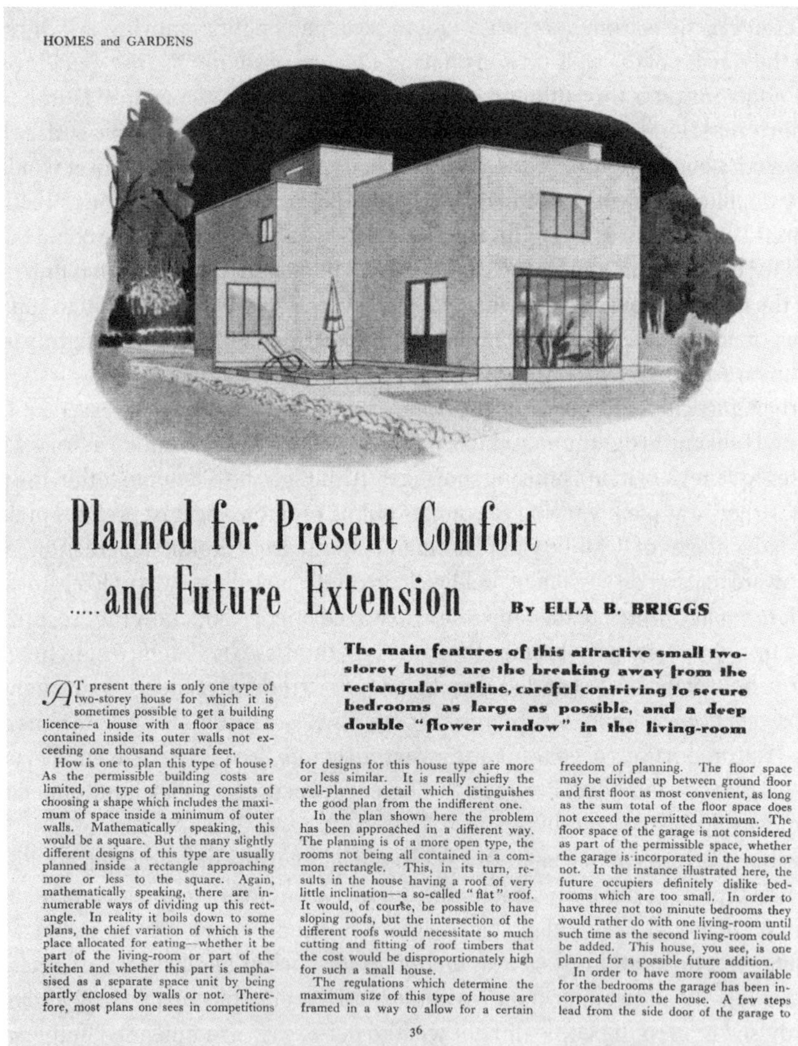

HOMES and GARDENS

Planned for Present Comfort .....and Future Extension

By ELLA B. BRIGGS

The main features of this attractive small two-storey house are the breaking away from the rectangular outline, careful contriving to secure bedrooms as large as possible, and a deep double "flower window" in the living-room

AT present there is only one type of two-storey house for which it is sometimes possible to get a building licence—a house with a floor space as contained inside its outer walls not exceeding one thousand square feet.

How is one to plan this type of house? As the permissible building costs are limited, one type of planning consists of choosing a shape which includes the maximum of space inside a minimum of outer walls. Mathematically speaking, this would be a square. But the many slightly different designs of this type are usually planned inside a rectangle approaching more or less to the square. Again, mathematically speaking, there are innumerable ways of dividing up this rectangle. In reality it boils down to some plans, the chief variation of which is the place allocated for eating—whether it be part of the living-room or part of the kitchen and whether this part is emphasised as a separate space unit by being partly enclosed by walls or not. Therefore, most plans one sees in competitions for designs for this house type are more or less similar. It is really chiefly the well-planned detail which distinguishes the good plan from the indifferent one.

In the plan shown here the problem has been approached in a different way. The planning is of a more open type, the rooms not being all contained in a common rectangle. This, in its turn, results in the house having a roof of very little inclination—a so-called "flat" roof. It would, of course, be possible to have sloping roofs, but the intersection of the different roofs would necessitate so much cutting and fitting of roof timbers that the cost would be disproportionately high for such a small house.

The regulations which determine the maximum size of this type of house are framed in a way to allow for a certain freedom of planning. The floor space may be divided up between ground floor and first floor as most convenient, as long as the sum total of the floor space does not exceed the permitted maximum. The floor space of the garage is not considered as part of the permissible space, whether the garage is incorporated in the house or not. In the instance illustrated here, the future occupiers definitely dislike bedrooms which are too small. In order to have three not too minute bedrooms they would rather do with one living-room until such time as the second living-room could be added. This house, you see, is one planned for a possible future addition.

In order to have more room available for the bedrooms the garage has been incorporated into the house. A few steps lead from the side door of the garage to

36

Fig. 20.2 Ella Briggs, design for a small two-story house with her signature deep double "flower window" in the living room published in *Homes and Gardens* in April 1946. This "extendible" design typifies Briggs's pragmatic responses to space limits set by building licenses and costs. It also shows how she did occasionally adopt the modern flat-roof style.

her to revisit another theme she had set out decades before for American readers: homes that would accommodate the full human life cycle. Future articles in *Homes and Gardens* would show her engaging more directly with the realities of generational change; people upsizing or downsizing, converting or moving on. Nevertheless, she would always lean toward arrangements that permitted self-sufficiency and privacy. There was little talk of cooperative or communal facilities of the kind that had made her reputation in Vienna.

In truth, her silence on these amenities is not all that remarkable. While opinionated, Briggs was never dogmatic: her ability to work in so many contexts was down to her willingness to adapt to suit client needs and audience expectations. As she had done when writing for American publications two decades before, Briggs now adopted a gentler approach in deference to her readership, in this case the middlebrow readers of *Homes and Gardens* who had a decided preference for the English garden cottage (plate 19).[13] Briggs understood the appeal of this type very well, having designed many suburban villas and houses for bourgeois clients over her long career. Indeed, at that moment she herself was inhabiting, apparently quite contentedly, an entirely conventional suburban house with its own back garden.

In spite of moving away from collectivism, however, Briggs was not abandoning modernism; instead, she seemed to wish to make it palatable to her readers, going to some lengths to persuade them that modern styles were not incommensurate with tradition. This emerged in her piece on a Swiss house designed by Werner M. Moser for an affluent family in the Tyrol, one of only two articles she wrote that focused on the work of another architect.[14] The article confirmed Briggs's ongoing allegiance to Continental European modernism, especially of the Swiss variety, but her article's purpose was to show readers that "many of the features regarded as so very new in some modern houses [she had Le Corbusier's in mind] are really based on tradition."[15] She explained that Moser's house actually just substituted new materials for old, and that, far from radical, its cantilevered upper stories were typical of the Tyrolian region, providing extra living space and views.

Briggs's conciliatory approach appears to have secured her place in *Homes and Gardens*, even as the magazine became glossier—photographs of celebrities and royals began to grace its covers—and thick with ads. Although never a leading writer, Briggs remained a regular contributor; for instance, she was in the lineup for the bumper issue of May 1951 that previewed the Festival of Britain, as well as in the issue devoted to the Queen's preparations for her coronation in November 1952. Despite the magazine's increasingly sophisticated look, Briggs's articles changed little, soberly cycling through permissible options for various types of houses and, very occasionally, flats. Briggs continued to develop her interest in accommodating generational change and housing old people independently. She enthusiastically promoted indoor gardens. And in 1953, she was allowed one grand flourish: her description of another Swiss house by fellow Munich Technical University alumnus, architect Max Kopp, was given the full-blown *Homes and Gardens* feature treatment, complete with pages of beautiful photos.[16]

The following year, however, Briggs slipped down the table of contents, from "Special Features" to "Decoration and Furnishing." In 1955, with stacks of articles under her belt, she departed the magazine. She went out as she came in, with a final piece on labor- and space-saving considerations and bungalows.[17] Indeed, for over a decade, Briggs's concerns, and her black-and-white renderings, remained remarkably consistent; she turned stringent postwar limits on costs and space standards into architectural opportunities. Under the guise of "making do," she was able to propose some innovative ideas, testing out new construction methods, flexible designs, and easier ways of living. As she mused about one home designed for a maximum of 1,000 square feet: "It was quite [a] good experience . . . to be compelled to realise in how small a space one could live comfortably."[18] But once rationing ended, it seemed the editors of *Homes and Gardens* no longer wished readers to feel so compelled.

Collectively, Briggs's articles testify to how deeply invested she was in her identity as an architect. Her last known commissions were in 1947; three years later she was diagnosed with chronic lymphatic leukemia, a condition that required constant monitoring.[19] (It also prompted a visit to a doctor in Switzerland, which helps explain her ongoing familiarity with the country's architecture.)[20] Yet her articles for *Homes and Gardens* did not read like the work of someone who was stepping back or slowing down. Briggs wrote as if tackling problems encountered in a still-active architectural practice, citing the specific needs of flesh-and-blood clients. You can just picture them: "The clients are plant-lovers and not quite young enough to potter about in a greenhouse and to bend down to their gardening tasks."[21] She always provided credible, detailed descriptions of site conditions, topography, and orientation. Whether or not these projects were ever built is beside the point: they were real insofar as they allowed Briggs to carry on designing, planning, and engaging some of the leading housing problems of the day.

It is hard to believe that Briggs gave up her column any less reluctantly than she did her architectural practice. Starting in 1953, however, she became absorbed in another project: seeking restitution from the German government, a lengthy legal process that required exceptional tenacity—fortunately, a quality Briggs possessed in spades. In 1953 her brother Friedrich died, and, as sole heir, Briggs took over his already-initiated claim for reparations.[22] This was ultimately successful and would result in a substantial, though not life-changing, settlement of over 15,000 deutsche mark. The first tranche of money would be paid to Briggs in 1956; the second, in 1959.[23]

In 1954 Briggs would also file claims on her own behalf. The first was for lost assets of various kinds. Briggs estimated she had left behind furnishings worth 80 pounds, consisting of a sofa and a cherry-wood cupboard and bookcase, made by "good craftsmen" to her designs (see plate 8).[24] Based on the sale price of her photographic prints to the Victoria and Albert Museum and the Courtauld, she also valued her abandoned plates of Italy at 300 pounds, reasoning, "I could have sold the collection to dozens of museums and universities in England and the United States, if I had had the plates." She even asked for 33 pounds for transport and storage costs associated with her 1937 move.[25] This claim would prove unsuccessful.

Her second restitution claim was to do with her lost career and the successful architectural practice she had left in Berlin. Setting out her case, she re-narrated many of the events covered in the previous chapter but cast them in a far more brutal light. She bitterly recalled her financial hardship in England as she tried to help her family emigrate and waited for a work permit: "Years passed before I was allowed to practice," she said. She described how, when she was classed an "enemy alien," a combination of inactivity and discrimination kept her from paid work. She ended by noting, "After the war I was 65 years old. Even though I found a few jobs that paid very little, . . . I no longer had the resilience to build up a practice that was as good as the one in Berlin."[26] Elsewhere, she claimed to be living primarily off a paltry welfare payment of four pounds per week from the National Assistance Board.[27] Citing her solid earnings between 1928 and 1932 (10,000–12,000 reichsmark a year), she demanded an overall figure of 63,707 reichsmark as compensation for lost income.[28] But the reams of documents mainly serve to highlight how impossible it was to value the loss that Briggs likely felt most deeply: the security, fulfillment, and status a flourishing practice would have brought her. In short, the future that should have been hers.

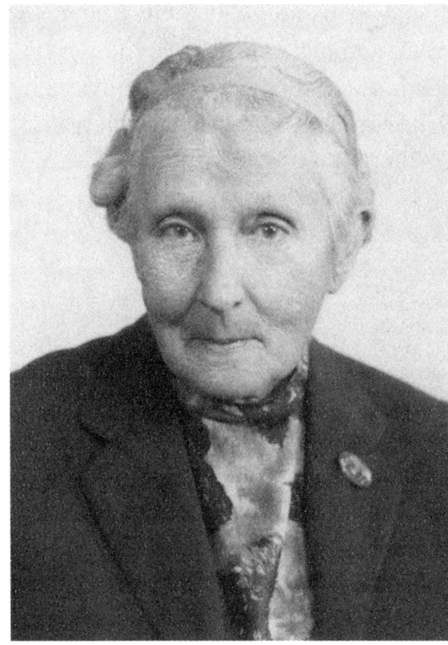

Fig. 20.3 Ella Briggs at eighty. This is the last known photograph of the architect, dated September 5, 1960.

This time, she won her claim. In October 1957, Briggs received a one-time payment of 2,500 deutsche mark from the German government. Although only a fraction of what she had requested, when added to her brother's claim, the sum likely made her final years a bit more comfortable (fig. 20.3).[29] By this point, however, her immediate family members had died: Frieda passed away in 1943; Friedrich in 1953. Life became quiet. Writing to her American grandniece, the educator Phylis Morrison, she confided, "I do not go out anymore and live on memories." Briggs followed this by dreamily recalling her mother's furniture, abandoned in Friedrich's flat in Berlin—lovely antique furniture, family portraits, clocks, silver, and china. But then, in a typical Briggs move, she shook off the nostalgia and recounted an outing she had made previously to visit ancient churches. "Have you never wondered why some churches have one spire and some two spires?" she mused, a true architect to the end.[30]

Briggs passed away the following year, on June 20, 1977, age ninety-seven. Her ashes were sent to lie beside Friedrich's at the South London Crematorium. Her will was thorough, carefully sharing the small number of remaining family possessions and personal photos between her heirs, Morrison in the United States, and her nephew

Theodore Baumfeld in Switzerland. These included her grandfather's portrait miniature and her mother's wedding ring, which was set with a "small brilliant clasp." Her home was sold for the benefit of her heirs; her furniture and books were left to the Architects Benevolent Society.[31]

There was no obituary.

PART II

Reflections on Ella Briggs

21. Family Bonds and Legacies: Ella Briggs and Phylis Morrison

Elana Shapira and Despina Stratigakos, in Conversation with Jeanne Paradise

In a letter written a year before her death, Ella Briggs, ill and housebound, confided to her grandniece Phylis Morrison, "I do not go out anymore and live on memories." Those memories—of family and friends, of work and travel, of building and writing, of war and peace, of migration and exile—were rich but also painful. Remembering her grandfather, Briggs remarked that the diamond trader's work brought him frequently to London, where she now resided. She proudly noted that he had translated a "famous English novel" into German, and that once on a visit he had witnessed "rioting outside parliament for the vote." But Briggs was also haunted by loss: she described how in fleeing Nazi terror in Germany, her family was forced to leave behind many of their cherished possessions, including artwork and family photographs. Of the heirlooms that remained in Ella's home, she promised them to Phylis "when I peg out."[1]

Although Briggs wrote the letter partly to clarify Morrison's inheritance, the stories about family were also about a different kind of legacy—about intangible connections that bind people across generations. Ella and Phylis shared a deep and abiding passion for learning and teaching. Briggs closed her letter with a discovery that she had made about church spires, which she recommended that her grandniece share with her students: "That's something to tell your pupils."[2]

Briggs's desire to relate to Morrison's educational work is not surprising given the prominent role education had played in both of their lives. Even as a refugee in England with diminished professional opportunities, Briggs found an educational outlet in writing about homes and interiors, offering to her mostly female British readers (as she had earlier to American and German-speaking audiences) a chance to explore and put into practice new ideas about architecture and living. Indeed, the set of ideas she gave readers to understand their domestic spaces and to make their own informed decisions about design could be considered a tool kit, broadly defined.[3] By the time Briggs wrote the advice to Morrison about instructing her pupils on architecture, she knew that Morrison, a progressive educator, was already engaged in developing educational kits and other creative methods to empower school children.

What Morrison thought of this advice we do not know, as her letters to Briggs have not been preserved. We catch glimpses of her distancing herself from her great aunt, however, in the letter Briggs wrote, a response to an earlier one from Morrison. Briggs expresses dismay that Morrison plans to visit Europe without stopping in London to see her, and she refuses her niece's apparent offer to give her share of the inheritance Briggs had set aside for her to her uncle, Theodore Baumfeld (Briggs's nephew), then living in Switzerland. Ella and Phylis's relationship was forged in tragedy, and even decades later, it seems, Phylis remained wary.[4]

Phylis Beatrice Hagen was born in 1927 in the city of Orange, New Jersey, to Angela Hagen, the daughter of Moritz Baumfeld, Ella's older brother, who had not lived to see his granddaughter's birth. Hans John Hagen, Phylis's father, travelled frequently between the United States and Europe on import business. The couple divorced in 1932. Angela and her young daughter were living in Salzburg when, in June 1935, at the age of thirty-nine Angela died suddenly of heatstroke. Phylis lived with relatives in Berlin or Vienna (possibly with Ella, who would soon begin her quest to leave Nazi Germany) until September of that year, when she was returned to the United States. Morrison remembered that "aunt Ella" frightened her as a child, and even late in life she referred to her as "the dragon lady." Yet despite these feelings, she and Briggs maintained a lifelong relationship.[5]

As an adult, and perhaps shaped by her early experiences of fear and bewilderment, Morrison dedicated herself to children's education. By the 1960s, she was working with the Boston Children's Museum, an institution that attracted educational innovators across a broad range of fields, from the arts to the sciences. Morrison advised the museum's Kit Department, which developed learning kits for children that it loaned to area schools. The kits covered hundreds of topics, including history, geography, and physics, and promoted hands-on learning.[6]

In 1969 Morrison met Jeanne Paradise. Initially her colleague at the museum, Paradise eventually became Morrison's friend. The two women developed their own teaching projects outside the museum, including a course on beads that considered their technology and design across human history and around the globe. As Paradise recalls, to prepare the course they went beyond merely looking at pictures and reading texts; they also gathered up a vast range of materials—such as clay, bone, seeds, stone, and glass—and learned by making beads themselves. They visited museum collections, talked to experts, and grew seeds in their gardens to harvest for use in the workshops. According to Paradise, Morrison's interests and talents were boundless. The resulting course, which had been Morrison's idea, deftly merged art, materials science, technology, ethnography, and history. It also captured Morrison's thought process: in making a bead you could travel the world. Whenever the two friends got together to work out their projects and ideas, they would use their hands. Paradise remembers that they did not discuss weaving, for example, without weaving together. Thinking back on their time, Paradise vividly recalls the flow of words and crafting hands generating inspiration and ideas.[7]

During the 1960s and 1970s, the Boston area was a hub of innovation in education, and women were at the heart of it. Paradise recounts how vibrant female networks, which included figures such as writer Joan Erikson and psychologist Carol Gilligan, sparked extraordinary conversations that encouraged the exploration of new pedagogies for children as well as new frameworks for women's development. Paradise was so inspired by this milieu that she later studied for her doctorate and worked in women's development and education.[8]

It was through her work as an educator that Phylis met her second husband, the Massachusetts Institute of Technology physicist Philip Morrison, whom she married in 1965. Renowned for his work on the Manhattan Project, quantum and nuclear physics, and high-energy astronomy, he was also intensely interested in how children learn science. He and Phylis collaborated on projects for the general public, including the immensely popular book *Powers of Ten.* The volume, which explores the relative size of things within the universe, reworked in printed form the subject of an earlier film by designers Charles and Ray Eames. Phylis also published the book *Spiders' Games*, which, much like the course on beads, explored weaving through materials, tools, history, and ethnography.[9]

Throughout all of that talking and making, there were some things Phylis Morrison never mentioned to Paradise: her childhood and aunt Ella. Morrison brimmed with energy and ideas for new projects and did not dwell on the trauma of her past. Today, reading Briggs's letter to her grandniece and especially her advice to "tell your pupils," Paradise is struck by the tone: the directives of an expert. As Paradise recalls, "'Telling' pupils was not something Phylis did. In our work together, and typically in Phylis's work, we created a materials-rich environment, including text and image, and engaged with students' questions, discoveries and ideas as they began exploring the materials and emerging ideas."[10]

Phylis herself had pursued a path of educational self-discovery: after her junior year of high school, she talked her way into college. When she left college to marry her first husband, she ended up with neither a high school nor a college diploma. But that did not stop her from forging a highly creative career as an educator. For Ella, who grew up in a different time and a different culture, educational credentials had an authority that opened doors. Whereas Ella felt entitled by those credentials and the license they conferred—and for that reason, fought fiercely for the right to obtain them—Phylis adopted a philosophy of "just do it and make it happen."[11]

And yet, despite these differences, one could make an argument about the bond that Briggs and Morrison shared: an extraordinary range of talents and interests, a deep curiosity for discovery and innovation, and a passion to empower others through "do-it-yourself" learning. Each originated new methods to make complex ideas, whether in the natural sciences or the arts, comprehensible to nonspecialist audiences. As Paradise notes, "They both were innovative learners and teachers, though in differing directions, each a part of the educational ferment of their separate communities and historical time."[12]

22.
Viennese Women's Art Schools and Their Communities in Ella Briggs's Time

Megan Brandow-Faller

In 1897, when the seventeen-year-old Ella Briggs set out to study art in Vienna, she had few options to pursue. Even schools that, in theory, stood open to women on equal terms with men—such as Vienna's Kunstgewerbeschule (School of Applied Arts), which she would later attend—in practice severely limited the range of possibilities open to women. This would begin to change in the years that immediately followed, and during Briggs's lifetime opportunities for studying not only art and design but also architecture would widen.

Briggs's professional training and career spanned a pivotal time in the evolution of women's education, when centuries-long systems that prevented access were dismantled, and new systems that served to maintain access—as well as ensure success—among her female cohort were created. Indeed, Briggs herself would come to play a foundational role in expanding access to and opportunities for women in architecture, and would pioneer a place for them within numerous educational and professional contexts. But at the turn of the century in Vienna, Briggs occupied a red-hot center of this cataclysmic change to come.

In 1899, members of the Secessionist movement led a coup at Vienna's School of Applied Arts, revolutionizing its educational programs and opening more of its course offerings to women. Women had been formally admitted from the school's 1868 founding but were excluded from "unfeminine" fields of study such as life drawing and figure painting. Felician Baron von Myrbach, a founding member of the Secession and the school's director, hired architect Josef Hoffmann and designer Koloman Moser, among other Secessionist artists, to implement a thorough program of ideological and artistic rejuvenation. Secessionist faculty reoriented the school's curriculum, away from its founders' focus on training designers to copy historical models and toward a reformist curriculum privileging nature study, individual expressiveness, spontaneity, and multidisciplinary experimentation. These methods drew on progressive currents in early childhood education that stressed the principle of "unlearning," whereby traditional means of instruction were discarded in favor of looser methods of guidance and noninterference.[1]

Myrbach's reforms granting full admission to women at the school stood in contrast to policies governing the city's leading art institution. Until 1920 women were not welcome at the Akademie der bildenden Künste Wien (Academy of Fine Arts Vienna). The men who controlled the academy repeatedly blocked inquiries and petitions to integrate female students. They pointed to the academy's supposed inability to provide appropriate facilities in which to offer separate life drawing classes, citing lack of space. Drawing from life played a central role in the academy's curriculum, and the possibility of men and (respectable) women sharing a studio while studying models' naked bodies was out of the question.[2]

The academy's ruse to exclude women had at its core two hierarchal systems of belief. The first system, which pervaded Viennese society, maintained the fundamental inequality of the sexes: men allegedly experienced a natural connection to higher intellectual and artistic pursuits, while women naturally gravitated toward instinctual and domestic matters. The second system, foundational to Austrian art schools and cultural institutions, ranked the arts according to their relative value, from high art to low art, major works to minor objects, the monumental to the merely decorative. Male artists dominated the "high," "major," "monumental" end of the scale, whereas female artists occupied its "low," "minor," "decorative" end. Somewhat ironically, although Vienna's two, mutually reinforcing hierarchical systems served to exclude women from the academy, they would facilitate women's admission to the School of Applied Arts—at least initially.

When the School of Applied Arts opened in 1868, its founders publicly stated that women had an inborn prowess for the decorative arts and design. According to deeply rooted cultural assumptions, women had an affinity for ornamenting the home, and themselves, as well as a tendency to be diligent and detail-oriented. These traits were thought to equip them for success in the applied arts. Further advancing the case for women's admission among design reformers—albeit not discussed openly—was a realization that women would potentially provide a cheap source of artistic labor.[3] The school thus admitted female students from the start and attracted notably large numbers of women (ranging from 13 to 27 percent of the total student enrollment) in the mid-1870s and early 1880s.[4]

Female students at the School of Applied Arts were typically of higher-class backgrounds than their male counterparts, a reflection in part of women's lack of other opportunities. In late Imperial Austria, women seeking state-run artistic training were largely limited to schools of applied arts.[5] Beginning in 1908, the state-run Graphische Lehr- und Versuchsanstalt (Graphic Arts Training and Research Institute) admitted women for vocational training in the graphic arts and photography. Alternatively, women could attend one of a variety of private art schools in Vienna. These were often short-lived, however, tethered as they were to their operators' career trajectories. The training they provided frequently relied on untested educational methods and idiosyncratic teaching styles, limited women's access to life classes, and produced uneven results.[6] A bridge between public and private could be found in the Kunstschule für Frauen und Mädchen (Art School for Women and Girls), which was founded in 1897 as a private institution but gained increasing levels of state support and accreditation after 1908.

Women's education at the School of Applied Arts proved less inclusive than many expected. Its prohibition of women taking life drawing classes resulted in their de facto exclusion from the concentrations of painting and sculpture. In open rebellion, female art students delivered a petition to the school's board in 1872. Art historian Rudolf von Eitelberger, a cofounder of the school's sister institution, the Österreichisches

Museum für Kunst und Industrie (Austrian Museum of Art and Industry), delivered a reply that insisted that the school existed to support Austria's applied arts industries and was *not* to be "misused [by] little young ladies who are dilettantes and want to pursue history, landscape, or genre painting."[7] This criticism reflected broader fears among design educators that the school had been co-opted by well-to-do female students, who had supposedly transformed it into a sort of *Damen-Winkelakademie* (backstreet ladies' academy). During the ensuing years, the school's male leadership instituted policies that eroded female students' access, culminating in more severe restrictions in the mid-1880s.[8] From 1886 until 1899, only a limited number of female students were permitted to study in one of the special "feminine" workshops, such as textiles, and only after completing extensive private training.

Myrbach's reforms of 1899 restored the more open attitude toward female students initially displayed by the School of Applied Arts, and female enrollment soared. The director took gender equality even further than the school's founders: for the first time, women joined the teaching staff of the school. This hardly translated to true equity, as the small cadre of female instructors—invariably concentrated in culturally "feminine" fields, with a very few given the title of *Professorin* (professor)—stood in stark contrast to its large numbers of female students. Nevertheless, the female instructors guided the female students, provided opportunities for them, and served as role models for imagining a life as a professional artist.

In the period after the Secessionist coup, the School of Applied Arts pulsed with new energy and opportunities for female art students. These women were invited to participate in the most important ventures of the Secessionist movement, including art exhibitions and public events. Their visibility was noted by contemporary critics, who spoke of the "new feminine strength" of the school, evident at international exhibitions such as the Universal Exposition of 1900 in Paris.[9] Ella Briggs's entry into the school in 1901 coincided with this triumph. There, Briggs gained a broad-based education in handcraft, attending courses in anatomy, technical drawing, chemistry, art history, embroidery, and lacework in addition to her concentration in painting and graphics with Koloman Moser. Briggs would have rubbed elbows with other rising female "stars" among Moser's students (such as Therese Trethahn and Jutta Sika), deriving strength from the shared professional and personal goals among this pioneering generation of female students. Such bonds of female collectivity were not unlike those operating at the state-accredited Art School for Women and Girls, where feminist philosopher Rosa Mayreder and Impressionist painter Tina Blau-Lang mentored a younger generation of artists—including Briggs, for a short period of time.[10]

Yet despite the doors that Secessionist and other reformers opened to women, gender biases remained. Within the School of Applied Arts's broader culture, female students were valued primarily for their industriousness and were discouraged from pursuing so-called masculine fields. Only a handful of women studied architecture with Hoffmann, whose classes remained overwhelmingly male. When the design collective Wiener Kunst im Hause (Viennese Art in the Home) staged interior design displays at the 1900 exposition in Paris and at the fifteenth Secessionist exhibition in

Vienna (1902), female students were expected to decorate and accessorize spaces designed by their male colleagues.[11] Unsurprisingly, few female graduates of the School of Applied Arts advertised themselves as "architects" proper. More common were careers in teaching (at craft, technical, and vocational schools); in fashion and interior design; or in production (in arts-and-crafts workshops; in particular, the Wiener Werkstätte, for which the school served as a talent pool).[12] Once established, however, these careers were often cut short, as even highly successful artist-craftswomen were expected to sacrifice their professional ambitions to care for their families and children.

Yet limited progress was made. One benchmark of female students' integration at the school and their greater role as coproducers of Viennese modernism ensued after Briggs had left the school and was professionally active as an interior designer in New York. At the 1908 *Vienna Kunstschau* (Art Show), organized by the Secession's most progressive artists and typically viewed as the highpoint of the Secessionists' attempts to unify art, architecture, and design, no less than one third of the exhibitors were women.[13] Further heightening their visibility, Briggs and her female colleagues frequently published their work in magazines such as *Ver Sacrum* and the experimental graphic portfolio *Die Fläche*.[14] Briggs took this lesson about the importance of magazines for introducing new ideas into her later architecture career, where she not only engaged professional audiences but also branched out into new territory largely left untouched by her male colleagues: popular women's magazines. Importantly, Hoffmann and Moser recruited female art students to design for the Wiener Werkstätte, where commissions for graphic art, ceramics, and textiles were considered a continuation of the school's "learning workshop," as they had been for its forerunner, Viennese Art in the Home. Unlike many of her colleagues in Moser's classes, Briggs was not linked to the Wiener Werkstätte, but her studies at the School of Applied Arts imbued her with a commercial savvy that would inform her future design initiatives. A few years after completing her studies, Briggs devised an idea for a commercial design outlet in New York City representing leading Austrian firms and serving American firms wishing to integrate Austrian handcraft and products into their commissions.[15] While never realized, Briggs's innovative proposal, drafted in collaboration with the leadership of the Museum for Art and Industry, foreshadowed the emergence of intense Austrian-American crosscurrents in design during the interwar years.

Although in some ways still shackled by gender stereotypes and hierarchical structures, Briggs's educational experience offers stunning proof of how women pushed the boundaries of artistic education at the School of Applied Arts. The school's curriculum, programs, and culture launched many women into dynamic artistic careers, the range and magnitude of which we are only just now beginning to document and appreciate. Briggs and her female peers came away having gained solid training in the applied arts and handcraft as well as professional and commercial contacts that would inform collaborations in Vienna. They used this foundation and milieu to open doors for themselves that might otherwise have remained shut. In some cases, they were able to deploy resources (courses, mentors, etc.) available to male students. In other cases, they operated both within and outside of those possibilities in forming their own networks and opportunities. What initially began within the context of Vienna's Secession movement would later exceed it, reaching other parts of Central Europe, New York, and well beyond.

If Briggs's early career would help tip the scale of acceptable female artistic practice from low art to higher art, minor or decorative arts to major works, then her subsequent career as a full-fledged architect would help rebalance the scale entirely. Close examination of the educational environments in which women like Briggs trained must factor into our assessment of their subsequent work. How, we must ask, did these institutions create not only the hurdles women initially faced but also the challenges they would rise to overcome? How did these places shape their habits and their thinking about design, both artistically and professionally?

More specifically, we must investigate how women associated with progressive art schools and movements, including the Secession, shaped modernist architecture and design culture in previously underappreciated ways. Exploring the path that Ella Briggs—one of the first female students at the School of Applied Arts to reap the benefits of its Secessionist coup—forged to create a successful career in architecture and design casts into relief the significant role played by the academic environment, student experiences, and educational and vocational training. Shaped by mentors, friendships, professional networks, and dreams, Briggs's pursuit of her own artistic and cultural revolutions would take Viennese modernism in a new, female-focused direction.

23.
The Interiors of Ella Briggs: International Crosscurrents and Modern Adaptations

Eva B. Ottillinger

Ella Briggs began her career as an interior designer during the first decade of the twentieth century. Having completed her applied art studies in Vienna, she was living in New York; it would be more than a decade before she would obtain her degree in architecture. Her first known commission—for the German Theater in 1908—emerged seemingly out of nowhere and now represents a long-forgotten gem of Secessionist design in New York. But Briggs did not simply transplant ideas from Vienna to New York; instead, she combined and adapted design trends and traditions with an eye toward capturing an American clientele. This begs a more general question: how did Briggs blend design traditions and modern trends from multiple sources to create fresh yet accessible interior designs and to position herself as a conduit of ideas across national frontiers?

An examination of the men's smoking rooms and ladies' parlors Briggs designed for the German Theater provides illumination. As is evident from photographs published in the journal *Kunst und Kunsthandwerk* (Art and Craft) in 1909 (see figs. 5.8 and 5.10), the walls of both the men's and women's rooms followed the same decorative scheme: wooden wainscoting, built-in furniture, and an inglenook chimneypiece with seats on either side.[1] The design of the inglenooks and wainscoting was influenced by British interiors that had emerged in the 1860s as part of the Arts and Crafts movement, which pursued social and aesthetic reform through handcraft. Initially shaped by the ideas and designs of William Morris, the movement later spread internationally, spawning new branches across the world.[2] Vienna Secessionists embraced this design movement and even exhibited the work of artists from England and Scotland in their eighth annual exhibition in 1900. British interiors inspired modern Viennese ones, such as the Vienna law office of Walter Briggs (Ella's future husband), designed by Josef Hoffmann in 1899.[3] As a student of the Kunstgewerbeschule (School of Applied Arts), Ella was exposed to these exchanges among designers in Austria and the United Kingdom and witnessed firsthand how they produced artistic expressions adapted to new contexts. When we look at Briggs's theater rooms, we see a similar process unfolding: the shape and ornamentation of her wainscoting was less radical than the wainscoting found in Secessionist interiors, such as those of Hoffmann. Thus, the adaptations already made to British designs in Vienna underwent yet another iteration in Briggs's theater rooms—British Arts and Crafts influences filtered through Vienna and adapted yet again for American users. Briggs clearly wanted to create interiors that were new and exciting, but without shocking her New York audience.

Although the wall decorations in the men's and ladies' rooms were similar to each other, the color schemes differed. The particular smoking room illustrated in *Kunst und Kunsthandwerk*, with its dark-green chimneypiece, gray-green wainscoting, and blue upholstery, was much darker than the ladies' parlor, also depicted in the journal, with its white walls, furniture in light gray and violet, and silver textile wall coverings with light gray and violet stencils.[4] The practice of varying the decoration of rooms by gender was well established, going back to the second half of the nineteenth century. At that time the housewife's sitting room in an upper-middle-class Austrian dwelling was often decorated in a neo-Rococo style with furnishings in light colors, while the husband's reading or smoking room was outfitted in a neo-Renaissance style with wood and textiles in dark colors (not least because smoke had a darkening effect on its surroundings).[5] In the theater rooms designed by Briggs, the lightness of the ladies' parlor and the darkness of the men's room would have thus been expected by their users. But the particular color combinations influenced by the Viennese Secession would have appeared fresh and unusual in New York.

Although Briggs did not vary the historical style of the rooms, she did use furniture to further differentiate them by gender. For the men's room, Briggs selected modern American Arts and Crafts furniture produced by Gustav Stickley at the Craftsman Workshops in Eastwood near Syracuse in New York State.[6] Stickley's heavy hardwood furniture was considered revolutionary at the time for its simplicity and comfort. In New York City, it would have been highly unusual to see this style used outside a domestic setting, and especially in a formal venue such as a theater. For the ladies' parlor, Briggs chose modern bentwood furniture produced by the Austrian firm Jacob & Josef Kohn, which maintained a showroom at 191 Canal Street in lower Manhattan.[7] The light bentwood furniture had been available in the city since around 1885, part of a growing European furniture, fashion, and art market catering to wealthy and upper-middle-class New Yorkers.[8] But at the time the theater decoration was completed, the Kohns' bentwood furniture was still rarely used in upper-class salons. Thus Briggs's furniture preferences, although once again following conventional design practice in terms of their gender associations, with heavy furniture for the men and light furniture for the women, would have struck visitors to the theater as starkly modern.

The German Theater catered to German and Austrian patrons who may well have been aware of the latest European design trends, including Alphonse Mucha's lavish stage sets for Parisian actress extraordinaire Sarah Bernhardt.[9] By contrast, the New York Press Club's members were more locally focused, and were looking for interiors that, while speaking to the members' modernity and awareness of global trends, created an appropriate setting for their professional and social activities. Briggs also used Jacob & Josef Kohn furniture for the ladies' reception room at the New York Press Club, which she decorated together with Minna Leigh Mercer in 1909 (see fig. 5.15). The rest of the club was outfitted with heavier furniture, as was characteristic of men's social and professional clubs. These familiar furnishings would have presumably appealed to male club members (see fig. 5.14).

After Briggs left New York, she established herself as an interior designer in Central Europe. In 1912 she designed the Breslau (today Wrocław) home of Otto and Lilly

Pringsheim, in-laws of Moritz Baumfeld (Ella's older brother). Given the family connection and Briggs's recent work, it is not surprising to see that the chimneypiece in the living room (see fig. 7.1) was similar to that of the men's smoking room at the German Theater. Briggs thus repurposed her own Viennese-influenced New York design, bringing new ideas back across the Atlantic. By contrast, the type of buffet she used was representative of Vienna around 1912. As in her New York commissions, here Briggs blended old and new, adapted to her clients and their specific contexts. Otto Pringsheim was a progressive economist and intellectual who supported the women's rights movement. We can well imagine how a salon designed by a professional female designer who introduced modern elements would have appealed to this patron's self-understanding.[10] A surviving Morris-style armchair (named after an early type of recliner developed by William Morris) designed by Briggs for the Pringsheims reveals this self-understanding quite clearly. (The chair is visible to the left of the fireplace; see fig. 7.1.) This sort of recliner was the quintessential man's reading armchair, a "tool" for the intellectual life of the owner or user, and Pringsheim made a statement about how he saw himself by asking Briggs to design it for him. (One can hardly imagine, for example, Sigmund Freud doing the same.) The design combines influences from British Arts and Crafts furniture with modern Central European precedents, such as the Morris chair that Henry van de Velde designed for his own Haus Hohe Pappeln (1907) in Weimar, Germany.[11] The recliner is the only known piece of furniture from this project to survive changes of address and Nazi persecution, and appears to have been of particular importance to the family.

Back in Vienna, Briggs collaborated with local cabinetmakers, for whom she designed furniture and interior decoration. This form of partnership was common in Austrian modernism around 1900. Initially leading architects worked closely with furniture makers to execute their designs for wealthy clients; but eventually, furniture firms began to hire graduates of Vienna's School of Applied Arts to serve as professional designers for their companies. Briggs, a school alumna with international experience, found willing partners among Viennese furniture makers. One such collaboration resulted in her design of a writing room published in 1914 in *Das Interieur*, which may have been part of her own interior design studio (see plate 8). The room was inspired by Biedermeier, a neoclassical style popular in Central Europe in the nineteenth century that came back into vogue in Vienna before the First World War.[12] Briggs's furniture was made of cherrywood, which had been very popular during the 1820s, with upholstery in yellow and green. It was executed by the cabinetmaker Johann Marek, whose workshop was located in a working-class neighborhood.[13] Interestingly, Briggs worked with small workshops rather than with major firms, as Josef Hoffmann had done. She presumably found more opportunities for collaboration there, in contrast to larger enterprises that already had their own established design teams in place. The same article in *Das Interieur* also included a middle-class dining room, the furniture for which was designed by Briggs and made by Lorenz Bogataj (fig. 23.1). Bogataj was known for his own furniture designs for workers' apartments.[14]

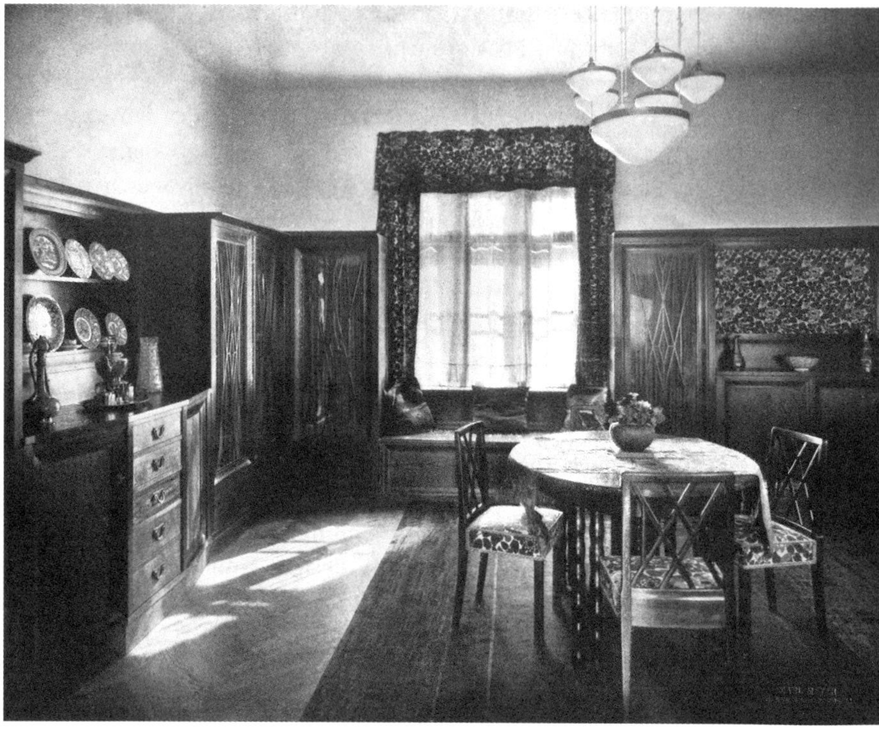

Fig. 23.1 Dining room with furniture designed by Ella Briggs and made by Lorenz Bogataj, c. 1914.

The built-in cupboards and buffets of the dining room illustrated in *Das Interieur* (see fig. 23.1) were made of dark-stained pinewood, the upper parts of the walls and the ceiling were painted green, and a colorful Backhausen fabric with a floral motif was used for the curtains, chair upholstery, and as wall covering.[15] The room conveyed a sense of unpretentious but elegant middle-class comfort. The chairbacks and the cupboards' glass doors were decorated with late eighteenth-century motifs in the style of the British cabinetmaker George Hepplewhite. Briggs may have been inspired by Adolf Loos's incorporation of historical objects, such as Chippendale chairs, into his modern ensembles, but she went further in blending furniture details into hybrids of old and new. The buffet (on the left), which was inspired by American Arts and Crafts furniture, recalls a similar buffet designed by Loos around 1900 for Hugo Haberfeld's Vienna apartment.[16] Like Briggs, Loos had spent time in the United States (in the 1890s) and incorporated influences from English and American interior design into his own furnishings after returning to Austria.[17] These borrowings were part of a larger ideological approach to the Westernization and modernization of Viennese domestic culture promoted by Loos, with which Briggs also identified.[18]

Briggs did not have a chance to fully develop her skills as a conduit of international design trends in Vienna as her career was interrupted by the First World War. The economic crisis that ensued meant that there were far fewer commissions available to an independent interior designer. Even had there been such opportunities, it is not clear that her global approach to stylistic influences would have been particularly well received in this era of heightened nationalism. In 1917 Briggs published an article that featured only the work of women designers in Berlin and Vienna, an artistic selection that mirrored the war's political alliance.[19] But this patriotic focus was a brief interlude, and by the 1920s Briggs was back to a transatlantic mixing and matching of influences in her American and Viennese designs.

During the First World War, Briggs was hired to work for Sigmund Járay's internationally known interior design firm. Járay had established his decoration and furniture workshop in Vienna around 1870 in collaboration with his brother Sádro Járay, a sculptor. The firm was well connected with the Viennese modernist movement.[20] Sigmund Járay and Briggs had similar design sensibilities, particularly in their detailed knowledge of historic interior styles, making the firm a useful outlet for Briggs's creative expression. Given the economic crisis triggered by the war, however, Briggs's employment with the workshop lasted only a year.[21]

The interior designs executed by Briggs before World War I reveal that she did not possess a distinctive "Briggs" style. Instead, she applied her international and professional experiences to her interest in local conditions and traditions, which resulted in highly adaptive solutions for public rooms and private spaces, calibrated to the needs of their users. This creative, user-focused, modern approach would form the foundation of her later work as an architect.

Briggs's interiors became a space for new mixtures of design ideas culled from local, national, and global sources. If we focus, as historians often have done, on the development of an individual and consistent aesthetic style as the hallmark of a great designer, then Briggs falls to the wayside, since she did not develop a recognizable personal style. But this misses the point of how Briggs employed her talent and keen attention to different trends and contexts to great effect. Arguably, Briggs's process, whereby she became a thoughtful and self-aware conduit of ideas across borders and created her interiors as places for experimenting with new blends of modern design trends and sources, *was* her style. What seemingly fascinated Briggs—and makes her such an intriguing figure—is her interest in the process of adaptation, one that made design fresh through unique blends that found just the right fit for her clients.

24. Jewish Women Architects in Vienna: Forging and Maintaining Networks of Support in the Interwar Period and Beyond

Ursula Prokop and Elana Shapira

Ella Briggs was not the only woman of Jewish descent who aspired to become an architect in Vienna during the interwar period. The names of many women from diverse Jewish cultural and social backgrounds fill the growing record of professional practice that scholars have amassed in recent times. What impetus gave rise to this striking phenomenon? What mechanisms worked to sustain it? And importantly, in the long run, how did these pathbreaking Jewish women architects fare?

In the early twentieth century, public education for girls and boys in Austria remained separate and unequal. Boys received instruction in mathematics and science, while girls received instruction in the modern languages, literature, and history. By 1910 the growth of private *Gymnasien* for girls in Vienna offered greater opportunities for rigorous secondary education. Propelled by economic prosperity, liberal values that prized modern advances in science and technology, and the desire for social mobility, Jewish middle-class families in Vienna tended to give their daughters higher levels of education than was the norm for most girls.[1] By the 1920s a generation of well-educated Jewish women had come of age and were confidently striving for economic independence.

Such empowering attitudes encouraged Jewish women to try their hand at architecture, even if within Austrian society more broadly it was still considered a "masculine" profession too difficult for women to undertake. Before and during the First World War, the primary option for women seeking to study design in Vienna was the Kunstgewerbeschule (School of Applied Arts), although few specialized in architecture.[2] Some Jewish women, like Briggs, pursued architecture degrees at German universities. When Austrian technical universities opened fully to women in 1919, a notably high percentage of female students were Jewish.[3] In the interwar period, the Jewish women taking architecture classes in Vienna at the School of Applied Arts, Academy of Fine Arts, and Technical University achieved varying degrees of success in the field.[4]

While this new cohort of designers may have encountered raised eyebrows and condescension in certain conservative architects' offices, they would have found encouragement and inspiration in Vienna's culturally engaged Jewish circles. Beginning at the turn of the twentieth century and continuing throughout the interwar period, Viennese patrons of modern architecture and design were largely (although not exclusively) progressive Jewish men and women. Early patrons who set an ambitious example of support for modern architecture, and were later followed by other members of the Viennese Jewish bourgeoisie, included the textile industrialist Fritz

Waerndorfer, who supported Josef Hoffmann and cofounded the Wiener Werkstätte; the tailor Leopold Goldman, who commissioned the Goldman & Salatsch Haus from Adolf Loos; and the author Helene Scheu-Riesz, who together with her (non-Jewish) husband, the lawyer and socialist Gustav Scheu, and her friend, the educator Eugenie Schwarzwald, were also loyal patrons of Loos.

With the rise of antisemitism at the end of the First World War, Jewish patrons began to exercise a preference for hiring Jewish architects. Among the leading patrons who supported modernism and Jewish architects in the interwar period were paper manufacturer Hugo Bunzl and rubber manufacturer Julius Beer, both of whom were loyal clients of Josef Frank; Margarethe Stonborough-Wittgenstein, daughter of the main patron of the Secession movement, Karl Wittgenstein, who commissioned her brother Ludwig Wittgenstein and Paul Engelmann to build a revolutionary modern villa; the textile industrialist Hans Moller, a patron of the arts whose wife Anny Wottitz studied at the Bauhaus, and who became a loyal client of Loos and his wife's friend and colleague Friedl Dicker; and the Ephrussi family, leading patrons of Vienna's Ringstrasse, who gave Liane Zimbler (née Juliana Fischer) her first major commission—the redesign of their bank building.

Leading art and design critics who supported modernism in the interwar period were also Jewish: Max Eisler, who supported (among others) Josef Hoffmann, Oskar Strnad, Josef Frank, and Oskar Wlach; and Berta Zuckerkandl, who continued her support of Hoffmann and the Wiener Werkstätte. Embedded within this milieu, Jewish women seeking to practice architecture had not only prominent sponsors in architectural circles but also influential contacts in social circles, through which they might obtain job leads and secure commissions.

And yet, despite these supportive networks, women still struggled to find their professional footing. Those graduating in the economically turbulent years immediately after the First World War could hardly count on independent architectural commissions. Some found opportunities in the field of interior design, while others secured employment in construction offices. Misogyny and antisemitism within Viennese society presented additional real and enduring barriers to professional advancement: in seeking career opportunities, Jewish women faced prejudice not only as women but also as Jews.[5] Julius Klinger, a leading Viennese illustrator and graphic designer, joined Loos in attacking the "feminization" of Wiener Werkstätte design. Klinger complained, in overtly sexualizing tones: "One immediately thinks of something splayed out, over-the-top, affected, titillating, bogus, fake, and above all, s u p e r f l u o u s: in a word, of a product of the WW, Wiener Weiberkunstgewerbe"—(Arts and Crafts of Vienna Broads; a play on the actual name, Wiener Werkstätte, or Vienna Workshops)—"who doesn't dread the feminine horror?"[6] Klinger admired critic Karl Kraus and may have been inspired by the latter's persistent mockery of the professional and cultural pretensions of Jewish women, whom Kraus portrayed as superficial, materialistic slaves to fashion and as untalented.[7]

Though Briggs herself did not publicly comment on such stereotypes, it does not mean she did not concern herself with their potential damage. In a 1911 letter she wrote to the director of the Austrian Museum of Art and Industry about her ambitious plan to open a retail store representing Austrian firms in New York, she had been careful to stress that she was also working on her own designs at the time and did not want to be seen as a "mere" retailer.[8] As an architect in the interwar period, Briggs steadfastly maintained a professional public image that emphasized her concerns for helping others through developing economical and practical forms of housing. This stance does genuinely capture her architectural philosophy. It also serves to undermine the broader prejudice against Jewish women, exemplified in Kraus's writings, for their supposed tendencies to pursue expensive, frivolous, and lavish design.

More broadly, Jewish women fought back against such obstacles with the help of women's rights advocates and writers, many of whom were Jewish themselves.[9] They included feminist Yella Hertzka, art magazine editor Else Hofmann, and publisher and journalist Gisela Urban. Hofmann and Urban were highly supportive of professional women in the arts, including Briggs, Zimbler, and Käthe Böhm.[10] Their journalistic efforts gave female designers the public exposure they needed to attract new commissions. Working together, journalists and architects formed a female collaborative of sorts within interwar Viennese society that bolstered one another's success.

And there were successes. After studying at the School of Applied Arts, Friedl Dicker continued her education in Weimar at the Bauhaus, becoming one of the few Viennese designers to attend the renowned German school. Upon graduating she returned to Vienna and, together with her fellow Bauhaus student Franz Singer, ran a busy architecture and interior design studio during the 1920s. In addition to architectural projects such as the Heller Tennis Club (1928) and the Auersperg-Hériot Guest House (c. 1933), the studio designed the furniture for the Montessori Kindergarten (c. 1932)—an innovative progressive educational institution—located within the Goethe-Hof municipal housing complex.[11]

Yet the period for such flourishing was all too short. Whereas in Germany women gained the right to matriculate by 1909, in Austria women had to wait until 1919 in order to earn a degree in architecture at a technical university.[12] That delay of a decade would prove decisive, and few of the early Jewish female graduates of Vienna's Technical University would go on to have thriving professional careers in Austria. The rise of National Socialism in Germany made an already difficult professional environment, plagued by prejudice and sexism, precarious. With Austria's annexation by the Nazis in 1938, it became downright dangerous. Jewish professors and students were expelled from all institutions of higher learning, with only a few dissertation candidates given short amounts of time to finish up. Architects and designers like Briggs turned to professional mentors and colleagues, as well as to social and familial networks, to seek work abroad. Many of those who remained in Austria and Central Europe would perish in the Holocaust. Among them was Dicker (married Dicker-Brandeis), who, having relocated to Czechoslovakia, was deported to the Theresienstadt concentration camp and later murdered at Auschwitz in 1944.[13] Briggs was one of the few Jewish women architects who started early enough and remained long enough to complete large-scale architectural projects in Austria and Germany.

And yet, what could not be accomplished at home sometimes became possible in exile. For some Viennese Jewish women designers, their careers expanded after their forced emigration. Hilde Blumberger (née Pick), a pupil of Josef Hoffmann, was one. Her cheerful, colorful textile designs became immensely popular with fashion companies. After fleeing to England during the Second World War, where she changed her name to Jacqueline Groag, she emerged as one of the most influential UK pattern designers of the postwar era.[14] Similarly, after moving to the United States in 1938, Zimbler ran a successful interior design firm in Los Angeles. Zimbler's daughter followed in her mother's footsteps and became an architect, and the two subsequently worked together.[15] Käthe Böhm, the first woman to graduate in electrical engineering from Vienna's Technical University, toured the United States in 1925 to learn about modern technology in the home. In the 1920s and 1930s, she showcased her own technological innovations for the home in building exhibitions in Munich and Vienna. In 1932 she opened a shop in Vienna where women could test out a model kitchen equipped with electric appliances.[16] After immigrating with her parents to Haifa (then in British Mandatory Palestine), she opened her own technical consulting office.[17]

Other Jewish women architects from Vienna experienced most of their professional success in exile. Elizabeth Scheu Close—daughter of Helene and Gustav Scheu—introduced Austrian modernist design principles to Minnesota in the United States, with a portfolio of hundreds of buildings.[18] After becoming the first female graduate in architecture from Vienna's Technical University in 1926, Helene Roth established a thriving interior design practice in British Mandatory Palestine, and later Israel, in partnership with German émigré Alfred Abraham. Dora Gad, too, found success there, enjoying a long and brilliant career as an architect and interior designer who developed her own original interpretation of modernism, showcased at the Israel Museum (with Al Mansfield) and National Library of Israel (with husband and partner Yehezkel Gad), both in Jerusalem, among other locations nationally and abroad.[19]

Yet rebuilding a creative career in exile was difficult work. Leonie Pilewski, whose life and work share significant parallels with Briggs's own, despite their age difference, was also among those who managed to do so through persistence and reinvention. Pilewski's family moved to Vienna from Vynnyky in Galicia (today western Ukraine) when she was a young adult, with the outbreak of the First World War. After auditing classes at the Technical University and being refused permission to matriculate, just as Briggs was, she obtained her diploma at the Technische Hochschule Darmstadt (Darmstadt Technical University) in 1922. Briggs received her diploma from the Technische Hochschule München (Munich Technical University) in 1920.

Early in her career, Pilewski worked in the Soviet Union, designing workers' housing in Moscow (1926–1928) and later publishing on new architectural developments in the Soviet Union.[20] Pilewski viewed communist ideology as having a positive influence on modern design as part of the broader reorganization of Soviet life and culture. In her writings, she praised the solutions she witnessed in the design of collective housing, such as the fact that the apartments were equipped with functional furniture and that the residents were not allowed to bring their own. Pilewski also appreciated

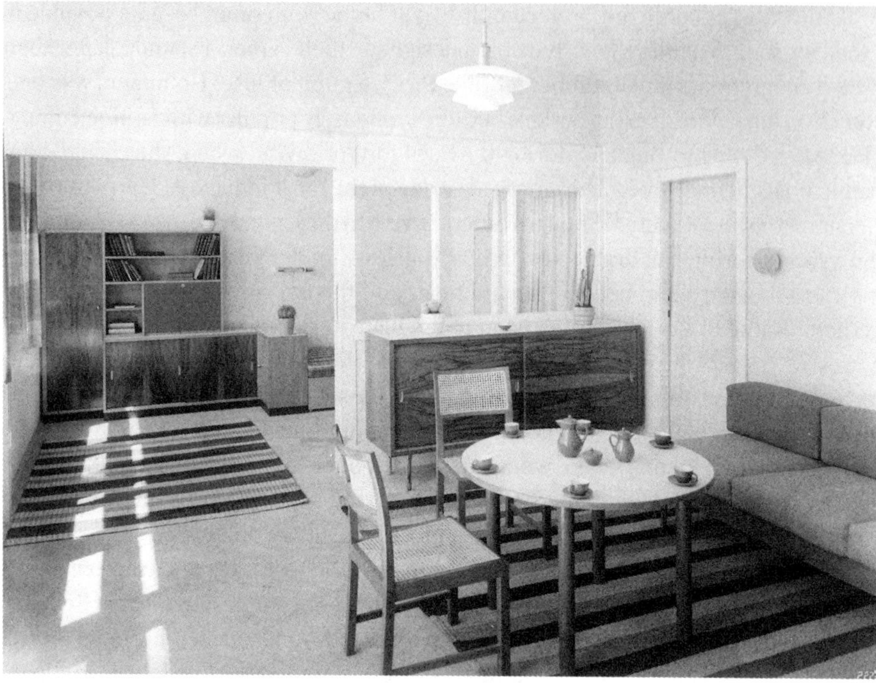

Fig. 24.1 Leonie Pilewski, interior of the Hugo Häring House No. 1, Vienna Werkbund Housing Settlement Exhibition, 1932. (Photograph by Julius Scherb.)

how Soviet design developments were used as a means to educate the new woman and man.[21] Although Briggs's views were less politically radical, her social housing in Red Vienna and her Mariendorf housing complex in Berlin demonstrate her adherence and commitment to Social Democratic values, as do her writings from this period.

After the Soviet Union, Pilewski worked briefly in Switzerland before returning to Vienna, where she designed interiors and furniture, published in architecture journals, and participated in modernist conferences and exhibitions. Like Briggs, who wrote about the rationalization of the household in women's magazines and technical journals, Pilewski advocated for design that eased housework, particularly for career and working-class women.[22] Both architects participated in major design exhibitions that brought their ideas to a broader sphere. In 1932 Pilewski designed the interiors of the Hugo Häring House No. 1 at the Werkbundsiedlung, a modernist housing settlement and exhibition in Vienna (fig. 24.1). A year earlier Briggs had exhibited at the *Deutsche Bauausstellung Berlin* (German Building Exhibition in Berlin), where her Mariendorf housing complex was featured alongside the work of celebrated modernist architects.

Confronting the dangers of life in Austria under Nazi rule, both Pilewski and Briggs chose exile. On the very day of Austria's annexation, March 12, 1938, Pilewski, wanted by the Gestapo, fled the country, eventually immigrating to Stockholm, where she continued a career as a painter, exhibiting regularly in Sweden and abroad.[23] Her choice of Stockholm may have grown out of an earlier experience: In 1934 Jewish socialist politician and future Austrian chancellor Bruno Kreisky had helped her to exhibit her designs in that city.[24] Briggs received some support from Jewish émigrés as well while she was in exile in London. Potentially benefitting from her earlier contact with the sociologist of Jewish descent Otto Neurath, she obtained a large housing commission in Bilston, extending her architectural career into the postwar period. Kreisky and Neurath formed part of Austria's political and cultural networks, respectively, that helped Jewish female émigrés to reestablish their professional careers on new soil.

Briggs's story shares elements with those of many different women who entered the male-dominated fields of architecture and design in Vienna during the interwar years. Looking back at that period and at the hurdles these architects faced, their successes are truly extraordinary. The contribution of Jewish women architects in particular to the development of modern design, both at home and in their adoptive lands, validates their enormous strengths and talents. It also attests to their professional savvy, as they maintained networks of support among their teachers, fellow students, patrons, and work colleagues, as well as their media savvy, as they continued to provide desirable content for the architectural press and for women's magazines.[25] Finally, it speaks to the power and persistence of their cultural connectedness, as they appealed to familial and social circles for critical support in order to secure work and maintain financial stability under challenging political circumstances. For decades, these designers had been all but forgotten; as research progresses and their life stories come to light, we note their accomplishments with awe.

25.
Under Different Circumstances: Ella Briggs and Margarete Schütte-Lihotzky

Monika Platzer

For a short time during the interwar period, the career paths of Austrian architects Ella Briggs and Margarete Schütte-Lihotzky converged in significant ways. Although Schütte-Lihotzky was seventeen years Briggs's junior, both reached important professional milestones. Political and social changes in Austria and Germany after the First World War created new professional opportunities for women, and Briggs and Schütte-Lihotzky seized them. In 1925 Briggs became the first female architect admitted to the Zentralvereinigung der Architekten Österreichs (Central Association of Austrian Architects). A year later, in 1926, Schütte-Lihotzky became the first female architect to be employed by Frankfurt's municipal building department.

The architects' paths would diverge, however, when Schütte-Lihotzky designed a fitted kitchen as part of Frankfurt's municipal housing program directed by Ernst May (fig. 25.1). The Frankfurt Kitchen, as it became known, was installed in large numbers between 1926 and 1932, its extreme functionality attracting the attention of consumers as well as the international media. Schütte-Lihotzky became one of the few women within the profession to achieve worldwide recognition.

In Schütte-Lihotzky's opinion, her kitchen design's celebrity came back to haunt her, because it obscured the view of her diverse body of work and also perpetuated a gendered stereotype that limited female architects to designing for certain spheres, such as children's rooms and kitchens. Late in life she remarked, "If I had known that everyone would keep talking about nothing else, I would never have built that damned kitchen!"[1]

Schütte-Lihotzky struggled in her own way, just as Briggs struggled in hers, to gain the recognition she desired within a profession overwhelmingly dominated by men and associated with masculinity. But while Schütte-Lihotzky became well-known as the poster girl of an architectural avant-garde, Briggs sank into oblivion. This raises the question, how did Schütte-Lihotzky escape Briggs's fate?

The pathways Schütte-Lihotzky followed to formal education, which she was able to pursue without interruption, and to professional practice, were contributing factors to her success. Like Briggs, she attended the Vienna School of Applied Arts; but in 1915, at the very beginning of her studies, she was admitted to Oskar Strnad's architecture class, which had been founded the previous year. Directly after completing her studies, Schütte-Lihotzky began working, shifting between various organizations: the municipal building department in Frankfurt, but also housing cooperatives in Vienna and various architecture and planning agencies in the Soviet Union. Chiefly a full-time employee until 1937, Schütte-Lihotzky became part of a network of (predominantly male) avant-garde architects. Through this network she gained access to other commissions.

By contrast, Briggs's pursuit of architectural education and practice took less straightforward routes. Structural discrimination meant that her educational journey was more indirect. It was not until 1920, at the age of forty, that she finished her architectural studies at Munich's Technical University. Briggs's willingness to relocate for her work, a sign of the high professional commitment already evident in her earlier career as an applied artist and interior designer, continued out of necessity after her graduation. Pursuing new projects, she travelled between the United States and Austria, as well as to Italy and Germany, before being forced to emigrate as National Socialism took hold in Central Europe. In England she found herself without strong connections to architects or government agencies willing or able to provide her with steady work. Admittedly, on a few early occasions, Briggs had received commissions through family

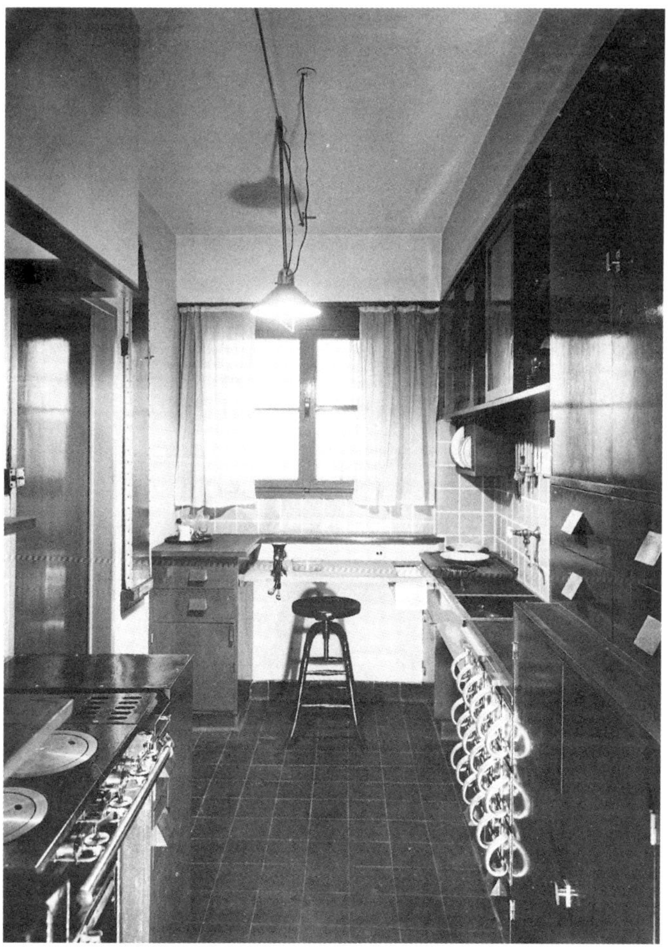

Fig. 25.1 Margarete Schütte-Lihotzky, Frankfurt Kitchen, Frankfurt, 1927.

connections; particularly, via her brother Moritz Baumfeld in New York and his in-laws in Breslau. But otherwise, she was among those women in architecture left to carve their own path and open their own doors.

Both Briggs and Schütte-Lihotzky used the political climate of Red Vienna as a testing ground for new ideas. In two articles published in 1928, journalist and women's rights activist Gisela Urban drew attention to the projects of the young and promising Schütte-Lihotzky, including her 1924 design for a wing of the Winarsky-Hof (a commission shared with other architects), as well as to those of the more experienced Briggs, whose solo-designed Pestalozzi-Hof was completed by 1927.[2] In addition to the innovative architectural aspects of their work, Urban emphasized the competencies of both architects in interior design. More broadly, if implicitly, the articles made the case for greater recognition of the two architects' work and their continued involvement in Viennese building activity. Yet by the time Urban's articles appeared, both women had already left Austria—Schütte-Lihotzky for Frankfurt, and Briggs for Berlin.

Following her departure, Briggs shifted her publishing efforts to German specialist building journals such as *Bauwelt* and *Deutsche Bauzeitung*. Presenting herself as an expert, her tone was sober and factually descriptive, in keeping with her professional self-image. Briggs's essays on the kitchen and the access-gallery apartment building in a 1930 handbook of housing commissioned by the German Association for Housing Reform attest not only to her architectural expertise but also to her social commitment to improve the housing conditions of the wider population.[3] Although no evidence has been found that the two architects ever met, Briggs clearly knew of Schütte-Lihotzky, whose Frankfurt Kitchen she discussed in the handbook. Of note are Briggs's critical comments on a design she otherwise viewed as a success. She pointed out that the haybox and the uniform sizes of the food storage bins did not correspond to actual consumption habits. In contrast to a complete rationalization of all processes, Briggs advocated a kitchen layout that allowed users to work in an individualized way.[4] Briggs's objection to the uniformity of the kitchen's built-in furniture and fittings has parallels to Josef Frank's critique of modernist dogma: he, too, voiced his opposition to utilitarian doctrines of housing reform by promoting variety and choice.

Despite Briggs's expressed commitment to and experimentation with the rationalization of housework during the interwar period (and beyond), she did not have the same opportunities to apply her ideas with a thoroughness or on a scale comparable to Schütte-Lihotzky's Frankfurt Kitchen. Moreover, in neither Briggs's writings on such processes nor in her realized architectural projects did she develop a prototypical image of a kitchen similar to that of Schütte-Lihotzky. By contrast, the Frankfurt Kitchen was immediately mediatized after its rollout. Focus on this prototype in later histories of the modern movement tended to overshadow the breadth and volume of work being done in this period by other architects in the realm of home economics.

Indeed, and as Schütte-Lihotzky herself maintained, this narrow focus, reinforced by historians, has overshadowed the complexity of Briggs's and Schütte-Lihotzky's work in the interwar period, including in social housing. Schütte-Lihotzky's designs for settler housing and especially her fully furnished core-house types (small settler dwellings that could be extended, when time and resources permitted) for the building office of the Österreichischer Verband für Siedlungs- und Kleingartenwesen (Austrian Association for Settlement and Allotment Gardens) reveal her intensive efforts to improve the housing conditions of working-class women. Briggs's innovative design for the Ledigenheim (adjoining the Pestalozzi-Hof), which became Vienna's first municipal student dormitory, reconceptualized domestic space for single people.[5] Later in Berlin, in 1931, Briggs's prototypes for a housing settlement of unemployed families offered exemplary ways to create cost-effective self-build construction that gave residents the opportunity for future growth.[6] Acknowledging how pressing a topic this was at the time, that same year *Bauwelt* announced a competition for "The Growing House."[7]

In the end, Schütte-Lihotzky's work became better known than that of Briggs for reasons that are varied and complex. The generational differences between the two women—Briggs ended her studies at the Vienna School of Applied Arts in 1906, almost a decade before Schütte-Lihotzky entered in 1915—influenced their circumstances. Importantly, Schütte-Lihotzky operated in a professional environment shaped by the influential architects of her time: Oskar Strnad, Adolf Loos, Wilhelm Schütte, Ernst May, Clemens Holzmeister, and Bruno Taut. Her oeuvre thus has been scrutinized in the contexts of their contributions, from the settlers' movement in Austria to *Neues Bauen* in Frankfurt and Moscow. Indeed, Schütte-Lihotzky's work has always been assessed within the framework of the pioneers of the modernist avant-garde. Until very late in life, she remained available to an international research community as a sought-after witness to—and protagonist of—this twentieth-century transnational movement.

Schütte-Lihotzky also made her own considerable efforts to write herself into this avant-garde history by constructing her own narrative. She published two books: a political memoir about her time in the communist resistance, and a reflection on her journey to becoming an architect.[8] These writings solidified Schütte-Lihotzky position as a communist and as an architect, and helped establish her as an exceptional female figure within a history of architecture mostly chronicled by—and about—men. Hailed as "Austria's first female architect," Schütte-Lihotzky's fame obscured the view of other early women practitioners—even Briggs, whose entry into professional practice actually predated that of her younger colleague.

In contrast to Schütte-Lihotzky's work, Briggs's oeuvre ranges across multiple disciplines. It encompasses works of craft, interior design, architecture, exhibition design, photography, and architectural criticism. Additionally, her oeuvre exhibits countless stylistic disruptions and discontinuities. Her domestic projects in the United States have been largely omitted from studies of her work, either out of ignorance of their existence or because her designs deviated from the modernist canon in their outward appearance. Ironically, her large-scale cooperative housing in Vienna and Berlin has been interpreted as conventional in the sense of its alleged strict adherence to the principles of *Neues Bauen*.[9] This assessment is based on the false assumption that the designs of the Pestalozzi-Hof and Ledigenheim in Vienna and the Mariendorf apartment building in Berlin are prescribed exclusively by the (supposedly standard) aesthetic principles of that movement. Viewed from this perspective, Briggs has been denied an independent contribution to the change and evolution within that very movement.

Unlike some *Neues Bauen* protagonists, Briggs never advocated for a uniform "style of the time." Her work was shaped by trends in architectural reform that emerged around the turn of the twentieth century and that rejected historicism in preference for a rootedness in local contexts. In the interwar period Briggs further simplified and rationalized her architectural designs in closer alignment with the *Neues Bauen* movement, which became known globally as the International Style. Yet this style was itself never uniform, incorporating local differences as well as diverse ideas about modern lifestyles and social relationships.

Over the course of her long career as a practicing architect, Briggs repeatedly devised strategies to adapt her designs to the diverse economic and cultural contexts within which she worked. Her stylistic pluralism, among other approaches, testifies to her ability to respond thoughtfully to each client and set of circumstances she encountered. To write a cultural history that can encompass these various complexities, including Briggs's gender, Jewish identity, and the political and social frameworks of the periods within which she operated, yields an outlook at odds with the linear narrative of "heroic modernity." The fact is that such complexities in the work of women architects have met with little understanding or even tolerance from architectural historians. Simply adding Briggs to the modernist canon, therefore, will not suffice; rather, it is a matter of shifting perspectives and rethinking frameworks in such a way that will prevent one type of architect or one type of architectural career from continually coming to the fore.

Briggs died in 1977 in England without, it seems, having returned to Austria or Germany after the war. Perhaps she was reluctant to travel because of illness or advancing age, or because those countries no longer resembled the ones she had known. In contrast to Schütte-Lihotzky, who had returned to Vienna in 1947, Briggs did not have much of an opportunity to influence how her architectural legacy would be interpreted by historians in the countries where she had once worked. In her later career, Briggs published regularly in *Homes and Gardens*, whereas earlier in her career, while in Germany, she contributed extensively to professional journals. Founded in 1919, *Homes and Gardens* was a successful home-interest magazine offering its readers trusted advice from experts. Briggs's articles provided design solutions to a broad range of client needs, from those of newly married couples to families with children to elderly people. She created exemplary, affordable floor plans, replete with built-in furniture. The exteriors she illustrated drew on a broad repertoire of types, ranging from English cottages to modernist villas.

Schütte-Lihotzky, too, rarely published in professional journals after 1945. Her texts appeared almost exclusively within the communist milieu, in magazines such as *Stimme der Frau* (Woman's Voice), published by the communist women's movement. In this journal she published a series of educational articles on the subject of housing comparable to those written by Briggs.[10] That both Briggs and Schütte-Lihotzky were writing for women's magazines (albeit for different socio-economic classes) after the war raises the question of whether this was by choice or because of gender limitation, as well as the question of what we miss when we overlook such sources in architectural history.

Even while fleeing Nazi terror, Briggs preserved what she could of her archive, bringing professional records—photographs, contracts, and more—to England. Drawing on this documentation, she filed a number of restitution claims with the Federal Republic of Germany in the 1950s. This process created its own kind of archive, which has been invaluable in reconstructing her biography. When Briggs died, most of the material she had with her in the United Kingdom sadly vanished.[11] When later, historians began to take an interest in her career, they had only fragments to work with and trouble reconstructing the international scope of her activities and influence. This earlier research remained stuck inside national boundaries and obscured the complex, border-crossing social and political realities of this pathbreaking woman.

By contrast, the scholarly reappraisal of Schütte-Lihotzky's work began during her own lifetime. Research on gender and women's histories emerging in the 1980s led to the 1993 exhibition *Margarete Schütte-Lihotzky: Soziale Architektur; Zeitzeugin eines Jahrhunderts* (Margarete Schütte-Lihotzky: Social Architecture; Eyewitness to a Century), which was accompanied by a catalog of work.[12] The breadth and depth of research on Schütte-Lihotzky, which continues to this day, was enabled by the fact that its subject managed to save her archive through tumultuous times. Over the years, Schütte-Lihotzky meticulously organized it and, following the exhibition, donated it to her alma mater, today's University of Applied Arts Vienna. The preservation of this archive represents a stroke of luck for gender and other researchers; the collection is one of the most frequently used among the university's holdings. Having been born nearly two decades after Briggs, Schütte-Lihotzky was not only able to witness her own rediscovery but also actively participate in it. In contrast to Briggs, who remained in exile without a strong support network, Schütte-Lihotzky received support from the Austrian Communist Party when she returned to Austria after the war. She had joined the party in 1939 and retained a strong connection to it for the rest of her life, receiving commissions from the party and continuing her journalistic work within its orbit. Yet it should not go unsaid that anti-communist sentiment in Austria did exert a detrimental effect on her architectural career.

A lack of adequate sources is often cited as the reason that women architects are written out of history. Briggs shares the fate of double discrimination with many of her female colleagues. Not only did structural inequalities minimize their professional opportunities, but also only those women whose architectural oeuvres were equal in form and measure to those of their male colleagues typically received recognition. Just how much has been missed as a result, even within Austria, is suggested by recent research that identified more than two hundred women enrolled in architecture at Austrian universities prior to 1938.[13] A global history of women architects (without men) requires new approaches and modes of inquiry.[14]

Indeed, new research methods and archival practices have already demonstrated that there are other paths we can follow to recover women's stories. The Architekturzentrum Wien has partnered with the transnational research collective that produced this volume, the first comprehensive biography of Ella Briggs, to ensure that the many disparate sources brought together with great effort from around the world will not disperse yet again. The extremely varied materials gathered by the researchers—including magazines, family heirlooms, photographs, plans, and even furniture, from public and private archival collections—have been assembled in a virtual and physical archive. Ultimately, these materials will be incorporated into the Architekturzentrum Wien's collections database and made available to the public.

The Architekturzentrum Wien's aim is not only to act as a focal point for future research on Briggs but also to make the Ella Briggs holdings in the Architekturzentrum Wien collection a prototype for female architects similarly lacking a robust physical archive. We see the interdisciplinary and collaborative research initiative we have undertaken with the authors in this volume as a model study of how to recognize and eliminate blind spots in archival collections and explore new directions. We hope this model will provide inspiration for how to deal in more innovative ways with those instances in which there is no surviving archive in the traditional sense.

In light of the social inequities women have faced and the tendency of many women architects to relocate across national borders, we must develop new approaches to collecting artifacts and information about their work. With the establishment of the archive and the publication of this volume, the immediate goal of shedding light on Ella Briggs's life, work, and influence has been accomplished. Yet the ultimate objective remains: to bring many more such women out of the shadows and into the realm of public knowledge.

26.
Why Ella Briggs Captivates Us: A Female Challenger of Modernism

Dörte Kuhlmann

In recent years, robust and meticulous research has unearthed materials about women in architecture once thought to have been lost forever. In the case of Ella Briggs, scattered and long-forgotten educational records, photographs, letters, project information, articles, and other pieces of her fascinating life-puzzle have come to light. Viewed as a collection, these fragments form a picture not only of her physical contribution to the emergence of modern architecture in the early twentieth century but also of the ideas, influences, theoretical concerns, and unique creativity she brought to that enterprise.

Briggs captivates us not only with her courageous personality but also with her innovative challenges to the male-dominated realm of modernism. Initially trained in the largely female sphere of graphic design, she managed to escape the gendered boundaries of artistic production to enter a professional field—architecture—then reserved for men. She succeeded in obtaining commissions and demonstrated that she could do much more than simply cope with her male competitors, developing and vocally asserting her own ideas as a woman architect.

When assessing Briggs's contributions, we need to consider her career in the context of Vienna at the turn of the twentieth century, when the city represented one of Europe's most important art and design centers. The flourishing metropolis was populated by artists and intellectuals of international repute and offered progressive new educational opportunities for women of Briggs's social class, particularly in the applied arts. In view of her proximity as a student to Vienna's artistic luminaries, especially those within the Secession and Wiener Werkstätte, should we regard Briggs as a typical representative of what would become known as Austrian modernism, or did she develop her own approach? Even a brief reflection on an early project suggests it was the latter, that in finding her own position as an artist and as a woman, she emancipated herself from her own gendered Viennese education.[1]

In 1908, while sharing the German Theater commission in New York with other artists, Briggs designed the theater's social rooms—the smoking salons, ladies' parlors, and dining room—independently. Despite collaborating with the famous artist Alphonse Mucha, who oversaw the auditorium's design, she did not subordinate her approach to his. Unlike Mucha's somewhat outdated Art Nouveau style, Briggs created architectural compositions far more progressive in their simplicity and restraint. Beyond her innovative color schemes, the more casual arrangement of the furniture itself drew on developing modernist ideas from Vienna. Yet her design does not constitute a direct importation of Viennese Secessionist design, with its preference for a seamless *Gesamtkunstwerk* (total work of art), to the New World. Rather,

Briggs contributed an interpretation of her own with a symbiosis of European interior design and American modernism.[2] Although Vienna's School of Applied Arts typically trained its graphic design students to create recognizable, repetitive patterns, Briggs produced something different and more fluid here. She realized that the American metropolis, with its own evolving identity, demanded from architects and artists a different strategy than that employed in Vienna.

Indeed, the American way of life appears to have had a lasting influence on the young Briggs, just as it did earlier on her renowned colleague Adolf Loos, whose works and writings readily referenced progressive American culture from a Viennese point of view. Briggs and Loos together occupied an important professional circle in Vienna. Both architects created seemingly "simple" small houses—Briggs, rural; Loos, modernist—and later devoted themselves to the development of large, modern, and visionary buildings within a democratic tradition. In 1910, toward the end of the monarchy, Loos designed the Goldman & Salatsch Haus, a commercial and residential building opposite the royal court at the center of the city, and the following decade Briggs designed the Pestalozzi-Hof in the nineteenth district as part of the ambitious Red Vienna housing reforms.[3] Both of these projects were part of evolving democratic discourses in Austria about the rights of citizens, expressed through design—for Loos, in the political meaning of his aesthetics; for Briggs, in the rationalization of the floor plan.[4] From the United States, both architects drew on American building culture, and particularly its advanced domestic technologies, as part of that search for greater equality.

Loos was one of the few Central European architects who had also experienced the advanced plumbing infrastructure of the United States and England. He realized its importance, claiming that water usage correlated with a society's level of progress. In an essay written in 1898, Loos advocated adopting these sanitary advances; he titled the essay "Die Plumber" (after the English), as at that time there was still no German term to describe the new technology.[5] Briggs endorsed the mission to raise awareness of the importance of integrating bathrooms into the home and the need for proper installation. Indeed, in her later exhibition work, she made the technology of plumbing a focal point of display (see fig. 16.4).[6]

In contrast to Loos, who experienced and admired the United States from a visitor's perspective, Briggs worked there professionally. Thus, she had the opportunity to export her Viennese artistic lineage to New York and, in turn, to bring the influences of New York back to Vienna. Wherever she travelled, Briggs collected ideas and concepts in order to incorporate them later in the appropriate place. After returning to Vienna from New York in the mid-1920s, she introduced a household amenity already typical in American households: the bathroom. Briggs incorporated a shower together with a toilet in her design for a 38-square-meter apartment, proposed for Vienna municipal housing. Praised in the September 15, 1926 issue of *Zentralblatt der Bauverwaltung* (the official journal of Berlin's Building Department), the bathroom was a novelty in Viennese social housing.[7] The inclusion of this amenity confirms the decisive impact the American kitchen and bathroom planning had on Briggs's experience. More than mere design concepts, the introduction of bathroom and kitchen improvements (including indoor plumbing, refrigeration, and laborsaving appliances) was transformative in domestic architecture of the twentieth century. Briggs's (ultimately unsuccessful) effort to introduce these into the apartments of Vienna's social housing program was just as radical an innovation as Margarete Schütte-Lihotzky's introduction of the Frankfurt Kitchen to social housing in Germany in the same period.[8] How truly revolutionary Briggs's idea was in 1920s Vienna can be deduced from the fact that the apartments in the city's most famous superblock, the Karl-Marx-Hof (1930), would not possess their own bathrooms until a renovation in 1989.

This comparison of Briggs's work and preoccupations to those of Loos might seem at first glance to be an attempt to embed Briggs within the Viennese artistic circle recognized today as pioneering early modernism. But this would be a simplification—one that would not fully address the complexities of gender and aesthetics in delineating boundaries between outsiders and insiders. Certainly, these circles were comprised of men, positioning the female Briggs as an outsider. But even Loos, while a leading architect in fin de siècle Vienna, also occupied the margins, albeit in a different way: as a notorious taunter, mocking his architectural colleagues.[9] Unlike Josef Hoffmann, who was a well-respected professor and leading figure of the Secession promoting the notion of the *Gesamtkunstwerk*, Loos was a provocateur who dared to challenge what he saw as the false cultural claims of the "inner circle" whenever he got the chance. Against their focus on their own artistic self-realization, he insisted on prioritizing the client's needs—a stance also shared by Briggs. In this sense, both Loos and Briggs were outsiders.

Another prominent member of Vienna's intimate circle with whom Briggs shared many experiences as well as some artistic ideas is Josef Frank. Like Loos, Frank received international recognition for his contribution to modern architecture and the applied arts. But whereas Loos was ten years older than Briggs and thus preceded her in many ways, Frank was five years younger, and yet able (because of his gender) to obtain his architecture degree ten years before her. Nevertheless, Briggs would share with Frank ideas and perspectives on stylistic eclecticism, as well as outspoken skepticism about orthodox modernism's rigidity.

Like Frank, Briggs possessed strong graphic and compositional abilities, and she worked comfortably at a variety of different scales, from small graphic projects as a young illustrator to large buildings as a mature architect. Her early interior designs are fashionable as an independent reworking of the Secessionist style, but also mainstream in the sense that they could be integrated successfully into any household, not just those of the elite. They were decidedly modern but not avant-gardist: in this sense, they seem to anticipate Frank's design ideology of "accidentism" in architecture, which, while rooted in modernism, at the same time sharply critiques its orthodox banality, arguing instead for greater pluralism in design inspired by the element of chance. It rebukes the idea of the *Gesamtkunstwerk*, of the architect as godlike creator. The writing room that Briggs designed around 1913, probably for herself (see plate 8), is a forerunner of accidentism: organized around a collection of cherished objects that appear to have been passed down within the family or acquired over the years, it is a distinctly personal space that integrates individuality, space, and time.[10]

Always client-oriented, both Briggs and Frank varied the stylistic approach to their architectural projects. Each developed a personal signature that transforms in a dialogical way, according to a given client and their environment. While skillfully combining different materials and textures, both exercised their passion for color and innovative spatial arrangements. Yet Briggs arrived at this interplay of ideas through her Viennese design training, together with her engagement with progressive home economics and her concern for women's domestic lives, distinguishing her work in terms of its ambition from Frank's, which overlooked specifically female needs in the pursuit of a pluralistic modernism.[11]

A notable similarity among all three architects was the role influential women played in their careers. Loos received the commission to design Rosa Mayreder's first women's club in Vienna, where he may have become acquainted with his lifelong supporter Eugenie Schwarzwald, a progressive Austrian reform educator. Briggs benefitted from her association with Yella Hertzka, creating an exhibition at her New Vienna Women's Club. Frank was fortunate to establish at a turning point in his career a long and economically profitable relationship with Estrid Ericson, whose Svenskt Tenn design collaborative enabled him to launch a highly successful second career in exile.[12]

More broadly, all three architects had at one time strong networks of patrons and friends who promoted their work. Loos, for example, relied on friends of his Viennese circle such as the critic Karl Kraus to promote his ideas, and influential and internationally renowned clients such as the owners of leading fashion salons Leopold Goldman (Goldman & Salatsch) and Gisela Wolff (Knize) to provide commissions.[13] Yet, in considering these networks of support, we are compelled to question their relative power. For despite being extremely adept at cultivating networks in many different places, Briggs needed to work harder than Loos or Frank to find those next commissions. In exile in England, she struggled professionally in light of her isolation, although insisting to the last on the achievements and fame she had once shared with her Viennese colleagues.

Loos, Frank, and Briggs were certainly unusual. All three were citizens of the world, Viennese trailblazers of early modernism, whose work diverged from the doctrinaire, international modernism that developed subsequently. For this reason, Loos and Frank have typically been grouped into the loosely defined but intriguing historiographical category of the "other modernists."[14] Briggs's career, by contrast, has largely eluded historical scrutiny until now, and she remains an outsider even among these "other" modernists. If, as the architectural historian Beatriz Colomina maintains, promoting one's ideas in mass media constitutes an important hedge against oblivion, then how might Briggs's obscurity today be explained, given that all three of these figures contributed publicly to the theoretical discourses of modernism, especially concerning housing issues?[15] That Briggs's contributions were appreciated in her own time is clear: her international activities, active participation in important exhibitions, and publication of many popular and professional journal articles provide evidence that her engagement in architectural discourses was visible, sought after, encouraged, and sustained. So why was she forgotten, whereas Loos's and (to a lesser extent) Frank's work is remembered in the histories of early modernism?

Today, as we recover her story, Briggs captivates us as a modernist innovator who demonstrated that, against all odds, a woman architect could succeed (to a degree) without being part of modernism's male inner sanctum. From early on she worked independently, in parallel with much more famous players but never subordinating herself to any of them. She actively sought out beneficial connections and patronage but did not ingratiate herself or imitate others to advance her career. Briggs's engagement throughout her life and work with questions about how modernity affected women, and her immersion in circles dedicated to advancing women's causes, from women's clubs to women's magazines, shows that Briggs's "otherness" emerges less out of formal issues than from a deeply personal and philosophical concern about what architecture meant to women's self-actualization. From a historical perspective, she is thus doubly "othered"—as an architect who does not fit neatly into prescribed modernist lines, and as a woman.

This publication and the new research it makes available give us a chance to reconsider Briggs's othering within the historiography of early Viennese modernism as well as broader questions about her pursuit of an architectural career in the first half of the twentieth century and her remarkable professional achievements. Briggs, it is clear, was an exceptionally determined character, whose focus on her artistic vocation and open-mindedness about what was possible contributed to a stunning degree of professional self-realization. Briggs's unflinching desire to escape narrow social conventions in order to realize her own dreams fascinates and inspires us. At the same time, that she never received the level of support that allowed other male architects to soar saddens us, as it leaves many questions about her potential unanswered. Nonetheless, in searching for those answers, there is also hope that history can teach us about building a future for the architectural profession—and its storytellers—that includes instead of others.

27.
The Stowlawn Estate at Bilston as Seen by Today's Residents

Sabrina Rahman

In 1947, Ella Briggs was at the heart of a pioneering development in the West Midlands town of Bilston. The vision of that project closely aligned with the radical housing projects of interwar Vienna she had earlier played a prominent role in creating. And yet, historians who have written about the wider cultural and historical context of the Bilston project have largely overlooked Briggs's contribution.[1] The early involvement of Austrian sociologist Otto Neurath in the planning of a new housing estate perhaps has overshadowed Briggs's work in executing the plan. Her housing designs, which effortlessly blend into the landscape of midcentury regional housing in Britain, may have seemed too ordinary to warrant inclusion in the canonical histories of modern architecture. But at the time Briggs's designs were constructed on the Stowlawn Estate (as it came to be known), their exteriors were remarkable for their light-colored facades, which brighten up the dark brick so characteristic of British vernacular housing from the Industrial Revolution onward, as well as for their interiors, which vastly improved the domestic lives of residents with their novel spatial arrangements (see fig. 19.5).[2] Stowlawn still functions today as a working-class suburb. Its personal stories have not been widely shared nor has Briggs's contribution been widely acknowledged. In 2015 the Bilston Craft Gallery hosted the exhibition *Bilston's Happy Housing: Otto Neurath's Vision for Postwar Modern Living*, cocurated by the author and Carol Thompson; the exhibition's critical reevaluation helped to correct this, by introducing Briggs and the central role she played in the redevelopment of Bilston to a contemporary audience (plate 20).

The seeds of the Stowlawn Estate were first sown in the early 1940s, amid debates about the reconstruction of deprived postindustrial towns in England's "Black Country," a name that reflects the region's long history of coal mining. Land in this region had been made essentially uninhabitable due to the environmental impacts of coal mining and heavy industrialization, and towns, including Bilston, suffered from pollution, poverty, and poor housing.[3] These dire circumstances led to the hiring in 1945 of Otto Neurath as a "Consultant for Happiness" charged with bringing renewal to Bilston.[4] The sociologist's sudden death from a heart attack that same year resulted in Briggs, among other architects, taking over the challenge of pursuing happiness through housing in the geographic center of the Black Country. Briggs would eventually design at least sixteen flats and sixty-six houses around a communal green for the Stowlawn Estate.[5]

Prior to his hiring, Neurath had delivered a talk in 1944 to the nearby Wolverhampton branch of the International Friendship League, an organization dedicated to the global exchange of ideas and cooperation. Neurath, who had fled Austria for the United

Kingdom in 1941, discussed the work on "happiness" he had undertaken in Red Vienna in the 1920s and 1930s, which aimed to create a community of individuals who would think for themselves, feel responsible for each other, and engage with their environment. In 1932 in *Die Form* (The Form), published by the German Werkbund, Neurath argued that it was essential that modern housing allow working-class individuals to achieve *Glücksmaximum* (a maximum of happiness) in real—as opposed to ideal—modern houses and apartments.[6] He asserted that domestic architecture had to react to the changing needs of the individual, who should always be given free choice: this, a critical response to the German modernist predilection for uniform sets of rigid tubular-steel furniture, which for Neurath failed to accommodate the vibrant diversity of modern life. Neurath explained to his listeners in Wolverhampton that his own efforts focused on client empowerment and intergenerational community building—two practices he pursued as a housing consultant in Vienna, especially in the context of the Vienna Werkbundsiedlung (Werkbund Housing Settlement) exhibition.[7]

Neurath's discussion about how client empowerment could lead to greater happiness within the community proved inspiring. In the summer of 1945, Robert Abbott, chairman of the West Midlands Development and Reconstruction Committee (a municipal body created to improve living standards in the region) commissioned Neurath to organize an exhibition on new housing and infrastructure possibilities in Bilston. Neurath visited the town in July and, seeing the social isolation of the elderly, suggested that, "maisonettes for pensioners . . . be scattered among other housing so that the tenants could share to the full in community life."[8] That fall, Neurath was invited to lead local health education initiatives and to consult on Bilston's replanning, which had been under discussion since the late war years.[9] Neurath's death upended these plans; others would step in, however, to continue this work.

Neurath's wife, the German science educator and illustrator Marie Reidemeister, took over the curation of the Bilston Housing Exhibition, which opened in early November 1946 in an empty storefront on Bilston's Oxford Street.[10] On display were Isotype charts featuring the pictorial language that Neurath and Reidemeister had developed in conjunction with the German graphic designer Gerd Arntz at the Gesellschafts- und Wirtschaftsmuseum (Museum of Society and Economy) in Vienna during the 1920s (see plate 14). The charts addressed a range of issues related to housing, health, and community-building in Bilston, including the environmental impact of coal mining on the landscape, the effects of air pollution on the town's children, possible housing solutions to allow more sunlight to enter homes, and leisure facilities to create happier living environments for intergenerational residents.[11] While there is no direct evidence to suggest that the exhibition made a tangible contribution to the subsequent construction of new housing in Bilston, its principles remained in the minds of local authorities as plans for the Stowlawn Estate materialized.

Briggs was hired to help develop the Stowlawn Estate, which had been intended as the culmination of Neurath's project for happier and healthier living in Bilston. Briggs was well versed in ideas of happiness and health and of client empowerment in housing; she espoused them in her writings and advanced them in her built projects. Unfortunately, little archival material remains to tell us about her involvement, or how that may have been shaped by Neurath's Bilston ideas. No evidence directly connects Briggs to Neurath regarding this project. We do know, however, that they corresponded a few years earlier. She certainly was familiar with his work in Vienna, where she had once met him, which in many ways conformed to her own philosophy of social housing. To understand Briggs's contributions, we must rely largely on two 1947 articles published in *The Architects' Journal* and *Homes and Gardens*, which documented the first stage of Stowlawn's planning. This stage focused on a communal green space (later known as Lawnside Green) and featured Briggs's designs exclusively.[12]

Further complicating our understanding of Briggs's role in the project is the involvement of another architect—the renowned British architect Charles Reilly, associated with the pioneering Liverpool School of Architecture. Reilly was initially invited to prepare sketches for Stowlawn as part of Bilston's redevelopment scheme in 1947. Bilston town clerk A. V. Williams, who had been involved in the early planning work with Neurath, was deeply impressed by Reilly's innovative approach to working-class housing—specifically the architect's championing of the use of oval-shaped greens to create a strong sense of community within social housing developments.[13] Although Reilly claimed not to know much about Neurath or his housing consultancy in interwar Vienna, both men shared a strong belief in the importance of communal facilities in creating meaningful modern housing, especially for marginalized groups of people.

Briggs bridged the social and spatial philosophies circulating among progressive British and Austrian reformers, bringing her own experience in public housing to bear on Stowlawn. Her involvement with the Bilston project is not only proof of the expertise that Briggs had gained through Viennese social housing projects in the 1920s but also indicative of her decades-long skills in translating Viennese design principles into new environments. The 1947 article in *The Architects' Journal* featuring Briggs's Bilston designs emphasized the reservation of land for "community buildings, day nurseries, schools, clinics and libraries" and the building of houses around the communal green space.[14] Decades later, Lawnside Green remains a much-beloved place for residents to meet or relax, and especially for children to play (see fig. 19.5, plate 18).

The articles in *The Architects' Journal* and *Homes and Gardens* (the latter written by Briggs herself) note how the architect integrated diverse users into her Stowlawn architectural plans.[15] Rental housing accommodated the elderly, single people, and childless couples, as well as large and small families. Importantly, the four-flat houses were interspersed among single-family homes with the intention of creating a supportive community of residents with diverse needs and backgrounds (see fig. 19.6). This emphasis on cultivating an integrative community derived directly from the approach taken to social housing estates in Red Vienna, which was influenced by Neurath's collaborative consultation work that featured in travelling exhibitions for the Museum of Society and Economy.[16]

If Briggs's site planning for the Stowlawn Estate aimed to preclude a sense of social isolation, in her designs for the house interiors, she promoted comfortable and self-sufficient modern living. In setting up options for both interdependence (on the estate) and independence (within individual homes), Briggs's designs captured Neurath's concept of the "maximum of happiness," which he had sought to bring to Bilston before his untimely death. Living on Stowlawn was thereby easily adaptable to the changing needs and moods of individual residents, with the notion of free choice at the center of Briggs's plans. Each home provided separate living and sleeping spaces, indoor bathrooms, and fully functional kitchens equipped with larders, cooking ranges, and hot water boilers (see fig. 19.7). Living-and-dining room layouts were open in plan to encourage an airy feel, but the rooms' separate functions were clearly marked by a framed recess that encompassed enough space for a dining table (see fig. 19.8). Entrances were private (even in the four-flat houses) and included a hallway intended for hanging outerwear. As a designer in the United States, Briggs had shown a shrewd sensitivity to local traditions and tastes. In Bilston, too, her designs for the house facades blended with the broader landscape of midcentury British vernacular architecture. They were constructed out of brick, clad with cement render, and often painted a neutral color, such as beige. The ground-floor units had small private gardens that could be accessed through the living room, a feature that is typical of many midcentury British homes. A good number of the kitchens, however, instead of being placed at the back of the houses, faced onto Lawnside Green, so that women could easily prepare meals while simultaneously watching their children play outside through a central window (see fig. 19.7). This was a clever design decision by Briggs, which reflects her considered approach to the practical needs of residents.

The rehousing of people in communities such as Bilston was intended in its day to rescue local populations living in poorly maintained and overcrowded industrial workers' housing. This meant that many of the town's low-quality nineteenth-century buildings were demolished and the area redeveloped with modern homes that met the needs of everyday life in the mid-twentieth century. The construction of the Stowlawn Estate, which exemplifies such practices, was met with ambivalence. While many residents appreciated the opportunity to escape the overcrowding and disrepair (as well as the outdoor toilets), others took offense at the assumption that their previous homes were inherently unhygienic—made explicit, for example, in the requirement that all used furniture be fumigated before it was moved into the new houses at Stowlawn. Furthermore, some residents were hesitant about leaving the intergenerational terraces that had fostered tight-knit communities over the decades, where people looked after each other's children in the back alleys.

The 2015 exhibition at the Bilston Craft Gallery documented the memories of Stowlawn's earliest residents through photographic albums as well as recorded oral testimonies that allowed visitors to hear of people's experiences moving from working-class terraces into one of Briggs's modern houses (plate 21). The recordings capture the residents' sense of joy and empowerment, as well as the marked shift in domestic living arrangements that Briggs's houses facilitated. Individuals recalled the excitement they felt as small children in the early 1950s in flipping electric light switches for the very first time. They spoke of the freedom and security they experienced in playing outside while their parents observed from the large front kitchen windows. Many of the recordings address the dire conditions that residents had left in anticipation of higher-quality modern housing. Joanne, who moved onto the estate as a small child, recalled that she had previously lived in a one-bedroom back-to-back terraced house with her grandparents, parents, and two sisters.[17] She described moving onto the estate as a life-changing event for the entire family:

> So when we moved to Stowlawn it was moving into a palace because we had three bedrooms, we had a bathroom, which we had not had before, and mum had this kitchen which she thought was wonderful. And we had a big front room that stretched the whole length of the house, from the window at the front, the window at the back, and a French door onto the back garden, which was a bit posh, really. . . . It was a really happy time because of the freedom that we'd got, and all the places we could play on Stowlawn.

In a particularly animated recording, David, another resident, spoke with great excitement about the modern amenities in his new childhood home: "I remember walking down, seeing where we were going to live: a new house! It's got a toilet upstairs and a toilet downstairs! And electric light! And a radio! That was a novelty. It was the height of luxury, it truly was." Alan, who lived in one of the first houses to have been built on Lawnside Green, had previously lived in a two-bedroom back-to-back house with ten family members: "You're coming from people who had nothing. They lived with their grandparents, their parents, ten to a house, with outside toilets. And then to come to Stowlawn—it was a different environment altogether!" He also credited Briggs's floor plans with helping him to recover from serious illness as a toddler: "The front room was a through room, with parquet tiles. I had meningitis when I was about two and nearly died. I was that weak that I couldn't walk, and me dad bought me a pedal car. And they shifted all the furniture back (it was a big room!), and I used to pedal up and down to get me legs strong." Lastly, Maureen, who moved onto the estate at the age of four, recalled: "We were one of the first in the street, and then across the street a family moved in with two girls, and we are all still friends today."[18]

Briggs helped to realize a shared dream of bringing happiness and health to Bilston. Today, Stowlawn remains the site of a close-knit community, where neighbors continue to meet on Lawnside Green and a variety of housing types still accommodate the diversity of the residents' lifestyles. Her houses at Stowlawn mark a pivotal moment in her architectural practice in Britain, demonstrating her striking ability to adapt Viennese housing principles to the distinctive needs of various people and their environments in her newly adopted land. The fact that the Stowlawn Estate continues to provide quality housing for a working-class community is a testament to the enduring human legacy of Briggs's designs.

Afterword.
Finding Ella Briggs: The Road Travelled

Despina Stratigakos and Elana Shapira

When we began this book project, we asked fourteen other scholars to take a leap of faith with us. Despite the seeming lack of historical materials to work with, we believed we could reconstruct the life and work of Ella Briggs if we tried a novel, team approach. As we conclude, the biggest surprise has been just how much we have been able to discover, even nearly fifty years after the architect's death. Indeed, it is hard to remember the paucity of information with which we began, although easy to recall the longing to know more—a feeling shared by every team member.

This leaves us wondering why an architect as talented and ambitious as Briggs, who had achieved considerable visibility before the Second World War, is not better known today—especially since others before us had kept her memory alive. In 1980, just three years after Briggs's death, the Marxist critic Manfredo Tafuri took note of Briggs's contributions to Vienna's social housing, albeit without expressing interest in the architect herself.[1] Scholars continued to focus on Briggs's work in the Austrian capital, although some have touched on her projects in the United States, Germany, and England.[2] These studies have helped us to understand pieces of Briggs's career. Yet a broader view—one that integrates into her work questions of personal biography, identity, the transatlantic flow of ideas, migration, and forms of patronage—has remained missing until now.

Although Ella Briggs does not represent all women in architecture and her story is very much her own, the challenges she poses to historians inevitably lead to questions about the subjects and methods of architectural history generally. Up until a few decades ago, it was hard to find any book written about a woman in architecture. This lacuna was often blamed on the subjects themselves: women lacked the talent or perseverance (or both) to get ahead in a demanding profession, it was said, and their absence in the history books only reflected their failure to achieve notable things. As feminist scholars have pushed back on this assertion to show just how many accomplished women in architecture have been overlooked by historians and left out of architecture's historiography, there remains a lingering tendency to lay blame elsewhere, rather than to confront the limitations of our own approaches.

Briggs's adaptability to different contexts and her centering of user needs, for example, go against conventional ideas of what makes for a "great" architect—particularly one worthy of inclusion in canonical formulations of modern design, laid out in the glossy tomes that line museum shop shelves. Even if historians like to decode the influences that guided an artist's development, their greatness is generally associated with the emergence of a style that is identifiable as the artist's own. Coherent as well as unique, that style absorbs and supersedes all other influences (including clients' tastes). An artist who refuses to choose one stylistic lane or decides to change lanes too often is perceived as problematic—unless, of course, the artist is Picasso.

For the defenders of a modernist canon thought to begin with the British Arts and Crafts and Viennese Secession movements of the turn of the century and to lead directly to the German Bauhaus, Briggs's apparent lack of concern with stylistic purity constituted a heresy.[3] (For example, she expressed no unwavering preference for the flat roof, and she incorporated both flat and slopping varieties in her work. This went against the dictates of modernism's proponents, such as Ludwig Mies van der Rohe.)[4] And yet, she directly contributed to modern architectural movements, including Viennese modernism and the International Style, both as a designer and as a critical voice in the public discourses that shaped them.

Briggs's Viennese social housing appeared in publications such as *Wasmuths Monatshefte für Baukunst* (Wasmuth's Monthly Magazine for Architecture), which contributed in the 1920s and 1930s to the codification of a modernist canon. But this integration of Briggs's Red Vienna buildings into a strict modernist narrative ultimately did not serve Briggs's career or reputation well, in that it set a precedent for interpreting the architect's work through a narrow, exclusionary lens. The broader arc of her production—works executed in different styles, within different cultural contexts and over the course of different decades—was excluded from view, fostering a fragmentation of her oeuvre.

Much is also lost in our understanding of Briggs's formally modernist projects when we fail to see their continuities with both her earlier and her later work. Indeed, Briggs was remarkably consistent across decades of production in seeing modern design—achieved through thoughtful and flexible planning, the incorporation of technological advances, and the empowerment of users through education—as the driver of individual happiness and social unity. In this sense, Briggs was a modernist through and through.

In laying out a canon of modernist architecture, historians have also overlooked how individual women as well as women's movements influenced design developments.[5] Even today, after fifty years of efforts by feminist architects, critics, and historians, architecture school curricula have a long way to go in integrating women's contributions into the histories and theories of modernist design.[6] Where we do find such attention tends to be where the project fits within a canonically modernist framework—such as Grete Schütte-Lihotzky's gleaming kitchen designs. The roles played by professional women in supporting each other, by female patrons in creating opportunities for aspiring women designers, and by women's organizations more broadly in advancing women's career ambitions, remains little discussed within architectural histories of modernism. This neglect extends to the vehicles women used to communicate and create audiences for their ideas. These include women's magazines, the content of which has long been considered outside the realm of "proper" architectural discourse.

That Briggs can float in and out of a modernist canon as defined from a male perspective adds to the challenges of writing about her. Even when her work seems to square with inherited ideas about modernism, a closer look reveals misalignments. Above all, Briggs focused on defining ways of living that centered women and their own ideas of modernity. This perspective fits poorly into a modernist pantheon, assembled by historians and critics, in which women—as users or designers—are either adjacent to or invisible in constructions of modern life and identity. Writing about Briggs inevitably poses the question, then, of whether we are trying to add her to a sanctioned modernist canon or to dismantle the canon altogether. It would seem, paradoxically, that we are trying to do both. Specifically, we explore the intersections where Briggs locates herself at the center of modernist discussions, but also how those intersections are neither precise meeting points nor divides. The paths Briggs took in her career do not align perfectly with male-focused accounts of modernism, but they also do not entirely diverge. Yet this does not make Briggs herself a paradox. Rather, we contend that the restrictive tools and narratives of architectural history produce the illusion of contradictions, where Briggs herself saw none.

Beyond exclusionary ideas of a modernist canon and who or what belongs, women's disappearance in architectural history is sometimes attributed to their so-called gendered passivity—that is, their willingness to stand in the shadows. Social norms do, in fact, tell women not to be "pushy," and some female practitioners in the past have chosen to quietly "let the work speak for itself"—which it usually does not.[7] This presumption assumes that a woman who steps out of the shadows will find a place in the limelight—meaning that erasure is the (deserved) result of her own avoidance of fame rather than a consequence of how we shine the limelight. Briggs, coming from a family of journalists and editors, masterfully used popular and professional venues to bring attention to her work and to educate the public. Given her fierce efforts to stay in the limelight and to remind everyone of her fame, it is hard to argue that she courted the oblivion that followed her death.

A more unique challenge to writing about Briggs, and one that also flies in the face of gendered expectations, is her peripatetic lifestyle. Briggs is arguably as much a traveler as she is an artist. Travel has long been considered an important path for an artist's development. But in the case of Briggs, she did not just pass through far-flung territories with sketchbook in hand: she stayed, joined local associations, made friends, and pursued commissions. This immersion into different cultural and artistic contexts profoundly shaped her work. It also transformed her into a conveyer of ideas about modernism, for example, by bringing Viennese ideas to New York, and American ideas to Austria. Yet following in Briggs's footsteps is not easy for an individual scholar, and not only because of the time and funding it involves. Researching Briggs also requires specialized knowledge of different eras, geographies, and cultures. Gilded Age New York is not Red Vienna; nor is it postwar England, for that matter. The challenge is further exacerbated by the sheer range of Briggs's talent and activities, which encompassed architecture, exhibition design, furniture making, graphic design, interior design, painting, photography, and writing. Then, too, there are the different languages in which Briggs operated. How could a lone historian keep up?

A conversation in the fall of 2019 about the obstacles to researching Briggs inspired us to try a tactic typically reserved for researching famous men. The International

James Joyce Symposium, for example, has held twenty-nine meetings on the writer to date. What if we organized a single event on Ella Briggs? Our idea was to bring historians from around the world who had studied aspects of Briggs's life and work into one room, to see if collectively we could piece together a larger whole. Then the COVID-19 global pandemic intervened, and international travel stopped. We continued to plan, and in June 2022 we convened a one-day workshop at the Architekturzentrum Wien, the national museum for architecture in Austria.[8] The library was filled to capacity, attesting to a curiosity about Briggs that went beyond our workshop presenters. In 2019, celebrations commemorating the one hundredth anniversary of Red Vienna had raised awareness among the Viennese about the city's "other" pioneering female architect.[9] While the workshop focused on Briggs's relationship to Viennese and Central European modernisms, she also emerged as a subject of interest as a travelling Viennese designer in the United States, and as an émigré in her late career in Britain. Many of the questions raised by participants took up broader issues relating to transnational movements of people and ideas. Some also considered Briggs's Jewish background and how it fit into local as well as wider historical contexts. By the end of the day, we had learned many more things about Ella Briggs, but it had also become clear that the fragments of her life and work would not assemble themselves. We needed a bigger, bolder strategy.

And that is how we became the Ella Briggs Detective Brigade. Sixteen of us scoured archives, libraries, and attics from Berlin to London, Munich, New York, and Vienna, as well as virtual resources, from online shopping venues to genealogy databases, for traces of Briggs. Thanks to the pandemic, we were all familiar with video conferencing platforms, and we used these to meet to share discoveries. Sometimes, in our virtual study room, as we pored over documents, these discoveries happened in real time. As we worked, we also uncovered more gaps in the research. We could not have succeeded in addressing these without the assistance of many archivists, curators, and librarians—from the Museum of Architecture in Wrocław, Poland, to the office of the assessor for the Village of Pelham in New York State—who dug into their own records to provide us with help. They, too, became a part of our international collaborative search brigade.

The ongoing support of the Architekturzentrum Wien proved crucial. They committed to establishing an Ella Briggs archive that would draw on our collaborative work: in the absence of a traditional archival collection, we would create a new one together. They also set up a virtual archive portal, to which all contributors had access and could add materials. We hope that the archive we have assembled, which digitalizes and centralizes sources once scattered across continents, will prove a useful resource for those seeking to further advance knowledge of Briggs.

The decision not to produce a standard edited volume but rather to collectively write Briggs's biography required not only new kinds of technological and institutional support but also—and most importantly—a generosity of time and spirit. Scientists understand that innovation depends on teamwork; universities, publishers, and grant organizations have long recognized and rewarded this kind of collaborative scientific work. In the humanities, by contrast, recognition and reward structures still rely on the increasingly outdated ideal of the lone scholar producing a single-authored work. We perceived that, institutionally speaking, there were potential risks for historians choosing to work in the truly collaborative manner this book required.

Among the questions we asked ourselves, for example, was how we could both join our voices in writing a collective biography and yet also ensure that individual effort be recognized. As a result, our names appear in chapter headings to credit authorship, singly or jointly, even if the feedback and materials shared by others in the team could not always be called out as clearly without overwhelming the endnotes. Although we valued the different timbres of our voices, creating a smoothly flowing biographical narrative did necessitate more stylistic aligning than would a conventional edited volume. We also had to navigate intellectual, cultural, and even linguistic differences among the institutions of knowledge (archives, universities, research centers) to which we belong, and differences in the ways we were used to crafting our scholarship and envisioning our audiences. Here, again, a generosity of spirit got us through the voyage, buoyed by the contributors' unwavering passion to tell Briggs's story in the manner she deserved.

In the past, biographies have been criticized as a model for writing about women in architecture: "By emphasizing an individual's activity within a discriminatory system, it cloaks the workings of discrimination."[10] More recently, there has been pushback against this viewpoint. Feminist scholars interested in the intersectionality of lived experience are turning to biography because it allows a more nuanced understanding of the many forces that impact a person's life and career. Similarly, in presenting Briggs's biography we have explored the circumstances she encountered, where she created and seized opportunities, and how she succeeded or failed. Here, Briggs's identity as a woman is a central component, but it is not the only one; her Jewish background, ethnicity, family networks, education, profession, middle-class status, marriage and divorce, citizenship, linguistic ability, engagement with women's culture, émigré status, and age also played determining roles. The structure of the book helps us to balance these layers: the main biographical section interweaves life and career along a chronological trajectory, while the subsequent reflections consider Briggs's legacies from different perspectives, from the familial to the historiographical. Most of these perspectives arguably inform any conventional biography, but by training additional focus on them in this manner, we call attention to the frameworks that have helped us to see Briggs as a complex individual—one who, propelled by her talent, personality, ambition, experiences, and networks, sometimes achieved remarkable things and other times could not overcome the forces arrayed against her.

Research discoveries about Briggs kept coming, right up to the point when we were required to submit the manuscript to the publisher. We know that more exists to be found and hope the book provides the foundation for new materials, when they appear, to be noticed and incorporated into future histories. Briggs spoke of clients and projects in Europe and the United States that remain mysteries. For example, we know that more of the houses she designed (on either side of the Atlantic) await identification. The reasons for some of her geographical relocations are also not yet clear. What was she doing in Paris? Why did she choose London when she fled the Nazis? We encourage others to pursue these and other yet-to-be-told stories, adding more layers to Briggs's biography and work.

The new projects we succeeded in bringing to light, as well as the greater depth and detail we were able to add to previously known works, challenge received ideas about modernism's development in Central Europe and America. Their stories demonstrate the disruptive power of histories once thought marginal. Considering Briggs's projects across time and place—as well as within varied contexts, including systems of female patronage and support, that are often neglected in traditional modernist histories—we weave together what had until now been single threads into a tapestry of surprising richness and complexity, even if that tapestry remains incomplete. Recovering Briggs's story was never just about her: in seeing her, we see differently.

We hope that, beyond the revelations themselves contained in this book, the methods used to arrive at those revelations will also leave their mark. New collaborative models and innovative partnerships with knowledge institutions (including archives and universities) are needed if humanities scholars are to make research breakthroughs that finally go beyond the limited women's histories that skeptics contend "can only go so far." We want histories of women in architecture that burst with new material and that burst our expectations, and we aim to have them. And indeed, they are coming. Astonishing new histories—in book, exhibition, and social media formats—are emerging through such collaborations, often with the intention of reaching the broader public.[11] These initiatives have instilled new energy and enlisted new audiences in the pursuit of recovering past women in architecture.

This project began with the refusal to believe that Briggs was lost to us forever. It ends with the hope—and conviction—that other intrepid detectives will carry her story even farther, challenging received ideas, discarding old methods, and making new discoveries as they go.

ACKNOWLEDGMENTS

In searching for Ella Briggs, the paths we followed were long and sometimes winding, and along the way we encountered many people who offered directions or accompanied us for a stretch of the journey. Bert Singer and Angela Kimberk were steady companions, providing artwork by Briggs and other family heirlooms that profoundly shaped the book, and that they later gave to the collection of the Architekturzentrum Wien as the foundation stone of its Ella Briggs Archive. (Briggs would have enjoyed the picture they sent us of her work boxed up and transported on a sleigh over Maine snow to the local shipping agent, on its way back to her cosmopolitan birthplace.) We are profoundly grateful for their help, our long conversations, and the connections they helped us make.

We owe an enormous debt to those on the receiving end of those heirlooms: the Architekturzentrum Wien, Austria's national architecture museum, under the leadership of Angelika Fitz and Karin Lux. They were our partners from start to finish, hosting the initial workshop that sparked this book, and then collaborating with us in the creation of the Ella Briggs Archive. They are truly a model for historians seeking new types of relationships with institutions so that we can produce new types of histories. The head of collections Monika Platzer has been an inspirational champion for the project, ensuring that the search for materials in reconstructing Briggs's biography would also stimulate new institutional ways of working. With the dedication of archivist Katrin Stingl, who brought her own expertise and passion to the project, they created a virtual and dynamic archive portal that became the research team's shared site for processing and sharing discoveries. We are deeply grateful to the Architekturzentrum Wien and its staff for their commitment, time, and resources, which helped us not only to achieve our goals but also to reimagine them in bigger and bolder ways.

Materials for this book and for the archive have passed through many helping hands. We received important information about Ella Briggs's commission for the Pringsheim family from Britta Schinzel, Professor Emerita of Mathematics and Computer Science at the University of Freiburg and partner of the artist Rudolf Schönwald, who was the Pringsheims' grandson. Indeed, Dr. Schinzel generously gave a Morris-style chair Briggs designed for the family to the Architekturzentrum Wien, adding plush physical heft to the Briggs archive. We are also grateful for the many hours in conversation with Jeanne Paradise, who shared memories of her friendship with Phylis Morrison, Briggs's grandniece.

We express our sincere thanks to archivists in many locations for digging into their own collections to provide information needed to stitch together Briggs's life and work. Daria Dorota Pikulska, curator of the Interwar Collection in the Nineteenth- and Twentieth-Century Architecture Department at the Museum of Architecture in Wrocław, helped to solve the mystery of Briggs's connection to this city through her own extensive research. We are grateful to the generous curators and archivists at the Museum of Applied Arts Vienna (MAK), with special thanks to Anne-Katrin Rossberg, curator of the MAK Metal Collection and Wiener Werkstätte Archive; Lara

Steinhäußer, curator of MAK Textiles and Carpets Collection; Rainald Franz, curator of MAK Glass and Ceramics Collection; and head of archive Walther Merk. University Archive Director Silvia Herkt of the University of Applied Arts Vienna supported the project with time and resources. At the Archive of the Technical University Vienna, we received help from director Paulus Ebner and historian Juliane Mikoletzky. Irma Wulz, head of the Archive of Vienna's Jewish Community, provided many valuable documents. We are also grateful to Andrea Pahlke of the Berlin Restitution Administration (Landesamt für Bürger- und Ordnungsangelegenheiten Abteilung I–Entschädigungsbehörde, Opfer des Nationalsozialismus); Renate Domnanich at the Austrian State Archives–War Archive; Birgit Ladinig at the Archive of the University of Vienna; Ursula Oswald-Graf of the Backhausen Archive, Leopold Museum in Vienna; Renáta Purnochová of the National Archives (Czech Republic) in Prague; Lynne Crowley of the Larchmont Historical Society, Town of Mamaroneck, New York; Barbara Maloney and John T. Pierpont in the Office of the Assessor, Town of Pelham, New York; and town historian Arthur Scinta, Pelham Town Hall, New York.

Many historians also responded to queries, pulling materials out of their own files to close research gaps and providing insights that gave us new directions to follow. We thank Lori Brown at Syracuse University; Christopher Burke at the University of Reading; S. E. Eisterer at Princeton University; Anca Lasc of the Pratt Institute; Christopher Long at the University of Texas at Austin; Mary McLeod at Columbia University; Pia Pedersen at the Royal Danish Academy; Mary Pepchinski, former professor at the Technical University Dresden; and Leslie Topp, former professor at Birkbeck College, University of London. We are deeply grateful to the anonymous historians who reviewed the manuscript for their excellent guidance.

For help tracking down images in books and journals, we would like to thank librarians at the Austrian National Library, Cambridge University, Carnegie Library of Pittsburgh, Columbia University, Getty Research Institute, Harvard University, Royal Institute of British Architects, Seattle Public Library, Syracuse University, Technical University Vienna, University at Buffalo, University of Chicago, University of Illinois Urbana-Champaign, University of Reading, and University of Texas at Austin. We are also grateful to photographer Benjamin von Radom for his images of Viennese buildings, and architect Paul Sutliff for redrawing a Bilston floorplan.

Along our journey, we were fortunate to find enthusiastic supporters who allowed us to realize our ambitions as the project grew. Funding from the Cultural Department of the City of Vienna made possible the initial workshop on Briggs. As we turned to writing a book, the Botstiber Institute for Austrian-American Studies provided a generous grant that supported the next phase of development. Julia Czerniak, dean of the University at Buffalo School of Architecture and Planning, understood the challenges and potential of this project and provided funding at a critical juncture. At the University of Applied Arts Vienna, former rector Petra Schaper Rinkel and director of publications Roswitha Janowski-Fritsch gave both encouragement and financial help. The support we received from Christie Henry, director of Princeton University Press, with a global equity grant, and from Victoria Wolcott, director of the University at Buffalo Gender Institute, with a faculty research grant, ensured we would cross the finish line.

We also thank Barb Carlson and Janelle Price at the University at Buffalo for their help administering these grants.

When it came time to assemble the manuscript, bringing together stories written by sixteen people in two different languages, we relied on experts to help us compose and calibrate. We are grateful for the diligent work of our translator, Elise Feiersinger. Nancy Eklund, our developmental editor, went above and beyond in working with us to find the logic and poetry of the book, guiding us as we tuned our many voices into a true ensemble. We thank her for her invaluable part in the making of the Ella Briggs story.

And in bringing that story to a broader public, we are immensely grateful for the enthusiasm and support of Michelle Komie, our brilliant editor at Princeton University Press. When we approached her with our idea about the Ella Briggs Detective Brigade, she embraced it and helped us navigate the process of writing a book together, as a team. Her wisdom in devising strategies and helping us to make choices when we hit forks in the road, and especially her unwavering belief that we would reach our final destination, made all the difference. We would also like to thank the many people affiliated with Princeton University Press who assisted along the way from manuscript to finished book, including Lachlan Brooks, Heather Hansen, Jessica Massabrook, Annie Miller, Steve Sears, and Jaden Young.

Finally, all the contributors would like to thank our families and friends for indulging our collective obsession with Ella Briggs and for their patience as we searched into the night for clues on that "one last thing" we needed to check. Sharing the journey with you was a joy.

NOTES

CHAPTER 1. FAMILY LIFE IN AN IMPERIAL CAPITAL: DREAMS OF BELONGING

1 Marsha L. Rozenblit, "A Note on Galician Jewish Migration to Vienna," *Austrian History Yearbook* 19, no. 1 (1983): 143–52.

2 Entry for Josef Baumfeld, *Adolph Lehmann's Allgemeiner Wohnungs-Anzeiger* (Vienna: Alfred Hölder, 1880), 161 [hereafter cited as *Lehmann's*]. Baumfeld held the title of "k. u. k. Advokat," the abbreviation for *kaiserlich und königlich* (imperial and royal), which meant that he served the Emperor of Austria and the King of Hungary and could work in all realms of the empire. In 1857 Ignaz Pisko cofounded the journal *Gerichtshalle* (Court Hall), through which he helped influence and reform legislation. See D. Ströher, "Ignaz Pisko (1828–1905), Jurist," *Österreichisches Biographisches Lexikon, 1815–1950*, vol. 8 (1980), 99–100. Briggs mentions her father's partnership with Pisko in her application for German citizenship: Ella Briggs to Polizei-Praesidium Berlin, March 5, 1932, APr.Br. Rep. 030–06, no. 11426, Landesarchiv Berlin, Germany.

3 Briggs noted her relatives' respectable professions in her application for German citizenship (Ella Briggs to Polizei-Praesidium Berlin, March 5, 1932, APr.Br. Rep. 030–06, no. 11426, Landesarchiv Berlin).

4 Karoline's date (June 6, 1845) and place of birth are recorded in Karoline Baumfeld residence registration, October 2, 1917, Meldearchiv Wien, Wiener Stadt- und Landesarchiv (MA 8), Vienna. For Jewish communities in Galicia, see Suzan F. Wynne, *The Galitzianers: The Jews of Galicia, 1772–1918* (Kensington, MD: pub. by author, 2006).

5 Marriage record of Philipp Bryk and Fanni Reis, June 25, 1871, Israelitische Kultusgemeinde Wien, Vienna, Austria [IKG].

6 Ella Briggs to Phylis Morrison, March 16, 1976, Bert Singer and Angela Kimberk Archive (Cambridge, MA), Architekturzentrum Wien, Collection, Vienna, Austria. Salomon Bryk (also written as Brick) was praised as a gifted author who wrote new Hebrew literature. See "Literarische Anzeige," *Wiener Mittheilungen*, April 1, 1865.

7 All four Baumfeld children were given Hebrew names in the Jewish community's birth records: Moriz יאיר Baumfeld, birth record 5126/1868 (October 6, 1868); Friedrich שְׁלֹמֹה Baumfeld, birth record 589/1870 (October 14, 1870); Friederike רִבְקָה Baumfeld, birth record 4852/1873 (March 5, 1873); and Elsa אֶסְתֵּר Baumfeld, birth record 5055/1880 (March 5, 1880), all from IKG. Note "Moriz" was the spelling used on the birth and Austrian military records of the Baumfelds' oldest child; Moriz later used the German spelling, "Moritz," and in America anglicized it to "Maurice." Elsa used the name "Ella" from her art student days in Vienna and perhaps even earlièr, although she does not appear to have changed it legally. To avoid confusion, we have used the name she came to adopt professionally—Ella Briggs—throughout the book.

8 The address was Schottenbastei 6 (*Lehmann's*, 1880, 161). On the building's history, see the Wien Geschichte Wiki, https://www.geschichtewiki.wien.gv.at/Schottenbastei_6.

9 Edmund de Waal, *The Hare with Amber Eyes* (New York: Farrar, Straus and Giroux, 2010).

10 Moriz Baumfeld, military personnel records (Grundbuchblätter Wien), AT-OeStA/KA Pers GB OuM KrL Wien 1868, 68; Friedrich Baumfeld, military personnel records (Grundbuchblätter Wien), AT-OeStA/KA Pers GB OuM KrL Wien 1870, 239; both held in the Österreichisches Staatsarchiv, Kriegsarchiv, Vienna, Austria.

11 "Verzichtleistung auf die Advokatie," *Neues Wiener Tagblatt*, June 17, 1890. Perhaps related to his illness, Josef Baumfeld visited the summer resort Bad Ischl, apparently alone, in the 1870s. He is listed as staying in the luxurious hotel Erzherzog Franz Carl in early summer 1875; see "Fremden-Liste," *Ischler Cur-Liste*, June 26, 1875.

12 Ella Briggs, Police Report, October 19, 1931, Application for German Citizenship, APr.Br. Rep. 030–06, no. 11426, Landesarchiv Berlin.

13 When Moritz came to visit his father, he stayed at the Gothensitz, presumably joining other family members there. His address ("Gothensitz: Moriz Baumfeld, Wien") is noted in "Angekommene Fremde," *Meraner Zeitung*, January 1, 1891. The *Meraner Zeitung* contains advertisements for luxury family apartments of different sizes for rent in this villa.

14 In 1890, almost 8,500 tourists visited Merano; see Werner Biersack, *Der Fremdenverkehr im Kurort Meran*, vol. 12 of *Schriftenreihe des Südtiroler Wirtschafts- und Sozialinstituts* (Bozen: Südtiroler Wirtschafts- u. Sozialinstitut, 1967), 168–69.

15 These included the writer Arthur Schnitzler in the 1880s. See Martin Anton Müller, "Reconstructing Arthur Schnitzler's Library: Literary and Biographical Sources for 'Die Frau des Weisen,'" *Austrian Studies* 27 (2019): 53.

16 Obituary of Josef Baumfeld, *Juristische Blätter* 21, no. 44 (1892): 525. The obituary remarked on Baumfeld's popularity in legal circles "because of his honesty and pleasant manners." It also noted his dedicated longtime service on the committee of the Lower Austrian Chamber of Lawyers.

17 The status of Karoline Baumfeld's finances remains unclear. In 1892, when Josef died, the family was still

living at Schottenbastei 6 in the prestigious first district. In 1896, Karoline had moved to Spörlingasse 4, in the business and commercial sixth district (*Lehmann's*, 1896, 45). In 1901, she was living at Lerchengasse 36, in the densely built eighth district (*Lehmann's*, 1901, 50). From 1902 to 1906, Karoline lived at Stammgasse 6, in the third district, close to Ella's design school (Karoline Baumfeld residence registration, November 20, 1902, to May 9, 1906, Meldearchiv Wien, Wiener Stadt- und Landesarchiv [MA 8], Vienna). In previous years, Karoline had spent time in Hinterbrühl, perhaps for health reasons. In 1906, she relocated there, and her address suggests an improvement in her finances, possibly from an inheritance. From 1906 to 1917, she rented a spacious and expensive apartment at Kalkstrasse 16 in Hinterbrühl (see *Illustrierter Wegweiser durch die österreichischen Kurorte, Sommerfrischen und Winterstationen* [Vienna: Elbemühl, 1914], 31; and Karoline Baumfeld residence registration, October 2, 1917, Meldearchiv Wien, Wiener Stadt- und Landesarchiv [MA 8], Vienna). Karoline may have purchased property in Hinterbrühl. Briggs mentions in her German citizenship application that she and her siblings owned "a house with large garden and land" in Hinterbrühl, which they presumably had inherited from their mother; Ella Briggs to Polizei-Praesidium Berlin, March 26, 1932, APr.Br. Rep. 030–06, no. 11426, Landesarchiv Berlin.

18 Ella would earn her *Matura* much later, at the age of thirty-nine, in order to matriculate in architecture studies.

19 Entry for Moriz Baumfeld in *Lehmann's* (1898), 48. Moritz Baumfeld does not appear to have completed his law studies at the University of Vienna, perhaps because of his father's illness and death. Whether he did so elsewhere is unclear. Email correspondence from Vienna University archivist Birgit Ladinig to Elana Shapira, March 15, 2024. Thanks to Ms. Ladinig for her research on this matter.

20 Their marriage date was May 23, 1895, as noted in the 1901 birth registration of their first son, Josef Baumfeld (June 25, 1897), in the IKG records.

21 Friedrich Baumfeld's military personnel records (Grundbuchblätter Wien), AT-OeStA/KA Pers GB OuM KrL Wien 1870, 239, Österreichisches Staatsarchiv, Kriegsarchiv, Vienna.

22 As far as can be determined, Ella's paternal grandparents, Moritz and Salomea Baumfeld, had three children: Josef, Isidor Theodor, and Franziska. Isidor Theodor Baumfeld (later Theodor Baumfeldt) entered the banking profession and made a fortune. His testament divided his assets among his own children and his sister Franziska, but did not include his brother Josef's three surviving children (Friedrich, Friederike and Ella), which perhaps indicates an earlier break between the families. Testament of Isidor Theodor Baumfeld(t), BG Döbling, A4/1 (died on November 21, 1929), Wiener Stadt- und Landesarchiv, Vienna, Austria.

23 Adolph Bryk also appears as Adolf Bryk in contemporary sources. Karoline had a third brother, Wilhelm Bryk, an engineer who left Vienna to work on the Suez Canal. His traces, however, are difficult to discern. On the genealogy of the Bryk family, see https://www.geni.com/family-tree/index/6000000010725590985, updated May 1, 2022.

24 Entry for Adolf Bryk and Philipp Bryk, *Lehmann's* (1879), 200; "Musik- und Gesangschulen" [advertisement], *Wiener Zeitung*, April 27, 1895. On the identification of Leopoldstadt as a predominantly Jewish neighborhood, see Lisa Silverman, "Leopoldstadt, Judenplatz, and Beyond: Rethinking Vienna's Jewish Spaces," *Journal of East Central Europe* 42, nos. 2–3 (2015): 249–67.

25 "Der Musik-Orchesterverein 'Lyra,'" *Deutsche Kunst- und Musik-Zeitung*, March 6, 1885; Monika Kornberger, "Bryk, Familie," in *Österreichisches Musiklexikon Online*, updated August 18, 2020, https://www.musiklexikon.ac.at/ml/musik_B/Bryk_Familie.xml.

26 In addition to being a lawyer, Adolph Bryk was copublisher of the satirical weekly *Wiener Caricaturen* (Viennese Caricatures). Bryk's two sons were also involved in publishing: Rudolf Bryk as a journalist, and Siegfried Bryk as an editor.

27 This distinction was clearly a source of pride: in 1932, Adolph's son (and Ella's cousin) Rudolf Bryk published a letter in Austria's largest newspaper recounting this family history, as well as his father's cofounding of *Wiener Caricaturen*. Rudolf Bryk, "Wie der 'Carneval in Rom' entstand" [letter to the editor], *Illustrierte Kronen Zeitung*, May 21, 1932.

28 For further insights on this issue, see Steven E. Aschheim, "The Modern Jewish Experience and the Entangled Web of Orientalism," in *Internal Outsiders—Imagined Orientals? Antisemitism, Colonialism and Modern Constructions of Jewish Identity*, ed. Ulrike Brunotte, Jürgen Mohn, and Christina Späti (Würzburg: Ergon, 2017), 11–34. For an antisemitic attack on Galician Jews as presumptuous "fake" Germans, see "Man sollte ihnen doch einmal auf den Zahn fühlen," *Kikeriki*, April 27, 1882.

29 The word *luftmentsh*, originally used by Yiddish writers to describe Jewish economic behavior, was also used by Jewish authors to reflect on their own vulnerability. Antisemites applied it as an anti-Jewish trope. On the *luftmentsh* and Galician Jews, see Nicolas Vallois and Sarah Imhoff, "'Floating Jews': The *luftmentsh* as an Economic Character," *Œconomia* 12, no. 2 (2022): 275–314; Piotr Wróbel, "The Jews of Galicia under Austrian-Polish Rule, 1869–1918," *Austrian History Yearbook* 25 (1994): 97–138; and Nicolas Berg, *Luftmenschen: Zur Geschichte einer Metapher* (Göttingen: Vandenhoeck and Ruprecht, 2008).

30 A few years before Ella was born, Adolph Bryk had successfully defended a twelve-year-old Jewish Galician boy accused of theft in a Leopoldstadt synagogue by pointing the finger at the immoral influence of a Jewish peddler from Lesko who had manipulated him. The case, covered by the press, suggests that Jewish emigrants themselves who had settled in Vienna from Galicia made distinctions between "better" and "worse" classes of Galician Jews. For the case about the boy who stole a liturgical silver chain decorating the Torah scrolls from a synagogue in Grosse Schiffgasse, see "Kriminal-Geschichten (Der Tempeldiebstahl in der Schiffgasse)," *Illustrirtes Wiener Extrablatt*, January 14, 1877.

31 Ella Briggs to Polizei-Praesidium Berlin, March 5, 1932, APr.Br. Rep. 030–06, no. 11426, Landesarchiv Berlin.

32 Felix Salten, *Das österreichische Antlitz: Essays* (Berlin: Fischer, 1910), 132. Salten's most famous work is *Bambi: Eine Lebensgeschichte aus dem Walde* (Bambi: A Life in the Woods; Berlin: Ulstein, 1923), a novel later adapted by Walt Disney into an animated film.

33 For years, Siegfried Bryk served as the right-hand man of Theodor Wolff, the renowned chief editor of Rudolf Mosse's *Berliner Tageblatt*. See Richard A. Bermann, Hans-Harald Müller, Brita Eckert, Werner Berthold, and Mechthild Hahner, *Richard A. Bermann alias Arnold Höllriegel: Österreicher–Demokrat–Weltbürger* (Munich: K. G. Saur, 1995), 22.

34 See, for example, Moritz Baumfeld, "Bühnenmoral?," *Wiener Montags-Journal*, December 2, 1895; Moriz Baumfeld, "Bei Charlotte Wolter," *Wiener Montags-Journal*, October 21, 1895; Moriz Baumfeld, "Regie (Ein Rundinterview)," *Wiener Montags-Journal*, February 17, 1896; and Moriz Baumfeld, "Künstelei," *Wiener Montags-Journal*, April 27, 1896.

CHAPTER 2. ART AND DESIGN STUDIES: A BEGINNING

1 Leo Hirschfeld, "Hofoperntheater," *Wiener Salonblatt*, June 13, 1897.

2 *Katalog der I. Kunst-Ausstellung der Vereinigung Bildender Künstler Österreichs* (Vienna: Vereinigung bildender Künstler Österreichs, 1898).

3 Margarethe Szeless, "To New Art a New House: Planning and Construction of the Building, 1897–1898," in *Secession: Die Architektur*, ed. Susanne Koppensteiner, trans. Aileen Derieg and Angela Parker (Vienna: Brandstätter, 2003), 24.

4 List of students: *Jahresbericht Verein Kunstschule für Frauen und Mädchen, 1897/1898* (Vienna: Verein Verlag, 1898), 18.

5 See Ella Briggs's request for permission to study architecture at Berlin's Technical University: Ella Briggs to Ministerium für Wissenschaft, Kunst und Volksbildung Berlin, December 2, 1918, HA-I, Rep. 76 Vb, Sekt. 4, Tit. 7, Nr. 6, Bd. 1, Geheimes Staatsarchiv, Berlin, Germany.

6 Harriet Pass Freidenreich, *Female, Jewish, and Educated: The Lives of Central European University Women* (Bloomington: Indiana University Press, 2002), 6.

7 Otto was the son of Karoline's brother Adolph and his wife Bettina. On Otto Bryk's teaching and support of the school, see *VI. Jahresbericht des Mädchenlyzeums der Frau Dr. Phil. Eugenie Schwarzwald* (Vienna, 1908), 94; and, *VIII. Jahresbericht der Schulanstalten der Frau Dr. Phil. Eugenie Schwarzwald* (Vienna, 1910), 24.

8 Bourgeois women's rights activists founded the Wiener Frauen-Erwerb-Verein (Association for the Employment of Women in Vienna) in 1866, which was the first major economic women's organization in Austria to campaign for better educational and employment opportunities for women. Marianne Hainisch, a leader of the Austrian feminist movement and member of the Wiener Frauen-Erwerb-Verein, cofounded the Verein der Schriftstellerinnen und Künstlerinnen Wien (Viennese Association of Women Writers and Artists) in 1885. Both associations encouraged and supported women pursuing employment and careers. See Harriet Anderson, *Utopian Feminism: Women's Movements in Fin-de-Siècle Vienna* (New Haven, CT: Yale University Press, 1992), 25–38.

9 Dora Peyser, "Alice Salomon: Ein Lebensbild," in *Alice Salomon: Die Begründerin des sozialen Frauenberufs in Deutschland: Ihr Leben und Ihr Werk*, ed. Hans Muthesius (Cologne: Heymanns, 1958), 17–18.

10 Elsa and Hugo were the children of Philipp and Fanni Bryk. Shortly after Ella's ninth birthday, the siblings gave their last concert; see "Theater, Kunst und Literatur," *Neues Wiener Tagblatt*, March 12, 1889. Elsa was sufficiently well-known as a music teacher that her return to Vienna and to teaching after a trip merited a mention in "Theater- und Kunstnachrichten," *Neue Freie Presse*, September 28, 1907.

11 Death announcement, Ange Baumfeld, *Neue Freie Presse*, November 29, 1898.

12 List of students: *Jahresbericht Verein Kunstschule für Frauen und Mädchen, 1899/1900* (Vienna: Verein Verlag, 1900), 18. Ella Baumfeld does not appear in the previous year's list (1898/1899), revealing her absence.

13 Ella Baumfeld, student registration form for the School of Applied Arts for 1901/1902: Kunstgewerbeschule [KGS] Nationale 1901/02, Kunstsammlung und Archiv, Universität für angewandte Kunst Wien, Vienna, Austria [this archive is hereafter cited as Archiv, Die Angewandte].

14 For a more detailed comparison of traditional versus emerging doctrines for art instruction in this period, see chapter 22, "Viennese Women's Art Schools and Their Communities in Ella Briggs's Time," in this volume.

15 A. F. Seligmann, "Secessionistisches," *Die Wage: Eine Wiener Wochenschrift* 1, no. 14 (1898): 233–34.

16 Elana Shapira, "'Our Great Josef Hoffmann': Undoing the Austrian Profile of a Celebrated Architect," in *Erasures and Eradications in Modern Viennese Art, Architecture and Design*, ed. Megan Brandow-Faller and Laura Morowitz (New York: Routledge, 2023), 58–62.

17 Ella Baumfeld, student registration form for the School of Applied Arts for 1901/02, KGS Nationale 1901/02, Archiv, Die Angewandte.

18 "Katalog der Kunstgewerbe-Schule, Anatomie, Schuljahr 1901/02," Archiv, Die Angewandte; Betty Kurth to Gertrud Kurth, April 16, 1945, Gertrud Kurth Collection, Leo Baeck Institute, New York, New York. Marianne Pisko (birth record 4575/1880, IKG) married Simon Walter Hausmann in 1905.

19 Ella Briggs's courses are noted on her registration forms (KGS Nationale 1901/02; KGS Nationale 1902/03; KGS Nationale 1903/04) as well as in the instructors' course catalogs; all in Archiv, Die Angewandte. See also Katrin Stingl, "Ella Briggs (-Baumfeld): Wohnbauten in Wien (1925/26) und in Berlin (1929/30)" (MA thesis, University of Vienna, 2008), 18–19.

20 Kunstgewerbeschule Wien, "Katalog Fachklasse Koloman Moser, Studienjahr 1903/04," Archiv, Die Angewandte.

21 Ella Baumfeld, design for embroidery in silk and metal threads, color lithograph, c. 1902, in *Die Fläche* 1, no. 3 (1902): 44.

22 "Die Ausstellung der Wiener Kunstgewerbeschule," *Wiener Mode* 14, no. 23 (1901): 969. Photograph reproduced in Rebecca Houze, *Textiles, Fashion, and Design Reform in Austria-Hungary before the First World War: Principles of Dress* (Farnham, UK: Ashgate, 2015), 164. Peyfuss and Briggs both attended Moser's class in 1903.

23 Gustav Klimt, *Fischblut*, in *Ver Sacrum*, no. 3 (1898): 6. This work was later adapted for his provocative painting *Goldfish* (also known as *To My Critics*, 1901–1902), in which he depicts a golden fish observing the viewer's (possibly shocked) reaction to the revealing pose of a naked woman.

24 The design was published in *Die Fläche* 1, no. 11 (1904): 168. This page contains four designs attributed to four students, without a clear indication of who did what. However, we know that Briggs was interested in aquatic animals (and frogs in particular) during this period. Moreover, the three other students listed on the page with Briggs had artistic styles that more closely align with the other illustrated work, leaving Briggs as the likeliest creator of the frog print. (Another pattern of frogs appears in the same issue with a similar problem of unclear attribution and may also be Briggs's work: *Die Fläche* 1, no. 11 [1904]: 169.) I thank Rainald Franz, curator of the Glass and Ceramics Collection, Museum of Applied Arts Vienna, for his help with attribution.

25 One of the early design journals, *Die Fläche* appeared intermittently from 1902 to 1911. Heralding a break with naturalism and the mimetic artistic conventions of the previous century, it offered instead modernist and flattened images of nature and the urban landscape. Among the artists who contributed to the journal's fourteen issues, one-third were women. See Diane V. Silverthorne, Dan Reynolds, and Megan Brandow-Faller, *Die Fläche: Design and Lettering of the Vienna Secession, 1902–1911* (San Francisco: Letterform Archive Books, 2023).

26 "Unser Preisausschreiben," *Dekorative Kunst* 11 (1903): 479.

27 Ella Briggs recorded Hinterbrühl as her address in her student registration form for her first year (starting October 1901) at the School of Applied Arts: KGS Nationale 1901/02, Archiv, Die Angewandte.

28 For further information on the artistic scene in Hinterbrühl, see Katya Krylova, "Hofmannsthal and 'die göttliche Briehl,'" in *Studia austriaca* 21 (2013): 117–30.

29 For the address change from Hinterbrühl to Vienna, compare Ella Baumfeld's student registration forms for the School of Applied Arts from 1901–1902 to 1902–1903: KGS Nationale 1901/02, and KGS Nationale 1902/03; both in Archiv, Die Angewandte. It is unclear whether Ella's mother also kept her Hinterbrühl apartment for the duration of Briggs's studies. If so, Ella may have split her time between the two homes. Prior to her mother renting an apartment in Vienna, Briggs stayed for a few weeks in the fall of 1902 at a Viennese charitable institution for single women, widows, and orphans, a first glimpse of her navigating the city's social institutions as an independent single woman. See chapter 13, endnote 22.

30 Vera [Betty Kris; later Betty Kurth], *Eine für Viele: Aus dem Tagebuche eines Mädchens* (Leipzig: Seemann, 1902), 11–12; Agatha Schwartz, *Shifting Voices: Feminist Thought and Women's Writing in Fin-de-Siècle Austria and Hungary* (Montreal: McGill-Queen's University Press, 2008), 148–50.

31 My translation of the original text by Vera cited in Bettina Fraisl, Heidrun Zettelbauer, and Bettina Rabelhofer, "Der weibliche Körper als Ort von Identitätskonstruktionen in der Moderne," in *Kultur–Identität–Differenz: Wien und Zentraleuropa in der Moderne*, ed. Moritz Csáky, Astrid Kury, and Ulrich Tragatschnig (Innsbruck: Studien, 2004), 288n88.

CHAPTER 3. NEW WORLD ENCOUNTERS: THE FIRST TRANSATLANTIC CROSSING

1 Entry for Ella Baumfeld, Ship Manifest listing saloon (or first-class) passengers, SS *Kaiser Wilhelm der Grosse*, Port of New York, November 18, 1903, accessed on heritage.statueofliberty.org. In a later document, Briggs gave the dates of her New York stay as October 1904 to spring 1906, but these do not align with other sources. See Ella Briggs, Police Report, October 19, 1931, Application for German Citizenship, APr.Br. Rep. 030-06, no. 11426, Landesarchiv Berlin.

2 Entry for Morris [*sic*] Baumfeld and his children Angela and Joseph, dated June 19, 1900, Borough of Manhattan, New York, 1900 US Census, Enumeration District no. 781, sheet 10, Family History Library microfilm 1241116, accessed on ancestry.com; entries for Maurice Baumfeld and Ida Hutter, passenger list for the SS *Fürst Bismarck*, departing Hamburg on June 20, 1901 for New York, Auswandererlisten VIII A1, vol. 120, p. 1246, microfilm no. K 1770, Staatsarchiv Hamburg, accessed on ancestry.com; Ida Baumfeld, US naturalization record, signed in Bridgeport, CT, on April 21, 1936, Naturalization Records, National Archives at Boston (Waltham, MA), accessed on ancestry.com; Maurice Baunfeld [*sic*] and Ida Hutter, marriage record, September 5, 1901, New York City Marriage Records, 1829–1940, accessed on familysearch.org; Theodore Baumfeld birth record, June 20, 1902, New York City Births, 1846–1909, accessed on familysearch.org; Elisabeth Ellen Baumfeld birth record, July 4, 1903, New York City Births, 1846–1909, accessed on familysearch.org; Elizabeth Ellen Baumfeld death record, November 6, 1904, and burial record, November 7, 1904, New York City Municipal Deaths, 1795–1949, accessed on familysearch.org; Janet R. Gilsdorf, *Continual Raving: A History of Meningitis and the People Who Conquered It* (New York: Oxford University Press, 2020), 112–13; and Beatrice Baumfeld birth record, May 18, 1905, New York City Births, 1846–1909, accessed on familysearch.org.

3 Entry for Walter Brix in Anna L. Staudacher, "*. . . meldet den Austritt aus dem mosaischen Glauben*": *18000 Austritte aus dem Judentum in Wien, 1868–1914: Namen—Quellen—Daten* (Frankfurt am Main: Peter Lang, 2009), 82, and 82n108; entry for Dr. Walter Johannes Briggs, *Das deutsche Element der Stadt New York: Biographisches Jahrbuch der Deutsch-Amerikaner New Yorks und Umgebung*, ed. Otto Spengler (New York: pub. by author, 1913), 77–78.

4 *Das Interieur* 1 (1900): 26, 27, and 51.

5 Walter J. Briggs, US passport application, November 21, 1922, no. 237115, Passport Applications, January 2, 1906–March 31, 1925, microfilm publication M1490, roll no. 2148, certificates: 236850–237225, December 13, 1922–December 15, 1922, General Records of the Department of State, record group 59, National Archives, Washington, DC, accessed on ancestry.com; "Flucht des Advokaten Dr. Walter Brix nach Amerika," *Ischler Wochenblatt*, March 15, 1903; "Ein lucratives Unternehmen," *Illustrirtes Wiener Extrablatt*, October 15, 1903; Karl Kraus, "Criminalist," *Die Fackel* 4, no. 131 (1903): 21–22; "Dr. Walter Brix in New York," *Neues Wiener Tagblatt*, November 11, 1904. Walter Briggs was sued by other clients and business partners and was reportedly heavily in debt at the time he fled to New York. "Dr. Walter Brix—in Amerika: Die Flucht vor dem Arrest," *Neues Wiener Tagblatt*, March 6, 1903.

6 Entry for Dr. Walter Brix, ship manifest for passengers on the SS *Zeeland*, arriving at the Port of New York on March 4, 1903, Passenger and Crew Lists of Vessels Arriving at New York, New York, 1897–1957, microfilm publication T715, Records of the Immigration and Naturalization Service, record group 85, National Archives, Washington, DC, accessed on ancestry.com; "Die Ausübung der Advokatur . . . ," *Juristische Blätter* 32, no. 13 (1903): 151; "Dr. Briggs—50 Jahre," *Washington Staatszeitung* [Seattle, Washington], January 24, 1915; entry for Dr. Walter Johannes Briggs, in *Das deutsche Element der Stadt New York*, 78.

7 "Dr. Walter Brix—in Amerika"; "Kapellmeister Advokat Doktor Fochler," *Neues Wiener Journal*, May 3, 1908.

8 Greg King, *A Season of Splendor: The Court of Mrs. Astor in Gilded Age New York* (Hoboken, NJ: John Wiley, 2009), 13.

9 Louis H. Sullivan, "The Tall Office Building Artistically Considered," *Lippincott's Magazine*, March 1896, 403–9.

10 Moritz and his family lived at 422 Central Park West. See entry for Ella Baumfeld, ship manifest listing saloon (or first-class) passengers, SS *Kaiser Wilhelm der Grosse*, Port of New York, November 18, 1903, accessed on heritage.statueofliberty.org.

11 Robert A. M. Stern, Gregory Gilmartin, and John Montague Massengale, *New York 1900: Metropolitan Architecture and Urbanism, 1890–1915* (New York: Rizzoli, 1983), 360ff; John Tauranac, *Elegant New York: The Builders and the Buildings, 1885–1915* (New York: Abbeville, 1985), 235–37; and Steven Gaines, *The Sky's the Limit: Passion and Property in Manhattan* (New York: Little, Brown and Company, 2005), 175.

12 "Big Ship Coming to Port," *New York Times*, September 26, 1897.

13 "Two Women's Model Tenement," *Windsor Ledger* [Windsor, NC], June 13, 1895; "A Model Tenement House," *Cincinnati Commercial Tribune*, February 20, 1898; "Successful Women Architects: Sixteen Tenements to Be Built on Their Plans," *New York Times*, February 25, 1895; "Miss Gannon Discusses the Model Tenement-House," *The World* [New York], February 13, 1898.

14 "As Others See Us: Viennese Newspaper Man Drops in on Boston," *Boston Daily Globe*, February 4, 1902.

15 "Children's World's Fair," *New York Times*, December 6, 1903.

16 "International Children's Exhibition," *London Standard*, December 7, 1903; *Österreich auf der Internationalen Wissenschaftlichen und Gewerblichen Ausstellung "Die Kinderwelt" in St. Petersburg, 1903/1904: Bericht der Österr. Kommission* (Vienna: pub. by author, 1904).

17 Christopher Long, "The Viennese *Secessionsstill* and Modern American Design," *Studies in the Decorative Arts* 14, no. 2 (2007): 9–12, 14–15; Leslie Topp, "Moments in the Reception of Early Twentieth-Century German and Austrian Decorative Arts in the United States," in *New Worlds: German and Austrian Art, 1890–1940*, ed. Renée Price with Pamela Kort and Leslie Elizabeth Topp (New York: Neue Galerie, 2001), 572–75.

18 "Austria's Pavilion Formally Opened," *St. Louis Republic*, June 3, 1904; William Howe Downes, "Art at St. Louis," *Boston Evening Transcript*, November 9, 1904; S. I. Smith, "Austrian Art at the World's Fair," *Brush and Pencil* [15, no. 1], January 1905, 9–11; "Features of the World's Fair: Austrian 'New' Art," *St. Louis Republic*, June 9, 1904; and Long, "The Viennese *Secessionsstill*," 14–16.

19 Emil Fischer, who wrote a report on the exposition for the Austrian Ministry of Trade, listed a bronze medal for Elsa Baumfeld (Ella Briggs) in "Group 33" of the "Manufactures" category. According to the *Official Catalogue of Exhibitors*, this group appeared in the Austrian Pavilion and encompassed individuals and schools, including the Vienna School of Applied Arts. Briggs, who was not named individually under this catalog entry, presumably exhibited with other students from the Vienna School of Applied Arts. Their contributions were identified collectively in the catalog as "works in marble, bronze and iron." Emil S. Fischer, *Rückblick auf die Beteiligung der österreichischen Regierung an der Louisiana Purchase Exposition World's Fair St. Louis 1904* (Vienna: Verlag des Niederösterreichischen Gewerbevereines, 1906), 31; *Official Catalogue of Exhibitors, Universal Exposition St. Louis U.S.A. 1904, Division of Exhibits, Department D Manufacturers* (St. Louis, MO: Published for the Committee on Press and Publicity by the Official Catalogue Company, 1904), 49.

20 "Foreign Correspondents," *World's Fair Bulletin* [5, no. 7], May 1904, 24.

21 "News and Notes," *American Printer* 40, no. 1 (1905): 70.

22 Ella Briggs does not appear in the 1905 New York Census, which recorded the state's inhabitants as of June 1, 1905. The census did include Moritz Baumfeld, his wife, four children, and the family's two live-in servants. Entry for Morris Baumfield [*sic*], family, and servants, Election District 45, Assembly District 21, Borough of Manhattan, County of New York, page 37, State Population Census Schedules, 1905, New York State Archives, Albany, New York, accessed on ancestry.com.

CHAPTER 4. A RETURN TO DESIGN EDUCATION IN VIENNA, IN AND OUT OF SCHOOL

1 Karoline Baumfeld then lived at Stammgasse 6. See chapter 1, endnote 17.

2 Female designers included Pauline Mandel, who presented carpets and tapestries, and Hermine Mittler, who offered bonnets, handbags, and cushions; see K. K. Österreichisches Museum für Kunst und Industrie in Wien, *Ausstellung Österreichischer Hausindustrie und Volkskunst November 1905–Februar 1906* (Vienna: Christoph Reisser's Söhne, 1905), 405.

3 In fall of 1905, Ella Baumfeld (Briggs) was registered as an auditor in Moser's *Fachschule für Malerei* (painting class). Ella Baumfeld enrollment forms, KGS Nationale 1905–06, Archiv, Die Angewandte.

4 B. Z. [Berta Zuckerkandl], "Die Rumpf-Sezession," *Wiener Allgemeine Zeitung*, June 14, 1905.

5 In 1905, Moser married Editha Mautner Markhof, the daughter of a wealthy industrialist family, and converted to Protestantism. Maria Rennhofer, *Koloman Moser: Leben und Werk 1868–1918* (Vienna: Brandstätter, 2002), 111.

6 Rennhofer, *Koloman Moser*, 163.

7 A. S. Levetus, "Modern Decorative Art in Austria," in *The Art-Revival in Austria*, ed. Charles Holme (London: Offices of The Studio, 1906), 505. In Austria itself, both liberal and conservative newspapers praised the exhibition; see for example, "Der Kaiser und die Londoner Ausstellung," *Illustrierte Kronen Zeitung*, April 27, 1906; "Die Eröffnung der Oesterreichischen Ausstellung in London," *Neue Freie Presse*, May 7, 1906; and, "Oesterreichische Ausstellung in London," *Neues Wiener Tagblatt*, May 19, 1906.

8 Alys X. George, *The Naked Truth: Viennese Modernism and the Body* (Chicago: University of Chicago Press, 2020), 44–45.

9 "Hygienische Ausstellung in Wien," *Das Interieur* 7 (1906): 101–2, 105.

10 "XVIII: Möbelausstellung 1906," *Das Interieur* 7 (1906): 44.

11 Alice Korvin-Müller's student work for a class taught by Freiherr von Myrbach, reproduced in *Kunst und Kunsthandwerk* 4, nos. 6–7 (1901): 294.

CHAPTER 5. A VIENNESE DESIGNER TAKES MANHATTAN

1 "Big Liner and Crowded Ferry Near Collison," *Evening World* [New York], April 9, 1907.

2 Entry for Ella Baumfeld, ship manifest for saloon (or first-class) passengers on the SS *Kaiserin Auguste Victoria*, arriving at the Port of New York on April 9, 1907, Passenger and Crew Lists of Vessels Arriving at New York, New York, 1897–1957, microfilm publication T715, Records of the Immigration and Naturalization Service, record group 85, National Archives, Washington, DC, accessed at ancestry.com.

3 Ella Baumfeld marriage certificate, September 16, 1907, certificate no. 24481, Index to New York City Marriages, 1866–1937, accessed on ancestry.com; "Married: Briggs—Baumfeld," *New York Times*, October 4, 1907; "Westchester Towns Developing Rapidly," *New York Times*, March 12, 1905. The stay in Mount Vernon was short lived, for less than a year later the couple was living at 3750 Broadway, in Washington Heights. Walter Johannes Brix, United States of America Petition for Naturalization, Supreme Court of the State of New York, no. 1505, sworn on April 29, 1908, accessed ancestry.com. Around this time, in April 1908, Walter and Ella Briggs legally changed their name from "Brix" to "Briggs." *Laws of the State of New York Passed at the One Hundred and Thirty-Second Session of the Legislature*, vol. 2 (Albany: J. B. Lyon, 1909), 1844.

4 "Westchester County Homes," *Sun* [New York], April 19, 1908.

5 "A 'Cabaret' at the Astor," *New York Times*, February 11, 1907.

6 Walter Briggs was a governor of the American Playgoers' Club, which met at the Hotel Astor. See "The Playgoers Choose Governors," *New York Times*, April 6, 1908.

7 Edwin G. Burrows and Mike Wallace, *Gotham: A History of New York City to 1898* (New York: Oxford University Press, 1999), 1111–12; "German Theatre's Plans: Irving Place Will See Well-Known Players and New Dramas," *New York Times*, June 14, 1907; "Succeeds Herr Conried: New Manager of Irving Place Theatre May Build Uptown," *New York Times*, April 10, 1907; "New German Theatre Plans," *New York Times*, April 25, 1907; "New Home Uptown for German Theatre," *New York Times*, March 1, 1908.

8 "The New German Theater," *Wall-Paper News and Interior Decorator* [32, no. 6], December 1908, 15.

9 "Art that Resembles Nature: The New Panorama of the Battle of the Merrimac and the Monitor," *New York Times*, January 10, 1886; "Proud of Their Countryman," *New York Times*, April 4, 1886; "A New Home of Melody: The Lenox Lyceum, New York's Magnificent New Musical Hall," *Philadelphia Inquirer*, December 30, 1889.

10 "Some Fine New Buildings: Grand Edifices Now Going Up in This City," *New York Times*, December 15, 1889.

11 "New Home Uptown for German Theatre."

12 Stern, Gilmartin, and Massengale, *New York 1900*, 209–11.

13 Karen J. Rigdon, "Eugene Schoen: Designs for Furniture, 1927–1936" (MA thesis, Parsons School of Design / Cooper Hewitt, Smithsonian Design Museum, 1986), 1–2; Eugene Schoen, Passport Application no. 83444, issued March 10, 1904, Passport Applications, 1795–1905, microfilm publication M1372, roll 645 (March 10, 1904–1921, March 21, 1904), General Records Department of State, record group 59, National Archives, Washington, DC, accessed at ancestry.com; "Jacob Schoen" [obituary], *Brooklyn Daily Eagle*, June 27, 1913. On Schoen's interwar designs, see Christopher Long, *Paul T. Frankl and Modern American Design* (New Haven, CT: Yale University Press, 2007), 61–62.

14 "A Chat with M. Mucha," *Sun* [New York], April 10, 1904; Jiří Mucha, *Alphonse Maria Mucha: His Life and Art* (New York: Rizzoli, 1989), 201ff; Anna Dvořák, "New Aspirations, 1900–1939," in *Alphonse Mucha: The Spirit of Art Nouveau*, ed. Victor Arwas, Jana Brabcová-Orlíková, and Anna Dvořák (Alexandria, VA: Art Services International, 1998), 30–39.

15 "Large Throng Opens Deutsches Theater," *New York Times*, October 2, 1908; H. W. Frohne, "The German Theatre in New York," *Architectural Record* 24, no. 6 (1908): 409–13; "The Decoration of the New German Theatre," *Architects' and Builders' Magazine* [10, no. 3], December 1908, 89.

16 "Decoration of the New German Theatre," 89.

17 "New German Theater."

18 "Vom neuen deutschen Musentempel in New York," *Der deutsche Vorkämpfer* [2, no. 12], December 1908, 24.

19 "Decoration of the New German Theatre," 89, 93; Mucha, *Alphonse Maria Mucha*, 227.

20 Frohne, "German Theatre in New York," 413–14.

21 Frohne, "German Theatre in New York," 416; "Decoration of the New German Theater," 89, 93; "Stage Curtain of the New German Theater," *Wall-Paper News and Interior Decoration* [33, no. 1], January 1909, 38.

22 "Women [*sic*] to Decorate Theatre," *Master Painter* [13, no. 6], September 1908, 29.

23 Klara Ruge, "Amerikanische Kunstausstellungen der Saison 1908 bis 1909," *Kunst und Kunsthandwerk* 12, no. 11 (1909): 581–82, ills. 579, 580.

24 Stern, Gilmartin, and Massengale, *New York 1900*, 212, 216; Frohne, "German Theatre in New York"; "Decoration of the New German Theatre."

25 "Women to Decorate Theatre."

26 Ruge, "Amerikanische Kunstausstellungen der Saison 1908 bis 1909," 581.

27 Anna Dvořák, catalog entry for "Comedy," in *Alphonse Mucha: The Spirit of Art Nouveau*, 291.

28 In the biography of his father, Jiří Mucha identified the figure as "a niece of Dr Baumfeld," but Moritz did not have a niece. The twelve-year age difference between the siblings undoubtedly caused the error. Mucha, *Alphonse Maria Mucha*, 227.

29 Mucha, *Alphonse Maria Mucha*, 231.

30 "New Home Uptown for German Theatre"; "Vom neuen deutschen Musentempel in New York"; "New Vaudeville Home Opens," *New York Times*, April 20, 1909; Ruth Crosby Dimmick, *Our Theatres To-day and Yesterday* (New York: H. K. Fly, 1913), 72; "Plaza Theatre Delights Patrons with 'Cannibals of the South Seas,'" *The Moving Picture World*, January 4, 1919, 87.

31 "Plaza Theatre Delights Patrons." The photograph accompanying this article shows the preservation of the original theater interior design, including Mucha's paintings.

32 Rudolph Rosenthal and Helena Ratzka, *The Story of Modern Applied Art* (New York: Harper, 1948), 158.

33 Entry for Dr. Walter Johannes Briggs, in *Das deutsche Element der Stadt New York: Biographisches Jahrbuch der Deutsch-Amerikaner New Yorks und Umgebung*, ed. Otto Spengler (New York: pub. by author, 1913), 77–78.

34 "Notes for Architects," *New York Architect* [4, no. 6], June 1910, n.p.; Christine M. Totten, *Lucy Mercer Rutherfurd: Eleanor's Rival, FDR's Other Love* (Clinton Corners, NY: Eliot Werner Publications, 2018), 5ff; "Glimpse at Society: Mrs. Carroll Mercer," *Brooklyn Citizen* [Brooklyn, NY], June 24, 1908.

35 "Contract to Decorate Press Club," *American Carpet and Upholstery Journal* 27, no. 1 (1909): 74; "Notes for Architects."

36 "Notes for Architects"; Ernest Greene, "The New York Press Club," *Architects' and Builders' Magazine* [10, no. 5], February 1910, 185.

37 "Notes for Architects"; Greene, "New York Press Club," 185, 189.

38 Klara Ruge, "Amerikanische Kunstausstellungen der Saison 1909–1910," *Kunst und Kunsthandwerk* 14, no. 1 (1911): 55.

39 Entry for Walter J. Briggs, 1910 United States Federal Census, Manhattan Ward 22, New York, enumerated on April 29, 1910, p. 21b, Thirteenth Census of the United States, 1910, NARA microfilm publication T624, Records of the Bureau of the Census, record group 29, National Archives, Washington, DC, accessed on ancestry.com.

CHAPTER 6. PARIS: A DETOUR

1 In a citizenship application filed with German authorities in 1931, Ella Briggs noted her previous places of residence. Among the entries is a period from November 10, 1910, to April 28, 1911, in Paris. Ella Briggs's application for German citizenship, "Erwerb der deutschen Staatsbuergerschaft," APr. Br. Rep. 030-06, no. 11426, Landesarchiv Berlin.

2 The article states: "Ella Briggs, who first studied architecture in Vienna and Paris, is to-day one of the foremost practicing women architects in New York." It provides no further details. See "'Step-Saving' Design by New York Woman," *New York Tribune*, February 17, 1924.

3 Fae Brauer, "Dealing with Cubism: Daniel-Henry Kahnweiler's Perilous Internationalism," in *Dealing Art on Both Sides of the Atlantic, 1860–1940*, ed. Lynn Catterson (Boston: Brill, 2017), 132; Meredith L. Clausen, *Frantz Jourdain and the Samaritaine: Art Nouveau Theory and Criticism* (Leiden: Brill, 1987), 150; Louis Vauxcelles, "Le Septième Salon des Artistes Décorateurs," *Art et Industrie*, April 1912, n.p.; Nancy Troy, "Toward a Redefinition of Tradition in French Design, 1895 to 1914," *Design Issues* 1, no. 2 (1984): 64–65.

4 In comparison to the decorative arts, a stronger women's culture in the fine arts existed in Paris from the end of the nineteenth century. See Tamar Garb, *Sisters of the Brush: Women's Artistic Culture in Late Nineteenth-Century Paris* (New Haven, CT: Yale University Press, 1994).

5 Penny Sparke and Mitchell Owens, *Elsie De Wolfe: The Birth of Modern Interior Decoration* (New York: Acanthus, 2005).

CHAPTER 7. OPENING AN INTERIOR DESIGN FIRM IN VIENNA

1 Ella Briggs to Eduard Leisching, July 6, 1911, "Protokoll Betreff: Bittet um Förderung eines beabsichtigten Unternehmens" [Protocol subject: Requests sponsorship of an intended business enterprise], AZ 1911–704; and, Ella Briggs to Eduard Leisching, July 19, 1911, "Protokoll Betreff: Betreffend die Errichtung einer amerikanischen Verkaufsstelle" [Protocol subject: Regarding the establishment of an American sales outlet], AZ 1911–739; both in Bibliothek und Kunstblättersammlung / Archiv, MAK Museum, Vienna, Austria [hereafter this archive is cited as MAK]. Briggs's July 6, 1911, letter describes a sales outlet for Austrian design goods that Briggs planned for New York and her search for firms she could represent. Although Briggs did not specifically mention opening her own interior design firm, it is hard to imagine that she would not have offered her design services to customers as well. Many thanks to Anne-Katrin Rossberg, head of the Metal Collection and Wiener Werkstätte Archive, and Walther Merk, archivist, both of the Museum of Applied Arts Vienna, for their support of my research.

2 Stefan Üner, "Jacob & Josef Kohn," in *Wagner, Hoffmann, Loos und das Möbeldesign der Wiener Moderne: Künstler, Auftraggeber, Produzenten*, ed. Eva B. Ottillinger (Vienna: Böhlau, 2018), 142. On Jacob & Josef Kohn, see also chapter 23, "The Interiors of Ella Briggs," in this volume.

3 Ella Briggs to Eduard Leisching, July 19, 1911, "Protokoll Betreff: Betreffend die Errichtung einer amerikanischen Verkaufsstelle" [Protocol subject: Regarding the establishment of an American sales outlet], AZ 1911–739, MAK.

4 Secretariat of the Chamber of Commerce and Industry for Austria to Eduard Leisching, October 31, 1911, "Protokoll Betreff: Betrifft die Abgabe eines Gutachtens über Frau Ella Briggs" [Protocol subject: Concerns the submission of a report on Mrs. Ella Briggs], AZ 1911–1003, MAK.

5 Adolf Vetter, "Die Bedeutung des Werkbundes für Österreich," *Österreichische Wochenschrift für den öffentlichen Baudienst* 18, no. 30 (1912): 548.

6 On Wiener Werkstätte of America, Inc., see Werner J. Schweiger, *Wiener Werkstaette: Design in Vienna, 1903–1932* (London: Thames and Hudson, 1984), 114–16.

7 Ella Briggs to Eduard Leisching, July 19, 1911, "Protokoll Betreff: Betreffend die Errichtung einer amerikanischen Verkaufsstelle" [Protocol subject: Regarding the establishment of an American sales outlet], AZ 1911–739, MAK.

8 A.F.S. [Adalbert Franz Seligmann], "Ausstellung Österreichischer Kunstgewerbe," *Neue Freie Presse*, November 7, 1911. As noted in chapter 1 of this volume, Seligmann was Briggs's former teacher at the Art School for Women and Girls.

9 Ella Briggs-Baumfeld residence registration from November 22, 1911, to January 23, 1912, Meldearchiv Wien, Wiener Stadt- und Landesarchiv (MA 8), Vienna. Briggs did not stay exclusively in Breslau but made frequent trips to Hinterbrühl and Vienna throughout 1912. Her final trip to Breslau was in December 1912.

10 My thanks to Irma Wulz of the Archive of the Jewish Community of Vienna (IKG) for help in clarifying the family connection between Ella Briggs and the Pringsheims in relation to her frequent visits to Breslau in 1912. Elisabeth (Lilly) Pringsheim (née Hutter) was murdered in Theresienstadt in 1942. See Nationalarchiv Prag, Institut Theresienstädter Initiative, online database of Holocaust victims (holocaust.cz). For more on the sisters Ida Baumfeld and Lilly Pringsheim, see also chapter 18, "Desperation in Vienna," in this volume.

11 Curt Brandt, plans of Lohensteinstrasse 15/17, Breslau, Signature MAt AB-139010, p. 5, Muzeum Architektury we Wrocławiu, Oddział Archiwum Budowlane [Museum of Architecture in Wrocław, Construction Archive], Poland. The buildings in this settlement were destroyed. I am grateful to Daria Dorota Pikulska of the Museum of Architecture in Wrocław for her assistance and extensive research on Ella Briggs's work in Wrocław.

12 See, for example, Otto Pringsheim, *Kultur und Wirtschaft: Studie* (Berlin: Prager, 1909). Werner Sombart mentions his friendship with Elisabeth and Otto Pringsheim in his letters. See *Werner Sombart: Briefe eines Intellektuellen, 1886–1937*, ed. Thomas Kroll, Friedrich Lenger, and Michael Schellenberger (Berlin: Duncker and Humblot, 2019), 269, 280, 288, 295.

13 In a letter to a friend written the same year Briggs spent time in Breslau, Otto Pringsheim discussed the ideas of Marie Stritt; see Britta Schinzel, "Otto Pringsheim und Alfred Ploetz - eine Freundschaft versiegt: Briefe aus dem Historischen Archiv des MPI für Psychiatrie in München," in *Rudolf Schönwald: Graphik Erzählt*, ed. Britta Schinzel (Vienna: Mandelbaum, 2018), 34–35. My thanks to Britta Schinzel for sharing her essay with me.

14 On modern architecture in Breslau, see Beate Störtkuhl, *Moderne Architektur in Schlesien 1900 bis 1939: Baukultur und Politik* (Munich: Oldenbourg, 2013). On the Jewish bourgeoisie in modern Breslau and how they chose to engage with art, and on an antibinary (modernist versus traditional) approach to German architecture in Breslau in this period, see Deborah Ascher Barnstone, *Beyond the Bauhaus: Cultural Modernity in Breslau, 1918–1933* (Ann Arbor: University of Michigan Press, 2016), 111, 122, 133.

15 Information on bequests made by the Schottländer family can be found in the online database of the Breslau Synagogue Community Archive, https://cbj.jhi.pl/.

16 Unfortunately, these photographs appear to no longer survive. E. F. [possibly Ernst Friedmann], "Aus dem Reiche der Frau: Ausstellung der Kunstgewerblerinnen," *Fremden-Blatt*, May 1, 1914. I thank Daria Dorota Pikulska for identifying the Schützendorf Palace in Wilamowice.

17 This information is based on a police report Ella Briggs completed for her 1931 German citizenship application, in which she listed her places of residence since birth. See Ella Briggs, police report, October 19, 1931, filed with her application "Erwerb der deutschen Staatsbuergerschaft" [Application for German Citizenship], APr.Br. Rep. 030-06, no. 11426, Landesarchiv Berlin.

18 See Friederike Baumfeld, "Moderne Schmuck- und Fächerkunst," *Wiener Hausfrauen-Zeitung*, November 3, 1912, 547–48; and Friederike Baumfeld, "Berliner Weihnachtsplauderei," *Wiener Hausfrauen-Zeitung*, December 22, 1912, 619–20.

19 "Ella Briggs: Eine Wiener Architektin," *Frau und Gegenwart* 4, no. 40 (1927): 12. Beginning in 1905, Friedrich worked for Nasicer Tanningfabrik und Dampfsäge A. G. in Berlin, a firm founded by the Jewish Viennese entrepreneur Hermann Rosenberg

and headquartered in Budapest. The company transported wood on the Hungarian railroad system between Zagreb, Bucharest, Budapest, and Linz. Briggs may have used Friedrich's industry connections to establish a relationship with a carpentry workshop in Berlin. See Friedrich Baumfeld's statement describing his career in his claim for compensation to the Entschädigungsamt Berlin, January 6, 1952, Reg. no 50.392 Friedrich Baumfeld, BEG-Akte (German Federal Compensation Act), State Office for Civil and Administrative Affairs (Landesamt für Bürger- und Ordnungsangelegenheiten or LABO), Berlin, Germany [this archive is hereafter cited as LABO]. NB: sources designated in the endnotes with "LABO" refer to postwar restitution or compensation claims arising from National Socialist persecution.

20 Ella Briggs to Eduard Leisching, March 10, 1912, "Protokoll Betreff: Briggs verabschiedet sich" [Protocol subject: Briggs says goodbye], AZ 1912–242, MAK.

21 The divorce between Ella and her husband Walter became official sometime between May and October 1912. In Ella Briggs's Viennese residence registration forms, in May she is still identified as married and in October she is identified as divorced. Ella Briggs, May 23, 1912, and October 18, 1912, both in Meldearchiv Wien, Wiener Stadt- und Landesarchiv (MA 8), Vienna.

22 As recalled by Phylis Morrison in 1996, the split occurred during the "stock crash." Walter came home one day and told Ella he had been fired, and she responded by telling him to leave. (Despina Stratigakos, notes from interview with Phylis Morrison, May 2, 1996, Cambridge, MA, deposited in Ella Briggs Archive, Architekturzentrum Wien, Collection, Vienna.) Morrison's retelling of the anecdote makes Ella out to be insensitive, at best. It may have been that Ella did not want to reveal more damaging details about Walter (such as his trial for fraud and fugitive status) to her grandniece, choosing instead to present him as simply useless.

The reference to the "stock crash" is intriguing. It may indicate the panic of 1907, which had severe and prolonged economic consequences. However, it may also refer to the stock market crash of 1929. By that time, Walter and Ella may have reconciled in Berlin; we know they lived for a short period in adjacent apartment buildings. By 1930 Ella had moved away, distancing herself. Was this the couple's second break up? See chapter 17, "Late Berlin Projects, Family Ties, and Growing Danger," in this volume.

23 Briggs stayed at the Lehrerhaus periodically from November 1911 to December 1912. See Ella Briggs residence registration forms for 1911 and 1912 in Meldearchiv Wien, Wiener Stadt- und Landesarchiv (MA 8), Vienna.

24 "Im Athenäum," *Der Bund: Zentralblatt des Bundes österreichischer Frauenvereine* 7, no. 7 (1912): 16.

25 "Vorträge und Versammlungen von heute," *Neues Wiener Journal*, October 23, 1912. On the Athenaeum, see Günter Fellner, "Athenäum: Die Geschichte einer Frauenhochschule in Wien," *Zeitgeschichte* 14, no. 3 (1986): 99–115.

26 Application letter of Ella Briggs to Austrian Museum of Art and Industry, June 20, 1912, AZ 1912–594; Letter of Royal and Imperial Court's Chief Chamberlain's Office to the Director of the Austrian Museum of Art and Industry, August 17, 1912, "Protokoll Betreff: Um Verleihung einer Subvention aus dem Hoftiteltaxenfonds" [Protocol subject: Application for an award subsidy from the court title tax fund], AZ1912–595; and, Ella Briggs-Baumfeld to Eduard Leisching, September 4, 1912, AZ 1912–594; all in MAK. See also *Jahresbericht des K. K. Österr. Museums für Kunst und Industrie für das Jahr 1912* (Vienna: Verlag des Museum: 1913), 7. In 1912, 4,000 kronen (crowns) would have been equivalent to around $30,000 today.

27 The address on her professional letterhead is Taubstummengasse 13, which is in the fourth district. See Ella Briggs-Baumfeld, application to Eduard Leisching, February 23, 1914, "Protokoll Betreff: Frau Ella Briggs-Baumfeld in Wien bittet um Verleihung einer Subvention aus dem Hoftiteltaxenfonds" [Protocol subject: Ella Briggs-Baumfeld in Vienna asks for a subsidy from the court title tax fund], AZ 1914–213, MAK. According to her registration records, as of December 1912, Briggs also lived at this same address, on the top floor (American fifth floor, Viennese fourth floor). In the *Lehmann's* Vienna directory, "Ella Briggs-Baumfeld, Architect" also appears at Taubstummengasse 13 from the years 1914 to 1916. Because there is no other known address for Briggs during this period, it seems probable that she combined her studio and residence. See Ella Briggs-Baumfeld registration form dated December 12, 1912, Meldearchiv Wien, Wiener Stadt- und Landesarchiv (MA 8), Vienna; and *Lehmann's* for the years 1914 (vol. 2, 135) and 1916 (vol. 2, 133).

28 "Schreibzimmer," *Das Interieur* 15, no. 6 (1914): plate 72. Although the article did not state the location of the writing room, it was probably part of Briggs's studio, given her registration records (see note 27 above) as well as her subsequent restitution claim (see note 32 below).

29 Biedermeier-era inspired striped upholstery patterns were in vogue in Vienna in this period.

30 Karl Walde, "Die Frau in der Innenarchitektur," *Das Interieur* 15, no. 6 (1914): 21–23.

31 The presence of the Venus figurine in this room may have been inspired by the 1908 discovery of the Venus of Willendorf, a prehistoric figurine, near the Austrian village of Willendorf, and the ensuing press coverage.

32 After eventually closing her studio, Briggs would integrate furniture and other items into her subse-

quent residences in Vienna and Berlin. Indeed, these pieces were so important to her that she arranged to ship some of them to London when she fled the Nazis, although she had to leave other beloved possessions behind. Decades later, Briggs submitted a photograph of the writing room published in *Das Interieur* to the Compensation Office in Berlin in relation to her claim for furniture lost from her five-room apartment in Berlin on Fasanenstrasse, documenting her retention and reuse of the furniture. Briggs attached the photo to a letter submitted by her lawyer: Manfred Meyer to the Entschädigungsamt Berlin, October 11, 1956, Reg. no. 251.039 Ella Briggs, Berlin, BEG-Akte (German Federal Compensation Act), LABO.

33 Briggs confirmed the furniture was after her own designs in her postwar restitution claims. See source in note 32 above.

34 See, for example, the entries for Briggs in the catalog *Ausstellung der österreichischen Tapeten-, Linkrusta- und Linoleum-Industrie verbunden mit einer Ausstellung von Tapeten-Entwürfen und von historischen Tapeten* (Vienna: K. K. Österr. Museum für Kunst und Industrie, 1913), 65–66. See also chapter 23, "The Interiors of Ella Briggs," in this volume.

35 The identification of this project is based on a photograph (see fig. 7.3) in the Bert Singer and Angela Kimberk Archive (Cambridge, MA) held by the Architekturzentrum Wien, Collection, Vienna. (This same room, without the client's name, was reproduced in *Das Interieur* 15, no. 6 [1914]: plate 74.) On the back side of the photograph, Briggs identified the project as the living room of Dr. Wengraf, Vienna, 1912. She further described the colors used in the room: wall yellow, furniture mahogany, fabric and stencils green-violet, carpet black-multicolored. Although not mentioned by Briggs, the textile patterns suggest Wiener Werkstätte influences. The upholstery used for the sofa and two armchairs in the seating area resembles the Wiener Werkstätte textile design "Meadow of Flowers" by Arthur Scharrisch. Briggs's design for the carpet may also have been inspired by the floral abstraction of Wiener Werkstätte graphic and textile designs.

36 *Lehmann's* for the year 1912 (vol. 2, 1438–39). Briggs's clients may have been Johann Wengraf, a medical doctor, and his wife, the feminist writer Alice Wengraf (née König), who also used the title "Dr." See "Allgemeiner österr. Frauenverein," *Neues Frauenleben*, no. 1 (January 1905): 2. If these were her clients, they may have heard of Briggs through Yella Hertzka. The couple lived in a beautiful Jugendstil building at Lainzer Strasse 31 in the thirteenth district, and the bay windows on the upper floors resemble those in a photograph (see fig. 7.2) of the interior designed by Briggs.

37 In the 1920s, the Ginzkey carpet factory attracted international attention for manufacturing the world's largest carpet. It was delivered from Maffersdorf to the Waldorf Astoria Hotel in New York City. But even before this, the firm was known for its elite client list and collaborations with artists. See Werner Michael Schwarz, "Die Faszination für Teppiche: Zu Felix Saltens literarischen und politischen Perspektiven nach 1918," in *Design Dialogue: Jews, Culture and Viennese Modernism*, ed. Elana Shapira (Vienna: Böhlau, 2018), 361.

38 Karl Walde, "Innenarchitektur und Textilkunst," *Textile Kunst und Industrie* 7 (1914): 182, 195. The caption incorrectly identifies the firm I. Ginzkey as S. Ginskey.

39 Emil signed exclusive contracts with the radically modern composers Arnold Schönberg and Franz Schreker. Making professional connections across borders, he also recruited composers Alfredo Casella (Paris), Joan Manén (Barcelona), Karol Szymanowski (Warsaw), and Ethel Smyth (London). See Hans Heinsheimer and Paul Stefan, *25 Jahre neue Musik: Jahrbuch 1926 der Universal-Edition* (Vienna: Universal Edition, 1926), 11–13.

40 Ella Briggs-Baumfeld, "Selbst ist die Frau! Ersatz für Tapeten—Herrichtung der Wohnung ohne den Tapezierer—Künstlerische Gestaltung der Wandflächen," *Blatt der Hausfrau* [27, no. 42], July 15, 1917, 8–9. In addition to her own work, Briggs's text was illustrated with the work of female designers from Berlin, although whether she or the magazine's editor was responsible for the selection is unknown.

41 Anne-Katrin Rossberg, "Ein neues Experimentierfeld: Die Wand gehört den Gestalterinnen," in *Gestalterinnen: Frauen, Design und Gesellschaft im Wien der Zwischenkriegszeit*, ed. Elana Shapira and Anne-Katrin Rossberg (Berlin: De Gruyter, 2023), 80–97.

42 Obituary of Maurice Baumfeld, *Brooklyn Citizen* [Brooklyn, NY], March 5, 1913.

43 Reports appeared over several days in the liberal *Neues Wiener Tagblatt*, where Baumfeld had been an editor. See "Moritz Baumfeld—gestorben," *Neues Wiener Tagblatt*, March 5, 1913; "Moritz Baumfeld gestorben," *Neues Wiener Journal*, March 6, 1913; and "Moritz Baumfeld," *Neues Wiener Tagblatt*, March 8, 1913. On his New York memorial, see "Baumfeld, Dr. Maurice," in *Das deutsche Element der Stadt New York: Biographisches Jahrbuch der Deutsch-Amerikaner New Yorks und Umgebung*, ed. Otto Spengler (New York: pub. by author, 1913), 51.

44 Karoline Baumfeld had moved in 1906 from Vienna to Kalkstrasse 16 in Hinterbrühl. (On Karoline's change of addresses, see chapter 1, endnote 17.) In a letter dating a few months after Moritz's death, the address Briggs used for her printed letterhead reveals she was then living with her mother. See Ella Briggs-Baumfeld to Eduard Leisching, July 25, 1913, "Protokoll Betreff: Ella Briggs-Baumfeld bittet um Empfehlung an den Bürgermeister von

Baden S. Trenner" [Protocol subject: Ella Briggs-Baumfeld asks to be recommended to the Mayor of Baden S. Trenner], AZ1913–666, MAK.

45 Ella Briggs-Baumfeld to Eduard Leisching, July 25, 1913, "Protokoll Betreff: Ella Briggs-Baumfeld bittet um Empfehlung an den Bürgermeister von Baden S. Trenner" [Protocol subject: Ella Briggs-Baumfeld asks to be recommended to the Mayor of Baden S. Trenner], AZ1913–666, MAK.

46 "Die heutige Eröffnung der Jahresausstellung der Vereinigung bildender Künstlerinnen Oesterreichs," *Neue Freie Presse*, January 4, 1914.

47 Ida Mauthner, "Die Fünfte Ausstellung der Vereinigung der bildenden Künstlerinnen Oesterreichs," *Österreichische Frauen-Rundschau*, no. 117 (1914): 2; Daisy Minor, "Ausstellung der bildenden Künstlerinnen Oesterreichs," *Der Bund: Zentralblatt des Bundes österreichischer Frauenvereine* 9, no. 2 (1914): 13. For further brief mentions of Briggs's work, see "Die Vereinigung bildender Künstlerinnen Oesterreichs," *Neues Wiener Tagblatt*, January 8, 1914; "Vereinigung bildender Künstlerinnen Oesterreichs," *Die Zeit*, January 10, 1914.

48 Ella Briggs-Baumfeld, application to Eduard Leisching, February 23, 1914, "Protokoll Betreff: Frau Ella Briggs-Baumfeld in Wien bittet um Verleihung einer Subvention aus dem Hoftiteltaxenfonds" [Protocol subject: Ella Briggs-Baumfeld asks for a subsidy from the court title tax fund], AZ 1914–213; SR. k. und k. Apostolischen Majestät Obersthofmeisteramt (Royal and Imperial Court, Chief Chamberlain's Office) to Eduard Leisching, May 12, 1914, "Protokoll Betreff: Nicht genehmigt Subventionen aus dem Hoftiteltaxenfonds" [Protocol subject: Not approved subvention from the court title tax fund], AZ 1914–385; both in MAK. On the building crisis in Vienna in late 1913, see Peter Feldbauer, *Stadtwachstum und Wohnungsnot* (Vienna: Verlag für Geschichte und Politik, 1977), 115–16.

49 Liese Schmeja received 3,000 kronen (crowns); Hedwig Schmidl received 2,000 kronen. Chief Chamberlain's Office to Eduard Leisching, May 12, 1914, AZ 1914–385, MAK.

50 E. F., "Aus dem Reiche der Frau." For more exhibit reviews, see "Kunstgewerbliche Ausstellung im Frauenklub," *Die Zeit*, May 1, 1914; C. P., "Wiener Kunstgewerblerinnen," *Neues Wiener Journal*, May 3, 1914; "Kunstgewerbliche Ausstellung im Frauenklub," *Neues Wiener Tagblatt*, May 4, 1914; and A.F.S., "Der Oesterreichische Frauenklub," *Neue Freie Presse*, May 8, 1914.

51 "Originelle Frauenberufe," *Blatt der Hausfrau* [24, no. 35], May 31, 1914, II–III.

52 Petition submitted by Ella Briggs to the Diploma Preliminary Examination Committee of the Munich Technical University, August 6, 1919, TUM.Archiv. PA.Stud. Briggs, Ella, Technische Universität München Archiv, Munich, Germany.

53 "Kriegsfürsorge: Kunstwerkeverlosung für Kriegshilfszwecke," *Fremden-Blatt*, February 16, 1915; "Kriegshilfsaktion 'Kunstwerkeverlosung,'" *Neue Freie Presse*, April 11, 1915.

54 Ella Briggs, poster design for the opening of the *War Music Exhibition*, May 5, 1915, Inv. no. AC10557212–4201, Collection Wienbibliothek im Rathaus, Vienna.

55 In her application to Berlin's Technical University, Briggs noted that she worked as an interior decorator in Vienna until 1916, and then took employment at various firms, including the interior decoration company Sigmund Járay. Ella Briggs to Ministerium für Wissenschaft, Kunst und Volksbildung, Berlin, December 2, 1918, HA-I, Rep. 76Vb, Sekt. 4, Tit. 7, Nr. 6, Bd. 1, Geheimes Staatsarchiv, Berlin. Briggs moved out of her studio/apartment at Taubstummengasse 13 in October 1915. Ella Briggs residence registration, December 11, 1912, to October 26, 1915, Meldearchiv Wien, Wiener Stadt- und Landesarchiv (MA 8), Vienna. She relocated to the third district, renting an apartment at Linke Bahngasse 15 in a new building designed by Max Theuer. Entry for Briggs-Baumfeld, Ella, in *Lehmann's* for the year 1917 (vol. 2, 132).

56 That Briggs was still designing interiors as late as 1917 is confirmed by a surviving photograph that shows a completed living room design for a client identified only as "Aschner" in Vienna in 1917, Bert Singer and Angela Kimberk Archive (Cambridge, MA), Architekturzentrum Wien, Collection, Vienna.

57 E. P., "VII. Ausstellung der Vereinigung bildender Künstlerinnen Oesterreichs," *Der Bund: Zentralblatt des Bundes österreichischer Frauenvereine* 12, no. 2 (1917): 15.

58 Lisa Silverman, *Becoming Austrians: Jews and Culture Between the World Wars* (Oxford: Oxford University Press, 2012), 20.

59 Taufbuch 75, 1918, 02-Taufe-0189, October 26, 1918, archive of the Lutherische Stadtkirche Wien, Vienna, Austria. Böhm may have been a former colleague of Briggs's father. On Jewish conversion, see Staudacher, *". . . meldet den Austritt aus dem mosaischen Glauben."*

CHAPTER 8. THE FIGHT TO INTEGRATE ARCHITECTURE STUDIES

1 Ella Briggs's employment in these architectural offices as well as by the Sigmund Járay company (see chapter 7, note 55 above) are described in Ella Briggs to Ministerium für Wissenschaft, Kunst und Volksbildung, Berlin, December 2, 1918, HA-I, Rep. 76Vb, Sekt. 4, Tit. 7, Nr. 6, Bd. 1, Geheimes Staatsarchiv, Berlin, Germany; Ella Briggs to the Rektorat der Kgl. technischen Hochschule München, c. August 1918, TUM.Archiv.PA.Stud.Briggs, Ella, Technische Universität München Archiv, Munich. For

biographies of Alfred Keller and Karl Holey, see the Architektenlexikon Wien, 1770–1945 database: www.architektenlexikon.at/de/290.htm (Keller), and www.architektenlexikon.at/de/238.htm (Holey). On Holey's approach to preserving monuments, see Karl Holey, "Erzherzog Franz Ferdinand und die Pflege der heimischen Denkmäler," *Wiener Allgemeine Zeitung*, July 3, 1914.

2 Despina Stratigakos, "'I Myself Want to Build': Women, Architectural Education and the Integration of Germany's Technical Colleges," *Paedagogica Historica* 43, no. 6 (2007): 727–56; Ute Maasberg and Regina Prinz, *Die Neuen kommen! Weibliche Avantgarde in der Architektur der zwanziger Jahre* (Hamburg: Junius, 2004), 31–42.

3 Juliane Mikoletzky, Ute Georgeacopol-Winischhofer, and Margit Pohl, *"Dem Zuge der Zeit entsprechend . . .": Zur Geschichte des Frauenstudiums in Österreich am Beispiel der Technischen Universität Wien* (Vienna: WUV-Universitätsverlag, 1997), 9, 82; Juliane Mikoletzky, "An Unintended Consequence: Women's Entry into Engineering Education in Austria," *History and Technology* 14 (1997), 40. For a broad overview of women's options for architectural study in Vienna, see Iris Meder, "Women Designers and Architects in Early Twentieth Century Vienna," in *Women's Creativity since the Modern Movement (1918–2018): Toward a New Perception and Reception*, ed. Helena Seražin, Caterina Franchini, and Emilia Garda (Ljubljana: ZRC SAZU, France Stele Institute of Art History, Založba ZRC, 2018), 50–57.

4 "Ella Briggs: Eine Wiener Architektin," 12.

5 AT TUWA, Rektoratsakten, RZl. 629-1916/17, Protokoll Nr. III der Sitzung des Professorenkollegiums vom 6. Dezember 1916, Tagesordnungspunkt 11, Archiv der Technischen Universität Wien, Vienna, Austria; Mikoletzky, Georgeacopol-Winischhofer, and Pohl, *"Dem Zuge der Zeit entsprechend . . ."*, 56–57. Although auditors (whether male or female [with permission]) could attend lectures, they could not matriculate. Education ministry regulations further stipulated that they were not allowed to take examinations; therefore, they did not receive examination certificates (which prove they passed the test). Ella Briggs, however, managed to obtain such certificates, perhaps with the support of Rector Bamberger. Her application to the Munich Technical University reveals that she had presented examination certificates from the Vienna Technical University, which were accepted in Munich. Mikoletzky, Georgeacopol-Winischhofer, and Pohl, *"Dem Zuge der Zeit entsprechend . . ."*, 57; Technische Hochschule in München, Anmeldebogen, Ella Briggs, January 28, 1919, TUM.Archiv.PA.Stud.Briggs, Ella, Technische Universität München Archiv, Munich.

6 It is unclear exactly when Briggs began attending architecture lectures at the Vienna Technical University. If she did so in the summer semester of 1917, she would have been joined by another female auditor: Margarethe von Heimerich (see below).

7 This story appears on a website documenting the March 8, 2012, dedication to Ella Briggs of a student drawing room at the Vienna Technical University. See Sarah Reisenbauer, "8. März 2012—Internationaler Frauentag," March 9, 2012, https://web.archive.org/web/20180412212046/https://htu.at/Frauen/FrauenTag2012.

8 Ministerium für Kultus und Unterricht to Rektorat der k.k. technischen Hochschule, January 3, 1918; and Ministerium für Kultus und Unterricht to Ella Briggs-Baumfeld, January 6, 1918; both AT TUWA, Rektoratsakten, RZl. 565-1917/18, Archiv der Technischen Universität Wien, Vienna.

9 Mikoletzky, Georgeacopol-Winischhofer, and Pohl, *"Dem Zuge der Zeit entsprechend . . ."*, 59, 217.

10 Urbanek attended, among other educational institutions, the Fachschule für Textilindustrie (Technical College for the Textile Industry) and the Technische Lehranstalt für das allgemeine Baufach und Vermessungswesen (Technical College for General Construction and Surveying) in Vienna. See Mikoletzky, Georgeacopol-Winischhofer, and Pohl, *"Dem Zuge der Zeit entsprechend . . ."*, 59–60.

11 Susanne Ihsen and Sabrina Gebauer, eds., "Brochure for the Liesel Beckmann Symposium," in *Frauen an der Technischen Universität München; Women at Technische Universität München* (Institute for Advanced Study, Munich Technical University, 2007), https://mediatum.ub.tum.de/doc/1638950/1638950.pdf.

12 K. Bayer, "Staatsministerium des Innern für Kirchen- und Schulangelegenheiten to Rektorat der K. Techn. Hochschule in München," September 24, 1918, "Betrefft: Zulassung als Zuhörerin an die Architekten-Abteilung der K. Technischen Hochschule in München," TUM.Archiv.PA.Stud.Briggs, Ella, Technische Universität München Archiv, Munich.

13 Ella Briggs to Ministerium für Wissenschaft, Kunst und Volksbildung, Berlin, December 2, 1918; Ministerium to Rektor der Technischen Hochschule in Charlottenburg, January 13, 1919; both in HA-I, Rep. 76Vb, Sekt. 4, Tit. 7, Nr. 6, Bd. 1, Geheimes Staatsarchiv, Berlin. In Briggs's letter to the ministry, the address she listed for her mother (Fürther Strasse 4) was that of her brother Friedrich, suggesting that the entire Baumfeld family would have been reunited in Berlin if Briggs's application had been accepted. Entry for Fritz Baumfeld, *Berliner Adressbuch 1918*, vol. 1 (Berlin: August Scherl Deutsche Adressbuch-Gesellschaft, 1918), 115.

14 Briggs took the exam at the Staatsrealschule in Salzburg (today Bundesrealgymnasium Salzburg or BRG Salzburg). Although no female students were admitted to this school as regular students, it was possible for her to pass the examination as an external student. See "Abschlussprüfungen 1918–19," in Gerald Stadlbauer, *150 Jahre Geschichte und Entwicklung des*

Bundesrealgymnasiums Salzburg 1851–2001 (Salzburg: BRG Salzburg, 2001), 131; and Gürtler to Sabine Plakolm-Forsthuber, November 26, 1992, Ella Briggs Archive, Architekturzentrum Wien, Collection, Vienna.

15 Petition submitted by Ella Briggs to the Diploma Preliminary Examination Committee of the Munich Technical University, August 6, 1919; response from the Committee Chair, August 7, 1919; both in TUM. Archiv.PA.Stud. Briggs, Ella, Technische Universität München Archiv, Munich.

16 Nonetheless, this female cohort remained a fraction of Munich's architecture student body as a whole, which numbered 299 students (282 men and 17 women). "Endgültige Übersicht über den Besuch der Technischen Hochschule in München im Winter-Halbjahr 1918/19," in *Technische Hochschule in München: Personalstand im Sommer-Halbjahr 1919* (Munich: J. Lindauerschen Universitätsbuchhandlung, 1919), 140.

17 Ella Briggs diploma, Technische Hochschule in München, Zeugnis über die Diplom-Hauptprüfung für Architekten, dated August 13, 1920, TUM.Archiv. PA.Stud.Briggs, Ella, Technische Universität München Archiv, Munich. For Briggs to attain the equivalent of eight university semesters, she must have received substantial credit for her coursework at the Vienna Technical University. Unfortunately, the incomplete archival records at the Vienna Technical University do not give us a full picture of her studies there.

18 Proceedings on the admission of the first female member from April 22, 1921, Verhandlungsschrift der 7. Sitzung des Verwaltungsrates 1921, Archiv Österreichischer Ingenieur- und Architektenverein, Vienna, Austria. The press also reported on Briggs's admission as the first female member. See "Kleine Chronik," *Neue Freie Presse*, April 27, 1921.

CHAPTER 9. THE VIENNA SETTLER MOVEMENT AND EARLY ARCHITECTURAL WORK

1 "Ella Briggs: Eine Wiener Architektin," 12.

2 Klaus Novy, Wolfgang Förster, Ernst Koch, and Verein für Moderne Kommunalpolitik, *Einfach Bauen: Genossenschaftliche Selbsthilfe nach der Jahrhundertwende: Zur Rekonstruktion der Wiener Siedlerbewegung* (Vienna: Picus, 1991); Eve Blau, *The Architecture of Red Vienna, 1919–1934* (Cambridge, MA: MIT Press, 1999), 88–133.

3 On Hans Kampffmeyer's role in the German garden city movement, see Teresa Harris, "The German Garden City Movement: Architecture, Politics and Urban Transformation, 1902–1931" (PhD diss., Columbia University, 2012).

4 Blau, *The Architecture of Red Vienna*, 97ff.

5 Blau, *The Architecture of Red Vienna*, 113–16; Christopher Long, *Josef Frank: Life and Work* (Chicago: University of Chicago Press, 2002), 58–61.

6 Sophie Hochhaeusl, "From Vienna to Frankfurt Inside Core-House Type 7: A History of Scarcity through the Modern Kitchen," *Architectural Histories* 1, no. 1 (2013): n.p., online at https://journal.eahn.org/article/id/7455/#!. (To avoid confusion, we use the name Margarete [or Grete] Schütte-Lihotzky throughout the book, including for projects completed before her marriage to Wilhelm Schütte in 1927.)

7 S. E. Eisterer, "On Settler Huts and Core-Houses: Margarete Lihotzky's Contribution to Cooperative Labor in the Vienna Settlement Movement," in *Margarete Schütte-Lihotzky: Architecture, Politics, Gender; New Perspectives on Her Life and Work*, ed. Marcel Bois and Bernadette Reinhold (Basel: Birkhäuser, 2023), 78–93.

8 Blau, *The Architecture of Red Vienna*, 106, 125–27.

9 Blau, *The Architecture of Red Vienna*, 109–13, 116.

10 Sophie Hochhäusl, "From Garden Settlement to Cooperative Economy: Housing, Labor, and Socialization Theory in Vienna and Berlin, 1920–1925," in *Landscapes of Housing: Design and Planning in the History of Environmental Thought*, ed. Jeanne Haffner (Abingdon, UK: Routledge, 2022), 86, 88; Blau, *The Architecture of Red Vienna*, 88, 92–93.

11 Günther Sandner, *Otto Neurath: Eine politische Biographie* (Vienna: Zsolnay, 2014). For more on Neurath and Briggs's relationship, see in this volume chapter 16, "Exhibition Design," and chapter 19, "London."

12 Ultimately, the competition was not held. See Blau, *The Architecture of Red Vienna*, 92–93.

13 "Abenteuer einer Wiener Architektin in Sizilien: Eine wissenschaftliche Arbeit bringt sie ins Gefängnis," *Der Tag*, December 24, 1925. Thank you to Christopher Long for helping to clarify Frank's relationship to Grundstein.

14 I. H., "Wie sich der 'Grundstein' die Zukunft denkt," *Allgemeine Bauzeitung* 5, no. 132 (1928): 1–3.

15 "Was das Volk sagt," *Salzburger Volksblatt*, July 28, 1923.

16 Novy, Förster, Koch, and Verein für Moderne Kommunalpolitik, *Einfach Bauen*, 57–58.

17 Ella Briggs, "How Austria Is Helping to Solve the Housing Problem," *Architecture* 46, no. 5 (1922): 351–52.

18 Briggs, "How Austria Is Helping to Solve the Housing Problem," 351.

19 Our thanks to S. E. Eisterer for raising this possibility.

20 Helmut Weihsmann, *Das rote Wien: Sozialdemokratische Architektur und Kommunalpolitik, 1919–1934* (Vienna: Promedia, 1985), 225.

21 "Ella Briggs: Eine Wiener Architektin," 12.

CHAPTER 10. BUILDING CLIENTS AND AVID READERS IN NEW YORK AND BEYOND

1 Ella Briggs, application form, Architects' Registration Council of the United Kingdom, March 2, 1940, copy deposited with the Ella Briggs Archive, Architekturzentrum Wien, Collection, Vienna, Austria; death certificate for Karoline Baumfeld, May 27, 1921, reg. no. 517/1921, Standesamt Charlottenburg-Wilmersdorf von Berlin, Germany.

2 Entry for Ella Briggs, list or manifest of alien passengers for the United States Immigration Officer at Port of Arrival, SS *Yorck* arriving at the Port of New York on May 5, 1922, Passenger and Crew Lists of Vessels Arriving at New York, New York, 1897–1957, Microfilm Publication T715, Records of the Immigration and Naturalization Service, 1787–2004, record group 85, National Archives, Washington, DC, accessed on ancestry.com; entry for Ella Briggs, Bremen Passenger Lists, archive identifier number AIII15-22.04.1922_N, page 7, Staatsarchiv Bremen, accessed on https://www.passagierlisten.de/. On Hella Felicitas Bernay, see Jim Macklin, *Notable New Yorkers of Manhattan's Upper West Side: Bloomingdale-Morningside Heights* (New York: Fordham University Press, 2021), 136–37.

3 Briggs, "How Austria Is Helping to Solve the Housing Problem." For further discussion of Briggs's article in the Viennese context, see chapter 9, "The Vienna Settler Movement and Early Architectural Work," in this volume.

4 Briggs, "How Austria Is Helping to Solve the Housing Problem," 351.

5 Ella Briggs, "For Hunting Lodge or Home in the Mountains These Simple Swiss Chalets Are Economical and Suitable," *Country Life* [43, no. 1], November 1922, 50–51. In the magazine's table of contents, this article was listed under the title "Swiss Chalets."

6 Ida Clyde Clarke, "Whom Do You Want for President Next Year," *Pictorial Review* [25, no. 1], October 1923, 1, 50.

7 Mae Savell Croy, "The New Kind of Farmhouse," *Pictorial Review* [24, no. 6], March 1923, 62; Ella Briggs, "Labor-Saving House Plan Wins National Women's Competition," *New York Tribune*, February 17, 1924; Mae Savell Croy, "Houses Planned by Women," *Pictorial Review* [25, no. 1], October 1923, 54, 67; Mae Savell Croy, "Houses Planned by Women," *Pictorial Review* [25, no. 2], November 1923, 35, 95, 96.

8 Susan R. Henderson, *Building Culture: Ernst May and the New Frankfurt Initiative, 1926–1931* (New York: Peter Lang, 2013), 151–52.

9 Ella Briggs, "The House with a Future," *Country Life* [44, no. 1], May 1923, 62–63. The following year Briggs published a revised version of this article: Ella Briggs, "A Little House that Grew," *Designer and the Woman's Magazine* [59, no. 2], January 1924, 54–55.

10 Briggs, "The House with a Future."

11 See chapter 9, "The Vienna Settler Movement and Early Architectural Work," in this volume.

12 Ella Briggs, "Groups of Families Can Build These Apartments," *Ladies' Home Journal* [40, no. 10], October 1923, 42, 103, 104. Given that this project conspicuously stands out from Briggs's focus on single-family homes, it raises the question of whether it was influenced not just by European precedents but also by the as-yet-unidentified Philadelphia conversion of single-family homes into a courtyard development that she undertook in the early 1920s. See Ella Briggs, undated submission form for the 1923 Künstlerhaus exhibition, Künstlerhaus-Archiv, Wiener Stadt- und Landesarchiv, Vienna, Austria.

13 "'Step-Saving' Design by New York Woman"; Briggs, "Labor-Saving House Plan Wins National Women's Competition"; Henry Atterbury Smith, *The Books of a Thousand Homes* [1923], cited in Alan Gowans, *The Comfortable House: North American Suburban Architecture, 1890–1930* (Cambridge, MA: MIT Press, 1986), 66.

14 Briggs, "A Little House that Grew," 54.

15 Despina Stratigakos, *Where Are the Women Architects* (Princeton, NJ: Princeton University Press, 2016), 5ff; Despina Stratigakos, "The Good Architect and the Bad Parent: On the Formation and Disruption of a Canonical Image," *Journal of Architecture* 13, no. 3 (2008): 291–92.

16 Ella Briggs, "Anmeldung zur Herbstausstellung 1924," Künstlerhaus-Archiv, Wiener Stadt- und Landesarchiv, Vienna.

17 Obituary of Ethel Doty Brown, *The Alumnae News* [Hunter College], January 1949, 5; Beatrice M. Hinkle, "Women and the New Morality," in *Our Changing Morality: A Symposium*, ed. Freda Kirchwey (New York: Albert and Charles Boni, 1924), 235–49.

18 In 1940, Briggs stated that she had "worked for some time at the architects' office of Kahn and Gregory, New York." She may have been referring to the architectural firm of Ely Jacques Kahn and Albert Buchman, with which Julius Gregory was associated, but more research is needed to identify the firm, determine the dates of her employment, and locate the projects she may have undertaken with them. See Ella Briggs, application to the Architects' Registration Council, March 2, 1940, source in note 1 above.

19 Entry for Mary K. Chapin, 1920 US Census, New York, Manhattan Assembly District 21, District 1424, National Archives and Records Administration, accessed at ancestry.com; *American Art Annual* 17 (Washington, DC: American Federation of the Arts, 1921), 416; "Active Lot Buying and Home Building in the Suburbs," *New York Times*, March 9, 1924. Chapin's house with floor plans was later published

and described at length in Ella Briggs, "Arbeitserleichterungen im amerikanischen Kleinhaus," *Der Tag*, June 8, 1925.

20 "Active Lot Buying and Home Building in the Suburbs," *New York Times*, March 9, 1924.

21 Mary K. Chapin, death date January 1, 1927, death certificate 248, Index to New York City Deaths, 1862–1948, accessed at ancestry.com.

22 Email message to Despina Stratigakos from Lynne Crowley, archivist of the Larchmont Historical Society, January 28, 2020. Crowley identified the location of Chapin's former house as 48 Ellsworth Road, Larchmont Gardens. The building on the site is contemporary with Briggs's design but different from the drawing published in the *New York Times*. It is unclear whether Briggs made the alterations or if they are the work of John Corbin, the builder who purchased the property. In building documents Corbin filed at the time, he listed himself as the architect. The resale of the house to Harvey D. Symonds, vice president of the George A. Fuller Company, is noted in "Corbin Construction Company," *Daily Times* [Mamaroneck, NY], July 8, 1926.

23 Ella Briggs, "We Plan a House for You," *Good Housekeeping*, March 1924, 35, 148, 150; Ella Briggs, "We Plan *Another* House," *Good Housekeeping*, February 1925, 69, 104.

24 Briggs, "We Plan *Another* House," 69; Ella Briggs, "A Comfortable New House," *Good Housekeeping*, April 1928, 96, 214, 216; Briggs, "We Plan a House for You," 35.

25 Photograph of the Pelham Manor house designed by Ella Briggs in the Hans and Lily Hildebrandt Papers, 1899–1979, Getty Research Institute, Los Angeles, California; Ella Briggs, "Anmeldung zur Herbstausstellung 1924," Künstlerhaus-Archiv, Wiener Stadt- und Landesarchiv, Vienna; obituary of Alfred L. Hammett, *New York Times*, August 21, 1937; 1024 Clay Avenue deed and valuation records, Records of the Office of the Assessor, Town of Pelham, Pelham, NY; entry for Alfred L. Hammett, 1930 US Census, New York, Westchester, Pelham Manor, District 0316, and Entry for Alfred D. Hammett, 1930 US Census, New Jersey, Bergen, Teaneck, District 0231, both in National Archives and Records Administration, accessed at ancestry.com.

26 Briggs, "We Plan a House for You," 35. Briggs's March 1924 *Good Housekeeping* house design was also built that same year at 133 South Park Avenue in Hinsdale, Illinois. Sadly, the house was demolished in 2024. Bethany Salmon, email to Despina Stratigakos, April 21, 2025.

27 Briggs, "We Plan *Another* House," 69.

28 Ella Briggs, "Amerikanische Einfamilienhäuser," *Zeitschrift des Österreichischen Ingenieur- und Architekten-Vereines* 80, no. 17–18 (1928): 146; Despina Stratigakos, in conversation with Phylis Morrison, November 21, 1999, Cambridge, MA.

29 Briggs, "We Plan *Another* House," 104.

30 Briggs, "Amerikanische Einfamilienhäuser."

31 List of works noted by Briggs in her entry application forms for the 1923, 1924, and 1926 exhibitions organized by the Genossenschaft der bildenden Künstler Wiens in the Künstlerhaus; all in Künstlerhaus-Archiv, Wiener Stadt- und Landesarchiv, Vienna; and, illustration of a wooden house in New Jersey, published in "Ella Briggs: Eine Wiener Architektin," 12.

32 Entry for Ella Briggs, "Record of Aliens Held for Special Inquiry," SS *Majestic White Star*, arrived at the Port of New York on November 2, 1927, Passenger and Crew Lists of Vessels Arriving at New York, New York, 1897–1957, microfilm T715, Records of the Immigration and Naturalization Service, 1787–2004, record group 85, National Archives, Washington, DC, accessed at ancestry.com; Jia Lynn Yang, *One Mighty and Irresistible Tide: The Epic Struggle over American Immigration, 1924–1965* (New York: Norton, 2020). Although there is no denying that Austria and Germany presented attractive opportunities for reform-minded architects in the mid-1920s, the passage of the US 1924 Immigration Act in May of that year raises the question of whether Briggs had the option of legally staying in the United States, given that she had never applied for citizenship. Briggs may have been both drawn to developments in Europe and concerned about her legal status in the United States. Both factors may have influenced her decision to leave the United States in late fall 1924.

33 Christina A. Ziegler-McPherson, *The Great Disappearing Act: Germans in New York City, 1880–1930* (New Brunswick, NJ: Rutgers University Press, 2022), 134ff.

34 "Germany Asks A.G.A. Aid," *American Gas Association Monthly* 10, no. 4 (1928): 243. For more on Briggs's exhibition designs, see chapter 16, "Exhibition Design," in this volume.

CHAPTER 11. RETURN TO VIENNA AND A BIG BREAK

1 Ella Briggs, "Anmeldung zur Ausstellung 1923, Künstlerhaus, Wien," n.d.; and jury minutes, November 22, 1923; both in the Künstlerhaus-Archiv, Wiener Stadt- und Landesarchiv, Vienna. See also the Künstlerhaus catalog entries in *Herbst-Ausstellung: Mit Gedächtnisausstellungen Robert Russ und Richard Drasche* (Vienna: Genossenschaft der bildenden Künstler Wiens, 1923), nos. 328, 329, 374, 375.

2 Hans Ankwicz-Kleehoven, "Herbst-Ausstellungen," *Wiener Zeitung*, November 7, 1923.

3 Briggs submitted photographic and facsimile prints of her work as exhibition entries. For her Herbstausstellung 1924 submission, she described the represented projects as follows: "Haus der Mrs. H. G. Chapin, Larchmont Gardens, New York; Haus der Mr. W. L. Hammett Residence, Pelham Manor, New

York; Kleines Wohnhaus; Landhaus; [and two separate entries for an] Einfamilienhaus." For her Jahresausstellung 1926 submission, she described the represented projects as "Amerikanisches Einfamilienhaus"; "Haus der Mrs. H. G. Chapin, Larchmont Gardens, New York"; and "Zwei in Pelham Manor New York und in Hinsdale bei Chicago ausgefuehrte Einfamilienhaeuser, amerikansiches Typenhaus." See Ella Briggs, "Anmeldung zur Herbstausstellung 1924, Künstlerhaus Wien," November 15, 1922[4?] (the 1922 date noted by Briggs cannot be correct as the fall exhibition opened on November 22, 1924); and Ella Briggs, "Anmeldung zur Jahresausstellung 1926," April 7, 1926; all in the Künstlerhaus-Archiv, Wiener Stadt- und Landesarchiv, Vienna.

4 Indicated on the 1923 Künstlerhaus application form; Ella Briggs, "Anmeldung zur Ausstellung 1923, Künstlerhaus, Wien," n.d., Künstlerhaus-Archiv, Wiener Stadt- und Landesarchiv, Vienna.

5 Tim Bonyhady, *Good Living Street: The Fortunes of My Viennese Family* (Crows Nest, Australia: Allen and Unwin, 2011), 122–23, 132–35; Sue Course, *Lost Letters from Vienna* (Melbourne, Australia: Wild Dingo Press, 2019), 199–208; Burkhardt Rukschcio and Roland L. Schachel, *Adolf Loos: Leben und Werk* (Salzburg: Residenz, 1982), 187.

6 From 1922 to 1924, Briggs travelled back and forth between New York and Vienna. See entry for Ella Briggs, list or manifest of alien passengers for the United States Immigration Officer at Port of Arrival, SS *Yorck*, arriving at the Port of New York on May 5, 1922, and entry for Ella Briggs, ship manifest for the SS *Reliance*, arriving at the Port of New York on October 12, 1923; both in Passenger and Crew Lists of Vessels Arriving at New York, 1897–1957, microfilm T715, Records of the Immigration and Naturalization Service, 1787–2004, record group 85, National Archives, Washington, DC, accessed on ancestry.com. In her 1924 Künstlerhaus exhibition application form, dated November 15, she gave a New York address as her permanent residence. See Ella Briggs, "Anmeldung zur Herbstausstellung 1924, Künstlerhaus Wien," November 15, 1922[4?], Künstlerhaus-Archiv, Wiener Stadt- und Landesarchiv, Vienna. For much of the time that she was living in New York and while travelling in Italy during the spring of 1925 (see chapter 12, "Italian Travels, Architectural Photography, and Jail," in this volume), she listed as her local Vienna address the pension "Peter" (Peter Jordan Strasse 8) on her Vienna residence registration forms. See Bauxi Mang to Helga Schmidt-Thomsen, June 13, 1984, Ella Briggs Archive, Architekturzentrum Wien, Collection, Vienna.

7 Briggs lived at Hofzeile 29 from March 25, 1925, to November 1, 1925. Bauxi Mang to Helga Schmidt-Thomsen, June 13, 1984, Ella Briggs Archive, Architekturzentrum Wien, Collection, Vienna. Salzer was a graduate of the *Höhere Gartenbauschule für Frauen*, the horticultural school for women founded by Yella Hertzka. See Ulrike Krippner and Iris Meder, "Verlässliche Gärtnerinnen heranzubilden: Wiens private Gartenbauschulen für Frauen vor 1938," *David: Jüdische Kulturzeitschrift*, no. 86 (2010): 64–65.

8 Bauxi Mang to Helga Schmidt-Thomsen, June 13, 1984, Ella Briggs Archive, Architekturzentrum Wien, Collection, Vienna.

9 Both Briggs and Dirnhuber were members of the Zentralvereinigung der Architekten Österreichs (Central Association of Austrian Architects). Dirnhuber joined in 1919; Briggs in 1925. See further discussion below.

10 Gisela Urban, "The Problem for Housing for Self-Supporting Women," *Time and Tide* [5, no. 14], April 4, 1924, 333.

11 Marie-Noëlle Yazdanpanah, "'Es lebe drum: Die Frau von heut!': Frauenpolitik im Roten Wien," in *Das Rote Wien 1919–1934: Ideen, Debatten, Praxis*, ed. Werner Michael Schwarz, Georg Spitaler, Elke Wikidal (Basel: Birkhäuser, 2019), 50–57.

12 Blau, *The Architecture of Red Vienna*, 5, 43.

13 On Karl Dirnhuber, see *Zivilarchitekt Dr. Ing. Karl Dirnhuber: Zehn Jahre freischaffender Architekt 1921–1931: Eine Auswahl von Entwürfen und ausgeführten Bauten*, foreword by Max Eisler (Vienna: Elbemühl, 1932).

14 Zentralvereinigung der Architekten Österreichs, 1907–1938, statutes, 7 May 1929, BKA-I BPDion Wien VB Signatur VIII-1665, Österreichisches Staatsarchiv, Archiv der Republik, Vienna, Austria; Ella Briggs to Ministerium für Wissenschaft, Kunst und Volksbildung, Berlin, December 2, 1918, HA-I, Rep. 76Vb, Sekt. 4, Tit. 7, Nr. 6, Bd. 1, Geheimes Staatsarchiv, Berlin; *Verzeichnis der Mitglieder der Zentralvereinigung der Architekten Österreichs nach dem Stande vom 1. Juni 1933* (Vienna: Verlag der Zentralvereinigung der Architekten Österreichs 1933), 30.

15 Sabine Plakolm-Forsthuber, "Leonie Pilweski 1897–1992," in *Pionierinnen der Wiener Architektur*, ed. Ingrid Holzschuh, Sabine Plakolm-Forsthuber, Zentralvereinigung der ArchitektInnen Österreichs (Basel: Birkhäuser, 2022), 86–97. For further discussion of Leonie Pilewski's career, see chapter 24, "Jewish Women Architects in Vienna," in this volume.

16 Emmy Freundlich, "Was sieht die Hausfrau in der Ausstellung Der neue Haushalt?," *Arbeiter-Zeitung*, May 12, 1925; George, *The Naked Truth*, 49; "Die Hygiene-Ausstellung," *Neues Wiener Tagblatt*, April 29, 1925.

17 Mary Nolan, *Visions of Modernity: American Business and the Modernization of Germany* (Oxford: Oxford University Press, 1994); Martina Hessler, "The Frankfurt Kitchen: The Model of Modernity and the 'Madness' of Traditional Users, 1926–1933," in *Cold War Kitchen: Americanization, Technology, and European Users*, ed. Ruth Oldenziel and Karin

Zachmann (Cambridge, MA: MIT Press, 2011), 163–84.

18 Christine Frederick, *The New Housekeeping: Efficiency Studies in Home Management* (Garden City, NY: Doubleday, Page and Co., 1913); Christine Frederick, *Die rationelle Haushaltführung: Betriebswissenschaftliche Studien*, trans. Irene M. Witte (Berlin: Springer, 1921).

19 Michael Wildt, "Technik, Kompetenz, Modernität: Amerika als zwiespältiges Vorbild für die Arbeit in der Küche, 1920–1960," in *Amerikanisierung: Traum und Alptraum im Deutschland des 20. Jahrhunderts*, ed. Alf Lüdtke, Inge Marßolek, Adelheid von Saldern (Stuttgart, Franz Steiner, 1996), 79–80.

20 Bruno Taut, *Die neue Wohnung: Die Frau als Schöpferin* (Leipzig: Klinkhardt and Biermann, 1924).

21 "Die Hauswirtschaft," *Der freie Genossenschafter* [23, no. 13], July 1, 1925, 6.

22 Gisela Urban, "Der neue Haushalt: Eine Ausstellung der österreichischen Frauenorganisationen," *Neue Freie Presse*, January 23, 1925; Gisela Urban, "Die rationelle Haushaltführung," *Rohö-Flugblatt* [5, no. 13], July 1, 1925, 1–2; "Tagung des Bundes österreichischer Frauenvereine," *Reichspost*, April 2, 1925.

23 The radio address was reprinted, without identifying the speaker, in "Der neue Haushalt," *Rohö-Flugblatt* [5, no. 8], April 15, 1925, 1. It may have been Emmy Freundlich; see below.

24 "Programm der Hygiene-Ausstellung von heute," *Der Tag*, June 16, 1925.

25 Briggs, "Arbeitserleichterung im amerikanischen Kleinhaus"; Ella Briggs, "Taylorisierungsbestrebungen in amerikanischen Küchen," *Arbeiter-Zeitung*, June 13, 1925. The latter was reprinted two weeks later in Linz's workers' newspaper: Ella Briggs, "Taylorisierungsbestrebungen in amerikanischen Küchen," *Tagblatt* [Linz], June 28, 1925.

26 Briggs, "Taylorisierungsbestrebungen in amerikanischen Küchen"; Briggs, "Arbeitserleichterung im amerikanischen Kleinhaus."

27 Briggs, "Taylorisierungsbestrebungen in amerikanischen Küchen."

28 Else Ehrlich, "Der neue Haushalt," *Der Tag*, May 4, 1925.

29 Emmy Freundlich, "Arbeitsgemeinschaften der Hausfrauen," *Arbeiter-Zeitung*, April 11, 1925. On the different ideological justifications given by American and European reformers for easing the burden of housewives' labor, see Barbara Penner, "Gender and Home: (Re)scripting Domestic Life and Design," in *A Cultural History of the Home in the Modern Age*, ed. Despina Stratigakos (London: Bloomsbury Academic, 2021), 137–60.

30 For recent examples of a growing body of scholarship that investigates how women architects engaged with home economics to advance modern design, see Jannie Rosenberg Bendsen, Svava Riesto, and Henriette Steiner, *Untold Stories: Women, Gender, and Architecture in Denmark* (Copenhagen: Strandberg, 2023); Marcel Bois and Bernadette Reinhold, eds., *Margarete Schütte-Lihotzky: Architecture, Politics, Gender; New Perspectives on Her Life and Work* (Basel: Birkhäuser, 2023); and Sigal Davidi, "Home Planning and Gender in Mandatory Palestine," *Journal of the Society of Architectural Historians* 82, no. 1 (2023): 46–62.

31 *Amtsblatt der Stadt Wien* [34, no. 65], August 15, 1925, 912. The resolution to build the Ledigenheim, which adjoins the Pestalozzi-Hof, was passed on October 29, 1926; *Amtsblatt der Stadt Wien* [35, no. 89], November 6, 1926, 1193.

32 "Zwei neue Wohnhausbauten," *Zeitschrift der Baumeister Oesterreichs* 12, no. 16 (1925): 5.

CHAPTER 12. ITALIAN TRAVELS, ARCHITECTURAL PHOTOGRAPHY, AND JAIL

1 Austin Whittlesey, *The Renaissance Architecture of Central and Northern Spain* (New York: Architectural Book Publishing Company, 1920); Louis Conrad Rosenberg, *The Davanzati Palace, Florence, Italy* (New York: Architectural Book Publishing Company, 1922); Louis Conrad Rosenberg, *Cottages, Farmhouses and Other Minor Buildings in England of the 16th, 17th and 18th Centuries* (New York: Architectural Book Publishing Company, 1923); Winsor Soule, *Spanish Farm Houses and Minor Public Buildings* (New York: Architectural Book Publishing Company, 1924); Harold Donaldson Eberlein, *Spanish Interiors, Furniture and Details: From the 14th to 17th Century* (New York: Architectural Book Publishing Company, 1925); William D. Foster and Louis C. Rosenberg, *Cottages, Manoirs and Other Minor Buildings of Normandy and Brittany* (New York: Architectural Book Publishing Company, 1926).

2 Guy Lowell, *Smaller Italian Villas and Farmhouses* (New York: Architectural Book Publishing Company, 1916); Guy Lowell, *More Small Italian Villas and Farmhouses* (New York: Architectural Book Publishing Company, 1920); "Abenteuer einer Wiener Architektin in Sizilien"; "Wie es einem in Italien ergehen kann: Frau Architektin Ella Briggs über ihre Haft in Palermo," *Allgemeiner Tiroler Anzeiger*, January 2, 1926. In 1925, the Architectural Book Publishing Company also published a travelog-style architectural book on Italy; see Marian O. Hooker, *Farmhouses and Small Provincial Buildings in Southern Italy* (New York: Architectural Book Publishing Co., 1925), which Briggs may have seen in advance.

3 Arthur L. Blakeslee, *Ornamental Details of the Italian Renaissance* (New York: Architecture Book Publishing Company, 1920); George Leighton Dahl, *Portals, Doorways and Windows of France* (New York: Architectural Book Publishing Company, 1925).

4 Briggs had some previous experience illustrating travelogs. In 1922, her watercolor sketches of buildings and street scenes illustrated an article about the historic architecture of the Wachau, a heavily touristed and picturesque Austrian valley along the Danube River. The essay appeared in the *Deutsch-Amerika*, an illustrated weekly published by the *New Yorker Staatszeitung*, and intended for a German-speaking American audience. "Wachaufahrt," *Deutsch-Amerika* 8, no. 23 (1922): 12–13.

5 Maurice Baumfeld, *Cruising in the Mediterranean* (New York: Emil L. Boas and the South Publishing Press, 1905).

6 See Andrea Nelson, *The New Woman behind the Camera* (Washington, DC: National Gallery of Art, 2020).

7 See Val Williams, *Women Photographers: The Other Observers, 1900 to the Present* (London: Virago Press, 1986); Naomi Rosenblum, *A History of Women Photographers* (New York: Abbeville Press, 1994); Christian Bouqueret, *Les Femmes Photographes: De la Nouvelle Vision en France 1920–1940* (Paris: Marval, 1998); Lena Johannesson, Gunilla Knape, Eva Dahlman, eds., *Women Photographers—European Experience* (Gothenburg: Acta Universitatis Gothoburgensis, 2004); Ulrich Pohlmann, ed., *Qui a peur des femmes photographes? 1839–1945*, exhibition catalog Musée d'Orsay and Musée de l'Orangerie (Paris: Hazan, 2015); Ulrike Matzer, ed., *Marianne Strobl, "Industrie-Photograph," 1894–1914* (Salzburg: Fotohof, 2017).

8 A sociologist, Gisèle Freund wrote her discipline's first academic study on photography; her dissertation, "La Photographie en France au dix-neuvième siècle," was published by La Maison des Amis de Livres [Paris] in 1936. While still a student, she also became active as a photojournalist and undertook reporting trips to England's industrial areas. See Gisèle Freund, *Gisèle Freund: Photographs and Memoirs*, foreword by Christian Caujolle (Munich: Schirmer/Mosel, 2008). In addition to pursuing photography, Lucia Moholy worked as an editor and proofreader for renowned publishing houses. Of her oeuvre, the Bauhaus photographs would subsequently receive the most acclaim. See Rolf Sachsse, *Lucia Moholy: Bauhaus Fotografin* (Berlin: Museumspädagogischer Dienst, 1995); and Jordan Troeller, ed., *Lucia Moholy: Exposures* (Prague: Kunsthalle Praha, and Berlin: Hatje Cantz, 2024).

9 See Iris Meder and Andrea Winklbauer, eds., *Vienna's Shooting Girls: Jüdische Fotografinnen aus Wien* (Vienna: Metroverlag, 2012).

10 Alice Schalek had been active as a journalist and traveler since 1903, and during the First World War she also worked as a war correspondent. Her best-known travel books include *Indienbummel* (Berlin: Concordia Deutsche Verlags-Anstalt, 1912); *In Buddhas Land: Ein Bummel durch Hinterindien* (Vienna: Rikola, 1922); *Japan, das Land des Nebeneinander: Eine Winterreise durch Japan, Korea und die Mandschurei* (Breslau: Hirt, 1925); and *An den Höfen der Maharadschas* (Zürich: Orell Füssli, 1929). On Schalek, see *Von Samoa zum Isonzo: Die Fotografin und Reisejournalistin Alice Schalek*, ed. Elke Krasny, Marcus Patka, Christian Rapp, and Nadia Rapp-Wimberger (Vienna: Jüdisches Museum, 1999); and Rebekka Grossmann, "Alice Schalek," in *A World History of Women Photographers*, ed. Luce Lebart and Marie Robert (London: Thames and Hudson, 2022), 82.

11 In the 1950s, Briggs claimed she had made three trips. See Manfred Mayer to Entschädigungsamt Berlin, October 11, 1956, and Ella Briggs, declaration regarding loss of property [Eidesstattliche Erklärung], May 13, 1957; both sources in Reg. no. 251.039 Ella Briggs, BEG-Akte (German Federal Compensation Act), LABO. Contemporary newspaper accounts, however, mention only two trips. See "Im Massengefängnis von Palermo! Die furchtbaren Erlebnisse der Wienerin Ella Briggs," *Wiener Allgemeine Zeitung*, December 31, 1925; and, "Sbirrengeist im heutigen Italien: Randbemerkungen zum Fall Ella Briggs," *Der Tag*, December 31, 1925. Her advance fee is mentioned in "Wie es einem in Italien ergehen kann," *Allgemeiner Tiroler Anzeiger*.

12 Given the geographical and chronological range of her architectural subjects, as evident from the surviving photographs, Briggs may have had in mind a separate, broader project on Italy's cultural landscapes.

13 Entry for Ella Briggs, ship manifest for the SS *Reliance*, arriving at the Port of New York on October 12, 1923, Passenger and Crew Lists of Vessels Arriving at New York, New York, 1897–1957, microfilm T715, Records of the Immigration and Naturalization Service, 1787–2004, record group 85, National Archives, Washington, DC, accessed on ancestry.com. The description of Briggs's height in this record may not be accurate; the information about her height and appearance varies across ship records. Briggs's camera, together with prints she made on her Italian journeys, are preserved in the collection of the Bert Singer and Angela Kimberk Archive (Cambridge, MA), Architekturzentrum Wien, Collection, Vienna.

14 Ella Briggs, "A Distinctive House Adapted from the Italian," *Ladies' Home Journal* [43, no. 6], June 1926, 42. One of her sketches from Taormina published in this article bears a date of January 25, 1925.

15 "Wie es einem in Italien ergehen kann," *Allgemeiner Tiroler Anzeiger*; "Verhaftung einer Wiener Dame in Palermo," *Neue Freie Presse*, December 24, 1925; "Wie es einem Wiener in Italien ergehen kann," *Arbeiter-Zeitung*, December 31, 1925; "Im Massengefängnis von Palermo!"

16 See, for example, "U.S. Woman Held as Spy," *Los Angeles Record*, December 24, 1925. Stories about

Briggs's imprisonment appeared in newspapers in Austria, Canada, France, Germany, and the United States, and possibly other countries as well.

17 Antonio Pizzuto is celebrated today as an experimentalist novelist, "the Italian Joyce." Gianfranco Contini quoted in Serenella Zanotti, "James Joyce among the Italian Writers," in *The Reception of James Joyce in Europe*, vol. 1, *Germany, Northern and East Central Europe*, ed. Geert Lernout and Wim Van Mierlo (London: Thoemmes Continuum, 2004), 346.

18 "Wie es einem in Italien ergehen kann," *Allgemeiner Tiroler Anzeiger.*

19 "Wie es einem Wiener in Italien ergehen kann," *Arbeiter-Zeitung*. The letter to the relative, addressed to "B.," was published in "Verhaftung einer Wiener Dame in Palermo."

20 "Wie es einem in Italien ergehen kann," *Allgemeiner Tiroler Anzeiger*; "Verhaftung einer Wiener Dame in Palermo." She later told her grandniece Phylis Morrison that her brother Friedrich had been on vacation at the time and had not received her letter asking for help. Despina Stratigakos, notes of telephone interview with Phylis Morrison (and email message from Morrison, n.d.), May 2, 1996, Ella Briggs Archive, Architekturzentrum Wien, Collection, Vienna.

21 "American Woman Held in Sicily; Accused as Spy," *Hollywood Daily Citizen*, December 24, 1925; "American Is Arrested in Sicily," *Cincinnati Enquirer*, December 25, 1925.

22 "Verhaftung einer österreichischen Architektin unter Spionageverdacht," *Neues Wiener Tagblatt*, December 24, 1925.

23 "Das Abenteuer einer österreichischen Architektin in Sizilien," *Neues Wiener Journal*, December 25, 1925; "Woman Believed to Have Been Held as Spy Freed in Italy," *Columbus Telegram* [Columbus, Nebraska], December 26, 1925; "Mrs. Briggs Freed by Italian Officials," *New York Times*, December 28, 1925; "Ella Briggs Freigelassen," *Tagblatt*, December 29, 1925. Paul Pallester is mentioned as a "brother-in-law" in the obituary of Moritz Baumfeld's first wife, Ange. See chapter 2, note 11.

24 "Woman Believed to Have Been Held as Spy Freed in Italy"; "Wie es einem in Italien ergehen kann," *Allgemeiner Tiroler Anzeiger*; Beatrice Baskerville, "New York Architect Is Still Befuddled," *Commercial Appeal* [Memphis, TN], December 28, 1925.

25 "Faschisten-Terror: Erlebnisse einer Wienerin in Sizilien," *Münchner Neueste Nachrichten*, December 31, 1925.

26 "Im Massengefängnis von Palermo!"; "Wie es einem Wiener in Italien ergehen kann," *Arbeiter-Zeitung.*

27 Briggs, "A Distinctive House Adapted from the Italian."

28 Ella Briggs, "Sizilianische Reisebilder," *Deutsche Bauzeitung* [64, no. 36], May 3, 1930, 281–86.

29 Briggs, "Sizilianische Reisebilder," 281.

30 Francesco Passanti, "The Vernacular, Modernism, and Le Corbusier," *Journal of the Society of Architectural Historians* 56, no. 4 (1997): 438–51; Jo Odgers, Flora Samuel, and Adam Sharr, eds., *Primitive: Original Matters in Architecture* (London: Routledge, 2006); Jean-François Lejeune and Michelangelo Sabatino, eds., *Modern Architecture and the Mediterranean: Vernacular Dialogues and Contested Identities* (Abingdon, UK: Routledge, 2010).

31 "Wie es einem in Italien ergehen kann," *Allgemeiner Tiroler Anzeiger*; "Die Abenteuer der Frau Ella Briggs," *Wiener Allgemeine Zeitung*, January 1, 1926; "Im Massengefängnis von Palermo!"

32 Despina Stratigakos, notes of telephone interview with Phylis Morrison (and email message from Morrison, n.d.), May 2, 1996, Ella Briggs Archive, Architekturzentrum Wien, Collection, Vienna.

CHAPTER 13. BUILDING FOR RED VIENNA: PESTALOZZI-HOF AND LEDIGENHEIM

1 On Red Vienna, see, among others, Werner Michael Schwarz, Georg Spitaler, and Elke Wikidal, eds., *Das Rote Wien, 1919–1934: Ideen, Debatten, Praxis* (Basel: Birkhäuser, 2019); Blau, *The Architecture of Red Vienna*; Wolfgang Hösl and Gottfried Pirhofer, *Wohnen in Wien, 1848–1938: Studien zur Konstitution des Massenwohnens* (Vienna: Deuticke, 1988); and Stingl, "Ella Briggs (-Baumfeld)."

2 Blau, *The Architecture of Red Vienna*, 180–85.

3 Blau, *The Architecture of Red Vienna*, 204.

4 Eve Blau, "From Red Superblock to Green Megastructure: Municipal Socialism as Model and Challenge," in *Architecture and the Welfare State*, ed. Mark Swenarton, Tom Avermaete, and Dirk Van Den Heuvel (Abingdon, UK: Routledge, 2015), 26–49.

5 Philip Oltermann, "The Social Housing Secret: How Vienna Became the World's Most Livable City," *Guardian*, January 10, 2024.

6 Stingl, "Ella Briggs (-Baumfeld)," 38–40.

7 Although the building permit was not officially issued until May 14, 1926, a newspaper article from December 1925 mentions that construction was well advanced by that point. See "Abenteuer einer Wiener Architektin in Sizilien." The occupancy permit was issued on November 19, 1926.

8 *Die Wohnhausanlage der Gemeinde Wien Pestalozzi-Hof im 19. Bezirk Philippovichgasse (früher Felix-Mottl-Straße)* (Vienna: Vorwärts, c. 1926–1927), 8, 10.

9 For more on the German Theater, see chapter 5, "A Viennese Designer Takes Manhattan," in this volume.

10 In the case of both the retail area and the kindergarten, Briggs marked these as special zones through the strong color of their facades. Additionally, both zones are framed by high cornices, which also form the parapet for the balconies above. Furthermore,

on the facades above, the impression of vertical columns is created by recessing the wall surfaces between the windows.

11 In an article published a few years later, Briggs described a more satisfactory model for a kindergarten: Ella Briggs, "Jugend-Tagesräume: Säuglingsheime—Kindergärten—Jugendhorte," *Bauwelt* [22, no. 8], February 9, 1931, 221–23.

12 Otto Neurath mentioned some of the disputes over the use of balconies in social housing in his article "Kommunaler Wohnungsbau in Wien," *Die Form* 6, no. 3 (1931): 110.

13 See Anita Aigner, "Der Schritt nach Draußen: Zur Phänomenologie des zugeordneten Außenraumes im Wiener Wohnbau, 1919–1934" (PhD diss., Vienna Technical University, 1998), 105, tab. 2.

14 Briggs, "We Plan a House for You"; Briggs, "We Plan *Another* House," 69, 103. See also chapter 10, "Building Clients and Avid Readers in New York and Beyond," in this volume.

15 "Ella Briggs: Eine Wiener Architektin," 13.

16 Despina Stratigakos, notes of telephone interview with Phylis Morrison (and email message from Morrison, n.d.), May 2, 1996, Ella Briggs Archive, Architekturzentrum Wien, Collection, Vienna.

17 Otto Polak-Hellwig, "Wohnungstypen: In den Wohnhausbauten der Gemeinde Wien," *Neues Wiener Tagblatt*, May 8, 1926, and May 22, 1926.

18 In addition, the apartments were provided with cold water only, so finding an appropriate location for a boiler would have been a prerequisite.

19 Ella Briggs, "Elektrizität im Haushalt," *Wohnungswirtschaft* 4, no. 1–2 (1927): 92.

20 The following description is based on Walter Müller-Wulckow, *Die Deutsche Wohnung der Gegenwart* (Königstein im Taunus: Langewiesche, 1932), 16, 17, and 23; and "Ella Briggs: Eine Wiener Architektin," 12–13.

21 See Blau, *Architecture of Red Vienna*, 105, 187ff.

22 The home (Verein "Witwen- und Waisenhort"), operating since 1900, was located at Eisengasse 23 in Vienna, and took in single women, poor widows, and orphans. Briggs stayed there from October 17 to November 14, 1902. We thank Elana Shapira for pointing out this early stay by Briggs in a social institution. See "Briefkasten," *Blatt der Hausfrau* [15, no. 33], 1904–5, 848; and address research supplied by the Magistratsabteilung 8, Wiener Stadt- U. Landesarchiv dated May 26, 1994, to Sabine Plakolm, attached to letter from Sabine Plakolm-Forsthuber to Despina Stratigakos, November 6, 1995; deposited in the Ella Briggs Archive, Architekturzentrum Wien, Collection, Vienna.

23 Ella Briggs's residence registration form, 1912, Vienna VIII, Josefsgasse 2, Lehrerhaus-Verein [residence of the teachers' association], Meldearchiv Wien, Wiener Stadt- und Landesarchiv (MA 8), Vienna. On Briggs's stay in the Lehrerhaus-Verein, see also chapter 7, "Opening an Interior Design Firm in Vienna," in this volume.

24 Ella Briggs's residence registration form, 1926–1929, Weimarer Strasse 1, Atelier 26, Meldearchiv Wien, Wiener Stadt- und Landesarchiv (MA 8), Vienna.

25 "Die Wohnhausanlage Pestalozzi-Hof: Das erste Wiener Ledigenheim," in *Die Neue Wirtschaft* 5, no. 8 (1927): 7; "Kommunale Studentenheime: Zur gestrigen Eröffnung des ersten Studentenhauses der Gemeinde Wien," *Der Tag*, May 13, 1928. For the building plans as well as the technical description of the Ledigenheim, see Building file EZ 2237, Magistratsabteilung 37, Baupolizei, nineteenth district, Vienna.

26 Briggs, "A Distinctive House Adapted from the Italian."

27 In a 1928 *Bauwelt* article, a photograph of the Ledigenheim's garden view was adjusted to make the courtyard facade appear brighter and more unified. Specifically, the flanking sections of the building on either end appear white, like the center. It remains uncertain if the adjustments for the trade journal were due to Briggs or the editor. See Ella Briggs, "Ledigenheim und Kleinstwohnungshäuser," *Bauwelt* [19, no. 48], November 19, 1928, 1132–33.

28 On color in modernist architecture, see Deborah Ascher Barnstone, *Color in German Architecture of the 1920s* (London: Bloomsbury Visual Arts, 2021).

29 In the interior, too, Briggs used decorative features, including color and patterns, to enliven otherwise functional spaces. In the Ledigenheim and Pestalozzi-Hof stairwells, the tile flooring was arranged in checkerboard patterns. In the Pestalozzi-Hof, she varied the design of the staircase railings according to the stairwell types.

30 "Techn. Beschreibung des Ledigenheims XIX., Billrothstr. 9," n.d. [c. April 1927], technical description included in the building file EZ 2237, Magistratsabteilung 37, Baupolizei, nineteenth district, Vienna.

31 Markus Eisen, "'Neues Wohnen' für 'Neue Menschen'. Ledigenheime als Programmbauten der Moderne in der späten Weimarer Republik," *RIHA Journal* (May 2018): https://doi.org/10.11588/riha.2018.1.

32 Briggs, "A Little House That Grew," 54; Briggs, "Ledigenheim und Kleinstwohnungshäuser," 1132.

33 Josef Bittner, "Neue Wohnhausbauten der Gemeinde Wien," *Statistische Mitteilungen der Stadt Wien*, nos. 10–12 (1926): 599; Karl Honay, "Eröffnung des Studentenheimes in der Billrothstrasse," *Rathauskorrespondenz* 137 (May 11, 1928), available online through the Vienna Library: https://www.digital.wienbibliothek.at/wbrobv/periodical/pageview/3618847; "Kommunale Studentenheime."

34 Briggs, "Ledigenheim und Kleinstwohnungshäuser," 1132.

35 Building file EZ 2237, Magistratsabteilung 37, Baupolizei, nineteenth district, Vienna.

36 "Kommunale Studentenheime." On the struggles of female students to find accommodations in Germany before the First World War, and the creation of a residence for female students by German architect Emilie Winkelmann, see Despina Stratigakos, "A Home of Our Own: Single Women and the New Domestic Architecture," in *A Women's Berlin: Building the Modern City* (Minneapolis: University of Minnesota Press, 2008), 53–96.

37 "Ella Briggs: Eine Wiener Architektin." The interview appeared in the October 4 issue of the magazine.

38 "Ella Briggs: Eine Wiener Architektin," 12.

39 "Ella Briggs: Eine Wiener Architektin," 12.

40 "Eröffnung des Pestalozzi-Hofes," *Neues Wiener Tagblatt*, February 28, 1927.

CHAPTER 14. AN OFFICE IN BERLIN: MODERNIST HOUSING BLOCKS

1 In documents pertaining to her application for German citizenship, Briggs is reported to have arrived in Berlin in April 1927. See letter to Oberregierungsrat Reiff, September 13, 1932; Konsularangelegenheit Oesterreichische Gesandtschaft Berlin to Polizeipräsidium Berlin, May 2, 1934; all in Ella Briggs's application for German citizenship, APr.Br. Rep. 030–06, no. 11426, Landesarchiv Berlin.

2 Iain Boyd Whyte and David Frisby, eds., *Metropolis Berlin: 1880–1940* (Berkeley: University of California Press, 2012), 1–2.

3 Celina Kress, "Gemeinnütziger Wohnungsbau bis 1933," in *100 Jahre Gross-Berlin: Wohnungsfrage und Stadtentwicklung*, ed. Harald Bodenschatz and Klaus Brake (Berlin: Lukas, 2017), 64–79.

4 In 1924, a new subsidy instrument called the *Hauszinssteuer* (a tax levied on the property wealth people accrued when they paid off their mortgages during the period of inflation, before the monetary stabilization of 1923), was put in place. In the initial phase, up to 90 percent of housing costs could be covered by *Hauszinssteuer* funds. The *Hauszinssteuer* gave municipalities the ability to demand quality standards. The federal states had the authority to stipulate how the tax would be levied. "Richtlinien für die Verwendung des für die Neubautätigkeit bestimmten Anteils am Hauszinssteueraufkommen," in Jacob Schallenberger and Hans Kraffert, *Berliner Wohnungsbauten aus öffentlichen Mitteln: Die Verwendung der Hauszinssteuer-Hypotheken* (Berlin: Bauwelt, 1926), 111–13; Christoph Bernhardt, "Aufstieg und Krise der öffentlichen Wohnungsbauförderung in Berlin 1900–1945," in *Wohnen in Berlin: 100 Jahre Wohnungsbau in Berlin*, ed. Lothar Juckel (Berlin: Stadtbaukunst, 1999), 61–63.

5 Celina Kress, *Adolf Sommerfeld / Andrew Sommerfield: Bauen für Berlin, 1910–1970* (Berlin: Lukas, 2011), 60.

6 Jacob Schallenberger and Hans Kraffert, *Berliner Wohnungsbauten aus öffentlichen Mitteln* (Berlin: Bauwelt, 1926).

7 Wagner had cofounded and directed the Verband sozialer Betriebe (Association of Social Enterprises, or VsB), an umbrella construction organization that included financing firms, construction companies, and housing agencies. Additionally, he cofounded and directed two collaborative housing enterprises: Gemeinnützige Heimstätten-, Spar- und Bau-Aktiengesellschaft (Community Home Savings and Building Company, or GEHAG) and Deutsche Wohnungsfürsorge-Aktiengesellschaft (German Housing Welfare Company, or DEWOG).

8 Martin Wagner, "Großsiedlungen, der Weg zur Rationalisierung des Wohnungsbaues," in *Wohnungswirtschaft* (1926), cited in Ludovica Scarpa, "Das Großsiedlungs-Modell: Von der Rationalisierung zum Städtebau," in *Vier Berliner Siedlungen der Weimarer Republik*, ed. Norbert Huse (Berlin: Argon, 1987), 24.

9 Martin Wagner, "Zivilisation, Kultur, Kunst" (1926), cited in Scarpa, "Das Großsiedlungs-Modell," 25. Emphasis in the original.

10 For further discussion of these projects, see chapter 13, "Building for Red Vienna," in this volume.

11 Leo Adler, "Wohnhausblock und Ledigenheim 'Pestalozzihof' in Wien," *Wasmuths Monatshefte für Baukunst* 12, no. 2 (1928): 72.

12 Werner Hegemann, *Reihenhaus-Fassaden: Geschäfts- und Wohnhäuser aus alter und neuer Zeit* (Berlin: Wasmuth, 1929), 94–95; Walter Müller-Wulckow, *Wohnbauten und Siedlungen* (Königstein im Taunus: Langewiesche, 1929), 96; Müller-Wulckow, *Die deutsche Wohnung der Gegenwart*, 16–17, 23; and Hans Hildebrandt, *Die Frau als Künstlerin* (Berlin: Rudolf Mosse, 1928), 151, 153. Hildebrandt's book, a survey of women artists, is viewed with ambivalence today in how it frames its subjects and their contributions. We know that Briggs sent Hildebrandt materials about her architectural projects for inclusion in the book (see Hans and Lily Hildebrandt Papers, 1899–1979, Getty Research Institute, Los Angeles). She did so even though she fundamentally resisted being given special treatment as a woman; see chapter 13, "Building for Red Vienna," in this volume, and Briggs's interview in "Ella Briggs: Eine Wiener Architektin," 12. Nevertheless, Hildebrandt's volume was the first comprehensive attempt to make women in art and architecture visible. Briggs appears to have owned the book, as she listed the page numbers of her entries on a 1936 resume submitted to Godfrey Samuel. See Ella Briggs, resume, 1936, Godfrey Samuel Papers [hereafter cited as GSP], SAG\83\2, folder 3, Royal Institute of British Architects (RIBA), London [hereafter cited as RIBA].

13 Ella Briggs, resume, February 12, 1954, submitted with her restitution claim, Reg. no. 251.039 Ella Briggs, BEG-Akte (German Federal Compensation Act), LABO. Briggs's account in this resume only mentions that she made inquiries, not where she made them. Martin Wagner's letter of introduction (note 14 below), noting that she had presented her work to him, suggests she approached him directly.

14 Martin Wagner, letter of introduction for Ella Briggs, May 6, 1927, Reg. no. 251.039 Ella Briggs, BEG-Akte (German Federal Compensation Act), LABO.

15 Briggs, "Elektrizität im Haushalt," 92.

16 On this research tour, see chapter 10, "Building Clients and Avid Readers in New York and Beyond," in this volume. Briggs had published earlier on American domestic technologies. See Briggs, "Taylorisierungsbestrebungen in amerikanischen Küchen."

17 Briggs, "Ledigenheim und Kleinstwohnungshäuser."

18 W-r., "Architekturzeitschriften," *Berliner Börsen-Zeitung*, March 18, 1928.

19 "Gesellschaft für Spezialbauausführungen mit beschränkter Haftung," *Berliner Börsen-Zeitung*, November 18, 1930. In a postwar restitution claim, Briggs identified Adolf Bloch (representing the Gesellschaft für Spezialbauausführungen) as her client for the Mariendorf project. Ella Briggs, resume, February 12, 1954, Reg. no. 251.039 Ella Briggs, BEG-Akte (German Federal Compensation Act), LABO. Bloch appears to have belonged to a network of Jewish critics and investors who shared a progressive ideology regarding Berlin's modernization and who became supporters of Briggs. More research needs to be done on Briggs's relationship to such networks in Berlin.

20 A 1929 letter from Boswau and Knauer reveals that the company paid Briggs's architectural fee. Boswau & Knauer Aktiengesellschaft to Ella Briggs, September 30, 1929, Reg. no. 251.039 Ella Briggs, BEG-Akte (German Federal Compensation Act), LABO.

21 Plans submitted for approval, dated November/December 1928, attic plans, spring 1929, building files "Alt und Neu," Rathausstrasse 82–83b, Königstrasse 42–43, Baupolizei Berlin-Tempelhof, Germany.

22 Matthias Donath, Gabriele Schulz, and Michael Hofmann, *Denkmale in Berlin: Bezirk Tempelhof-Schöneberg—Ortsteile Tempelhof, Mariendorf, Marienfelde und Lichtenrade* (Petersberg: Michael Imhof, 2007), 61–62, 165–66.

23 It is possible the client intended to build an addition to the apartment block on the fourth side of the courtyard at a later date. For some time after the completion of the building, tenants questioned the soundness of the gable wall on the short northern wing, contending that their apartments were susceptible to moisture and cold temperatures because no stucco had been applied: this is perhaps another indication that further construction was planned at this end of the wing but never realized. See building files "Alt und Neu," Rathausstrasse 82-83b, Königstrasse 42-43, Baupolizei Berlin-Tempelhof.

24 Ella Briggs, "Wohnbau in Berlin-Mariendorf," *Bauwelt* [21, no. 18], May 1, 1930, 11. (This article appears within its own section, with different pagination, used here.)

25 Ella Briggs, "Bauen und Wohnen: Zur Ausstellung in Zehlendorf," *Berliner Tageblatt*, September 11, 1928. See below for further discussion of her positive review of the Waldsiedlung.

26 Briggs, "Wohnbau in Berlin-Mariendorf"; "Block of Flats in Berlin, Designed by Ella Briggs," *Architects' Journal* (July 1936): 89.

27 The Housing Welfare Society funding guidelines required a minimum floor area for kitchens of 10 square meters.

28 Harry J. Carman, "Germany's Economic Fluctuations in 1928," *Current History* 29, no. 5 (1929): 862–65. On the electrified kitchen, Briggs, "Taylorisierungsbestrebungen in amerikanischen Küchen"; Briggs, "Elektrizität im Haushalt," 92; and Ella Briggs, "Küche," in *Handwörterbuch des Wohnungswesens*, ed. Gerhard Albrecht et al. (Jena: Gustav Fischer, 1930), 449–51.

29 Dr. Buer, "Mietshausblock im Süden Berlins: Architektin Dipl.-Ing. Ella Briggs (Berlin)," *Deutsche Bauhütte* [35, no. 7], April 1, 1931, 114–15.

30 "Block of Flats in Berlin, Designed by Ella Briggs," 89.

31 Elevations submitted in November 1928 and subsequently pasted over, notations by the building authorities, building files "Alt und Neu," Rathausstrasse 82-83b, Königstrasse 42-43, Baupolizei Berlin-Tempelhof.

32 Briggs, "Bauen und Wohnen: Zur Ausstellung in Zehlendorf."

33 "Block of Flats in Berlin, Designed by Ella Briggs," 90.

34 Boswau & Knauer Aktiengesellschaft to Ella Briggs, September 30, 1929, Reg. no. 251.039 Ella Briggs, BEG-Akte (German Federal Compensation Act), LABO; Gebrauchsabnahmeverhandlung [occupancy permit hearing], November 26, 1929, building files "Alt und Neu," Rathausstrasse 82-83b, Königstrasse 42-43, Baupolizei Berlin-Tempelhof.

35 Dipl.-Ing. Ella Briggs's membership card, no. 414, which noted that she was admitted on July 1, 1929, Reg. no. 251.039 Ella Briggs, BEG-Akte (German Federal Compensation Act), LABO.

36 For further discussion, see chapter 15, "Publishing Endeavors," in this volume.

37 Ella Briggs resume, February 12, 1954, submitted with her restitution claim, Reg. no. 251.039 Ella Briggs, BEG-Akte (German Federal Compensation Act), LABO.

38 Ella Briggs, "Zwei Kleinwohnungsgrundrisse," *Bauwelt* [21, no. 18], May 1, 1930, 577.

39 In a letter of January 10, 1930, Jean Krämer advised Ella Briggs to contact the Primus housing association herself, since the latter had already informed him "that it had no money available now to pay the fees." Jean Krämer to Ella Briggs, January 10, 1930, Reg. no. 251.039 Ella Briggs, BEG-Akte (German Federal Compensation Act), LABO.

CHAPTER 15. PUBLISHING ENDEAVORS

1 Briggs, "Ledigenheim und Kleinstwohnungshäuser."
2 Gerhard Albrecht et al., eds., *Handwörterbuch des Wohnungswesens* (Jena: Gustav Fischer, 1930).
3 Briggs, "Küche."
4 Briggs, "Küche," 451.
5 See Briggs, "Taylorisierungsbestrebungen in amerikanischen Küchen"; and chapter 11, "Return to Vienna and a Big Break," in this volume.
6 Ella Briggs, "Laubenganghaus," in *Handwörterbuch des Wohnungswesens*, ed. Gerhard Albrecht et al. (Jena: Gustav Fischer, 1930), 500–503.
7 Briggs, "Bauen und Wohnen: Zur Ausstellung in Zehlendorf"
8 Briggs, "Sizilianische Reisebilder."
9 For more on Briggs's Italian trip, see chapter 12, "Italian Travels, Architectural Photography, and Jail," in this volume.
10 For more on Müllerstrasse, see chapter 14, "An Office in Berlin," in this volume.
11 Briggs, "Zwei Kleinwohnungsgrundrisse."
12 Adler, "Wohnhausblock und Ledigenheim 'Pestalozzihof' in Wien," 69–73.
13 Leo Adler, ed., *Neuzeitliche Mietshäuser und Siedlungen* (Berlin: Pollak, 1931), x, 255.

CHAPTER 16. EXHIBITION DESIGN: TRADE FAIRS IN BERLIN

1 Briggs's 1914 commission for the New Vienna Women's Club appears to have been her first opportunity to curate and design an exhibition. Since no photographs exist of the exhibition space, it is difficult to evaluate the design. Nevertheless, contemporary descriptions indicate she achieved a unifying arrangement that also allowed the objects displayed to be appreciated in their own right; that is, a comprehensive decorative scheme that was not hegemonic in the traditional *Raumkunst* sense. Reviewers also noted her inclusion of photographs of her interior design ensembles. See chapter 7, "Opening an Interior Design Firm in Vienna," in this volume.
2 Ella Briggs, "Ausstellungs-Gestaltungen," *Bauwelt* [22, no. 19], May 7, 1931, 648–50. My thanks to Astrid Böck at the TU Wien Library for her help obtaining journals.
3 Günther Sandner, "Otto Neurath und die Wiener Methode der Bildstatistik," in *Die Konturen der Welt: Geschichte und Gegenwart visueller Bildung nach Otto Neurath*, ed. Gernot Waldner (Vienna: Mandelbaum, 2021), 26–29. On Frank's design for the museum, see Long, *Josef Frank: Life and Work*, 166.
4 Ella Briggs to Otto Neurath, n.d. [ca. March 1943], Otto and Marie Neurath Isotype Collection, University of Reading, UK. Many thanks to Christopher Burke for pointing me to this correspondence.
5 Briggs, "Ausstellungs-Gestaltungen," 649.
6 *Die Ernährung: Ausstellung für gesunde und zweckmäßige Ernährung* (Berlin: Gersbach, 1928). My thanks to Celina Kress for information from this catalog. Briggs may also have been commissioned to design a "modern American kitchen" for this exhibition. In 1927, she toured the United States to study the latest American kitchen designs. She was commissioned to do so by the German government for an unnamed three-month 1928 exhibition that began in April, coinciding almost exactly with the dates of the Ernährung exhibition. Unfortunately, we have no further information on this project. See "Germany Asks A.G.A. Aid," *American Gas Association Monthly* 10, no. 4 (1928): 243.
7 Briggs, "Ausstellungs-Gestaltungen," 649.
8 Deutsches Kupfer Institut Berlin Halensee to Ella Briggs, May 1, 1929, Reg. no. 251.039 Ella Briggs, BEG-Akte (German Federal Compensation Act), LABO.
9 Briggs, "Bauen und Wohnen: Zur Ausstellung in Zehlendorf." For further discussion of Moholy-Nagy's work at the *Bauen und Wohnen* exhibition, see Kress, *Adolf Sommerfeld / Andrew Sommerfield*, 158–59.
10 Ausstellungs-Messe und Fremdenverkehrs-Amt der Stadt Berlin to Ella Briggs, August 8, 1930, Reg. no. 251.039 Ella Briggs, BEG-Akte (German Federal Compensation Act), LABO.
11 Briggs, "Ausstellungs-Gestaltungen," 648–49.
12 *Grüne Woche* Berlin Exhibition Manager to Ella Briggs, January 14, 1931, Reg. no. 251.039 Ella Briggs, BEG-Akte (German Federal Compensation Act), LABO.
13 Briggs, "Ausstellungs-Gestaltungen," 650.
14 *Deutsche Bauausstellung Berlin 1931: Amtlicher Katalog und Führer* (Berlin: Bauwelt, 1931). Briggs was also invited to present a lecture on her work, entitled "The Dwelling of Our Time," at the exhibition. See Eliza Ichenhaeuser, "Im 'Ring der Frauen,'" *Kölnische Zeitung*, July 1, 1931.
15 "Die Bauwirtschaftlichen Verbände auf der deutschen Bauausstellung in Berlin," *Deutsche Bauzeitung* 65, nos. 57–58 (1931): 170–71; Wohnungsfürsorgegesellschaft Berlin m.b.H. to Ella Briggs, March 20, 1931, Reg. no. 251.039 Ella Briggs, BEG-Akte (German Federal Compensation Act), LABO.

16 Corinna Isabel Bauer, *Architekturstudentinnen in der Weimarer Republik: Bauhaus und Tessenow Schülerinnen* (PhD diss., University of Kassel, 2003), 198, 334; *Deutsche Bauausstellung Berlin 1931*, 154, 156; Josef Gantner, "Deutsche Bauausstellung Berlin 1931: Abteilung 'das Bauwerk unserer Zeit,'" *Zentralblatt der Bauverwaltung vereinigt mit Zeitschrift für Bauwesen* 51, nos. 49–50 (1931): 727–28.

17 Briggs, "Ausstellungs-Gestaltungen," 650.

18 In 1931, for her exhibition work Briggs received 5,600 reichsmark from the *Grüne Woche* fair and 5,863.90 reichsmark from the Wohnungsfürsorgegesellschaft (Housing Welfare Society). This amounted to almost the total of her income for that year (12,518.90 reichsmark or roughly $70,000 in today's values). Ella Briggs to the Polizei-Praesidium Berlin, March 26, 1932, [income statement for 1931 submitted as part of her German citizenship application], APr.Br. Rep. 030-06, no. 11426, Landesarchiv Berlin.

CHAPTER 17. LATE BERLIN PROJECTS, FAMILY TIES, AND GROWING DANGER

1 Tobias Straumann, *1931: Debt, Crisis, and the Rise of Hitler* (Oxford: Oxford University Press, 2019), xxii.

2 Rudolf Baade, *Kapital und Wohnungsbau in Berlin 1924 bis 1940* (Berlin: Berliner Wissenschafts-Verlag, 2004), 138.

3 Straumann, *1931: Debt, Crisis, and the Rise of Hitler*, 195; C. W. Gray, "Germany to Construct 16,000 Houses for Unemployed," *Commerce Reports*, no. 16 (April 18, 1932), 147; Timothy Moss, *Remaking Berlin: A History of the City through Infrastructure* (Cambridge, MA: MIT Press, 2020), 96; Tilman Harlander, Katrin Hater, and Franz Meiers, *Siedeln in der Not: Umbruch von Wohnungspolitik und Siedlungsbau am Ende der Weimarer Republik* (Hamburg: Christians, 1988); Gerd Kuhn, "Suburbanisierung: Planmäßige Dezentralisierung und 'wildes' Siedeln," in *Villa und Eigenheim: Suburbaner Städtebau in Deutschland*, ed. Tilman Harlander (Stuttgart: Deutsche Verlangs-Anstalt, 2001), 164–73; Gerd Kuhn, "Wohnungspolitik: Flachbausiedlungen für 'Minderbemittelte,'" in *Villa und Eigenheim*, ed. Harlander, 174–83, Gerd Kuhn, "Städtebau: Heimstätten, Kleinhäuser und Kleinsiedlungen," in *Villa und Eigenheim*, ed. Harlander, 184–97.

4 Ella Briggs, "Praktische Fragen zur Erwerbslosensiedlung," *Bauwelt* [22, no. 44], October 29, 1931, 1394–96.

5 Briggs, "How Austria Is Helping to Solve the Housing Problem." For further discussion of Briggs's involvement in the Vienna "wild settlement" movement, see chapter 9, "The Vienna Settler Movement and Early Architectural Work," in this volume.

6 In a 1936 resume, Briggs listed the ninety-five houses as completed. See Ella Briggs resume submitted to Godfrey Samuel, 1936, Godfrey Samuel Papers, SAG\83\2, folder 3, RIBA. (My thanks to Barbara Penner for sharing her research materials.) In 1932, Briggs presented this project as advancing: Ella Briggs to the Polizei-Praesidium Berlin, March 26, 1932, German citizenship application, APr.Br. Rep. 030-06, no. 11426, Landesarchiv Berlin.

7 "Die Stadtrandsiedlung Berlin-Blankenfelde: Entstehung und Entwicklung," Stadtrandsiedlung Berlin-Blankenfelde e.V., accessed December 1, 2024, https://stadtrandsiedlung.com/verein/die-chronik/; Bernd Wähner, "Bewohner der Stadtrandsiedlung Blankenfelde feiern 85. Geburtstag ihrer Siedlung," *Berliner Woche*, June 2, 2017, https://www.berliner-woche.de/event/blankenfelde/c-sonstiges/bewohner-der-stadtrandsiedlung-blankenfelde-feiern-85-geburtstag-ihrer-siedlung_e32612.

8 Gemeinnützige Baugesellschaft Berlin-Ost to Ella Briggs, March 20, 1930; and Ella Briggs, resume, February 12, 1954; both submitted with her restitution claim, Reg. no. 251.039 Ella Briggs, BEG-Akte (German Federal Compensation Act), LABO. On the Primus housing estate in Wedding, see chapter 14, "An Office in Berlin," in this volume.

9 Briggs, "Jugend-Tagesräume: Säuglingsheime—Kindergärten—Jugendhorte"; Briggs, "Praktische Fragen zur Erwerbslosensiedlung"; Ella Briggs, "Stockwerkswohnungs-Teilungen," *Bauwelt* [23, no. 50], December 15, 1932, 1273–74; Ella Briggs, "Einbaumöbel," *Deutsche Bauzeitung* [66, no. 33], August 10, 1932, 658–60.

10 Ella Briggs to the Polizei-Praesidium Berlin, March 26, 1932, in her citizenship application file, APr.Br. Rep. 030-06, no. 11426, Landesarchiv Berlin. Moniac was co-owner of the Moniac metalware company. In 1932, she was listed as a widow as well as owner and resident of the building at Schwäbische Strasse 26. See entry for "Moniac & Co. (Metallw.)," in the *Berliner Handels-Register*, vol. 64 (Berlin: Ullstein, 1928), 329; and *Berliner Adressbuch 1932* (Berlin: August Scherl Deutsche Adressbuch-Gesellschaft, 1932), 1551.

11 Ella Briggs resume submitted to Godfrey Samuel, 1936, Godfrey Samuel Papers, SAG\83\2, folder 3, RIBA.

12 Ella Briggs resume, February 12, 1954, submitted with her restitution claim, Reg. no. 251.039 Ella Briggs, BEG-Akte (German Federal Compensation Act), LABO; Ella Briggs resume submitted to Godfrey Samuel, 1936, Godfrey Samuel Papers, SAG\83\2, folder 3, RIBA. The Karlshorst project, which has yet to be identified, appears to have been Briggs's last Berlin project, as she emigrated shortly thereafter.

13 The building plans for these two houses are held by the Gemeinde Kleinmachnow Bauamt in Kleinmachnow, Germany. Haus Widera, on Fontanestrasse, was commissioned by Arthur Widera, a businessman, and constructed in 1933. Haus Hielscher, on Langendreesch, was commissioned by Paul Hielscher, a banker, and constructed in 1934–1935. On Haus Widera, see "House Near Berlin Designed by Ella Briggs," *Architects' Journal*, February 2, 1939, 211.

14 Entry for Ella Briggs on Emser Strasse 23, in the "Architekten, Architektenbüros" section, *BTB Branchen-Fernsprechbuch für Gross-Berlin und Umgegend*, vol. 8 (Berlin: Deutsche Reichs-Postreklame, 1928), 19.

15 Entry for F. Baumfeld on Fürther Strasse 4, *Berliner Adressbuch 1928* (Berlin: August Scherl Deutsche Adressbuch-Gesellschaft, 1928), part 4, 325. Ida Baumfeld settled in Berlin in 1915 and was registered in the Berlin address book from 1916 to 1932; see entries for Ida Baumfeld in *Berliner Adressbuch 1916* (Berlin: August Scherl Deutsche Adressbuch-Gesellschaft, 1916), 121, and *Berliner Adressbuch 1932* (Berlin: August Scherl Deutsche Adressbuch-Gesellschaft, 1932), 139. She returned to the United States in 1933 (see chapter 18, "Desperation in Vienna," in this volume). On the Bryks, see chapter 1, "Family Life in an Imperial Capital," and chapter 2, "Art and Design Studies," both in this volume.

16 Boswau & Knauer to Ella Briggs, September 30, 1929, Reg. no. 251.039 Ella Briggs, BEG-Akte (German Federal Compensation Act), LABO.

17 Hilda L. Briggs, United States passport application, January 16, 1922, Certificate 122386, Passport Applications, January 2, 1906–March 31, 1925, microfilm M1490, roll no. 1842, General Records of the Department of State, Record Group 59, National Archives in Washington, DC, accessed on ancestry.com; Walter J. Briggs, United States passport application, November 21, 1922, Certificate 237115, Passport Applications, January 2, 1906–March 31, 1925, microfilm M1490, roll no. 2148, General Records of the Department of State, Record Group 59, National Archives in Washington, DC, accessed on ancestry.com; obituary of Hilda Landes Briggs, *Editor & Publisher* 55, no. 39 (1923): 25.

18 See chapter 7, note 22 in this volume.

19 Listing for Walter J. Briggs in Berlin-Charlottenburg, *Commercial Law League Journal* 34 (1929): 122; "Berliner Faschingsfeste," *Sport im Bild* [35, no. 5], March 8, 1929, 304.

20 "Ella Briggs Polizeiliche Ummeldung," November 15, 1930; and "Ella Briggs, Polizeiliche Abmeldung," September 27, 1933; both in Reg. no. 251.039 Ella Briggs, BEG-Akte (German Federal Compensation Act), LABO.

21 For her interior design office in Vienna, she did hire at least one employee, and as a busy architect she would have required staff.

22 Ella Briggs to Polizei-Praesidium Berlin, March 5, 1932; letter to Oberregierungsrat Reiff, September 13, 1932; Polizeipräsident von Berlin to Ella Briggs, September 16, 1932; Konsularangelegenheit Oesterreichische Gesandtschaft Berlin to Polizeipräsidium Berlin, May 2, 1934; all in Ella Briggs's application for German citizenship, APr.Br. Rep. 030–06, no. 11426, Landesarchiv Berlin.

23 Ella Briggs mentioned a client who was a member of the SA in her letter to the Entschädigungsamt Berlin, February 12, 1954, submitted as part of her postwar restitution claim (Reg. no. 251.039 Ella Briggs, BEG-Akte [German Federal Compensation Act], LABO). Although Briggs did not name Bauer, she did state that the work for the client took place in the Berlin district of Johannisthal. In March 1934, Briggs was at work on a project located at Lindhorstweg 65 in Johannisthal; *Amtsblatt der Reichshauptstadt Berlin* 75, no. 11 (1934): 394. Hans Bauer is identified as the client. Bauer's stunningly swift career rise from toolmaker to technical employee to cost accountant revealed by entries in the Berlin address book for the years 1935 to 1938 (*Berliner Adressbuch 1935* [Berlin: August Scherl Deutsche Adressbuch-Gesellschaft, 1935], part 1, 103; *Berliner Adressbuch 1936* [Berlin: August Scherl Deutsche Adressbuch-Gesellschaft, 1936], part 1, 105; *Berliner Adressbuch 1938* [Berlin: August Scherl Deutsche Adressbuch-Gesellschaft, 1938], part 1, 109) strongly suggest the kind of political favors and promotion that came with membership in the Nazi party.

24 Ella Briggs to the Entschädigungsamt, February 12, 1954, submitted as part of her restitution claim, Reg. no. 251.039 Ella Briggs, BEG-Akte (German Federal Compensation Act), LABO.

CHAPTER 18. DESPERATION IN VIENNA

1 Ella Briggs's residence registration record on file with the Viennese authorities implied that she lived at her former apartment and studio in Vienna's eighteenth district until 1932. In fact, since 1927, Briggs had been living in Berlin. It is possible that she kept her Viennese studio and made short visits there during this period. See Ella Briggs's residence registration form, January 11, 1925, to April 1, 1935, eighteenth district, Weimarer Strasse 1 (Atelier 26), Meldearchiv Wien, Wiener Stadt- und Landesarchiv (MA 8), Vienna. When she returned in 1935, she stayed at a different address. See Ella Briggs's residence registration form, February 5, 1935, to March 5, 1935, nineteenth district, Linnéplatz 5, Meldearchiv Wien, Wiener Stadt- und Landesarchiv (MA 8), Vienna.

2 Kjäer's lecture was reviewed favorably in R. U., "Die Frau im Kunstgewerbe," *Neues Wiener Tagblatt*,

November 22, 1930. The lecture gave an overview of the historical development of women in the arts. In addition to Briggs, among the contemporary practitioners Kjäer discussed were Tina Blau-Lang and Olga Prager, founders of the Art School for Women and Girls, where Briggs had studied.

3 For more on this period, see Janek Wasserman, *Black Vienna: The Radical Right in the Red City, 1918–1938* (Ithaca, NY: Cornell University Press, 2017); and John W. Boyer, "The Catholic Dictatorship and the Nazi Occupation, 1933–1945," in *Austria, 1867–1955* (Oxford: Oxford University Press, 2022), 759–860.

4 Shapira, "'Our Great Josef Hoffmann,'"; Long, *Josef Frank: Life and Work*, 187–191. The interior design store Haus & Garten opened by Josef Frank and Oskar Wlach continued to operate during this period. See Christopher Long, "Refuge and Respite: Oskar Wlach, Max Eisler, and the Culture of the Modern Jewish Interior," in *Designing Transformation: Jews and Cultural Identity in Central European Modernism*, ed. Elana Shapira (London: Bloomsbury Visual Arts, 2021), 157–71.

5 Entry for Walter Briggs, departing on March 14, 1935, on the SS *Stuttgart* from Bremen, Archive no. AIII5–14.03.1935_N, accessed on Bremen Passenger Lists, www.passengerlists.de; see also chapter 17, "Late Berlin Projects, Family Ties, and Growing Danger," in this volume.

6 Ella Briggs's statement for the Entschädigungsamt Berlin dated August 4, 1954, Reg. no. 251.039 Ella Briggs, BEG-Akte (German Federal Compensation Act), LABO.

7 Ella Briggs's residence registration form, March 13, 1936, to June 9, 1936, eighteenth district, Bastiengasse 56/4, Meldearchiv Wien, Wiener Stadt- und Landesarchiv (MA 8), Vienna.

8 Ella Briggs to Godfrey Samuel, April 3, 1936; Godfrey Samuel to Ella Briggs, April 7, 1936; Ella Briggs to Godfrey Samuel, May 21, 1936; all in Godfrey Samuel Papers, SAG\83\2, folder 3, Drawings and Archives Collections, RIBA. Briggs asked Samuel about getting work with Tecton, the practice he had cofounded in 1932.

9 Else Hofmann, "25 Jahre Vereinigung Bildender Künstlerinnen Österreichs," *Österreichische Kunst* 7, no. 11 (1936), 20–21; "Möbel von Arch. Leonie Pilewski," *Österreichische Kunst* 7, no. 11 (1936): 26. For further discussion of Pilewski and other Jewish women architects, see chapter 24, "Jewish Women Architects in Vienna," in this volume.

10 The apartment was originally designed by Adolf Loos for the Goldman family, clients of the Goldman & Salatsch Haus. See Sabine Plakolm-Forsthuber, "'Loos Remodeled': Zum Umbau der Wohnung Leopold Goldman durch die Architektin Liane Zimber 1936," in *Design Dialogue: Jews, Culture and Viennese Modernism*, ed. Elana Shapira (Vienna: Böhlau, 2018), 263–80.

11 "Ausstellungen," *Das interessante Blatt* 55, no. 40 (1936): 10.

12 Ella Briggs's residence registration form, February 9, 1937, to February 15, 1937, nineteenth district, Weimarer Strasse 90/4, Meldearchiv Wien, Wiener Stadt- und Landesarchiv (MA 8), Vienna. In her application for German citizenship, Briggs mentioned that she and her siblings owned a house in Hinterbrühl near Vienna. It is possible that she returned to Vienna to sell this property in advance of her emigration to England. Ella Briggs to the Polizei-Praesidium Berlin, March 26, 1932, German citizenship application, APr. Br. Rep. 030–06, no. 11426, Landesarchiv Berlin.

13 For example, Berta Zuckerkandl wrote to her grandson Emile Zuckerkandl in March 1937 about the looming danger of Austria's annexation to Nazi Germany, asking rhetorically, "What then if you are a Jew?" Quoted in Gertrude Enderle-Burcel, ed., *Berta Zuckerkandl–Gottfried Kunwald: Briefwechsel, 1928–1938* (Vienna: Böhlau, 2018), 37.

14 Ida Baumfeld, United States of America Declaration of Intention, no. 35540, State of Connecticut, County of Fairfield, April 21, 1936, Naturalization Record Books, 12/1893-9/1906, Records of District Courts of the United States, Record Group 21, National Archives at Boston, Waltham, MA, accessed on ancestry.com. Ida arrived back in the United States in September 1933 with her daughter Beatrice, who, born in the United States, had been issued a US passport in Berlin. Ida listed her sister Lilly Pringsheim in Breslau as her nearest European relative. Entries for Ida and Beatrice Baumfeld, list or manifest of Alien Passengers for the United States Immigration Officer at Port of Arrival, MS *St. Louis*, passengers arriving at the Port of New York, September 13, 1933, Passenger and Crew Lists of Vessels Arriving at New York, New York, 1897–1957, microfilm T715, Records of the Immigration and Naturalization Service, Record Group 85, National Archives, Washington, DC, accessed on ancestry.com. On Pringsheim, see chapter 7, "Opening an Interior Design Firm in Vienna," in this volume. Unlike her sister, Pringsheim was unable to escape and was murdered in Theresienstadt in 1942. See Czech Terezín Initiative Institute's holocaust database, https://www.holocaust.cz/en/database-of-victims/victim/27927-elisabeth-pringsheim.

15 Doris L. Bergen, *War and Genocide: A Concise History of the Holocaust*, 3rd ed. (Lanham, MD: Rowman and Littlefield, 2016), 98.

16 In mid-August 1942, Löwenthal was among the 1,000 Jewish deportees, most elderly, transported from Vienna to the Theresienstadt concentration camp. She died there on October 17, 1942. See Lilli (Cornelia) Löwenthal's death notice from the Theresienstadt ghetto, published online on the Czech Terezín Initiative Institute's holocaust database, https://www.holocaust.cz/de/opferdatenbank/opfer/54655-lilli

-cornelia-l-wenthal. Theresienstadt served as a transit point for many Viennese Jews who were imprisoned there before being sent to Nazi death camps, including the designer Friedl Dicker.

CHAPTER 19. LONDON: STRUGGLES, NEW BEGINNINGS, AND A COMMISSION

1 Ella Briggs to Phylis Morrison, March 16, 1976, Bert Singer and Angela Kimberk Archive (Cambridge, MA), Architekturzentrum Wien, Collection, Vienna.

2 My chapters on Briggs's life and work in the United Kingdom were written with the generous assistance of many scholars and archivists. In addition to those specifically acknowledged in the notes, I would like to thank the following: John Allan, Iain Boyd Whyte, Valerie Carullo, Mark Crinson, Elizabeth Darling, Kelvin MacDonald, Lynn Walker, and Volker M. Welter. With true generosity, Frank Sharman toured me around Bilston. I am also most grateful to Despina Stratigakos and Elana Shapira for sharing many sources and reflections.

3 An excellent summary of developments is provided by Charlotte Benton, *A Different World: Emigre Architects in Britain, 1928–1958* (London: RIBA Heinz Gallery, 1995), 33–43. See also Barbara Miller Lane, *Architecture and Politics in Germany, 1918–1945* (Cambridge, MA: Harvard University Press, [1968] 1985), 169–85.

4 Ella Briggs, application form, Architects' Registration Council UK, March 2, 1940, copy deposited with the Ella Briggs Archive, Architekturzentrum Wien, Collection, Vienna, Austria.

5 This account is taken from a letter written by Ella Briggs to an unknown recipient, February 12, 1954. In the letter Briggs reviews her career in Austria, Germany, and England, setting out her claims for restitution from the German government. See Reg. no. 251.039 Ella Briggs, BEG-Akte (German Federal Compensation Act), LABO. For further details regarding Briggs's encounters with the SA officer, see chapter 17, "Late Berlin Projects, Family Ties, and Growing Danger," in this volume.

6 On Viennese Jews' Anglophilia, see Liliane Weissberg, "The Promised Land: Freud's Dream of England," in *Freud and the Émigré: Austrian Émigrés, Exiles and the Legacy of Psychoanalysis in Britain, 1930s–1970s*, ed. Elana Shapira and Daniela Finzi (London: Palgrave Macmillan, 2020), 46. On Salomon Bryk, see Ella Briggs to Phylis Morrison, March 16, 1976, Bert Singer and Angela Kimberk Archive (Cambridge, MA), Architekturzentrum Wien, Collection, Vienna.

7 Briggs gave the departure date of September 1935 in a statement for the Entschädigungsamt Berlin dated August 4, 1954, Reg. no. 251.039 Ella Briggs, BEG-Akte (German Federal Compensation Act), LABO. She mentions her residence permit in a letter to Godfrey Samuel, noting it has been extended to July 31, 1936. See Ella Briggs to Godfrey Samuel, April 3, 1936, Godfrey Samuel Papers, SAG\83\2, folder 3, Drawings and Archives Collections, RIBA.

8 On the review of candidates for work permits by the RIBA's Practice Standing Committee, see Benton, *A Different World*, 46–50.

9 The leading British social housing expert Elizabeth Denby proclaimed Vienna's program as "the greatest housing achievement of the century." Elizabeth Denby, *Europe Re-housed* (London: George Allen and Unwin, 1938), 253.

10 The arrival of the first wave of European émigrés in 1933 had triggered an openly fascist backlash. (See "Alien Architects Invade Britain," *Architects' Journal* [February 1934]: 244.) The RIBA more neutrally attributed architects' "apprehensiveness" about competition to the 7 percent fall in building activity in 1937–1938. This same report also claimed that, out of twelve thousand architects, there were only twenty-five refugee architects then working with permission in the UK. Although these numbers are disputed, it is clear the figure was proportionately small. "Refugees Committee: Report to Council," *Journal of the Royal Institute of British Architects* [26], June 1939, 827; and Benton, *A Different World*, 224n103.

11 The Schüttes arrived in London from the Soviet Union in April 1938. See "Margarete Schütte-Lihotzky—Biography," in *Margarete Schütte-Lihotzky: Architecture, Politics, Gender; New Perspectives on Her Life and Work*, ed. Marcel Bois and Bernadette Reinhold (Basel: Birkhauser, 2023), 344.

12 E. N. Cooper to Ella Briggs, March 11, 1936, GSP, SAG\83\2, folder 3, Drawings and Archives Collections, RIBA.

13 Briggs was definitely not alone in this. It was, ironically, harder to get work as an architectural assistant than as an architectural principal, due to the RIBA's preference to accept only leading practitioners. Benton notes that another route by which architects could secure a work permit was to claim specialist skills, which resulted in much massaging of credentials. See Benton, *A Different World*, 49–50.

14 Ella Briggs to Godfrey Samuel, April 3, 1936, GSP, SAG\83\2, folder 3, Drawings and Archives Collections, RIBA.

15 Samuel's help was enlisted via many routes: friends wrote refugees notes of introduction to him; or organizations such as the Congrès internationaux d'architecture moderne or the Professional Committee for German Jewish Refugees asked for his assistance. Berger was directed to him by Walter Gropius. Fiona MacCarthy, *Walter Gropius: Visionary Founder*

of the Bauhaus (London: Faber and Faber, 2019), 387. See also Tanya Harrod, "Otti Berger in England 1936–38: Hope and Disappointment," in *Otti Berger: Weaving for Modernist Architecture*, ed. Judith Raum (Berlin: Bauhaus-Archiv Berlin, 2024), 244–55.

16 Ella Briggs to Godfrey Samuel, April 3, 1936, GSP, SAG\83\2, folder 3, Drawings and Archives Collections, RIBA. One hundred and fifty pounds is a modest sum: around £13,300 in 2024 values. See "UK Inflation Calculator: GBP from 1751 to 2022," April 10, 2024, Official Inflation Data, Alioth Finance, https://www.officialdata.org/UK-inflation.

17 Godfrey Samuel to Ella Briggs, April 7, 1936; and Ella Briggs to Godfrey Samuel, May 21, 1936; both in GSP, SAG\83\2, folder 3, Drawings and Archives Collections, RIBA.

18 Ella Briggs to Godfrey Samuel, May 21, 1936, GSP, SAG\83\2, folder 3, Drawings and Archives Collections, RIBA.

19 Briggs's Viennese residence registration records, which note her entry and exit dates from Austria, indicate that she stayed three months in Vienna, from March 13 to June 9, 1936. See Ella Briggs's residence registration form from March 13, 1936, to June 9, 1936, eighteenth district, Bastiengasse 56/4, Meldearchiv Wien, Wiener Stadt- und Landesarchiv (MA 8), Vienna.

20 "Block of Flats in Berlin: Designed by Ella Briggs," *Architects' Journal* (July 16, 1936): 89–90.

21 Volker M. Welter, *Ernst L. Freud, Architect: The Case of the Modern Bourgeois Home* (New York: Berghahn, 2012), 120.

22 Compare this article with Briggs, "Wohnbau in Berlin-Mariendorf." For further discussion of the Mariendorf project, see chapter 14, "An Office in Berlin," in this volume.

23 In her "Exemption from Internment" form of 1939, for instance, she describes herself as self-employed. Card for Elsa Brix [*sic*], "Female Enemy Alien—Exemption from Internment—Refugee," HO 396 WW2 Internees (Aliens) Index Cards 1939–1947, ref. no. Ho 396/219, National Archives, Kew, London, UK, accessed on ancestry.com.

24 Entry for Ella B. Briggs, Electoral Register, 1937, Parliamentary Borough of Holborn, Parish of Holborn, North St. Giles Ward, Polling District A, p. 14; London Metropolitan Archives; London, UK; accessed on ancestry.com. In addition to Briggs, 3 Gower Street housed seven other residents.

25 For a map of German-speaking refugees and relief organizations, see Clare George, "On the trail of refugees in 1930s Bloomsbury," Research Centre for German and Austrian Exile Studies (EXILE), Institute of Languages, Cultures and Societies, School of Advanced Study, University of London, November 2020, https://ilcs.sas.ac.uk/sites/default/files/institute_modern_languages_research/bloomsbury-on-the-trail-map%20%281%29.pdf.

26 Along with Liverpool University, the AA was then the leading architecture school in England. It was a reasonably welcoming place for female architectural students; between 1935 and 1939, women made up between 15 and 19 percent of the student body, and they were very socially engaged. (On these years, see Elizabeth Darling, "Becoming Truly Alive," in *AA Women in Architecture, 1917–2017*, ed. Elizabeth Darling and Lynne Walker [London: AA Publications, 2017], 28–43.) Briggs, however, never appeared to teach there and is not on membership lists. Email correspondence between Edward Bottoms, AA Head of Archives, and Barbara Penner, September 20, 2022.

27 Thanks to Edward Bottoms for pointing this out, as well as the proximity of another architect at 7 Gower Street, Robert Furneaux Jordan, who organized the AA's Architects Czech Refugee Relief Fund. Email correspondence between Edward Bottoms and Barbara Penner, September 20, 2022.

28 Leverkus is best known for her work with the Women's Pioneer Housing association from 1923 on, a suffragist-led initiative to provide women of "moderate means" with decent places to live. While she and Briggs had much in common, it cannot be confirmed if they were acquainted, and they did not overlap for long: Leverkus closed her Gower Street office soon after Briggs arrived as work dried up with the war. She joined the Women's Voluntary Service, Borough of Holborn, and aided refugees in that capacity. Bonnie Emmett, *Housing for Single Working Women in Inter-War London 1919–1939* (PhD diss., Open University, 2023), 115–18.

29 Briggs's letterhead shows that, at this point, she was residing in the Kensington Gardens Hotel in west London, while she waited to occupy her own flat. She told Samuel that she had to provide the Home Office a satisfactory account of her work by November 1937. Ella Briggs to Godfrey Samuel, March 8, 1937, GSP, SAG\83\2, folder 2, Drawings and Archives Collections, RIBA. On struggles with work permits, see Benton, *A Different World*, 50–51.

30 "I am sorry if I gave you the impression that we have more small house work than we care to do; what I meant was that we have less large work than we would like." Godfrey Samuel to Ella Briggs, March 8, 1937, GSP, SAG\83\2, folder 3, Drawings and Archives Collections, RIBA.

31 Unfortunately, apart from Shell Mex, Briggs provides no dates or names for these commissions. Ella Briggs, application form, Architects' Registration Council, March 2, 1940, Ella Briggs Archive, Architekturzentrum Wien, Collection, Vienna.

32 "House Near Berlin: Designed by Ella Briggs," *Architects' Journal* (February 2, 1939): 211.

33 Price and details of sale confirmed in Arthur Wheen, Keeper of the Library, Victoria and Albert Museum

(London), to Ella Briggs, May 1, 1957, Reg. no. 251.039 Ella Briggs, BEG-Akte (German Federal Compensation Act), LABO.

34 The claim about the sale in 1937 appears in a letter from Manfred Meyer (regarding the case of Ella Briggs), October 11, 1956, Reg. no. 251.039 Ella Briggs, BEG-Akte (German Federal Compensation Act), LABO. The details of the sale or subsequent fate of these prints cannot currently be confirmed. Email correspondence between Tom Bilson, Head of Digital Media, The Courtauld Institute of Art, and Barbara Penner, November 9, 2022.

35 Affidavit from Ella Briggs, May 13, 1957, Reg. no. 251.039 Ella Briggs, BEG-Akte (German Federal Compensation Act), LABO.

36 Letter from Ernst Freud, September 21, 1939, to unnamed recipient; it is assumed that the letter was presented at Briggs's Internment Tribunal, held in October 1939. See Reg. no. 251.039 Ella Briggs, BEG-Akte (German Federal Compensation Act), LABO.

37 Many Category "C" men, like Briggs's brother, were interned following the Nazi occupation of Denmark, Norway, Holland, Belgium, and France. Friedrich was interned between June 21 and August 1, 1940. Card for Friedrich Baumfeld, "Revised Decision: Male Enemy Alien—Exemption from Internment—Refugee," ref. no. Ho 396/166, HO 396 WW2 Internees (Aliens) Index Cards 1939–1947, National Archives, Kew, London, UK, accessed on ancestry.com.

38 Ella Briggs, application form, Architects' Registration Council, March 2, 1940, Ella Briggs Archive, Architekturzentrum Wien, Collection, Vienna.

39 Both serious and service-oriented men, MacDonald and Samuel were founding members of the Architectural Science Group (1939–1941) and served on the convening committee of its successor, the RIBA Architectural Science Board, so it is certain they knew each other. See GSP, SaG\99\1–4, SaG\100\1–2, Drawings and Archives Collections, RIBA. Another possible broker between Briggs and MacDonald was the RIBA Librarian Bobby Carter, who sometimes arranged for members to vouch for refugees' credentials to support their work permit applications to the Home Office. See Benton, *A Different World*, 47.

40 On MacDonald's pacifism and his career, see Susan MacDonald, "Obituary: Alister MacDonald," *Independent*, March 27, 1993.

41 Grahame B. Tubbs, who supported her ARC application with MacDonald, was also a successful *moderne* architect. Max R. Hofler, who seconded Briggs's later application for an RIBA licentiate (again with MacDonald), had spent four years during the First World War as estate architect to the disowned Crown Princess Stephanie of Austria. Lettice Rathbone, the witness for Briggs's licentiate application, was wealthy, educated, and a member of the Women's Institute. She may have been related to independent MP Eleanor Rathbone, a notable campaigner on behalf of refugees and a member of the Committee for Intellectual Liberty, which sublet offices at 23 Haymarket from Godfrey Samuel. See GSP, SAG\83\2, folder 2, Drawings and Archives Collections, RIBA.

42 Monica Bohm-Duchen, "Modernist Sanctuary: Hampstead in the 1930s and 1940s," in *Insiders Outsiders: Refugees from Nazi Europe and Their Contribution to British Visual Culture*, ed. Monica Bohm-Duchen (London: Lund Humphries, 2019), 157–63; Leyla Daybelge and Magnus Englund, *Isokon and the Bauhaus in Britain* (London: Batsford, 2019), 159–64; Leyla Daybelge and Stefanie Pirker, *Through a Bauhaus Lens: Edith Tudor-Hart and Isokon* (London: Isokon Gallery / Fotohof Edition, 2024). It is worth noting, however, that other female émigré artists who came alone to England, such as the Bauhauslers Otti Berger and Lucia Moholy, also ended up in Bloomsbury. See Harrod, "Otti Berger in England 1936–38," 250; Robin Schuldenfrei, "Images in Exile: Lucia Moholy's Bauhaus Negatives and the Construction of the Bauhaus," *History of Photography* 37, no. 2 (2013): 182–203.

43 Deirdre Fernand, "Peter Moro and the Men from Mars," in *Applied Arts in British Exile from 1933*, ed. Marian Malet, Rachel Dickson, Sarah MacDougall, and Anna Nyburg (Leiden: Brill, 2019), 27.

44 Otti Berger, who was not included in the "New Architecture" show either, consoled herself by observing that it seemed "a little outdated" anyway (Harrod, "Otti Berger in England 1936–38," 251). On the MARS Group's show, and Samuel's role in it, see John R. Gold, "'Commoditie, firmenes and delight': Modernism, the Mars Group's 'New Architecture' Exhibition (1938) and Imagery of the Urban Future," *Planning Perspective* 8, no. 4 (1993): 357–76.

45 Betty Kurth to Gertrud Kurth, April 16, 1945, and Betty Kurth to Gertrud Kurth, April 29, 1946; both letters in Gertrud Kurth Collection, 1877–1996, Series V, Family Papers, 1877–1971, subseries Bettina (Betty) Kurth—Personal Correspondence, Leo Baeck Institute, New York. Thank you to Vivian Zech, who discovered these letters in her research for her master's thesis. Vivian Zech, "Betty Kurth: Annäherung an eine Biographie" (MA thesis, University of Applied Arts Vienna, 2024).

46 Although Bloomsbury was heavily bombed, it does not seem that 3 Gower Street was hit. We do not know if Briggs remained in London during the Blitz as most people who had the means or chance to evacuate did so. But Briggs claimed to have been employed in "local government offices" during wartime, which suggests she may have stayed on to work. Ella Briggs, application to be admitted a licentiate of the Royal Institute of British Archi-

tects, September 23, 1947, Ella Briggs, Biographical File, RIBA Library, London. For a record of wartime destruction, see the Bomb Damage Map (1945), produced by the London County Council: https://www.layersoflondon.org/map/overlays/bomb-damage-1945?overlayGroup.

47 Vera [Betty Kris; later Kurth], *Eine für Viele*. For more on *Eine für Viele*, see chapter 2, "Art and Design Studies," in this volume.

48 Good summaries of these artists' careers are provided in Anna Nyburg, "Emigré Designers," in *Insiders Outsiders: Refugees from Nazi Europe and Their Contribution to British Visual Culture*, ed. Monica Bohm-Duchen (London: Lund Humphries, 2019), 50–61 and Michael Berkowitz, "Emigré Photographers," in *Insiders Outsiders: Refugees from Nazi Europe and Their Contribution to British Visual Culture*, ed. Monica Bohm-Duchen (London: Lund Humphries, 2019), 62–73. Rie's archive, sadly, yields no trace of Briggs. Email correspondence between Greta Bertram, Curator, Crafts Study Centre, University for the Creative Arts and Barbara Penner, September 7, 2022.

49 Benton, *A Different World*, 7–8.

50 Tanja Poppelreuter has uncovered further details about Frommer, a German Jewish refugee, who fled Germany, came to London in 1936, and continued on to New York in 1939. In light of Briggs's relationships with women's magazines, it is interesting to note how Frommer also actively used women's professional networks to cultivate business. Tanja Poppelreuter, "Sustaining Independence: Marie Frommer's Networks and Architectural Practices in Berlin and in New York," in *Designing Transformation: Jews and Cultural Identity in Central European Modernism*, ed. Elana Shapira (London: Bloomsbury Visual Arts, 2021), 221–36.

51 S. E. Eisterer has tracked the story of Hedwig Adler, and I thank her for sharing this information with me. Email correspondence between S. E. Eisterer and Barbara Penner, December 31, 2023. See S. E. Eisterer, "'Invisible Hands': Architecture, Historiography, and Memory in the Loosely Entangled Lives of Hedwig Adler and Margarete Schütte-Lihotzky, 1930–1933," in *How to Build a Better World? The Architects Hans and Hedwig Adler between Germany and the USSR (1920–1930)*, ed. Federica Rossi (Florence: Firenze University Press, 2024).

52 Ella Briggs, application to be admitted a licentiate of the Royal Institute of British Architects, RIBA; Ella Briggs to Otto Neurath, October 26, 1945, held in Otto and Marie Neurath Isotype Collection, University of Reading, UK.

53 Ella Briggs to Otto Neurath, c. March 1943; Otto Neurath to Ella Briggs, March 30, 1943; and Ella Briggs to Otto Neurath, April 13, 1943; all in Otto and Marie Neurath Isotype Collection, University of Reading, UK.

54 For accounts of Neurath's career in Britain, see Iain Boyd Whyte, "Otto Neurath and the Sociology of Happiness," in *Man-Made Future: Planning, Education and Design in Mid-Twentieth Century Britain*, ed. Iain Boyd Whyte (Abingdon: Routledge, 2007), 16–37; and Mark Crinson, *Rebuilding Babel: Modern Architecture and Internationalism* (London: I. B. Tauris, 2017), 88–90. On Neurath's friendship with Margarete Schütte-Lihotzky, see Günther Sandner, "Friendship and Estrangement: Margarete Schütte-Lihotzky and Otto Neurath," in *Margarete Schütte-Lihotzky: Architecture, Politics, Gender; New Perspectives on Her Life and Work*, ed. Marcel Bois and Bernadette Reinhold (Basel: Birkhauser, 2023), 186–95.

55 Ella Briggs to Otto Neurath, c. March 1943; Otto Neurath to Ella Briggs, March 30, 1943; and Ella Briggs to Otto Neurath, April 13, 1943; all in Otto and Marie Neurath Isotype Collection, University of Reading, UK. For more on the 1931 exhibition, see chapter 16, "Exhibition Design," in this volume.

56 Neurath (1937) quoted in Boyd Whyte, "Otto Neurath and the Sociology of Happiness," 26. See also Derek Wragge Morley, "Sociological Approach to Town Planning: The Bilston Experiment—A Problem in Social Engineering," *Discovery* 8, no. 8 (1947): 250–51.

57 The most thorough published accounts of Bilston are: Elain Harwood, "Neurath, Riley and Bilston, Pasmore and Peterlee," *Twentieth Century Architecture*, no. 9 (2008): 84–96; and Peter J. Larkham, "People, Planning and Place: The Roles of Client and Consultants in Reconstructing Postwar Bilston and Dudley," *Town Planning Review* 77, no. 5 (2006): 563–64. Due to the unusual happiness-driven nature of this housing experiment, there has been a resurgence of interest in it, reflected in media coverage and exhibitions. See, for instance, Stuart Jeffries, "Bilston's Revival: the Pursuit of Happiness in a Black Country Town," *Guardian*, August 2, 2016; and, in this volume, Sabrina Rahman's discussion in chapter 27 ("The Stowlawn Estate at Bilston as Seen by Today's Residents") of the exhibition she cocurated on *Bilston's Happy Housing: Otto Neurath's Vision for Post-War Modern Living* (Bilston Craft Gallery, Wolverhampton, March 7, 2015 to May 2, 2015). Sincere thanks to Rahman and Frank Sharman for sharing their Bilston research.

58 Williams quote ("international repute") from Larkham, "People, Planning and Place," 562.

59 On the German POWs' involvement (according to the Bilston Council Housing Committee minutes), see Frank Sharman, "The Early History of Stowlawn; Part 8, The Council Then Started Building," from the Archives of The Black Country Memories Club, n.d., https://bilstononline.co.uk/stowlawn8.html.

60 Reilly was one of those who appealed for Berger's release from the Isle of Man internment camp; see "Biographical/Administrative History," Margarete Berger-Hamerschlag Papers, University of London, https://archives.libraries.london.ac.uk/resources/MBH_catalogue.pdf.

61 For more on Reilly's role, see Harwood, "Neurath, Riley and Bilston, Pasmore and Peterlee," 84–96; and Larkham, "People, Planning and Place," 563–64. The only known interaction of Briggs and Reilly was in December 1946, when they met at the RIBA at Briggs's instigation. Sincere thanks to Simon Pepper for confirming this detail in the Papers of Professor Sir Charles Reilly, University of Liverpool Special Collections and Archives, Liverpool, UK.

62 The completed units consisted of eight two-bedroom, eight four-bedroom, and fifty three-bedroom houses. There were also sixteen flats. "Houses and Flats on the Stowlawn Park Estate for the Bilston Borough Council: Ella B. Briggs, L.R.I.B.A., Architect," *Builder* [177, no. 5564], October 7, 1949, 448–51. Harwood claims that Briggs designed the homes on nearby Church Green as well, but this attribution is not substantiated; instead, local historians such as Frank Sharman attribute them to Bilston Borough Architect Wallace Lofthouse. Harwood, "Neurath, Riley and Bilston, Pasmore and Peterlee," 89.

63 "Houses and Flats on the Stowlawn Park Estate for the Bilston Borough Council," 450.

64 Charles Reilly quoted in Harwood, "Neurath, Riley and Bilston, Pasmore and Peterlee," 89.

65 After his death, the Bilston exhibition was completed by Neurath's wife, Marie, and went on display in November 1946, though the results were not felt to be satisfactory. See Pia Pedersen, "Marie Neurath: Design Bilston's Housing Exhibition," *Journal of Design History* 36, no. 2 (2023): 157–74.

66 "Houses at Bilston, Notts: Designed by Ella B. Briggs," *Architects' Journal* [105, no. 2710], January 2, 1947, 15–16; Ella Briggs, "A Four-Flat House," *Homes and Gardens* [29, no. 4], October 1947, 28.

67 Briggs, "A Four-Flat House," 28. For more on her concern for "urban image," see chapter 14, "An Office in Berlin," in this volume.

68 On the Ledigenheim, see chapter 13, "Building for Red Vienna," in this volume.

69 Quoted in Morley, "Sociological Approach to Town Planning," 250.

70 Briggs, "A Four-Flat House." See also Ella Briggs, "Flats with Private Balcony Access," *Homes and Gardens* [34, no. 6], December 1952, 41.

71 Interestingly, Gary A. Boyd notes that dedicated miners' housing had long dispensed with front parlors in the name of economy, space, and women's labor. See Gary A. Boyd, *Architecture and the Face of Coal: Mining and Modern Britain* (London: Lund Humphries, 2023), 184–85.

72 Briggs, "A Four-Flat House," 29.

73 See, for example, Briggs, "Taylorisierungsbestrebungen in amerikanischen Küchen." For more on Briggs's advocacy for architects designing with housewives in mind, see the chapters in part I, section 3 of this volume.

74 The plan for all-male domestic help was noted approvingly in Alison Settle, "From a Woman's Viewpoint," *Observer* [London], July 7, 1946.

75 On the residents' responses to the new housing, see chapter 27, "The Stowlawn Estate at Bilston as Seen by Today's Residents," in this volume.

76 "Houses at Bilston, Notts"; "Houses and Flats on the Stowlawn Park Estate," 448–51.

77 The date of her naturalization was likely May 15, 1947. Card for Elsa Brix [*sic*], "Female Enemy Alien—Exemption from Internment–Refugee," HO 396 WW2 Internees (Aliens) Index Cards 1939–1947, ref. no. Ho 396/219, National Archives, Kew, London, UK, accessed on ancestry.com.

78 The licentiate certifies that Briggs had shown professional competence without having sat for the RIBAs architectural exams. (Those who passed the RIBA exams were awarded an A.R.I.B.A.; they often regarded themselves as superior to the L.R.I.B.A.s). The highest category was fellow (F.R.I.B.A), for which some L.R.I.B.A.s would apply, though Briggs appears not to have done so. Thanks to Simon Pepper for guiding me through the history and nuances of these professional categories. Email correspondence between Simon Pepper and Barbara Penner, February 6, 2023.

79 Thanks to Daniel Croughton, Community Library Officer at Camden Local Studies and Archives Centre, for confirming this detail in the Holborn Borough Council Minutes, June 25, 1947, 280. Email correspondence between Daniel Croughton and Barbara Penner, August 30, 2022.

CHAPTER 20. WRITING, DESIGNING, AND FIGHTING FOR RESTITUTION

1 See chapter 15, "Publishing Endeavors," in this volume.

2 It is not known how Briggs secured this job. To Neurath, Briggs said that *Homes and Gardens* had given her "a small contract doing house designs." Ella Briggs to Otto Neurath, October 26, 1945, Otto and Marie Neurath Isotype Collection, University of Reading, UK.

3 *Homes and Gardens* felt expertise was a major selling point, often boasting of the quality of advice provided by its columnists, described as "the most famous women experts of the day"; see "The Editor's Page," *Homes and Gardens* 23, no. 11 (1942): 11.

4 Briggs opened many articles by reminding readers that the maximum size of a private house that could

receive a license was 1,500 square feet. In 1953 the Minister of Housing decreed that houses up to 1,000 square feet could be built without a permit; this number was upped to 1,500 square feet in 1954. Ella Briggs, "A House on a Hill," *Homes and Gardens* [32, no. 3], September 1950, 44–45; Ella Briggs, "A Family Bungalow—To Be Built without a License," *Homes and Gardens* [34, no. 10], April 1953, 45.

5 On the flat roof controversy in Berlin, see chapter 15, "Publishing Endeavors," in this volume.

6 Ella Briggs, "Essentials of House Planning," *Homes and Gardens* [25, no. 11], April 1944, 36–37.

7 The other reigning "small homes" expert was a man, R. Randall Phillips, author of *The Book of Bungalows* (London: Country Life, 1920). Later, the architect H. Dalton Clifford, author of *Plan Your Own Home Decoration* (London: Country Life, 1955), appeared on the roster. Neither paid attention to laborsaving as Briggs did.

8 Ella Briggs, "Ella B. Briggs Plans a Small Labour- and Space-Saving House," *Homes and Gardens* [27, no. 12], May 1946, 32–33; and Ella Briggs, "Planned for Modern Requirements," *Homes and Gardens* [27, no. 9], February 1946, 34–35, 69.

9 Ella Briggs, "Bungalow Home from Prefabricated Huts," *Homes and Gardens* [26, no. 11], April 1945, 32–33. Briggs championed the flower window most overtly in Ella Briggs, "Planned for Present Comfort and Future Extension," *Homes and Gardens* [27, no. 11], April 1946, 37; and Ella Briggs, "A Plant-Lovers' Bungalow," *Homes and Gardens* [35, no. 10], April 1954, 87.

10 Briggs, "Bungalow Home from Prefabricated Huts."

11 Ella Briggs, "Victorian House into Two Labour-Saving Homes," *Homes and Gardens* [27, no. 5], October 1945, 20–21; Briggs, "Ella B. Briggs Plans a Small Labour- and Space-Saving House," 33. On the extendible houses, see Briggs, "Planned for Present Comfort and Future Extension," 36–37; and Ella Briggs, "House of the Future," *Homes and Gardens* [31, no. 11], May 1950, 45.

12 On Briggs's previous explorations of extendible houses, see chapter 10, "Building Clients and Avid Readers in New York and Beyond" (particularly on the 1924 article "A Little House That Grew"); and chapter 17, "Late Berlin Projects, Family Ties, and Growing Danger," both in this volume.

13 For instance, the *Homes and Gardens* house at the *Daily Mail* Ideal Home Exhibition in 1949 was a two-story "modern cottage," built by the architect W. M. Carter. See "Our House at the Ideal Home Exhibition," *Homes and Gardens* 30, no. 10 (1949): 30–31. Although *Homes and Gardens* often contributed to the *Daily Mail* Ideal Home Exhibition, there is no evidence they involved Briggs.

14 Briggs, "A Four-Flat House"; Ella Briggs, "A Modern Swiss Home," *Homes and Gardens* [29, no. 11], May 1948, 32–23, 69–70; and Ella Briggs, "A Swiss Country House," *Homes and Gardens* [35, no. 2], August 1953, 33–37.

15 Briggs, "A Modern Swiss Home," 33.

16 Briggs, "A Swiss Country House."

17 Ella Briggs, "Space- and Labour-Saving Bungalow," *Homes and Gardens* [36, no. 9], March 1955, 103.

18 Briggs, "A Plant-Lovers' Bungalow," 87.

19 We know of this diagnosis through Briggs's later claims for compensation for lost income. In a letter, her doctor confirmed the leukemia diagnosis, noting that, while benign, it was "liable to flare up at any time." Given this, he did not regard her as being "in a fit condition to undertake any employment at the present time." Letter from Dr. P.M.S. Gillam (regarding Ella Briggs) to H. H. Marcus, Esq., September 21, 1955, Reg. no. 251.039 Ella Briggs, BEG-Akte (German Federal Compensation Act), LABO.

20 Letter from Prof. Dr. Med. Walther Gloor-Meyer (Zurich) regarding Ella Briggs, September 17, 1952, Reg. no. 251.039 Ella Briggs, BEG-Akte (German Federal Compensation Act), LABO. Switzerland also held other lures for Briggs, including her nephew, Theodore Baumfeld, who resided there.

21 Briggs, "A Plant-Lovers' Bungalow," 87.

22 When he died, Friedrich was living in Epsom Surrey. He also left the sum of £220 19s. 3d. to his sister. Entry for "Baumfeld, Friedrich," 1953, p. 495, Principal Probate Registry, Calendar of all Grants of Probate and Letters of Administration made in the Probate Registries of the High Court of Justice in England, Wills and Administrations 1953, accessed on ancestry.com.

23 I am very grateful to Mrs. Pahlke of the Berlin compensation office for her support and for the photocopied documents; to Katrin Stingl (Az W) for her help in pointing out relevant documents; and to Elana Shapira for piecing this complex story together. Briggs received the first payment of 12,500 deutsche mark in June 1956 (about $40,000 today; see Historical Dollar-to-Mark Currency Conversion Page created by Harold Marcuse, UC Santa Barbara, https://marcuse.faculty.history.ucsb.edu/projects/currency.htm). In February 1959, she received the remaining payment of 2,826 deutsche mark (about $8,500 today). Compensation office to Dr. Georg Schmidt [representative of the claim of Friedrich Baumfeld for Ella Briggs], February 12, 1959, Reg. no. 50 392 Ella Briggs, BEG-Akte (German Federal Compensation Act), LABO.

24 Briggs claimed that this furniture was built in 1913 with a grant of 3,000 kronen from the Obersthofmeisteramt (Office of the Grand Master of the Court), the body responsible for managing the imperial estates, and arranged by Eduard Leisching, director of the Austrian Museum of Art and Industry. Letter from Manfred Meyer (regarding the case of Ella Briggs), October 11, 1956, Reg. no. 251.039 Ella Briggs, BEG-Akte (German

Federal Compensation Act), LABO. In fact, Briggs received 4,000 kronen at the time to open her design studio. The furniture was probably part of the studio arrangement. See discussion in chapter 7, "Opening an Interior Design Firm in Vienna," in this volume.

25 Affidavit from Ella B. Briggs, May 13, 1957, Reg. no. 251.039 Ella Briggs, BEG-Akte (German Federal Compensation Act), LABO.

26 Letter from Ella Briggs, February 12, 1954, Reg. no. 251.039 Ella Briggs, BEG-Akte (German Federal Compensation Act), LABO.

27 Power of Attorney signed by the Consulate Secretary of the Diplomatic Mission of the Federal Republic of Germany in London for Dr. Manfred Mayer (Hamburg), authorized to represent Ella Briggs to the Compensation Office, Berlin, March 31, 1954, Reg. No. 251.039 + 251.040 Ella Briggs, BEG-Akte (German Federal Compensation Act), LABO.

28 Letter from Ella Briggs, February 12, 1954, Reg. no. 251.039 Ella Briggs, BEG-Akte (German Federal Compensation Act), LABO. Overall claim figure provided in Ella Briggs, "Schaden im beruflichen Fortkommen," May 7, 1954, Reg. no. 251.039 Ella Briggs, BEG-Akte (German Federal Compensation Act), LABO. Briggs's declared income at the end of the Weimar Republic of 10,000–12,000 reichsmark a year is equivalent to approximately $60,000 to $70,000 today, modestly calculated (Historical Dollar-to-Mark Currency Conversion Page created by Harold Marcuse, UC Santa Barbara, https://marcuse.faculty.history.ucsb.edu/projects/currency.htm).

29 Compensation Office Report on the compensation sum for Ella Briggs, November 4, 1957, Reg. 251.039 Ella Briggs, BEG-Akte (German Federal Compensation Act), LABO. In 1957, 2,500 deutsche mark was not a huge sum; it is equivalent to under $10,000 today (Historical Dollar-to-Mark Currency Conversion Page created by Harold Marcuse, UC Santa Barbara, https://marcuse.faculty.history.ucsb.edu/projects/currency.htm).

30 Ella Briggs to Phylis Morrison, March 16, 1976, Bert Singer and Angela Kimberk Archive (Cambridge, MA), Architekturzentrum Wien, Collection, Vienna.

31 Ella Briggs, "Last Will," February 20, 1973, Enfield, Middlesex; Ella Briggs, "Death Certificate," Barnet Registration District, registered on June 22, 1977; both Ella Briggs Archive, Architekturzentrum Wien, Collection, Vienna. According to the death certificate, Briggs died in the Ellern Mede Nursing Home in Totteridge, in the London Borough of Barnet.

CHAPTER 21. FAMILY BONDS AND LEGACIES: ELLA BRIGGS AND PHYLIS MORRISON

1 Ella Briggs to Phylis Morrison, March 16, 1976, Bert Singer and Angela Kimberk Archive (Cambridge, MA), Architekturzentrum Wien, Collection, Vienna. Ella's maternal grandfather was Salomon Bryk, identified as a jeweler in the marriage record of Philipp Bryk and Fanni Reis, June 25, 1871, Israelitische Kultusgemeinde Wien, Vienna, Austria.

2 Ella Briggs to Phylis Morrison, March 16, 1976, Bert Singer and Angela Kimberk Archive (Cambridge, MA), Architekturzentrum Wien, Collection, Vienna.

3 See, for example, Ella Briggs, "Three Ways to Plan a House," *Homes and Gardens* [34, no. 4], October 1952, 45; and Briggs-Baumfeld, "Selbst ist die Frau!"

4 Ella Briggs to Phylis Morrison, March 16, 1976, Bert Singer and Angela Kimberk Archive (Cambridge, MA), Architekturzentrum Wien, Collection, Vienna.

5 Phylis Beatrice Hagen, US Social Security Applications and Claims Index, 1936–2007, Death Report for Angela Eleonore Hagen, July 16, 1935, Report of the Death of an American Citizen, American Foreign Service, Death Reports of US Citizens Abroad, 1920–1962, Publication A1 205, General Records of the Department of State, Record Group 59, National Archives at College Park, MD; entry for Franziska Baumfeld and Phillys [*sic*] Hagen, ship manifest SS *Westernland*, List of United States Citizens, arriving at the port of New York on September 23, 1935, Passenger and Crew Lists of Vessels Arriving at New York, New York, 1897–1957, microfilm T715, Records of the Immigration and Naturalization Service, Record Group 85, National Archives, Washington, DC; all accessed on ancestry.com; Bert Singer, telephone communication with Jeanne Paradise, November 26, 2022, as described in Jeanne Paradise, email message to Elana Shapira and Despina Stratigakos, November 27, 2022; Despina Stratigakos, interview with Phylis Morrison, November 21, 1999, Cambridge, MA.

6 Archives Finding Aid, Kits Collection 1928–2011, Accession #A 2019.9, Boston Children's Museum, Boston, MA, accessed online at https://bostonchildrensmuseum.org/sites/default/files/pdfs/museumarchives/A%202019.9-Kits%20Collection.pdf. The interactive learning program was initiated by Boston Children's Museum director Michael Spock, son of Dr. Benjamin Spock. Sean Plaistowe (Boston Children's Museum archivist), email message to Elana Shapira, September 17, 2022.

7 Jeanne Paradise, "Beads," Phylis Morrison Memorial Day, October 6, 2002, Massachusetts Institute of Technology, accessed online at https://www.bcmstories.com/pdfs/beads.pdf; Jeanne Paradise, conversation with Elana Shapira and Despina Stratigakos, November 22, 2022.

8 Jeanne Paradise, conversation with Elana Shapira and Despina Stratigakos, November 22, 2022; Jeanne Paradise, email messages to Elana Shapira and Despina Stratigakos, January 17, 2023, and January 30, 2023.

9 Philip Morrison, Phylis Morrison, and the Office of Charles and Ray Eames, *Powers of Ten: A Book about the Relative Size of Things in the Universe and the Effect of Adding Another Zero* (Redding, CT: W. H. Freeman, distributed on behalf of Scientific American Library, 1982); Phylis Morrison, *Spiders' Games: A Book for Beginning Weavers* (Seattle: University of Washington Press, 1979).

10 Jeanne Paradise, conversation with Elana Shapira and Despina Stratigakos, November 22, 2022; Jeanne Paradise, email message to authors, December 16, 2022.

11 Bert Singer, email message to Elana Shapira and Despina Stratigakos, January 7, 2024.

12 Jeanne Paradise, email message to Elana Shapira and Despina Stratigakos, December 16, 2022.

CHAPTER 22. VIENNESE WOMEN'S ART SCHOOLS AND THEIR COMMUNITIES IN ELLA BRIGGS'S TIME

1 Secessionist pedagogical reforms arguably established nothing less than a Viennese "proto-Bauhaus," anticipating developments in the early expressionist stages of the celebrated German design school and forming direct antecedents to instructional methods used by Johannes Itten in his famous *Vorkurs* (preliminary course) at the Weimar Bauhaus. See Rainer K. Wick, "Die Wiener Kunstgewerbeschule und die Wiener Werkstätte—Ein Bauhaus vor dem Bauhaus?," in *Bauhaus: Kunst und Pädagogik* (Oberhausen: Athena, 2009), 56–74.

2 See Megan Brandow-Faller, *Female Secession: Art and the Decorative at the Viennese Women's Academy* (University Park, PA: Penn State University Press, 2020), 29–30.

3 Bernadette Reinhold, "'Weibliche artistische Arbeitskräfte' in spe—Frauenstudium an der frühen Kunstgewerbeschule: Ein unbequemer Rückblick," in *150 Jahre Universität für angewandte Kunst Wien: Ästhetik der Veränderung*, ed. Gerald Bast, Anja Seipenbusch-Hufschmied, and Patrick Werkner (Berlin: de Gruyter / Edition Angewandte, 2017), 159.

4 Brandow-Faller, *Female Secession*, 29.

5 Brandow-Faller, *Female Secession*, 29.

6 For a comprehensive list of private art schools in late Imperial Vienna, see Megan Brandow-Faller, "An Art of Their Own: Reinventing *Frauenkunst* in the Female Academies and Artist Leagues of Late-Imperial and First Republic Austria, 1900–1930" (PhD diss., Georgetown University, Washington, DC, 2010), 112n334.

7 Rudolf von Eitelberger, "Zur Regelung des Kunstunterrichts für das weibliche Geschlecht," *Mittheilungen des k.k. Museum für Kunst und Industrie* 4, no. 78 (1873): 61.

8 Armand Freiherr von Dumreicher, *Vertrauliche Denkschrift über die Lage am k.k. österreichischen Museum für Kunst und Industrie* (Reichenberg: pub. by author, 1885), 15–16.

9 See Houze, *Textiles, Fashion, and Design Reform*, 160–61.

10 See Brandow-Faller, *Female Secession*, 34–35.

11 Houze, *Textiles, Fashion, and Design Reform*, 167–70; and Brandow-Faller, *Female Secession*, 36.

12 *Kunstgewerbeschule Wien: 60. Bestandsjahr: Ausstellung von Schülerarbeiten aus Anlass der Vollendung des 60. Bestandsjahres der Anstalt* (Vienna: Austrian Museum for Art and Industry, 1929), n.p.

13 Brandow-Faller, *Female Secession*, 113.

14 See discussion in chapter 2, "Art and Design Studies," in this volume.

15 See discussion in chapter 7, "Opening an Interior Design Firm in Vienna," in this volume.

CHAPTER 23. THE INTERIORS OF ELLA BRIGGS: INTERNATIONAL CROSSCURRENTS AND MODERN ADAPTATIONS

1 Ruge, "Amerikanische Kunstausstellungen der Saison 1908 bis 1909," 581–82, ills. 579, 580.

2 On William Morris, the rise of the Arts and Crafts movement, and its international manifestations, see, for example, Monica Penick and Christopher Long, eds., *The Rise of Everyday Design: The Arts and Crafts Movement in Britain and America* (Austin and New Haven: Harry Ransom Center, The University of Texas at Austin and Yale University Press, 2019); Andrzej Szczerski, *Views of Albion: The Reception of British Art and Design in Central Europe* (Oxford: Peter Lang, 2015); Karen Livingstone and Linda Parry, *International Arts and Crafts* (London: V&A Publishing, 2005); and Linda Parry, *William Morris* (New York: Abrams, 1996).

3 Eduard F. Sekler, *Josef Hoffmann: Das architektonische Werk* (Salzburg: Residenz, 1982), entry at the end of the book of Hoffmann's catalog of works, 258, WV 30.

4 Ruge, "Amerikanische Kunstausstellungen der Saison 1908 bis 1909," 581.

5 Eva B. Ottillinger and Lieselotte Hanzl, *Kaiserliche Interieurs: Die Wohnkultur des Wiener Hofes und die Wiener Kunstgewerbereform* (Vienna: Böhlau, 1997), 335ff.

6 On Stickley see, David M. Cathers, *Gustav Stickley* (London: Phaidon, 2010); and, *Gustav Stickley and*

the American Arts and Crafts Movement (Dallas and New Haven: Dallas Museum of Art and Yale University Press, 2010).

7 Giovanni Renzi, *Il mobile moderno: Gebrüder Thonet Vienna, Jacob & Josef Kohn* (Milan: Silvana, 2008), 50. Briggs's furniture selections for the ladies' salon in the theater and the ladies' reception room in the New York Press Club can be identified in a later 1916 Kohn's catalog: table number 728 with chair, bench, and armchair numbers 415, 415/2, and 415/F. See Graham Dry, ed., *Jacob & Josef Kohn: Bugholzmöbel; Der Katalog von 1916* (Munich: Graham Dry, 1980), 37 and 46.

8 A reference to a J. & J. Kohn branch on Broadway Avenue in New York is noted in an announcement of the firm winning a gold medal in the New Orleans Exposition; see "Awarded First Prize," *Democrat and Chronicle* [Rochester, NY], July 24, 1885.

9 Although better known for his posters, Mucha also designed stage sets for Sarah Bernhardt in the Art Nouveau style.

10 On the Pringsheims and Briggs's project for them, see chapter 7, "Opening an Interior Design Firm in Vienna," in this volume.

11 Henry van de Velde, *Das Haus unter den hohen Pappeln*, ed. Antje Neumann and Thomas Föhl (Wiesbaden: Weimarer Verlagsgesellschaft in der Verlagshaus Römerweg GmbH, 2016), 45. Briggs's Morris-type chair from the Pringsheim apartment survived within the family, and family members credit the design to Briggs herself. Britta Schinzel, interviewed by Monika Platzer and Elana Shapira, September 26, 2023, Vienna.

12 Walde, "Die Frau in der Innenarchitektur," 21–23. Biedermeier was considered the last authentic style to emerge in Austria before the rise of historicism and inspired designers such as Josef Hoffmann and Adolf Loos as well.

13 The workshop was near the Westbahnhof at Illekgasse 22, Vienna. See *Lehmann's* for the year 1909 (vol. 2, 728).

14 Walde, "Die Frau als Innenarchitektin," pl. 73. Bogataj exhibited his own designs at the Preiskonkurrenz für Arbeiterwohnungen (competition for workers' apartments) in 1910 in Vienna.

15 The Backhausen fabric was designed by Rudolf Hejda: RH (Rudolf Hejda), Drawing, BA03148, Musterbuchseite (pattern book page) 7732–1, MB30_055, and Dessinbuchseite (design book page) 7732, D4_029; all in the Backhausen Archive, bequest from Dr. Louise Kiesling, on permanent loan to the Leopold Museum, Vienna, Austria.

16 Eva B. Ottillinger, *Adolf Loos: Wohnkonzepte und Möbelentwürfe* (Salzburg: Residenz, 1994), 102, fig. 127.

17 Eva B. Ottillinger, ed., *Wagner, Hoffmann, Loos und das Möbeldesign der Wiener Moderne: Künstler, Auftraggeber, Produzenten* (Vienna: Böhlau, 2018), 96–107.

18 Adolf Loos, "Die Plumber," *Neue Freie Presse*, July 17, 1898.

19 See Briggs-Baumfeld, "Selbst ist die Frau!"

20 "Sándor Jaráy, k. und k. Hof-Kunstmöbelfabrik und Decorations-Atelier," in *Die Gross-Industrie Oesterreichs: Festgabe zum glorreichen fünfzigjährigen Regierungs-Jubiläum seiner Majestät des Kaisers Franz Josef I*, vol. 3 (Vienna: Leopold Weiss, 1898), 319; Vera J. Behal, *Möbel des Jugendstils: Sammlung des Österreichischen Museums für angewandte Kunst in Wien* (Munich: Prestel, 1981), 60–61.

21 Ella Briggs to Ministerium für Wissenschaft, Kunst und Volksbildung, Berlin, December 2, 1918, HA-I, Rep. 76Vb, Sekt. 4, Tit. 7, Nr. 6, Bd. 1, Geheimes Staatsarchiv, Berlin; Ella Briggs to the Rektorat der Kgl. technischen Hochschule München, c. August 1918, TUM.Archiv.PA.Stud.Briggs, Ella, Technische Universität München Archiv, Munich.

CHAPTER 24. JEWISH WOMEN ARCHITECTS IN VIENNA: FORGING AND MAINTAINING NETWORKS OF SUPPORT IN THE INTERWAR PERIOD AND BEYOND

1 Alison Rose, *Jewish Women in Fin de Siècle Vienna* (Austin: University of Texas Press, 2008), 11–17; and Freidenreich, *Female, Jewish, and Educated.*

2 On women's options for architectural study in Vienna more broadly, see Meder, "Women Designers and Architects in Early Twentieth Century Vienna."

3 Mikoletzky, Georgeacopol-Winischhofer, and Pohl, *"Dem Zuge der Zeit entsprechend . . ."*, 139–42.

4 For example, among the successful Jewish female students who studied under Oskar Strnad at the Kunstgewerbeschule were Liane Zimbler, Ilse Bernheimer, and Ada Gomperz; among those who studied under Clemens Holzmeister at the Academy of Fine Arts were Susanne Bánki, Marya Lilien, Grete Weiss, and Judith Zweig. Prominent graduates of the Technical University's architecture program, such as Dora Gad and Helene Roth, are discussed in this chapter. See also Ursula Prokop, *On the Jewish Legacy in Viennese Architecture: The Contribution of Jewish Architects to Building in Vienna, 1868–1938* (Vienna: Böhlau, 2016), 152–53; and, Beatrix Bastl, *Die jüdischen Studierenden der Akademie der bildenden Künste Wien, 1848–1948* (Vienna: Kovač, 2019), 79, 170–71, 242–43, 254.

5 Lisa Silverman writes, "Jewish women were often doubly disadvantaged, particularly if they transgressed prescribed gender roles as women and as Jews. And if they were Jewish women from Eastern Europe, they might face yet a third disadvantage, particularly if their looks and affect pinned them as

representative of what was considered an unpalatable form of visible Jewish culture." See Silverman, *Becoming Austrians*, 102.

6 "Mäda! [. . .] man denkt sofort an etwas Gesprageltes, Ueberspitztes, Affektiertes, Gekitzeltes, Falsches, Unechtes und vor allem U e b e r f l ü s s i g e s, mit einem Wort an ein Erzeugnis der WW, Wiener Weiberkunstgewerbe, wem graust da nicht weiblich!" Julius Klinger, "Ein angenehmer Gast: Schmuckkunst: Mäda," *Das Tribunal*, May 12, 1927, 10; held in Wiener Werkstätte Archiv 85-1419-2, MAK. Although Klinger's title refers to Mäda, the non-Jewish Mäda Primavesi, patron of the Wiener Werkstätte, he also cites the nicknames of Jewish women designers, such as Vally Wieselthier.

7 On Kraus's criticism of the so-called materialistic consumerism of Jewish women, see Steven Beller, "Dis-Oriented Jews? Orientalism, Assimilation, and Modernism in Vienna 1900," in *Design Dialogue: Jews, Culture and Viennese Modernism*, ed. Elana Shapira (Vienna: Böhlau, 2018), 306; on Klinger, see Anne-Katrin Rossberg, "Brought to Light: Art and Life of the Wiener Werkstätte Women," in *Die Frauen der Wiener Werkstätte: Women Artists of the Wiener Werkstätte*, ed. Christoph Thun-Hohenstein, Anne-Katrin Rossberg, and Elisabeth Schmuttermeier (Basel: Birkhäuser, 2020), 13.

8 See chapter 7, "Opening an Interior Design Firm in Vienna," in this volume.

9 For a broader discussion of the mutually beneficial relationships among feminist art circles in Vienna, see Elana Shapira, "Professional Women in the Arts and Media in Vienna–Kulturschaffende Frauen in Wien," in *Gestalterinnen: Frauen, Design und Gesellschaft im Wien der Zwischenkriegszeit*, ed. Elana Shapira and Anne-Katrin Rossberg (Berlin: De Gruyter, 2023), 9–27.

10 On Hofmann, see Sabine Plakolm-Forsthuber, "Else Hofmann: Eine arrivierte Kunstpublizistin," in *Gestalterinnen: Frauen, Design und Gesellschaft im Wien der Zwischenkriegszeit*, ed. Elana Shapira and Anne-Katrin Rossberg (Berlin: De Gruyter, 2023), 194–212. For an example of Urban's writings on women architects, including Briggs, see Gisela Urban, "Die Frau als Architektin: Ihre Arbeit in Oesterreich und anderwärts," *Neues Wiener Journal*, May 13, 1928. In 1932 Urban organized an exhibition, *Das Wiener Heim vor hundert Jahren und Heute* (The Viennese Home a Hundred Years Ago and Today) at Gerngroß, one of Vienna's largest department stores. It featured a kitchen with electrical appliances designed by the engineer Käthe Böhm; see "Das Wiener Heim vor hundert Jahren und Heute," *Der Tag*, October 25, 1932.

11 On these and other projects, see Katharina Hövelmann, *Bauhaus in Wien? Möbeldesign, Innenraumgestaltung und Architektur der Wiener Ateliergemeinschaft von Friedl Dicker und Franz Singer* (Vienna: Böhlau, 2021). Neither Dicker nor Singer had an architecture degree. They hired other architects, including the non-Jewish Leopoldine Schrom, who studied architecture at the Vienna Technical University. Schrom worked in the design studio from 1929. See Georg Schrom and Peter Stuiber, "Georg Schrom über Friedl Dicker und Franz Singer: 'Sie waren der Gegenpol zur Wiener Architekturszene,'" *Wien Museum Magazin*, June 12, 2022, https://magazin.wienmuseum.at/georg-schrom-ueber-friedl-dicker-und-franz-singer.

12 See chapter 8, "The Fight to Integrate Architecture Studies," in this volume; Despina Stratigakos, "'I Myself Want to Build.'"

13 Hövelmann, *Bauhaus in Wien?*, 168.

14 Ursula Prokop, *Jacques and Jacqueline Groag, Architect and Designer: Two Hidden Figures of the Viennese Modern Movement*, trans. Jonee Tiedemann and Laura McGuire (Los Angeles: DoppelHouse Press, 2019).

15 Sabine Plakolm-Forsthuber, "Ein Leben, Zwei Karrieren: Die Architektin Liane Zimbler," in Matthias Boeckl, *Visionäre und Vertriebene: Österreichische Spuren in der modernen amerikanischen Architektur* (Berlin: Ernst and Sohn, 1995), 295–309.

16 Our thanks to Sabine Plakolm-Forsthuber for this information. Conrad, "Eine elektrische Musterküche in Wien," *Zeitschrift der Österreichischen Gesellschaft für Technik im Haushalt* 6, no. 4 (1932): 28; and the advertisement for Käthe Böhm's shop: "Der Hoover klopft," *Oesterreich-ungarische Maschinenwelt* 21, no. 2010 (1937): 7. The shop was located in her apartment at Mariahilfer Strasse 97 in the sixth district. In the early 1930s, it was the only woman-run shop for electric appliances in Vienna.

17 Susanne Breuss, "Unter Strom: Frauen, Arbeit und Technik im Nachkriegs- und 'Wirtschaftswunder'-Österreich," in *1919–2019: 100 Jahre Frauen an der Technischen Universität Wien*, ed. Marion Krammer and Margarete Szeless (Vienna: Promedia, 2019), 109–12.

18 Jane King Hession, *Elizabeth Scheu Close: A Life in Modern Architecture* (Minneapolis: University of Minnesota Press, 2020).

19 Sabine Plakolm-Forsthuber, "Helene Roth, 1904–1995," *Pionierinnen der Wiener Architektur: Das Archiv der Zentralvereinigung der ArchitektInnen Österreichs (ZV)*, ed. Ingrid Holzschuh, Sabine Plakolm-Forsthuber, and Zentralvereinigung der ArchitektInnen Österreichs (Basel: Birkhäuser, 2022), 128–39; Sigal Davidi, "Reclaiming the Work of Women Architects in Mandatory Palestine," in *The Routledge Companion to Women in Architecture*, ed. Anna Sokolina (New York: Routledge, 2021), 154–55, 160, 162.

20 It is unclear if Leonie Pilewski joined the communist party. She is mentioned as a speaker at the founding congress of the Austrian League of Friends of the Soviet Union in "Kongreß des österreichischen Bundes der Freunde der

Sovietunion," *Die Rote Fahne*, November 24, 1928. On Pilewski, see Plakolm-Forsthuber, "Leonie Pilewski, 1897–1992."

21 Leonie Pilewski, "Neuer Wohnungsbau in der Sowjet-Union," *Die Form*, no. 3 (1931): 99. In an earlier article, Pilewski praised the collaboration between architects and the broadest segments of the Soviet population: Leonie Pilewski, "Neue Bauaufgaben in der Sowjet-Union," *Die Form*, no. 9 (1930): 233.

22 Leonie Pilewski, "Was hat die moderne Architektin der modernen Frau zu sagen," *Arbeiter-Zeitung*, January 17, 1933.

23 Plakolm-Forsthuber, "Leonie Pilewski, 1897–1992," 96.

24 Bauer, "Bauhaus- und Tessenow-Schülerinnen," 384.

25 Facilitating this process, the art magazine editor Else Hofmann settled in New York, where she wrote about Austrian émigrés in the United States.

CHAPTER 25. UNDER DIFFERENT CIRCUMSTANCES: ELLA BRIGGS AND MARGARETE SCHÜTTE-LIHOTZKY

1 Wojciech Czaja, "Margarete Schütte-Lihotzky: 'Diese verdammte Küche!,'" *Der Standard*, January 20, 2017, https://www.derstandard.at/story/2000051238694/margarete-schuette-lihotzky-diese-verdammte-kueche.

2 Urban, "Die Frau als Architektin"; Gisela Urban, "Wiener Architektinnen," *Tages-Post* [Linz], September 23, 1928.

3 Briggs, "Küche"; Briggs, "Laubenganghaus."

4 Briggs, "Küche," 451. For further discussion of Briggs's essay on kitchens for the *Handwörterbuch des Wohnungswesens*, see chapter 15, "Publishing Endeavors," in this volume.

5 On the Ledigenheim, see chapter 13, "Building for Red Vienna," in this volume.

6 Briggs, "Praktische Fragen zur Erwerbslosensiedlung."

7 "Entscheidung des Wettbewerbes 'Das wachsende Haus,'" *Bauwelt* 23, no. 1 (1932): 3–7.

8 Margarete Schütte-Lihotzky, *Erinnerungen aus dem Widerstand, 1938–1945* (Berlin: Volk und Welt, 1985). This memoir became a manifesto of communist resistance, a counter-narrative to the anti-communism that has prevailed in Austria since 1945. Margarete Schütte-Lihotzky, *Warum ich Architektin wurde* (Salzburg: Residenz, 2004); see selected text from this book in Margarete Schütte-Lihotzky, trans. Juliet Kinchin, "Passages from *Why I Became an Architect*," *West 86th: A Journal of Decorative Arts, Design History and Material Culture* 18, no. 1 (2011): 86–96.

9 Maasberg and Prinz, *Die Neuen Kommen!*, 97–99.

10 Margarete Schütte-Lihotzky, "Euch Frauen geht es an"; "Wie stelle ich meine Möbel auf"; "Hubers bekommen ein Kind"; "Wohnküche, Kochküche oder Eßküche"; "Frauenarbeit—Schwerarbeit und wie man sie erleichtert?"; "Ohne Badezimmer"; "Die Poldi zieht nach Wien und wo soll sie wohnen?"; "Ein Fall aus meiner Praxis": undated article clippings from the magazine *Stimme der Frau*, estate of Margarete Schütte-Lihotzky, 281–327, Archiv, Die Angewandte.

11 Some materials that survived within the family are now a part of the Bert Singer and Angela Kimberk Archive (Cambridge, MA), Architekturzentrum Wien, Collection, Vienna.

12 Peter Noever, ed., *Margarete Schütte-Lihotzky: Soziale Architektur: Zeitzeugin eines Jahrhunderts*, 2nd ed. (Vienna: Böhlau, 1996). For a critical reappraisal of Schütte-Lihotzky's work, see Bois and Reinhold, eds., *Margarete Schütte-Lihotzky*.

13 See the Viennese research project "Architektur Pionierinnen" (Pioneering Female Architects), led by Christine Zwingl, Sabina Riss, Carmen Trifina, and Christine Oertel, accessible online at https://architekturpionierinnen.at/en/research-project/.

14 Karen Burns and Lori Brown, "Telling Transnational Histories of Women in Architecture, 1960–2015," *Architectural Histories* 8, no. 1 (2020): 1–11. For an art historical perspective, see Katy Hessel, *The Story of Art without Men* (London: Hutchinson Heinemann, 2022).

CHAPTER 26. WHY ELLA BRIGGS CAPTIVATES US: A FEMALE CHALLENGER OF MODERNISM

1 Although the Kunstgewerbeschule embraced professional education for women in the applied arts, for decades the field of architecture was reserved (by unwritten rule) for men; see chapter 22, "Viennese Women's Art Schools and Their Communities in Ella Briggs's Time," in this volume.

2 For further discussion on the German Theater design, see chapter 5, "A Viennese Designer Takes Manhattan," and chapter 23, "The Interiors of Ella Briggs," both in this volume.

3 On Briggs's Red Vienna projects, see chapter 13, "Building for Red Vienna," in this volume.

4 On the political meanings of the Goldman & Salatsch Haus, see Leslie Topp, *Architecture and Truth in Fin-de-Siècle Vienna* (Cambridge: Cambridge University Press, 2004); and, Elana Shapira, "Portrait of a Jewish Tailor as a Viennese Gentleman: Goldman and Loos Fashioning Vienna," in *Buy from Jews! Story of a Viennese Store Culture*, ed. Astrid Peterle (Vienna: Amalthea, 2017), 130–49.

5 Loos, "Die Plumber." The term "plumber" had been used in Austrian and Viennese professional journals since the early nineteenth century.

6 See the discussion of Briggs's design installation for the German Copper Institute in chapter 16, "Exhibition Design," in this volume.

7 [Alfred] Grotte, "Wiener Kleinwohnungstypen von 27 bis 66 qm," *Zentralblatt der Bauverwaltung* 46, no. 37 (1926): 425–27. For more on Briggs's efforts to include individual bathrooms in her Vienna social housing projects, see chapter 13, "Building for Red Vienna," in this volume.

8 Although both Schütte-Lihotzky and Briggs acted as bold agents seeking to advance professional design, they did not receive the same support or subsequent recognition for those efforts. For more on this, see chapter 25, "Under Different Circumstances," in this volume.

9 Loos was well connected in Viennese intellectual circles but his personal and professional antipathy to Josef Hoffmann and his followers prevented him from becoming part of Vienna's design establishment.

10 Christopher Long, "Apostle and Apostate: Josef Frank's Modernist Vision," *Places Journal* (February 2018): https://placesjournal.org/article/josef-franks-modernist-vision-accidentism/; Hermann Czech and Sebastian Hackenschmidt, "Josef Frank: Against Design," in *Josef Frank: Against Design; The Architect's Anti-Formalist Oeuvre*, ed. Christoph Thun-Hohenstein, Hermann Czech, and Sebastian Hackenschmidt (Basel: Birkhäuser/MAK, 2016), 14–27; and, Mikael Bergquist and Olof Michélsen, *Accidentism: Josef Frank* (Basel: Birkhäuser, 2005). For an analysis of Briggs's interior design philosophy and the writing room, see chapter 7, "Opening an Interior Design Firm in Vienna," in this volume. On Josef Frank more broadly, see Tano Bojankin, Christopher Long, and Iris Meder, eds., *Josef Frank: Schriften/Writings* (Vienna: Metroverlag, 2012); and, Long, *Josef Frank: Life and Work*.

11 The development of home economics in the nineteenth century by leading female figures such as Catherine Beecher in the United States and Ida von Kortzfleisch in Germany (founder of the Reifenstein Schools) helped to give rise to many ideas central to modernism, such as functional design, practicality, simplicity, and hygiene, to name but a few. Briggs's position as one of the few female architects at the time allowed her to demonstrate her professional skills and authority at the intersection of home economics and domestic design in a way different from her male colleagues, who rarely acknowledged their debt to home economists. For further discussion of Briggs's engagement with home economics, see chapter 11, "Return to Vienna and a Big Break," in this volume.

12 Estrid M. Ericson (1894–1981) was a Swedish designer and founder of the interior decorating company Svenskt Tenn, known for its modern, Swedish design. Her collaboration with Josef Frank helped the company expand in new directions.

13 Elana Shapira, "Die kulturellen Netzwerke der Wiener Moderne: Loos, Hoffmann und ihre Klienten," in *Wagner, Hoffmann, Loos und das Möbeldesign der Wiener Moderne: Künstler, Auftraggeber, Produzenten*, ed. Eva B. Ottillinger (Vienna: Böhlau, 2018), 123–33.

14 While Loos, Frank, and Briggs can be characterized as important innovators of early Austrian modernism, they do not quite fit into the selection of orthodox modernists that would be promoted some years later under the label of the International Style. Their deviations from mainstream modernism arguably demonstrated their individual creativity and skills to a greater extent than those who adhered to strict doctrines. In addition, by shifting the focus from the architect to the client, they displayed a better grasp of what was to come in future architectural developments.

15 In *Privacy and Publicity: Modern Architecture as Mass Media* (Cambridge, MA: MIT Press, 1994), Beatriz Colomina argues that modern architecture, rather than having been formed in opposition to mass culture, was actually produced within the emerging mass media systems of the twentieth century. She demonstrates how architectural discourses were shaped by media representations such as drawings, models, photographs, books, films, and exhibitions. Briggs's own public interventions indicate she was well aware of the expanding sites of architectural production.

CHAPTER 27. THE STOWLAWN ESTATE AT BILSTON AS SEEN BY TODAY'S RESIDENTS

1 See, for example, Marco Amati, "Engagement and Exhibitionism in the Era of High Modernism: Otto Neurath and the Example of 1940s Bilston," in *Exhibitions and the Development of Modern Planning Culture*, ed. Marco Amati and Robert Freestone (Farnham: Ashgate, 2014), 149–62; Boyd Whyte, "Otto Neurath and the Sociology of Happiness"; Harwood, "Neurath, Riley and Bilston, Pasmore and Peterlee"; Michelle Henning, "The Pig in the Bath: New Materialisms and Cultural Studies," *Radical Philosophy* 145 (2007): 11–19; Larkham, "People, Planning and Place"; Sybilla Nikolow, "Planning, Democratization and Popularization with ISOTYPE, ca. 1945: A Study of Otto Neurath's Pictorial Statistics with the Example of Bilston, England," *Vienna Circle Institute Yearbook* 11 ([2003] 2004): 299–329; and Pia Pedersen, "Behind Isotype Charts: The Design of

Number-Fact Pictures," *Visible Language* 51, no. 1 (2017): 12–37.

2 For further discussion of Briggs's Bilston designs, see chapter 19, "London," in this volume.

3 Larkham, "People, Planning and Place," 558.

4 Otto Neurath to Josef Frank, November 27, 1945, Autogr. 1219/5-8, Manuscript Collection, Austrian National Library, Vienna, Austria.

5 Larkham, "People, Planning and Place," 563. I focus on Lawnside Green because it was the only section of Stowlawn that ever truly functioned around a communal green, and which can be confirmed as Briggs's work. While there were also houses built on Church Green at an early stage in the estate's development, Briggs's involvement with these designs remains unverified in archival records.

6 See Otto Neurath, "Glückliches Wohnen: Die Bedeutung der Werkbundsiedlung für die Zukunft," *Arbeiter-Zeitung*, June 19, 1932; and Otto Neurath, "Die Internationale Werkbundsiedlung Wien 1932 als 'Ausstellung,'" *Die Form* 7, no. 7 (1932): 208–17.

7 See Sabrina Rahman, "'Out of All That Is Alive and Felt': The Austrian Werkbund and the Design of Social Democracy," *Journal of Design History* 32, no. 4 (2019): 340–55.

8 Harwood, "Neurath, Riley and Bilston, Pasmore and Peterlee," 87.

9 Bilston town clerk A. V. Williams to Otto Neurath, CMB-BIL/14/1/Box 20, C29, Wolverhampton City Archives, UK.

10 On Marie Reidemeister and Otto Neurath's collaborative work, see Christopher Burke and Günther Sandner, "Marie Reidemeister und Otto Neurath: Eine Lebens- und Arbeitspartnerschaft," in *Gestalterinnen: Frauen, Design und Gesellschaft im Wien der Zwischenkriegszeit*, ed. Elana Shapira and Anne-Katrin Rossberg (Berlin: De Gruyter, 2023), 213–23.

11 For a detailed examination of the exhibition and the use of Isotype charts in relation to the redevelopment of Bilston, see Pedersen, "Behind Isotype Charts"; and Pedersen, "Marie Neurath: Designing Bilston's Housing Exhibition." For a discussion of the exhibition in its historical context, see Marie L. Neurath, "An Isotype Exhibition on Housing," *Journal of the Royal Institute of British Architects* 54, no. 13 (1947): 600–603. The exhibition also included a formicarium in the street-facing display window, which was intended as a real-life illustration of how ants, as social creatures, worked together to build their own houses and community structures. The formicarium was popular with children, but it was widely panned by the few adults who attended, who resented being compared to insects. Ultimately this resulted in the premature closure of the exhibition, despite Reidemeister's best intentions. See "Ants Will Guide This Town to Healthier Living," *Birmingham Gazette*, November 2, 1946.

12 "Houses at Bilston, Notts," 15; Briggs, "A Four-Flat House." A third article, published in 1949 in *The Builder*, contains helpful plans, photographs, and technical details. "Houses and Flats on the Stowlawn Park Estate." On Briggs's correspondence with Neurath, see chapter 19, "London," in this volume. Some vestiges of Neurath's ideas remained in the Welsh town planner Thomas Alwyn Lloyd's preliminary plans for what would become the Stowlawn Estate, which had been commissioned by the Bilston Town Council in 1945; see John Boughton, *A History of Council Housing in 100 Estates* (London: RIBA Publishing, 2023), 103. Future stages that did not include Briggs were executed throughout the 1960s. These included construction of high-rise housing on another green located on the site. I would like to thank local resident Paul Quigley for a series of site visits in 2015, during which he clarified the developmental stages of the estate.

13 On A. V. [Arthur Vivian] Williams, see Larkham, "People, Planning and Place," 561. On Reilly, see Harwood, "Neurath, Riley and Bilston," 87ff.

14 "Houses at Bilston, Notts," 15.

15 "Houses at Bilston, Notts," 15; Briggs, "A Four-Flat House," 28.

16 For a detailed discussion of these activities, see Eve Blau, "Isotype and Architecture in Red Vienna: The Modern Projects of Otto Neurath and Josef Frank," *Austrian Studies* 14 (2006): 227–59.

17 All residents have been pseudonymized.

18 Former residents of the Stowlawn Estate, interviews by Sabrina Rahman and Carol Thompson, February 2015, Bilston.

AFTERWORD

1 Manfredo Tafuri, *Vienna Rossa: La politica residenziale nella Vienna socialista* (Milan: Electa, [1980] 1995), 84, 191, 277, 278.

2 For previous scholarship on Briggs's work in Vienna, see Sabine Plakolm-Forsthuber, *Künstlerinnen in Österreich, 1897–1938: Malerei, Plastik, Architektur* (Vienna: Picus, 1994); and, Blau, *The Architecture of Red Vienna*. On her work in Vienna and Berlin, see Stingl, "Ella Briggs (-Baumfeld)"; Robert Schmid, "Ella Briggs (1880–1977): Beiträge der österreichischen Architektin zum Bauen in turbulenten Zeiten" (MA thesis, Vienna Technical University, 2019); Myra Warhaftig, *Deutsche jüdische Architekten vor und nach 1933* (Berlin: Reimar, 2005); Kerstin Dörhöfer, *Pionierinnen in der Architektur: Eine Baugeschichte der Moderne* (Berlin: Wasmuth, 2004); and, Bauer, "Bauhaus und Tessenau Schülerinen." On Briggs's work in Britain, see Benton, *A Different World*; Boughton, *A History of Council Housing in 100 Estates*.

3 Three important early publications in this formation of the modernist canon are Henry-Russell Hitchcock and Philip Johnson, *The International Style: Architecture Since 1922* (New York: Norton, 1932); Nikolaus Pevsner, *Pioneers of the Modern Movement from William Morris to Walter Gropius* (London: Faber and Faber, 1936); and Siegfried Giedion, *Space, Time and Architecture: The Growth of a New Tradition* (Cambridge, MA: Harvard University Press, 1941). For critiques on canon formation, see, for example, Jennifer Kaufmann-Buhler, Victoria Rose Pass, and Christopher Wilson, eds., *Design History beyond the Canon* (London: Bloomsbury, 2023); Vikramaditya Prakash, Maristella Casciato, and Daniel E. Coslett, eds., *Rethinking Global Modernism: Architectural Historiography and the Postcolonial* (Abingdon, UK: Routledge, 2022); Irene Cheng, Charles L. Davis II, and Mabel O. Wilson, eds., *Race and Modern Architecture: A Critical History from the Enlightenment to the Present* (Pittsburgh: University of Pittsburgh Press, 2020); and, Anna Brzyski, ed., *Partisan Canons* (Durham, NC: Duke University Press, 2007).

4 See Richard Pommer, "The Flat Roof: A Modernist Controversy in Germany," *Art Journal* 43, no. 2 (1983): 158–69. See also chapter 15, "Publishing Endeavors," in this volume.

5 This absence is being challenged by recent scholarship on the role of gender, women's movements, and modern design, notably in the German and Austrian context. See, for example, Elana Shapira and Anne-Katrin Rossberg, eds., *Gestalterinnen: Frauen, Design und Gesellschaft im Wien der Zwischenkriegszeit* (Berlin: De Gruyter, 2023); Sabine Wieber, *Jugendstil Women and the Making of Modern Design* (London: Bloomsbury Visual Arts, 2021); Brandow-Faller, *The Female Secession*; Madhavi Desai, *Women Architects and Modernism in India: Narratives and Contemporary Practices* (Abingdon, UK: Routledge, 2017); Mary Pepchinski and Mariann Simon, eds., *Ideological Equals: Women Architects in Socialist Europe, 1945–1989* (Abingdon, UK: Routledge, 2017); Ruth Oldenziel and Karin Zachmann, eds., *Cold War Kitchen: Americanization, Technology, and European Users* (Cambridge, MA: MIT Press, 2009); Susan R. Henderson, "Housing the Single Woman: The Frankfurt Experiment," *Journal of the Society of Architectural Historians* 68, no. 3 (2009): 358–77; Stratigakos, *A Women's Berlin*; Despina Stratigakos, "Women and the Werkbund: Gender Politics and German Design Reform, 1907–14," *Journal of the Society of Architectural Historians* 62, no. 4 (2003): 490–511.

6 Catherine W. Zipf, "Surveys, Seminars, and Starchitects: Gender Studies and Architectural History Pedagogy in American Architectural Education," in *A Gendered Profession: The Question of Representation in Space Making*, ed. James Benedict Brown, Harriet Harriss, Ruth Morrow, and James Soane (London: RIBA, 2016), 200–208.

7 Despina Stratigakos, "Unforgetting Women Architects: A Confrontation with History and Wikipedia," in *Where Are the Women Architects?* (Princeton, NJ: Princeton University Press, 2016), 65–76.

8 The workshop took place on June 9, 2022, with generous funding from the Cultural Department of the City of Vienna and the dedicated support of the Architekturzentrum Wien staff. We worked with Monika Platzer to conceptualize and organize this event and express our deep gratitude for her foundational role. We also extend our heartfelt thanks to the symposium participants who brought their knowledge and enthusiasm to the event.

9 Among the events to mark the anniversary, the Wien Museum held the exhibition *Das Rote Wien* (Red Vienna) from April 2019 to January 2020. The exhibition catalog and related events, such as the renaming of a contemporary social housing project (at Philippovichgasse 6–10, in the nineteenth district) as the Ella Briggs Hof, brought greater public awareness of Briggs's participation in the Red Vienna movement.

10 Abigail A. Van Slyck, "Women in Architecture and the Problems of Biography," in "Gender and Design," special issue, *Design Book Review* 25 (Summer 1992): 19. For a more recent analysis of the strategic use of biography, particularly concerning intersectional identities, see Burns and Brown, "Telling Transnational Histories of Women in Architecture, 1960–2015," 6–8.

11 For examples of recent groundbreaking collaborative projects on the histories of women in architecture, see Bendsen, Ricoto, and Steiner, *Untold Stories*; Mary McLeod and Victoria Rosner, codirectors, *Pioneering Women of American Architecture*, online profiles of fifty women in American architecture, hosted by the Beverly Willis Architectural Foundation (https://pioneeringwomen.bwaf.org/); and, Lori A. Brown and Karen Burns, eds., *The Bloomsbury Global Encyclopedia of Women in Architecture, 1960–2015* (London: Bloomsbury, 2025).

SELECTED BIBLIOGRAPHY

"Abenteuer einer Wiener Architektin in Sizilien: Eine wissenschaftliche Arbeit bringt sie ins Gefängnis." *Der Tag*. December 24, 1925.

Adler, Leo. *Neuzeitliche Mietshäuser und Siedlungen.* Berlin: Pollak, 1931.

———. "Wohnhausblock und Ledigenheim 'Pestalozzihof' in Wien." *Wasmuths Monatshefte für Baukunst* 12, no. 2 (1928): 69–73.

Amati, Marco. "Engagement and Exhibitionism in the Era of High Modernism: Otto Neurath and the Example of 1940s Bilston." In *Exhibitions and the Development of Modern Planning Culture*, edited by Marco Amati and Robert Freestone, 149–62. Farnham: Ashgate, 2014.

Amati, Marco, and Robert Freestone, eds. *Exhibitions and the Development of Modern Planning Culture.* Farnham: Ashgate, 2014.

Anderson, Harriet. *Utopian Feminism: Women's Movements in Fin-de-Siècle Vienna.* New Haven, CT: Yale University Press, 1992.

Aschheim, Steven E. "The Modern Jewish Experience and the Entangled Web of Orientalism." In *Internal Outsiders—Imagined Orientals? Antisemitism, Colonialism and Modern Constructions of Jewish Identity*, edited by Ulrike Brunotte, Jürgen Mohn, and Christina Späti, 11–34. Würzburg: Ergon, 2017.

Baade, Rudolf. *Kapital und Wohnungsbau in Berlin 1924 bis 1940*. Berlin: Berliner Wissenschafts-Verlag, 2004.

Barnstone, Deborah Ascher. *Beyond the Bauhaus: Cultural Modernity in Breslau, 1918–1933*. Ann Arbor: University of Michigan Press, 2016.

———. *Color in German Architecture of the 1920s*. London: Bloomsbury Visual Arts, 2021.

Bastl, Beatrix. *Die jüdischen Studierenden der Akademie der bildenden Künste Wien, 1848–1948*. Vienna: Kovač, 2019.

Bauer, Corinna Isabel. "Architekturstudentinnen in der Weimarer Republik: Bauhaus und Tessenow Schülerinnen." Dr.-Ing. diss., University of Kassel, 2003.

Baumfeld, Maurice. *Cruising in the Mediterranean.* New York: Emil L. Boas and the South Publishing Press, 1905.

Beller, Steven. "Dis-Oriented Jews? Orientalism, Assimilation, and Modernism in Vienna 1900." In *Design Dialogue: Jews, Culture and Viennese Modernism*, edited by Elana Shapira, 299–311. Vienna: Böhlau, 2018.

Bendsen, Jannie Rosenberg, Svava Riesto, and Henriette Steiner. *Untold Stories: Women, Gender, and Architecture in Denmark.* Copenhagen: Strandberg, 2023.

Benton, Charlotte. *A Different World: Emigre Architects in Britain, 1928–1958*. London: RIBA Heinz Gallery, 1995.

Bergquist, Mikael, and Olof Michélsen. *Accidentism: Josef Frank.* Basel: Birkhäuser, 2005.

Bernhardt, Christoph. "Aufstieg und Krise der öffentlichen Wohnungsbauförderung in Berlin 1900–1945." In *Wohnen in Berlin: 100 Jahre Wohnungsbau in Berlin*, edited by Lothar Juckel, 45–87. Berlin: Stadtbaukunst, 1999.

Blau, Eve. *The Architecture of Red Vienna, 1919–1934*. Cambridge, MA: MIT Press, 1999.

———. "From Red Superblock to Green Megastructure: Municipal Socialism as Model and Challenge." In *Architecture and the Welfare State*, edited by Mark Swenarton, Tom Avermaete, and Dirk Van Den Heuvel, 26–49. Abingdon, UK: Routledge, 2015.

———. "Isotype and Architecture in Red Vienna: The Modern Projects of Otto Neurath and Josef Frank." *Austrian Studies* 14 (2006): 227–59.

"Block of Flats in Berlin, Designed by Ella Briggs." *Architects' Journal.* July 16, 1936, 89–90.

Bodenschatz, Harald, and Klaus Brake, eds. *100 Jahre Gross-Berlin: Wohnungsfrage und Stadtentwicklung*. Berlin: Lukas, 2017.

Bohm-Duchen, Monica, ed. *Insiders Outsiders: Refugees from Nazi Europe and Their Contribution to British Visual Culture*. London: Lund Humphries, 2019.

Bois, Marcel, and Bernadette Reinhold, eds. *Margarete Schütte-Lihotzky: Architecture, Politics, Gender; New Perspectives on Her Life and Work.* Basel: Birkhäuser, 2023.

Bonyhady, Tim. *Good Living Street: The Fortunes of My Viennese Family.* Crows Nest, Australia: Allen and Unwin, 2011.

Boughton, John. *A History of Council Housing in 100 Estates.* London: RIBA Publishing, 2023.

Boyd, Gary A. *Architecture and the Face of Coal: Mining and Modern Britain.* London: Lund Humphries, 2023.

Boyer, John W. *Austria, 1867–1955*. Oxford: Oxford University Press, 2022.

Brandow-Faller, Megan. *Female Secession: Art and the Decorative at the Viennese Women's Academy.* University Park, PA: Penn State University Press, 2020.

Brandow-Faller, Megan, and Laura Morowitz, eds. *Erasures and Eradications in Modern Viennese Art, Architecture and Design.* New York: Routledge, 2023.

Briggs-Baumfeld, Ella. "Selbst ist die Frau! Ersatz für Tapeten—Herrichtung der Wohnung ohne den

Tapezierer—Künstlerische Gestaltung der Wandflächen." *Blatt der Hausfrau* [27, no. 42]. July 15, 1917, 8–9.

Briggs, Ella. "Amerikanische Einfamilienhäuser." *Zeitschrift des Österreichischen Ingenieur- und Architekten-Vereines* 80, no. 17–18 (1928): 146.

———. "Arbeitserleichterungen im amerikanischen Kleinhaus." *Der Tag*. June 8, 1925.

———. "Ausstellungs-Gestaltungen." *Bauwelt* [22, no. 19]. May 7, 1931, 648–50.

———. "Bauen und Wohnen: Zur Ausstellung in Zehlendorf." *Berliner Tageblatt*. September 11, 1928.

———. "Bungalow Home from Prefabricated Huts." *Homes and Gardens* [26, no. 11]. April 1945, 32–33.

———. "A Comfortable New House." *Good Housekeeping*. April 1928, 96, 214, 216.

———. "A Distinctive House Adapted from the Italian." *Ladies' Home Journal* [43, no. 6]. June 1926, 42.

———. "Einbaumöbel." *Deutsche Bauzeitung* [66, no. 33]. August 10, 1932, 658–60.

———. "Elektrizität im Haushalt." *Wohnungswirtschaft* 4, nos. 1–2 (1927): 92.

———. "Ella B. Briggs Plans a Small Labour-and Space-Saving House." *Homes and Gardens* [27, no. 12]. May 1946, 32–33.

———. "Essentials of House Planning." *Homes and Gardens* [25, no. 11]. April 1944, 36–37.

———. "A Family Bungalow—To Be Built without a License." *Homes and Gardens* [34, no. 10]. April 1953, 45.

———. "Flats with Private Balcony Access." *Homes and Gardens* [34, no. 6]. December 1952, 41.

———. "For Hunting Lodge or Home in the Mountains These Simple Swiss Chalets Are Economical and Suitable." *Country Life* [43, no. 1]. November 1922, 50–51.

———. "A Four-Flat House." *Homes and Gardens* [29, no. 4]. October 1947, 28–29.

———. "Groups of Families Can Build These Apartments." *Ladies' Home Journal* [40, no. 10]. October 1923, 42, 103, 104.

———. "House of the Future." *Homes and Gardens* [31, no. 11]. May 1950, 45.

———. "A House on a Hill." *Homes and Gardens* [32, no. 3]. September 1950, 44–45.

———. "The House with a Future." *Country Life* [44, no. 1]. May 1923, 62–63.

———. "How Austria Is Helping to Solve the Housing Problem." *Architecture* 46, no. 5 (1922): 351–52.

———. "Jugend-Tagesräume: Säuglingsheime—Kindergärten—Jugendhorte." *Bauwelt* [22, no. 8]. February 19, 1931, 221–23.

———. "Küche." In *Handwörterbuch des Wohnungswesens*, edited by Gerhard Albrecht et al., 449–51. Jena: Gustav Fischer, 1930.

———. "Labor-Saving House Plan Wins National Women's Competition." *New York Tribune*. February 17, 1924.

———. "Laubenganghaus." In *Handwörterbuch des Wohnungswesens*, edited by Gerhard Albrecht et al., 500–503. Jena: Gustav Fischer, 1930.

———. "Ledigenheim und Kleinstwohnungshäuser." *Bauwelt* [19, no. 48]. November 19, 1928, 1132–33.

———. "A Modern Swiss Home." *Homes and Gardens* [29, no. 11]. May 1948, 32–23, 69–70.

———. "Planned for Modern Requirements." *Homes and Gardens* [27, no. 9]. February 1946, 34–35, 69.

———. "Planned for Present Comfort and Future Extension." *Homes and Gardens* [27, no. 11]. April 1946, 36–37.

———. "A Plant-Lovers' Bungalow." *Homes and Gardens* [35, no. 10]. April 1954, 87.

———. "Praktische Fragen zur Erwerbslosensiedlung," *Bauwelt* [22, no. 44]. October 29, 1931, 1394–96.

———. "Sizilianische Reisebilder." *Deutsche Bauzeitung* [64, no. 36]. May 3, 1930, 281–86.

———. "Space- and Labour-Saving Bungalow." *Homes and Gardens* [36, no. 9]. March 1955, 103.

———. "Stockwerkswohnungs-Teilungen." *Bauwelt* [23, no. 50]. December 15, 1932, 1273–74.

———. "A Swiss Country House." *Homes and Gardens* [35, no. 2]. August 1953, 33–37.

———. "Taylorisierungsbestrebungen in amerikanischen Küchen." *Arbeiter-Zeitung*. June 13, 1925.

———. "Three Ways to Plan a House." *Homes and Gardens* [34, no. 4]. October 1952, 45.

———. "Victorian House into Two Labour-Saving Homes." *Homes and Gardens* [27, no. 5]. October 1945, 20–21.

———. "We Plan a House for You." *Good Housekeeping*. March 1924, 35, 148, 150.

———. "We Plan *Another* House." *Good Housekeeping*. February 1925, 69, 102, 104.

———. "Wohnbau in Berlin-Mariendorf." *Bauwelt* [21, no. 18]. May 1, 1930, 11–12.

———. "Zwei Kleinwohnungsgrundrisse." *Bauwelt* [21, no. 18]. May 1, 1930, 577–78.

Briggs, Ella B. "A Little House That Grew." *Designer and the Woman's Magazine* [59, no. 2]. January 1924, 54–55.

Brown, James Benedict, Harriet Harriss, Ruth Morrow, and James Soane, eds. *A Gendered Profession: The Question of Representation in Space Making*. London: RIBA, 2016.

Brown, Lori A., and Karen Burns, eds. *The Bloomsbury Global Encyclopedia of Women in Architecture, 1960–2015*. London: Bloomsbury, 2025.

Brzyski, Anna, ed. *Partisan Canons*. Durham, NC: Duke University Press, 2007.

Buer, Dr. "Mietshausblock im Süden Berlins: Architektin Dipl.-Ing. Ella Briggs (Berlin)."

Deutsche Bauhütte [35, no. 7]. April 1, 1931, 114–15.
Burke, Christopher, and Günther Sandner. "Marie Reidemeister und Otto Neurath: Eine Lebens- und Arbeitspartnerschaft." In *Gestalterinnen: Frauen, Design und Gesellschaft im Wien der Zwischenkriegszeit*, edited by Elana Shapira and Anne-Katrin Rossberg, 213–23. Berlin: De Gruyter, 2023.
Burns, Karen, and Lori Brown. "Telling Transnational Histories of Women in Architecture, 1960–2015." *Architectural Histories* 8, no. 1 (2020): 1–11.
Burrows, Edwin G., and Mike Wallace. *Gotham: A History of New York City to 1898*. New York: Oxford University Press, 1999.
Cheng, Irene, Charles L. Davis II, and Mabel O. Wilson, eds. *Race and Modern Architecture: A Critical History from the Enlightenment to the Present*. Pittsburgh: University of Pittsburgh Press, 2020.
Colomina, Beatriz. *Privacy and Publicity: Modern Architecture as Mass Media*. Cambridge, MA: MIT Press, 1994.
Course, Sue. *Lost Letters from Vienna*. Melbourne, Australia: Wild Dingo Press, 2019.
Crinson, Mark. *Rebuilding Babel: Modern Architecture and Internationalism*. London: I. B. Tauris, 2017.
Croy, Mae Savell. "Houses Planned by Women." *Pictorial Review* [25, no. 1]. October 1923, 54, 67.
———. "Houses Planned by Women." *Pictorial Review* [25, no. 2]. November 1923, 35, 95, 96.
Czech, Hermann, and Sebastian Hackenschmidt. "Josef Frank: Against Design." In *Josef Frank: Against Design: The Architect's Anti-Formalist Oeuvre*, edited by Christoph Thun-Hohenstein, Hermann Czech, and Sebastian Hackenschmidt, 14–27. Basel: Birkhäuser/MAK, 2016.
Darling, Elizabeth. "Becoming Truly Alive." In *AA Women in Architecture, 1917–2017*, edited by Elizabeth Darling and Lynne Walker, 28–43. London: AA Publications, 2017.
Davidi, Sigal. "Home Planning and Gender in Mandatory Palestine." *Journal of the Society of Architectural Historians* 82, no. 1 (2023): 46–62.
———. "Reclaiming the Work of Women Architects in Mandatory Palestine." In *The Routledge Companion to Women in Architecture*, edited by Anna Sokolina, 154–64. New York: Routledge, 2021.
"The Decoration of the New German Theatre." *Architects' and Builders' Magazine* [10, no. 3]. December 1908, 89–93.
Denby, Elizabeth. *Europe Re-housed*. London: George Allen and Unwin, 1938.
Deutsche Bauausstellung Berlin 1931: Amtlicher Katalog und Führer. Berlin: Bauwelt, 1931.
"Die Abenteuer der Frau Ella Briggs." *Wiener Allgemeine Zeitung*. January 1, 1926.
Die Wohnhausanlage der Gemeinde Wien Pestalozzi-Hof im 19: Bezirk Philippovichgasse (früher Felix-Mottl-Straße). Vienna: Vorwärts, c. 1926–1927.
Donath, Matthias, Gabriele Schulz, and Michael Hofmann. *Denkmale in Berlin: Bezirk Tempelhof-Schöneberg—Ortsteile Tempelhof, Mariendorf, Marienfelde und Lichtenrade*. Petersberg, Germany: Michael Imhof, 2007.
Dörhöfer, Kerstin. *Pionierinnen in der Architektur: Eine Baugeschichte der Moderne*. Berlin: Wasmuth, 2004.
E. F. "Aus dem Reiche der Frau: Ausstellung der Kunstgewerblerinnen." *Fremden-Blatt*. May 1, 1914.
Eisen, Markus. "'Neues Wohnen' für 'Neue Menschen': Ledigenheime als Programmbauten der Moderne in der späten Weimarer Republik." *RIHA Journal*, May 2018.
Eisterer, S. E. "On Settler Huts and Core-Houses: Margarete Lihotzky's Contribution to Cooperative Labor in the Vienna Settlement Movement." In *Margarete Schütte-Lihotzky: Architecture, Politics, Gender; New Perspectives on Her Life and Work*, edited by Marcel Bois and Bernadette Reinhold, 78–93. Basel: Birkhäuser, 2023.
"Ella Briggs: Eine Wiener Architektin." *Frau und Gegenwart* [4, no. 40]. October 4, 1927, 12–13.
"Eröffnung des Pestalozzi-Hofes." *Neues Wiener Tagblatt*. February 28, 1927.
Fernand, Deirdre. "Peter Moro and the Men from Mars." In *Applied Arts in British Exile from 1933*, edited by Marian Malet, Rachel Dickson, Sarah MacDougall, and Anna Nyburg, 27–48. Leiden: Brill, 2019.
Frederick, Christine. *Die rationelle Haushaltführung: Betriebswissenschaftliche Studien*. Translated by Irene M. Witte. Berlin: Springer, 1921.
———. *The New Housekeeping: Efficiency Studies in Home Management*. Garden City, NY: Doubleday, Page and Co., 1913.
Freidenreich, Harriet Pass. *Female, Jewish, and Educated: The Lives of Central European University Women*. Bloomington: Indiana University Press, 2002.
Freundlich, Emmy. "Arbeitsgemeinschaften der Hausfrauen." *Arbeiter-Zeitung*. April 11, 1925.
Frohne, H. W. "The German Theatre in New York." *Architectural Record* [24, no. 6]. December 1908, 408–16.
Gaines, Steven. *The Sky's the Limit: Passion and Property in Manhattan*. New York: Little, Brown and Company, 2005.
Garb, Tamar. *Sisters of the Brush: Women's Artistic Culture in Late Nineteenth-Century Paris*. New Haven, CT: Yale University Press, 1994.
George, Alys X. *The Naked Truth: Viennese Modernism and the Body*. Chicago: University of Chicago Press, 2020.

Greene, Ernest. "The New York Press Club." *Architects' and Builders' Magazine* [10, no. 5]. February 1910, 185–89.
Harlander, Tilman, ed. *Villa und Eigenheim: Suburbaner Städtebau in Deutschland.* Stuttgart: Deutsche Verlags-Anstalt, 2001.
Harlander, Tilman, Katrin Hater, and Franz Meiers. *Siedeln in der Not: Umbruch von Wohnungspolitik und Siedlungsbau am Ende der Weimarer Republik.* Hamburg: Christians, 1988.
Harwood, Elain. "Neurath, Riley and Bilston, Pasmore and Peterlee." *Twentieth Century Architecture,* no. 9 (2008): 84–96.
Hegemann, Werner. *Reihenhaus-Fassaden: Geschäfts- und Wohnhäuser aus alter und neuer Zeit.* Berlin: Wasmuth, 1929.
Henderson, Susan R. *Building Culture: Ernst May and the New Frankfurt Initiative, 1926–1931.* New York: Peter Lang, 2013.
———. "Housing the Single Woman: The Frankfurt Experiment." *Journal of the Society of Architectural Historians* 68, no. 3 (2009): 358–77.
Hessel, Katy. *The Story of Art without Men.* London: Hutchinson Heinemann, 2022.
Hession, Jane King. *Elizabeth Scheu Close: A Life in Modern Architecture.* Minneapolis: University of Minnesota Press, 2020.
Hessler, Martina. "The Frankfurt Kitchen: The Model of Modernity and the 'Madness' of Traditional Users, 1926–1933." In *Cold War Kitchen: Americanization, Technology, and European Users,* edited by Ruth Oldenziel and Karin Zachmann, 163–84. Cambridge, MA: MIT Press, 2011.
Hildebrandt, Hans. *Die Frau als Künstlerin.* Berlin: Rudolf Mosse, 1928.
Hochhäusl, Sophie. "From Garden Settlement to Cooperative Economy: Housing, Labor, and Socialization Theory in Vienna and Berlin, 1920–1925." In *Landscapes of Housing: Design and Planning in the History of Environmental Thought,* edited by Jeanne Haffner, 77–99. Abingdon, UK: Routledge, 2022.
———. "From Vienna to Frankfurt Inside Core-House Type 7: A History of Scarcity through the Modern Kitchen." *Architectural Histories* 1, no. 1 (2013). https://journal.eahn.org/article/id/7455/#!.
Holzschuh, Ingrid, Sabine Plakolm-Forsthuber, and Zentralvereinigung der ArchitektInnen Österreichs, eds. *Pionierinnen der Wiener Architektur.* Basel: Birkhäuser, 2022.
Hösl, Wolfgang, and Gottfried Pirhofer. *Wohnen in Wien, 1848–1938: Studien zur Konstitution des Massenwohnens.* Vienna: Deuticke, 1988.
"House Near Berlin Designed by Ella Briggs." *Architects' Journal.* February 2, 1939, 211.
"Houses and Flats on the Stowlawn Park Estate for the Bilston Borough Council: Ella B. Briggs, L.R.I.B.A., Architect." *Builder* [177, no. 5564]. October 7, 1949, 448–51.
"Houses at Bilston, Notts: Designed by Ella B. Briggs." *Architects' Journal* [105, no. 2710]. January 2, 1947, 15–16.
Houze, Rebecca. *Textiles, Fashion, and Design Reform in Austria-Hungary before the First World War: Principles of Dress.* Farnham, UK: Ashgate, 2015.
Hövelmann, Katharina. *Bauhaus in Wien? Möbeldesign, Innenraumgestaltung und Architektur der Wiener Ateliergemeinschaft von Friedl Dicker und Franz Singer.* Vienna: Böhlau, 2021.
Huse, Norbert, ed. *Vier Berliner Siedlungen der Weimarer Republik.* Berlin: Argon, 1987.
"Im Massengefängnis von Palermo! Die furchtbaren Erlebnisse der Wienerin Ella Briggs." *Wiener Allgemeine Zeitung.* December 31, 1925.
Johannesson, Lena, Gunilla Knape, and Eva Dahlman, eds. *Women Photographers—European Experience.* Gothenburg: Acta Universitatis Gothoburgensis, 2004.
Juckel, Lothar, ed. *Wohnen in Berlin: 100 Jahre Wohnungsbau in Berlin.* Berlin: Stadtbaukunst, 1999.
Kaufmann-Buhler, Jennifer, Victoria Rose Pass, and Christopher Wilson, eds. *Design History Beyond the Canon.* London: Bloomsbury, 2023.
King, Greg. *A Season of Splendor: The Court of Mrs. Astor in Gilded Age New York.* Hoboken, NJ: John Wiley, 2009.
"Kommunale Studentenheime: Zur gestrigen Eröffnung des ersten Studentenhauses der Gemeinde Wien." *Der Tag.* May 13, 1928.
Krammer, Marion, and Margarete Szeless, eds. *1919–2019: 100 Jahre Frauen an der Technischen Universität Wien.* Vienna: Promedia, 2019.
Kress, Celina. *Adolf Sommerfeld / Andrew Sommerfield: Bauen für Berlin, 1910–1970.* Berlin: Lukas, 2011.
———. "Gemeinnütziger Wohnungsbau bis 1933." In *100 Jahre Gross-Berlin: Wohnungsfrage und Stadtentwicklung,* edited by Harald Bodenschatz and Klaus Brake, 64–79. Berlin: Lukas, 2017.
Lane, Barbara Miller. *Architecture and Politics in Germany, 1918–1945.* Cambridge, MA: Harvard University Press, [1968] 1985.
Larkham, Peter J. "People, Planning and Place: The Roles of Client and Consultants in Reconstructing Postwar Bilston and Dudley." *Town Planning Review* 77, no. 5 (2006): 557–82.
Lebart, Luce, and Marie Robert, eds. *A World History of Women Photographers.* London: Thames and Hudson, 2022.
Lejeune, Jean-François, and Michelangelo Sabatino, eds. *Modern Architecture and the Mediterranean: Vernacular Dialogues and Contested Identities.* Abingdon, UK: Routledge, 2010.
Livingstone, Karen, and Linda Parry. *International Arts and Crafts.* London: V&A Publishing, 2005.

Long, Christopher. *Paul T. Frankl and Modern American Design.* New Haven, CT: Yale University Press, 2007.

———. "Refuge and Respite: Oskar Wlach, Max Eisler, and the Culture of the Modern Jewish Interior." In *Designing Transformation: Jews and Cultural Identity in Central European Modernism,* edited by Elana Shapira, 157–71. London: Bloomsbury Visual Arts, 2021.

———. "The Viennese *Secessionsstill* and Modern American Design." *Studies in the Decorative Arts* 14, no. 2 (2007): 6–44.

Lüdtke, Alf, Inge Marßolek, and Adelheid von Saldern, eds. *Amerikanisierung: Traum und Alptraum im Deutschland des 20. Jahrhunderts.* Stuttgart: Franz Steiner, 1996.

Maasberg, Ute, and Regina Prinz. *Die Neuen kommen! Weibliche Avantgarde in der Architektur der zwanziger Jahre.* Hamburg: Junius, 2004.

Malet, Marian, Rachel Dickson, Sarah MacDougall, and Anna Nyburg. *Applied Arts in British Exile from 1933.* Leiden: Brill, 2019.

Matzer, Ulrike, ed. *Marianne Strobl, "Industrie-Photograph," 1894–1914.* Salzburg: Fotohof, 2017.

Meder, Iris. "Women Designers and Architects in Early Twentieth Century Vienna." In *Women's Creativity since the Modern Movement (1918–2018): Toward a New Perception and Reception,* edited by Helena Seražin, Caterina Franchini, and Emilia Garda, 50–57. Ljubljana: ZRC SAZU, France Stele Institute of Art History, Založba ZRC, 2018.

Meder, Iris, and Andrea Winklbauer, eds. *Vienna's Shooting Girls: Jüdische Fotografinnen aus Wien.* Vienna: Metroverlag, 2012.

Mikoletzky, Juliane, Ute Georgeacopol-Winischhofer, and Margit Pohl. *"Dem Zuge der Zeit entsprechend . . .": Zur Geschichte des Frauenstudiums in Österreich am Beispiel der Technischen Universität Wien.* Vienna: WUV-Universitätsverlag, 1997.

Moss, Timothy. *Remaking Berlin: A History of the City through Infrastructure.* Cambridge, MA: MIT Press, 2020.

Mucha, Jiří. *Alphonse Maria Mucha: His Life and Art.* New York: Rizzoli, 1989.

Müller-Wulckow, Walter. *Die deutsche Wohnung der Gegenwart.* Königstein im Taunus: Langewiesche, 1932.

———. *Wohnbauten und Siedlungen.* Königstein im Taunus: Langewiesche, 1929.

Nelson, Andrea. *The New Woman behind the Camera.* Washington, DC: National Gallery of Art, 2020.

Neurath, Marie L. "An Isotype Exhibition on Housing." *Journal of the Royal Institute of British Architects* 54, no. 13 (1947): 600–603.

"The New German Theater." *Wall-Paper News and Interior Decorator* [32, no. 6]. December 1908, 15, 16.

Nikolow, Sybilla. "Planning, Democratization and Popularization with ISOTYPE, ca. 1945: A Study of Otto Neurath's Pictorial Statistics with the Example of Bilston, England." *Vienna Circle Institute Yearbook* 11 ([2003] 2004): 299–329.

Noever, Peter, ed. *Margarete Schütte-Lihotzky: Soziale Architektur: Zeitzeugin eines Jahrhunderts.* 2nd edition. Vienna: Böhlau, 1996.

Nolan, Mary. *Visions of Modernity: American Business and the Modernization of Germany.* Oxford: Oxford University Press, 1994.

"Notes for Architects." *New York Architect* [4, no. 6]. June 1910, n.p.

Novy, Klaus, Wolfgang Förster, Ernst Koch, and Verein für Moderne Kommunalpolitik. *Einfach Bauen: Genossenschaftliche Selbsthilfe nach der Jahrhundertwende; Zur Rekonstruktion der Wiener Siedlerbewegung.* Vienna: Picus, 1991.

Odgers, Jo, Flora Samuel, and Adam Sharr, eds. *Primitive: Original Matters in Architecture.* London: Routledge, 2006.

Oldenziel, Ruth, and Karin Zachmann, eds. *Cold War Kitchen: Americanization, Technology, and European Users.* Cambridge, MA: MIT Press, 2009.

Ottillinger, Eva B. *Adolf Loos: Wohnkonzepte und Möbelentwürfe.* Salzburg: Residenz, 1994.

———. *Wagner, Hoffmann, Loos und das Möbeldesign der Wiener Moderne: Künstler, Auftraggeber, Produzenten.* Vienna: Böhlau, 2018.

Ottillinger, Eva B., and Lieselotte Hanzl. *Kaiserliche Interieurs: Die Wohnkultur des Wiener Hofes und die Wiener Kunstgewerbereform.* Vienna: Böhlau, 1997.

Pedersen, Pia. "Marie Neurath: Design Bilston's Housing Exhibition." *Journal of Design History* 36, no. 2 (2023): 157–74.

Penick, Monica, and Christopher Long, ed. *The Rise of Everyday Design: The Arts and Crafts Movement in Britain and America.* Austin and New Haven: Harry Ransom Center, The University of Texas at Austin and Yale University Press, 2019.

Penner, Barbara. "Gender and Home: (Re)scripting Domestic Life and Design." In *A Cultural History of the Home in the Modern Age,* edited by Despina Stratigakos, 137–60. London: Bloomsbury Academic, 2021.

Pepchinski, Mary, and Mariann Simon, eds. *Ideological Equals: Women Architects in Socialist Europe 1945–1989.* Abington, UK: Routledge, 2017.

Pilewski, Leonie. "Was hat die moderne Architektin der modernen Frau zu sagen." *Arbeiter-Zeitung.* January 17, 1933.

Plakolm-Forsthuber, Sabine. "Else Hofmann: Eine arrivierte Kunstpublizistin." In *Gestalterinnen: Frauen, Design und Gesellschaft im Wien der Zwischenkriegszeit,* edited by Elana Shapira and Anne-Katrin Rossberg, 194–212. Berlin: De Gruyter, 2023.

———. "Helene Roth, 1904–1995." In *Pionierinnen der Wiener Architektur: Das Archiv der Zentralvereinigung der ArchitektInnen Österreichs (ZV)*, edited by Ingrid Holzschuh, Sabine Plakolm-Forsthuber, and Zentralvereinigung der ArchitektInnen Österreichs, 128–39. Berlin: De Gruyter, 2023.

———. *Künstlerinnen in Österreich, 1897–1938: Malerei, Plastik, Architektur.* Vienna: Picus, 1994.

———. "Leonie Pilweski 1897–1992." In *Pionierinnen der Wiener Architektur: Das Archiv der Zentralvereinigung der ArchitektInnen Österreichs (ZV)*, edited by Ingrid Holzschuh, Sabine Plakolm-Forsthuber, and Zentralvereinigung der ArchitektInnen Österreichs, 86–97. Basel: Birkhäuser, 2022.

———. "'Loos Remodeled': Zum Umbau der Wohnung Leopold Goldman durch die Architektin Liane Zimber 1936." In *Design Dialogue: Jews, Culture and Viennese Modernism*, edited by Elana Shapira, 263–80. Vienna: Böhlau, 2018.

Pohlmann, Ulrich, ed. *Qui a peur des femmes photographes? 1839–1945.* Exhibition catalog, Musée d'Orsay and Musée de l'Orangerie. Paris: Hazan, 2015.

Poppelreuter, Tanja. "Sustaining Independence: Marie Frommer's Networks and Architectural Practices in Berlin and in New York." In *Designing Transformation: Jews and Cultural Identity in Central European Modernism*, edited by Elana Shapira, 221–36. London: Bloomsbury Visual Arts, 2021.

Prakash, Vikramaditya, Maristella Casciato, and Daniel E. Coslett, eds. *Rethinking Global Modernism: Architectural Historiography and the Postcolonial.* Abingdon, UK: Routledge, 2022.

Price, Renée, with Pamela Kort, and Leslie Elizabeth Topp, eds. *New Worlds: German and Austrian Art, 1890–1940.* New York: Neue Galerie, 2001.

Prokop, Ursula. *Jacques and Jacqueline Groag, Architect and Designer: Two Hidden Figures of the Viennese Modern Movement.* Translated by Jonee Tiedemann and Laura McGuire. Los Angeles: DoppelHouse Press, 2019.

———. *On the Jewish Legacy in Viennese Architecture: The Contribution of Jewish Architects to Building in Vienna 1868–1938.* Vienna: Böhlau, 2016.

Rahman, Sabrina. "'Out of All That Is Alive and Felt': The Austrian Werkbund and the Design of Social Democracy." *Journal of Design History* 32, no. 4 (2019): 340–55.

Reinhold, Bernadette. "'Weibliche artistische Arbeitskräfte' in spe—Frauenstudium an der frühen Kunstgewerbeschule: Ein unbequemer Rückblick." In *150 Jahre Universität für angewandte Kunst Wien: Ästhetik der Veränderung*, edited by Gerald Bast, Anja Seipenbusch-Hufschmied, and Patrick Werkner, 158–63. Berlin: de Gruyter / Edition Angewandte, 2017.

Rennhofer, Maria. *Koloman Moser: Leben und Werk 1868–1918.* Vienna: Brandstätter, 2002.

Rose, Alison. *Jewish Women in Fin de Siècle Vienna.* Austin: University of Texas Press, 2008.

Rosenblum, Naomi. *A History of Women Photographers.* New York: Abbeville Press, 1994.

Rossberg, Anne-Katrin. "Brought to Light: Art and Life of the Wiener Werkstätte Women." In *Die Frauen der Wiener Werkstätte: Women Artists of the Wiener Werkstätte*, edited by Christoph Thun-Hohenstein, Anne-Katrin Rossberg, and Elisabeth Schmuttermeier, 12–21. Basel: Birkhäuser, 2020.

———. "Ein neues Experimentierfeld: Die Wand gehört den Gestalterinnen." In *Gestalterinnen: Frauen, Design und Gesellschaft im Wien der Zwischenkriegszeit*, edited by Elana Shapira and Anne-Katrin Rossberg, 80–97. Berlin: De Gruyter, 2023.

Ruge, Klara. "Amerikanische Kunstausstellungen der Saison 1909–1910." *Kunst und Kunsthandwerk* 14, no. 1 (1911): 39–61.

———. "Amerikanische Kunstausstellungen der Saison 1908 bis 1909." *Kunst und Kunsthandwerk* 12, no. 11 (1909): 562–82.

Sandner, Günther. *Otto Neurath: Eine politische Biographie.* Vienna: Zsolnay, 2014.

"Sbirrengeist im heutigen Italien: Randbemerkungen zum Fall Ella Briggs." *Der Tag.* December 31, 1925.

Schmid, Robert. "Ella Briggs (1880–1977): Beiträge der österreichischen Architektin zum Bauen in turbulenten Zeiten." MA thesis, Vienna Technical University, 2019.

Schütte-Lihotzky, Margarete. *Erinnerungen aus dem Widerstand, 1938–1945.* Berlin: Volk und Welt, 1985.

———. *Warum ich Architektin wurde.* Salzburg: Residenz, 2004.

Schwartz, Agatha. *Shifting Voices: Feminist Thought and Women's Writing in Fin-de-Siècle Austria and Hungary.* Montreal: McGill-Queen's University Press, 2008.

Schwarz, Werner Michael, Georg Spitaler, and Elke Wikidal, eds. *Das Rote Wien 1919–1934: Ideen, Debatten, Praxis.* Basel: Birkhäuser, 2019.

Schweiger, Werner J. *Wiener Werkstaette: Design in Vienna, 1903–1932.* London: Thames and Hudson, 1984.

Sekler, Eduard F. *Josef Hoffmann: Das architektonische Werk.* Salzburg: Residenz, 1982.

Seražin, Helena, Caterina Franchini, and Emilia Garda, eds. *Women's Creativity since the Modern Movement (1918–2018): Toward a New Perception and Reception.* Ljubljana: ZRC SAZU, France Stele Institute of Art History, Založba ZRC, 2018.

Shapira, Elana, ed. *Design Dialogue: Jews, Culture and Viennese Modernism.* Vienna: Böhlau, 2018.

———, ed. *Designing Transformation: Jews and Cultural Identity in Central European Modernism.* London: Bloomsbury Visual Arts, 2021.

———. "Die kulturellen Netzwerke der Wiener Moderne: Loos, Hoffmann und ihre Klienten." In *Wagner, Hoffmann, Loos und das Möbeldesign der Wiener Moderne: Künstler, Auftraggeber, Produzenten,* edited by Eva B. Ottillinger, 123–33. Vienna: Böhlau, 2018.

———. "'Our Great Josef Hoffmann': Undoing the Austrian Profile of a Celebrated Architect." In *Erasures and Eradications in Modern Viennese Art, Architecture and Design,* edited by Megan Brandow-Faller and Laura Morowitz, 58–73. New York: Routledge, 2023.

———. "Portrait of a Jewish Tailor as a Viennese Gentleman: Goldman and Loos Fashioning Vienna." In *Buy from Jews! Story of a Viennese Store Culture,* edited by Astrid Peterle, 130–49. Vienna: Amalthea, 2017.

———. "Professional Women in the Arts and Media in Vienna–Kulturschaffende Frauen in Wien." In *Gestalterinnen: Frauen, Design und Gesellschaft im Wien der Zwischenkriegszeit,* edited Elana Shapira and Anne-Katrin Rossberg, 9–27. Berlin: De Gruyter, 2023.

Shapira, Elana, and Daniela Finzi. *Freud and the Émigré: Austrian Émigrés, Exiles and the Legacy of Psychoanalysis in Britain, 1930s–1970s.* London: Palgrave Macmillan, 2020.

Shapira, Elana, and Anne-Katrin Rossberg, eds. *Gestalterinnen: Frauen, Design und Gesellschaft im Wien der Zwischenkriegszeit.* Berlin: De Gruyter, 2023.

Silverman, Lisa. *Becoming Austrians: Jews and Culture between the World Wars.* Oxford: Oxford University Press, 2012.

———. "Leopoldstadt, Judenplatz, and Beyond: Rethinking Vienna's Jewish Spaces." *Journal of East Central Europe* 42, no. 2–3 (2015): 249–67.

Silverthorne, Diane V., Dan Reynolds, and Megan Brandow-Faller. *Die Fläche: Design and Lettering of the Vienna Secession, 1902–1911.* San Francisco: Letterform Archive Books, 2023.

Sparke, Penny, and Mitchell Owens. *Elsie De Wolfe: The Birth of Modern Interior Decoration.* New York: Acanthus, 2005.

Spengler, Otto. *Das deutsche Element der Stadt New York: Biographisches Jahrbuch der Deutsch-Amerikaner New Yorks und Umgebung.* New York: pub. by author, 1913.

"'Step-Saving' Design by New York Woman." *New York Tribune.* February 17, 1924.

Stern, Robert A. M., Gregory Gilmartin, and John Montague Massengale. *New York 1900: Metropolitan Architecture and Urbanism, 1890–1915.* New York: Rizzoli, 1983.

Stingl, Katrin. "Ella Briggs (-Baumfeld): Wohnbauten in Wien (1925/26) und in Berlin (1929/30)." MA thesis, University of Vienna, 2008.

Störtkuhl, Beate. *Moderne Architektur in Schlesien 1900 bis 1939: Baukultur und Politik.* Munich: Oldenbourg, 2013.

Stratigakos, Despina, ed. *A Cultural History of the Home in the Modern Age.* London: Bloomsbury Academic, 2021.

———. "The Good Architect and the Bad Parent: On the Formation and Disruption of a Canonical Image." *Journal of Architecture* 13, no. 3 (2008): 283–96.

———. "'I Myself Want to Build': Women, Architectural Education and the Integration of Germany's Technical Colleges." *Paedagogica Historica* 43, no. 6 (2007): 727–56.

———. *Where Are the Women Architects?* Princeton, NJ: Princeton University Press, 2016.

———. "Women and the Werkbund: Gender Politics and German Design Reform, 1907–14." *Journal of the Society of Architectural Historians* 62, no. 4 (2003): 490–511.

———. *A Women's Berlin: Building the Modern City.* Minneapolis: University of Minnesota Press, 2008.

Straumann, Tobias. *1931: Debt, Crisis, and the Rise of Hitler.* Oxford: Oxford University Press, 2019.

Sullivan, Louis H. "The Tall Office Building Artistically Considered." *Lippincott's Magazine.* March 1896, 403–9.

Swenarton, Mark, Tom Avermaete, and Dirk Van Den Heuvel. *Architecture and the Welfare State.* Abingdon, UK: Routledge, 2015.

Szczerski, Andrzej. *Views of Albion: The Reception of British Art and Design in Central Europe.* Oxford: Peter Lang, 2015.

Tafuri, Manfredo. *Vienna Rossa: La politica residenziale nella Vienna socialista.* Milan: Electa, [1980] 1995.

Tauranac, John. *Elegant New York: The Builders and the Buildings, 1885–1915.* New York: Abbeville, 1985.

Taut, Bruno. *Die neue Wohnung: Die Frau als Schöpferin.* Leipzig: Klinkhardt and Biermann, 1924.

Thun-Hohenstein, Christoph, Hermann Czech, and Sebastian Hackenschmidt, eds. *Josef Frank: Against Design—Das anti-formalistische Werk des Architekten / The Architect's Anti-Formalist Oeuvre.* Basel: Birkhäuser/MAK, 2016.

Topp, Leslie. *Architecture and Truth in Fin-de-Siècle Vienna.* Cambridge: Cambridge University Press, 2004.

———. "Moments in the Reception of Early Twentieth-Century German and Austrian Decorative Arts in the United States." In *New Worlds: German and Austrian Art, 1890–1940,* edited by Renée Price, 572–82. New York: Neue Galerie, 2001.

Urban, Gisela. "Die Frau als Architektin: Ihre Arbeit in Oesterreich und anderwärts." *Neues Wiener Journal*. May 13, 1928.

———. "The Problem for Housing for Self-Supporting Women." *Time and Tide*. [5, no. 14]. April 4, 1924, 332–33.

———. "Wiener Architektinnen." *Tages-Post* [Linz]. September 23, 1928.

"U.S. Woman Held as Spy." *Los Angeles Record*. December 24, 1925.

Vera [Betty Kris; later Betty Kurth]. *Eine für Viele: Aus dem Tagebuche eines Mädchens*. Leipzig: Seemann, 1902.

"Verhaftung einer Wiener Dame in Palermo." *Neue Freie Presse*. December 24, 1925.

"Vom neuen deutschen Musentempel in New York." *Der deutsche Vorkämpfer* [2, no. 12]. December 1908, 24.

"Wachaufahrt." *Deutsch-Amerika* [8, no. 23]. July 8, 1922, 12–13.

Walde, Karl. "Die Frau in der Innenarchitektur." *Das Interieur* 15, no. 6 (1914): 21–23.

Waldner, Gernot, ed. *Die Konturen der Welt: Geschichte und Gegenwart visueller Bildung nach Otto Neurath*. Vienna: Mandelbaum, 2021.

Warhaftig, Myra. *Deutsche Jüdische Architekten vor und nach 1933*. Berlin: Reimar, 2005.

Wasserman, Janek. *Black Vienna: The Radical Right in the Red City, 1918–1938*. Ithaca, NY: Cornell University Press, 2017.

Welter, Volker M. *Ernst L. Freud, Architect: The Case of the Modern Bourgeois Home*. New York: Berghahn, 2012.

Whyte, Iain Boyd, ed. *Man-Made Future: Planning, Education and Design in Mid-Twentieth Century Britain*. Abingdon, UK: Routledge, 2007.

Whyte, Iain Boyd, and David Frisby, eds. *Metropolis Berlin: 1880–1940*. Berkeley: University of California Press, 2012.

"Wie es einem in Italien ergehen kann: Frau Architektin Ella Briggs über ihre Haft in Palermo." *Allgemeiner Tiroler Anzeiger*. January 2, 1926.

Wieber, Sabine. *Jugendstil Women and the Making of Modern Design*. London: Bloomsbury Visual Arts, 2021.

Wildt, Michael. "Technik, Kompetenz, Modernität: Amerika als zwiespältiges Vorbild für die Arbeit in der Küche, 1920–1960." In *Amerikanisierung: Traum und Alptraum im Deutschland des 20. Jahrhunderts*, edited by Alf Lüdtke, Inge Marßolek, Adelheid von Saldern, 78–95. Stuttgart: Franz Steiner, 1996.

"Women [*sic*] to Decorate Theatre." *Master Painter* [13, no. 6]. September 1908, 29.

Yang, Jia Lynn. *One Mighty and Irresistible Tide: The Epic Struggle over American Immigration, 1924–1965*. New York: Norton, 2020.

Yazdanpanah, Marie-Noëlle. "'Es lebe drum: Die Frau von heut!': Frauenpolitik im Roten Wien." In *Das Rote Wien 1919–1934: Ideen, Debatten, Praxis*, edited by Werner Michael Schwarz, Georg Spitaler, and Elke Wikidal, 50–57. Basel: Birkhäuser, 2019.

Zech, Vivian. "Betty Kurth: Annäherung an eine Biographie." MA thesis, University of Applied Arts Vienna, 2024.

Ziegler-McPherson, Christina A. *The Great Disappearing Act: Germans in New York City, 1880–1930*. New Brunswick, NJ: Rutgers University Press, 2022.

ARCHIVAL SOURCES

Architekturzentrum Wien, Vienna, Austria
Archiv der TU Wien, Vienna, Austria
Archiv der Universität Wien, Vienna, Austria
Archiv des Österreichischen Ingenieur- und Architektenvereins, Vienna, Austria
Austrian National Library, Vienna, Austria
Baupolizei Berlin-Tempelhof, Germany
Baupolizei Planarchiv, Magistratsabteilung 37, Vienna, Austria
Bibliothek und Kunstblättersammlung / Archiv, MAK Museum, Vienna, Austria
Geheimes Staatsarchiv, Berlin, Germany
Gemeinde Kleinmachnow Bauamt, Kleinmachnow, Germany
Getty Research Institute, Los Angeles, United States
Israelitische Kultusgemeinde Wien, Vienna, Austria
Kunstsammlung und Archiv, Universität für angewandte Kunst Wien, Vienna, Austria
Landesamt für Bürger- und Ordnungsangelegenheiten [LABO], Berlin, Germany
Landesarchiv Berlin, Germany
Leo Baeck Institute, New York, United States
Leopold Museum, Vienna, Austria
Österreichisches Staatsarchiv, Archiv der Republik, Vienna, Austria
Österreichisches Staatsarchiv, Kriegsarchiv, Vienna, Austria
Otto and Marie Neurath Isotype Collection, University of Reading, United Kingdom
Royal Institute of British Architects, London, United Kingdom
Standesamt Charlottenburg-Wilmersdorf von Berlin, Germany
Technische Universität München Archiv, Munich, Germany
Wienbibliothek im Rathaus, Vienna, Austria
Wiener Stadt- und Landesarchiv, Vienna, Austria
Wolverhampton City Archives, United Kingdom

CONTRIBUTORS' BIOGRAPHIES

Megan Brandow-Faller is Professor of History at Kingsborough Community College, The City University of New York. She is the author of *The Female Secession: Art and the Decorative at the Viennese Women's Academy* (2020) and *Child Creativity in the Visual Arts from Secessionist Vienna to Postwar America* (2025), editor of *Childhood by Design: Toys and the Material Culture of Childhood, 1700–Present* (2018), and coeditor of *Erasures and Eradications in Viennese Modern Art, Architecture and Design, 1900–1938* (2022).

Celina Kress is an architect and urban planning historian based in Berlin, with a special focus on the history and theory of urban development as well as twentieth-century housing construction. She is an associate researcher at the Center for Metropolitan Studies of the Berlin Technical University and a founding partner of BEST, an urban design team active in the fields of architecture, urban development, and art. She has published extensively on Berlin architecture and is the author of *Adolf Sommerfeld / Andrew Sommerfield: Bauen für Berlin, 1910–1970* (2011).

Dörte Kuhlmann is Professor in the Faculty of Architecture and Planning at the Technical University of Vienna, with a focus on architecture theory and history. She is the author of *Gender Studies in Architecture: Space, Power, and Difference* (2013), *Emotion in Architecture* (2011), and *Lebendige Architektur: Metamorphosen des Organizismus* (1998), and coeditor of *Basic Design Methods* (2017) and *The Art of ReCreation: Sweden/Austria* (2014). In 2023, she and Heimo Schimek designed the Austrian Pavilion at the International Book Fair in Leipzig, Germany.

Ulrike Matzer is an art historian and critic based in Vienna. She is the director of the Margarete Schütte-Lihotzky Center in Vienna and lecturer at the University of Zurich in the program of Advanced Studies in Theory and History of Photography. Her publications on photography, feminism, and architecture include her edited book *Marianne Strobl, "Industrie-Photograph," 1894–1914* (2017) and "Photography Research from a Feminist Perspective," in *Fotografie als Motiv / Photography as Motif*, edited by Caroline Heider, Ruth Horak, Lisa Rastl, and Claudia Rohrauer (2021).

Christine Oertel is a Vienna-based historian of contemporary Austria. She worked for many years with Simon Wiesenthal and participated with a team of historians commissioned to investigate forced labor practices in the Austrian electrical industry during the Nazi period. She is a collaborator on the Female Pioneers in Austrian Architecture project of the Margarete Schütte-Lihotzky Center in Vienna. Her publications include "Die Geschichte neu schreiben: Architektur-Pionierinnen in Österreich," *Architektur Aktuell*, no. 512 (2022); "Rudolf Hermann Eisenmenger and His Safety Curtain," *museum in progress* (2017), and *Juden auf der Flucht durch Austria: Jüdische Displaced Persons in der US-Besatzungszone Österreichs* (1999).

Eva B. Ottillinger is an art historian and chief curator of the Möbelmuseum Wien. Her research, exhibitions, and publications have explored a broad range of Austrian furniture, from modernist designs to bentwood and wicker furniture to furniture produced for children, the kitchen, and the bathroom. Her publications include *Wagner, Hoffmann, Loos und das Möbeldesign der Wiener Moderne: Künstler, Auftraggeber, Produzenten* (2018), *Wohnen zwischen den Kriegen: Wiener Möbel, 1914–1941* (2009), *Ernst Plischke: Modern Architecture for the New World* (2004, with August Sarnitz), *Kaiserliche Interieurs: Die Wohnkultur des Wiener Hofes im 19. Jahrhundert* (1997, with Lieselotte Hanzl), and *Adolf Loos: Wohnkonzepte und Möbelentwürfe* (1994).

Barbara Penner is Professor in Architectural Humanities at the Bartlett School of Architecture, University College London. She is the author of *Bathroom* (2013) and *Newlyweds on Tour: Honeymooning in Nineteenth-Century America* (2009). She has coedited numerous books on gender and domestic architecture, including *Sexuality and Gender at Home* (2017), *Ladies and Gents: Public Toilets and Gender* (2009), and *Gender Space Architecture* (2000). She is a contributing editor to the architectural journal *Places*. She recently received a Leverhulme Major Research Fellowship to work on a new book, *Subject to Design: Social Sciences in the Home* (forthcoming).

Sabine Plakolm-Forsthuber is Associate Professor of Art History at the Institute of Art History, Building Archeology, and Restoration at the Technical University of Vienna. She has published broadly on modern Austrian art and architecture, with a focus on exhibition architecture and women artists and architects, as well as on Renaissance Italian convents and art policy under National Socialism. She is the author of *Künstlerinnen in Österreich, 1897–1938: Malerei–Plastik–Architektur* (1994) and coeditor of *Pionierinnen der Wiener Architektur: Das Archiv der Zentralvereinigung der ArchitektInnen Österreichs (ZV)* (2022).

Monika Platzer is head of collections and curator at the Architekturzentrum Wien. Her research focuses on transnational architectural history, twentieth-century

Austrian architecture, and cultural history. Her exhibitions and accompanying publications include *Cold War and Architecture: The Competing Forces that Reshaped Austria* (2020), *Lessons from Bernard Rudofsky: Life as a Voyage* (2007), and *Shaping the Great City: Modern Architecture in Central Europe, 1890–1937* (2000).

Ursula Prokop is an architectural and design historian in Vienna focused on Austria in the modern period. She is the author of *Jacques and Jacqueline Groag, Architect and Designer* (2019), *On the Jewish Legacy in Viennese Architecture* (2016), *Margaret Stonborough-Wittgenstein* (2003), and *Wien, Aufbruch zur Metropole* (1994). She has collaborated on numerous research projects, including a database of Viennese architects, and exhibitions (including on Otto Wagner and Josef Frank), and is a contributor to the magazine *David*.

Sabrina Rahman is Senior Lecturer in Art History and Visual Culture at the University of Exeter. She has published widely on themes related to visual culture in Central and Eastern Europe, including in *Camera Austria*, *Journal of Design History*, and the *Museum History Journal*. She coedited *Imagining Blackness in Germany and Austria* (2012) and the forthcoming *Routledge Companion to Race and Design*. In 2015 she curated the exhibition *Bilston's Happy Housing: Otto Neurath's Vision for Post-War Modern Living* at the Bilston Craft Gallery, Wolverhampton, UK.

Elana Shapira is a design and cultural historian and Lecturer in Cultural Studies at the University of Applied Arts Vienna. She is the author of *Style and Seduction: Jewish Patrons, Architecture and Design in Fin de Siècle Vienna* (2016), editor of *Designing Transformation: Jews and Cultural Identity in Central European Modernism* (2021) and *Austrian Identity and Modernity: Culture and Politics in the 20th Century* (2025), and coeditor of *Émigré Cultures in Design and Architecture* (2017) and *Gestalterinnen: Frauen, Design und Gesellschaft im Wien der Zwischenkriegszeit* (2023).

Katrin Stingl is the archivist at the Architekturzentrum Wien, where she is active in the fields of collection management, exhibitions, and knowledge production. She earned a graduate degree in art history from the University of Vienna, with her master's thesis on Ella Briggs-Baumfeld (2008).

Despina Stratigakos is SUNY Distinguished Professor of Architecture at the University at Buffalo. She is the author of *Hitler's Northern Utopia: Building the New Order in Occupied Norway* (2020), *Where Are the Women Architects?* (2016), *Hitler at Home* (2015), and *A Women's Berlin: Building the Modern City* (2008). She has been a fellow at the Institute for Advanced Study in Princeton, Ludwig Maximilian University of Munich, Rice University, the University of Copenhagen, and the University of Michigan. From 2018 to 2022, she served as UB Vice Provost for Inclusive Excellence.

Carmen Trifina is an architect and researcher based in Vienna. She received her Diplom-Ingenieur in Architecture from the Technical University of Vienna. Her research focuses on early female practitioners in Austrian architecture and the kindergartens designed by Margarete Schütte-Lihotzky. For several years she was part of the research team for the Female Pioneers in Austrian Architecture project of the Margarete Schütte-Lihotzky Center.

Christine Zwingl, an architect who works and lives in Vienna, is the founder and inaugural director of the Margarete Schütte-Lihotzky Center in Vienna. Located in the former apartment of Schütte-Lihotzky, the MSL Center is open to the public and serves as the foundation for the Female Pioneers in Austrian Architecture project. Zwingl is the editor of *Margarete Schütte-Lihotzky: Spuren in Wien* (2021), and she led the conceptual and design work for the groundbreaking 1993 exhibition *Margarete Schütte-Lihotzky: Soziale Architektur; Zeitzeugin eines Jahrhunderts*. She also contributed to the catalog.

ILLUSTRATION CREDITS

© American Printer 39, no. 6 (1905): 488 (plate 5)

© Barbara Penner (plates 15–18)

© Benjamin von Radom (plates 1, 2, 7)

© Bert Singer and Angela Kimberk Archive (Cambridge, MA), Architekturzentrum Wien, Collection, Vienna, Austria (plates 9, 11, 13; figs. 7.2, 7.3, 7.5, 7.6, 12.1, 12.2, 12.4, 19.3, 19.8, 20.3)

© Bibliothek und Kunstblättersammlung / Archiv, MAK – Museum of Applied Arts, Vienna, Austria, Photo © MAK (fig. 7.7)

© "Block of Flats in Berlin: Designed by Ella Briggs," *Architects' Journal* (July 16, 1936): 89–90 (figs. 14.1, 14.2, plate 12 with colorization by Katrin Stingl)

© Britta Schinzel (fig. 7.1)

© Building file EZ 2237, Magistratsabteilung 37, Baupolizei, 19th District, Vienna, Austria (plate 10)

© *Das Interieur* 15, no. 6 (1914–1915), plate 73. Collection University of Applied Arts Vienna Library, Austria (fig. 23.1)

© "The Decoration of the New German Theatre," *Architects' and Builders' Magazine* [10, no. 3], December 1908, 91–92. Collection Cornell University Library, Ithaca, NY (figs. 5.1, 5.2)

© *Dekorative Kunst* 11 (1903): 479. Collection MAK – Museum of Applied Arts, Vienna, Austria (fig. 2.2)

© "Die Bauwirtschaftlichen Verbände auf der deutschen Bauausstellung in Berlin," *Deutsche Bauzeitung* 65, no. 57–58 (1931): 171. © Bildrecht, Wien 2025. Photographs by Arthur Köster (figs. 16.6, 16.7)

© "Die Ernährung Ausstellung," *Berliner Leben* 31, no. 3 (1928): 10. Collection Digitale Landesbibliothek Berlin, Germany (fig. 16.1)

© *Die Fläche* 1, no. 3 (1902): 44. Collection, MAK – Museum of Applied Arts, Vienna, Austria (plate 3)

© *Die Fläche* 1, no. 11 (1904): 168. Collection MAK – Museum of Applied Arts, Vienna, Austria (plate 4)

© *Die Woche für die Deutsche Jugend* (1906): 176 (plate 6)

© *Die Wohnhausanlage der Gemeinde Wien Pestalozzi-Hof im 19: Bezirk Philippovichgasse (früher Felix-Mottl-Straße)* (Vienna: Vorwärts, c. 1926–1927), 9, 10 (figs. 13.2, 13.3)

© Dr. Buer, "Mietshausblock im Süden Berlins: Architektin Dipl.-Ing. Ella Briggs (Berlin)," *Deutsche Bauhütte* [35, no. 7], April 1, 1931, 115 (fig. 14.3)

© E. E., "Vom neuen deutschen Musentempel in New York," *Der deutsche Vorkämpfer* 2, no. 12 (1908): 24. Collection Harvard University Library, Cambridge, MA (fig. 5.5)

© Ella Briggs, "A Distinctive House Adapted from the Italian," *Ladies' Home Journal* [43, no. 6], June 1926, 42 (fig. 12.3)

© Ella Briggs, "Arbeitserleichterungen im amerikanischen Kleinhaus," *Der Tag*, June 8, 1925. Picture Archives, Inv. 544.502-D, Austrian National Library Vienna, Austria (fig. 10.7)

© Ella Briggs Archive, Architekturzentrum Wien, Collection, Vienna, Austria (fig. 17.2)

© Ella Briggs, "Ausstellungs-Gestaltungen," *Bauwelt* [22, no. 19], May 7, 1931, 649, 650. Collection Harry Ransom Center, The University of Texas at Austin (figs. 16.2–16.5)

© Ella Briggs, "Essentials of House Planning," *Homes and Gardens* [25, no. 11], April 1944, 36. Courtesy Future Publishing Ltd. (fig. 20.1)

© Ella Briggs, "For Hunting Lodge or Home in the Mountains These Simple Swiss Chalets Are Economical and Suitable," *Country Life* [43, no. 1], November 1922, 51 (fig. 10.1)

© Ella Briggs, "Groups of Families Can Build These Apartments," *Ladies' Home Journal* [40, no. 10], October 1923, 42, 103 (fig. 10.6)

© Ella Briggs, "The House with a Future," *Country Life* [44, no. 1], May 1923, 62, 63 (figs. 10.3–10.5)

© Ella Briggs, "How Austria Is Helping to Solve the Housing Problem," *Architecture* 46, no. 5 (1922): 351–52 (figs. 9.1–9.4)

© Ella Briggs, "Planned for Present Comfort and Future Extension," *Homes and Gardens* [27, no. 11], April 1946, 36. Courtesy Future Publishing Ltd. (fig. 20.2)

© Ella Briggs, "Praktische Fragen zur Erwerbslosensiedlung," *Bauwelt* [22, no. 44], October 29, 1931, 1394. Collection Harry Ransom Center, The University of Texas at Austin (fig. 17.1)

© Ella Briggs, "Taylorisierungsbestrebungen in amerikanischen Küchen," *Arbeiter-Zeitung*, June 13, 1925, ANNO/Austrian National Library, Vienna, Austria (fig. 11.3)

© Ella Briggs, "We Plan a House for You," *Good Housekeeping* 78 (March 1924): 35 (fig. 10.9)

© Ella Briggs, "Zwei Kleinwohnungsgrundrisse," *Bauwelt* [21, no. 18], May 1, 1930, 577. Collection Harry

Ransom Center, The University of Texas at Austin (fig. 14.4)

© Ernest Greene, "The New York Press Club," *Architects' and Builders' Magazine* [10, no. 5], February 1910, 186, 188. Collection Cornell University Library (figs. 5.12, 5.14)

© Estate of W. Suschitzky, courtesy Fotohof, Vienna, Austria (fig. 19.1)

© "Handarbeiten," *Das Blatt der Frau*, October 3, 1915, 13. Picture Archives, Inv. 394.566-D, Austrian National Library, Vienna, Austria (fig. 7.8)

© Hans and Lily Hildebrandt Papers, 1899–1979, Getty Research Institute, Los Angeles, California (850676) (fig. 10.8)

© H. B., "Handwerker- und Kunstgewerbeschule zu Bielefeld," *Textile Kunst und Industrie* 5 (1914): 195. Collection MAK – Museum of Applied Arts, Vienna, Austria (fig. 7.4)

© *Homes and Gardens* 29, no. 11 (1948). Courtesy Future Publishing Ltd. (plate 19)

© "House Near Berlin: Designed by Ella Briggs," *Architects' Journal* (February 2, 1939): 211 (fig. 17.3)

© "Houses and Flats on the Stowlawn Park Estate for the Bilston Borough Council: Ella B. Briggs, L.R.I.B.A., Architect," *Builder* [177, no. 5564], October 7, 1949, 448, 450, 451. Collection British Architectural Library, Royal Institute of British Architects, London, UK (figs. 19.4, 19.5, 19.7)

© H. W. Frohne, "The German Theatre in New York," *Architectural Record* [24, no. 6], December 1908, 410 (fig. 5.3)

© Joseph Urban Collection, Rare Book and Manuscript Library, Columbia University, New York (fig. 3.2)

© Klara Ruge, "Amerikanische Kunstausstellungen der Saison 1908 bis 1909," *Kunst und Kunsthandwerk* 12 (1909): 580, 579, 581. Collection University of Chicago Library (figs. 5.8, 5.10, 5.11)

© Klara Ruge, "Amerikanische Kunstausstellungen der Saison 1909–1910," *Kunst und Kunsthandwerk* 14, no. 1 (1911): 49, 51. Collection University of Chicago Library (figs. 5.15, 5.13)

© Leonie Pilewski, Interior of the Hugo Häring House No. 1, 1932. Picture Archives, Inv. 423001-D, Austrian National Library, Vienna, Austria. Photograph by Julius Scherb (fig. 24.1)

© Mae Savell Croy, "Houses Planned by Women," *Pictorial Review* [25, no. 2], November 1923, 35 (fig. 10.2)

© Margarete Schütte-Lihotzky, Frankfurter Küche, 1927, Inv. No. 50/29/FW, Collection and Archive, University of Applied Arts Vienna, Austria; © Bildrecht, Wien 2025. Photograph by Hermann Traugott Collischonn (fig. 25.1)

© Norman B. Leventhal Map and Education Center at the Boston Public Library, MA (06_01_012247) (fig. 3.1)

© Otto and Marie Neurath Isotype Collection, University of Reading, UK. Digital image file colored by Pia Pedersen (plate 14)

© Otto Polak-Hellwig, "Wohnungstypen: In den Wohnhausbauten der Gemeinde Wien," *Die Welt der Technik, Neues Wiener Tagblatt*, May 8, 1926. Picture Archives, Inv. 394.205-D, Austrian National Library, Vienna, Austria (fig. 13.7)

© Paul Sutliff, redrawn plans after Ella Briggs from "Houses and Flats on the Stowlawn Park Estate for the Bilston Borough Council: Ella B. Briggs, L.R.I.B.A., Architect," *Builder* [177, no. 5564], October 7, 1949, 451 (fig. 19.6)

© "Refugees Committee: Report to Council," *Journal of the Royal Institute of British Architects* (June 26, 1939): 829. Collection British Architectural Library, Royal Institute of British Architects, London, UK (fig. 19.2)

© Reg. no. 251.039 Ella Briggs, BEG-Akte (German Federal Compensation Act), State Office for Civil and Administrative Affairs [LABO], Berlin, Germany (plate 8, fig. 11.2)

© Sabrina Rahman (plates 20, 21)

© "Stage Curtain at the New German Theater," *Wall-Paper News and Interior Decoration* [33, no. 1], January 1909, 38 (fig. 5.6)

© Technical University of Munich Archives, Germany (fig. 8.1)

© *Ver Sacrum*, no. 3 (1898): 6. Collection MAK – Museum of Applied Arts, Vienna, Austria (fig. 2.1)

© *Wall-Paper News and Interior Decorator* 32, no. 6 (1908): 15, 33, 39 (figs. 5.4, 5.7, 5.9)

© Walter Müller-Wulckow, *Die Deutsche Wohnung der Gegenwart* (Königstein im Taunus: Langewiesche, 1932), 17, 23 (figs. 13.8, 13.9)

© Wien Museum, Vienna, Austria, inv. no. 57962/421 (fig. 11.1)

© Wiener Stadt- und Landesarchiv, Vienna, Austria, 3.3.2 – Fotoarchiv Gerlach, 1925–1972; Philippovichgasse 2–4: FC1.1230fM, FB2.794, FC1.0795M, FC1.1846M (figs. 13.1, 13.4–13.6); Billrothstraße 9: FC1.1407M (fig. 13.10)

INDEX

Note: Page numbers in italic type indicate illustrations.

NEW OBJECTIVITY

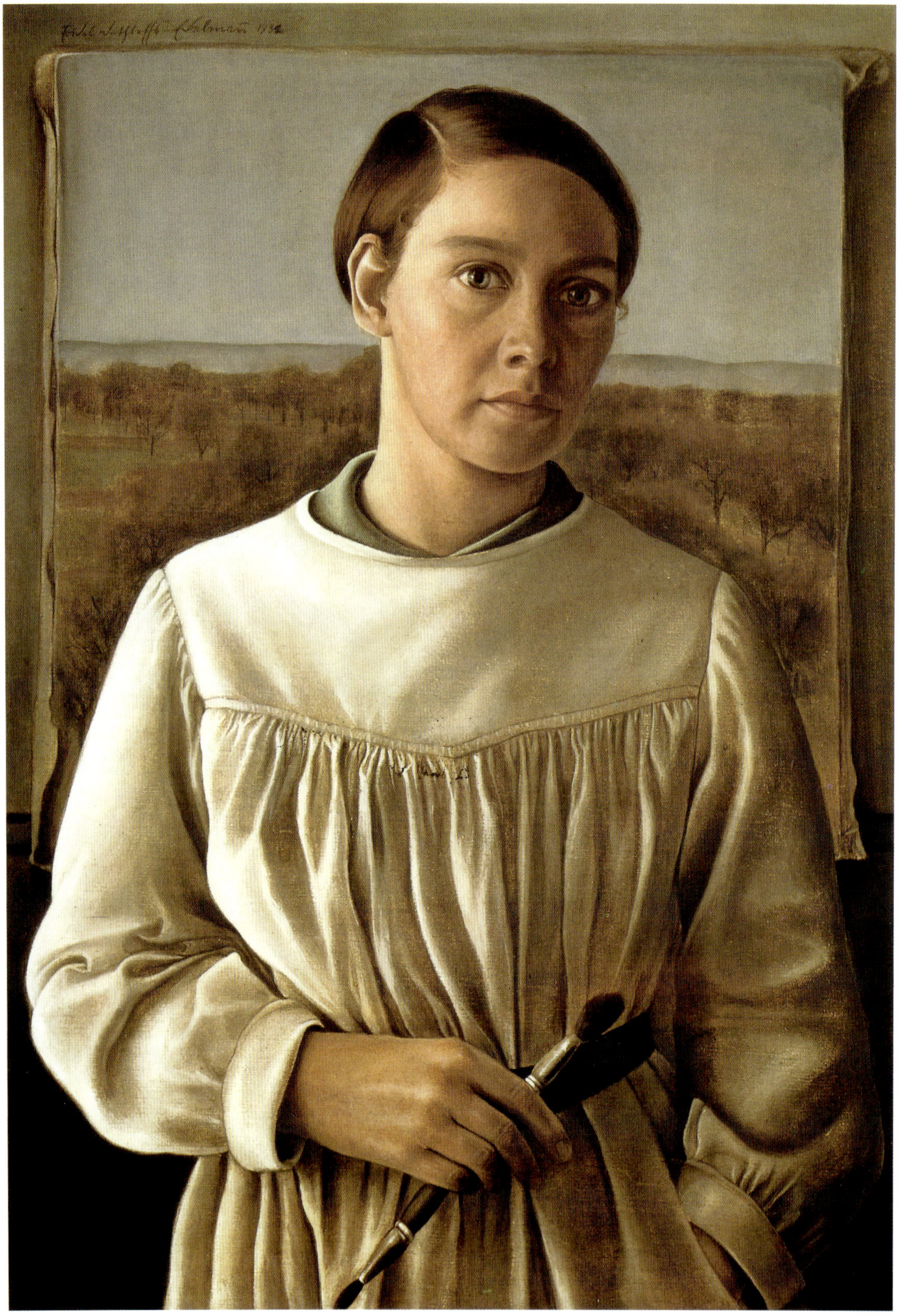

Sergiusz Michalski

NEW OBJECTIVITY

Painting, Graphic Art and Photography
in Weimar Germany 1919–1933

TASCHEN

KÖLN LONDON LOS ANGELES MADRID PARIS TOKYO

FRONT COVER:
Christian Schad
Count St. Genois d'Anneaucourt, 1927
Graf St. Genois d'Anneaucourt
Oil on wood, 86 x 63 cm
Private collection

Photo: akg-images / Erich Lessing

BACK COVER:
Carl Grossberg
Vision: Steam Boiler with Bat, 1928
Traumbild: Dampfkessel mit Fledermaus
Oil on wood, 55 x 66 cm
Bonn, on loan to the Rheinisches Landesmuseum

ILLUSTRATION PAGE 2:
Fridel Dethleffs-Edelmann
Self-Portrait Wearing an Artist's Smock, 1932
Selbstbildnis in der Malkutte
Oil on canvas, 74 x 55 cm
Augsburg, Bayerische Staatsgemäldesammlungen, Kunsthalle Augsburg

Hohenzollernring 53, D–50672 Köln
www.taschen.com

Edited by Rolf Taschen, Cologne
English translation by Michael Claridge, Bamberg
Cover design: Angelika Taschen, Claudia Frey, Cologne

Printed in Italy
ISBN 3–8228–2372–4

Contents

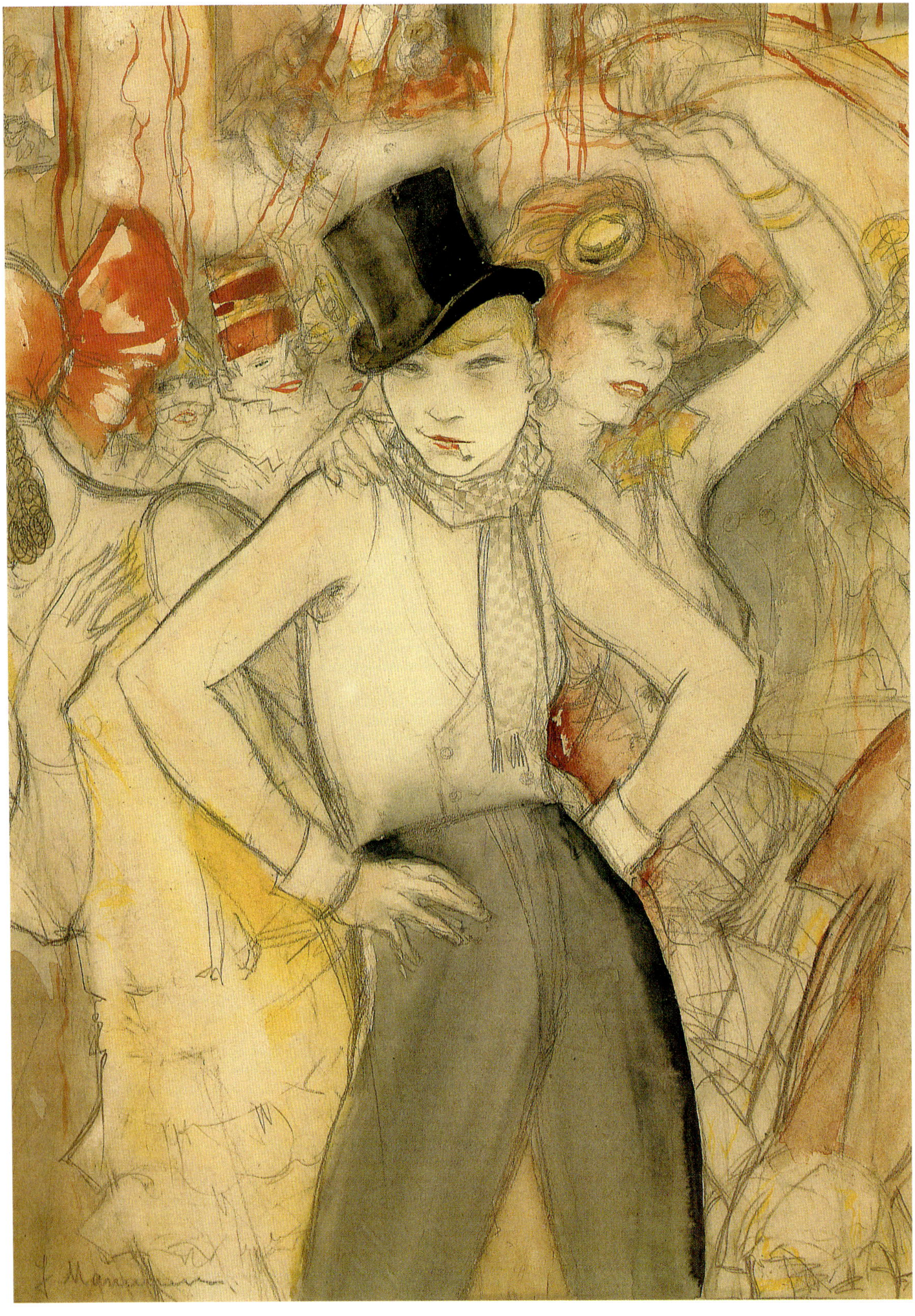

Weimar Contrasts

Culture and Politics 1919–1933

Looking back at the Weimar Republic, one is struck even today, sixty years on, by the stark contrasts that it presented: a democratic state, constituting the prelude to the most violent dictatorship in German history, yet at the same time a period of extraordinary cultural creativity, one that would end in such works as the nude paintings of Adolf Ziegler and the Thing Festivals. The heights and depths of the human soul could be found – side by side. In venerable Weimar, where the Republic had been born and which symbolized the German cultural tradition, a National Socialist minister of culture was already in office by 1930. In Munich, the same artists' cafés that were frequented by Thomas Mann and Erich Mühsam also numbered Hitler among their regular clients. In monarchist, right-wing, conservative Potsdam, where even Art Nouveau was still frowned upon, the Expressionist solitaire of Erich Mendelsohn's Einstein Tower had stood since 1921. Weimar culture boasted left-wing intellectuals of European status – Ernst Bloch, Walter Benjamin, Max Horkheimer and many others – yet it was simultaneously moulding such figures as Alfred Kurella and Johannes R. Becher, the dogmatic advocates of Stalinist cultural policy who were subsequently instrumental in delaying the acceptance of Weimar culture by the German Democratic Republic.

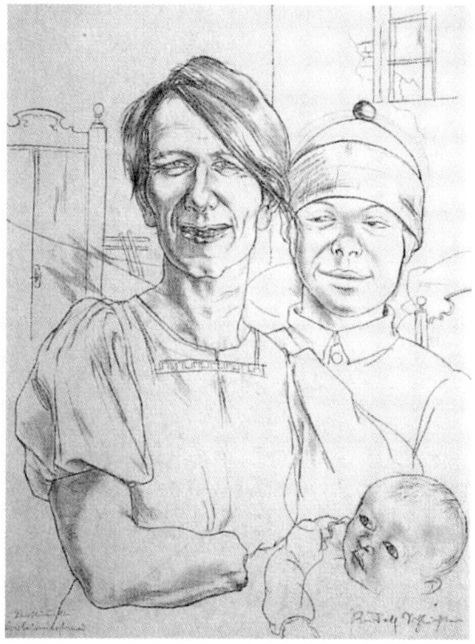

Rudolf Schlichter
Maimed Proletarian Women, c. 1924
Verstümmelte Proletarierfrauen
Pencil drawing, 63 x 48 cm
Berlin, Berlinische Galerie

The fifteen-year history of the Weimar Republic can be divided into three sections of roughly equal length. In the first, turbulent phase from 1918 to 1923, it was only with the greatest of effort that the young state was able to assert itself. With Germany's defeat and the corresponding burdens and restrictions imposed upon the country by the Treaty of Versailles casting a gloomy shadow over its birth, the Republic was actively supported by only a minority among the German people. However, the tactical alliance formed in November 1918 between the SPD (German Social Democratic Party) and parts of the Reichswehr (German army) and the old bureaucratic structures of power created a foundation which, even in times when the SPD was not directly in power, enabled the Republic to survive attacks from the left (Spartacus revolt, 1919; Central German rebellion, 1921) and the more dangerous putsches from the right (Kapp-Lüttwitz, 1920; Hitler putsch, 1923). 1923, a year that saw the occupation of the Ruhr by the French, spiralling inflation, separatist activities, and a number of workers' uprisings (Hamburg), brought things once again to a dramatic head.

Late in the autumn of 1923, a coalition of the centre under Gustav Stresemann succeeded not only in halting inflation but even – following the introduction of the rentenmark – in overcoming it. The heavy burden

Jeanne Mammen
She represents, c. 1927
Sie repräsentiert
Watercolour and pencil, 40 x 30 cm
Private collection

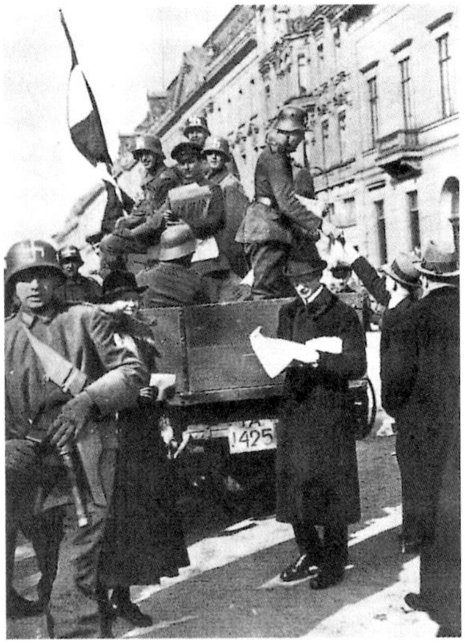

Soldiers of the putsch troops with swastikas, Potsdamer Platz, 1920

of reparations was partly relieved by the Dawes Plan, announced in 1924; the French began their withdrawal from the Ruhr, with further departures scheduled from the occupied territories in the west. This second phase of the Weimar Republic was one of relative stabilization, lasting until the end of the 1920s. These six years (1924–1929) are often summed up by the popular tag "the Golden Twenties" – a description, however, which reflects more a horror of what had gone before and was later to follow than the reality of life at the time for large sections of the population. In the field of foreign affairs, Stresemann's diplomacy in this period brought a limited arrangement with the western powers. The sphere of internal politics saw a return to a more peaceful state of affairs, with passions cooling: "Sachlichkeit" (objectivity or functionality) became the watchword. Similarly, people spoke of a "Neue Sachlichkeit" (New Objectivity, New Functionality) in politics and art, using this as a means of distancing themselves from the excesses of Expressionism and the years of inflation.

Germany was governed during these years by alternating centre-right coalitions with colourless chancellors (with the SPD also involved again from 1928 onwards). However, these coalitions were unable to fundamentally overcome the structural divides within the Republic. The state of political polarization continued, with the extremists from right and left alike waiting for their moment to come. Only a few people were willing to identify themselves clearly and unreservedly with the Republic; nor was the number of what might be called "Republicans of convenience" particularly high. The 1925 elections for the state presidency brought the Republic what was effectively a substitute monarch, in the person of Paul von Hindenburg. The considerable authority placed in the hands of the president would prove fateful in the second crisis of the Weimar Republic, after 1930.

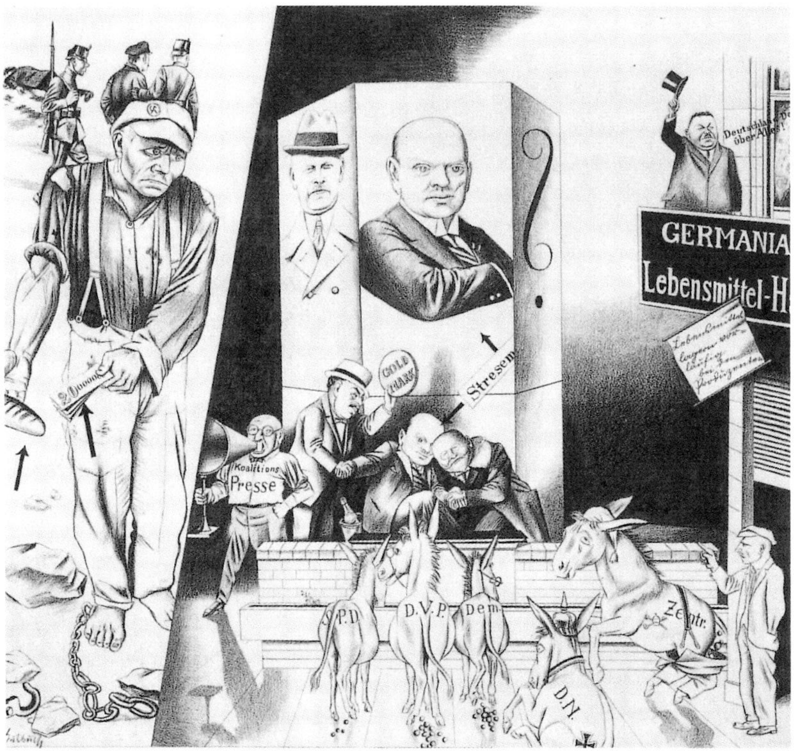

Karl Hubbuch
Herr Stresemann and a Piece of Black Bread, c. 1923
Herr Stresemann und ein Stück Schwarzbrot
Chalk, 37.8 x 41.4 cm
Munich, Staatliche Graphische Sammlung

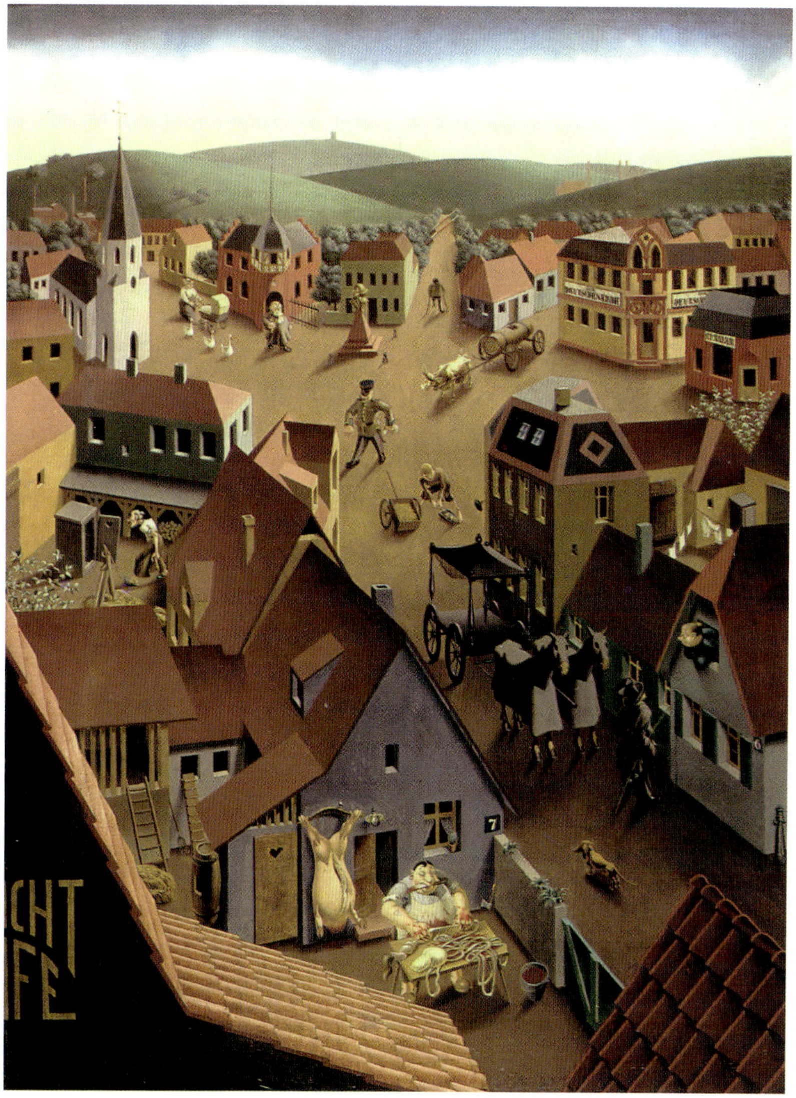

Georg Scholz
Small Town by Day: The Butcher, 1922/23
Kleinstadt bei Tag: Der Metzger
Watercolour and pencil on paper, 31 x 24 cm
Private collection

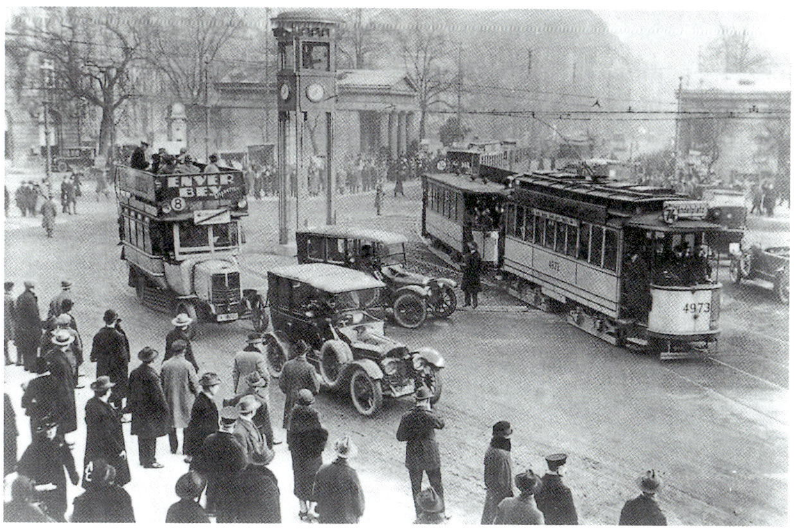

City traffic on Potsdamer Platz looking towards Leipziger Platz, c. 1925

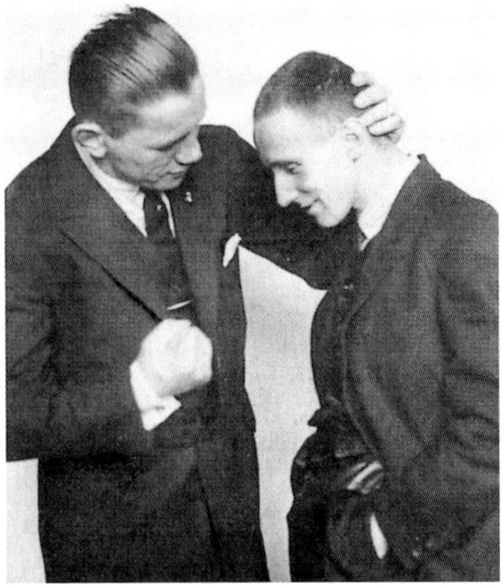

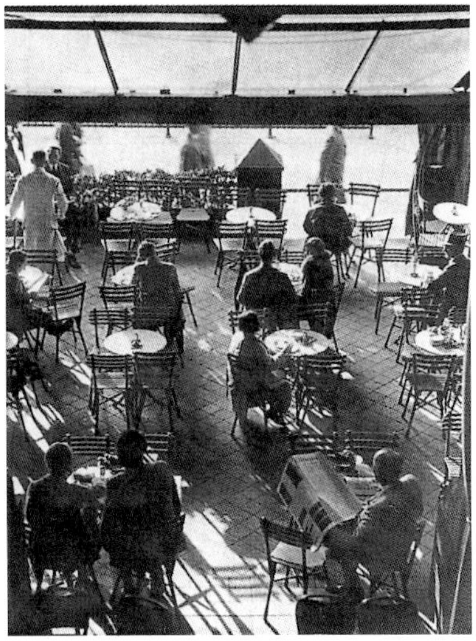

Within the economy, numerous American loans fostered a relative industrial boom; indeed, in the context of the rapidly developing enthusiasm for technology after 1924, seemed to be radical change in the air promising a better life for millions of people. Yet this limited upturn had already passed its peak by the winter of 1928/29, scarcely a year before the crisis in the world economy.

The autumn of 1929 saw the death of Gustav Stresemann, the guarantor of a reliable foreign policy. Shortly afterwards came the beginning of the acute phase of the world economic crisis. The American loans were called in, countless companies went out of business, and the number of those unemployed began to rise dramatically, fuelling radical sentiment amongst the masses. The Republic found itself in difficulties both at home and abroad, the latter visible in conflicts with Poland and France. In 1930, the last Weimar coalition, under SPD Chancellor Hermann Müller, collapsed. The resulting parliamentary elections brought great gains for the extremist parties, the National Socialists becoming the second most powerful party in the Reichstag. At this point, alternative courses of action were still open; all the options for the beset Republic had not been tried out. A two-year presidential cabinet, headed by centrist Heinrich Brüning and governing on the basis of emergency decrees issued by the president, attempted to stabilize the economy by means of deflationary measures. However, such measures were insufficient to deal with the crisis. Violence on the streets increased, and the clashes between the party militias – usually provoked by the Nazis – plunged the country into a state similar to that of civil war.

By 1932, the Republic was in a cul de sac. The numerous elections held in this year signalled a steady growth in political extremism; following Brüning's dismissal, two short-lived right-wing governments (led by von Papen and von Schleicher respectively) destabilized the remaining institutions of the Republic. Sectors of the economy were now turning to support the Nazis, regarding them as the lesser evil. On 30th January 1933, Hindenburg appointed Adolf Hitler as Chancellor. The demagogue had achieved his ambition; the Weimar Republic was at an end. The state – upholder of the law – was on the way to becoming a systematic law-breaker.

TOP:
Bertolt Brecht and the boxer Samson-Körner (left), 1928

BOTTOM:
Romanisches Café, interior view

RIGHT:
Romanisches Café from the outside, before 1939

Berlin's artists and literati met in the Romanisches Café, where they would read newspapers, play chess, critically discuss the theatre, argue and debate endlessly.

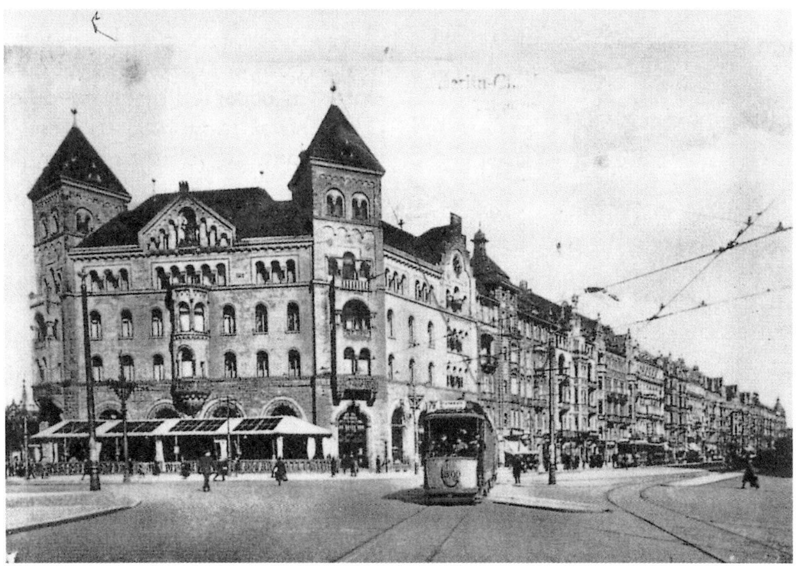

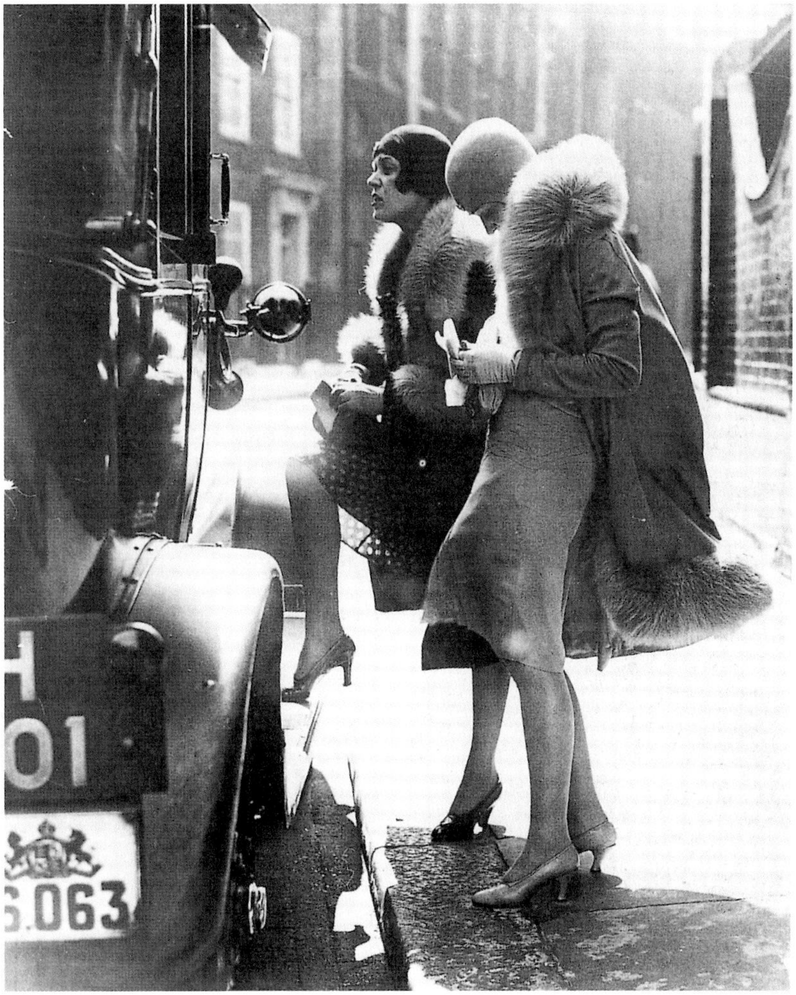

Sex for sale
Berlin streetscene, 1929

Despite the fact that many cultural phenomena came about through the political situation, politics and the arts remained as it were on separate levels under the Weimar Republic. For eight years, the position of head of state was occupied by an aged field-marshal who – as he himself stated – had never read a book, other than the Bible and the military service regulations. And other prominent politicians – Walther Rathenau excepted – also had no contact with the cultural scene. The promotion of culture remained the domain of enlightened communal politicians.

The typical representatives of Weimar culture are such personalities as Marlene Dietrich, Fritz Lang, Erwin Piscator, George Grosz and Walter Gropius. Film, theatre, architecture and design – and not least caricature – succinctly represent the process by which culture was opening itself up to the masses, a phenomenon characteristic of the Weimar period. In this manner, a process of cultural democratization was begun only a decade after the late-Wilhelminian class culture. What was theatrical and visually striking, the dominant element in the public awareness of culture, pushed pure literature and pure painting into the background. Bertolt Brecht himself enjoyed experimenting with multimedia forms in the 1920s, such as radio concerts in the form of a theatre performance, before concentrating on

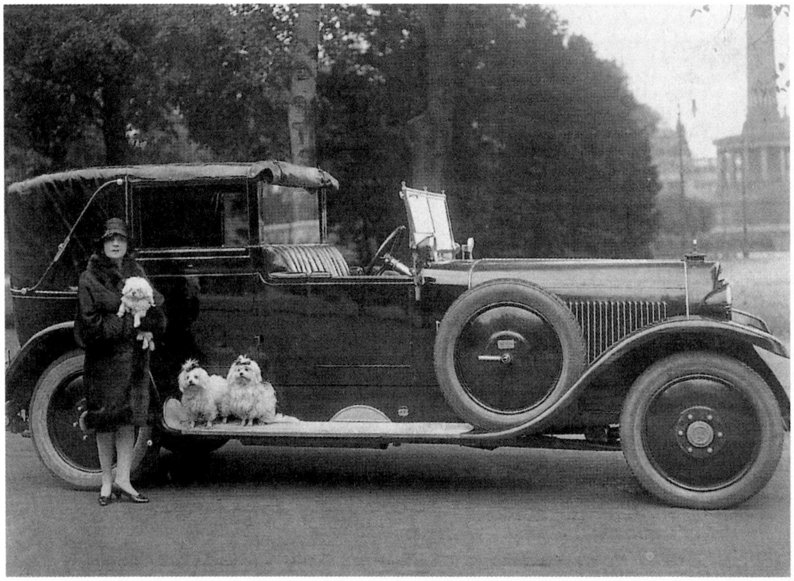

Fritzi Massary, the operetta star, with her convertible and Maltese dogs, 1926

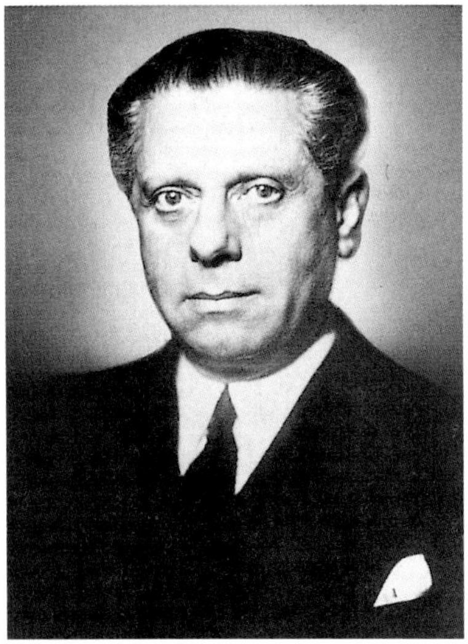

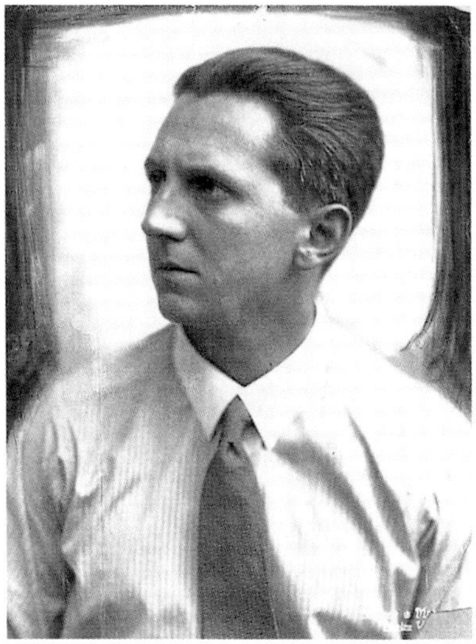

LEFT:
Max Reinhardt, director and actor

RIGHT:
Erwin Piscator, stage and theatre director, c. 1927

Reinhardt and Piscator represented the two directions in the German theatre of the 1920s, one of them bourgeois, liberal and aesthetic, the other antibourgeois and revolutionary.

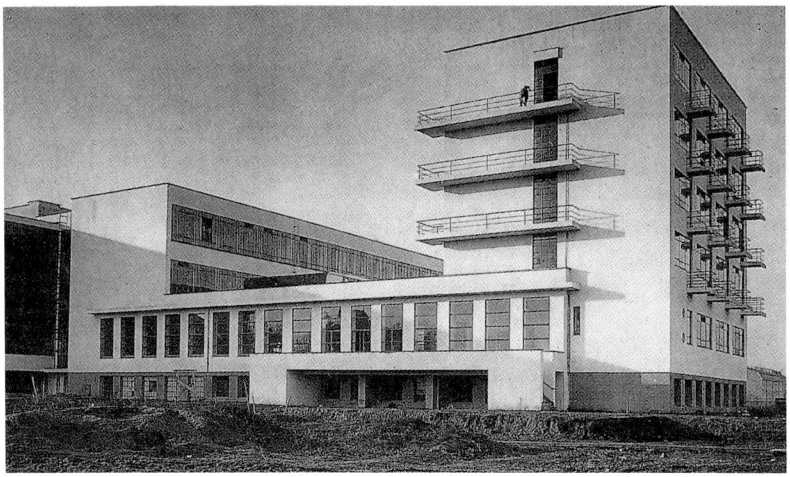

The Bauhaus building in Dessau by Walter Gropius, 1925/26, view from the southeast

Rudolf Arnheim wrote in 1927 concerning the Bauhaus: "The desire for cleanliness, clarity and spaciousness has won a victory here."

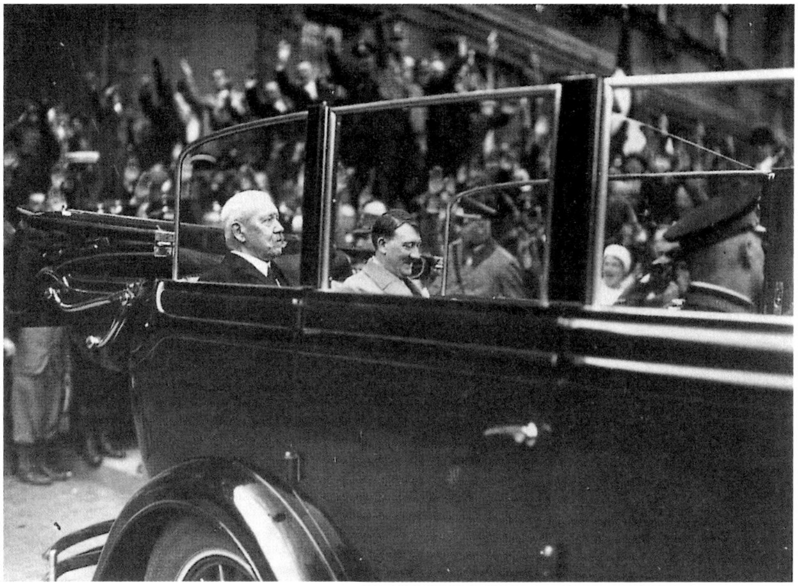

RIGHT:
President von Hindenburg and Chancellor Hitler, 1933

BOTTOM:
Torchlight procession to the Chancellery by Nazi storm troopers and Stahlhelm detachments, 1933

Joseph Goebbels speaking to German National Socialist Party (NSDAP) propagandists, Kroll Opera, Berlin, 1938

Storm trooper guarding prisoners, 1933

work for the stage in its conventional form. The Bauhaus, with its functional architecture and purpose-orientated design, is a particularly good representative of the attempt to overcome the specialist element within the individual arts.

Although the cultural achievements of the Weimar Republic may since have received international recognition, at the time they made little impact on large sections of the population. The objectivity and the claim to realism of the artistic avantgarde in the Weimar period hardly corresponded to the need still felt by many Germans – and by no means only those of a Nazi frame of mind – for generally binding aesthetic norms and the mystical transformation of reality. "This diagnosis can be more broadly applied to the structure of life, changing awareness and changing lifestyle of wide sectors of the population. What signified progress and the expansion of the individual's possibilities to one person, an escape from outdated commitments and a liberation from tiresome chains, represented the decay of culture and excessive libertinism to the other, who blamed the political system of the Weimar democracy for making it possible. In this way, attitudes of cultural pessimism received considerable impetus, amplifying the hostility towards the state of Weimar which was already deep-rooted in the conservative nationalist camp."[1]

Despite its great achievements, therefore, Weimar culture was in no position to exert a stabilizing effect upon the system. Following the Allies' victory in the First World War, cultural developments in France and Britain were dominated for a decade by the deceptive feeling that the world was still – or once again – in order. Germany, in contrast, was still suffering from its defeat and from political unrest. Weimar culture bore greater similarities in this respect to the revolutionary culture of Soviet Russia in the first years after 1917, albeit without the latter's utopian dimensions. Ultimately, it was a reflection of German society at that time, torn between a desire for and simultaneous fear of unconditional modernity, between sober, objective rationality and residues of Expressionist and rationalist irrationalities.

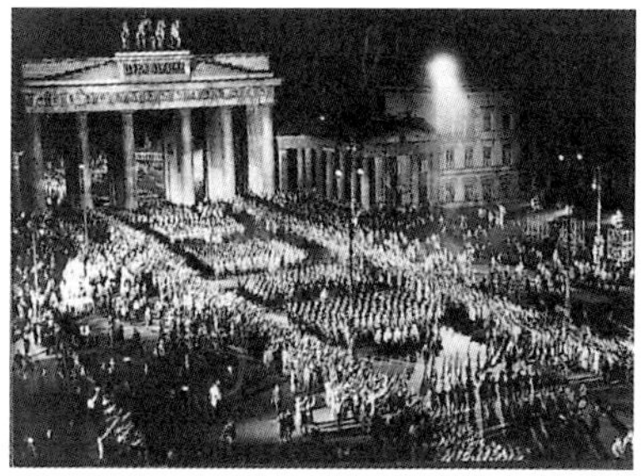

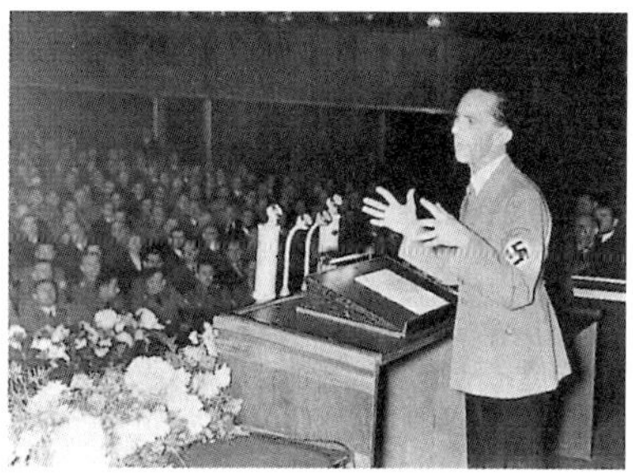

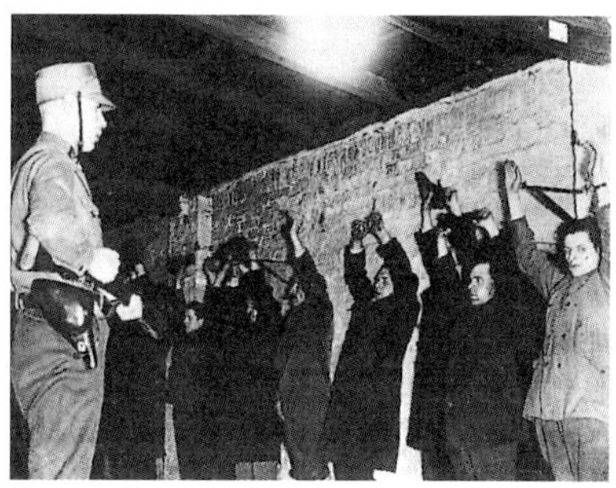

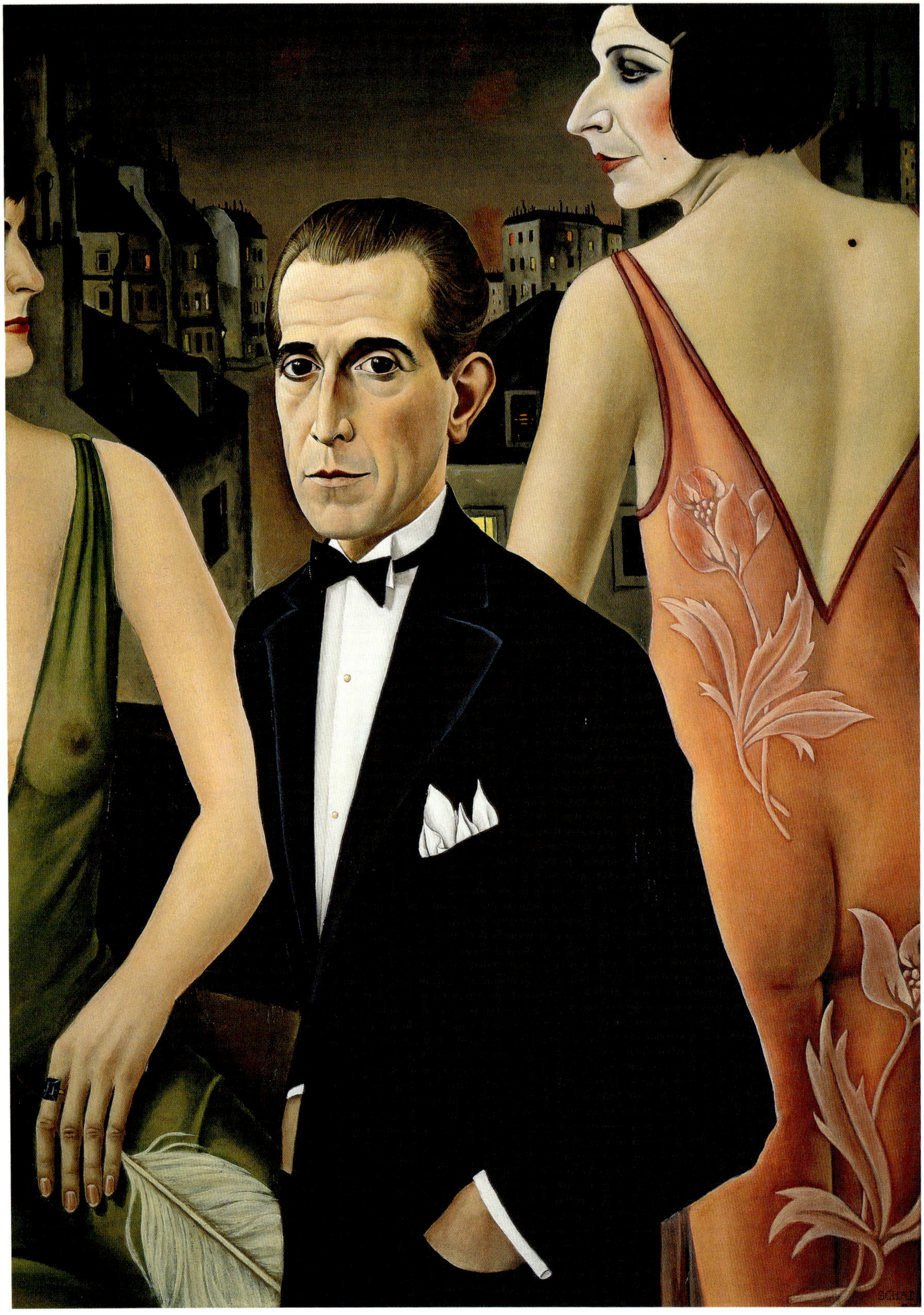
SCHAD

Neue Sachlichkeit
A Style and Its Name

By the early 1920s, Expressionism had exhausted itself. The decline and fall of a style which had been so dominant only a short time before was ascertained not only by the art critics – among them such famous names as Wilhelm Hausenstein and Wilhelm Worringer – but also by the art-loving public, pleased by the fact that the period of an art of neo-emotional expression was over. The November Revolution of 1918 had given Expressionism renewed impetus, with it spreading to cinematic art, while even provincial bars and dance cafés were decorated around 1920 in Expressionist style with indentations and facets. Yet this very widening of its impact led to its being downgraded to the level of mere stylization, causing it to lose its importance as a characteristic stylistic direction within painting.

In 1919, the Expressionist Ludwig Meidner had indicated a new direction in his "Septemberschrei" manifesto: "What will matter tomorrow, what I and all the others need, is a fanatical, fervent naturalism."[2] Thus was the decisive keyword uttered that would determine the course of the debate concerning art theory for the following three years, even if the term itself did not become the label for the new style that was to succeed Expressionism. Indications of the portrayal of the representational world had already been increasing in number within European painting during the final years of the First World War. In France around 1920, Picasso was following the "rappel à l'ordre" (call to order). French painting was being increasingly characterized by a new representationalism and figurative classicism, a development to which artists of different schools contributed, among them former Cubists such as Jean Metzinger and Fauvists such as André Derain.

In Italy, the path to representationalism had been taken since 1917 by the Pittura metafisica painters – Giorgio de Chirico, Carlo Carrà and their fellows – in a manner that was first of all surrealistically excessive, then adopted the tectonic plastic realism of such artists as Masaccio or Ucello in a reversion to the Early Renaissance. An example was set for German artists in the 1920s not only by de Chirico and Carrà, their output publicized through the magazine "Valori Plastici", but also by the painters of the Novecento group (Achille Funi, Mario Sironi, Ubaldo Oppi and Felice Casorati), founded in Milan in 1922. Their synthesis of realism and traditional classicism was admired, and certain elements were borrowed from their works.

In Germany, the indications were increasing around 1920 of a return on the part of the younger artistic generation, born in the 1890s, to a distanced manner of observing and painting things, one based upon representation-

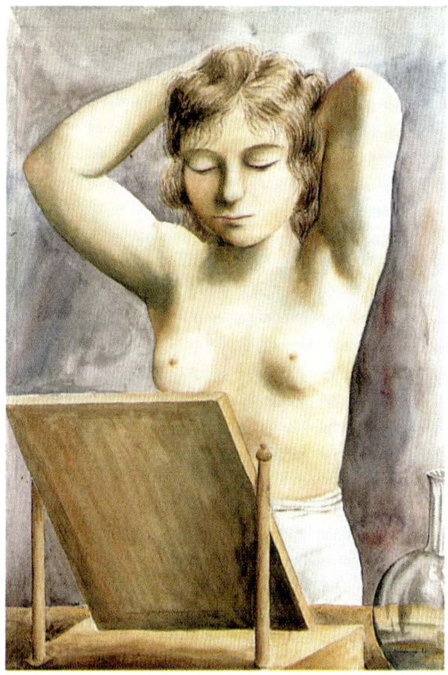

Georg Schrimpf
Girl in front of a Mirror, 1926
Mädchen vor dem Spiegel
Watercolour over pencil, 45 x 32.3 cm
Cologne, Museum Ludwig

Christian Schad
Count St.Genois d'Anneaucourt, 1927
Graf St.Genois d'Anneaucourt
Oil on wood, 86 x 63 cm
Private collection

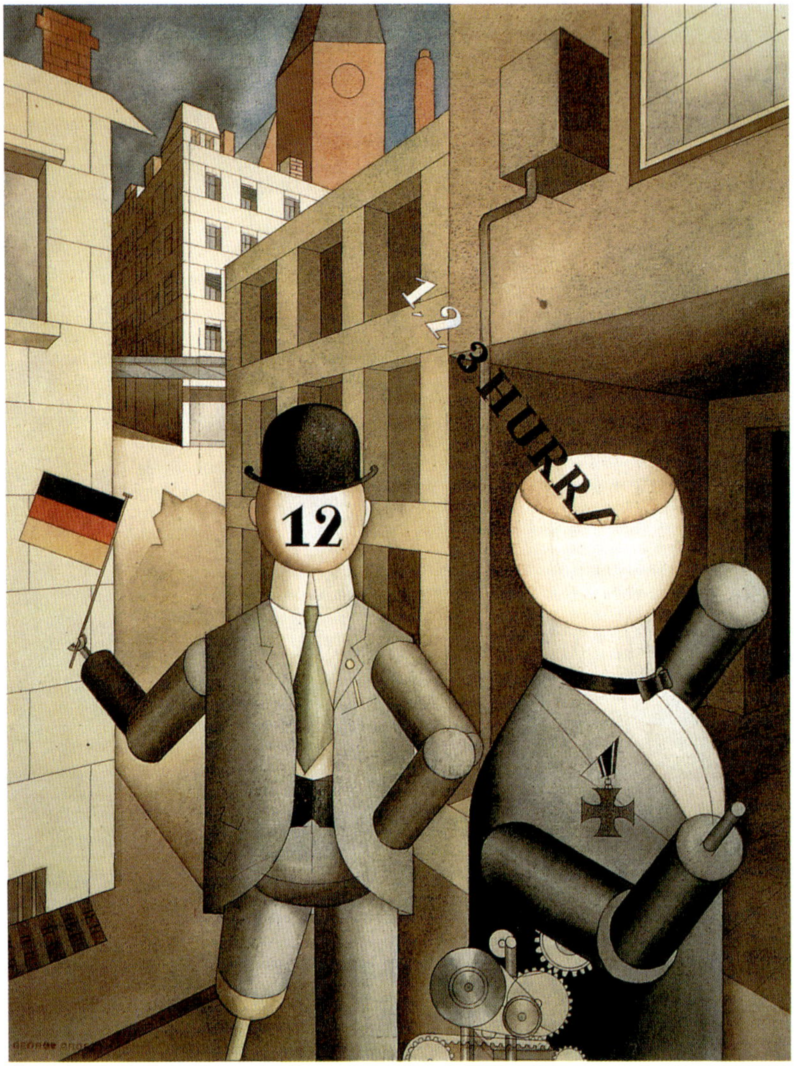

George Grosz
Republican Automatons, 1920
Republikanische Automaten
Watercolour, pen and Indian ink on card, 60 x 47.3 cm
New York, Collection, The Museum of Modern Art, Advisory Committee Fund

Giorgio de Chirico
The Prodigal Son, 1922
Il figlio prodigo
Oil on canvas, 87 x 59 cm
Milan, Civica Galleria d'Arte Moderna

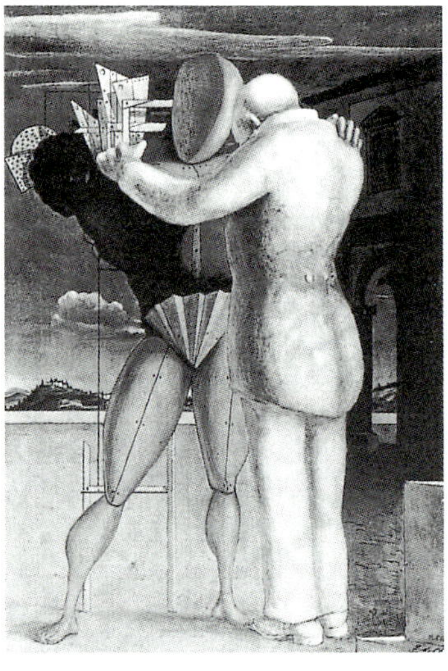

alism. This process was almost continuous, with an absence of great leaps or manifest events, and was fed by many sources. The tendency towards representationalism could be observed not only in Berlin but also in the provinces, developing between 1922 and 1924 into a new style, one already recognized as such by contemporaries and broadly understood as a reaction to Expressionism, a form of post- or even anti-Expressionism.

This stance had its roots in the new awareness of life found in the early 1920s. The fantastic dreams and the pathos of Expressionism were giving way to a new rationality of vision, a feeling for what was down-to-earth, feasible, real. Against Expressionism's promises of the future were set the banal, small-scale happiness of an unassuming life, against cosmic ecstasy the insight into earthly and social restraints. The surrounding world appeared in a new light: "The important thing was to focus one's gaze upon the here-and-now, upon the view out of the window, upon everyday life taking place in front of one's house, upon the alleyways and gutters, upon the factory floor and the shipyard, upon the scene in the operating theatre and the brothel – even if it should sometimes fall merely upon someone's

Rudolf Schlichter
Dada Roof Studio, c. 1920
Dada-Dachatelier
Watercolour and pen drawing,
45.8 x 63.8 cm
Berlin, Galerie Nierendorf

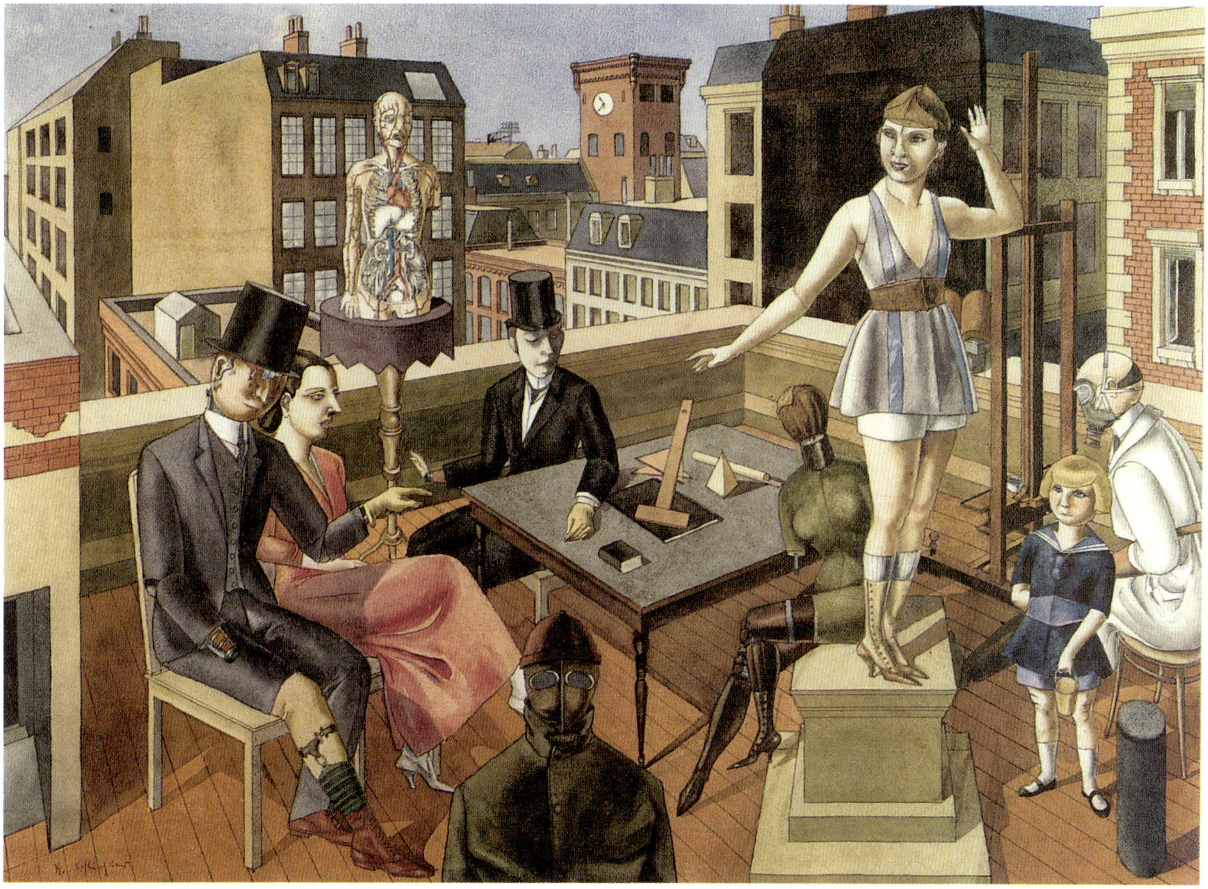

allotment, or on a level-crossing keeper's hut, or on happiness in the corner, or be caught by the washing-line perspective of the backyard milieu."[3]

This comparison with Expressionism enabled the new elements contained in the style of new objectivity to take on form. In 1925 Franz Roh, the art critic, brought together an entire list of such contrasting characteristics in his book "Nachexpressionismus. Magischer Realismus" (Post-Expressionism. Magic Realism) in a summary in tabular form. Instead of using the term "Neue Sachlichkeit" (New Objectivity), he spoke of "Nachexpressionismus" (Post-Expressionism), something characterized by "down-to-earth objects", something "miniature-like, cool to cold", characterized in terms of painting technique by "a thin layer of paint, smooth, even, like brightly polished metal", the manner of composition "of a more right-angled nature, more parallel to the frame"[4] – to mention here but a few of the characteristics observed by Roh.

Three years previously – in 1922 – a survey bearing the title "Ein neuer Naturalismus?" (A new Naturalism?) had been carried out by the Berlin art magazine "Das Kunstblatt" (1917–1932), inviting leading personalities

The works of the Pittura metafisica – of Carlo Carrà and Giorgio de Chirico – impressed many German artists around 1920. The typical mechanical jointed dolls occur in numerous pictures, often in connection with humans wearing artificial limbs, together with an architecture that is eerie in its uninhabited quality.

to give their thoughts on emerging stylistic trends. Among the 45 replies, the analysis submitted by Gustav Friedrich Hartlaub, art historian and director of the Kunsthalle in Mannheim, is particularly significant. Hartlaub adopted a bipolar schema, applying the political concepts of "right-wing" and "left-wing" to the artists' relationship to reality and then utilizing the result to classify and categorize them: "I see a right and a left wing. The first, so conservative as to be equal to Classicism, rooted in that which is timeless, is seeking once again to sanctify that which is healthy, corporeal, sculptural, through pure drawing from nature, possibly even exaggerating the earthly, well-rounded element, after so much fantasy and chaos. It regards Michelangelo, Ingres, Genelli, and even the Nazarenes as its main authority. The other wing, incandescently contemporary in its lack of belief in art, born rather from a denial of art, is attempting to expose chaos, the true feeling of our days, by means of a primitive obsession with assessment, a nervous obsession with the exposure of the self."[5] We are concerned here with a text that provides the key to the contemporary reception accorded the new style. Hartlaub's bipolar schema – one not without justification in the early 1920s, to be sure – has had a considerable influence upon the manner in which art history tends to look back on Neue Sachlichkeit. The present book will once again undertake the attempt to free itself from the confines of oversimplifying "political" polarity.

Hartlaub's activities as a museum director also played a part in determining the fate of the new artistic movement. In May 1923, he sent a circular bearing the title "Neue Sachlichkeit" to artists, art dealers and museums, informing them of his plans to organize an exhibition of new contemporary painting in Mannheim in the autumn of that year: "It is my concern to bring together representative works by those artists who in the last few years have been neither exhaustedly Impressionist nor abstractly Expressionist, neither purely concerned with the senses externally nor purely constructive internally. I would like to exhibit those artists who have remained true – or have reaffirmed their loyalty – to the positive, concrete reality and who display an element of conviction in what they do... Both wings will be taken into consideration, that of the 'right' (neo-Classicists etc.) as well as that of the left, the 'Verist' wing, which may be seen as including such artists as Beckmann, Grosz, Dix, Drexel, Scholz etc."[6]

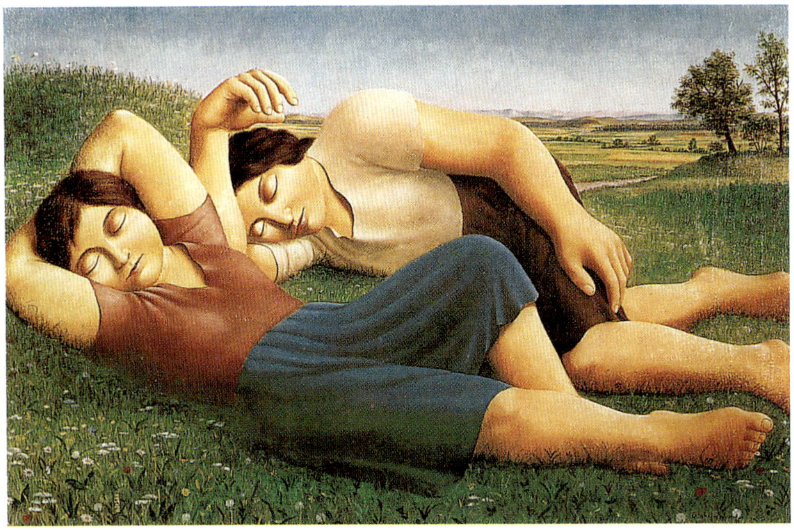

Georg Schrimpf
Sleeping Girls, 1926
Schlafende Mädchen
Oil on canvas, 55 x 85.5 cm
Private collection

Georg Schrimpf and Alexander Kanoldt, on the one hand, and Otto Dix and George Grosz, on the other, were considered the prominent representatives of 1920s right-wing – neo-Classicist – and left-wing – Verist – Realist painting. Despite their ideological and stylistic differences, their works were subsumed in the important Mannheim exhibition of 1925 under the title of "Neue Sachlichkeit".

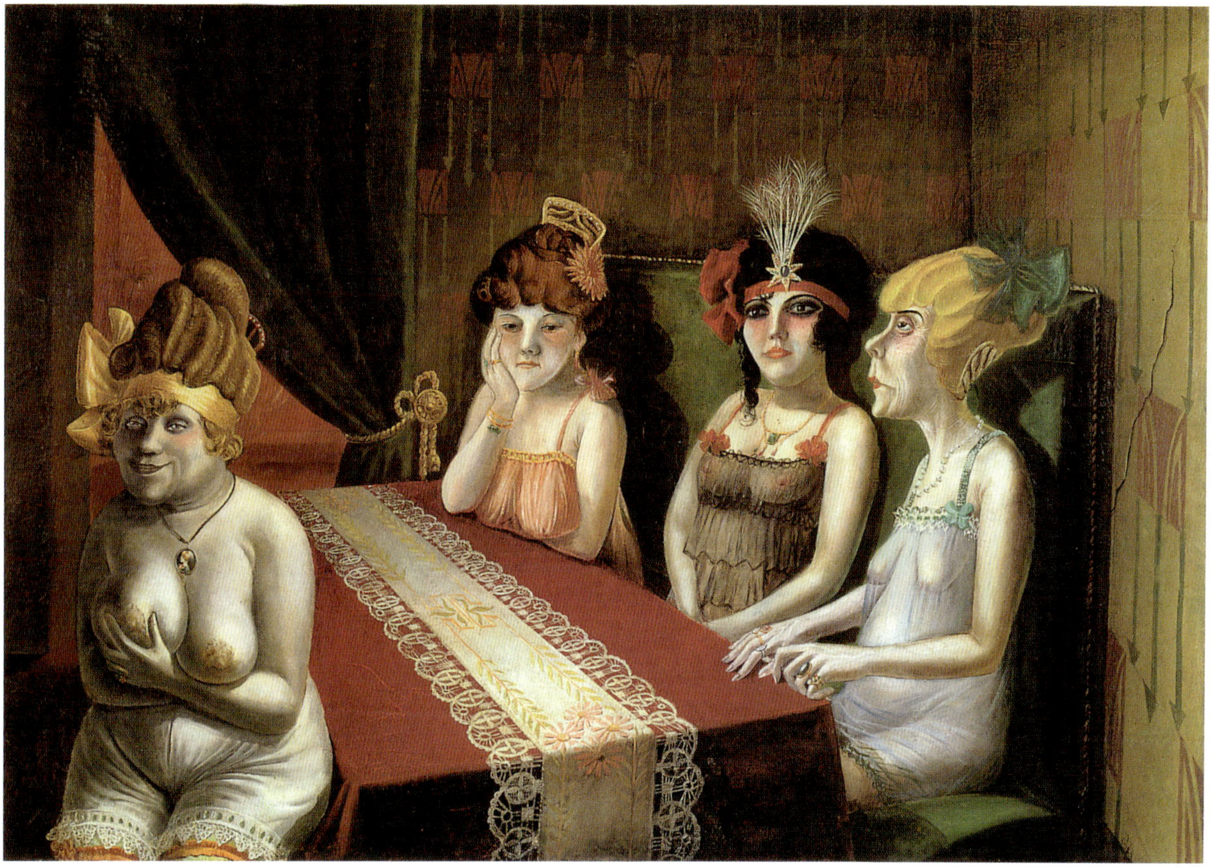

Otto Dix
The Salon I, 1921
Der Salon I
Oil on canvas, 86 x 120.5 cm
Stuttgart, Galerie der Stadt Stuttgart

The term "Neue Sachlichkeit" is used here by Hartlaub as a generic stylistic term to cover the entire range stretching from the neo-Classical wing on the right to the Verist wing on the left. At the same time, however, "Neue Sachlichkeit" is also frequently used as a Synonym for the neo-classical tendency. The decisive problem underlying Hartlaub's analytical and terminological construction thus lies in the ambivalence between the use of Neue Sachlichkeit as a generic term and its simultaneous function as the description of the right wing subsumed under it.

It proved impossible to stage the intended exhibition in the autumn of 1923. Mannheim lay in the occupied zone and there were fears of transportation difficulties; furthermore, the general political and economic situation was anything but encouraging. The exhibition was postponed, not opening until June 1925 under the title "Neue Sachlichkeit. Deutsche Malerei seit dem Expressionismus" (The New Objectivity. German painting since Expressionism). Hartlaub showed 124 works by representational artists, predominantly those of the "right wing". The spectrum of the exhibition was nevertheless very broad, with Hartlaub including works by Max Beckmann and two painters who are less well known today, Niklaus Stöcklin and Kay H. Nebel. The exhibition was a great success with both the public and the art critics, and later transferred to several cities in Saxony and Thuringia, helping to spread the new style's popularity.

So it was that the term "Neue Sachlichkeit" became established – if not unchallenged. This "new objectivity" thereby described not only the ob-

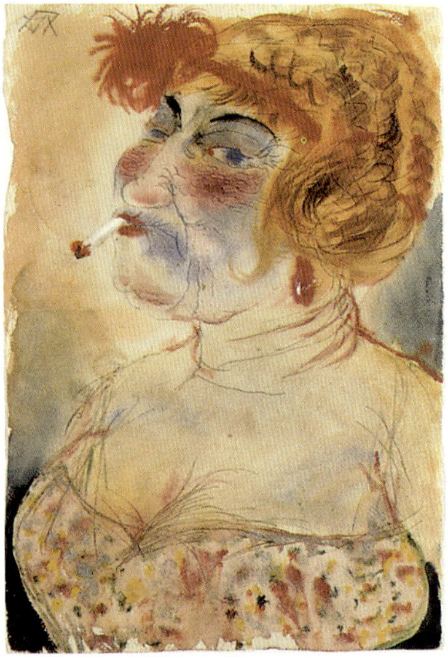

Otto Dix
Brothel Mama, c. 1923
Puffmutter
Watercolour, 50 x 35 cm
Vaduz, Otto Dix Foundation

Bar girls and prostitutes, often worn-out women marked by their way of life, were among the preferred subjects for pictures by the Verist painters, who concerned themselves particularly intensively with the repressed, ugly side of reality. Such portrayals generally caricature the male customer more strongly than the female personnel of the amusement business.

jective element within the artist's attitude to reality but also "object-ivity" representationalism – as a general term for the content of art. There was no lack of alternative suggestions for naming the new style, among them some intended ironically. People spoke of neo-Realism, new painting from nature, the neo-Nazarenes, German neo-Romanticism, Naturalism – but only two terms could be regarded as serious contenders, namely those of Magic Realism and Verism. The first of these, suggested by Roh, was unable to achieve universal acceptance, despite its literary quality. Unlike the semantically more diffuse Neue Sachlichkeit, it cannot be applied to the works of the socially critical left wing; it was also eclipsed in terms of what it was seeking to convey by the emerging concept of Surrealism. With regard to the latter objection, one could argue that the precision of Roh's term is to be preferred, since in Magic Realism, unlike Surrealism, "the secret is not a part of the depicted world but rather remains in the background of this world"[7]. However, the fact remains that many Neue Sachlichkeit pictures have nothing of a "background" or "secret" nature about them.

The exponents of Verism (the name is derived from Latin "verus", meaning true, or Italian "verismo", a Naturalist trend within Italian opera) mostly came to Neue Sachlichkeit via Expressionism and Dada, attempting to transfer the ideological impetus of these two movements to the new representationalism. However, Verism is but a limited variant of Neue Sachlichkeit, rather than forming any stylistic alternative. With regard to the extreme stance expressed in its works, it represents inconsistency within a style rather than the formation of a new style. The involvement of the artists in social criticism, and the resulting intensification of representational form, reveal a tendency towards caricature; this in turn imposes a clear limitation upon the possible subject-matter for portrayal in Verist works. Not one of the Neue Sachlichkeit artists has left a purely Verist œuvre; for many, Verism was but a stopover on the way to Neue Sachlichkeit pictures. Georg Scholz' work may be seen as a good example of this, his output undergoing the development in the space of a few years from bitter sarcasm to a placid Baden idyll.

Neue Sachlichkeit was a style with no particular artistic programmes or manifestos. In this respect, too, a reaction may be seen to the exuberant announcements of Expressionism. It lacked the central formative influence of an outstanding artistic figure, a position filled in other artistic movements by a Picasso, a Kirchner, a Kandinsky. The Neue Sachlichkeit artists were spread over various centres within the Weimar Republic. For this reason, the present book, diverging from the conventional division into stylistic variants and ideological groupings – Neue Sachlichkeit, Verism, political Constructivists, proletarian-revolutionary art etc. – the heuristic value of which appears to be more than limited, proposes to orient itself around these geographical centres. It is not our intention to overrate the role of a supposed *genius loci*; nevertheless, such an approach will permit a precise definition of the respective formal and iconographic elements for each place. In contrast to the case with other artistic movements, groups of artists played no particular role in Neue Sachlichkeit, and here its art cannot be approached from this angle. Attention will be directed here primarily to a presentation of the entire style, of its great variety, together with the provincial variants. It has proved necessary within this context to limit somewhat the portrayal of the leading artistic personalities, such as George Grosz or Otto Dix, when compared with their importance. It is the author's hope that this will result in the presentation of a more balanced picture within this volume.

Elfriede Lohse-Wächtler
Lissy, 1931
Watercolour on paper, 68 x 49 cm
Milwaukee, Marvin and Janet Fishman Collection

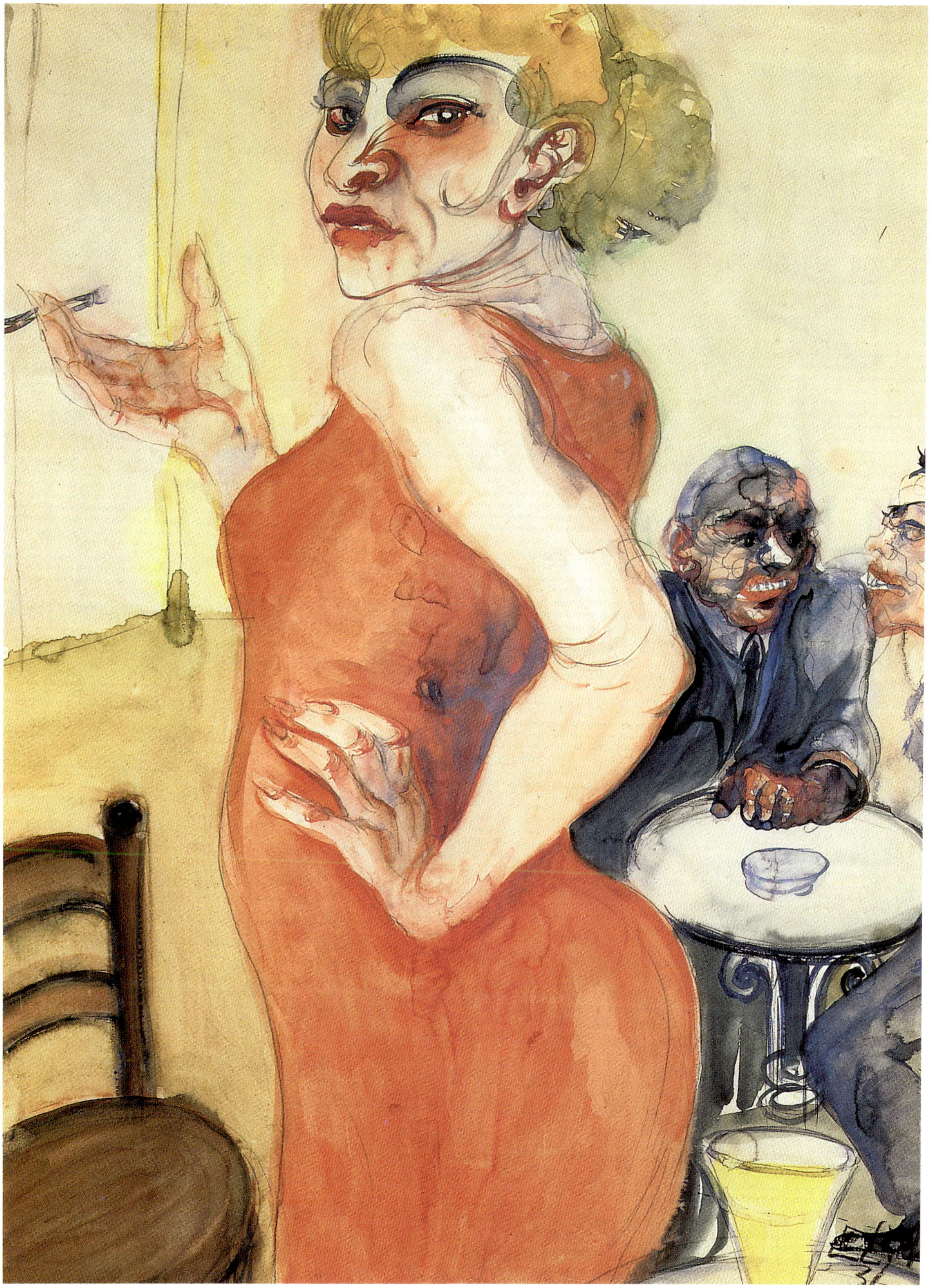

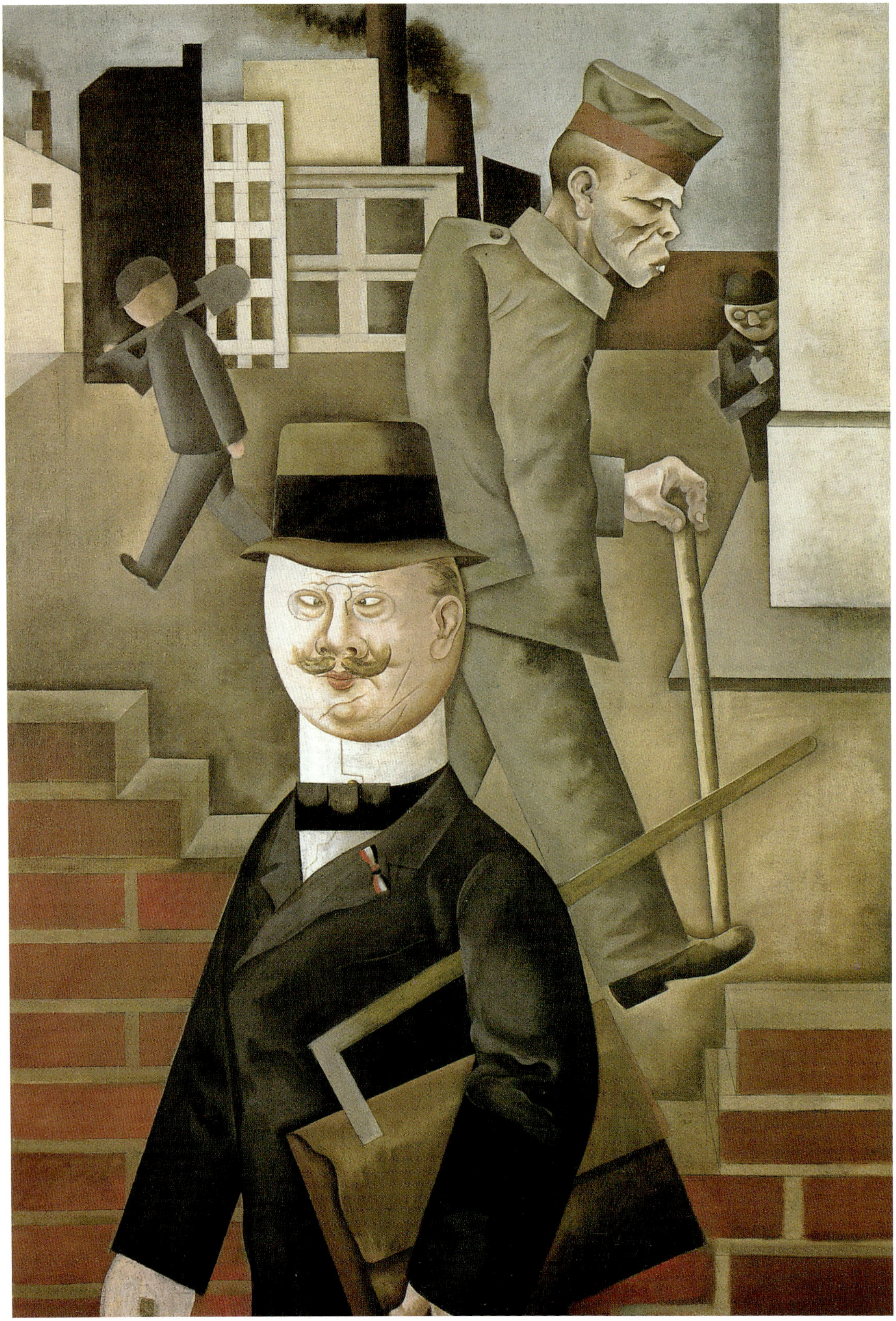

The Berlin Metropolis
The Verist School

It can hardly be expected of any cosmopolitan city that it should develop and nurture one style alone – and that for a period of some years – or even but one variant of that style. How much more must this apply to the legendary Berlin of the 1920s, of which it has been said with regard to the fields of "theatre, music, literature, architecture, film – indeed, in practically every area of the free and applied arts... [it] had been outstripping Paris and London for the duration of a decade".[8] (The Berlin night life, an important theme within fine art, was also perfectly capable of holding its own against that of Paris during the 1920s, and was absolutely unmatched anywhere else in Germany.) To be sure, objectivity as a psychological attitude, with its mixture of scepticism, curiosity, and rationality, may be seen as belonging to the particular characteristics to be found in the citizens of a metropolis; it may even be that the oft-quoted Berlin quality of cool cockiness reflects the deeper significance of the term. However, it would be an exaggeration to speak of objectivity as a way of life peculiar to Berlin. Correspondingly, the "New Objectivity" in art was but one of many trends within the contemporary Berlin scene. Considered from the viewpoint of stylistic categories, this scene covered a range stretching from late Expressionism and Dadaism, via Constructivism, to the Realism to be encountered in Heinrich Zille's "Kiez-Milljö"[9] or that of Otto Nagel.

Compared with the other centres – with the exception of Cologne – the picture presented by the Berlin Neue Sachlichkeit artists was less unified. A central focal point, along the lines of the Academy in Karlsruhe or the group around Georg Schrimpf in Munich, was not to be found here. The number of Neue Sachlichkeit artists based in Berlin or living in the metropolis for any considerable period of time was by no means small, yet for some of them (Otto Dix, Franz Radziwill, Heinrich Maria Davringhausen, Gert Wollheim), the city on the Spree was nothing more than a stopover, a place where one sought commissions or staged exhibitions, and then travelled onwards. At any rate, the sense of having close ties to a place, a productive factor within Neue Sachlichkeit that should not be underestimated, was weaker in Berlin than in the provincial centres. Yet this is astonishing, given the fact that the city's atmosphere appeared to correspond to and nurture the hard and isolating manner in which the Neue Sachlichkeit artists looked at things. This at least was George Grosz' view: "...you won't find a Matisse flourishing in Eastern Pomerania or Berlin. But so what! The air and everything is hard, a bit uncomfortable and good for drawing. It's easy to catch cold and get cold feet there..."[10]

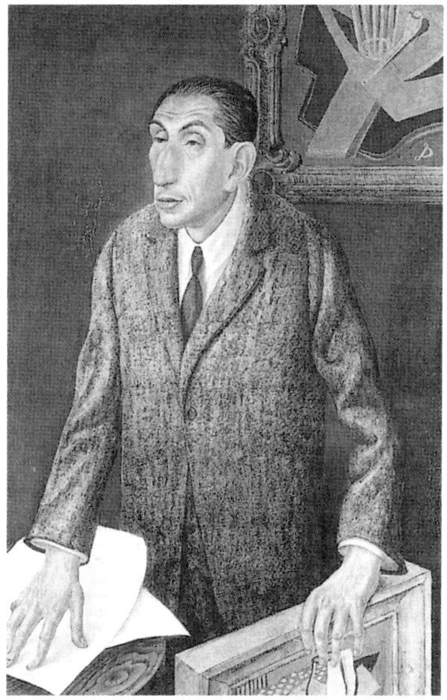

Otto Dix
Portrait of the Art Dealer Alfred Flechtheim, 1926
Bildnis des Kunsthändlers Alfred Flechtheim
Mixed media on wood, 120 x 80 cm
Berlin, Staatliche Museen zu Berlin – Preußischer Kulturbesitz, Nationalgalerie

George Grosz
Grey Day, 1921
Grauer Tag
Oil on canvas, 115 x 80 cm
Berlin, Staatliche Museen zu Berlin – Preußischer Kulturbesitz, Nationalgalerie

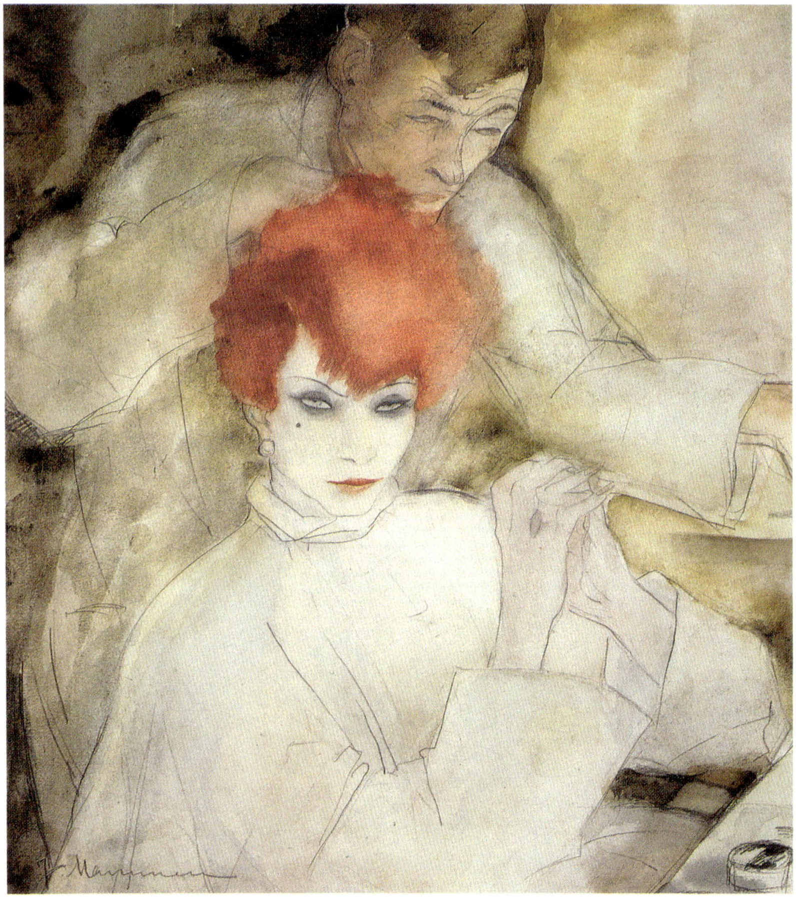

Jeanne Mammen
The Redhead, c. 1928
Die Rothaarige
Pencil drawing with watercolour, 34 x 31 cm
Berlin, Berlinische Galerie

The principal galleries and art dealers in Berlin – Herwarth Walden's Sturm Galerie until the mid–1920s, thereafter the galleries of Bruno Cassirer and Alfred Flechtheim – exhibited no Neue Sachlichkeit works apart from those by Grosz and Dix; indeed, their general attitude towards the movement was rather negative. *The* gallery for Neue Sachlichkeit in the city was "Neumann-Nierendorf", run by Karl Nierendorf. While extremely active and of reliable opinion with regard to what was good art, the former banker and later co-founder of the famous "Katakombe" cabaret did not possess the numerous connections – including those abroad – of the likes of Cassirer or Flechtheim. A medium-sized exhibition dedicated to Neue Sachlichkeit was staged in the Galerie Nierendorf from February to March 1927. It was to be the only comprehensive exhibition of its kind in Berlin, evidence perhaps of a reticence – cause or effect? – on the part of the art-loving public. Perhaps we can learn more from the ambivalent attitude exhibited by Flechtheim, who, while closing his gallery to the Neue Sachlichkeit artists, nevertheless helped them to achieve a certain popularity in his function as editor of the magazine "Der Querschnitt". Did he – and, with him, the bourgeois art-loving public – thus regard the style as finding its legitimacy within the realm of lifestyle illustration? Given the popularity of Christian Schad's pictures, and also Jeanne Mammen's depictions of moral practices, this could indeed be the case. On the other hand, the art review "Das Kunstblatt" appeared in Berlin, edited by art critic Paul Westheim and encompassing in Neue Sachlichkeit every artistic centre, together

Kurt Tucholsky paid homage in the "Weltbühne" of August, 1929, to the work of Jeanne Mammen as follows: "The gentle, gossamer-light watercolours which you publish in magazines and comic papers surpass the undisciplined scribblings of the majority of your professional colleagues to such an extent that one owes you a little declaration of love. Your figures feel clean, yet are simultaneously graceful and austere; they spring out from the paper, their skin and hair almost tangible ..."

Christian Schad
Two Girlfriends, 1928
Zwei Freundinnen
Oil on canvas, 109.5 x 80 cm
Private collection

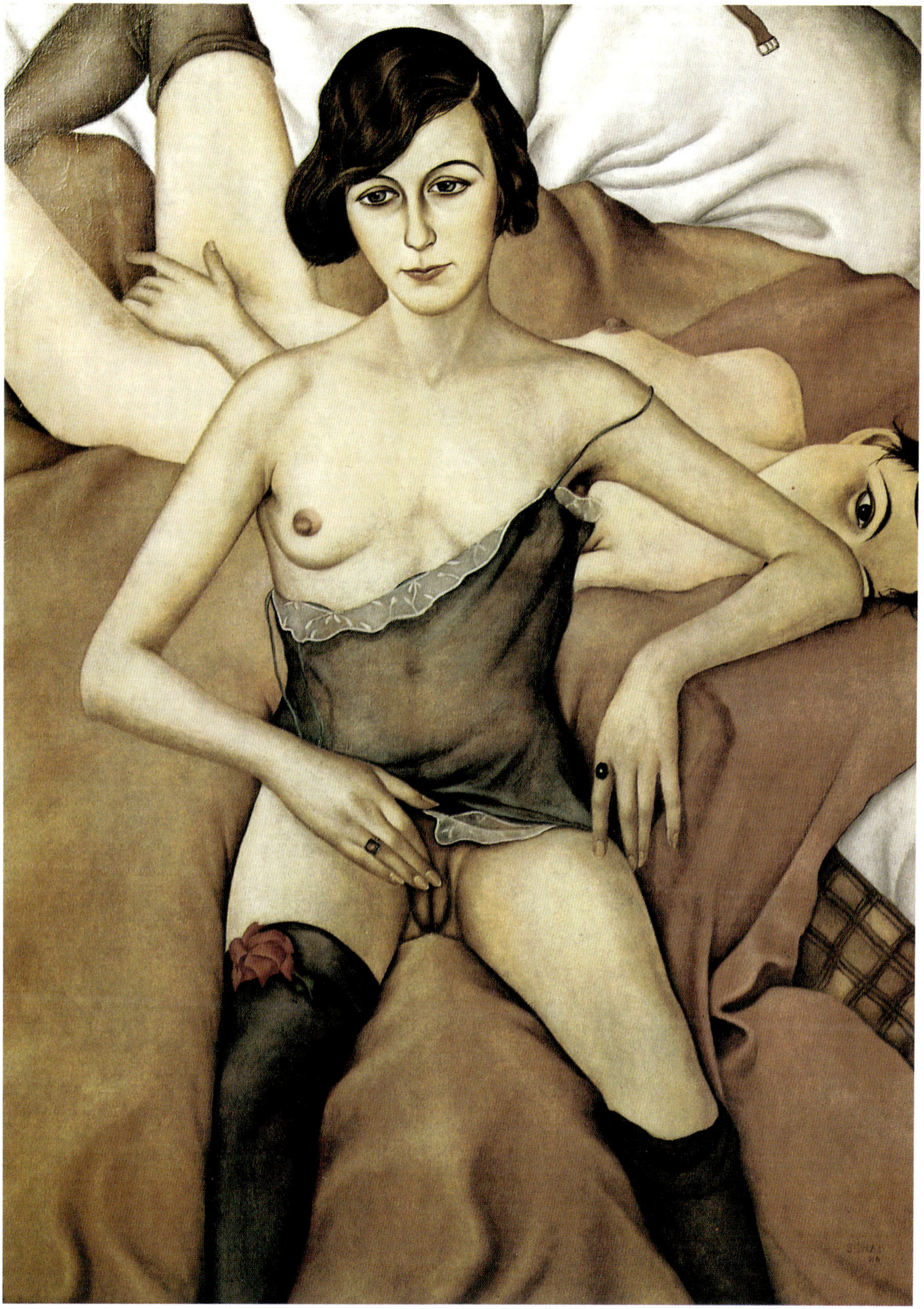

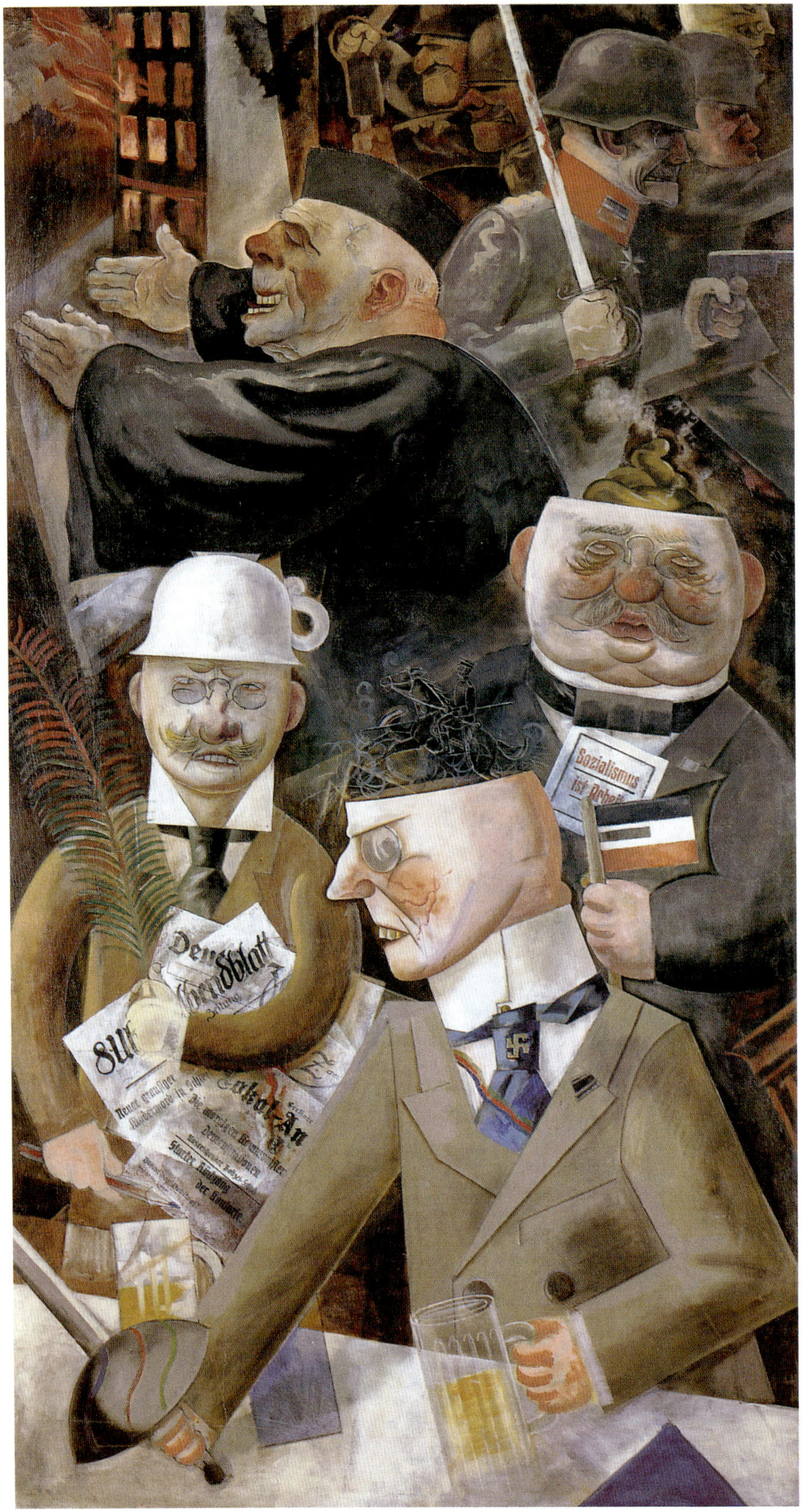
Sozialismus

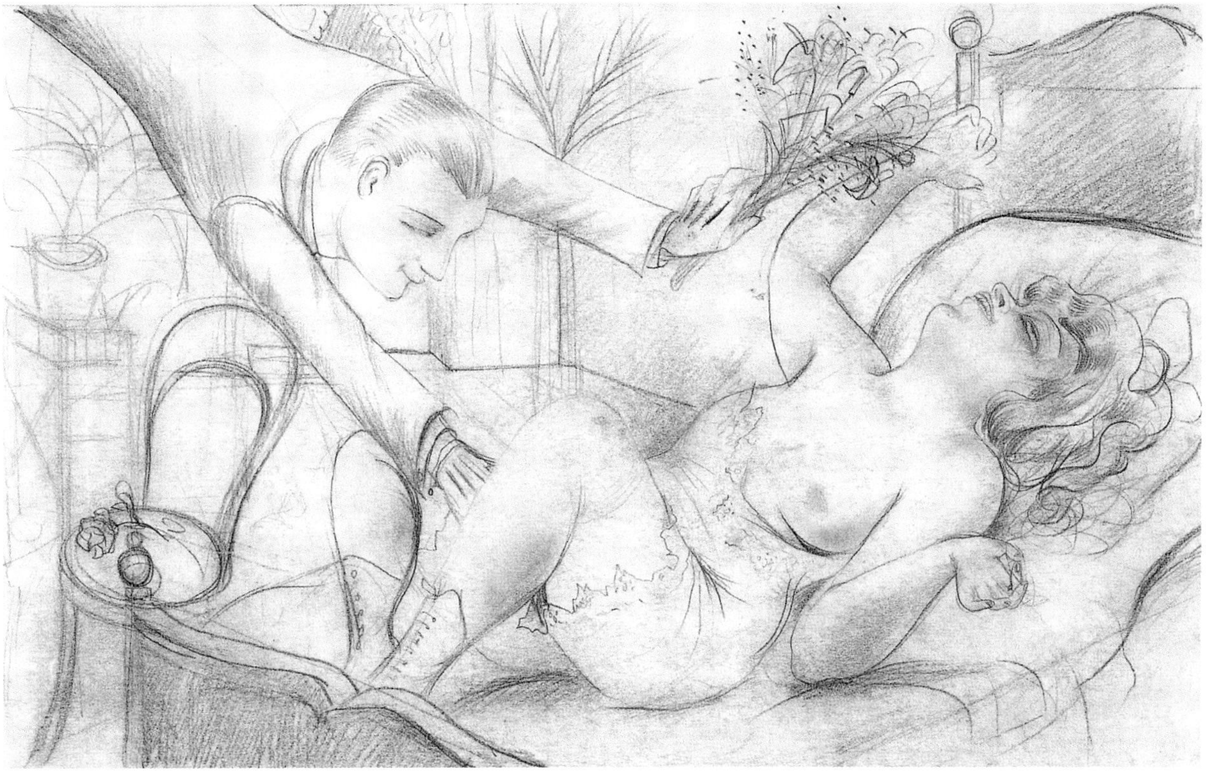

Otto Dix
The Annunciation, 1921/23
Verkündigung
Pencil, 50 x 60 cm
By kind permission of the Galerie Huber-Nising, Frankfurt am Main

with critiques, surveys, and exhibition and book reviews. While not claiming the status of a theoretical organ, it nevertheless remained the most important Neue Sachlichkeit publication.

George Grosz

Alongside Dix, Georg Ehrenfried Grosz (George Grosz from 1916 on) is regarded as the most important Verist artist. His work as graphic artist, painter, and designer of costumes and stage sets, along with his involvement as co-founder and advocate of new artistic movements, teacher, writer, and political commentator, all underline his versatility. At the centre of his œuvre, however, stand his political, critically-engaged drawings; it is through them that Grosz became famous. His name is as closely linked to art in the Berlin of the Twenties as are the names Bert Brecht and Kurt Tucholsky to literature and Max Reinhardt and Erwin Piscator to theatre.

Like Wieland Herzfelde, his friend and publisher (Malik-Verlag), and in common with many other artists, Grosz joined the Communist Party after the First World War. However, his relations with the German Communist Party were not uncomplicated, and he had great difficulty bowing to party doctrine. Following his trip to Russia late in the summer of 1922 – including an audience with Lenin – it was clear to him that he could no longer subscribe to the positive image of the happy, liberated worker. His view of the world was too sceptical and ultimately too pessimistic for that. He wrote in 1925, at the peak of his creativity, as an apologist for an artistic movement directed against the political and militarist reaction: "The Verist holds up a mirror to the faces of his contemporaries. My drawings and

George Grosz
The Pillars of Society, 1926
Die Stützen der Gesellschaft
Oil on canvas, 200 x 108 cm
Berlin, Staatliche Museen zu Berlin – Preußischer Kulturbesitz, Nationalgalerie

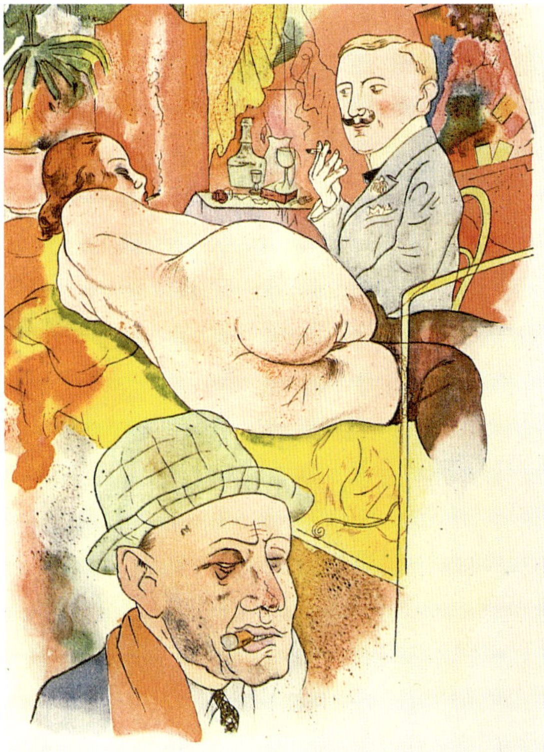

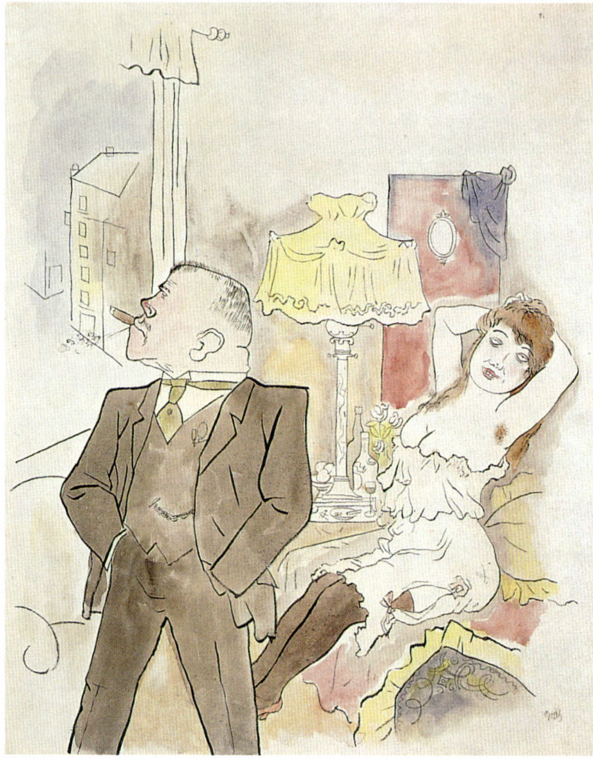

LEFT:
George Grosz
Ecce Homo, 1921
Watercolour, 35 x 26 cm
Berlin, Staatliche Museen zu Berlin – Preußischer Kulturbesitz, Nationalgalerie

RIGHT:
George Grosz
Strength and Grace, 1922
Kraft und Anmut
Watercolour, 35 x 26 cm
Cologne, Museum Ludwig

"It is a mistake to believe if you paint circles, cubes or some profound jumble of lines that you are being revolutionary – in comparison to Makart, perhaps. (...) Your brushes and pens, which should be your weapons, are empty straws. Go out of your rooms, (...) allow yourselves to be captured by the ideas of working people, and help them in the struggle against a rotten society."

George Grosz, 1920/21

paintings were done as an act of protest; I was trying by means of my work to convince the world that it is ugly, sick and hypocritical."[11]

The violent excesses of city life had preoccupied Grosz since 1916. Common everyday crime struck him as the reflex to and continuation of the lunacy of war: "The catastrophe had begun. I drew drunks, people throwing up, men shaking their fists at the moon as they cursed it, the murderers of women, playing at cards while sitting on a crate in which the murder victims could be seen ... I drew a man looking around him fearfully, washing his hands, which had blood on them ..."[12]

Grosz' style of drawing gradually lost its initial debt to Expressionism, becoming terser and more succinct. In an early autobiographical note, Grosz refers to the doodles found in pissoirs as representing an important source of inspiration for his drawings. By 1918, his characteristic linear style of drawing had fully developed, resulting in the "political" portfolios "Gott mit uns" (God with us) (1920) and "Das Gesicht der herrschenden Klasse" (The face of the ruling class) (1921), together with the satirical caricatures for the Dadaist magazine "Die Pleite", which established his fame. Grosz' style strikes the balance between depictive and symbolic elements, the two forming the prerequisite for the hard, isolating manner of looking at things so characteristic of Neue Sachlichkeit. The obvious similarities between his style of drawing and that seen in Klee's early works are a further argument in favour of applying the term of Verism more to an artist's intentions with regard to content than to the formal peculiarities of his style of drawing.

Grosz and his drawings accompanied the period covering Germany's defeat in war, the November Revolution, the Spartacus League's street battles, politically motivated murders, and the cold days of inflation. Style

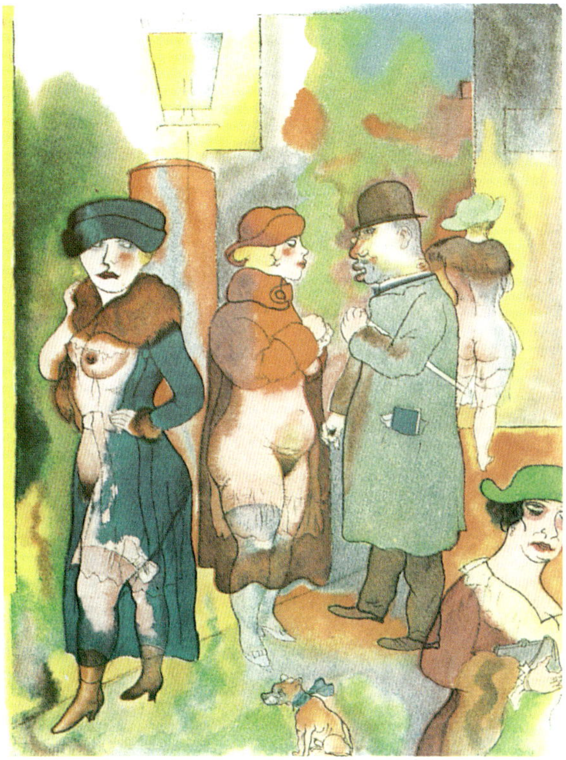

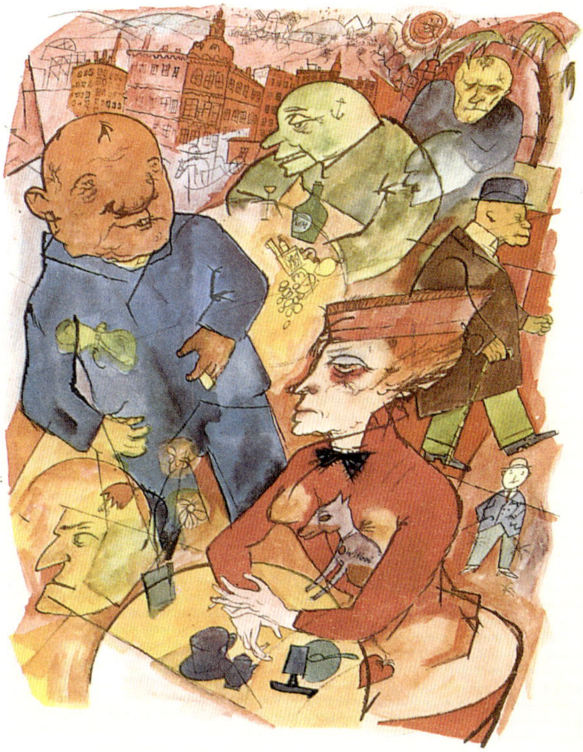

and political commitment make up an unmistakable unity in his work from these years; they create an overstated and biased effect, and the power of their expression was feared. This is clearly visible from the court cases conducted against Grosz on charges of insulting the German Army (1921), attacking on public morality (1924) and blasphemy (1928), each of which resulted in his being sentenced to payment of a fine. For long phases within his creative output, Grosz saw himself less as an artist than as an aggressive pictorial journalist.

From 1920 onwards, Grosz' works bear clear references to Pittura metafisica. He began to produce Constructivist paintings, of stereotype streets along which human automatons, tailor's dummies and figures with artificial limbs are strolling. His political stance is expressed in such titles as *Republican Automatons* (illus. p. 16). The people in these pictures are portrayed not as individuals but rather as a "collectivist, almost mechanical concept". In order to intensify this effect, Grosz decided to number his soulless creations. His links with Dadaism, too, can still be felt – perhaps most obviously in his self-parodying commentary upon his own wedding in the picture title: "Daum marries her pedantic automaton George in May 1920, John Heartfield is very glad of it."[13]

Grosz' incorporation of Italian elements into his painting represented an important stage along his way to Neue Sachlichkeit: "Once again, I am attempting to present an absolutely realistic picture of the world... In endeavouring to form a clear, simple style, one inevitably finds oneself drawn to that of Carrà... I restrain my use of colour. Lines are drawn on an individual, photography- like basis; construction is carried out that plastic art be created. Stability, structure, efficacy once again... control over line and form is being reintroduced – It's no longer a question of

LEFT:
George Grosz
Oh, Crazy World, You Blessed Freak Show, 1916
Ach, knallige Welt, du seliges Abnormitätenkabinett
Watercolour, 35 x 26 cm
Berlin, Staatliche Museen zu Berlin – Preußischer Kulturbesitz, Kupferstichkabinett

RIGHT:
George Grosz
Before Sunrise, 1922
Vor Sonnenaufgang
Watercolour, 35 x 26 cm
Berlin, Staatliche Museen zu Berlin – Preußischer Kulturbesitz, Kunstbibliothek

Grosz, having taken up overtly political topics in his portfolios "Gott mit uns" (1920), "Das Gesicht der herrschenden Klasse" (1921) and "Abrechnung folgt" (1923), turned in "Ecce Homo" (1923) – from which the above illustrations are taken – to a demasking of the private life of the bourgeoisie, his target above all their erotic excesses and obsessions. The result was a panorama of moral decay, its intention both accusatory and "educational".

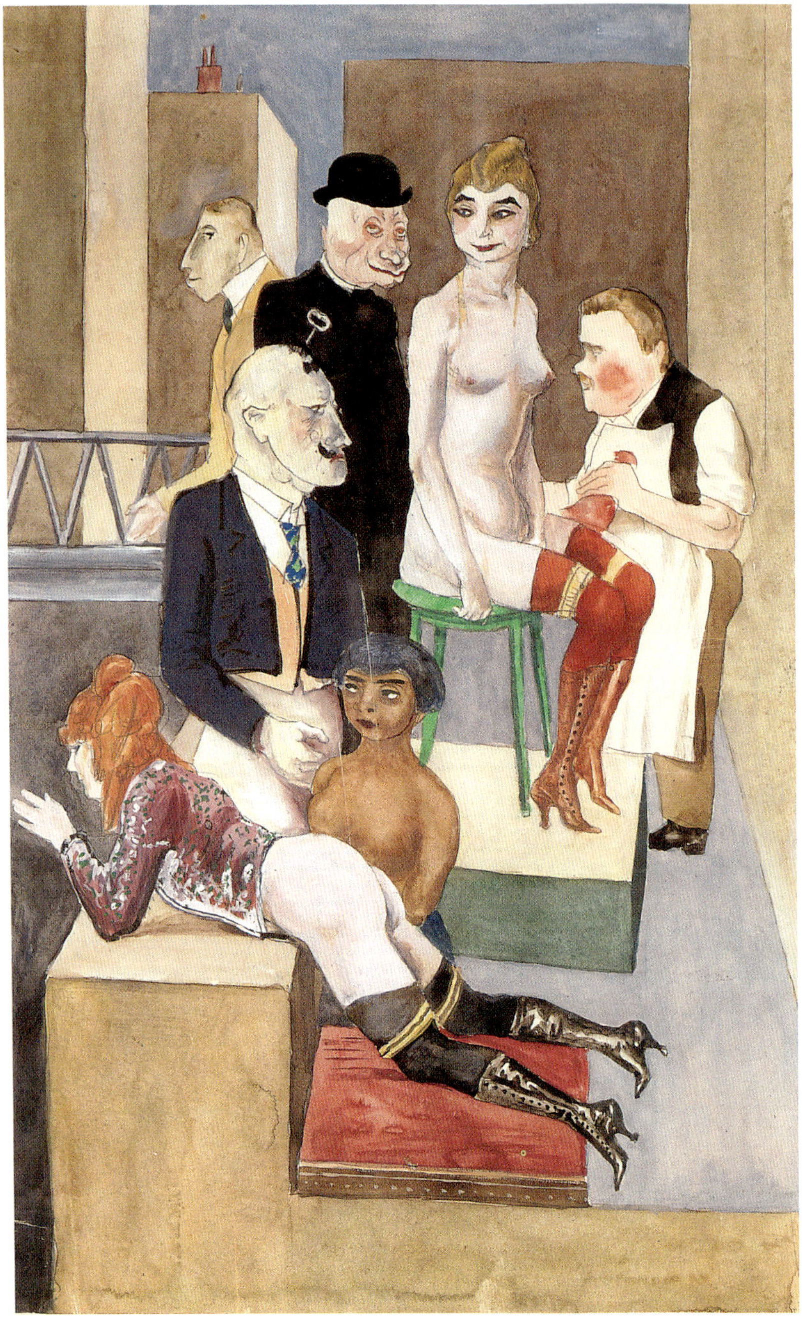

Rudolf Schlichter
Meeting of Fetishists and maniacal Flagellants, c. 1921
Treffen von Fetischisten und manischen Flagellanten
Watercolour, 43.9 x 27.3 cm
Private collection

Women in tight-fitting boots with high heels appear again and again in Schlichter's pictures. The painter was himself a pronounced shoe fetishist, a passion in which his wife, Speedy, willingly obliged him. We may read in "World Between Worlds – an Intermezzo", his autobiographical novel: "After a pause in the converation, he asked her, his voice trembling, if she might possibly be inclined, even today, despite the unusual nature of the fashion, to do something for his pleasure and torment, namely to put on high button-up boots with delicately slender Pompadour heels. How astonished and shaken he was when she not only agreed on the spot to his request but even suggested herself in return, with great interest and empathy, that she deal with this important matter the very next day ..."

Otto Dix
Three Women, 1926
Drei Weiber
Mixed media on wood, 181 x 105.5 cm
Stuttgart, Galerie der Stadt Stuttgart

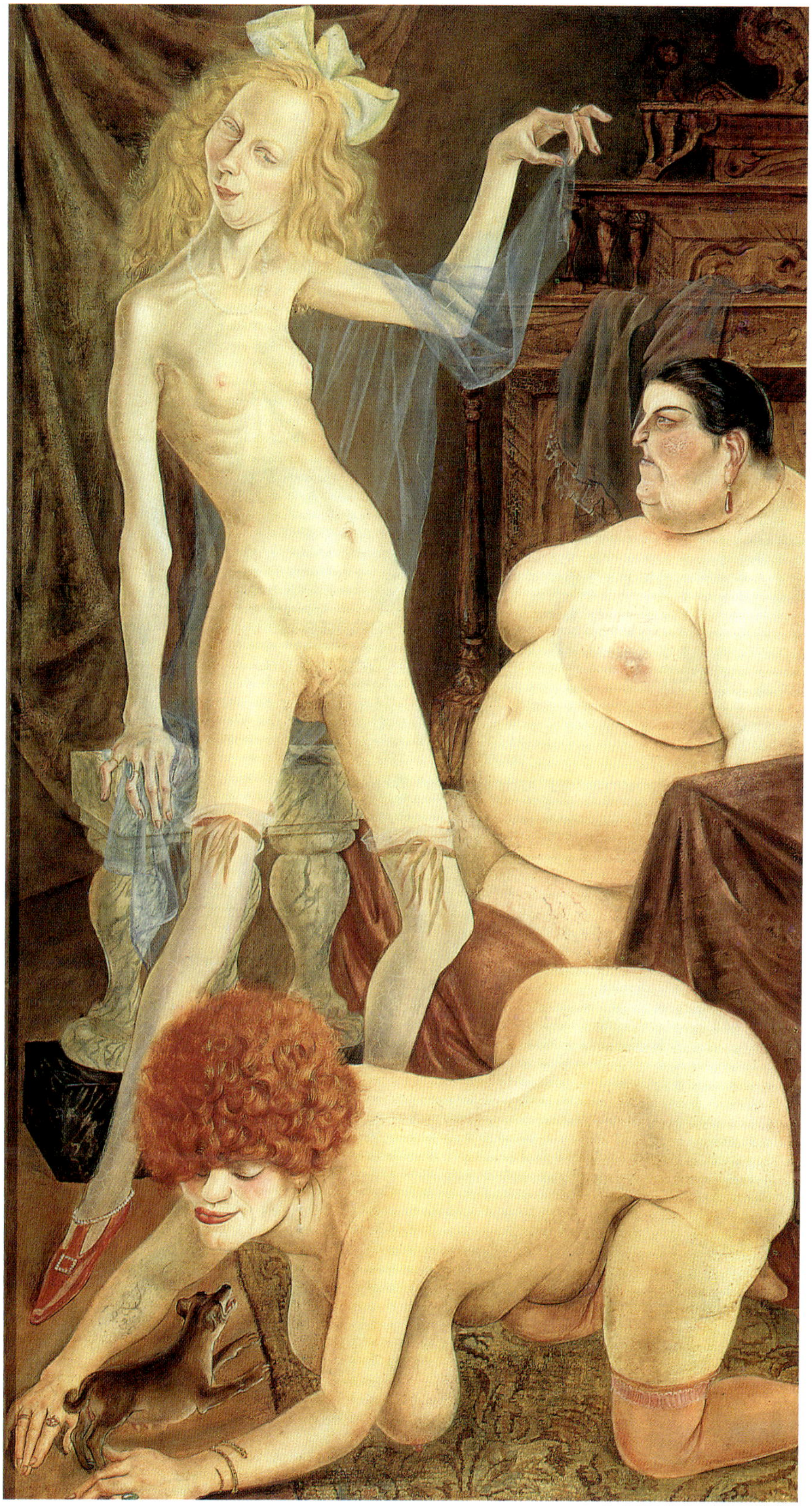

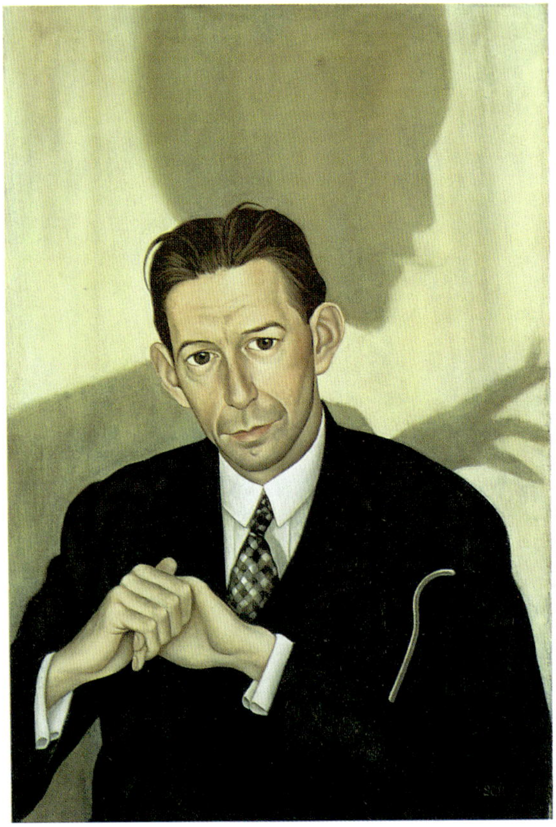

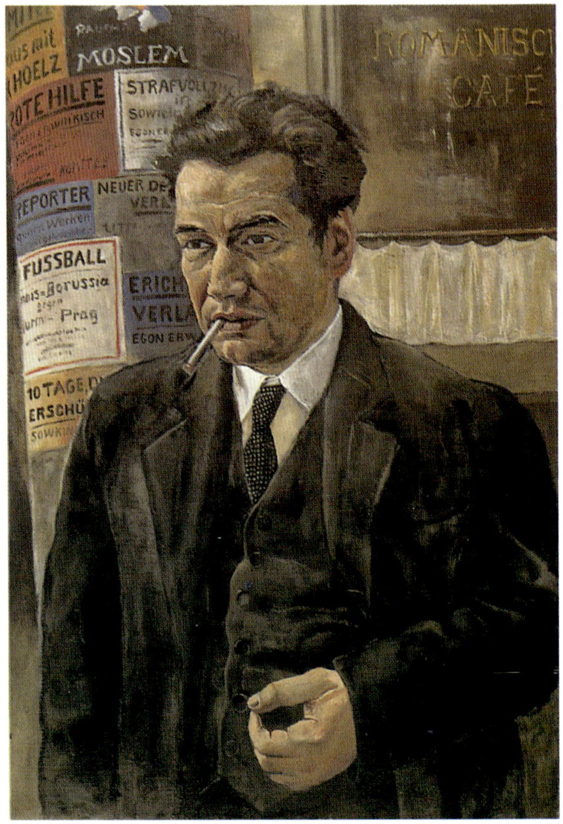
MOSLEM
HOELZ
ROTE HILFE
REPORTER
FUSSBALL
Borussia
Prag
CAFÉ

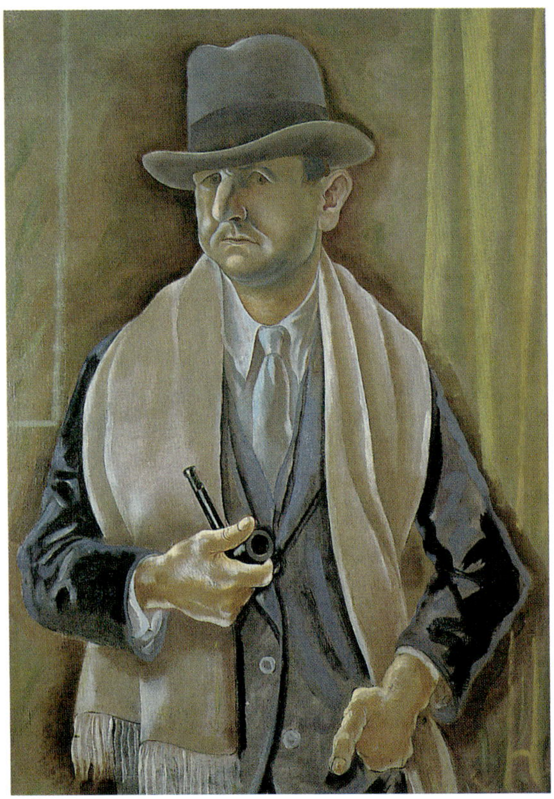

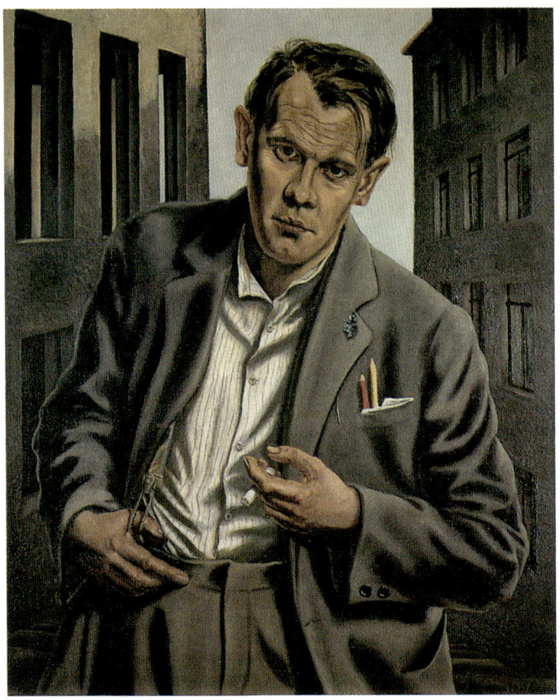

George Grosz
Portrait of the Poet Max Herrmann-Neisse, 1925
Porträt des Schriftstellers Max Herrmann-Neisse
Oil on canvas, 100 x 101 cm
Mannheim, Städtische Kunsthalle

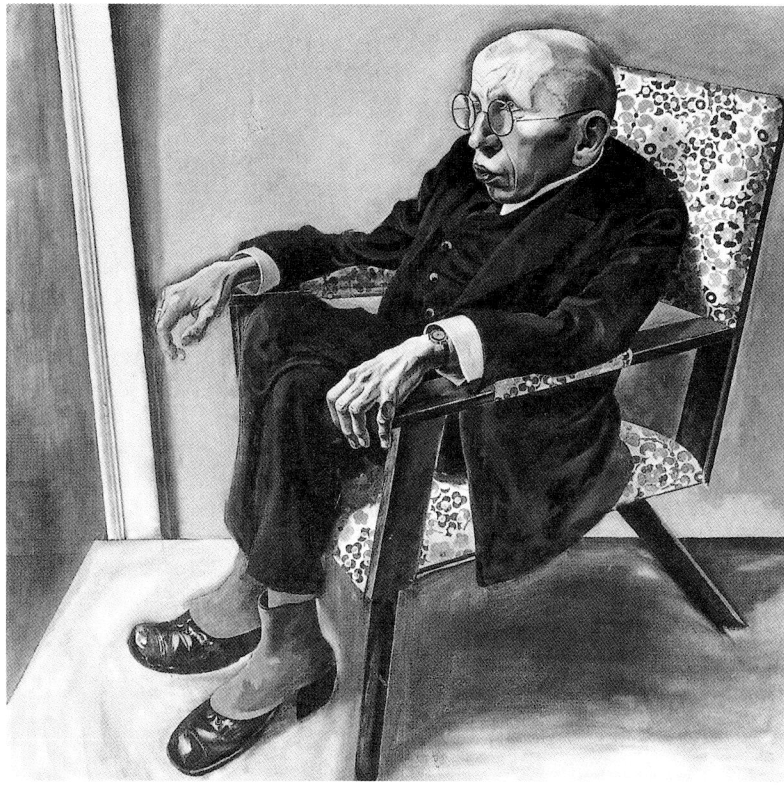

ILLUSTRATIONS PAGE 32
TOP LEFT:
Christian Schad
Portrait of Dr. Haustein, 1928
Bildnis Dr. Haustein
Oil on canvas, 80.5 x 55 cm
Lugano, Thyssen-Bornemisza Collection

TOP RIGHT:
Rudolf Schlichter
Portrait of Egon Erwin Kisch, 1928
Bildnis Egon Erwin Kisch
Oil on canvas, 62 x 88 cm
Mannheim, Städtische Kunsthalle

BOTTOM LEFT:
George Grosz
Self-Portrait, 1928
Selbstbildnis
Oil on canvas, 109.5 x 79 cm
Berlin, Berlinische Galerie

BOTTOM RIGHT:
Walter Schulz-Matan
Portrait of Oskar Maria Graf, 1927
Bildnis Oskar Maria Graf
Oil on canvas, 90 x 74 cm
Oldenburg, Landesmuseum

colourfully conjuring Expressionist tapestries of the soul onto the canvas – The functionality [Grosz uses the term "Sachlichkeit" in the original] and clarity of an engineer's drawings present a better model than the uncontrollable wafflings of Kabbala and metaphysics and religious ecstasy."[14]

The significant use of the word "Sachlichkeit" – Grosz was later generally to avoid the term – turns these remarks into a document of transition. Grosz is sketching out here the essential elements of a programme for a Constructivist realism. However, the references to Pittura metafisica broke off in 1921; perhaps their binding power struck him as too great for an adopted stylistic formula. But in the years that followed, Grosz was to consistently pursue the task he had set himself of developing a fashion of painting that was realistic and functional. His "metaphysical" intermezzo had an effect upon many of the Neue Sachlichkeit artists. Davringhausen and Räderscheidt adopted the monotonous backdrop of the urban landscape, while Heinrich Hoerle, the Rhineland painter, would quote the artificial-limb motif from *Republican Automatons* in as late as 1930.

In the three years that followed, Grosz was to concentrate once again upon political caricatures and portfolios of graphic art. New Year 1922/23 saw the appearance of his celebrated "Ecce Homo" (illus. pp. 28/29), comprising 16 watercolours with 84 lithographs and published by Berlin's Malik-Verlag, which had also been responsible for publishing most of his other folders previously. The first traces of a softening were visible in Grosz' style of drawing, a contributory element being the choice of a new medium, namely brush drawing, whose black-and-white contrasts produced a more painterly effect. The adoption of a further graphic medium, the pencil, led to Grosz' transition to Neue Sachlichkeit in 1924. Use of the pencil enabled

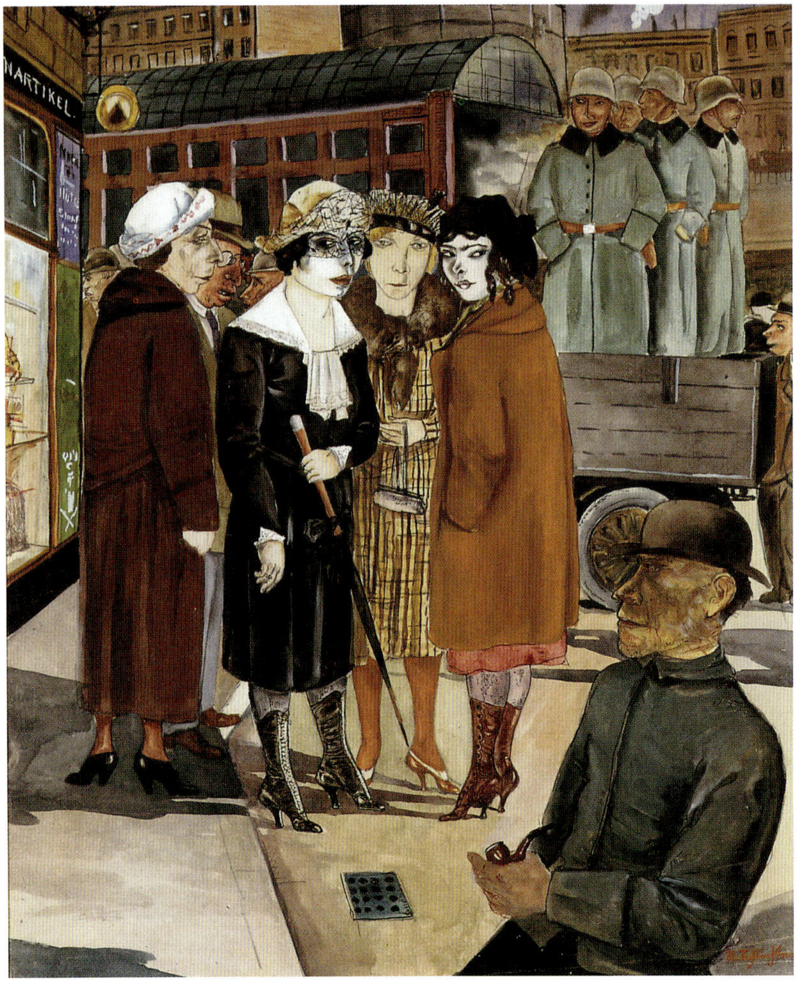

Rudolf Schlichter
Passers-by and the Imperial Army, 1925/26
Passanten und Reichswehr
Watercolour, 58 x 40 cm
Karlsruhe, Kunstkabinett Mirko Heipek

him to create shadings and bring out three-dimensional quality. The hard abbreviations peculiar to the pen were increasingly absent, being replaced by illustratively depictive elements.

The subject-matter of his works was also changing, the classical incarnations fossilized into the caricaturist's standard clichés of capitalists, inflation profiteers, generals and judges now appearing with growing rarity. The direct impression of political exposure in his works receded. Grosz was turning increasingly to the sociologically more interesting types found in the new Weimar cultural smart set, as seen for example in the portfolio "Der Spießerspiegel" (The Philistine's Mirror) of 1925. It was also in this year that Grosz began to devote himself to portrait painting, resulting in a whole series of portraits depicting people close to him, such as the *Portrait of the Poet Max Herrmann-Neisse* (illus. p. 33) or that of Eduard Plietzsch, the art historian. The portrait of Herrmann-Neisse, with its diagonal arrangement of the sitter, established a new compositional type within portrait painting. The subject's hands and face have been captured with Verist vividness. In the portrait of his mother, as well as in that of Felix Weil, his friend and patron – both of them diagonal views as well – Grosz toned

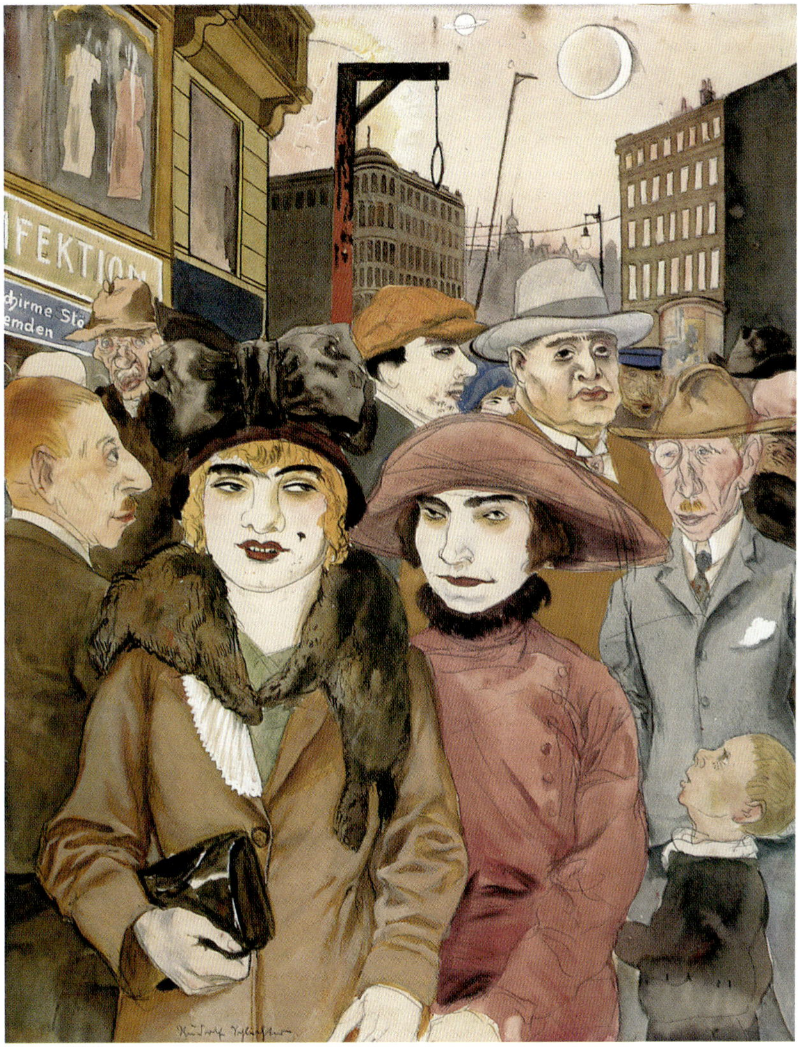

The two women in the foreground of the picture are completely surrounded by male passers-by, to whose gaze and bodily proximity they are exposed. Schlichter's street scene is dominated by a threatening atmosphere, the most obvious expression of which may be found in the bloody gallows rising up behind the pushing and shoving of the crowd. The heavenly bodies in the sky – Sun and Moon appearing in unusual manifestations, along with Saturn, the planet of melancholics – heighten the general impression, achieving an effect that verges on the apocalyptic.

Rudolf Schlichter
Hausvogteiplatz, c. 1926
Watercolour, 66.5 x 51.5 cm
By kind permission of the Galerie Huber-Nising, Frankfurt am Main

down the tensions arising from the composition, thereby also reducing the Verist elements in the depictions. A desire for harmonious solutions was making itself increasingly apparent in his work.

The majority of his paintings and watercolours after 1926 were characterized by an essentially Neue Sachlichkeit-like conception of form, one lacking Verist intensification. However, Grosz was unable to come to terms with the figural plasticity of Neue Sachlichkeit. The forms in his pictures from the second half of the 1920s seem rather to be modelled along a softer pattern, calling to mind watercolours by the French artist Jules Pascin as well as works by Schlichter. Towards the end of the 1920s, Grosz expanded his stylistic repertoire within the Neue Sachlichkeit spectrum. His less well-known *Cityscape*, to give but one example, is a shooting-gallery idyll in the manner of the naive cityscapes by the Hanover Neue Sachlichkeit artists. Grosz' works were now taking on an increasingly sentimental quality, something that would lead them away again from Neue Sachlichkeit. The wheel was beginning to turn full circle, with the one-time aggressive Verist searching for a new, lyrical ideal. In 1928, speaking to Harry Count Kessler, Grosz revealed himself as an apologist for precisely that higher "Kunscht"

The self-assurance displayed by Margot, a prostitute often painted by Schlichter and becoming well-known in the process, appears to equal that of Brecht, the writer, in every way. Her casual posture and facial expression indicate her determination to hold her own in the fight for survival against men.

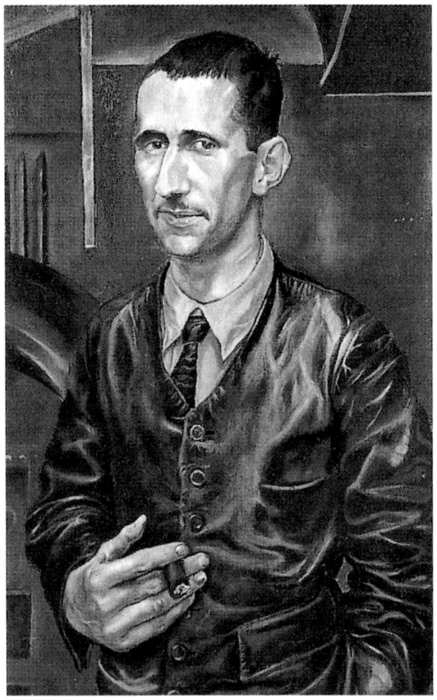

Rudolf Schlichter
Portrait of Bert Brecht, c. 1926/27
Bildnis Bert Brecht
Oil on canvas, 75.5 x 46 cm
Munich, Städtische Galerie im Lenbachhaus

Rudolf Schlichter
Portrait of Margot, 1924
Bildnis Margot
Oil on canvas, 110.5 x 75 cm
Berlin, Märkisches Museum

(combining "Kunst", art, with "Kitsch", rubbish) which he himself had once scorned: "What is real is not sufficient for me. Look, I'm what you could call an artistic chap, I'm striving after fairytales."[15]

This transition, one that was to become increasingly manifest following Grosz' emigration to America in January 1933, was doubtless also the result of his disappointment about the powerlessness of art in the face of politics. The advance of National Socialism, which forced an end to Grosz' activities in Germany, made him aware of the futility of his years of political commitment, particularly against German militarism. Yet harder still than this defeat was the suffering which Grosz inflicted upon himself, arising from the boundless hatred which both he and others have diagnosed again and again in his works. For years this hatred was the source of his artistic powers of expression. Numerous remarks that he made, together with the path taken by his art, indicate that from the mid–1920s onwards he had been searching for new creative impulses – a search that was ultimately to prove futile.

Rudolf Schlichter

Born in Württemberg, Schlichter studied before the war at the Karlsruhe Academy, one of the birthplaces of the Neue Sachlichkeit movement. He was called up in 1916, but was able to obtain his release from military service in the same year by means of a hunger-strike. The young artist developed views that became noticeably ever more radical, his antipathy towards bourgeois conventions clearly eclipsing the political element within his work. In his autobiographies "The Wilful Flesh" and "Feet of Clay", Schlichter refers to the emphatically anti-bourgeois roots of his childhood: "How I suffered under the unimaginative dullness and profound hypocrisy of the modern bourgeoisie – a bourgeoisie which hid its base, materialistic aspirations behind the phrases of the might and greatness of the nation, the worshipper of quantity, which desecrated the German cityscape with the abominations spawned by a terrible monumental style of architecture, which considered the profound sayings of German poets and thinkers just about good enough to serve as captions and trademarks for the advertising brochures of its export articles."[16]

In 1919, Schlichter, together with Georg Scholz and others in Karlsruhe, founded the "Rih" group, which regarded itself as an offshoot of the Berlin Novembergruppe. This latter had come into being at the end of 1918 as a product of the November Revolution, and comprised an amalgam of architects, artists, writers, film-makers and composers, whose aim it was to democratize the art business and support the "young, free Germany". Wall graffiti with the contraction "Rih" covered Karlsruhe; ultimately, however, the group achieved more provocative uproar than artistically significant work. At the end of 1919, Schlichter, bane of the bourgeoisie and erotic shoe fetishist, moved to Berlin, to the "centre of art against petit-bourgeois conformism", as he thought. Here he came to know Grosz and joined the Berlin Dada movement, producing the beautiful watercolour *Dada Roof Studio* (illus. p. 17), with the jointed doll and desolate urban backdrop typical of Pittura metafisica. A T-square and triangles may be observed on the table; de Chirico had described them in 1919 in his essay "Metaphysical Aesthetics" as frightening magical symbols.

In the initial period of his time in Berlin, Schlichter went through a brief, intensive phase of fascination with city life. The hated bourgeois morality

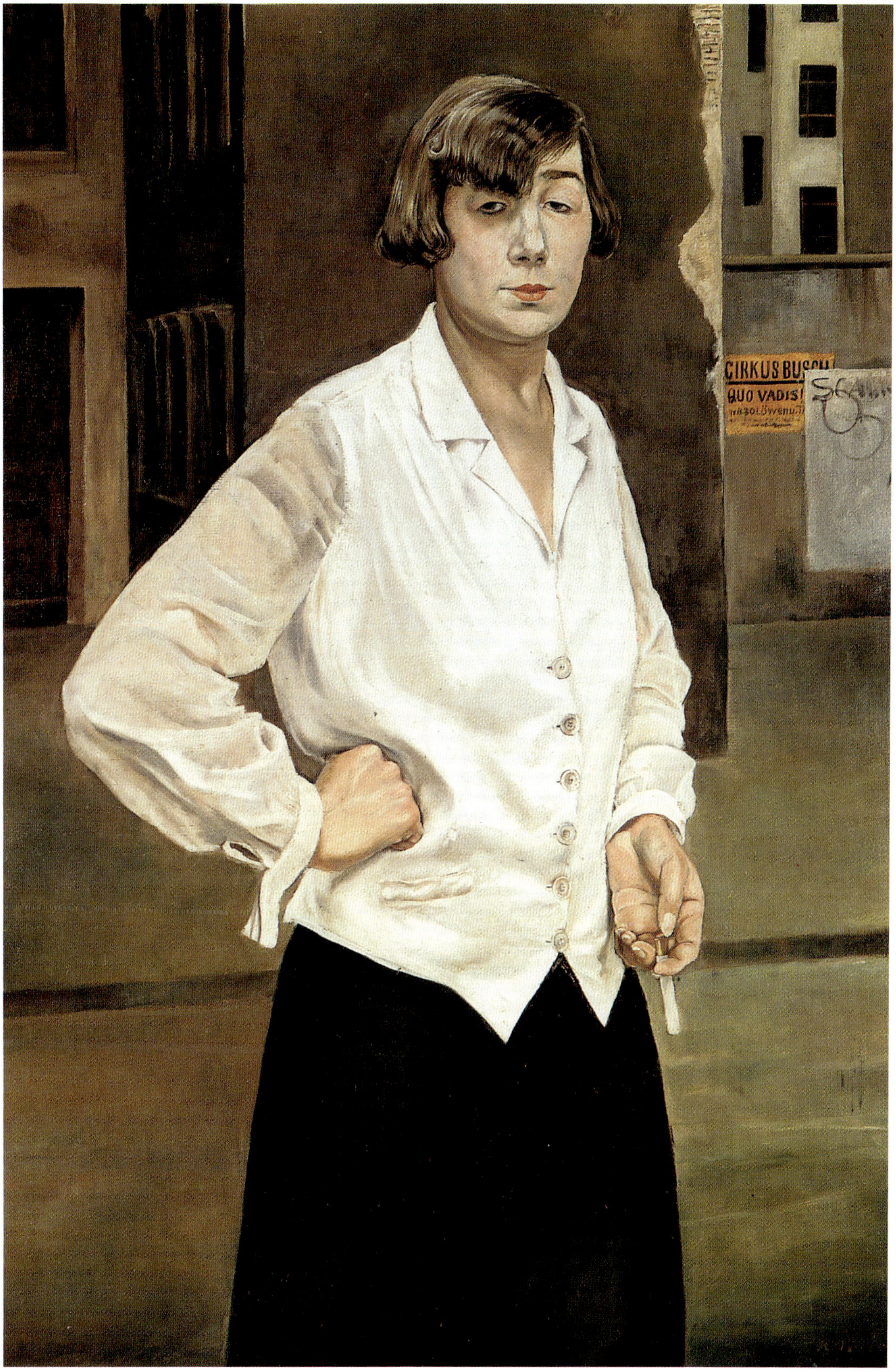
CIRKUS BUSCH
QUO VADIS!

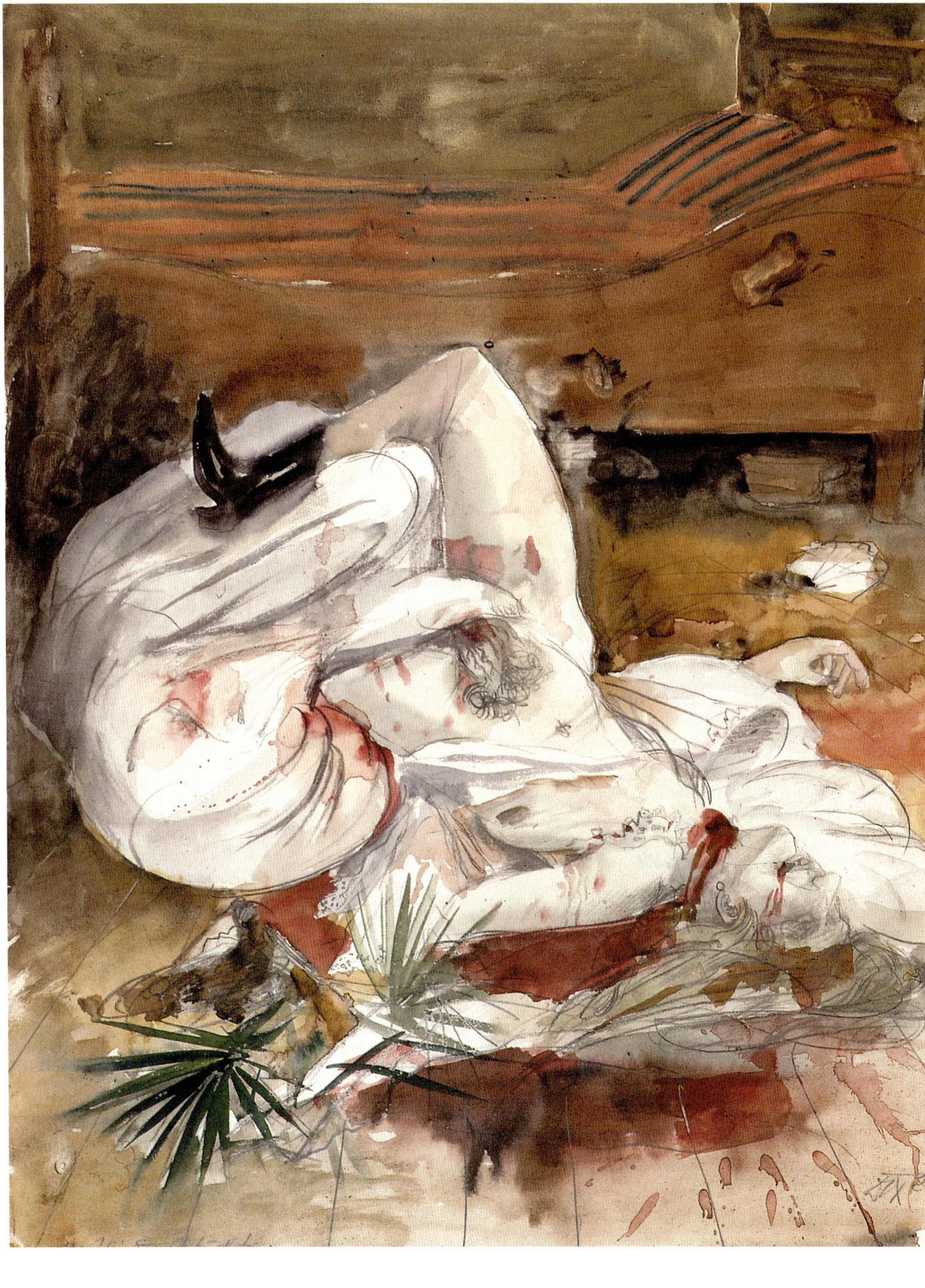

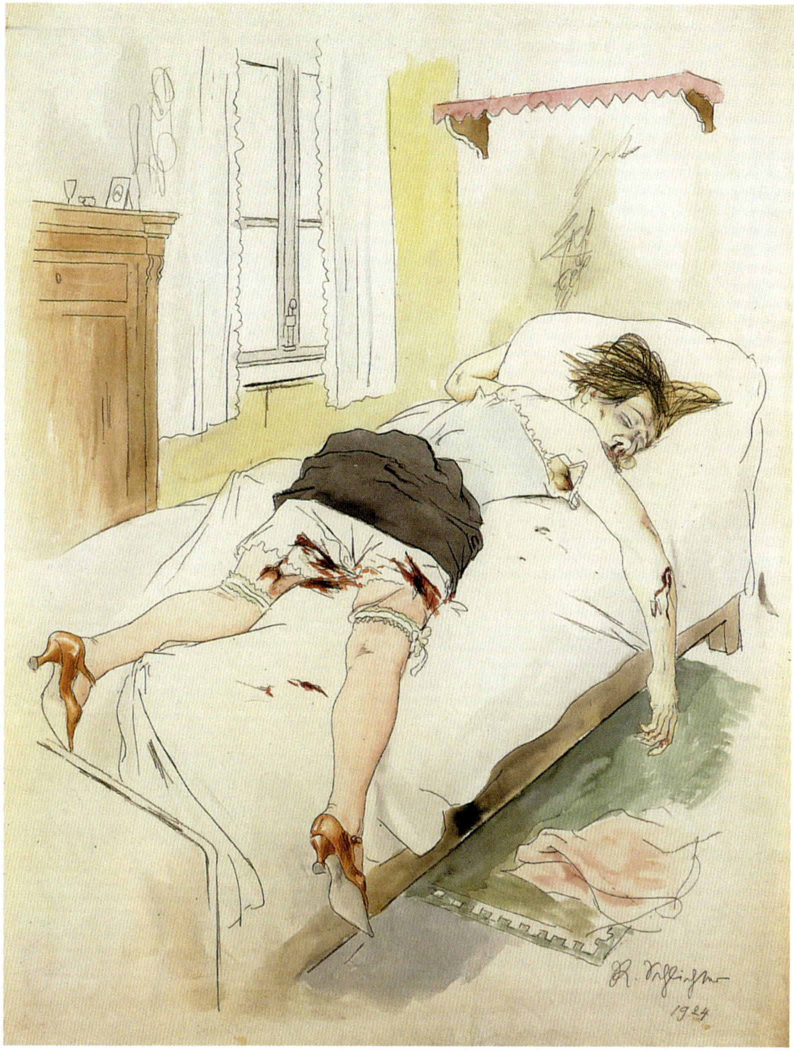

Rudolf Schlichter
Sex Murder, 1924
Lustmord
Watercolour and black crayon, 69 x 53 cm
Private collection

The drastic, brutal subject of sex murder was introduced into the Expressionist iconography by Kirchner and Grosz. Dix and Schlichter developed it further in the course of the 1920s in the realist spirit of Neue Sachlichkeit.

Otto Dix
Scene II, Murder, 1922
Scene II, Mord
Watercolour, 62 x 47.5 cm
Vaduz, Otto Dix Foundation

seemed to him to have been defeated once and for all in the voracious giant that Berlin represented. Here it was possible to live out one's fantasies and sexual preferences. It did not take long for disillusion to set in, however: Berlin, he was to say later when looking back in his autobiography on his time there, was a "well-organized asphalt desert", one in which everything functioned perfectly and where even vice had been organized down to the last detail, rendering it a positive institution for the good of society. If it is true that a sober, disillusioned way of looking at things is a favourable quality for Neue Sachlichkeit, then Schlichter was ready for this style by 1921. He became a cold, analytical chronicler of 1920s vice-ridden Berlin. His drawings and watercolours often call to mind Grosz' works, yet they clearly have a quality of their own. The numerous drawn figure-studies are more three-dimensional; the depictions of unemployed or socially disadvantaged people reveal human characters captured in nuances, without one isolated, predominant trait being brought out and intensified, as in the works of Grosz or Dix. His watercolours betray the influence of the wash technique employed by Jules Pascin, the French artist, whose impact upon Schlichter's art was greater than on that of Grosz. In brief, Schlichter

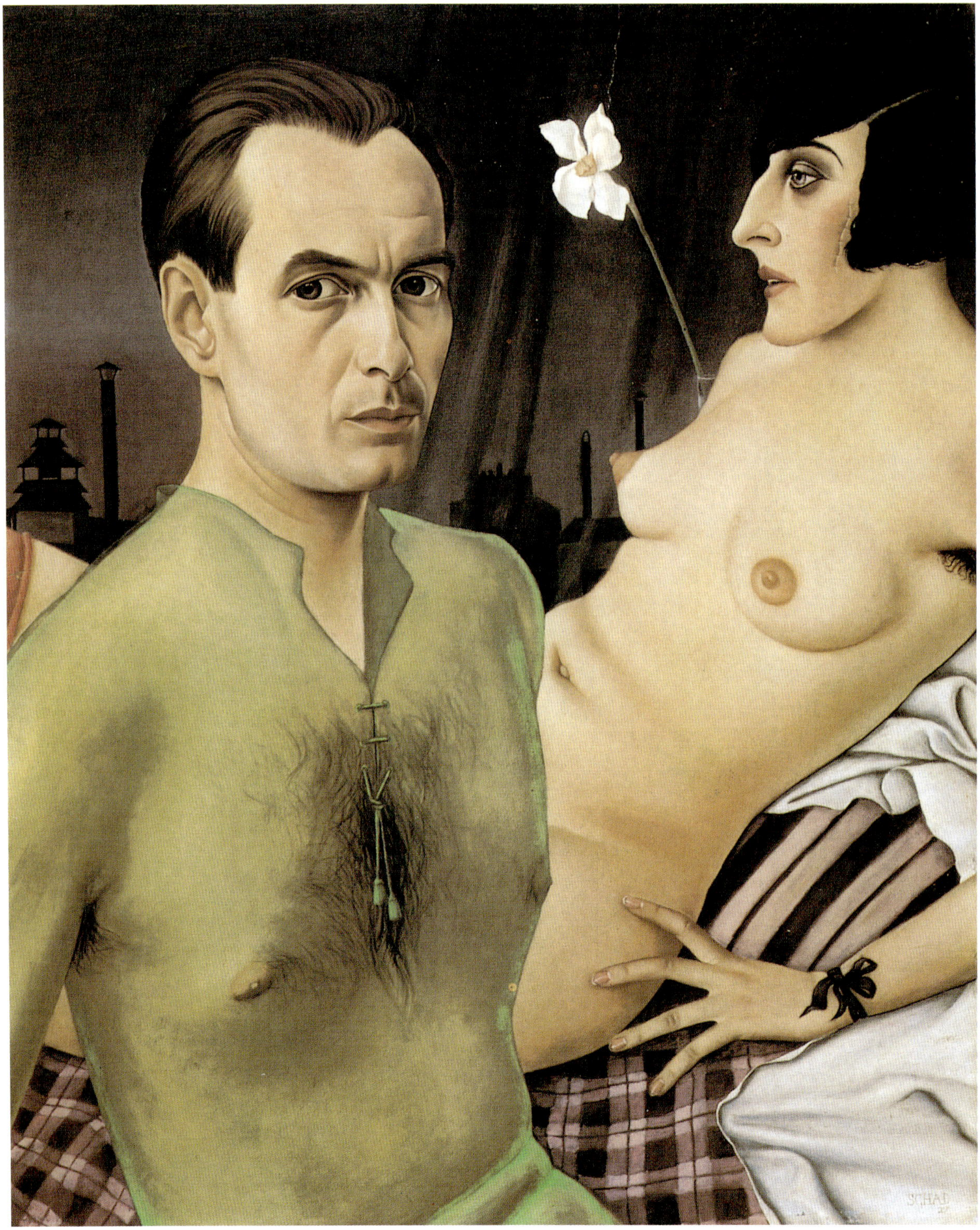
SCHAD

lacked the early bitterness, but also the maudlin sentimentality, that characterizes Grosz' later works.

Schlichter did not recoil from erotic graphicness. The washed bloodstains in *Sex Murder* (illus. p. 39), applied spontaneously and confidently, create an unambiguous, horrifying eye-catcher. Schlichter further varies this theme, one beloved of the Verists, in other works, and indeed the theme of sexuality and violence frequently occurs in his output. A sense for the ironic is revealed in his picture *Meeting of Fetishists and maniacal Flagellants* (illus. p. 30).

However, his Verist gaze was capable of perceiving more beneath the frequently dull surface that people presented than merely their ugly, violent and nasty qualities. The large-scale *Portrait of Margot* (illus. p. 37) depicts a Berlin "professional" who modelled for Schlichter on several occasions. The observer is struck by the cold, unsentimental attitude of the prostitute, her evident self-assurance asserting itself against the seedy backdrop. The broken white of her blouse and the deep black skirt have been rendered with firm, hard strokes of the brush and gain in clarity of colour through the contrast with the grey background. In this picture, Schlichter takes as his central theme the contradiction between the social status of the prostitute and her personal professional pride and self-esteem. The difficulty involved in combining the one with the other is further suggested by the poster caption "Quo vadis!", one loaded with meaning.

The painter depicts leading intellectual figures of contemporary Berlin in two further portraits, namely Bert Brecht and Egon Erwin Kisch, the so-called "Rushing Reporter". In his portrait of Brecht (illus. p. 36), Schlichter has adopted the undoubtedly vain writer's self-projection of noble proletarianism – yet Brecht's suppressed smile signals at the same time a certain self-mockery and a distancing from the image that he presents. The abstract outlines of bodywork fragments in the background refer to Brecht's passion for fast cars. Kisch (illus. p. 32), a reporter admired and feared for his harshness in criticizing social conditions, is depicted in front of the sign of the well-known Romanisches Café, a meeting-place for artists and literati. Concentrated and seemingly about to leave for some appointment, his gaze is directed towards a point behind the observer. The captions on the advertising column refer to various phases in Kisch's life. The picture is disappointing, not only from a formal point of view but also with respect to its content: the purely illustrative conception of the portrait's subject and the background, together with the idea of visually combining a person and his life in one work, suggest that the painter was experiencing an artistic and intellectual crisis.

Schlichter was also undergoing problems of identity in the political sphere. A member of the German Communist Party and left-wing artistic groupings in the 1920s, he joined the right-wing nationalist Ernst-Jünger-Kreis in 1930 for a short period. He describes the process in a further autobiographical account, not without a certain self-defensiveness: "The basic substance of his life, which had remained unchanged, violently broke through the hard crust of Marxist dogmas, the artificial wall of intellectualist constructs."[17] Soon afterwards, Schlichter converted to Catholicism, thereafter remaining in touch with Catholic intellectuals, and also with the anti-Nazi circle centred around the magazine "Hochland" during the Third Reich. The left-wing "Weltbühne" sarcastically ridiculed the "rejoicing in Heaven over a convert from Neue Sachlichkeit".[18] Such individual reorientations reflect the altered political climate at the beginning of the 1930s.

Schlichter left Berlin in 1932, moving back to Württemberg. Admittedly a purely superficial examination of the studies of nature which he produced

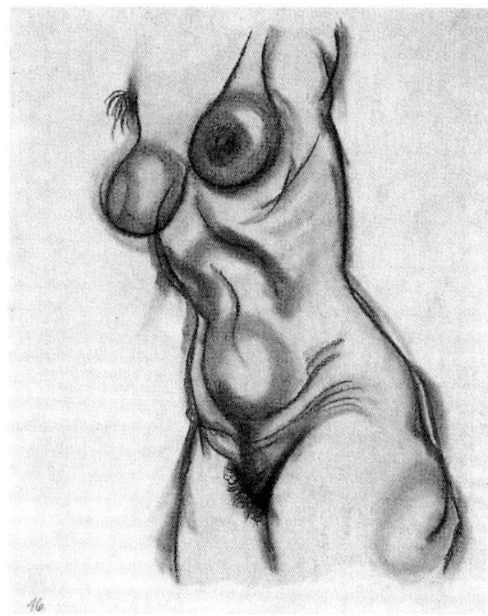

George Grosz
Nude Torso, 1916
Halbakt
Watercolour and carpenter's pencil,
32.3 x 26.6 cm
Private collection

"Man stands alone, with no possibility of establishing contact with his own neighbour: no bridge exists to connect one individual with another; even that of the sexual instinct is a fictitious bond: it is impossible for man and woman to fuse and overcome the metaphysical enmity which separates them ... "
Walter Serner, 1915/16

Christian Schad
Self-Portrait with Model, 1927
Selbstbildnis mit Modell
Oil on wood, 76 x 71.5 cm
Private collection

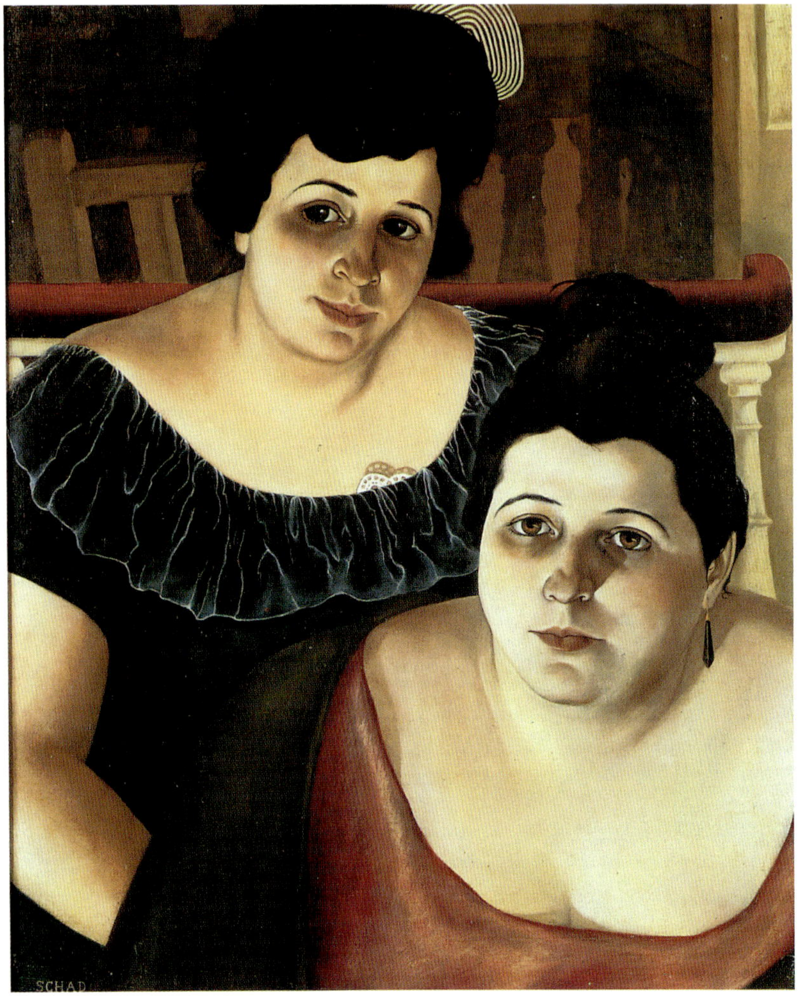

Schad painted his impressive Neue Sachlichkeit portraits between 1923 and 1930. Compared with Maria and Annunziata, the two Neapolitan women, Sonja from Berlin appears chic. Her few attributes and fashionable short hairstyle characterize her as a typical modern female figure on the nighttime stage of the city.

Christian Schad
Maria and Annunziata from the Harbour, 1923
Maria und Annunziata vom Hafen
Oil on canvas, 67.5 x 55.5 cm
Lugano, Thyssen-Bornemisza Collection

there could suggest that the artist had become transformed into a painter of regional idylls. (He considered the people of Württemberg to be "the most revolting specimens possible of Germans".) Schlichter kept a critical distance between himself and the National Socialists. His painting *Blind Power* of 1937, an allegory of destruction in a mixture of Old-Master and Surrealist styles, led to a stern reprimand from the Reichskulturkammer (the authority responsible for culture under the National Socialists). This impressive picture marks Schlichter's transition from Neue Sachlichkeit to Surrealism, the latter characterizing the artist's later – and less significant – work.

Christian Schad

Schad's artistic career began with his working his way through contemporary art movements and trends: his works from 1915 and 1916 reveal Cubist and Futurist traits, while Expressionist influences make themselves visible from 1917 onwards. The pacifist artist rode out the world war in Switzerland, in intellectual and artistic avant-garde circles. Schad had moved from Munich in 1915, initially to Zurich and then on to Geneva, the two centres of Dada

Christian Schad
Sonja, 1928
Oil on canvas, 90 x 60 cm
Private collection

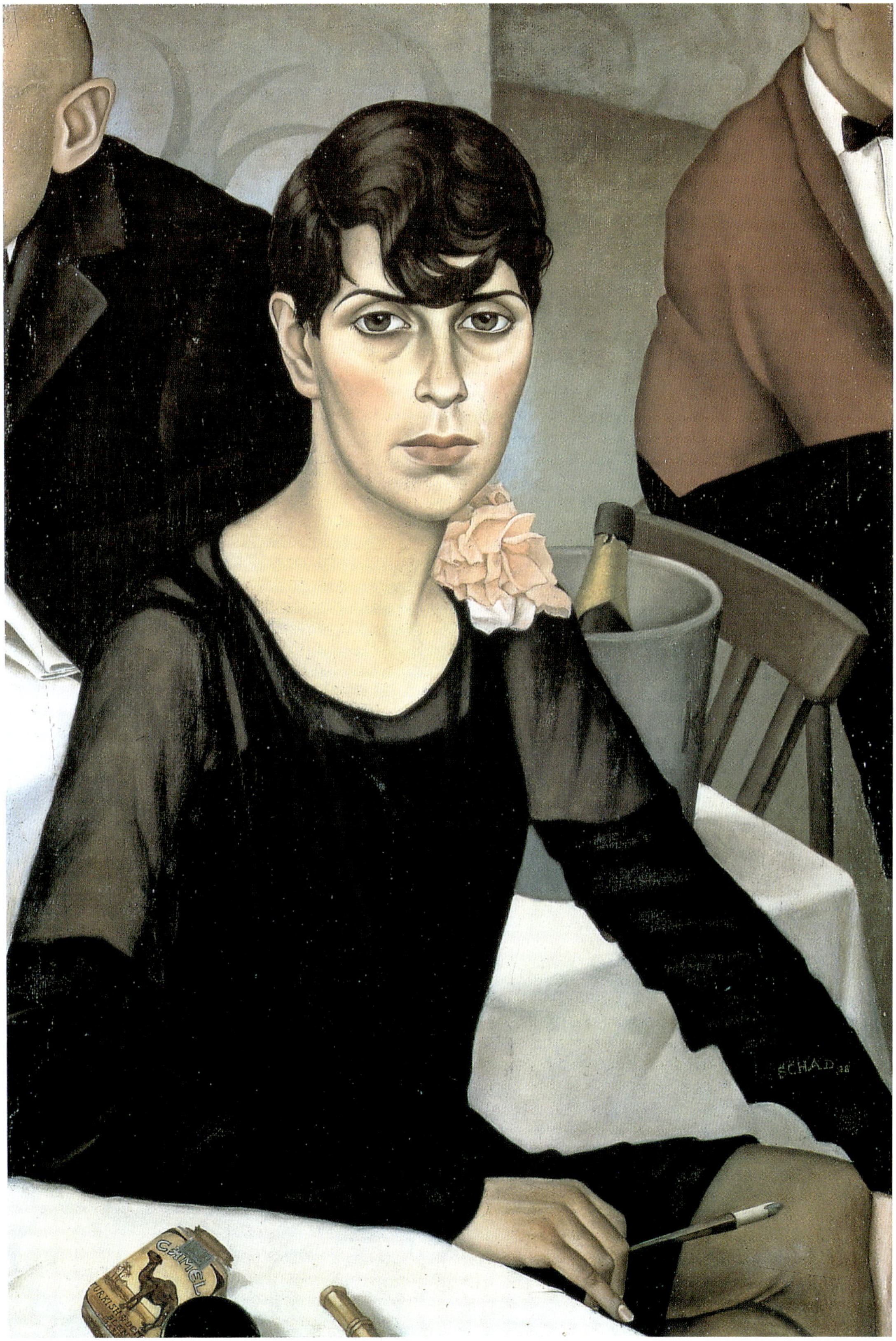
SCHAD

in Switzerland. In 1917, Schad himself became a Dadaist and also the close comrade-in-arms of Walter Serner, the eccentric Dada writer, with whom he had been friends since 1915. The artistic fruits of this period were to be seen principally in his "photography without a camera" (the so-called Schadographs), which he had discovered while experimenting with "objets trouvés", along with some Dadaist wood reliefs. Serner and Schad, together with Tristan Tzara, Alexander Archipenko and others, also provoked Geneva's conservative citizens. The duo never missed a single one of the numerous tumultuous Dadaist functions and balls. The opening in February 1920 of an exhibition of Schad's pictures in a Geneva gallery ended in a particularly spectacular incident: after Serner had overtaxed the audience with an interminable speech and a suddenly executed tango, the enraged guests tore Schad's pictures from the walls and trampled them to pieces.

Serner, the leader of the Geneva Dadaists, embodies the extremely individualistic Dadaist type of artist. He represents a particularly fine example of the provocative, calculatedly irrationalist attitude displayed by a Dadaist actionist. His favoured "stylistic means is the satirizing of social events in direct contact with the members of 'high society', poking fun at their decadence by letting them enjoy the perversions of etiquette with lascivious horror – a precursor of the Happening. He does this by making use of slapstick effects, gags and tricks, all with the distanced, superior gestures of a first-class salon conjurer. Serner is a master of skilfully calculated provocation. His misanthropy, as with the other Dadaists the traumatic result of bourgeois self-hatred, has become intensified in his case into an idiosyncrasy towards his social environment."[19]

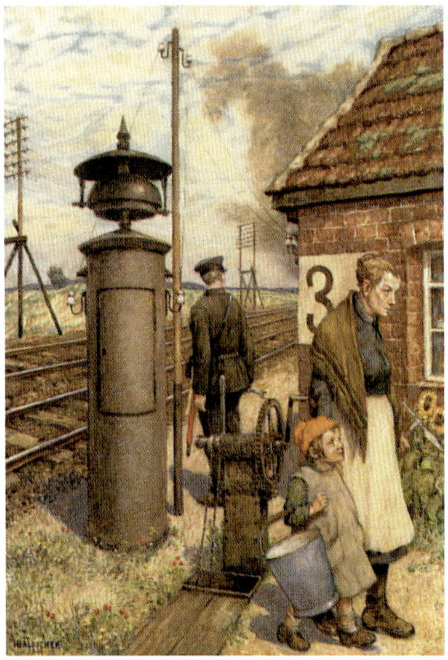

Hans Baluschek
By the Railway Track, 1932
An der Bahnstrecke
Tempera, oil crayons on card,
98 x 68.3 cm
Berlin, Bröhan Museum

Provocation as an artistic principle exhausted itself with time, an experience shared by many among the Dadaist artists at the beginning of the 1920s. Schad cast off actionist Dadaism in favour of a chic observer pose, without abandoning Dadaism's individualist ideas. From 1920 to 1925, he lived for the most part in Italy, for a while together with Serner. Preferring the unusual, they selected Naples – run-down and seldom visited by artists and writers – as the their principal place of residence. Schad's style underwent a change during his period in Italy. He painted scenes from cafés and the theatre, gipsy children and ordinary girls with realistic intensity; a few firmly placed lines came together in his drawings to form impressive heads. A short stay in Germany brought Schad together again with Georg Schrimpf, whom he had known since his time as a student in Munich. The latter's artistic output had come under strong Italian influence. There can be no doubt that the encounter with Schrimpf was not without influence on Schad's moving closer to the stylistic forms of Neue Sachlichkeit. Certain echoes of Schrimpf's type of figure may be detected in *Maria and Annunziata from the Harbour* (illus. p. 42), a very early work in the Neue Sachlichkeit style; however, it abstains from every one of Schrimpf's Classicist elements. Schad later maintained that he had had no knowledge of the artistic circle grouped around the magazine "Valori plastici" while living in Italy, something that seems amazing when one studies his works from this period. In 1925, the former bane of the bourgeoisie painted a portrait of Pope Pius XI, a subdued work full of respect. Schad lived in Vienna for the following two years; then came his period of greatest artistic productivity, in Berlin.

From 1928 onwards, no trace was to be found of his friend Serner. He was regarded as missing for some considerable period, resulting in rumours that he had supposedly gone underground. We know in the meantime that Serner retired into anonymity, worked in Prague as a teacher, married there – and fell victim to the Nazis in 1942.

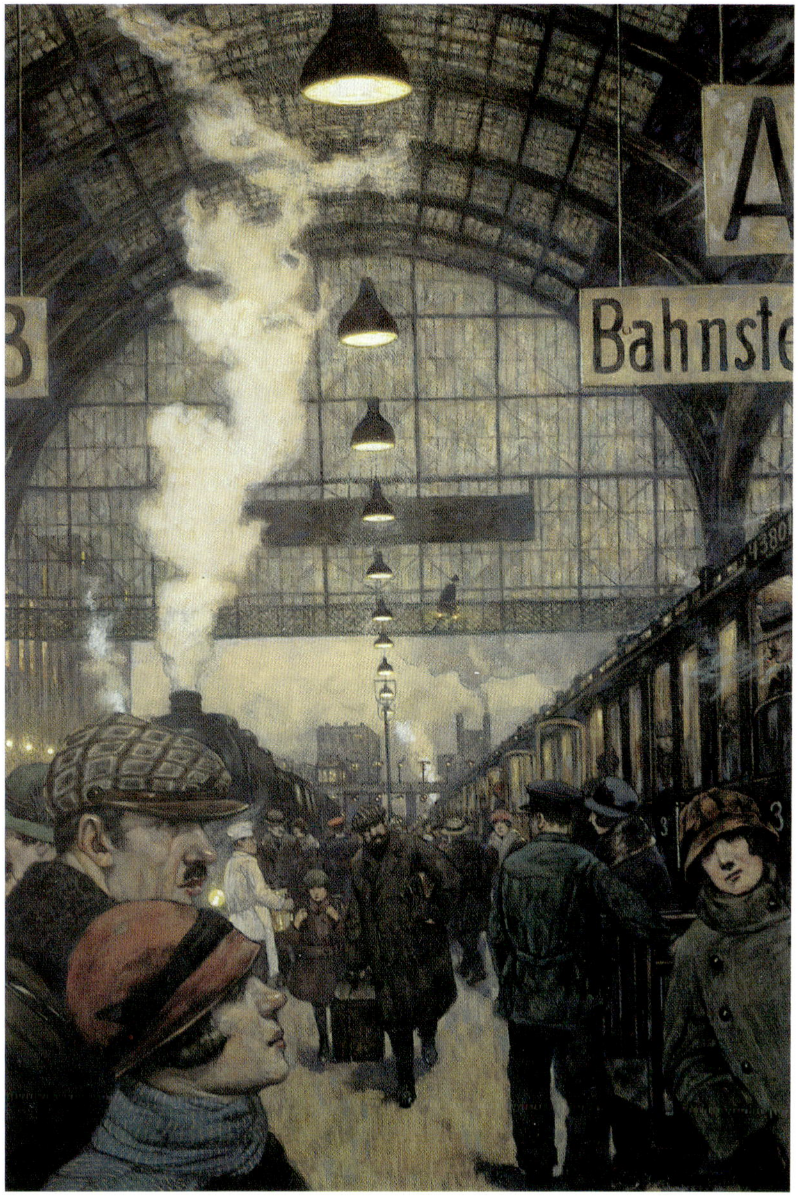

Hans Baluschek
Station Concourse (Lehrter Station), 1929
Bahnhofshalle (Lehrter Bahnhof)
Watercolour and gouache on paper and cardboard, 99 x 70 cm
Berlin, Berlinische Galerie

"The order which I maintain in my thinking apparatus made it possible for me not to pass by the machine in an unappreciative manner... In addition, it strikes me as a positive beauty – and I too become positive in depicting it."

Hans Baluschek

Schad was already painting in the style of Neue Sachlichkeit towards the end of his period in Italy, having discovered in this style his own form of the realistic manner of painting that he so admired in the works of Raphael. In his famous *Self-portrait* of 1927 (illus. p. 40), one of the best-known examples of Neue Sachlichkeit, Schad presents himself in provocative self-stylization as the cold lover, radiating post-coital disillusionment. The fine, transparent shirt indicates that his devotion is limited, that the relationship between the two is no more than "skin-deep" as far as he is concerned. The woman with the attribute-like scar inflicted by another in a fit of jealousy is portrayed as an object. She may have been the object of his desire prior to their encounter; now, however, seen in the harsh light, she appears ugly and without appeal. The picture is distinguished by the Old-Master nature of the smoothness with which the paint has been applied,

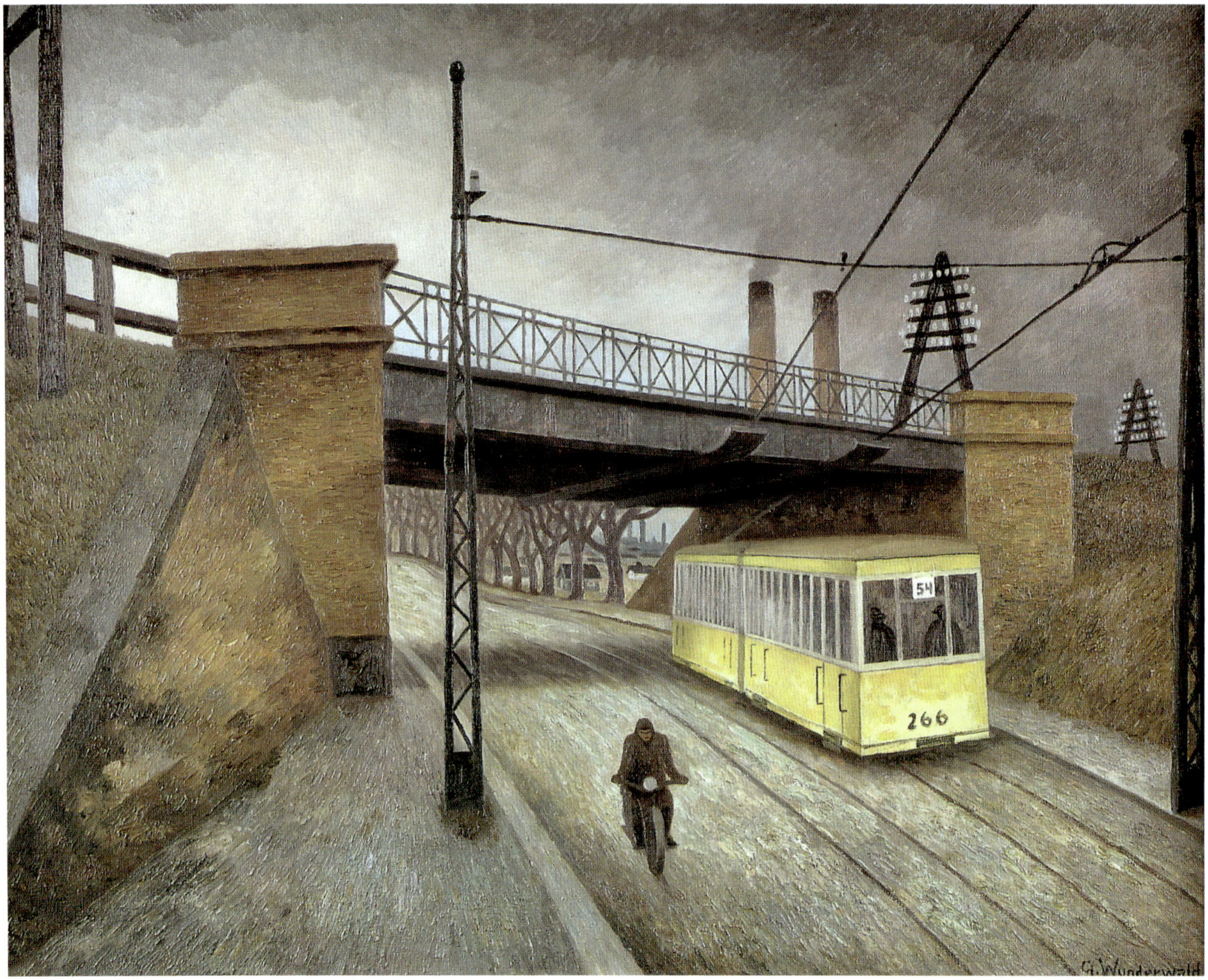

Gustav Wunderwald
Underpass in Spandau, c. 1927
Unterführung in Spandau
Oil on canvas, 66.3 x 83.7 cm
Milwaukee, Marvin and Janet Fishman Collection

Wunderwald's 1920s urban pictures are sober physiognomical studies of that side of the metropolis which is turned away from glamour. "I am attracted by the most dreary things, which prey on my mind. Moabit and Wedding grip me the most, with their interesting soberness and wretchedness…", Wunderwald wrote in a letter of 1926.

together with the glass-like hardness of the whole. It takes as its central theme the problem of the lovers' loneliness, the problem of narcissism. The narcissus rearing up against the picture's black background provides the cue in symbolic form for the work's interpretation.

In his picture *Two Girlfriends* (illus. p. 25), Schad radicalizes the theme of narcissistic egocentricity. The separation of sex and feelings, and the emotional non-relevance of the partner, leads the individual to address their erotic interest to their own body. Self-gratification in the presence of the not-included partner further heightens the feeling of loneliness. Each of the two masturbating women is totally preoccupied with herself, denying the observer, too, any illusion of involvement.

Nothing was more interesting for Schad than man as an individual. Man as the representative of a class, for example as exploiter or exploited, bears no interest for him. His sociology is that of private and semi-private relationships governed by sexuality, even if the public context sometimes appears to conceal this. Thus in *Count St. Genois d'Anneaucourt* (illus. p. 14), Schad depicts an elegantly dressed, distinguished roué between a transvestite and a woman, the latter looking over her male rival for the Count's favour with unconcealed enmity. The transvestite is returning her gaze, with the hint of a sympathetic smile; clearly, he is more certain of his sexual attraction for the Count than she. Schad succeeds in this picture in compressing the erotic ambivalence of the situation, founded in the Count's latent homosexuality, into a minidrama of frozen passions.

Schad knew his way around the Berlin establishments; it was here that he encountered some of the subjects for his portraits, whom he transferred in his pictures into the typical surroundings for the person in question. A strange conflict may be observed again and again between the sociable, social aspect of the portraits' subjects – suggested in the pictures by the respective location – and the sense of their being alone or content with their own company. If we look at the female portraits of *Sonja* (illus. p. 43) and *Lotte*, it appears that coolness, the conscious quality of refusing to be impressed by others as a means of expressing one's own strength of character and personality, was already extremely popular in 1920s Berlin. Schad's portraits express much of the modern liberal-libertarian spirit of the age, of the awareness of life of people who really began to live – whose interesting life started – only with the onset of night. The following poem, by the Berlin poet Max Kolpe[20], likewise deals with this aspect:

Feelings in neutral

You talk to each other – just met for the first time.
You fix a rendezvous for the following day.
You pass up the first one, and the second, so as to go
straight to bed with the third.
She doesn't spend much time asking why.

You go to bed. Well, what else is there to do...?
You don't know each other – that's interesting.
You keep on formal terms, but also use other formulations...
You think of your parents, too, and have to laugh:
They still love each other. Amazing!

You went to bed. Well, that doesn't mean anything.
The next day, you're two strangers again.
You greet each other as you would anyone else.

Oskar Nerlinger
To Work, 1929
An die Arbeit
Casein tempera, 120 x 80 cm
Halle, Staatliche Galerie Moritzburg

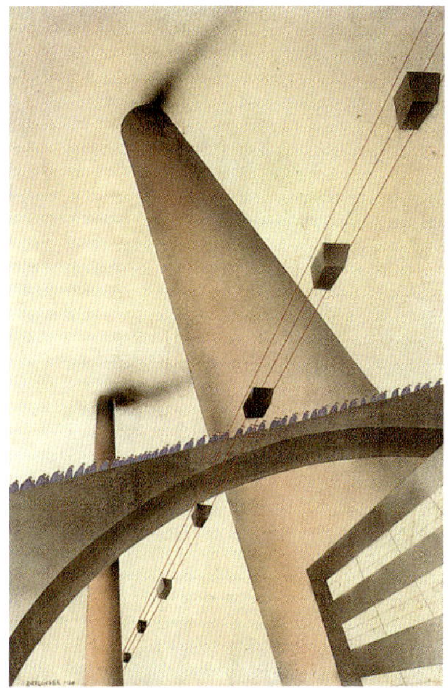

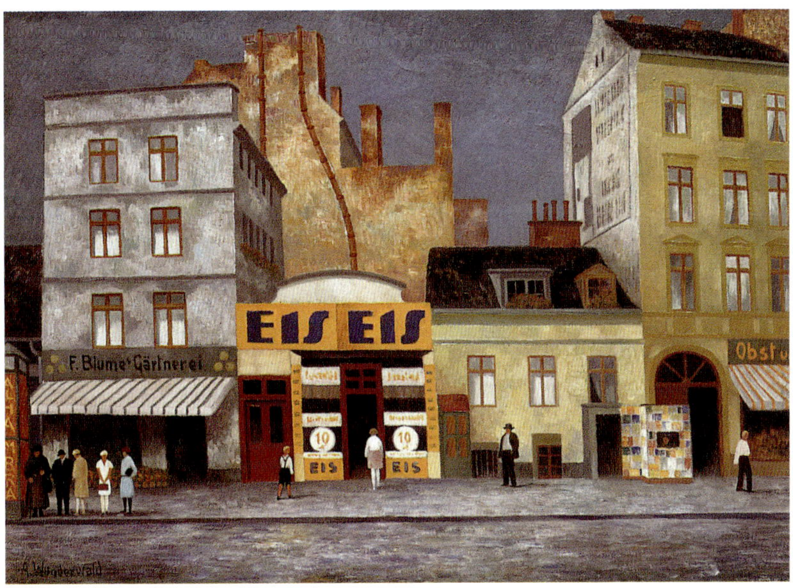

Gustav Wunderwald
Corner, Müllerstraße-Seestraße, Berlin-Wedding, 1928
Müllerstraße – Ecke Seestraße Berlin-Wedding
Oil on canvas, 60.5 x 85.5 cm
Berlin, Staatliche Museen zu Berlin – Preußischer Kulturbesitz, Nationalgalerie

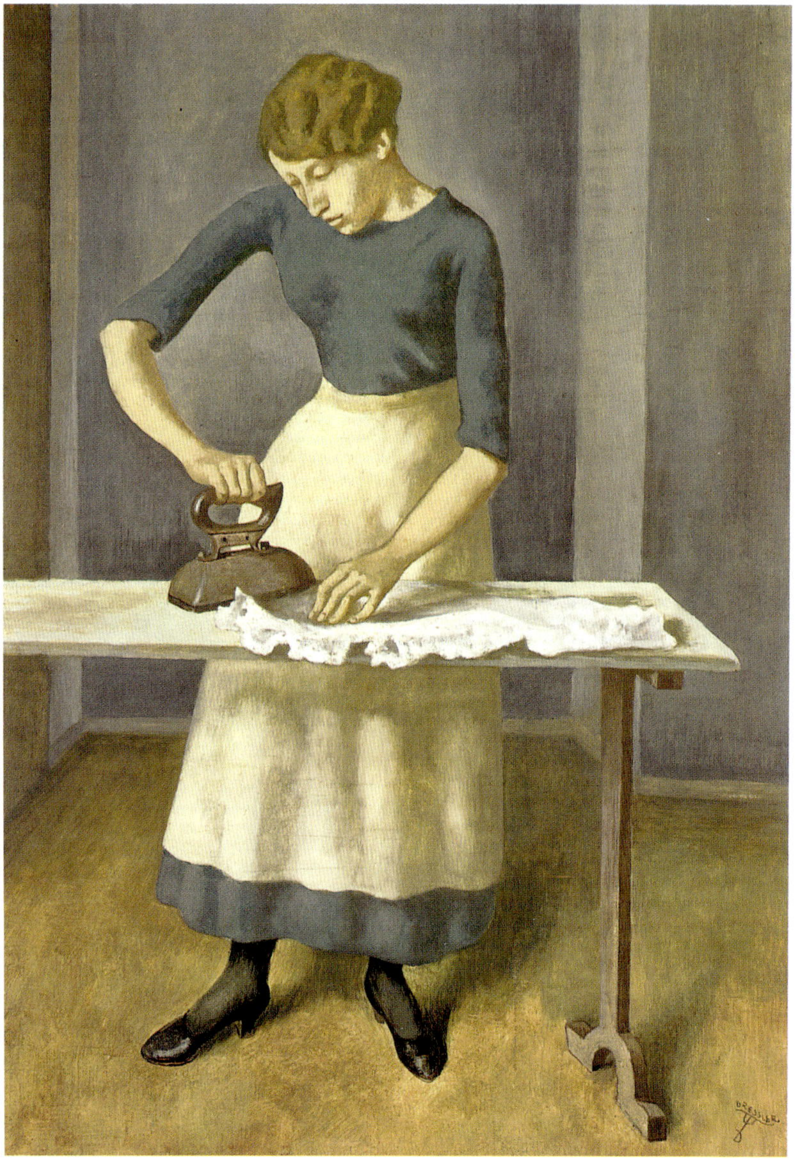

August Wilhelm Dressler
The Ironer, 1923
Die Plätterin
Oil on canvas, 84 x 60 cm
Berlin, Staatliche Museen zu Berlin – Preußischer Kulturbesitz, Nationalgalerie

You meet, the same way that you would any girl.
You kept your options open. And you're footloose and fancy-free.

You talk to each other – just met for the first time.
You hope – in vain – that this time it'll be different.
You let love take whatever course it will, your heart's not really involved.
If you had to chose, you'd jump into the water now...
But you go dancing. And it's impossible to understand
why you are sad whenever you go dancing.[21]

Little is known with regard to the extent to which Schad himself participated in the metropolitan hustle and bustle of late-Twenties Berlin. What is surprising is the abrupt decline in his artistic productivity at the beginning of the 1930s, after the appearance of his illustrations for Curt Morek's

"Guide to 'vice-ridden' Berlin" (1920). Schad was becoming involved with Far Eastern philosophy, which could indicate that his interests were indeed moving in another direction. He was experiencing increased financial problems, and found himself more and more isolated from 1932 onwards. He produced only a handful of works after the National Socialists seized power, with those works that did appear sadly lacking in expressive force when compared with the Neue Sachlichkeit pictures from the late 1920s.

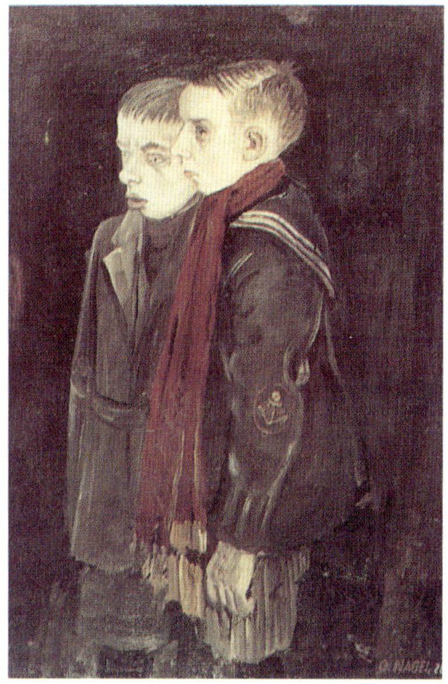

Otto Nagel
Boys from Wedding, 1928
Weddinger Jungen
Oil on canvas, 91 x 62 cm
Berlin, Staatliche Museen zu Berlin – Preußischer Kulturbesitz, Nationalgalerie

Other Berlin Painters

Compared to Grosz, Schlichter and Schad, such painters as Hans Baluschek, Gustav Wunderwald, August Wilhelm Dressler, Otto Nagel and Franz Lenk all make a more restrained impression. The themes depicted in their works are less spectacular; nonetheless, their realistic portrayals of people and urban landscapes have a particular forcefulness.

Hans Baluschek's extensive œuvre embraces scenes of squalor and injustice, portraits of harmonious family life among the lower social strata, depictions of bustling city life, and – above all – industry. The son of a railway engineer, he was one of the first to discover the "positive beauty" of technology. "Over and over again he painted trains, stations, factory sites and buildings, scaffolding, bridges, dams, sets of signals; the result is an unemotional reproduction of places of technology, in which man lives in reconciled companionship with factory and machine."[22] From the iconographical point of view, Baluschek's pictures have much in common with Neue Sachlichkeit, yet their composition and figural representation still look back to French late Impressionism.

Gustav Wunderwald's passion was reserved for the cityscape. Paul Westheim named him the "Berlin Utrillo";[23] one year older than Utrillo, Wunderwald would of course never achieve the popularity of his French counterpart. Essentially, he remained the retiring, solitary "wanderer" that he had been for ten years in Berlin. When he was on one of his walks through the city, it was the dreary things and areas that had a particular appeal for him, everyday Berlin life away from the city centre, escaping attention through

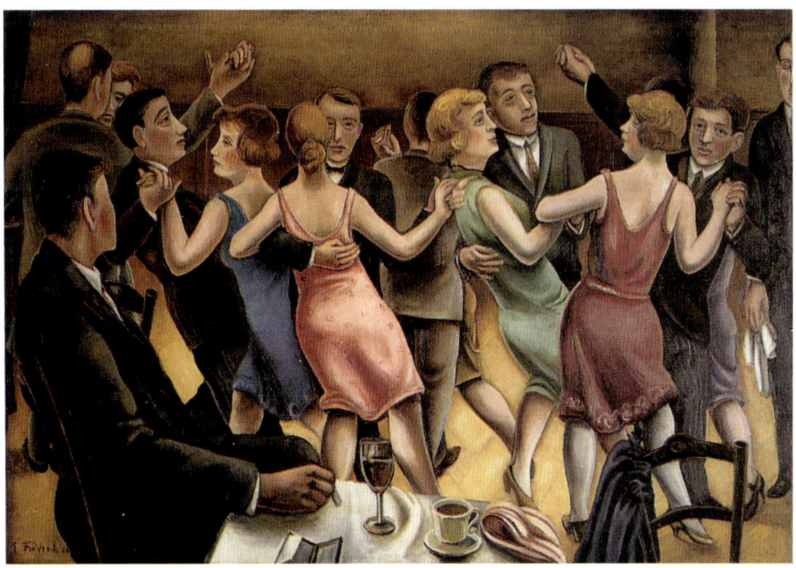

Ernst Fritsch
Jeunesse dorée, 1926
Oil on canvas, 103 x 148 cm
Private collection

The men and women depicted here evidently do not belong to the refined echelons of Berlin society: the dancers lack elegance and their dress any fashionable finesse. The ambience of the establishment also calls to mind the dullness of suburbia, rather than the sparkle of the metropolis.

its common banality. In Wunderwald's picture *Underpass in Spandau* (illus. p. 46) – as in the majority of his urban landscapes – man recedes completely behind his creations within civilization. He appears but fleetingly – as a passer-by or, as in this picture, as a road-user. After all, a railway underpass is hardly a place where one would wish to linger, but is rather a functional construction, its purpose to enable movement in different directions at one point. This place, one which the observer is customarily aware of merely in passing – and thus only fleetingly – is for Wunderwald the ideal place in which to pause, so as to safeguard it from being forgotten.

Franz Lenk, who studied at the Dresden Academy, began from 1922 onwards to shape his Neue Sachlichkeit style. During the following decade, he was to develop all the themes which would thereafter characterize his work, the classical themes of landscape, still life and portrait. Lenk's painting tended more towards the conservative. In 1926, he moved from Lausa, near Dresden, to Berlin, where exhibition opportunities would regularly

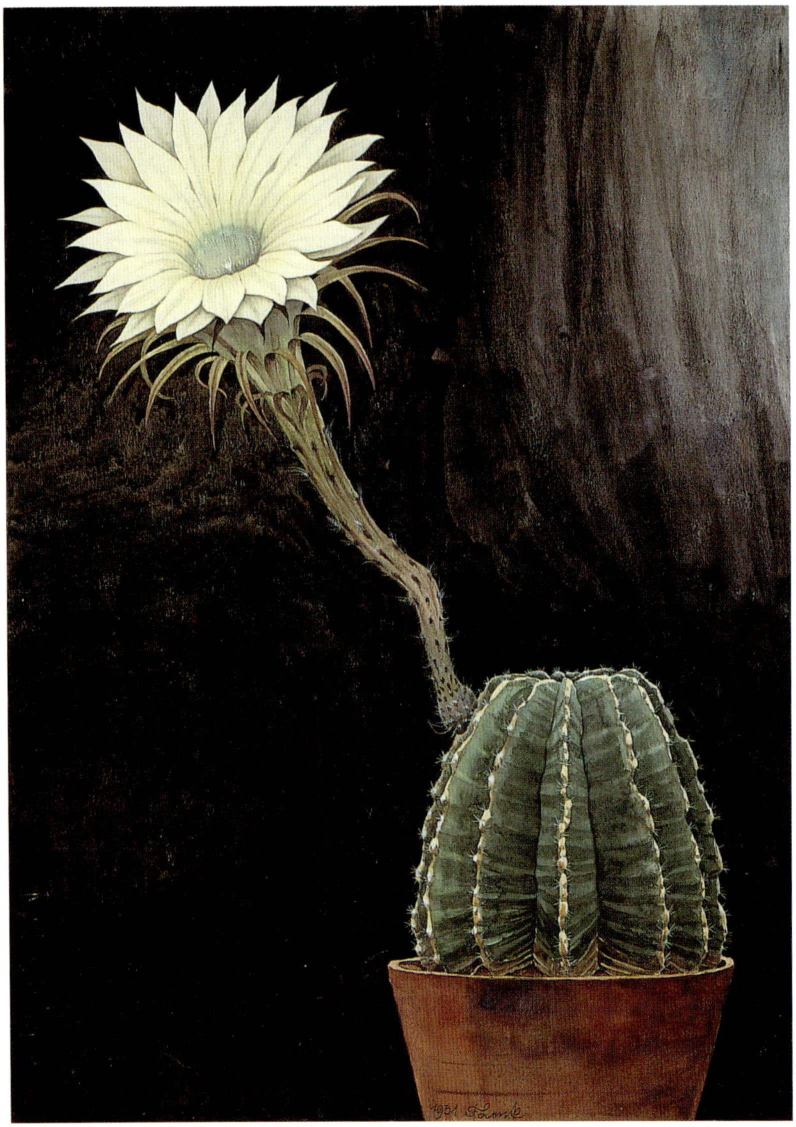

Franz Lenk
Flowering Cactus, 1931
Blühender Kaktus
Watercolour on paper, 40.8 x 29.2 cm
Milwaukee, Marvin and Janet Fishman Collection

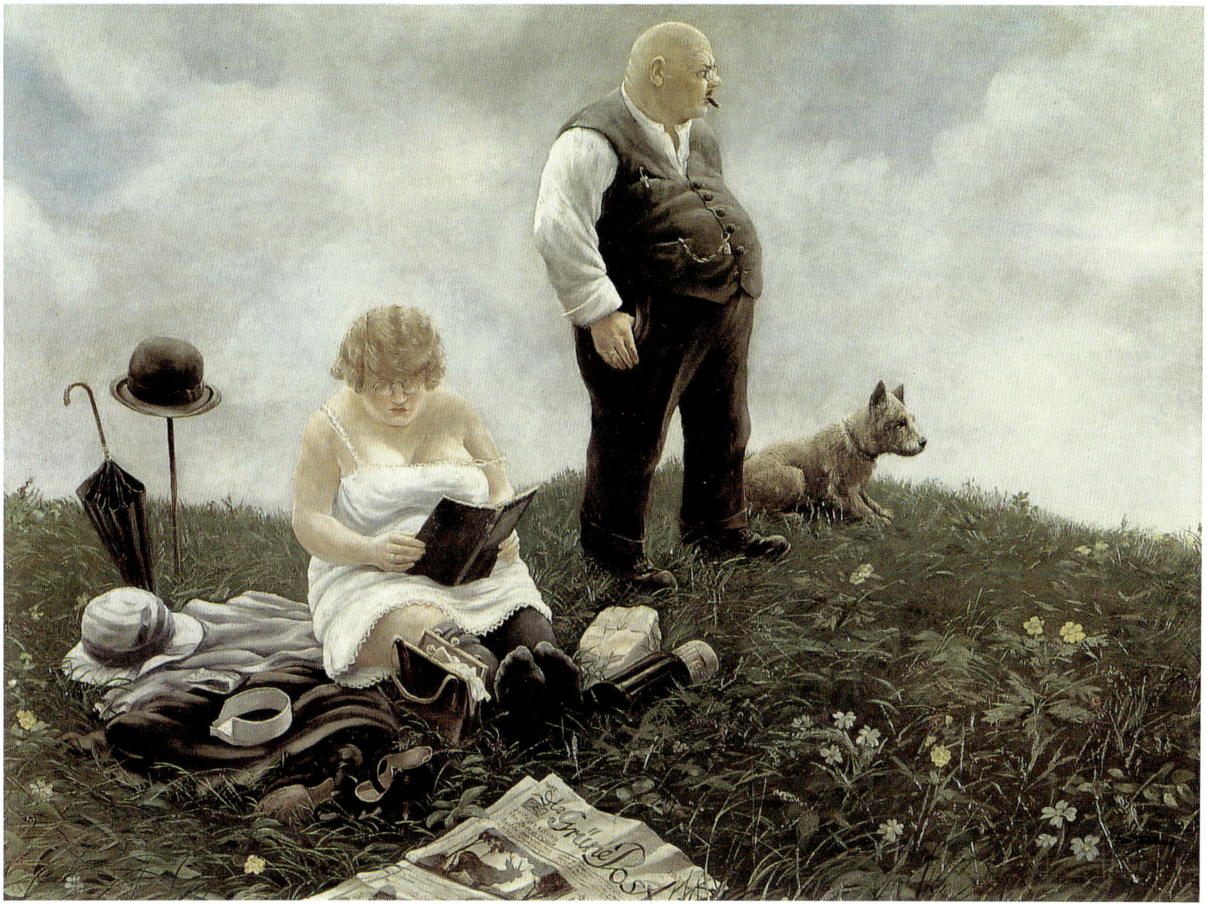

Fred Goldberg
Sunday Afternoon, 1930
Sonntagnachmittag
Oil on plywood, 97.5 x 133.5 cm
Karlsruhe, Staatliche Kunsthalle

come his way in the course of the years that followed. His pictures found a public, and also purchasers, while even the National Socialists were kindly disposed towards his works. However, in 1938, Lenk gave up the professorship of landscape painting which he had taken up in 1933, in protest against the politicizing of art and the persecution of his colleagues: "The total restriction of every artistic freedom, however small, had also served to take away any enjoyment that I had from teaching",[24] he wrote in his workbook in 1940. In her book on Lenk, Susanne Thesing emphasizes that the motif of being confined occurs again and again in Lenk's still-lifes. Of his 1929 *Cellar Still-Life* (illus. p. 163), in which the composition is dominated by an axe lying ready to hand in the middle of the picture, she writes: "The ambivalence of compact objects trying to unfold and powerless, wounded props is staged in front of the backdrop of the cellar dungeon almost as a form of fateful hopelessness."[25] Nostalgic, homely elements also play an important part in Lenk's works; hidden behind them, however, there is often something threatening, as can be seen in the *Flowering Cactus* (illus. p. 50) in front of the dark background, for example. This picture goes together very well with *Sunday Afternoon* (illus. p. 51) by the little-known Fred Goldberg, castigating the petit bourgeois' joy of picnicking. Events after 1933 would demonstrate in a frightening manner how unpleasant the lower middle-class could become if it appeared politically opportune to do so.

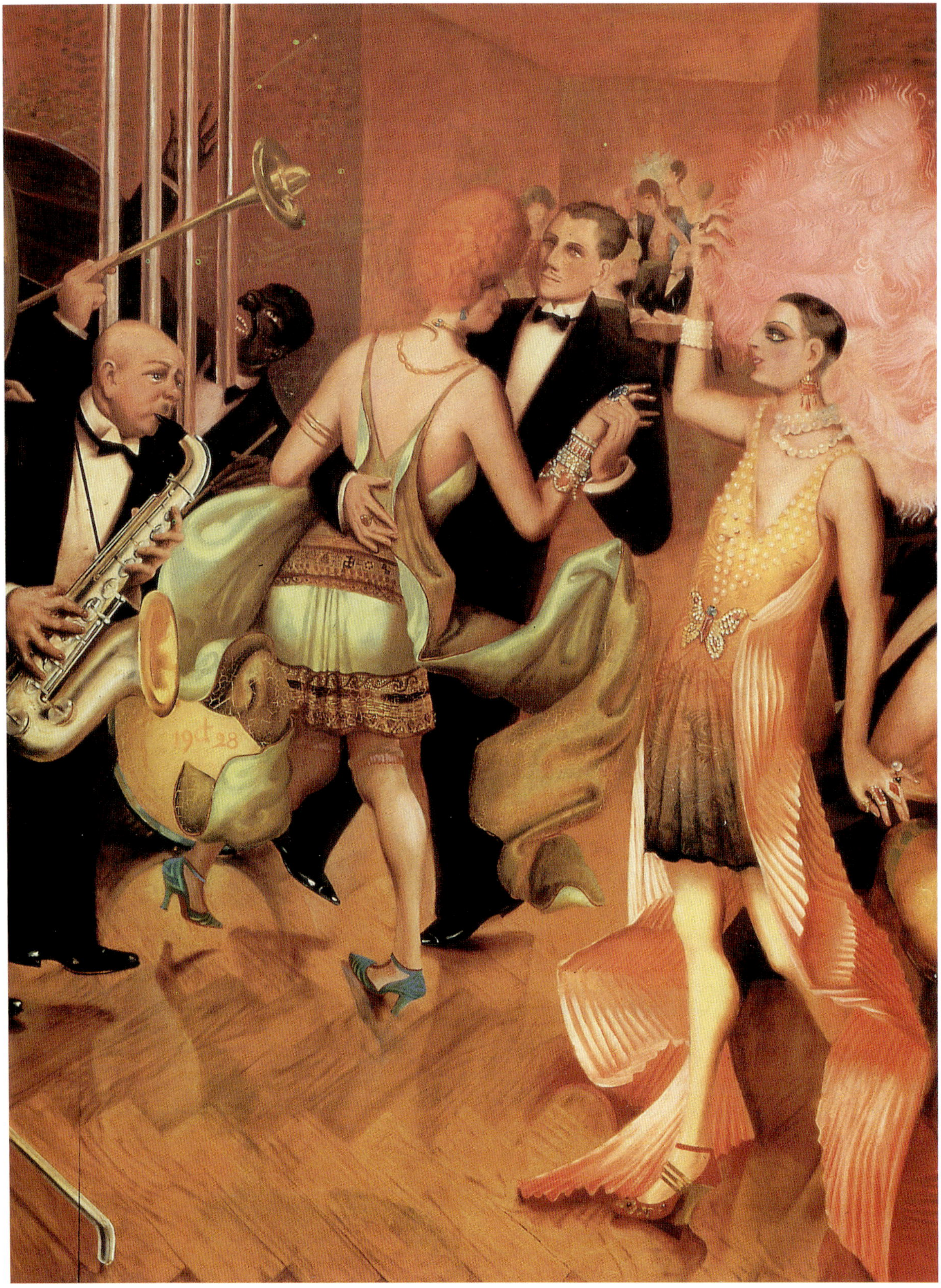

Dresden
Otto Dix and the Proletarian Realists

Otto Dix is one of the central figures of Neue Sachlichkeit; indeed, to many he is Neue Sachlichkeit personified. He always regarded Dresden as his home, even if he spent part of the 1920s working first in Düsseldorf and later in Berlin. He had studied in Dresden since 1909, at the School of Arts and Crafts and the Academy of Art. In 1927, he was given a professorship at the Academy, and left his mark upon the younger generation of painters working in the city.

The works that Dix produced in the 1920s have had a lasting effect upon the picture that we have of this epoch. His interest during this period was focussed solely upon people, in a constant search for personalities who could provide information about their time. The result was a depiction in many individual portraits of metropolitan society during the Twenties. Only in extremely rare instances were his portraits commissioned works, Dix preferring to seek out his models himself in cafés, in the street, and within his circle of friends. Sylvia von Harden, the journalist, recalls how Dix addressed her excitedly in the street: "I must paint you! I simply must! . . . You are representative of an entire epoch!"[26]

Dix depicted Sylvia von Harden (illus. p. 56) as the emancipated Weimar Republic female intellectual per se; Anita Berber (illus. p. 57), the notorious dancer, as the very epitome of the man-slaying vamp; Ivar von Lücken, the poet, as the typical failed artistic character; and Alfred Flechtheim (illus. p. 23), the art dealer, as the inflexible and strong-willed dictator of art. Dix was especially interested in striking personalities from the bohemian world, from his personal circle; however, he also depicted a side of society which many preferred to overlook, namely that of war cripples, depraved proletarian youths, and pregnant working-class women in misery and squalor.

The fundamental element to be found within his portrayals is always a sober observation of things as they really are, attention being paid especially to details: Dix emphasizes particular characteristics and attributes, sometimes exaggerating them in such a way that individuals become types. Yet he also calls clichés into question by rendering people's inner tensions perceptible, for example through the use of psychologically calculated, shrill arrangements of colour.

On looking at Dix' work, one is particularly struck by his emphasis of the ugly side of man. He admitted that his experience of war – he had spent four years in a machine-gun company at the front – had made him aware of this side: "War is so bestial: hunger, lice, mud, those insane

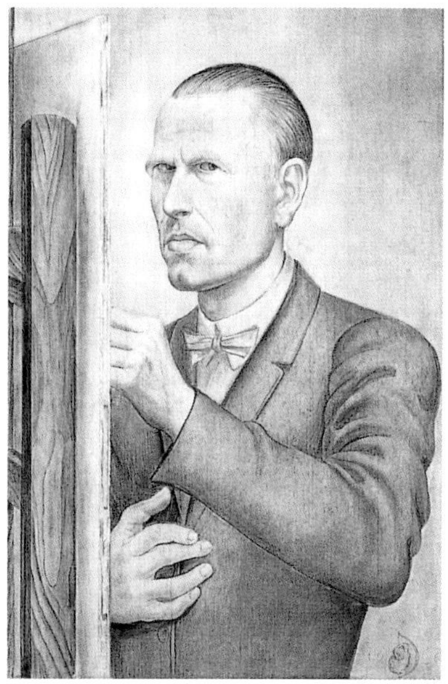

Otto Dix
Self-Portrait with Easel, 1926
Selbstbildnis mit Staffelei
Mixed media on plywood, 80 x 55 cm
Düren, Leopold-Hoesch-Museum

Otto Dix
Metropolis (Triptych), detail from the central panel, 1927/28
Großstadt (Triptychon)
Mixed media on wood, 181 x 200 cm
Stuttgart, Galerie der Stadt Stuttgart

noises ... I had the feeling, on looking at the pictures from my early years, that I had completely missed one side of reality so far, namely the ugly aspect."[27]

Dix' experience of war also served to make him particularly sensitive to the hypocrisy of post-war bourgeois society, a hypocrisy which he recognized as the product of (mental) suppression. People did not want to see the innumerable war cripples lining the streets, not wishing to be reminded of the disastrous years. People dressed up, donned masks, did anything to avoid being themselves, and lost themselves in the temples of pleasure. Dix created a monument to this society in his *Metropolis Triptych* (illus. p. 59), one pushed to extremes through its employment of the sacred form of the triptych. The division of the picture enabled him to set off the pleasure-craving bourgeoisie in the centre against the prostitutes in the side wings. He himself appears, in admonishing manner, as a war cripple in the left wing. One group consciously dresses up so that it may make its intentions clear and serve the process of forgetting; the other dresses up so as to become anything but what it is.

As with others, so also in the case of Dix the turning to Neue Sachlichkeit was motivated by a rejection of Expressionist emotion, something he himself had practised for many years. This rejection manifested itself around 1919, at first in a pronounced Dadaist phase and stylistic variants, beginning with a gentle mocking of Sunday painting (*Sunday Stroll*) and ranging as

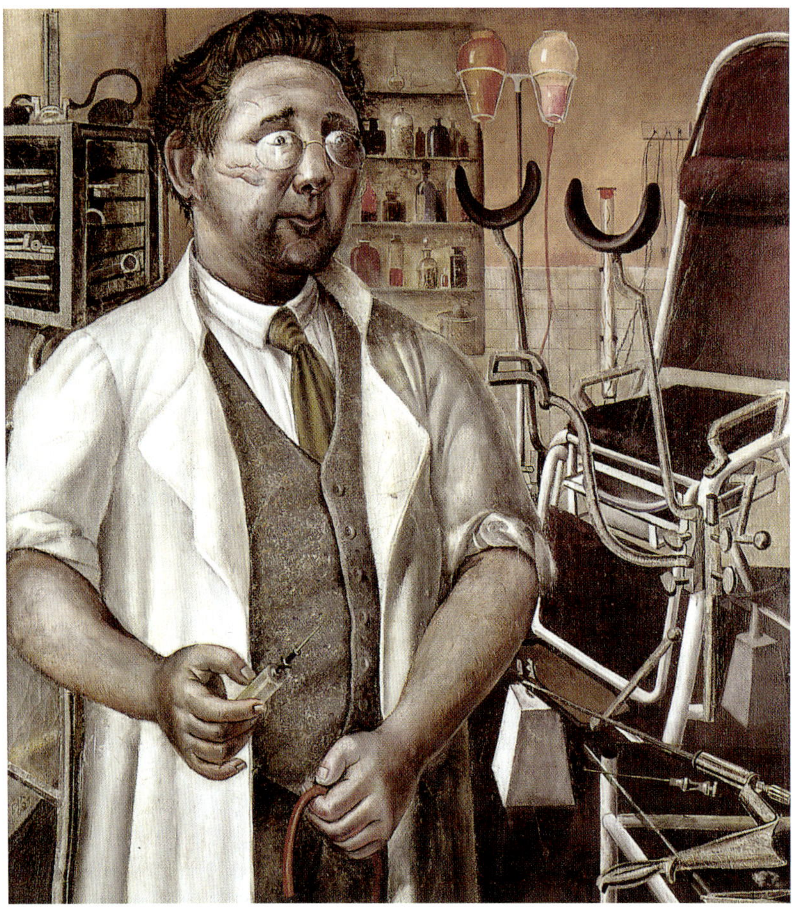

Otto Dix
Dr. Hans Koch, Dermatologist and Urologist, 1921
Der Dermatologe und Urologe Dr. Hans Koch
Oil on canvas, 100.5 x 90 cm
Cologne, Museum Ludwig

ILLUSTRATION PAGE 55:
Otto Dix
To Beauty, 1922
An die Schönheit
Oil on canvas, 139.5 x 120.5 cm
Wuppertal, Von der Heydt-Museum

The telephone in the hand of the central figure, a self-portrait of the artist, indicates that he sees himself as a reporter, communicating facts, completely devoted to the objects and events of reality. However, an examination of the picture reveals that this Realist credo is not to be taken entirely seriously.

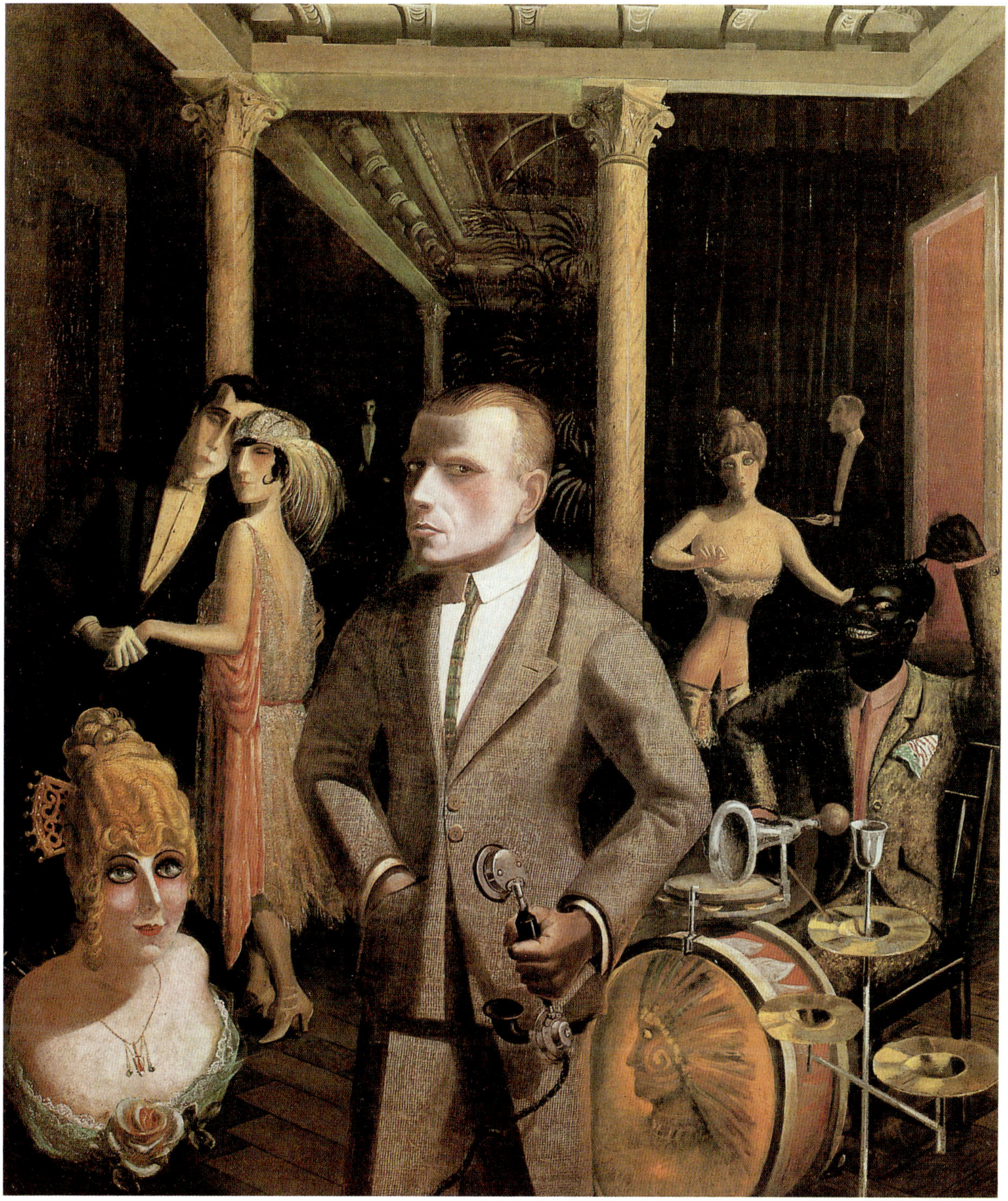

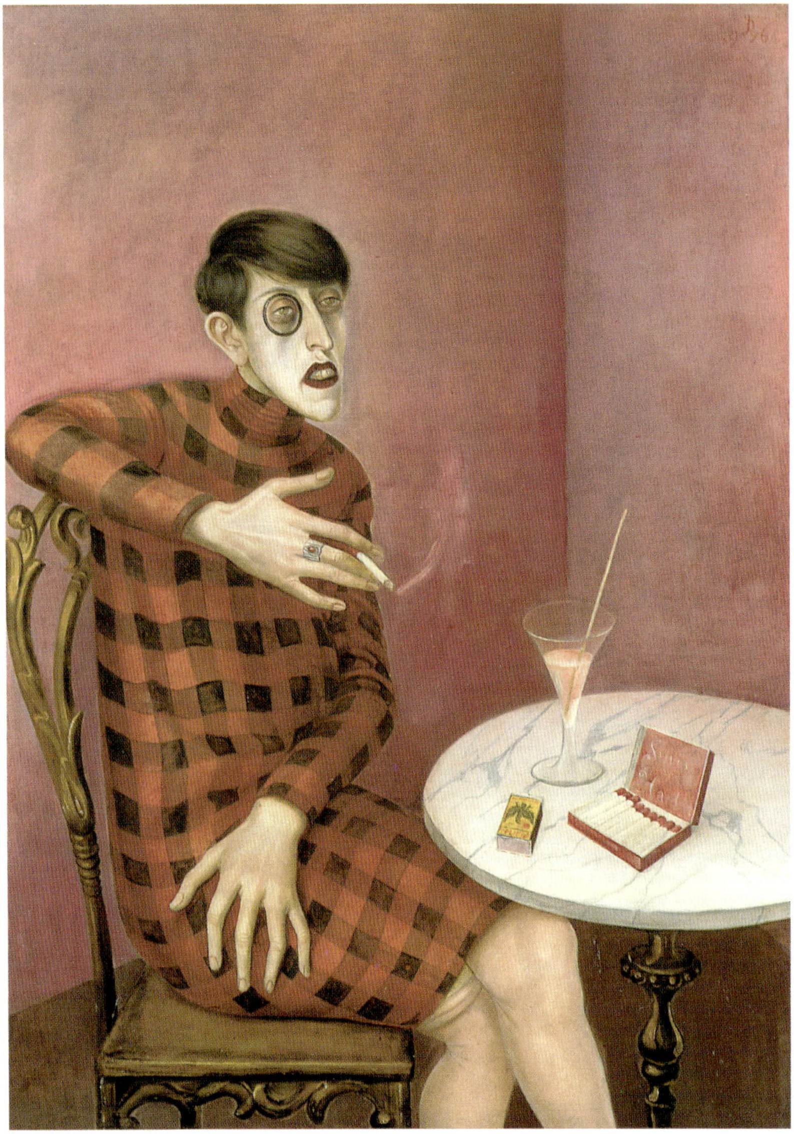

Otto Dix
Portrait of the Journalist Sylvia von Harden, 1926
Bildnis der Journalistin Sylvia von Harden
Mixed media on wood, 120 x 88 cm
Paris, Musée National d'Art Moderne, Centre Georges Pompidou

far as a folksy, naive proto-Surrealism (*God of the Hairdressers*). This was followed by a phase of painting in shades of grey: "To a certain extent . . . it was a contradiction of the Expressionists' colossal colourfulness . . . I said to myself: Things actually aren't as colourful as all that. Everything is much darker, the shades of colour much quieter, much simpler. In short, I wanted to show things as they really are."[28]

Dix developed his Neue Sachlichkeit style somewhere around 1920. An early example may be seen in the portrait of *Dr. Hans Koch, Dermatologist and Urologist* (illus. p. 54), who, incidentally, was also the first husband of the artist's wife. It is an instance of the Neue Sachlichkeit professional portrait, showing the subject of the picture surrounded by attributes such as provide information concerning his profession. Hans Koch was a dermatologist and urologist, as indicated by the numerous utensils in the picture. These are given almost the same status within the portrait as the

Dix addressed Sylvia von Harden on the street: "I must paint you! I simply must! . . . You are representative of an entire epoch!"

"So, you want to paint my lacklustre eyes, my ornate ears, my long nose, my thin lips; you want to paint my long hands, my short legs, my big feet – things which can only scare people off and delight no-one?"

"You have brilliantly characterized yourself, and all that will lead to a portrait representative of an epoch concerned not with the outward beauty of a woman but rather with her psychological condition."

Sylvia von Harden, Erinnerungen an Otto Dix

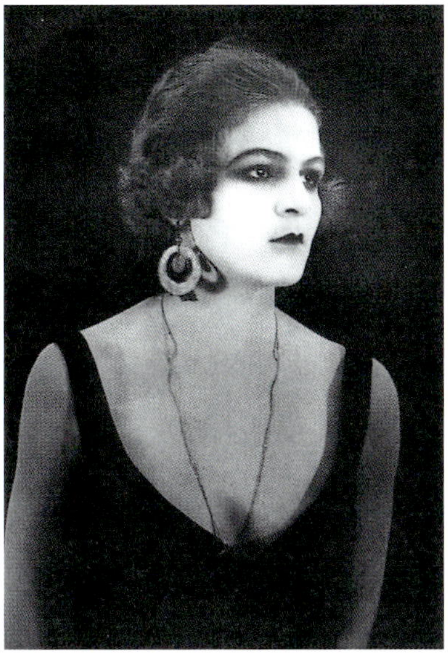

Anita Berber, 1920
Berlin, Archiv Lothar Fischer

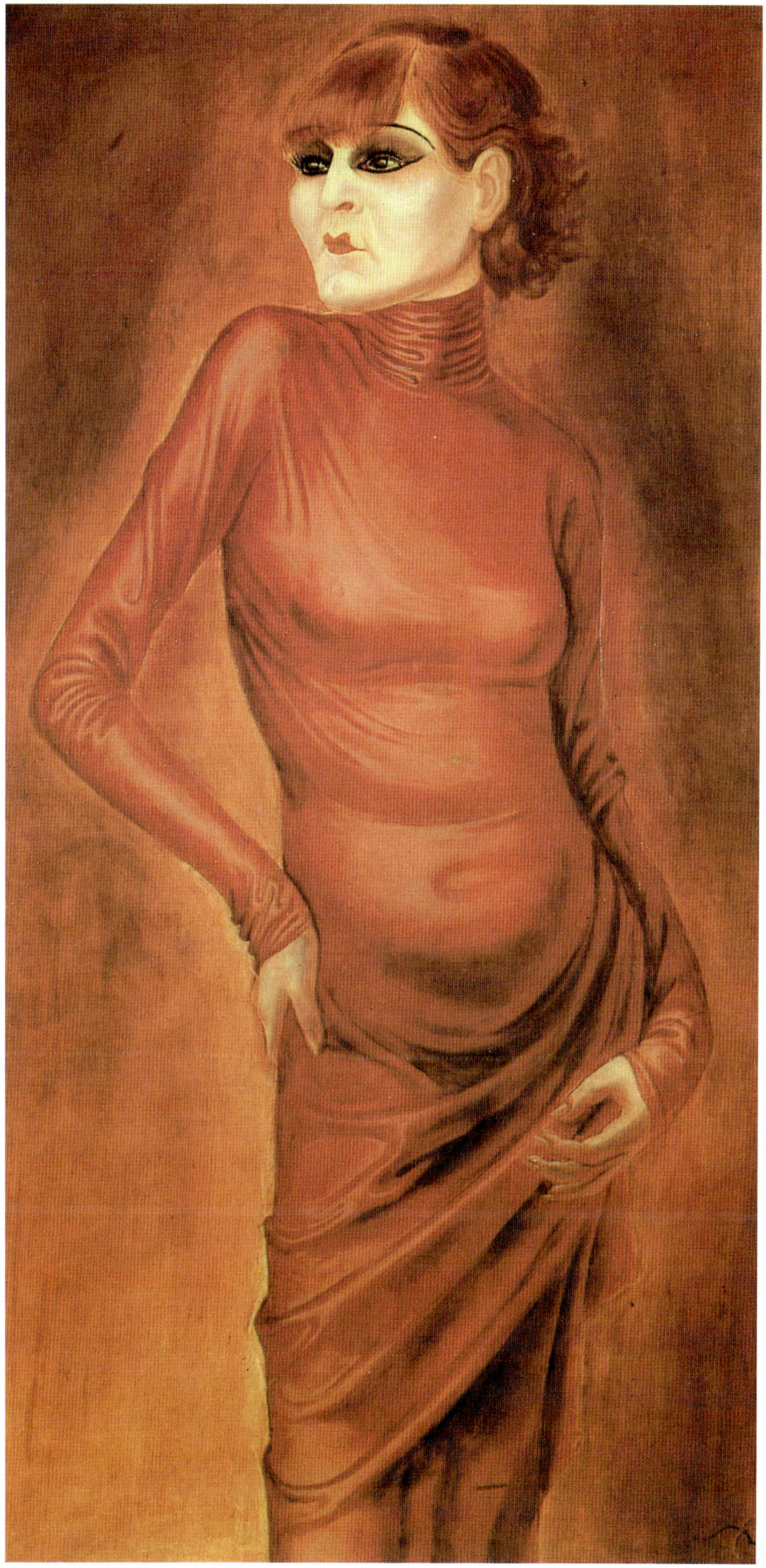

Otto Dix
Portrait of the Dancer Anita Berber, 1925
Bildnis der Tänzerin Anita Berber
Tempera on plywood, 120 x 65 cm
Stuttgart, Galerie der Stadt Stuttgart

Anita Berber, actress, nude dancer, and queen of Berlin's bohemian world, was a representative of her times of the kind for which Dix was constantly on the lookout for his portraits. She was as popular in early-1920s Berlin as Marlene Dietrich; unlike the latter, however, she died young (1928), after an ecstatic life of excess.

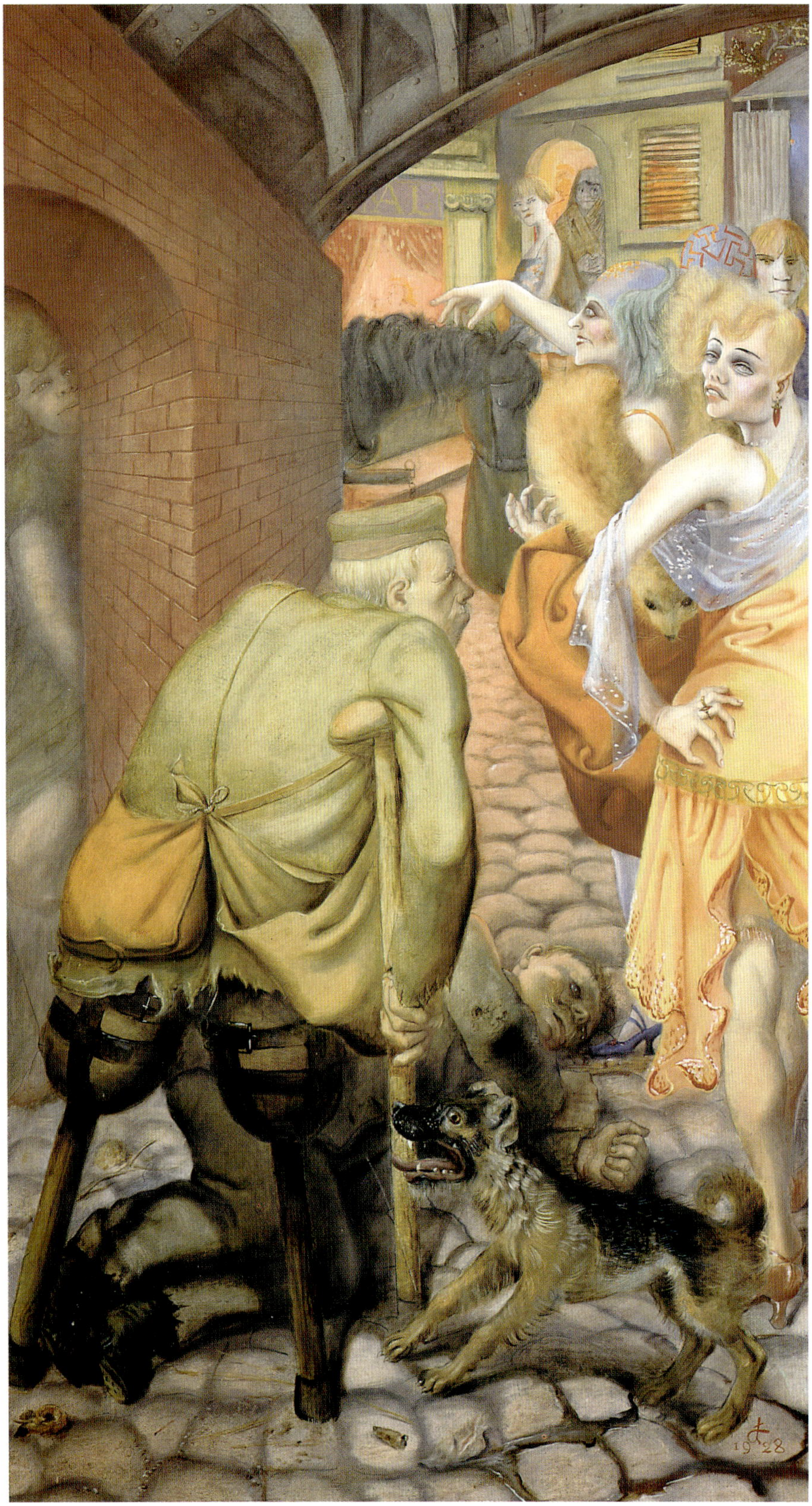

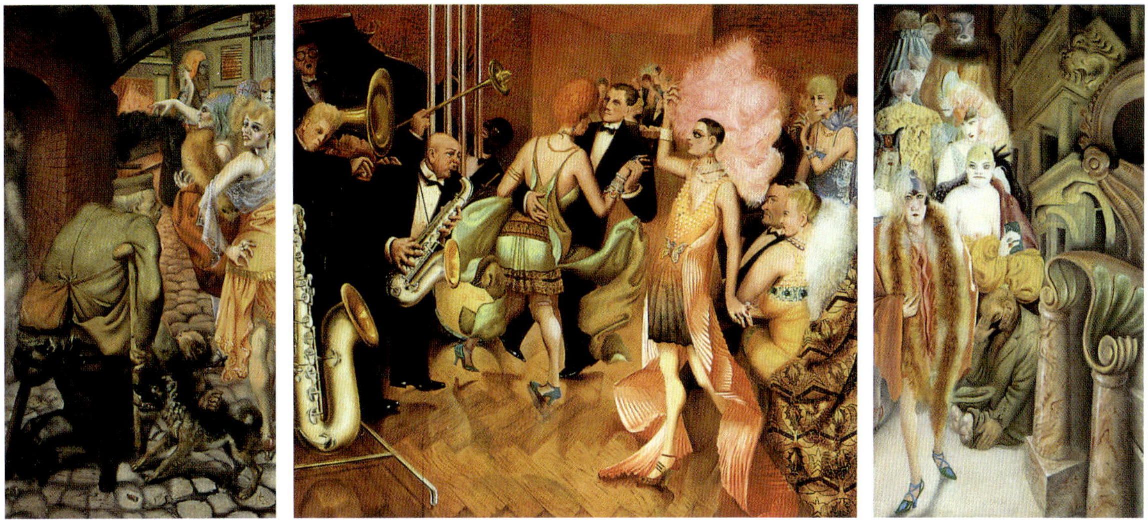

Otto Dix
Metropolis (Triptych), overall view, 1927/28
Großstadt (Triptychon)
Mixed media on wood, l. and r. panels 181 x 101 cm, central panel 181 x 200 cm
Stuttgart, Galerie der Stadt Stuttgart

The pleasure-addicted bourgeois society was among its own in the restaurants and dance bars. When its members went home at night along the streets, however, they were reminded by the cripples and beggars – beings living on the borderline of existence – of the horrors of war. These human wrecks expose the bourgeois pleasures as productions of the attempt to forget.

person himself. In later portraits, Dix was to concentrate upon fewer informative details and characteristics.

In 1924, Dix turned to the Old-Master technique of applying transparent layers of colour, something that would become characteristic of many Neue Sachlichkeit artists. Dix even painted on wood, a base that had fallen out of custom some centuries before. It offered him a smoother and flatter foundation upon which to build up his composition, using a succession of fine layers of paint to achieve the high glaze of the Old Masters; it was for this reason that he was also given the nickname "Otto Holbein from Dresden". This Old-Master manner of painting creates the impression of great coolness and distance, something corresponding to the Neue Sachlichkeit concern to take stock of things around them in a sober, unemotional manner.

Dix had already studied the Old Masters in Dresden's famous Gemäldegalerie during his studies. Now, however, his orientation towards artistic tradition assumed a central importance, one going far beyond painting technique alone. In his *Self-Portrait with Easel* (illus. p. 53), for example, Dix not only portrays himself in the traditional artist's pose but thereby quotes Albrecht Dürer's famous Munich self-portrait in the positioning of his hands. On the one hand, Dix was looking to the Old Master tradition to help determine his own role as an artist in society; on the other hand, he was aiming to harness Old Master timelessness to ensure that his painting went beyond the mere documentation of its own time. He even designed the emblem of a snake biting itself in its tail for the O and a bow for the D, following Lucas Cranach's winged serpent. With this highly unusual signature, Dix proclaimed his allegiance to tradition.

Self-portraits were a particularly important subject for the artists of the 1920s, especially in the cases of Otto Dix and Max Beckmann. The artists were constantly questioning both themselves and their role within society. They were uncertain as to what role befitted them, and thus were in great need of self-affirmation. Dix takes as his theme in the picture *To Beauty* (illus. p. 55) the isolated position of the artist, one going beyond the solitude of man as depicted by so many artists during these years. Instead of brush and easel, the artist as portrayed here is holding a telephone receiver in

Otto Dix
Metropolis (Triptych), left-hand panel, 1927/28
Großstadt (Triptychon)
Mixed media on wood, 181 x 101 cm
Stuttgart, Galerie der Stadt Stuttgart

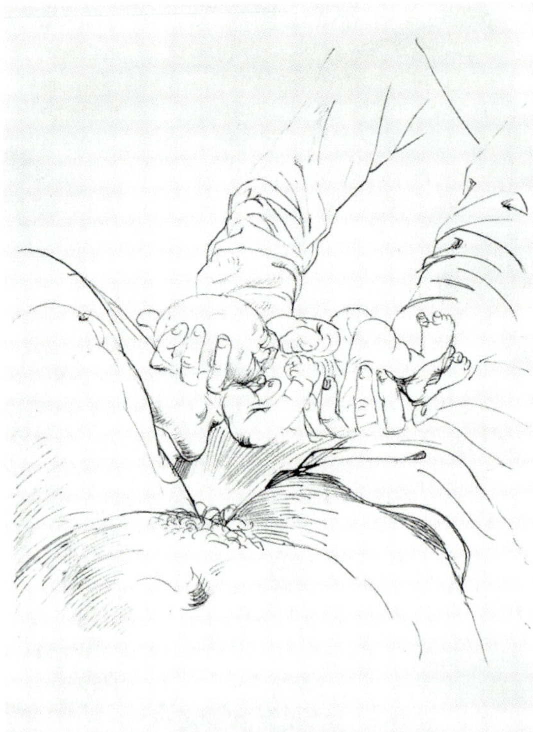

Dix' depictions of his new-born son Ursus reveal a pitiless "Sachlichkeit" (objectivity). In his drawing of the birth, the sober visual approach serves to emphasize the new-born babe's exposed state. In the picture from 1927, the pitiful and helpless nature of young Ursus Dix is underlined once again, while the more balanced "Nelly amongst Flowers" consciously refers back to the child portraits by Philipp Otto Runge.

TOP LEFT:
Otto Dix
Birth, 1928
Geburt
Pen, 45.3 x 38.2 cm
Vaduz, Otto Dix Foundation

BOTTOM RIGHT:
Otto Dix
Nelly amongst Flowers, 1924
Nelly in Blumen
Oil on canvas, 81 x 55.5 cm
Vaduz, Otto Dix Foundation

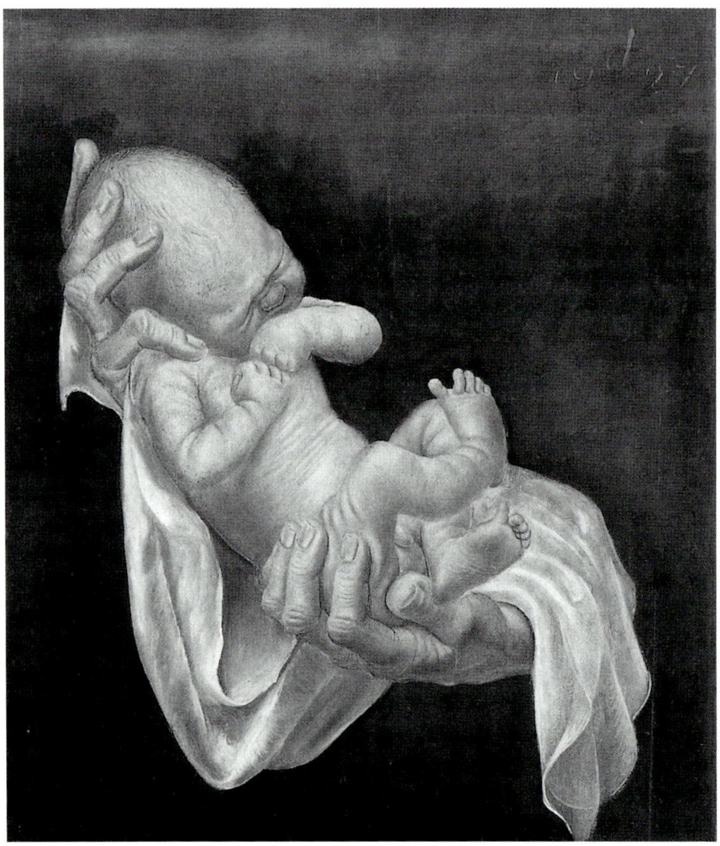

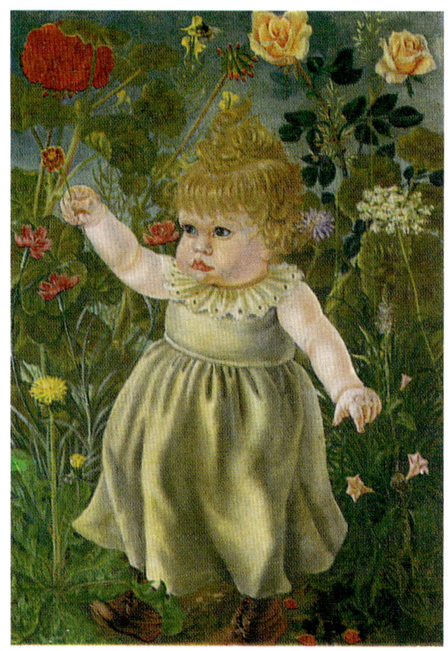

BOTTOM LEFT:
Otto Dix
New-Born Baby in Hands (Ursus Dix), 1927
Neugeborenes auf Händen (Ursus Dix)
Mixed media on wood, 50 x 43.5 cm
Vaduz, Otto Dix Foundation

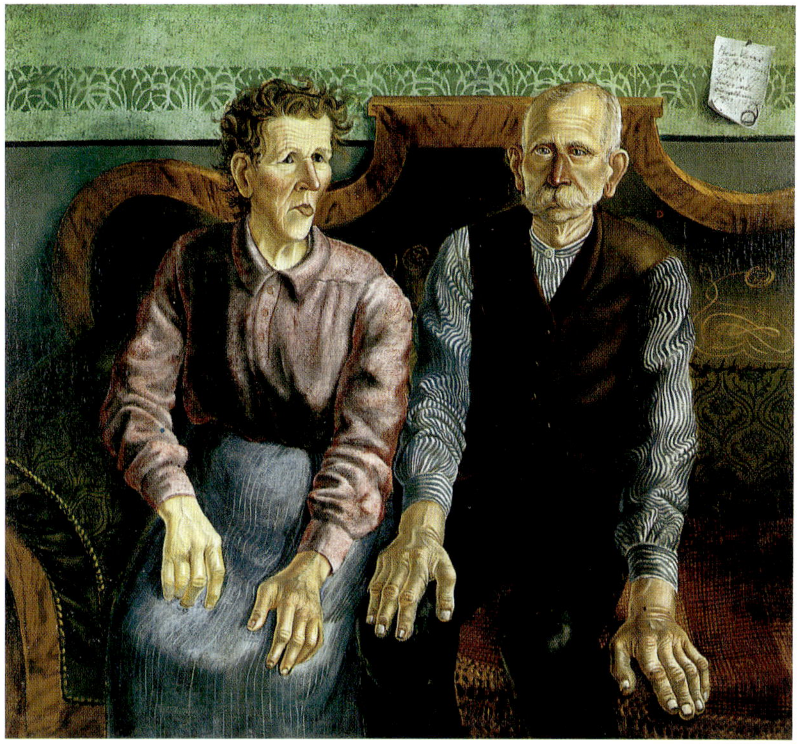

Otto Dix
The Artist's Parents II, 1924
Die Eltern des Künstlers II
Oil on canvas, 118 x 130.5 cm
Hanover, Sprengel Museum

"Behind every good likeness lies a vision: the nature of every person is expressed in his external appearance; the external appearance is the expression of the internal being; thus, external and internal nature are identical. This goes so far that even the folds of a garment, the posture of the person, his hands, his ears, immediately convey information to the painter regarding his model's emotional state, something more often the case with the latter two features than with eyes and mouths." *Otto Dix*

his hand, something that is tantamount to a programmatic statement: Dix sees himself as a reporter, giving an objective account of what he is observing. It is not the subjectivist viewpoint of the artist which is given predominance in his work, but rather the facts which it is necessary to record. The rejection of Expressionism is formulated anew here. "The Expressionists produced enough art. We wanted to see things totally naked and clear, almost without art."[29]

Even Dix' drawings of his own children are executed with a merciless "Sachlichkeit" (objectivity). His son Ursus, as a *New-Born Baby in Hands* (illus. p. 60), becomes a small, ugly monster, because Dix, not content with leaving it at a simple, sober stock-taking of the situation, contrasts the twisted, wrinkled, pale body with the dark background, black as night. The hands holding the newborn child as if in front of a void seem disconnected from any person, something further accentuating the loneliness and exposed state of the infant. However, Dix' love and admiration for his children often won, coaxing out of the artist a quite different side and resulting in many loving portrayals of happy childhood. Dix is orientating himself in his depiction of *Nelly amongst Flowers* (illus. p. 60) towards the style of Philipp Otto Runge, the most important painter of German Romanticism after Caspar David Friedrich. Nelly is portrayed in a heavenly garden as a "blossom of mankind among blossoms in the garden"[30], with no signs of any dissonance. However, the artificial nature of the composition clearly reveals that this is merely a vision of a harmonious life, of an intact world. Despite such dreams, painting for the Dix of the 1920s was "a means of cold-blooded execution", as Carl Einstein said in 1923.[31] It is for this reason that Dix, with his cool, reserved manner of looking at reality with markedly critical potential, is regarded as the most important advocate, alongside George Grosz, of the Verist direction within Neue Sachlichkeit.

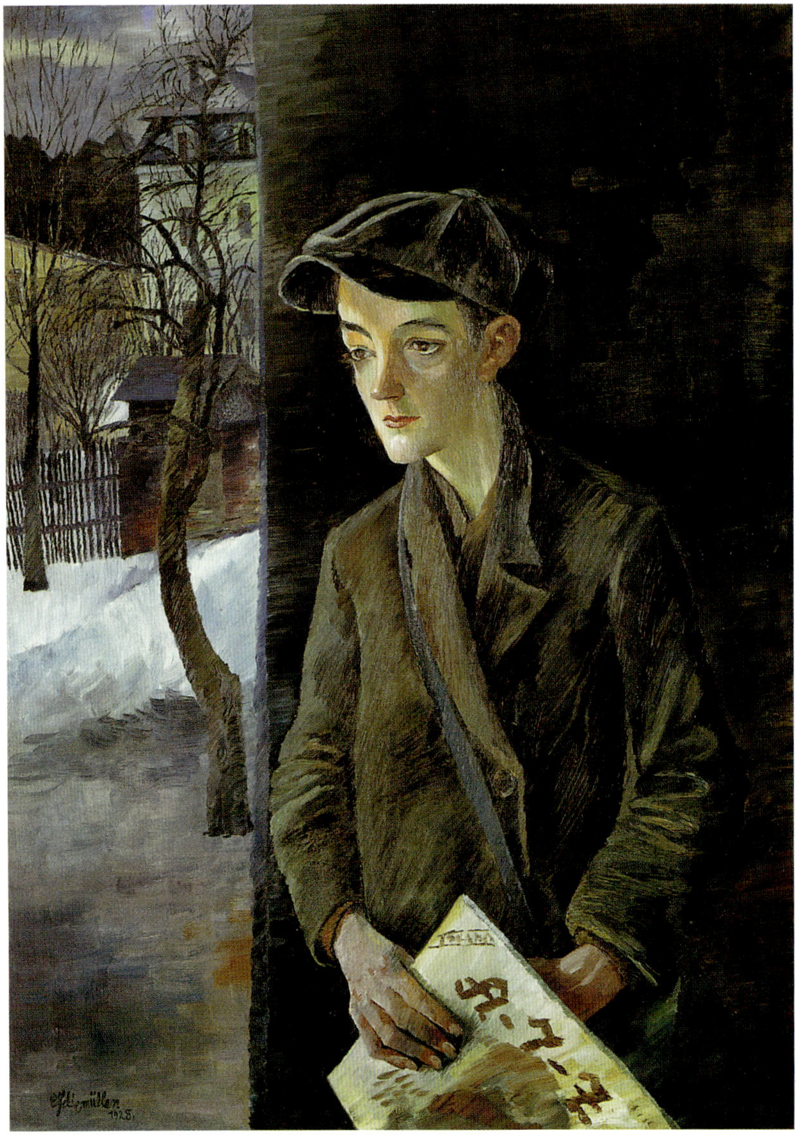

LEFT:
Conrad Felixmüller
Newspaper boy, 1928
Zeitungsjunge
Oil on canvas, 105 x 75 cm
Altenburg, Staatliches Lindenau Museum

ILLUSTRATION PAGE 63:
Conrad Felixmüller
Lovers from Dresden, 1928
Liebespaar von Dresden
Oil on canvas, 161 x 103 cm
Dresden, Staatliche Kunstsammlungen
Dresden, Gemäldegalerie Neue Meister

Yet Dix' "execution" was never determined by hate, as was the case with Grosz. In spite of his wartime experiences, Dix never lost his respect for mankind, although he portrayed its ugly side. Grosz constantly focussed on the sociopolitical dimension, searching for the guilty and for those responsible, accusing the military, the capitalists, the church, in his de-individualizing caricatures. Dix's criticism, in contrast, is not obvious. A differentiating eye and a deep understanding for mankind lie behind his depiction of reality. It is true that he came from the proletariat – his father was a moulder in an iron foundry – and this class left its mark on him and sharpened his social awareness, yet he never embraced the cause of party politics. When Conrad Felixmüller, his Dresden friend, asked him to join the German Communist Party, he merely replied: "I don't want to hear about your stupid politics – I'd rather spend the 5 marks' membership fee on a whore."[32]

"It has become increasingly clear to me that the only necessary goal is to depict the direct, simple life which one has lived oneself, also involving the design of colour as painting – in the manner in which it was cultivated by the Old Masters for centuries, until Impressionism and Expressionism, infected by the technical and industrial delusions of grandeur, rejected every affinity for tradition, ability and results, committing harakiri."
Conrad Felixmüller, 1929

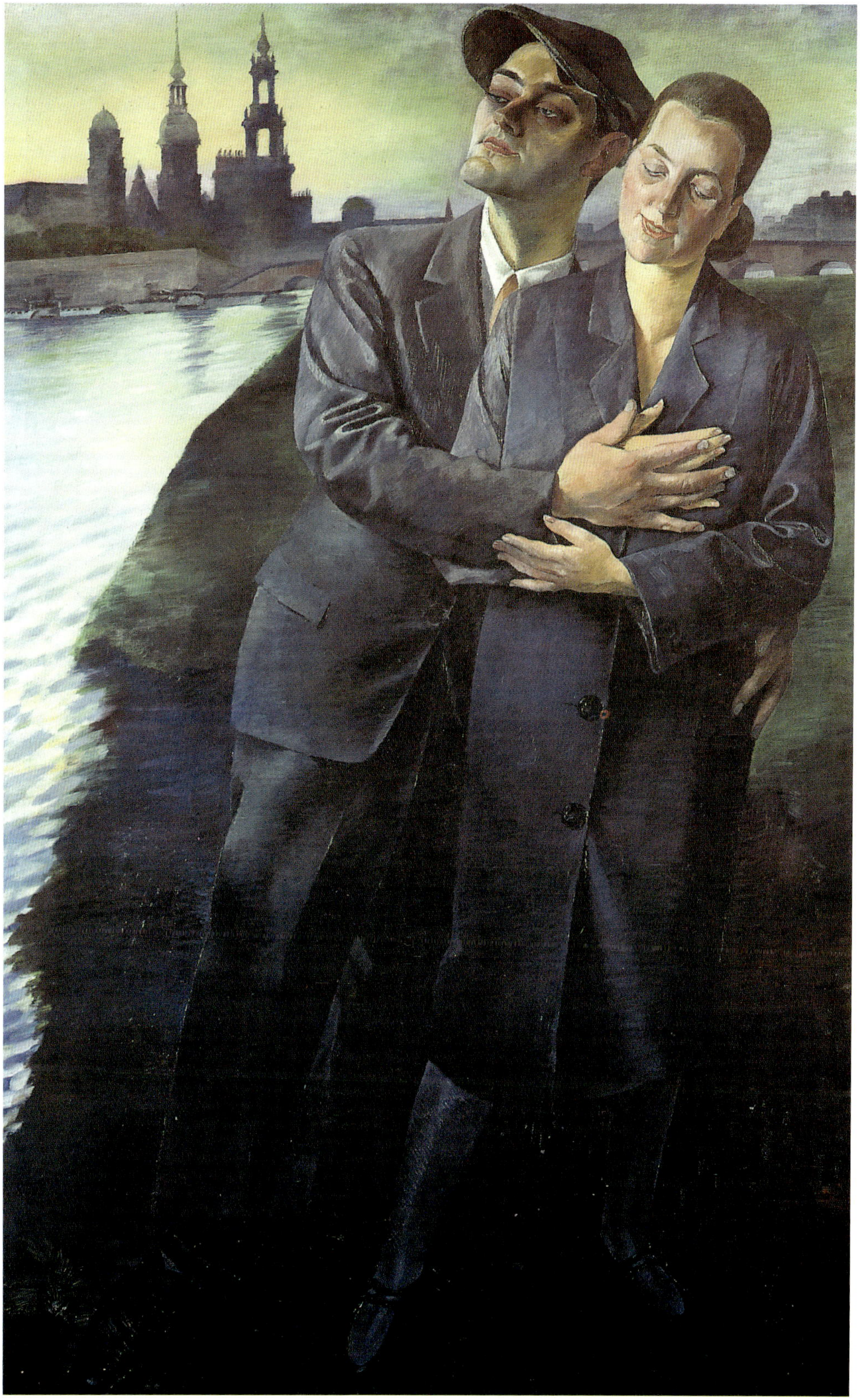

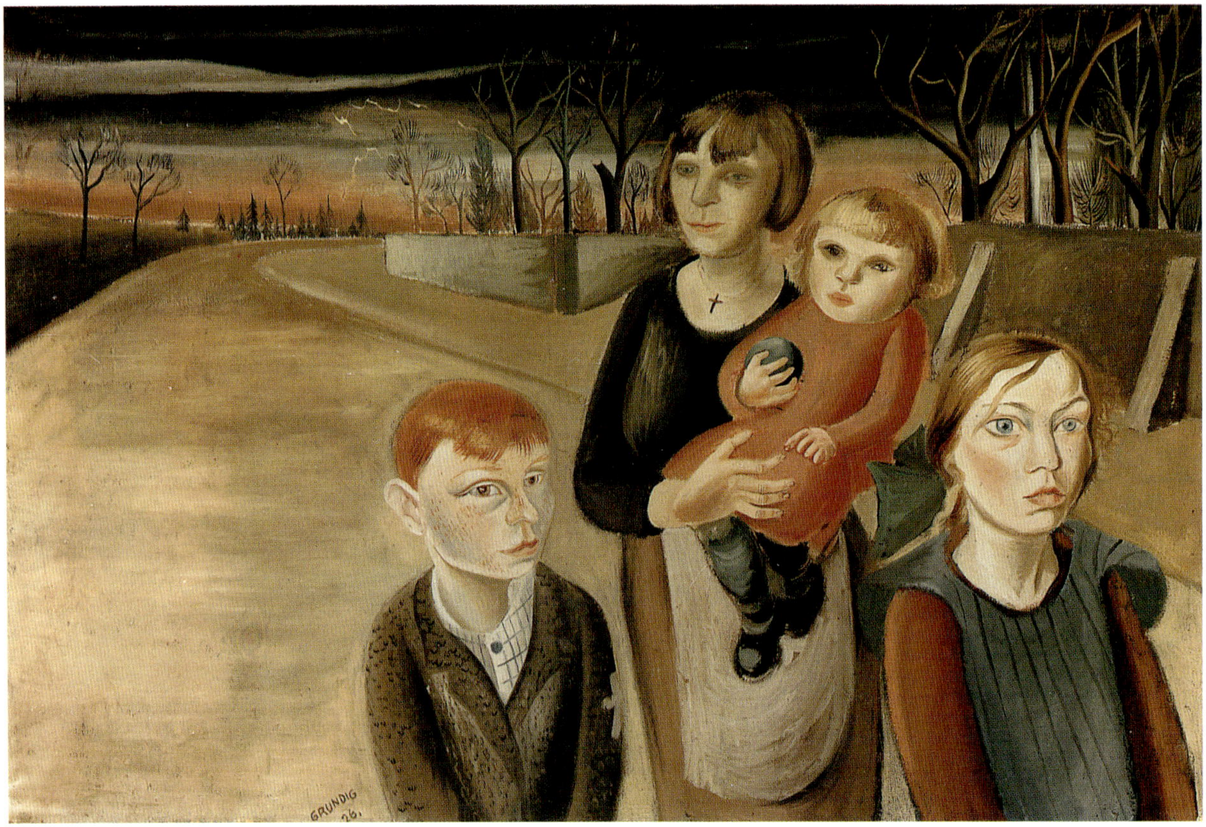

Hans Grundig
City Outskirts, 1926
Am Stadtrand
Oil on canvas, 80 x 118 cm
Berlin, Staatliche Museen zu Berlin – Preußischer Kulturbesitz, Nationalgalerie

Grundig's pictures were initially influenced by Dix. Thereafter, living in a working-class environment, the artist developed his own realistic manner of depiction, one in which the elements of social criticism recede behind what is more a descriptive, sympathetic view of ordinary people. Such a view is also encountered in Curt Querner's portrayals of farmers.

Conrad Felixmüller and Other Dresden Painters

The very thing which Otto Dix so vehemently rejected – socio-revolutionary, party political involvement – was the prime concern of Felixmüller, and with him the majority of the Dresden Realists. They were determinedly left-wing and pro-communist, most of them were members of the German Communist Party, and in 1928 they joined the newly founded "German Association of Proletarian and Revolutionary Artists" – known as ASSO – a component of the German Communist Party's cultural front. Otto Dix represents an exception among the Dresden artists in this respect, even if his painting provided themodel for many. Dix said everything that he wanted to say through his art – something with which the others were not prepared to be satisfied. "We must play an active role in life. This duty will confront us sooner or later, and it is of greater importance than painting pictures if we would see ourselves as something more than mere Romanticists ousted from life as it really is", declared Hans Grundig.[33]

Although younger than Dix, Felixmüller occupied an influential position in Dresden before the former, thanks to the considerable success which had already come his way at a very early stage. By 1920, he was held in national esteem. He was awarded the State Prize of Saxony but turned down the period of study in Rome that accompanied it, travelling instead to the German industrial region of the Ruhr to study the lives of the miners there. The impressions that he received would form his central subject-matter over the following years, especially in graphic works. Subsequent to his wartime experiences, Felixmüller had joined radical groupings; he was an extremely enthusiastic utopian and fighter for the cause of the workers, and attempted to convince his Dresden colleagues of the importance of socio-revolutionary commitment. It was under his influence that Dix painted his proletarian subjects around 1920, although they were not to hold his interest for long. Yet Felixmüller too changed his interests from the mid–1920s onwards, making use of an objective, sober manner of expression and painting predominantly portraits of people from his circle of friends and family, reflecting his years of private happiness without any material worries. Even in such a proletarian subject as that of the *Newspaper Boy* (illus. p. 62), however, he dispenses with agitatory elements, restricting himself to a descriptive realism.

The Dresden painters focussed their interest primarily upon workers and peasants within their milieu – not the intellectuals and literati, the bohemians or the demimonde, the prostitutes and beggars, but rather the ordinary people. Whereas Dix' Verism becomes a biting accusation, a note of sympathy for the simple, straightforward life is often to be found in the works of his colleagues and pupils. "Indeed, that is the wonderful thing about this young generation . . ., they don't let things get them down, they still say 'Yes' to life", as Hildebrand Gurlitt characterized the Dresden group in 1926.[34]

Felixmüller was partnered by Otto Griebel as spokesman for the Dresden artists; during Dix' absence, it was Griebel who set the tone in painting. For a long time, he maintained a close friendship with Dix, something also visible in his art, for example in the watercolour *The Naked Tart* (illus. p. 67) from 1923. However, it is also possible to detect the influence of Schlichter here, Griebel having come to know him in Berlin in 1921. In addition, his art was waylaid from time to time by his socio-revolutionary commitment, leading Dix to say once: "You and your damned politics . . . why don't you

Hans Grundig
Girl in Studio, 1925
Mädchen im Atelier
Oil on canvas, 105 x 66 cm
Weimar, Staatliche Kunstsammlungen zu Weimar

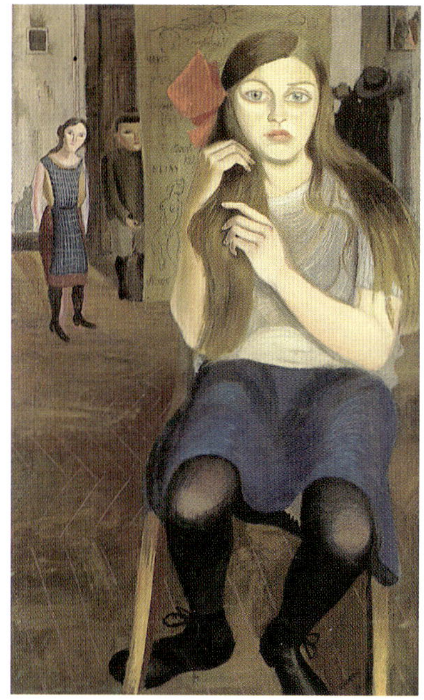

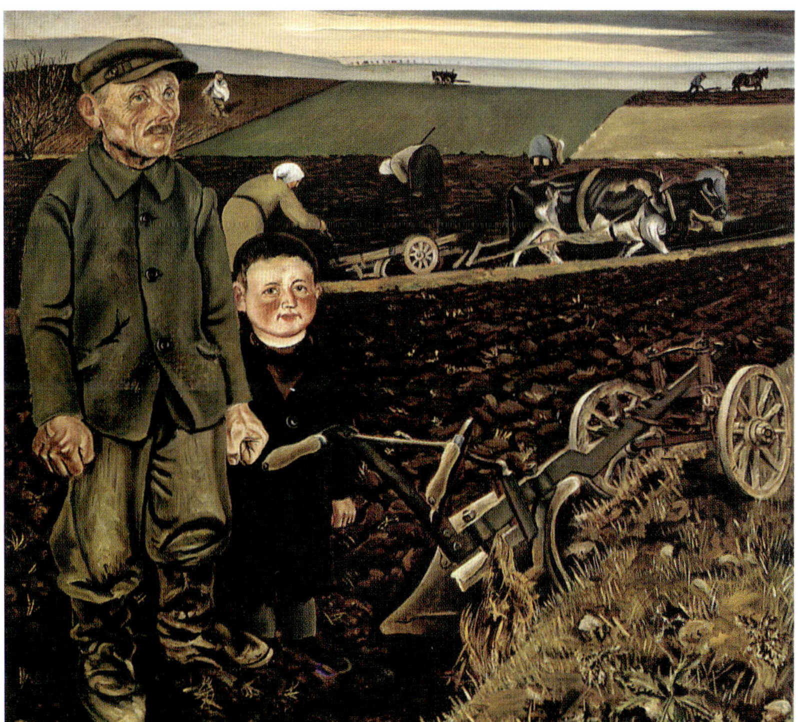

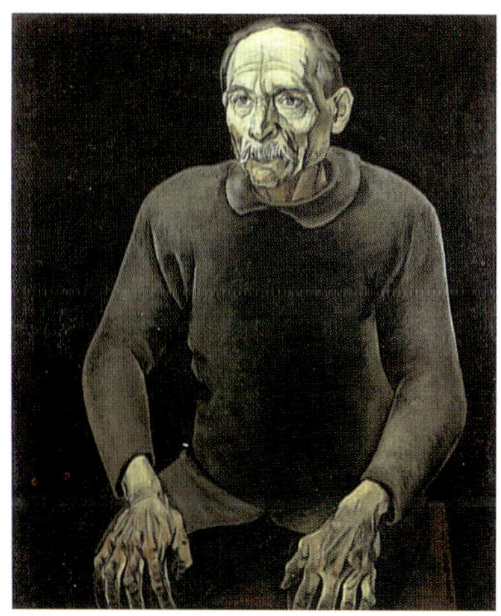

Wilhelm Rudolph
The Artist's Father, 1920/21
Oil on canvas, 109 x 93 cm
Dresden, Staatliche Kunstsammlungen Dresden, Gemäldegalerie Neue Meister

Curt Querner
Work in the Fields, 1933
Oil on canvas, 135 x 148.5 cm
Halle, Staatliche Galerie Moritzburg

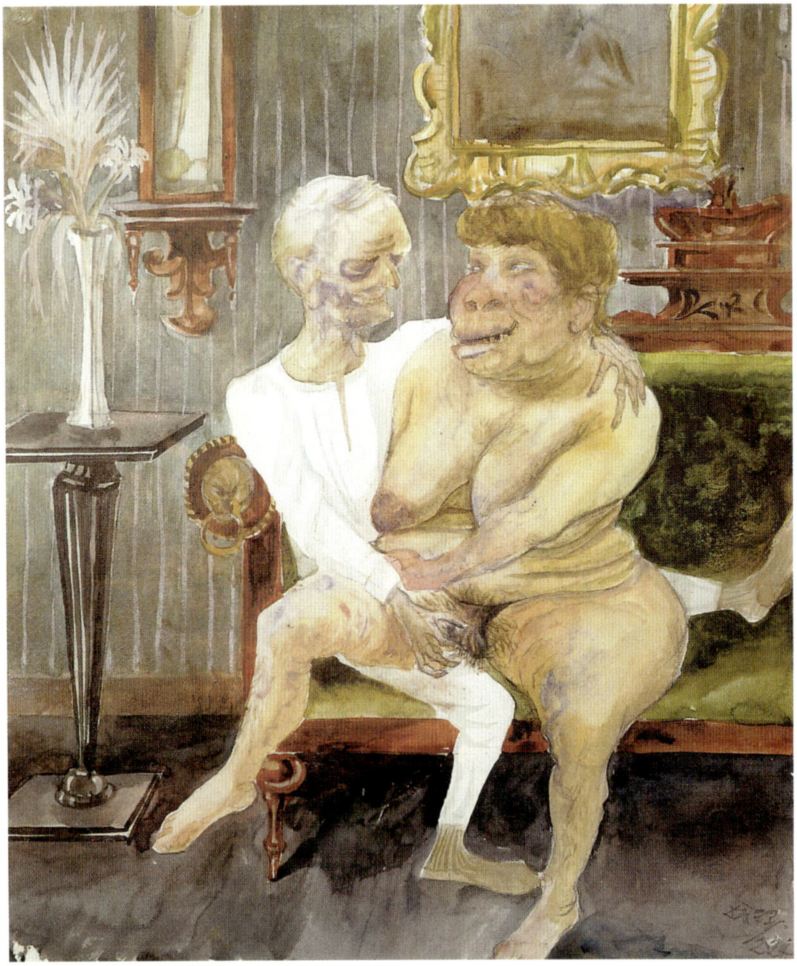

Otto Dix
Elderly Couple, 1923
Älteres Liebespaar
Watercolour, 39 x 33.5 cm
Private collection

sit down on your arse and paint instead".[35] In his well-known picture *The Internationale* (illus. p. 69), Griebel is marching in the front row – for workers' rights. This picture summed up his message in a manifesto-like manner: art, for him, was in the service of political and social aims. *The Internationale* has thereby become one of the incunabula of socialist Realism; it is a symbol of that which the term revolutionary "working masses" once represented yet has since degenerated through its inflationary use into a mere linguistic shell. While it is true that Griebel indeed gave the faces of his subjects individual features, they are nonetheless characterized primarily by their membership of a particular class – that of the workers.

Along with Griebel, it was Hans Grundig who was largely responsible for founding the ASSO in Dresden. Himself from the proletariat, he lived together with his wife, the artist Lea Grundig, in this milieu, since he was unable to achieve enduring recognition during the 1920s. It was thus quite natural that he should depict the world where his sympathies lay. His pictures (illus. pp. 64/65) are without pity, simple, and forthright – like the people portrayed in them.

Although he was committed politically, Wilhelm Lachnit was by nature quieter and more reserved, tending towards melancholy and depressive moods. Accordingly, his pictures were created in a less crude manner,

Where Dix exaggerates the ugly element in his watercolour "Elderly Couple" until it becomes repulsive – the woman's face has something bestial about it, while that of the man seems already marked by death – Griebel, for his part, is more concerned with an admittedly comical yet undoubtedly realistic depiction of an ageing prostitute. What the body lacks in appeal must be compensated for in attraction by the signal-red hat.

Otto Griebel
The Naked Tart, 1923
Die nackte Nutte
Pencil, watercolour on paper,
40.6 x 29.1 cm
Milwaukee, Marvin and Janet Fishman Collection

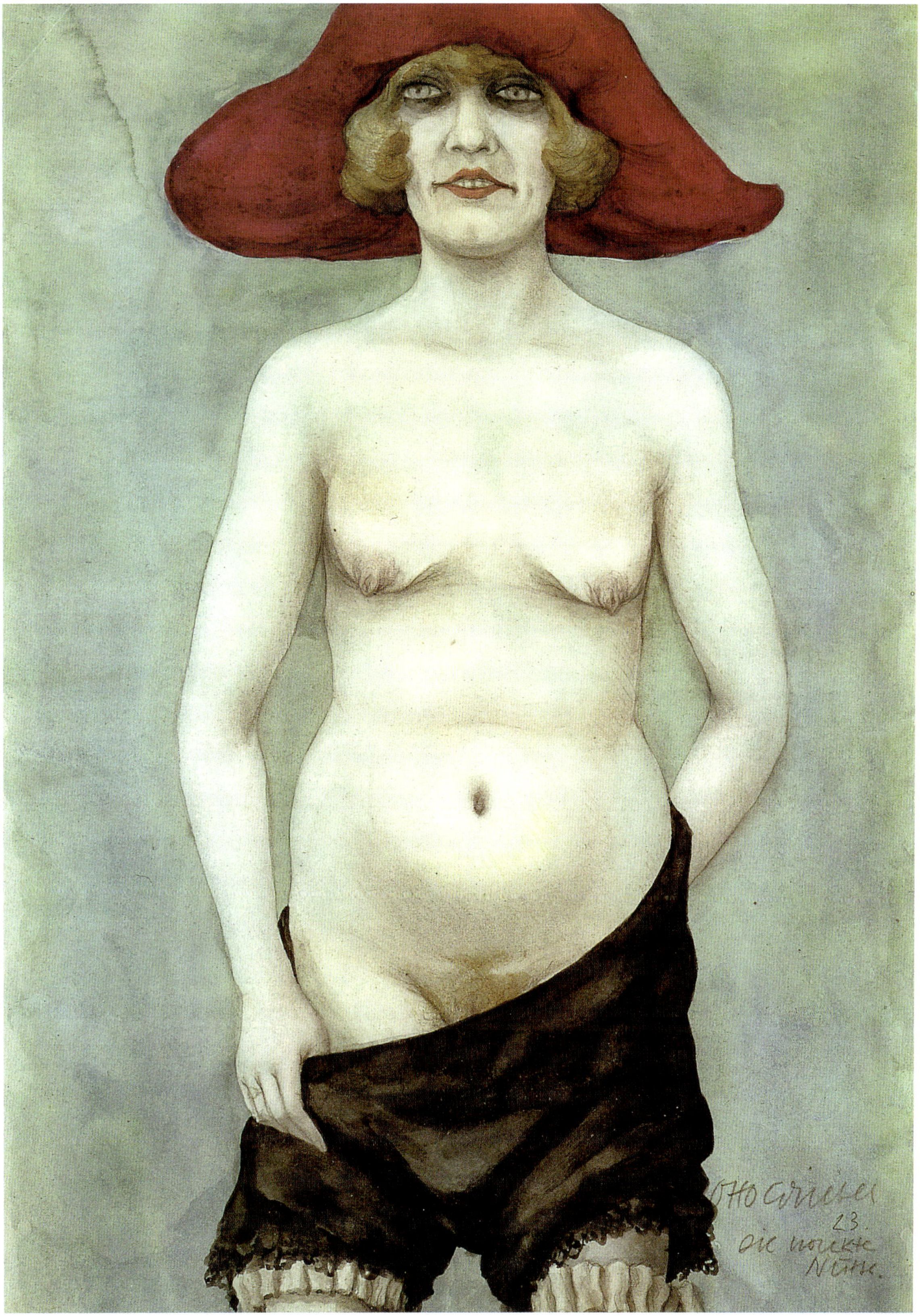
23.

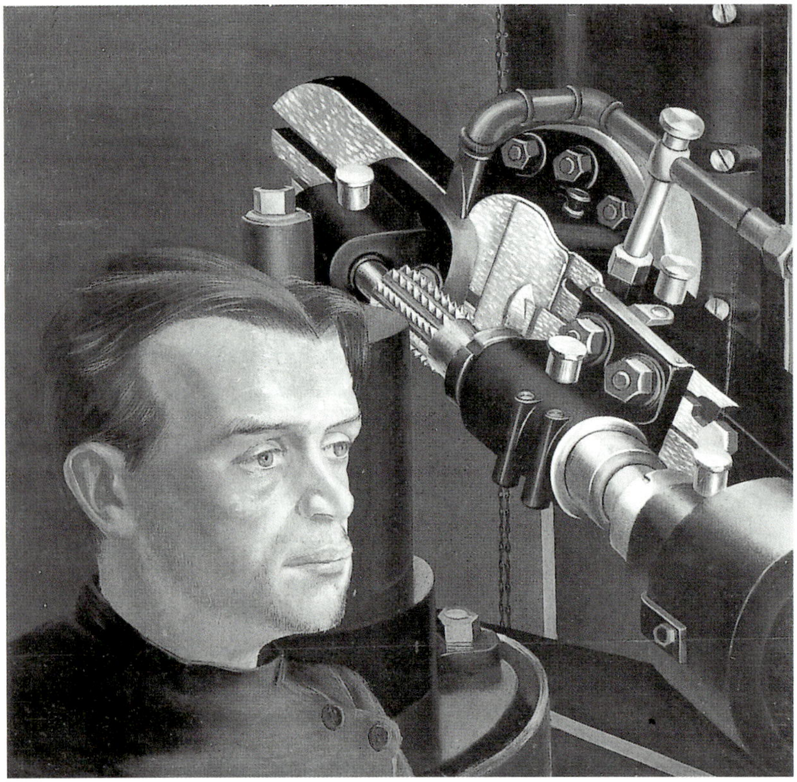

Wilhelm Lachnit
The Communist Frölich, 1924/28
Der Kommunist Frölich
Oil on wood, 50 x 52 cm
Berlin, Staatliche Museen zu Berlin – Preußischer Kulturbesitz, Nationalgalerie

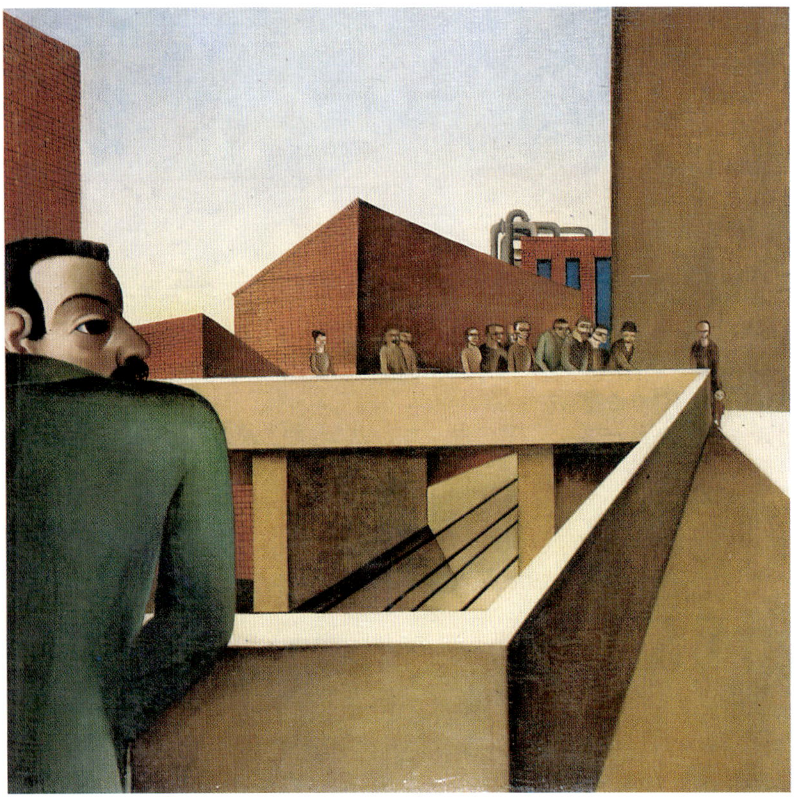

Karl Völker
Industrial Picture, 1923
Industriebild
Oil on canvas, 93 x 93 cm
Halle, Staatliche Galerie Moritzburg

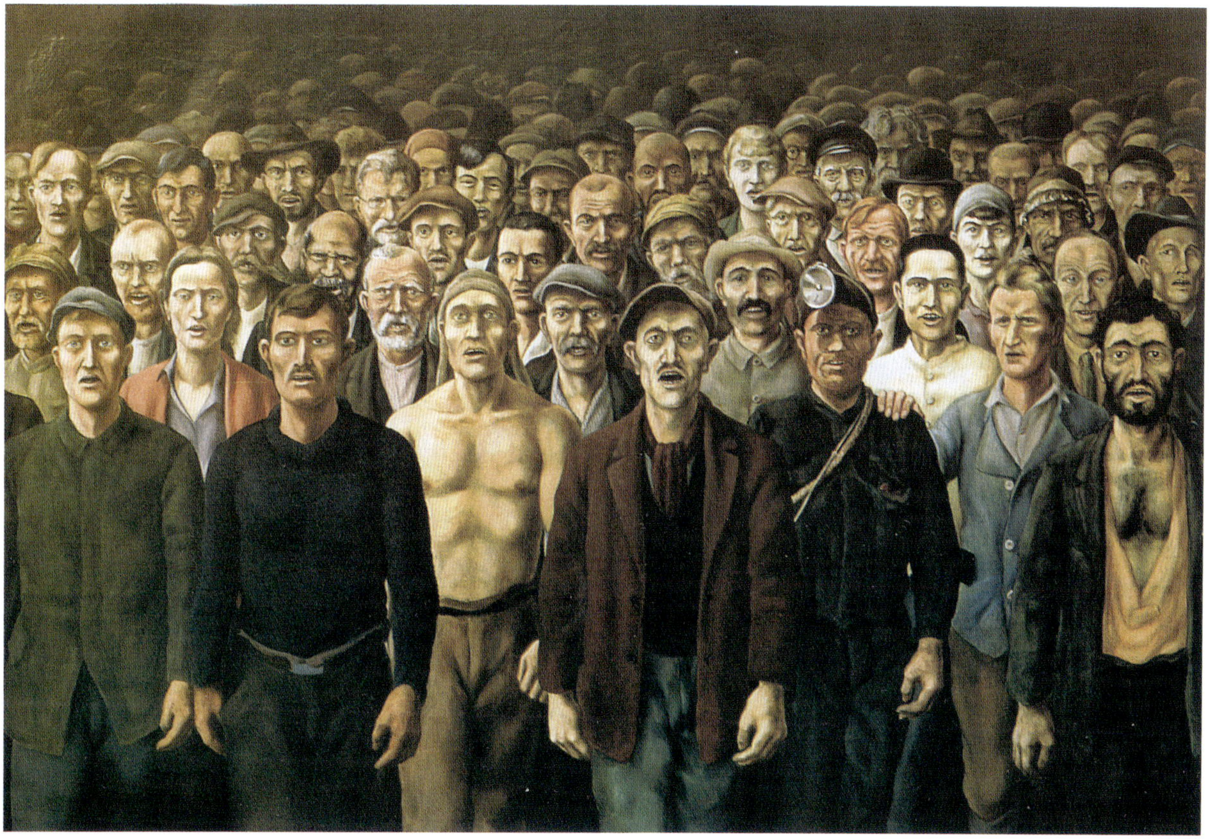

Otto Griebel
The Internationale, 1928/30
Die Internationale
Oil on canvas, 127 x 186 cm
Berlin, Deutsches Historisches Museum

The world of industrial workers and communism form the thematic brackets around these paintings by Lachnit, Völker and Griebel. Griebel's "Internationale" is a proletarian picture that possesses unusual power of expression, calling to mind the communist hope in the revolutionary potential of the "working masses" – a hope that, like the picture itself, has passed into history.

reflecting his desire for harmony and beauty, something that led more radical intellects to reproach him that his working-class girls looked like Madonnas. Lachnit made use of an extremely refined Old-Master technique to achieve a certain idealization of his subject, one generally creating a reserved and spiritualized effect, as in his *Woman with Rose* (illus. p. 203). It is for this reason that Lachnit is often described as the lyricist among the Dresden artists.

Wilhelm Rudolph found his métier in woodcuts, although he did paint a few portraits of workers. The majority of the Dresden artists particularly favoured the graphic media, not least because they made a greater distribution possible and were easier to sell. Rudolph's portrait of his father (illus. p. 65) thus also has something of the coarse nature common to the woodcut, corresponding to the artist's "hand".

Curt Querner belongs to the second generation of Dresden Realists. Living in a small village outside Dresden, he had to walk a considerable number of kilometres to the Academy every day. He earnt his living working for the farmers along his way. He took the life of the small-scale farmer (illus. p. 65) as his main theme. Querner's paintings of farmers are far removed from any "blood and soil" style of art;[36] they arise from sympathy for ordinary people, yet abstain from any false idealization, bearing witness to the hardships inherent in their existence. Only a very small part of the pre-war work of almost all the Dresden Realists has survived – the hail of bombs that fell in 1945 claimed the majority – rendering it very difficult to evaluate their output today to any adequate extent.

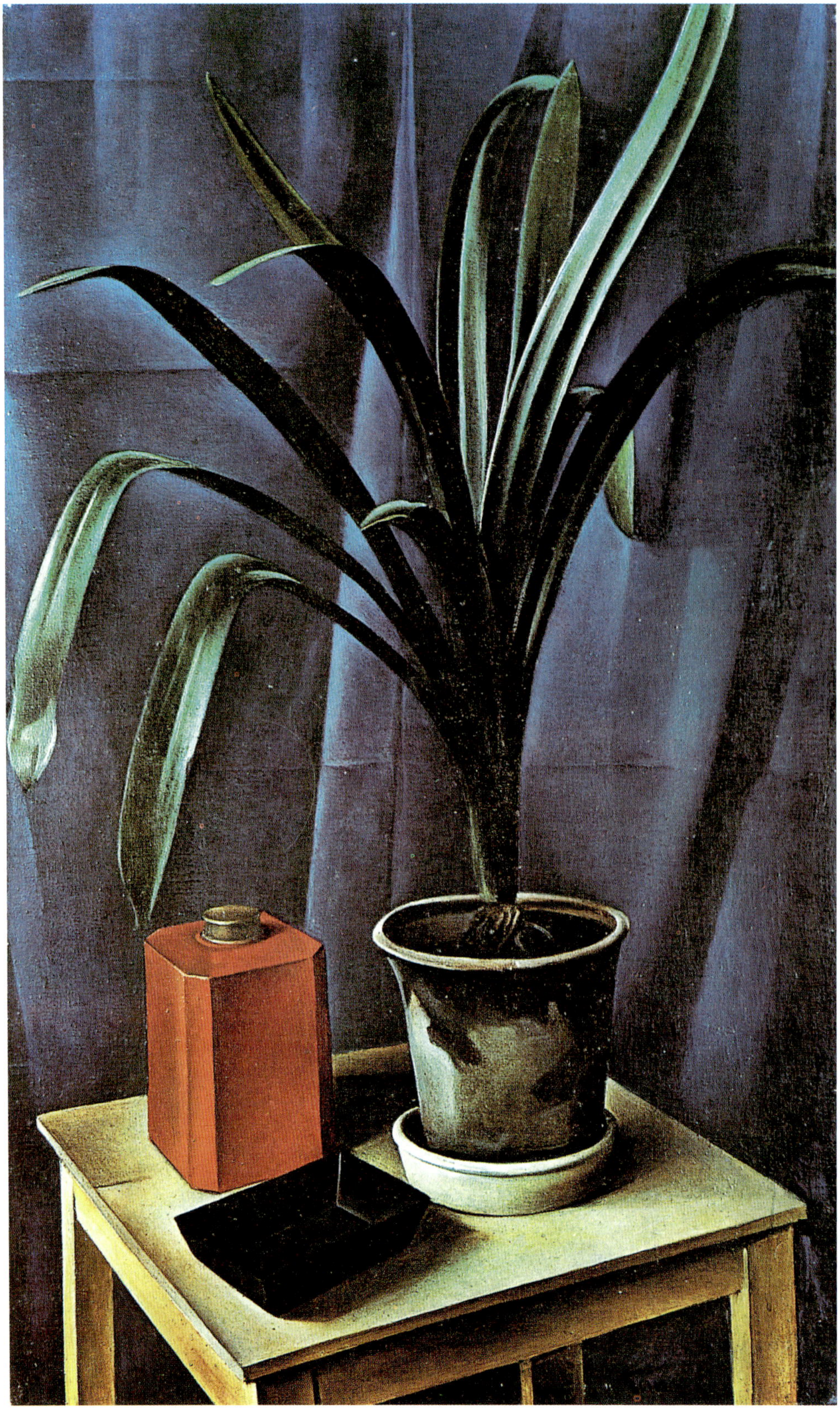

Munich
A Return to Order

A mere quarter of a century lies between two comments upon the role of Munich as a city of culture, Thomas Mann's "Munich glowed", on the one hand, and Eugen Roth's biting observation to the effect that it was "one of the stupidest cities anywhere", on the other. This period of time saw the inexorable decline of what had once been a German cultural metropolis, from the heights reached under the Prince Regents to what was to a large extent an insignificant provincial city towards the end of the 1920s, one staring with a mixture of disgust and secret admiration at the exuberant cultural life in Berlin.[37] This decline affected every sphere, that of literature as much as that of the theatre, yet nowhere was it perhaps as noticeable as in the support by state and city of the fine arts. Formerly so sure of their instinct and quality, always a few steps ahead of stuffy Wilhelminian Berlin, the people of Munich were to achieve no large or even middling success after 1900. Even the Darmstadt variant of Jugendstil (the German manifestation of Art Nouveau) was deemed too modern, while "Der Blaue Reiter" (The Blue Rider)[38], which Munich was only later – after 1945 – to claim as its historical contribution to modern art, was an absolute foreign body, one tolerated as hotel guests are tolerated who pay and make no fuss during their stay.

In this rather depressing situation the Munich grouping of Neue Sachlichkeit artists – Georg Schrimpf, Carlo Mense, Alexander Kanoldt, Heinrich Maria Davringhausen, and also Richard Seewald for a while – found itself having to play the role of a substitute for a genuine artistic avant-garde. The fact that it was precisely during their period of artistic activity in Munich that these four painters established the classicizing wing of Neue Sachlichkeit – the "right" wing in terms of Hartlaub's classification – has been attributed by some to the conservative *genius loci*. This may appear true from a general point of view; however, the group met with no success at all in its efforts to establish itself in the Munich art world.

The group's sole genuine backing came from Hans Goltz, owner of a gallery, although his efforts in Munich were the subject of constant hostility, culminating in his being accused of cultural Bolshevism. Goltz published the magazine "Valori Plastici" from 1919 onwards, and it provided a source of inspiration for the group's artists that should not be underestimated, even if the first large-scale exhibition in Germany of works by de Chirico and Carrà, in 1921, was restricted to Berlin, Hanover and Hamburg, bypassing Munich. In 1920, Goltz devoted an entire exhibition to the works of Grosz – the artist's debut one-man show – but the reaction of the Munich

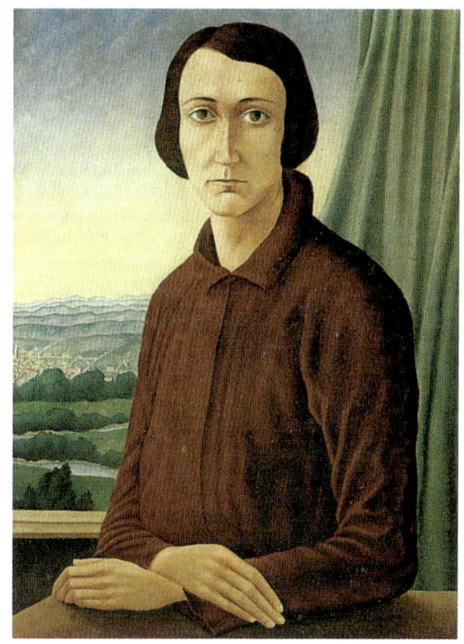

Georg Schrimpf
Hedwig Schrimpf, 1922
Oil on hardboard, 69 x 50 cm
Munich, Städtische Galerie im Lenbachhaus

Alexander Kanoldt
Still Life against a Blue Background, 1926
Stilleben vor blauem Hintergrund
Oil on canvas, 103 x 65 cm
Dresden, Staatliche Kunstsammlungen Dresden, Gemäldegalerie Neue Meister

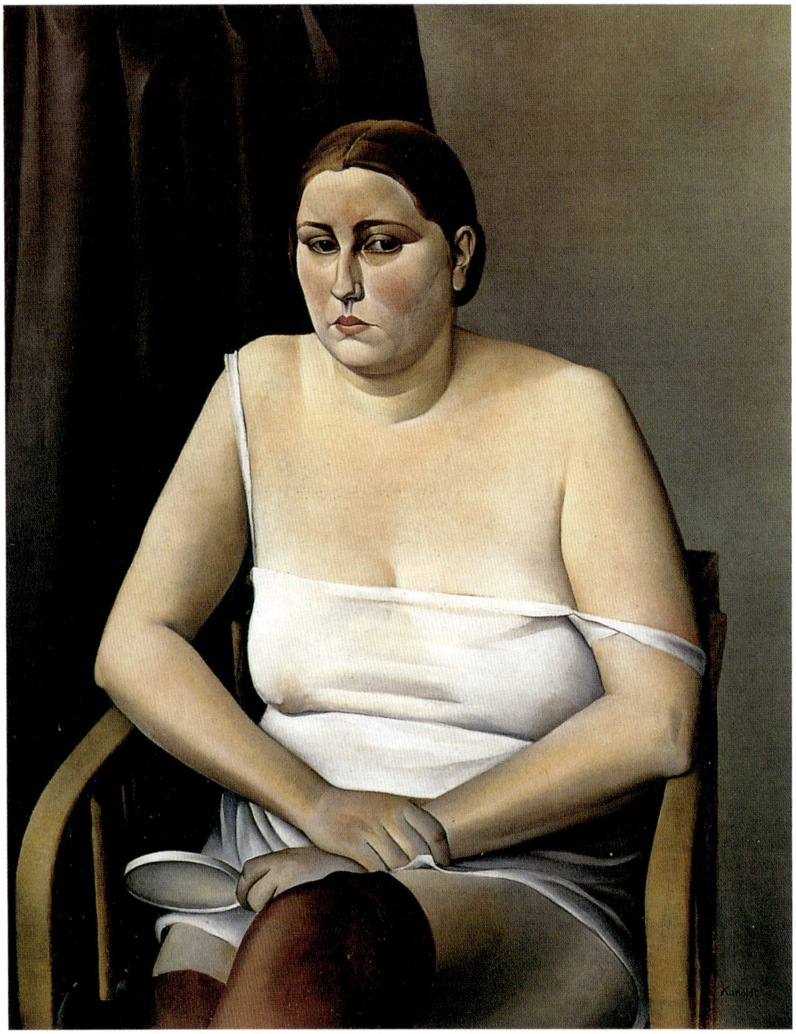

Alexander Kanoldt
Half-Length Nude II, 1926
Halbakt II
Oil on canvas, 90.5 x 71 cm
Munich, Bayerische Staatsgemälde-sammlungen

art critics was malicious; nor was Verism later to come to fruition here. Davringhausen also had a one-man show in Goltz' gallery, and the latter exhibited works by Schrimpf on a number of occasions within the context of general exhibitions. Finally, in 1921, an important exhibition took place embracing almost the entire group, one that really did justice to their artistic profile. Kanoldt alone was not represented here.

Looking back from a later perspective tends to reduce distances, and in particular those of a personal nature. Close links – personal as well as stylistic and iconographical – existed between Mense, Schrimpf and Davringhausen for a time, Kanoldt for his part keeping rather to himself. An important role was played by Oskar Maria Graf, the author, who was friendly with Mense and Schrimpf and would later become the mentor of the younger generation of Neue Sachlichkeit painters as well. He propagated their works in reviews appearing in the early 1920s, above all in "Cicerone". In 1923 he published a slender volume on Schrimpf; in 1950 he would dedicate a moving literary obituary to his deceased friend. Extended drinking sessions in the Nymphenburg villa of Anthony van Hoboken, the eccentric Dutchman, further reinforced these friendships. An important role was also played by the important Neue Sachlichkeit art critic Franz Roh while Wilhelm Hausenstein's friendship was more with Kanoldt, resulting in sensitive analyses to accompany the artist's works. Gustav Hartlaub, in his exhibition of Neue Sachlichkeit in Mannheim, showed 50 "Munich" works, comprising almost half of the total of 124 works on display. Even if this selection was biased – Hartlaub revealing himself clearly prejudiced against Verism – it nevertheless represented a "triumph on the part of the Munich variety of French Neoclassicism"[39], as Paul Westheim, the art critic, was to formulate it. This did not serve to endear the Munich artists to the public; nonetheless, they increasingly came to be regarded as a homogeneous group, one attributed a more intense reception of Italian realism's intensity and a higher degree of classicism than was actually the case.

Munich, the conservative city of art, once again found itself in an ambivalent position, identified with a stylistic trend which was too progressive for the tastes even of Munich's artistic élite. Those on the left – and also Weimar's avant-gardist art critics – saw this as further evidence of the decline in the fine arts within the city on the River Isar. This identification of Munich with Neue Sachlichkeit found particularly harsh expression in the irritable words of Herwarth Walden, as recorded in the magazine "Der Sturm": "The attempt to provoke a reaction under the Neue Sachlichkeit label is pitiful . . . Neue Sachlichkeit resides in Munich – but sufficient idiots can also be found elsewhere."[40]

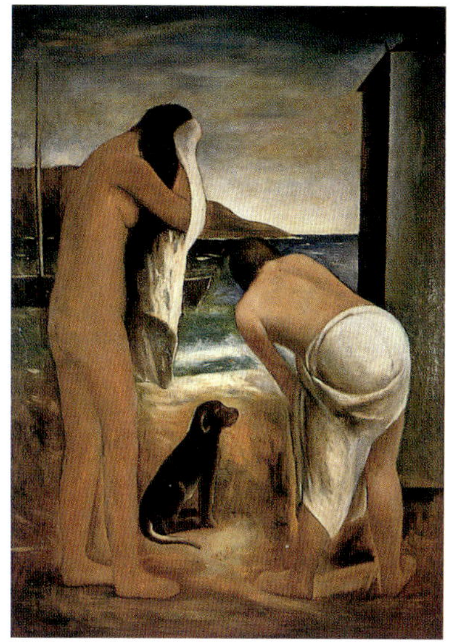

Carlo Carrà
Summer (Estate), 1930
Der Sommer (Estate)
Oil on canvas, 166 x 121.5 cm
Milan, Civica Galleria d'Arte Moderna

Georg Schrimpf

Georg Schrimpf owes his historical role to one single artistic decision, namely his adoption in 1920 of the world of forms found in the works of Carlo Carrà, the Italian artist. With this decision, something akin to a claim to the artistic leadership of the developing Munich group devolved upon

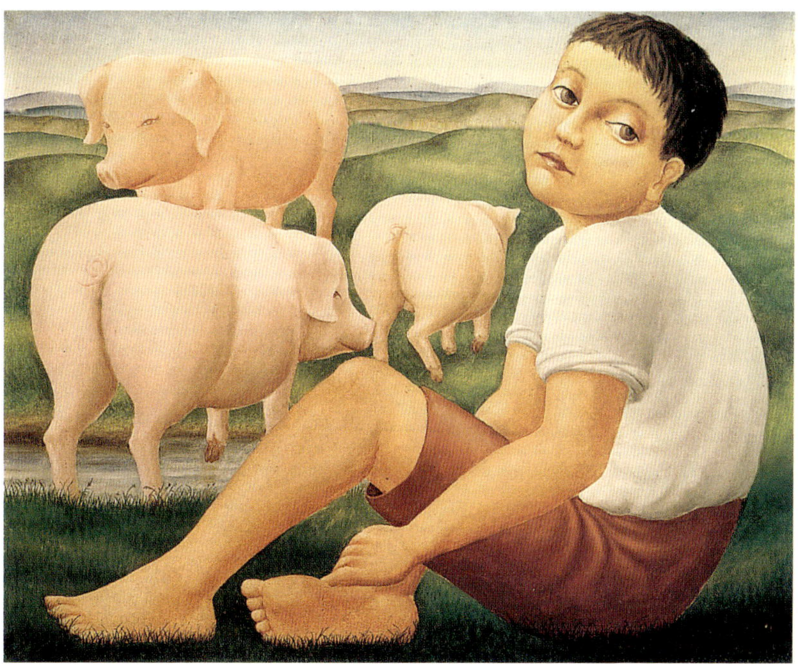

Georg Schrimpf
Swineherd, 1923
Schweinehirt
Oil on canvas, 39 x 60.5 cm
Cologne, Museum Ludwig

Through his leanings towards Carrà, Schrimpf's pastoral landscapes attain the block-like solidity and melancholic grace found in early paintings of the Madonna. The overlarge heads, seemingly stuck onto the bodies, imbue the figures with a sentimental insistence.

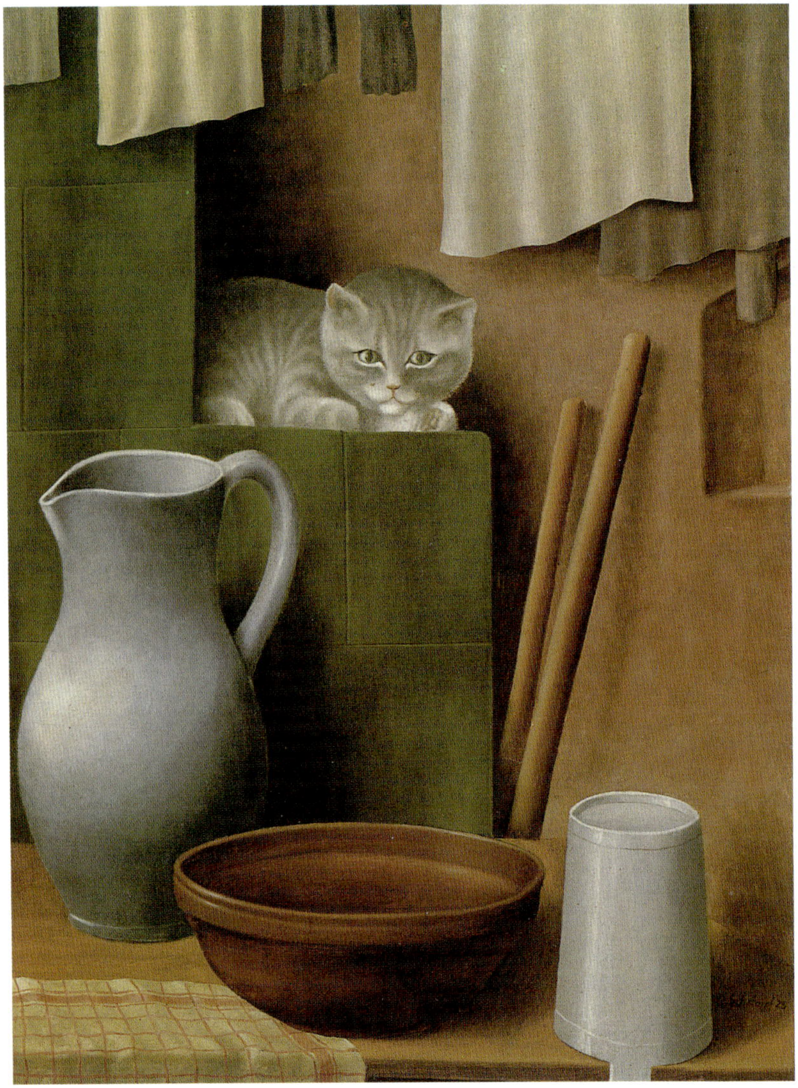

Georg Schrimpf
Still Life with Cat, 1923
Stilleben mit Katze
60.7 x 45.5 cm
Munich, Bayerische Staatsgemälde-sammlungen

him. However, this was no role in the term for such a sensitive painter, a man often out of touch with reality. Schrimpf's encounter in 1913 with the pictures of the "Blaue Reiter" in Munich provided the initial impetus to his artistic career. He was influenced by Franz Marc's spiritual world of animals, something that was also in keeping with his desire for harmony and his attachment to nature. It was also owing to the "Blaue Reiter" that he had access to the decorative primitivism of Henri Rousseau. Schrimpf, a declared antimilitarist, successfully employed every possible trick to avoid military service; in so doing, however, he ruined his health. It was during the period of the war that he found acceptance into the Expressionist circle in Berlin focussed around the "Der Sturm", and it was here that he came to know his future wife, Maria Uhden, herself a painter. The influence of her lyrical, decorative paintings upon Schrimpf was more decisive than that of the Expressionism found in the group around Herwarth Walden, which remained basically alien to him.

In 1918, Schrimpf moved to Munich, establishing contact with Goltz, the

"What is it, then, that gives these pictures, this simplicity, this quiet power, these mothers, children, animals and landscapes such a deep magic?... Let's say it straight out for once and despite its being spoilt and distorted – let's simply say it: it is the German element which works in the nature of this artistry, of these pictures; it is that quality which rings out so ever-present, eternally fresh, and reaching the uttermost depths of one's soul, as in a poem by Claudius. It is the indestructible power of the German disposition." *Oskar Maria Graf, 1923*

Carlo Mense
Mother with Children, 1925
Mutter mit Kindern
Oil on canvas, 99 x 60 cm
Marburg, Universitätsmuseum Marburg

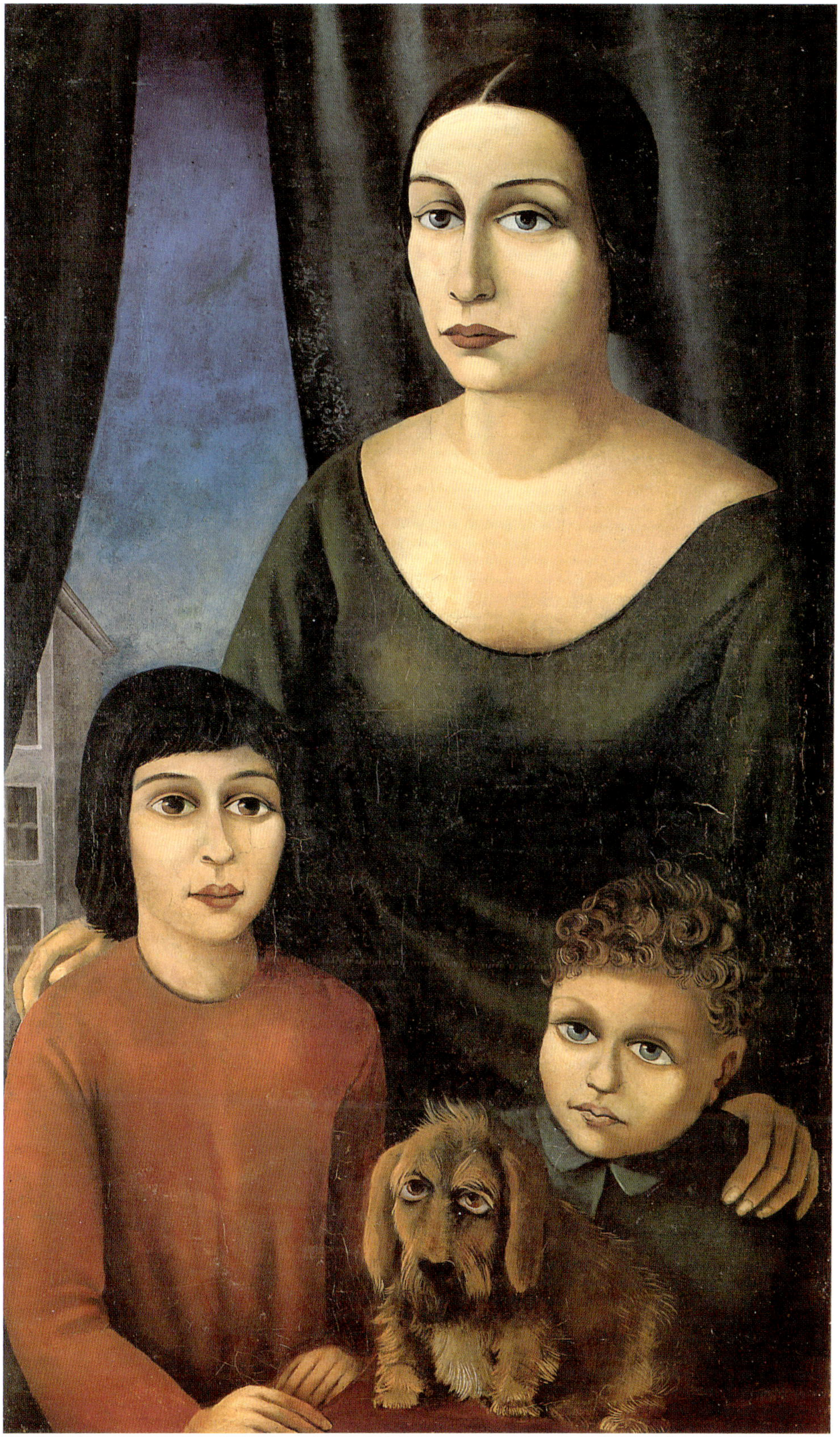

In his portrait of Davringhausen (1922), Mense portrays his artist friend as the bearer of a Chirico-esque secret, while his "Portrait of Underberg", with its chessboard pattern in the background, presents an obvious stage prop from Pittura metafisica.

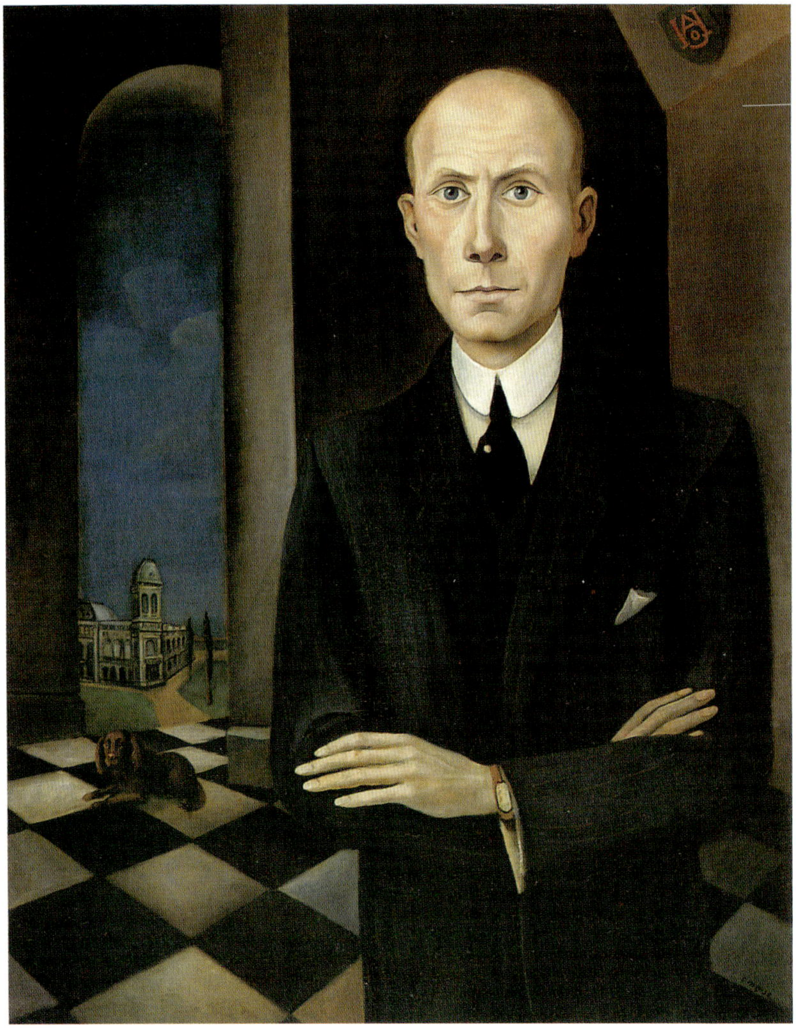

Carlo Mense
Portrait of Underberg, c. 1922
Bildnis Underberg
Oil on canvas, 97 x 77.5 cm
Private collection

gallery owner, to whom he was to grant the exclusive rights to his current artistic production from 1918 to 1921. It was through Goltz that Schrimpf came into contact with the works of de Chirico and Carrà, probably as early as in 1920; Franz Roh's account, according to which this did not occur until 1921, would seem unlikely. Schrimpf selected Carrà as his model. Conservative at this point in time, Carrà was proclaiming a return – not without a religious basis – to the Italian painting of the trecento and quattrocento. Schrimpf thereafter extended the referential scope of his art to include the painting of the Nazarenes – primarily that of Overbeck – along with Philipp Otto Runge's child portraits and, after 1930, the works of Caspar David Friedrich as well. His reception of the Nazarenes was even to temporarily eclipse the Italian influences, to such a great extent that Franz Roh – someone otherwise allied with him – spoke, not without

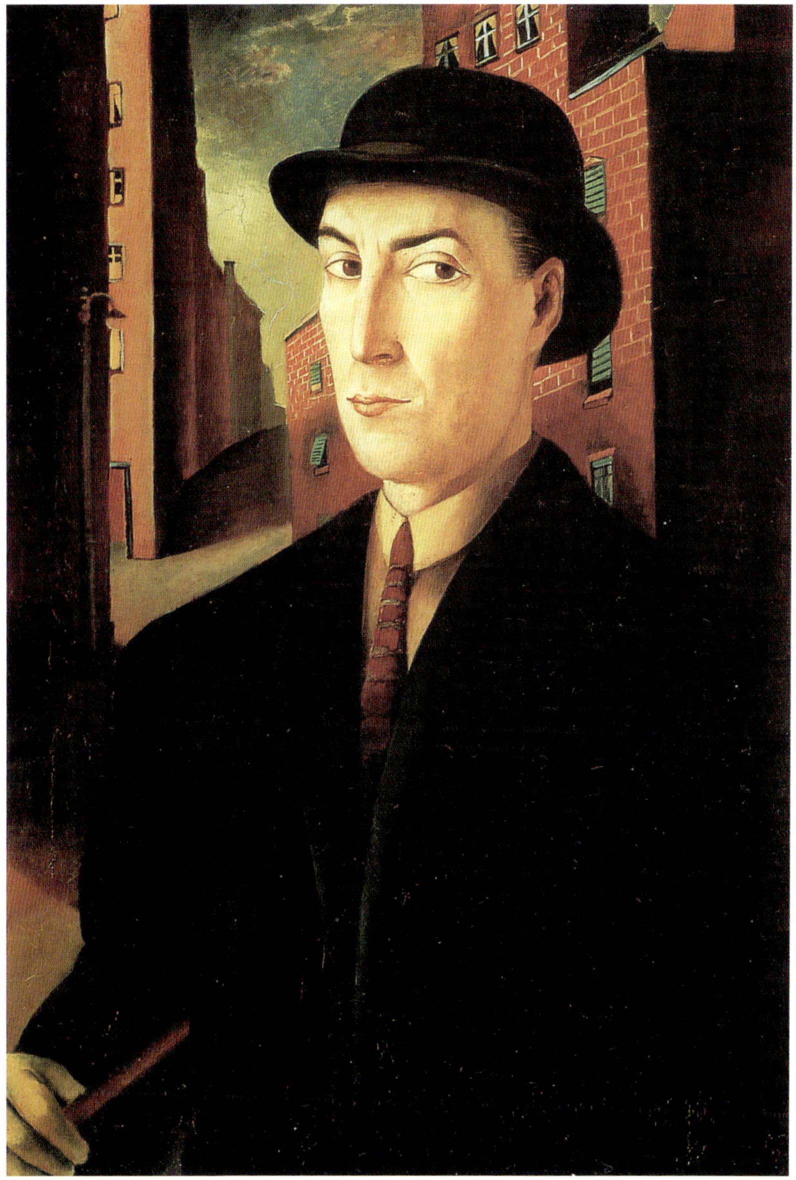

Carlo Mense
The Painter Heinrich Maria Davringhausen, 1922
Der Maler Heinrich Maria Davringhausen
Oil on canvas, 86.5 x 59.5 cm
Cologne, Museum Ludwig

an element of disassociation, of "Neo-Nazarenedom". This process of acquisition, one characterized by the reception of Carrà and his "italianità", was of significance for the entire Munich group, although it is of course important to draw a distinction between direct and indirect acquisition.

The classical works of this stylistic period appeared between 1922 and 1926. The subjects depicted in these pictures can be briefly summarized. The portraits with a landscape view repeated patterns from the portraits of the quattrocento, superimposing light Nazarene touches upon these. Schrimpf painted swineherds (illus. p. 73), young women (illus. p. 18), either sitting or lying, meditating or silently sharing one another's company, or girls in garrets (illus. p. 161), in front of tiny windows or views, awaiting an imminent bundle of joy. These pictures were restrained in their use of colour, concerned to achieve an unobtrusive rhythm. Oskar Maria Graf,

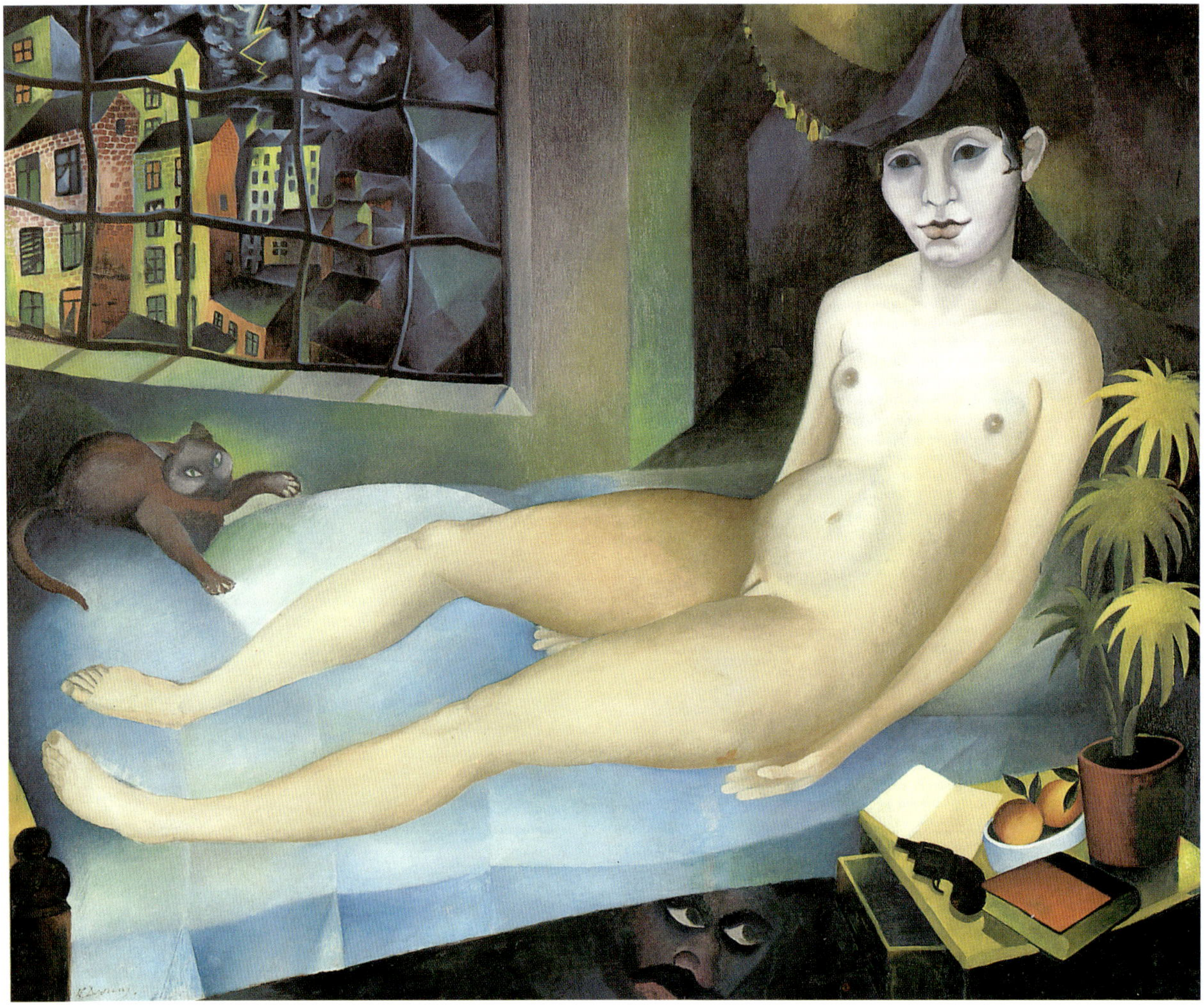

Heinrich Maria Davringhausen
The Sex Murderer, 1917
Der Lustmörder
Oil on canvas, 119.5 x 148.5 cm
Munich, Bayerische Staatsgemälde-sammlungen

The peaceful posture of the woman and the cat arching its back at her feet are a homage to Manet's "Olympia". The murderer is still lying in wait under her bed, as the approaching storm already heralds the impending murder. Despite the fact that the deed has been performed in "The Dreamer", the murder here quite definitely has something of the imaginary about it; it is more colourfully evoked than performed in reality. Deed and imaginary dreamworld diverge.

a friend of Schrimpf's, described this type of picture, if not without a certain irony, as "unutterably chaste girl-forms and landscapes of a compelling peacefulness"[41]. For his part, Franz Roh saw in Schrimpf's naivety a form of piousness, one founded in an excessive sense of inwardness.

A high point during this period may be seen in the book written by Carlo Carrà about Schrimpf, published in Rome in 1924 by the "Valori Plastici" press. Critical accents are unmistakable in Carrà's analyses, shedding a significant light upon the different traditions and formal conceptions of German and Italian artists. For example, Carrà finds Schrimpf's work "simultaneously attractive and repellant". He criticizes the as yet "undeveloped, brittle... childish design", observing with the self-assurance of an Italian classicist that Schrimpf's art is basically "mute and monotonous in its expression"[42]. With this more than dissonant attempt at appreciation, what was without a doubt the artist's most creative period came to an end.

Schrimpf's feeling for the tectonics of his figures was thereafter to become more superficial, with the result that they appear more decorative. The accordance of their proportions with the space in which they find themselves is missing. Their overlarge heads, apparently simply stuck onto their bodies, give them a sentimental obtrusiveness. Furthermore, the south-

Heinrich Maria Davringhausen
The Dreamer, 1919
Der Träumer
Oil on canvas, 120 x 119 cm
Darmstadt, Hessisches Landesmuseum

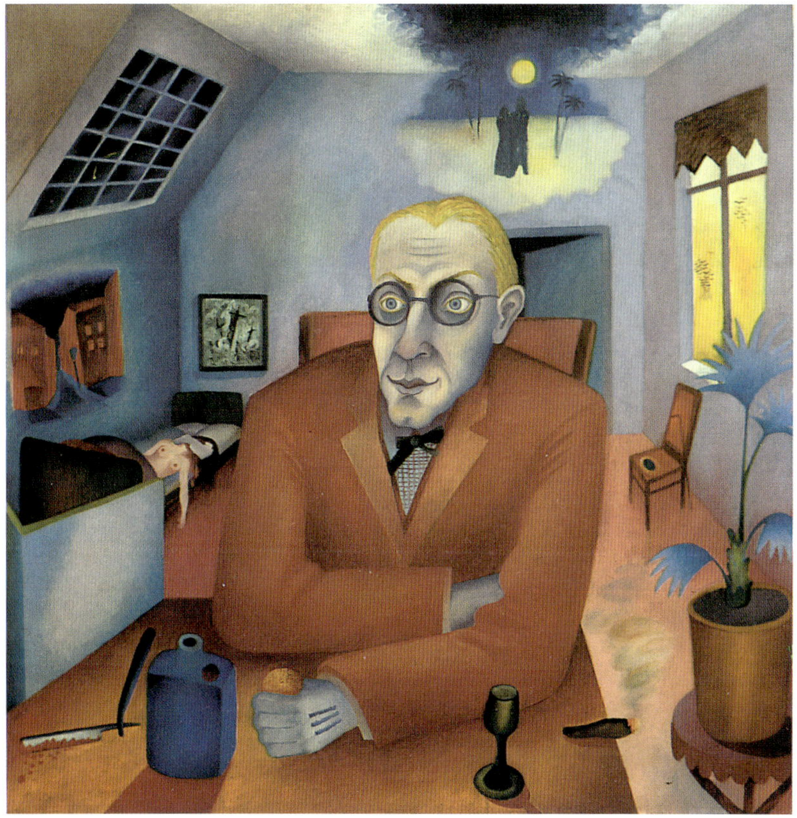

ern pastoral landscape metamorphoses into a pictorial type similar to that of Caspar David Friedrich: "In the course of time, something of an Old-Master nature appeared in his groupings of trees. It is true that the distant perspective lacked a piercingly analytical element . . . everything was more cheerful, more balanced . . ."[43] In the year in which the National Socialists came to power, Schrimpf, as a "German Romanticist", was appointed to a professorship at the College of Art Education in Berlin-Schöneberg. The protection of Rudolf Hess, Hitler's deputy, who liked the artist's late landscape pictures, continued to provide him with a considerable measure of freedom for a while, despite the onset of the first attacks on his work. Hess was even able to obtain the immediate removal of an early Expressionist-Cubist picture by Schrimpf from the "Entartete Kunst" (Degenerate Art) exhibition in Munich.[44] However, Schrimpf was overtaken by his past at the end of 1937, by which time his position in Berlin had become untenable in the light of his involvement in the Munich soviet republic of 1919 – for which documentary evidence existed – and his brief membership of the German Communist Party. The new year saw him dismissed from his position. In 1938, the artist died in Berlin, a broken man far away from his beloved Munich.

Carlo Mense

Mense's work is usually mentioned in the same breath as that of Schrimpf. For a time, their output bore close stylistic similarities, with Mense initially taking more than he gave. He was to make the acquaintance of Schrimpf and Davringhausen in 1914, on the occasion of a period of residence in the artists' colony at Ascona. From 1921 onwards, he would come increasingly under the influence of Schrimpf and the Italians, even exhibiting in 1922 at a Florence exhibition of the "Valori Plastici". He travelled around Italy in the course of several study trips, primarily painting landscapes the nature of which tended towards the pastoral idyll, albeit somewhat ponderous in their effect. Mense's real achievement lies in a series of portraits, all of which came into being in the first half of the 1920s.

Thereafter, Mense's style became more solid, more classical. In *Mother with Children* (illus. p. 75), a work linking Italian models (Carrà, Sironi) with Schrimpf's arrangement of figures and space, he was to create a masterpiece of sentimental Classicism. No work produced by the Munich circle is so closely bound up with "italianità" – yet this also represented the conclusion of the Italian formal element in Mense's work. In 1925, he was appointed to a professorship at the Academy in Breslau, as was Kanoldt. Their hopes of establishing an artistic counterpole there to the avant-gardist circle around Oskar Moll, the Academy's principal, proved impossible to fulfil, and no independent centre of Neue Sachlichkeit painting emerged in Breslau. Shortly after the move, Mense fell into a crisis of creativity; his portraits from this time – more linear in conception – and diffuse still-lifes demonstrate his artistic decline, after a relatively brief heyday.

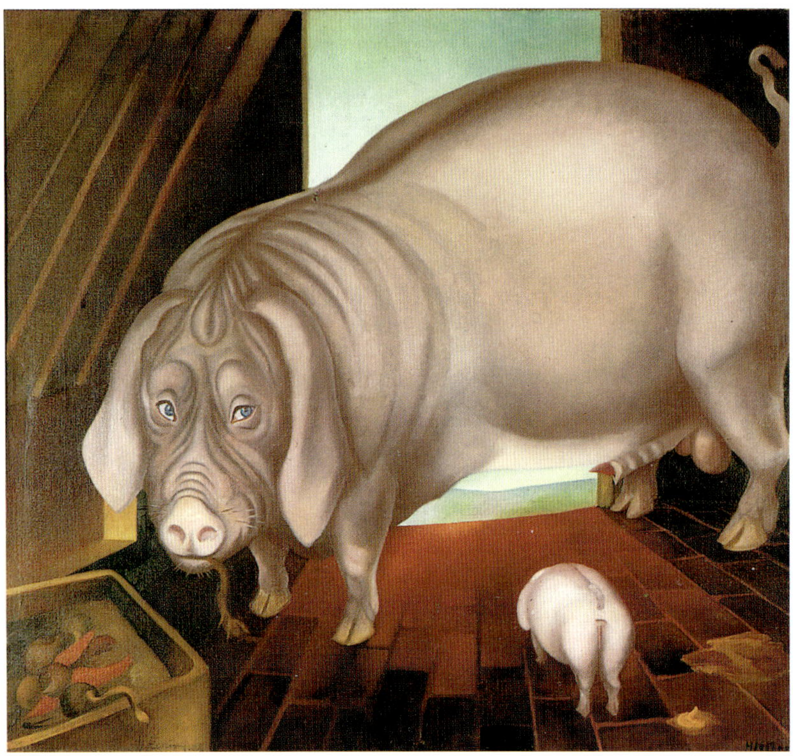

The modern speculator is working in a bare, impersonal room, tensed like a predator lying in wait for its prey. Davringhausen compresses into this composition the anonymity of modern capital, the interchangeability of people.

Heinrich Maria Davringhausen
Sunday Morning, 1922
Sonntagmorgen
Oil on canvas, 100 x 110 cm
Hagen, Karl Ernst Osthaus-Museum

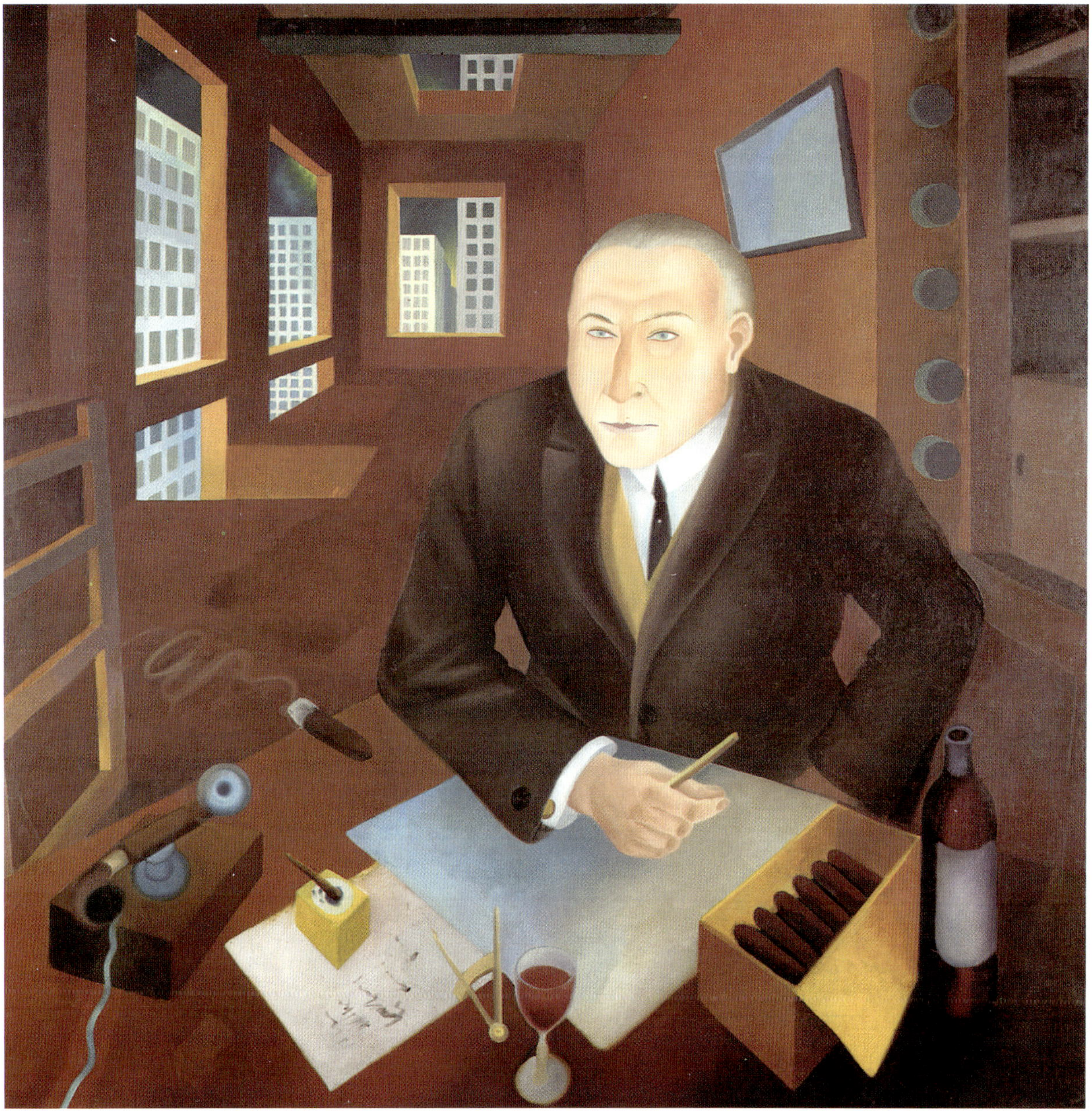

Heinrich Maria Davringhausen

Born in Aachen, Heinrich Maria Davringhausen was basically self-taught, his brief time at the Academy there notwithstanding. Falling early under the spell of the Rhineland Expressionists around August Macke, he strengthened his links with the artistic and intellectual avant-garde through a stay in Ascona during 1914/15. From 1915 onwards, exempted from military service, he lived in Berlin, quickly finding acceptance into the left-wing revolutionary circle of artists and poets around Herwarth Walden, Ludwig Meidner, Franz Jung, Else Lasker-Schüler and the so-called "H brothers" (John Heartfield and Wieland Herzfelde). His Expressionist pictures from this period are marked by a somewhat noncommittal humanist-religious

Heinrich Maria Davringhausen
The Black-Marketeer, 1920/21
Der Schieber
Oil on canvas, 120 x 120 cm
Düsseldorf, Kunstmuseum Düsseldorf im Ehrenhof

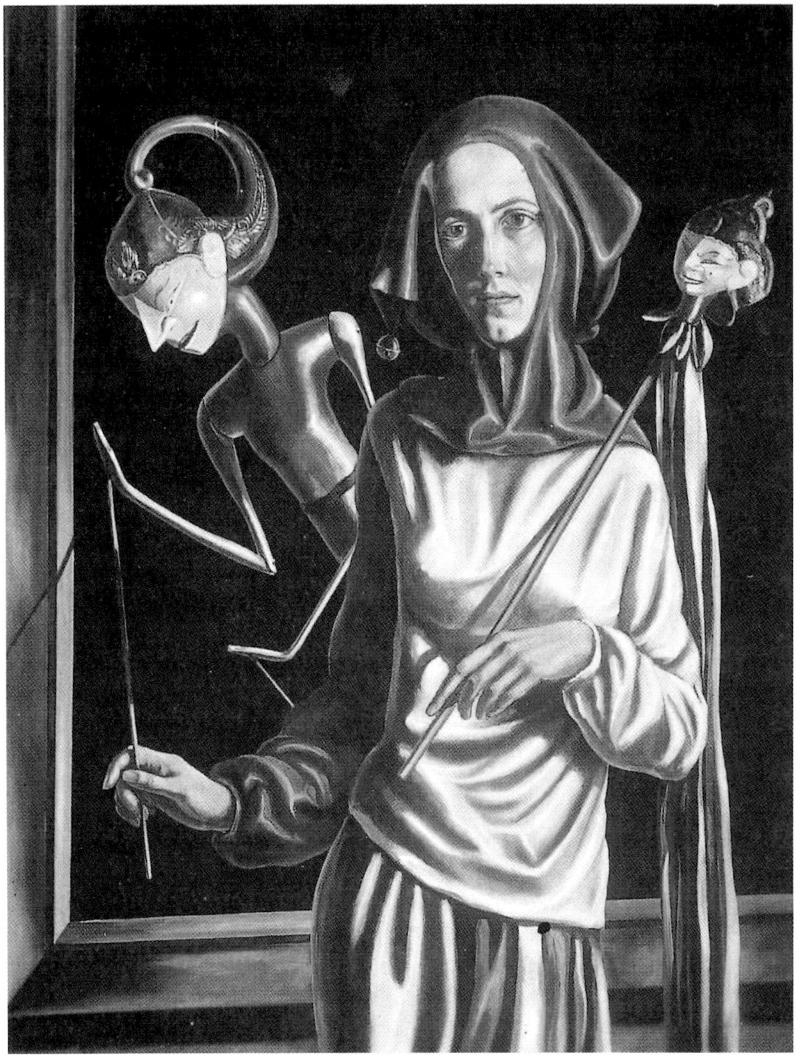

subject-matter. In his private life, he behaved in a dandyish manner, as an aesthete. Else Lasker-Schüler described him, with erotic infatuation, as a "young Trojan priest, his lips kissed a fair maid of God"; she also liked the "godlike restraint"[45] that characterized his pictures. In contrast, the politically well-versed Wieland Herzfelde deeply regretted the fact that Davringhausen felt himself "unattracted by any ideological ism[46].

Walter Schulz-Matan
"Soebodra", 1927
Oil on canvas, 101 x 81 cm
Private collection

Davringhausen's pictures from the years 1914 to 1918, with their restrained elements of lyrical sentimentality, owe a considerable amount to Chagall. Angular and softly flowing forms are integrated into a decorative, magical whole. From 1915/16 on, however, soberly and realistically portrayed objects appear in his works, individually and in groups, heralding the emerging Neue Sachlichkeit conception of form. Davringhausen was not to accomplish a Neue Sachlichkeit vocabulary of form that could be termed his own until 1920/21, contemporaneously with the first Neue Sachlichkeit artists. He was receptive to new motifs and styles, yet he neglected his work on the further development of series of forms. It is perhaps here that the cause of the paradoxes in his development should be sought.

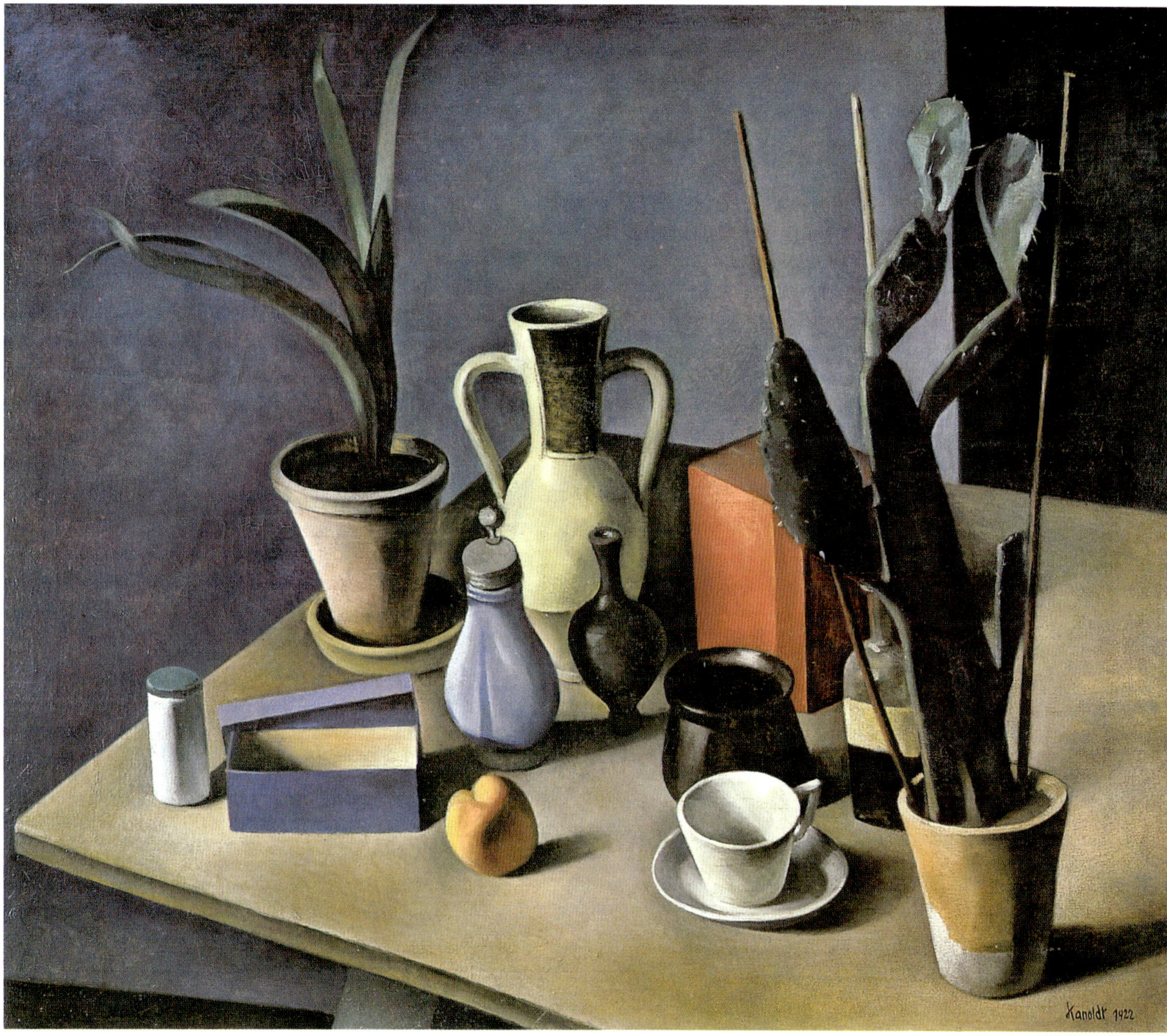

Davringhausen's *The Sex Murderer* (illus. p. 78) is striking for its restraint – one might almost speak of a lyrical approach to the subject, albeit one not without parodistic undertones. The picture is dominated by the girl's indifferent pose. The still-life fragment at the side of the bed would seem to anticipate Kanoldt's still lifes from around 1920, while the view out of the window is a boring compilation of Expressionist elements. All in all, therefore, we have three clearly delineated areas in terms of style and motif. Blood has already flowed in *The Dreamer* (illus. p. 79), painted in 1919 following the artist's move to Munich. A woman lies in bed, her throat cut, while the perpetrator (we may assume) sits at the table, seemingly at a loss, with the razor, dripping with blood, and a lighted cigar before him. The box-like space with its dramatically expanding perspective graphically demonstrates the tension between the near and the distant view; it is structured by means of colours which are all intended to be psychologically significant. In the transition from Expressionism to Neue Sachlichkeit, the new stylistic elements sometimes appear exaggerated, almost caricatured, yet they carry unambiguous authority.

Alexander Kanoldt
Still Life with Jugs and Red Tea-Caddy, 1922
Stilleben mit Krügen und roter Teedose
Oil on canvas, 77.5 x 88.5 cm
Karlsruhe, Staatliche Kunsthalle

In Kanoldt's "Subiaco" and in the numerous landscape-format views of Olevano from 1924 on, the town appears as an additive entity of geometrical bodies, an impression created by the rhythmical ranging of the buildings. The backdrop is provided by a landscape recorded without individual characteristics and unable to serve as a counterpole to the rigid solidity of the town.

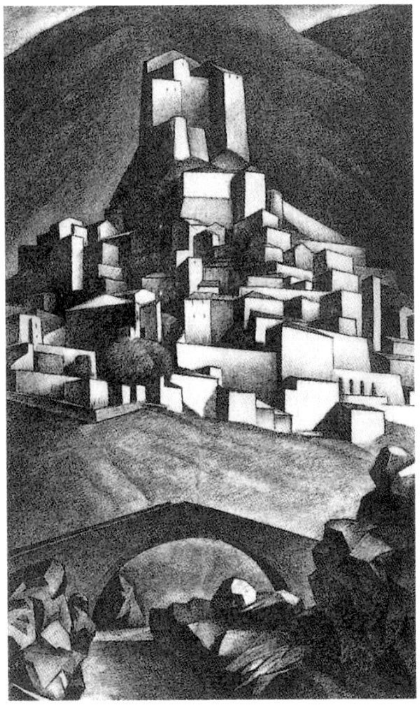

Alexander Kanoldt
Subiaco, 1924
Lithograph, 50.7 x 37.1 cm
Karlsruhe, Staatliche Kunsthalle

With *The Black-Marketeer* (illus. p. 81) – a socio-critical subject, something very rare for Davringhausen – the artist created the classic pictorial symbol of the period of inflation that was commencing. We are concerned here with money, yet it is precisely that which is absent from the picture: now information is becoming money. The picture was inspired by the Italian Pittura metafisica and Grosz' *Diabolo Player*, in particular in its monotonous urban backdrop. The room recedes in strongly linear perspective to give a view out onto the city, communicating with it, itself an anonymous part of the equally anonymous urban business structure. The geometrizing treatment of the room deceives, however, as does the related sense of something well-ordered and rational: the abrupt foreshortenings create compositional tensions, intensified still further by the conscious dissonances of a venom-charged palette. The speculator also belongs to the series of sexual offenders in the broader sense, without possessing their individuality as illustrated by their environment or deed. This important work marked the beginning of Davringhausen's Neue Sachlichkeit period as such.

The pictures in still-life manner from this Munich period favour drastic foreshortenings and diagonal angles. Around 1922, Davringhausen also fused new window views à la Schrimpf (illus. p. 80) with still lifes which take up Kanoldt's work from around 1920/21. In contrast, the numerous still lifes of toys demonstrate a poetic feeling for the quiet unreality of a child's world. The artist subsequently lived in Berlin and Cologne. It is impossible to detect any further clear development after 1923, merely indicating a withdrawal from what had become a sterile canon of Neue Sachlichkeit forms. In March 1933, Davringhausen left Germany for good, to make a contribution to French Abstraction under the name of Henri Davring.

Alexander Kanoldt

"He loves everything which reveals a constructive plan behind the order of things. He loves order itself."[47] Thus Wilhelm Hausenstein, the art critic, characterized his former Karlsruhe schoolfriend, Alexander Kanoldt. In Germany, a country that had suffered more as a result of the excesses of order than from those of anarchy, this was undoubtedly ambiguous praise; nonetheless, it does justice in its own way to Kanoldt's artistic bent.

The painter grew up in a house steeped in artistic tradition. His father, the painter Edmund Kanoldt, was one of the last important Nazarenes, and the classical 19th-century pictures of Italy hung in the family home. The young, Kanoldt, however, wished to leave the path of late academic art. After studying in Karlsruhe, he went to Munich, where a stroke of good fortune brought him into immediate contact with the current avant-garde. In 1909, he became secretary of the recently founded "Neue Künstlervereinigung" (New Artists' Association), whose members included Jawlensky, Kandinsky and – later – Marc. Kanoldt took part in the Association's first exhibition in the Galerie Thannhauser in Munich in December 1909, showing early paintings clearly indebted to French Pointillism and van Gogh.

One year later, he would become acquainted with the works of Derain, Braque, Picasso and Vlaminck at an exhibition in Munich. This precipitated his decisive transition to a manner of painting that cited Cubist forms, together with his search for a strictly disciplined compositional structure. Since Kanoldt rejected pure abstraction, however, his path was to depart from that of Kandinsky and Marc in 1911. While the latter two left the New Artists' Association and founded the "Blaue Reiter", the conflict between

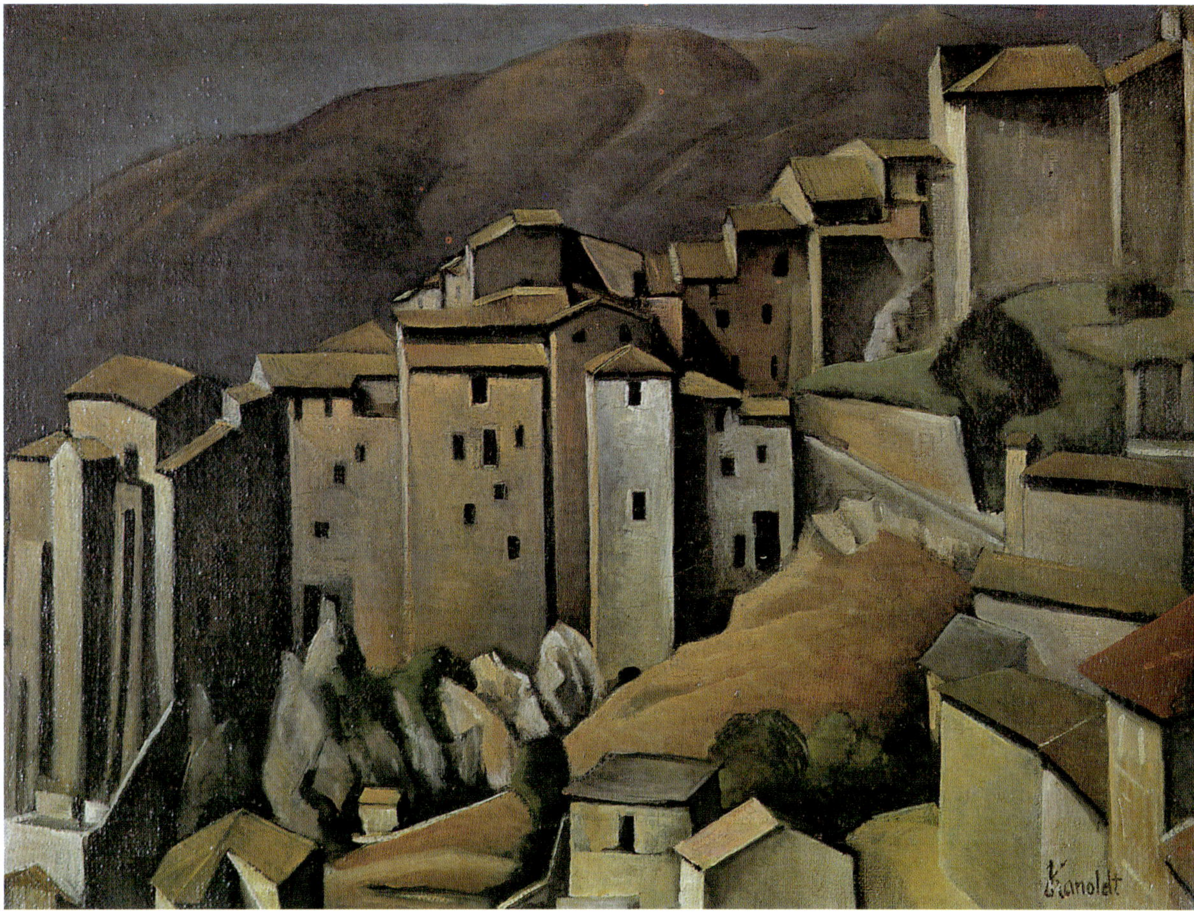

Kanoldt and the artistic avant-garde smouldered on unresolved and would reach a sad climax in the years between 1925 and 1930, with Kanoldt bitterly fighting the Bauhaus tendencies of the progressive Breslau Academy of Art.

The still lifes painted by Kanoldt after 1918 likewise reveal Cubist elements, but also the influence of Derain and late Cézanne. It was not until the beginning of the 1920s that the development of a Neue Sachlichkeit style became evident, one shaped by the remnants of a Cubist compositional manner and a strictly structured pictorial composition. Kanoldt joined the front view with the view from above in a polyperspective manner, shifting and overlapping zones and levels within the picture. Despite this, he remained closely attached to the model offered by nature, seeking to purify and transcend it but not cause its concreteness to disappear.

In 1922, he was to develop a new type of still life (illus. pp. 70, 83). The portrayed objects – including rubber plants and potted plants, but predominantly jugs and angular containers – are positioned apart from one another; in the atmosphere of restrained colour, they acquire increased tranquillity and an apparently magical value of their own through a muted, smooth application of paint. Spatial relations of an unclear perspective further heighten the tension between the obtrusive super-reality and a no less marked unreality within the ensemble, the latter only initially giving the impression of a collection of familiar household objects. In some cases, the selection and placing of the objects portrayed is at first pleasing; even

Alexander Kanoldt
Olevano II, 1925
Oil on canvas, 61 x 82 cm
Essen, Museum Folkwang

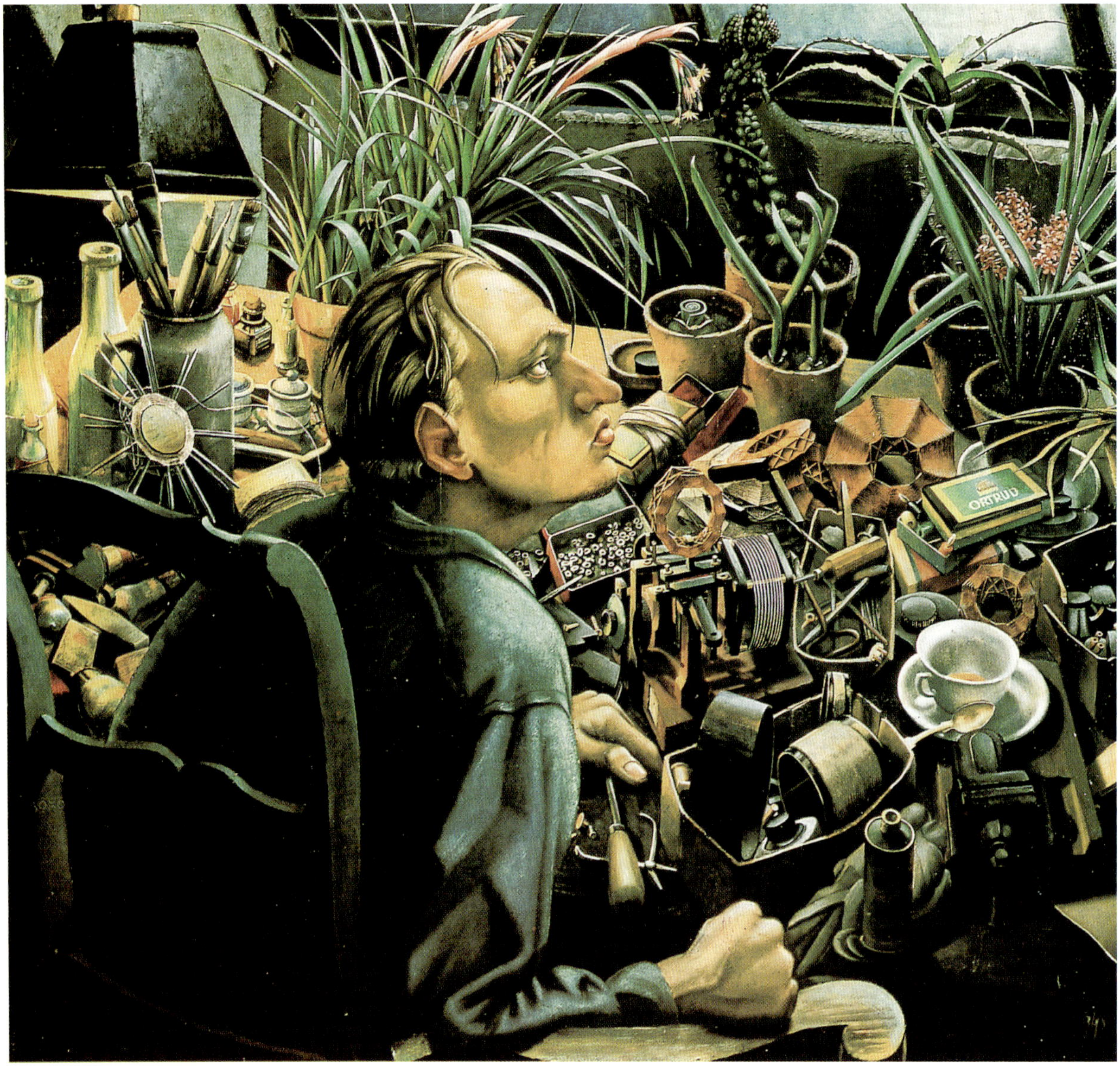

Wilhelm Heise
Fading Spring (Self-Portrait at Work-table), c. 1926
Verblühender Frühling (Selbstbildnis am Basteltisch)
Oil on wood, 84 x 90 cm
Munich, Städtische Galerie im Lenbachhaus

here, however, such an impression is only of very limited duration. The distance to the observer remains too obvious. The numerous imitators of this still-life type, one which would later become very popular, were to break through this barrier relatively easily with a scarcely nuanced, delicate application of paint, although they would never achieve anything remotely resembling the quality of Kanoldt's pictures.

Kanoldt painted numerous views of small Italian towns, both shortly before the war and in the years 1924–1926. He himself said that he was thereby attempting to discover "the soul of the town", that he wanted to find the internal order of the urban organism and avoid everything "manifestly impressional". In 1913/14, he rendered the towers of San Gimignano in Tuscany as building cubes; in 1924, he turned his attention to two mountain towns in Latium, Olevano (illus. p. 85) and Subiaco (illus. p. 84. His father had already depicted Olevano and Serpentara wood, favourite spot of the Nazarenes. In the mid–1920s, at the peak of his Neue Sachlichkeit period, Kanoldt produced an impressive series of paintings, lithographs and drawings of these two towns. In the second half of the 1920s, the constructive order within Kanoldt's pictures froze into a pictorial cliché, one suppressing any artistic sensitivity. Nor could Kanoldt's unfortunate efforts to accept cultural politics after 1933 conceal the progressive loss of substance in his art. The artist himself was dissatisfied with the harmless Neo-Romanticism of his work after 1930, and embarked around 1937 upon the search for new forms and subjects. But his confidence in pictorial order as an analogon of world order had been, leading the painter Kurt Rössing, on visiting Kanoldt shortly before his death, to note despondently: " . . . painting had become a matter of uncertainty for him."[48]

Munich after 1925

In 1925 – the very year, ironically, of the Munich group's success at the Mannheim exhibition – Munich was to lose its short-lived status as the centre of Neue Sachlichkeit painting, following the departure of Davringhausen for Berlin and Kanoldt and Mense taking up their appointments in Breslau. No further impulses of any great significance were to come from Schrimpf, who remained behind, although only until 1933. Franz Roh complained bitterly about the total disinterest on the part of the state and city cultural bureaucracy, which had countenanced the exodus quite unmoved. None of the new-generation Neue Sachlichkeit painters still resident in Munich were invited to participate in the second large Neue Sachlichkeit exhibition, held in Amsterdam in 1929. However, whole series of painters were working in Munich after 1925, and should be taken into consideration within a topographical portrayal of Neue Sachlichkeit art.

Wilhelm Heise, for example, who had been living in Munich since 1918, promulgated a stylistic variant of Neue Sachlichkeit in which a precise design, one somewhat affected in places, produced an unconscious tension between the seemingly clumsy figures and the luxuriant if soon wilting nature surrounding them. His unreal natural details occasionally call to mind the late Pre-Raphaelites. An inexplicable sense of threat exudes from the plants and objects bathed in gleaming light in *Fading Spring* (illus. p. 86), painted with dry application of paint on plywood; he also fashioned *Farewell to Summer* as a symbol of the threat inherent in the plant-world. Unchallenged by the Nazis, Heise continued to develop his style in the 1930s (*Stiglmaierplatz in Munich*, illus. p. 176), despite a waning in creative power.

Young Walter Schulz-Matan created the astonishing portrait of a *Faïence Collector* (illus. p. 87). The finely veined head of the collector, placed directly adjacent to the edge of the picture and overlapped by one of his objects, enjoys the same coldly shimmering texture as may be seen in the collector's items surrounding it. Among the many portraits of Oskar Maria Graf, a man closely linked with the Munich Neue Sachlichkeit painters, that by Schulz-Matan (illus. p. 32) particularly strikes the observer on account of its realistic effect and its renunciation of the otherwise obligatory folkloric stylization of the portrait's subject as the epitome of a Bavarian.

A further aspect of the Neue Sachlichkeit formal spectrum is presented by the paintings of Max Radler, the technology enthusiast. He employed the same unobtrusive objectivity in his paintings of railway lines (illus. p. 173) as in those of half-timbered idylls, the latter revealing traces of a lingering Cubist formal vocabulary reduced to the level of naive decoration.

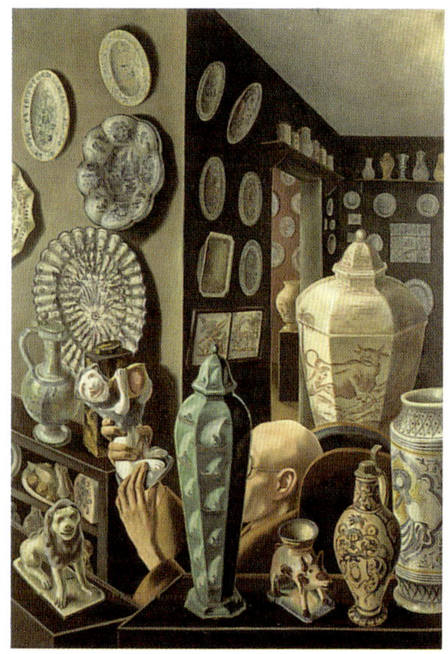

Walter Schulz-Matan
Faïence Collector, 1927
Fayencesammler
Oil on canvas, 100 x 142 cm
Munich, Stadtmuseum

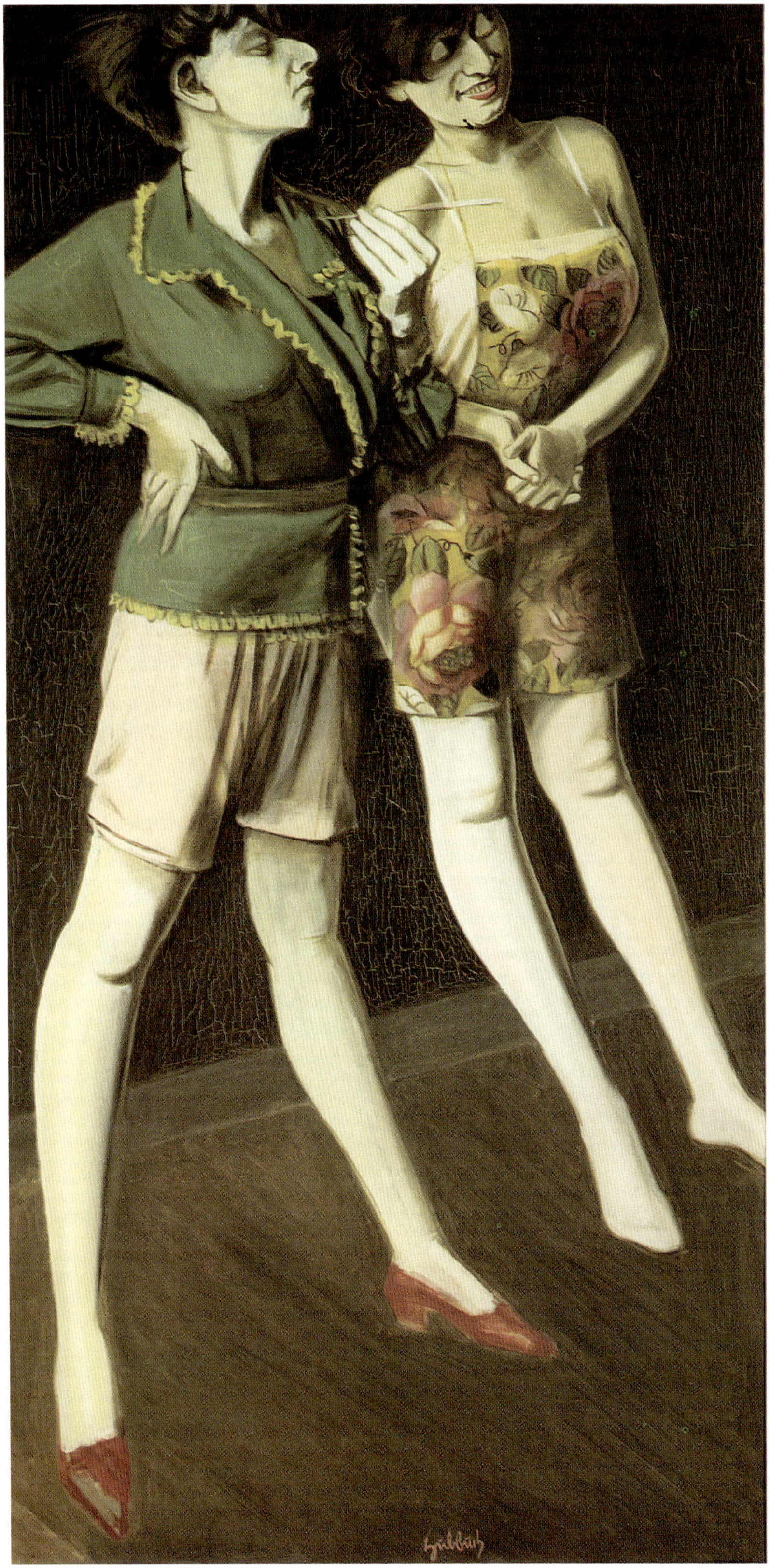

Karlsruhe

Drawing Takes Priority

The tranquil city of Karlsruhe, historical residency of the Baden rulers, was to become one of the most important provincial centres of Neue Sachlichkeit. The common stylistic features of the Karlsruhe Neue Sachlichkeit artists predominantly derive from the formal elements instilled during their academic training, something true not only of the artists of the older generation, those who studied before 1914, but also of those younger artists studying in the 1920s. The Karlsruhe Academy and its large studios were the constant point of reference – in the material sense as well – for the artists living there. Even Schlichter and Kanoldt, former pupils of the Academy active in Berlin and Munich respectively in the 1920s, felt linked to the city of their alma mater; in addition, Kanoldt had been born in Karlsruhe. The Academy had possessed a school of etching and an institute of lithography since the turn of the century. In contrast to many other German seats of learning, Karlsruhe students received excellent instruction in the techniques of graphic art, and practised drawing unceasingly.[49]

Apart from the Academy (reformed in 1920 as the Baden State School of Art), the capital of Baden offered no fertile ground for modern art. Only for a short time, during the eventful years from 1918 to 1920, did it appear that an emotional Expressionism might be able to arouse the artistic life of the city from its blissful daydreams of the sentimental scenes painted by Hans Thoma. Soon after, however, the conservative status quo reasserted itself. The widespread taste for late-German romanticism concealed a dull provinciality containing pre-fascistoid seeds. This would become evident in dramatic form as early as in 1933, when leading figures in the local Nazi group, in close collaboration with painters from the Thoma school, brought off the first "Degenerate Art" exhibition in April – without any directive from Berlin! – utilizing this show and its malicious attitude towards the Kunsthalle's purchasing policy to attack above all the classic German Impressionists and, among the works of the 1920s, the Neue Sachlichkeit movement in particular. This was an unusual event in the early years of Nazism, even with regard to the objects that were the subject of the complaints; it produced a strained situation, one which could only be defused after fierce intervention by Kanoldt, at that time a figure of considerable influence.

Wilhelm Schnarrenberger had been teaching at the Academy since 1920, and was joined in 1925 by Karl Hubbuch and Georg Scholz, their excellent final examinations resulting in their being appointed to the staff from within the Academy. Among the Academy pupils to gather around this Verist-Neue

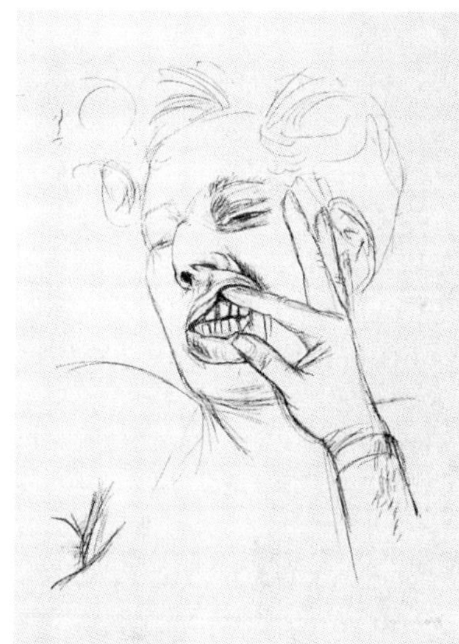

Karl Hubbuch
At the Doctor's, 1930
Beim Arzt
Lithograph, 41.3 x 30 cm
Private collection

Karl Hubbuch
Hilde Twice, 1923
Zweimal Hilde
Oil on canvas, 150 x 77 cm
Munich, Bayerische Staatsgemälde-sammlungen

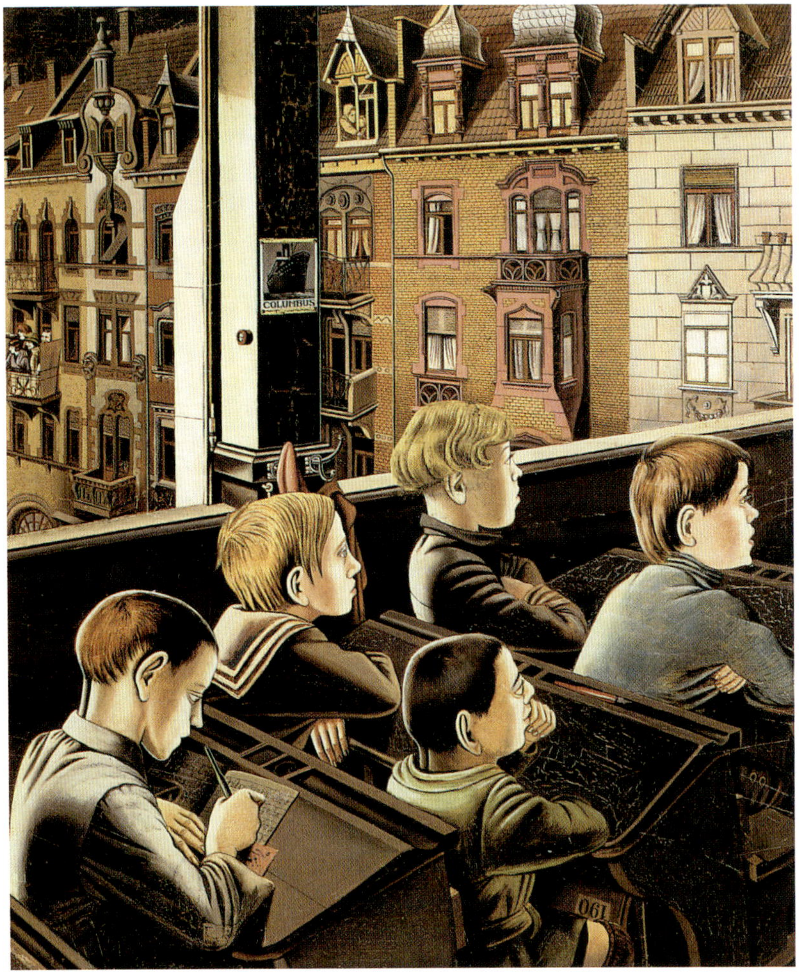

Karl Hubbuch
The Classroom, 1925
Die Schulstube
Oil on hardboard, 75 x 63 cm
Karlsruhe, Helmut Goettl

Sachlichkeit troika were Rudolf Dischinger, Hermann Sprauer, Hanna Nagel and Willi Müller-Hufschmid. From an official point of view, the dismissal of Schnarrenberger, Hubbuch and Scholz in 1933 marks the end of Neue Sachlichkeit in Karlsruhe, although a weakening of its formal innovation may already be detected at an earlier point, roughly from 1929 onwards. The works of the Karlsruhe artists were characterized by the hard style of drawing with precisely sketched outlines, as developed by Hubbuch and Scholz and adopted by Dischinger, Nagel and Sprauer. Hubbuch, who ran the drawing class, taught his pupils to record the chance occurrences and unspectacular aspects of everyday life. He also encouraged them to draw subjects whose pictorial organization was not already predetermined by the unambiguity of their form, but for which it was first of all necessary to find an ordering structure – for example dilapidated huts, piles of wood, the ends of railway tracks, and so forth. Hubbuch, as head of the Academy's drawing class, held the decisive teaching post among the Karlsruhe artists. Yet he must also have exerted a great influence upon his pupils as a person. He was generous, for example in the acceptance of pupils into his drawing class, and liberal – yet also most concerned to achieve discipline. He knew how to motivate his pupils.

Karl Hubbuch

Hubbuch had not grown up in an atmosphere with any artistic connections: his grandfathers were farmers and craftsmen, his father first an army officer and then a civil servant. Hubbuch himself had studied in Karlsruhe from 1908 to 1912, forming friendships there with Scholz and Schlichter. In 1912/13, he consolidated his studies at the School of Arts and Crafts in Berlin under Emil Orlik, the important Art Nouveau artist; here he also met Grosz. It might appear that Hubbuch's later Verism had already been prescribed through these early friendships; however, he would work it out for himself in a highly individual manner.

Hubbuch's interest was directed from early on towards the graphic arts. Beginning with drawings, he later adopted etchings and lithographs as his favoured techniques. According to the account given by his friend Rudolf Schlichter, Hubbuch had already developed the essential elements of his style, one exaggerating and thereby alienating reality, while at the Karlsruhe Academy: "For a long time, we saw nothing of his work apart from his well-drawn heads. It was not until we had been acquaintances for roughly half a year that Zack happened one day upon some strange drawings of his in an art shop. Our interest aroused, we examined the curious sheets that he had done. They depicted mysterious, empty rooms, with pieces of bizarre furniture standing in them or dreadful instruments lying around, crumpled beds resembling the ectoplasm of spiritualist manifestations rather than genuine places of human rest. (...) Other sheets depicted desolate urban courtyard tenement houses, façades covered with repulsive ornaments

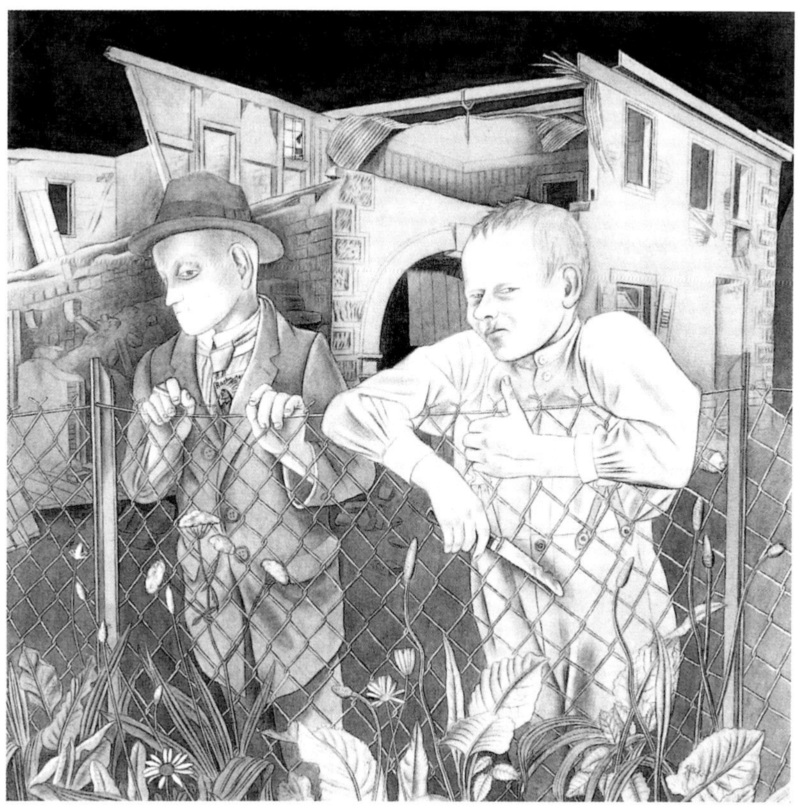

Karl Hubbuch
Duck Poachers, c. 1924/25
Entenräuber
Pencil and watercolour, 43 x 43.2 cm
Stuttgart, Graphische Sammlungen, Staatsgalerie Stuttgart

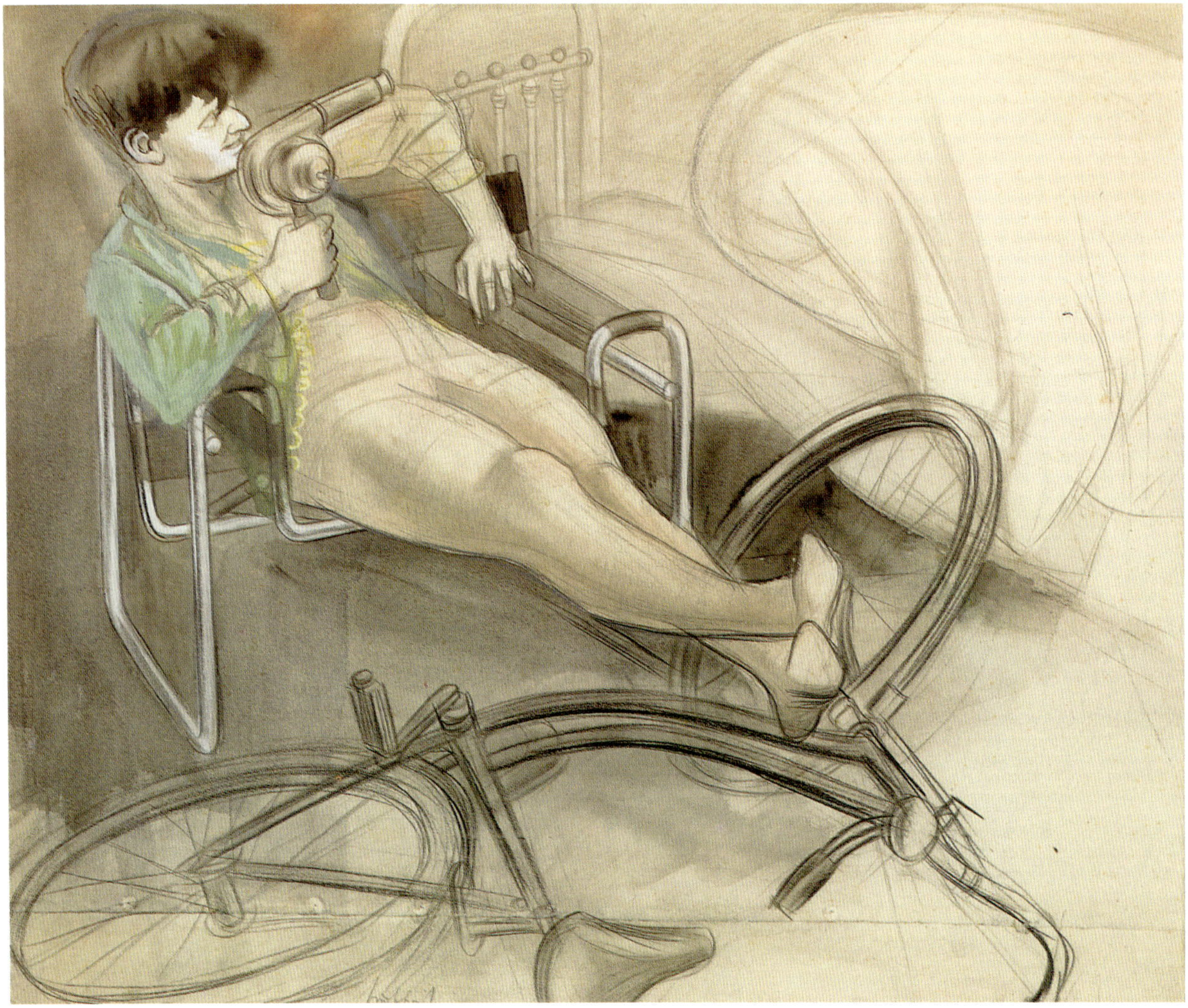

Karl Hubbuch
With Bicycle and Hair Dryer, 1929/30
Mit Fön und Fahrrad
Chalk and watercolour, 57 x 74 cm
By kind permission of the Galerie Huber-Nising, Frankfurt am Main

with gaping, staring black windows. All this had been drawn with thin, extremely exact strokes of the pencil, elevated to a ghostly plane by means of light colouring."[50]

After the war, Hubbuch continued to study in Karlsruhe in a master class. He visited Berlin for a second time in 1922, meeting Schlichter and Grosz. The fast-moving metropolis made a great impression upon him, although without leading him to sever his provincial connections. The political topics that were exercising people at this time of crisis were reflected in his work, where he occupied himself with a critical treatment of inflation and the harsh social conditions. While it is still possible to detect the influence of Art Nouveau and Expressionism in these works, a dominant, sharp Verist characterization is already present. In contrast to the contemporaneous political allegories by his friend Scholz, Hubbuch's sheets reveal a multiscene structure, similar to the French "croquis" (sketches) of the 19th century or the later "complex pictures" of left-wing provenance. In *Herr Stresemann and a Piece of Black Bread* (illus. p. 8), an allegory concerning the 1923

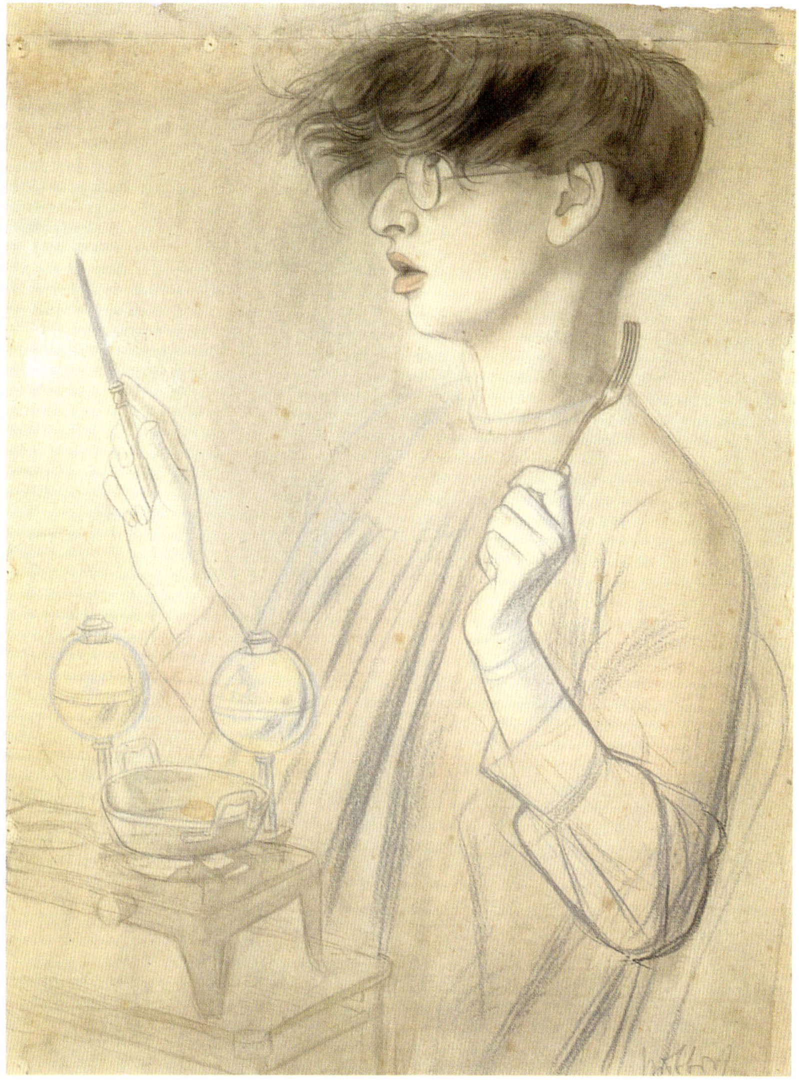

Karl Hubbuch
The Fried Egg, 1929/30
Das Spiegelei
Pencil, coloured pencil, 63.1 x 47.8 cm
Private collection

autumn of inflation, Hubbuch adopts in uninhibited manner the didactic means of the school blackboard, with black arrows pointing to the most important associations from the point of view of content. The despairing proletarian is holding a piece of bread in his right hand and the corresponding pecuniary "value" in his left, a banknote with a never-ending row of zeros. At the top, a policeman is leading away a worker, followed in the middle of the composition by the political spectacle of the formation of the Cabinet, while on the right-hand side a satisfied President Ebert is greeting the German people. The arrangement of the scenes itself provides whatever commentary is required.

Hubbuch's Berlin city pictures are without didactic intention and are aesthetically more attractive. Here the artist celebrates a view of urban events which, while appearing superficially naive, is in fact highly sophisticated from a formal point of view. In his watercolour *Berlin City Scene with Circus Caravans* (illus. p. 96), Hubbuch depicts himself wide-eyed, as if he were the Berlin embodiment of the naive "Paysan de Paris" (Aragon), while

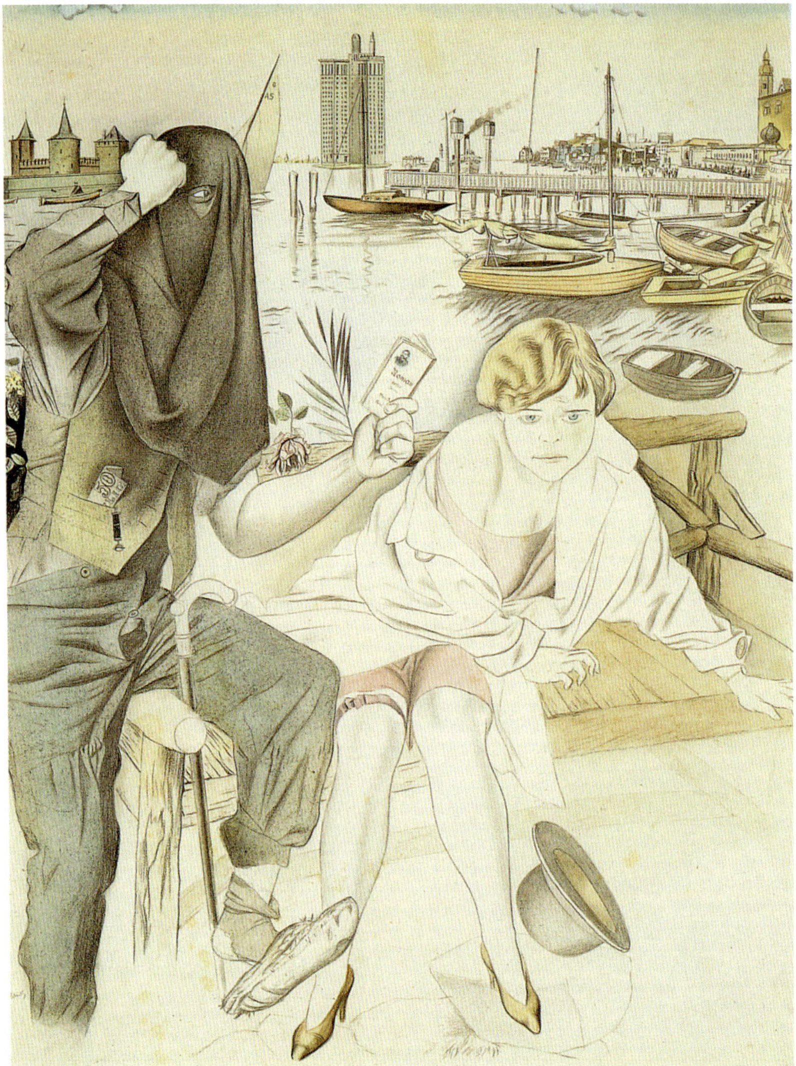

Karl Hubbuch
Detective Story, c. 1924
Leichter Krimi
Pencil and watercolour, 52 x 39.5 cm
Milwaukee, Marvin and Janet Fishman Collection

a group of people sitting near him demonstrate how to enjoy the moment – or kill time. 1924, the year in which this work was executed, saw a whole series of such role-playing self-portraits. In each case their particularly striking feature is the artist's intense gaze which fixes itself upon the observer.

The following could be read in a newspaper review of Hubbuch's work, published on the occasion of an exhibition in Frankfurt's Galerie Trittler in October 1924: "A cold observer, a philosophical mind full of ideas, an uncompromising talent that satirizes the contemporary scene, and finally a draftsman of quite extraordinary quality. A wealth of pencil drawings, lithographs and etchings reveals the great range of his art, embracing equally a most exact observation of reality and bold speculations of fantastic symbolism."[51] "Coldness", "exactness" and "precision" – these are the terms which appear again and again in characterizations of the stylistic qualities to be found in Hubbuch's drawings. Empty spaces alternate in them with areas that are unusually clearly worked out, Hubbuch successfully managing the transition with a few brief strokes.

Karl Hubbuch
The Cologne Swimmer, 1923
Die Schwimmerin von Köln
Pencil and watercolour, 66.3 x 48 cm
Mannheim, Städtische Kunsthalle

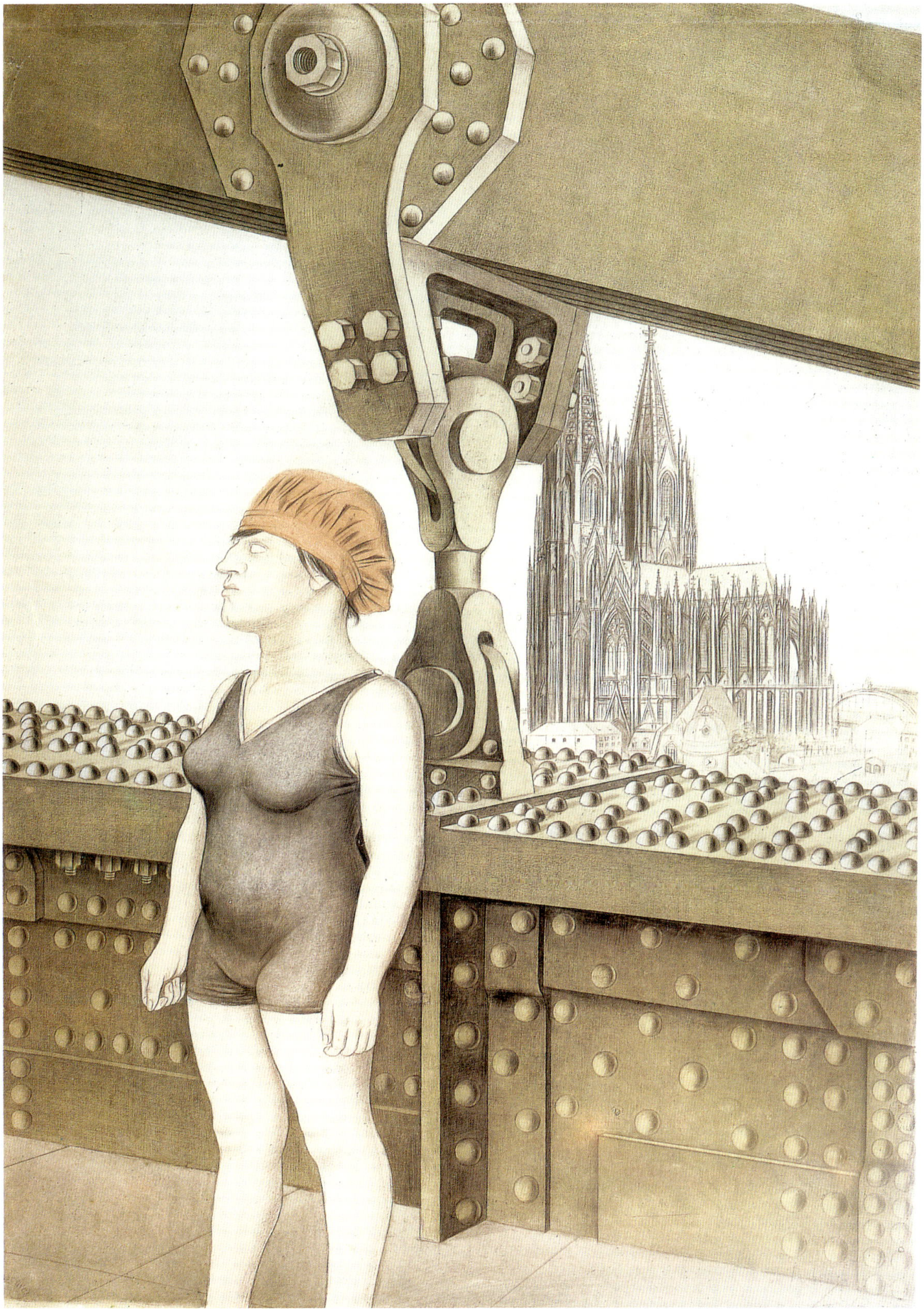

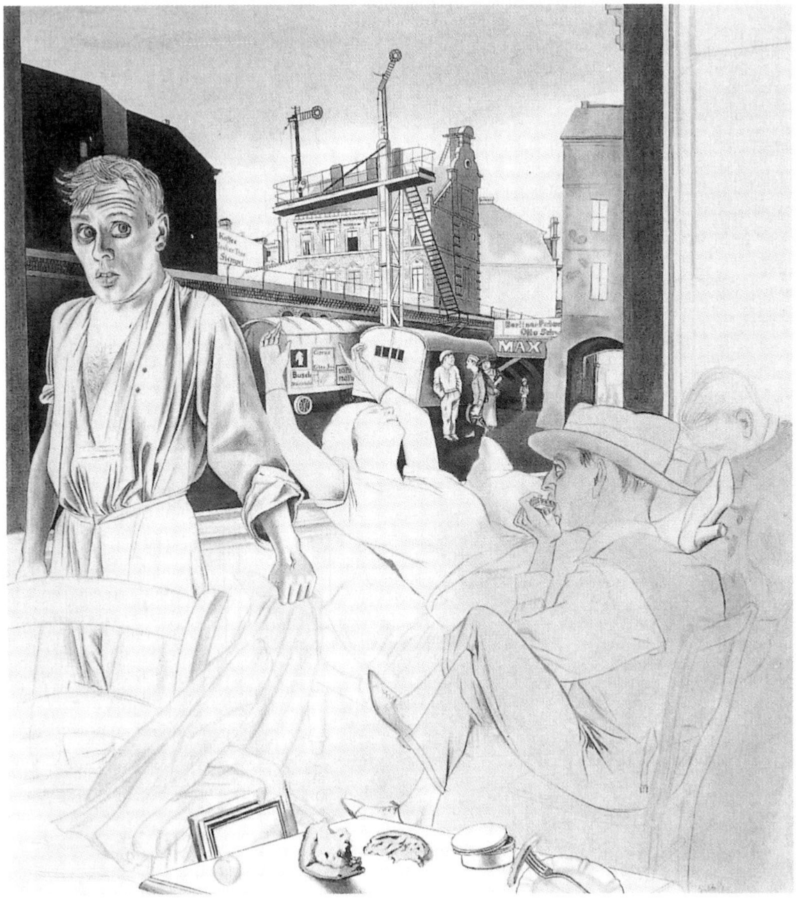

Karl Hubbuch
Berlin City Scene with Circus Caravans, c. 1924
Berliner Großstadtszene mit Zirkuswagen
Watercolour, 52.1 x 40.9 cm
Karlsruhe, Staatliche Kunsthalle

In 1925, Hubbuch became head of the drawing class at the Karlsruhe Academy. He participated in Hartlaub's Mannheim exhibition of "Neue Sachlichkeit" in this year, and also at regular intervals from this point on in nationwide exhibitions. The Mannheim exhibition included not only drawings and prints but also his first oil painting, *The Classroom* (illus. p. 90). In this work, Hubbuch depicts a group of schoolboys in one small section of a classroom who are attentively following the lesson in progress. The fact that the boys' gaze is directed forwards points to the presence of a figure of authority, one who, whilst not actually in the picture, nonetheless clearly has the scene under his or her control. One of the pupils alone is not participating in what is going on, but is writing in his exercise book, looking grimly determined as he does so as if he wished thereby to assert his stubbornness. The entire picture exudes restriction and a lack of freedom, an impression reinforced by many details.

Among Hubbuch's most important pictures is his watercolour *The Cologne Swimmer* (illus. p. 95), in which a determined-looking woman in bathing costume may be seen on a railway bridge in front of a gigantic iron construction component. Cologne Cathedral stands in the background – a third element which, according to a more recent interpretation, enjoys a significance beyond that of merely indicating the location. The picture, it suggests, could "be read as man's alienation from handed-down concepts through the technological orientation of modern times. This view is further

Many of the artists who had initially tended towards Verism and later towards Neue Sachlichkeit had become increasingly moderate by the beginning of the 1930s. In contrast, Hubbuch's works from this period had still lost nothing of their – subject-dependent – sharpness. The relationship between the sexes, as in these two pictures, is fundamentally disturbed. Whether the man makes himself subservient to the woman or keeps her as an object, both are objectified relationships.

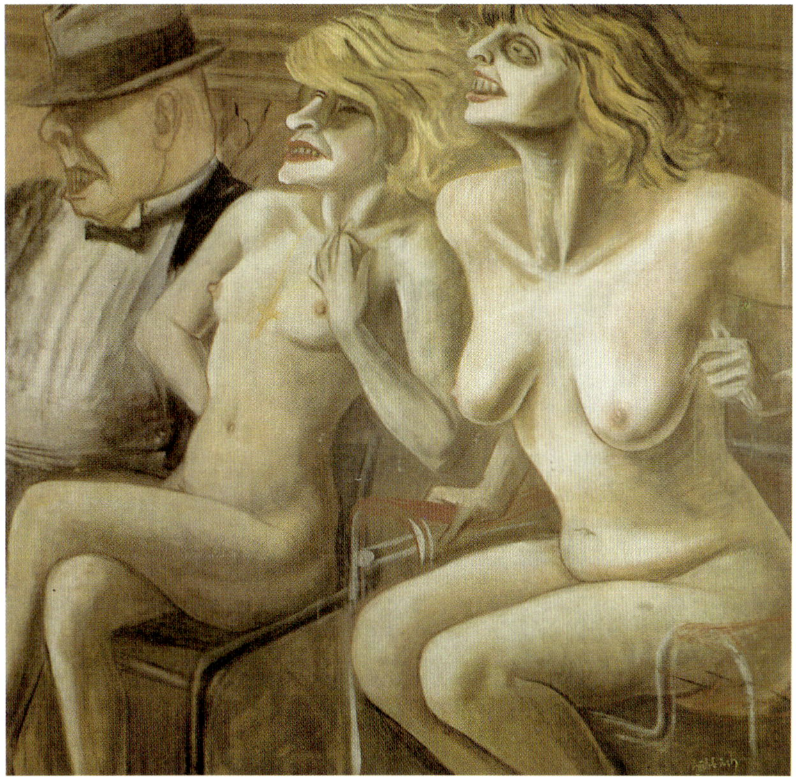

Karl Hubbuch
Everyone Shows What He Has (Bruno and his Ladies), c. 1930
Jeder zeigt, was er hat (Bruno und seine Damen)
Oil on canvas, 152 x 158 cm
Private collection

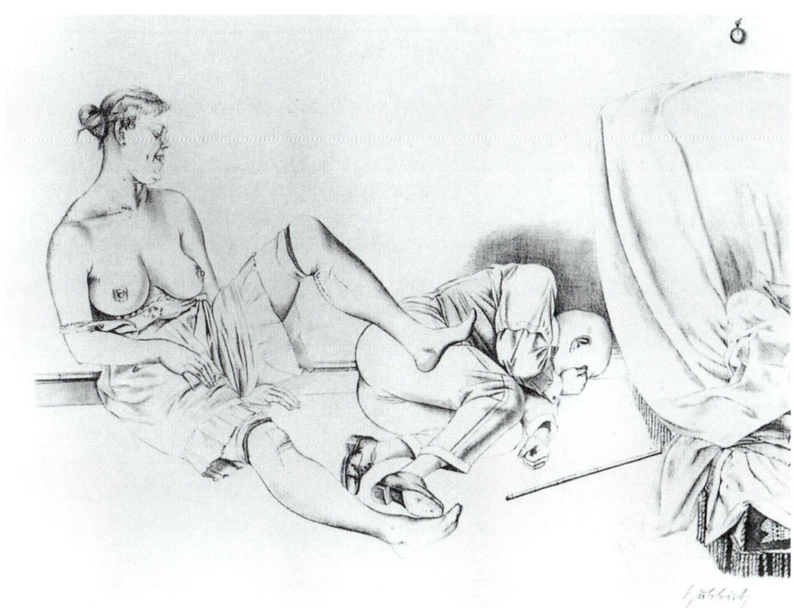

Karl Hubbuch
The Underling, 1923
Der Untertan
Lithograph, 33.8 x 48 cm
Private collection

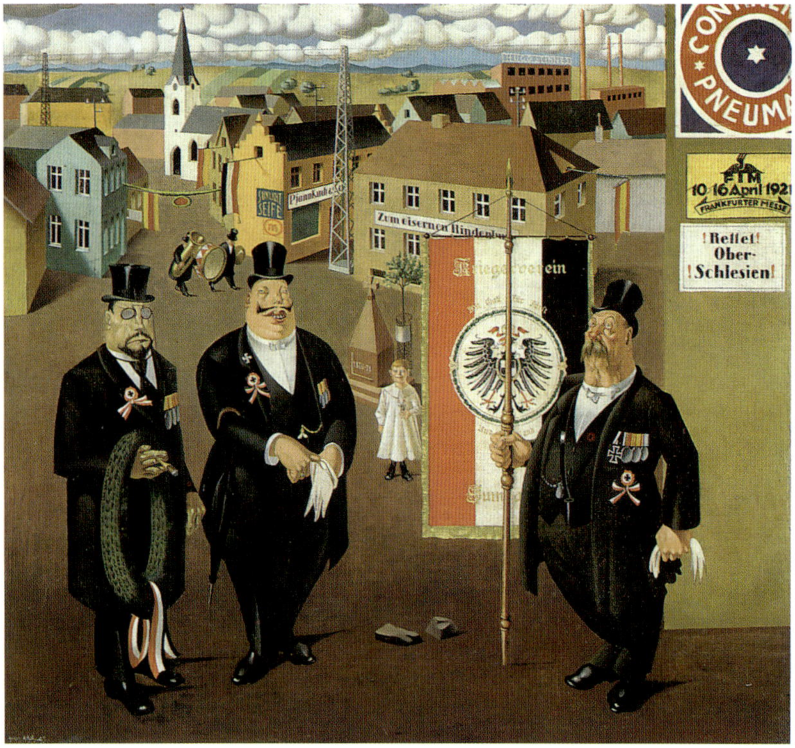

Georg Scholz
War Veterans' Association, 1921
Kriegerverein
Oil on wood, 69 x 75 cm
Karlsruhe, Staatliche Kunsthalle

supported by the position of the woman, who, considerably diminished in stature when seen against the parapet, is standing to the left of the Cathedral, visible some distance behind. A further separation of the two is effected by the axis of the girder construction, which, running through the exact centre of the picture, thereby assigns the woman to the left-hand half and the Cathedral to the right-hand half of the picture."[52]

Hubbuch changed his drawing style after 1925, although his pupils would continue to practise his former style until roughly 1930. Hubbuch was concentrating at this time upon figure studies in which the work process is made visible with a new type of stroke. His drawing from the years 1926 to 1928 would anticipate an astonishingly large number of elements from the so-called "reporting style" of early 1970s West German graphic art. One of his few panel paintings from the 1920s, a study of his wife (*Hilde Twice*, illus. p. 88), who often modelled for him, also reveals his new-found interest in studying poses. Hubbuch fell into a crisis of creativity after 1929, one which would later become intensified as a result of the political difficulties to which he was exposed from 1933 onwards.

Georg Scholz

"We should desire not art, but life"; "Mankind is bad".[53] By means of these striking, programmatic sentences, the young Scholz attempted to distance himself not only from the aestheticism of Art Nouveau, which he had become adequately aware of while studying at the Karlsruhe Academy, but also from the pathos of Expressionism. After returning from the war, he joined the short-lived "Rih" group around Schlichter in 1919, and produced pictures of a Cubist-Futurist nature for a time. Through Schlichter,

Georg Scholz
Industrial Farmers, 1920
Industriebauern
Oil and collage on plywood, 98 x 70 cm
Wuppertal, Von der Heydt-Museum

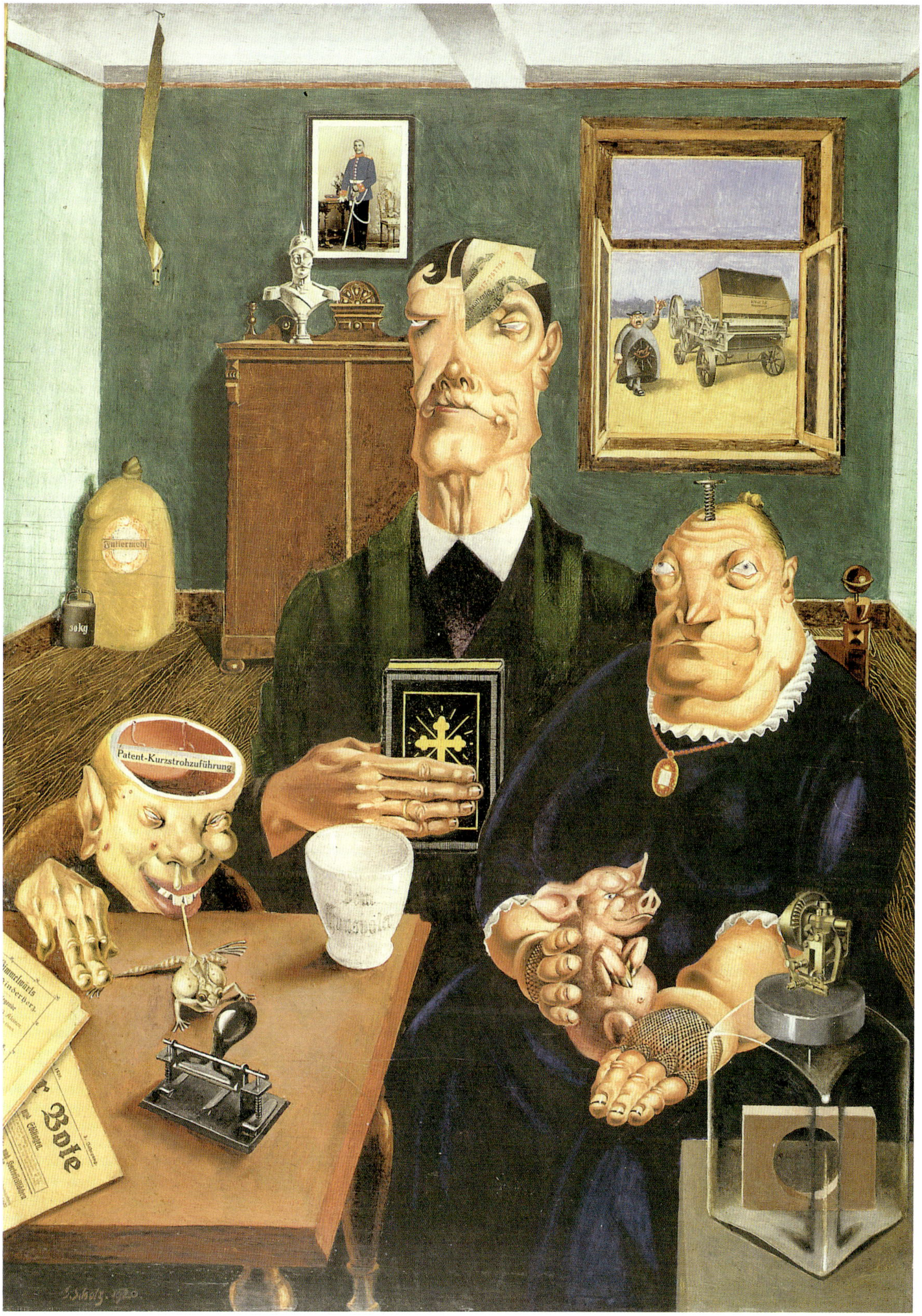
Patent-Kurzstrohzuführung
Futtermehl
30kg

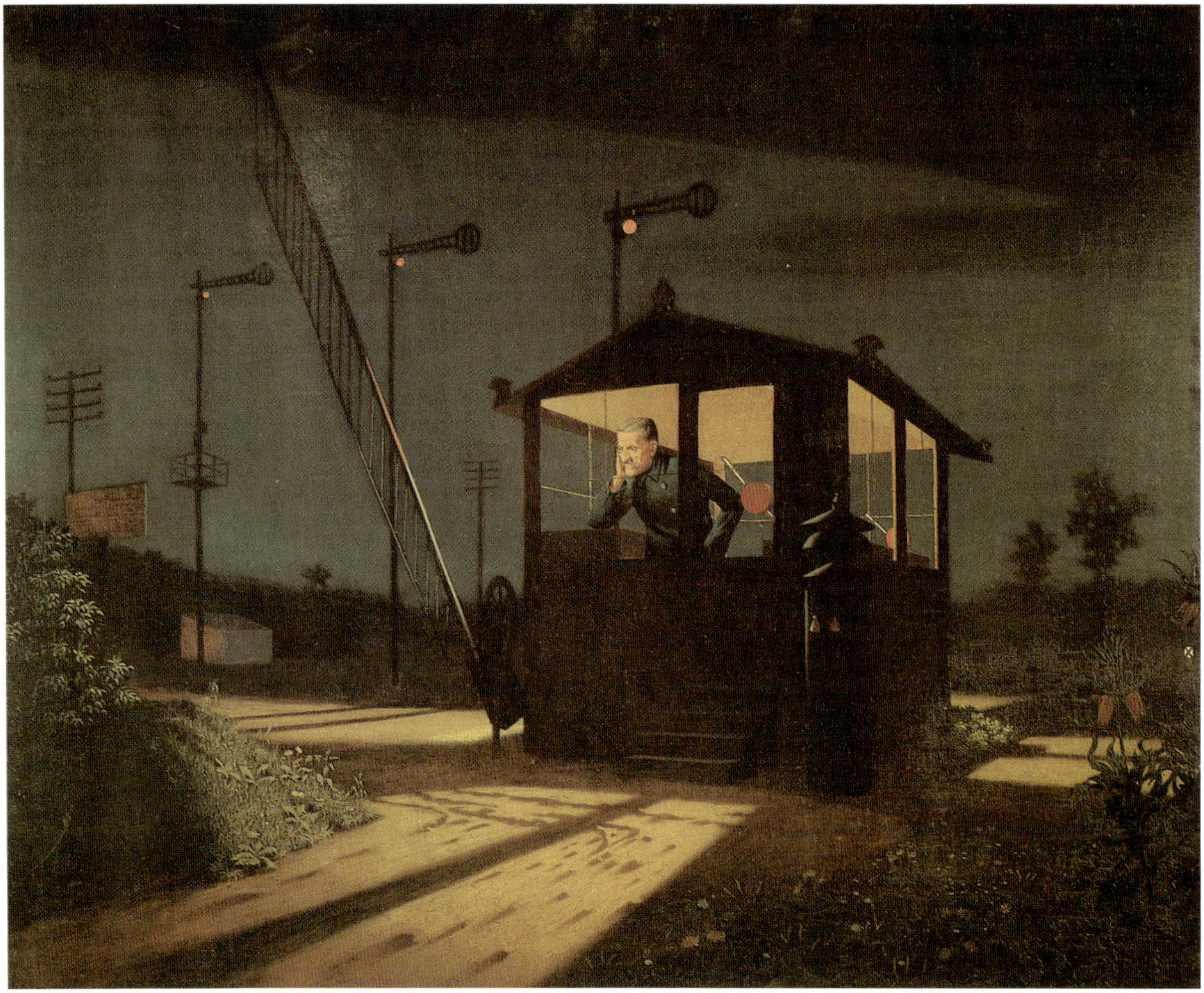

Georg Scholz
Level-Crossing Keeper's Hut, 1924
Bahnwärterhaus
Oil on cardboard, 63 x 83 cm
Düsseldorf, Kunstmuseum Düsseldorf im Ehrenhof

Scholz came into contact with other Verists, in particular Grosz. "Yesterday George Grosz came to visit me from Baden-Baden. Schlichter and Jenny were here as well... We spent an interesting and amusing day together. Grosz is one of the most decent and sensible people I know",[54] Scholz noted down in a diary entry of August 1923. After concluding his studies at the Karlsruhe Academy, he was appointed to a professorship there in 1925 – something, given the work which he had produced up to that time, which speaks for the liberal spirit of the Academy in this period.

Scholz' early works were determinedly critical of society. One of them goes back to a painful personal experience, when, on returning hungry from the war, he attempted to buy something to eat for himself and his family, only to be pointed by a farmer in the direction of the compost heap. It was this sort of heartless individual to whose meanness the artist erected a lasting monument in his *Industrial Farmers* of 1920 (illus. p. 99). Even the feeble-minded-looking boy, a good-for-nothing tormentor of frogs, is characterized as the monstrous product of stupidity. Despite obvious references to the art of Dix and Grosz, Scholz found here an individual form of expression, one marked by discreet sprinklings of collage and the inclusion of elements of a discursive and illustrative nature. At the time, the picture

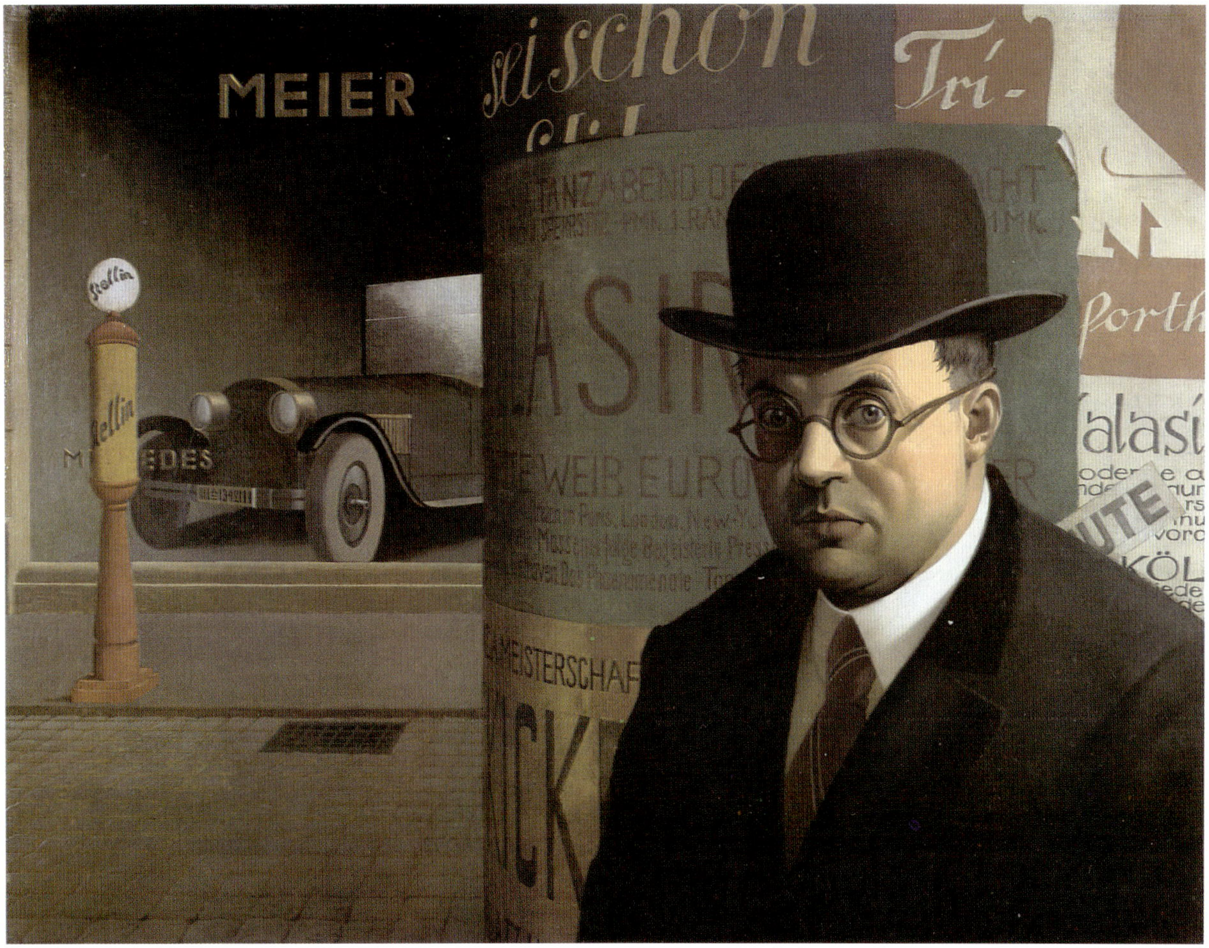

provoked a small Parliamentary question in the Reichstag, it being considered that the work ridiculed the farming community.

Scholz continued the Verist line of his work with his *War Veterans' Association* (illus. p. 98). In this work, he is not only attacking the royalists' tendency to revel in their veteran status but also revealing that what appears to belong to the past in fact contains the seeds of ominous new developments: one of the three petit bourgeois in frock-coats is already wearing the swastika, the symbol of his new political denomination, on his lapel. At the same time, Scholz uses the name of the pub, "Zum eisernen Hindenburg" (Iron Hindenburg), to point to the connection between commercial advertizing and political propaganda.

Between 1922 to 1923, he fell back on an Expressionist motif to mock the apparently healthy world of the small town, in which everyone goes about his harmless business (illus. p. 9). As the well-ordered day draws to an end, the petit bourgeois dare to come out onto the streets ... Scholz was later to grow fond of the Baden small-town idyll, as a refuge from the Nazis. The element of threat behind the idyllic façade, shown in the figure of the butcher in *Small Town by day*, may also be detected in Scholz' *Level-Crossing Keeper's Hut* (illus. p. 100). The official, basically a harmless

Georg Scholz
Self Portrait in front of an Advertising Column, 1926
Selbstbildnis vor der Litfaßsäule
Oil on pasteboard, 59.5 x 78.5 cm
Karlsruhe, Staatliche Kunsthalle

Spitzweg-like character, has acquired a touch of the demonic through the way in which the lighting is stage-managed. Other interpretations, in contrast, emphasize the "pointsman's troubled, starving expression", believing it to contain an allusion to the disparity between responsibility and payment.[55]

After 1924, Scholz was increasingly to dispense with Verism. His *Self-Portrait in front of an Advertizing Column* (illus. p. 101) from 1926 reveals a pronouncedly bourgeois artist – Scholz had become a professor shortly before – parading in front of the typical symbols of the time for information (the advertising column) and speed (the car showroom). His face simultaneously conveys a sceptical reserve and a melancholy consent. The almost invisible glass pane fronting the car showroom, indicated only by the lettering it carries, underlines the ambivalence between distance and proximity. The works of the following years would reveal growing indications that Scholz was undergoing a transition to a "Latinity" often previously embraced in Baden. The pictorial concept of his *Seated Nude with Plaster Bust* (illus. p. 103) goes back to works by de Chirico and Casorati, whom Scholz had probably encountered in the magazine "Valori Plastici". The classical aura emanating from the bust and the nude model is so dominating that the significance of the long black stockings (a prostitute) – and with it the ironic break in the picture's message – recedes.

Scholz travelled in 1928 to Paris, and in 1930 to the Matisse exhibition in Berlin. He expressed himself enthusiastic about French painting. In 1929, he declined an invitation from Hartlaub to participate in the "Contemporary Artistic Works in Baden" exhibition. "He says that he has not exhibited for two years. He speaks of the experimental character of his recent pictures, adding that his work has led him away from Neue Sachlichkeit to new formulations."[56] He had hardly enough time in the remaining years until 1933 to shape these experiments into a recognizable new style, although it is possible to identify an orientation in the direction of the modern French artists, in particular Pierre Bonnard. Following the Nazis' rise to power, Scholz retired to Waldkirch so that he might escape from them.

Georg Scholz
Seated Female Nude, Head propped in Hand, 1925
Sitzender weiblicher Akt, sich aufstützend
Pencil drawing, paper, 60 x 45 cm
Private collection

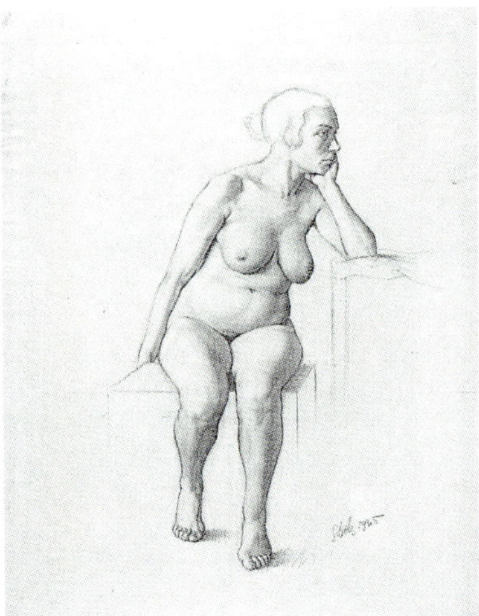

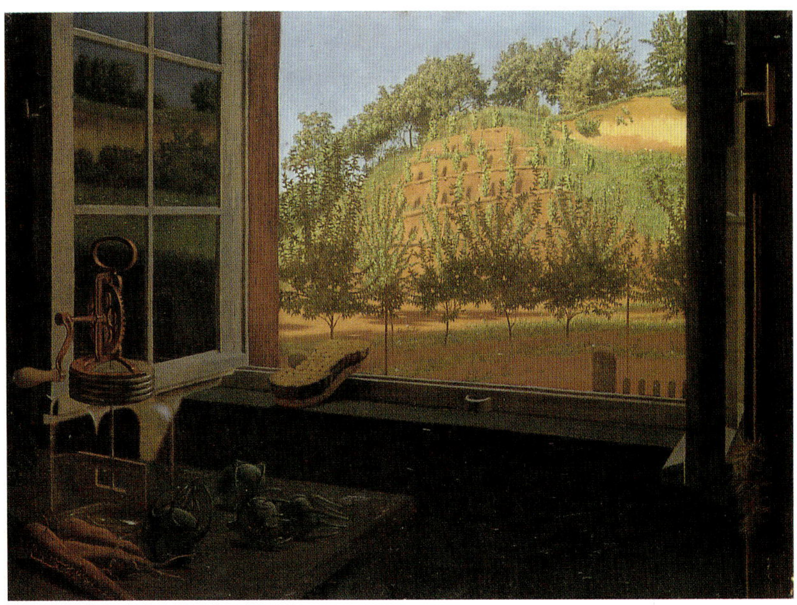

Georg Scholz
View from the Kitchen Window, 1926
Blick aus dem Küchenfenster
Oil on pasteboard, 73 x 98 cm
Karlsruhe, Staatliche Kunsthalle

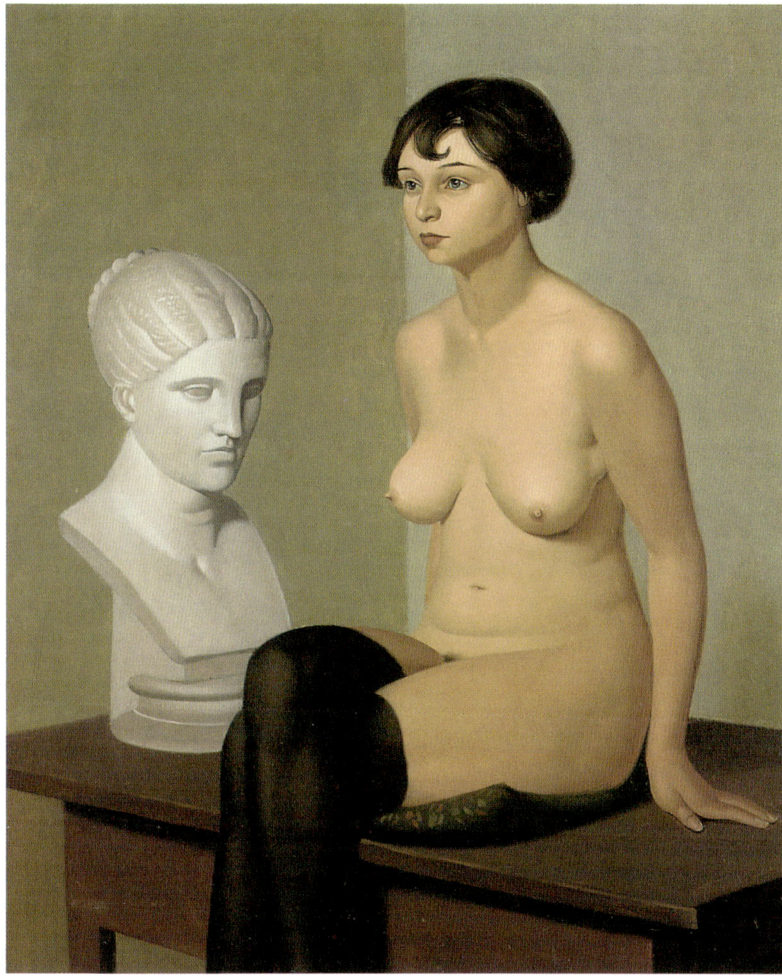

Georg Scholz
Seated Nude with Plaster Bust, 1927
Sitzender Akt mit Gipskopf
Oil on canvas, 49.5 x 67.5 cm
Karlsruhe, Staatliche Kunsthalle

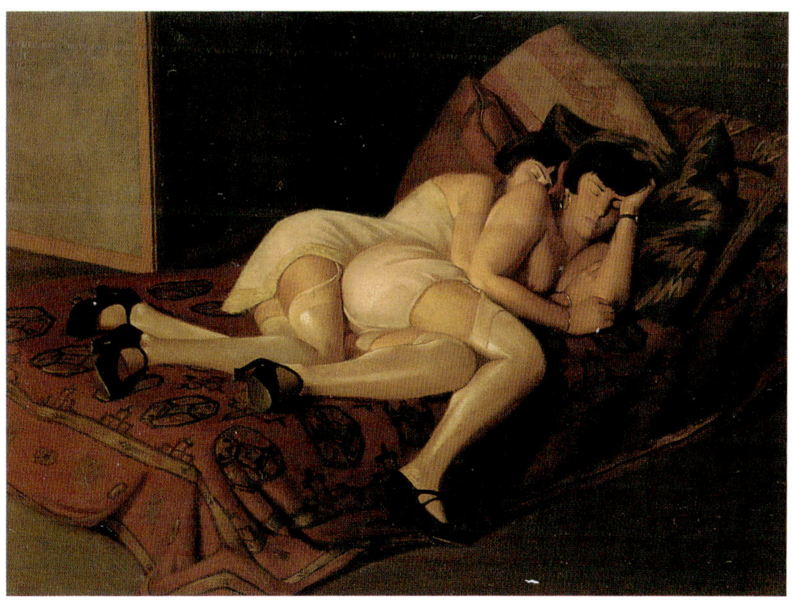

Georg Scholz
The Sisters, 1928
Die Schwestern
Oil on canvas, 70.5 x 95 cm
Waldkirch, Georg Scholz-Haus

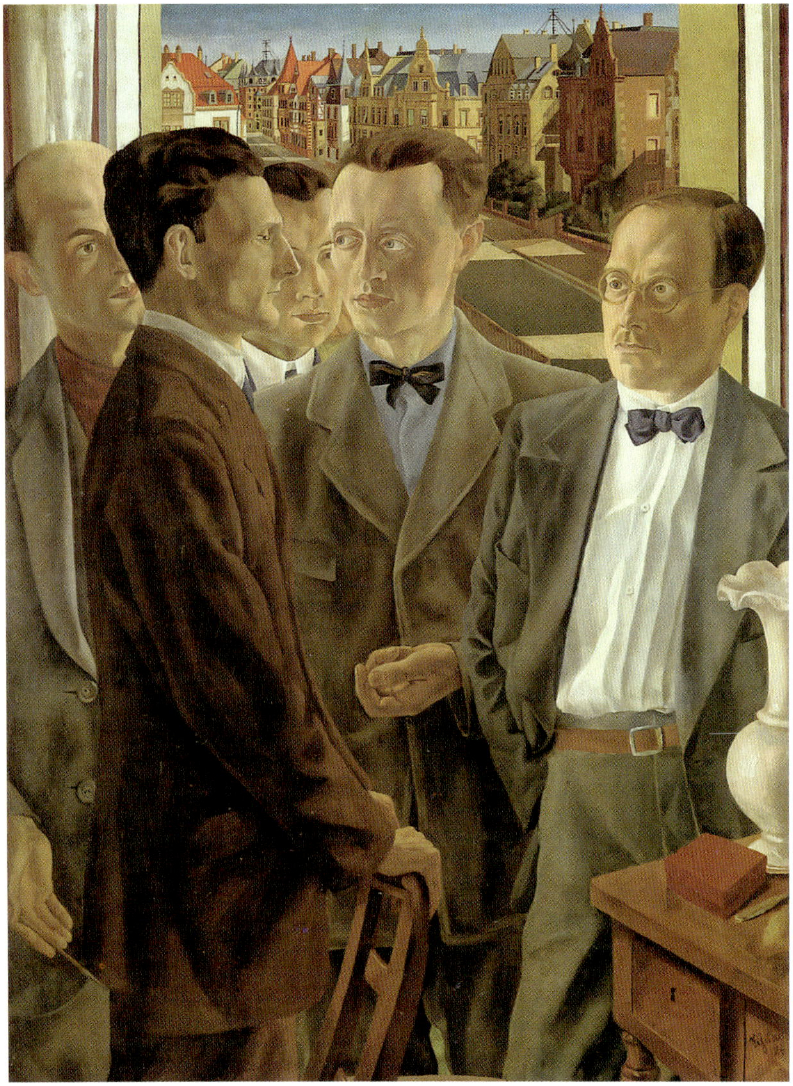

Wilhelm Schnarrenberger
The Friends, 1924
Die Freunde
Oil on canvas, 120.5 x 90.5 cm
Karlsruhe, Staatliche Kunsthalle

Wilhelm Schnarrenberger

The doyen of the Karlsruhe Neue Sachlichkeit artists, Wilhelm Schnarrenberger, who taught at the Academy from 1920, was lastingly influenced by his studies in Munich. He went through a phase of intense fascination with Rousseau's works in the early 1920s, as can be seen in his Munich urban vedute and – even more clearly – in his painting *Old Men Going for a Walk* of 1922. The intermeshing of spatial layers unrelated to each other with regard to perspective, the intentionally naive portrayal of the figures, the stage-like stiffness of the composition – all may be traced back to inspirations from the great customs official, once again confirming the role of German Rousseauism as a morphological variant and a roundabout route in the transitional phase towards Neue Sachlichkeit.

1924 was the year in which Schnarrenberger would definitively reveal Neue Sachlichkeit principles of style in his work. In his picture *The Friends* (illus. p. 104), he created an exceptional group portrait characterized by the combination of restrained colour with sharp contours. In contrast to the

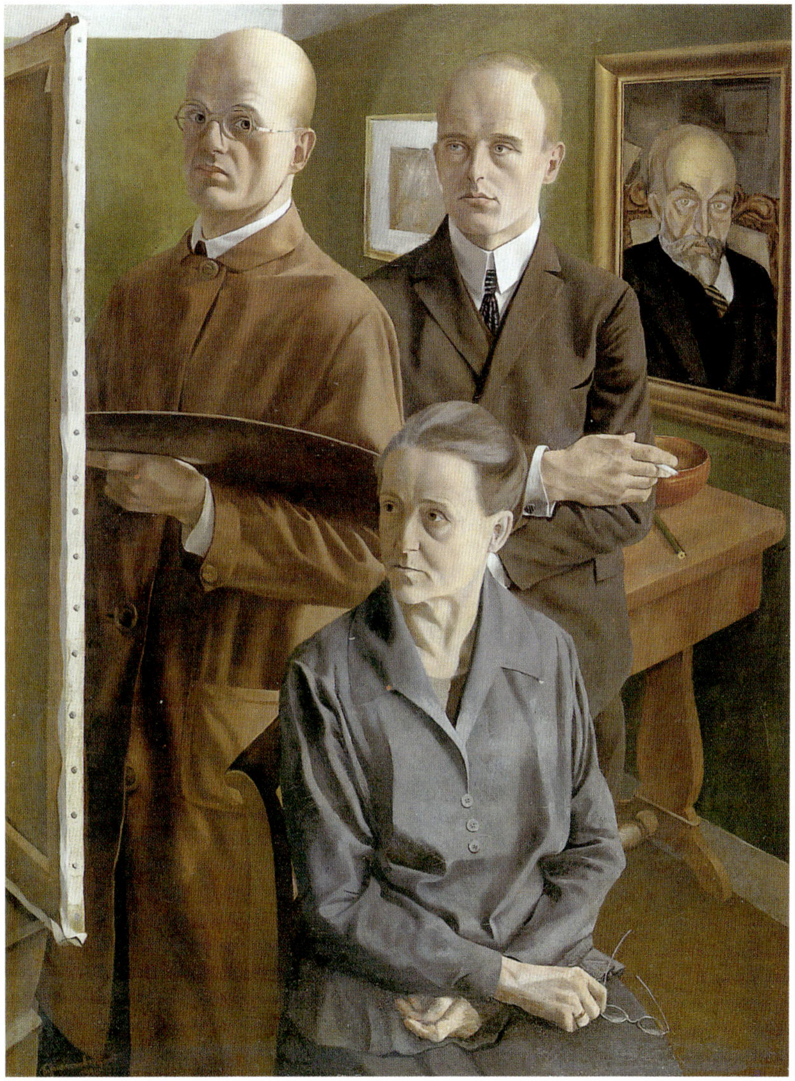

Wilhelm Schnarrenberger
Large Family Portrait, 1925
Großes Familienbild
Oil on canvas, 125.5 x 95.5 cm
Stuttgart, Galerie der Stadt Stuttgart

Romanticists' depictions of friends, the distant ancestors of this iconographical type, Schnarrenberger almost demonstratively refrains from portraying any emotional link between the persons in the picture. The staggered arrangement within the composition and the overlapping of the isocephalously portrayed figures is particularly striking, making them appear demonstratively out of place in the room, their postures merely adopted. In contrast, Schnarrenberger's *Large Family Portrait* (illus. p. 105), painted only a year later, reveals the first traces of a sentimental element. One is also struck by the presence of certain similarities to Nazi art, for example with Udo Wendel's *Kunstzeitschrift* (Art Magazine) of 1939. Repeated reference was made to such similarities at a time when it was a matter of importance to underline elements suggesting a continuity between Neue Sachlichkeit painting and that of the Nazis. However, the considerable differences between the two are just as important, the event objectified by the artist's searching, cool gaze, questioning the observer. A counterpole to the emerging effort to portray inwardness in the picture continues to be present in the implied dialogue between artist and observer.

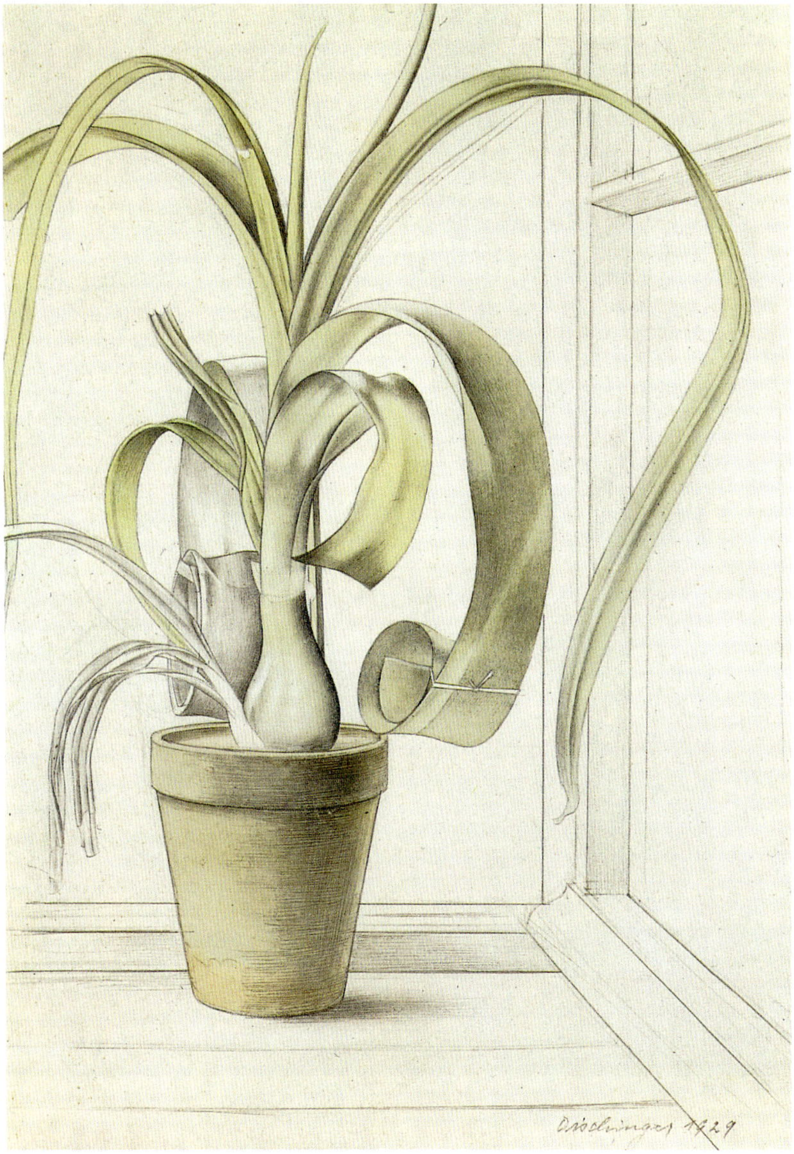

Rudolf Dischinger
Foliage Plant by the Window, 1929
Blattpflanze am Fenster
Pencil and watercolour,
49.9 x 35.9 cm
Freiburg, Städtische Museen Freiburg,
Museum für Neue Kunst

Around 1928/29 Schnarrenberger's precise brushwork gave way to a looser style suggestive of late Impressionism. He was one of the first artists to adopt this course. While thus departing from the formal canon of Neue Sachlichkeit, he remained true to its iconographical types until the 1940s.

Rudolf Dischinger

Scholz and Hubbuch, Dischinger's teachers at the Karlsruhe Academy, moulded his precise, hard style, one graphically isolating objects and denying itself every spontaneous gesture. It was not until 1925 that the artist arrived at Neue Sachlichkeit, without first going through a Verist phase. The drawing technique employed in his initial works, such as *Suburbs with Tram* (illus. p. 108), still shows clear echoes of the shading used in

Rudolf Dischinger
Gramophone, 1930
Grammophon
Oil on plywood, 79 x 64 cm
Freiburg, Städtische Museen Freiburg,
Museum für Neue Kunst

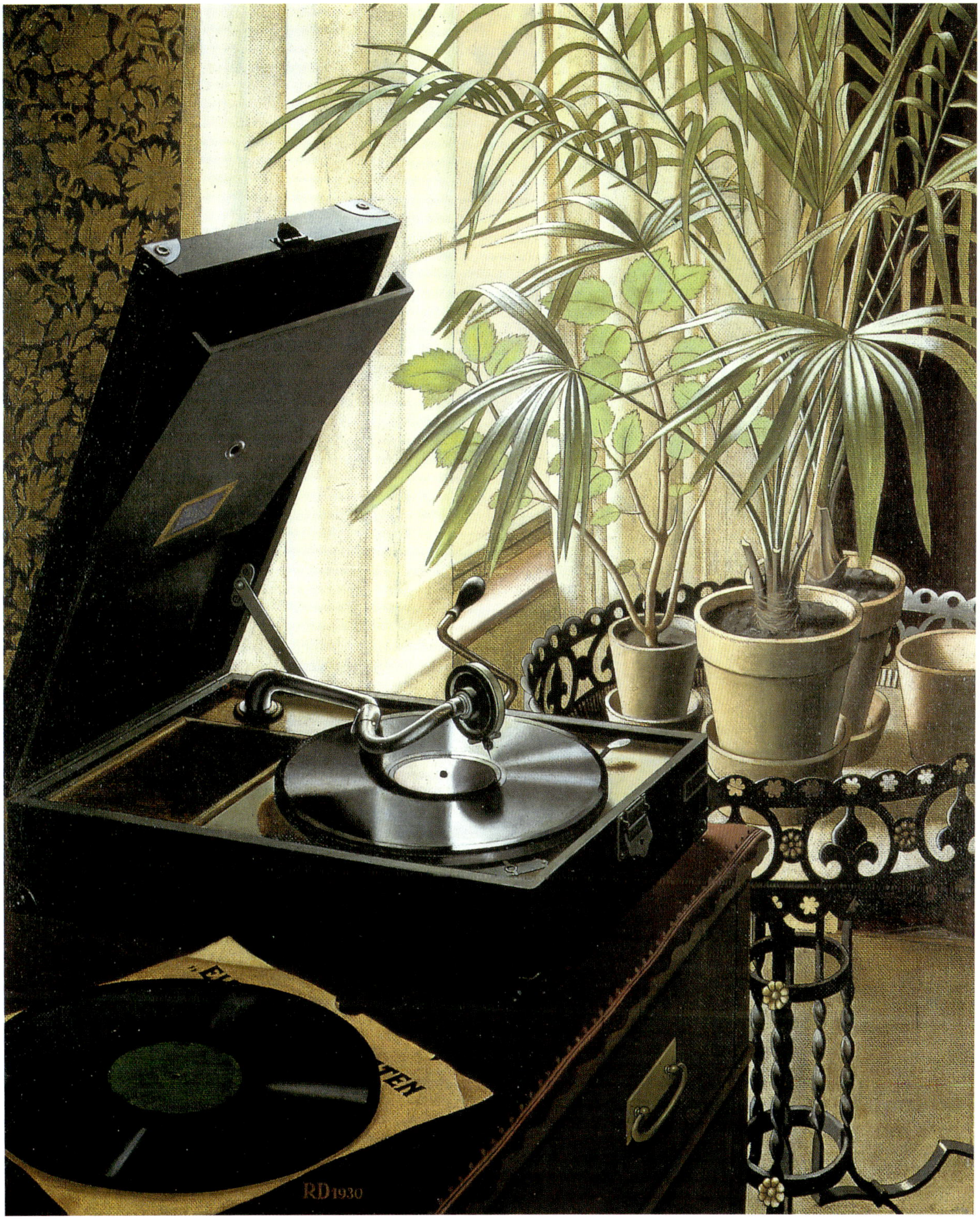
RD1930

TOP RIGHT:
Rudolf Dischinger
Suburbs with Tram, 1926
Vorstadt mit Straßenbahn
Coloured pencil, 48 x 65 cm
Karlsruhe, Staatliche Kunsthalle

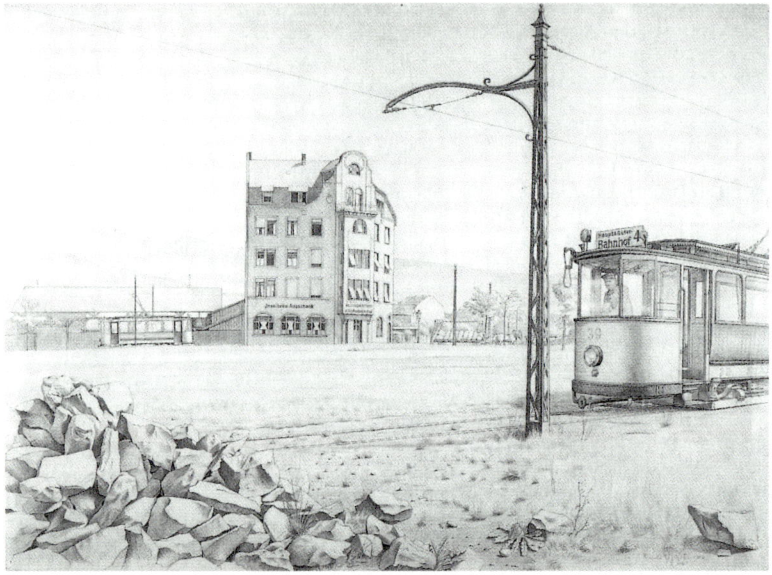

BOTTOM LEFT:
Rudolf Dischinger
Still Life with Amaryllis, 1935/36
Stilleben mit Amaryllis,
Oil on canvas, 71 x 54 cm
Freiburg, Städtische Museen Freiburg,
Museum für Neue Kunst

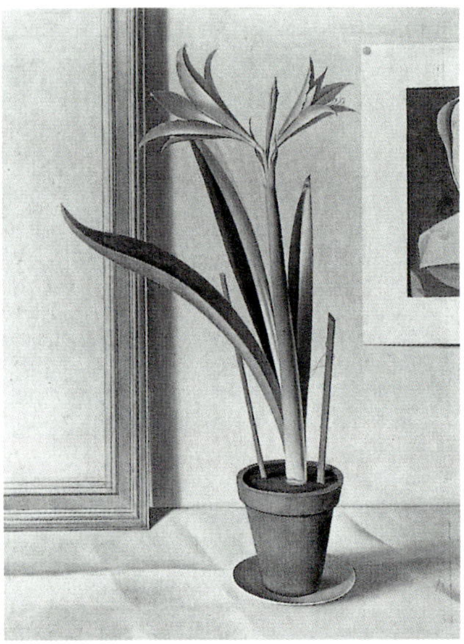

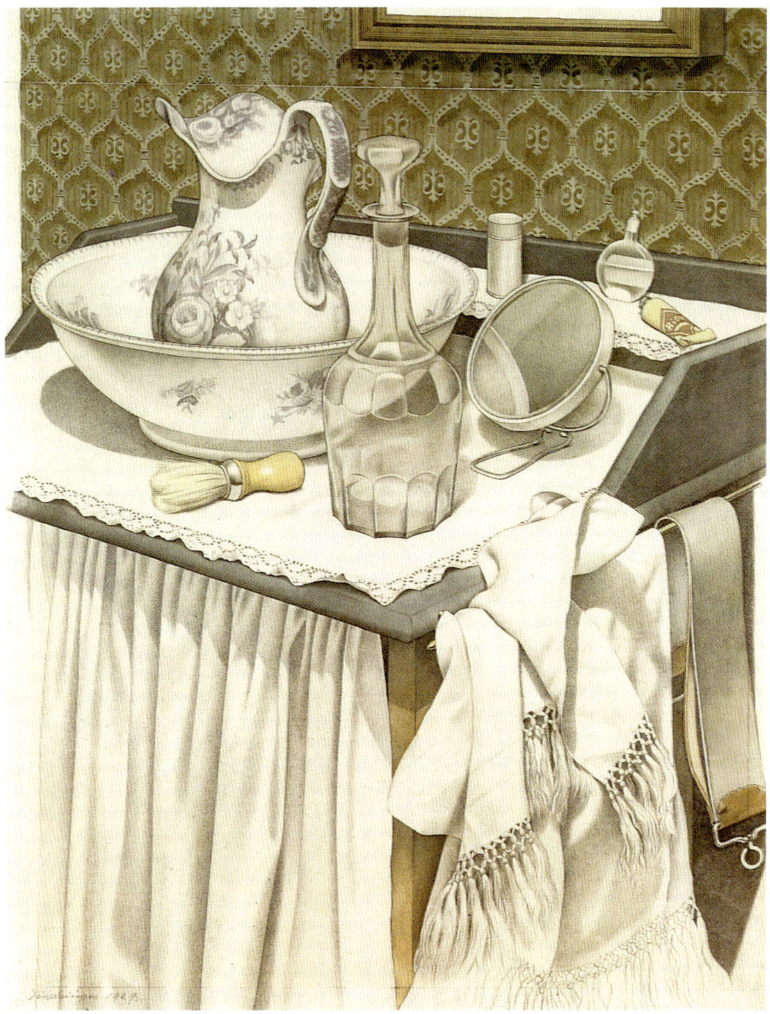

BOTTOM RIGHT:
Rudolf Dischinger
Wash-Stand, 1929
Waschtisch
Pencil, watercolour and brush-and-ink,
63.1 x 48 cm
Freiburg, Städtische Museen Freiburg,
Augustinermuseum

Rudolf Dischinger
"Joiner's Workshop", 1931
"Schreinerei"
Pencil, 65.8 x 89.5 cm
Löffingen, Inge Sigwarth

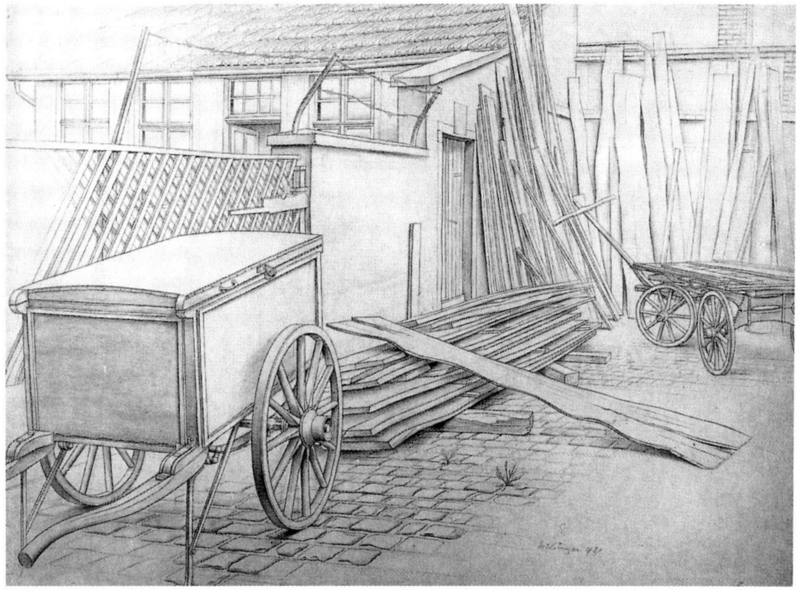

Rudolf Dischinger
Boats, 1926
Boote
Pencil, 43 x 54.5 cm
Löffingen, Inge Sigwarth

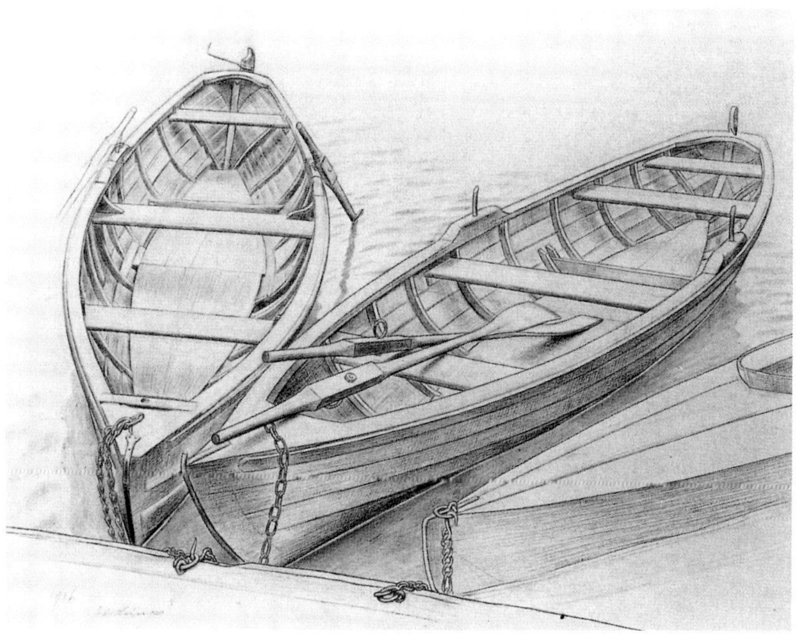

19th-century post-Nazarene drawing. After 1926, Dischinger turned to austere studies of object structures (*"Joiner's Workshop"*, illus. p. 109). His *Electric Kettle* (illus. p. 189), bears a striking similarity to Neue Sachlichkeit photographic studies, such as those by Hans Finsler.

Trousers (illus. p. 159), a work in which the prosaic is particularly emphasized, is among Dischinger's best drawings. It illustrates one of the most important traits of Neue Sachlichkeit, namely its ability to three-dimensionalize and monumentalize chance constellations of material whose appearance is essentially amorphous. Dischinger's model in this case was undoubtedly his teacher Hubbuch. Dischinger writes in his notebooks of the influence exerted upon him by Hubbuch and Scholz: "The works of the

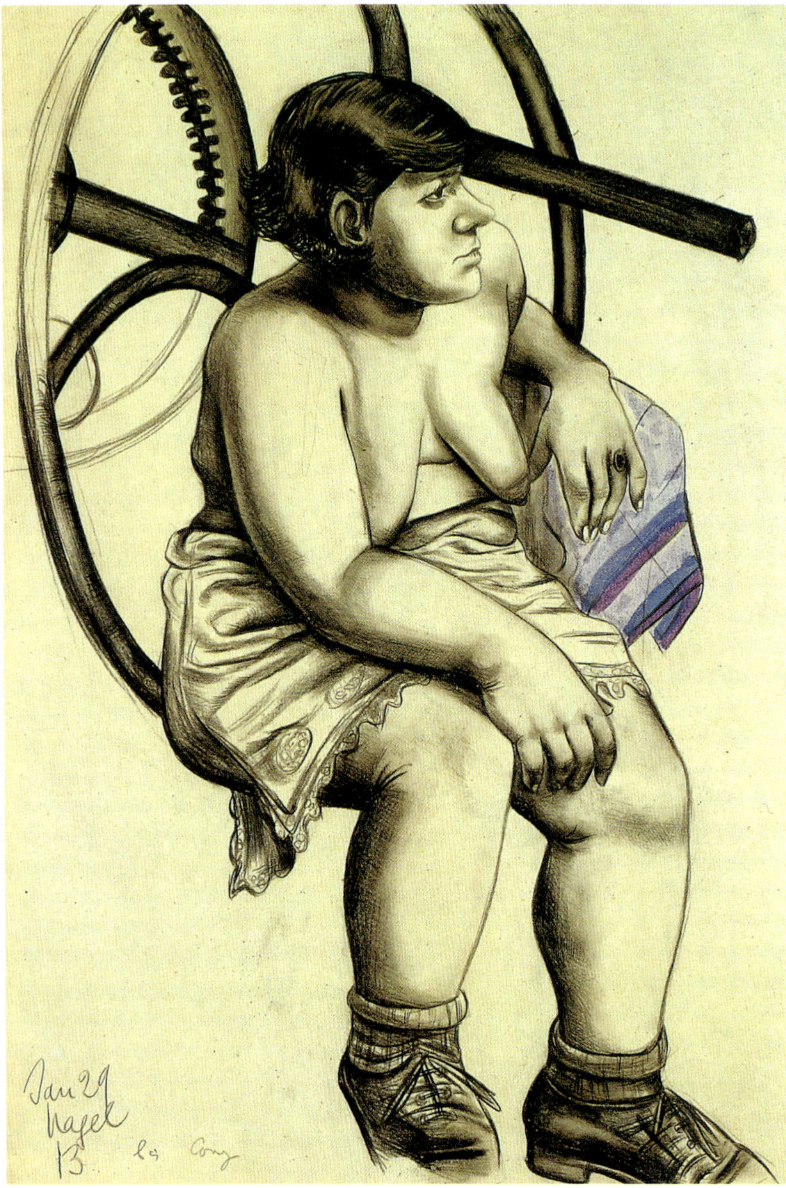

Hanna Nagel
Half-Naked Woman in front of a Printing Press, 1929
Halbnackte Frau vor Druckerpresse
Pencil and watercolour
Karlsruhe, Irene Fischer-Nagel

two teachers, which were based on solid craftsmanship, appealed to me ... greatly, both through the precision of their forms and also because of their overall conception (attitude), their world view; something I'd been completely unconscious of before – this world partly from the perspective of the 'suburban atmosphere', something which would later characterize my work too, very familiar."[57]

Dischinger did relatively few paintings. *Gramophone* (illus. p. 107), without doubt the most important of them, evokes the aura and magic of the isolated object in a special manner, one differing somewhat from the usual Neue Sachlichkeit still life. A slight hint of Art Deco preciousness and the plywood base shimmering through alleviate the customary hardness of the palette, a hardness and plasticity that would return a few years later in *Still Life with Amaryllis* (illus. p. 108). Dischinger's notes on Neue Sachlichkeit reflect his own artistic thinking: "Penetrating observation of the (consciously selected!) visual scene. Cold, interested, seeking the visual 'shock' in drawing, the aggressiveness of precise reproduction, wherever possible going into even the most insignificant details, without losing the larger from. No claim to great gestures, not momentary, not excited, not loud, quietly reserved, seeking illusions in work rather than in the content of what is to be reproduced. Contemplative . . . non-political, no criticism,no judgement of others (no social criticism)."[58]

Dischinger's artistic development after 1933 deserves brief mention. Three different stylistic modi co-exist in an astonishing manner in his work: references back to the Primitivist-decorative style of 1920 which heralded Neue Sachlichkeit; a continuation of Neue Sachlichkeit composition in still-life pictures of plants; and finally, in his graphic art, a surrealism imitating classical forms, infused with Pittura metafisica reminiscences.

Other second-generation artists

The bombs which fell on Karlsruhe during WW2 destroyed almost the entire Verist œuvre of Willi Müller-Hufschmid, continuing the unlucky streak of a man who had already endured six years of captivity and deportation to Siberia in the First World War. To judge from his few surviving works, and especially the (regrettably equally incomplete) photographic documentation of his output, the painter quite clearly belonged to the more interesting Neue Sachlichkeit artists. Although his exhibitions were well received in Karlsruhe, no wider response was forthcoming.

The work of Hanna Nagel was also largely destroyed in the war. The earliest surviving pictures date from 1926, a number of drypoint engravings revealing the influence of her teacher, Conz. But it was Hubbuch, her teacher in figure drawing, who imparted to her the medium she would make her own. She subsequently did neither engravings nor lithographs, bestowing upon drawing an almost existential significance: "Drawing is my form of existing . . . My drawing is my passion. It's what I live for."[59]

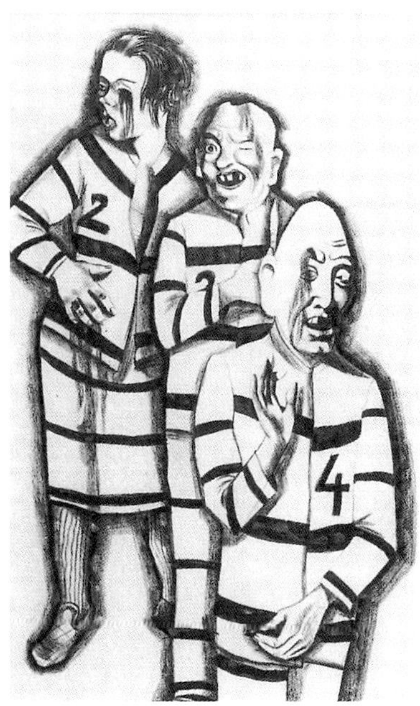

Hanna Nagel
In Prison Uniform, 1927
In Zuchthauskleidung
Lithographic chalk, lithographic ink, 35.5 x 19.5 cm
Karlsruhe, Irene Fischer-Nagel

Hanna Nagel used her drawing to create works of a singular conciseness, individuals isolated from any kind of surroundings that may be conceived in concrete terms, individuals who – apparently depicted realistically – illustrate the central theme of a social and personal reality to be felt under the surface. Thus, the arms and legs of the model in the drawing *Half-Naked Woman in front of a Printing Press* (illus. p. 110) seem to be proportionally larger than her trunk, emphasizing through their clumsy obtrusiveness the model's indifference towards the aesthetic expectations of the observer. This impression of listlessness is further increased by the printing press rising up behind the woman and the use of strong contour, causing the figure to stand out sharply against the background.

In this drawing, Hanna Nagel highlights the situation in which the sitter finds herself: the wearying work of modelling, her impersonal relationship to the artists making use of her – a picture of everyday art academy life. However, the artist did not only draw scenes of prosaic, sober reality. Using the same technique, she also portrayed dreams and bizarre images (*In Prison Uniform*, illus. p. 111). Many of Hanna Nagel's works only became known after her death, since she hid her works of the 1930s from the public eye for fear of being labelled a "degenerate" artist; this would have cost her the numerous illustration commissions by means of which she secured her family's existence.

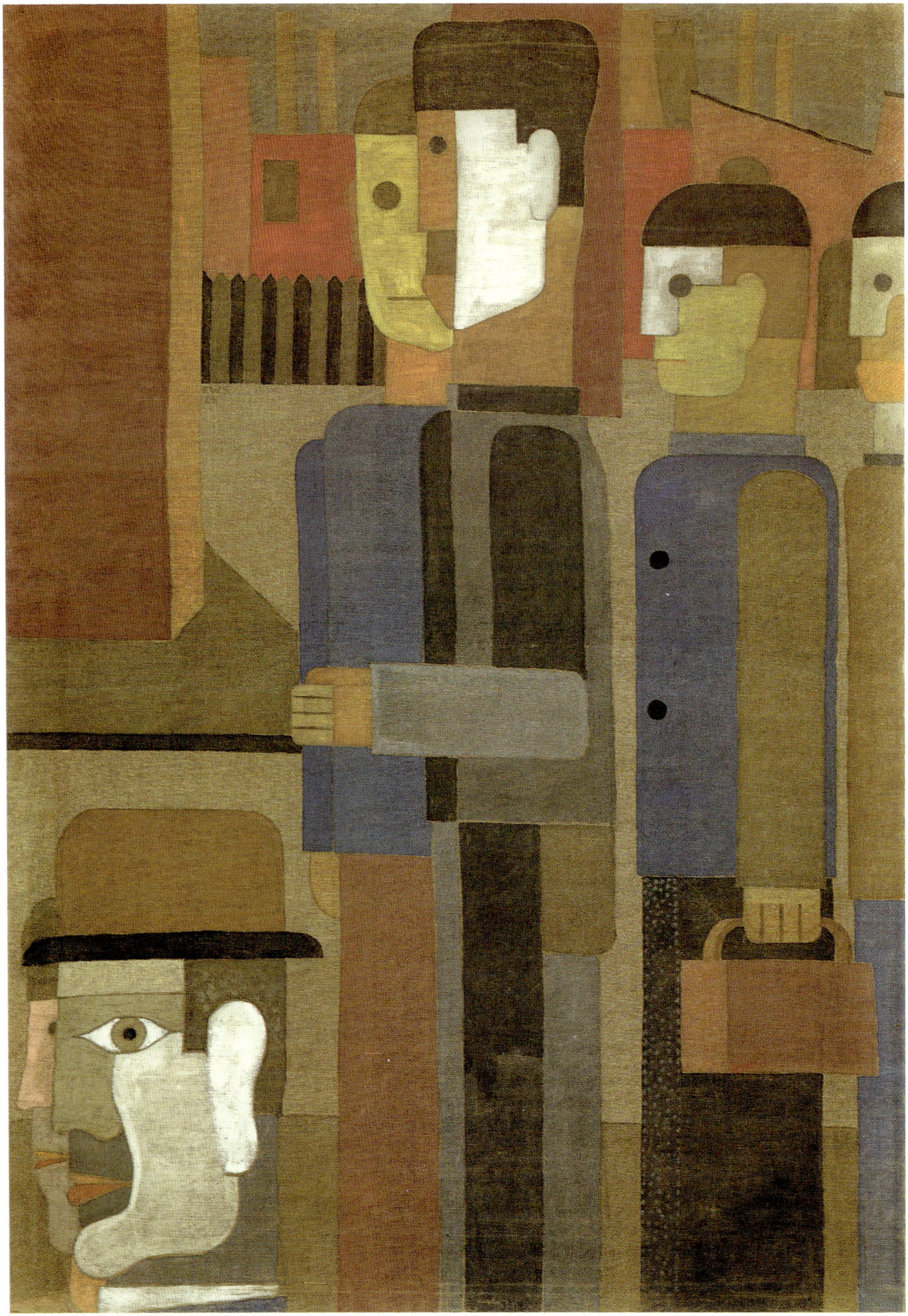

Cologne
Figural Constructivism

Weimar Cologne under Konrad Adenauer, its mayor, was a rather conservative city, one not particularly receptive to modern art. The Dadamax activities of Max Ernst, which coincided with the shock of defeat and the post-war occupation of the Rhineland, were hardly the means best suited to counteract the reserve of the Rhenish bourgeoisie. Even moderate varieties of modern art were greeted at best with muted enthusiasm. Despite all this, however, the city represented fertile terrain artistically between the metropolises of Paris and Berlin. In the 1920s, talk focussed particularly on the "Gruppe progressiver Künstler, Köln" (Group of Progressive Artists, Cologne) around Franz Wilhelm Seiwert and Heinrich Hoerle, a circle of politically committed left-wing artists, primarily working in a figural style of Constructivism. While not every member of the group worked in Cologne, the city nevertheless clearly constituted their centre.

A number of other important artists besides the Progressiver were also active in the city. In first place was Anton Räderscheidt, who spent the entire period of the Weimar Republic in his home town before going to Berlin in 1934, from whence he would later flee to France. Räderscheidt was closely linked with the Progressives for a number of years. The same was true of the young Gottfried Brockmann, whose representations of cripples and dolls belong to the catalogue of Neue Sachlichkeit motifs, albeit given a pronounced Constructivist character. He broke with the Progressives in 1926, and moved to Düsseldorf. Forceful dolls and mannequins – in part revealing a clear Italian influence – also characterize the work of Ludwig Ronig, an even less well-known Cologne artist. In contrast, Josef Mangold, the conservative painter of lyrical-romantic still lifes, shows no evidence of contact with the other artists mentioned here; the same is true of Barthel Gilles, who found his most powerful expression in Verist works portraying the class struggle.

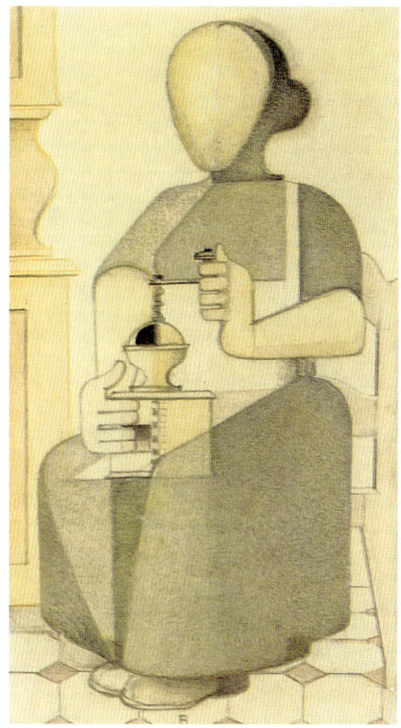

Gottfried Brockmann
Woman with Coffee-Mill, 1924
Frau mit Kaffeemühle
Pencil and watercolour, on paper, mounted on cardboard, 30 x 17 cm
Wuppertal, Von der Heydt-Museum

The "Group of Progressive Artists"

In common with many artists whose principal creative phase lay in the 1920s and early 1930s and whose work would be abruptly interrupted in 1933, the Progressives had also been fundamentally influenced by the experiences of the First World War and the 1918/1919 Revolution. Some of them had gone through a Dada phase, thereafter turning to non-representational or abstract-constructivist works. The initiative to found the

Franz Wilhelm Seiwert
Knocking-Off Time, 1925
Feierabend
Oil on burlap, 140 x 200 cm
Hamburg, Hamburger Kunsthalle

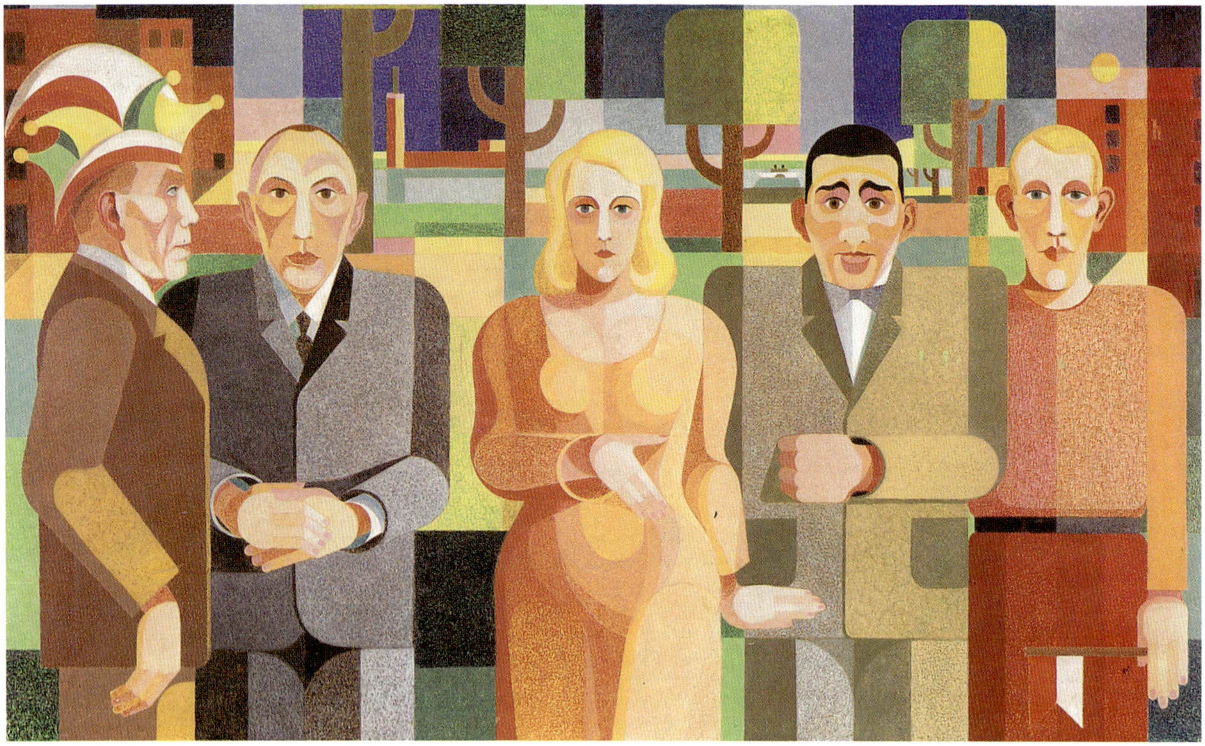

Heinrich Hoerle
The Contemporaries, 1931
Die Zeitgenossen
Wax on plywood, 120 x 200 cm
Cologne, Kölnisches Stadtmuseum

Heinrich Hoerle puts up his motifs in a pictorial framework of horizontal and vertical lines. The pictures appear to consist of a combination of finished parts. Thus Hoerle complies with his own demand that artists understand themselves as engineers. Nevertheless, the portrayal of man ultimately asserts itself in his world of schematized pictorial signs.

"Group of Progressive Artists, Cologne" came in 1924, from Seiwert, Hoerle and Otto Freundlich. The core was made up of these three, together with Gerd Arntz, Hans Schmitz and Stanislav Kubicki, while Augustin Tschinkel and Peter Alma were included in the outer circle. Of those belonging to or associated with the group who were neither painters nor sculptors, only August Sander, one of the greatest Neue Sachlichkeit photographers, will be mentioned here (cf. pp. 180 f.).

The common ground shared by the Cologne artists with their colleagues from Düsseldorf who would become representative of 1920s art – meaning particularly the artists of "Young Rhineland group" (cf. pp. 124 f.) – "was extremely limited; nor did the Cologne group make any secret of their distance from the artistic activities in the neighbouring city."[60] Unlike Cologne, Düsseldorf was in a position to offer its artists markets of no mean potential; accordingly, hardly any radical or revolutionary tendencies were to be detected in the art done there. Düsseldorf had the reputation of being a "city of art". "It was naturally impossible that such a reputation ... could originate with the Progressives, and equally so that the Cologne artists could be included in the Düsseldorf art scene or provide the basis for an advertising slogan of 'city of art' for the city of Cologne. Their art was completely dependent upon its own resources – its source of pride, but also its fate."[61]

The fact that the Progressives are treated at all within the context of this book can be justified by the realistic tendency underlying their figurative Constructivism and pictogram-like picture-language. "In using this pictorial form, I am attempting to depict a reality stripped of any sentimental and accidental element, attempting to render visible its function, its legitimacy, its relations and tensions within the picture frame and its regularity."[62] This statement by Seiwert regarding his work could be considered the leitmotiv

Heinrich Hoerle
Three Invalids, c. 1930
Drei Invaliden
Oil on plywood, 100 x 50 cm
Private collection

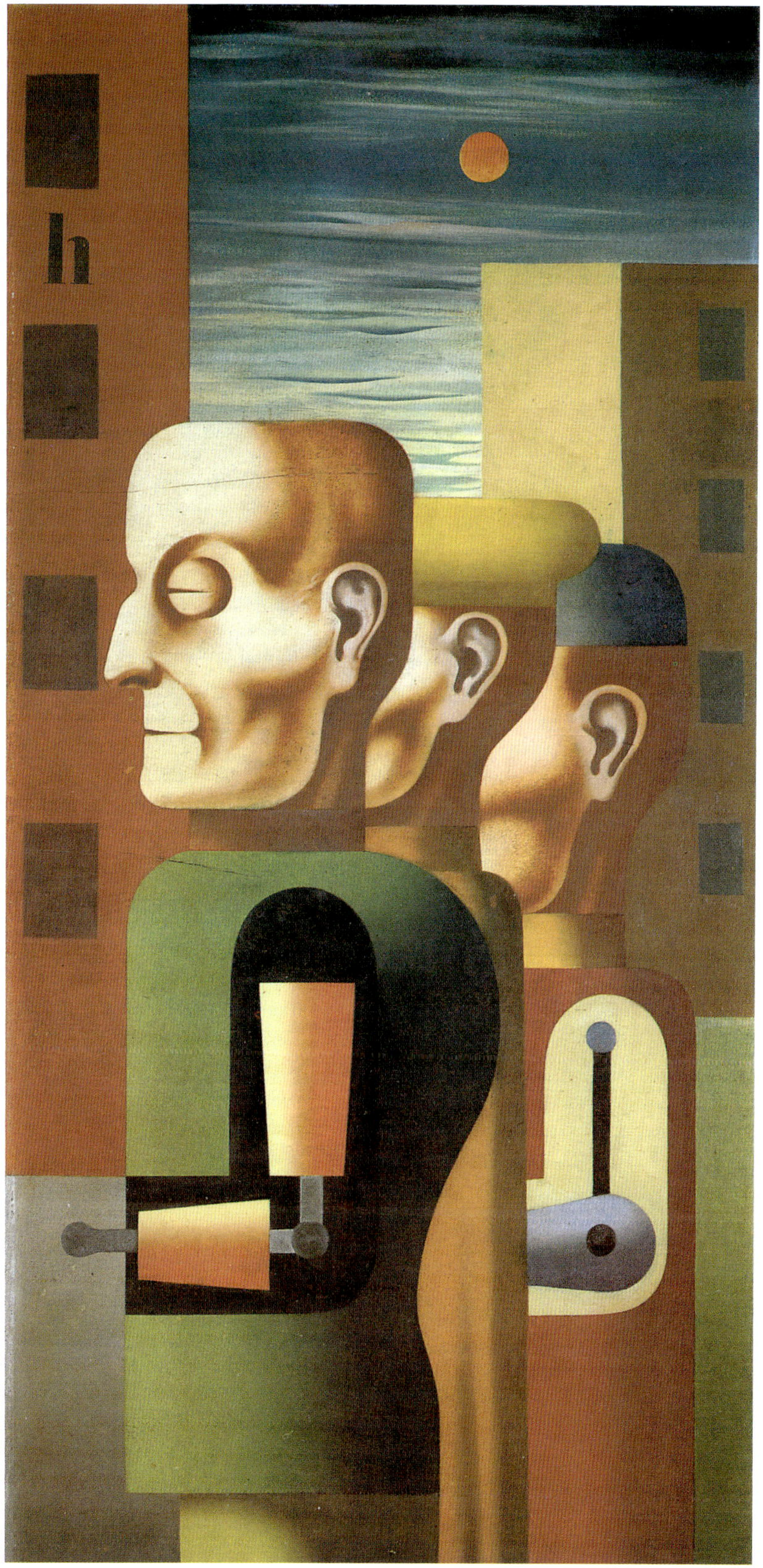
h

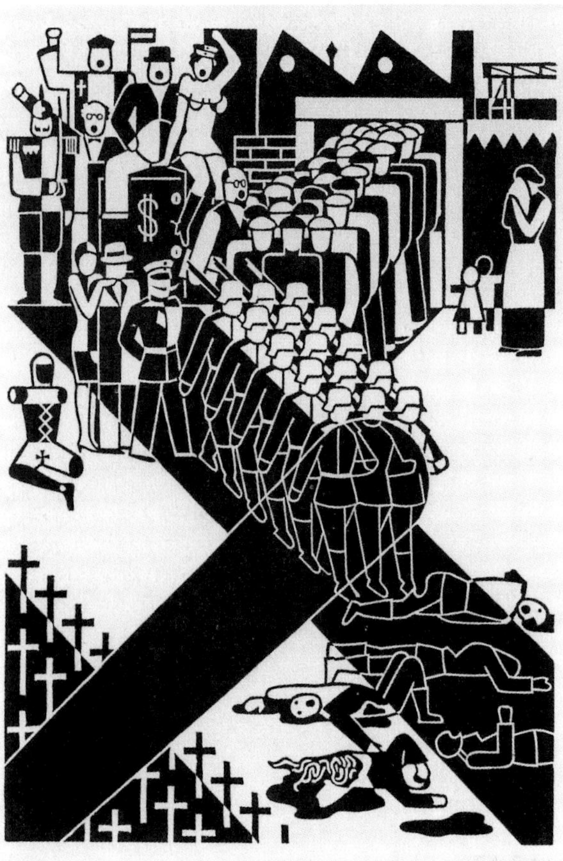

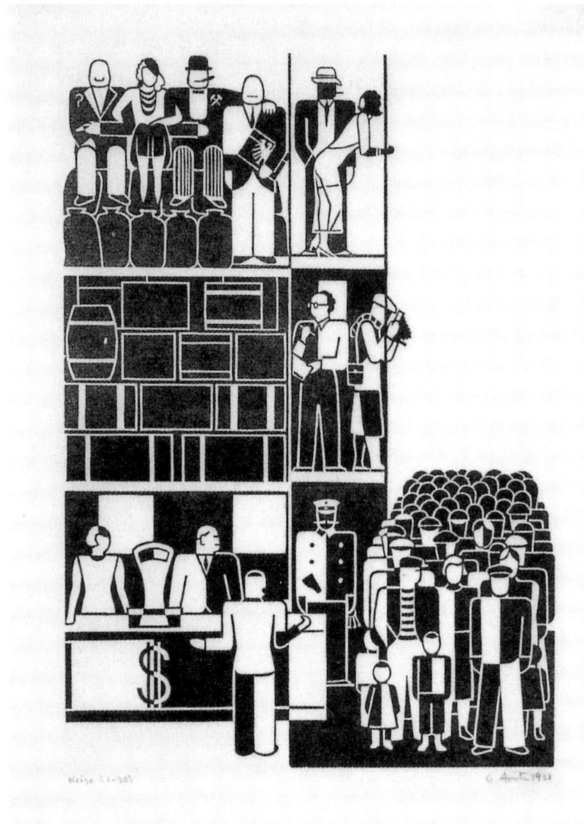

LEFT:
Gerd Arntz
War, 1931
Krieg
Woodcut, 43.5 x 32.5 cm
Amsterdam, Stedelijk Museum

RIGHT:
Gerd Arntz
Crisis, 1931
Krise
Woodcut, 43.5 x 32.5 cm
The Hague, Collection Haags Gemeentemuseum

"Genuinely socially conscious art is also formally tendentious. Only in this way can it portray man as the product of his circumstances. Only in this way will it maintain its value when its content too belongs to the past. The factory picture shows individual people as real components of a firm, components which can be totalled up by the entrepreneur like other items in his inventory. It is more important to show that than to show wrinkles and drops of sweat."

Augustin Tschinkel, 1930

for the aesthetic and political intentions of the Progressives – with the important qualification that the members followed no common programmatic line either politically or artistically. "What united the closer and wider circle of friends was the recognition of the individual's freedom. Every political system that threatened to limit this freedom was rejected, especially Party communism. Even intellectual communism, where it did not separate itself from the Party, was regarded with suspicion."[63]

The figurative Constructivism of the Progressives was a particular offshoot of European Constructivism, initially influenced by the Russian Constructivism of such artists as Vladimir Tatlin and El Lissitzky and also by the Dutch group De Stijl. The approach adopted by the group towards the Russians was directed primarily by Seiwert, the group's leader in theoretical matters. Many of his contributions appeared in the magazine "a-z", an organ of the Progressives published by Hoerle, which appeared between 1929 and 1933. Like many contemporary Marxist artists, Seiwert was concerned with doing away with the distinction between manual and clerical work. This required a fundamental social restructuring of work, of everyday life and everyday objects through art or following the model of art as "creative work". It was the artist's job to make an active contribution to this. Seiwert wrote in a letter to Kubicki: "as far as I am concerned, 'useless' art is a side-effect of times of cultural crisis and a consequence of individualistic isolation. In a time of collective commitment, there can be only purpose-oriented art, and a time in which we once again have purpose-oriented art strikes me as something to aim for, since in my view artistic work – like any kind of work – is not an end in itself but must have an effect upon society. If the existing society is hostile to it, because the reason behind artistic creation is hostile to society, then artistic work must desire social change."[64]

It may appear surprising that the Progressives followed a completely different path to that taken by the Verists, seeking to maintain their claim to be critical of society by Constructivist means. They rejected the socially critical or proletarian revolutionary art of the likes of Grosz and the ASSO artists as "petit bourgeois", on the grounds that such art was directed via its content at the feelings of the observer. The Progressives, in contrast, employing a conception of form that is not always easy to comprehend, focussed on the rational means of the form, a means fostering insight. "Current art may be divided into the content represented and the form utilized for the representation of that content. The content may well have a 'proletarian' tendency, may well make a statement about the struggle, solidarity and class-consciousness of the proletariat; nevertheless, bourgeois art has not yet become the art of the proletariat. Content must remodel form until it fits in with the content . . ."[65] The Progressives developed a "vocabulary" of simplified symbols of reality with which to comply with this demand. Again and again one encounters the pictorial symbols of factories, chimneys, blast furnaces, traction wheels and transmission belts, hammers, sickles, ships, locomotives, high-rise buildings, trees, simplified bodies and faces, but also numbers, question marks and letters. The majority of these symbols concern the sphere of work and belong to the political concepts relating to capitalism and communism – although this does not mean that one should read the fabric of symbols contained in a picture as a one-dimensional message. The "functions" and "laws" of social reality depicted nevertheless generally reveal a certain tendency.

This becomes apparent – indeed, even didactically trenchant – in the political graphic art of Arntz, Tschinkel and Alma. Arntz' woodcuts in particular were distinguished by "an absence of sentimentality unusual in

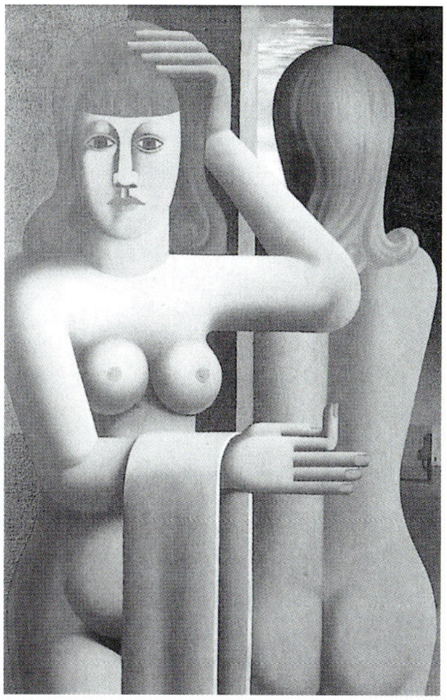

Heinrich Hoerle
Two Female Nudes, 1930/31
Zwei Frauenakte
Oil on wood, 108 x 73 cm
Cologne, Museum Ludwig

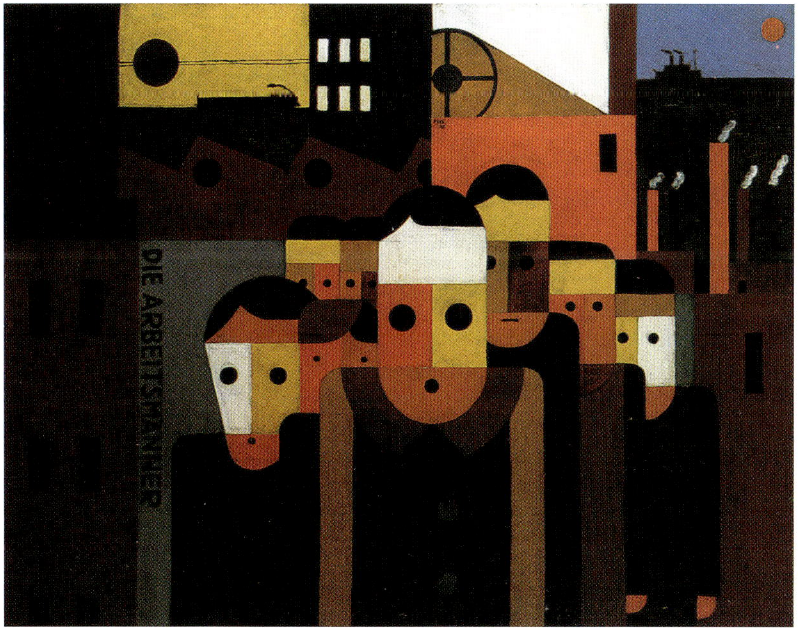

Franz Wilhelm Seiwert
Working Men, 1925
Arbeitsmänner
Oil on wood, 68 x 89 cm
Düsseldorf, Kunstmuseum Düsseldorf im Ehrenhof

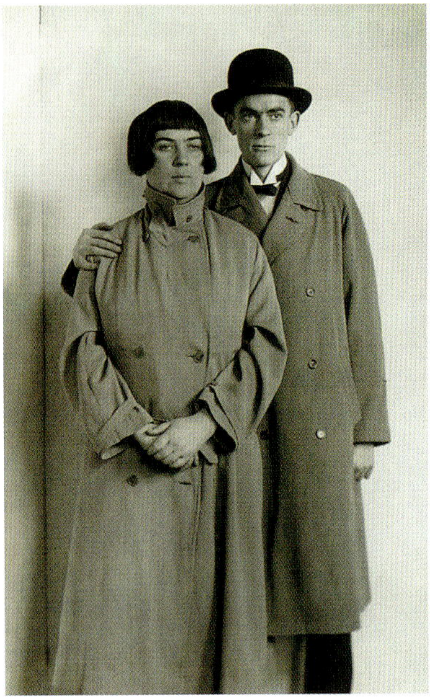

Germany".[66] This had also struck Otto Neurath, the director of the Museum of Industry and Society in Vienna, who in 1929 appointed Arntz as head of the museum's department of graphic art. It was while at this decisively didactically orientated museum that Arntz would develop the so-called "Viennese method of pictorial statistics", a method attempting to depict economic and political interrelations by means of austere, simple symbols. The programmatic difference between the Progressives and the Verists is particularly apparent in Arntz's woodcut *War* (illus. p. 116), in which he exposes the representatives of State, Church, politics, industry and the military as warmongers. In tending towards the academic-scientific – that is, towards political and social analysis – the Progressives were attempting to overcome the antipathy-fanning characterizations of the typical capitalist, the typical general etc., as were to be seen in Grosz' decadent physiognomies.

In comparison with Seiwert's pictures, Hoerle's works are distinguished by a certain lightness; the didactic element within them is not as direct and seems to be less forced. The forms and colours in *The Contemporaries* (illus. p. 114), for example, have developed a life of their own and a quality of colour such as is generally somewhat dark and forbidding in Seiwert's work. Hoerle's pictures gain in compositional quality through their lighter didacticism.

TOP:
August Sander
Anton Räderscheidt und Martha Hegemann, 1925
Black-and-white photograph
Cologne, August Sander Archiv

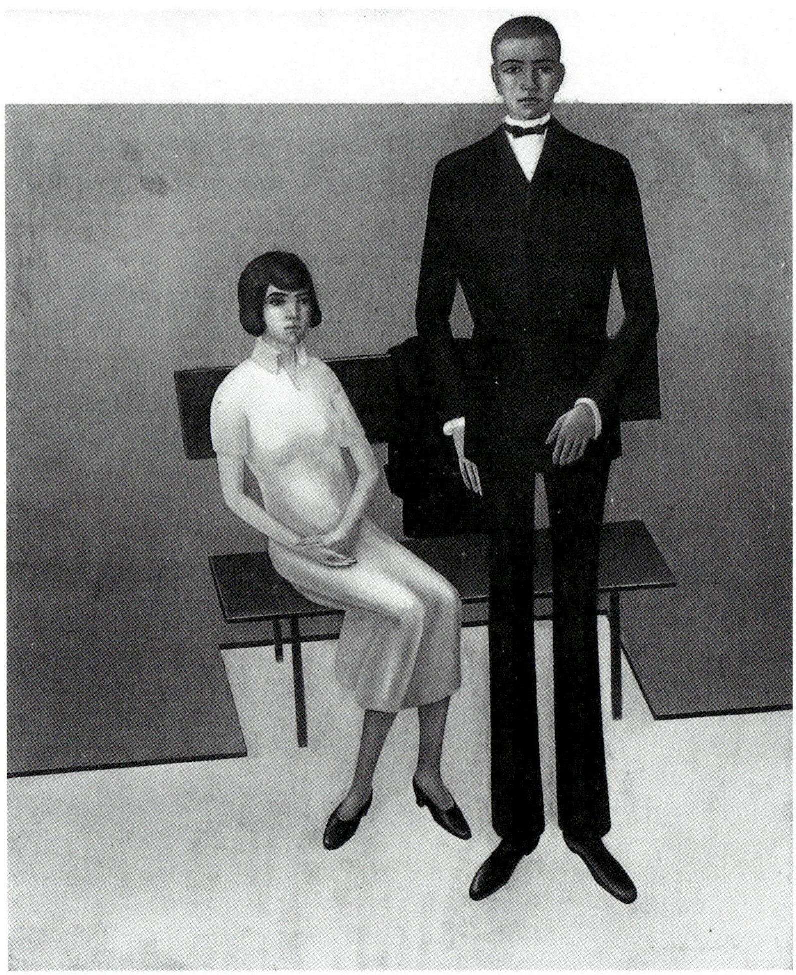

BOTTOM:
Anton Räderscheidt
The Lawn Bench, 1921
Die Rasenbank
Oil on wood
Private collection

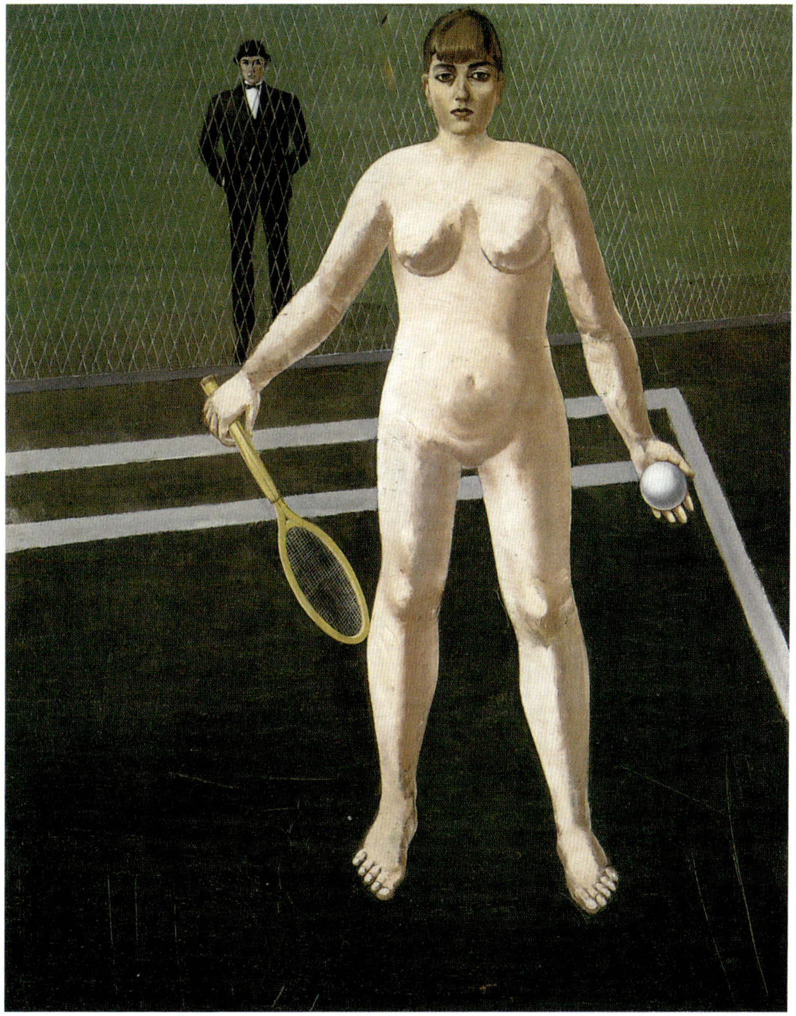

Anton Räderscheidt
The Tennis-Player, 1926
Tennisspielerin
Oil on canvas, 100 x 80 cm
Munich, Bayerische Staatsgemälde-sammlungen

Anton Räderscheidt

Räderscheidt, an artist who, while close to the Rhenish Constructivists, nonetheless was to go his own way artistically as early as the beginning of the 1920s, was occupied with a quite different subject. He made the relationship between man and woman, encapsulated in the pictorial formula of the lonely couple, the thematic centre of his output from the 1920s, to an extent unmatched by any other painter of his time. His artistic career began with a brief Dadaist episode in 1919. This was followed a year later by a Constructivist phase, in close contact with Hoerle and Seiwert, that would be equally brief but of greater importance for the formal development of his work. In 1921, the subject-matter and style of his pictures changed once again, taking on a character that was specifically Neue Sachlichkeit – or, surely more accurately in this case, Magic Realist – in nature.[67] It was at this time that the first pictures were done portraying the clumsy, stiffly standing couples engaged in silent communication with which Räderscheidt became well-known.[68] The frequently encountered empty street-scene is derived from Pittura metafisica, which Räderscheidt had found particularly impressive according to his own account. The figures throw no shadow, creating a highly disconcerting effect. The impression of loneliness and alienation is further heightened by the bare, empty squares and uninhabited architecture.

Räderscheidt's philosophy of life, shaped by his readings of Arthur Schopenhauer and Max Stirner, had clearly solipsistic features. With grim determination, he makes his conception of man as a loner the central theme of his pictures. His pictures of couples are generally stylized self-portraits of Räderscheidt and his wife, the painter Martha Hegemann. In view of the heavily symbolic transcendence of the motif, however, the suggested self-revelation tends in the direction of an empty gesture. A series of photographs from this period by August Sander, the Cologne photographer, in accordance with the artist's own suggestion, shows Räderscheidt and his wife in the familiar pose encountered in his pictures (illus. p. 118).

The so-called "sports pictures" (*Nude at the Parallel Bars* and *The Tennis Player*, illus. p. 119), which Räderscheidt commenced in the mid–1920s, see the battle of the sexes taking on a new interpretation: the woman, portrayed in provocative nudity, is adopting a dominant pose, while the man appears, taciturn, in the background. The natural power of the woman, as demonstrated by her physical exercises, is opposed to the self-referential focus of the man, whose self-awareness is reacting to the challenge of the "relentless nakedness of the woman"[69] by retiring into its shell.

In the "studio pictures", a further series done between 1926 and 1928, the conflict's resolution is demonstrated on a – in the dialectic sense – third, higher plane, namely that of the pictorial power of art. Not until the woman is banished to a picture within the picture (*Self-Portrait*, illus. p. 121), not until her object-ification as a tailor's dummy or compliant painter's model, is the conflict resolved with an apotropaic gesture. Not until this "Pictorial magic"[70] has robbed the woman of her latent power to threaten is the artist free to turn to the observer and engage in dialogue with him, open and relaxed. The man's self-assertion as artist brings to an end the ritual isolation which had begun in 1921 with Räderscheidt's *Young Man with Yellow Gloves* (illus. p. 120), an icon of male loneliness.

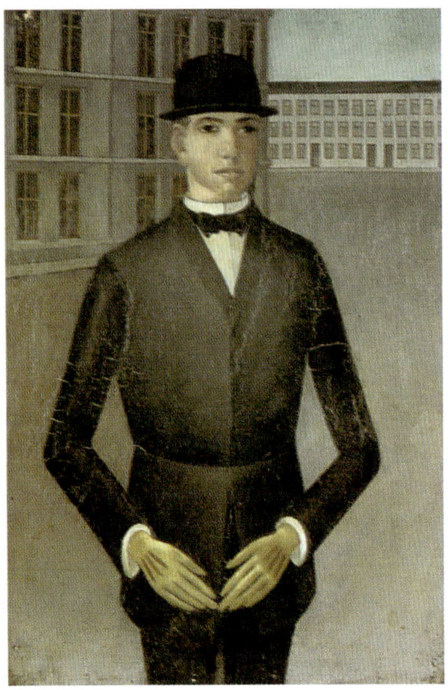

Anton Räderscheidt
Young Man with Yellow Gloves, 1921
Junger Mann mit gelben Handschuhen
Oil on wood, 27 x 18.5 cm
Private collection

Barthel Gilles

It was not until the 1980s that the work produced by Gilles, whose initially Expressionist and decorative-Primitivist paintings were followed in the second half of the 1920s by some notable Neue Sachlichkeit pictures, was rediscovered by art historians and the public. His first Neue Sachlichkeit works, such as *The Bride*, from 1926, in which decorative elements of French Art-Deco poster graphics could still be detected, hardly led one to suspect that Gilles would later "articulate" himself in such a clear political manner. In 1929, he joined both the German Communist Party and the ASSO, the association of "proletarian-revolutionary" artists.

The impressive picture *Ruhr Battle* (illus. p. 123), the last highpoint of Weimar Verism, bears unmistakable witness to Gilles' political partisanship. The composition, spatially extremely compressed, enables the observer to participate directly in what is going on. The open mouth and the look on the face of the worker loading his rifle possess an entreating urgency, while the cramped space behind the barricade and the absence of any sight of the opposition further heighten the psychological effect of the situation. The three individuals are depicted in a rising, rhythmic, staggered

Anton Räderscheidt
Self-Portrait, 1928
Selbstbildnis
Oil on canvas, 100 x 80 cm
Private collection

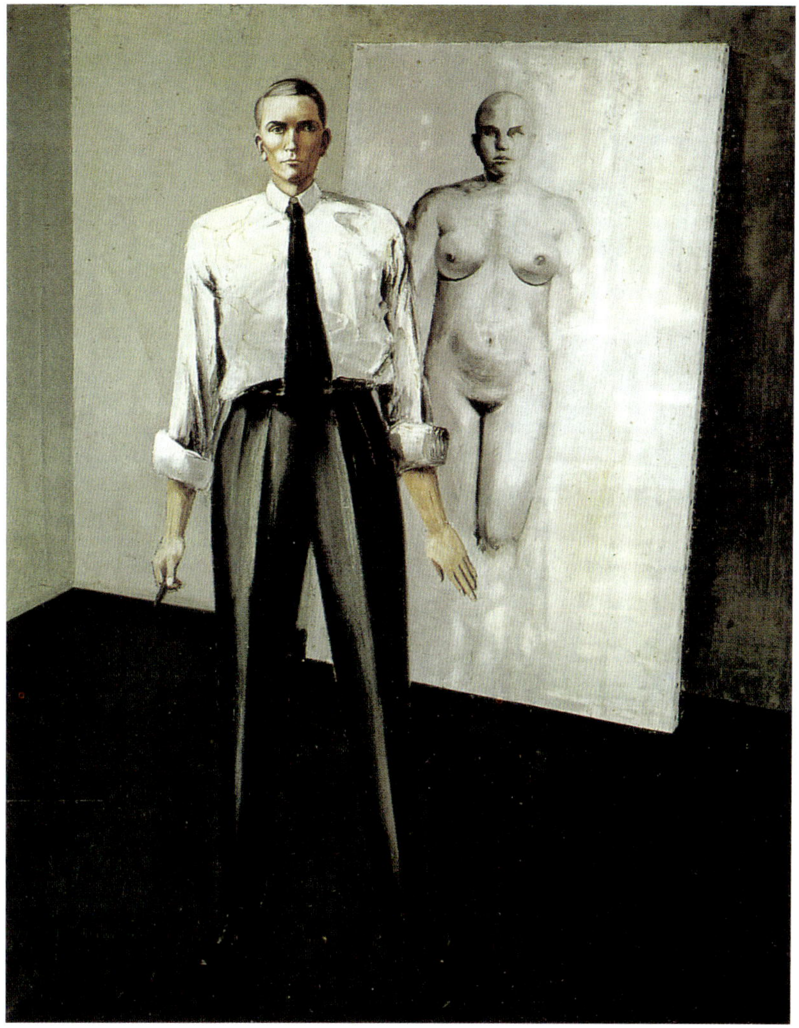

Anton Räderscheidt's most famous self-portrait, a combination of self-portrait and studio painting, shows the artist in front of a large canvas featuring a female nude bearing the features of the painter. Are we concerned here with the banishment of an ideal, or with the pictorial doubling of identity? Whatever the case, Räderscheidt here presents a résumé of his art.

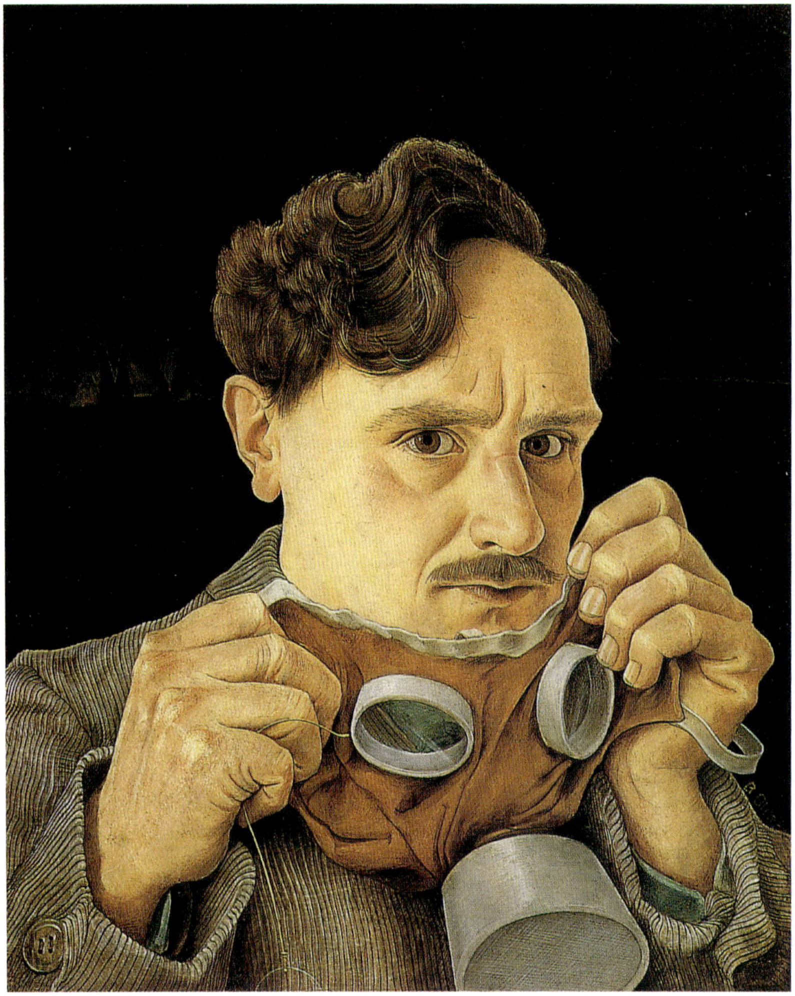

Barthel Gilles
Self-Portrait with Gas Mask, 1930
Selbstbildnis mit Gasmaske
Egg tempera on wood, 50 x 39.5 cm
Aachen, Suermondt-Ludwig-Museum

arrangement, together portraying the act of shooting. The immediate presence of those fighting in front of the observer – and also on his behalf, the painter suggests, – is intensified by a cool glazing technique. Gilles undoubtedly look his inspiration for one of the three workers from Grosz' *Storm Clouds* (from the 1930 portfolio "The new face of the ruling class"). A challenge to our present-day reception of this picture emerges from the biographical fact that this portrayal of the time around 1930, perhaps the most impressive depiction of the class struggle from the artistic viewpoint, was done by an artist who would later deny his communist connections after the assumption of power by the Brownshirts and participate unmoved in exhibitions of Nazi art.

With this in mind, Gilles' *Self-Portrait with Gas Mask* (illus. p. 122), which recalls his traumatic experiences in the First World War and is apparently a prophetic premonition of the new horrors to come (Cologne can be seen burning in the background), might be interpreted with hindsight in a more personal light. It is almost as if the artist, his face filled with fear, wished to admit simultaneously to the weakness of his convictions. His hands clenched, he is about to put on a gas mask, transforming the latter into a modern symbol of the memento mori.

Barthel Gilles
Ruhr Battle, 1930
Ruhrkampf
Egg tempera on wood, 69.5 x 100.5 cm
Aachen, Suermondt-Ludwig-Museum

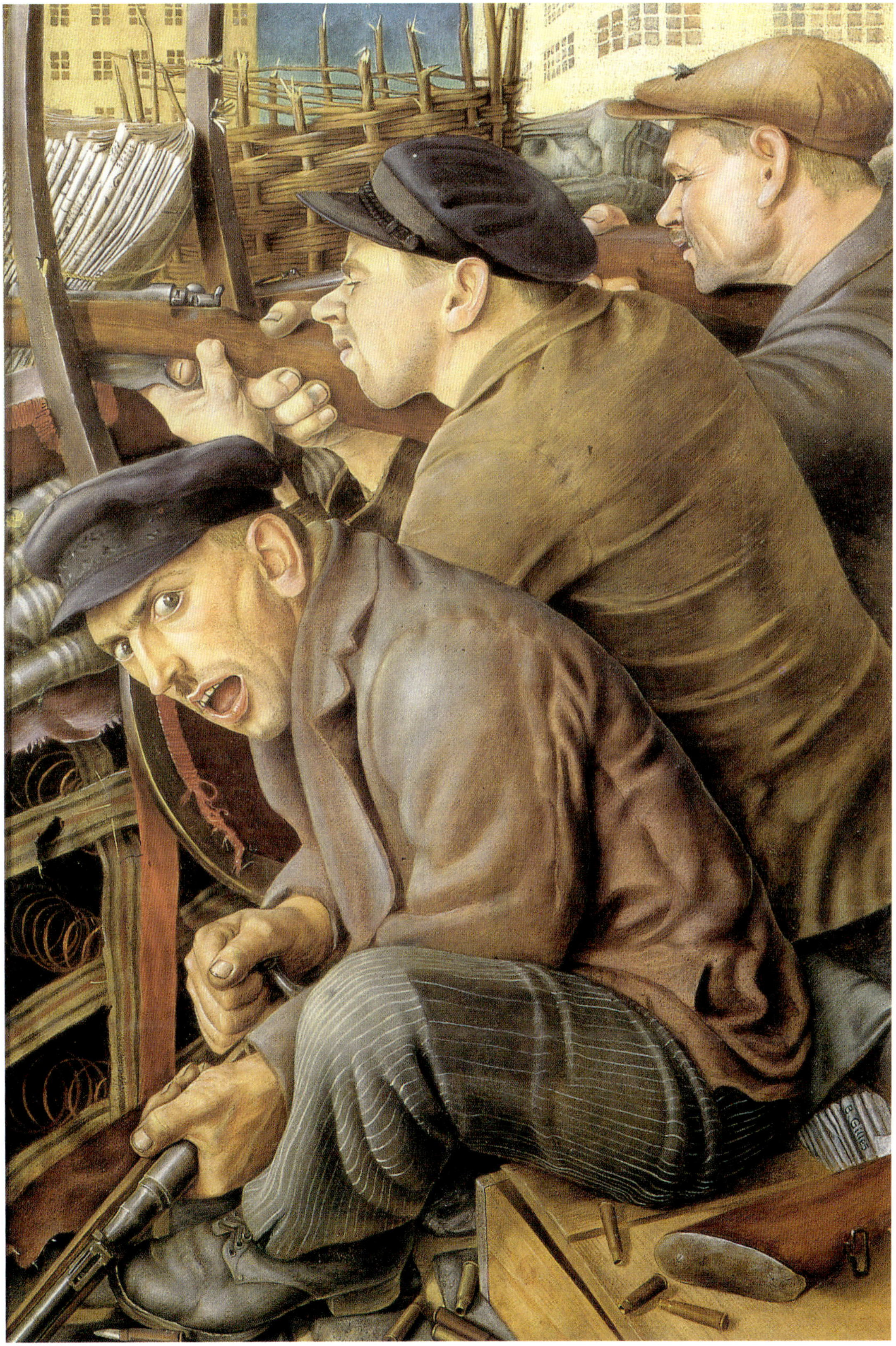
B. GILES

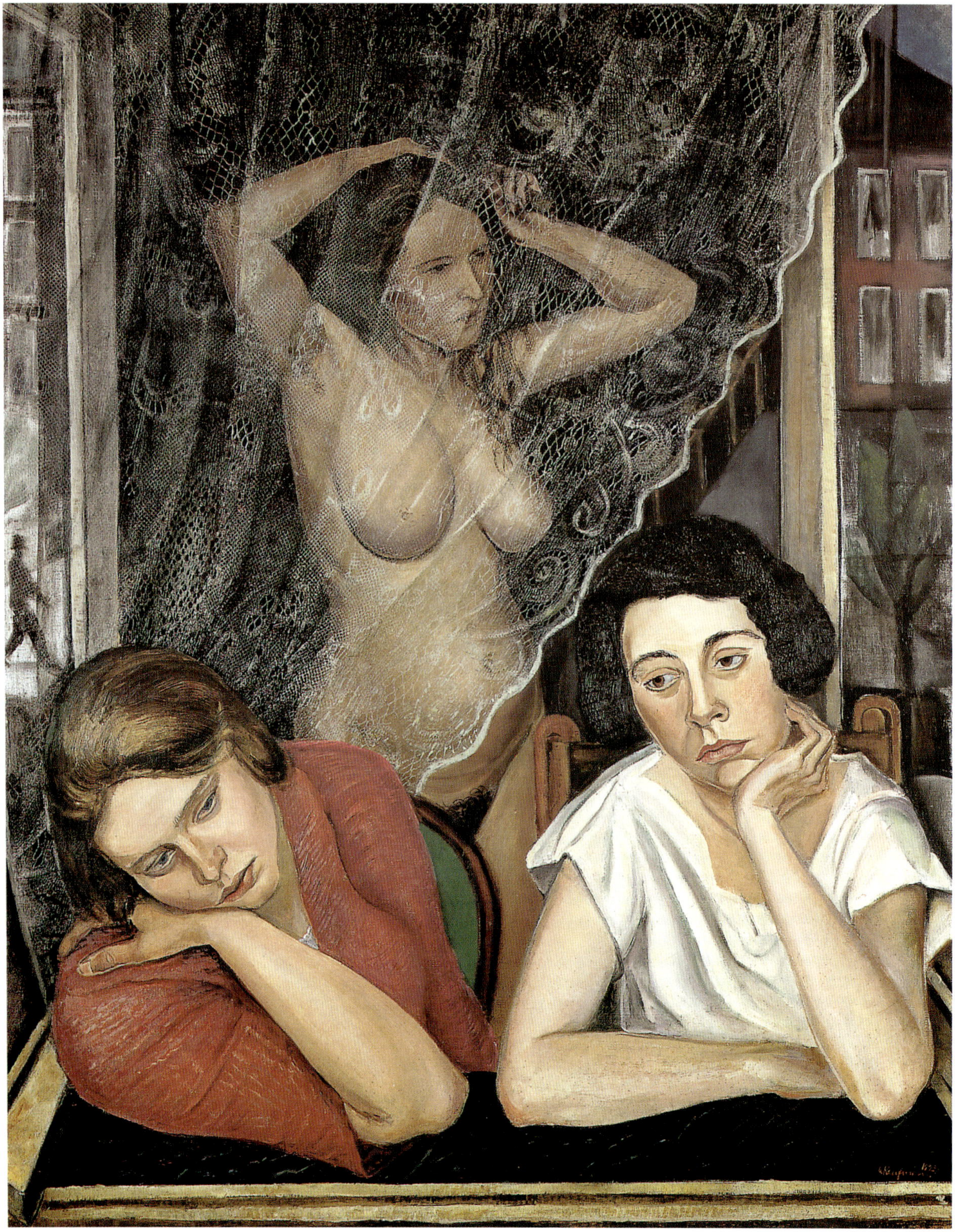

Düsseldorf

Mother Ey and the Young Rhineland Movement

Like Cologne, Düsseldorf was also to become a centre of modern art in the 1920s. While the war was still on, Arthur Kaufmann, Adolf Uzarski and Herbert Eulenberg had appealed to 45 artists to join together in order to give a chance to modern, progressive art, which had been suppressed in Düsseldorf for so long. Like all other institutions, the Düsseldorf Academy had become fossilized in tradition. The result was the foundation in 1919 of the "Junge Rheinland" (Young Rhineland), an interest group of artists with no particular stylistic commitment. The only condition of membership was that one should produce "young" art. The field of participants was correspondingly large – 113 artists were involved in the first exhibition – and the output correspondingly heterogeneous. A group style never emerged in Düsseldorf; while most of the artists worked initially in an Expressionist manner, many of them turned in the course of time to Neue Sachlichkeit forms of artistic articulation.

An important figure in the Düsseldorf art world was the doctor Hans Koch (illus. p. 54), who ran a gallery in addition to his medical practice. He did great service for young artists, as well as establishing initial contacts with artists living elsewhere, among them Felixmüller and Dix. It was through Felixmüller that contact with the Dresden Secession was maintained. The fact that the graphic media were of such great importance for the Düsseldorf artists is also attributable to his influence. Their graphic works were then published in the magazines "Das Junge Rheinland" and "Das Ey", enabling the artists to make themselves known more easily than would have been the case with exhibitions alone.

In addition to this, the Galerie Flechtheim, already renowned at this time, supported some members of the Young Rhineland group, displaying them in honorable proximity to the great names of the fathers of modern art such as van Gogh and Cézanne. However, Flechtheim was soon to fall out with the genuinely radical artists, who had banded together to form the "Aktivistenbund 1919" (1919 Activists' League).

Yet precisely these artists were able to rely upon the boundless support of Johanna Ey, the legendary "Mutter Ey" (Mother Ey), who would become a magnet for radical artists. Her gallery developed into the centre for young artists who were not understood, especially as Flechtheim increasingly turned his attention away from Düsseldorf in the course of the Twenties, concentrating upon his branches in other cities, and particularly upon Berlin. The Young Rhineland group took up residence in Mother Ey's coffee shop behind the gallery; all activities were directed from here.

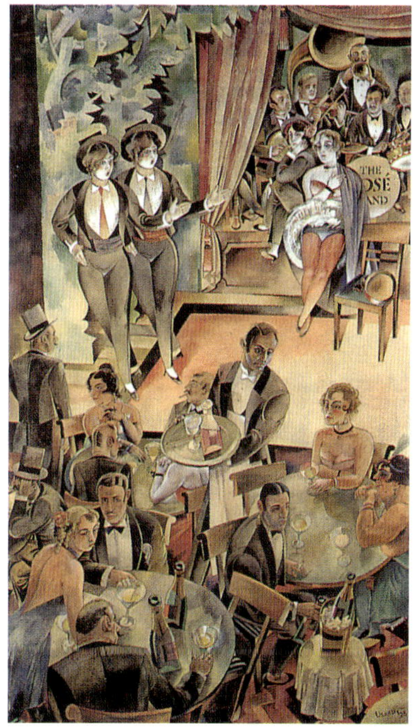

Adolf Uzarski
Cabaret Café, 1928
Kabarett-Café
Watercolour, 70 x 40 cm
Düsseldorf, Stadtmuseum

Arthur Kaufmann
Three Girls at the Window, 1927
Drei Mädchen am Fenster
Oil on canvas, 125 x 94.5 cm
Düsseldorf, Stadtmuseum

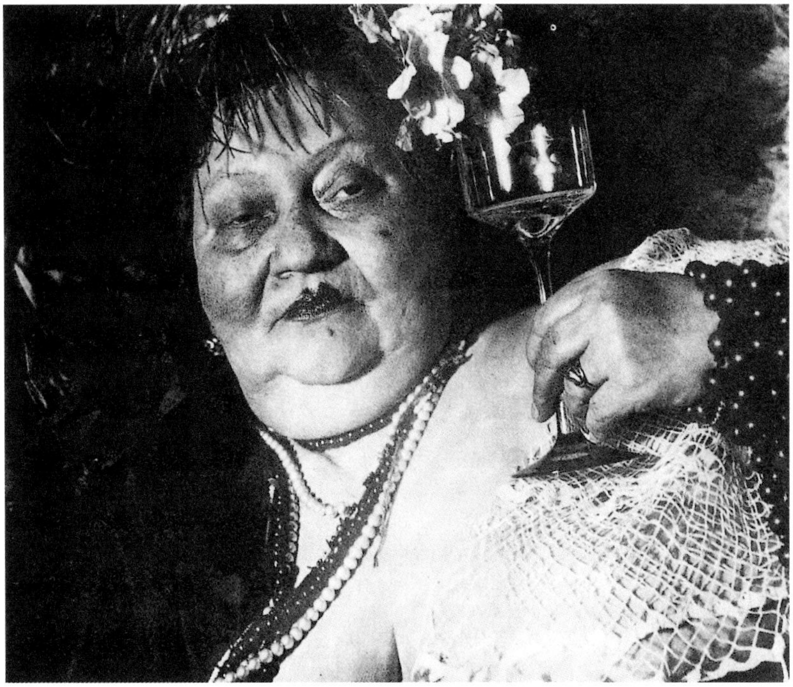

Max Peiffer-Watenphul
Portrait of Johanna Ey, 1930/31
Porträt Johanna Ey
Black-and-white photograph
Private collection

Johanna Ey had come to Düsseldorf from her home in the country before the First World War, in order to make a new life for herself following the birth of her twelve children and her divorce from her husband. She came into contact with young artists through the bakery which she ran in the neighbourhood of the Academy, and became an art collector on declaring herself prepared to take pictures as payment in lieu of money. After the war, she opened her own gallery, becoming increasingly a protagonist of new art, where her sympathies intuitively lay. Many artists owed their survival to her energetic and motherly support during their difficult initial years. Mother Ey not only darned the socks of her protégés but even defended them in court, as on the occasion when Wollheim and Dix were charged with immorality. Dix, full of sympathy and gratitude, painted a portrait of her as Queen, a picture of quietly smiling irony yet also revealing a dignity meant in all seriousness (illus. p. 127).

The strong desire for a sense of community at this time is reflected in the numerous portraits, which formed a principal theme of the Düsseldorf artists. Everybody painted everyone else, and Johanna Ey's portrait was painted more often than that of any other woman in Germany. Arthur Kaufmann's double portrait of *Betty Kohlhaas and Jankel Adler* (illus. p. 131) conjures up unity through the woman's hand placed comfortingly upon the artist's shoulder, assuring him of her support. The group portrait of the legendary circle around Mother Ey (illus. p. 131) is also by Kaufmann. It follows the style of Max Ernst's *Rendezvous des amis*, and displays a similar self-confidence, as also expressed in the picture's subtitle, *Düsseldorf's Intellectual Scene*. Dix was in very close contact with Kaufmann during his years in Düsseldorf, the two travelling together to Italy in 1923/24.

Adolf Uzarski was gifted in many different directions. A trained commercial artist, he had been head of the advertising department of the Tietz department store during the First World War. At the time of the Young Rhineland foundation, he was already established and financially secure.

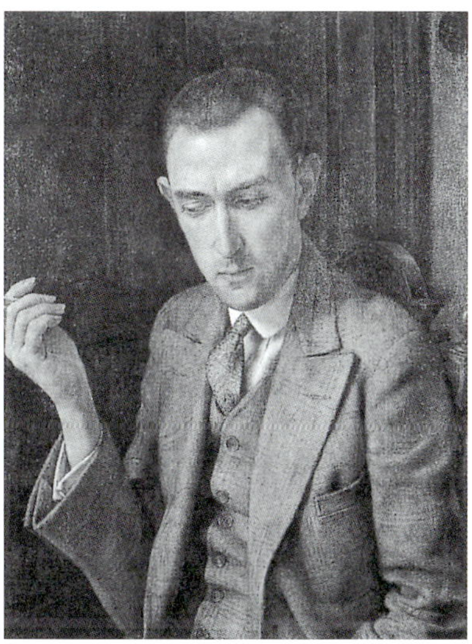

Albert Henrich
Portrait of Willi Henrich, 1930
Porträt Willi Henrich
Oil on canvas, 76 x 59 cm
Düsseldorf, Stadtmuseum

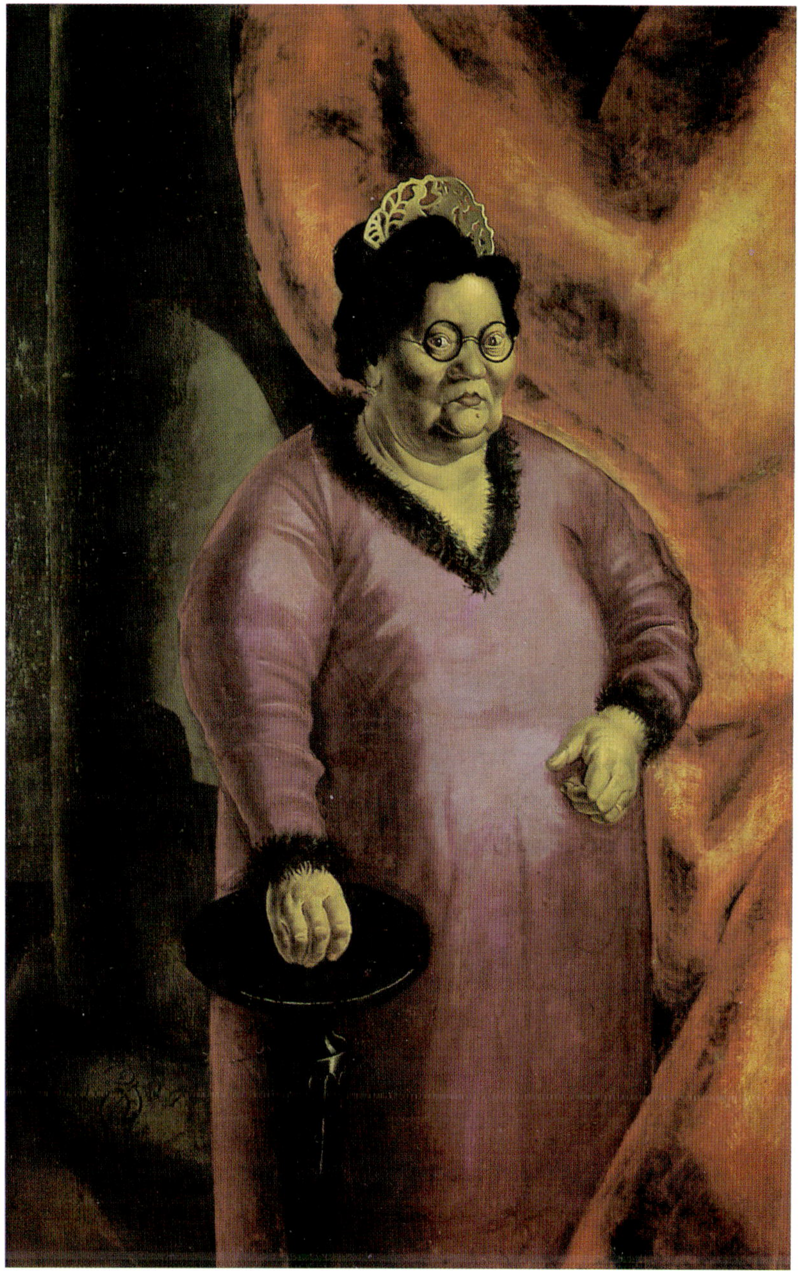

Otto Dix
Portrait of Johanna Ey, 1924
Bildnis Johanna Ey
Oil on canvas, 138 x 89 cm
Private collection

With her open support of modern art, gallery owner Johanna Ey, affectionately called "Mother Ey" by her artists, became the legendary focal point of the Young Rhineland group. As such, she had her portrait painted time and again, and was even given the honour in Arthur Kaufmann's 1925 group portrait of being made the centre of the Düsseldorf intellectual scene.

Hanns Kralik's view from his window opens onto the paralysing quiet of an almost deserted city under a dark and gloomy sky. The shop windows have already been emptied and the doors stand open. Disconsolate passers-by and an elderly couple are awaiting the departure of the tram, which seems locked in place under the heavy shadows. Kralik, who became municipal official for cultural affairs in Düsseldorf for a short time after the war, shows the Nordstraße below as an oppressive, dead landscape.

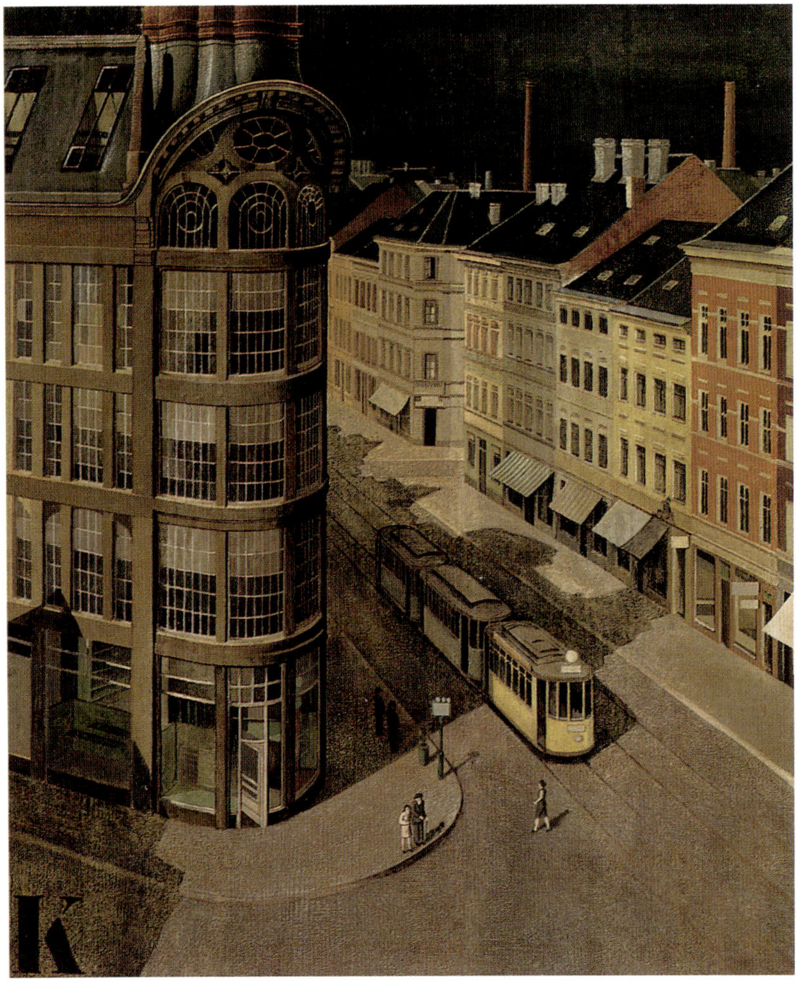

Hanns Kralik
From My Window, 1930
Aus meinem Fenster
Oil on canvas, 58.5 x 50 cm
Düsseldorf, Stadtmuseum

Furthermore, his numerous contacts contributed in no small way to the promotion of the Young Rhineland, some exhibitions taking place in the aforementioned department store, for example. Uzarski often illustrated works of literature – something which he did with great enthusiasm – among them his own works of poetry. His literary œuvre may be placed on an equal far with his depictive work. In addition to innumerable articles in magazines, he also published novels and stories.

His work is characterized by a satirical, humorous keynote, which he employed to convey his biting social criticism. Himself from a solid middle-class background, Uzarski focussed his critical attention on the German petit bourgeois. In his watercolour *German Family* (illus. p. 132), of 1932, the members of the family proudly present themselves in the parlour, where everything is gathered together such as secures the status of a good middle-class citizen. The motherly matron, as calming influence, and the father,

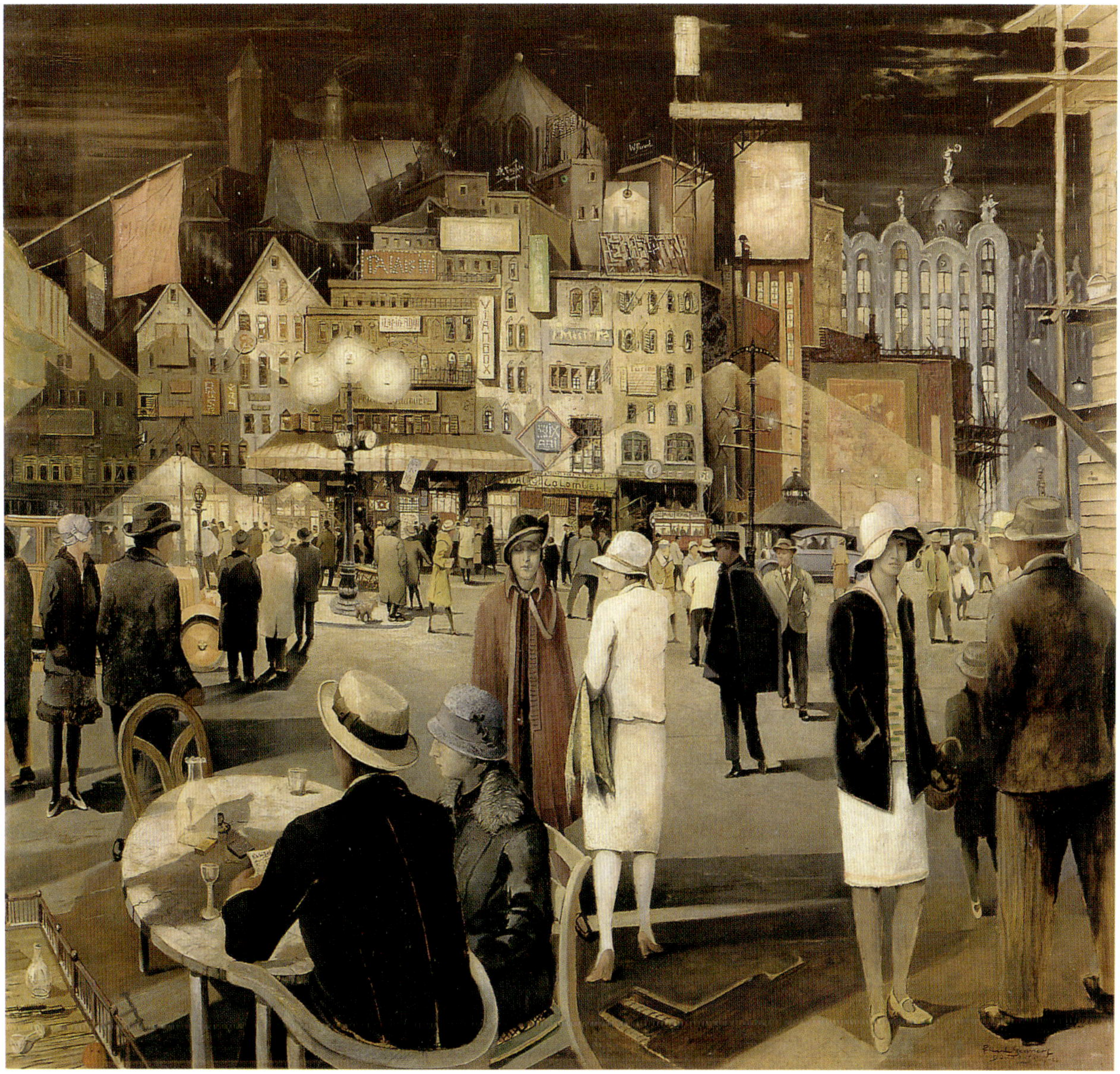

vested with the self-assurance of a Prussian official, are endeavouring to pose like aristocrats. The well-bred daughter, coy to the point of flirtatious; the junior member of the family, full of enthusiasm for the army – everything is as it should be. The picture's decisive message is conveyed by numerous details, however, the significance of which within Uzarski's work as a whole can be explained by his predilection for illustrations and caricatures. They serve here to reveal the complete absurdity of this perfect example. The girth of the lady of the house is stretching her dress almost to bursting point, while the suit worn by the paterfamilias, for its part, is distinctly a few sizes too large – and, moreover, incorrectly buttoned up; nevertheless, both are anxious to maintain the required dignity. The family presents itself in the surroundings of its antiquated ambience of Wilhelminian paraphernalia. Every centimetre of the room – even the ambiguous window catch – is decorated with projecting, ornamental elements. Thus does Uzarski

Richard Gessner
Paris by Night, 1927/28
Paris bei Nacht
Oil on canvas, 185 x 200 cm
Düsseldorf, Kunstmuseum Düsseldorf im Ehrenhof

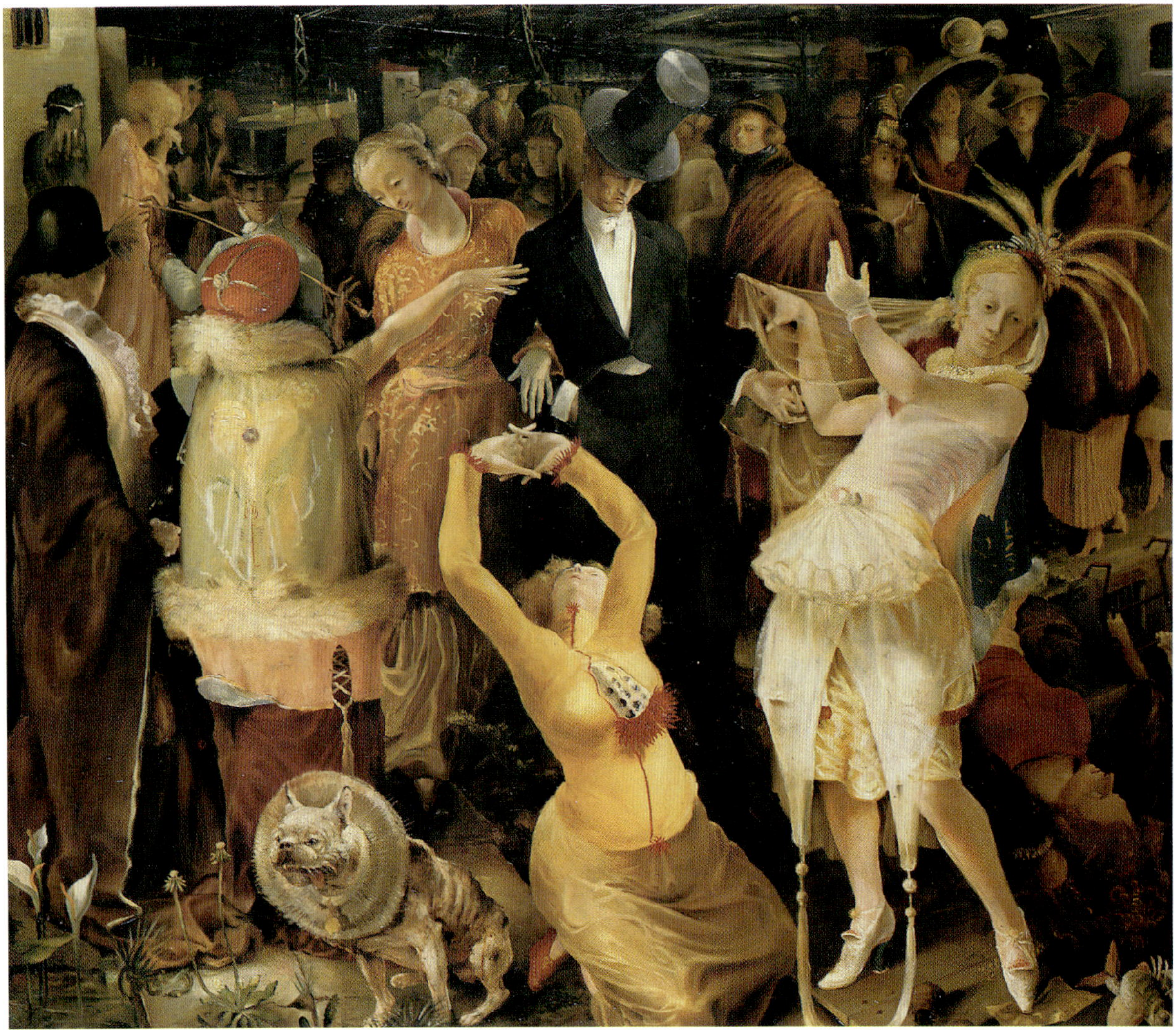

Gert Wollheim
Taking Leave of Düsseldorf, 1924
Abschied von Düsseldorf
Oil on canvas, 160 x 185 cm
Düsseldorf, Kunstmuseum Düsseldorf im Ehrenhof

allegorically presents the dandyish self-assurance of this family, whose members are hard-pressed to find room in which to move among all the homely objects – as made clear to the point of ridicule by the accentuated central perspective. Uzarski is sketching in this work the caricature of a family of the old order on the eve of National Socialism, living in its world of lies, pushed more or less unwillingly into the corner. Only the picture hanging over the sideboard, with its Neue Sachlichkeit austerity, represents a contrasting world to the confinement of the parlour. The dove appears to be trying to fly out of the picture – and not merely out of the picture within the picture – to fly to freedom.

Although no Rhinelander himself, Gert Wollheim must be considered one of the leading figures in the Düsseldorf scene. Mother Ey had grown fond of Wollheim and his friend Otto Pankok, and spontaneously put their portraits of each other on show in the display window of her gallery. "The effect was catastrophic... All that could be heard was laughter, abuse, a crowd of people as if someone had been murdered... And so a decision crystallized within me to exhibit the works of the Modernists, at this very moment", Mother Ey recorded.[71] Wollheim was a pugnacious fighter in word, deed and artistic output against the established and bigoted art world. Max Ernst came from Cologne to hear one of his fiery speeches, thereby also entering the circle around Mother Ey. Wollheim's motto was "Epater le bourgeois" – he wanted to violate norms and break taboos.

His style in the course of these years varies between expressive elements, surreal inspirations influenced by Max Ernst, and forms of expression taken from Neue Sachlichkeit. A constant feature running through his work, however, is that of the theatrical, of the pose – seen not only in his work but also in his appearance. Like Dix, he moved to Berlin in 1925. He depicted himself in his mysterious painting *Taking Leave of Düsseldorf* (illus. p. 130) as an elegant gentleman in the midst of a demimonde bidding him farewell amid great lamentations. Theatrical poses, fantastic costumes, simultaneous scenes and completely impenetrable spatial relationships give the picture the appearance of the portrayal of a dream. It is Wollheim's farewell to his "wild years", for now he, too, like so many of his comrades-in-arms, was gradually becoming established.

Karl Schwesig was a close friend of Wollheim's, and the two formed a pugnacious duo. Like Uzarski, Schwesig was highly extrovert. His œuvre from these years consists almost exclusively of portraits. As in the case of Wollheim, he, too, regarded self-presentation as principal to every artistic statement, as for example in his *Self-Portrait during the Carnival Season* (illus. p. 133). He portrays himself in a casual pose, surrounded by scantily clad ladies and a gentleman with a paunch, whereby these latter are sliced by the edges of the picture, serving to underline his dominating role. Schwesig's application of colour is always pastose and wildly animated.

The majority of the Düsseldorf artists regarded man as the focal point of interest. Some of them, however, also concerned themselves with other subjects. Theo Champion devoted himself to peaceful landscapes and urban views, for which he cultivated an Old-Master technique. Richard Gessner focussed particulary on industrial scenes, although his cityscape

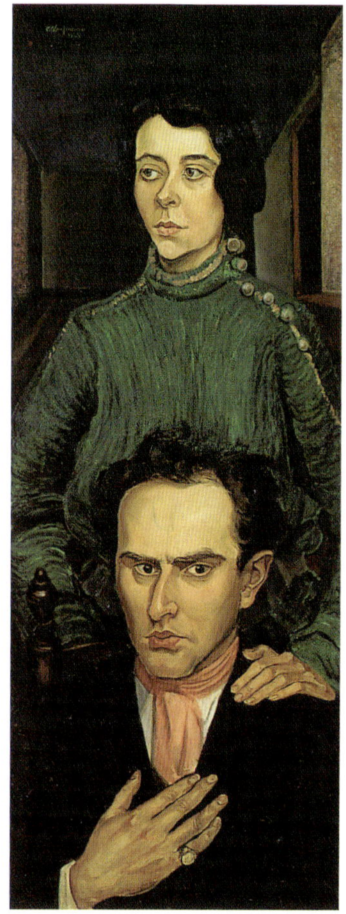

TOP:
Arthur Kaufmann
Betty Kohlhaas and Jankel Adler, 1927
Oil on canvas, 125 x 94.5 cm
Düsseldorf, Stadtmuseum

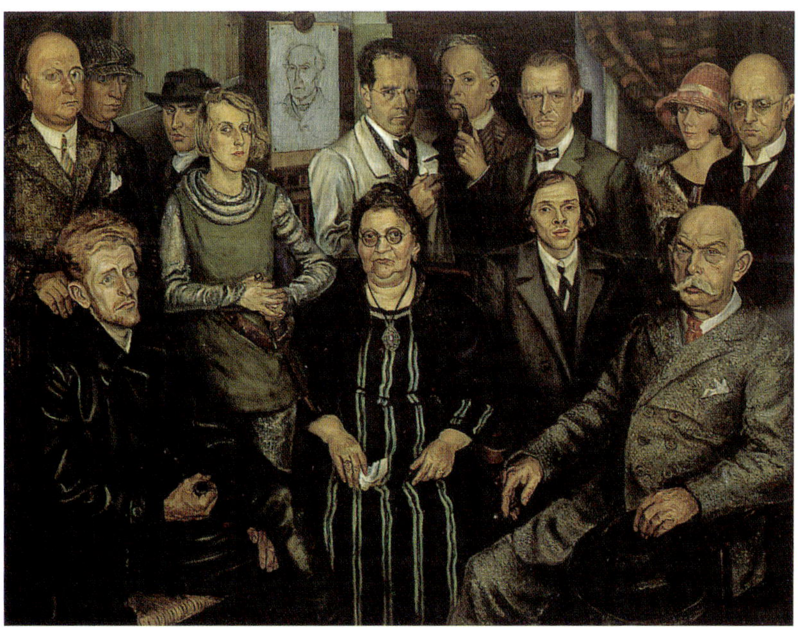

BOTTOM:
Arthur Kaufmann
Contemporaries (Düsseldorf's Intellectual Scene), 1925
Zeitgenossen (Das geistige Düsseldorf)
Oil on canvas, 182 x 245.5 cm
Düsseldorf, Stadtmuseum

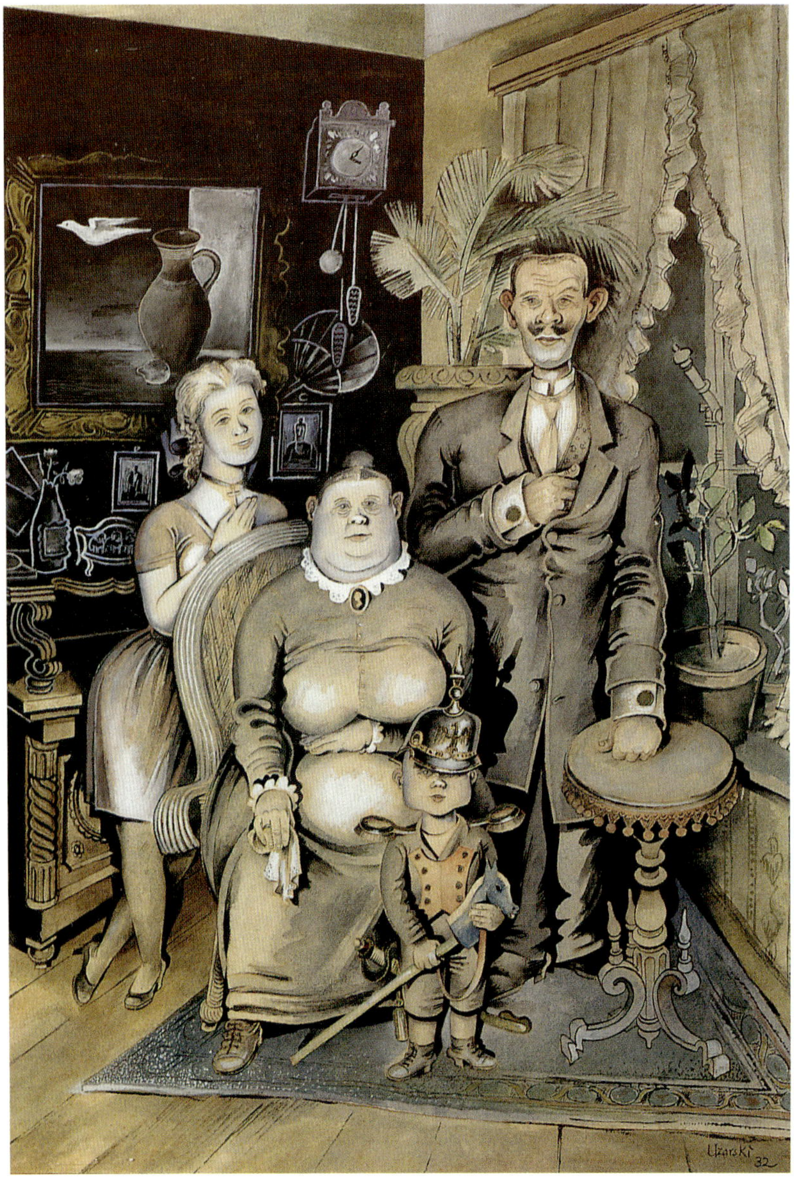

Uzarski also used his position as secretary of the Young Rhineland group to express his biting and ironic criticism of the bourgeoisie that supported the far-right German Nationalist People's Party: "I've written some hundred of the best German novels under the name of Courths-Mahler. Politically, I'm a dyed-in-the-wool German Nationalist and an honorary member of the German Nationalist Protection and Defence Alliance."

Adolf Uzarski
German Family, 1932
Deutsche Familie
Watercolour, 67 x 48.8 cm
Düsseldorf, Stadtmuseum

Paris by Night (illus. p. 129), also became well-known, with its alienating atmosphere of a stage set populated with dolls and floodlit with artificial light, producing strange, harsh shadows.

The cohesion of the Young Rhineland group was subjected to constant and exacting tests as a result of the great differences between the personalities and convictions of the various artists. A far-reaching break occurred as early as in 1923, Uzarski falling out with Mother Ey, who made no secret of the fact that she had grown particularly fond of certain artists. During an exhibition of Uzarski's work in her gallery, she revealed herself more interested in selling visitors pictures by Max Ernst and Wollheim in her little room at the back. This led to a split in the Young Rhineland, and the formation of the "Rheingruppe" (Rhine group) around Uzarski. The bitterness ran so deep that Uzarski refused to let himself be depicted with Wollheim

Theatrical appearances, poses and self-staging accompanied the work of Gert Wollheim and Karl Schwesig: "My soul is a chameleon", Wollheim remarked, while Schwesig ironically described himself as "a painter of ladies, a poet, and a leader of the dance".

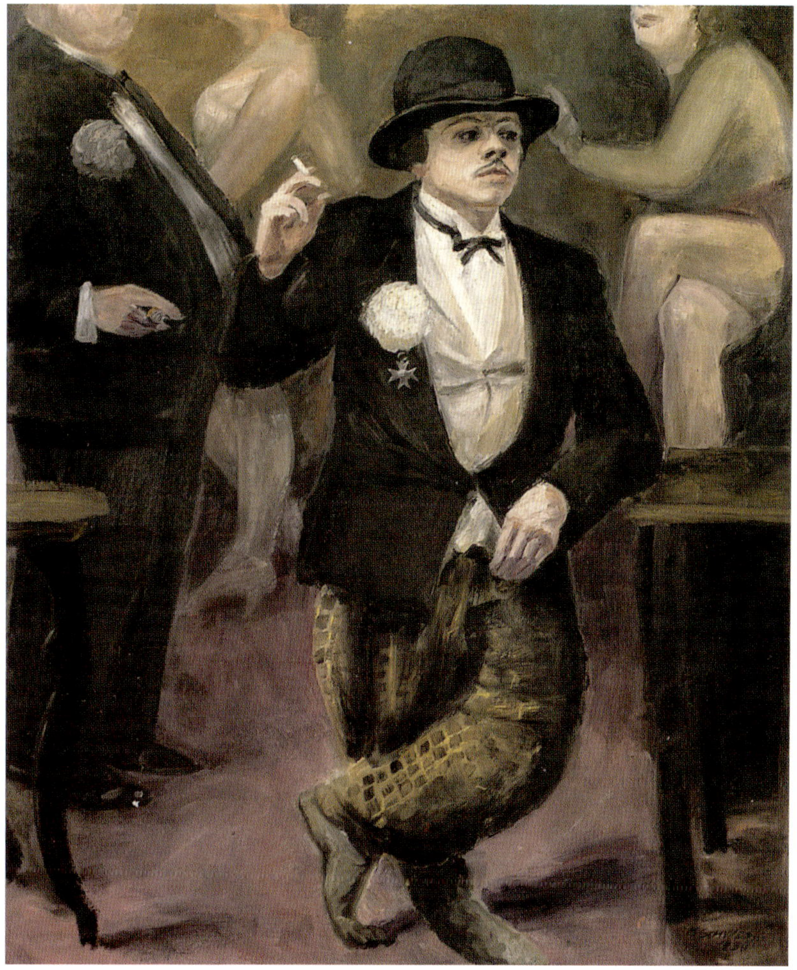

Karl Schwesig
Self-Portrait during the Carnival Season, 1930
Selbstbildnis im Karneval
Oil on canvas, 134 x 114 cm
Düsseldorf, Kunstmuseum Düsseldorf im Ehrenhof

in Kaufmann's portrait of the circle around Mother Ey. His place was subsequenlty taken by the actress Schewior.

While the radical artists gradually became established around the mid-Twenties and lost their quarrelsomeness – even Mother Ey turning into an advertisement for the city – a new generation of artists was growing up in Düsseldorf's lively atmosphere, a generation consciously seeking a sober distance from the concrete world. The city views of Hanns Kralik, for example, are dominated by an ominous, unreal atmosphere, similar to that in Radziwill's works. People appear unable to live in Kralik's cities; they are simply tin figures to be moved backwards and forwards. However, these younger artists – whose number included Carl Barth, Will Küpper and Frans Monjau – were barely able to develop further before the seizure of power by the National Socialists.

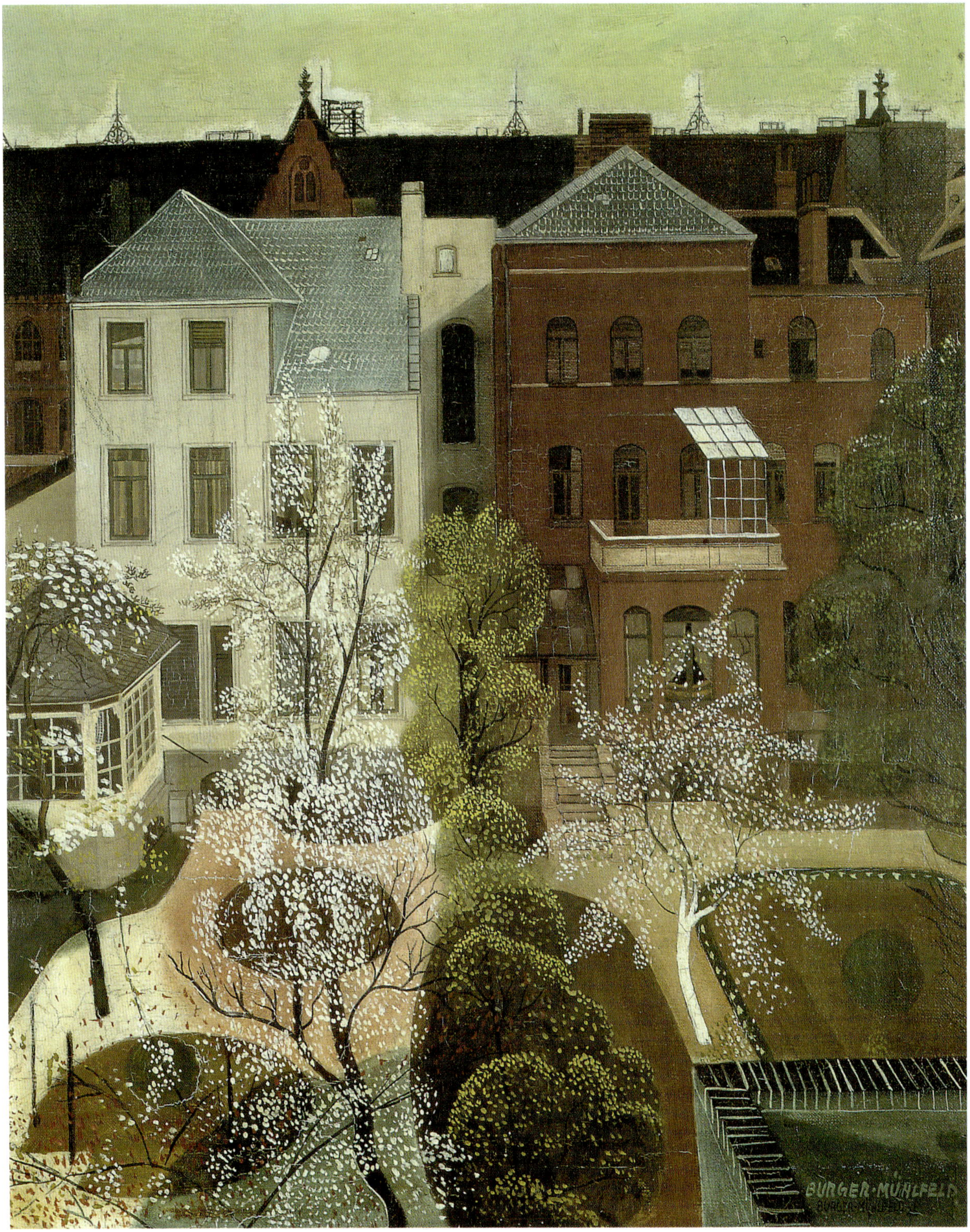
BURGER-MÜHLFELD

Hanover
Disillusion and Middle-Class Mentality

The city on the River Leine, always somewhat aloof in nature, has only ever been kissed once by the Muses, namely in the 1920s. The placid metropolis, historic seat of the Guelph dynasty, had been turned completely upside down after the end of the war and during the period of high inflation. Profiting from its central location between Berlin, the occupied Rhineland, and the harbours of northern Germany, Hanover soon became a great centre of black marketeering. Traders, crooks, prostitutes and other colourful characters hung around on the corners and in the winding streets of the quaint Old Town. The comfy world of the middle class was threatened by extremes: Kurt Schwitters, the Dadaist, on the one side, together with Anna Blume and company, and the infamous sex murderer Haarman on the other, the latter helping Hanover to a dubious renown and a brilliant description by Theodor Lessing.

In the midst of this fascinating hustle and bustle arose the astonishingly homogeneous group of Hanover Neue Sachlichkeit painters (Ernst Thoms, Grethe Jürgens, Friedrich Busack, Gerta Overbeck, Erich Wegner, Hans Mertens, and Karl Rüter), all of whom belonged to the generation of 1900. They documented this Hanover-turned-upside-down in various ways, yet it was never to become their world. While they naturally knew Schwitters, their respectable provinciality did not fit in with the international ambience of his circle. They remained bound up with the pleasant facets of provincial life, rather than with Schwitters' REVONNAH. The Hanover Neue Sachlichkeit artists were therefore deliberately ignored by the Kestner-Society and the Kunstverein, organisations which were patronizing Schwitters at the time. The Hanover painters, all of whom were studying at the city's School of Arts and Crafts at the beginning of the 1920s, found their strongest backing in Fritz Burger-Mühlfeld, the gifted head of the graphic-arts class, who became their artistic mentor and, thanks to their influence, himself underwent a stylistic transition to Neue Sachlichkeit, something rather unusual within teacher-pupil relationships.

The Hanover painters represent an exception among Neue Sachlichkeit artists, in that they all – without exception – pursued a second profession, working as commercial artists, decorators or stage-set painters in order to earn a living. This graphically illustrates the restricted nature of local conditions, particularly after the end of the "wild times" at the close of the Twenties, as Hanover fell back once again into its provincial stuffiness. They did not maintain contact with any other Neue Sachlichkeit artists or groupings; Ernst Thoms alone was able to establish himself in Berlin – at

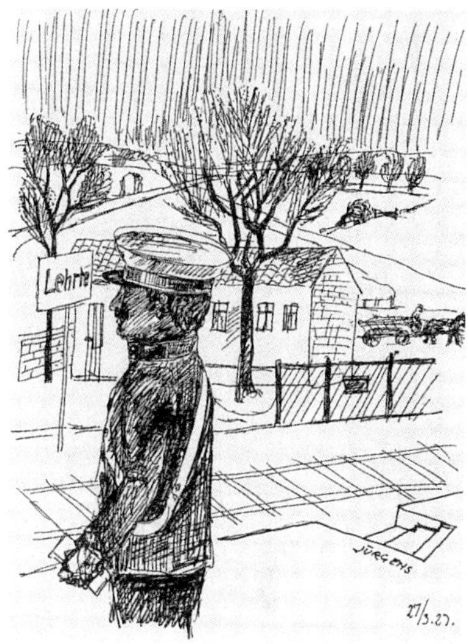

Grethe Jürgens
Station-Master, 1927
Bahnvorsteher
Pen drawing, 28 x 12 cm
Private collection

Fritz Burger-Mühlfeld
Houses in the Dieterichstraße, 1925
Häuser in der Dieterichstraße
Oil on canvas, 70 x 59.7 cm
Hanover, Sprengel Museum

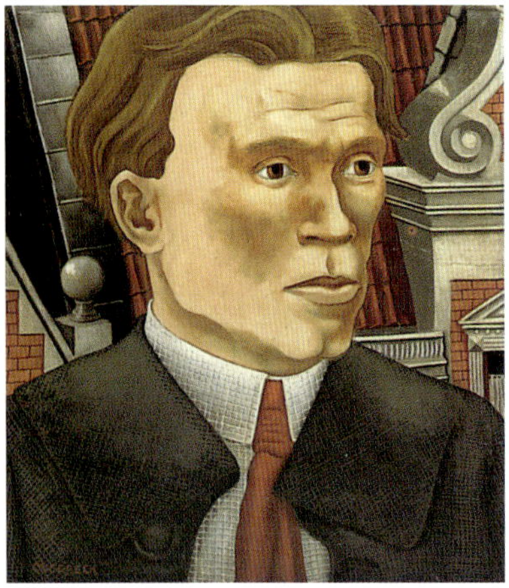

Gerta Overbeck-Schenk
Portrait of Ernst Thoms, 1926
Bildnis Ernst Thoms
Oil on canvas, 40.5 x 35.5 cm
Hanover, Sprengel Museum

least for a time – attaining higher Neue Sachlichkeit orders with an exhibition at the Galerie Nierendorf. On the other hand, the Hanover artists knew the French Realists of the 1920s relatively well, presumably primarily through publications; this further contributed to their special status within German Neue Sachlichkeit.

The Neue Sachlichkeit painters of Hanover pursued a style that was completely lacking in sentimentality, albeit one that often reveals moods of a lyrical and fairy-tale-like nature. One might be inclined to see this unusual combination of disillusionment and a manifestly middle-class mentality as characteristic of the "clerk culture" (Siegfried Kracauer)[72], the segment of society that played such an important part within the Weimar Republic. While not avoiding social issues in their pictures – their ever-precarious financial position undoubtedly served to shape their ideas – the Hanover artists nonetheless documented these without malice or condemnation.

The best attempt at characterizing the group's attitude from the viewpoint of art theory is perhaps to be found in a short essay by Grethe Jürgens in the magazine "Der Wachsbogen", of which she was the editor: "We are discovering an entirely new world . . . One paints a landscape, trees, houses, vehicles, and sees the world in a new way. Unemployed people, tramps, or beggars are painted, not because they are 'interesting characters' . . . or through a desire to appeal to the sympathy of society, but because one suddenly realizes that it is in these people that the most powerful expression of the present time is to be found."[73] This disassociation from motifs of social condemnation, articulated here with unusual explicitness, but also the disassociation from the type of profession or status-related picture otherwise predominating in Neue Sachlichkeit, remained binding for the work of the group.

From an artistic perspective, Ernst Thoms stood out from the rest of the seven painters. He was also the only one of them to be supported by the Kestner-Society. *Attic* (illus. p. 137) picks up one of the key motifs of Neue

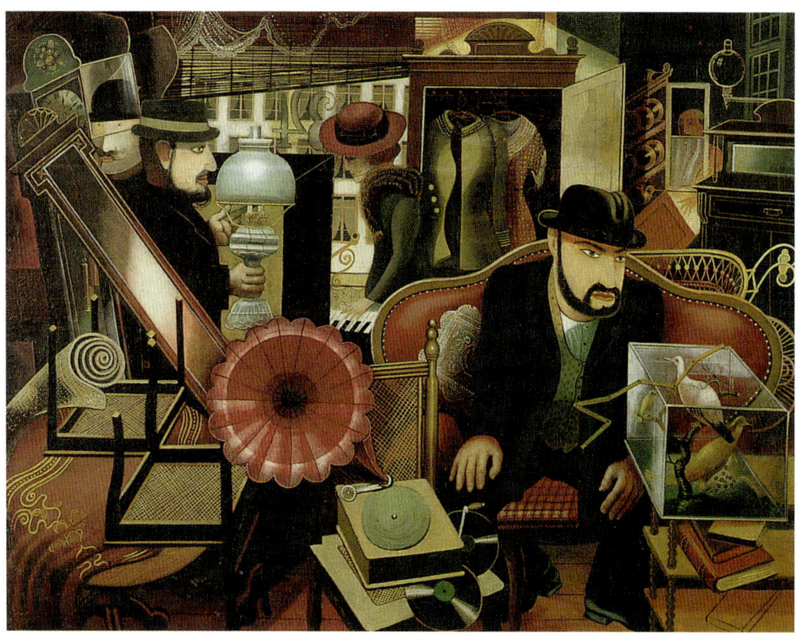

Ernst Thoms
Junk Shop, 1926
Trödelladen
Oil on canvas, 100 x 130.8 cm
Hanover, Sprengel Museum

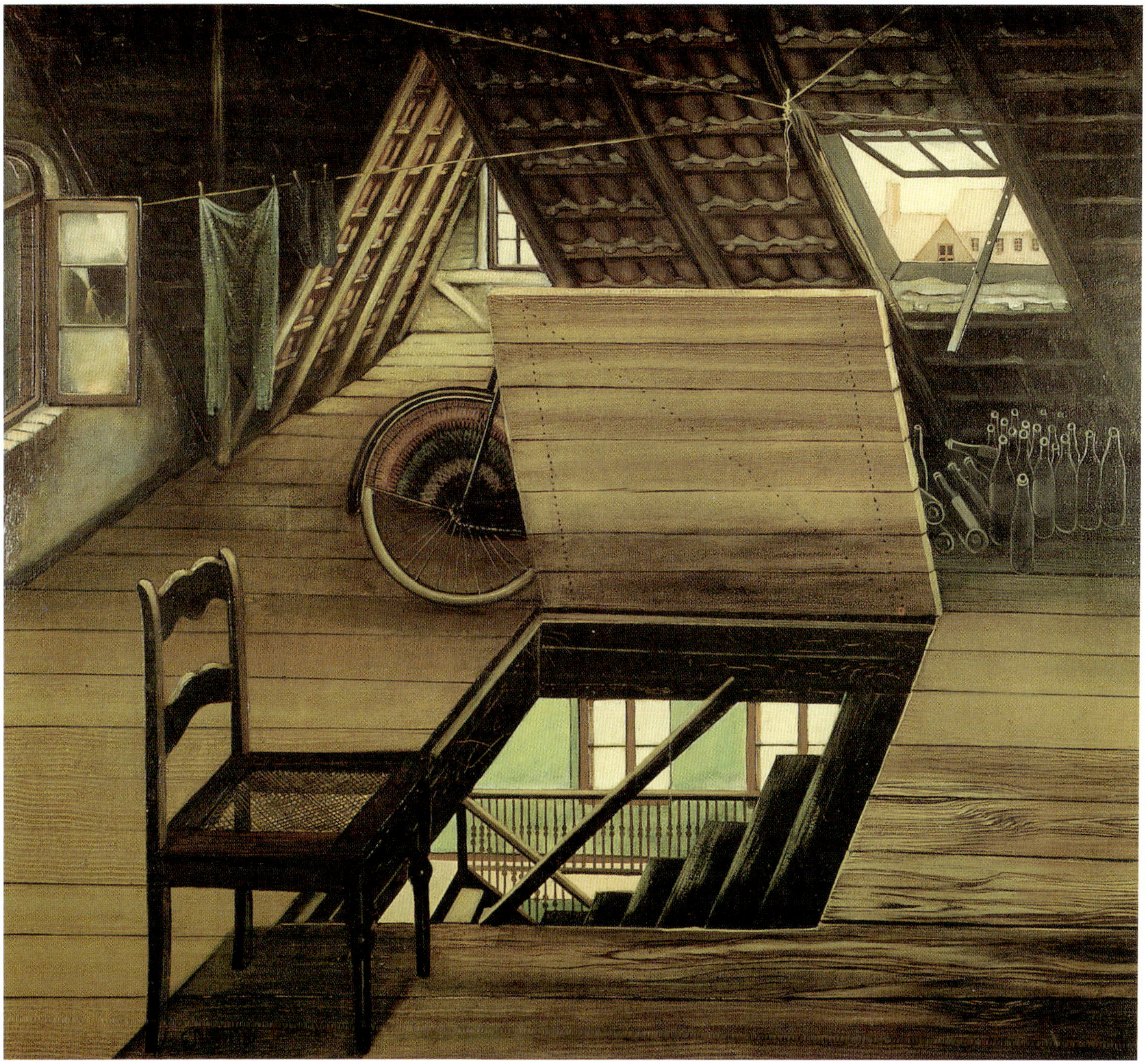

Sachlichkeit, presenting it in its full psychological ambivalence: attics may well have something romantic and homely about them, yet they are also confined and the view from them is narrow and remote. The motif functions as a perhaps all-too-obvious metaphor for the various pressures with which the individual is surrounded on all sides. Thoms deliberately renders the spatial conditions unclear, not so much by using a consciously deformed perspective à la Davringhausen as through a cunning combination of the view down through the raised trapdoor in the floor with a variety of views and vistas inside and out of the attic. Our eyes are presented with a spatial conglomeration of immense complexity, the faint hint of a secret. The finely shaded coloration attains a unique brilliance in the darker areas, for example in the case of the shadowy bottles. In *Junk Shop* (illus. p. 136), Thoms conjures up the dreamlike atmosphere of a gallery of curiosities, in which objects and figures of the character found in a Rousseau painting interweave with and merge into each other. Here, too, Thoms appears as

Ernst Thoms
Attic, 1926
Dachboden
Oil on canvas, 88 x 99 cm
Hanover, Sprengel Museum

"Attic", by the loner Ernst Thoms, takes up a key motif of Neue Sachlichkeit. However, he sees this not as a loft with everyday objects but rather as the enigmatic picture of an emptied, complex space, connected by its windows and trapdoors both to the interior of the house and to the outside world.

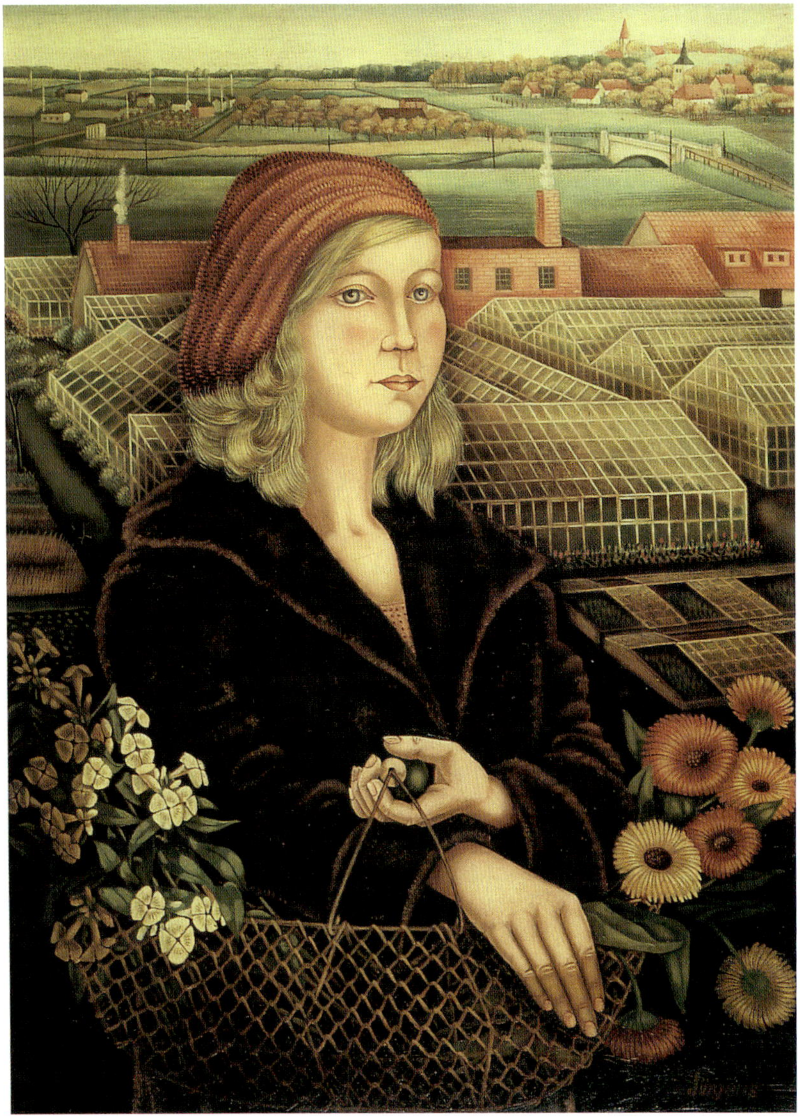

Grethe Jürgens
Flower-Girl, 1931
Blumenmädchen
Oil on canvas, 72.5 x 51.8 cm
Hanover, Sprengel Museum

a virtuoso of complex interlocking forms: while it is possible to draw a spatial distinction between the various objects, yet together, unreally illuminated in the midst of the predominant shades of red, they form a mystery of unbridled banality.

In his early paintings of pubs and seamen, reflecting the atmosphere of the "wild" inflationary years in Hanover, Erich Wegner was consciously seeking to take up the satirizing style of Otto Dix' pictures of sailors. By the mid–1920s, however, this subject-matter had been played out. In 1928, Wegner did a work of classical severity using almost geometrical black-white contrasts, namely *Winter Landscape* (illus. p. 141), among the most beautiful Neue Sachlichkeit landscape depictions. Its only superficially naive appearance seems to anticipate the pseudo-naive landscapes of the "Yugoslav Naives" (those of Ivan Generalič, for example), which enjoyed a certain popularity some time ago.

The same subject was taken up by Wegner's colleague Karl Rüter (*Winter*

Friedrich Busack drew the village level-crossing keeper's hut with its barrier again and again. Viewed from a naive perspective, things are shown and contrasted with each other according to their importance: the hut and the signal bells, the sunflowers behind the fence and the sky crisscrossed by wires. Railway pictures constitute the largest group of Neue Sachlichkeit pictures linking technology and landscape with each other.

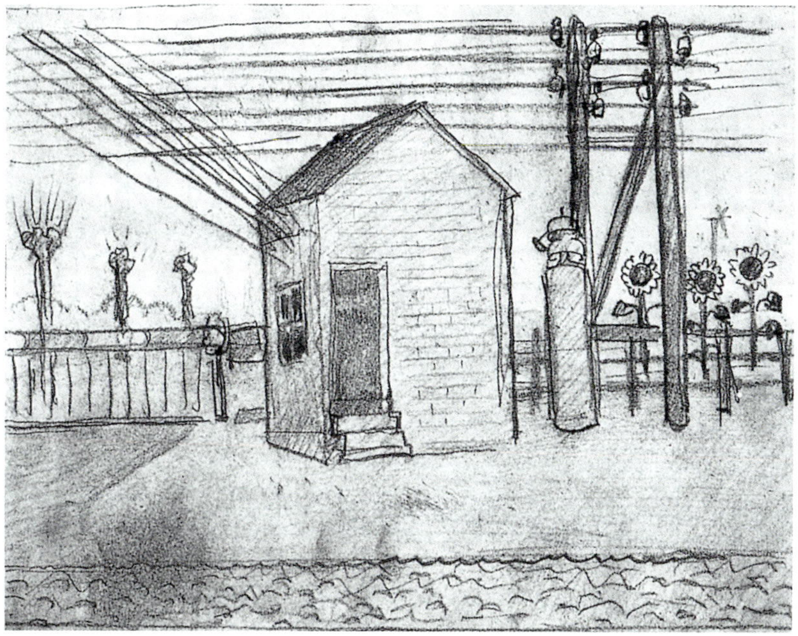

Friedrich Busack
Level-Crossing Keeper's Hut, c. 1929
Bahnwärterhäuschen
Charcoal drawing, 21 x 27 cm
Private collection

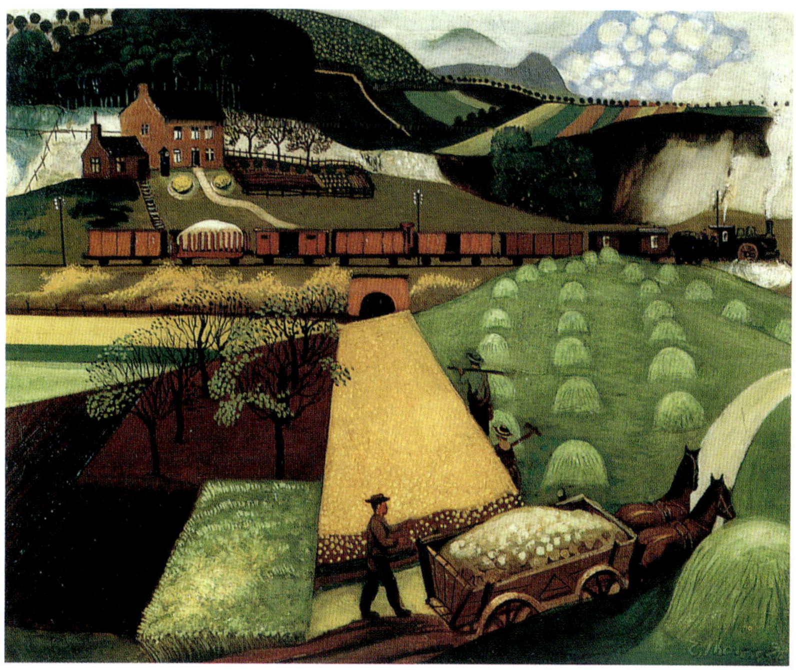

Ernst Thoms
Train, 1926
Eisenbahn
Oil on cardboard, 53 x 68 cm
Hanover, Kunstsammlung der Stadtsparkasse Hannover

The snow-bound landscapes by Wegner and Rüter are not so much pictures determined by the winter season but rather unsentimental transferences into nature of suburban dreariness. The broken wires of the telegraph pole in Rüter's picture symbolize the lack of contact that the suburban inhabitants have to the outside world.

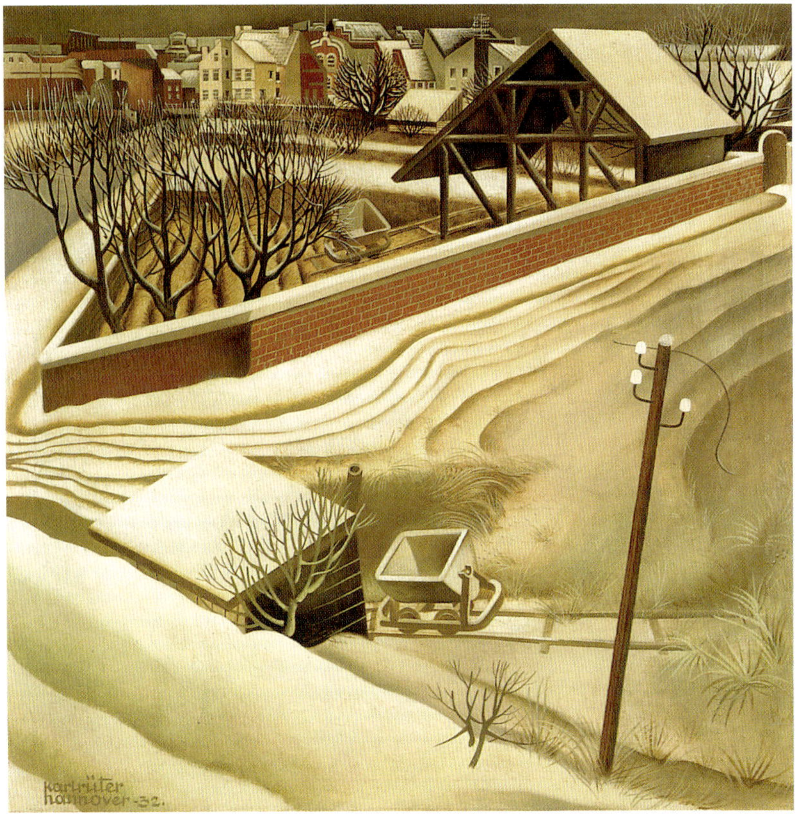

Karl Rüter
Winter Landscape, 1932
Winterlandschaft
Oil on nettle-cloth, 75 x 75 cm
Hanover, Sprengel Museum

Landscape, illus. p. 140). The diverging diagonals of the brick wall and the railway line serve to make the picture seem wider, counteracting the vanishing-line. The calligraphic broken wire of the telegraph pole functions as a symbol for dreary suburban life in wintertime. The particular genre of winter landscapes (Karl Zerbe, the Munich artist, may also be mentioned in this context) would later turn out to constitute a form of connection between Neue Sachlichkeit and moderate trends of painting during the Nazi period. The latter, while admittedly falling back on Breughel and Caspar David Friedrich to a greater extent, were on the whole not very far removed from the Neue Sachlichkeit formulations of this subject.

Still lifes of considerable note may also be found among the works of the Hanover artists. Wegner's *Pub Bar* (illus. p. 142), painted with thinly applied colours on unprimed canvas, betrays a hint of Art Deco. When the artist repeated the picture as a silk screen at the end of the 1960s, associations with Pop Art immediately sprang to mind, unintentionally revealing one of the latter's more distant lines of tradition. The observer is captivated in Hans Mertens' *Still Life with Household Articles* (illus. p. 143) by the nuanced shades of coloration with which the material of each object is rendered. The surfaces of these prosaic articles become a

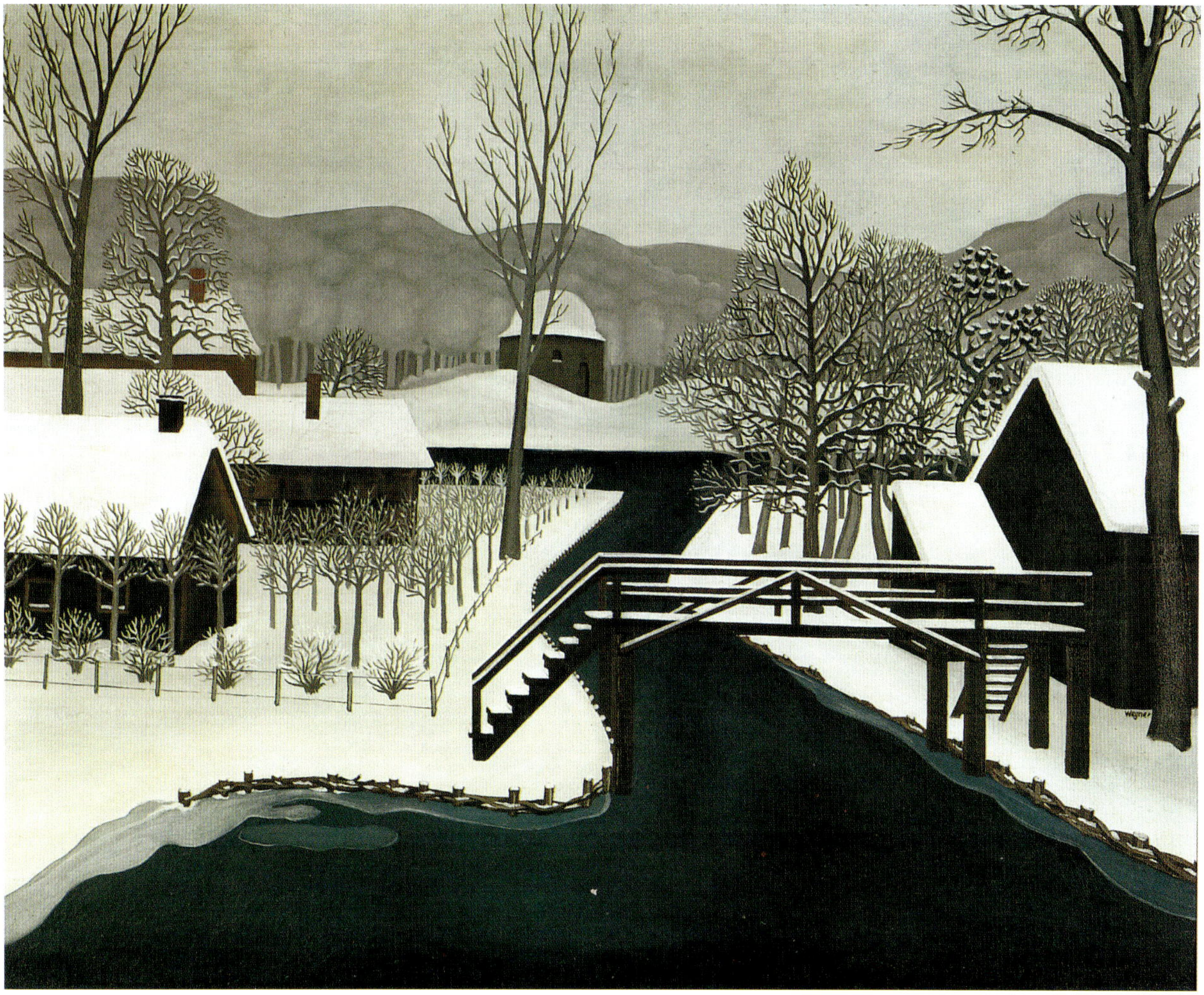

Erich Wegner
Winter Landscape, 1928
Winterlandschaft
Oil on canvas, 71 x 87 cm
Hanover, Sprengel Museum

source of unsuspected appeal. When looking at this picture, one finds oneself instinctively reminded of the analyses of form by Georg Scholz, the Karlsruhe professor of art: "Depending upon the manner in which they are employed, the interaction of opaque and glaze paints can express proximity and distance: smoothly painted surface – raw structure. Changes in the manner in which the paint is applied enable one to achieve not only light-and-shade but also material effects . . ."[74]

Grethe Jürgens is – together with Thoms – perhaps the group's best-known painter. Her *Employment Exchange* (illus. p. 145) is an impressive documentation of the social miseries of the 1920s, one into which autobiographical elements have been mixed: the artist herself is visible in the background, leaving the comfortless office after receiving a small sum of unemployment benefit. The influence of the French Realists is very apparent here, and of these primarily that of Auguste Herbin, the figures in his *Boules Players* (1923) having a similar arrangement. In addition, the figures in this painting, formed with firm yet flowing strokes of the brush and standing out black against the ground of the picture, also call to mind 19th-century photography with its distinct breaks between foreground and background. *Garden Picture*, in contrast, which Jürgens painted in 1928, can be seen almost as a tribute to the garden and park depictions of Henri Rousseau, following the sensational success of a large-scale exhibition of Rousseau's work in Germany two years before. Jürgens' picture demonstrates the contrast between the romantic ruined house and the modern building with a subliminal detachment, one which incorporates the fragility of the supposed idyll behind the wire into the artist's calculations. The artist's *Self-Portrait* reveals her knowledge of light-and-dark contrast photography in the style of an artist such as Hilmar Lerski. The fragile tulips and the overbright light-bulbs have been depicted with an almost penetrating lack of affection, their symbolism exposing the artificiality of the entire arrangement. There is very little that this work still has in common with the Neue Sachlichkeit portrait type and its concept of the "appropriate attribute".

Working together with, the author Gustav Schenk, the many-sided Grethe Jürgens edited the aforementioned magazine "Der Wachsbogen" from 1931 to 1932. This attempt to create a theoretical organ for the group and for her variety of Neue Sachlichkeit was doomed to failure, given the

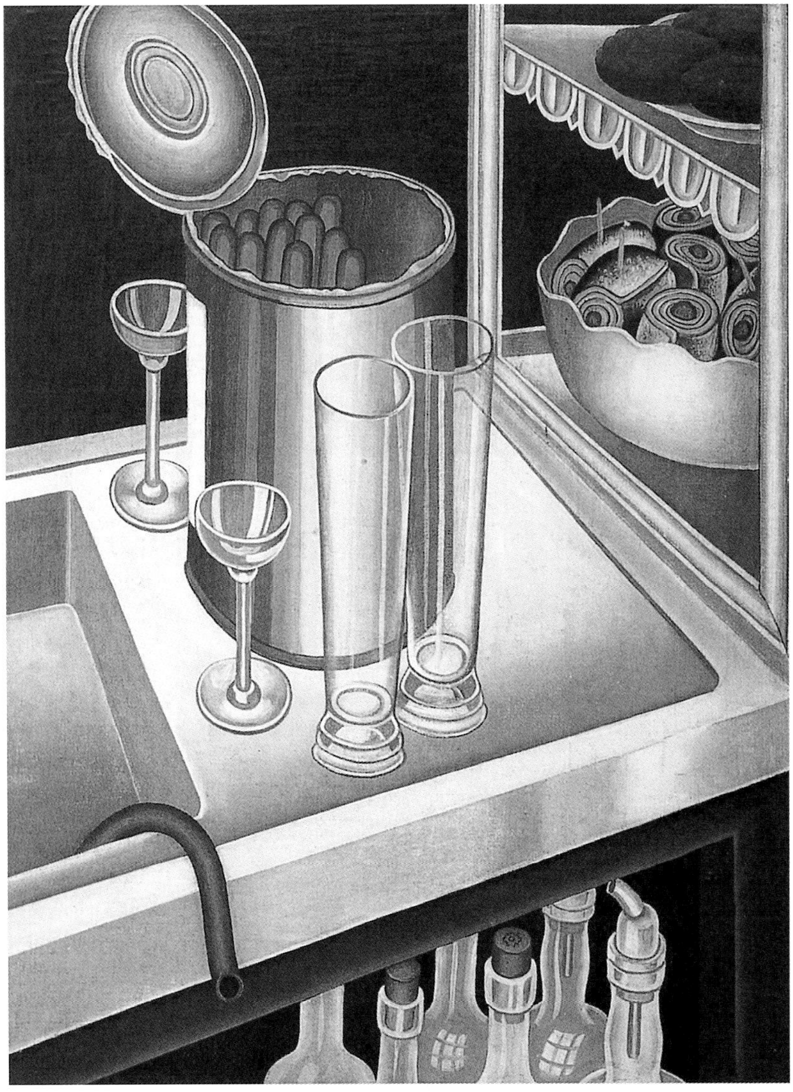

Erich Wegner
Pub Bar, c. 1927
Wirtshaustheke
Oil on canvas, 62 x 46.5 cm
Wuppertal, Von der Heydt-Museum

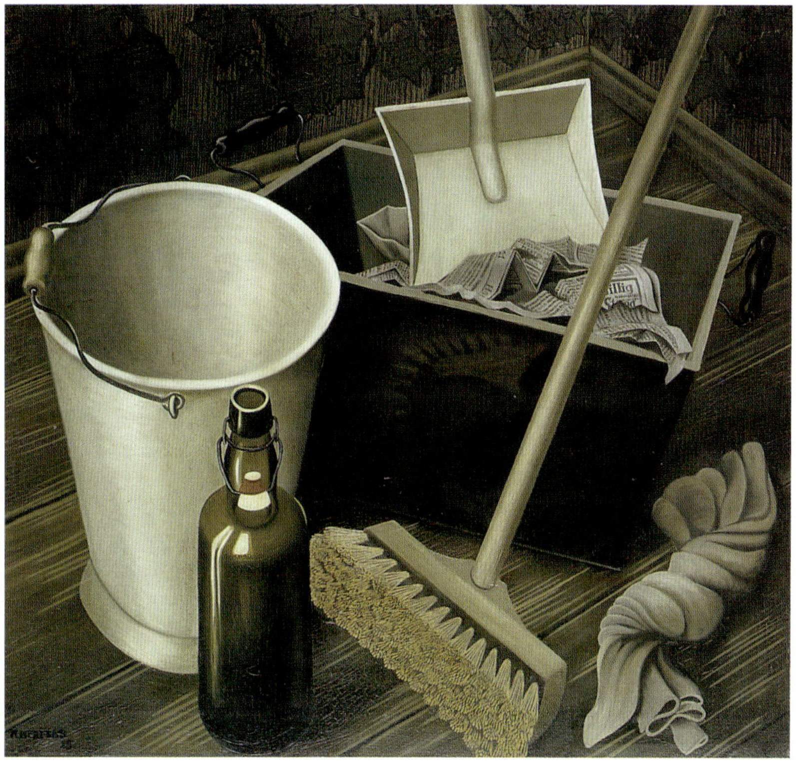

Hans Mertens
Still Life with Household Articles, 1928
Stilleben mit Hausgeräten
Oil on canvas, 65.2 x 70.3 cm
Hanover, Sprengel Museum

prevailing conditions. After twelve numbers, with only minimal sales, the magazine folded. The number of copies printed never exceeded 200, all of which were delivered by Jürgens and Greta to the individual subscribers by bicycle, since they did not have enough money to send them by post. Gerta Overbeck, a close friend of Grethe Jürgens, portrayed primarily the milieu of the common people in her works. Her concentrated, by no means unsympathetic painting of the *Card Players* goes back to French inspirations, while her visually particularly effective *Portrait of Ernst Thoms* (illus. p. 136) consciously contrasts the portrait's subject with the confusing conglomeration of sections of roofing, windowsills and volutes in the background. It is possible to detect here something of the representational manner of naive sign-painting, something that was being rediscovered at this time. However, the shadows on the subject's face are also influenced by photography.

A disruption for the Hanover artists came in 1933, just as something like a process of artistic maturation was becoming apparent and the first modest external successes were coming, among them an exhibition of some considerable size in Brunswick in 1932 of the group's work. Secluded in the country, without the limited space which some Berlin galleries were still able to offer unpopular artists until 1937, they nonetheless reveal no concessions in their works to Nazi tastes. The need correspondingly grew for all of them to switch to their non-artistic professions. The talented Friedrich Busack died in 1933; Mertens fell in 1944. A considerable proportion of the works from the Neue Sachlichkeit period, including almost the entire œuvre of Karl Rüter, was destroyed by the especially heavy bombing raids on Hanover. The majority of the Hanover painters experienced the general movement in the direction of Abstraction after 1945 as fruitless from the artistic viewpoint.

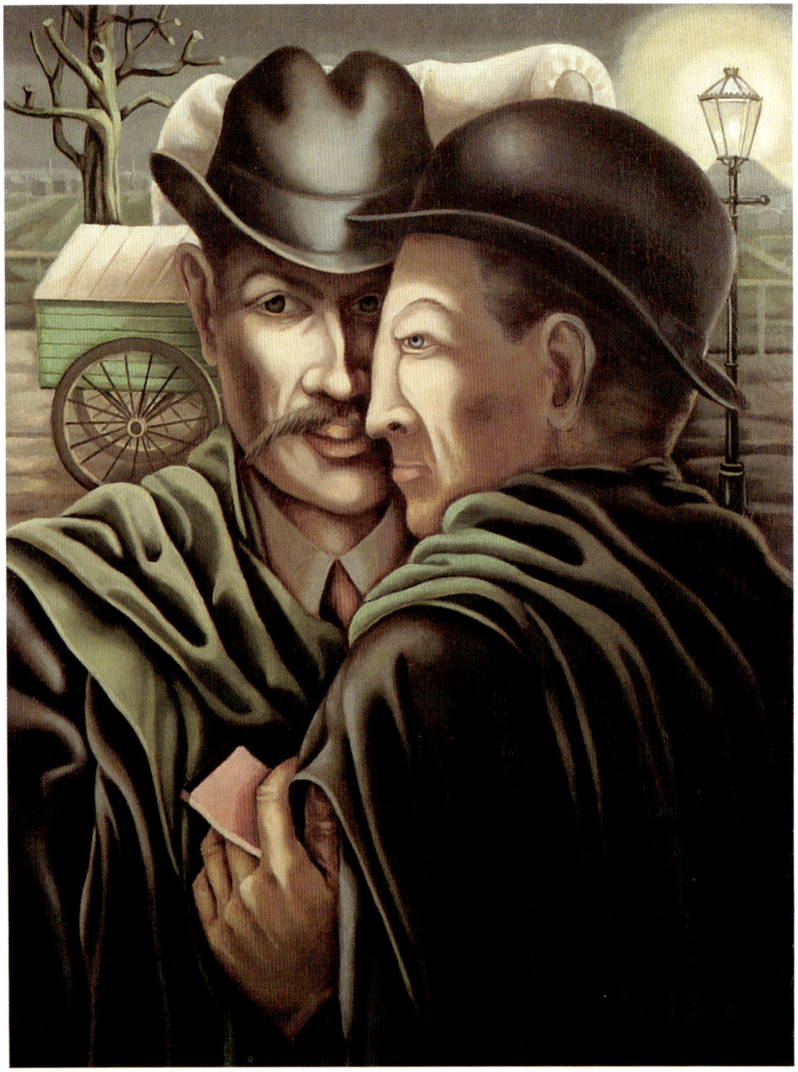

Grethe Jürgens
Cloth Merchant, 1932
Stoffhändler
Oil on canvas, 52.5 x 40.5 cm
Hanover, Sprengel Museum

Thus it was that their end as an informal group in the year of the Nazis' assumption of power was followed by thirty years of almost total oblivion. Once the artistic tradition had been broken, hardly anyone felt inclined to express an interest in these artists. It was not until 1962 that their partial rediscovery occurred, followed in the 70s by a comprehensive exhibition and research into their œuvre – markedly later than the reception granted other Neue Sachlichkeit artists. Despite this, however, some art historians continue to include them among the – not to be despised – genre of "amateur painters". The most important arguments against such a verdict have been advanced above. (Incidentally, Grethe Jürgens herself took up the subject of this scant regard for the Hanoverians work, pointing to the necessity of a historical understanding representational painting.) Art historians in the former East Germany, despite the great intensity with which they investigated every aspect of social criticism within the Weimar Republic, also had great problems with regard to these works, for it was – and still is – impossible to judge Hanover's Neue Sachlichkeit painters by conventional means of assessment.

"In the days when art seemed representational and comprehensible for everyone, no matter how slow he might be, every step that went further in the direction of the abstract was hard-won. Today it's the other way around. Suspicion of everything that is naive, of everything that a tram conductor can understand, is great, and we are accused of producing reactionary art."

Grethe Jürgens, 1932

Grethe Jürgens
Employment Exchange, 1929
Arbeitsamt
Oil on canvas, 66 x 50 cm
Hanover, Sprengel Museum

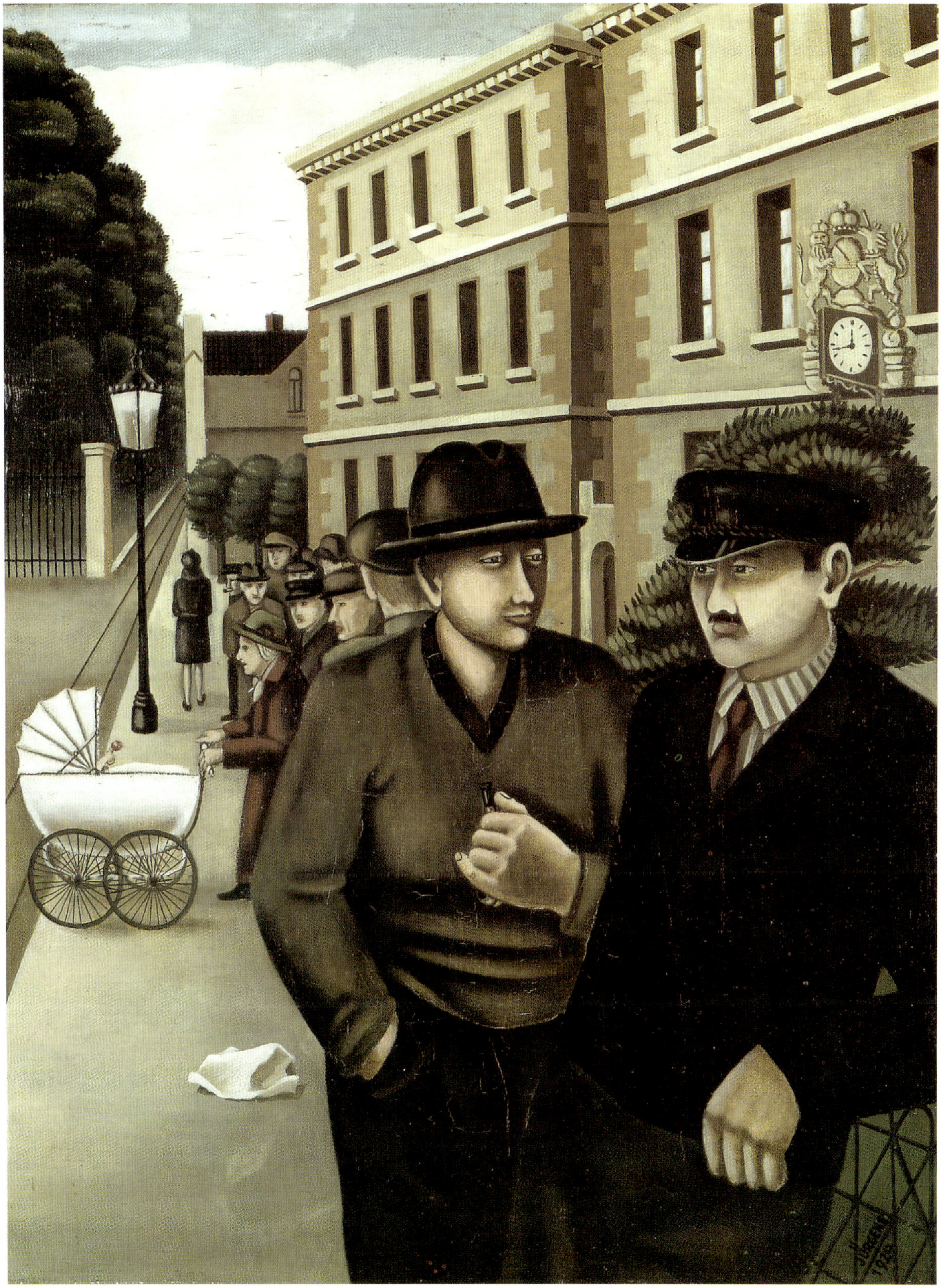

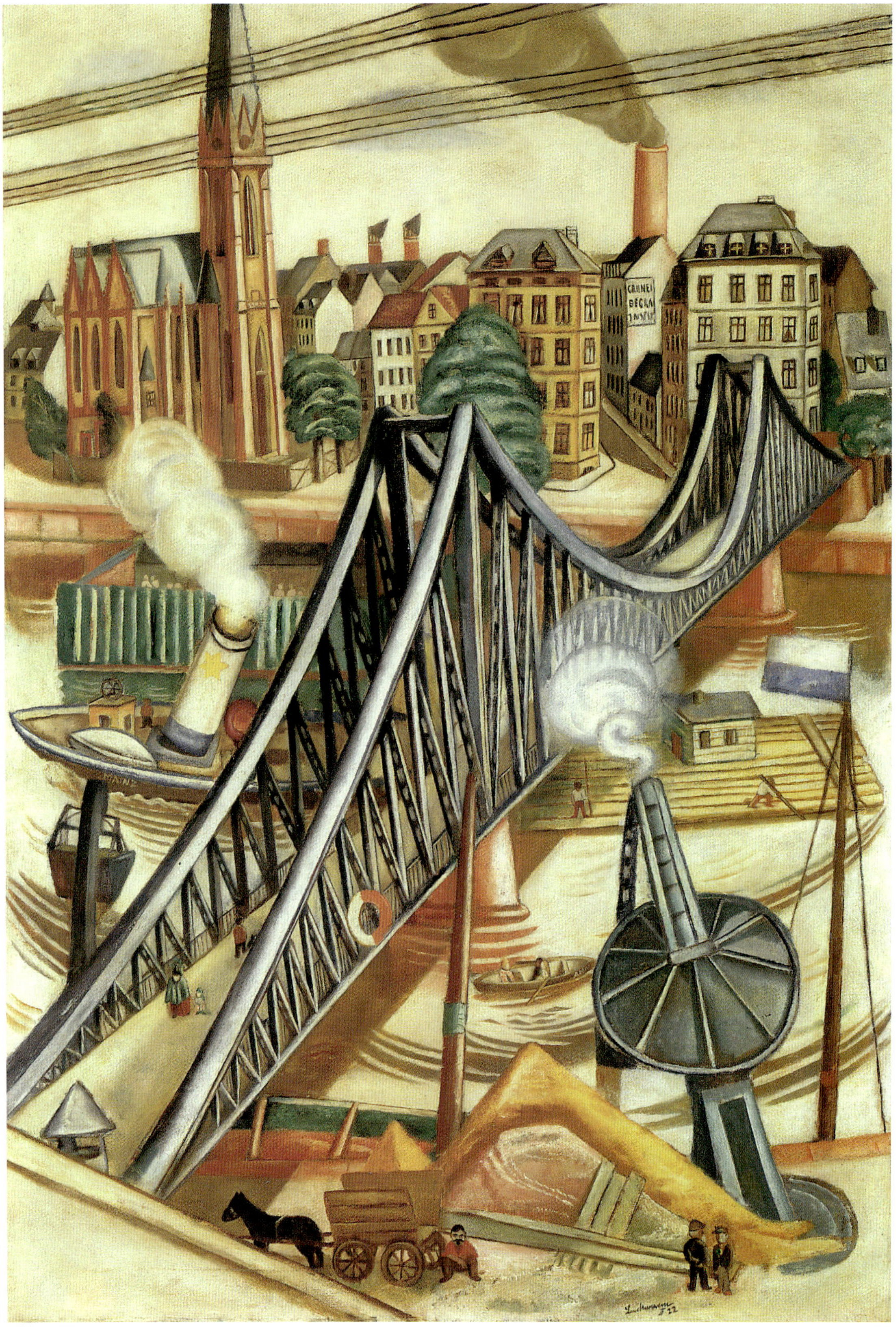

Outsiders

Max Beckmann, Karl Hofer, Franz Radziwill

Within Neue Sachlichkeit as a whole, there were no instances of artists joining together in stylistic associations such as Expressionism's "Die Brücke".[75] Nonetheless, all Neue Sachlichkeit works were considerably influenced both by the climate prevailing in the respective city in which they were done and by a given painter's contacts with other artists living there, something that explains the regional approach adopted in this book. However, there are certain artists whom it is impossible to incorporate into such a regional approach – if for no other reason than that they lived at some distance from the centres of Neue Sachlichkeit art, as was the case with Franz Radziwill in Dangast and Max Beckmann in Frankfurt. Choosing a solitary existence devoid of close contact with other artists, Beckmann followed a path of his own in Frankfurt. The same may be said of Karl Hofer, who, despite living in Berlin, reveals quite different elements in his work than may be seen in the output of the majority of Realist painters working in Berlin. It is nevertheless impossible to overlook an affinity to the subjects and style of Neue Sachlichkeit art in Beckmann and Hofer's output, for which reason they have been and continue to be mentioned in this context. Once again, however, it is important to stress their separate status: no one style can be said to dominate their art.

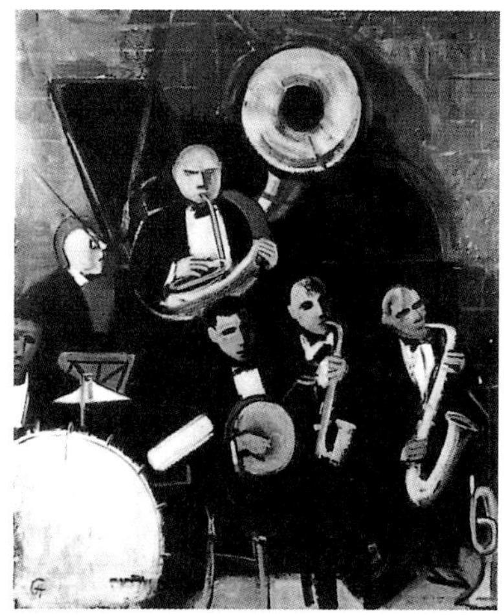

Karl Hofer
Jazz Band, 1926/27
Oil on canvas, 75 x 64 cm
Dortmund, Karl-Hofer-Dokumentation

Max Beckmann

The majority of the pictures included in Hartlaub's pioneering exhibition of 1925 were by Beckmann, who was regarded by the organizer of the exhibition as undisputedly the leading force within Neue Sachlichkeit. However, contemporary press reviews of the exhibition soon observed the extent to which this artist stood outside of the main stream. The distress caused to Beckmann by his experience of war found initial expression in his pictures in splintered forms, chaotic spatial relationships, twisted postures, and the horrified expressions on the faces of the individuals depicted. Yet he was already admitting by 1919: "What I'm trying to achieve is an ever clearer and more definite form."[76]

Beckmann was anticipating certain stylistic characteristics of Neue Sachlichkeit in these years. His views of Frankfurt am Main (illus. pp. 146, 148), for example, give the impression of stage-set landscapes made of papier-mâché. Atmospheric effects are completely absent; houses and trees are simplified, interpreted almost in the manner of naive painting; people seem

Max Beckmann
The Iron Footbridge, 1922
Der eiserne Steg
Oil on canvas, 120.5 x 84.5 cm
Düsseldorf, Kunstsammlung Nordrhein-Westfalen

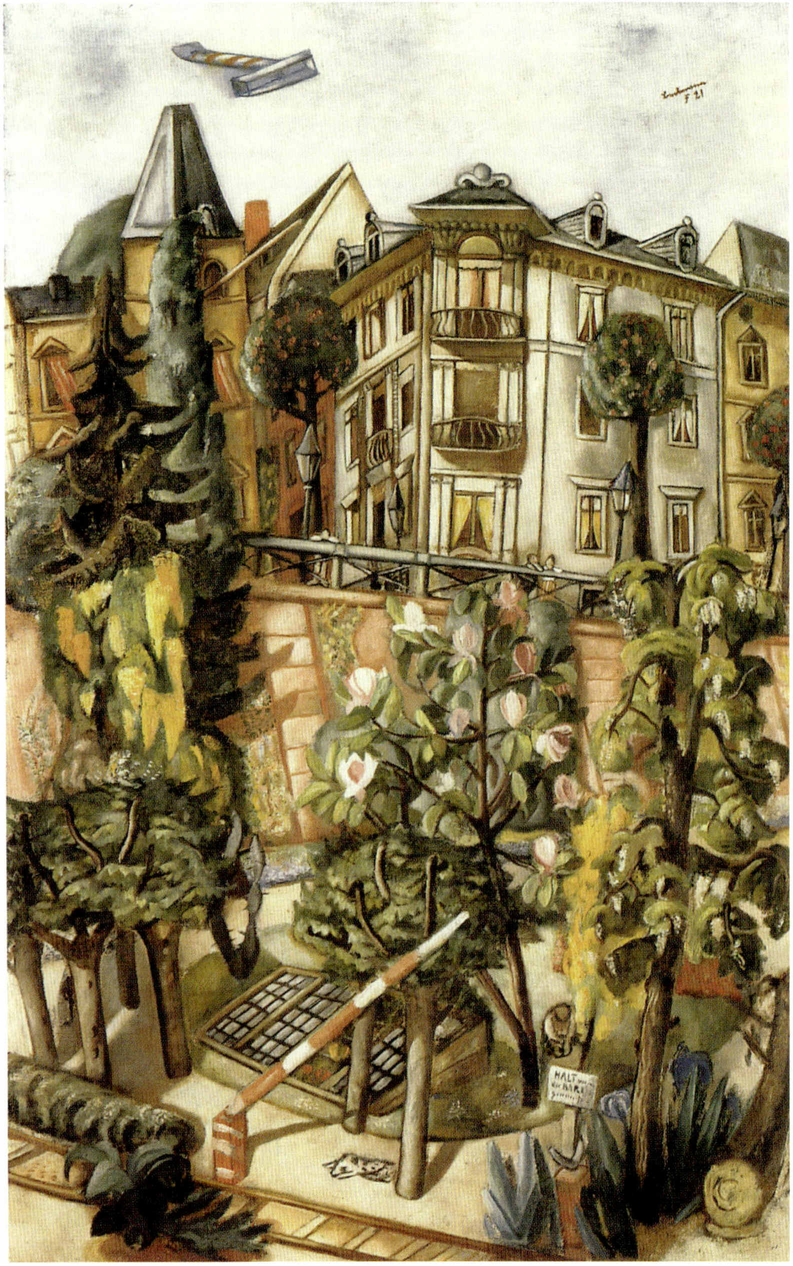

At the beginning of the 1920s, Max Beckmann frequently anticipated subjects and stylistic elements of Neue Sachlichkeit art. However, he demanded in his declaration of 1920 that one should come to "a transcendental objectivity" (Sachlichkeit), "one which can follow from a deeper love of nature and of people". Through its compression and fossilization, the depiction of the park on the banks of the Main, crowned by town houses and called "Nizza" (Nice) in the Frankfurt vernacular, takes on the character of a dream landscape.

Max Beckmann
"Nizza" (Main Riverbank in Frankfurt), 1921
"Nizza" (Mainufer in Frankfurt)
Oil on canvas, 100.5 x 65.5 cm
Basle, Öffentliche Kunstsammlung Basel, Kunstmuseum

to be toy figures, far too small in relation to their surroundings. The pictorial elements follow no superordinate perspective, nor is the observer granted a clear vantage point. Despite the sense of insecurity that the picture conveys, however, it is still possible to detect the attempt to achieve a certain austerity of approach and a searching for firmness; the elements within the picture remain inflexible and stiff, resulting in a stock-taking of reality in great detail.

Beckmann's portrait of his first wife, *Minna Beckmann-Tube* (illus. p. 150), painted in 1924, is regarded as one of the most magnificent portraits to emerge from Neue Sachlichkeit. The figure, adopting a quiet, relaxed pose,

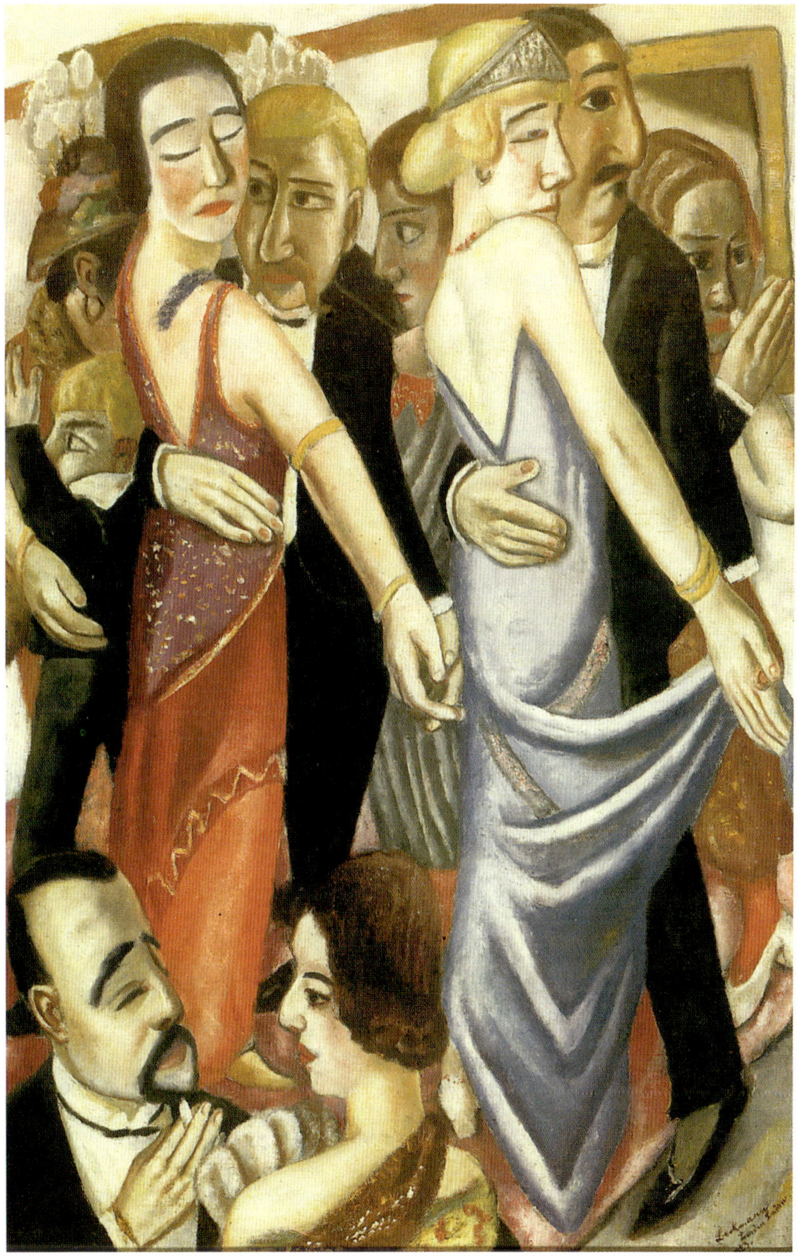

Max Beckmann
Dance in Baden-Baden, 1923
Tanz in Baden-Baden
Oil on canvas, 100.5 x 65.5 cm
Munich, Bayerische Staatsgemälde-sammlungen

is given firmness by the artist's restricting himself to a few large areas of restrained colour. In so doing, Beckmann achieves an enormous plasticity of form, while giving the figure a presence such as can hardly be surpassed, brought about in particular through a glazing technique peculiar to him involving a thick application of paint without varnish.

Beckmann's *Dance in Baden-Baden* (illus. p. 149) is characterized by similar stylistic features. The artist depicts the chic society of the health resort, people indulging in civilized pleasure yet seemingly frozen in the process in their unrelatedness to each other. He has painted here a picture of his times, constituting something of an exception in his œuvre. Beckmann is interested in statements concerning man's fundamental condition, in the timeless regularity of his existence, and not so much in the people themselves of his – or, for that matter, of any particular – time. Unlike such artists as George Grosz, he does not seek to change people; rather, he wishes to demonstrate the constraints and conditions of human existence.

However, there is a particular reason behind his interest in the blasé nouveaux riches. Dressed up as they are, they appear rather ridiculous, the individual couples merely giving rise to pity. Packed together in the smallest possible space, they are dancing on a sloping floor of such a nature as to render it practically impossible for them to remain on their feet. Nevertheless, they are attempting at all costs, in spite of everything, to maintain their dignity and keep their composure. This picture has been seen as depicting a "masked ball without the disguise"[77], and it is indeed the case that these people are playing roles, that they are not themselves. Beckmann was especially fond of lingering in the lobbies of the chic hotels, since it was here that he could observe the social stratum which constantly adopts roles, continually dons masks.

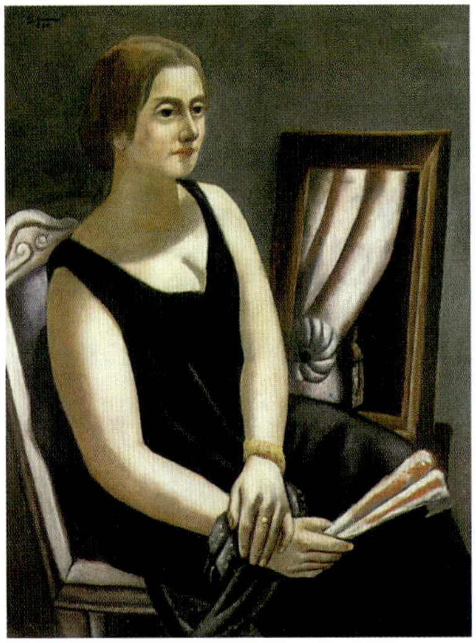

Max Beckmann
Minna Beckmann-Tube, 1924
Oil on canvas, 92.5 x 73 cm
Munich, Bayerische Staatsgemälde-sammlungen

The masquerade was a central subject for Max Beckmann from the 1920s on. He often depicted scenes from the context of the carnival season or commedia dell'arte that express the artificiality of earthly existence. In the artist's world view, people are attached to threads held by unknown powers; marionette-like, they are fated to play their roles for the amusement of those in power. All the world's a stage, the entire world a theatre. Yet this masking can also indicate the freedom of the Fool to do as he wishes. Beckmann portrays himself in his 1921 *Self-Portrait as Clown* (illus. p. 151) as a Fool who not only knows more but is also willing to communicate what he knows. For Beckmann, the artist possesses a special understanding of the human situation. From the security offered by his mask, he can undertake the demasking process and see the reality clearly.

The excerpts of reality portrayed in Neue Sachlichkeit, each of them concerned to achieve constructive validity, contradicted Beckmann's conception of the artistic world theatre, one which he sought to realize in ever-new disguises and ever-new symbols. For Beckmann, the subordinate objects in the picture always exist as aids to explaining the meaning behind the picture; for Neue Sachlichkeit, they explain the reality of the picture itself – a significant difference. Despite this, the model represented by Beckmann's painting would play an important role, especially in the crisis that was to beset Neue Sachlichkeit around 1930.

Karl Hofer

A view detached from time and directed at fundamental issues was also of central importance for Hofer; he, too, was seeking primarily a timeless validity for his view of mankind. The artist lived in the 1920s in the middle of the seething metropolis that was Berlin, yet created works that seemingly portray another world to that recorded by artists such as Dix, Grosz, Schad and Schlichter from the life of this city. Hofer's subject is man, in a sense that is more philosophical than sociological or psychological. Portraits are accordingly rare, while even his self-portraits do not necessarily depict a particular person. The facial expression of the individuals portrayed is usually stereotyped, preserving their anonymity and frequently even turning them into masks. In addition, they often radiate a melancholy mood, making them appear curiously serious.

Max Beckmann
Self-Portrait as Clown, 1921
Selbstbildnis als Clown
Oil on canvas, 100 x 59 cm
Wuppertal, Von der Heydt-Museum

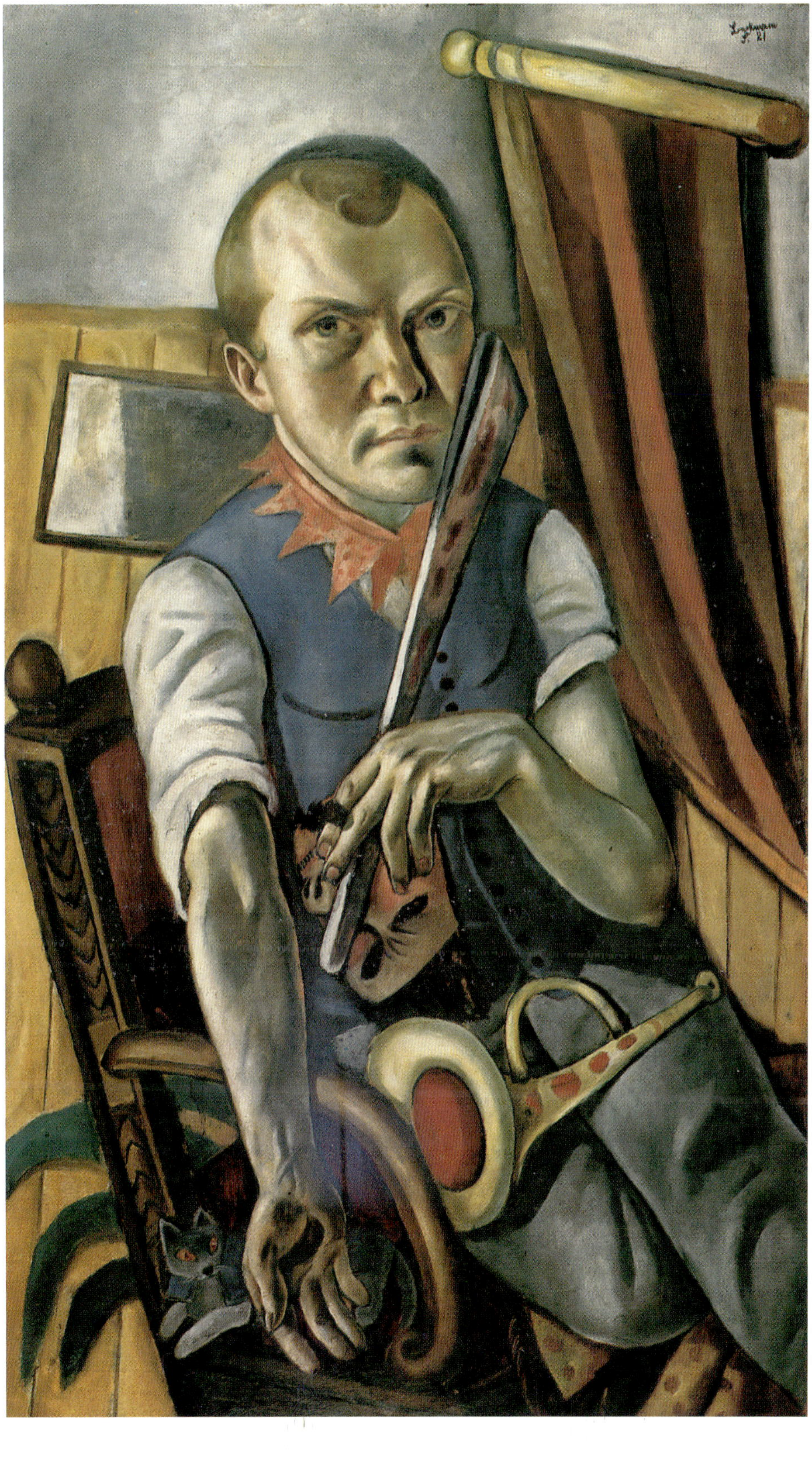

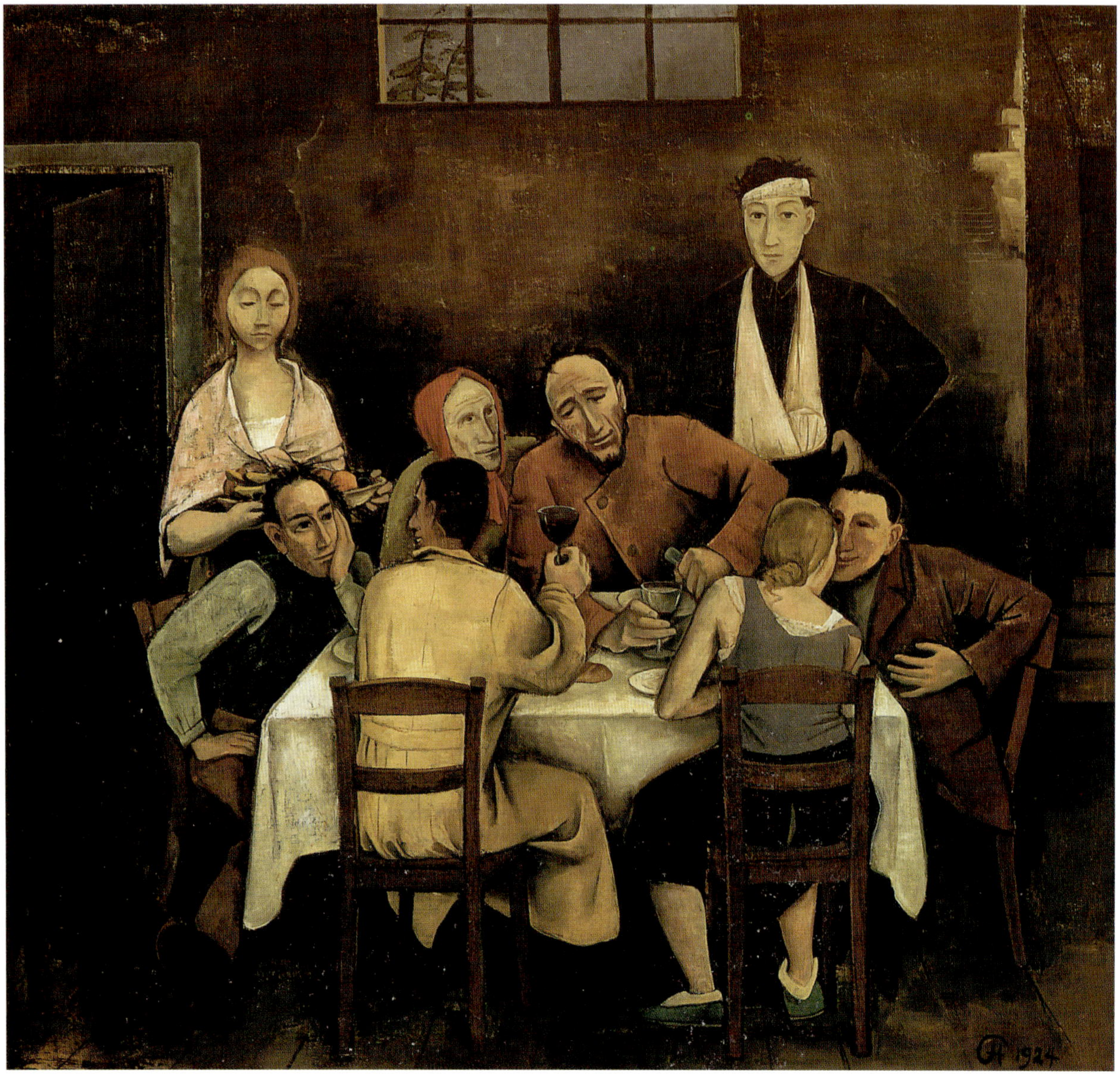

Karl Hofer
Dinner Party, 1924
Tischgesellschaft
Oil on canvas, 180 x 192 cm
Winterthur, Kunstmuseum, presented in 1951 by the heirs of Dr. Theodor Reinhart

A puzzling significance is suggested by the strange atmosphere of the *Dinner Party* (illus. p. 152). The oddly serious, pensive mood indicates that what we are confronted with here is not simply the prosaic depiction of a meal. Rather, the people would appear to have congregated in order to discuss serious matters. The situation is given a particularly insistent and admonishing quality by the visual contact that the injured man establishes with the observer. In this way, Hofer gives his pictures a certain underlying symbolism: indeed, they may be seen as metaphors. He distanced himself correspondingly from Neue Sachlichkeit, which he regarded as a style of art "too close to mere reproduction".[78]

Similarly, the special atmosphere of his *Woman with Flower* makes it evident that this is no mere depiction of a genre scene, but that something more significant is in fact taking place. The young woman, her eyes closed, is holding the flower in a very solemn, reverential manner. This flower clearly takes on symbolic meaning, apparently an allegory for the woman – yet ultimately it remains enigmatic, especially since it cannot be definitively identified. Even when Hofer turns his attention to such topical subjects as a *Jazz Band* (illus. p. 147), the scene seems at a curious remove. Where Dix reproduces the jazz band in his *Metropolis Triptych* with heightened realism, Hofer distances himself from reality, using simplified forms and abstracted faces. All lively animation is thus removed from the setting, which seems almost frozen.

From 1925 on, Hofer spent his summers in the Ticino (illus. p. 153). The Italian landscape enabled him to transpose into his own work the clear principles of composition adopted by Cézanne, whom he admired. His views reveal a similar "constructed" quality to that encountered in Kanoldt's Olevano landscapes. However, the latter appear dead, unable to incorporate people, whereas Hofer emphasizes the natural harmony and peacefulness of the landscape in his pictures, giving it – as with his depictions of people – a solemn touch.

Franz Radziwill

In contrast to Hofer's pictures, with their celebration of harmonious peacefulness, the landscapes of Franz Radziwill offer rather gloomier visions. From 1922 onwards, Radziwill lived a secluded existence in the small coastal town of Dangast, far away from the centres of art. The attention of the young autodidact had been drawn to the village on the Jadebusen by Karl Schmidt-Rottluff, who had found Dargast, a valued place of refuge both for himself and the other painters of "Die Brücke" around 1910.

Franz Radziwill dedicated himself entirely to the landscape of northern Germany. The sea, the coast and the countryside around Oldenburg became an inexhaustible source of inspiration for his mysterious landscapes. Like many other Neue Sachlichkeit painters, Radziwill renders his subjects in a

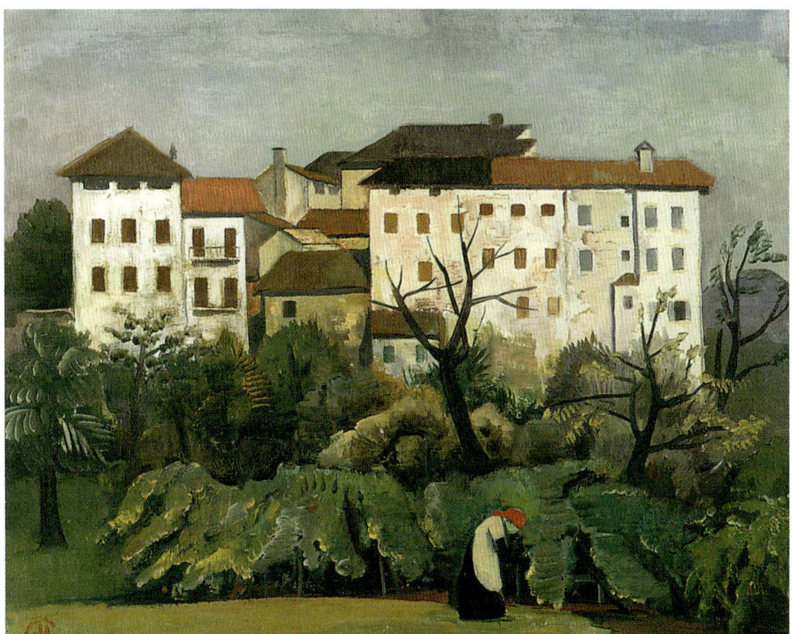

Hofer processed the impressions of his first trip to Italy, in 1925, in a series of Ticino landscapes. He considered this "... a simple reproduction of what I have experienced in this region, consciously without any artistic ambition or any kind of exaggeration, and consequently hideously un-modern." Hofer occupied himself in these pictures with Cézanne's principles of composition and adopted something of the latter's palette.

Karl Hofer
Houses near Montagnola, 1926
Häuser bei Montagnola
Oil on canvas, 65.3 x 81 cm
Hanover, Sprengel Museum

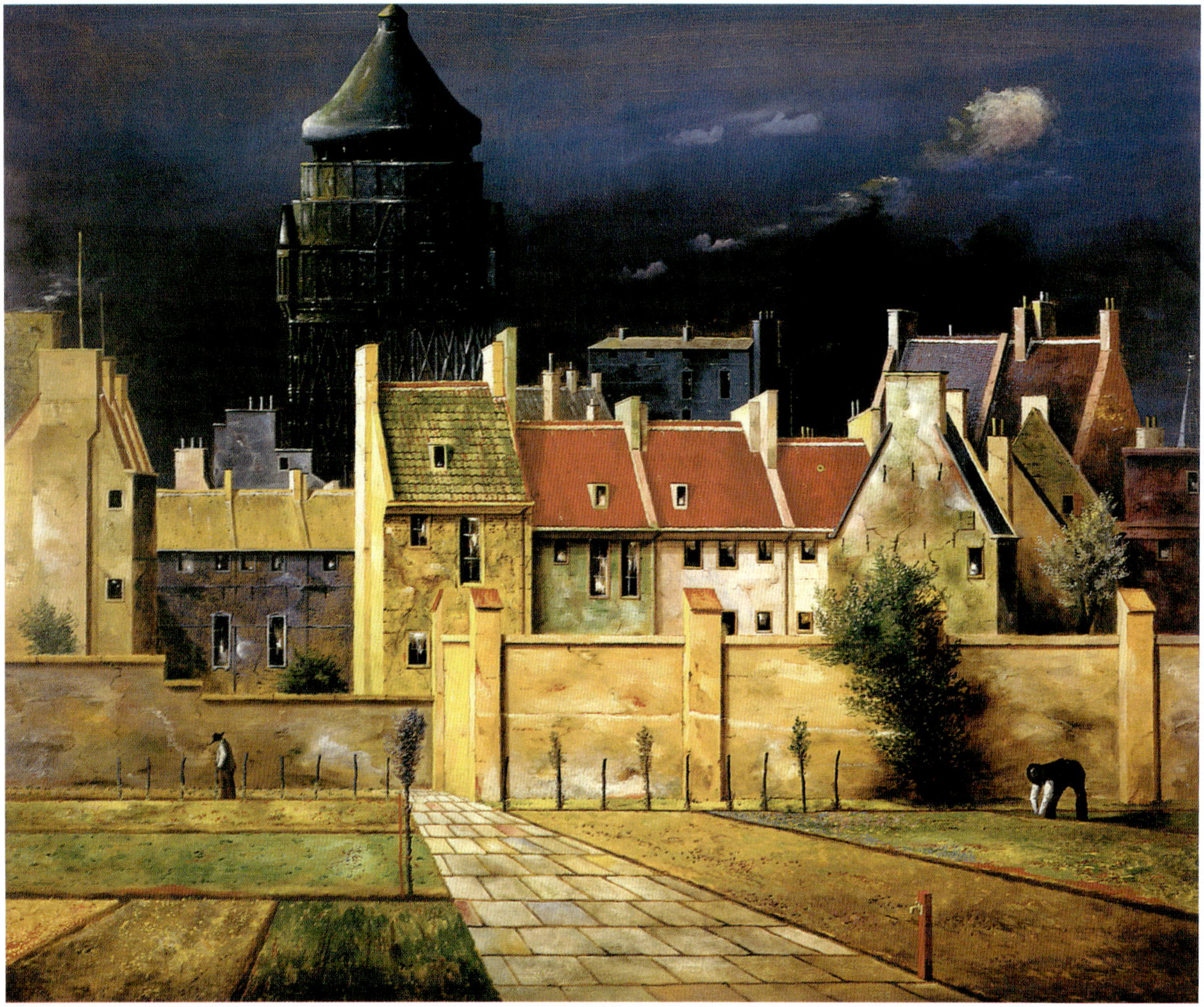

Franz Radziwill
Water Tower in Bremen, 1931
Der Wasserturm in Bremen
Oil on wood, 99.5 x 80 cm
Private collection

distanced manner. Using an Old-Master glaze coupled with precise drawing, he concentrates upon a meticulous depiction of the world, engrossed in every detail. However, he places this cold stock-taking in an atmospheric landscape loaded with meaning, an unusual combination distinguishing his landscapes and rendering them unmistakable. The civilized world is dazzlingly – almost supernaturally – illuminated, set against a dark sky announcing imminent disaster. By means of this magic effect, the city and landscape motifs that Radziwill is depicting, of themselves familiar, are rendered strangely alien and sinister.

Such an effect is achieved in his *Water Tower in Bremen* (illus. p. 154). The sense of estrangement is heightened by the composition: the city rises like a barrier in front of the observer, preventing him from passing yet also refusing him entry, closing itself off like a fortified settlement. No people seem to live in it; it appears deserted, a ghost city. The entire scenery in Radziwill's pictures, like the houses in this city, often appears merely a backdrop, a drama stage between thin papier-mâché walls. The people who have strayed into these landscapes are lost in the eerie vacuum, which is created not least by the enormous force of suction which so many of Radziwill's landscapes exert.

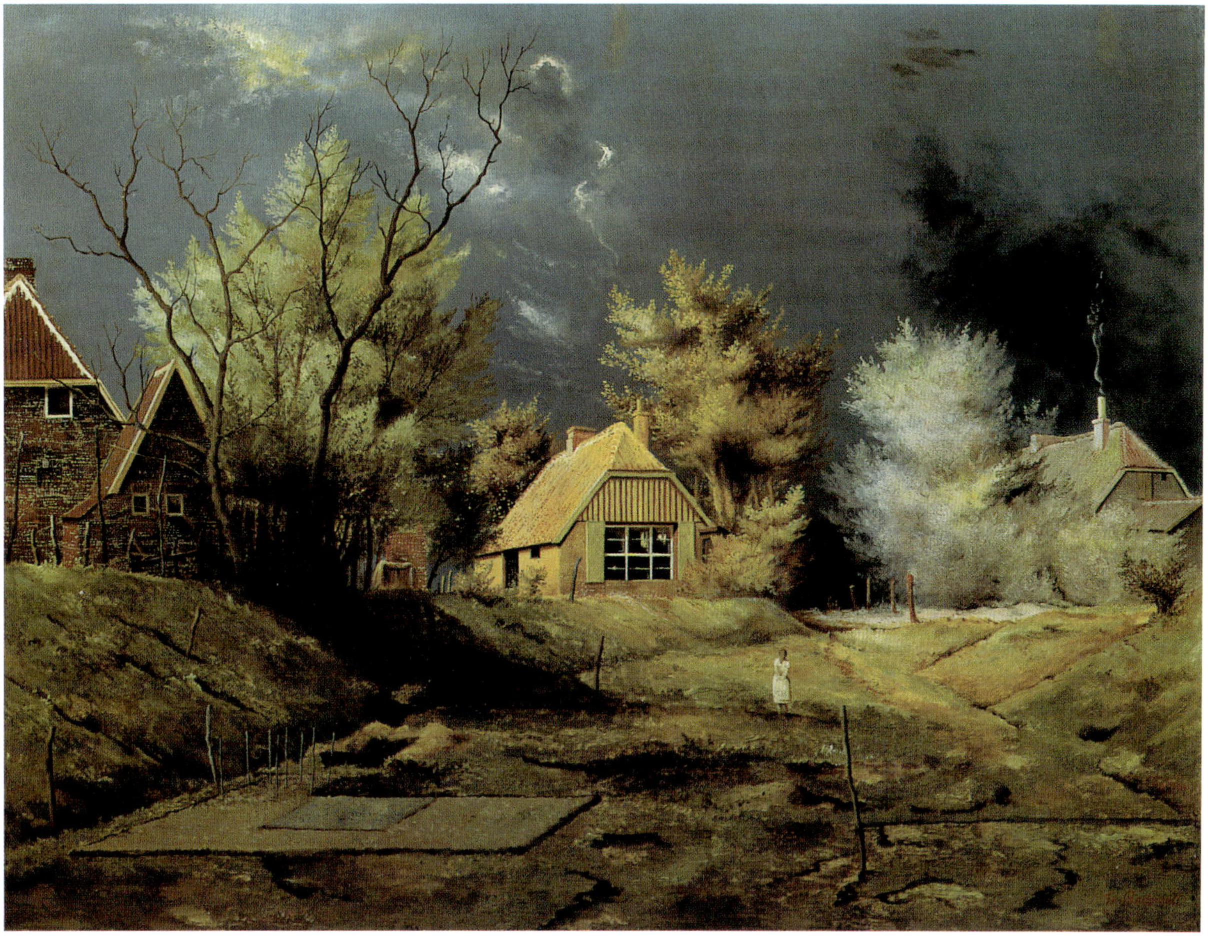

Franz Radziwill
Landscape with the Artist's House, 1930
Landschaft mit dem Haus des Künstlers
Oil on canvas on wood, 75 x 99 cm
Private collection

Yet it is not only the stormy atmosphere and strange emptiness in his pictures which threaten the observer. Radziwill also often includes elements referring directly to death, such as cemetery walls, crosses, and gallow-like beams, together with such motifs of transience as dead trees. Thus, in *Landscape with the Artist's House* (illus. p. 155), for example, instead of the homely village idyll we might expect, we see but one solitary individual, abandoned by God and the world, in the midst of emptiness. Despite the surrounding houses and the smoking chimney, there would appear to be no other people anywhere.

Radziwill was to take this situation of an idyll overtaken by catastrophe as his subject again and again in his work.[79] It becomes especially clear in a picture tellingly entitled *Demons* (illus. p. 199). We see the front door and window of a small, neat, brick house, in which a laundry may be found. The little house has obviously seen happy days – a sign above the door wishes blessings upon a bridal couple, and a flower blooms in the window. Yet these are only the remnants of the idyll: the house has meanwhile been overtaken by catastrophe. A mysterious maxim on the wall of the house makes this clear: "In the light of the state's ideas, or, each will kill the other." This picture clearly expresses the philosophy that Radziwill carried around with him. Here – in the year 1933 – it is obviously referring to political circumstances; in general, however, the artist adopts a subtler approach when introducing sinister and threatening elements.

One theme which Radziwill took up again and again in his pictures was that of technical achievements in the modern world. Harbour scenes and ships may often be found in his paintings. Above all, however, he populated his skies with aircraft, often looking like large insects. He had grown up in the immediate vicinity of the Bremen-Neuland airport, and these dream

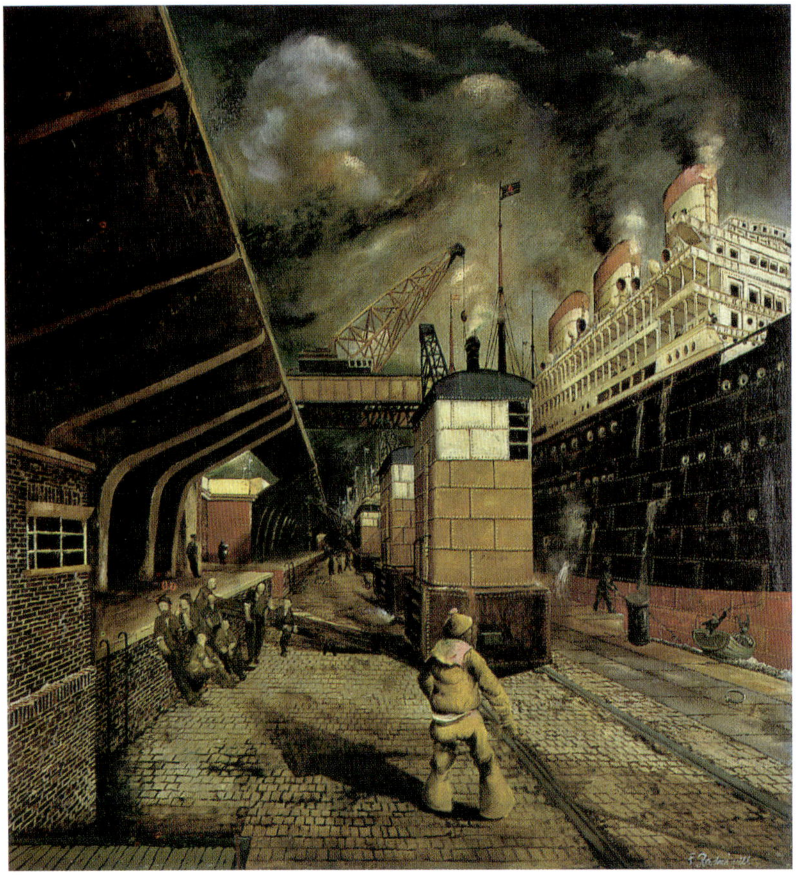

Franz Radziwill
Harbour with the "Cap Populonia" and a Sailor in Yellow, 1921
Hafen mit der Cap Populonia und gelbem Matrosen
Oil on canvas, 85 x 80 cm
Private collection

machines of mankind became a passion of his. In his well-known *Karl Buchstätter's Fatal Dive* (illus. p. 157) of 1928, the scene is dominated by electricity pylons and level-crossing barriers. The houses are spotlit as if in the depths of night, while the sea – a lane seemingly sucked out to it – shimmers magically on the horizon. The two barriers point like the barrels of a gun at the aircraft in the sky, which is already spinning into a dive. The pilot Karl Buchstätter was killed in 1911 during a test-flight; the event was witnessed by the 16-year-old Radziwill and was clearly to prove one of the key experiences of his life. The artist is also referring in his picture to the legend of Icarus, the embodiment of human hubris, who paid for his presumptuousness with his life. Radziwill's cold, sober depiction of the technical elements reflects his ambivalent relationship towards a technology that threatens to escape from man's control.

Franz Radziwill's magic realism combines a sharply observed reality with visionary lighting effects. The buildings in their glowing colours, set against eerily dark skies in his demonizing depictions of technology and cities, radiate a threatening atmosphere.

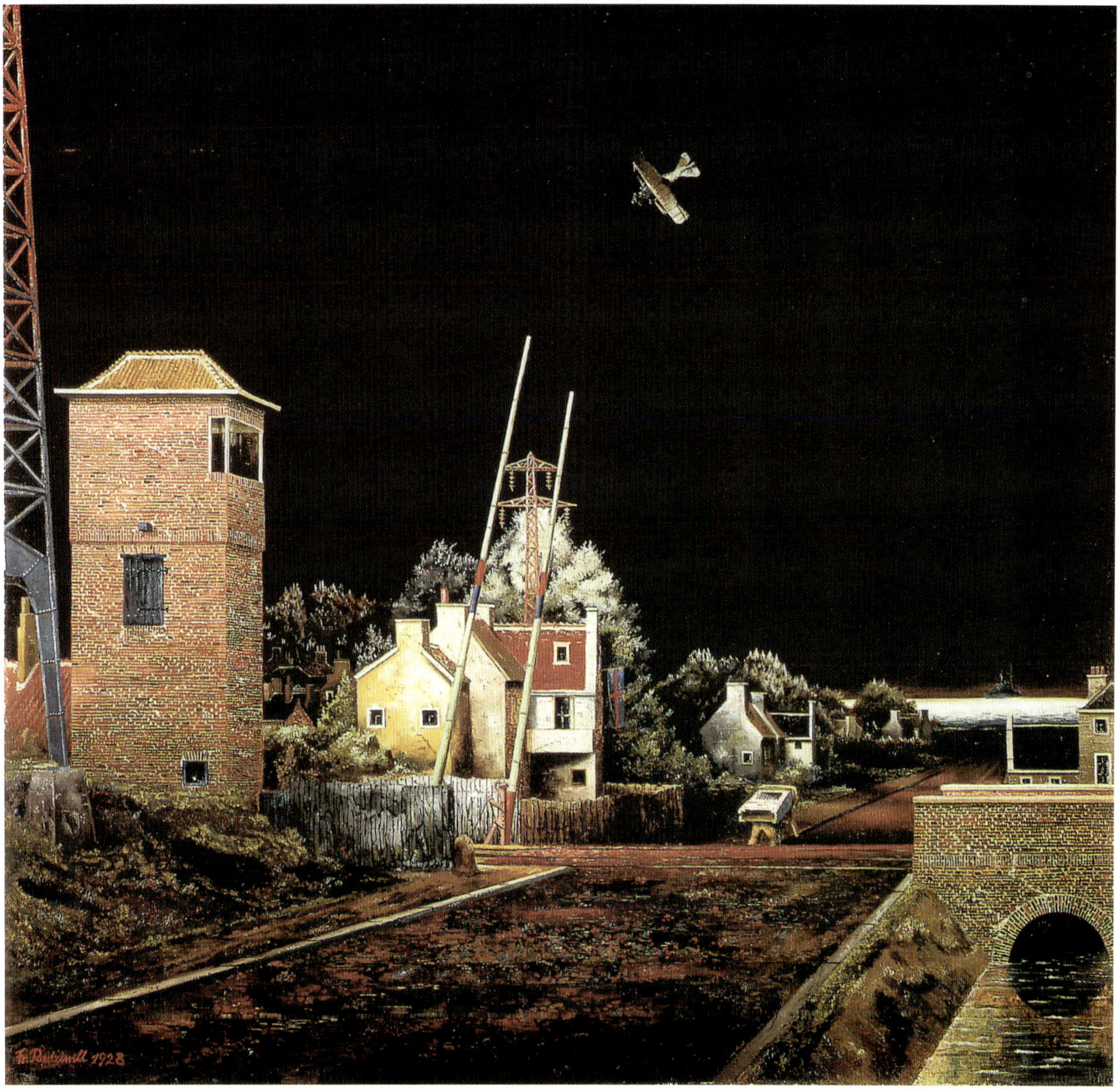

However much Franz Radziwill achieved an unreal atmosphere in his settings, inexplicable, alien, estranged from reality, one is still struck by his unconditional orientation towards a reality the precise observation of which he emphasized through a wealth of detail, his glaze technique, and precise drawing. "Reality represents the greatest miracle imaginable. I had to capture this realization, which I felt rather than knew, in pictures."[80] Radziwill is thus no Surrealist, despite his strange, fantastic-seeming landscapes. He charges what is visible with a magic in which familiar reality appears sinister and disconcerting; as in the case of Räderscheidt, Radziwill may most appropriately be described as a "Magic Realist". There is no security for humankind to be found in Radziwill's world; like the organ-grinder in the centre of Karl Buchstätter's death scene, he goes on his way.

Franz Radziwill
Karl Buchstätter's Fatal Dive, 1928
Todessturz Karl Buchstätters
Oil on hardboard, 90 x 95 cm
Essen, Museum Folkwang

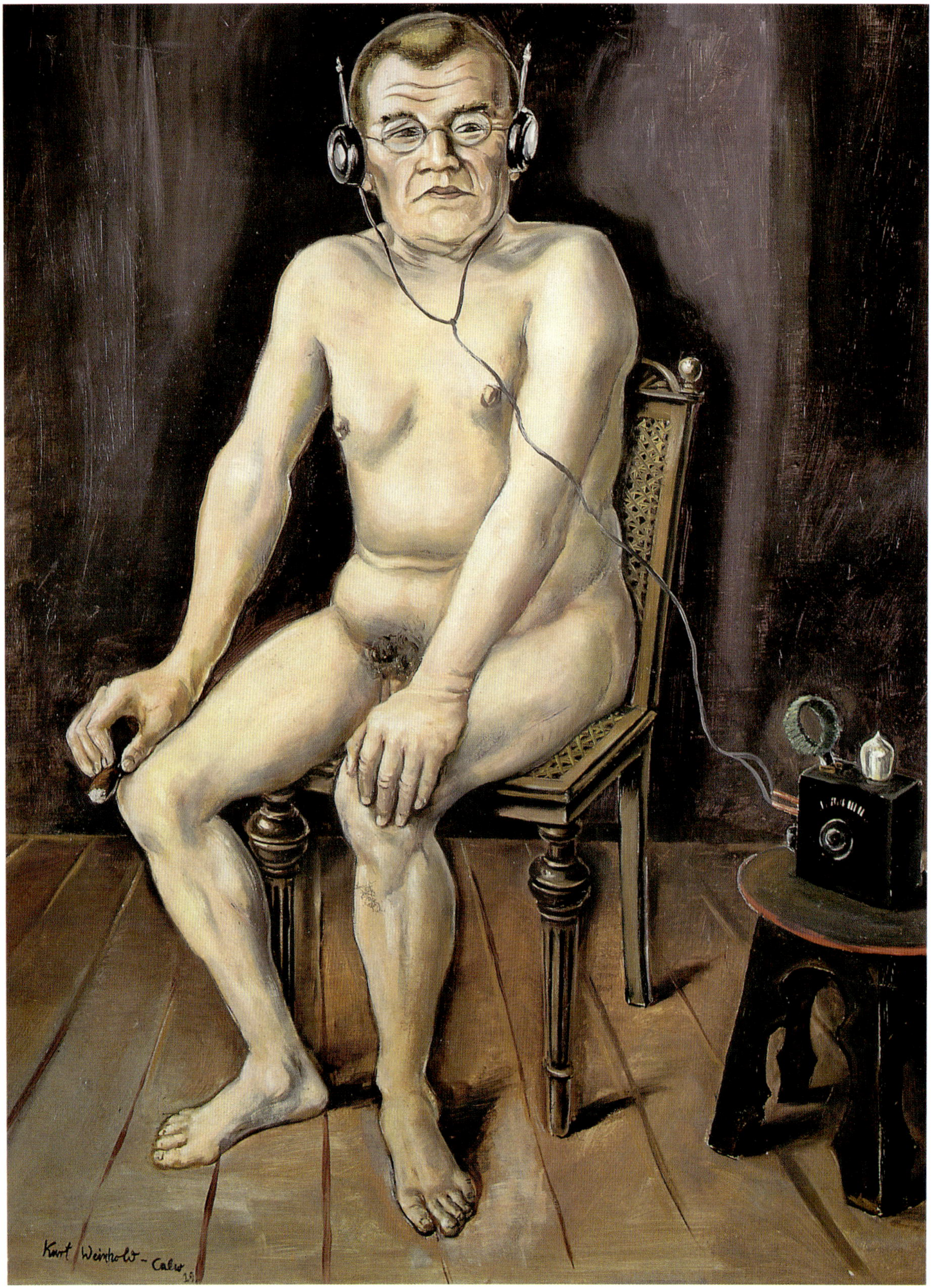
Kurt Weinhold – Calw

Neue Sachlichkeit Iconography

An Isolating View of Things

Neue Sachlichkeit painting displays a distinct preference for certain groups of subjects and motifs; it has an iconography of its own. It may be assumed that the motifs selected accorded in a particular way with its understanding of life and its philosophy. However, the frequency with which certain motifs were given relatively similar form by different artists points to the predominance of aesthetic concerns over aspects relating purely to content. Neither the Neue Sachlichkeit artists nor the Verists were after a topical relevance in the sense of reportage. Nonetheless, Neue Sachlichkeit, insofar as it was seeking – and indeed found – symbols that condensed entire complexes of subjects, was to become an important contemporary witness to the events and attitudes of the times. *Hartmannsweilerkopf*, by the Swiss Neue Sachlichkeit painter Niklaus Stöcklin, and Davringhausen's *The Black-Marketeer* (illus. p. 81) bear witness to the consequences of war and inflation in a manner that is no less succinct than the Verist Berlin street scenes by such as George Grosz or Otto Dix; the absence of subjectivity in the representational treatment of these processes of worldwide impact, their far-reaching anonymity, is frighteningly evident.

Neue Sachlichkeit counters the Expressionist exuberance of unlimited possibilities with an insight into the constraints imposed by reality. Man's environment is depicted shorn of illusion. Attics, garrets and skylights function as direct – but also metaphorical – references to the constricted nature of human life. Courtyards bear silent witness to a marginal existence. While the desire to extend one's horizons in life, to break out, might emerge, the Neue Sachlichkeit artists nevertheless all remained realists. Georg Schrimpf's garret pictures and Ottohans Beier's *View* (illus. p. 160) – in all other respects a mediocre work – are excellent examples of this melancholic subjugation to constraints, a demonstration of the culture of self-moderation in all things, of a happiness that, however small, can still be grasped.

The relationship between figure and space is of pre-eminent importance for a psychological evaluation of these pictures. In spite of the oft-invoked classicism, the figures in Neue Sachlichkeit pictures never shape the space in which they find themselves. Instead, the space reveals their inner and outer dimensions; it determines the relationship between man and his environment. This occasionally results in claustrophobic spatial conditions, comparable to the sense of restricted space commonly found in 1920s literature. Even in situations in which man initially appears free from constriction, he is separated from reality by a glass dome that is no less

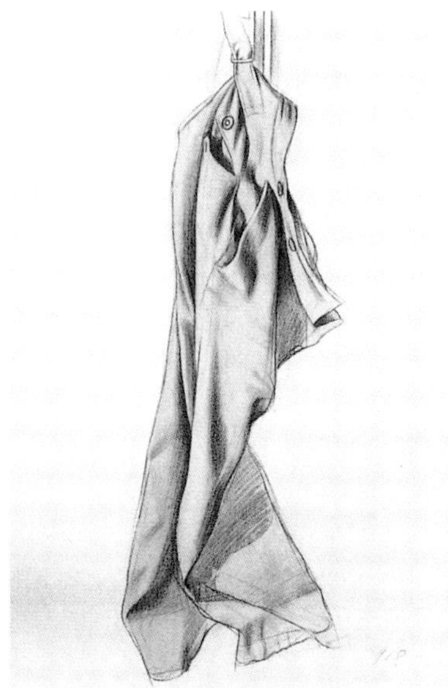

Rudolf Dischinger
Trousers, 1928
Die Hose
Pencil (coloured in), 51 x 35 cm
Löffingen, Inge Sigwarth

Kurt Weinhold
Man with Radio (Homo sapiens), 1929
Mann mit Radio (Homo sapiens)
Oil on canvas, 121 x 90 cm
Grafenau, Galerie Schlichtenmaier

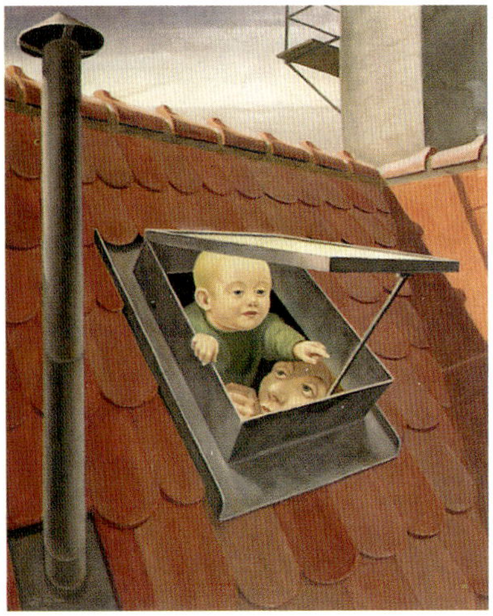

restrictive, for all that it is transparent. This visual metaphor from Erich Kästner's "Fabian" – the archetypal Neue Sachlichkeit novel – may be understood as a characterization of the particular mood to be encountered in many Neue Sachlichkeit pictures. It is the abstention from any atmospheric element, together with the constant clarity in the depiction of the objects – despite considerable distances of depth – that give rise to the particular feeling of simultaneous vacuum and distance between the world seen in the picture and the observer.

Alfred Neumeyer, the art historian, recognized in as early as 1928 that the sense of space, and its depiction, in Neue Sachlichkeit art have little in common with centralized perspective. [81] Nevertheless, the unreflected thesis of a post-Expressionist "return to perspective order" still persists in the literature. In fact, however, a construction made up of various perspectives underlies Neue Sachlichkeit pictures. They often show two spatial layers unconnected to each other by any gradation and merging seamlessly with each other. This is a process which could have been influenced by the pictures of Rousseau, the customs officer (references to Rousseau have already been indicated a number of times elsewhere in this work). Only in a very few cases are we concerned with a box space of the conventional

TOP:
Ottohans Beier
View
Der Ausblick
Oil on canvas, 74 x 60 cm
Munich, Städtische Galerie im Lenbachhaus

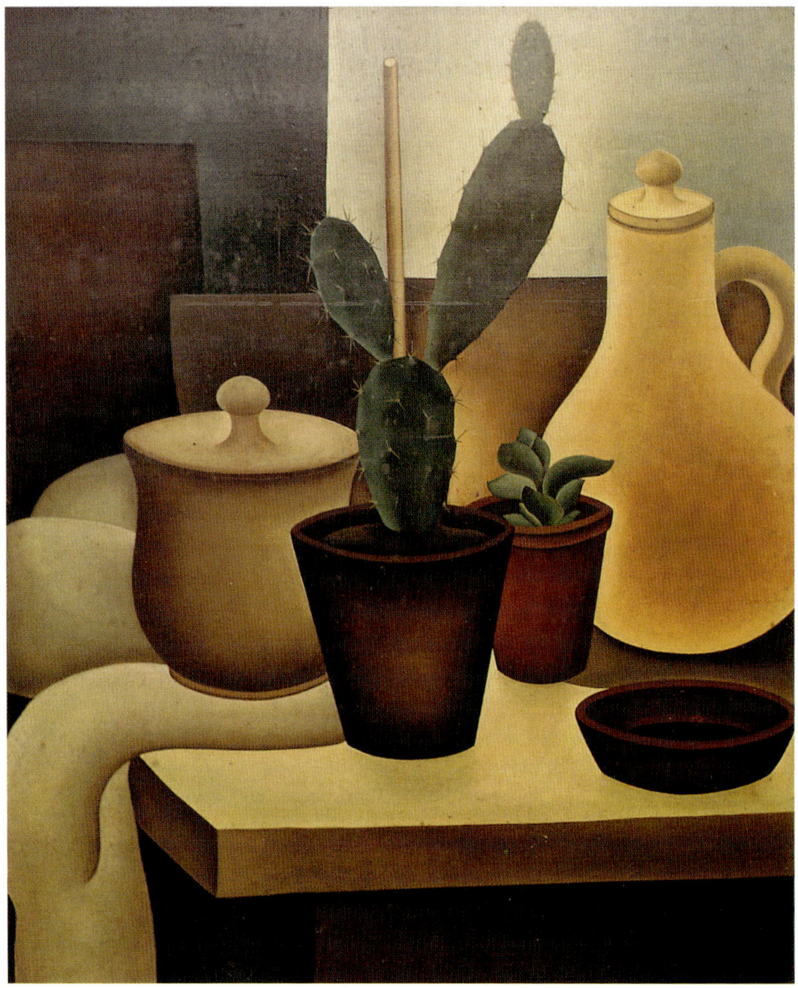

BOTTOM:
Eberhard Viegener
Cactus and Yellow Jug, 1927
Kaktee und gelber Krug
Oil on wood, 58 x 48 cm
Dortmund, Museum am Ostwall

Georg Schrimpf
Girl at the Window, 1925
Mädchen am Fenster
Oil on canvas, 77.5 x 48.5 cm
Basle, Öffentliche Kunstsammlung
Basel, Kunstmuseum

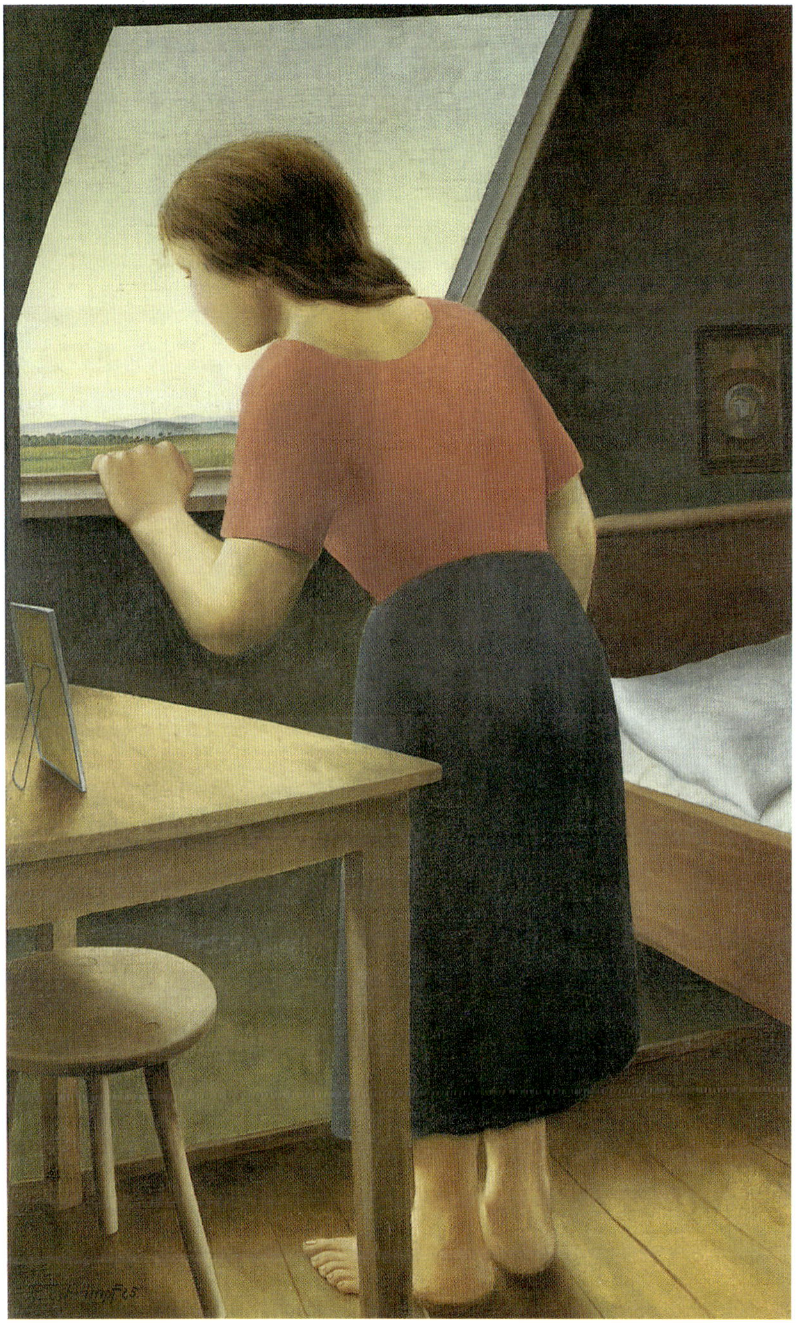

Attics and garrets were among the favourite motifs of Neue Sachlichkeit, not merely as spaces containing discarded or banished items to which the painter devote his attention. Ever since the Biedermeier period (c. 1815–1848) and the art of Carl Spitzweg, the attic room had also functioned as a subject by means of which an artist could establish his professional allegiance, an image of his attic existence and his failure on the fringes of society.

type; the majority of pictures reveal side views from a sharp angle of sight, or a diagonal perspective of the inner space. Converging and/or diverging vanishing lines form the sharp boundaries of the field of the picture. All in all, this occasionally calls to mind the tentative, intuitive perspective constructions of northern European painting in the first half of the 15th century, as seen in the Master of Flémalle and Konrad Witz, with whose works many of the Neue Sachlichkeit artists may have been acquainted.

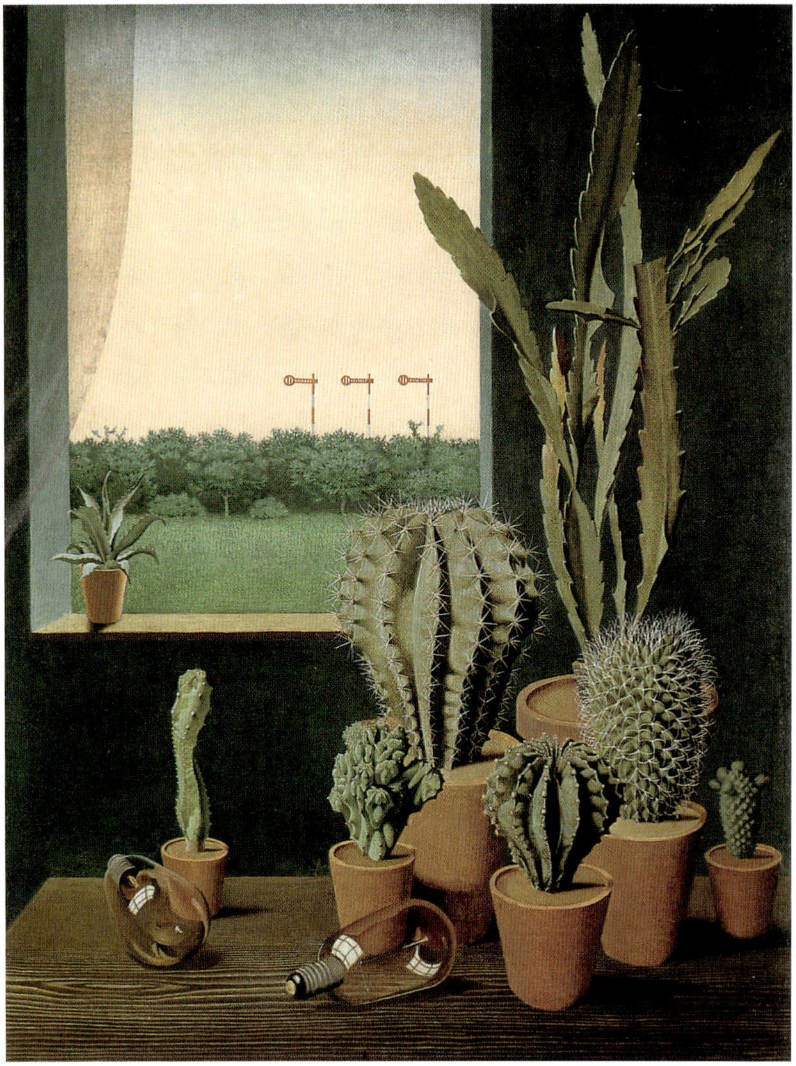

Georg Scholz
Cacti and Semaphore, 1923
Kakteen und Semaphore
Oil on hardboard, 69 x 52,3 cm
Münster, Westfälisches Landesmuseum für Kunst und Kulturgeschichte

Still Lifes

Still lifes often convey the illusion of a purely accidental arrangement of portrayed objects; however, this is not the case in Neue Sachlichkeit painting. The artists' efforts to achieve a constructive, ordering pictorial composition were especially evident here. The isolating austerity of the view was to become the analogon of its compositional principles, as if it were a matter of exploring the particular ambiguity of the concept of "objectivity" – precisely an unemotional, objective recording of items – in the pictorial form of the still life. An overdefined presentation of frozen life, concentrated upon the objects, emerges from the Neue Sachlichkeit still-lifes. The sense of harmony is achieved through a levelling assimilation within an often undefined vacuum. Nonetheless, the artificial and forced nature of the whole cannot be overlooked, nor can the inorganic dissonance in the nature and effect of some of the plants. Hence the predilection for rubber plants and cacti, which now stage a triumphal entry into the world of art.

Franz Lenk
Cellar Still Life, 1929
Kellerstilleben
Oil and egg tempera on canvas, 106 x 76 cm
Private collection

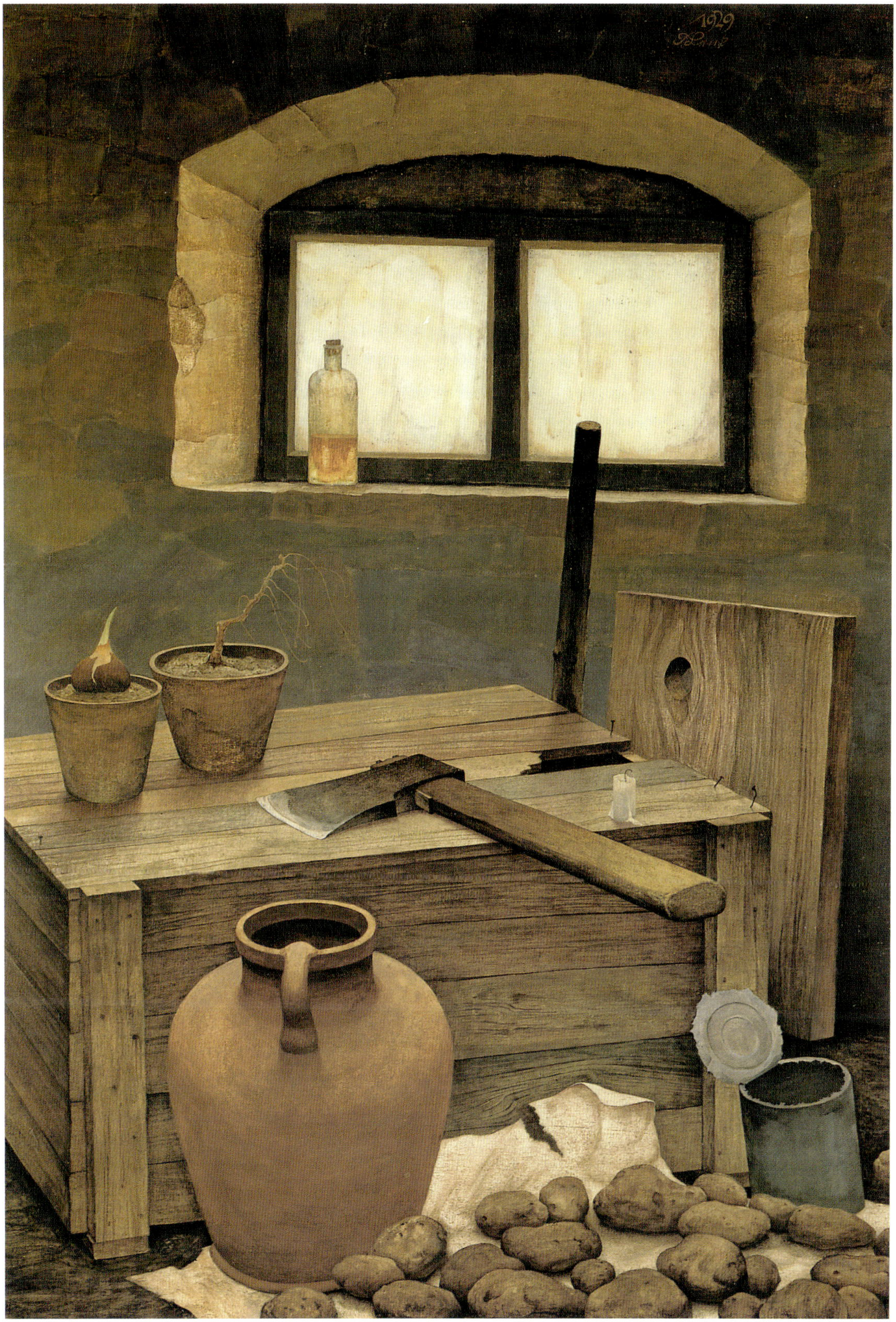
1929

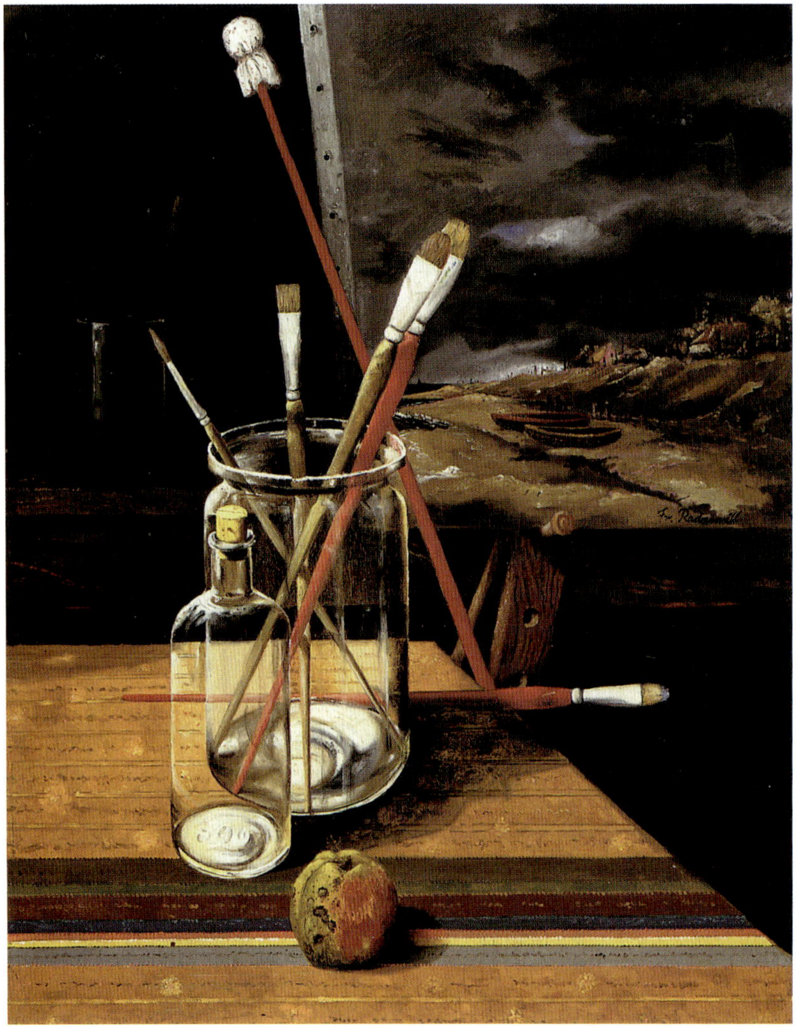

Franz Radziwill
Still Life, 1929
Stilleben
Oil on plywood, 56 x 43 cm
Regensburg, Museum Ostdeutsche Galerie

The cactus in particular becomes Neue Sachlichkeit's pictorial motif par excellence. The model here was Giorgio Morandi's *Il Cactus* from 1917. He received no emulation in Italy; in Germany, on the other hand, a curious succession of motifs would follow, beginning in 1920. The cactus became a metaphor for the human condition in Scholz' *Mestizos*, a work which is regrettably lost. Cacti, lined up in a threatening manner, surround the lonely, homeless half-caste. The prickly plants, the desolate blocks of flats, and the gas container combine within the depiction to present an exaggerated form of dissonant life. The picture gives rise to an inhospitable, rejective quality, the daily experience of this human being accepted by no one. Yves Tanguy, the Surrealist, was later to take up similar possibilities of expression with regard to cacti, but the metonymic poetry of Surrealism had little time for Neue Sachlichkeit's prosaic gatherings of symbolic objects.

The cactus appears in the first half of the 1920s in many still lifes by Kanoldt, Schrimpf, Scholz and Fritz Burmann. Alfred Wortmann, the art critic, speculated in 1925 with regard to this motif's significance as follows: "Are cacti not vegetable crystals, living architecture? Sphere and cylinder, dimension and number? May our newly awakened love for abstract, ge-

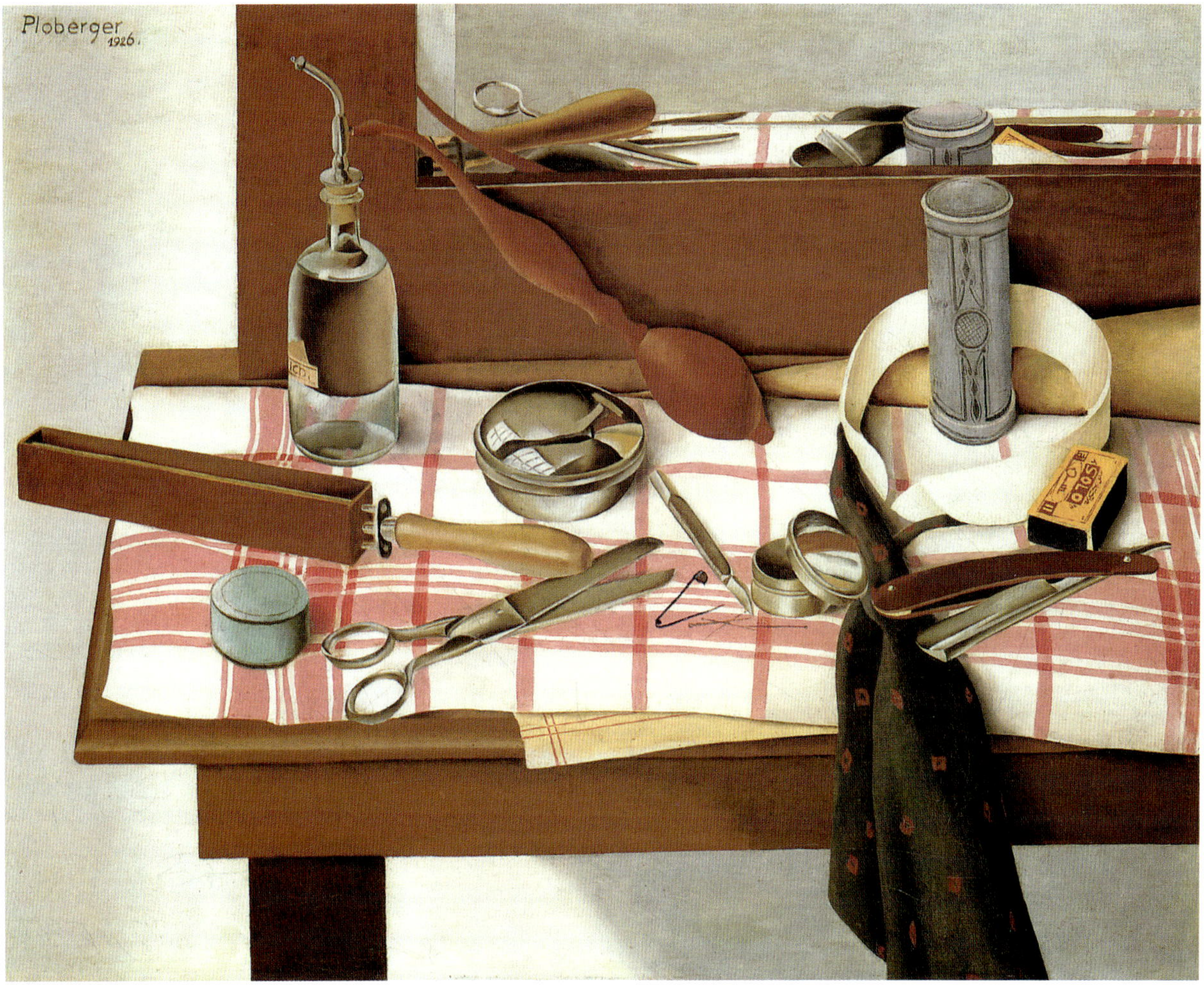

Herbert Ploberger
Dressing Table, 1926
Toilettentisch
Oil on canvas, 45 x 70 cm
Private collection

ometric plants not be compared with our efforts to shape space from the timeless forms of limitedness, sphere and cube?"[82] This is a remarkably lucid analysis, despite the echoes of Expressionist rhetoric: Wortmann sees the cactus as a symbol of the crystalline and geometric, but also of the inorganic. The crystalline element is decoratively exaggerated in Lenk's *Flowering Cactus* (illus. p. 50); in Burmann's case (illus. p. 192), the uneven surface structure of the paper lampshade is compared with the cactus. Scholz went even further in his *Cacti and Semaphore* (illus. p. 162), playing off the perception of glassy coldness against something inorganic in a virtuoso manner. It is perhaps herein that the Neue Sachlichkeit quintessence of the artificial element in plant still lifes is to be found.

Neue Sachlichkeit regarded numerous prosaic objects as worthy of inclusion in a still life: angular bottles and containers, instruments, even surgical appliances. Many of these arrangements are not without appeal. The emphatically ugly is avoided, yet the selection of objects itself creates a curious split in the way in which one perceives such a picture. The works depict useful objects, objects of such a nature, however – like the axe or the scalpel – that they neither can nor wish to deny their not always

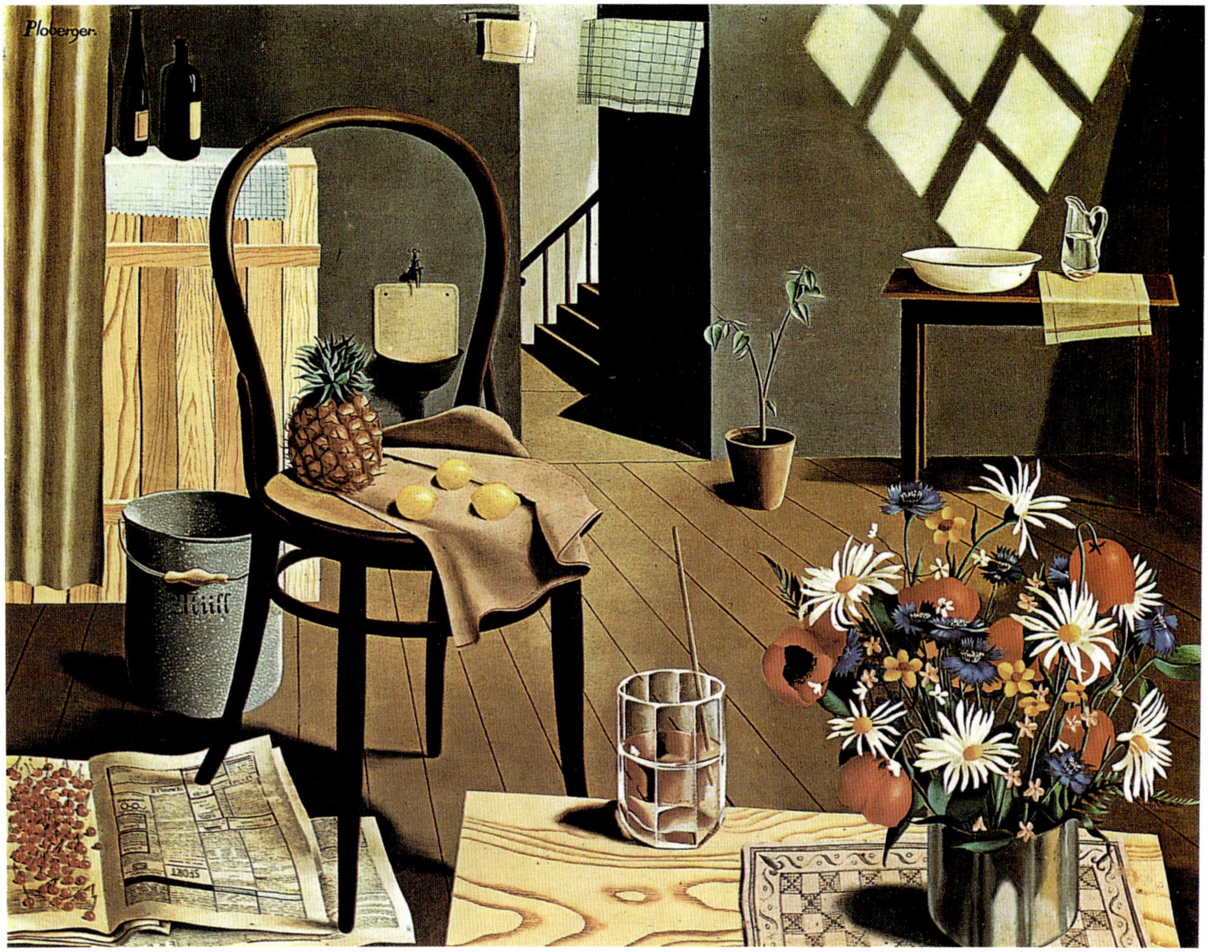

Herbert Ploberger
Still Life, 1926
Stilleben
Oil on canvas, 56 x 52 cm
Vienna, Österreichische Galerie

harmonious associations. At any rate, Neue Sachlichkeit is a long way away from the associative agreeableness of French post-Cubist still lifes, with their endlessly varied pieces of fruit, picturesque cans, or guitars. Only Eberhard Viegener from Soest appears to mediate between these two worlds, even the cactus acquiring a purely decorative touch in his work (illus. p. 160).

Technology and the city

With Neue Sachlichkeit, the world of technology finds its way into photography, and also – to a lesser extent – into painting. The new technological civilization, the contours of which gradually became apparent after the First World War, was accepted without illusion by the Neue Sachlichkeit artists, without their being overtaken by a passion for all things technological. They recognized the presence of two disparate elements in the world of machines, the one constructive, bringing order, the other demonic, unpredictable. In correlating humankind with the functional procedures and requirements of machines, and analytically surveying and isolating a particular aspect, their pictures express the hope that it will be possible to govern and control this world. Neue Sachlichkeit painting was not completely

Adolf Dietrich
Amaryllis and Crocus in a Greenhouse, 1930
Amaryllis und Krokus im Gewächshaus
Oil on canvas, 70 x 84 cm
Basle, Thomas Dietschy

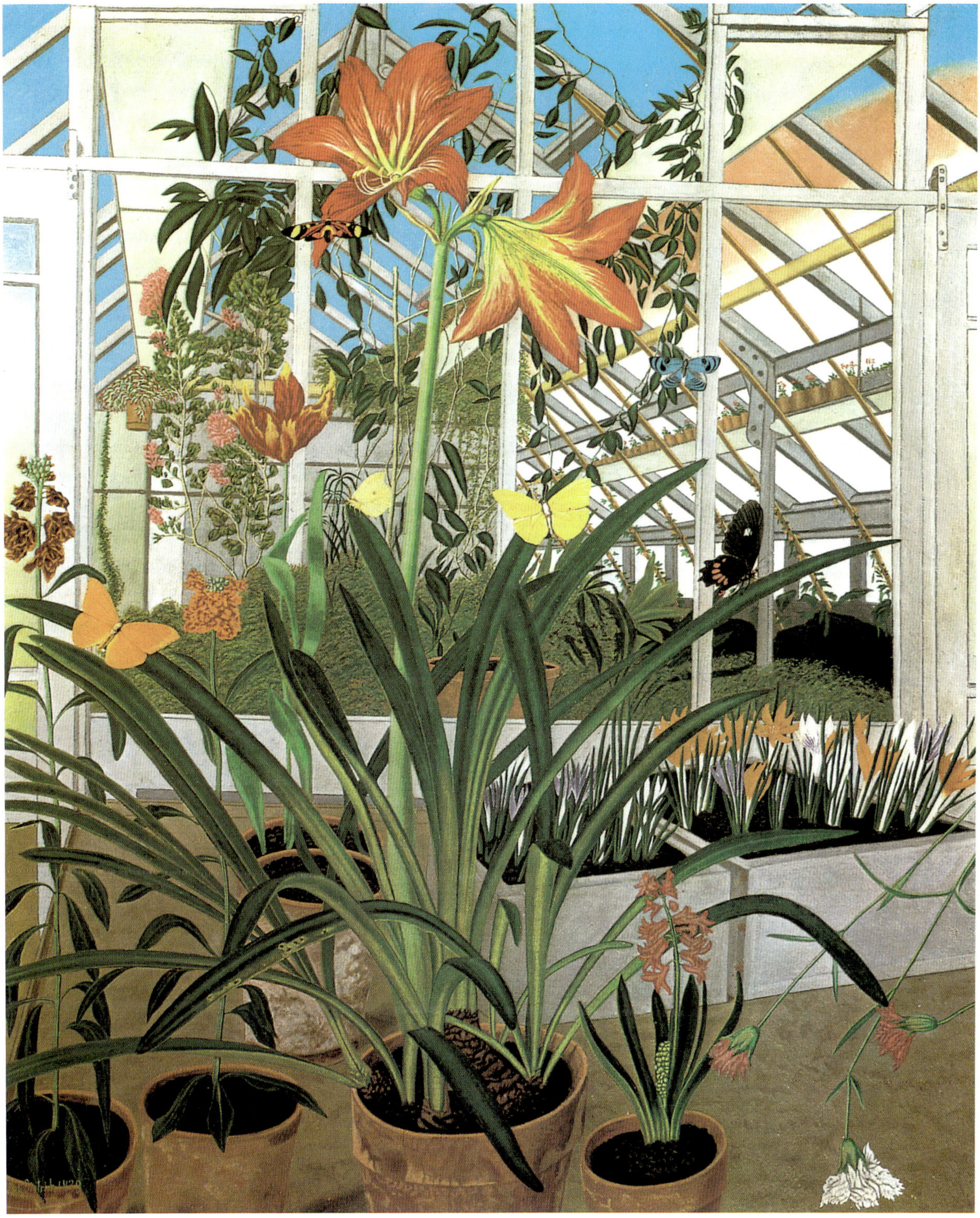

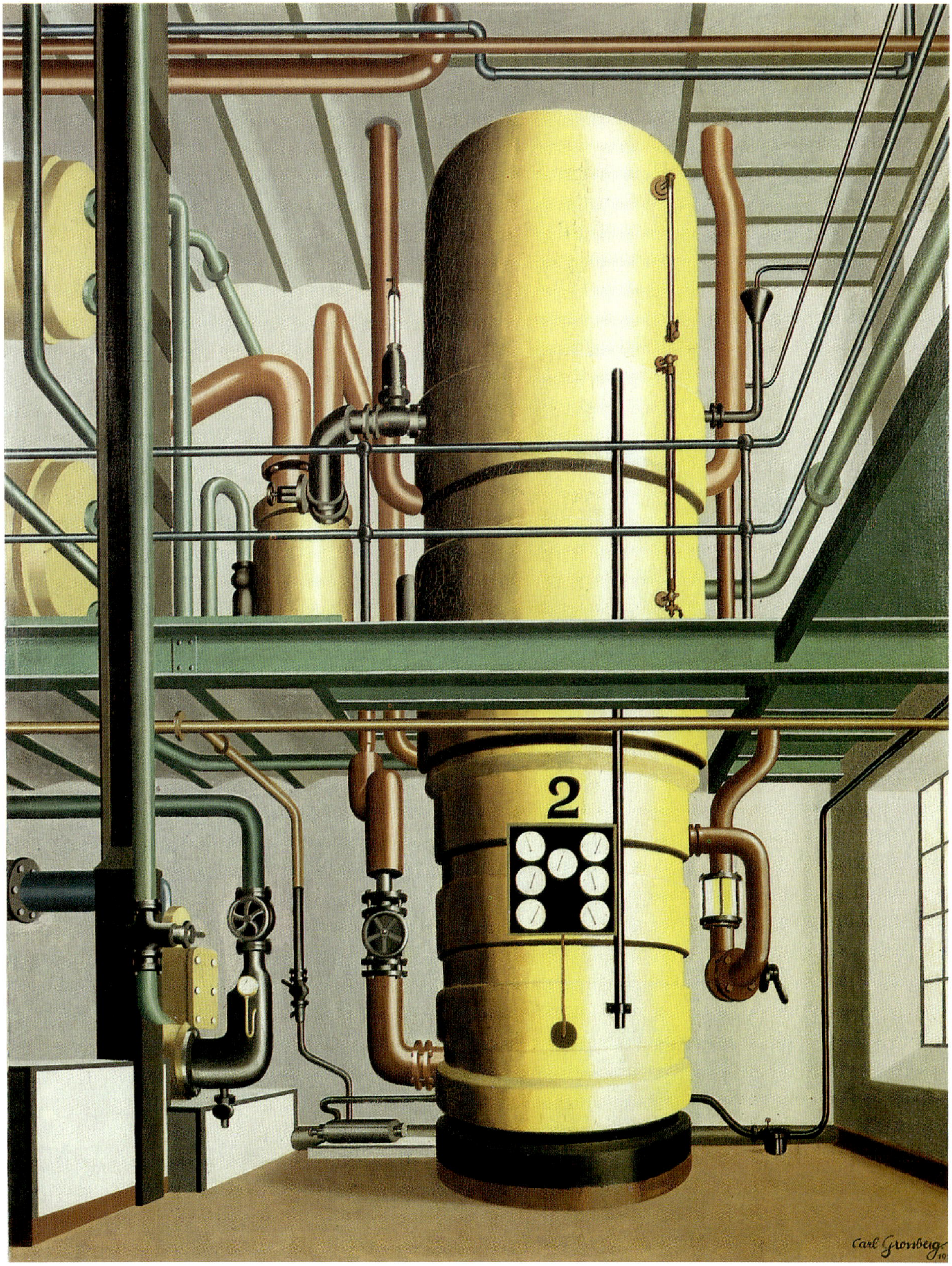
2
Carl Grossberg

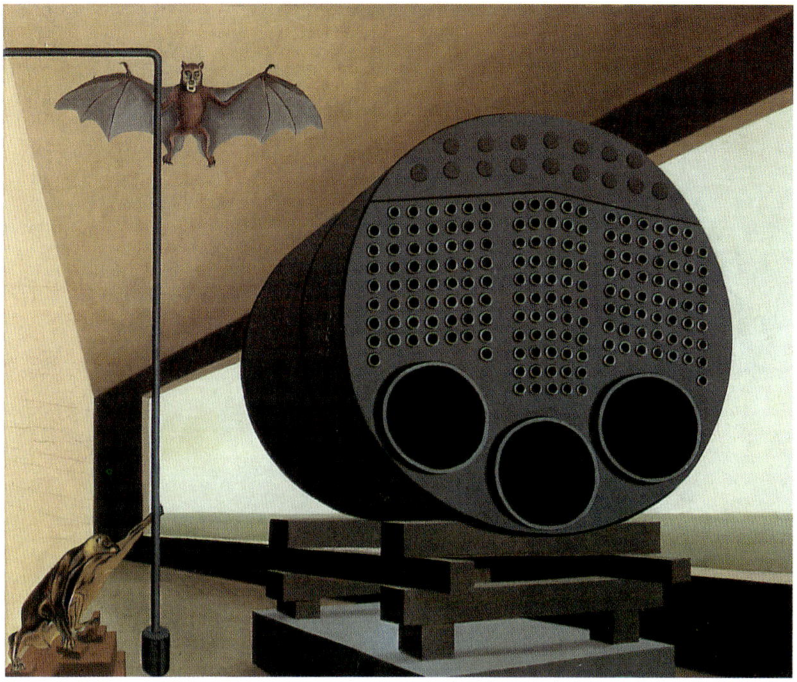

Carl Grossberg
Vision: Steam Boiler with Bat, 1928
Traumbild: Dampfkessel mit Fledermaus
Oil on wood, 55 x 66 cm
Bonn, on loan to the Rheinisches Landesmuseum

Carl Grossberg's cold interior views and deserted factory halls show oversized technological motifs detached from their functions, symbols of industrial power. His machine world, fundamentally static despite its perspective dynamic, bears the apparatus, exaggerated to memorial proportions, away from the observer, yet simultaneously presents it quite clearly before his eyes.

captivated by a Constructivist utopia, nor did it believe naively in the compatibility of nature, man and technology, as did Léger, the optimistic disciple of progress. It maintained an equal distance between itself and technology, on the one hand, and itself and man, on the other, both ultimately striking it as unpredictable. The deserted industrial pictures of Carl Grossberg, among others, bear witness to this attitude.

Grossberg had studied architecture before the war, in Aachen and Darmstadt. He resumed his studies in 1919 at the Academy of Art in Weimar, and, for a few months in 1920/21, also at the Bauhaus. In 1921, he settled down in the Franconian town of Sommerhausen near Würzburg, and it was to here that he always withdrew during the time that followed whenever he needed peace and quiet. The style of Grossberg the painter, not uninfluenced by the functional ethos of Grossberg the architect, underwent a clear development from 1922 onwards in a Neue Sachlichkeit direction. Cityscapes initially predominated, revealing "toy-towns" in the manner of Scholz, his Karlsruhe painting colleague. These were already characterized by interesting perspective views and technological motifs. In the years that followed, technology would be given ever more weight, as in the depiction of the Berlin Avus race track and his views of industrial Wuppertal, Grossberg's home town, for example.

This same period gave rise to his series of "Visions", in which a delight in the detail of technical depictions is combined with an almost Surrealist fantasy. Monkeys, birds and bats appear in the tension-filled emptiness and silence of great engine-rooms, no further indication being present within the picture as to their symbolic significance. A fine example of these visions may be seen in the picture of the boiler drum (illus. p. 169). Grossberg himself emphatically rejected either any intention of Verist criticism or any cult of the technological: "I am not aware of having begun as an engineer. There are no doubt other reasons for my interest in the forms assumed by

Carl Grossberg
The Yellow Boiler, 1933
Der gelbe Kessel
Oil on wood, 90 x 70 cm
Wuppertal, Von der Heydt-Museum

technology." "The progress made by technology has always attracted my attention; however, I have been aware of how certain important things have slipped away from us because of this development."[83]

From 1931 to 1939, Grossberg's visions were executed only in the form of sketches; thereafter he began painting them again. His realistic works from the 1930s abstain from any distracting combination such as merely obeys dream logic. His outside views of factories and industrial complexes reveal a clear affinity to Neue Sachlichkeit industrial photography. The inside views of the industrial plants are often characterized by the tension-laden contrast between the monolithic, static effect radiating from machines or enormous tanks, and a labyrinthine, "dynamic" system of pipes. The space is given depth by scaffolding and pipes, the visual impression being further heightened by the shading on those parts with

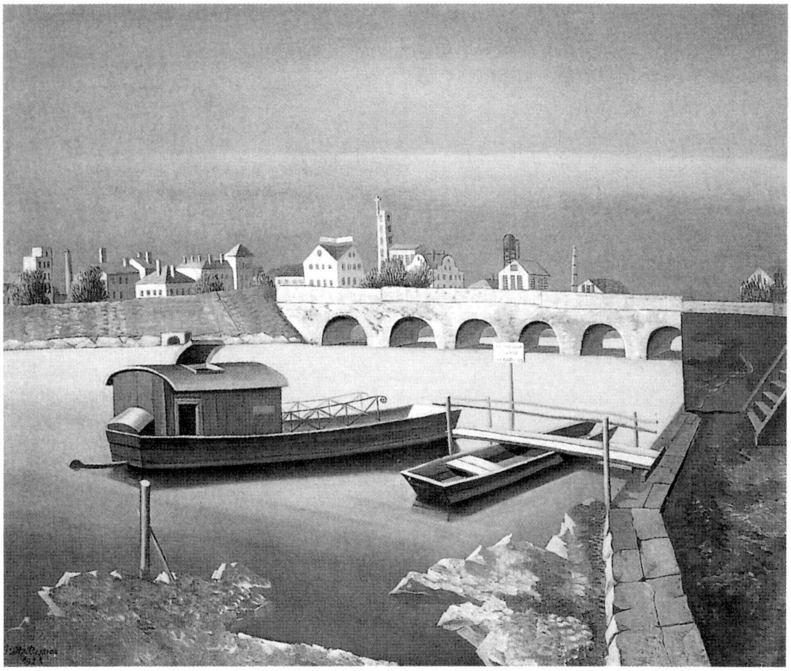

Julius Bissier
Rhine Ferry, 1928
Rheinfähre
Oil on canvas, 70 x 80 cm
Freiburg, Städtische Museen Freiburg, Museum für Neue Kunst

extensive surfaces. Grossberg did his best pictures of this type in 1933, the majority of them as works commissioned by firms, such as *The Yellow Boiler* (illus. p. 168). This period saw Grossberg's interest in technology reaching encyclopaedic dimensions. In 1934, he began to put into effect his industry-painting plan, namely the depiction of the most important industrial types and factories in Germany. However, this ambitious project would not be continued.

People play either merely a subordinate role or no role at all in Grossberg's pictures. At most, they serve as staffage in the world of technological artefacts. One can hardly maintain on this basis that they express any special attitude on the part of the painter. Nevertheless, the supposition that the austere, occasionally even lonely mood that radiates from the artist's pictures will not have been totally alien to him is not without foundation. "My hair stands up on end when I think of the future of Germany and

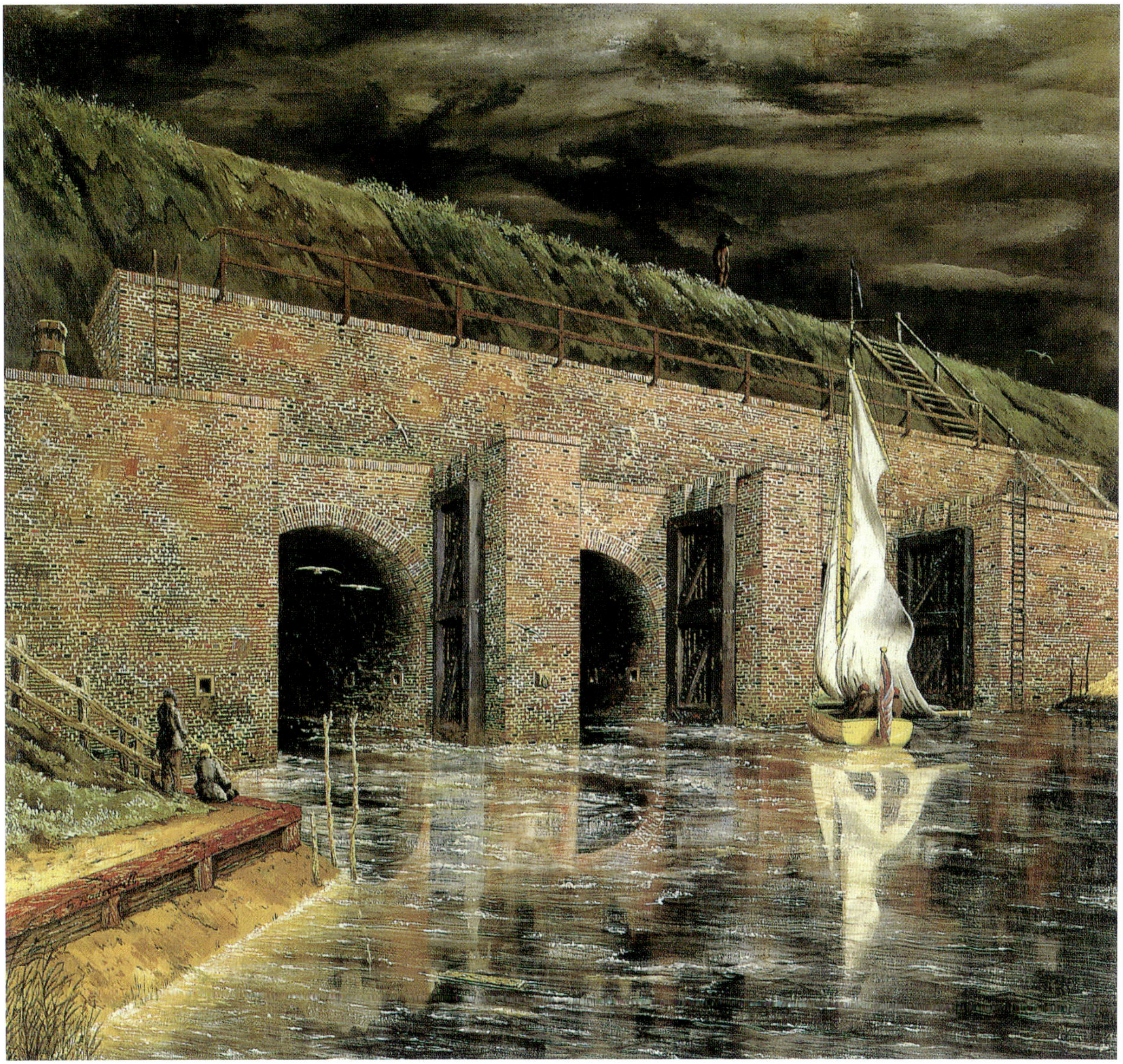

Europe", he wrote to a friend in 1931. And we may read in a letter from 1934, "Despite every ideational success, my basic mood is one of indescribable pessimism, something which I can no longer throw off."[84] In the same year, Grossberg was offered – and accepted – a contract from the Berlin Ministry of Propaganda to create a monumental mural on the subject of "Industrial landscape". No further works were forthcoming from him in this connection – in the same way that he kept his distance from politics, and especially from National Socialism.

No other among the Neue Sachlichkeit painters could rival Grossberg in his field. Nonetheless, mention should be made in this context of the industrial pictures by Karl Völker, the early Constructivist from Halle, and the railway pictures by Max Radler from Munich, as well as the technical works of architecture by Reinhold Nägele from Stuttgart and the magical œuvre of Franz Radziwill. The other artists generally left technology on

Franz Radziwill
Floodgate near Petershörn, 1927
Siel bei Petershörn
Oil on canvas on wood, 85 x 79.5 cm
Private collection

one side, however, something that is also true of the Rhineland Constructivists, astonishingly enough, who schematized people instead of machines.

Radziwill's harbours with warships and passenger liners, and his aircraft depictions, emphasize the surreal strangeness of such creations in the midst of an indifferent landscape. The artist rejects any structuring analysis of technology; his gaze, displaying a demonstrative indifference with respect to technology's internal laws, is directed towards its observable exterior, as seen in the precisely painted rivets on the ship in *Harbour*, for example. In his pictures of the naval harbour in Wilhelmshaven, he does not conceal the cold, reptilian quality that comes from the crouching silhouette of a cruiser, despite – or perhaps precisely because of – his friendship with senior naval officers. The observer is struck again and again by the attention to detail seen in the application with which Radziwill devotes himself to his pictorial representations, something visible in the manner in which he records a brick façade brick by brick, for instance, as in *Floodgate, near Petershörn* (illus. p. 171), a picture which takes on a Magic Realism in a special way.

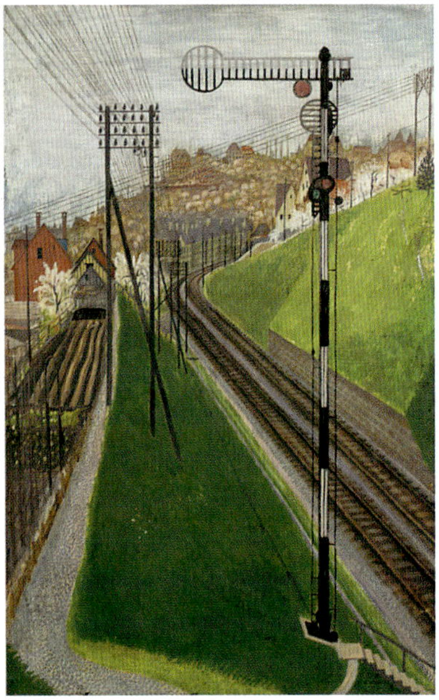

Reinhold Nägele
Railway Line, 1922
Bahnlinie
Tempera on cardboard, 55.5 x 36 cm
Berlin, Staatliche Museen zu Berlin – Preußischer Kulturbesitz, Nationalgalerie

The magical, demonic element conjured up by Radziwill is completely alien to the pictures of technology and architecture by Reinhold Nägele, the Swabian artist. He became famous through his – rather overrated – view of the Stuttgart *Weißenhof Housing Estate* (illus. p. 175), still under construction at that time, in which the controversial buildings become unfamiliar, box-like structures. At any rate, he does not do justice to the technical aesthetics of the "Neues Bauen" (New Building), for the harshly isolating manner of looking at things adopted by Neue Sachlichkeit did not accord with Nägele's artistic nature. It is thus due to similarities in motif, rather than in style, that his works have been classified as belonging to 1920s Neue Sachlichkeit. The decisive factor here was Nägele's interest in technology, and in particular in New Building. His early *Railway Line* (illus. p. 172) also took up a Neue Sachlichkeit motif – yet the effect of the linear network of tracks and wires within the green landscape in front of a hillside village creates more of a homely feeling than a sense of order, while the signal in the foreground – a favourite Neue Sachlichkeit motif – becomes

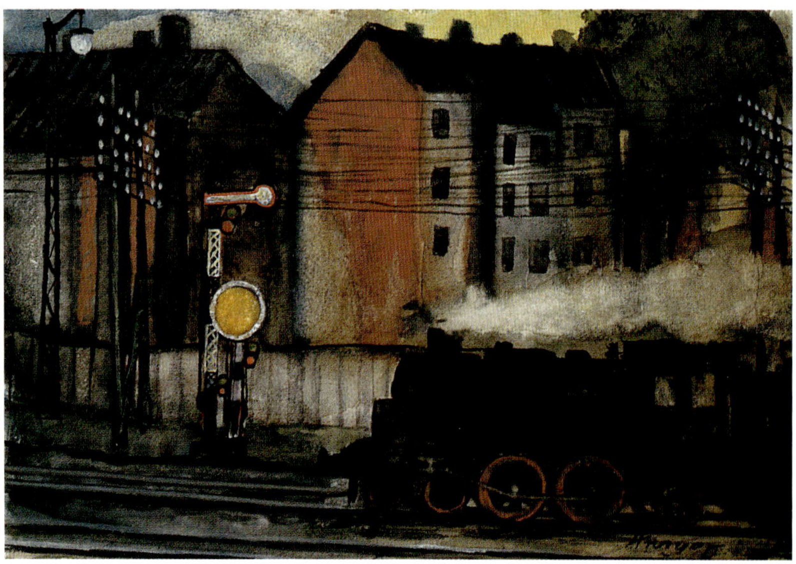

Immanuel Knayer
Locomotive, 1927
Watercolour, brush and ink,
13.6 x 19.5 cm
Milwaukee, Marvin and Janet Fishman Collection

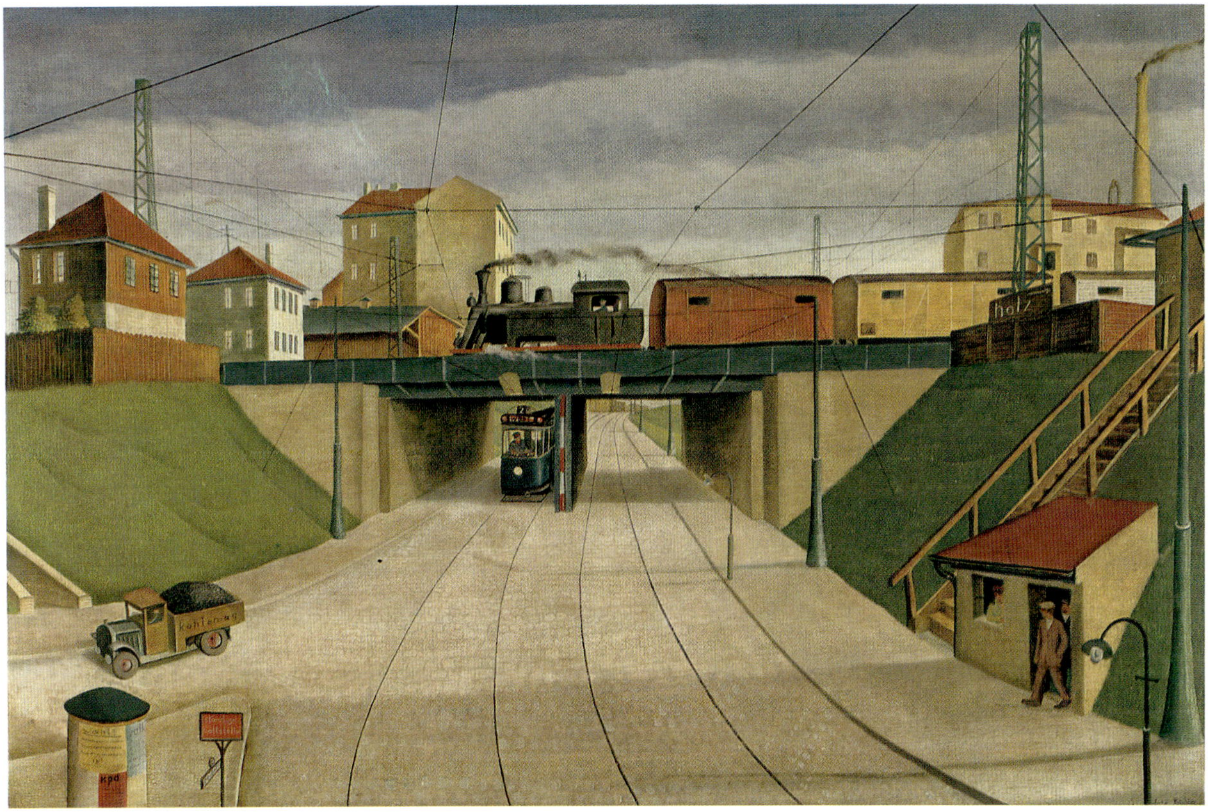

Max Radler
Railway Underpass, 1932
Bahnunterführung
Oil on wood, 53.5 x 80.5 cm
Bremen, Kunsthalle Bremen

an overlarge toy. Nägele's Swabian good-naturedness subdues the cold gleam of technology. However, this painting achieved a surprisingly great influence in southern Germany, even the 1932/33 views by Volker Böhringer, the Stuttgart artist, being indebted to this model.

The architectural and urban pictures done by Nägele in the 1920s were characterized by elements of Art Nouveau in the Japanese style, carried over from his early work, along with a certain degree of absurdity. *Pressa (Cologne), from the Hohenzollernbrücke* (illus. p. 174) once again shows an important building in the new style of architecture.[85] The painting contains captivatingly decorative features shaped by a Far-Eastern linearity, while the chains of lights, made up of many dots, demonstrate Nägele's alert eye for the new aspects presented by an aerial perspective. Incidentally, his night views of Stuttgart, done in the early 1930s, reveal a similar perception of the metropolitan night to that presented in Wilhelm Heise's *Stiglmaierplatz in Munich* (illus. p. 176).

The architectural and individual studies of technical objects (Grossberg, Dischinger, and Guido Kern with his *Beelitz Station Building*) constitute a separate area of the Neue Sachlichkeit reception of technology, its hard stylization consciously seeking an affinity with technical drawing. Inversely, Ferdinand Porsche's first preliminary study (1934) for the Volkswagen car undoubtedly reveals formal features taken from Neue Sachlichkeit. Astonishingly, Neue Sachlichkeit almost completely overlooked the car itself as a pictorial motif. Even in Barthel Gilles' painting *The Bride*, it functions purely as a form of precious setting for the woman getting out. Those few pictures in which it is visible as a background motif, such as the self-portraits

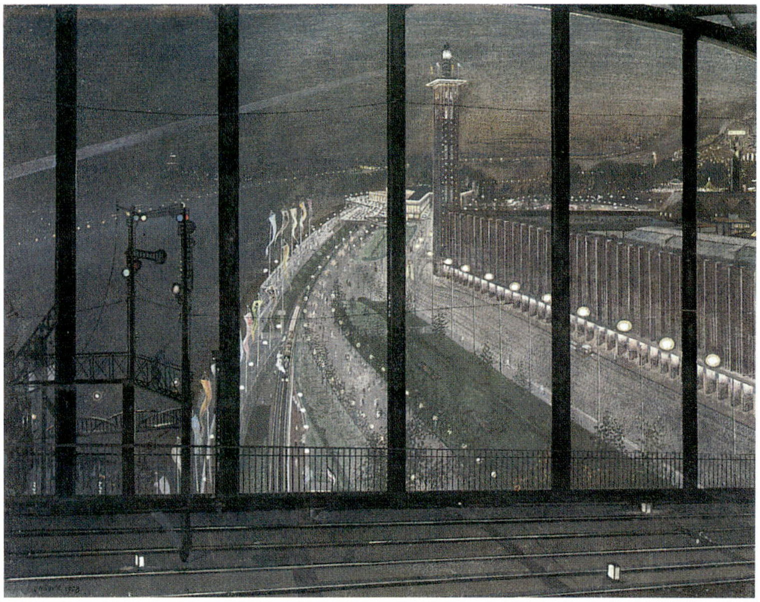

Reinhold Nägele
Pressa (Cologne), from the Hohenzollern-brücke, 1928
Pressa (Köln) von der Hohenzollernbrücke
Tempera on paper, 38.5 x 50.5 cm
Stuttgart, Galerie der Stadt Stuttgart

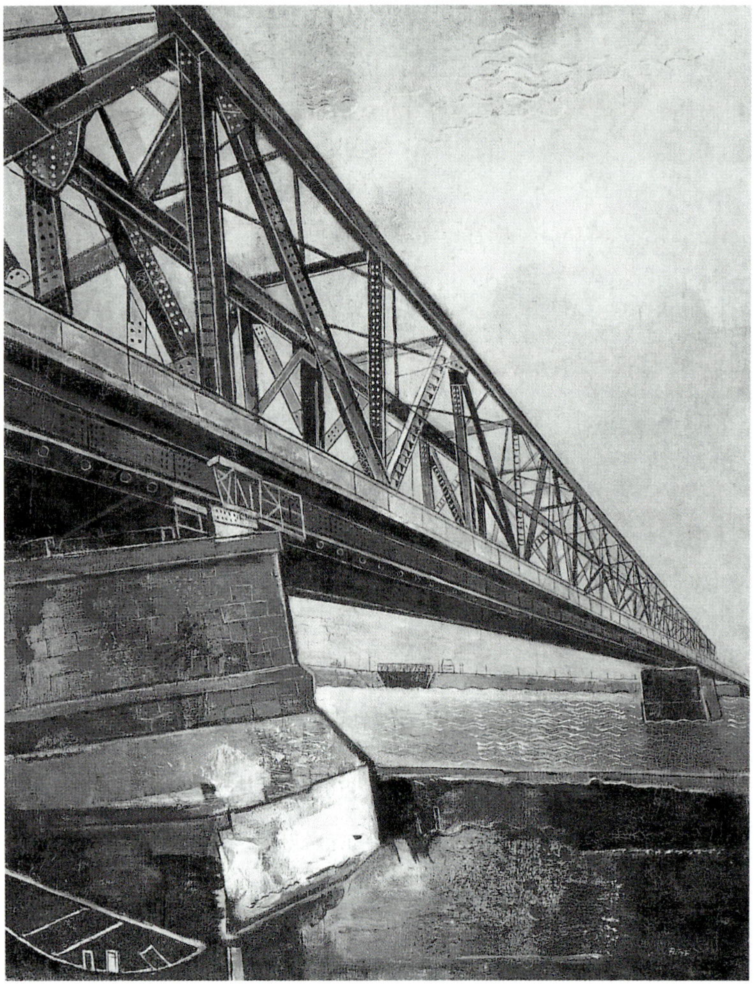

Xaver Fuhr
Iron Bridge, 1928
Eisenbrücke
Oil on canvas, 97.5 x 77 cm
Essen, Museum Folkwang

by Georg Scholz and Werner Hofmann, cannot give it a specific function or character.

Things were different with the radio, which aroused immense fascination in the Twenties, not as a social medium – that, unfortunately, would come later with the Nazis and their "Volksempfänger" (People's Receiver) – but primarily as a technological manifestation of the removal of frontiers. In Ernst Toller's play "Hoppla, wir leben", staged by Erwin Piscator in Berlin in 1927, the radio became the epitome of the " . . . soul-destroying fantasticalness of the technological age. Via the radio station, Toller lets us hear the heartbeat of an aircraft! Toller is romanticizing the mechanical".[86] Those Neue Sachlichkeit painters who took up the motif of the radio listener (Max Radler, Kurt Günther, Max Ackermann, Kurt Weinhold) exploited the contrast between the barrier-removing, apparently unlimited possibilities offered by the radio set and the obvious limitations – both spatial and psychological – of human existence. Kurt Günther's *Radio Listener* (illus. p. 178) caricatures a petit bourgeois in Wilhelminian dress surrounded by the new world of technology – a satire on the "Sunday citizen, who, fed up with the world, has walled himself in between his wheezing radio, his too-tight headphones, his opera libretto and his cigar,

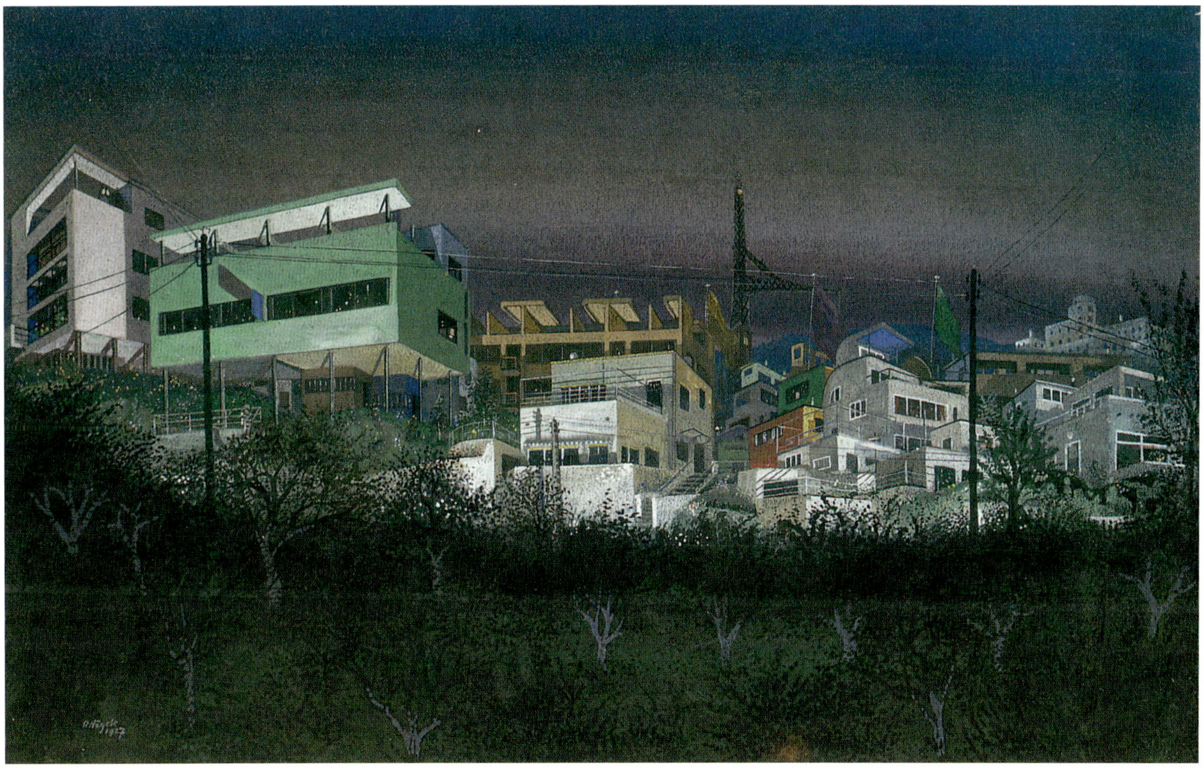

Reinhold Nägele
Weißenhof Housing Estate, Stuttgart, 1927
Weißenhofsiedlung Stuttgart
Tempera on cardboard, 31.5 x 50 cm
Stuttgart, Graphische Sammlungen,
Staatsgalerie Stuttgart

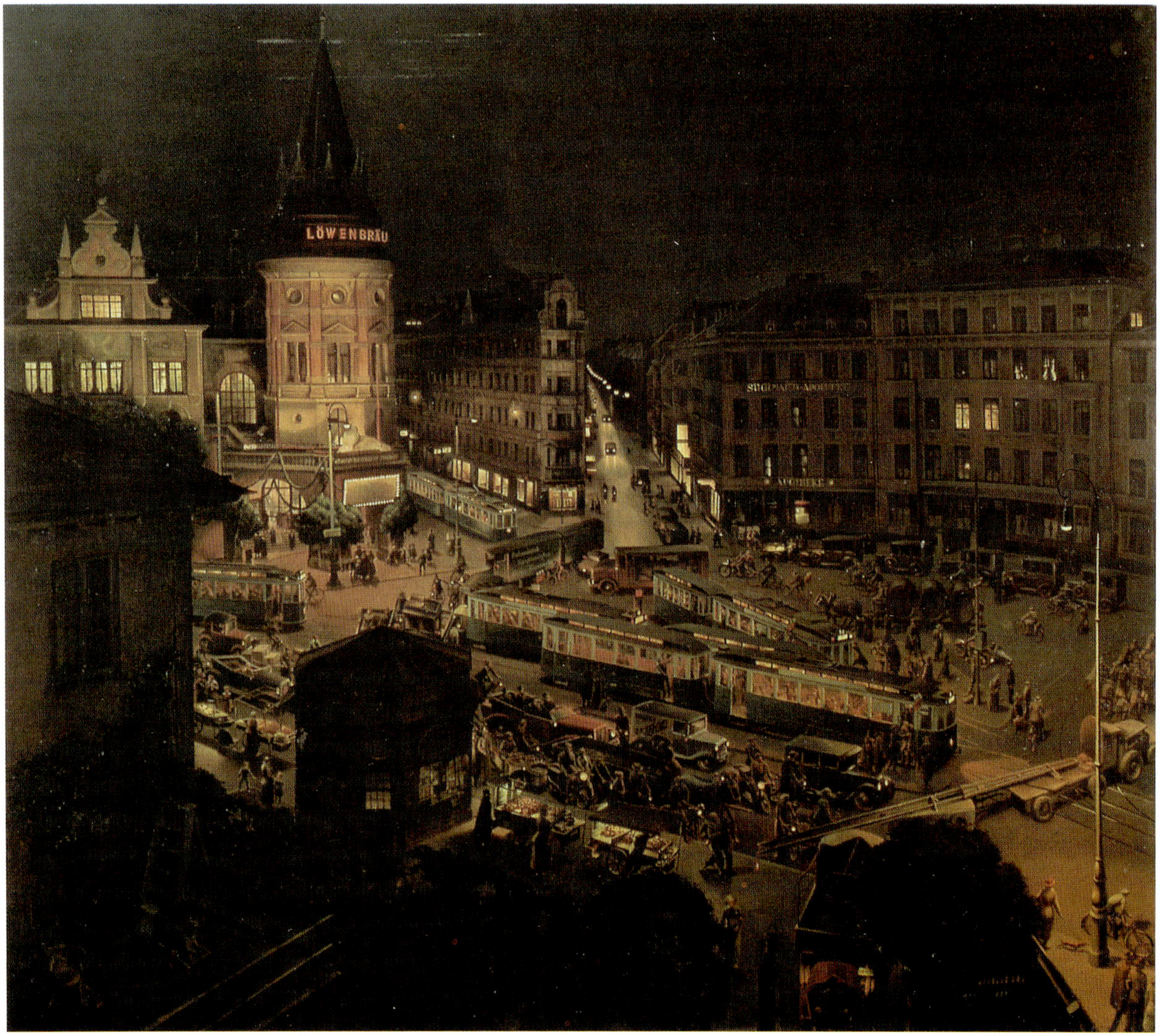

Wilhelm Heise
Stiglmaierplatz in Munich, 1935
Stiglmaierplatz in München
Oil on wood, 107 x 122 cm
Munich, Stadtmuseum

in a vindictive bachelor idyll of our epoch, a musical fortification glittering with hostility."[87]

Neue Sachlichkeit conspicuously emphasizes the presence of technology in the city and the countryside. Among its most frequent motifs here were level crossings, underpasses, telegraph poles and telephone wires, bridges, and gasometers. While the level crossings and railway signals were given a rather playful, somewhat twee form, in the case of telegraph poles and telephone wires the Constructivist, ordering element was also emphasized from the compositional respect. The heavily solid level crossings and bridges represented an attempted synthesis of tectonics with an unconcealed fascination for the Constructivist. Gasometers functioned as ciphers for the element of threat. In no way did the Neue Sachlichkeit painters deny the village or small-town idyll – indeed, they depicted it in some of their works – yet the modern city was their true, ever-present field of reference. After the Expressionist city pictures, visionary if apocalyptic, by Ludwig Meidner and the early Grosz (*Dedication to Oskar Panizza*), they searched for a

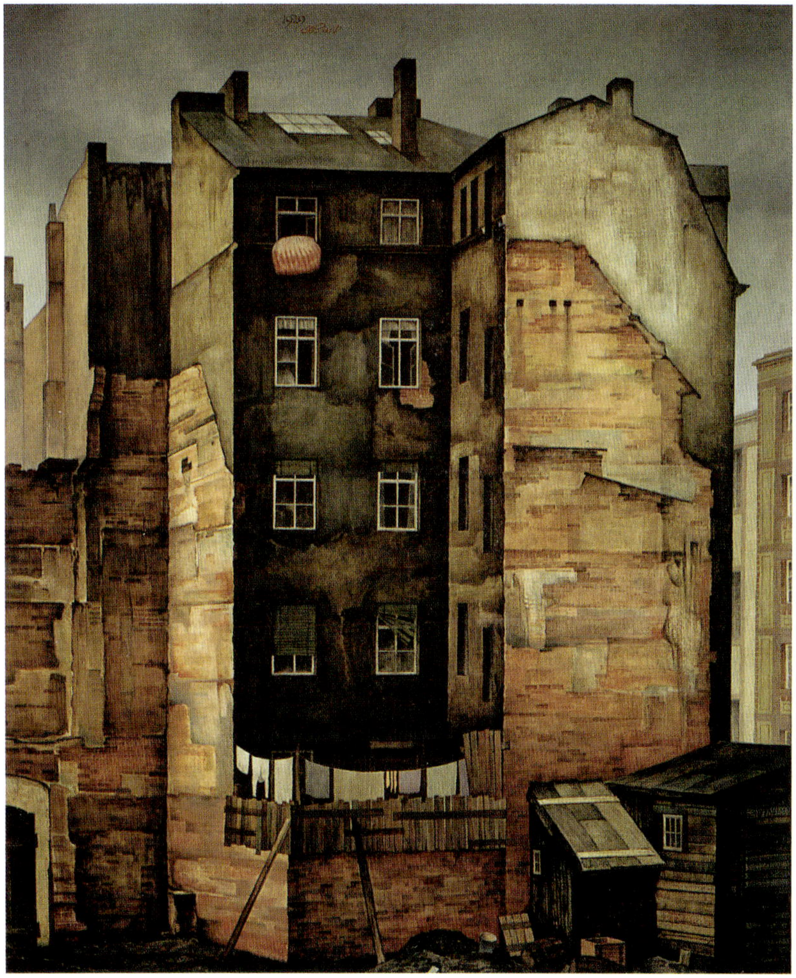

Franz Lenk
Berlin Tenements, 1929
Berliner Hinterhäuser
Oil on canvas on plywood, 113.5 x 94 cm
Berlin, Berlinische Galerie

Neue Sachlichkeit painting regarded the city less as the embodiment of a cheerfully greeted modernity; instead, it was seen first and foremost as the scene of the disintegration of social order. It is not the sophisticated side of the city which is displayed, but rather the cramped environment with its obstructed view of the sky, an accumulation of tenement houses and desolate corners. Comparable with Alfred Döblin's novel "Berlin Alexanderplatz" (1929), this critical view of the city portrays a chaos to which all experience bears no relation.

new form in which to present this subject. It is only in Rudolf Schlichter's *Hausvogteiplatz* (illus. p. 35) that the city is portrayed as doomed – yet this verdict is hinted at without Expressionist pathos and solely by means of hidden symbols, the crumbling sun, the planet Saturn, the gallows.

Neue Sachlichkeit avoided presenting the city subject in its full form: with the exception of Reinhold Nägele's Stuttgart cityscapes, no veritable urban panoramas were forthcoming. Slightly fairy-tale-like urban vedute predominate, in no small way indebted to Rousseau (for example Schnarrenberger, or Beckmann's Frankfurt pictures of around 1920). One variant of this pictorial type was the so-called "building-block vedutà", to be seen in the early works by Scholz, for example; despite the evident deliberateness of its construction, it also reveals a simultaneous tendency towards trivialization. The achievements of Neue Sachlichkeit itself in the field of urban vedute are to be found in Grossberg's deserted Wuppertal pictures, as mentioned earlier, and in Wunderwald's Berlin cityscapes (illus. pp. 46, 47), as well as in the special type of street view at night. Richard Gessner's

After 1923, the number of radio owners increased to reach a figure of more than two million. The cultural changes due to the radio became a theme in painting: the radio listener: the radio, technical manifestation of the removal of barriers, contrasting sharply with the limitations of human existence.

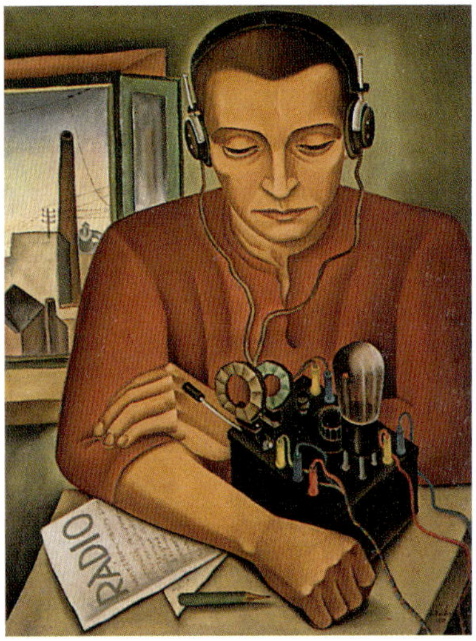

Paris by Night (illus. p. 129), Wilhelm Heise's *Stiglmaierplatz in Munich* (illus. p. 176), and Reinhold Nägele's views of night-time Stuttgart all accentuate street sections illuminated by sharp cones of light, each of which constitutes an artificially delimited, overbright zone of human communality in the midst of the threatening blackness. The basic psychological impressions and topoi of Neue Sachlichkeit are evident here. With respect to the graphic arts, mention should be made of Hubbuch's Berlin lithographs of 1922/23, which conjure up the hidden secrets and unrealities of the city; however, a distant echo of Art Nouveau may still be detected in these works.

Neue Sachlichkeit was interested first and foremost in the world of objects, irrespective of whether the items depicted belonged to technology or not. The object itself was of primary importance, its isolation and formalization through artistic means the aim. Through this stylistic characterization of objects, the articles and objects depicted could occasionally take on a remarkable resemblance to one another. Despite the obvious disparity of the objects in Hubbuch's drawing *Ironing Board*, Dischinger's *Trousers* (illus. p. 159) and Aereboe's *Red Jacket* (illus. p. 179), the central regard is one and the same, namely to form an amorphous piece of material in a hard, visually voluminous manner, in order that its meaning be tectonically heightened. We are concerned in these three works with the quintessence of the Neue Sachlichkeit style of drawing, and perhaps even with the style's formal centre itself.

Neue Sachlichkeit was not least a visual barometer of fashion, lifestyle, and the changing objects of everyday existence, something to be seen from

TOP:
Max Radler
Radio Listener, 1930
Radiohörer
Oil on canvas, 63 x 49 cm
Munich, Städtische Galerie im Lenbachhaus

Egon Friedell wrote in 1927: "The bioscope is killing human gesticulation, as sound film is killing the human voice – and the same is true of the radio; at the same time, it is freeing us of the necessity of concentration, and we are now able to enjoy Mozart and sauerkraut, or the Sunday sermon and a game of cards, at one and the same time. The human voice has achieved omnipresence, human gesticulation eternity – but at the cost of the soul."

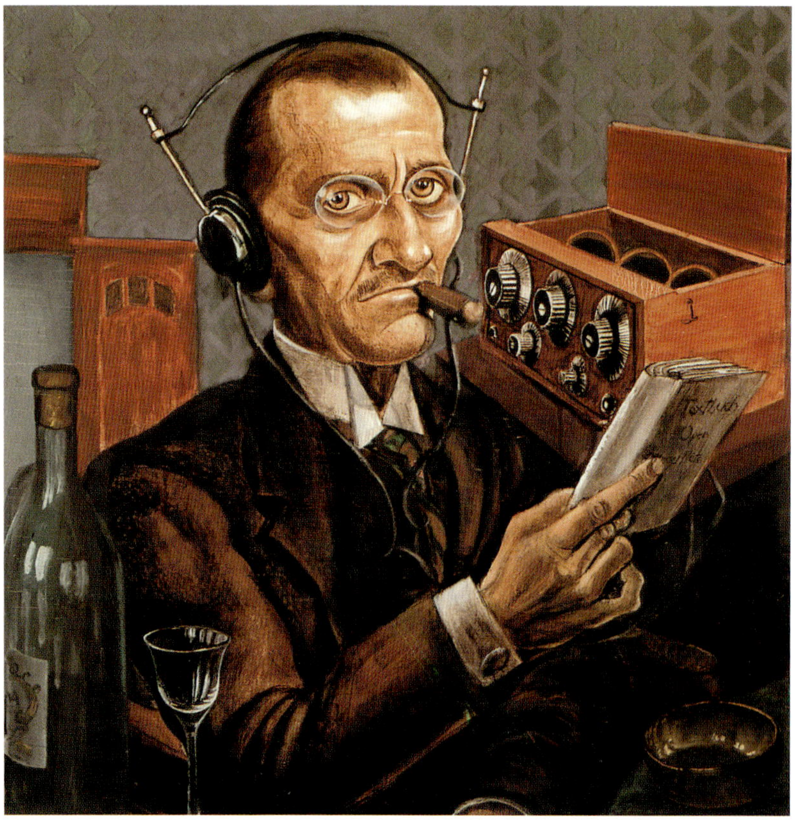

BOTTOM:
Kurt Günther
Radio Listener, 1927
Radionist
Tempera on wood, 55 x 49 cm
Berlin, Staatliche Museen zu Berlin – Preußischer Kulturbesitz, Nationalgalerie

Albert Aereboe
The Red Jacket, 1924
Oil on canvas on wood, 52 x 39 cm
Lübeck, Museum für Kunst und Kulturgeschichte der Hansestadt Lübeck

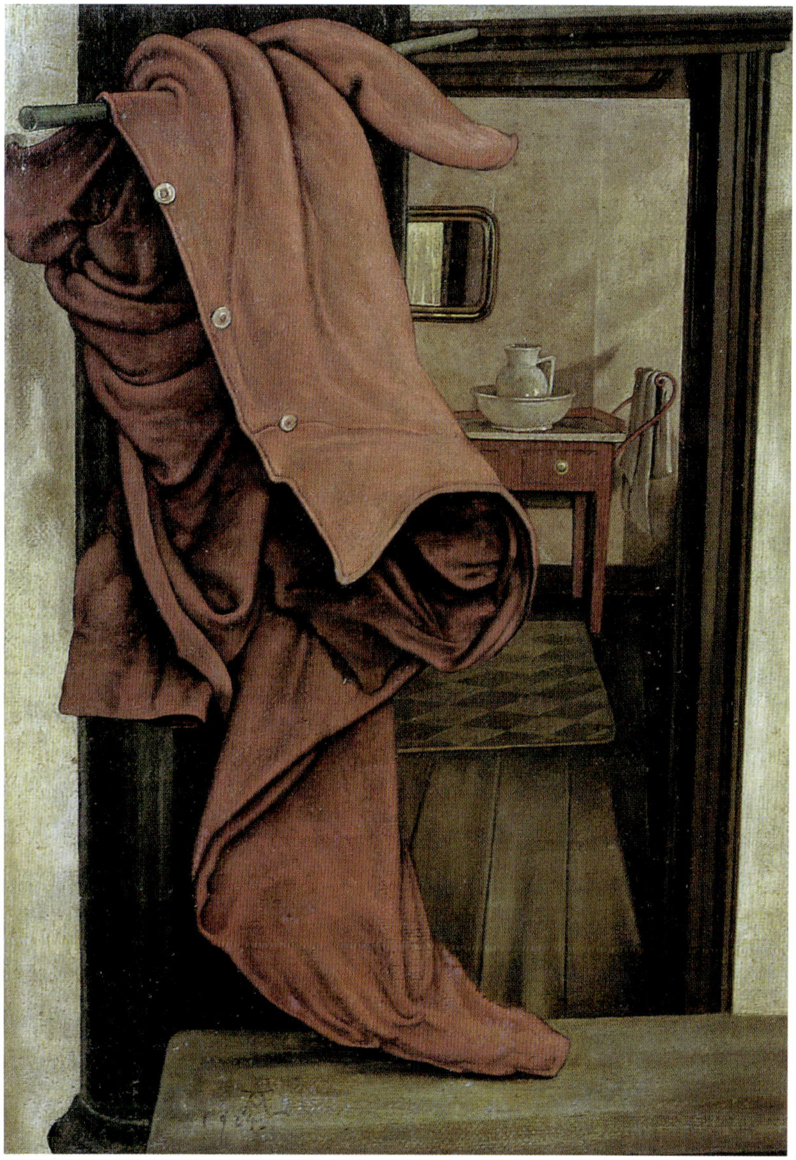

the fact that the leading magazines on 1920s lifestyle – "Der Querschnitt" and "Der Uhu" (The Owl) – frequently used Neue Sachlichkeit pictures as illustrations. Such pictures present us with fashionable cafés and bars, short-lived leading figures from high society such as dancers and boxers, and also the "Bubikopf", the bobbed haircut popular at the time. And even such eccentric motifs as tattoos, which were immensely popular for a time, took on greater importance through their appearance in Neue Sachlichkeit works, as in Dix's ironic *Suleika*, Griebel's *Sailor*, and, finally, Schad's portrait of *Egon Erwin Kisch*.

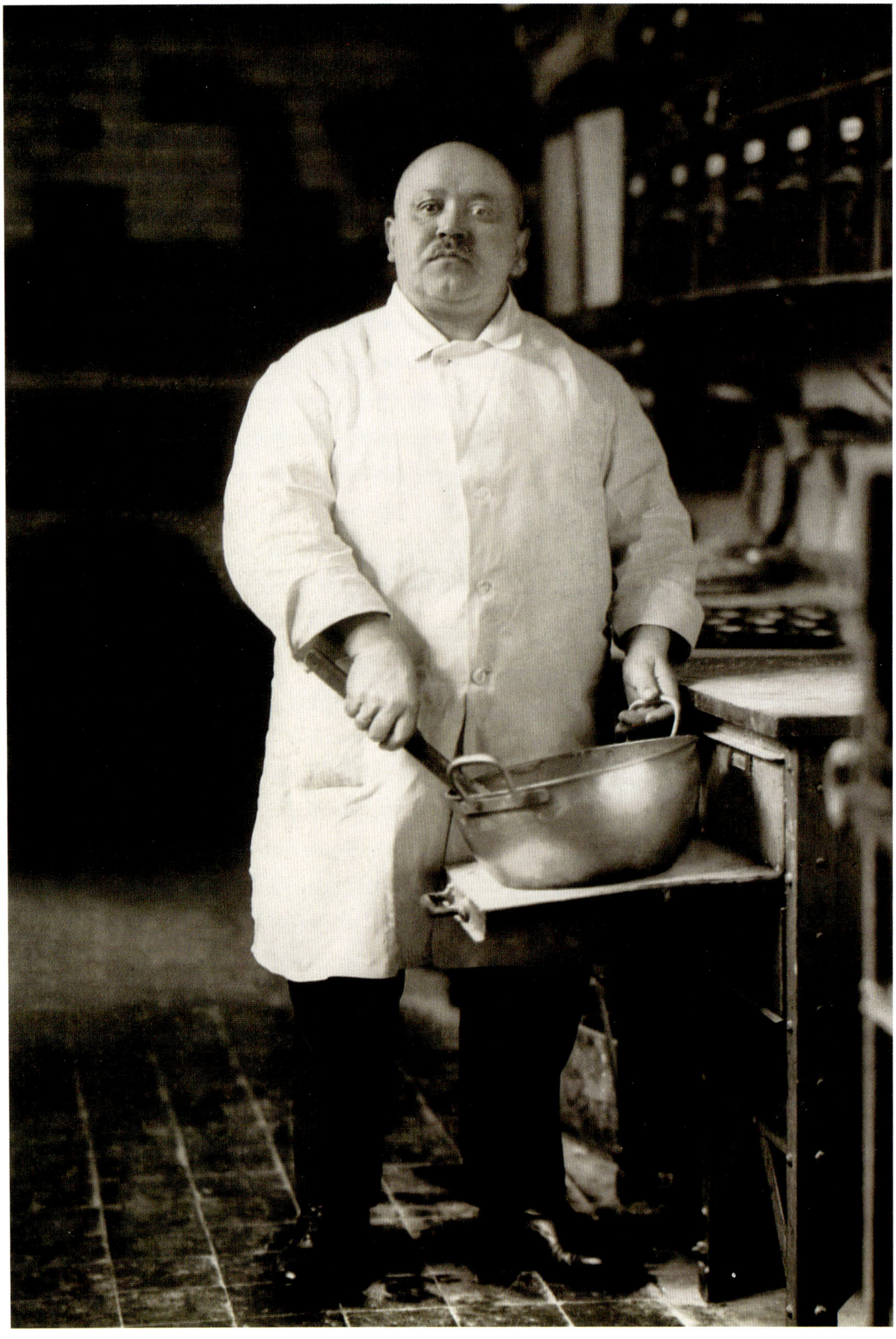

Painting and Photography
An Affinity

An abrupt break occurred in European photography after 1920, away from the previously predominant direction of so-called art photography. This took the form of a final departure from a style aiming at picturesque effects and seeking to imitate post-Impressionist painting by means of soft-focus lenses and the bromoil process. The important prerequisites for the emergence of a Neue Sachlichkeit direction in photography were the development of a visual approach to things that presented its subjects in sharp detail and isolated the figures and objects, bound up with the new fascination in the aesthetic aspects of technology and the possibilities of scientific documentation that photography offered.

Close links existed between Neue Sachlichkeit painting and German photography in the years from 1926 to 1932, even if no definite double talents emerged in Germany as in the case of certain artists among the Surrealists or Charles Sheeler in America. However, photography in Germany – as in France – was still dominated in the first half of the 1920s by an experimental approach to the medium. The success of the Realist movement was delayed for some years by Abstract and Constructivist "photograms" (for example by Moholy-Nagy), Man Ray's "Rayograms", and the "Schadograms" of Christian Schad, the last dabbling in this field with no great success. On the other hand, Neue Sachlichkeit photography also owed certain inspirations to these experiments.

It was not until the second half of the 1920s, a few years after the appearance of Neue Sachlichkeit painting, that a correspondingly orientated photographic style came onto the German scene, quickly asserting itself against not only the antiquated art photography but also avant-gardist experimenting. The years from 1928 to 1930 would bring the high point of this development, with the publication of important volumes of photographs and crucial theoretical programmes. Significantly, Walter Petry's "Bindung an die Dinge" (Attachment to Things), perhaps the most important manifesto of Neue Sachlichkeit photography, appeared in 1929 in the central organ of art criticism for Neue Sachlichkeit painting, the "Kunstblatt".

"We are concerned here with the clear and unambiguoustructure of things, with their meaning more than with their appearance. It is precisely to this aspect that art's efforts are addressed. Art takes the object out of its context, frees its object, gives it a wealth of meaning – yet with what medium? It subjectivizes the object, and the limits of the respective subjectivity become the limits of the artistic depiction, right down to the last little detail. It is here that the purely objective element of the photographic

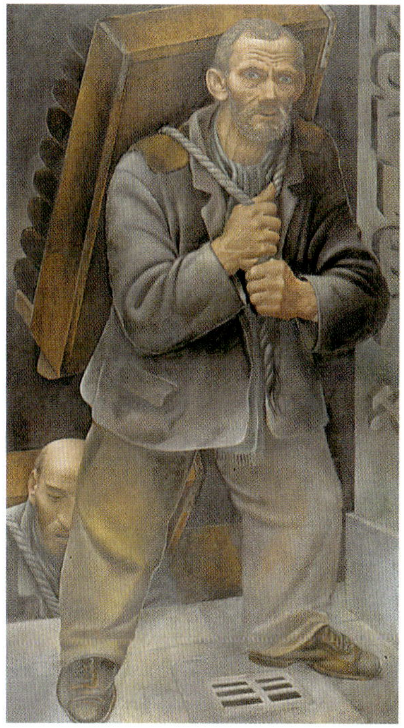

Leo Breuer
The Coal Man, 1931
Der Kohlenmann
Oil on wood, 150.5 x 86 cm
Bonn, Rheinisches Landesmuseum

August Sander
The pastry-Cook, 1928
Der Konditor
Black-and-white photograph
Cologne, August Sander Archiv

picture becomes evident, with no further clarification necessary. The object, clearly recorded, reproduced without any artistic transformation, must communicate with its meaning exclusively the objective meaning of its self, in so far as its reproduction gets beyond the reproductive element of a flat black-and-white suggestion of nature."[88] Petry – totally in tune with Neue Sachlichkeit art theory – is suggesting here that photography is capable of demonstrating the structural significance of the objects that it has isolated, and that, in a kind of interpretative circular argument, this recognition of the object's inner order would also retrospectively objectify the procedure of recording it. This would banish the subjective element from photography. In avoiding that which is accidental and transitory, photography gives us access to the "real, persisting world".[89]

In the same year, the photography critic Wilhelm Kästner wrote: "Here, too, by analogy with painting, we could speak of a 'Neue Sachlichkeit' (New Objectivity), although the relationship between photograph and painting is more the reverse of that which it was before, in that Neue Sachlichkeit painting endeavours precisely to achieve more photographic faithfulness in the representational reproduction within the picture. This objectivity is expressed in the case of photographs in the focussed reproduction of the object, in its clear emphasis – indeed, almost in the penetrating, all-round lighting, which completely banishes the shadows wherever possible or makes use of them as firmly outlined pictorial elements – and above all in the preference for solid, clearly recordable objects with a readily apparent formal structure as pictorial motifs".[90] Kästner highlights the important common characteristics to be found in the photography and painting of Neue Sachlichkeit: a clear and sharp recording of things, extreme close and in-depth perspective, the isolation of details, the filtering out of abstract structures, and the emphasis of the material's character. However, it proved impossible to reproduce not only the particular spatial conception of Neue Sachlichkeit painting in photography but also the sharpness in the depiction of the objects, one remaining constant despite a considerable increase in the depth of field.

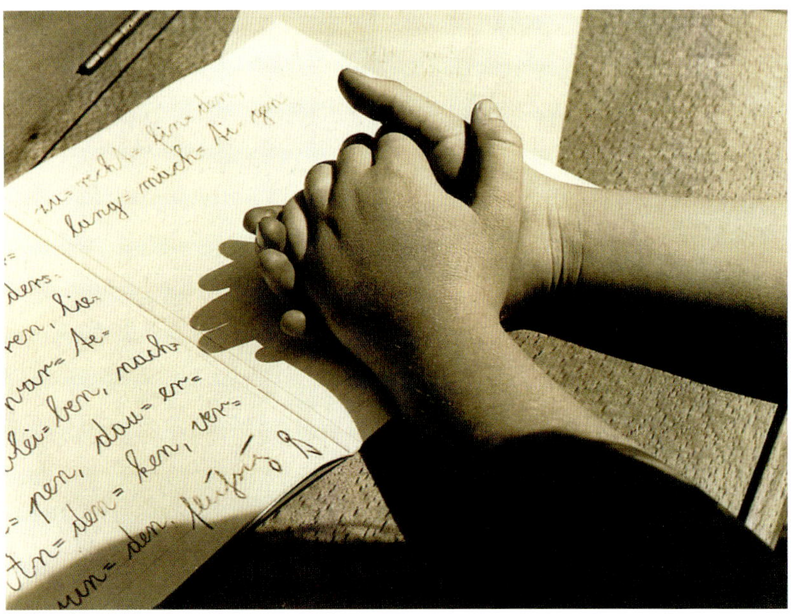

Aenne Biermann
Child's hands, 1928
Kinderhände
Black-and-white photograph
Essen, Museum Folkwang

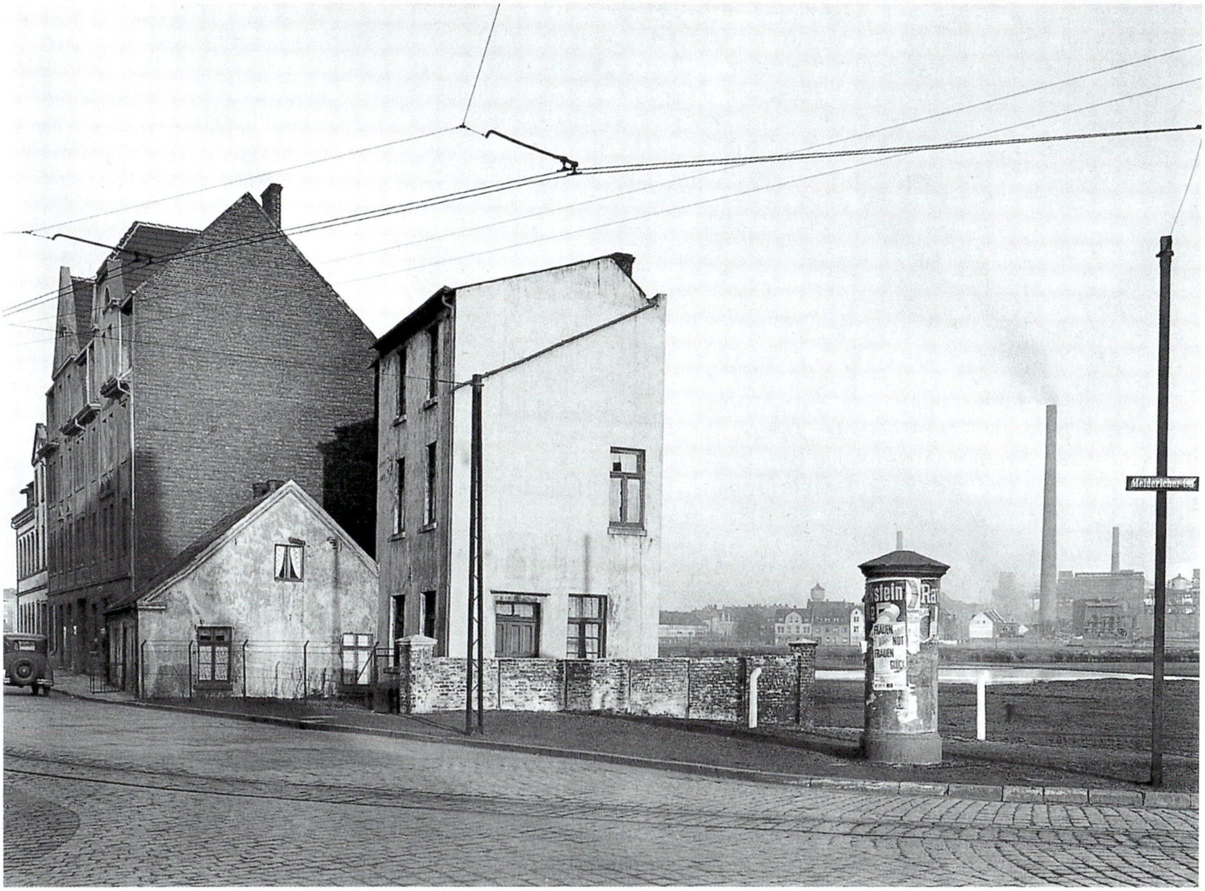

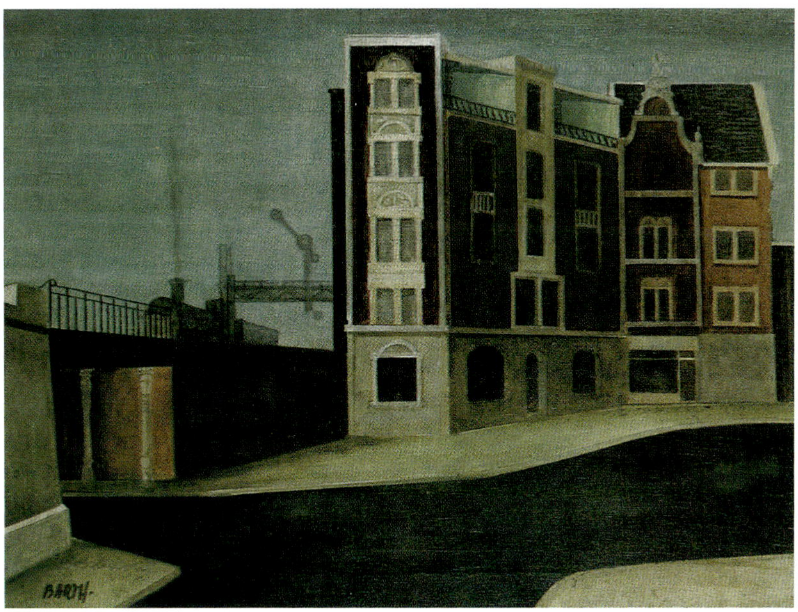

TOP:
Albert Renger-Patzsch
Ruhr Valley: Meidericher Straße in Mülheim-Ruhr, 1930
Ruhrgebiet: Meidericher Straße in Mülheim-Ruhr
Black-and-white photograph
Zülpich, Albert Renger-Patzsch Archiv, Ann and Jürgen Wilde

BOTTOM:
Carl Barth
Houses along the Railway Embankment, 1932
Häuser am Bahndamm
Oil on canvas, 60 x 80 cm
Düsseldorf, Stadtmuseum

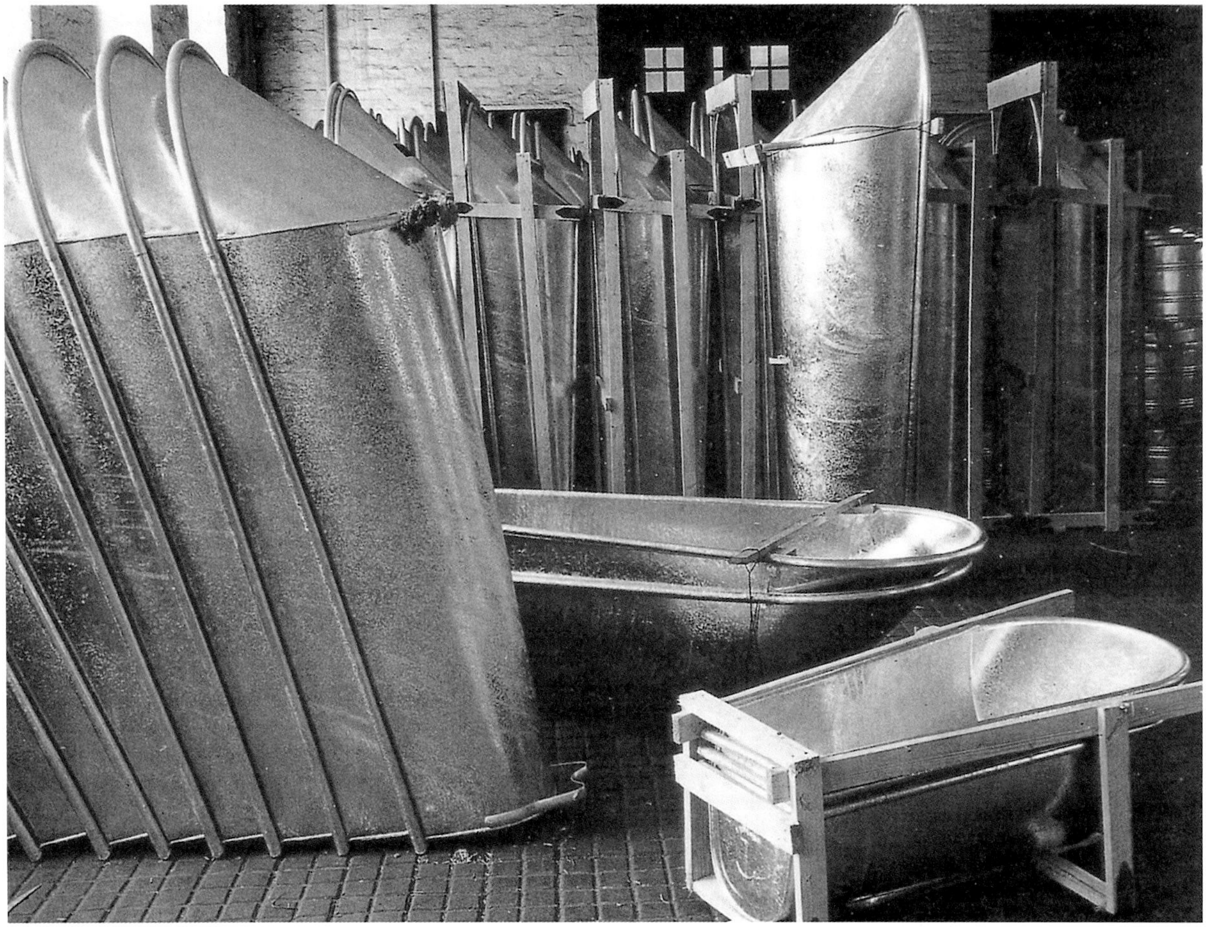

TOP:
Albert Renger-Patzsch
Zinc bathtub warehouse at the Krauss Works, Schwarzenberg, 1926
Zinkbadewannenlager der Krausswerke, Schwarzenberg
Black-and-white photograph
Zülpich, Albert Renger-Patzsch Archiv, Ann and Jürgen Wilde

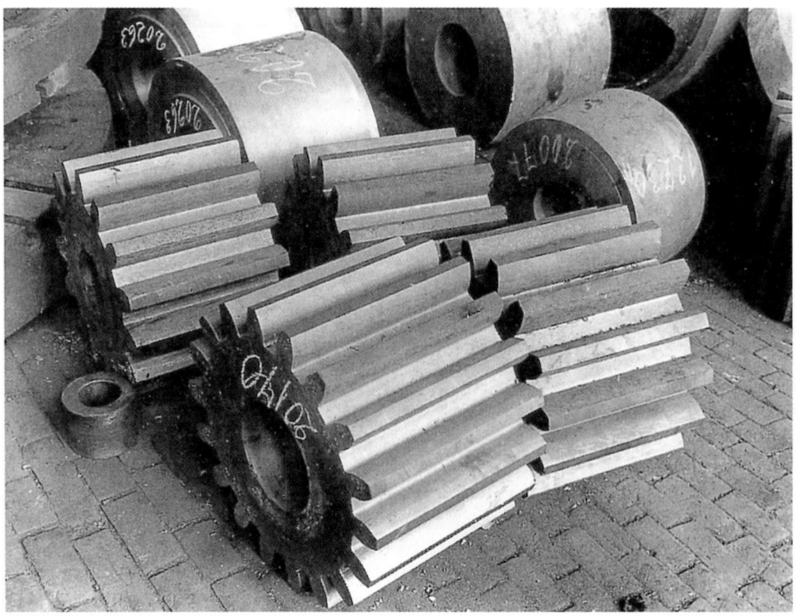

BOTTOM:
Albert Renger-Patzsch
Pinion and gear wheels, Lindener Iron and Steel Works, 1928
Ritzel und Zahnräder, Lindener Eisen-und Stahlwerke
Black-and-white photograph
Zülpich, Albert Renger-Patzsch Archiv, Ann and Jürgen Wilde

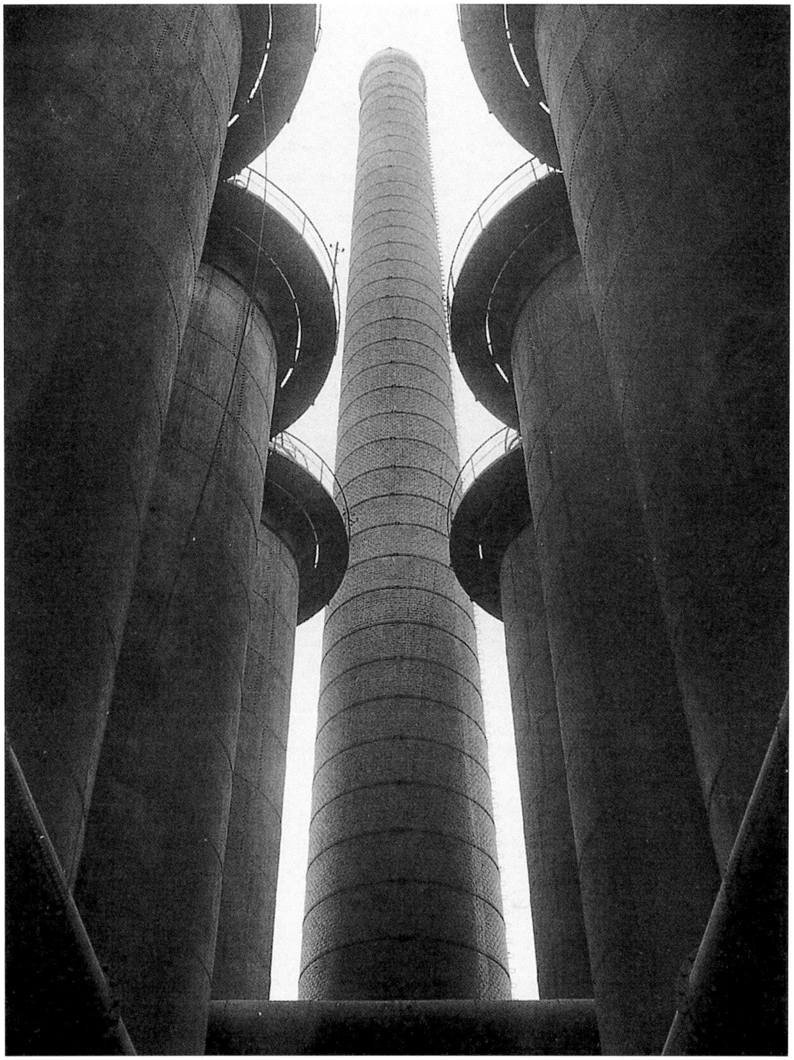

Albert Renger-Patzsch
Regenerator, 1927
Kauper
Black-and-white photograph
Zülpich, Albert Renger-Patzsch Archiv, Ann and Jürgen Wilde

"Surely only photography is capable of doing justice to the rigid linear structure of modern technology, the airy latticework of cranes and bridges, the dynamics of 1000-horse-power engines. That which its supporters – inasmuch as they support the 'painter's style' – lay to the charge of photography, namely, the mechanical reproduction of form, renders it superior here to all other means of expression." *Albert Renger-Patzsch, 1927*

Above all, however, it was the fruitful tension between pictorial material and picture that was lacking in photography, a tension also discernible in those Neue Sachlichkeit works where the optical impression could be described as an oleograph-like smoothness. Even here, the structure gives the impression of a materially saturated vehicle, plastic to the point of tangibility, of the pictorial image. But there are other limitations to the comparison. For example, the conservative current within Neue Sachlichkeit art had very few counterparts in Neue Sachlichkeit photography. It is significant in this respect that Munich, which was after all the centre of what Hartlaub would regard as "right-wing" Neue Sachlichkeit painting, remained extremely tradition-bound with regard to photography. A picturesque, Impressionist style of photography, including the bromoil process, continued here right up to 1930, and the renowned Bavarian State Institute of Photography attempted in a 1929 exhibition to counteract Neue Sachlichkeit ideas in photography.

The French advocates of the New Photography – such as Germaine Krull – were nearer to Constructivism, the Germans nearer to Neue Sachlichkeit,

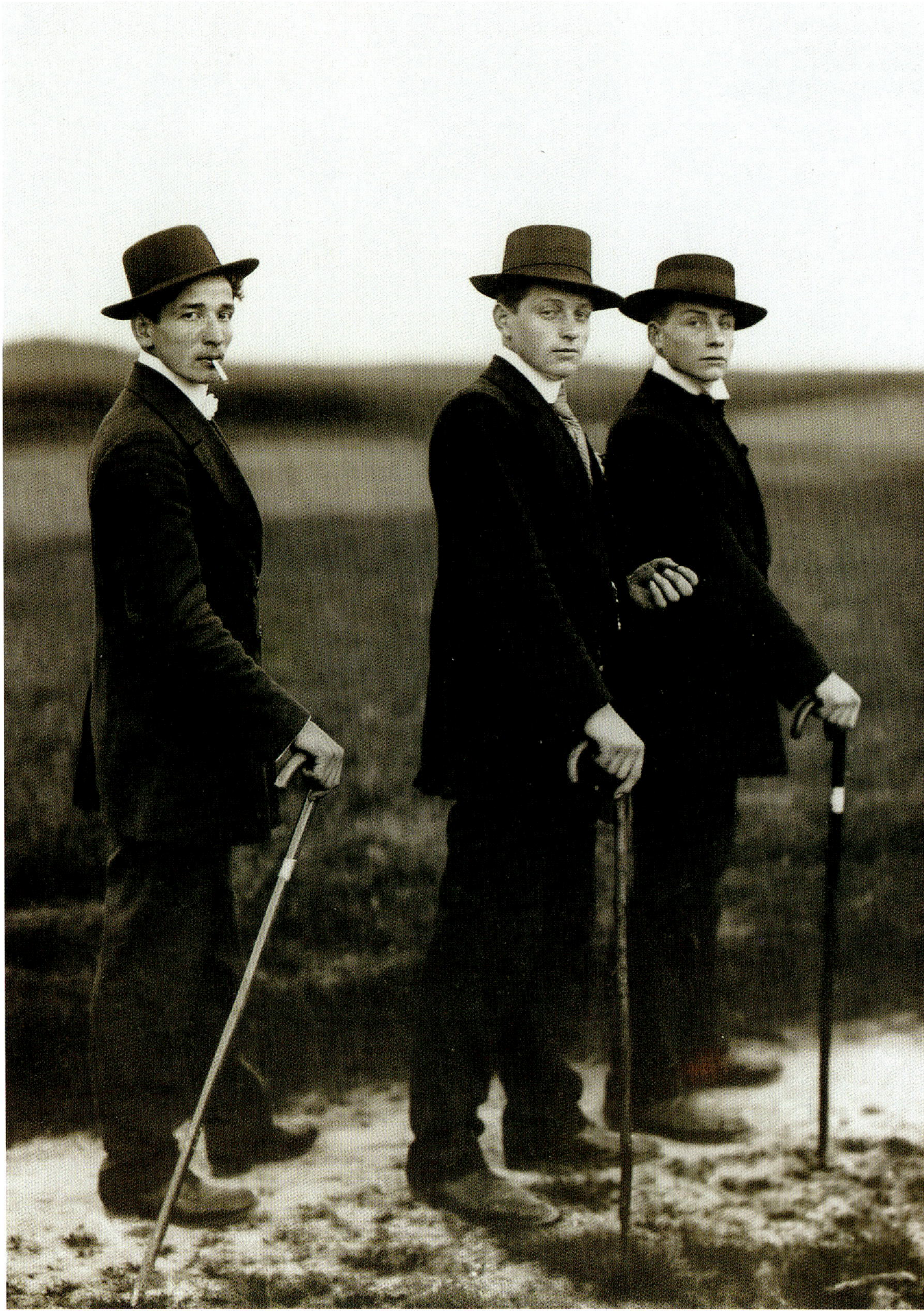

August Sander
Berlin coal-heaver, 1929
Berliner Kohlenträger
Black-and-white photograph
Cologne, August Sander Archiv

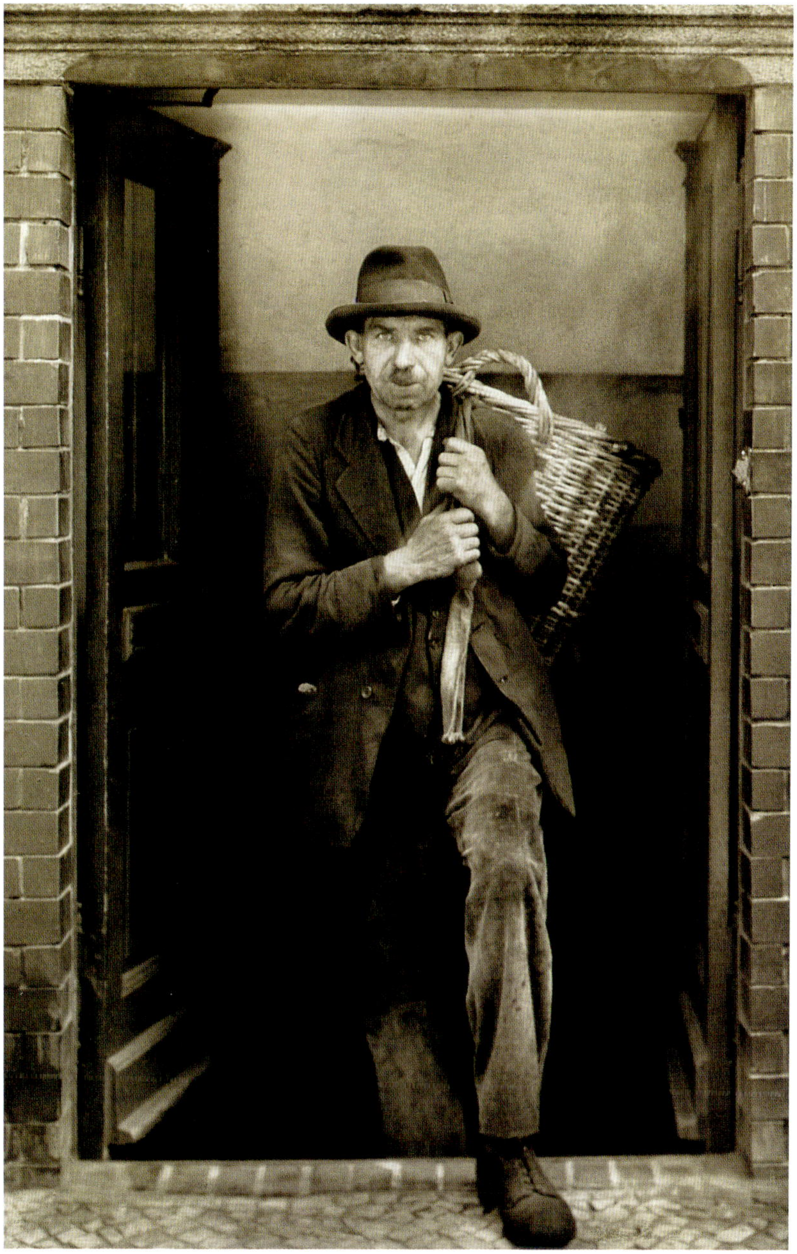

The people in Sander's photographs are "heart-and-soul" farmers, craftsmen, workers and industrialists. Their profession is not alien to their nature; rather, it serves to characterize them also as private individuals. The photographer was concerned to enable the subjects of his portraits to appear as representatives of social strata and professions, such a view therefore rejecting the upper-class ideal of the "autonomous personality".

August Sander
Young farmers, Westerwald, 1914
Jungbauern, Westerwald
Black-and-white photograph
Cologne, August Sander Archiv

without it being necessary to impose strict delimitations here. Added to this were Russian influences stemming from the photography of the Revolution and its 1920s propaganda, as well as impulses from the developing Surrealist movement. However, a fascination for the "beauty of technology" was typical of every variant of new photography. There were also many personal links connecting painting and photography. One of the two "founding fathers" of Neue Sachlichkeit, the art critic Franz Roh who has been mentioned several times, edited an important volume of selected Neue Sachlichkeit and avant-gardist photography ("Foto-Auge", 1929), in collaboration with the typographer Jan Tschichold. Otto Dix, for his part, was a friend of the

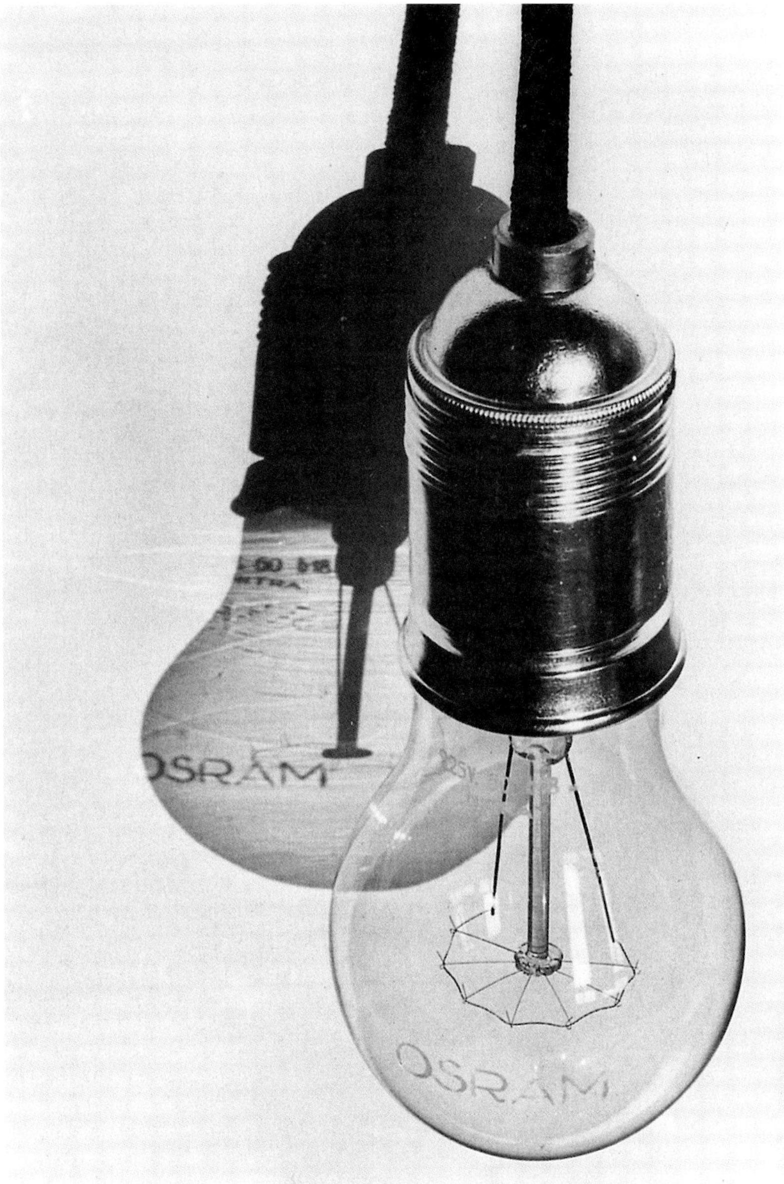

Neue Sachlichkeit photographer Hugo Erfurth, and the two did portraits of each other. More will be said below about the links between Karl Nierendorf, the leading Neue Sachlichkeit gallery-owner, and Karl Blossfeldt, the photographer.

Blossfeldt, Hans Finsler, Albert Renger-Patzsch and August Sander are among the most important Neue Sachlichkeit photographers. Hans Finsler was responsible from 1926 to 1932 for the important class of object photography at the School of Arts and Crafts in Burg Giebichenstein, Halle. His imaginative still lifes create variations upon those exactly recorded objects which are also to be found in Neue Sachlichkeit painting, such as the electric lightbulb (illus. p. 188). Its emphatic linearity shows analogies to drawings by Dischinger (illus. p. 189) and Hubbuch. Incidentally, Finsler

Hans Finsler
Electric lightbulb, 1928
Elektrische Birne
Black-and-white photograph
Halle, Staatliche Galerie Moritzburg

The "aggressiveness of precise reproduction, wherever possible going into even the most insignificant details", seen by Rudolf Dischinger as an important stylistic element of Neue Sachlichkeit, is particularly characteristic of his own work. In this respect it is every bit the equal of photography, as can be seen from his "Electric Kettle". The differentiated shading is remarkable, imbuing the objects with a high degree of plasticity.

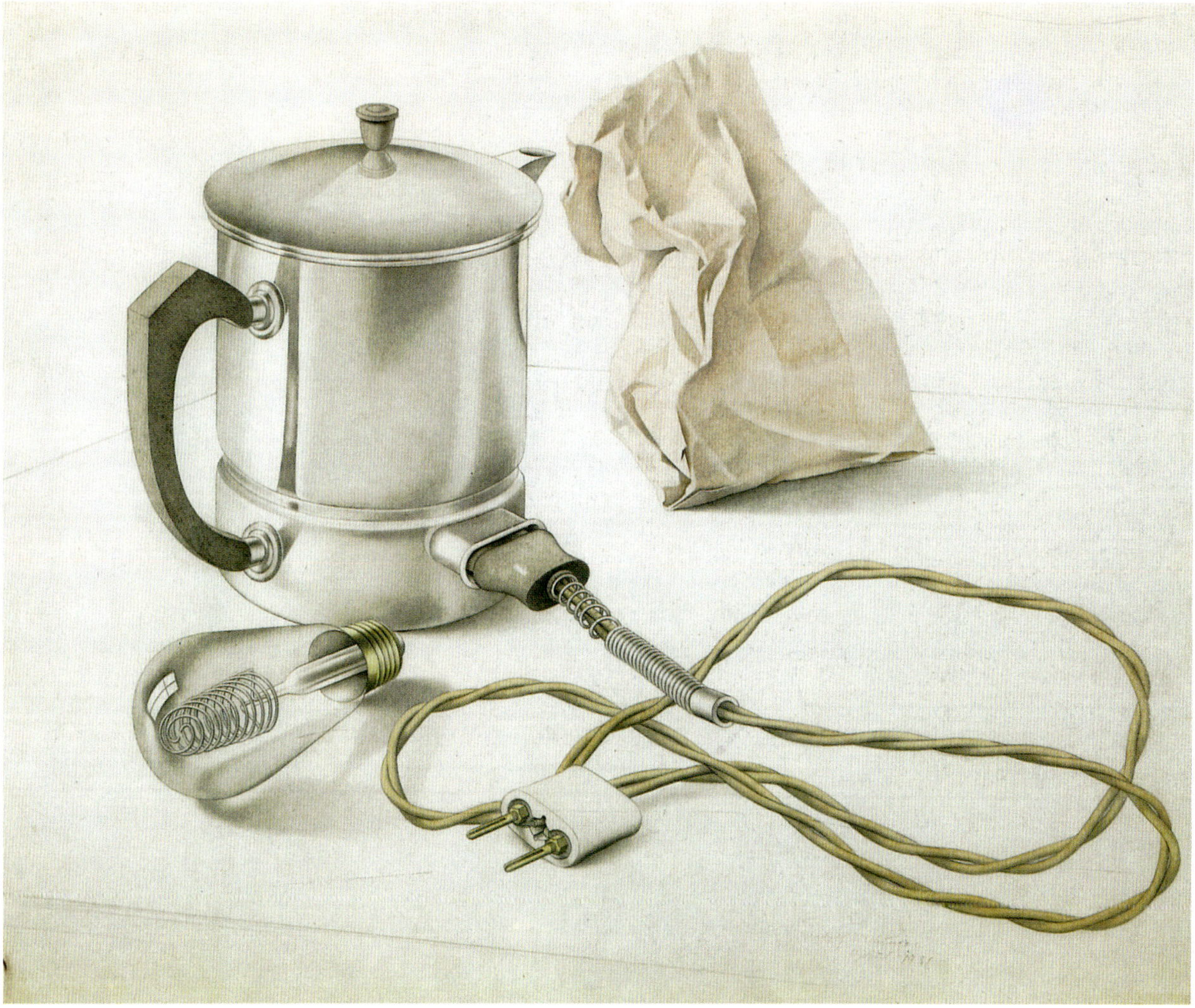

Rudolf Dischinger
Electric Kettle, 1931
Elektro-Kocher
Pencil, 57 x 68.5 cm
Stuttgart, Graphische Sammlungen, Staatsgalerie Stuttgart

was to organize a legendary school ball at Burg Giebichenstein in December 1925 entitled the "Neue Sachlichkeit Ball".

The year 1928 saw the publication of "Die Welt ist schön" (The World is Beautiful), a large volume of photographs by Albert Renger-Patzsch. The title became a symbol for the Neue Sachlichkeit attitude to the world, and the volume itself a showcase for photography from the Neue Sachlichkeit tendency. Its fame was further increased through a favourable review by Thomas Mann, who gave an astonishingly precise programmatic description of photographic objectivity in confirming that Renger-Patzsch had "... identified what is individual and objective out of the to-ing and fro-ing of the world perceived through the senses, isolated it, elevated it, intensified it, rendered it significant, given it a soul".[91] The slogan of the "beautiful world" inevitably became the target of a good many foolish remarks, such as that by Walter Benjamin; however, these were directed at the wrong person, since Renger-Patzsch's original suggestion for the volume's title – one discarded by the publishers – had been quite simply "Die Dinge" (Things). Renger-Patzsch photographed appliances, machines, and individual machine parts (illus. p. 184), as well as gigantic coke ovens in the Ruhr valley, and from time to time even plants. His photographs make an impression upon the observer either through the massiveness of the forms (*Regenerator*, illus. p. 185) or – as in his plant studies – through his imaginative isolation of the details.

The portrait studies by August Sander, the Rhenish photographer, have been regarded for some time as the stylistic and iconographic epitome; in fact, however, purely formal motifs were far from his mind. Living in a charming Rhenish provincialism, Sander had already decided in the years prior to the First World War to undertake a large-scale project entitled "Menschen des 20. Jahrhunderts" (20th-Century People), prompted by a particular combination of encyclopaedic and commercial interests. His intention was to document human types, grouped according to class, profession, sex and age. Sander's unerring eye and his feeling for what was typical and unusual created an incomparable portrait gallery, one which says a very great deal about the social conditions and the spirit of the German people[92] in the first thirty years of our century. It proved impossible to complete the immense project; the only part to be published – in 1929 – was the introductory volume, "Antlitz der Zeit" (Countenance of the Times). It included an enthusiastic foreword by Alfred Döblin, who was of the opinion that the reader was presented here with "a kind of cultural history – or rather, sociology – of the past thirty years".[93] The astonishing fact that two great writers – Mann and Döblin – had thus commented upon volumes of photography within the space of one year is vivid evidence of the sharp increase in the prestige of photography during the Weimar period.

While August Sander's initial photographs, appearing around 1914,

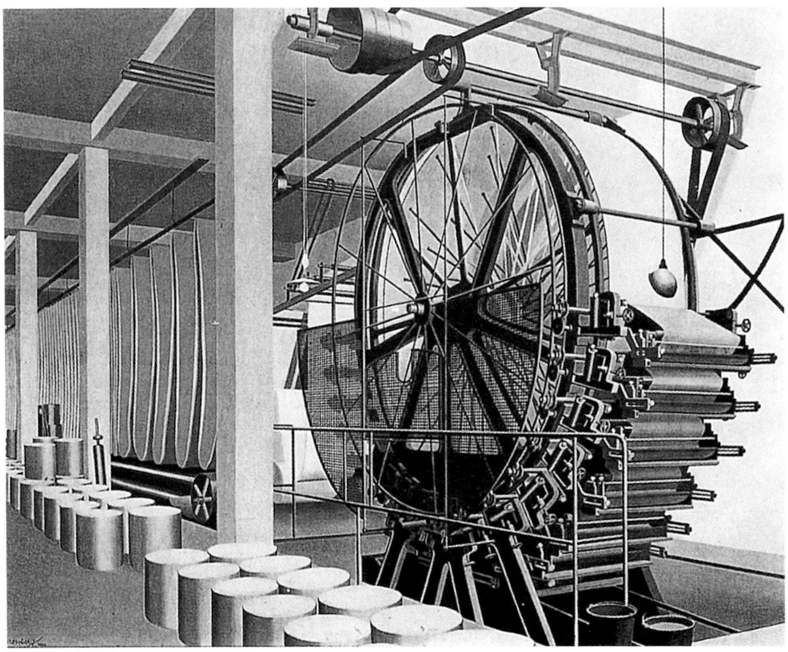

Carl Grossberg
Paper Machine, 1934
Papiermaschine
Oil on wood, 90 x 118 cm
Private collection

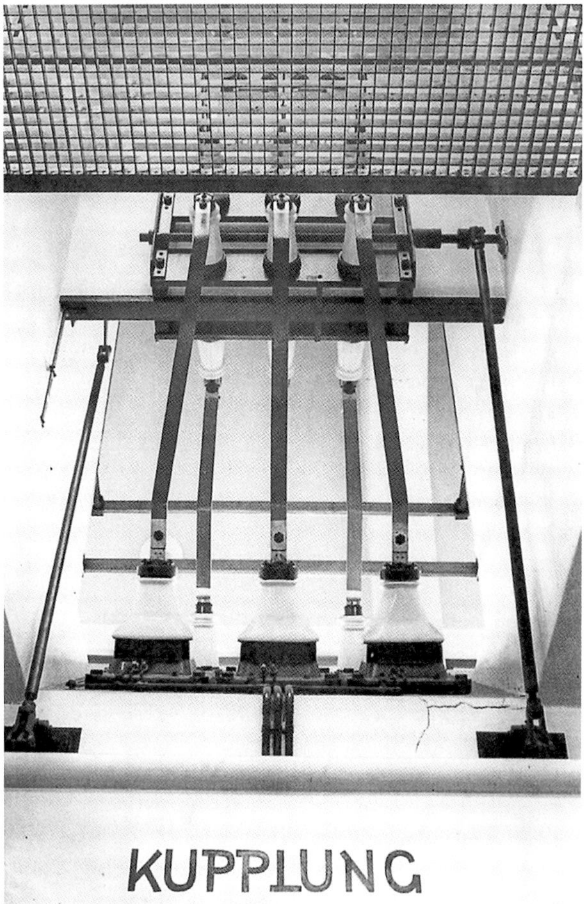

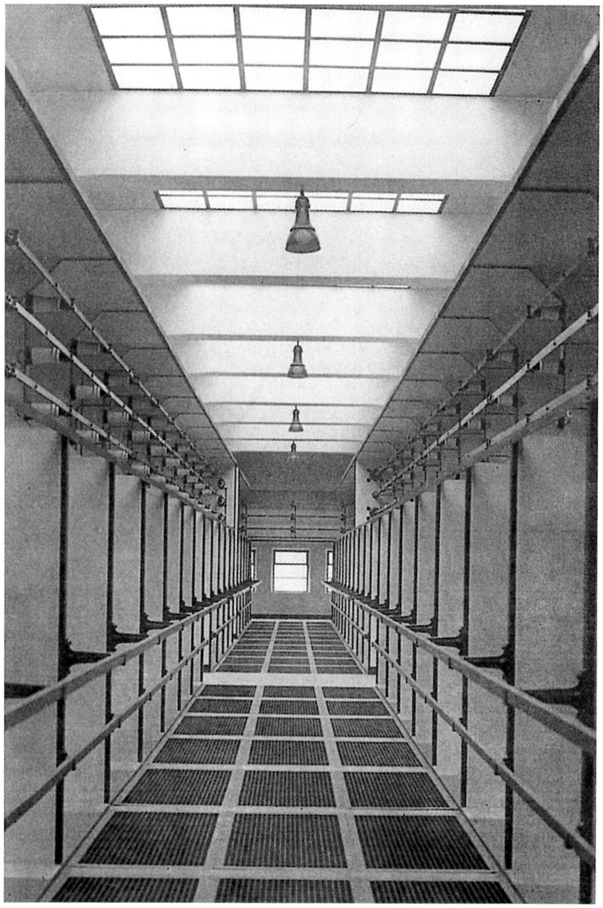

were still indebted to the art photography of Impressionism, the portrait studies which he did in the 1920s owe much in their spatial conception and figure isolation to the stylistic principles of Neue Sachlichkeit. His photograph *Unemployed Man*, for example, reveals the familiar diagonal perspective, sliced in characteristic fashion. Sander's photographs are linked with the painted portraits of Neue Sachlichkeit art above all through his infallible feeling for the class-specific element in pose and clothing. More: as a rule, his likenesses reveal greater concentration and greater expression than the painted portraits; they are able to do without attributive, characterizing additions. Furthermore, Sander's acquaintance with Räderscheidt, the Cologne painter, led to a special connection between painting and photography. Where the 1925 portrait series of the Räderscheidt couple celebrates, with psychological exhibitionism, the inner alienation between husband and wife, Sander's *Portrait Photograph of the Räderscheidts* of 1927 is a pastiche-like reference back to the painter's hidden self-portraits of the early 1920s.

The situation with regard to Karl Blossfeldt is similar to that of Molière's Monsieur Jourdain: without being aware of doing so, he created photographs for purely scientific reasons which anticipated many formal principles of Neue Sachlichkeit. Blossfeldt had been conducting intensive photobotanical studies since 1896, and would later dabble in questions of aesthetics, albeit without daring to reveal his work to a wider public. It was

LEFT:
Hans Finsler
Klosterstraße transformer, detailed circuit view from above, "Coupler", 1929
Transformator Klosterstraße, Schaltdetail von oben nach unten, "Kupplung"
Black-and-white photograph
Halle, Staatliche Galerie Moritzburg

RIGHT:
Hans Finsler
Klosterstraße transformer, central corridor above, 1929
Transformator Klosterstraße, zentraler Gang oben
Black-and-white photograph
Halle, Staatliche Galerie Moritzburg

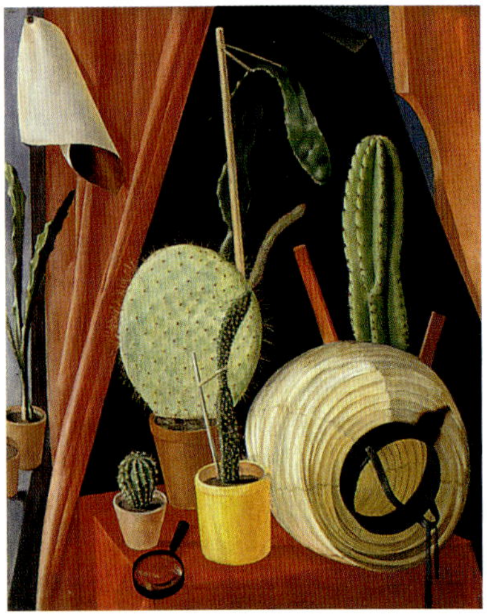

Fritz Burmann
Still Life with Cacti, 1925
Stilleben mit Kakteen
Oil on wood, 66.5 x 53.5 cm
Berlin, Staatliche Museen zu Berlin – Preußischer Kulturbesitz, Nationalgalerie

not until the end of the 1920s that the artist's photographs of plants and flowers (illus. p. 193) became well-known, among them examples that he had combined in diagrams with architectonic forms of art for purposes of comparison ("Urformen der Kunst" – Prototypes of Art, 1928; "Wundergarten der Natur" – Nature's Garden of Wonders, 1932). Blossfeldt's work was discovered and promoted by Karl Nierendorf, the well-known Berlin gallery-owner, who had dedicated himself above all to Neue Sachlichkeit. Following the publication of "Urformen", Blossfeldt's œuvre became the embodiment of Neue Sachlichkeit photography, including works which had come into being in the course of the search for simple scientific documentation a decade or more before the style had emerged. This paradoxical circumstance may be seen as pointing to the unusual quality of Neue Sachlichkeit photography, in which – under certain conditions – detail and object could themselves contribute to the style's formation. Bound up with this is also the particular ambivalence between those elements which characterize a form and those documenting it: for Blossfeldt, objectivity ("Sachlichkeit") is used as a label with which to refer to the documented objects, while the observer perceives these objects in the first place as formal pictorial compositions.

Numerous other parallels between painting and Neue Sachlichkeit photography can be drawn. In the sphere of sociologically orientated photography, a comparison of Leo Breuer's *Coal Man* (illus. p. 181) with August Sander's *Berlin coal-heaver* (illus. p. 187), published two years previously, points to a direct process of inspiration, with the photograph as its starting-point. Charles Sheeler, the American Neue Sachlichkeit painter, while often photographing ships' funnels, also did numerous painted studies of this motif (*Upper Deck*, 1923). A comparison here with Hans Finsler's *Ship's Funnels* is also instructive. The same holds true for the realm of machinery depictions, where Carl Grossberg's painting *Transmission Belts* is strongly reminiscent of Renger-Patzsch' *Pulleys*. A comparison of plant still lifes by Dischinger, Lenk and Burmann, among others, with Blossfeldt's botanical photographs (illus. p. 193) points to a possible – albeit not conclusive – influence by the plant photographs upon the design of the painted flower motifs. The field of portraiture reveals especially close connections to have existed. Such a list could easily be continued. The idea behind Ilse Bing's *Self-Portrait in Mirrors* is the same as that which may be found in Willi Müller-Hufschmid's *Self-Portrait in front of a Mirror*. And, finally, several photographic counterparts may be found for Rudolf Wacker's depictions of dolls, despite the rarity of the motif.

A satisfactory study of the connections between painting and Neue Sachlichkeit photography has not yet appeared.[94] It is difficult to draw hard-and-fast delimitations between direct influences and similarities which can be traced back to a common visual approach to things within this brief period of art. It would certainly be very rewarding to conduct a more precise survey, one which also included the important field of film and theatre photography. Be that as it may, this was a time which discovered the seemingly unlimited possibilities of photography for itself and also played them off now and again against painting. Lajos Kassak, the Hungarian Constructivist, attacked the links between Neue Sachlichkeit painting and photography in the name of the strict mechanical objectivity of illustration: "The painter's eye sees things from a subjective angle, the lens of a camera from an objective angle. This objective manner of seeing things and the anti-emotional nature of the camera set photography today ... above the recently advanced style of painting in the spirit of 'New Objectivity'."[95]

ILLUSTRATIONS PAGE 193
TOP LEFT:
Karl Blossfeldt
Acer rufinerve, maple, winged fruit

TOP RIGHT:
Karl Blossfeldt
Orchidaceae, orchid, young shoot

BOTTOM LEFT:
Karl Blossfeldt
Cynara scolymus L., artichoke, young head

BOTTOM RIGHT:
Karl Blossfeldt
Dryopteris filix mas., wood fern, curled-up young frond

Zülpich, Karl Blossfeldt Archiv, Ann and Jürgen Wilde

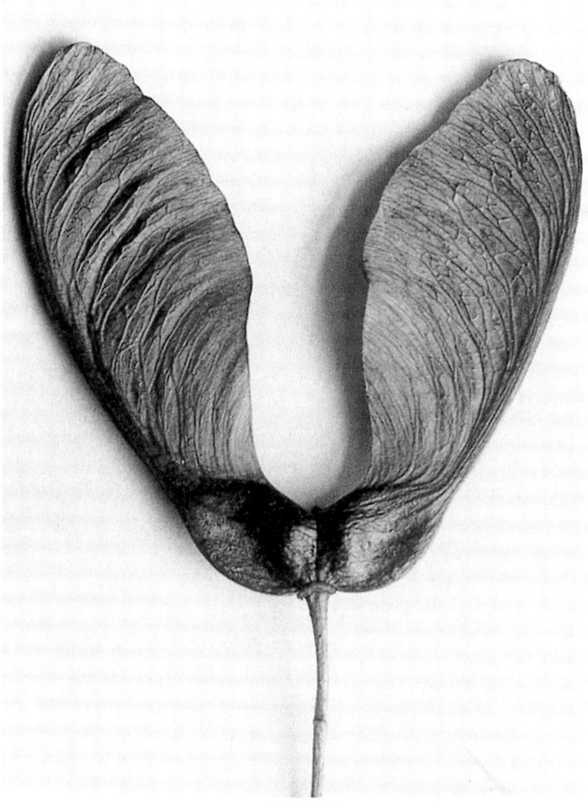

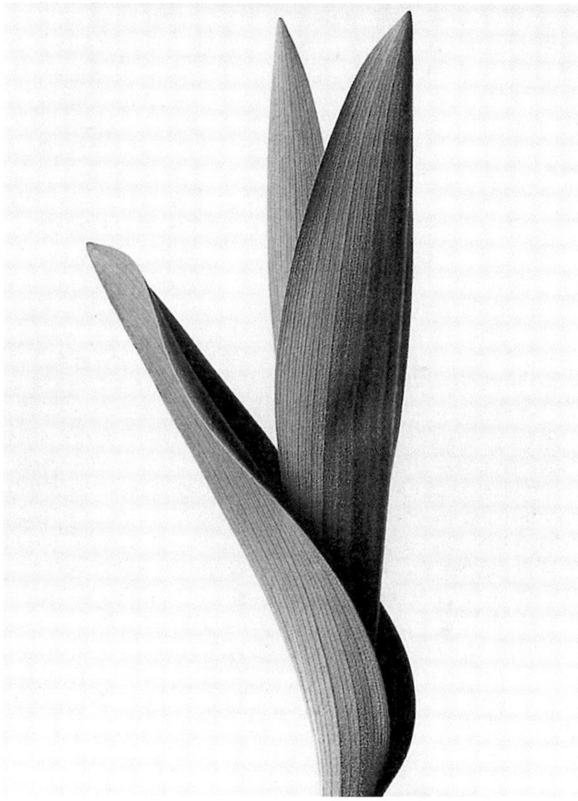

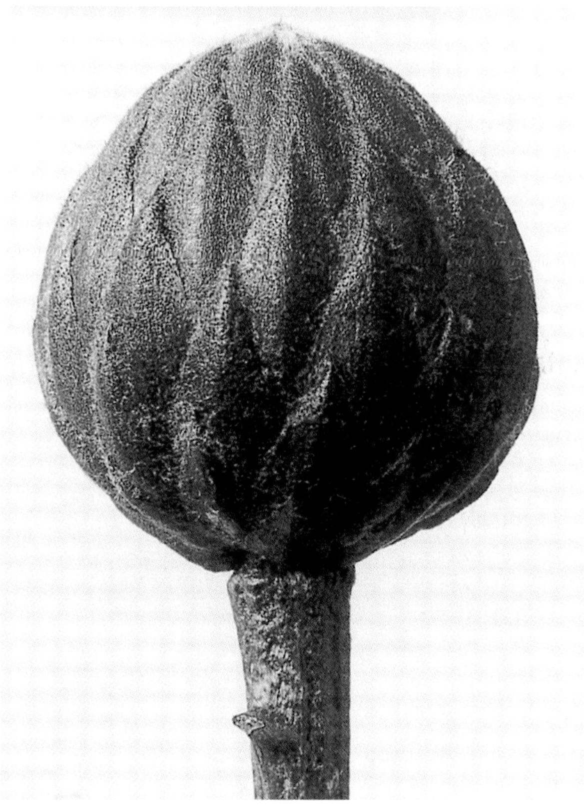

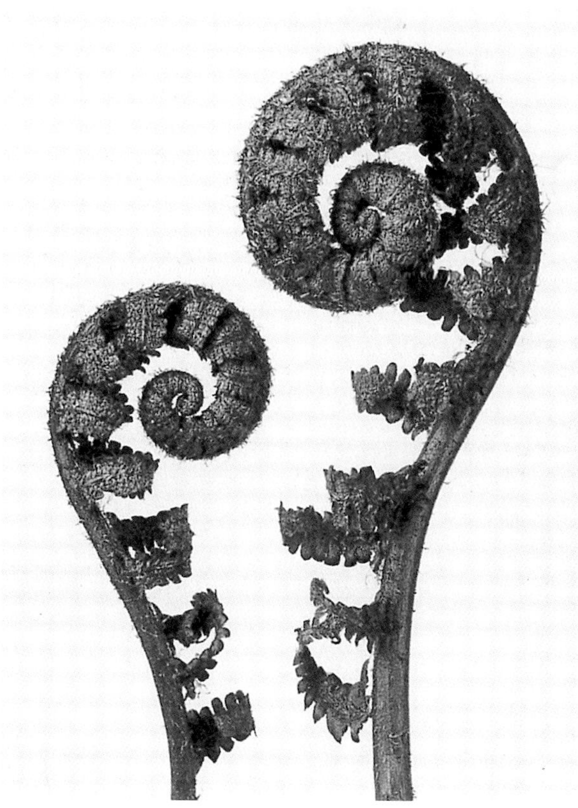

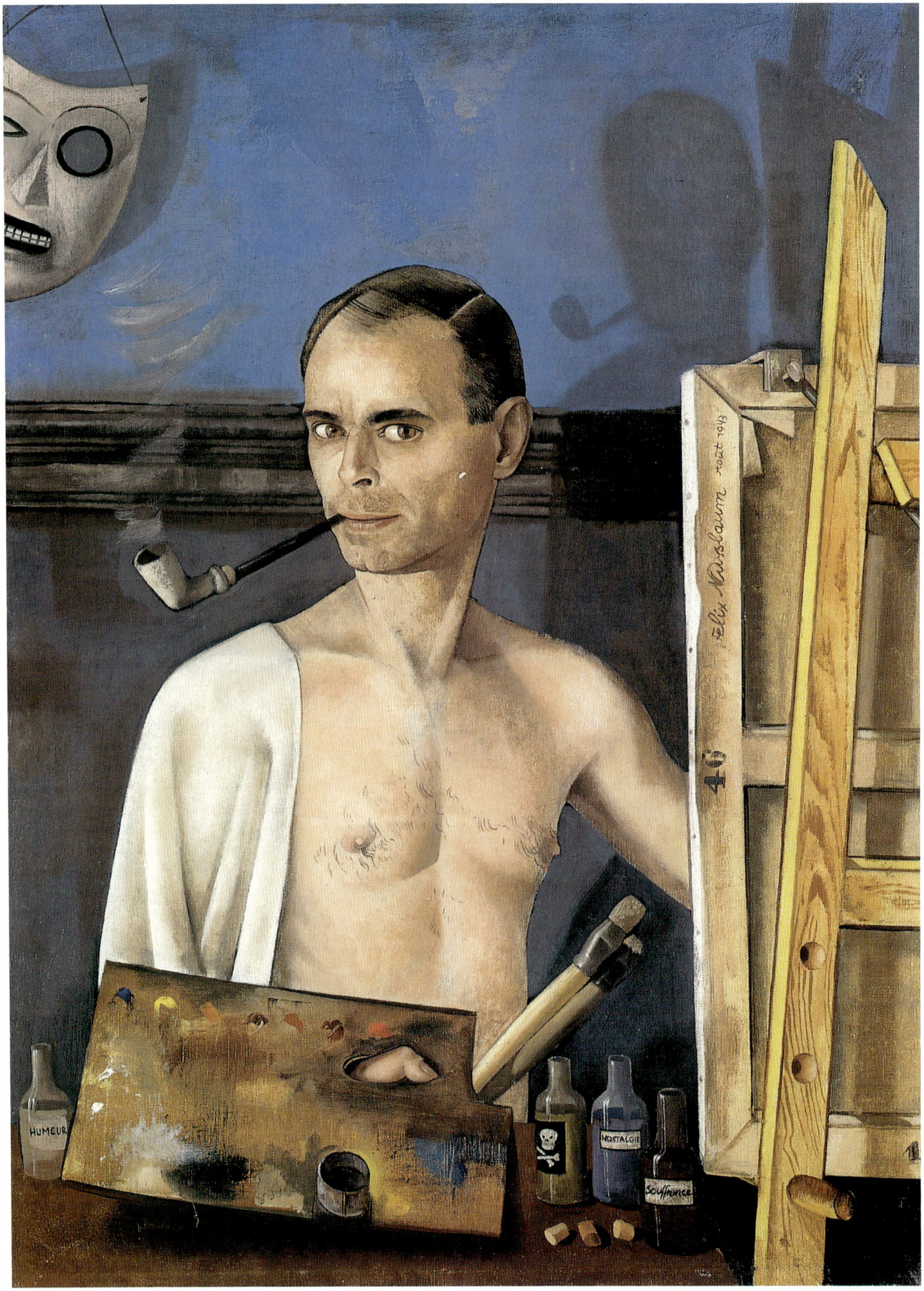
HUMEUR
NOSTALGIE
Souffrance
46

The End of the New Objectivity

The political and financial crisis of the years from 1930 to 1933 had a direct negative effect upon artistic life. During the Weimar Republic's first period of crisis, from 1919 to 1923, many speculative purchases of artistic objects had nevertheless taken place; however, the consistently deflationist policy that had followed now led to a dramatic crisis on the art market. In contrast to the years around 1920 in which Verism was born, the current aggravated political climate seemed merely to repel the artists; however, their great material need brought with it a susceptibility on the part of some of them to the social demagoguery of National Socialism. Not until the shocking fact of the assumption of power by the Nazis on 30th January 1933 would an end be put to this kind of fatalistic lethargy.

The year 1933 began with a tactical manœuvre by the old art establishment. The Kestner Society in Hanover – hitherto one-sidedly dedicated to avant-gardist art – organized a large-scale exhibition in March, significantly entitled "Neue Deutsche Romantik" (New German Romanticism). What had formerly been the stronghold of Schwitters and abstract art was thereby taking up a type of exhibition which, with varying succes, had been pursued under this selfsame name since 1929 by art associations and provincial museums of a rather conservative tendency. The Hanover show displayed pictures by Kanoldt, Schrimpf and Radziwill. In his foreword to the catalogue, Justus Bier, the important art historian, emphasized the elements that the works of these three artists had in common with Runge and Caspar David Friedrich. Neither Bier, who would later be forced to emigrate, nor the renowned Kestner Society can be accused of hyper-German or even directly fascist tendencies, yet there was already more than a trace of conformity in the air. Were all these merely rearguard actions, or also attempts at deceptive packaging in which fundamental connections between declining Neue Sachlichkeit and emerging Nazi art could be recognized? Put another way, does Neue Sachlichkeit in fact belong indirectly to the precursors of a fascist style of painting which in 1933 was as yet present only in barest outline, as is often maintained?

The answer to this question can only be a clear, flat negative. It is true that, in the case of the aforementioned painters of "New German Romanticism", their Neue Sachlichkeit allegiances become evident only on second glance. Within the band of second-rate artists, too, there were cases of a personal union of Neue Sachlichkeit and Nazism, seen for example in those instances in which fascist painting overlays or makes use of Neue Sachlichkeit elements. However, one cannot and should not speak of a

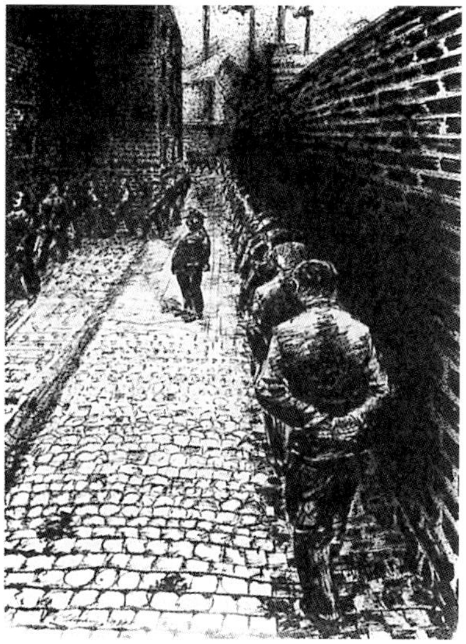

Karl Schwesig
Daily Exercise, from the "Schlegelkeller" cycle, 1937
Täglicher Spaziergang, aus dem Zyklus "Schlegelkeller"

Felix Nussbaum
Self-Portrait at the Easel, 1943
Selbstbildnis an der Staffelei
Oil on canvas, 51 x 39.5 cm
Osnabrück, Kulturgeschichtliches Museum

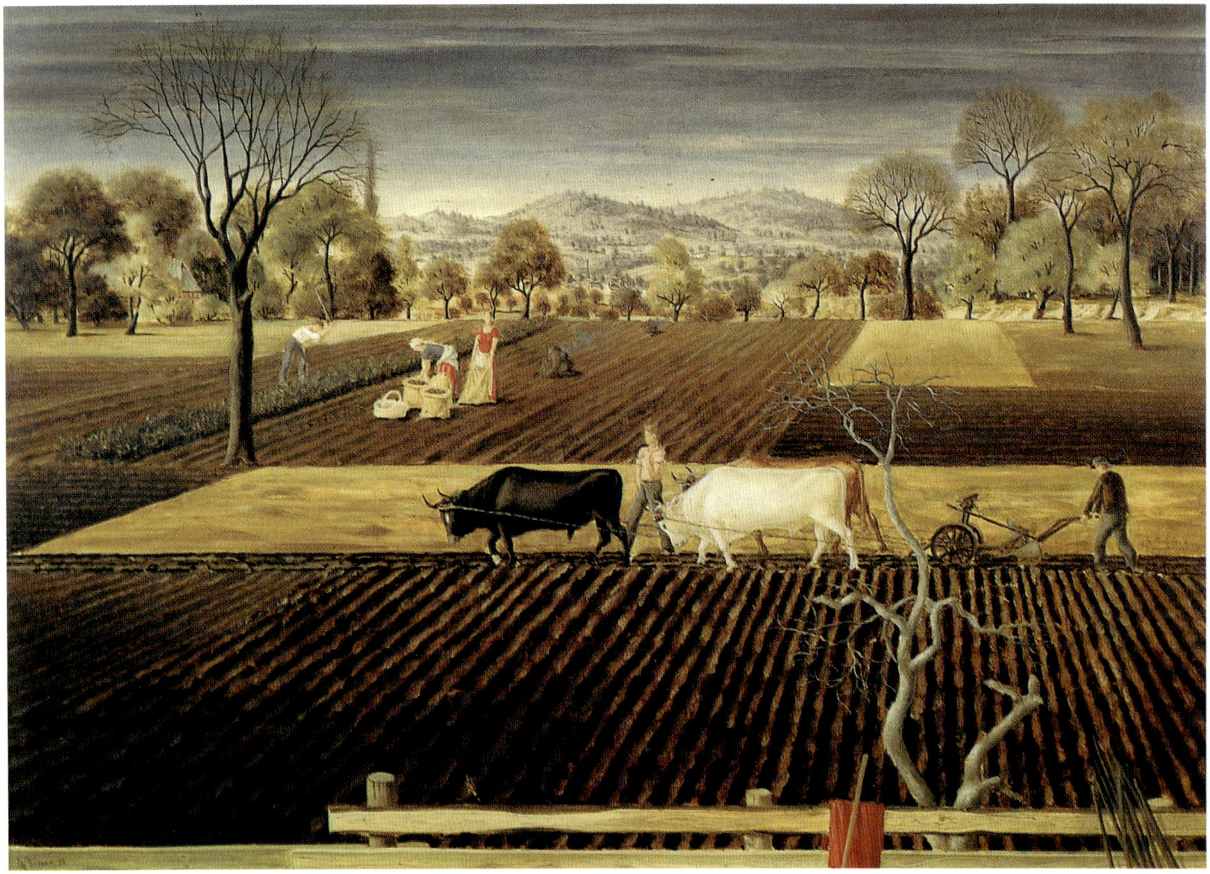

Werner Peiner
Working in the Fields, 1931
Feldarbeit
Oil on wood, 55 x 70 cm
Düsseldorf, Kunstmuseum Düsseldorf im Ehrenhof

synthesis of these two directions. The leading Nazi art theoreticians regarded Neue Sachlichkeit as a *quantité négligeable*, a second-rate movement within the general structure of the hated "art of the Weimar system". There was an ongoing – at times heated – argument between Joseph Goebbels and Alfred Rosenberg regarding the evaluation of Expressionism, decided in 1934 by Hitler's decree in favour of the conservatives. The Bauhaus was immediately anathemized, as were all "isms" of French origin. Nazi opposition to the early Verist works and proletarian revolutionary art arose to a certain extent automatically, if for no other reason than because of their content. Throughout all these polemics, Neue Sachlichkeit for its part continued to eke out a somewhat shadowy existence.

It was not until October 1933 that the nationalist attitude was laid down, in a speech by Wilhelm Frick, Minister of the Interior. Making his debut in the sphere of art, he demanded: "Away with the spirit of subversion... those ice-cold, completely un-German constructions that do business under the name of Neue Sachlichkeit must surely be at the end of their useful life by now..."[96] The emotive word was above all that of objectivity itself, an attitude completely unacceptable for an ardent National Socialist artist. Hitler also helped to finish off the movement in a sentence inimitable in its compactness from his Nuremberg party-conference speech of September 1935, in which he settled the score with "all those who blather on about Dadaist-Cubist and Futurist experience and objectivity".[97] In contrast to the other degenerate "isms", the National Socialists were concerned in the case of Neue Sachlichkeit less with questions of form than with the artistic attitude as such; thus, a side door remained open.

However, the verdict against Neue Sachlichkeit was substantiated very soon by concrete administrative decisions. The majority of the Neue Sachlichkeit painters and graphic artists lost their positions at art schools and art academies in 1933 or soon thereafter. Some from the younger generation of Neue Sachlichkeit made careers for themselves under the Nazi rulers (Albert Henrich, Georg Siebert, Werner Peiner, Bernhard Dörries), although they could easily be identified in the aggressive phalanx of Nazi artists as a whole through a certain degree of restraint. Remnants of Neue Sachlichkeit forms were able to survive in Nazi pictures of landscapes, families and farmers, trimmed with a striving after inwardness. The transition to a Romantic or Old High German-Dutch stylization in painting did not of itself have to be Nazi. It first required a certain formal and ideological intensification – for example through a title such as *German Soil* – before it could appear as such, as can be seen from the complexity of the content in Peiner's landscape pictures (illus. p. 196). The break was occasionally visible in the work of an individual artist. Bernhard Dörries' family pictures, for instance, are characterized by the insistent National Socialist ideal of motherhood, among other elements, whereas his still lifes and studio pictures from the 1930s could also have been done in the 1920s.

Whereas the majority of the Neue Sachlichkeit artists lost their posts, Kanoldt, the naive and idealistic Party member, and Radziwill, who had become such in 1933 from opportunistic motives, were appointed to new teaching positions. Lenk and Schrimpf, aligned with no particular party, also received posts at art academies. By a curious stroke of fate, Schrimpf, a former pacifist, came under the protection of Rudolf Hess. However one might judge the extent to which they conformed to or collaborated with Nazi cultural policy, they maintained their integrity in the narrow sense of the word. Kanoldt fought a battle – for a while even successfully – against scheming leading figures of the "Heimatstil"[98] from the same mould as Hans-Adolf Bühler, the Baden Nazi, until he himself increasingly fell foul

The painter Adolf Wissel was following the line of the Nazis in the content of his farmer pictures, the Nazis demanding that art provide a "demonstration of the German people's creative will to live". Discussing such idealizing pictures, Nazi art criticism praised "the artistic portrayal of German life: German people, work, its powerful men, the German landscape, farming life, the grace and beauty of German women". There are unmistakable formal references to Neue Sachlichkeit in the "Kalenberg Farmer's Family", a picture acquired by Hitler; what distinguishes it from Neue Sachlichkeit ist its content and its ideological criteria.

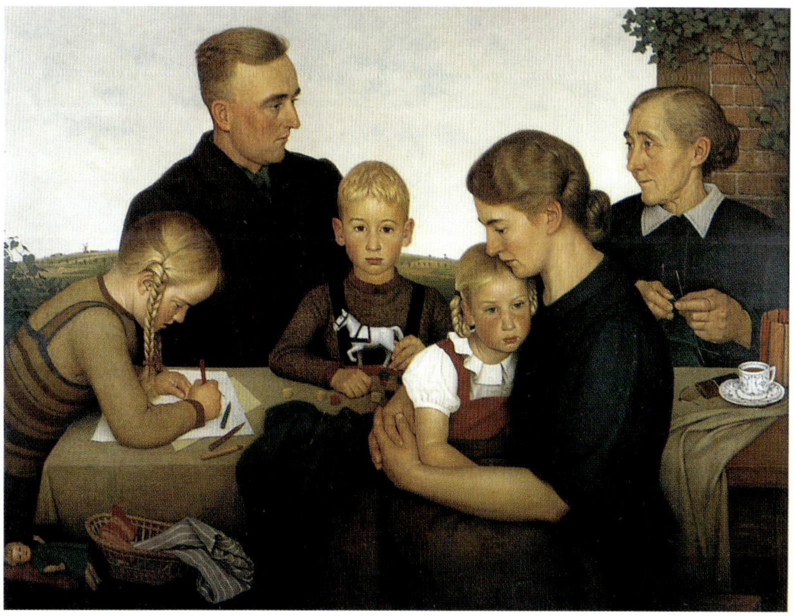

Adolf Wissel
Kalenberg Farmer's Family, 1939
Kalenberger Bauernfamilie
Oil on canvas, 150 x 200 cm
Munich, Oberfinanzdirektion

of the system. He and Lenk also attempted to help persecuted colleagues, Lenk, for example, demonstratively exhibiting in a two-man Berlin show with the ostracized Otto Dix in 1935.

The persecuted artistic avant-garde naturally saw all this differently. In 1934, a desperate Oskar Schlemmer, upon enquiring of Count Baudissin, the notorious director of the Essen Museum, which modern artists the Nazis were prepared to accept, was given the clear and disarming answer: Kanoldt, Schrimpf, Lenk. This led him to make this slightly malicious note in his diary, "The instinct of the National Socialists is thinking first of all of the Sachlichkeit painters ... this puritanism that paints nature cannot satisfy them in the long run."[99] Schlemmer would of course prove to be right. In 1937 and 1938, Nazi cultural policy was to become radically stricter. The time for compromise of any nature was past, and the last areas of freedom (with the exception of the legendary DAF factory exhibitions) were eliminated. The close season was also over for those few Neue Sachlichkeit painters who were still acceptable. Seventeen works by Kanoldt were removed from public museums and collections in the course of the confiscations stemming from the "Degenerate Art" campaign. He left the Academy of Fine Art in Berlin-Schöneberg, now having only a master's studio at the Prussian Academy of Arts. In 1937, Schrimpf's works appeared in the "Degenerate Art" exhibition at the end of 1937, he, too, was forced out of the Academy in Berlin-Schöneberg. A completely broken man, he died in 1938, followed a year later by Kanoldt, the "degenerate Party member". Lenk, in protest at Nazi cultural policy, also withdrew in 1938 from public life. Radziwill, who had already been reprimanded previously, was expelled from the ranks of the NSDAP in 1938, Hitler's party unerringly ridding itself of its last artist of any importance.

The decisive factor in the break between Neue Sachlichkeit and National Socialist painting could be seen in the premisses on which a work's content rested. Even at its most classicist, Neue Sachlichkeit was never an art picturing blonde youths with bodies of steel; it demonstrated little predilection for farmers close to nature, a class which it tended to depict with a certain

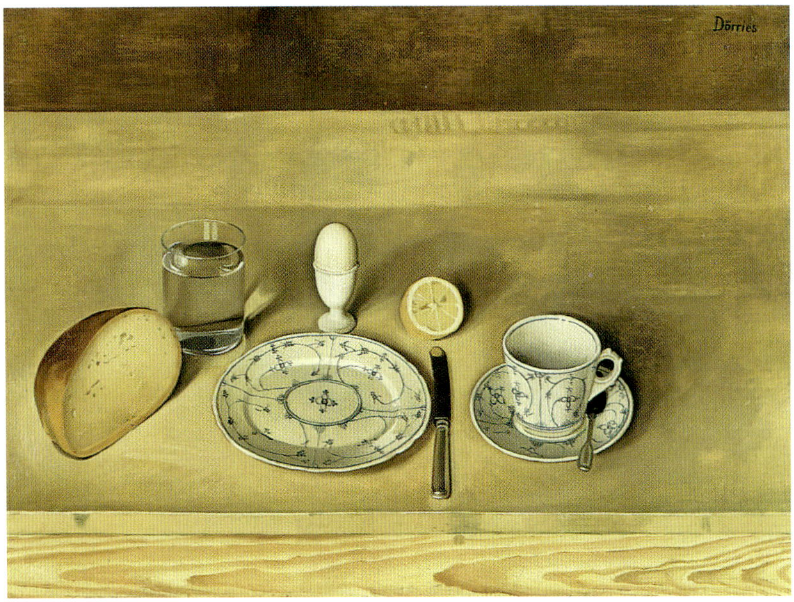

Bernhard Dörries
Breakfast Still Life, 1927
Frühstücksstilleben
Oil on hardboard, 51 x 70 cm
Hanover, Sprengel Museum

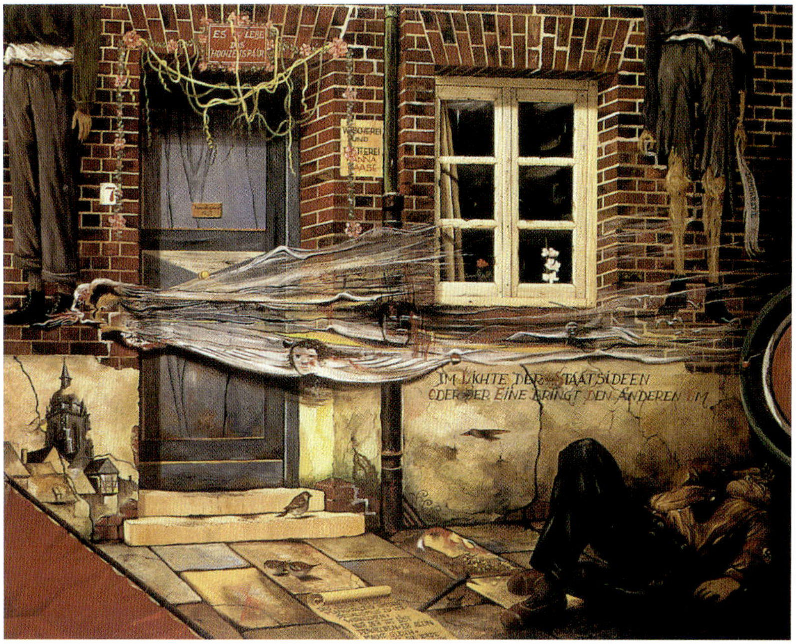

Franz Radziwill
Demons, 1933
Dämonen
Oil on canvas, 99 x 125 cm
Private collection

degree of malice, nor for blonde Amazons awaiting a Teutonic warrior. Nor did the petit-bourgeois voyeurism of Nazi nude painting find its echo even in the Neue Sachlichkeit idyllists. Of the intellectual leitmotifs to be found in Nazi art – pure-bloodedness, the sense of community, the truth embodied in the soil, strength, racial purity, the sense of security – only the last mentioned had certain points of contact with the fundamental themes of Neue Sachlichkeit art. With the possible exception of such works as the frescoes done by Kay Nebel in the Schleswig district assembly building (1926), moreover, there was absolutely nothing that Neue Sachlichkeit had to offer in the way of the monumental style of painting held in such high regard by the new rulers.

Felix Nussbaum

The pictures by Felix Nussbaum from Osnabrück stand out among the Neue Sachlichkeit works of the period after 1930. Of Jewish descent, this German painter emigrated for good in 1933. Between 1940 and 1944, living under terrible threat mostly in a garret hiding-place in Brussels, he did a series of moving pictures based on his situation. One of these shows the artist with the compulsory yellow Star of David and Jewish identity card (1943). It is of course difficult to discuss these powerful pictures, marked by growing desperation and the outright fear of death, in purely stylistic terms; nonetheless, a brief attempt will help to establish Nussbaum's position in the succession of Neue Sachlichkeit.

His paintings, run through with revealing references to Italian Pittura metafisica and to Surrealism, clearly take up Neue Sachlichkeit elements. The painter owes these to his art studies in late-1920s Germany. Nussbaum's Brussels *Self-Portrait with Felicia Platek* is a moving allegory of the power of erotic bonds, a power which triumphs over the elemental instinct of self-preservation. Nussbaum stayed in Brussels at the urging of Felicia

The Jewish painter Felix Nussbaum spent the last four years of his life in a hiding-place in Brussels to escape persecution by the Nazis. His pictures from this period are marked by fear and a wavering between hope and resignation. Every trace of hope has been erased in "The Damned": only a few months before his death, the painter (the man in the foreground wearing a cap) anticipates with horror his end in Auschwitz.

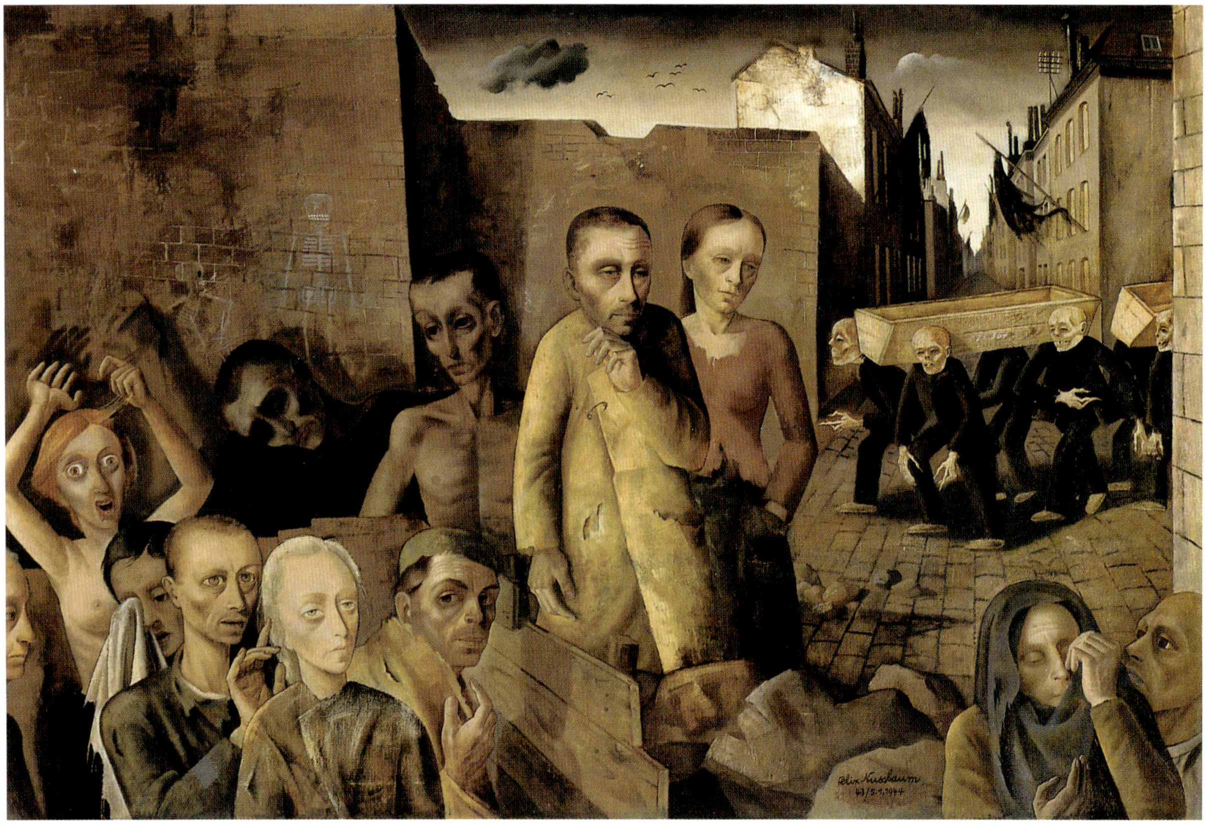

Felix Nussbaum
The Damned, 1944
Die Verdammten
Oil on canvas, 101 x 155 cm
Osnabrück, Kulturgeschichtliches Museum

Platek – who was already inwardly resigned to her fate – although the situation in the city was becoming ever more threatening for him. The artist adapts elements from Neue Sachlichkeit and Pittura metafisica influences in virtuoso style, although van Eyck's famous Arnolfini portrait and Christian Schad's works also acted as models for his composition. The work reveals a last flaring up of human sensuality, while at a deeper level the metaphysically substantiated alienation of man and woman simultaneously becomes evident – something previously observed as a major motif in the works of both Schad and Räderscheidt. And, finally, an allegory of constant threat is present, the daily, frightening, bad news, as symbolized by the antisemitic political smear-sheet of the German occupying powers, "Le Soir", lying on the floor.

Nussbaum spent the last four years of his life in a hiding-place in Brussels. He was attempting in his pictures from this time to overcome his nightmares, the terror of isolation, and the sense of being at the mercy of others: displaced persons, the kitchen in his hiding-place, sparse Neue Sachlichkeit still lifes, but also dramatic danses macabres. The motif of a bare tree with pruned branches became a particularly frequent cipher in Nussbaum's

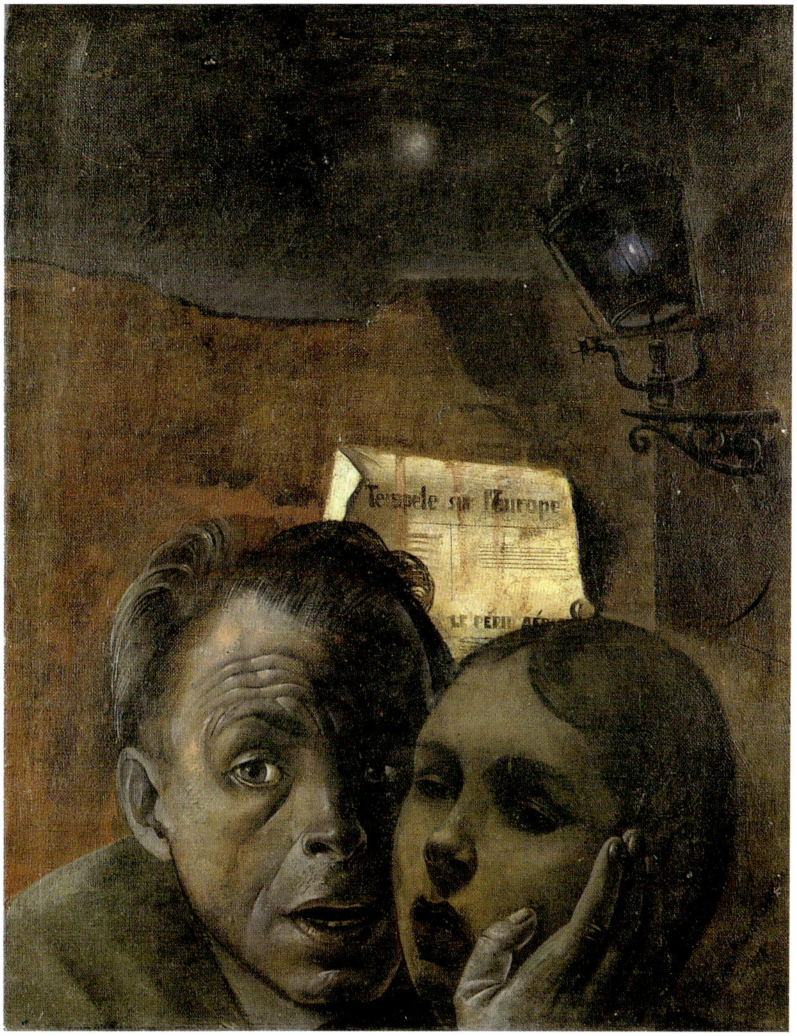

Felix Nussbaum
Fear (Self-portrait with Niece Marianne), 1941
Angst (Selbstbildnis mit seiner Nichte Marianne)
Oil on canvas, 75 x 55 cm
Osnabrück, Kulturgeschichtliches Museum

work for the feeling of being locked in, seen for example in the distinctly Neue Sachlichkeit work *Prison Compound* and in *Loneliness*, a picture that reveals especially strong associations with Pittura metafisica.

The Neue Sachlichkeit motif of the jointed doll appears again and again in Nussbaum's later works, reinterpreted as a symbol of helplessness. The artist leaves a shocking testimony to his desperate situation in his *Self-portrait with Niece Marianne* (illus. p. 201). Torn between a paralyzing sense of fear and a defiant will to live, Nussbaum awaited his fate in his hiding-place. His dark premonitions, expressed unmistakably in his picture *The Damned* (illus. p. 200), would prove only too well-founded: in June 1944, as the result of a denunciation, Nussbaum and Platek were tracked down and arrested. The last deportation train to succeed in leaving occupied Brussels ahead of the approaching Allies carried them to the death chambers of Auschwitz.

Influences on Later Art

By the end of the Second World War, Neue Sachlichkeit had disappeared from the scene. It was not until the 1960s, with a socially inspired realism once again becoming generally presentable in the west, that a reconsideration of its legacy took place. This began in West Germany with the 1961 exhibition in West Berlin organized by Eberhard Marx, and has continued – with a brief interruption during the 1980s – up to the present. Neue Sachlichkeit served as an important source of inspiration for several contemporary artistic movements between 1960 and the end of the 1970s, in particular in the cases of the pictorial world of Pop Art and Photorealism. Nevertheless, the revival of Neue Sachlichkeit art in Germany has been somewhat limited in nature.

The legacy of Neue Sachlichkeit was all the more noticeable in the painting of what was then the other half of Germany: the history of East German painting between 1968 and 1980 is also a history of constant reference to Neue Sachlichkeit painting. Volker Stelzmann from Leipzig was among the first to have turned, around 1968, to a Neue Sachlichkeit art previously branded as petit-bourgeois and reactionary. Stelzmann's Neue Sachlichkeit *Welder* of 1971, isolated in its cold monumentality from the socialist work process, became the showpiece of this new direction. Many other Neue Sachlichkeit formulations were to follow, above all in the so-called Leipzig School (Ulrich Hachulla, Günther Richter). It is certain that the Neue Sachlichkeit works from 1968 to 1972 helped to break up the dogmatic encrustations covering East German painting. An official art discussion in the publication "Bildende Kunst" of 1972 – including a significant delimitation from Surrealism – brought the final confirmation of a change of course. The approval of the Party aestheticists also had a tactically instrumental aim: borrowings from Neue Sachlichkeit were to serve as an antidote or corrective against possible future influence by western Pop Art and Photorealism.

After 1980, with the last impulses drawn from the artistic legacy of Neue Sachlichkeit fading away in the process of art criticism, the movement finally became a closed chapter of the classical modern age, the historical style of the Weimar Republic. Indebted equally to tradition and to the avant-garde, Neue Sachlichkeit wished to advance to the position of the realist art style of the epoch in which it lived. Its openness towards both sides of the artistic and political spectrum, a feature which initially constituted its strength, would ultimately prove to be its undoing. The reliable mirror of a fascinating and creative society, it was to share that society's historical – and historic – fate. It may be that neither the Weimar Republic, nor a Neue Sachlichkeit so much a part of it, really had a chance, that the challenges that the age posed both the political and the aesthetic figures of the time were quite simply too great for them. Their central dilemma was put in a nutshell back at the beginning of the 1930s by Wilhelm Michel, the Neue Sachlichkeit critic: "From an objective point of view, we have been besieged with too much that is new. Our powers of comprehension have been unable to keep pace with it... We stand, not in front of machines but rather in front of the machine culture, exactly as if before a war: dragged in mid-speech into the midst of the turmoil, lacking distance from what is going on around us, without the secure sense of our humanity, forced to make a virtue out of the 'experience' and the observation of details, since we cannot continue to exist as whole – that is, as experiencing and seeing and comprehending – human beings in the face of the reality rising up all around us."[100]

Wilhelm Lachnit
Woman with Rose, 1936
Frau mit Rose
Oil on wood, 92 x 74 cm
Private collection

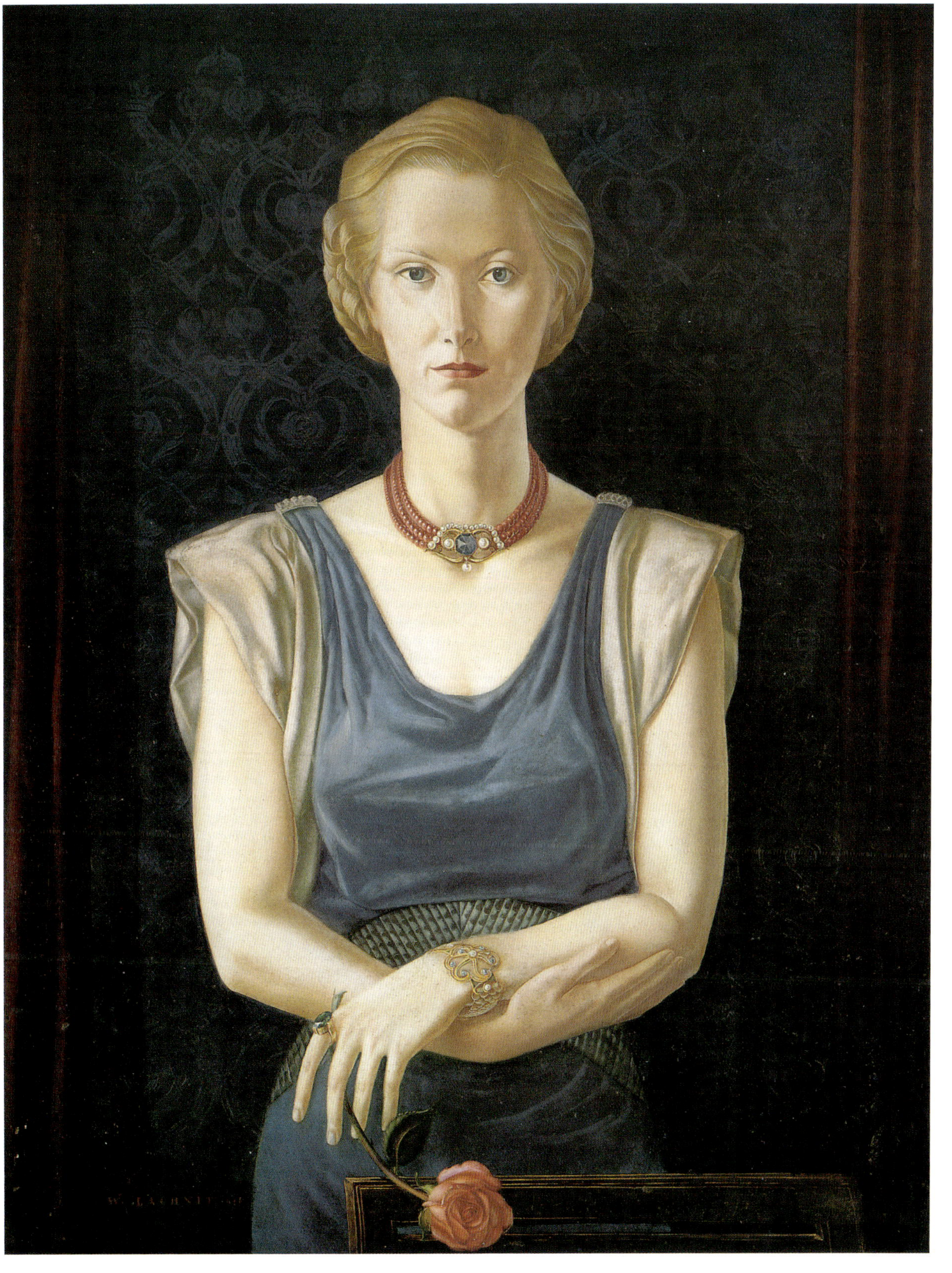

Notes

1 Eberhard Kolb: Die Weimarer Republik, in: E. Kolb, E. Roters, W. Schmied: Kritische Graphik in der Weimarer Zeit, Stuttgart 1985, p. 12

2 Kunstblatt, 3, 1919, p. 332

3 Wieland Schmied: Neue Sachlichkeit und Magischer Realismus in Deutschland 1918–1933, Hanover 1969, p. 13

4 Franz Roh: Nachexpressionismus – Magischer Realismus, Leipzig 1925, p. 119

5 Kunstblatt, 6, 1922, pp. 369–414

6 Ibid., p. 390

7 Roh, cf. note 4, Foreword

8 Realismus und Sachlichkeit. Aspekte deutscher Kunst 1919–1933. East Berlin, Staatliche Museen, 1974, p. 177

9 The "red-light district", named after a district of Berlin – Translator's note

10 Unter anderem ein Wort für deutsche Tradition (1931), quoted from G. Metken (ed.): Realismus zwischen Revolution und Reaktion 1919–1939, Munich 1981, p. 162

11 Quoted from Uwe M. Schneede: George Grosz, Cologne 1978, pp. 16–63

12 Georg Grosz: Ein kleines Ja und ein großes Nein, Hamburg 1974, p. 102

13 Collage, 1920, Galerie Nierendorf Berlin. [The commentary has not been translated here, but is in Grosz' original English – Translator's note]

14 Zu meinen Bildern, in: Kunstblatt, 5, 1921, p. 14

15 Harry Count Kessler, Tagebücher 1918–1937, Frankfurt am Main 1971, p. 577

16 Rudolf Schlichter: Tönerne Füße, Berlin 1933, p. 290

17 Rudolf Schlichter: Zwischenwelt. Ein Intermezzo, Berlin n.d., p. 25

18 Anonymous, Weltbühne, 8th November 1932, p. 704

19 Eberhard Roters: Dada Genf, in: Tendenzen der Zwanziger Jahre, 15. Europäische Kunstausstellung Berlin 1977, chap. 3, p. 57

20 Max Kolpe in: Herbert Günther (ed.): Hier schreibt Berlin, Berlin 1929, pp. 102 f.

21 Leerlauf der Gefühle
Man spricht sich an. Man hat sich kaum gesehen.
Man hat am nächsten Tag ein Rendezvous.
Man läßt die erste laufen und die zweite stehen,
um mit der dritten gleich ins Bett zu gehen.
Sie fragt nicht lang: wozu?!
Man geht ins Bett. Was soll man sonst schon machen ...?
Man kennt sich nicht. Und das ist interessant.
Man sagt sich "Sie" und noch ganz andere Sachen.
Man denkt auch an die Eltern und muß lachen:
Die lieben sich noch heute. Allerhand!
Man ging ins Bett. Das will noch nichts bedeuten.
Am nächsten Tag ist man sich wieder fremd.
Man grüßt sich wie mit andern Leuten.
Man trifft sich wie mit allen Bräuten.
Man ließ sich frei. Und man ist ungehemmt.
Man spricht sich an. Man hat sich kaum gesehen.
Man hofft vergebens, daß es einmal anders geht.
Man läßt die Liebe laufen, und das Herz bleibt stehen.
Man möcht' am liebsten gleich ins Wasser gehen ...
Doch man geht tanzen. Und kein Mensch versteht,
warum man traurig ist, wenn man zum Tanzen geht.

22 Margrit Bröhan: Hans Baluschek 1870–1935, Berlin 1985, p. 14

23 In: Hamburger Fremdenblatt, 10th February 1927

24 Quoted from Susanne Thesing: Franz Lenk, Recklinghausen 1986, p. 8

25 Ibid., p. 18

26 Sylvia von Harden: Erinnerungen an Otto Dix, in: Frankfurter Rundschau, 25th March 1959

27 Quoted from Diether Schmidt: Otto Dix – Maler und Werk, Dresden 1977, p. 252

28 Ibid., p. 269

29 Quoted from Lothar Fischer: Otto Dix. Ein Malerleben in Deutschland, Berlin 1981, p. 28

30 Heinz Lüdecke: Otto Dix, Dresden 1958, p. 10

31 In: Das Kunstblatt, 1923, pp. 97 f.

32 Quoted from Peter Barth: Otto Dix und die Düsseldorfer Künstlerszene, Düsseldorf 1983, p. 16

33 Quoted from Günter Feist: Hans Grundig, Dresden 1979, p. 47

34 Quoted from Wilhelm Lachnit, exhibition catalogue. Akademie der Künste der DDR, Berlin 1990, p. 49

35 Quoted from Peter Barth: Die Dresdener Künstlerszene 1913–1933, Düsseldorf 1987, p. 59

36 "Blut und Boden" (literally, blood and soil) was the label given to the Nazi idea whereby political stability and power are seen as dependent upon the unification of race and territory – Translator's note

37 Winfried Nerdinger: Die "Kunststadt" München, in: Christoph Stölzl: Die zwanziger Jahre in München. Exhibition catalogue, Munich 1979, pp. 93–120

38 The "Blauer Reiter", or "Blue Rider", involved a loose group of Expressionist artists who were reacting against late Impressionism and the tendency to view art from an (over-)academic standpoint. Founded by Wassily Kandinsky and Franz Marc in Munich in 1911, it centred around a desire to express spiritual values in the artist's work, embracing spiritual and mythological speculation, folkloric elements, and children's drawings. The group broke up with the onset of the First World War, but may be regarded during its short existence as the high point of German Expressionism – Translator's note

39 Paul Westheim: Kunst im deutschen Westen, in: Kunstblatt, 9, 1925, p. 266

40 Herwarth Walden: Amtliche Kunst, in: Der Sturm, 17, 1927, p. 146

41 Oskar Maria Graf: Ein barockes Malerporträt, in: Ibid.: Mitmenschen, Berlin 1950, p. 214

42 Quotation from Wieland Schmied: Georg Schrimpf und Italien, in: W. Storch (ed.): Georg Schrimpf und Maria Uhden, Berlin 1985, p. 11

43 Graf, cf. note 41, p. 214

44 "Entartete Kunst" (Degenerate Art) was the pejorative label used by the Nazis to discredit any contemporary art that did not correspond to the party's ideological line on racial theory, and especially those areas of modern art which seemed to promote "political and cultural anarchy". The artists responsible were forbidden to produce any further works. A speech by Hitler in Nuremberg in 1934 against "Entartete Kunst" was followed by a series of exhibitions intended to ridicule modern art. These culminated in 1937 in a show by the same name of "degenerate" works confiscated from German museums and displayed alongside works done by the inmates of lunatic asylums. In addition to the Expressionists, who featured prominently, the show included works by Dix, Grosz, Beckmann, Grundig, Schrimpf and – from outside Germany – van Gogh, Matisse and Picasso. – Translator's note

45 Else Lasker-Schüler: Heinrich Maria Davringhausen (1916), in: idem: Sämtliche Gedichte, Munich 1977, pp. 154 f.

46 Quoted from Joachim Heusinger von Waldegg: Heinrich Maria Davringhausen 1894–1970, catalogue. Bonn 1977, p. 19

47 Wilhelm Hausenstein: Alexander Kanoldt, in: Die Horen, I, 1925, p. 39

48 Letter from Rössing to Michael Koch, 1980, cf. Michael Koch: Der "entartete Parteigenosse". Alexander Kanoldt im Dritten Reich, in: Alexander Kanoldt 1881–1939. Exhibition catalogue, Freiburg im Breisgau 1987, p. 60

49 Günter Metken: "Gesund realistisch ohne abstossend zu sein." Der Beitrag Karlsruhes: zwei Generationen realistischer Zeichner, in: P. Nisbet (ed.): German Realist Drawings of the 1920s. Harvard University Art Museum 1986, pp. 47–50

50 Ibid., p. 49

51 R. Diehl in: Deutsche Allgemeine Zeitung, 28th October 1924, quoted from: H. Goettl et al. (eds.): Karl Hubbuch 1891–1979, Munich 1981, p. 91

52 Marlene Angermeyer-Deubner: Neue Sachlichkeit und Verismus in Karlsruhe 1920 bis 1933. Karlsruhe 1988, p. 29

53 Quoted from: Georg Scholz. Malerei, Zeichnung, Druckgraphik, catalogue, Waldkirch 1990, pp. 6 f.

54 Ibid., p. 11

55 Paul Westheim: Kunst Sachlichkeit, in: Kunstblatt, 9, 1925, p. 267

56 Angermeyer-Deubner, cf. note 52, p. 50

57 Quoted from: Rudolf Dischinger 1904–1988, catalogue, Freiburg 1991, p. 220

58 Ibid., p. 221

59 Quoted from: Hanna Nagel – Das frühe Werk, catalogue, Freiburg 1975, p. 21

60 H. U. Bohnen: Das Gesetz der Welt ist die Änderung der Welt. Die rheinische Gruppe progressiver Künstler, Berlin 1976, p. 44

61 Ibid.

62 Seiwert quoted from: Neue Gesellschaft für bildende Kunst (ed.): Politische Konstruktivisten. Die "Gruppe progressiver Künstler" Köln, Berlin 1975 (without pagination)

63 Hans Schmitt-Rost, cf. note 62

64 Seiwert, cf. note 62. The English translation has aimed at a reproduction of Seiwert's style, meaning principally his sentence structure and his complete refusal to use capital letters; the latter is even more striking in German, where nouns customarily begin with a capital letter – Translator's note

65 Seiwert quoted from Bohnen, cf. note 60, p. 63

66 cf. note 62

67 This is emphasized by Günter Herzog as well, in: idem: Anton Räderscheidt, Cologne 1991, p. 20

68 The pictures of the couples have been the subject of two attempts at interpretation which will be taken into consideration here: Joachim Heusinger von Waldegg: Zur Ikonographie der "einsamen Paare" bei Anton Räderscheidt, in: Pantheon, 37, 1979, pp. 59–68; Maria Walter: Anton Räderscheidts Paarbilder in den 20er Jahren, in: Anzeiger des Germanischen Nationalmuseums, 1991, pp. 275–302

69 Franz Roh: Anton Räderscheidt, Zwei Menschen, 1925, in: Kunstblatt, 14, 1930, p. 103

70 With regard to the term "Bildzauber" (pictorial magic), which I offer here as a possible solution, cf. – among others – Wolfgang Brückner: Bildzauber, in: Handwörterbuch der deutschen Rechtsgeschichte, Berlin 1971, vol. 1, pp. 428–430

71 Quoted from Friedrich W. Heckmann: Freunde in Düsseldorf, in: Ulrich Krempel (ed.): Am Anfang: Das junge Rheinland, Düsseldorf 1985, p. 45

72 In German, the "Angestelltenkultur": Siegfried Kracauer: Die Angestellten. Aus dem Neuesten Deutschland. Frankfurt am Main 1930

73 Der Wachsbogen No. 5/6, 1932, quoted from Wieland Schmied, cf. note 3, p. 253

74 Georg Scholz: Die Elemente zur Erzielung der Wirkung im Bilde, in: Kunstblatt, 8, 1924, p. 77

75 "Die Brücke" (The Bridge) was a group of German Expressionists, founded in Dresden in 1905 by the painters Ernst Ludwig Kirchner, Erich Heckel and Karl Schmidt-Rottluff. Moving to Berlin in 1910, the group broke up in 1913. They saw their work as constituting a "bridge" between the art of the past and that of the future. They worked in the area of the graphic arts, and especially that of the woodcut – Translator's note

76 Quoted from Peter Beckmann: Max Beckmann. Leben und Werk, Stuttgart 1989, p. 52

77 Cornelia Stabenow in: Max Beckmann – Retrospektive, Haus der Kunst München et. al., exhibition catalogue, Munich 1984, p. 221

78 Quoted from: Karl Hofer, exhibition catalogue, Schloß Cappenberg, Unna 1991, p. 14

79 cf. Peter Winter: Protokolle aus einer möglichen Wirklichkeit – Sieben Stichpunkte zum Werk des Malers Franz Radziwill, in: Franz Radziwill, exhibition catalogue, Hans-Thoma-Gesellschaft, Reutlingen 1975

80 Franz Radziwill in: Art, No. 1, January 1980, p. 108

81 Alfred Neumeyer: Zur Raumpsychologie der Neuen Sachlichkeit, in: Zeitschrift für Bildende Kunst, 1927/28, pp. 66–72

82 Kunstblatt, 9, 1925, p. 30 (summary of an article in the Frankfurter Zeitung)

83 Conflation of two passages from two letters by Großberg (from 1932 and 1934), quoted from: Carl Grossberg, Gemälde, Aquarelle, Zeichnungen und Druckgraphik 1914–1940, exhibition catalogue, Darmstadt 1976, pp. 12, 14

84 Ibid., p. 10

85 The "Pressa" was a trade fair for printing machines, held in 1928 in the Cologne trade centre, to be seen on the right of the picture on p. 174 – Translator's note.

86 Herbert Ihering in: Berliner Börsen-Courier, 5th September 1927

87 Franz Roh: Kurt Günther, Berlin 1928, p. 14

88 Kunstblatt, 13, 1929, p. 247

89 Ibid.

90 Fotographische Rundschau, No. 5, 1929, p. 93

91 Thomas Mann (1928), cf.: Thomas Mann: Reden und Aufsätze, vol. II, (Stockholm edition) Frankfurt 1965, p. 776

92 The expression in the original German text – "der Geist des deutschen Volkes"- has strong National Socialist associations, as the author notes, adding, however, that this should not hinder us from using it – Translator's note

93 Quoted from Döblin's Foreword in: August Sander: Antlitz der Zeit, Munich 1929 (new edition 1990), p. 13

94 Hans Gotthard Vierhuff's attempt (idem: Die Neue Sachlichkeit. Malerei und Photographie, Cologne 1980) can really only be seen as an initial approach

95 Quoted from Metken (ed.): Realismus zwischen Revolution und Reaktion 1919–1939, Munich 1981, p. 154

96 Völkischer Beobachter, 20th October 1933, p. 2

97 Quoted from Berthold Hinz: Die Malerei im deutschen Faschismus, Munich 1974, p. 140

98 "Heimatstil" (lit. "homeland style")is used here to refer – somewhat pejoratively – to those painters following a highly naturalistic line, keeping closely to their subject and painting everything exactly as it looked, with no attempt at "interpretation" – a form of art much favoured by the National Socialists – Translator's note

99 Oskar Schlemmer: Idealist der Form. Briefe, Tagebücher, Schriften 1912–43, Leipzig 1990, pp. 287, 294

100 Wilhelm Michel: Dichtung und Gegenwart, in: Neue Rundschau, No. 7, 1931, p. 122

Bibliography

The Culture of the Weimar Period

Gay, Peter: Weimar Culture: the outsider as insider. London 1969

Laqueur, Walter: Weimar: a Cultural History 1918–1933. London 1974

Wem gehört die Welt? Kunst und Gesellschaft in der Weimarer Republik, exhibition catalogue, Neue Gesellschaft für Bildende Kunst. Berlin 1977

Willett, John: Art and Politics in the Weimar Period. The New Sobriety 1917–1933. New York 1978

The History of the Term Neue Sachlichkeit

Adkins, Helen: Neue Sachlichkeit – Deutsche Malerei seit dem Expressionismus, in: Stationen der Moderne, exhibition catalogue, Berlinische Galerie. Berlin 1988

Hermand, Jost: Einheit in der Vielfalt. Zur Geschichte des Begriffes "Neue Sachlichkeit", in: idem: Stile, Ismen, Etikette. Zur Periodisierung der modernen Kunst. Wiesbaden 1978, pp. 80–94

Schmalenbach, Fritz: The Term "Neue Sachlichkeit" in: Art Bulletin, No. 22. 1940, pp. 161–165

General Surveys of Neue Sachlichkeit

Bertonati, Emilio: Neue Sachlichkeit in Deutschland. Herrsching 1988

Eberle, Matthias: Otto Dix und die Neue Sachlichkeit, in: Deutsche Kunst im 20. Jahrhundert – Malerei und Plastik 1905–1985, exhibition catalogue, Staatsgalerie Stuttgart. Stuttgart 1986

Heller, Reinhold (ed.): Art in Germany 1909–1936. From Expressionism to Resistance. The Marvin and Janet Fishman Collection. Munich 1990

Kolb, Eberhard, Roters, Eberhard, Schmied, Wieland (eds.): Kritische Grafik in der Weimarer Zeit. Stuttgart 1985

Liska, Pavel: Die Malerei der Neuen Sachlichkeit in Deutschland. Osnabrück 1976

März, Roland: Die Malerei der Neuen Sachlichkeit. Leipzig 1983

Matt, Georgia: Das Menschenbild der Neuen Sachlichkeit. Konstanz 1989

Oellers, Adam C.: Ikonographische Untersuchungen zur Bildnismalerei der Neuen Sachlichkeit. Mayen 1983

Paz de, Alfredo: Realismo Tedesco, Critica Sociale, Oggetività, Ideologia. Bologna 1981

Revolution und Realismus. Revolutionäre Kunst in Deutschland 1917–1933. Exhibition catalogue, Staatliche Museen zu Berlin. Berlin 1978

Roh, Franz: Nach-Expressionismus, Magischer Realismus, Leipzig 1925

Schmalenbach, Fritz: Die Malerei der Neuen Sachlichkeit. Berlin 1973

Schmied, Wieland: Neue Sachlichkeit und Magischer Realismus in Deutschland 1918–1933. Hanover 1969

Schneede, Uwe M.: Neue Sachlichkeit, Verismus, Figurativer Konstruktivismus, in: Propyläen Kunstgeschichte, G.C. Argan: Die Kunst des 20. Jahrhunderts. Berlin 1984, pp. 255–263

Schuster, Peter-Klaus: Neo-Neo-Klassizismus – Neusachliche Tendenzen im Vergleich Italien – Deutschland, in: Mythos Italien – Wintermärchen Deutschland, exhibition catalogue, Haus der Kunst. Munich 1988

Catalogues on Neue Sachlichkeit

Der Realismus der zwanziger Jahre. Niedersächsische Landesgalerie. Hanover 1977

Die zwanziger Jahre im Porträt. Porträts in Deutschland 1918–1933. Rheinisches Landesmuseum. Bonn 1976

German Realism of the Twenties. The Artist as Social Critic. Institute of Art. Minneapolis 1980

German Realist Drawings of the 1920s. University Art Museum. Harvard 1986

Kunst und Technik in den 20er Jahren. Neue Sachlichkeit und gegenständlicher Konstruktivismus. Städtische Galerie im Lenbachhaus. Munich 1980

Magischer Realismus in Deutschland 1920–1933. Kunst- und Museumsverein. Wuppertal 1967

Neue Sachlichkeit and German Realism of the Twenties. Hayward Gallery. London 1978

Neue Sachlichkeit und Realismus. Museum des 20. Jahrhunderts. Vienna 1977

Neue Sachlichkeit. Haus am Waldsee. Berlin 1961

Neue Sachlichkeit. Magischer Realismus. Kunsthalle. Bielefeld 1990

Politische Konstruktivisten: Die "Gruppe progressiver Künstler". Catalogue, Neue Gesellschaft für bildende Kunst. Berlin 1975

Réalismes en Allmagne 1919–1933. Musée d'Art et Industrie. St. Etienne 1974

Realismus der zwanziger Jahre. Galerie Hasenclever. Munich 1973

Realismus in der Malerei der zwanziger Jahre. Kunstverein. Hamburg 1968

Realismus und Sachlichkeit. Aspekte deutscher Kunst 1919–1933. Staatliche Museen. Berlin 1974

Realismus zwischen Revolution und Machtergreifung 1919–1933. Württembergischer Kunstverein. Stuttgart 1971

Realismus zwischen Revolution und Reaktion 1919–1933. Staatliche Kunsthalle. Berlin 1981 (French edition Centre Pompidou, Paris 1980)

Tendenzen der zwanziger Jahre. 15. Europäische Kunstausstellung des Europarates. Berlin 1977

The Artistic Centres of Neue Sachlichkeit

Angermeyer-Däubner, Marlene: Neue Sachlichkeit und Verismus in Karlsruhe 1920–1933. Karlsruhe 1988

Avantgarde gestern, Das Junge Rheinland und seine Freunde 1919–1925. Exhibition catalogue, Kunsthalle Düsseldorf. Düsseldorf 1970

Barth, Peter: Otto Dix und die Düsseldorfer Künstlerszene. Düsseldorf 1983.

– Johanna Ey und ihr Künstlerkreis. Düsseldorf 1984

Das Junge Rheinland, Eine Friedenssache. Exhibition catalogue. Düsseldorf 1988

Hannoversche Maler der Neuen Sachlichkeit. Catalogue, Stadtsparkasse Hannover, Sprengel Museum. Hanover 1991

Klapheck, Anna: Mutter Ey. Düsseldorf 1977

Koch, Michael: Neue Sachlichkeit – Magischer Realismus. Der Beitrag Münchens zur nachexpressionistischen Malerei und Graphik, in: Die zwanziger Jahre in München. Catalogue, Münchner Stadtmuseum. Munich 1979, pp. 121–139

Krempel, Ulrich (ed.): Am Anfang: Das Junge Rheinland. Zur Kunst und Zeitgeschichte einer Region 1918–1945. Düsseldorf 1985

Kunst in Karlsruhe 1900–1950. Catalogue, Kunsthalle. Karlsruhe 1981

Malerei der zwanziger und dreißiger Jahre in Sachsen. Exhibition catalogue, Kunststiftung Hohenkarpfen. Hausen ob Verena 1990

Neue Sachlichkeit in Hannover. Catalogue. Hanover 1974

Remmert, Herbert, Barth, Peter: Die Dresdner Künstlerszene 1913–1933. Düsseldorf 1987

Kunst im Aufbruch, Dresden 1918–1933. Exhibition catalogue, Staatliche Kunstsammlungen Dresden, Gemäldegalerie Neue Meister. Dresden 1980/81

Richter, Horst: Neue Sachlichkeit in Köln, in: Vom Dadamax bis zum Grüngürtel. Köln in den zwanziger Jahren. Kölner Kunstverein. Cologne 1975, p. 132 f.

Roters, Eberhard: Berlin 1910–1933. Die visuellen Künste. Berlin 1983

Painting and Photography

Mellor, David: Germany. The New Photography 1927–1933. London 1978

Molderings, Herbert: Überlegungen zur Photographie der Neuen Sachlichkeit, Kritische Berichte, No. 2/3. 1977, pp. 67–88

Vierhuff, Hans Gotthard: Die Neue Sachlichkeit. Malerei und Fotografie. Cologne 1988

The Artists of Neue Sachlichkeit

Maass-Spielman, B.: Der Maler Albert Aereboe 1889–1970. Kiel 1983

Hans Baluschek 1870–1935. Exhibition catalogue, Staatliche Kunsthalle Berlin. Berlin 1991

Hyman, Th.: Max Beckmann and the Neue Sachlichkeit. Artscribe, No. 15. 1978, pp. 29–36

Max Beckmann, Retrospektive. Exhibition catalogue, Haus der Kunst, ed. by Carla Schulz-Hoffmann and Judith C. Weiss. Munich 1984

Beckmann, Peter: Max Beckmann – Leben und Werk. Stuttgart 1989

Schmalenbach, W.: Julius Bissier. Cologne 1974

Hofstätter, Hans: Julius Bissier. Catalogue, Augustinermuseum Freiburg. Freiburg 1981

Gottfried Brockmann: Gemälde, Zeichnungen, Graphik. Catalogue, Karl-Ernst-Osthaus-Museum Hagen and the Kunsthalle zu Kiel. Kiel 1976

Heusinger von Waldeck, Joachim: Heinrich Maria Davringhausen 1894–1970. Monographie mit Werkkatalog 1912–1932. Rheinisches Landesmuseum Bonn 1977

Heinrich Maria Davringhausen. Exhibition catalogue, Leopold-Hoesch-Museum. Düren 1991

Hofstätter, Hans: Die Malerin F. Dethleffs-Edelmann, ed. by Bodenseemuseum, Friedrichshafen. n. p., n.d.

Ammann, Heinrich: Adolf Dietrich. Berne, Zurich 1977

Rudolf Dischinger 1904–1988. Exhibition catalogue, Museum für Neue Kunst. Freiburg i. Br. 1990

Barton, Brigid S.: Otto Dix und die Neue Sachlichkeit 1918–1925. Ann Arbor 1981

Dix. Exhibition catalogue to mark the artist's 100th birthday in 1991, Galerie der Stadt Stuttgart. Stuttgart 1991

Karcher, Eva: Otto Dix 1891–1969. Cologne 1989
Löffler, Fritz: Otto Dix 1891–1969. Œuvre der Gemälde. Recklinghausen 1981
Pfäffle, Suse: Otto Dix. Werkverzeichnis der Aquarelle und Gouachen. Stuttgart 1991
Kinkel, Hans: August Wilhelm Dressler. Munich 1970
Frenzel, Ursula: Chronik des Lebens Conrad Felixmüllers, in: Catalogue of the large-scale Conrad Felixmüller retrospective, 1990/91, in Schleswig, Düsseldorf, Brunswick and Halle
Heisberg, Dieter: Conrad Felixmüller, Dresden 1982
Barth, Peter: Conrad Felixmüller, Die Dresdner Jahre 1913–1933. Düsseldorf 1987
Rathke, Conrad: Conrad Felixmüller, in: Catalogue of the large-scale Conrad Felixmüller retrospective, 1990/91, in Schleswig, Düsseldorf, Brunswick and Halle
Söhn, Gerhart (ed.): Conrad Felixmüller, von ihm – über ihn. Düsseldorf 1977
Hans Finsler: Neue Wege der Photographie, ed. for the Staatliche Galerie Moritzburg Halle by Klaus E. Göltz. Leipzig 1991
Zienicke, Axel Hubertus: Xaver Fuhr 1898–1973. Recklinghausen 1984
Richard Gessner, Gemälde, Aquarelle 1927–1974. Exhibition catalogue, Städtische Kunsthalle Düsseldorf. Düsseldorf 1974
Oellers, Adam C., Euler-Schmidt, Michael: Barthel Gilles 1891–1877. Leben und Werk. Recklinghausen 1987
Otto Griebel: Ich war ein Mann der Straße – Lebenserinnerungen eines Dresdner Malers. Halle, Leipzig, Frankfurt am Main 1968
Schmidt, Diether: Otto Griebel. Berlin 1973
Carl Großberg, Gemälde, Aquarelle, Zeichnungen und Druckgraphik 1914–1940. Exhibition catalogue, Hessisches Landesmuseum Darmstadt. Darmstadt 1976
Flavell, M. Kay: George Grosz: A Biography. New Haven, London 1988
Drückers, Alexander: George Grosz. Das druckgraphische Werk. Berlin 1979
Hess, Hans: George Grosz. Dresden 1982
Schneede, Uwe M.: George Grosz. Der Künstler in seiner Gesellschaft. Cologne 1989
Feist, Günter: Hans Grundig. Dresden 1984
Hans Grundig: Zwischen Karneval und Aschermittwoch – Erinnerungen eines Malers. Berlin 1958
Wilhelm Heise, Memorial exhibition. Städelsches Kunstinstitut. Frankfurt 1972
Backes, D. et al: Heinrich Hoerle. Leben und Werk 1895–1936. Cologne 1981
Carl Hofer, ed. by Jürgen Schilling, exhibition catalogue, Schloß Cappenberg. Unna 1991
Karl Hubbuch 1891–1979. Exhibition catalogue, Badischer Kunstverein. Karlsruhe 1981
Hartmann, Wolfgang: Karl Hubbuch. Der Zeichner. Stuttgart 1991
Jochimsen, Margarethe (ed.): Grethe Jürgens, Gerta Overbeck, exhibition catalogue, Kunstverein. Bonn 1982
Alexander Kanoldt 1881–1939, Gemälde, Zeichnungen, Lithographien. Exhibition catalogue, Museum für Neue Kunst. Freiburg i. Br. 1987
Wilhelm Lachnit 1899–1962, Gemälde, Graphik, Zeichnungen. Exhibition catalogue, Akademie der Künste der DDR. Berlin 1990
– Memorial exhibition, exhibition catalogue, Staatliche Kunstsammlungen Dresden, Gemäldegalerie Neue Meister. Dresden 1965/66
Weidemann, F.: Wilhelm Lachnit, Maler und Werk. Dresden 1983
Franz Lenk, Retrospektive und Dokumentation. Cologne 1976
Thesing, Susanne: Franz Lenk. Recklinghausen 1986
Jeanne Mammen: Köpfe und Szenen. Exhibition catalogue, Kunsthalle Emden, Stiftung Henri Nannen and the Jeanne-Mammen-Gesellschaft in Berlin. Place n.d., 1991
Ertel, K.F.: Carlo Mense. Krefeld 1960
Hanna Nagel: Das frühe Werk, ed. Hans Hofstätter. Freiburg 1975
Musik, Rudolf: Hanna Nagel – Zeichnerin und Illustratorin, in: Illustration 63, No. 3. Memmingen 1975
Ruhmer, Eberhard: Hanna Nagel. Munich 1965
Otto Nagel, Gemälde, Pastelle, Zeichnungen. Exhibition catalogue, Nationalgalerie. Berlin 1984
Frommhold, Erhard: Otto Nagel. Berlin 1974
Reinhardt, B.: Reinhold Nägele 1884–1972. Stuttgart 1984
Felix Nußbaum – Gemälde, Zeichnungen und Dokumente. Exhibition catalogue, Wilhelm Lehmbruck-Museum. Duisburg 1988
Berger, Eva et al.: Felix Nußbaum. Verfemte Kunst-Exilkunst-Widerstandskunst. Exhibition catalogue. Osnabrück 1990
Reinhardt, Hildegard: Gerta Overbeck. Eine westfälische Malerin der Neuen Sachlichkeit, in: Niederdeutsche Beiträge zur Kunstgeschichte, 18. 1979, pp. 225 f.
Curt Querner 1904–1976, Gemälde, Aquarelle, Zeichnungen. Exhibition catalogue, Künstlerhaus. Vienna 1979
Dittrich, Christian: Werkverzeichnis Curt Querner. Berlin 1984
Heinz, Hellmuth: Curt Querner. Dresden 1968
Max Radler 1904–1971, Gemälde, Aquarelle, Zeichnungen, Karikaturen. Catalogue, Ostdeutsche Galerie. Regensburg 1976
Herzog, Günter: Anton Räderscheidt. Cologne 1991
Heusinger von Waldegg, Joachim: Zur Ikonographie der "einsamen Paare" bei Anton Räderscheidt, in: Pantheon, 33, No. 1. 1979, pp. 59–68
Walter, Maria: Anton Räderscheidts Paarbilder in den 20er Jahren, in: Anzeiger des Germanischen Nationalmuseums. Nuremberg 1991, pp. 275–302
Kaiser, H.W., Schulze, R.W.: Franz Radziwill. Der Maler. Munich 1975
Franz Radziwill. Exhibition catalogue, Kunsthalle Berlin. Berlin 1982
Radziwill, Konstanze, Maaß-Radziwill, Hans-Heinrich: Franz Radziwill. Raum und Haus. Munich 1988
August Sander: Menschen des 20. Jahrhunderts, ed. Gunther Sander, introduction by Ulrich Keller. Munich 1980
Eberle, Matthias (ed.): Christian Schad. Exhibition catalogue, Staatliche Kunsthalle Berlin. Berlin 1982
Christian Schad, Zeichnungen 1918–1977. Catalogue by Günter A. Richter. Rottach-Egern 1990
Horn, G., Klein, C.: Rudolf Schlichter 1890–1955. Exhibition catalogue, Staatliche Kunsthalle Berlin. Berlin 1984
Nedo, Ingrid: Wilhelm Schnarrenberger 1892–1966. Tübingen 1982
Wilhelm Schnarrenberger 1892–1966. Exhibition catalogue, City of Buchen (Odenwald), to mark the artist's 100th birthday. Buchen 1992
Georg Scholz 1890–1945, Malerei, Zeichnung, Druckgraphik. Waldkirch 1990
Holsten, Siegmar: Georg Scholz, Gemälde, Zeichnungen, Druckgraphik. Staatliche Kunsthalle Karlsruhe. Karlsruhe 1990
Oellers, Adam C.: Künstler, Freund und Zeitgenosse. Zur Porträtdarstellung bei Georg Schrimpf und seinem Umkreis in den 20er Jahren, in: Aachener Kunstblätter, 54/55, 1986/87, pp. 283–292
Storch, Wolfgang: Georg Schrimpf und Maria Uhden. Berlin 1985
Karl Schwesig: Ausgewählte Werke 1920–1955, ed. by Galerie Remmert und Barth. Düsseldorf 1985
Karl Schwesig: Leben und Werk, ed. by Galerie Remmert und Barth. Exhibition catalogue, Stadtmuseum Düsseldorf et al. Berlin, Düsseldorf 1984
Franz W. Seiwert 1894–1933, kritische grafiek en typografie. Catalogue, Gemeentemuseum. The Hague 1978
Ernst Thoms, ein Hannoveraner Maler der Neuen Sachlichkeit. Exhibition catalogue, Landesmuseum Oldenburg 1982
Adolf Uzarski 1885–1970, Gemälde – Grafik. Exhibition catalogue, Stadtmuseum Düsseldorf. Düsseldorf 1988
Lauter, Marlene: Bilder zum Lesen, das graphische und malerische Werk Adolf Uzarskis. Cologne, Vienna 1990
Eberhard Viegener 1890–1967. Exhibition catalogue. Soest 1990
Karl Völker, Leben und Werk. Exhibition catalogue, Galerie Moritzburg. Halle 1974
Taschenmacher, A.F.: Erich Wegner. Brunswick 1983
Gert H. Wollheim: Die wilden Jahre 1919–1925, ed. by Galerie Remmert und Barth. Düsseldorf 1984
Wollheim, Mona: Gert H. Wollheim, Gedanken und Werk. Munich 1977
Gert H. Wollheim 1894–1974, Gemälde, Zeichnungen, Dokumente. Exhibition catalogue, Stadtmuseum Düsseldorf. Düsseldorf 1984
Reinhardt, Hildegard: Gustav Wunderwald (1882–1945). Hildesheim 1988

Neue Sachlichkeit and Afterwards

Aust, Günter: Traditionalismus und Trivialität, in: Golo Mann (ed.): Die Dreißiger Jahre. Schauplatz Deutschland. Munich 1977, pp. 65–93
Hoffmann-Curtius, Kathrin: Die Kampagne "Entartete Kunst" – Die Nationalsozialisten und die moderne Kunst, in: Funkkolleg Moderne Kunst, Studienbegleitbrief 9, ed. by Monika Wagner et al. Weinheim, Basle n.d.
Oellers, Adam C.: Zur Frage der Kontinuität von Neuer Sachlichkeit und nationalsozialistischer Kunst, in: Kritische Berichte, No. 6, 1978, pp. 42–55
Sager, Peter: Neue Formen des Realismus. Cologne 1973

Biographies of the Artists

Albert Aereboe
1889 Lübeck –1970 Lübeck
1909 Apprenticeship as church painter in Berlin **1914–16** Studies under Hugo von Habermann at Munich Academy of Art (Kunstakademie) **1916–20** Active military service **1919–20** Member of the Secession and the Novembergruppe in Berlin **1920** Teacher at the State Werkbund School (Staatliche Werkbundschule), Kassel **1923** Appointed professor at the Werkbund School **1939** Moves to Berlin **1943** Flees to island of Sylt following destruction of studio **1959** Returns to Lübeck

Gerd Arntz
1900 Remscheid –1988 The Hague
1919 Trains as art teacher at the Atelier Kunowski **1922** First exhibition in Elberfeld, together with Heinrich Hoerle and Franz Seiwert **1928** Works with Seiwert for the Cologne "Pressa" (international press fair) **1929** Appointed head of graphic arts department at the Wirtschafts- und Gesellschaftsmuseum in Vienna; develops the "Viennese method of pictorial statistics"; collaborates on the magazine "a-z" **1934** Moves to The Hague; employed until 1940 at the Mundaneum Institute, thereafter head of the department of graphic art at the Dutch Statistics Foundation **1935** Contact with the soviet communist group "De arbeidersraad" **1943** Drafted into the German army **1944** Transfers to the Résistance, taken prisoner of war **1950** "Totentanz" (Danse macabre) series **1951–62** Works for Unesco in the field of pictorial statistics **1970** Honorary membership of "De Grafische"

Hans Baluschek
1870 Breslau –1935 Berlin
1889–94 Begins studies at the Royal Academy of Arts (Königliche Akademie der Künste), Berlin **1897** Takes part in the "Great Berlin Exhibition of Art" (Große Berliner Kunstausstellung) **1898** Drawing cycles "Sylt" and "Eisenbahn" (Railway) **1898/99** Collaborates on the satirical magazine "Das Narrenschiff" **1899** Exhibits with the group "Die XXI"; co-founder of the Berlin Secession **c. 1900** Teacher at the School of Women Artists (Künstlerinnenschule), Berlin, together with Käthe Kollwitz et al. **1923** Lithograph cycle "Porträts asozialer Frauen" (Portraits of Asocial Women) **1924** Chairman of the "Great Berlin Exhibition of Art" **1925** Co-organizer of the "Berlin Art" (Berliner Kunst) exhibition in the Deutsche Oper, Charlottenburg **1926** Cofounder of relief fund for Berlin artists **1927–31** Series of cityscapes commissioned by the Greater Berlin municipal authorities **1929** Examiner at the picture and film archives of the Central Institute of Education and Teaching (Zentralinstitut für Erziehung und Unterricht)

Carl Barth
1896 Haan/Rhineland –1976 Düsseldorf
1910–15 Apprenticeship as bookbinder **1916–18** Active military service **1919–20** Düsseldorf School of Arts and Crafts (Kunstgewerbeschule) **1921** Continues studies at the Munich School of Arts and Crafts **1923** Publishes set of woodcuts to lansquenet songs at own expense **1925** Commences studies at the Düsseldorf Academy of Art **1926** Participates in the Düsseldorf "Great Exhibition of Art" (Große Kunstausstellung) and the "Young Rhineland" (Junges Rheinland) exhibition **1929** Takes part in the Rhenish Succession jubilee exhibition and the exhibition by the group "The Juryless" (Die Juryfreien) in Berlin **1930** Active as freelance artist **1931** One-man show at the Düsseldorf Kunsthalle **1935** Elected to the committee of the Rhenish Secession **1936** Trip to the US **1937** Woodcuts seized **1938** Cornelius Prize from the Düsseldorf Academy of Art **1938–39** Scholarship to the Villa Massimo (German Academy) in Rome **1940** Studio in the Klever Tor, Xanten **1941** Exhibition of pre-Rome works prohibited **1942–43** Destruction of Düsseldorf studio and numerous pictures **1944** Moves to Haan **1946** One-man show in what is today the Von der Heydt-Museum, Wuppertal **1946–76** Numerous exhibitions

Max Beckmann
1884 Leipzig –1950 New York
1899/1900–03 Studies at the Weimar Academy of Art **1904** Settles in Berlin **1906** Participates in the exhibition in the Berlin Secession; Villa Romana Prize: six-month scholarship to Florence **1907** Returns to Berlin **1910** Appointed to the committee of the Berlin Secession **1911** Resigns from the Secession **1914** Active military service **1915** Released from army following a nervous breakdown; moves to Frankfurt am Main **1925** Teaching post at the Städel Art College (Städel-Kunstschule); takes part in the "Neue Sachlichkeit" exhibition held at the Staatliche Kunsthalle, Mannheim **1929** Appointed professor of free painting at the Städel Art College **1933** Dismissed from post; moves back to Berlin **1937** Ten of his pictures shown in the "Degenerate Art" (Entartete Kunst) exhibition; flees to Amsterdam **1947** Goes to US; 1st prize at the "International Exhibition of Contemporary Art", San Francisco **1949** Teacher at the Brooklyn Museum Art School, New York; Conte Volpi Prize at the Venice Biennale; Honorary doctorate from Washington University, St. Louis

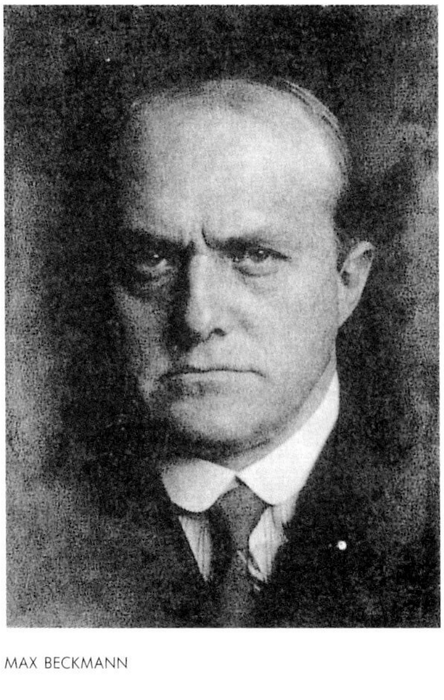

MAX BECKMANN

Ottohans Beier
1892 Karlsruhe –1979 (?) Munich
1913–14 Studies at the Karlsruhe School of Arts and Crafts **1914–18** Active military service and prisoner of war **1919 onwards** Apartment in Munich; trips to Denmark, Rumania and Sicily **1930** City of Nuremberg Dürer Prize **1937** Gold Medal at the World Exhibition in Paris

Aenne Biermann
1898 Goch/Niederrhein –1933 Gera As Aenne Sternefeld, trains as a pianist **1919** Marries Herbert Biermann from Gera **1922** Gives up music studies, commences autodidactic training as a photographer; numerous photographs published in such magazines as "Das Kunstblatt", "Die Form" and "Das neue Frankfurt" **1930** Publication of a study on Aenne Biermann by Franz Roh

Julius Bissier
1893 Freiburg –1965 Ascona
1913 Briefly studies art history at Freiburg University **1914** Continues studies for a few months at the Karlsruhe Academy of Art **1914–18** Active military service **1918** Resumes painting studies in Munich **1928** Gold Medal, Düsseldorf **1929–33** Teaching post at Freiburg University **1934** Fire at the University destroys his entire oeuvre **1935–38** Several trips to Italy **1939** Moves to Hagnau, Lake Constance **1955/56** Begins "Miniaturen" (Miniatures) series **1958** Retrospective at the Kestner-Gesellschaft, Hanover **1959** City of Düsseldorf Cornelius Prize; takes part in "documenta II", Kassel **1959/60** Wall-painting for Freiburg University; retrospective in the Gemeentemuseum, The Hague, and the Palais des Beaux-Arts, Brussels **1964** Awarded Grand Art Prize by the Federal State of North Rhine-Westphalia

Karl Blossfeldt
1865 Schielo/Harz Mountains –1932 Berlin
1881–84 Apprenticeship as sculptor and modeller in an ironworks **1886–90** Studies at the Royal Museum of Arts and Crafts School (Unterrichtsanstalt des Königlichen Kunstgewerbemuseums), Berlin **1891** Scholarship for trips to Italy, Greece and North Africa **1896** Works under Prof. Ernst Ewald at the Royal College of Art (Königliche Kunstschule) **1899** Lecturer on

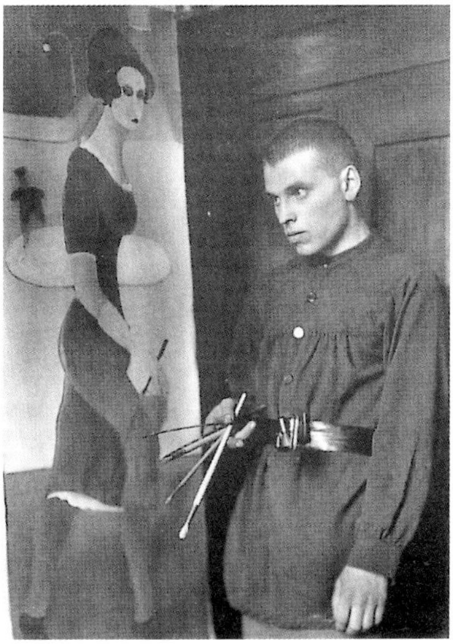

GOTTFRIED BROCKMANN Cologne, August Sander Archiv

plant modelling, Royal Museum of Arts and Crafts School; following the school's conversion into a college, appointed a professor there **1928** Publication of his book "Urformen der Kunst" (Prototypes of Art) **1932** Publication of his book "Wundergarten der Natur" (Nature's Garden of Wonders)

Leo Breuer
1893 Bonn –1975 Bonn
1912–15 School of Arts and Crafts in Cologne, then active military service and prisoner of war **1919–21** Resumes studies at the School of Arts and Crafts in Cologne **1921–22** Studies at the Academy of Fine Arts (Akademie der bildenden Künste), Kassel **1923–26** Studios in Bonn and Beuel **1927–34** Periods of residence in Düsseldorf, Koblenz and Berlin; member of the Rhenish Secession; teacher at the Diesterweg College (Diesterweg-Hochschule), Berlin; contributes to the magazine "Der Querschnitt" **1934** Emigrates to the Netherlands (The Hague) **1935** Moves to Brussels; works as a picture restorer **1940–45** Internment in southern France **1945–52** Lives in Paris; member of the "Salon des Nouveaux Réalistes"

Gottfried Brockmann
1903 Cologne –1983 Kiel
1920 Practical architect's training and painter's apprenticeship **1922** Member of the "Group of Progressive Artists, Cologne" (Gruppe Progressiver Künstler, Köln); first exhibition, Cologne Kunstgewerbemuseum **1926–32** Studies at the State Academy of Art (Staatliche Kunstakademie) Düsseldorf **1931** Member of the ASSO; takes part in the "Société Anonyme" exhibition, New York **1933** Member of the Rhenish Secession; moves to Berlin **1934** Contributes to the supplement for the weekly paper "Blick in die Zeit", which is subsequently banned in **1935. 1942–45** Active military service and prisoner of war in American hands **1945–52** Runs a lithograph company in Hof an der Saale **1952** Cultural advisor to the City of Kiel **1955–70** Head of the department for free and applied painting at the Muthesius School of Arts and Crafts (Muthesius-Werkkunstschule), Kiel **1964** Arts Prize from the Federal State of Schleswig-Holstein **1975** Appointed professor

Fritz Burger-Mühlfeld
1882 Augsburg –1969 Hanover
Studies under Franz von Stuck at the Munich Academy **1909–47** Teacher at the School of Arts and Crafts (Werkkunstschule), Hanover **1917–33** Co-founder and member of the Hanover Secession; stylistic transition to Neue Sachlichkeit painting inspired by his pupils Ernst Thoms, Gerta Overbeck, Friedrich Busack and Grethe Jürgens

Friedrich Busack
1899 Hanover –1933 Hanover
Training at the Hanover School of Arts and Crafts under Fritz Burger-Mühlfeld; death through complications resulting from a war wound

Fritz Burmann
1892 Wiedenbrück/Westphalia –1945 Berlin
1905 Begins studies under August Deusser at the Düsseldorf Academy **1912** Training continues under Heinrich Knirr in Munich **1913** Trips to Italy, Belgium, the Netherlands, France and Dalmatia **1914–18** Active military service **1921** Participates in the "Religious Art" (Religiöse Kunst) exhibition, Cologne; commissions for church painting and designs for church windows **1925** Takes part in the "Neue Sachlichkeit" exhibition at the Mannheim Kunsthalle **1926** Appointed professor at the Königsberg Academy of Art **1928** Participates in a touring exhibition of contemporary realist art **1936** Appointed professor at the Berlin-Charlottenburg Art College

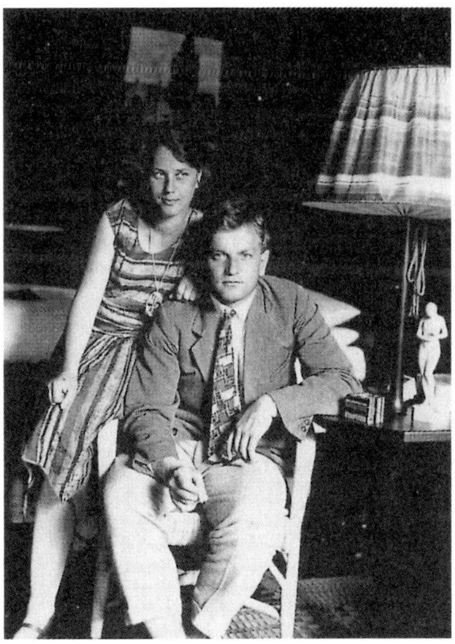

RUDOLF DISCHINGER

Heinrich Maria Davringhausen
1894 Aachen –1970 Nice
1913–14 Studies at the Düsseldorf Academy of Art; private tuition with Wilhelm Eckstein **1914** Exhibition in Alfred Flechtheim's Düsseldorf gallery; period of residence in Ascona with Carlo Mense **1915–18** Lives in Berlin **1918** Moves to Munich; takes part in the "New Religious Art" (Neue religiöse Kunst) exhibition, Mannheim Kunsthalle **1919** One-man show at Hans Goltz' Galerie Neue Kunst, Munich; participates in the first "Young Rhineland" exhibition, Düsseldorf Kunsthalle **1922** Moves back to Berlin **1923** One-man show at the Galerie Alfred Flechtheim **1924/25** Trip to Spain **1925** Takes part in the "Neue Sachlichkeit" exhibition at the Mannheim Kunsthalle **1927** Moves to Cologne; friendship with Anton Räderscheidt **1928** Takes part in the "Space and Wall-painting" (Raum und Wandbild) exhibition staged by the Kölner Kunstverein and "Neue Kunst" in Düsseldorf **1933** Flees to France **1939/40** Internment in Cagnes-sur-Mer and renewed flight from the Germans **1945** Returns to Cagnes-sur-Mer

Fridel Dethleffs-Edelmann
1899 Isny –1982 Isny
1916–18 Attends the Grand-Ducal Academy for Women (Großherzogliche Damenakademie), Karlsruhe; continues studies at the State Academy of Art, Karlsruhe; study-trip to Paris, Florence, Belgium, The Netherlands and many other countries by caravan **1930** Wins 1st State Prize **1931** 2nd Prize and Silver Medal in the "Southern German Art" (Süddeutsche Kunst) exhibition **1938** Apartment in Isny/Allgäu **1947** Founds the Upper Swabia/Lake Constance Secession **1975** Federal Cross of Merit

Adolf Dietrich
1877 Berlingen –1957 Berlingen
1893–10 Works in a textile factory in Berlingen; autodidactic training as a painter **1910** Forestry worker **1912** Plate-layer for the national railways **1913** First exhibition in the Wessenberhaus, Constance **1916–17** Book illustrations for the "Bodenseebücher" (Lake Constance Books) published by Walter Jerven **1917** Exhibition in the Galerie Goltz, Munich **1918** Participates in the "Baden in Pictures" (Das badische Land im Bild) exhibition, Mannheim Kunsthalle **1922** First one-man show at Dr. H. Tannenbaum's Kunsthaus gallery in Mannheim **1928** One-man show at the Galerie Flechtheim and Kahnweiler, Frankfurt **1932** Takes part in the exhibition by "The Seven" (Die Sieben), in the exhibition "New German Romanticism" (Neue Deutsche Romantik); numerous other exhibitions in Germany and abroad up until his death

Rudolf Dischinger
1904 Freiburg –1988 Freiburg
1924–27 Studies at the Baden State Academy of Art (Badische Landeskunstschule) in Karlsruhe under Georg Scholz, Karl Hubbuch and Ernst Würtenberger: participates in the "Latest Avenues in Painting and Drawing" (Die neuesten Wege der Malerei und der Zeichnung) exhibition in Leipzig **1927–39** Teaching post at Freiburg Junior High School for Girls

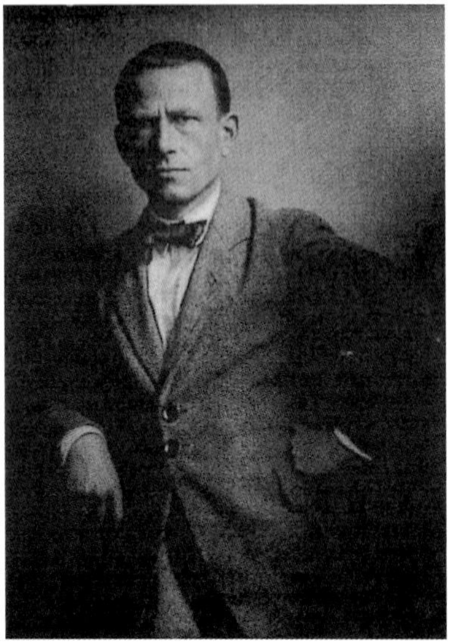

OTTO DIX

(Mädchenrealschule) **1934** Establishes own studio **1939–42** Active military service **1943–46** Having been wounded, works as freelance artist in Landshut **1946** Returns to Freiburg **1949** Teaching post at the Freiburg State Academy of Art **from 1954** Professorship **1956** After closure of the Academy, teaches at the Goethe Grammar School (Goethegymnasium) in Freiburg **1976** Awarded City of Freiburg Reinhold Schneider Prize

Otto Dix
1891 Unterhaus –1969 Hemmenhofen
1905–09 Apprenticeship as interior decorator in Gera **1910–14** School of Arts and Crafts in Dresden **1913** Study-trip to Italy **1914–18** Active military service **1919–22** Studies at the Dresden Academy of Art; founder-member of the "1919 Group" (Gruppe 1919), part of the New Dresden Secession **1922–24** Lives in Düsseldorf; in contact with the "Young Rhineland" and the circle of artists around the gallery owner Johanna Ey **1925** Takes part in the "Neue Sachlichkeit" exhibition at the Mannheim Kunsthalle **1926** Lives in Berlin **1927–33** Professor at the Dresden Academy of Art **1933** Dismissed from the Academy, forbidden to exhibit, forced out of the Prussian Academy of Arts (Preußische Akademie der Künste) for political reasons **1933** Moves to Randegg **1936** Moves to Hemmenhofen **1937** More than 200 works seized as "degenerate" ("entartet") **1939** Temporary arrest on grounds of alleged participation in the Munich assassination attempt on Hitler; many paintings classified as "degenerate" and consequently burnt **1943** Start of alla prima painting phase **1945** Called up for German territorial army; prisoner of war under the French **after 1946** Takes part in numerous exhibitions in Germany and abroad **1948** Participates in the "Painting and Sculpture" exhibition, Museum of Modern Art **1954** President of the Upper Swabia/Lake Constance Secession **1959** Awarded City of Düsseldorf Cornelius Prize and the Federal Cross of Merit (1st Class) **1962** Guest at the Villa Massimo, Rome **1964** Honorary membership of the Accadèmia delle Arti del disegno, Florence; Carl von Ossietzky Medal **1966** City of Hamburg Lichtwark Prize; City of Dresden Martin Andersen Nexö Prize **1967** Ernst Thoma Prize from the Federal State of Baden-Württemberg **1968** Honorary membership of the Karlsruhe Academy of Art; takes part in the "L'Art en Europe 1918–1968" exhibition, Straßburg

Bernhard Dörries
1898 Hanover –1978 Bielefeld
1917/18 Architectural studies at the Hanover Technical College (Technische Hochschule) **1919** Member of the Hanover Secession **1919–21** Exhibition at the Kestner-Society **1924** Member of the Hanover Kunstverein executive committee **1925** Rome Prize; trip to Paris and Pontoise/Seine **1926** Exhibition in the Kestner-Society **1937** Grand Prix at the World Exhibition, Paris, for child portraits **1938–45** Professor at the College of Fine Arts (Hochschule für Bildende Künste), Berlin, succeeding Georg Schrimpf **1945–55** Lives in Hanover **1955–67** Professor at the College of Fine Arts, Berlin **1971** Takes part for the first time in exhibitions by the German Federation of Artists (Deutscher Künstlerbund) **1973** Member of the German Federation of Artists

August Wilhelm Dressler
1886 Bergesgrün/Bohemia –1970 Berlin
1900–04 Training as a lithographer, Chemnitz **1906–13** Studies at the art academies in Dresden and Leipzig **1913** Moves to Berlin; works as a freelance artist; in contact with the "Novembergruppe" **1924** Joins the "Novembergruppe" **1927** Rome Prize from the Prussian Academy of Arts; takes part in the "Neue Sachlichkeit" exhibition at the Galerie Neumann-Nierendorf **1928** City of Nuremberg Dürer Prize **1929** Participates in the "De onafhangelijken" (Neue Sachlichkeit) exhibition at the Stedelijk Museum, Amsterdam **1930–31** Residence in the Villa Massimo, Rome **1934–38** Teaching post at the United State School (Vereinigte Staatsschule), Berlin; dismissal following classification as "degenerate" **1955** Retrospective; City of Berlin Art Prize **1956** Teaching post at the Master Craftsmen's School of Applied Arts (Meisterschule für angewandte Kunst, Berlin **1967** Exhibition in the Galerie Nierendorf, Berlin

Conrad Felixmüller
1897 Dresden (as Conrad Felix Müller) – 1977 Berlin
1911–12 Drawing classes at the Dresden School of Arts and Crafts **1912** Training in the private painting school run by Ferdinand Dorsch; begins studies at the Dresden Academy of Art under Carl Bantzer **from 1915** Commences work in Dresden as a freelance artist; contributes to the magazines "Der Sturm" and "Aktion" **1917** Co-editor of the art and literature magazine "Menschen"; publication of the art-theoretical pamphlet "Postulat", and the special issue "Felixmüller" in the magazine "Die schöne Rarität"; active military service as a male nurse following temporary arrest; founder-member of the Dresden Expressionist Alliance (Expressionistische Arbeitsgemeinschaft Dresden) **1918** Moves to Klotsche near Dresden **1918–1922** Member of the German Communist Party **1919** Co-founder and chairman of the "1919 Group" within the New Dresden Secession; member of the "Novembergruppe"; resigns from the Dresden Secession at year's end **1920** Grand State Prize for painting **1923–33** Numerous exhibitions and prizes **1934** Moves to Berlin **1937** Admitted to the Association of Berlin Artists (Verein Berliner Künstler); Prize for Painting at the VBK's spring exhibition; later expelled from the VBK **1937–38** A total of 151 works seized and destroyed **1944** Loses apartment in Berlin **1944–64** Converts a barn into a house and studio in Tautenhain near Leipzig **1945** Prisoner of war in Soviet hands **1951** Professor on the educational faculty of Halle University; takes part in an exhibition at the Staatliche Galerie Moritzburg, Halle **1957** Exhibition in the Düsseldorf Kunstmuseum **1962** Made emeritus professor **1964–77** Lives first in East Berlin, then – until his death – in Berlin-Zehlendorf; exhibitions at home and abroad **1973** First comprehensive general exhibition of his painting in the Verein Bildender Künstler, Berlin **1974** Gold Medal at the IV International Biennale of Graphic Arts, Florence

Hans Finsler
1891 Heilbronn –1972 Zurich
1911 Studies architecture at Stuttgart Technical College; moves to Munich; active military service **1915** Studies art history under Heinrich Wölfflin and Paul Frankl **1921** Moves to Halle; doctorate under Frankl's tutelage; teaching post at the School of Arts and Crafts (Handwerker- und Kunstgewerbeschule), Burg Giebichenstein, initially as art historian, later for publicity and photography **1928** "New Avenues in Photography" (Neue Wege in der Photographie) exhibition, Halle **1930** Appointed head of the photography department by Halle's City Council **1932** Transfers to the Zurich Technical College (Gewerbeschule); joins the Swiss Werkbund **1938** Elected to the Werkbund's Central

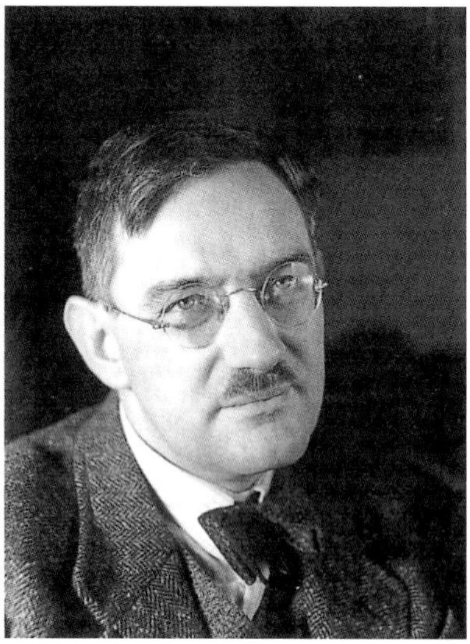

CONRAD FELIXMÜLLER

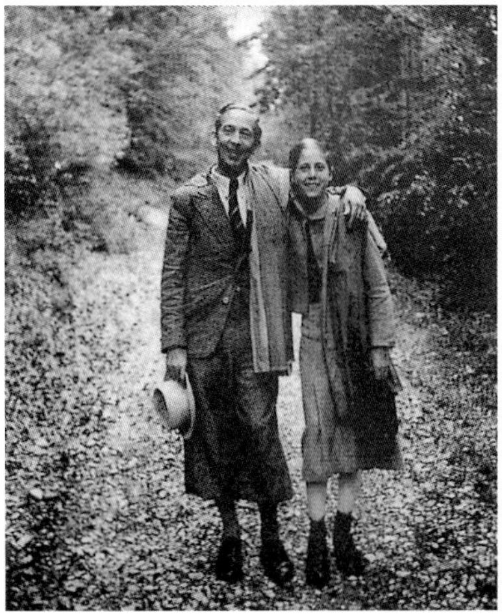

HANS FINSLER

Committee **1958/59** Lectures at the Zurich Adult Education College (Volkshochschule) and the University Contemporary Art Group (Hochschulgruppe für zeitgenössische Kunst) **1964** His lectures are published in the magazine "Du", entitled "Das Bild der Photographie" (The Picture of Photography) **1969** Exhibition in Josef Müller-Brockmann's Galerie 58 in Rapperswil, near Zurich

Ernst Fritsch
1892 Berlin –1965 Berlin
1911–14 Studies at the Berlin Museum of Arts and Crafts School **1914–18** Active military service **1919–21** Teacher in Berlin, **1919–32** Member of the Berlin Secession; participates in its exhibitions **1921** Joins the "Novembergruppe" **1923–33** Takes part in exhibitions at the Prussian Academy of Arts, Berlin **1925** Begins exhibiting at the Munich Secession **1927** Rome Prize **1928** Participates in the Düsseldorf "Great Exhibition of Art" **1928–29** Trips to Paris and Italy **1933** Large-scale retrospective at the Berlin Secession; forbidden to exhibit **1937** Eight works seized as "degenerate" **1939–42** Provisional teaching post at the School of Arts and Crafts (Kunst- und Werkschule), Berlin **1942–45** Active military service and prisoner of war **1946** Appointed professor at the College of Fine Arts, Berlin **1956** Member of the Academy of Arts **1960** Guest of honour at the Villa Massimo

Xaver Fuhr
1898 Mannheim, Neckarau –1973 Regensburg
Autodidact as painter **1930–31** Villa Romana Prize; period of residence in Florence **1937** Forbidden to paint **1943** Moves to Nabburg **1946–66** Appointed to the State Academy of Fine Arts (Staatliche Akademie der bildenden Künste), Munich **1950** Moves to Regensburg **1963** Hans Thoma Prize from the Federal State of Baden-Württemberg

Richard Gessner
1894 Augsburg –1989 Düsseldorf
1913 Commences studies at the Düsseldorf Academy of Art **1915–18** War artist in Macedonia **1918–21** Continues studies at the Düsseldorf Academy **1919** Founder-member of the "Young Rhineland" group; contact with the circle around the gallery owner Johanna Ey **1921–23** Trips to Finland, Italy and North Africa **1924** Exhibition in Alfred Flechtheim's Düsseldorf and Berlin galleries **1924–26** Lives in Paris **1928** Joins the Rhenish Secession **1929** Member of the German Federation of Artists; takes part in the "10 German Painters " (10 deutsche Maler) exhibition in Lübeck **1933** and **1935** Exhibitions in the Galerie Nierendorf **1937** City of Nuremberg Dürer Prize **1937–45** Moves to apartment in Schloß Kalkum **1941** City of Düsseldorf Cornelius Prize **1946** Returns to Düsseldorf **1953** Publication of book "Ein Maler sieht das Ruhrgebiet" (A Painter's View of the Ruhr Valley), with 80 industrial watercolours **1955** Participates in the "Exposition Internationale les Mines, les Forges et les Arts" exhibition in the Musée des Travaux Publiques, Paris **1975** Retrospective in the Städtische Kunsthalle, Düsseldorf

Barthel Gilles
1891 Rendsburg –1977 Wees
1905–08 Apprenticeship as interior decorator **1907** Moves to Cologne; attends evening classes at the Cologne School of Arts and Crafts (Kunstgewerbe- und Handwerkerschule) **1909–11** Studies at the Düsseldorf Academy of Art under Wilhelm Döringer and Ludwig Hempel-Siegen **1912–18** Voluntary and thereafter active military service **1919** Earns living as interior decorator **1921** Participates in an exhibition by the Düsseldorf section of the General German Art Co-operative (Allgemeine Deutsche Kunstgenossenschaft) **1923** Exhibition in the Suermondt Ludwig Museum, Aachen **1924** Joins the Cologne Painters' Exhibition Society (Ausstellungsgemeinschaft Kölner Maler) **1927** Moves to Ingersauelermühle, Bröltal **1929** Joins the German Communist Party and the ASSO **1931** City of Nuremberg Dürer Prize; begins encaustic painting **1933** Participates in two National Socialist exhibitions, "A Healthy Woman, A Healthy People" (Gesunde Frau, Gesundes Volk) in Cologne and "Western Front" (Westfront) in Essen **1930** Takes regular part in exhibitions by the "German Working Front, National Socialist 'Strength Through Joy' Fraternity" (Deutsche Arbeitsfront, NS-Gemeinschaft Kraft durch Freude) **1943** Loses apartment and numerous works through bombing **1954–55** Employed as a draughtsman on an infrastructural programme for the Belgian occupation authorities **1957–76** Lives variously in Bremerhaven, Berlin, Hooksiel near Bremerhaven, and Glücksburg

Fred Goldberg
1889 Berlin – unknown
Autodidact **1926–31** Known to have been working as a painter in Berlin, after which all trace of him disappears.

Otto Griebel
1895 Meerane (Saxony) –1972 Dresden
1909 Apprenticeship as interior decorator and fine-art painter **1911–15** Studies at the Dresden School of Arts and Crafts **1915–18** Active military service, seriously wounded; returns to Dresden; member of the Soldiers' Soviet (Soldatenrat) during the November Revolution **1919** Joins the German Communist Party; member of the "Novembergruppe" and the Dada group **1919–22** Studies at the Dresden Academy of Art; joins the Dresden Secession; first exhibition with Pol Cassel in the Kunstsalon Emil Richter **1922** Joins the "Young Rhineland" **1923** Works as a street-paver **1924** Founds the "Red Group" (Rote Gruppe), Dresden **1926** Participates in the "International Art Exhibition" (Internationale Kunstausstellung), Dresden; exhibition in the Galerie Neumann-Nierendorf, Berlin **1929** Founder-member of the Dresden section of the ASSO; takes part in the "De onafhangelijken" exhibition at the Stedelijk Museum, Amsterdam **1933** Arrested by the Gestapo, released after protests by the Dresden Secession **1936** Works as exhibition planner for the Dresden Hygiene-Museum **1937** His paintings are condemned as "degenerate" and removed from German museums **1939–40** Active military service **1941–43** Works as exhibition planner in occupied Cracow **1945** Works destroyed by bombing **1946–60** Professor at the Dresden Art College (Kunsthochschule)

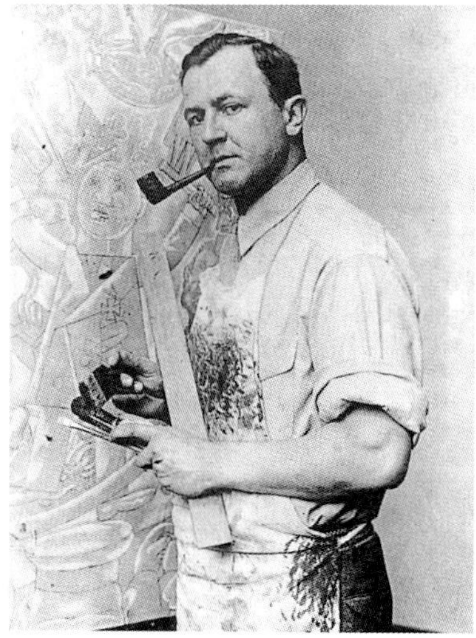

GEORGE GROSZ

Carl Grossberg
1894 Elberfeld –1940 Laon
1913–14 Architectural studies in Aachen and Darmstadt **1914–18** Active military service **1919–21** Studies at the Weimar Academy of Art and at the Bauhaus under Lyonel Feininger et al. **1921** Moves to Sommerhausen near Würzburg **1925** Trip to the Netherlands (Amsterdam, Zandvoort) **1926** First one-man shows in the Galerie Neumann-Nierendorf and the Kunsthaus Schaller in Stuttgart **1929** Participates in the "De onafhangelijken" exhibition at the Stedelijk Museum, Amsterdam **1931** Rome Prize from the Prussian Academy of Arts; scholarship to the Villa Massimo, Rome **1934** Retrospective in the Kestner-Society, Hanover **1935** Retrospective in the Folkwang Museum, Essen **1939–40** Active military service

George Grosz
1893 Berlin –1959 Berlin
1909–12 Studies at the Dresden Academy of Art **1910** First caricatures published in "Ulk", the supplement to the Berliner Tageblatt **1912–1916** Moves to Berlin; studies at the School of Arts and Crafts under Emil Orlik **1913** Spends several months in Paris **1914–16 and 1917–18** Active military service, court martial on charges of resistance **1918** Co-founder of the Berlin Dada group; joins the German Communist Party **1919–24** Co-editor of the magazine "Die Pleite" **1920** First one-man show at Hans Goltz's gallery in Munich; charged with attacking the military in his portfolio "Gott mit uns" (God with us) **1922** Trip to the Soviet Union **1923** charged with obscenity following the publication of his "Ecce Homo" portfolio; one-man show at Alfred Flechtheim's gallery **1924** Chairman of the "Red Group", Berlin; contributes to the magazines "Der Knüppel" and "Der Querschnitt" **1925** Takes part in the "Neue Sachlichkeit" exhibition at the Mannheim Kunsthalle; publishes "Der Spießer-Spiegel" (The Philistine's Mirror) **1928** Joins the ASSO; charged with blasphemy for his portrayal of Christ in a gas mask in the portfolio "Hintergrund" (Backcloth) **1929** Participates in the "De onafhangelijken" exhibition at the Stedelijk Museum, Amsterdam; one-man show at the Galerie Bruno Cassirer, Berlin; takes part in the "Novembergruppe's" jubilee exhibition **1932** Guest lecturer at the Art Students' League, New York **1933** Emigration to the US; lecturer at the Art Students' League; opens own school of art, the Sterne-Grosz School **1937** Stipend from the Guggenheim Fellowship; included in the "Degenerate Art" exhibition, Munich; 385 works seized **1940** Carol H. Beck Medal **1954** Large-scale retrospective at the Whitney Museum of American Art, New York; elected member of the American Academy of Arts and Letters **1958** Elected member of the Academy of Arts, Berlin **1959** Gold Medal of the United States National Institute of Arts and Letters

Hans Grundig
1901 Dresden –1958 Dresden
Apprenticeship as interior decorator **1920–21** Studies at the Dresden School of Arts and Crafts **1922–23** Transfers to the Dresden Academy; first exhibition with Hugo Erfurth, Dresden **1926** Joins the German Communist Party; takes part in the International Art Exhibition, Dresden **1927** Abandons studies and takes over his father's artisan business **1929** Joins the ASSO; wins Ilgen Prize; participates in "The Juryless" exhibitions; also in the "De onafhangelijken" exhibition at the Stedelijk Museum, Amsterdam **1933** First etchings **1936** Excluded from the National Chamber of Arts (Reichskulturkammer), forbidden to practise profession; trip to Switzerland; first – brief – period of arrest **1937** Works included in the "Degenerate Art" exhibition **1938** Renewed arrest, compelled to separate from Lea Grundig **1940–44** Sachsenhausen concentration camp, placed in the punitive division; later joins Red Army **1945** Attends an anti-fascist school in Moscow **1946** Returns to Berlin; organizes the large-scale "General German Art Exhibition" (Allgemeine Deutsche Kunstausstellung) **1947** Rector of the newly-opened Dresden Academy of Fine Arts (Akademie der bildenden Künste), professor of a painting class **1957** Publication of autobiography "Zwischen Karneval und Aschermittwoch" (Between Shrovetide carnival and Ash Wednesday); GDR Fatherland Order of Merit **1958** Large-scale retrospective of Hans and Lea Grundig, Dresden Albertinum

Kurt Günther
1893 Gera –1955 Gera
Studies at the Dresden Academy of Art; active military service; following period of convalescence in Davos, resumes studies in Dresden under Otto Dix and Richard Müller **after 1933** Pictures seized as "degenerate"; forbidden to exhibit **1944–45** Called up for active military service **after 1945** Professor at the Gera Art College (Kunstschule)

Wilhelm Heise
1892 Wiesbaden –1965 Munich
1912 Studies under H. Olde in Kassel; studies continued in Weimar **1918** Moves to Munich Takes part in the "Neue Sachlichkeit" exhibition at the Mannheim Kunsthalle **1926–28** Lives on Lake Starnberg; joins the Secession **1928** Participates in the "Young German Artists" (Junge Deutsche Künstler) exhibition at the Galerie Wiltschek, Berlin **1929** Scholarship to the Villa Massimo, Rome **1937** City of Nuremberg Dürer Prize **1937–43** Professor at the State Master Craftsmen's School (Staatliche Meisterschule), Königsberg, thereafter at the Städel Art College, Frankfurt **1953–58** Lecturer, Munich Academy of Fine Arts

Albert Henrich
1899 Düsseldorf –1971 Düsseldorf
1913 Studies at the Düsseldorf Academy of Art **1917** Active military service **1927** Study-trip to southern France **1930–40** Regular exhibitions in Munich, Rome and Paris **1949** Founder and for many years president of the "1949" group of artists

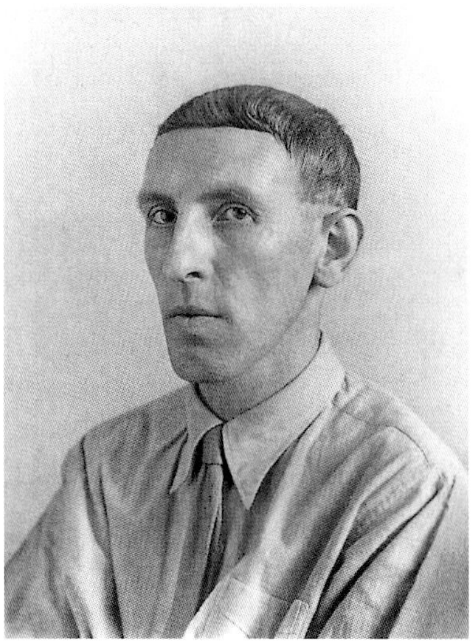

HEINRICH HOERLE Cologne, August Sander Archiv

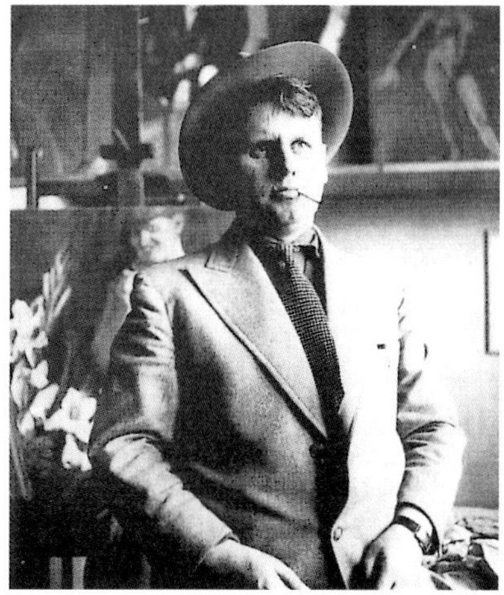

KARL HUBBUCH

Heinrich Hoerle
1895 Cologne –1936 Cologne
Autodidact, attending the Cologne School of Arts and Crafts only at irregular intervals **1913–14** Member of the "Lunisten" group (Max Ernst, Otto Freundlich, Karl Nierendorf et al.) **1914** Active military service **1919** Co-founder of the Group of Progressive Artists; collaborates on the magazine "Ventilator", published by Johannes Theodor Baargeld and Max Ernst **1920** Publishes his "Krüppelmappe" (Cripples' Portfolio) **1929** Founds the magazine "a-z" **1933** Trip to Majorca; art condemned as "degenerate"

Karl Hofer
1878 Karlsruhe –1955 Berlin
1898 Studies at the Karlsruhe Academy of Art **1900–02** Pupil of Hans Thoma **1902** Transfers to the Stuttgart Academy of Art under von Kalckreuth **1903–08** Lives in Rome **1908–13** Lives in Paris **1911** Trips to India **1913** Moves to Berlin **1914–17** Active military service and prisoner of war in France **1917** Lives in Zurich **from 1919** Lecturer at the United State Schools (Berlin Academy), Berlin **1923** Member of the Prussian Academy of the Arts **1933** Dismissed from post **1937** Numerous works seized **1940** Moves to Constance **1943** Studio and many works destroyed during a bombing raid on Berlin **1948** Awarded honorary doctorate by the Humboldt University, Berlin; made honorary member of the Karlsruhe Academy of Art **1950** Elected first president of the German Federation of Artists

Karl Hubbuch
1891 Karlsruhe –1979 Karlsruhe
1908–12 Studies at the Karlsruhe Academy **1912–14** Studies continued at the Berlin Museum of Arts and Crafts School under Emil Orlik **1914–18** Active military service, contracts malaria **1918–20** Convalescence in Neuenbürg at his parents' house **1920–22** Renews studies at the Karlsruhe Academy under Walter Conz **1922** Studies continued in Berlin, thanks to financial support from Otto Oppenheimer, a cloth wholesaler from Bruchsal **1924** Assistant teacher, lithography class, Karlsruhe Academy

1925 Head of the drawing class; takes part in the "Neue Sachlichkeit" exhibition at the Mannheim Kunsthalle **1928** Appointed professor in Karlsruhe; member of the ASSO **1929** Participates in the "De onafhangelijken" exhibition at the Stedelijk Museum, Amsterdam **1930** Co-founder of the "Monatsschrift für Zeitkunst, Zeitbetrachtung, Satire und Karikatur" ("Zakpo") of which two numbers appear **1931** 40 drawings and sketches published under the title "La France" **1932–33** A further collection of drawings is published under the title "Deutsche Belange" (German Concerns); dismissed from post for reasons of "artistic policy"; forbidden to paint **1939–45** Works as a flower painter at a Karlsruhe majolica factory and the Schmid-Schlenker cuckoo-clock company in Schwenningen **1945–47** Works for anti-fascist associations **1947** Teaching post in the department of architecture at Karlsruhe Technical College, **1947/48–57** Professor of painting, Karlsruhe Academy of Fine Arts

Grethe Jürgens
1899 Holzhausen –1981 Hanover
1918 Commences architectural studies at the Berlin Technical College **1919–22** Studies at the Hanover School of Arts and Crafts under Fritz Burger-Mühlfeld **1923–27** Advertising draughtswoman for the Hackethal wire factory in Hanover; thereafter freelance artist **1931–32** Co-editor of the magazine "Der Wachsbogen", of which 12 numbers appear **1932** Participates in the "Neue Sachlichkeit in Hanover" exhibition at the Herzog Anton Ulrich-Museum, Brunswick **1933** Exhibition in the Galerie Abels, Cologne; active during the following years as a book illustrator **1951** Retrospective in the Wilhelm-Busch-Museum, Hanover

Alexander Kanoldt
1881 Karlsruhe –1939 Berlin
1899–1900 Studies at the Karlsruhe School of Arts and Crafts **1901–04** Studies continued at the Karlsruhe Academy **1908** Move to Munich; trips to England, France, Italy and Switzerland **1909** Co-founder of the "New Artists' Association" (Neue Künstlervereinigung) in Munich, together with Alexei Jawlensky, Wassily Kandinsky and Gabriele Münter **1913** Co-founder of the Munich New Secession **1914–18** Active military service as officer **1924** Longer periods of residence in Italy (Olevano, Subiaco etc.) **1925** Takes part in the "Neue Sachlichkeit" exhibition at the Mannheim Kunsthalle; appointed professor at the Breslau Academy **1927** Participates in the "Neue Sachlichkeit" exhibition in the Galerie Neumann-Nierendorf, Berlin **1931** Gives up Breslau professorship, opens private school of painting in Garmisch **1932** Joins the Munich artists' group "The Seven" and participates in their touring exhibition through the Rhineland **1933** Appointed professor at the Berlin Academy of Art; takes part in the "New German Romanticism" exhibition organized by the Kestner-Gesellschaft, Hanover **1937** Some works seized as "degenerate"

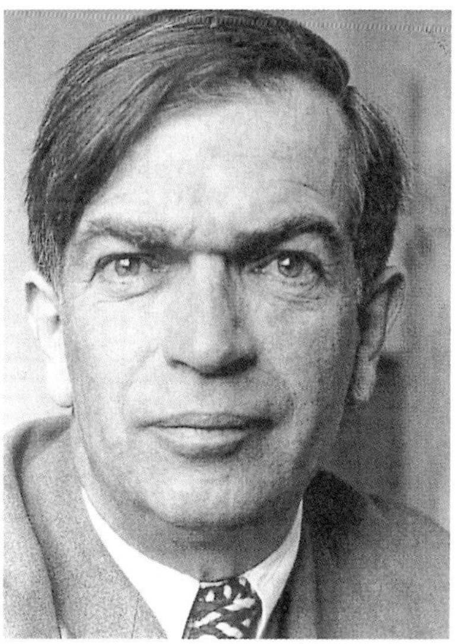

ALEXANDER KANOLDT

Arthur Kaufmann
1888 Mülheim/Ruhr –1971 Nowa Friburgo, Brazil
1905 Commences studies at the Düsseldorf Academy **1906–12** Periods of residence in Paris, England, and Italy **1913** Exhibition in Alfred Flechtheim's gallery, Düsseldorf **1914–15** Active military service **1919** Co-founder of the "Young Rhineland" group; member of the circle of artists around the Düsseldorf gallery owner Johanna Ey **1923–24** Trip to Italy with Otto and Martha Dix **1929** Director of the Municipal School of Decorative Art (Städtische Schule für dekorative Kunst), Düsseldorf **1933** Dismissed from position as a consequence of antisemitic policy; flees to The Netherlands (Scheveningen); begins antifascist work **1935–36** Trip and later emigration to the US, where he is given a teaching post after the war at the School of Art, Washington **1946–49** Period of residence in Brazil; two exhibitions there, in the Ministry of Education and the Arts (1946) and the Institute of Architecture in São Paulo (1948) **1976** Contributes to the catalogue accompanying the exhibition "Avant-garde of yesterday – the 'Young Rhineland' and its friends" (Avant-garde gestern – Das junge Rheinland und seine Freunde)

Immanuel Knayer
1896 Schöneberg/Enz –1962 Stuttgart
1914–18 Active military service, seriously wounded **1919–21** Studies at the Stuttgart School of Arts and Crafts **1921–22** Lives in Düsseldorf **1922–28** Studies continued at the Stuttgart Academy under Robert Breyer **1929–32** Takes part in the exhibitions of the Stuttgart Secession and the Stuttgart New Secession **1941** Forbidden to paint **1945** Stuttgart studio destroyed by bombs

Hanns Kralik
1900 Neufeld –1971 Düsseldorf
1920 Studies at the Krefeld School of Arts and Crafts **1924** Studies continued at the Düsseldorf Academy **1928** Works as a freelance artist; member of the ASSO, the German Communist Party and the "Young Rhineland" **1933** Compulsory labour in the Börger-Moor concentration camp **1934** Flees to the Netherlands and on to Paris; works with the Résistance **1939** Arrest and later escape **1945** Returns to Düsseldorf; appointed municipal official (departmental head) for cultural affairs **1951** Dismissed from post because of membership of the German Communist Party; resumes artistic activities

Wilhelm Lachnit
1899 Gittersee/Dresden –1962 Dresden
1914–20 Apprenticeship as interior decorator in Dresden; takes evening classes at the Dresden School of Arts and Crafts **1921–23** Studies at the Dresden Academy under Richard Dreher **1924** Member of the "Red Group"; participates in the "First General German Art Exhibition" in the USSR **1925** Joins the German Communist Party **1927** Co-founder of the Dresden "Aktion" group, which in **1932** becomes the Dresden Secession **1928** Trips to North Africa, southern France, Italy and Switzerland **1929** Founder member of the Dresden section of the ASSO; takes part in the "De onafhangelijken" exhibition at the Stedelijk Museum, Amsterdam **1933** Arrested by the Gestapo; restriction on artistic activities; four works seized as "degenerate" **1944–45** Called up for active military service **1945** Dresden studio destroyed by bombs **1947–54** Appointed professor at the Dresden Art College

Franz Lenk
1898 Langenbernsdorf/Vogtland –1968 Schwäbisch Hall
1912 Apprenticeship as interior decorator **1912–15** Apprenticeship as lithographer **1916–18** Active military service **1918** Studies at the Dresden Academy of Art under Richard Müller, Ferdinand Dorsch and Robert Sterl **1925** Participates in the last exhibition by the Dresden Secession "1919 Group" **1926** Teaching post at the Berlin Art College **1927 and 1928** Takes part in exhibitions by the Berlin Secession **1931** Exhibition in the Galerie Neumann-Nierendorf, Berlin **1932** Participates in the Rhineland touring exhibition of "The Seven" (in Barmen etc.) **1933/34** Appointed professor at the United State Schools, Berlin **1938** Gives up post in protest at the persecution of his colleagues; moves to Orlamünde **1944** Moves to Württemberg **1959–68** Officer for cultural affairs for the City of Schwäbisch Hall

Elfriede Lohse-Wächtler
1899 Dresden –1940 Brandenburg concentration camp
1916 Studies at the Dresden School of Arts and Crafts **1919** Contact with the Dresden Secession; adopts the pseudonym Nikolaus Wächtler; involved in the Spartacus group **1921** Studio together with Kurt Lohse, her husband, and Otto Griebel **1926–27** Period of residence in Hamburg **1929** Nervous breakdown, admitted to Friedrichsberg psychiatric institute; "Friedrichsberger Köpfe" (Friedrichsberg Heads) exhibited in the Galerie Maria Kunde, Hamburg **1930** One-woman show in the Vereinigter Stadtclub der Hamburger Frauenverbände, Hamburg **1931** Lives with a band of gipsies **1932** Returns to Dresden **1933**

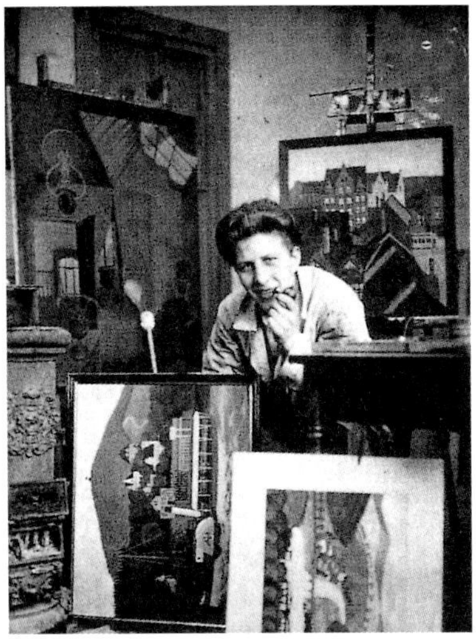

HANS MERTENS

Work condemned as "degenerate"; admitted to and interned in the Arnsdorf "clinic", near Dresden; numerous works done there destroyed **1940** Gassed as part of the fascist "cleansing" programme

Jeanne Mammen
1890 Berlin –1976 Berlin
1906–07 Studies at the Académie Julian, Paris **1908–10** Studies at the Académie Royale des Beaux-Arts, Brussels **1911** Studies continued at the Scuola Libera Academica, Rome, Villa Medici **1912** Return to Paris; shares studio with sister; participates in the "Salon des Indépendants", Paris **1913** Exhibits with the "Indépendants" in Brussels **1914** The Mammen family flees from Paris to the Netherlands (The Hague) **1917** First book of illustrations published **1919** Moves into studio on the Kurfürstendamm, Berlin **1921** Cinema posters for the Universum film company (Ufa) **1922–33** Illustrations for fashion magazines and advertising material, and for "Ulk", "Der Querschnitt" and "Simplicissimus" **1930** First one-woman show in the Galerie Fritz Gurlitt, Berlin **1931** Book illustrations **1932** Trip to the Soviet Union **1933/34–45** Illustration commissions cease **1933** Takes part in exhibition by the Association of Women Artists in Berlin (Verein der Künstlerinnen zu Berlin) **1938** Exhibition in the California Institute of Technology, Pasadena **1948** Takes part in the "Zone 5" group exhibition in the Galerie Franz, Berlin **1960** One-woman show in the Academy of Arts, Berlin **1967** Publication of the translation of Arthur Rimbaud's "Illuminations" **1970** One-woman show in the Neuer Berliner Kunstverein

Carlo Mense
1886 Rheine/Westphalia –1965 Königswinter
1905–08 Studies at the Düsseldorf Academy **1909** Studies continued at the Berlin Academy under Lovis Corinth **1910** Trips to the Netherlands, England and Italy **1912** Takes part in the Sonderbund exhibition, Cologne **1913** Participates in the Berlin Autumn Salon and the "Rhenish Expressionists" (Rheinische Expressionisten) exhibition in Bonn **1914** Period of residence in Ascona; called up for active military service **1918** Joins the "Novembergruppe"; moves to Munich **1922** Participates in the "Primavera fiorentina" exhibition, Florence, along with the "Valori plastici" group **1923** Member of the New Secession in Munich **1925–1932** Professor at the Breslau Academy of Art; takes part in the "Neue Sachlichkeit" exhibition at the Mannheim Kunsthalle **1929** Participates in the "De onafhangelijken" exhibition at the Stedelijk Museum, Amsterdam **1933** Rome Prize, followed by longer period of residence in Rome **1937** Numerous works seized as "degenerate" **1939–45** Lives in Bad Honnef **1961** One-man show at the Städtische Kunstsammlung, Bonn

Hans Mertens
1906 Hanover –1944 Albi (Alby)
1925–26 Studies at the Hanover School of Arts and Crafts; works as a restorer in Hanover's Provinzialmuseum and Kestner-Museum **1939** Called up for active military service

Hanna Nagel
1907 Heidelberg –1975 Heidelberg
1924 Apprenticeship as bookbinder **1925–29** Studies at the Karlsruhe Academy under Karl Hubbuch and Wilhelm Schnarrenberger et al. **1929** Transfers to Berlin; studies continued under Emil Orlik and Hans Meid **1933–34** Rome Prize and subsequent period of residence in Rome **1935** City of Nuremberg Dürer Prize scholarship and second period of residence in Rome **1936** First book illustrations **1937** Kassel Prize; Silver Medal for Graphic Art at the World Exhibition in Paris **1945** Moves to Heidelberg; works as graphic artist **1960** Drexel Prize, Nuremberg

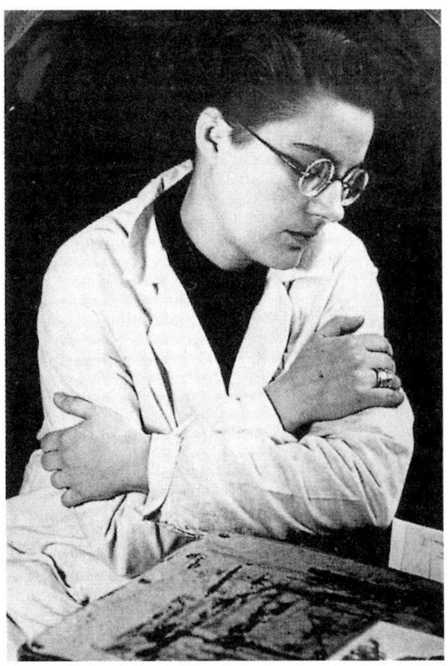

HANNA NAGEL

Otto Nagel
1894 Berlin –1967 Berlin
1908–10 Apprenticeship in the Gottfried Heinersdorf Mosaic and Glass-painting Workshops (Werkstätten für Mosaik- und Glasmalerei Gottfried Heinersdorf) in Berlin **1911/12** Attends the Municipal Evening College (Städtische Abendschule) **1913–17** Repeated active military service; member of Spartacus and the Independent Social Democratic Party of Germany **1919** Receives support from the "Art Soviet" (Arbeitsrat für Kunst) **1921** Works as a freelance artist; lithograph portfolio "Karree Weddings" (The Squares of Berlin-Wedding); takes part in Free Secession and "Juryless Art Show" (Juryfreier Kunstschau) exhibitions; founds "Artists' Aid" (Künstlerhilfe) **1924** Joins the "Red Group" **1927** contributes to "AIZ" and the "Rote Fahne" **1928** Co-founder of "Eulenspiegel" **1930** Trade-union work in the National Association of Artists (Reichsverband der bildenden Künstler) **1931** Co-organizer of "Women in Need" (Frauen in Not) exhibition **1933** House searched on numerous occasions, at times imprisoned **1934** Forbidden to paint; organizes an exhibition in Amsterdam and the Hague with works by Heinrich Zille, Käthe Kollwitz and himself; renewed arrest **1935/36** Founds a private painting school; sent to Sachsenhausen concentration camp **1937/38** 27 works seized as "degenerate" **1941** Flees to Forst **1945** Compulsory evacuation to Berlin; co-founder and chairman of the Brandenburg regional branch of the Arts Federation (Kulturbund) **1946** Member of the regional parliament **1948** Awarded professorship **1950/51** Founder member of the German Academy of Arts in Berlin (Deutsche Academy der Künste zu Berlin); National Prize; retrospective at the Academy of Arts **1957** City of Berlin Goethe Prize **1958** Exhibitions in Berlin, Stockholm, Moscow, Amsterdam and other cities **1959** Honorary member of the USSR Academy of Arts **1964** Fatherland Order of Merit (Gold)

Reinhold Nägele
1884 Murrhardt –1972 Stuttgart
1899–04 Training as interior decorator in his father's business **1904–05** Continues training in the workshops of the Stuttgart School of Arts and Crafts under Bernhard Pankok and Rudolf Rochga **1905–09** Works as interior decorator and church painter in Berlin **1907** Exhibition in Bruno Cassirer's gallery, Berlin **1909–10** Works as a freelance artist in Stuttgart **1910–11** Periods of residence in Munich and Paris **1915** Works as a church painter in Breslau; active military service **1919** Returns to Stuttgart **1923** Co-founder of the Stuttgart Secession **1937** Excluded from the National Chamber of Arts as a consequence of its antisemitic policy **1939** Emigrates to England **1940** Period of residence in New York **1952** "Honoris causa" professorship from the Baden-Württemberg Ministry of the Arts; moves to the Netherlands **1963** Returns to Murrhardt

Felix Nussbaum
1904 Osnabrück –1944 (presumed) Auschwitz
1922–23 Studies at the State School of Arts and Crafts, Hamburg, under Fritz Behnke **1923** Moves to Berlin **1924/25–29** Studies continued

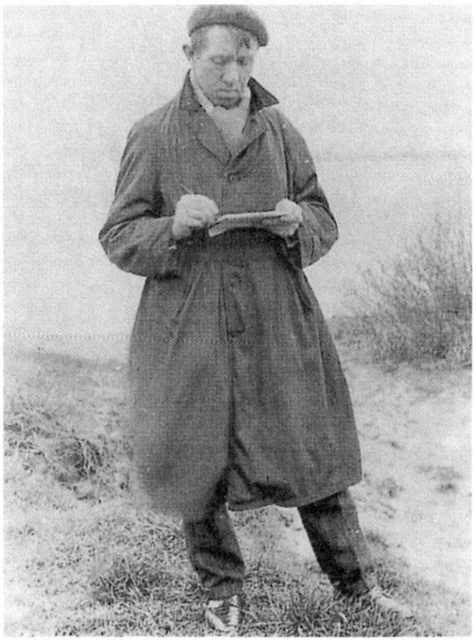

FRANZ RADZIWILL

at the United State School for Free and Applied Art under Cesar Klein and Paul Plonthe **1929** Works as a freelance artist **1932** Grand State Prize from the Prussian Academy of Fine Arts brings a scholarship and a period of residence in Rome; guest student at the Villa Massimo **1932** Works destroyed by a fire in his Berlin studio; contributes to the magazine "Der Querschnitt"; takes part in the Berlin Secession exhibition **1933** Studies in Rome continued; moves to Alassio as antisemitic feeling grows **1934** Flees to Belgium **1940** Registered in Brussels as an enemy foreigner and imprisoned in Saint-Cypres; later transferred to Bordeaux, from where he flees to Brussels **1944** Arrest and internment in the Villa Quatre Bras, Brussels; deportation to Auschwitz

Gerta Overbeck-Schenk
1898 Dortmund –1977 Lünen
1915–18 Training as an art teacher in Düsseldorf **1918–19** Trial appointment as an art teacher in Dortmund **1919–22** Studies at the Hanover School of Arts and Crafts under Fritz Burger-Mühlfeld **1922–31** Works as an art teacher in Dortmund **1931–38** Works as a freelance artist in Hanover **1931–32** Collaborates on the magazine "Der Wachsbogen" **1932** Participates in the "Neue Sachlichkeit in Hannover" exhibition in the Herzog Anton Ulrich-Museum, Brunswick **1937** Moves to Worpswede **1938** Moves to Cappenberg

Werner Peiner
1897 Düsseldorf –1984 Kronenburg/Eifel
1914–18 Active military service **1919** Commences studies at the Düsseldorf Academy **1920** Member of the "Three-man Federation" (Dreimannbund) together with Richard Gessner and Fritz Burmann **1923** Period of residence in Vienna; trips to the Netherlands, Spain, Italy and Austria **1933** Professor of monumental painting, Düsseldorf Academy **1935** Trip to Africa **1936** Founds own school of painting in the Eifel region; takes regular part in the "Great German Exhibition of Art" (Große Deutsche Kunstausstellung), Munich

Herbert Ploberger
1902 Wels/Upper Austria –1977 Munich
Studies at the Vienna School of Arts and Crafts under Böhm and Zischek; studies continued in Paris **1927** Moves to Berlin **1945–46** Works as a stage-set designer in Linz and Vienna **1950–77** Works as a stage-set and costume designer in Munich

Curt Querner
1904 Börnchen, near Dresden –1976 Kreischa
Apprenticeship as metalworker **1926–30** Studies at the Dresden Academy **from 1929** Studies continued under Otto Dix; member of the ASSO and the German Communist Party **1930–32** Cordage business in the Erz Mountains; house in Dresden **1933** Arrested at the "Degenerate Art" exhibition in front of Otto Dix' war triptych **1932–37** Out of work **1940–45** Active military service **1945** House and studio destroyed, only a part of his work recovered **1945–47** Prisoner of war in French hands; following his return, works as a freelance artist **1959** City of Freital Art Prize **1971** Käthe Kollwitz Prize from the Academy of Arts **1972** Awarded GDR National Prize **1973** Exhibition in Vienna **1975** Exhibitions in Amsterdam and the Hague

Max Radler
1904 Breslau –1971 Munich
1918 Apprenticeship as stone-mason and stuccoer **1919** Works as an interior decorator in Zeitz **1923/24** Moves to Munich; works as an interior decorator **1928** Studies at the Institute of Applied Arts and Related Trades (Lehranstalt für Angewandte Kunst und Verwandte Berufe an der Westen-Rieder-Straße) under Georg Schrimpf et al. **1938** Joins and exhibits with "The Juryless" group **1939–45** Active military service and prisoner of war; almost all his works are destroyed in bombing raids on Munich; participates after the war in the exhibitions by the "New Group", Munich; collaborates on "Simpl und Simplicissimus"

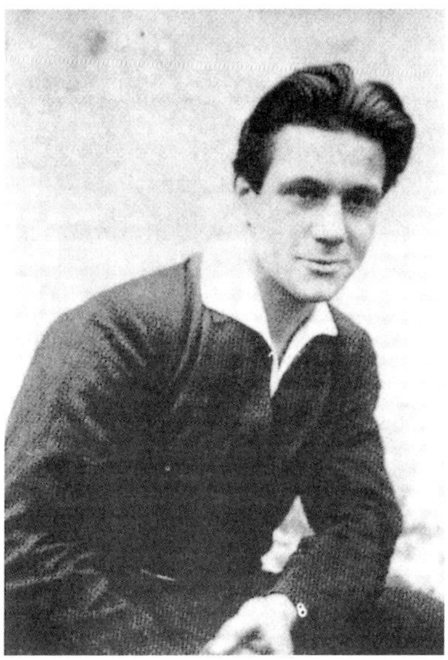

KARL RÜTER

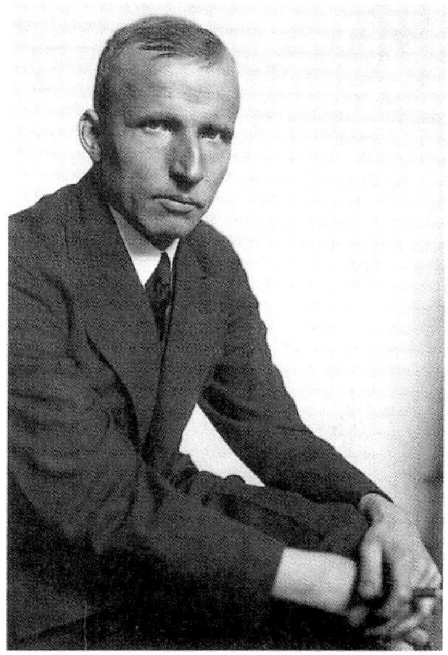

ALBERT RENGER-PATZSCH

Franz Radziwill
1895 Strohhausen –1983 Wilhelmshaven
1909–13 Apprenticeship as builder; studies architecture at the State Insitute of Higher Technology (Höhere Technische Staatslehranstalt) and at the same time takes evening classes in commercial drawing and design at the Bremen School of Arts and Crafts **1915–17** Active military service and prisoner of war **1919** Returns from captivity **1920–23** Lives in Berlin; joins the Secession **1923** Moves to Dangast **1925** First one-man show in Oldenburg **1927** Exhibition in Bruno Cassirer's Berlin gallery **1927/28** Uses a studio at Otto Dix's home in Dresden **1929** Participates in the "De onathangelijken" exhibition at the Stedelijk Museum, Amsterdam **1931** Joins the Novembergruppe **1931** Appointed professor at the Düsseldorf Academy of Art (assuming Paul Klee's chair); takes part in the "New German Romanticism" exhibition at the Kestner-Gesellschaft, Hanover **1935** Dismissed from post; forbidden to practise profession **1937** Work condemned as "degenerate" **1939–45** Called up for military service **1963** Rome Prize and period of residence in the Villa Massimo

Anton Räderscheidt
1892 Cologne –1970 Cologne
1910 Commences studies at the Cologne School of Arts and Crafts **1911–14** Studies continued at the Düsseldorf Academy of Art; trains as an art teacher at the Art Teachers' Seminar (Zeichenlehrerseminar) **1914–17** Active military service **1917–19** Teaching practice at the Cologne-Mülheim secondary school (Realgymnasium); thereafter works as a freelance artist **1919** Co-founder and member of the Cologne

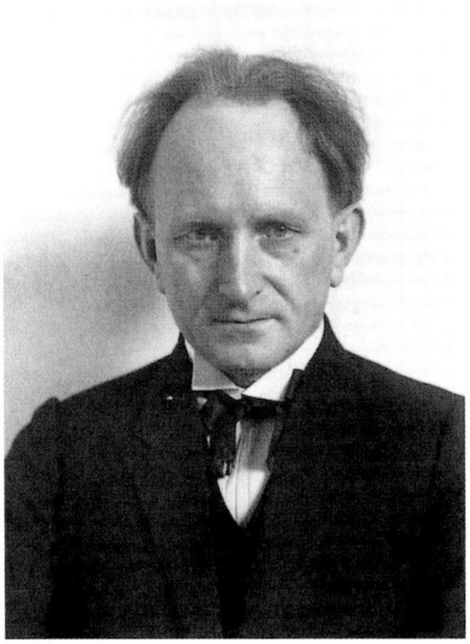

AUGUST SANDER Cologne, August Sander Archiv

group "Stupid" **1925** Takes part in the "Neue Sachlichkeit" exhibition at the Mannheim Kunsthalle **1934–35** Moves to Berlin **1936** Flees to France **1937** Takes part in the exhibitions of the "Salon des Surindépendants"; one-man show at the Galerie Billiét-Vorms **1938** Participates in the "Free German Art" (Freie Deutsche Kunst) exhibition by the Federation of Free Artists (Freier Künstlerbund) in the Maison de la Culture, Paris, organized as a counter-event to the fascist propagandist "Degenerate Art" exhibition **1939–42** Internment in Toulon and Les Milles; Paris studio seized **1942** Flees to Switzerland **1947** Moves to Paris **1949** Returns to Cologne **1952** Retrospective in the Kölner Kunstverein **1953** Participates in the "3rd German Exhibition of Art" (III. Deutsche Kunstausstellung) in Dresden **1960** Exhibits with the German Federation of Artists in the Baden-Baden Kunsthalle **1962** Exhibition in the Kölner Kunstverein and the rooms of the Kunsthaus Lempertz

Albert Renger-Patzsch
1897 Würzburg –1966 Wamel
1916–18 Active military service; chemistry studies at the Dresden Technical College **1922–25** Press photographer for the Chicago Tribune; collaborates with Ernst Fuhrmann on the latter's book series "Die Welt der Pflanze" (The World of Plants) **1924–25** Plant studies and essays in the "Deutscher Kamera Almanach" **1925** Works as a freelance photographer; first exhibition; joins the German Werkbund **1928** Own studio in the Folkwang Museum; publication of "Die Welt ist schön" (The World is Beautiful), edited by Kurt Wolff and with a foreword by Carl Georg Heise; works for industry and in advertising; his archives are destroyed during World War II **1944** Moves to Wamel

Karl Rüter
1902 Hanover –1986 Bremen
1920–23 Training at the Hanover School of Arts and Crafts under Richard Schlösser and Carl Wiederhold; trips to Italy, to Spain and Prague **1932** Participates in the "Neue Sachlichkeit in Hanover" exhibition, Herzog Anton Ulrich-Museum, Brunswick **1937** Exhibition at the Kunstverein; simultaneously, two of his works are removed from the museum as being "degenerate" **1943** Works destroyed by bombs **around 1955** Works as a stage-set designer in "Die Brücke", the theatre directed by his brother **1961** Retrospective in the Haus am Waldsee, Berlin **1964** Designs for tapestries; moves to Bremen **1974** Large-scale special exhibition of the Federation of Fine Artists (Bund Bildender Künstler) in Hanover

Wilhelm Rudolph
1889 Chemnitz –1982 Dresden
Apprenticeship as lithographer **1908–14** Studies at the Dresden Academy of Art under Robert Sterl and Carl Bantzer **from 1920** Freelance artist; member of the Dresden Association of Artists (Künstlervereinigung) **1924** Participates in the "First General German Exhibition of Art", USSR **1932–38** Professor at the Dresden Academy **1938** Dismissed from post on political grounds **1945** Works destroyed by bombs **1947–49** Professor at the Dresden College of Fine Arts (Hochschule für Bildende Künste) **1981** Honorary senator of the College

August Sander
1876 Herdorf a.d. Heller –1964 Cologne
1890–96 Works as a pithead boy at the "San Fernando" mine near Herdorf; first photographic equipment of his own **1896** Called up for military service; works for the Trier photographer Georg Jung **1898–1900** Journeyman years as photographic assistant; attends the Dresden Academy of Art **1901** Works for the "Fotographische Kunstanstalt Greiff" (Greiff Photographic Art Studio) in Linz **1902** Takes over Greiff studio with Franz Stuckenberg **1904** Assumes the running of the studio single-handedly; Gold Medal in Wels; Stifter Prize in Leipzig; Gold Medal and Cross of Honour at an exhibition in the Palais des Beaux-Arts, Paris **1909** Sells Linz studio **1910** Moves to Cologne; briefly employed as manager in the Atelier Blumenberg and Hermann; begins Westerwälder portraits **1914** Participates in exhibition at the German Werkbund, Cologne **1914–18** Active military service **1920** Develops idea for an artistic and documentary survey of different human types, to comprise 45 portfolios in 7 groups of 12 photographs each **1929** Publishes "Antlitz der Zeit" (Countenance of the Times) – 60 photographs of German people – intended as a preview of the complete work "Menschen des 20. Jahrhunderts" (20th-Century People) involving c. 550 pictures **1931** Series of lectures on the nature and development of photography on Cologne Radio **1933–37** Publication of the series "Deutsche Lande – Deutsche Menschen" (German Lands – German People) with photographs by August Sander **1934** "Antlitz der Zeit" is withdrawn from shops on the orders of the National Socialists and the plates are destroyed **1939** Photographic works secured; gradual move to Kuchhausen **1944** Cologne apartment destroyed by bombs **1951** Exhibits at the 1st "Photokina" show, Cologne **1954** Participates in the "Family of Men" exhibition, Museum of Modern Art, New York **1959** Own special issue of the magazine "Du" ("You") with a selection of portraits **1960/61** Federal Cross of Merit (1st Class) and Deutsche Gesellschaft für Photographie Art Prize **1962** Publication of the book "Deutschenspiegel" (German Mirror); exhibition in Mexico

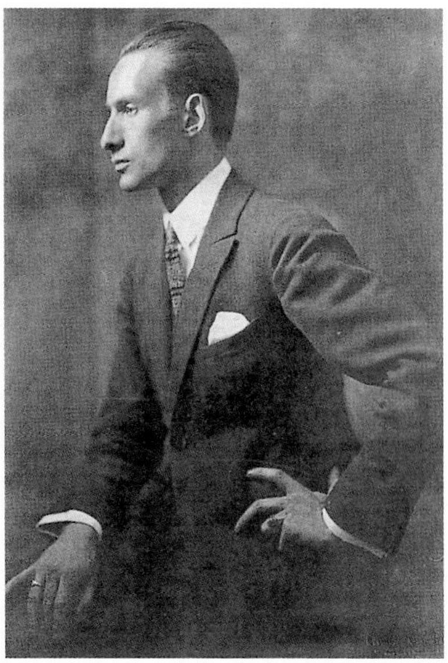

CHRISTIAN SCHAD

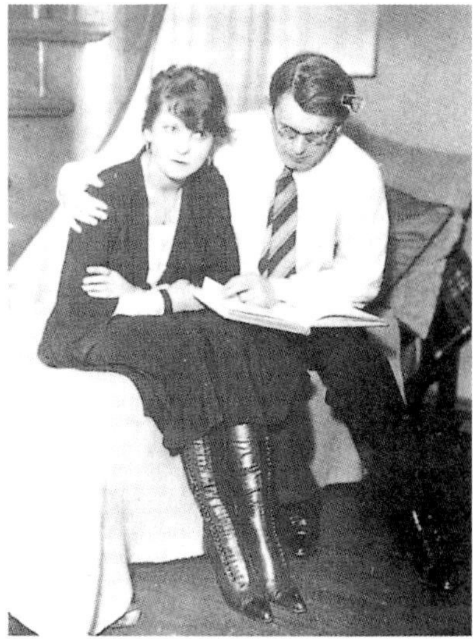

RUDOLF SCHLICHTER

Christian Schad
1894 Miesbach –1982 Keilberg
1913 Studies at the Munich Academy **1915** Participates in an exhibition by the New Munich Secession **1915–20** Periods of residence in Zurich and Geneva; takes part in Dada activities **1919** First photograms, or "Schadographs" **1920–27** Period of residence in Italy, primarily

in Naples **1925** Moves to Vienna **1927** First one-man show in the Galerie Würthle, Vienna **1929** Participates in the "De onafhangelijken" exhibition at the Stedelijk Museum, Amsterdam **1930** Special exhibition in the rooms of the "The Juryless" group, Berlin **1935–42** Commissions and exhibitions, incl. in the Verein Berliner Künstler **from 1935** Works in commercial business **1936** First exhibition in the Museum of Modern Art, New York: "Fantastic Art, Dada, Surrealism"; this is followed by others **1942** Moves to Aschaffenburg; produces a copy of the Stuppach Madonna, commissioned by the City of Aschaffenburg **1962** Moves to Keilheim; numerous one-man and group shows **1968** Takes part in the "Dada, Surrealism and their Heritage" exhibition, Museum of Modern Art, and in the "Aspects of Neue Sachlichkeit" (Aspekte der Neuen Sachlichkeit) exhibition at the Galleria del Levante, Milan, Munich, and Rome **1971** Takes part in the "Metamorphoses of the Object" (Metamorphosen des Dinges) touring exhibition in Brussels, Rotterdam, Berlin and Milan, and in the "Realismus 1919–1930" exhibition in the Württembergischer Kunstverein, Stuttgart **1972** Large-scale retrospective of his works from 1915 to 1971 in the Palazzo Reale, Milan **1976** Takes part in "The Thirties – The German Arena" (Die 30er Jahre – Schauplatz Deutschland) touring exhibition in Munich, Essen and Zurich **1978** Participates in the "1900–1933" exhibition, Centre Georges Pompidou, Paris **1979** Takes part in the "Neue Sachlichkeit and German Realism of the Twenties" exhibition by the Arts Council of Great Britain, Hayward Gallery, London

Rudolf Schlichter
1890 Calw (Württemberg) –1955 Munich
1904 Apprenticeship as enamel painter in a factory in Pforzheim **1907–10** Attends the Stuttgart School of Arts and Crafts **1910** Commences studies at the Karlsruhe Academy **1916** Called up for active military service, early release following hunger strike **1919** Co-founder of the "Rih" group in Karlsruhe; moves to Berlin; joins the "Novembergruppe" and the German Communist Party **1920** Takes part in the "1st International DADA Fair (1. Internationale DADA-Messe); works as an illustrator for various publishing houses **1924** Founder member of the Berlin "Red Group" **1925** Takes part in the "Neue Sachlichkeit" exhibition at the Mannheim Kunsthalle **1927** One-man show in the Galerie Neumann-Nierendorf, Berlin **1928** Member of the ASSO **1929** Takes part in the "De onafhangelijken" exhibition at the Stedelijk Museum, Amsterdam **1931** Publication of his novel "Zwischenwelt" (Intermediate World) **1932/33** Moves to Rottenburg am Neckar; Rowohlt publishes his two-volume autobiography, "Das widerspenstige Fleisch" and "Tönerne Füße" (The Wilful Flesh; Feet of Clay) **1937** Works seized as "degenerate" **1939** Moves to Munich; contact with the Catholic circle around the magazine "Hochland" **1942** Studio destroyed in bombing raids **1946** Participates in the "1st German Exhibition of Art" (I.Deutsche Kunstaustellung), Dresden **1949** Rowohlt publishes his essay "Das Abenteuer der Kunst" (The Adventure of Art); joins the "New Group"; participates in the "Great Munich Exhibition of Art" (Große Münchner Kunstausstellung)

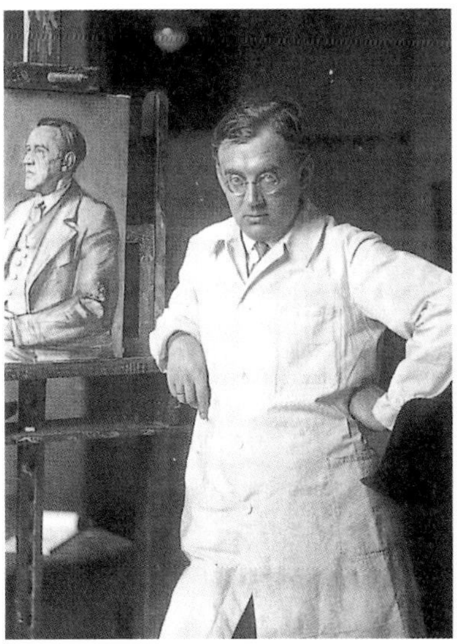

GEORG SCHOLZ

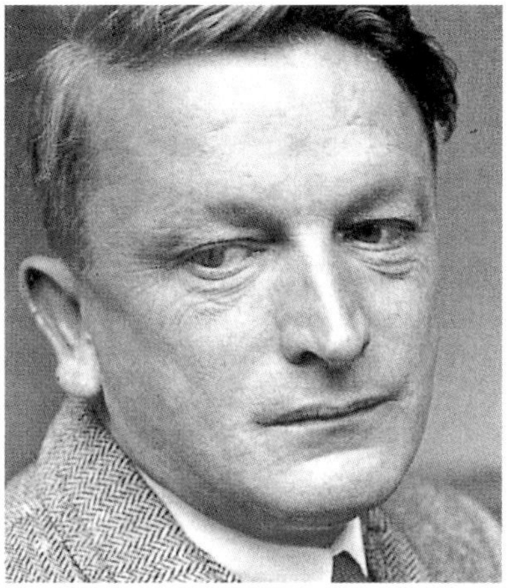

GEORG SCHRIMPF

Wilhelm Schnarrenberger
1892 Buchen (Baden) –1966 Karlsruhe
1911–16 Attends the Munich School of Arts and Crafts **from 1912** Parallel architectural studies at the Ludwig Maximilian University, Munich **1916** First one-man show at Hans Goltz' gallery in Munich; called up for active military service **1919/20** Returns to Munich, works as a freelance artist; contributes to the magazines "Simplicissimus", "Wieland", "Der Weg" and others; exhibits with the Munich New Secession for the first time **1921** Appointed professor of commercial art at the Karlsruhe Academy; member of the "Rih" group **1924** Together with the architect Hans Wingler, founds the "ORNA Workshops for All Areas of Commercial Art, Advertising Architecture and Interior Decoration" (ORNA-Werkstätten für alle Bereiche der Werbekunst, der Reklamearchitektur und der Innendekoration) **1925** Takes part in the "Neue Sachlichkeit" exhibition at the Mannheim Kunsthalle **1927** Participates in "The Juryless" exhibition, Berlin, the Cologne "Pressa" and the "German Art of the Present Day" (Deutsche Kunst der Gegenwart) exhibition in Nuremberg **1933** Dismissed from post; moves to Berlin **1934/35** Period of residence in Rome as guest of the Villa Massimo **1937** Works condemned as "degenerate" **1938–47** Period of residence in Lenzkirch, Black Forest **1947** Reappointed professor at the Karlsruhe Academy; member of the Baden Secession **1948** Moves to Karlsruhe **1955** Exhibits with the Baden-Württemberg Federation of Artists (Baden-Württemberg Künstlerbund) for the first time **1958** Elected onto the Baden-Württemberg Federation of Artists' "Council of Ten" (Rat der Zehn) **1962** Hans Thoma State Prize

Georg Scholz
1890 Wolfenbüttel –1945 Waldkirch
1908 Commences studies at the Karlsruhe Academy under Hans Thoma et al. **1912–14** Studies for one semester under Lovis Corinth in Berlin **from 1914** Works as a freelance artist **1915–18** Active military service **1919** Moves to Grötzingen, near Karlsruhe; member of the German Communist Party and the Berlin "Novembergruppe"; co-founder of the "Rih" group **1920** Collaborates on the magazine "Der Gegner"; takes part in the "1st Internationale DADA Fair" in Berlin **1920–23** Exhibitions and work as a book illustrator **1923** Assistant at the Baden State Academy of Art, Karlsruhe; collaborates on the magazine "Die Pleite" **1924** Head of an preparatory class at the State Academy of Art; participates in "The Juryless" exhibition, Berlin **1925** Appointed professor at the State Academy of Art; takes part in the "Neue Sachlichkeit" exhibition at the Mann-

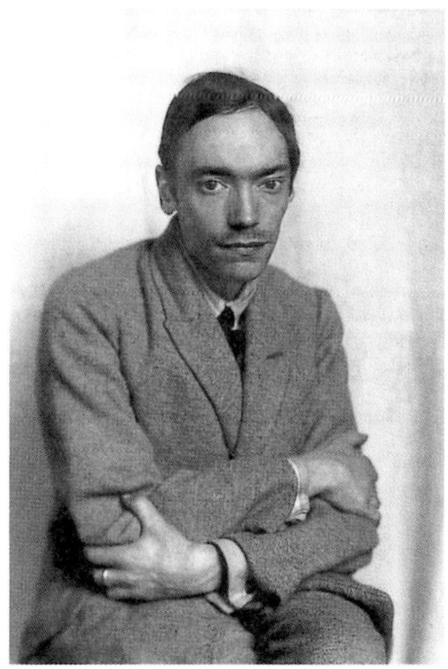

FRANZ WILHELM SEIWERT Cologne, August Sander Archiv

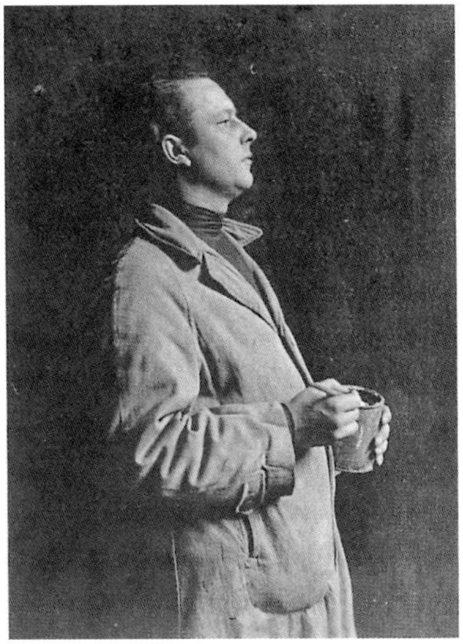

WALTER SCHULZ-MATAN

heim Kunsthalle **1926** Starts contributing to the magazine "Simplicissimus" **1927** Member of the executive committee of the newly-founded Arts and Crafts Institute (Institut für das Kunsthandwerk) **1928** His picture "Fleisch und Eisen" (Flesh and Iron) is removed from the exhibition "Art and Technology" (Kunst und Technik) at the Folkwang Museum, Essen, on "moral grounds" **1933** Dismissed from teaching post; moves to Hassmersheim **1935** Moves to Waldkirch; converts to Catholicism **1937** Pictures seized as "degenerate" **1939** Forbidden to practise profession **1945** Appointed mayor of Waldkirch by the French occupation forces

Georg Schrimpf
1889 Munich –1938 Berlin
1902 Apprenticeship as baker; autodidact as painter **1915** Active military service, released following illness **1915–18** Lives in Berlin; works as a freelance artist **1918** Moves to Munich **1921** Joins the New Secession **1922** Lives in Italy; in contact with the "Valori plastici" group **1924** Publication of a small monograph on Georg Schrimpf by Carlo Carrà **1925** Takes part in the "Neue Sachlichkeit" exhibition at the Mannheim Kunsthalle **1927** Professor at the Master Craftsmen's School of Interior Decoration (Meisterschule für Dekorationskunst), Munich **1929** Participates in the "De onafhangelijken" exhibition at the Stedelijk Museum, Amsterdam **1932** Period of residence in Rome **1933–38** Professor at the College of Art Education (Hochschule für Kunsterziehung), Berlin **1933** Takes part in the "New German Romanticism" exhibition at the Kestner-Society, Hanover **1937** Dismissed from teaching post by the National Socialists

Karl Schwesig
1898 Gelsenkirchen –1955 Düsseldorf
1914–15 Works as a gardener's assistant **1916–18** Military service as a clerk **1918** Attends the Düsseldorf Academy **1921** Member of the "Young Rhineland" group and the artistic circle around the gallery owner Johanna Ey; takes part in exhibitions **1924** Co-founder of the magazine "Die Peitsche" **1928** Co-founder of the Rhenish Secession **1930** Period of study in Sanary, Côte d'Azur **1933–34** Arrested and tortured by the Gestapo in Düsseldorf **1934** Trial before the Hamm Higher Regional Court; convicted of high treason **1934–35** Lives in Düsseldorf **1935** Flees to Antwerp; political asylum **1940** Captured by German army, deported to France and interned in the St. Cyprien camp **1940–43** Internment in various camps in France; moved to Paris and imprisoned in Romainville fortress **1943** Transportation back to Düsseldorf; compulsory labour; release under police observation **1943–44** In hiding in Lohne/Oldenburg, Zeltingen and Wehlen a.d. Mosel; return to Düsseldorf following end of the war

Walter Schulz-Matan
1889 Apolda –1965 Schiers/Switzerland
Apprenticeship as interior decorator in Mittweida **1912** Briefly attends the Munich School of Arts and Crafts; further training as autodidact **1914–18** Active military service **1919/20** Lives in Munich; takes part in exhibitions in Hans Goltz' gallery and with "The Juryfree" group **1923** Exhibition in the rooms of the Munich New Secession **1924/25** Study-trip to Italy and Germany **1925** Takes part in the "Neue Sachlichkeit" exhibition at the Mannheim Kunsthalle; participates in the "Novembergruppe" exhibition in Berlin **1927** Periods of residence in Paris and Brittany **1928** Joins the Munich artists' group "The Seven" **1932/33** Travel scholarship from the City of Munich, period of residence in Spain and Portugal **1934** Commission for a series of paintings of German motorways, covering the stretch from Munich to Salzburg **1949–64** Renewed participation in exhibitions **1989** Memorial exhibition in the Munich Stadtmuseum on the occasion of his 100th birthday

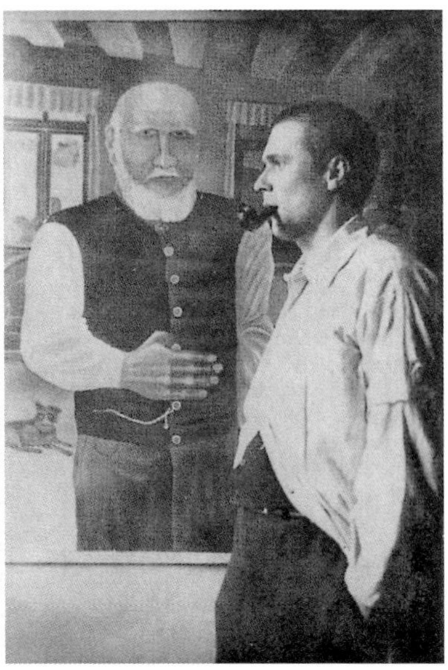

ERICH WEGNER

Franz Wilhelm Seiwert
1894 Cologne –1933 Cologne
1910–14 Attends the Cologne School of Arts and Crafts **1917** Collaborates on the magazine "Die Aktion" **1919** Participates in Dada activities, but not in the Dada exhibition; publication of the woodcut series "Welt zum Staunen" (A World To Be Amazed At); joins the "Stupid" group **1923** First large-scale one-man show, Kölner Kunstverein **1929** Founds the magazine "a-z" as the organ of the "Group of Progressive Artists"; takes part in the "asb (architectuur, schilderwerk, beeldhouwwerk)" exhibition, Stedelijk Museum, Amsterdam **1930** Participates in the "Socialistische kunst heden", Stedelijk Museum **1931–32** Collaborates on the interior design of the Cologne Kunstgewerbemuseum; design for a glass mosaic (later destroyed by the National Socialists)

Ernst Thoms
1896 Nienburg –1938 Nietzen (near Nienburg)
1911–14 Apprenticeship as painter **1914–19** Active military service and prisoner of war **1920** Studies at the Hanover School of Arts and Crafts under Fritz Burger-Mühlfeld **1924–25** Works as a stage-set painter in the opera house **1926** One-man show in the Kestner-Society, Hanover **1928** One-man show in the Galerie Neumann-Nierendorf, Berlin **1930** Member of the German Federation of Artists **1931** Member of the Hanover Secession **1939–40** Active military service **1943** Studio and house destroyed by bombs, numerous pictures lost **1950** Returns to Hanover **1957** Retrospective in the Hanover Kunstverein **1964** Grand Cross of Merit of the Lower-Saxony Order of Merit

Adolf Uzarski
1885 Ruhrort bei Duisburg –1970 Düsseldorf
Building apprenticeship and training at the Cologne School of Architecture (Baugewerbeschule) **1906** Commences studies at the Düsseldorf School of Arts and Crafts **1909–10** Participates in exhibitions by the "Ring" association of artists in Hagen, and in further exhibitions in Berlin and Hagen **1916** First exhibition with Arthur Kaufmann in the Düsseldorf Kunsthalle **1916/17** "Totentanz" (danse macabre) lithograph portfolio **1917/18** Takes part in the "Great Berlin Exhibition of Art" in Düsseldorf **1919** Co-founder of the "Young Rhineland" group **1922** "1st International Exhibition of Art" staged in the Tietz department store, having been turned down by the Düsseldorf Kunsthalle **1925** A split in the "Young Rhineland" leads to the formation of the "Rhine Group" (Rheingruppe), with whom Udarski exhibits until **1930**. **1929–30** Collaboration with the newly founded Rhenish Secession **1942** Forbidden to paint; moves to Stromberg/Sieg; in hiding in Robertville, Belgium **1945** Returns to Düsseldorf **1954–56** Contributes to the magazine "Der neue Michel" **1967** Retrospective in the Academy of Arts, Berlin

Eberhard Viegener
1890 Soest/Westphalia –1967 Bilme
1904–07 Apprenticeship as painter **1907** Attends the painting class at the Commercial School of Further Education (Gewerbliche Fortbildungsschule), Hagen **1912–14** Lives in Zu-

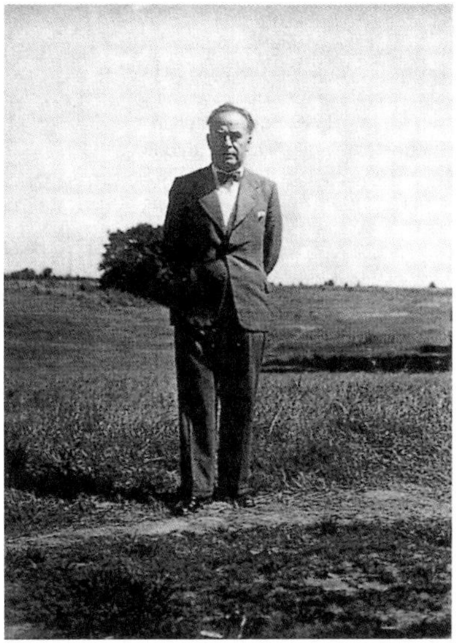

GUSTAV WUNDERWALD

rich and Klosters **1914–17** Lives in Soest **1928** Trip to Paris **1934** Foundation of the Eberhard-Viegener-Gesellschaft in Dortmund **1936** Period of residence in Berlin **1937** Pictures seized as "degenerate" **1945** Joins the Westphalian Secession **1946–54** President of the West German Federation of Artists (Westdeutscher Künstlerbund) **1947** City of Hagen Osthaus Prize **1960** "Honoris causa" professorship on the occasion of his 70th birthday

Karl Völker
1889 Halle –1962 Halle
1904–10 Apprenticeship as interior decorator **1912–13** Training at the Dresden School of Arts and Crafts; thereafter works as a freelance artist **1918** First one-man show at the Halle Kunstverein **1919** Foundation of the Halle Artists' Group (Hallische Künstlergruppe), link-up with the Berlin "Novembergruppe" and participation in exhibitions **1921** Takes part in the "Great Berlin Exhibition of Art" **1922** Participates in the "1st International Exhibition of Art" in Düsseldorf **1923–25** Contributes to the weekly paper "Das Wort" **1924** Joins the Berlin "Red Group"; participates in the "First General German Art Exhibition", USSR **1927** Submits an entry in the competition for a design for the Palace of the League of Nations, Geneva **1928–32** Works as an architect, primarily in the field of social housing **1930** Participates in the "International Exhibition of Socialist Art", Amsterdam **1933–43** Commissions to restore historical monuments **1944–45** Active military service and prisoner of war **1946–62** Works as architect and painter **1949** Retrospective in the Moritzburgmuseum, Halle **1961** City of Halle Art Prize

Erich Wegner
1899 Gnoien/Mecklenburg –1980 Hanover
1919–21 Studies at the Hanover School of Arts and Crafts under Fritz Burger-Mühlfeld **1921–25** Periods of residence at various places; works as house painter, commercial artist and stage-set painter **1929** Participates in the "De onafhangelijken" exhibition at the Stedelijk Museum, Amsterdam **1946** Teaching post at the Hanover College of Adult Education **1951–79** Numerous exhibitions at home and abroad; retrospective in the Wilhelm-Busch-Museum, Hanover **1972** Medal for Services to the City of Hanover **1979** Cross of Merit (2nd Class) of the Lower-Saxony Order of Merit

Kurt Weinhold
1896 Berlin –1965 Calw
Initial training as painter from father and as autodidact; moves to Munich **1915** Active military service and release **1917** Called up again, he refuses to comply **1922** Moves to Calw **From 1928** takes regular part in the spring exhibitions of the Prussian Academy in Berlin and the Berlin Federation of Artists **1929** Trip to Paris **1930** Takes part in the "Socialistische kunst heden" exhibition, Stedelijk Museum, Amsterdam, and in exhibitions by the Berlin Secession **1932** Converts to Catholicism **1934** Rome Prize and period of residence at the Villa Massimo in Rome **1937** Mentioned by name at the "Degenerate Art" exhibition in Munich **1939** Drafted into a construction unit as a draughtsman and sent to Baden-Baden and Freudenstadt **1940** Release from active military service **1942** Exhibition in the Frankfurter Kunstverein **1944** Hidden by friends in Weil der Stadt **1945** Member of the administrative council of the town of Calw appointed by the French occupation forces **1945** Participates in the "Art against the War" (Kunst gegen den Krieg) exhibition at the Württembergische Staatsgalerie, Stuttgart **1950–58** Commissioned works (frescoes) in Freudenstadt, Calw, Basle, Esslingen and other locations **1951–56** Exhibits with the "Red Rider" (Roter Reiter) group **1955–61** Exhibits with the Baden-Württemberg Federation of Artists

Gert Heinrich Wollheim
1894 Dresden-Loschwitz –1974 New York
1911–13 Studies at the College of Fine Arts, Weimar **1914–17** Active military service; wounded **1917–19** Lives in Berlin **1919** Lives in Remels, East Friesia, as one of a "painters' colony" with Otto Pankok, Ulfert Lüken and Hermann Hundt; moves to Düsseldorf; foundation of the "Young Rhineland" group; member of the artists' circle around gallery owner Johanna Ey **1922** Taken to court for his picture "Lenkbares Stück Festland passiert unter wehender Fahne den Raum von Omega" (Steerable Piece of Mainland Passes the Expanse of Omega with Fluttering Flag; since lost) **1925** Moves to Berlin **1926** Member of the exhibition committee for the Gesolei exhibition **1927** Trip to El Arenal, Majorca **1930** Participates in the "German Exhibition" (Deutsche Ausstellung), Munich **1933** Flees to France, active there in the Résistance; co-founder of the German Artists' Collective (Kollektiv Deutscher Künstler); committee member of the Federation of Free German Artists (Freier Deutsche Künstlerbund) **1933** Works destroyed as "degenerate" **1939–42** Arrest and internment in the labour camp in Camp du Ruchard and Septfonds, near Montauban **1942** Flees and is hidden in Nay/Basses Pyrénées **1945** Returns to France **1947** Moves to New York **1951–72** Trips to South America and Europe

Gustav Wunderwald
1882 Cologne/Kalk –1945 Berlin
1896–98 Apprenticeship as painter **1904–07** Works as stage-set painter; stage-set designer at the Royal Opera, Stockholm **1907–08** Member of the Düsseldorf Schauspielhaus committee **1908** Moves to the Villa Brand, Tegernsee **1910** Works as stage-set designer in Freiburg **1911** Participates in an exhibition by the Freiburger Kunstverein **1912–15** Interior decorator at the Deutsches Opernhaus, Berlin **1915–18** Active military service **1925 and 1926** Takes part in the "Great Berlin Exhibition of Art" **1925–30** Produces Berlin city vedute **1929–31** Commissions for the magazines "Sendung" and "Der Heimatdienst" **1936–43** Colouring of promotional films for Ufa and Mars-Film

The publishers would like to express their gratitude to Dr. Annette Baumeister, Michael Hasenclever and Richard Leibinger for their expert advice and support in the production of this book. We would also like to thank those of the artists' heirs who made portrait photographs of the artists available to us and generously provided us with informative material.

The contemporary documentary photographs in the first chapter (with the exception of the Bauhaus photograph), together with the portrait photographs of Grosz, Kanoldt and Schrimpf in the appendix, were supplied by Ullstein-Bilderdienst, Berlin.

In addition to the owners of photographs mentioned by name in the captions, the following are also listed here as sources/photographers for the original pictures, where they are not identical with the former: Thomas Adel (illus. p. 197); Archiv für Kunst und Geschichte, Berlin (illus. p. 16); Artothek, Peissenberg (illus. pp. 18, 72, 74, 78, 88, 119, 149, 150); Günther Barz (illus. 139, bottom); Bildarchiv Marburg, Marburg (illus. p. 75); Bildarchiv Preußischer Kulturbesitz, Berlin (illus. pp. 22, 26, 28, 29, 47, 48, 49, 53, 64, 68, 172, 178, 192); R. Boemke/D. Nagel, Berlin (illus. p. 69); Colorphoto Hans Hinz (illus. pp. 148, 160, top); Fedener, Halle (illus. p. 68); Foto-Studio-Grünke, Hamburg (illus. p. 14); Fotostudio Otto, Vienna (illus. p. 166); Foto Santvoort, Wuppertal (illus. pp. 99, 142, 151); Peter Frese, Wuppertal (illus. p. 113); Anne Gold, Aachen (illus. pp. 122, 123); Galerie Hasenclever, Munich (illus. pp. 49, bottom, 89, 93, 97, bottom); Reinhard Hentze, Halle (illus. p. 65, bottom left); Jürgen Karpinski, Dresden (illus. p. 65, bottom right); Walter Klein, Düsseldorf (illus. pp. 129, 196); Gerhard Reinhold, Leipzig (illus. p. 63); Rheinisches Bildarchiv, Cologne (illus. pp. 28, 54, 73, 74, 77, 117, 118); Friedrich Rosenstiel, Cologne (illus. p. 80); Wolfram Schmidt, Regensburg (illus. p. 164); Foto Strenger, Osnabrück (illus. pp. 194, 200); Elke Walford, Hamburg (illus. p. 112); Antje Zeis-Loi, Wuppertal (illus. p. 168)

Art

Petra Lamers-Schütze / p.lamers-schuetze@taschen.com
Gilles Néret / g.neret@taschen.com
Ingo F. Walther / ingofwalther@compuserve.de

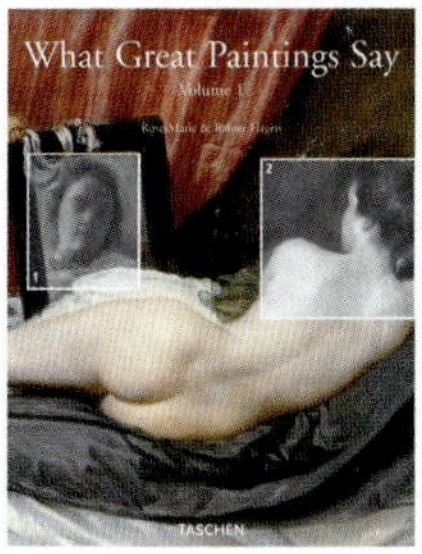

WHAT GREAT PAINTINGS SAY VOL. I
Rose-Marie & Rainer Hagen / Flexi-cover, format: 19.6 x 24.5 cm (7.7 x 9.6 in.), 496 pp. /
€ 29.99 / $ 39.99 / £ 19.99 / ¥ 4.900

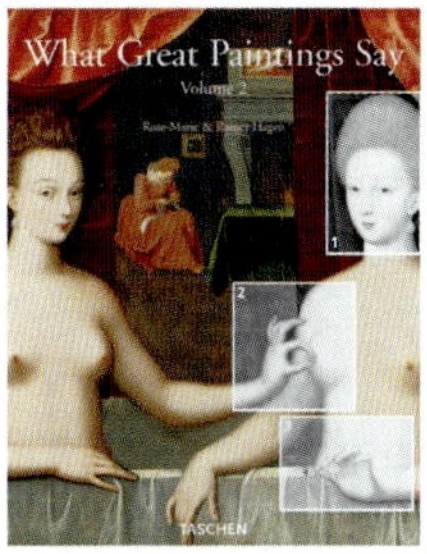

WHAT GREAT PAINTINGS SAY VOL. II
Rose-Marie & Rainer Hagen / Flexi-cover, format: 19.6 x 24.5 cm (7.7 x 9.6 in.), 432 pp.
€ 29.99 / $ 39.99 / £ 19.99 / ¥ 4.900

All Flexi-covers

ONLY € 29.99 / $ 39.99 / £ 19.99 / ¥ 4.900

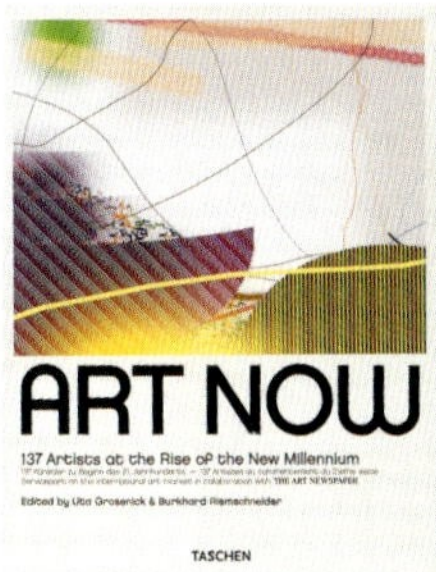

ART NOW
Ed. Uta Grosenick, Burkhard Riemschneider / Flexi-cover, format: 19.6 x 24.9 cm (7.7 x 9.8 in.), 640 pp. /
€ 29.99 / $ 39.99 / £ 19.99 / ¥ 4.900

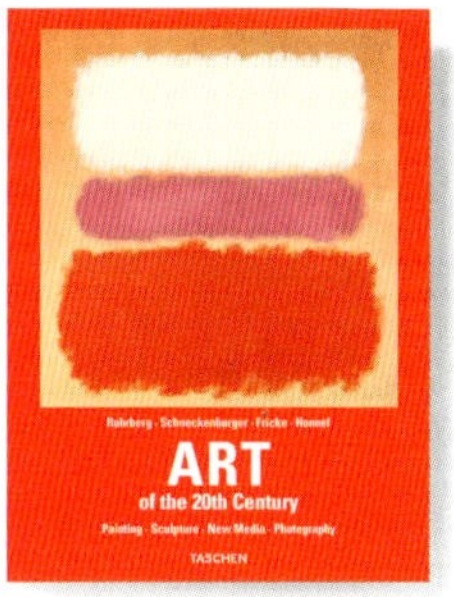

ART OF THE 20TH CENTURY
K. Ruhrberg, M. Schneckenburger, C. Fricke, K. Honnef / Ed. Ingo F. Walther / Flexi-cover, format: 19.6 x 25.8 cm (7.7 x 10.1 in.), 840 pp.
€ 29.99 / $ 39.99 / £ 19.99 / ¥ 4.900

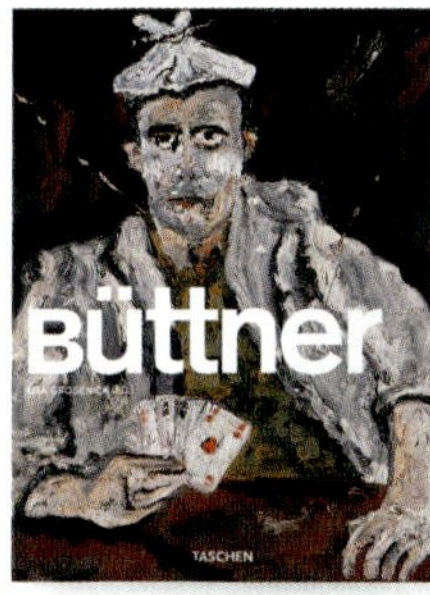

WERNER BÜTTNER
Ed. Uta Grosenick / Flexi-cover, format: 18.4 x 24.5 cm (7.2 x 9.6 in.), 192 pp.
€ 14.99 / $ 19.99 / £ 9.99 / ¥ 2.900

"S'approche si intelligemment des toiles qu'il nous fait les aimer.... Magique."

—*La Provence de l'économie*, Paris, on *What Great Paintings Say Vol. II*

"Le guide incontournable de l'art contemporain.... Indispensable."

—*Joyce*, Paris, on *Art Now*

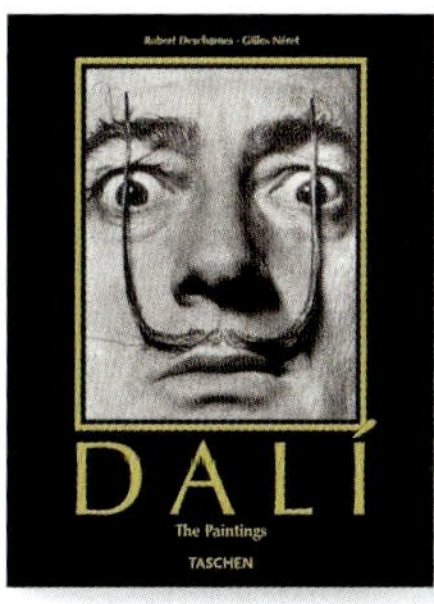

DALÍ. THE PAINTINGS
Robert Descharnes, Gilles Néret / Flexi-cover, format: 19.6 x 25.8 cm (7.7 x 10.1 in.), 780 pp. /
€ 29.99 / $ 39.99 / £ 19.99 / ¥ 4.900

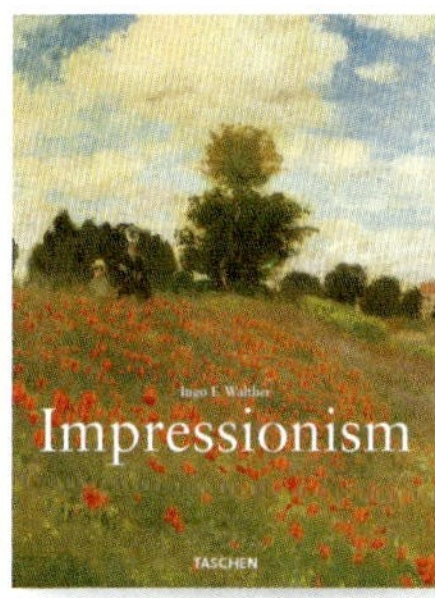

IMPRESSIONISM
Peter H. Feist / Ed. Ingo F. Walther / Flexi-cover, format: 19.6 x 25.8 cm (7.7 x 10.1 in.), 712 pp.
€ 29.99 / $ 39.99 / £ 19.99 / ¥ 4.900

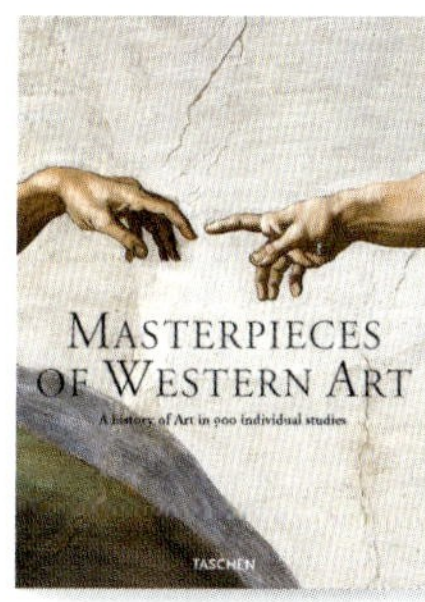

MASTERPIECES OF WESTERN ART
Ed. Ingo F. Walther / Flexi-cover, format: 19.6 x 25.8 cm (7.7 x 10.1 in.), 768 pp.
€ 29.99 / $ 39.99 / £ 19.99 / ¥ 4.900

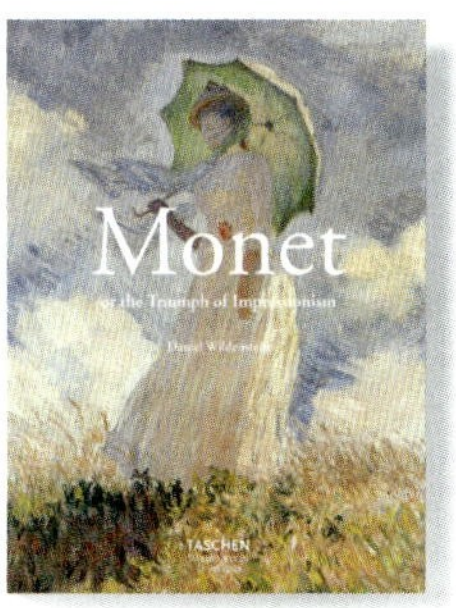

MONET OR THE TRIUMPH OF IMPRESSIONISM
Daniel Wildenstein / Ed. Gilles Néret / Flexi-cover, format: 19.6 x 25.8 cm (7.7 x 10.1 in.), 480 pp.
€ 29.99 / $ 39.99 / £ 19.99 / ¥ 4.900

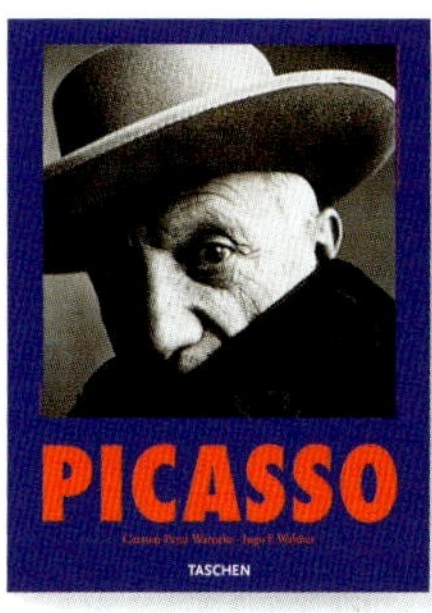

PICASSO
Carsten-Peter Warncke / Ed. Ingo F. Walther / Flexi-cover, format: 19.6 x 25.8 cm (7.7 x 10.1 in.), 740 pp.
€ 29.99 / $ 39.99 / £ 19.99 / ¥ 4.900

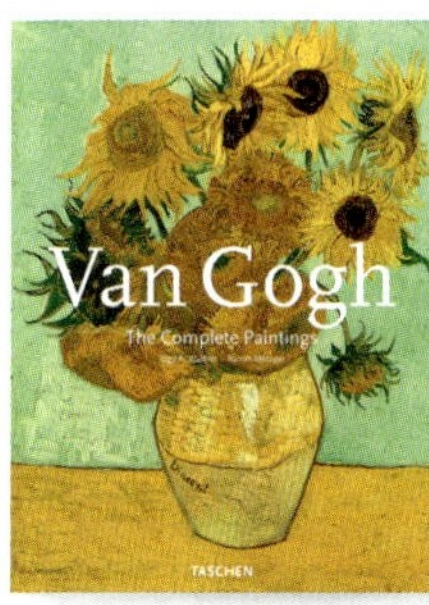

VAN GOGH – THE COMPLETE PAINTINGS
Ingo F. Walther / Rainer Metzger / Flexi-cover, format: 19.6 x 25.8 cm (7.7 x 10.1 in.), 740 pp.
€ 29.99 / $ 39.99 / £ 19.99 / ¥ 4.900

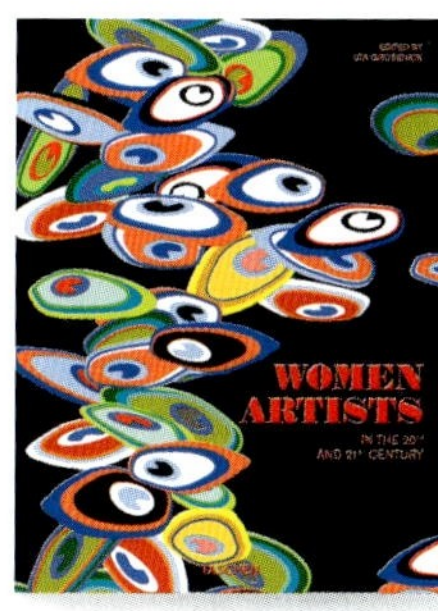

WOMEN ARTISTS
Ed. Uta Grosenick / Flexi-cover, format: 19.6 x 24.9 cm (7.7 x 9.8 in.), 576 pp.
€ 29.99 / $ 39.99 / £ 19.99 / ¥ 4.900

Art

Petra Lamers-Schütze / p.lamers-schuetze@taschen.com
Gilles Néret / g.neret@taschen.com
Ingo F. Walther / ingofwalther@compuserve.de

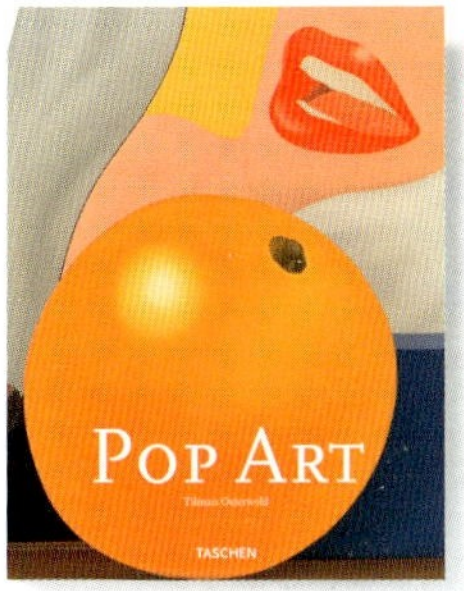

New edition!

POP ART
Tilman Osterwold / Flexi-cover, format: 19.6 x 24.5 cm (7.7 x 9.6 in.), 240 pp.
€ 14.99 / $ 19.99 / £ 9.99 / ¥ 2.900

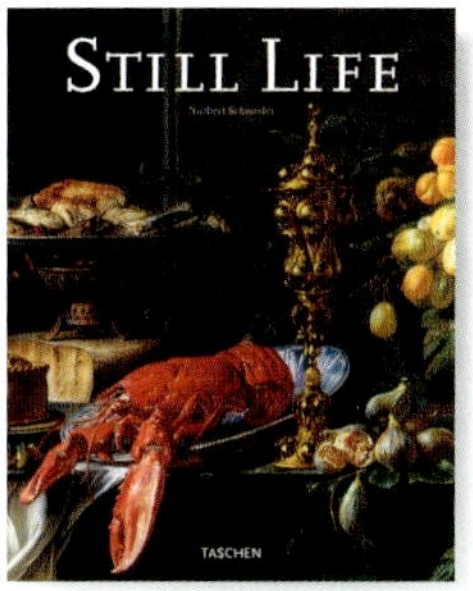

New edition!

STILL LIFE
Norbert Schneider / Flexi-cover, format: 19.6 x 24.5 cm (7.7 x 9.6 in.), 216 pp.
€ 14.99 / $ 19.99 / £ 9.99 / ¥ 2.900

"La alta costura del arte hecha prêt a porter editorial."
—*El País Semanal*, Madrid

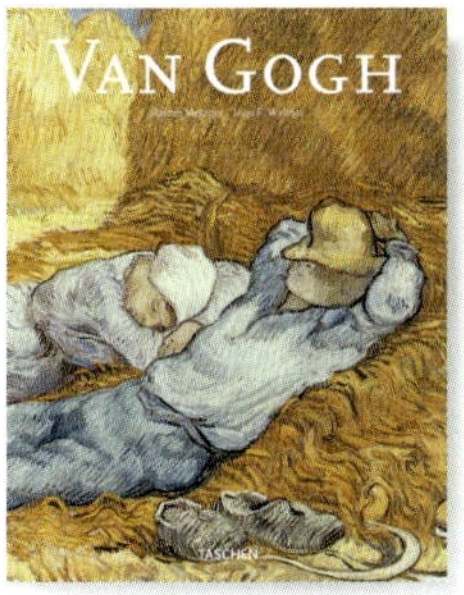

VAN GOGH
Rainer Metzger, Ingo F. Walther / Flexi-cover, format: 19.6 x 24.5 cm (7.7 x 9.6 in.), 256 pp.
€ 14.99 / $ 19.99 / £ 9.99 / ¥ 2.900

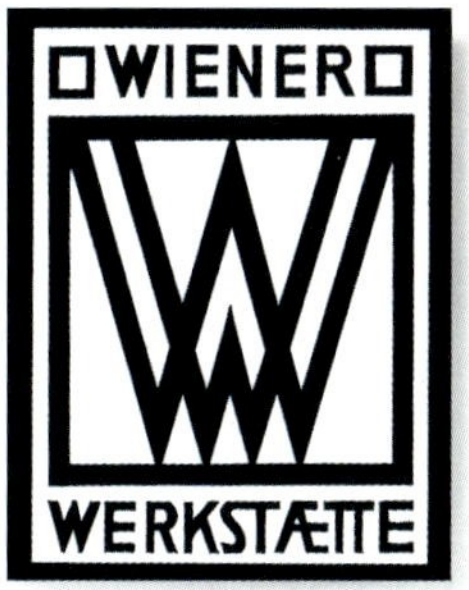

New edition!

WIENER WERKSTÄTTE
Gabriele Fahr-Becker / Ed. Angelika Taschen / Flexi-cover, format: 18.4 x 24.5 cm (7.2 x 9.6 in.), 240 pp.
€ 14.99 / $ 19.99 / £ 9.99 / ¥ 2.900

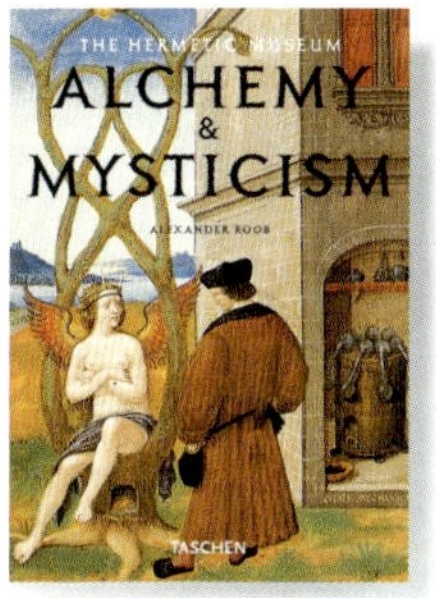

ALCHEMY & MYSTICISM
The Hermetic Museum / Alexander Roob / Flexi-cover, Klotz, format: 14 x 19.5 cm (5.5 x 7.7 in.), 712 pp.
€ 19.99 / $ 29.99 / £ 16.99 / ¥ 3.900

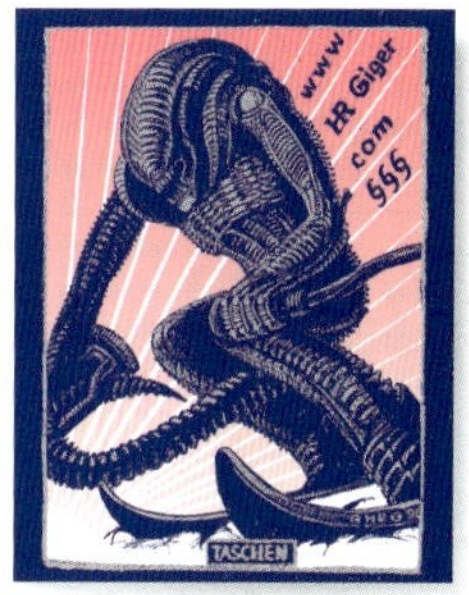

WWW HR GIGER COM
HR Giger / Hardcover, format: 23.8 x 29.7 cm (9.3 x 11.7 in.), 240 pp.
€ 19.99 / $ 29.99 / £ 16.99 / ¥ 3.900

This edition, the last book created by Friedensreich Hundertwasser, includes:

* **Two volumes in a slip case designed by Hundertwasser, lavishly printed in ten colors on rounded, black-edged pages**
* **Hundertwasser's original layout design**
* **1.792 pages and over 2.000 illustrations, documenting Hundertwasser's life and œuvre from 1928 to 2000, with many personal notes and comments by the artist**
* **An original 24 x 20 cm color etching (9.4 x 7.9 in.), specially created for this edition, numbered and marked with the Hundertwasser estate stamp**
* **Limited edition of worldwide 10.000 copies**

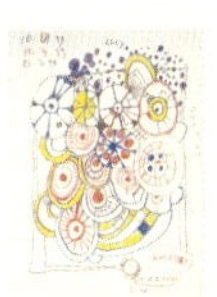

Each *Catalogue Raisonné* comes with one of five limited-edition color etchings, printed on deckle-edged paper (300 g/qm), 24 x 20 cm (9.4 x 7.9 in.), numbered and provided with the Hundertwasser estate stamp.

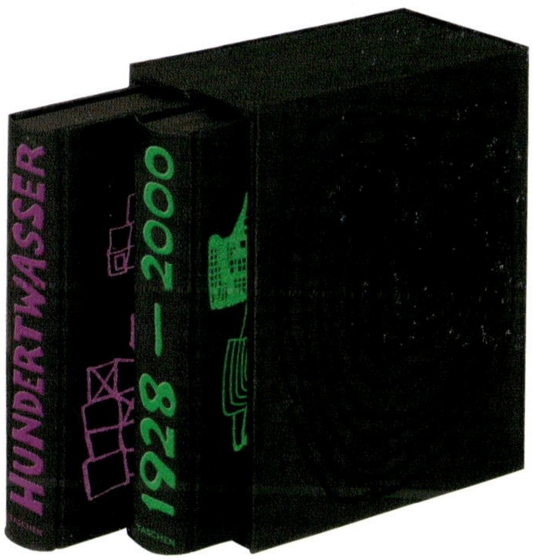

CATALOGUE RAISONNÉ
FRIEDENSREICH HUNDERTWASSER 1928–2000
Wieland Schmied / Hardcover, 2 volumes in a box, format: 21 x 25 cm (8.3 x 9.8 in.), 1.792 pp.
€ 750 / $ 750 / £ 500 / ¥ 90.000

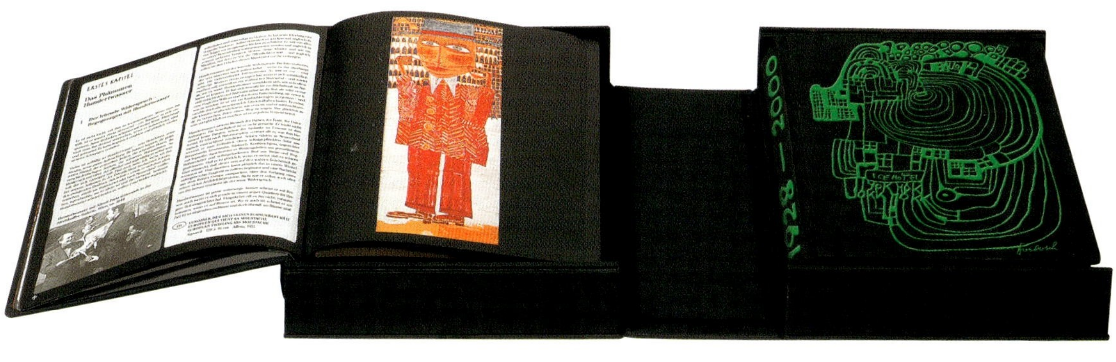

Design

Charlotte & Peter Fiell / Charlotte.Fiell@btopenworld.com

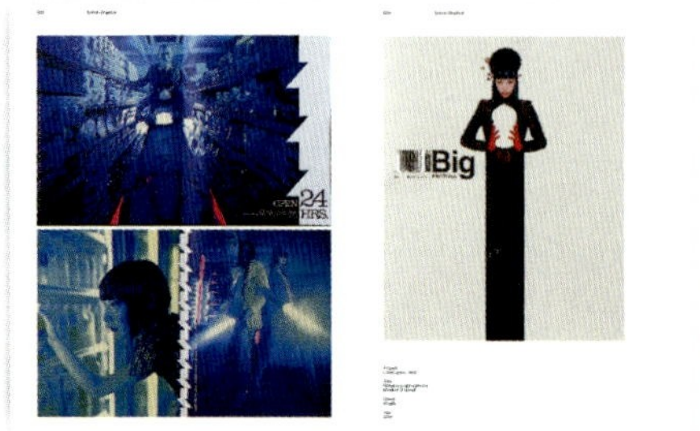

"A sweeping look at some of the most progressive designers."

—*Blue Print*, London, on *Graphic Design for the 21st Century*

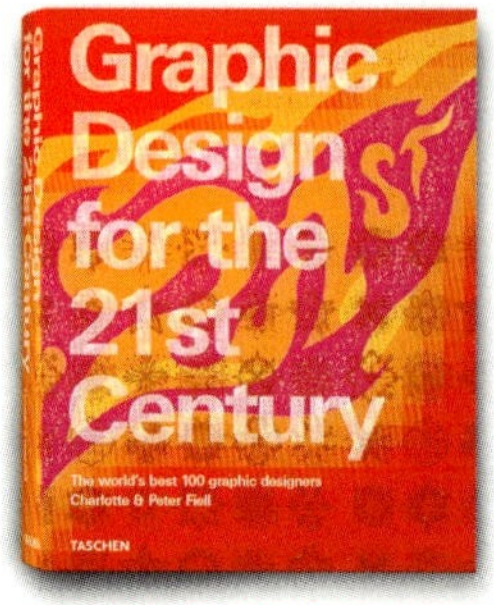

GRAPHIC DESIGN FOR THE 21ST CENTURY
Charlotte & Peter Fiell / Flexi-cover, format: 19.6 x 24.9 cm (7.7 x 9.8 in.), 640 pp.
€ 29.99 / $ 39.99 / £ 19.99 / ¥ 4.900

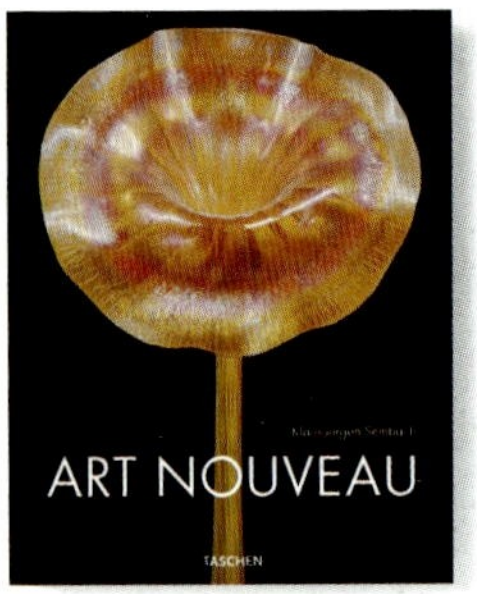

ART NOUVEAU
Klaus-Jürgen Sembach / Flexi-cover, format: 19.6 x 24.5 cm (7.7 x 9.6 in.), 240 pp.
€ 14.99 / $ 19.99 / £ 9.99 / ¥ 2.900

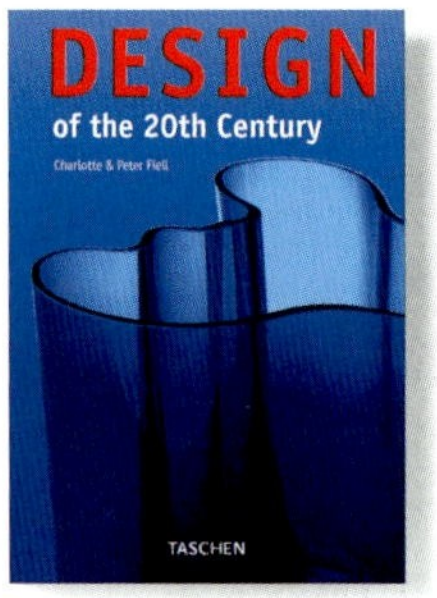

DESIGN OF THE 20TH CENTURY
Charlotte & Peter Fiell / Flexi-cover, Klotz, format: 14 x 19.5 cm (5.5 x 7.7 in.), 768 pp.
€ 19.99 / $ 29.99 / £ 14.99 / ¥ 3.900

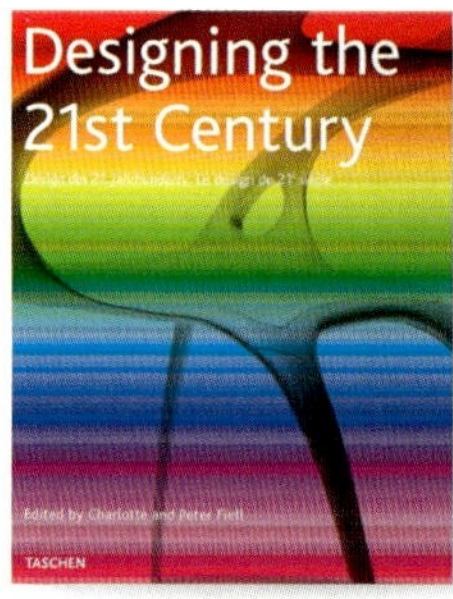

DESIGNING THE 21st CENTURY
Ed. Charlotte & Peter Fiell / Flexi-cover, format: 19.6 x 24.9 cm (7.7 x 9.8 in.), 576 pp.
€ 29.99 / $ 39.99 / £ 19.99 / ¥ 4.900

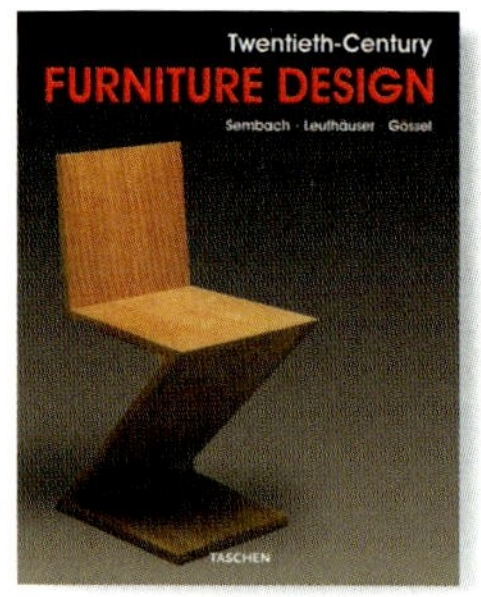

FURNITURE DESIGN
Klaus-Jürgen Sembach, Gabriele Leuthäuser, Peter Gössel / Flexi-cover, format: 19.6 x 24.5 cm (7.7 x 9.6 in.), 256 pp.
€ 14.99 / $ 19.99 / £ 9.99 / ¥ 2.900

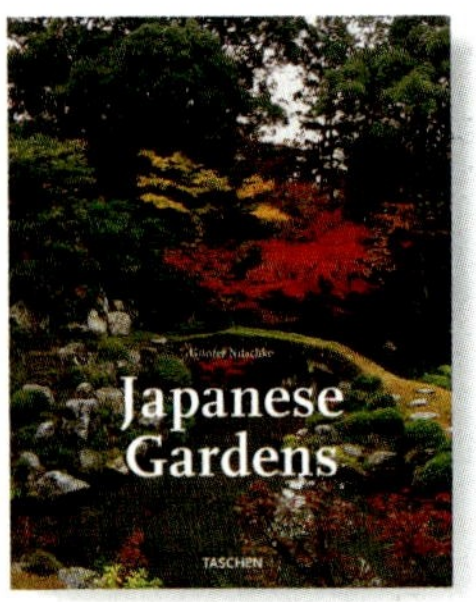

JAPANESE GARDENS
Günter Nitschke / Flexi-cover, format: 19.6 x 24.5 cm (7.7 x 9.6 in.), 240 pp.
€ 14.99 / $ 19.99 / £ 9.99 / ¥ 2.900

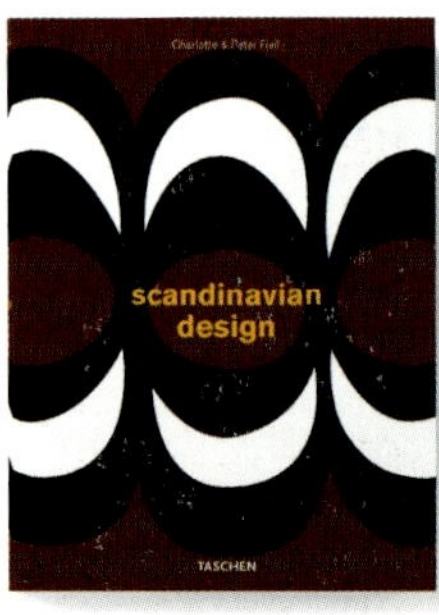

SCANDINAVIAN DESIGN
Charlotte & Peter Fiell / Flexi-cover, format: 19.6 x 25.2 cm (7.7 x 9.8 in.), 704 pp.
€ 29.99 / $ 39.99 / £ 19.99 /¥ 4.900

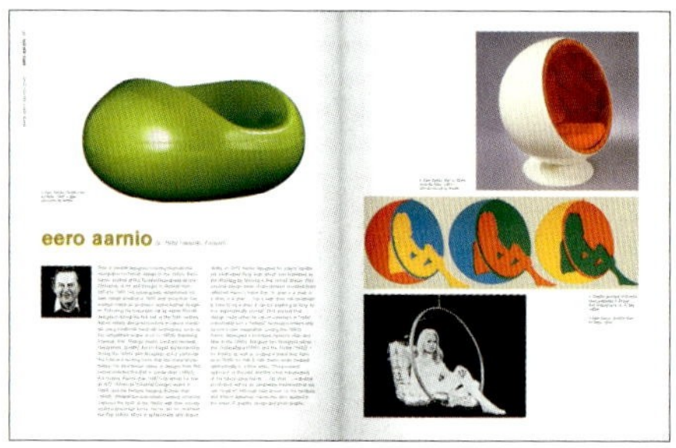

"[I]mmediately appealing… take this book and drink a toast to it."

—*Blue Print*, London, on *Scandinavian Design*

"Packed as tight as herring with design companies and artists from 1900 to the present."

—*Vanity Fair*, New York, on *Scandinavian Design*

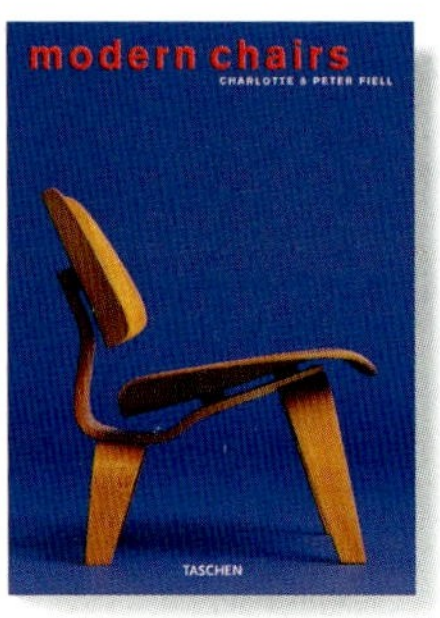

MODERN CHAIRS
Charlotte & Peter Fiell / Flexi-cover, format: 18.4 x 24.5 cm (7.2 x 9.6 in.), 160 pp.
€ 14.99 / $ 19.99 / £ 9.99 / ¥ 2.900

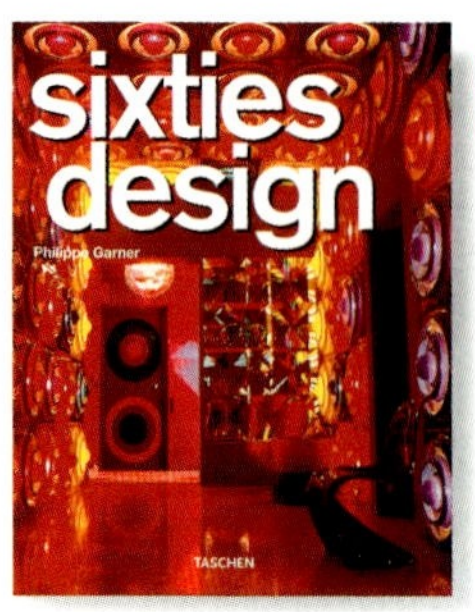

New edition!

SIXTIES DESIGN
Philippe Garner / Flexi-cover, format: 18.4 x 24.5 cm (7.2 x 9.6 in.), 176 pp.
€ 14.99 / $ 19.99 / £ 9.99 / ¥ 2.900

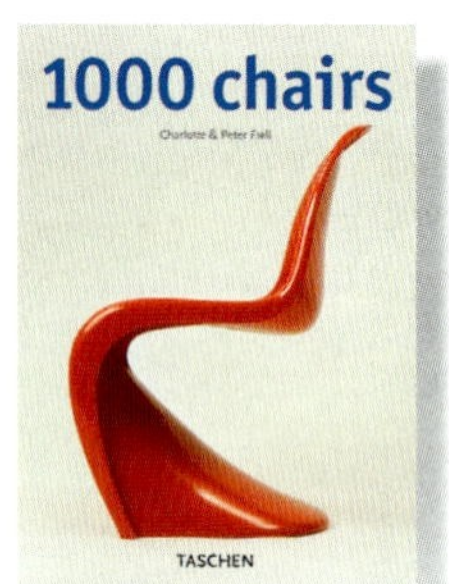

1000 CHAIRS
Charlotte & Peter Fiell / Flexi-cover, Klotz, format: 14 x 19.5 cm (5.5 x 7.7 in.), 768 pp.
€ 19.99 / $ 29.99 / £ 14.99 / ¥ 3.900